Web Resources Offer Online Support

Needles Accounting Resource Center: visit it at http://accounting.college.hmco.com to access a variety of educational resources, including:

For Students

- NEW! **ACE,** an online self-quizzing program, with over 700 new questions, that allows students to check their mastery of the topics covered in each chapter.

- **Research activities** based on the material covered in each chapter.

- **Toys "R" Us Annual Report Activities** that make use of the latest Toys "R" Us financial statements.

- **Links** to the web sites of over 200 real companies and annual reports referenced in the book.

- **Business readings** from leading periodicals.

- **Accounting Transaction Tutor,** with tutorials for every chapter to reinforce understanding of both accounting concepts and procedures.

- NEW! **Check Figures** for end-of-chapter problems.

For Instructors

- NEW! A brand new set of **PowerPoint Slides** that will enhance classroom presentation of text material. The new slides explain the accounting process in clear, easy-to-follow steps.

- **Text previews,** which highlight new features and provide demonstrations of supplements.

- **Sample syllabi** from other first-year accounting faculty.

- *Accounting Instructors' Report* newsletter, which explores a wide range of contemporary teaching issues.

- **Teaching Accounting Online,** a training program from Faculty Development Programs, which provides suggestions for integrating new technologies into accounting education.

- NEW! A series of 16 **Essays** (one for each chapter) on timely accounting issues, with two sets of questions and suggested answers.

- **Electronic Solutions,** which are fully functioning Excel spreadsheets for all text exercises, problems, and cases.

Real-Time Online Tutoring From SmarThinking: In partnership with SmarThinking, we offer personalized, online tutoring during typical homework hours. Every new text comes with a one-semester pass key that will allow access to three types of services:

- **Live help** provides access to 20 hours a week of real-time, one-on-one instruction. With Internet access, students may interact live online with an experienced SmarThinking "e-structor" (online tutor) between 9 PM and 1AM EST, every Sunday through Thursday.

- **Questions anytime** enables students to submit questions 24 hours a day, 7 days a week, for response by an e-structor within 24 hours. Students can even submit spreadsheets for personalized feedback within 24 hours.

- **Independent Study Resources** are available around the clock and provide access to additional educational services, ranging from interactive web sites to Frequently Asked Questions posed to SmarThinking e-structors.

Participate in Teaching Accounting Online: This online training course from Faculty Development Programs provides suggestions for integrating new technologies into accounting education. Available within Blackboard.com, the course includes the following modules: Designing Course Basics; Be the Student; Common Online Tools; Designing Teaching Strategies; Designing Learning Activities; Designing Outcomes Assessment; and Delivering a Course. For more information, contact your Houghton Mifflin sales representative or our Faculty Services Center at (800) 733-1717.

Financial Accounting

2004e

Eighth Edition

Belverd E. Needles, Jr., Ph.D., C.P.A., C.M.A.
DePaul University

Marian Powers, Ph.D.
Northwestern University

Houghton Mifflin Company   Boston   New York

To Annabelle and Abigail Needles
In memory of Mr. and Mrs. Belverd E. Needles, Sr., and
   Mr. and Mrs. Benjamin E. Needles
To Mr. and Mrs. Thomas R. Powers

Senior Sponsoring Editor: Bonnie Binkert
Senior Development Editor: Margaret M. Kearney
Editorial Associate: James R. Dimock
Project Editor: Claudine Bellanton
Editorial Assistant: Rachel B. Zanders
Senior Production/Design Coordinator: Sarah L. Ambrose
Senior Manufacturing Coordinator: Priscilla J. Bailey
Marketing Manager: Steven Mikels

Cover illustration © Sean Kane/Stock Illustration Source.

PHOTO CREDITS: page 3, © Edward Holub/CORBIS; page 5, Footage featuring Intel Corporation Courtesy of
Intel Corporation; page 107, © DigitalVision/PictureQuest; page 149, ©1999-2002 Getty Images, Inc.; page 189,
AP/Wide World Photos; page 239, © Mark Richards/PhotoEdit; page 287, ©1999-2002 Getty Images, Inc.; page 289,
Footage featuring Claire's Boutiques, Inc. Courtesy of Futures Media Development, Inc.; page 333, © Jose Luis
Pelaez, Inc./CORBIS; page 375, © BananaStock/BananaStock, Ltd., PictureQuest; page 377, Footage featuring
J.C. Penney Courtesy of J.C. Penney Company, Inc.; page 413, © 1999-2002 Getty Images, Inc.; page 449, © Ed
Young/CORBIS; page 451, Footage featuring Fermi National Accelerator Laboratory Courtesy of Fermi National
Accelerator Laboratory; page 495, ©1999-2002 Getty Images, Inc.; page 535, AP/Wide World Photos; page 537,
Footage featuring Lotus Development Corporation Courtesy of Lotus Development Corporation; page 571, © Todd
Gipstein/CORBIS; page 611, © DigitalVision/PictureQuest; page 613, Footage featuring Goodyear Courtesy of
Goodyear Tire & Rubber Company; page 653, AP/Wide World Photos; page 695, Getty Images.

The Toys "R" Us Annual Report (excerpts and complete) for the year ended February 2, 2002, which appears at the
end of Chapter 1, pages 59–90, is reprinted by permission of Toys "R" Us.

The 2001 Annual Report from Walgreens, which appears at the end of Chapter 1, pages 91–105, is reprinted with
permission from Walgreen Co., Deerfield, IL.

Printed in the U.S.A.
Library of Congress Control Number: 2002109652
ISBN: 0-618-31074-6

123456789-VH-07 06 05 04 03

BRIEF CONTENTS

CONTENTS

1 Uses of Accounting Information and the Financial Statements 2

Supplement to Chapter 1 How to Read an Annual Report 49

4 Accounting Information Systems

5 Financial Reporting and Analysis

6 Merchandising Operations and Internal Control

7 Short-Term Financial Assets

10 Long-Term Assets   448

11 Long-Term Liabilities   494

12 Contributed Capital

13 The Corporate Income Statement and the Statement of Stockholders' Equity

14 The Statement of Cash Flows

15 Financial Performance Evaluation

16 Long-Term Investments and International Accounting

PREFACE

Financial Accounting, 2004e continues a long tradition of teaching students that a company's financial statements tell a story. For investors and analysts, they reveal such things as a company's financial health, prosperity, and future. For management, they guide a company's progress and profitability. Our goal is to improve students' understanding of the "story" revealed in a company's financial statements, and never has that goal been as critical as in current times, with business events underscoring the fact that accounting really matters.

In order to read financial statements and follow the "story," students have to learn how to think. *Financial Accounting*, 2004e teaches students to think about what they are reading, how they might make a financial decision, and what roles they might play as future users of financial statements. Students also have to learn how to analyze and interpret the numbers in the financial statements—where did the numbers come from? What is the meaning behind the numbers? What do the numbers say about the financial health of the company? Today, financial accounting students need to learn more than how to prepare financial statements; they also must learn how to find meaningful information in them. *Financial Accounting*, 2004e focuses on teaching students to do just that.

Financial Accounting continues to be the leading text for students with no previous training in accounting or business. This textbook is intended for use at both the undergraduate and graduate levels. It has proved successful in a traditional one-quarter or one-semester course and has been used equally well in a two-quarter course in financial accounting.

Financial Accounting was revised with these major objectives in mind:

- **To support new instructional technologies in today's business environment**

- **To provide a framework for making successful and ethical business decisions**

- **To present real-world events and relevant business practices**

- **To develop skills and abilities critical to life-long learning**

NEW INSTRUCTIONAL TECHNOLOGIES IN TODAY'S BUSINESS ENVIRONMENT

New technologies are a driving force behind business growth and accounting education today. We have therefore developed an integrated text and technology program dedicated to helping instructors take advantage of the opportunities created by new instructional technologies. Whether an instructor wants to present a user or procedural orientation, incorporate new instructional strategies, develop students' core skills and competencies, or integrate technology into the classroom, the new 2004 edition provides a total solution, making it the leading choice among instructors of first-year financial accounting courses.

Web Resources

The Needles Accounting Resource Center (http://accounting.college.hmco.com/students) provides a wealth of resources for students. For example, students can access ACE, an online self-testing program that allows them to take sample quizzes and check their mastery of the chapter material. Over 700 new questions have been added to the ACE quizzes. An ACE icon 🌐 at the end of each learning objective section reminds students to check out the ACE online review quizzes.

Houghton Mifflin and SmarThinking have partnered to provide state-of-the-art, live, online tutoring with new textbooks purchased from Houghton Mifflin. Tutors can assist students with all examples, problems, and activities found in the text and related student supplements. An interactive interface allows tutors and students to share, annotate, and manipulate resources in real time to help illustrate concepts.

Other student web resources include:

■ Links to the web sites of over 200 real companies

■ Relevant readings from leading business and accounting periodicals (such as *BusinessWeek*, *Forbes*, *The Wall Street Journal*, and *The Journal of Accountancy*), which examine current business issues, the accounting profession, and career options in a broad context

■ Research activities, which present extended investigations of topics covered in the text

■ Toys "R" Us annual report activities, which make use of the latest Toys "R" Us financial statements

For instructors, the Needles Accounting Resource Center (http://accounting. college.hmco.com/instructors) contains a variety of resources designed to facilitate instruction, both within the traditional classroom and outside of it. A new feature is a series of 16 essays (one for each chapter) that relate timely accounting issues to the text. Each essay has two sets of questions and suggested answers. Students can answer the first set by reading the essay and related text chapter. The second set requires students to do additional research. The instructor can use these questions for final exams or as extra credit assignments. Topics include "How Accounting Numbers Affect the Stock Market" (Chapter 2), "Investor Protection and the Accounting Information System" (Chapter 4), "Fraudulent Financial Reporting: The Enron Case" (Chapter 5), "The Nature and Importance of Goodwill" (Chapter 10), "Stock Options: A Controversial Issue" (Chapter 12), and "Improving the Quality of Earnings" (Chapter 13).

Other instructor web resources include:

■ Sample syllabi, which show how your colleagues organize and teach the financial accounting course

■ The *Accounting Instructors' Report* newsletter, which explores a wide range of contemporary teaching issues

■ Teaching Accounting Online, an online training program from Faculty Development Programs, which provides suggestions for integrating new technologies into accounting education

■ A completely revised set of PowerPoint slides, which contain classroom presentation materials, discussion questions, and figures from the text

■ Electronic solutions, which are fully functioning Excel spreadsheets for all exercises, problems, and cases in the text, available both on the web site and on the HMClassPrep with HMTesting CD-ROM

Additional Technology Supplements

HMClassPrep with HMTesting   This instructor CD contains the computerized version of the test bank. It allows instructors to select, edit, and add questions, or generate randomly selected questions to produce a test master for easy duplication. The 2004 edition of the computerized test bank also contains algorithms and the ability to compile tests using key terms from the text. Online Testing and Gradebook functions allow instructors to administer tests via their local area network or the Web, set up classes, record grades from tests or assignments, analyze grades, and compile class and individual statistics. This program can be used on both PCs and Macintosh computers. The instructor CD also includes the complete Course Manual, the Solutions Manual (also available in print), PowerPoint slides, Video Cases, check figures for end-of-chapter problems, and web links to the Accounting Transaction Tutor and the Needles Accounting Resource Center Web Site.

Student CD-ROM This CD contains the Accounting Transaction Tutor (Chapters 1–16) and the Houghton Mifflin General Ledger Software for Windows.

- Accounting Transaction Tutor (ATT) is an easy-to-use Windows software program that reinforces accounting concepts and procedures through abundant exercises tied to Learning Objectives. It includes an online glossary and diagnostic tests that allow students to monitor their progress through the course material. The ATT software can also be downloaded from the student web site by accessing the Needles Accounting Resource Center at http://accounting.college.hmco/students.

- The Houghton Mifflin General Ledger Software for Windows is designed to function as a commercial package. It contains preliminary data for most of the problems in the text. This CD offers complete coverage of accounting concepts and procedures in a straightforward, user-friendly Windows environment.

The student CD also contains check figures for the end-of-chapter problems, selected video cases, and a link to the Needles Accounting Resource Center Web Site.

Peachtree Educator's Edition This popular accounting software tool is now available to students. The educational version is the same as the professional version sold to businesses.

Mastering the Accounting Cycle: A Bridge Tutorial This new, stand-alone CD-ROM tutorial emphasizes accounting transactions, reviews the debit and credit mechanism, and provides a foundation for the preparation and use of financial statements. Four demonstration problems show the connections between the balance sheet, income statement, and cash flow statement. The tutorial also features an interactive quizzing function and a built-in glossary.

Fingraph® Financial Analyst™ CD-ROM This CD contains the educational version of a patented software program used by financial analysts and certified public accountants to analyze and summarize the financial performance of companies. The financial data reported by over 20 well-known companies have been summarized and loaded into Microsoft Excel spreadsheets that can be accessed through the Needles Accounting Resource Center Web Site at http://accounting.college.hmco.com. Students can also enter data obtained from the annual report of any company. The Fingraph software enables students to prepare financial analyses of real companies in a very short time. The software accommodates a variety of learning styles: analyses are presented in tabular, graphic, and written formats. In addition, each chapter of *Financial Accounting*, 2004e contains a case, designed to be worked in conjunction with Fingraph, in which students analyze balance sheets, income statements, and statements of cash flows of real companies.

Introduction to Financial Accounting: The Language of Business Developed by Belverd Needles and Marian Powers with Learning Insights, Inc., this interactive, multimedia product is designed to teach accounting to students with little or no background, especially business majors and nonfinancial managers who need to understand the financial impact of business decisions. The CD combines video, audio, and text in an interactive simulation. Students learn accounting by recording a series of business transactions for a real-world company. Each transaction is described and recorded in everyday business language and reconciled to financial statements prepared in accordance with GAAP. As students proceed through the program, they are tutored by an accounting coach. The program is designed to help students understand fundamental accounting principles and understand how to become intelligent readers of financial statements.

Electronic Working Papers CD   Excel-based templates for exercises, problems, and selected cases in the text enable students to learn both accounting and the basic skills required for spreadsheet applications.

A FRAMEWORK FOR SUCCESSFUL AND ETHICAL DECISION MAKING

We know that most instructors want to place more emphasis on the analysis and use of accounting information by management, and on decisions that management makes with the help of accounting information. We also know that *ethical* decision making is an important topic in light of the accounting scandals that have headlined financial news. *Financial Accounting* has a long tradition of emphasizing ethical decision making, both in its Focus on Business Ethics boxes and in its end-of-chapter cases. The 2004 edition continues that tradition. The text reflects this emphasis on successful and ethical decision making in the following ways:

Workplace Ethics

With the new focus on corporate governance and ethical decision making, we present short cases, based on real, public companies, in which students must address an ethical dilemma directly related to the chapter content. The cases reveal how managers must account for their business decisions. Also, several new Focus on Business Ethics boxes within the text feature examples of real companies that have faced ethical issues.

Management Sections

Reflecting our increased emphasis throughout the book on the use and analysis of accounting information by management, we continue to address management's reliance on accounting information for successful decision making. In most cases, this discussion can be found in each chapter's first Learning Objective where we focus the students' attention on the purpose of the chapter; we then expand upon these management issues in the body of the chapter, frequently drawing examples from real companies.

Comparative Financial Analysis

We have expanded the concept of using financial information in performance evaluation and measurement by introducing a new comparison case at the end of each chapter. Students compare Walgreens and Toys "R" Us, referring to both companies' financial statements, which appear in the text at the end of Chapter 1. The comparison cases require students to compute ratios, make assumptions, report on the effect of seasonal sales, and describe each company's inventory management system, to name a few tasks. Again, *Financial Accounting*, 2004e continues to stress the importance of using the financial statements to obtain useful information about a company, in this case with a focus on performing comparative analyses.

Cash Flow

We emphasize the effect of business activities on cash flow throughout the text. Beginning in Chapter 1, we introduce the statement of cash flows. We also point out the difference between income measurement and cash flow in various chapters, and reinforce the concept through assignments. A cash flow icon 🖳 in the margin indicates a discussion of cash flow.

Key Ratios

Starting in Chapter 5, we examine financial analysis ratios and continue to integrate them in subsequent chapters, as appropriate. These ratios are usually discussed in the "management issues" section at the beginning of each chapter, and where appropriate, appear as components of the review problems. We bring all the ratios together in a comprehensive financial analysis of Sun Microsystems, Inc., in Chapter 15. A key ration icon % in the margin indicates an instance of a key ratio.

REAL-WORLD EVENTS AND BUSINESS PRACTICES

Working toward our goal of reflecting current business practice in a context that is relevant and exciting to students, we have incorporated the following real-world elements into the text.

Actual Financial Statements

To enhance students' appreciation for the usefulness and relevance of accounting information, we include excerpts from annual reports of real companies and articles about them from business journals. In total, we cite more than 200 publicly held companies so that students can apply the concepts to real examples. These companies are identified by a URL in the margin of the text or by a URL within the cases in the end-of-chapter material.

The complete annual report of Toys "R" Us and the financial statements and notes of Walgreen Company are printed in the book at the end of Chapter 1. Walgreens' financial statements also appear in Chapter 1 to illustrate the structure and interrelationships of financial statements. Chapter 5 presents the financial statements of Dell Computer Corporation in graphical form using the Fingraph Financial Analysis CD-ROM software. Chapter 15 features the most recent financial statements of Sun Microsystems, Inc., to illustrate comprehensive financial analysis. Several of the Financial Reporting and Analysis Cases ask students to select real companies and access their financial statements on the Internet or through the Needles Accounting Resource Center Web Site at http://accounting.college.hmco.com/students to research the information needed to answer the questions.

Updated Decision Points

Every chapter begins with a Decision Point based on excerpts from a real company's annual report or from articles in the business press. In addition to introducing the concepts to be covered in the chapter, the Decision Point presents a situation that requires a decision by management and then demonstrates how the decision can be made using accounting information. The 2004 edition features several new Decision Points, among them Walgreens, Kelly Services, Cisco, Sun Microsystems, and PepsiCo. All of the other Decision Points have been revised and updated with the most recent financial information available.

New Focus on Business Boxes

Always a popular feature in the Needles accounting series, the Focus on Business boxes have been redesigned and over a third of them have been replaced with newsworthy feature stories. These boxes contain short summaries of items that show the relevance of accounting in four areas:

- Focus on Business Practice
- Focus on International Business
- Focus on Business Technology
- Focus on Business Ethics

Real-World Graphic Illustrations

We present graphs and tables illustrating how actual business practices relate to chapter topics. Many of these illustrations are based on data from studies of 600 annual reports published in *Accounting Trends & Techniques*. Beginning with Chapter 5, we display selected ratios in graphic form for selected industries based on Dun & Bradstreet data. Service industry examples include advertising agencies and interstate trucking companies. Merchandising industry examples include auto and home supply companies and grocery stores. Manufacturing industry examples include machinery and computer companies. We have updated all graphs and tables with the most recent data available.

International Accounting

Recognizing the global economy in which all businesses operate today, we introduce international accounting examples in Chapter 1 and incorporate them throughout the text. Each chapter includes a Financial Reporting and Analysis Case that features an international company. Some examples include Harrods (British), Heineken (Dutch), Pioneer Corporation (Japanese), and Roche (Swiss). Chapter 16, "Long-Term Investments and International Accounting," covers foreign exchange rates, restatement of foreign subsidiaries' financial statements in U.S. dollars, and international accounting standards.

Video Cases

We have added three new 5-minute video vignettes (Claire's Stores, Inc., J.C. Penney Company, Inc., and Goodyear Tire & Rubber Company) to the series of video cases. Each video highlights a real company and is accompanied by an in-text case that serves as an introduction to the chapter. The videos work equally well as individual or group assignments, and all six include a written, critical-thinking component. The following video cases are included in the 2004 edition:

Intel Corporation (Chapter 1) examines the business goals of liquidity and profitability and the business activities of financing, investing, and operating.

Claire's Stores, Inc. (Chapter 6) describes a merchandising business that offers trendy costume jewelry, accessories, and cosmetics to teens and young adults. The case emphasizes the company's successful marketing practices and efficient distribution system.

J.C. Penney Company, Inc. (Chapter 8) focuses on how this major department store retailer manages its inventory.

Fermi National Accelerator Laboratory (Chapter 10) demonstrates the importance of long-term assets to a unique scientific laboratory.

Lotus Development Corporation (Chapter 12) tells the history of Lotus from its beginning as a small start-up company through its growth to one of America's most successful companies and finally to its sale to IBM. The case emphasizes the equity financing needs Lotus has encountered along the way.

Goodyear Tire & Rubber Company (Chapter 14) describes the vision and objectives of the world's largest tire and rubber company and illustrates how Goodyear will need strong cash flows to carry out its objectives.

COMPETENCY-BASED SKILL DEVELOPMENT FOR LIFE-LONG LEARNING

Our goal is to provide the most comprehensive and flexible set of assignments to promote the development of critical skills and abilities while still providing the necessary technical skills required of future managers and accountants. Whether you favor more traditional assignments or cases that enhance a broader set of student skills, or a combination of both, we provide ample competency-based assignments.

We also continue to integrate conceptual learning with procedural learning, especially in our end-of-chapter problems. We have added an analysis component to the requirements for most of our problems so students learn why a transaction was recorded or how the information in a particular financial statement can be used to evaluate financial performance. We continue to focus on the meaning behind the numbers in the financial statements—the message they contain, the story they tell. Assignment material is organized as follows:

Building Your Knowledge Foundation

This section consists of a variety of questions, exercises, and problems designed to develop basic knowledge, comprehension, and application of the concepts and techniques in the chapter.

- Questions (Q): Fifteen to 25 review questions cover the essential topics of the chapter.

- Short Exercises (SE): These 10 brief exercises are suitable for classroom use.

- Exercises (E): An average of 15 single-topic exercises stress application.

- Problems (P): Five problems provide extensive applications of chapter topics, often covering more than one Learning Objective. Many of the problems in the 2004 edition contain analysis components in which students are asked to explain how the numbers relate to the concepts covered in the chapter. Most problems can be solved using our General Ledger Software for Windows. These problems are marked with the following icon: ▊

- Alternate Problems (P): We provide an alternate set of the most popular problems based on feedback from our study of users' syllabi.

Skills Development (SD) Cases and Financial Reporting and Analysis (FRA) Cases

The Accounting Education Change Commission, the American Accounting Association, the American Institute of CPAs, and the Institute of Management Accountants have all called for the development of a broader set of skills among business and accounting graduates. The 10 or more cases in this section respond to this need by requiring students to work on their critical-thinking and communication skills, analytical skills, and writing skills. Most of the cases are based on real companies. All require critical-thinking and communication skills in the form of writing. At least one assignment in each chapter requires students to practice good business communication skills by writing a memorandum reporting results and offering recommendations. In addition, all cases are suitable for the development of interpersonal skills through group activities. Certain cases are especially appropriate for group activities and have specific instructions for applying a group methodology. We use icons to identify these cases, as well as to highlight the skill sets emphasized in other assignments. The following is a list of those icons:

Cash Flow icons indicate assignments dealing with cash flow; they also indicate text discussions of cash flow.

Communication icons identify assignments designed to help students develop their ability to understand and to communicate accounting information successfully.

Critical Thinking icons indicate assignments intended to strengthen students' critical-thinking skills.

Ethics icons identify assignments that address ethical issues.

Group Activity icons identify assignments appropriate for groups or teamwork.

International icons indicate international company cases.

Key Ratio icons indicate the presence of financial analysis ratios in both the text and assignments.

Memorandum icons identify cases that require students to write short business memorandums.

Each case has a specific purpose, as described in the following paragraphs:

Conceptual Analysis Designed so that a written solution is appropriate, these short cases are based on real companies and address conceptual accounting issues.

Ethical Dilemma Including ethics training in the business and accounting curriculum has become increasingly important in light of the accounting scandals that have rocked corporate America. Every chapter in *Financial Accounting*, 2004e contains a short case, often based on a real company, in which students must address an ethical dilemma directly related to the chapter content.

Research Activity Each chapter contains a case that asks students to do research using business periodicals, annual reports, newspaper articles, the library, and the Internet. Some cases are designed to improve students' interviewing and observation skills through field activities at actual businesses.

Decision-Making Practice Students practice decision making after extracting relevant data from a case and making computations as necessary. Students' decision-making role may be from the perspective of a manager, investor, analyst, or creditor.

Interpreting Financial Reports These short cases are abstracted from business articles and annual reports of well-known companies such as Kmart, Sears, IBM, Toys "R" Us, Chrysler, and many others. All require students to extract relevant data, make computations, and interpret the results.

International Company Each chapter contains an international case focusing on a foreign company that has had an accounting experience compatible with chapter content.

Toy "R" Us Annual Report Students read and analyze the actual annual report of Toys "R" Us, which is printed at the end of Chapter 1.

Comparison Case: Toys "R" Us and Walgreens This is a new case in which students are asked to compare Toys "R" Us and Walgreens in a number of different ways. Using Toys "R" Us's and Walgreens' financial statements, both of which appear at the end of Chapter 1, students learn how to find information, perform various financial analyses, and then compare the results.

Fingraph Financial Analyst Each chapter includes a case that requires students to use the Fingraph Financial Analyst CD-ROM. Students can use the Fingraph software to do tabular, graphic, or written analyses. Students can obtain financial data from more than 20 companies by accessing the Needles Accounting Resource Center Web Site at http://accounting.college.hmco.com/students, or they can obtain data from any company of their choice.

Internet Case Each chapter features an Internet case, which asks students to research a topic on the Internet, answer critical- and analytical-thinking questions, and then prepare a written or oral report on their findings.

The Annual Report Project Because the use of real companies' annual reports is the most rapidly growing type of term project in the financial accounting course, we provide an annual report project that we have used in our own classes for several years. Depending on how comprehensive you want the project to be, we have developed four assignment options, including the use of the Fingraph Financial Analyst CD-ROM software.

ORGANIZATION OF THE 2004 EDITION

The chapter organization reflects, first, an early introduction of financial statements and, second, the relationship of financial accounting to the major activities of a business. For example, we have positioned a supplement entitled "How to Read an Annual Report" (which includes the entire Toys "R" Us annual report and Walgreens' financial statements and notes) after Chapter 1 to facilitate the presentation, early in the course, of published financial statements. We introduce performance measurements, cash flow effects, and ratio analysis in Chapters 1–5, making possible the integration of these key management techniques throughout the text. Chapters 6–9 emphasize operating activities. Chapters 10–12 focus on investing in long-term assets and long-term financing activities. Chapters 13–16 discuss advanced statements and analyses.

All 16 chapters of *Financial Accounting*, 2004e have been thoroughly reviewed and edited. The book is quite a bit shorter, a goal the authors have long been striving for. A new and fresh design will engage students as they proceed through the text.

Pedagogical Color

A consistent color scheme throughout the text presents inputs to the accounting system (source documents) in orange, the processing of accounting data (working papers and accounting forms) in green, and outputs of the system (financial statements) in blue.

Stop and Think Questions

We have introduced a series of "Stop and Think" questions in the margins of the text to motivate students to read actively and think critically. These questions, accompanied by a short answer, can also serve as a valuable review device or as the basis for class discussions.

Pedagogical Annotations

These annotations appear in Chapter 1 only. They introduce each pedagogical element of the text—Learning Objectives, Decision Points, Content Annotations, and Chapter Reviews, to name a few. They describe the purpose of the pedagogy and provide usage suggestions so that students can derive maximum benefit when reading and studying the text.

Content Annotations

These marginal annotations appear throughout the text, offering material that enriches the text discussion as well as strategies and tips for mastering text content. Content Annotations fall into the following categories:

- *Key Points* briefly summarize main concepts or ideas.
- *Enrichment Notes* offer interesting insights—such as historical perspectives— to heighten students' appreciation of the material.
- *Terminology Notes* provide succinct definition of key terms and concepts used in the text discussion.
- *Business-World Examples* are short anecdotes drawn from real businesses to help students see the day-to-day relevance of accounting in real companies.
- *Ethical Considerations* highlight practices or behaviors that might engender ethical concern.
- *Study Notes* provide useful strategies and tips to help students avoid common pitfalls.

Related Text Assignments

In the 2004 edition, we have added a list of related text assignments to each learning objective. Students can now see which questions (Q), short exercises (SE), exercises (E), Problems (P), Skills Development Cases (SD), and Financial Reporting and Analysis Cases (FRA) reinforce a particular learning objective.

ACKNOWLEDGMENTS

A successful textbook is a collaborative effort. We are grateful to the many professors, other professional colleagues, and students who have taught and studied from our book, and we thank all of them for their constructive comments. With the knowledge that we cannot mention everyone who has been helpful, we wish to recognize in the following paragraphs those who made special contributions to our efforts in preparing the 2004 edition of *Financial Accounting*.

We wish to express our deep appreciation to colleagues at DePaul University, who have been extremely supportive and encouraging.

The thoughtful and meticulous work of Edward H. Julius (California Lutheran University) is reflected not only in the Study Guide, but in many other ways as well. We would also like to thank Marion Taube (University of Pittsburgh) for her contribution to the Test Bank and Gail Mestas for creating the PowerPoint slides. Sarah Evans deserves special recognition for her thoroughness and clarity in copyediting the 2004 edition. Further thanks go to Jacquie Commanday for her assistance with the Course Manual.

Also very important to the quality of this book is the supportive collaboration of our senior sponsoring editor, Bonnie Binkert. We further benefited from the ideas and guidance of our senior development editor, Margaret Kearney, the production expertise of our project editor, Claudine Bellanton, and the organizational skills of our editorial associate, Jim Dimock.

Others who have been supportive and have had an impact on this book through their reviews, suggestions, and class testing are:

Gregory D. Barnes *Clarion University*
Mohamed E. Bayou *The University of Michigan—Dearborn*
Charles M. Betts *Delaware Technical and Community College*
Michael C. Blue *Bloomsburg University*
Gary R. Bower *Community College of Rhode Island*
Lee Cannell *El Paso Community College*
Nancy Cassidy *Texas A&M University*
Michael Cornick *University of North Carolina, Charlotte*
John D. Cunha *University of California—Berkeley*
Mark W. Dawson *Duquesne University*
Patricia A. Doherty *Boston University*
Lizabeth England *American Language Academy*
David Fetyko *Kent State University*
Micah Frankel *California State University, Hayward*
Sue Garr *Wayne State University*
Roxanne Gooch *Cameron University*
Christine Uber Grosse *The American Graduate School of International Management*
Dennis A. Gutting *Orange County Community College*
John Hancock *University of California—Davis Graduate School of Management*
Marianne James *California State University, Los Angeles*
Edward H. Juilus *California Lutheran University*
Howard A. Kanter *DePaul University*
Stacy Kovar *Kansas State University*
Cathy X. Larson
Elliott S. Levy *Bentley College*
Kevin McClure *ESL Language Center*
George McGowan
Gail A. Mestas
Melanie Middlemist *North Colorado State University*
Michael F. Monahan
Jenine Moscove
Glenn Owen *Alan Hancock College*
Beth Brooks Patel *University of California—Berkeley*
LaVonda Ramey *Schoolcraft College*
Roberta Rettner *American Ways*
James B. Rosa *Queensborough Community College*
Donald Shannon *DePaul Univeristy*
S. Murray Simons *Northeastern University*
Marion Taube *University of Pittsburgh*
Kathleen Villani *Queensborough Community College*
John Weber *DeVry Institute*
Kay Westerfield *University of Oregon*
Carol Yacht
Glenn Allen Young *Tulsa Junior College*
Marilyn J. Young *Tulsa Junior College*

B.N. AND M.P.

TO THE STUDENT

HOW TO STUDY ACCOUNTING SUCCESSFULLY

The introductory accounting course is fundamental to the business curriculum and to success in the business world beyond college. Whether you are majoring in accounting or in another business discipline, it is one of the most important classes you will take. The course has multiple purposes because its students have diverse interests, backgrounds, and reasons for taking it. What are your goals in studying accounting? Being clear about your goals can contribute to your success in this course.

Success in this class also depends on your desire to learn and your willingness to work hard. It depends on your understanding of how the text complements the way your instructor teaches and the way you learn. A familiarity with how this text is structured will help you to study more efficiently, make better use of classroom time, and improve your performance on examinations and other assignments.

To be successful in the business world after you graduate, you will need a broad set of skills, which may be summarized as follows:

Technical/Analytical Skills   A major objective of your accounting course is to give you a firm grasp of the essential business and accounting terminology and techniques that you will need to succeed in a business environment. With this foundation, you then can begin to develop the higher-level perception skills that will help you acquire further knowledge on your own.

An even more crucial objective of this course is to help you develop analytical skills that will allow you to evaluate data. An important aspect of analytical skills is the ability to use technology effectively in making analyses. Well-developed analytical and decision-making skills are among the professional skills most highly valued by employers and will serve you well throughout your academic and professional careers.

Communication Skills   Another skill highly prized by employers is the ability to express oneself in a manner that others correctly understand. This can include writing skills, speaking skills, and presentation skills. Communication skills are developed through particular tasks and assignments and are improved through constructive criticism. Reading skills and listening skills support the direct communication skills.

Interpersonal Skills   Effective interaction between two people requires a solid foundation of interpersonal skills. The success of such interaction depends on empathy, or the ability to identify with and understand the problems, concerns, and motives of others. Leadership, supervision, and interviewing skills also facilitate a professional's interaction with others.

Personal/Self Skills   Personal/self skills form the foundation for growth in the use of all other skills. To succeed, a professional must take initiative, possess self-confidence, show independence, and be ethical in all areas of life. Personal/self skills can be enhanced significantly by the formal learning process and by peers and mentors who provide models upon which one can build. Accounting is just one course in your entire curriculum, but it can play an important role in your skill development. Your instructor is interested in helping you gain both a knowledge of accounting and the more general skills you will need to succeed in the business world. The following sections describe how you can get the most out of this course.

The Teaching/Learning Cycle™

Both teaching and learning have natural, parallel, and mutually compatible cycles. This teaching/learning cycle, as shown in Figure 1, interacts with the basic structure of learning objectives in this text.

The Teaching Cycle   The inner (tan) circle in Figure 1 shows the steps an instructor takes in teaching a chapter. Your teacher *assigns* material, *presents* the subject in lecture, *explains* by going over assignments and answering questions, *reviews* the subject prior to an exam, and *assesses* your knowledge and understanding using examinations and other means of evaluation.

The Learning Cycle   Moving outward, the next circle (green) in Figure 1 shows the steps you should take in studying a chapter. You should *preview* the material, *read* the chapter, *apply* your understanding by working the assignments, *review* the chapter, and *recall* and *demonstrate* your knowledge and understanding of the material in examinations and other assessments.

Integrated Learning Objectives   Your textbook supports the teaching/learning cycle through the use of integrated learning objectives. Learning objectives are simply statements of what you should be able to do after you have completed a chapter. In Figure 1, the outside (blue) circle shows how learning objectives are integrated into your text and other study aids and how they interact with the teaching/learning cycle.

1. Learning objectives listed at the beginning of each chapter aid your teacher in making assignments and help you preview the chapter.
2. Each learning objective is referenced in the margin of the text at the point where that subject is covered. A list of related text assignments below each learning objective identifies the end-of-chapter exercises, problems, and cases that relate to that objective.
3. Every exercise, problem, and case in the end-of-chapter assignments shows the applicable learning objective(s) so you can refer to the text if you need help.
4. A summary of the key points for each learning objective, a list of new concepts and terms referenced by learning objectives, and a review problem covering key learning objectives assist you in reviewing each chapter. The Study Guide, also organized by learning objectives, provides additional review.

Why Students Succeed   Students succeed in their accounting course when they coordinate their personal learning cycle with their instructor's cycle. Students who do a good job of previewing their assignments, reading the chapters before the instructor is ready to present them, preparing homework assignments before they are discussed in class, and reviewing carefully will ultimately achieve their potential on exams. To ensure that your learning cycle is synchronized with your instructor's teaching cycle, check your study habits against the following suggestions.

Previewing the Chapter

1. Read the learning objectives at the beginning of the chapter. These learning objectives specifically describe what you should be able to do after completing the chapter.
2. Study your syllabus. Know where you are in the course and where you are going. Know the rules of the course.
3. Realize that in an accounting course, each assignment builds on previous ones. If you do poorly in Chapter 1, you may have difficulty in Chapter 2 and be lost in Chapter 3.

FIGURE 1
The Teaching/Learning Cycle™ with integrated Learning Objectives

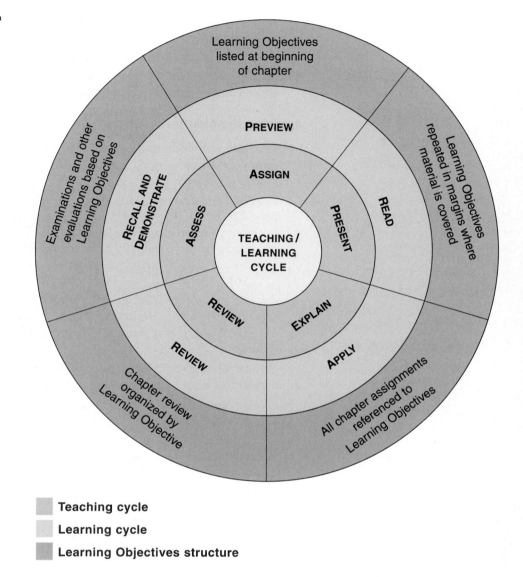

Teaching cycle

Learning cycle

Learning Objectives structure

Reading the Chapter

1. As you read each chapter, be aware of the learning objectives in the margins. They will tell you why the material is relevant.

2. Allow yourself plenty of time to read the text. Accounting is a technical subject. Accounting books are so full of information that almost every sentence is important.

3. Strive to understand not only how each procedure is done, but also why it is done. Accounting is logical and requires reasoning. If you understand why something is done in accounting, there is little need to memorize.

4. Relate each new topic to its learning objective and be able to explain it in your own words.

5. Be aware of colors as you read. They are designed to help you understand the text. (For handy reference, the use of color is also explained on the back cover of the book.)

    Orange: All source documents and inputs are in orange.

    Green: All accounting forms, working papers, and accounting processes are shown in green.

Blue: All financial statements, the output or final product of the accounting process, are shown in blue.

6. If there is something you do not understand, prepare specific questions for your instructor. Pinpoint the topic or concept that confuses you. Some students keep a notebook of points with which they have difficulty.

Applying the Chapter

1. In addition to understanding why each procedure is done, you must be able to do it yourself by working exercises, problems, and cases. Accounting is a "do-it-yourself" course.

2. Read assignments and instructions carefully. Each assignment has a specific purpose. The wording is precise, and a clear understanding of it will save time and improve your performance. Acquaint yourself with the end-of-chapter assignment materials by reading the description of them in the Preface.

3. Try to work exercises, problems, and cases without referring to their discussions in the chapter. If you cannot work an assignment without looking in the chapter, you will not be able to work a similar problem on an exam. After you have tried on your own, refer to the chapter (based on the learning objective reference) and check your answer. Try to understand any mistakes you may have made.

4. Be neat and orderly. Sloppy calculations, messy papers, and general carelessness cause most errors on accounting assignments.

5. Allow plenty of time to work the chapter assignments. You will find that assignments seem harder and that you make more errors when you are feeling pressed for time.

6. Keep up with your class. Check your work against the solutions presented in class. Find your mistakes. Be sure you understand the correct solutions.

7. Note the part of each exercise, problem, or case that causes you difficulty so you can ask for help.

8. Attend class. Most instructors design classes to help you and to answer your questions. Absence from even one class can hurt your performance.

Reviewing the Chapter

1. Read the summary of learning objectives in the chapter review. Be sure you know the definitions of all the words in the review of concepts and terminology.

2. Review all assigned exercises, problems, and cases. Know them cold. Be sure you can work the assignments without the aid of the book.

3. Determine the learning objectives for which most of the problems were assigned. They refer to topics that your instructor is most likely to emphasize on an exam. Scan the text for such learning objectives and pay particular attention to the examples and illustrations.

4. Look for and scan other similar assignments that cover the same learning objectives. They may be helpful on an exam.

5. Review quizzes. Similar material will often appear on longer exams.

6. Attend any labs or visit any tutors your school provides, or see your instructor during office hours to get assistance. Be sure to have specific questions ready.

Taking Examinations

1. Arrive at class early so you can get the feel of the room and make a last-minute review of your notes.

2. Have plenty of sharp pencils and your calculator (if allowed) ready.

3. Review the exam quickly when it is handed out to get an overview of your task. Start with a part you know. It will give you confidence and save time.

4. Allocate your time to the various parts of the exam, and stick to your schedule. Every exam has time constraints. You need to move ahead and make sure you attempt all parts of the exam.

5. Read the questions carefully. Some may not be exactly like your homework assignments. They may approach the material from a slightly different angle to test your understanding and ability to reason, rather than your ability to memorize.

6. To avoid unnecessary errors, be neat, use good form, and show calculations.

7. Relax. If you have followed the above guidelines, your effort will be rewarded.

Preparing Other Assignments

1. Understand the assignment. Written assignments, term papers, computer projects, oral presentations, case studies, group activities, individual field trips, video critiques, and other activities are designed to enhance skills beyond your technical knowledge. It is essential to know exactly what your instructor expects. Know the purpose, audience, scope, and expected end product.

2. Allow plenty of time. "Murphy's Law" applies to such assignments: If anything can go wrong, it will.

3. Prepare an outline of each report, paper, or presentation. A project that is done well always has a logical structure.

4. Write a rough draft of each paper and report, and practice each presentation. Professionals always try out their ideas in advance and thoroughly rehearse their presentations. Good results are not accomplished by accident.

5. Make sure that each paper, report, or presentation is of professional quality. Instructors appreciate attention to detail and polish. A good rule of thumb is to ask yourself: Would I give this work to my boss?

ABOUT THE AUTHORS

Central to the success of any accounting text is the expertise of its author team. This team brings a wealth of classroom teaching experience, relevant business insight, and pedagogical expertise, as well as first-hand knowledge of today's students.

Belverd E. Needles, Jr., PhD, CPA, CMA
DePaul University

Belverd E. Needles, Jr. received his BBA and MBA degrees from Texas Tech University and his Ph.D. degree from the University of Illinois. Dr. Needles teaches auditing and financial accounting at DePaul University, and is an internationally known expert in international auditing and accounting education. He has published in leading journals in these fields and is the author or editor of more than 20 books and monographs. He has served in a leadership capacity in many U.S. and international academic and professional accounting associations.

During his more than 30 years of teaching beginning accounting students, Belverd Needles has been an acknowledged innovator in accounting education. He has won teaching and education awards from DePaul University, the American Accounting Association, the Illinois CPA Society, the American Institute of CPAs, and the national honorary society, Beta Alpha Psi. The Conference on Accounting Education, started by Dr. Needles and sponsored by Houghton Mifflin, is in its 19th year; it has helped more than 2,000 beginning accounting instructors improve their teaching. Dr. Needles is editor of the *Accounting Instructors' Report*, in its 18th year, a newsletter that thousands of accounting teachers rely on for new ideas in accounting education.

Marian Powers, PhD
Northwestern University

Marian Powers earned her BS in business from Chicago State University and her Ph.D. in accounting from the University of Illinois at Urbana. With more than 20 years of teaching experience, Marian Powers has taught beginning accounting at every level, from large lecture halls of 250 students to small classes of graduate students. She is a dynamic teacher who incorporates a variety of instructional strategies designed to broaden students' skills and experiences in critical thinking, group interaction, and communication. Consistently, Dr. Powers receives the highest ratings from students. She also brings practical experience to her students, including examples of how managers in all levels of business use and evaluate financial information. In recent years, Dr. Powers has concentrated on executive education. She has taught thousands of executives from leading companies around the world how to read and analyze the financial statements of their own companies and those of their competitors.

CHECK FIGURES

These check figures provide a key number in the solutions to the problems at the end of each chapter.

Chapter 1 Problems
P 1.   Total Assets: $10,820
P 2.   Total Assets: $70,600
P 3.   Total Assets: $15,920
P 4.   Total Assets: $71,900
P 5.   Total Assets: $5,120
P 6.   Total Assets: $9,150
P 7.   Total Assets: $143,800
P 8.   Total Assets: $48,750

Chapter 2 Problems
P 1.   No check figure
P 2.   Trial Balance: $16,450
P 3.   Trial Balance: $7,400
P 4.   Trial Balance: $11,550
P 5.   Trial Balance: $23,515
P 6.   No check figure
P 7.   Trial Balance: $10,540
P 8.   Trial Balance: $30,710

Chapter 3 Problems
P 1.   No check figure
P 2.   No check figure
P 3.   Adjusted Trial Balance: $125,792
P 4.   Adjusted Trial Balance: $31,578
P 5.   Adjusted Trial Balance: $654,209
P 6.   No check figure
P 7.   No check figure
P 8.   Adjusted Trial Balance: $109,167

Chapter 4 Problems
P 1.   Net Income: $83,150
P 2.   Total Assets: $113,616
P 3.   Net Income for May: $431; Net Income for June: $467
P 4.   Net Income: $78,622
P 5.   Net Income: $25,196
P 6.   Net Income: $42,739
P 7.   Total Assets: $6,943
P 8.   Net Income: $22,893

Chapter 5 Problems
P 1.   No check figure
P 2.   Income from Operations: 20x4, $66,426; 20x3, $110,628
P 3.   Total Assets: $397,143
P 4.   Return on Equity: 20x4, 25.2%; 20x3, 21.7%
P 5.   Net Income: $72,260; Total Assets: $1,083,800
P 6.   No check figure
P 7.   Income from Operations: 20x5, $34,320; 20x4, $84,748
P 8.   Return on Equity: 20x4, 15.6%; 20x3, 12.2%

Chapter 6 Problems
P 1.   Net Income: $2,761
P 2.   No check figure

P 3.   Net Income: $56,823
P 4.   No check figure
P 5.   No check figure
P 6.   No check figure
P 7.   Net Income: $26,870
P 8.   No check figure
P 9.   Net Income: $2,435
P 10. No check figure

Chapter 7 Problems
P 1.   Short-term investments (at market): $354,000
P 2.   No check figure
P 3.   Amount of adjustment: $73,413
P 4.   No check figure
P 5.   Adjusted book balance: $149,473.28
P 6.   Short-term investments (at market): $903,875
P 7.   No check figure
P 8.   Adjusted book balance: $54,485.60

Chapter 8 Problems
P 1.   1. Cost of goods available for sale: $157,980
P 2.   1. Cost of goods sold: March, $4,578; April, $15,457
P 3.   1. Cost of goods sold: March, $4,560; April, $15,424
P 4.   Estimated inventory shortage: At cost, $6,052; At retail, $8,900
P 5.   Estimated loss of inventory in fire: $653,027
P 6.   Cost of goods available for sale: $10,560,000
P 7.   1. Cost of goods sold: April, $9,660; May, $22,119
P 8.   1. Cost of goods sold: April, $9,580; May, $21,991

Chapter 9 Problems
P 1.   No check figure
P 2.   No check figure
P 3.   1.b. Estimated Product Warranty Liability: $20,160
P 4.   No check figure
P 5.   Fund Balance: $3,310,000; Annual Payment: $327,600; Cost of Buyout: $317,000; Fund Balance: $798,600
P 6.   No check figure
P 7.   1.b. Estimated Product Warranty Liability: $10,800
P 8.   Fund Balance: $58,300; Initial Deposit: $110,250; Purchase Price: $399,300; Annual Payments: $136,355.89

Chapter 10 Problems
P 1.   Totals: Land, $361,950; Land Improvements, $71,000; Building, $691,800; Furniture and Equipment, $105,400
P 2.   1. Depreciation, Year 3: a. $165,000; b. $132,000; c. $90,000
P 3.   Total Depreciation Expense: 20x5, $13,280; 20x6, $18,760; 20x7, $15,728
P 4.   a. Gain on Sale of Road Grader: $1,800; b. Loss on Sale of Road Grader: $2,200; c. Gain on Exchange of Road Grader: $1,800; d. Loss on Exchange of Road Grader: $2,200; e. No gain recognized

P 5.   Part A. c. Amortization Expense: $492,000;
       d. Loss on Exclusive License: $1,476,000; Part B.
       d. Leasehold Amortization Expense: $1,575;
       e. Leasehold Improvements Amortization Expense:
       $2,500
P 6.   Totals: Land, $852,424; Land Improvements,
       $333,120; Buildings, $1,667,880; Machinery,
       $2,525,280; Expense, $36,240
P 7.   1. Depreciation, Year 3: a. $54,250; b. $81,375;
       c. $53,407
P 8.   Total Depreciation Expense: 20x1, $71,820; 20x2,
       $103,092; 20x3, $84,072

Chapter 11 Problems

P 1.   2. Bond Interest Expense: Nov. 30, $1,597,500;
       Dec. 31, $266,250
P 2.   1. Bond Interest Expense: Sept. 1, $754,400; Nov.
       30, $377,071
P 3.   Bond Interest Expense: June 30, 20x4, $144,666;
       Sept. 1, 20x4, $93,290
P 4.   2. Loss on early retirement: $2,261,293
P 5.   Bond Interest Expense: Jan. 31, 20x4, $2,400,000;
       June 30, 20x4, $2,000,000
P 6.   2. Bond Interest Expense: Sept. 1, $192,800; Nov.
       30, $96,400
P 7.   1. Bond Interest Expense: Nov. 30, $520,150; Dec.
       31, $86,651
P 8.   Bond Interest Expense: June 30, 20x3, $46,598;
       Sept. 30, 20x3, $96,900

Chapter 12 Problems

P 1.   2. Total stockholders' equity: $175,700
P 2.   1. 20x5 Total dividends: Preferred, $60,000;
       Common, $34,000
P 3.   No check figure
P 4.   2. Total stockholders' equity: $950,080
P 5.   2. Total stockholders' equity: $330,375
P 6.   2. Total stockholders' equity: $1,488,000
P 7.   1. 20x3 Total dividends: Preferred, $420,000;
       Common, $380,000
P 8.   2. Total stockholders' equity: $475,040

Chapter 13 Problems

P 1.   2. Difference in net income: $48,800
P 2.   1. Income before extraordinary items and cumula-
       tive effect of accounting change: $108,000
P 3.   1. Income from continuing operations, December
       31, 20x3: $551,250
P 4.   2. Total stockholders' equity, December 31, 20x3:
       $1,157,000
P 5.   2. Retained earnings: $231,500; Total stockholders'
       equity: $1,321,500

P 6.   1. Income before extraordinary items and cumula-
       tive effect of accounting change: $205,000
P 7.   2. Total stockholders' equity, December 31, 20x5:
       $2,964,000
P 8.   2. Retained earnings: $207,500; Total stockholders'
       equity: $1,257,500

Chapter 14 Problems

P 1.   No check figure
P 2.   1. Net cash flows from: operating activities,
       $126,600; investing activities, ($25,800); financing
       activities, $14,000
P 3.   1. Net cash flows from: operating activities,
       ($32,600); investing activities, ($7,200); financing
       activities, $51,000
P 4.   1. Net cash flows from: operating activities,
       ($106,000); investing activities, $34,000; financing
       activities, $24,000
P 5.   No check figure
P 6.   1. Net cash flows from: operating activities,
       $274,000; investing activities, $3,000; financing
       activities, ($130,000)
P 7.   1. Net cash flows from: operating activities,
       $46,800; investing activities: ($14,400); financing
       activities, $87,000

Chapter 15 Problems

P 1.   No check figure
P 2.   Increase: d, h, i
P 3.   1.c. Receivable turnover, 20x5: 13.9 times; 20x4:
       15.6 times; 1.e. Inventory turnover, 20x5: 3.9
       times; 20x4: 3.8 times
P 4.   1.b. Quick ratio, Reynard: 0.4 times; Bouche: 1.0
       times; 2.d. Return on equity, Reynard: 11.8%;
       Bouche: 8.8%
P 5.   Increase: a, b, e, f, l, m
P 6.   1.a. Current ratio, 20x6: 1.9 times; 20x5: 1.0 times;
       2.c. Return on assets, 20x6: 8.4%; 20x5: 6.6%

Chapter 16 Problems

P 1.   No check figure
P 2.   Investment in Mitgang Corporation, Ending
       Balance: $367,000
P 3.   Total Assets, Consolidated Balance Sheet:
       $3,310,000
P 4.   Total Assets, Consolidated Balance Sheet:
       $2,645,000
P 5.   No check figure
P 6.   No check figure
P 7.   Investment in Macree Company, Ending Balance:
       $320,000

Financial Accounting

1

Chapter 1 explores the nature and environment of accounting, with special emphasis on the users and uses of accounting information.

Uses of Accounting Information and the Financial Statements

LEARNING OBJECTIVES

LO1 Define *accounting,* identify business goals and activities, and describe the role of accounting in making informed decisions.

LO2 Identify the many users of accounting information in society.

LO3 Explain the importance of business transactions, money measure, and separate entity to accounting measurement.

LO4 Describe the corporate form of business organization.

LO5 Define *financial position,* state the accounting equation, and show how they are affected by simple transactions.

LO6 Identify the four financial statements.

LO7 State the relationship of generally accepted accounting principles (GAAP) to financial statements and the independent CPA's report, and identify the organizations that influence GAAP.

LO8 Define *ethics* and describe the ethical responsibilities of accountants.

Look to the learning objectives (LOs) as a guide to help you master the material. You will see many references to LOs throughout each chapter.

Look in the margin for reminders of key concepts or ideas.

KEY POINT: Management must have a good understanding of accounting to set financial goals and to make financial decisions. Management not only must understand how accounting information is compiled and processed but also must realize that accounting information is imperfect and should be interpreted with caution.

Walgreen Co. <www.walgreens.com>, a nationwide chain of more than 3,500 drugstores and pharmacies, has been a retailing success story, with 27 years of record sales and earnings. Why is Walgreens considered successful? Customers appreciate the quality of the products that the company sells and the large selection and good service that its stores offer. Investment companies and others with a financial stake in Walgreens evaluate the success of the company and its management in financial terms, such as those contained in the Financial Highlights from the company's annual report, shown on the opposite page.[1]

Net sales, net earnings, total assets, and stockholders' equity are common financial measures of all companies, large or small. These measures are used to evaluate a company's management and to compare the company to other companies. It is easy to see the large increases at Walgreens over the years in these measures, but what do the terms mean? What financial knowledge do Walgreens' managers need to measure progress toward their financial goals? What financial knowledge does anyone who is evaluating Walgreens in relation to other companies need to understand these measures?

Walgreens' managers must have a thorough knowledge of accounting to understand how the operations for which they are responsible contribute to the firm's overall financial health. People with a financial stake in the company, such as owners, investors, creditors, employees, attorneys, and governmental regulators, must also know accounting to eval-

What kind of information do the people with a financial stake in Walgreens need to have?

uate the financial performance of a business. Anyone who aspires to any of these roles in a business requires mastery of accounting terminology and concepts, the process of producing financial information, and how that information is interpreted and analyzed. The purpose of this course and this textbook is to assist you in acquiring that mastery.

Walgreens' Financial Highlights
(In millions)

	2001	2000	1999	1998	1997
Net sales	**$24,623**	$21,207	$17,839	$15,307	$13,363
Net earnings	886	777	624	511	437
Total assets	8,834	7,104	5,907	4,902	4,207
Stockholders' equity	**5,207**	4,234	3,484	2,849	2,373

ACCOUNTING AS AN INFORMATION SYSTEM

LO1 Define *accounting,* identify business goals and activities, and describe the role of accounting in making informed decisions.

RELATED TEXT ASSIGNMENTS
Q: 1, 2, 3, 4
E: 1
P: 4, 7
SD: 1, 5
FRA: 2, 4, 6, 7, 8

Each LO is stated in the margin to introduce the related text material. The list of Related Text Assignments will guide you to the appropriate questions, exercises, problems, and cases for that LO.

Today's accountant focuses on the ultimate needs of decision makers who use accounting information, whether those decision makers are inside or outside the business. **Accounting** "is not an end in itself,"[2] but *an information system that measures, processes, and communicates financial information about an identifiable economic entity.* An economic entity is a unit that exists independently—for example, a business, a hospital, or a governmental body. The central focus of this book is on business entities and business activities, although other economic units, such as hospitals and governmental units, are mentioned at appropriate points in the text and assignment material.

Accounting provides a vital service by supplying the information that decision makers need to make "reasoned choices among alternative uses of scarce resources in the conduct of business and economic activities."[3] As shown in Figure 1, accounting is a link between business activities and decision makers. First, accounting measures business activities by recording data about them for future use. Second, the data are stored until needed and then processed to become useful information. Third, the information is communicated, through reports, to decision makers. We might say that data about business activities are the input to the accounting system and that useful information for decision makers is the output.

BUSINESS GOALS, ACTIVITIES, AND PERFORMANCE MEASURES

Key terms are highlighted in blue and are followed by their definition.

A **business** is an economic unit that aims to sell goods and services to customers at prices that will provide an adequate return to its owners. The list on the opposite page contains the names of some very well-known businesses and the principal goods or services that they sell:

FIGURE 1
Accounting as an Information System

Figures illustrate relationships between concepts and/or processes.

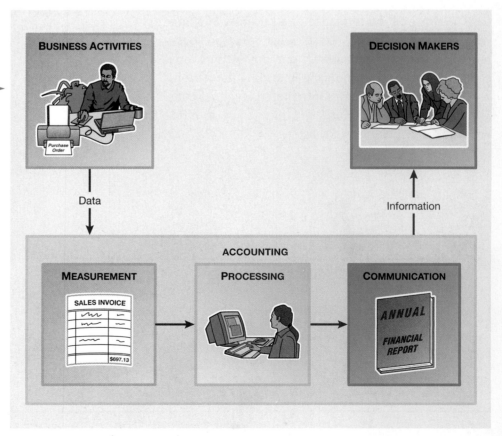

Intel Corporation   <www.intel.com>

OBJECTIVES

- To examine the principal activities of a business enterprise: financing, investing, and operating.
- To explore the principal performance goals of a business enterprise: liquidity and profitability.
- To relate these activities and goals to the financial statements.

BACKGROUND FOR THE CASE

Intel Corporation is one of the most successful companies in the world. In 1971, Intel introduced the world's first microprocessor, which made the personal computer (PC) possible. Today, Intel supplies the computing industry with chips, boards, systems, and software. Its principal products include:

- **Microprocessors.** Also called central processing units (CPUs), these are frequently described as the "brains" of a computer because they act as the central control for the processing of data in PCs. This category includes the famous Pentium® processor.

- **Networking and Communications Products.** These products enhance the capabilities and ease of use of PC systems by allowing users to talk to each other and to share information.

- **Semiconductor Products.** Semiconductors facilitate flash memory, making possible easily reprogrammable memory for computers, mobile phones, and many other products. Included in this category are embedded control chips that are programmed to regulate specific functions in such products as automobile engines, laser printers, disk drives, and home appliances.

In addition to PC users, Intel's customers include manufacturers of computers and computer systems, automobiles, and a wide range of industrial and telecommunications equipment.

For more information about Intel Corporation, visit the company's web site directly or access it through the Needles Accounting Resource Center Web Site at **http://accounting.college.hmco.com/students**.

REQUIRED

View the video on Intel Corporation that accompanies this book. As you are watching the video, take notes related to the following:

1. All businesses engage in three basic activities—financing, investing, and operating—but how they engage in them differs from company to company. Describe in your own words the nature of each of these activities and give as many examples as you can of how Intel engages in each activity.

2. To be successful, all businesses must achieve two performance objectives—liquidity and profitability. Describe in your own words the nature of each of these goals and describe how each applies to Intel.

3. Four financial statements apply to business enterprises. Which statements are most closely associated with the goal of liquidity? Which statement is most closely associated with the goal of profitability? Which statement shows the financial position of the company?

> Video cases introduce key concepts and techniques presented in the chapter in the context of a real company.

www.generalmills.com	General Mills, Inc.	Food products
www.reebok.com	Reebok International Ltd.	Athletic footwear and clothing
www.sony.com	Sony Corp.	Consumer electronics
www.wendys.com	Wendy's International Inc.	Food service
www.hilton.com	Hilton Hotels Corp.	Hotels and resorts service
www.southwest.com	Southwest Airlines Co.	Passenger airline service

Despite their differences, all these businesses have similar goals and engage in similar activities, as shown in Figure 2. Each must take in enough money from customers to pay all the costs of doing business, with enough left over as profit for the owners to want to stay in the business. This need to earn enough income to attract and hold investment capital is the goal of **profitability**. In addition, businesses must meet the goal of liquidity. **Liquidity** means having enough cash available to pay debts when they are due. For example, Toyota may meet the goal of profitability by selling many cars at a price that earns a profit, but if its customers do not pay for their cars quickly enough to enable Toyota to pay its suppliers and employees, the

> Icons are visual guides to key features of text and supporting study aids.

www.toyota.com

FIGURE 2
Business Goals and Activities

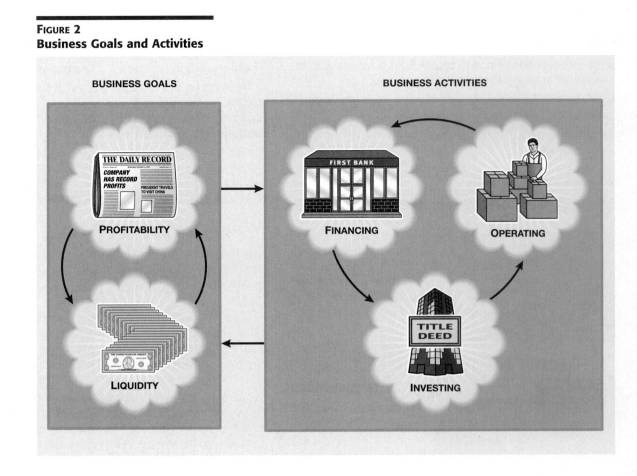

BUSINESS GOALS

PROFITABILITY

LIQUIDITY

BUSINESS ACTIVITIES

FINANCING

OPERATING

TITLE DEED

INVESTING

KEY POINT: Multiple financial goals signal that more than one measure of performance is of interest to users of accounting information. For example, lenders are concerned primarily with cash flow, and owners are concerned with earnings and dividends.

The cash flow icon highlights discussion of cash as a measure of liquidity.

The key ratio icon highlights discussion of a measure used to evaluate a company's performance.

company may fail to meet the goal of liquidity. Both goals must be met if a company is to survive and be successful.

All businesses pursue their goals by engaging in similar activities. First, each business must engage in **financing activities** to obtain adequate funds, or capital, to begin and to continue operating. Financing activities include obtaining capital from owners and from creditors, such as banks and suppliers. They also include repaying creditors and paying a return to the owners. Second, each business must engage in **investing activities** to spend the capital it receives in ways that are productive and will help the business achieve its objectives. Investing activities include buying land, buildings, equipment, and other resources that are needed in the operation of the business, and selling these resources when they are no longer needed. Third, each business must engage in **operating activities**. In addition to the selling of goods and services to customers, operating activities include such actions as employing managers and workers, buying and producing goods and services, and paying taxes to the government.

An important function of accounting is to provide **performance measures**, which indicate whether managers are achieving their business goals and whether the business activities are well managed. It is important that these performance measures align with the goals of the business. For example, earned income is a measure of profitability, and cash flow is a measure of liquidity. Ratios of accounting measures are also used as performance measures. For instance, one performance measure for operating activities might be the ratio of expenses to the revenue of the business. A performance measure for financing activities might be the ratio of money owed by the business to total resources controlled by the company. Because managers are usually evaluated on whether targeted levels of specific performance measures are achieved, they must have a knowledge of accounting to understand

FOCUS ON BUSINESS PRACTICE

How Do Performance Measures Relate to Executive Bonuses?

A study of chief executive officers' bonus contracts shows that almost all companies use financial performance measures for determining annual bonuses. The most frequent measures are earnings per share, net income, operating income, return on equity, and cash flow. About one-third of the companies studied also use nonfinancial performance measures to determine bonuses. Examples of nonfinancial measures are customer satisfaction, product or service quality, nonfinancial strategic objectives, efficiency or productivity, and employee safety.[4]

Notations like this indicate that a direct link to the company's web site is available on the Needles Accounting Resource Center Web Site at **http://accounting.college.hmco.com/students**.

www.gap.com

www.walgreens.com

Focus on Business boxes highlight the relevance of accounting in four different areas: business practice, business technology, business ethics, and international business.

how they are evaluated and how they can improve their performance. Further, because managers will act to achieve the targeted performance measures, these measures must be crafted in such a way as to motivate managers to take actions that are in the best interests of the owners of the business.

FINANCIAL AND MANAGEMENT ACCOUNTING

Accounting's role of assisting decision makers by measuring, processing, and communicating information is usually divided into the categories of management accounting and financial accounting. Although there is considerable overlap in the functions of management accounting and financial accounting, the two can be distinguished by who the principal users of their information will be. **Management accounting** provides internal decision makers who are charged with achieving the goals of profitability and liquidity with information about financing, investing, and operating activities. Managers and employees who conduct the activities of the business need information that tells them how they have done in the past and what they can expect in the future. For example, The Gap, a retail clothing business, needs an operating report on each mall outlet that tells how much was sold at that outlet and what costs were incurred, and it needs a budget for each outlet that projects the sales and costs for the next year. **Financial accounting** generates reports and communicates them to external decision makers so that they can evaluate how well the business has achieved its goals. These reports to external users are called **financial statements**. Walgreens, whose stock is traded on the New York Stock Exchange, sends its financial statements to its owners (called *stockholders*), its banks and other creditors, and government regulators. Financial statements report directly on the goals of profitability and liquidity and are used extensively both inside and outside a business to evaluate the business's success. It is important for every person involved with a business to understand financial statements. They are a central feature of accounting and are the primary focus of this book.

PROCESSING ACCOUNTING INFORMATION

To avoid misunderstandings, it is important to distinguish accounting itself from the ways in which accounting information is processed by bookkeeping, computers, and management information systems.

FOCUS ON BUSINESS PRACTICE

What Does Walgreens Have to Say about Itself?

Walgreens <www.walgreens.com> reports its performance in meeting the major business objectives in its annual report.[5]

Liquidity: "Based on the company's credit rating, . . . short-term borrowings are readily available to support . . . growth."

Profitability: "The company's profitability is the principal source for providing funds for expansion and remodeling programs, dividends to shareholders and funding for various technological improvements."

Walgreens' main business activities are shown at the right.

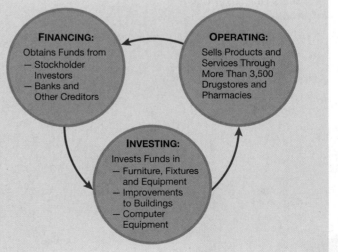

FINANCING: Obtains Funds from — Stockholder Investors — Banks and Other Creditors

OPERATING: Sells Products and Services Through More Than 3,500 Drugstores and Pharmacies

INVESTING: Invests Funds in — Furniture, Fixtures and Equipment — Improvements to Buildings — Computer Equipment

FOCUS ON BUSINESS PRACTICE

How Did Accounting Develop?

Accounting is a very old discipline. Forms of it have been essential to commerce for more than five thousand years. Accounting, in a version close to what we know today, gained widespread use in the 1400s, especially in Italy, where it was instrumental in the development of shipping, trade, construction, and other forms of commerce. This system of double-entry bookkeeping was documented by the famous Italian mathematician, scholar, and philosopher Fra Luca Pacioli. In 1494, Pacioli published his most important work, *Summa de Arithmetica, Geometrica, Proportioni et Proportionalita,* which contained a detailed description of accounting as practiced in that age. This book became the most widely read book on mathematics in Italy and firmly established Pacioli as the "Father of Accounting."

People often fail to understand the difference between accounting and bookkeeping. **Bookkeeping** is the process of recording financial transactions and keeping financial records. Mechanical and repetitive, bookkeeping is only a small—but important—part of accounting. Accounting, on the other hand, includes the design of an information system that meets the user's needs. The major goals of accounting are the analysis, interpretation, and use of information.

The **computer** is an electronic tool used to collect, organize, and communicate vast amounts of information with great speed. Accountants were among the earliest and most enthusiastic users of computers, and today they use microcomputers in all aspects of their work. It may appear that the computer is doing the accountant's job; in fact, it is only a tool that is instructed to do routine bookkeeping and to perform complex calculations.

KEY POINT: Computerized accounting information is only as reliable and useful as the data that go into the system. The accountant must have a thorough understanding of the concepts that underlie accounting to ensure the data's reliability and usefulness.

With the widespread use of the computer today, a business's many information needs are organized into what is called a **management information system (MIS)**. A management information system consists of the interconnected subsystems that provide the information needed to run a business. The accounting information system is the most important subsystem because it plays the key role of managing the flow of economic data to all parts of a business and to interested parties outside the business.

 Check out ACE for a Review Quiz at http://accounting.college.hmco.com/students

DECISION MAKERS: THE USERS OF ACCOUNTING INFORMATION

LO2   Identify the many users of accounting information in society.

RELATED TEXT ASSIGNMENTS
Q: 5, 6, 7, 8, 9
E: 1, 2
SD: 1, 2, 5

As shown in Figure 3, the people who use accounting information to make decisions fall into three categories: (1) those who manage a business; (2) those outside a business enterprise who have a direct financial interest in the business; and (3) those people, organizations, and agencies that have an indirect financial interest in the business. These categories apply to governmental and not-for-profit organizations as well as to profit-oriented ventures.

FIGURE 3
The Users of Accounting Information

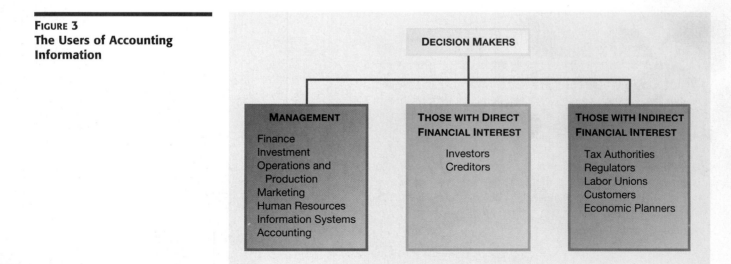

MANAGEMENT

Management refers to the people who have overall responsibility for operating a business and for meeting its profitability and liquidity goals. In a small business, management may consist solely of the owners. In a large business, management more often consists of people who have been hired to do the job. Managers must decide what to do, how to do it, and whether the results match their original plans. Successful managers consistently make the right decisions based on timely and valid information. To make good decisions, managers need answers to such questions as: What was the company's net income during the past quarter? Is the rate of return to the owners adequate? Does the company have enough cash? Which products are most profitable? What is the cost of manufacturing each product? Because so many key decisions are based on accounting data, management is one of the most important users of accounting information.

In carrying out its decision-making process, management performs a set of functions that are essential to the operation of the business. Although large businesses have more elaborate operations than small ones, the same basic functions must be accomplished in all cases, and each requires accounting information for decision making. The basic management functions are:

Financing the business. Financial management obtains financial resources so that the company can begin and continue operating.

Investing the resources of the business. Asset management invests the financial resources of the business in productive assets that support the company's goals.

Producing goods and services. Operations and production management develops and produces goods and services.

Marketing goods and services. Marketing management sells, advertises, and distributes goods and services.

Managing employees. Human resource management encompasses the hiring, evaluation, and compensation of employees.

Providing information to decision makers. Information systems management captures data about all aspects of the company's operations, organizes the data into usable information, and provides reports to internal managers and appropriate outside parties. Accounting plays a key role in this function.

USERS WITH A DIRECT FINANCIAL INTEREST

Another group of decision makers who need accounting information are those with a direct financial interest in a business. They depend on accounting to measure and report information about how a business has performed. Most businesses periodically publish a set of general-purpose financial statements that report their success in meeting the goals of profitability and liquidity. These statements show what has happened in the past, and they are important indicators of what will happen in the future. Many people outside the company carefully study these financial reports. The two most important outside groups are investors and creditors.

■ **INVESTORS** Those who invest or may invest in a business and acquire a part ownership are interested in its past success and its potential earnings. A thorough study of a company's financial statements helps potential investors judge the prospects for a profitable investment. After investing, they must continually review their commitment, again by examining the company's financial statements.

■ **CREDITORS** Most companies borrow money for both long- and short-term operating needs. Creditors, those who lend money or deliver goods and services before being paid, are interested mainly in whether a company will have the cash to pay interest charges and to repay debt at the appropriate time. They study a company's liquidity and cash flow as well as its profitability. Banks, finance companies, mortgage companies, securities firms, insurance firms, suppliers, and other lenders must analyze a company's financial position before they make a loan.

USERS WITH AN INDIRECT FINANCIAL INTEREST

In recent years, society as a whole, through governmental and public groups, has become one of the largest and most important users of accounting information. Users who need accounting information to make decisions on public issues include tax authorities, regulatory agencies, and various other groups.

■ **TAX AUTHORITIES**   Government at every level is financed through the collection of taxes. Under federal, state, and local laws, companies and individuals pay many kinds of taxes, including federal, state, and city income taxes; social security and other payroll taxes; excise taxes; and sales taxes. Each tax requires special tax returns and often a complex set of records as well. Proper reporting is generally a matter of law and can be very complicated. The Internal Revenue Code, for instance, contains thousands of rules governing the preparation of the accounting information used in computing federal income taxes.

■ **REGULATORY AGENCIES**   Most companies must report periodically to one or more regulatory agencies at the federal, state, and local levels. For example, all public corporations must report periodically to the **Securities and Exchange Commission (SEC)**. This body, set up by Congress to protect the public, regulates the issuing, buying, and selling of stocks in the United States. Companies listed on a stock exchange also must meet the special reporting requirements of their exchange.

www.sec.gov

■ **OTHER GROUPS**   Labor unions study the financial statements of corporations as part of preparing for contract negotiations; a company's income and costs often play an important role in these negotiations. Those who advise investors and creditors—financial analysts, brokers, underwriters, lawyers, economists, and the financial press—also have an indirect interest in the financial performance and prospects of a business. Consumer groups, customers, and the general public have become more concerned about the financing and earnings of corporations as well as the effects that corporations have on inflation, the environment, social problems, and the quality of life. And economic planners, among them the President's Council of Economic Advisers and the Federal Reserve Board, use aggregated accounting information to set and evaluate economic policies and programs.

GOVERNMENTAL AND NOT-FOR-PROFIT ORGANIZATIONS

● **STOP AND THINK!**

Why do managers in governmental and not-for-profit organizations need to understand financial information as much as managers in profit-seeking businesses?

Like managers of profit-seeking businesses, managers of governmental and not-for-profit organizations must report to those who fund them, and they must operate their organizations in a financially prudent way. ■

More than 30 percent of the U.S. economy is generated by governmental and not-for-profit organizations (hospitals, universities, professional organizations, and charities). The managers of these diverse entities need to understand and to use accounting information to perform the same functions as managers in businesses. They need to raise funds from investors, creditors, taxpayers, and donors, and to deploy scarce resources. They need to plan to pay for operations and to repay creditors on a timely basis. Moreover, they have an obligation to report their financial performance to legislators, boards, and donors, as well as to deal with tax authorities, regulators, and labor unions. Although most of the examples throughout this text focus on business enterprises, the same basic principles apply to governmental and not-for-profit organizations.

✔ Check out ACE for a Review Quiz at http://accounting.college.hmco.com/students.

ACCOUNTING MEASUREMENT

LO3 Explain the importance of business transactions, money measure, and separate entity to accounting measurement.

RELATED TEXT ASSIGNMENTS
Q: 10
SE: 1
E: 3, 4, 5
SD: 3

TERMINOLOGY NOTE:

Measurement means the analysis of transactions in terms of recognition, valuation, and classification. That is, it answers the question: How is this transaction best represented in the accounting records?

Terminology notes define terms used in the text.

⬡ **STOP AND THINK!**

Are all economic events business transactions?

No, because not all economic events involve exchanges of value between a business and someone else. For example, when a customer places an order, it is an economic event, but until the order is fulfilled, no exchange of value has taken place. ■

www.acehardware.com

Accounting is an information system that measures, processes, and communicates financial information. In this section, you begin the study of the measurement aspects of accounting. Here you learn what accounting actually measures and how certain transactions affect a company's financial position.

To make an accounting measurement, the accountant must answer four basic questions:

1. What is measured?
2. When should the measurement be made?
3. What value should be placed on what is measured?
4. How should what is measured be classified?

All these questions deal with basic assumptions and accepted accounting practice, and their answers establish what accounting is and what it is not. Accountants in industry, professional associations, public accounting, government, and academic circles debate the answers to these questions constantly, and the answers change as new knowledge and practice require. But the basis of today's accounting practice rests on a number of widely accepted concepts and conventions, which are described in this book. We begin by focusing on the first question: What is measured?

WHAT IS MEASURED?

The world contains an unlimited number of things to measure and ways to measure them. Consider a machine that makes bottle caps. How many measurements of this machine could you make? You might start with size and then go on to location, weight, cost, and many other units of measurement. Some of these measurements are relevant to accounting; some are not. Every system must define what it measures, and accounting is no exception. Basically, financial accounting uses money measures to gauge the impact of business transactions on separate business entities. The concepts of business transactions, money measure, and separate entity are discussed in the next sections.

BUSINESS TRANSACTIONS AS THE OBJECT OF MEASUREMENT

Business transactions are economic events that affect the financial position of a business entity. Business entities can have hundreds or even thousands of transactions every day. These business transactions are the raw material of accounting reports.

A transaction can be an exchange of value (a purchase, sale, payment, collection, or loan) between two or more independent parties. A transaction also can be an economic event that has the same effect as an exchange transaction but does not involve an exchange. Some examples of "nonexchange" transactions are losses from fire, flood, explosion, and theft; physical wear and tear on machinery and equipment; and the day-by-day accumulation of interest.

To be recorded, a transaction must relate directly to a business entity. Suppose a customer buys a shovel from Ace Hardware but has to buy a hoe from a competing store because Ace is out of hoes. The transaction in which the shovel was sold is entered in Ace's records. However, the purchase of the hoe from the competitor is not entered in Ace's records because even though it indirectly affects Ace economically, it does not involve a direct exchange of value between Ace and the customer.

MONEY MEASURE

All business transactions are recorded in terms of money. This concept is termed **money measure**. Of course, information of a nonfinancial nature may be recorded,

TABLE 1.   **Examples of Foreign Exchange Rates**

Country	Price in $ U.S.	Country	Price in $ U.S.
Britain (pound)	1.43	Hong Kong (dollar)	0.13
Canada (dollar)	0.63	Japan (yen)	0.008
Europe (euro)	0.89	Mexico (peso)	0.10

Source: The Wall Street Journal, December 3, 2001.

Tables give factual information referred to in the text.

but it is through the recording of monetary amounts that the diverse transactions and activities of a business are measured. Money is the only factor common to all business transactions, and thus it is the only practical unit of measure that can produce financial data that are alike and can be compared.

KEY POINT: The common unit of measurement in the United States for financial reporting purposes is the dollar.

The monetary unit a business uses depends on the country in which the business resides. For example, in the United States, the basic unit of money is the dollar. In Japan, it is the yen; in Europe, the euro; and in the United Kingdom, the pound. In international transactions, exchange rates must be used to translate from one currency to another. An **exchange rate** is the value of one currency in terms of another. For example, a British person purchasing goods from a U.S. company and paying in U.S. dollars must exchange British pounds for U.S. dollars before making payment. In effect, the currencies are goods that can be bought and sold. Table 1 illustrates the exchange rates for several currencies in dollars. It shows the exchange rate for British pounds as $1.43 per pound on a particular date. Like the prices of most goods, these prices change daily according to supply and demand for the currencies. For example, a few years earlier the exchange rate for British pounds was $1.65. Although our discussion in this book focuses on dollars, selected examples and certain assignments will be in foreign currencies.

THE CONCEPT OF SEPARATE ENTITY

Study notes provide useful tips on ways to avoid common pitfalls.

STUDY NOTE: For accounting purposes, a business is *always* separate and distinct from its owners, creditors, and customers. Note, however, that there is a difference between separate economic entity and separate legal entity.

For accounting purposes, a business is a **separate entity**, distinct not only from its creditors and customers but also from its owner or owners. It should have a completely separate set of records, and its financial records and reports should refer only to its own financial affairs.

For example, the Jones Florist Company should have a bank account separate from the account of Kay Jones, the owner. Kay Jones may own a home, a car, and other property, and she may have personal debts, but these are not the Jones Florist Company's resources or debts. Kay Jones also may own another business, say a stationery shop. If she does, she should have a completely separate set of records for each business.

✔ Check out ACE for a Review Quiz at http://accounting.college.hmco.com/students.

THE CORPORATION AS A SEPARATE ENTITY

LO4   Describe the corporate form of business organization.

RELATED TEXT ASSIGNMENTS
Q: 11, 12
SE: 2
E: 2, 4

There are three basic forms of business enterprise: the sole proprietorship form, the partnership form, and the corporate form. Regardless of its form, a business should be viewed for accounting purposes as a separate entity, and all its records and reports should be developed separately and kept apart from those of its owners.

CORPORATIONS DIFFERENTIATED FROM SOLE PROPRIETORSHIPS AND PARTNERSHIPS

A **sole proprietorship** is a business owned by one person. The individual receives all profits or losses and is liable for all obligations of the business. Sole proprietor-

Focus on Business Practice

Are Most Corporations Big or Small Businesses?

Most people think of corporations as large national or global companies whose shares of stock are held by thousands of people and institutions. Indeed, corporations can be huge and have many stockholders. However, of the approximately 4 million corporations in the United States, only about 15,000 have stock that is publicly bought and sold. The vast majority of corporations are small businesses privately held by a few stockholders. Illinois alone has more than 250,000 corporations. Thus, the study of corporations is just as relevant to small businesses as it is to large ones.

● **Stop and Think!**

Sole proprietorships, partnerships, and corporations differ legally; how and why does accounting treat them alike?

Accounting treats sole proprietorships, partnerships, and corporations as entities separate and apart from their owners because each form represents a business for which financial performance must be measured and reported. ■

KEY POINT: A key disadvantage of the partnership is the unlimited liability of its owners. Unlimited liability can be avoided by organizing the business as a corporation.

ships represent the largest number of businesses in the United States, but typically they are the smallest in size. A **partnership** is like a sole proprietorship in most ways, but it has two or more owners. The partners share the profits and losses of the partnership according to an agreed-upon formula. Generally, any partner can obligate the partnership to another party, and the personal resources of each partner can be called on to pay obligations of the partnership. A partnership must be dissolved if the ownership changes, as when a partner leaves or dies. If the business is to continue as a partnership after this occurs, a new partnership must be formed. Both the sole proprietorship and the partnership are convenient ways of separating the business owners' commercial activities from their personal activities. But legally there is no economic separation between the owners and the businesses. (Accounting for sole proprietorships and partnerships is discussed in an appendix to this book.)

A **corporation**, on the other hand, is a business unit chartered by the state and legally separate from its owners (the stockholders). The stockholders, whose ownership is represented by shares of stock, do not directly control the corporation's operations. Instead, they elect a board of directors to run the corporation for their benefit. In exchange for their limited involvement in the corporation's actual operations, stockholders enjoy limited liability; that is, their risk of loss is limited to the amount they paid for their shares. Thus, stockholders are often willing to invest in risky, but potentially profitable, activities. Also, because stockholders can sell their shares without dissolving the corporation, the life of a corporation is unlimited and not subject to the whims or health of a proprietor or a partner.

The characteristics of corporations make them very efficient in amassing capital, which enables them to grow extremely large. Even though corporations are fewer in number than sole proprietorships and partnerships, they contribute much more to the U.S. economy in monetary terms (see Figure 4). For example, in 1999,

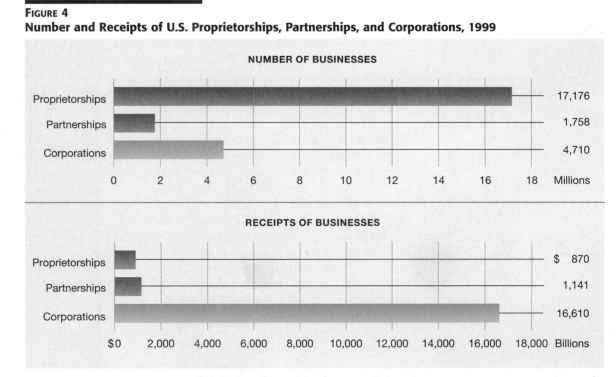

Figure 4
Number and Receipts of U.S. Proprietorships, Partnerships, and Corporations, 1999

Source: U.S. Treasury Department, Internal Revenue Service, *Statistics of Income Bulletin,* Spring 2000.

FIGURE 5
The Corporate Form of Business

www.exxonmobil.com ExxonMobil generated more revenues than all but 30 of the world's countries. Because of the economic significance of corporations, this book emphasizes accounting for the corporate form of business.

FORMATION OF A CORPORATION

To form a corporation, most states require individuals, called incorporators, to sign an application and file it with the proper state official. This application contains the **articles of incorporation**. If approved by the state, these articles, or company charter, become a contract between the state and the incorporators. The company is then authorized to do business.

ORGANIZATION OF A CORPORATION

The authority to manage the corporation is delegated by the stockholders to the board of directors and by the board of directors to the corporate officers (see Figure 5). That is, the stockholders elect the board of directors, which sets company policies and chooses the corporate officers, who in turn carry out the corporate policies by managing the business.

■ **STOCKHOLDERS**   A unit of ownership in a corporation is called a **share of stock**. The articles of incorporation state the maximum number of shares of stock that the corporation is authorized to issue. The number of shares held by stockholders is the outstanding capital stock; this may be less than the number authorized in the articles of incorporation. To invest in a corporation, a stockholder transfers cash or other resources to the corporation. In return, the stockholder receives shares of stock representing a proportionate share of ownership in the corporation. Afterward, the stockholder may transfer the shares at will. Corporations may have more than one kind of capital stock but the first part of this book will refer only to common stock—the most universal form of capital stock.

■ **BOARD OF DIRECTORS**   As noted, the stockholders elect the board of directors, which in turn decides on the major business policies of the corporation. Among the specific duties of the board are authorizing contracts, setting executive salaries, and arranging major loans with banks. The declaration of dividends is also an important function of the board of directors. Only the board has the authority to declare dividends. Dividends are distributions of resources, generally in the form of cash, to the stockholders. Paying dividends is one way of rewarding stockholders for their investment when the corporation has been successful in earning a profit. (The other way is through a rise in the market value of the stock.) Although there is usually a delay of two or three weeks between the time the board declares a dividend and the date of the actual payment, we shall assume in the early chapters of this book that declaration and payment are made on the same day.

The composition of the board of directors varies from company to company, but in most cases it includes several officers of the corporation and several outsiders. Today, the formation of an **audit committee** with several outside directors is encouraged in order to ensure that the board will be objective in evaluating management's performance. One function of the audit committee is to engage the company's independent auditors and review their work. Another is to make sure that proper systems exist to safeguard the company's resources and that reliable accounting records are kept.

■ **MANAGEMENT**   The board of directors appoints managers to carry out the corporation's policies and run day-to-day operations. The management consists of the operating officers, who are generally the president, vice presidents, controller, treasurer, and secretary. Besides being responsible for running the business, management has the duty of reporting the financial results of its administration to the board of directors and the stockholders. Though management must, at a minimum, make a comprehensive annual report, it generally reports more often. The annual reports of large public corporations are available to the public. Excerpts from many of them are used throughout this book.

 Check out ACE for a Review Quiz at http://accounting.college.hmco.com/students.

FINANCIAL POSITION AND THE ACCOUNTING EQUATION

LO5   Define *financial position,* state the accounting equation, and show how they are affected by simple transactions.

RELATED TEXT ASSIGNMENTS
Q: 13, 14, 15, 16
SE: 3, 4, 5, 6, 7, 8, 9
E: 6, 7, 8, 9, 10, 11
P: 1, 2, 3, 5, 6, 8
SD: 6
FRA: 6, 8

Financial position refers to the economic resources that belong to a company and the claims against those resources at a point in time. Another term for claims is *equities.* Therefore, a company can be viewed as economic resources and equities:

$$\text{Economic Resources} = \text{Equities } (\text{claims})$$

Every company has two types of equities, creditors' equities and owners' equity:

$$\text{Economic Resources} = \text{Creditors' Equities} + \text{Owners' Equity}$$

In accounting terminology, economic resources are called *assets* and creditors' equities are called *liabilities.* So the equation can be written like this:

$$\text{Assets} = \text{Liabilities} + \text{Owners' Equity}$$

This equation is known as the **accounting equation.** The two sides of the equation always must be equal, or "in balance." To evaluate the financial effects of business activities, it is important to understand their effects on this equation.

ASSETS

Assets are economic resources owned by a business that are expected to benefit future operations. Certain kinds of assets—for example, cash and money owed to the company by customers (called *accounts receivable*)—are monetary items. Other assets—inventories (goods held for sale), land, buildings, and equipment—are non-monetary, physical items. Still other assets—the rights granted by patents, trademarks, or copyrights—are nonphysical.

LIABILITIES

Liabilities are present obligations of a business to pay cash, transfer assets, or provide services to other entities in the future. Among these obligations are debts of the business, amounts owed to suppliers for goods or services bought on credit (called *accounts payable*), borrowed money (for example, money owed on loans payable to banks), salaries and wages owed to employees, taxes owed to the government, and services to be performed.

As debts, liabilities are claims recognized by law. That is, the law gives creditors the right to force the sale of a company's assets if the company fails to pay its debts. Creditors have rights over owners and must be paid in full before the owners receive anything, even if payment of a debt uses up all the assets of a business.

OWNERS' EQUITY

Owners' equity represents the claims by the owners of a business to the assets of the business. It equals the residual interest, or *residual equity*, in the assets of an entity that remains after deducting the entity's liabilities. Theoretically, it is what would be left over if all the liabilities were paid, and it is sometimes said to equal **net assets**. By rearranging the accounting equation, we can define owners' equity this way:

$$\text{Owners' Equity} = \text{Assets} - \text{Liabilities}$$

The owners' equity of a corporation is called **stockholders' equity**, or *shareholders' equity*. Thus the accounting equation becomes

$$\text{Assets} = \text{Liabilities} + \text{Stockholders' Equity}$$

Stockholders' equity has two parts, contributed capital and retained earnings:

$$\text{Stockholders' Equity} = \text{Contributed Capital} + \text{Retained Earnings}$$

Contributed capital is the amount that stockholders invest in the business. Their ownership in the business is represented by shares of capital stock. Figure 6 is a Toys "R" Us stock certificate, which represents such ownership.

Typically, contributed capital is divided between par value and additional paid-in capital. Par value is an amount per share that is entered in the corporation's capital stock account and is the minimum amount that can be reported as contributed capital. When the value received is greater than par value, the amount over par value is called additional paid-in capital. In the initial chapters of this book, contributed capital will be shown as common stock that has been issued at par value.

Retained earnings represent the equity of the stockholders generated from the income-producing activities of the business and kept for use in the business. As you

---

FIGURE 6
A Toys "R" Us Stock Certificate

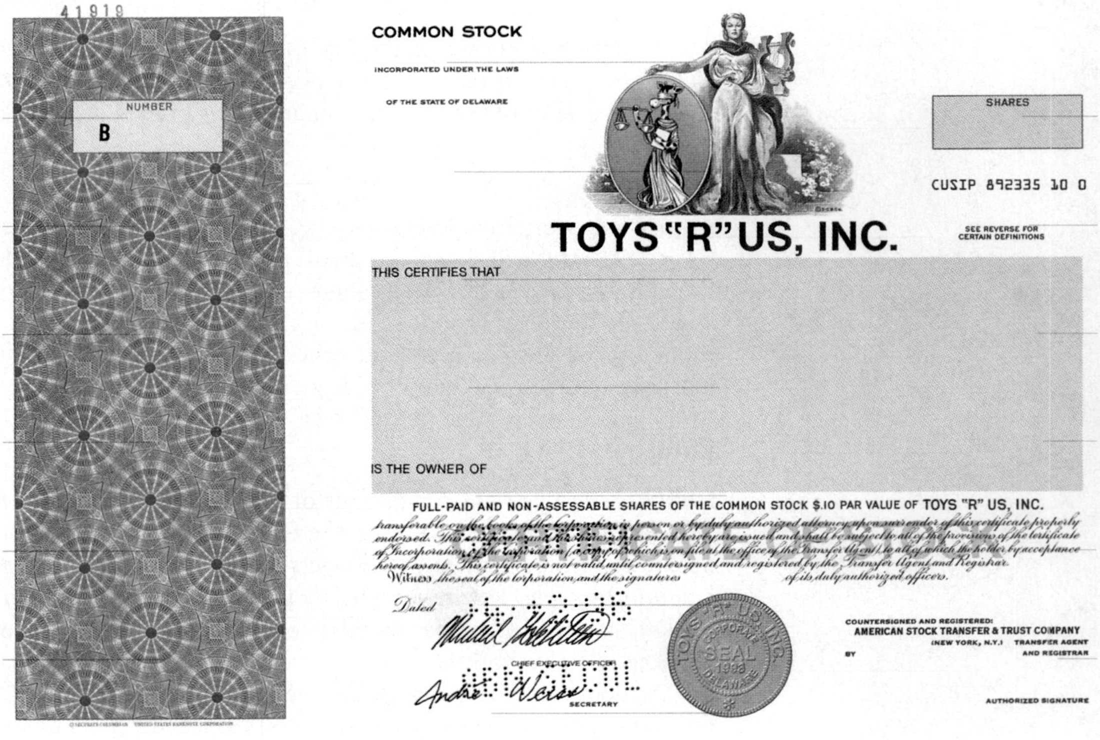

Source: Reprinted by permission of Toys "R" Us.

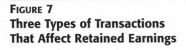

FIGURE 7
Three Types of Transactions That Affect Retained Earnings

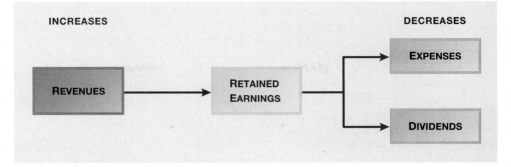

can see in Figure 7, retained earnings are affected by three kinds of transactions: revenues, expenses, and dividends.

Simply stated, **revenues** and **expenses** are the increases and decreases in stockholders' equity that result from operating a business. For example, the amount a customer pays (or agrees to pay in the future) to a company in return for a service provided by the company is a revenue to the company. The assets (cash or accounts receivable) of the company increase, and the stockholders' equity in those assets also increases. On the other hand, the amount a company pays out (or agrees to pay in the future) in the process of providing a service is an expense. In this case, the assets (cash) decrease or the liabilities (accounts payable) increase, and the stockholders' equity decreases. Generally speaking, a company is successful if its revenues exceed its expenses. When revenues exceed expenses, the difference is called **net income**; when expenses exceed revenues, the difference is called **net loss**. **Dividends** are distributions to stockholders of assets (usually cash) generated by past earnings. It is important not to confuse expenses and dividends, both of which reduce retained earnings. In summary, retained earnings is the accumulated net income (revenues − expenses) less dividends over the life of the business.

SOME ILLUSTRATIVE TRANSACTIONS

Let us now examine the effect of some of the most common business transactions on the accounting equation. Suppose that James and Jessica Shannon open a real estate agency called Shannon Realty, Inc., on December 1. During December, their business engages in the transactions described in the following paragraphs.

■ **OWNERS' INVESTMENTS**   James and Jessica Shannon file articles of incorporation with the state and receive their charter. To begin their new business, they invest $50,000 in Shannon Realty, Inc., in exchange for 5,000 shares of $10 par value stock. The first balance sheet of the new company would show the asset Cash and the contributed capital (Common Stock) of the owners:

Assets	=	Stockholders' Equity (SE)	
Cash		Common Stock	Type of SE Transaction
1. $50,000		$50,000	Stockholders' Investments

At this point, the company has no liabilities, and assets equal stockholders' equity. The labels Cash and Common Stock are called **accounts**. These are used by accountants to accumulate amounts that result from similar transactions. Transactions that affect stockholders' equity are identified by type so that similar types may later be grouped together on accounting reports.

■ **PURCHASE OF ASSETS WITH CASH**   After a good location is found, the company pays cash to purchase a lot for $10,000 and a small building on the lot for $25,000.

This transaction does not change Shannon Realty's total assets, liabilities, or stockholders' equity, but it does change the composition of the assets—it decreases Cash and increases Land and Building:

		Assets		=	Stockholders' Equity	
	Cash	Land	Building		Common Stock	Type of SE Transaction
bal.	$50,000				$50,000	
2.	−35,000	+$10,000	+$25,000			
bal.	$15,000	$10,000	$25,000		$50,000	

$50,000

KEY POINT: The purchase of an asset does not affect stockholders' equity.

■ **PURCHASE OF ASSETS BY INCURRING A LIABILITY**   Assets do not always have to be purchased with cash. They may also be purchased on credit, that is, on the basis of an agreement to pay for them later. Suppose the company buys some office supplies for $500 on credit. This transaction increases the assets (Supplies) and increases the liabilities of Shannon Realty. This liability is designated by an account called Accounts Payable:

		Assets			=	Liabilities	+	Stockholders' Equity	
	Cash	Supplies	Land	Building		Accounts Payable		Common Stock	Type of SE Transaction
bal.	$15,000		$10,000	$25,000				$50,000	
3.		+$500				+$500			
bal.	$15,000	$500	$10,000	$25,000		$500		$50,000	

$50,500 $50,500

Notice that this transaction increases both sides of the accounting equation to $50,500.

KEY POINT: Payment of a liability does not affect stockholders' equity or the asset purchased on credit.

■ **PAYMENT OF A LIABILITY**   If Shannon Realty later pays $200 of the $500 owed for the supplies, both assets (Cash) and liabilities (Accounts Payable) decrease, but Supplies is unaffected:

		Assets			=	Liabilities	+	Stockholders' Equity	
	Cash	Supplies	Land	Building		Accounts Payable		Common Stock	Type of SE Transaction
bal.	$15,000	$500	$10,000	$25,000		$500		$50,000	
4.	−200					−200			
bal.	$14,800	$500	$10,000	$25,000		$300		$50,000	

$50,300 $50,300

Notice that both sides of the accounting equation are still equal, although now at a total of $50,300.

■ **REVENUES**   Shannon Realty earns revenues in the form of commissions by selling houses for clients. Sometimes these commissions are paid to Shannon Realty immediately in the form of cash, and sometimes the client agrees to pay the commission later. In either case, the commission is recorded when it is earned and Shannon Realty has a right to a current or future receipt of cash. First, assume that Shannon Realty sells a house and receives a commission of $1,500 in cash. This transaction increases both assets (Cash) and stockholders' equity (Retained Earnings):

	Assets				=	Liabilities	+	Stockholders' Equity		
	Cash	Supplies	Land	Building		Accounts Payable		Common Stock	Retained Earnings	Type of SE Transaction
bal.	$14,800	$500	$10,000	$25,000		$300		$50,000		
5.	+1,500								+$1,500	Commissions
bal.	$16,300	$500	$10,000	$25,000		$300		$50,000	$1,500	Earned

$51,800 $51,800

KEY POINT: Revenues are recorded when they are earned, not necessarily when payments are received.

Now assume that Shannon Realty sells a house, in the process earning a commission of $2,000, and agrees to wait for payment of the commission. Because the commission has been earned now, a bill or invoice is sent to the client, and the transaction is recorded now. This revenue transaction increases both assets and stockholders' equity as before, but a new asset account, Accounts Receivable, shows that Shannon Realty is awaiting receipt of the commission:

	Assets					=	Liabilities	+	Stockholders' Equity		
	Cash	Accounts Receivable	Supplies	Land	Building		Accounts Payable		Common Stock	Retained Earnings	Type of SE Transaction
bal.	$16,300		$500	$10,000	$25,000		$300		$50,000	$1,500	
6.		+$2,000								+2,000	Commissions
bal.	$16,300	$2,000	$500	$10,000	$25,000		$300		$50,000	$3,500	Earned

$53,800 $53,800

As you progress in your study of accounting, you will be shown the use of separate accounts for revenues, like Commissions Earned.

■ **COLLECTION OF ACCOUNTS RECEIVABLE** Let us assume that a few days later Shannon Realty receives $1,000 from the client in transaction **6.** At that time, the asset Cash increases and the asset Accounts Receivable decreases:

	Assets					=	Liabilities	+	Stockholders' Equity		
	Cash	Accounts Receivable	Supplies	Land	Building		Accounts Payable		Common Stock	Retained Earnings	Type of SE Transaction
bal.	$16,300	$2,000	$500	$10,000	$25,000		$300		$50,000	$1,500	
7.	+1,000	−1,000									
bal.	$17,300	$1,000	$500	$10,000	$25,000		$300		$50,000	$3,500	

$53,800 $53,800

Notice that this transaction does not affect stockholders' equity because the commission revenue was already recorded in transaction **6.** Also, notice that the balance of Accounts Receivable is $1,000, indicating that $1,000 is still to be collected.

■ **EXPENSES** Just as revenues are recorded when they are earned, expenses are recorded when they are incurred. Expenses can be paid in cash when they occur, or they can be paid later. If payment is going to be made later, a liability—for example, Accounts Payable or Wages Payable—increases. In both cases, stockholders' equity decreases. Assume that Shannon Realty pays $1,000 to rent some equipment for the office and $400 in wages to a part-time helper. These transactions reduce assets (Cash) and stockholders' equity (Retained Earnings):

	Assets					= Liabilities +	Stockholders' Equity		
	Cash	Accounts Receiv- able	Supplies	Land	Building	Accounts Payable	Common Stock	Retained Earnings	Type of SE Transaction
bal.	$17,300	$1,000	$500	$10,000	$25,000	$300	$50,000	$3,500	
8.	−1,000							−1,000	Equipment Rental Expense
9.	−400							−400	Wages Expense
bal.	$15,900	$1,000	$500	$10,000	$25,000	$300	$50,000	$2,100	
	$52,400					$52,400			

Now assume that Shannon Realty has not paid a $300 bill for utilities expense incurred for December. In this case, the effect on stockholders' equity is the same as when the expense is paid in cash, but instead of a reduction in assets, there is an increase in liabilities (Accounts Payable):

	Assets					= Liabilities +	Stockholders' Equity		
	Cash	Accounts Receiv- able	Supplies	Land	Building	Accounts Payable	Common Stock	Retained Earnings	Type of SE Transaction
bal.	$15,900	$1,000	$500	$10,000	$25,000	$300	$50,000	$2,100	
10.						+300		−300	Utilities Expense
bal.	$15,900	$1,000	$500	$10,000	$25,000	$600	$50,000	$1,800	
	$52,400					$52,400			

As you progress in your study of accounting, you will be shown the use of separate accounts for expenses, like Equipment Rental Expense, Wages Expense, and Utilities Expense.

STUDY NOTE: Dividends do not qualify as expenses because they do not generate revenue; they are simply distributions to stockholders.

■ **DIVIDENDS** A dividend of $600 is declared, and it is paid by taking $600 out of the company's bank account and paying it to the stockholders for deposit in their personal bank accounts. The payment of dividends reduces assets (Cash) and stockholders' equity (Retained Earnings). Note that even though these dividends reduce retained earnings in the same way as the expenses in transactions 8, 9, and 10, they perform a different function. They are distributions of assets (Cash) to the stockholders, whereas the function of the expenses is to pay for services that helped produce the revenues in transactions 5 and 6.

	Assets					= Liabilities +	Stockholders' Equity		
	Cash	Accounts Receiv- able	Supplies	Land	Building	Accounts Payable	Common Stock	Retained Earnings	Type of SE Transaction
bal.	$15,900	$1,000	$500	$10,000	$25,000	$600	$50,000	$1,800	
11.	−600							−600	Dividends
bal.	$15,300	$1,000	$500	$10,000	$25,000	$600	$50,000	$1,200	
	$51,800					$51,800			

■ **SUMMARY** Exhibit 1 summarizes these 11 illustrative transactions.

✓ Check out ACE for a Review Quiz at http://accounting.college.hmco.com/students.

EXHIBIT 1

Summary of Effects of Illustrative Transactions on Financial Position

	Assets					=	Liabilities	+	Stockholders' Equity		Type of Stockholders' Equity Transaction
	Cash	Accounts Receivable	Supplies	Land	Building		Accounts Payable		Common Stock	Retained Earnings	
1.	$50,000								$50,000		Stockholders' Investments
2.	−35,000			+$10,000	+$25,000						
bal.	$15,000			$10,000	$25,000				$50,000		
3.			+$500				+$500				
bal.	$15,000		$500	$10,000	$25,000		$500		$50,000		
4.	−200						−200				
bal.	$14,800		$500	$10,000	$25,000		$300		$50,000		
5.	+1,500									+$1,500	Commissions Earned
bal.	$16,300		$500	$10,000	$25,000		$300		$50,000	$1,500	
6.		+$2,000								+2,000	Commissions Earned
bal.	$16,300	$2,000	$500	$10,000	$25,000		$300		$50,000	$3,500	
7.	+1,000	−1,000									
bal.	$17,300	$1,000	$500	$10,000	$25,000		$300		$50,000	$3,500	
8.	−1,000									−1,000	Equipment Rental Expense
9.	−400									−400	Wages Expense
bal.	$15,900	$1,000	$500	$10,000	$25,000		$300		$50,000	$2,100	
10.							+300			−300	Utilities Expense
bal.	$15,900	$1,000	$500	$10,000	$25,000		$600		$50,000	$1,800	
11.	−600									−600	Dividends
bal.	$15,300	$1,000	$500	$10,000	$25,000		$600		$50,000	$1,200	

$51,800

$51,800

Exhibits illustrate financial information.

COMMUNICATION THROUGH FINANCIAL STATEMENTS

LO6 Identify the four financial statements.

RELATED TEXT ASSIGNMENTS
Q: 17, 18, 19, 20, 21
SE: 10
E: 11, 12, 13, 14, 15
P: 4, 5, 7, 8
SD: 6
FRA: 3, 5, 7

KEY POINT: Businesses communicate financial information to decision makers in the form of four major financial statements.

Financial statements are the primary means of communicating important accounting information about a business to those who have an interest in the business. It is helpful to think of these statements as models of the business enterprise because they show the business in financial terms. As is true of all models, however, financial statements are not perfect pictures of the real thing. Rather, they are the accountant's best effort to represent what is real. Four major financial statements are used to communicate accounting information about a business: the income statement, the statement of retained earnings, the balance sheet, and the statement of cash flows.

Exhibit 2 illustrates the relationship among the four financial statements by showing how they would appear for Shannon Realty, Inc., after the eleven sample transactions shown in Exhibit 1. The time period covered is the month of December 20xx. Notice that each statement is headed in a similar way. Each heading identifies the company and the kind of statement. The income statement, the statement of retained earnings, and the statement of cash flows give the time period to which they apply; the balance sheet gives the specific date to which it applies. Much of this book deals with developing, using, and interpreting more complete versions of these basic statements.

THE INCOME STATEMENT

TERMINOLOGY NOTE:
The income statement is also called the *statement of earnings,* the *statement of operations,* or the *profit and loss statement.* Its purpose is to measure a company's performance over an accounting period.

The **income statement** summarizes the revenues earned and expenses incurred by a business over a period of time. Many people consider it the most important financial report because it shows whether or not a business achieved its profitability goal of earning an acceptable income. In Exhibit 2, Shannon Realty had revenues in the form of commissions earned of $3,500 ($2,000 of revenue earned on credit and $1,500 of cash). From this amount, total expenses of $1,700 were deducted (equipment rental expense of $1,000, wages expense of $400, and utilities expense of $300), to arrive at a net income of $1,800. To show that it applies to a period of time, the statement is dated "For the Month Ended December 31, 20xx."

THE STATEMENT OF RETAINED EARNINGS

The **statement of retained earnings** shows the changes in retained earnings over a period of time. In Exhibit 2, the beginning retained earnings is zero because the company was started in this accounting period. During the month, the company earned an income (as shown on the income statement) of $1,800. Deducted from this amount are the dividends for the month of $600, leaving an ending balance of $1,200 of earnings retained in the business.

Many companies use the **statement of stockholders' equity,** or shareholders' equity, in place of the statement of retained earnings. The statement of stockholders' equity is a more comprehensive statement that not only incorporates the components of the retained earnings statement but also includes the changes in all the stockholders' equity accounts. The statement of stockholders' equity will be explained in greater detail in a later chapter.

THE BALANCE SHEET

TERMINOLOGY NOTE:
The balance sheet is also called the *statement of financial position.* It represents two different views of a business: The left side shows the resources of the business; the right side shows who provided those resources (the creditors and the owners).

The purpose of a **balance sheet** is to show the financial position of a business on a certain date, usually the end of the month or year. For this reason, it often is called the *statement of financial position* and is dated as of a certain date. The balance sheet presents a view of the business as the holder of resources, or assets, that are equal to the claims against those assets. The claims consist of the company's liabilities and the stockholders' equity in the company. In Exhibit 2, Shannon Realty, Inc., has several categories of assets, which total $51,800. These assets equal the total liabilities of $600 (Accounts Payable) plus the ending balance of stockholders' equity of

EXHIBIT 2

Income Statement, Statement of Retained Earnings, Balance Sheet, and Statement of Cash Flows for Shannon Realty, Inc.

Shannon Realty, Inc.
Income Statement
For the Month Ended December 31, 20xx

Revenues		
Commissions earned		$3,500
Expenses		
Equipment rental expense	$1,000	
Wages expense	400	
Utilities expense	300	
Total expenses		1,700
Net income		$1,800

Shannon Realty, Inc.
Statement of Retained Earnings
For the Month Ended December 31, 20xx

Retained earnings, December 1, 20xx	$ 0
Net income for the month	1,800
Subtotal	$1,800
Less dividends	600
Retained earnings, December 31, 20xx	$1,200

Shannon Realty, Inc.
Statement of Cash Flows
For the Month Ended December 31, 20xx

Cash flows from operating activities		
Net income		$ 1,800
Adjustments to reconcile net income to net cash flows from operating activities		
Increase in accounts receivable	($ 1,000)*	
Increase in supplies	(500)	
Increase in accounts payable	600	(900)
Net cash flows from operating activities		$ 900
Cash flows from investing activities		
Purchase of land	($10,000)	
Purchase of building	(25,000)	
Net cash flows from investing activities		(35,000)
Cash flows from financing activities		
Investments by stockholders	$50,000	
Dividends	(600)	
Net cash flows from financing activities		49,400
Net increase (decrease) in cash		$15,300
Cash at beginning of month		0
Cash at end of month		$15,300

Shannon Realty, Inc.
Balance Sheet
December 31, 20xx

Assets		Liabilities	
Cash	$15,300	Accounts payable	$ 600
Accounts receivable	1,000		
Supplies	500	**Stockholders' Equity**	
Land	10,000	Common	
Building	25,000	stock $50,000	
		Retained earnings 1,200	
		Total stockholders' equity	51,200
		Total liabilities and stockholders'	
Total assets	$51,800	equity	$51,800

KEY POINT: Notice the sequence in which these financial statements must be prepared. The statement of retained earnings is a link between the income statement and the balance sheet, and the statement of cash flows is prepared last.

*Parentheses indicate a negative amount.

EXHIBIT 3
Walgreen Co.'s Income Statements

> Many excerpts from the annual reports of leading businesses illustrate key concepts.

Consolidated Statements of Earnings*
Walgreen Co. and Subsidiaries
for the Years Ended August 31, 2001, 2000 and 1999
(Dollars in Millions, except per share data)

> The word *consolidated* means all companies owned by Walgreens are combined.

> Walgreens' fiscal year ends on August 31.

	Earnings	2001	2000	1999
Net Sales	Net Sales	$24,623.0	$21,206.9	$17,838.8
Costs and Deductions	Cost of sales	18,048.9	15,465.9	12,978.6
	Selling, occupancy and administration	5,175.8	4,516.9	3,844.8
		23,224.7	19,982.8	16,823.4
Other (Income) Expense	Interest income	(5.4)	(6.1)	(12.3)
	Interest expense	3.1	.4	.4
	Other income	(22.1)	(33.5)	—
		(24.4)	(39.2)	(11.9)
Earnings	Earnings before income tax provision	1,422.7	1,263.3	1,027.3
	Income tax provision	537.1	486.4	403.2
	Net Earnings	$ 885.6	$ 776.9	$ 624.1
Net Earnings per Common Share	Basic	$ .87	$ .77	$ .62
	Diluted	$ .86	$ .76	$ .62
	Average shares outstanding	1,016,197,785	1,007,393,572	1,000,363,234
	Dilutive effect of stock options	12,748,828	12,495,236	13,918,481
	Average shares outstanding assuming dilution	1,028,946,613	1,019,888,808	1,014,281,715

> Income taxes (Income Tax Provision) are shown separately.

> Net earnings figure moves to statements of stockholders' equity.

Source: Walgreen Co., *Annual Report,* 2001 (year ended August 31, 2001).

*Note that in Walgreen Co.'s actual annual report, the consolidated statements of earnings are combined with the consolidated statements of shareholders' equity.

$51,200. Notice that the Retained Earnings account on the balance sheet comes from the ending balance on the statement of retained earnings.

THE STATEMENT OF CASH FLOWS

Whereas the income statement focuses on a company's profitability goal, the **statement of cash flows** is directed toward the company's liquidity goal. **Cash flows** are the inflows and outflows of cash into and out of a business. Net cash flows are the difference between the inflows and outflows. The statement of cash flows shows the cash produced by operating a business as well as important investing and financing transactions that take place during an accounting period. Notice in Exhibit 2 that the statement of cash flows for Shannon Realty explains how the Cash account changed during the period. Cash increased by $15,300. Operating activities pro-

EXHIBIT 4
Walgreen Co.'s Statements of Stockholders' Equity

Consolidated Statements of Shareholders' Equity*
Walgreen Co. and Subsidiaries
for the Years Ended August 31, 2001, 2000 and 1999
(Dollars in Millions, except per share data)

> Each stockholders' equity account has a column that explains the change from year to year.

> Net earnings (loss) from Income Statement

Shareholders' Equity	Common Stock Shares	Amount	Paid-in Capital	Retained Earnings
Balance, August 31, 1998	996,487,044	$77.8	$118.1	$2,653.0
Net earnings	—	—	—	624.1
Cash dividends declared ($.13 per share)	—	—	—	(130.1)
Employee stock purchase and option plans	7,535,214	.6	140.8	—
Balance, August 31, 1999	1,004,022,258	78.4	258.9	3,147.0
Net earnings	—	—	—	776.9
Cash dividends declared ($.135 per share)	—	—	—	(136.1)
Employee stock purchase and option plans	6,796,632	.6	108.3	—
Balance, August 31, 2000	1,010,818,890	79.0	367.2	3,787.8
Net earnings	—	—	—	885.6
Cash dividends declared ($.14 per share)	—	—	—	(142.5)
Employee stock purchase and option plans	8,606,162	.6	229.5	—
Balance, August 31, 2001	**1,019,425,052**	**$79.6**	**$596.7**	**$4,530.9**

Source: Walgreen Co., *Annual Report,* 2001 (year ended August 31, 2001).

The accompanying Statement of Major Accounting Policies and the Notes to Consolidated Financial Statements are integral parts of these statements.
*Note that in Walgreen Co.'s actual annual report, the consolidated statements of earnings are combined with the consolidated statements of shareholders' equity.

KEY POINT: The purpose of the statement of cash flows is to explain the change in cash in terms of operating, investing, and financing activities over an accounting period. It provides valuable information that cannot be determined in an examination of the other three financial statements.

www.walgreens.com

duced net cash flows of $900, and financing activities produced net cash flows of $49,400. Investing activities used cash flows of $35,000.

This statement is related directly to the other three statements. Notice that net income comes from the income statement and that dividends come from the statement of retained earnings. The other items in the statement represent changes in the balance sheet accounts: Accounts Receivable, Supplies, Accounts Payable, Land, Building, and Common Stock. Here we focus on the importance and overall structure of the statement. Its construction and use are discussed in a later chapter.

FINANCIAL STATEMENTS OF WALGREEN CO.

The financial statements of Shannon Realty, Inc., are relatively simple and easy to understand. While significantly more complex, the financial statements of a large corporation like Walgreen Co. are based on the same concepts and structure. The financial statements for Walgreens are shown in Exhibits 3 through 6. Although you will not yet understand some of the terms in these statements, you can comprehend the structure and interrelationships of the statements.

These statements present data for either two or three years. They are called *comparative financial statements* because they enable the reader to compare

EXHIBIT 5
Walgreen Co.'s Balance Sheets

Consolidated Balance Sheets
Walgreen Co. and Subsidiaries
at August 31, 2001 and 2000
(Dollars in Millions)

Assets		2001	2000
Current Assets	Cash and cash equivalents	$ 16.9	$ 12.8
	Accounts receivable, net	798.3	614.5
	Inventories	3,482.4	2,830.8
	Other current assets	96.3	92.0
	Total Current Assets	4,393.9	3,550.1
Non-Current Assets	Property and equipment, at cost, less accumulated depreciation and amortization	4,345.3	3,428.2
	Other non-current assets	94.6	125.4
	Total Assets	$8,833.8	$7,103.7

Liabilities and Shareholders' Equity

		2001	2000
Current Liabilities	Short-term borrowings	$ 440.7	$ —
	Trade accounts payable	1,546.8	1,364.0
	Accrued expenses and other liabilities	937.5	847.7
	Income taxes	86.6	92.0
	Total Current Liabilities	3,011.6	2,303.7
Non-Current Liabilities	Deferred income taxes	137.0	101.6
	Other non-current liabilities	478.0	464.4
	Total Non-Current Liabilities	615.0	566.0
Shareholders' Equity	Preferred stock, $.0625 par value; authorized 32 million shares; none issued	—	—
	Common stock, $.078125 par value; authorized 3.2 billion shares; issued and outstanding 1,019,425,052 in 2001 and 1,010,818,890 in 2000	79.6	79.0
	Paid-in capital	596.7	367.2
	Retained earnings	4,530.9	3,787.8
	Total Shareholders' Equity	5,207.2	4,234.0
	Total Liabilities and Shareholders' Equity	$8,833.8	$7,103.7

Walgreens categorizes certain assets as current assets.

Walgreens categorizes certain liabilities as current liabilities.

Balances from the statements of stockholders' equity.

Source: Walgreen Co., *Annual Report,* 2001 (year ended August 31, 2001).

The accompanying Statement of Major Accounting Policies and the Notes to Consolidated Financial Statements are integral parts of these statements.

◆ **STOP AND THINK!**
How are Walgreens and Toys "R" Us comparable?

Although their merchandise differs, their operations are similar. They sell closely related products efficiently at reasonable prices in large buildings in many different locations. Thus, from an operating standpoint, they are very comparable. ■

Walgreens' performance from year to year. Also note that the year-end date of Walgreens' business, or the fiscal year, in these financial statements is August 31. A company usually may end its business year on any day it likes as long as it is consistent from year to year. Finally, note that the data are given in millions, so that net revenues for 2001, shown as $24,623.0, are actually $24,623,000,000. For purposes of readability and for showing meaningful relationships, it is not necessary for Walgreens to show the last five digits of the numbers.

The income statements for Walgreens, which are shown in Exhibit 3, are called *consolidated statements of earnings.* "Earnings before income tax provision" is computed before deducting "income tax provision" to arrive at "net earnings" (rather

EXHIBIT 6
Walgreen Co.'s Statements of Cash Flows

Consolidated Statements of Cash Flows
Walgreen Co. and Subsidiaries
for the Years Ended August 31, 2001, 2000 and 1999
(In Millions)

Fiscal Year		2001	2000	1999
Cash Flows from Operating Activities	Net earnings	$ 885.6	$ 776.9	$ 624.1
	Adjustments to reconcile net earnings to net cash provided by operating activities—			
	Depreciation and amortization	269.2	230.1	210.1
	Deferred income taxes	46.9	21.0	(9.4)
	Income tax savings from employee stock plans	67.3	38.5	26.8
	Other	2.1	13.6	12.2
	Changes in operating assets and liabilities—			
	Inventories	(651.6)	(368.2)	(435.7)
	Trade accounts payable	182.8	233.7	223.4
	Accounts receivable, net	(177.3)	(135.4)	(106.0)
	Accrued expenses and other liabilities	82.2	101.2	103.7
	Income taxes	(5.4)	28.6	8.6
	Other	17.4	31.7	(5.8)
	Net cash provided by operating activities	719.2	971.7	652.0
Cash Flows from Investing Activities	Additions to property and equipment	(1,237.0)	(1,119.1)	(696.3)
	Disposition of property and equipment	43.5	22.9	41.7
	Net proceeds from corporate-owned life insurance	59.0	58.8	9.1
	Net cash used for investing activities	(1,134.5)	(1,037.4)	(645.5)
Cash Flows from Financing Activities	Proceeds from short-term borrowings	440.7	—	—
	Cash dividends paid	(140.9)	(134.6)	(128.6)
	Proceeds from employee stock plans	126.1	79.2	105.0
	Other	(6.5)	(7.9)	14.5
	Net cash provided by (used for) financing activities	419.4	(63.3)	(9.1)
Changes in Cash and Cash Equivalents	Net increase (decrease) in cash and cash equivalents	4.1	(129.0)	(2.6)
	Cash and cash equivalents at beginning of year	12.8	141.8	144.4
	Cash and cash equivalents at end of year	$ 16.9	$ 12.8	$ 141.8

Cash flows are shown for operating activities, investing activities, and financing activities.

Cash and cash equivalents to Balance Sheets

Source: Walgreen Co., *Annual Report,* 2001 (year ended August 31, 2001).
The accompanying Statement of Major Accounting Policies and the Notes to Consolidated Financial Statements are integral parts of these statements.

than arriving at net income in one step, as was done in Shannon Realty's income statement). Because the company is a corporation, a provision is made for income taxes that Walgreens must pay. The statements show net earnings per common share, the net earnings divided by the weighted-average shares outstanding.

The consolidated statements of stockholders' equity for Walgreens in Exhibit 4 differ from Shannon Realty's statement of retained earnings in that they explain the changes in all the stockholders' equity accounts, including retained earnings.

In Exhibit 5, the ending balances of stockholders' equity accounts, including retained earnings, carry over to the stockholders' equity section of Walgreen Co.'s balance sheets. Walgreens' balance sheets present two years of data and are structured similarly to Shannon Realty's balance sheet. The only difference is that some assets are categorized as current assets and some liabilities as current liabilities. Generally speaking, current assets are assets that will be realized as cash or used up in the next year, as opposed to property, plant, and equipment and other assets, which will benefit the company for a longer time. Similarly, current liabilities are obligations that generally must be fulfilled within the next year, whereas noncurrent liabilities represent obligations to be paid more than one year from the balance sheet date. Walgreens has deferred income taxes and other noncurrent liabilities that the company will have to pay in future years, which is explained in the notes to the financial statements. From Walgreens' balance sheet, the equality of the accounting equation may be proven:

$$\text{Assets} \quad = \quad \text{Liabilities} \quad + \text{Stockholders' Equity}$$
$$\$8{,}833{,}800{,}000 = \$3{,}626{,}600{,}000 + \quad \$5{,}207{,}200{,}000$$

Finally, Walgreens' cash flow statements, shown in Exhibit 6, like those of Shannon Realty, Inc., show the changes in cash. These statements are very similar to those of Shannon Realty except that here "cash" is called "cash and cash equivalents," which means that it includes certain accounts or securities that are very similar to cash. The totals of cash and cash equivalents carry over to the balance sheet.

✔ Check out ACE for a Review Quiz at http://accounting.college.hmco.com/students

GENERALLY ACCEPTED ACCOUNTING PRINCIPLES

LO7 State the relationship of generally accepted accounting principles (GAAP) to financial statements and the independent CPA's report, and identify the organizations that influence GAAP.

RELATED TEXT ASSIGNMENTS
Q: 22, 23, 24
E: 1, 16
SD: 2
FRA: 1, 6

⬡ **STOP AND THINK!**
How do generally accepted accounting principles (GAAP) differ from the laws of science?
GAAP differ from the laws of science in that they are not unchanging but rather are constantly evolving. They may change as business conditions change or as improved methods are introduced. ∎

To ensure that financial statements will be understandable to their users, a set of practices, called **generally accepted accounting principles (GAAP)**, has been developed to provide guidelines for financial accounting. Although the term has several meanings in the literature of accounting, perhaps this is the best definition: "Generally accepted accounting principles encompass the conventions, rules, and procedures necessary to define accepted accounting practice at a particular time."[7] In other words, GAAP arise from wide agreement on the theory and practice of accounting at a particular time. These "principles" are not like the unchangeable laws of nature found in chemistry or physics. They are developed by accountants and businesses to serve the needs of decision makers, and they can alter as better methods evolve or as circumstances change.

In this book, we present accounting practice, or GAAP, as it is today. We also try to explain the reasons or theory on which the practice is based. Both theory and practice are important to the study of accounting. However, you should realize that accounting is a discipline that is always growing, changing, and improving. Just as years of research are necessary before a new surgical method or lifesaving drug can be introduced, it may take years for new accounting discoveries to be implemented. As a result, you may encounter practices that seem contradictory. In some cases, we point out new directions in accounting. Your instructor also may mention certain weaknesses in current theory or practice.

FINANCIAL STATEMENTS, GAAP, AND THE INDEPENDENT CPA'S REPORT

Because financial statements are prepared by the management of a company and could be falsified for personal gain, all companies that sell ownership to the public and many companies that apply for sizable loans have their financial statements audited by an independent certified public accountant. **Certified public accountants (CPAs)** are licensed by all states for the same reason that lawyers and doctors are—to protect the public by ensuring the quality of professional service. One

TABLE 2. Large International Certified Public Accounting Firms

Firm	Home Office	Some Major Clients
Deloitte & Touche	New York	General Motors, Procter & Gamble, Sears
Ernst & Young	New York	Coca-Cola, McDonald's
KPMG	New York	General Electric, Xerox
PricewaterhouseCoopers	New York	Du Pont, ExxonMobil, IBM, Ford

KEY POINT: The purpose of an audit is to lend credibility to a set of financial statements. The auditor does *not* attest to the absolute accuracy of the published information or to the value of the company as an investment. All he or she renders is an opinion, based on appropriate testing, about the fairness of the presentation of the financial information.

ETHICAL CONSIDERATION: To lend credibility to the work of the independent auditor, the profession has developed the AICPA Code of Professional Ethics, a set of guidelines that dictate appropriate professional behavior. The current guidelines were adopted in 1988 and are based on earlier standards. LO 8 covers the topic of ethics in detail.

KEY POINT: The FASB is the primary source of GAAP.

KEY POINT: The AICPA is considered the primary organization of certified public accountants.

important attribute of CPAs is independence: They have no financial or other compromising ties with the companies they audit. This gives the public confidence in their work. The firms listed in Table 2 employ about 25 percent of all CPAs.

An independent CPA performs an **audit**, which is an examination of a company's financial statements and the accounting systems, controls, and records that produced them. The purpose of the audit is to ascertain that the financial statements have been prepared in accordance with generally accepted accounting principles. If the independent accountant is satisfied that this standard has been met, his or her report contains the following language:

In our opinion, the financial statements . . . present fairly, in all material respects . . . in conformity with generally accepted accounting principles.

This wording emphasizes the fact that accounting and auditing are not exact sciences. Because the framework of GAAP provides room for interpretation and the application of GAAP necessitates the making of estimates, the auditor can render an opinion or judgment only that the financial statements *present fairly* or conform *in all material respects* to GAAP. The accountant's report does not preclude minor or immaterial errors in the financial statements. However, it does imply that on the whole, investors and creditors can rely on those statements. Historically, auditors have enjoyed a strong reputation for competence and independence. As a result, banks, investors, and creditors are willing to rely on an auditor's opinion when deciding to invest in a company or to make loans to a company. The independent audit is an important factor in the worldwide growth of financial markets.

ORGANIZATIONS THAT INFLUENCE CURRENT PRACTICE

Many organizations directly or indirectly influence GAAP and so influence much of what is in this book. The **Financial Accounting Standards Board (FASB)** is the most important body for developing and issuing rules on accounting practice. This independent body issues *Statements of Financial Accounting Standards*. The **American Institute of Certified Public Accountants (AICPA)** is the professional association of certified public accountants and influences accounting practice through the activities of its senior technical committees. The Securities and Exchange Commission (SEC) is an agency of the federal government that has the legal power to set and enforce accounting practices for companies whose securities are offered for sale to the general public. As such, it has enormous influence on accounting practice. The **Governmental Accounting Standards Board (GASB)**, which was established in 1984 under the same governing body as the Financial Accounting Standards Board, is responsible for issuing accounting standards for state and local governments.

With the growth of financial markets throughout the world, worldwide cooperation in the development of accounting principles has become a priority. The **International Accounting Standards Board (IASB)** has approved more than 30 international standards.

U.S. tax laws that govern the assessment and collection of revenue for operating the federal government also influence accounting practice. Because a major source of the government's revenue is the income tax, the tax laws specify the rules for determining taxable income. These rules are interpreted and enforced by the **Internal Revenue Service (IRS)**. In some cases, the rules conflict with good accounting practice, but they still are an important influence on that practice. Businesses use certain accounting practices simply because they are required by the tax laws. Sometimes companies follow an accounting practice specified in the tax laws to take advantage of rules that can help them financially. Cases in which the tax laws affect accounting practice are noted throughout this book.

Check out ACE for a Review Quiz at http://accounting.college.hmco.com/students.

PROFESSIONAL ETHICS AND THE ACCOUNTING PROFESSION

LO8   Define *ethics* and describe the ethical responsibilities of accountants.

RELATED TEXT ASSIGNMENTS
Q: 25
SD: 4

Ethical issues are discussed in each chapter; they relate to real business situations that require ethical judgments.

◆ **STOP AND THINK!**
What are some unethical ways in which a business may do its accounting or prepare its financial statements?

Unethical ways of accounting include recording business transactions that did not occur or being dishonest in recording those that did occur. Financial statements are unethically prepared when they misrepresent a company's financial situation or contain false information. ■

Ethics is a code of conduct that applies to everyday life. It addresses the question of whether actions are right or wrong. Ethical actions are the product of individual decisions. You are faced with many situations involving ethical issues every day. Some may be potentially illegal—the temptation to take office supplies from your employer to use when you do homework, for example. Others are not illegal but are equally unethical—for example, deciding not to tell a fellow student who missed class that a test has been announced for the next class meeting. When an organization is said to act ethically or unethically, it means that individuals within the organization have made a decision to act ethically or unethically. When a company uses false advertising, cheats customers, pollutes the environment, treats employees poorly, or misleads investors by presenting false financial statements, members of management and other employees have made a conscious decision to act unethically. In the same way, ethical behavior within a company is a direct result of the actions and decisions of the company's employees.

Professional ethics is a code of conduct that applies to the practice of a profession. Like the ethical conduct of a company, the ethical actions of a profession are a collection of individual actions. As members of a profession, accountants have a responsibility, not only to their employers and clients but to society as a whole, to uphold the highest ethical standards. Historically, accountants have been held in high regard. For example, a survey of over one thousand prominent people in business, education, and government ranked the accounting profession second only to the clergy as having the highest ethical standards.[8] It is the responsibility of every person who becomes an accountant to uphold the high standards of the profession.

To ensure that its members understand the responsibilities of being professional accountants, the AICPA and each state have adopted codes of professional conduct that certified public accountants must follow. Fundamental to these codes is responsibility to the public, including clients, creditors, investors, and anyone else who relies on the work of the certified public accountant. In resolving conflicts among these groups, the accountant must act with integrity. **Integrity** means that the accountant is honest and candid and subordinates personal gain to service and the public trust. The accountant must also be objective. **Objectivity** means that he or she is impartial and intellectually honest. Furthermore, the accountant must be independent. **Independence** means avoiding all relationships that impair or even appear to impair the accountant's objectivity.

One way in which the auditor of a company maintains independence is by having no direct financial interest in the company and by not being an employee of the company. The accountant must exer-

FOCUS ON BUSINESS ETHICS

Good Ethics = Good Business!

Ethics is good business. Many companies, especially those that engage in international trade, adopt codes of ethics. Management sees such self-regulation as a way of avoiding fraud and litigation. A recent survey of 124 companies in 22 countries found that 78 percent of boards of directors had established ethics standards, a fourfold increase over a ten-year period. The study also found that codes of ethics help promote tolerance of diverse practices abroad. In addition, research has shown that over time, companies with codes of ethics tend to do much better in the stock market than those that have not adopted such codes.[9] The recent Enron bankruptcy is an example of the tragic results that can occur when a company's ethical system breaks down.

cise **due care** in all activities, carrying out professional responsibilities with competence and diligence. For example, an accountant must not accept a job for which he or she is not qualified, even at the risk of losing a client to another firm, and careless work is not acceptable. These broad principles are supported by more specific rules that public accountants must follow. (For instance, with certain exceptions, client information must be kept strictly confidential.) Accountants who violate the rules can be disciplined or even suspended from practice.

A professional association, the **Institute of Management Accountants (IMA)**, has adopted the Code of Professional Conduct for Management Accountants. This ethical code emphasizes that management accountants have a responsibility to be competent in their jobs, to keep information confidential except when authorized or legally required to disclose it, to maintain integrity and avoid conflicts of interest, and to communicate information objectively and without bias.[10]

✓ Check out ACE for Review Quiz at http://accounting.college.hmco.com/students.

Chapter Review ←

The Chapter Review restates each learning objective and its main ideas.

REVIEW OF LEARNING OBJECTIVES

LO1 Define *accounting,* identify business goals and activities, and describe the role of accounting in making informed decisions.

Accounting is an information system that measures, processes, and communicates financial information about an identifiable entity for the purpose of making economic decisions. An important type of entity is the business which engages in operating, investing, and financing activities for the purpose of achieving the goals of profitability and liquidity. Management accounting focuses on the preparation of information primarily for internal use by management. Financial accounting is concerned with the development and use of accounting reports that are communicated to those outside the business as well as to management. Accounting is a tool that provides the information necessary to make reasoned choices among alternative uses of scarce resources in the conduct of business and economic activities.

LO2 Identify the many users of accounting information in society.

Accounting plays a significant role in society by providing information to managers of all institutions and to individuals with a direct financial interest in those institutions, including present or potential investors or creditors. Accounting information is also important to those with an indirect financial interest in the business—for example, tax authorities, regulatory agencies, and economic planners.

LO3 Explain the importance of business transactions, money measure, and separate entity to accounting measurement.

To make an accounting measurement, the accountant must determine what is measured, when the measurement should be made, what value should be placed on what is measured, and how what is measured should be classified. The objects of accounting measurement are business transactions that are measured in terms of money and are for separate entities. Relating these concepts, financial accounting uses money measure to gauge the impact of business transactions on a separate business entity.

LO4 Describe the corporate form of business organization.

Corporations, whose ownership is represented by shares of stock, are separate entities for both legal and accounting purposes. The stockholders own the corporation and elect the board of directors, whose duty it is to determine corporate policy. The corporate officers or management of the corporation are appointed by the board of directors and are responsible for the operation of the business in accordance with the board's policies.

LO5 Define *financial position,* state the accounting equation, and show how they are affected by simple transactions.

Financial position refers to the economic resources that belong to a company and the claims against those resources at a point in time. The accounting equation shows financial position as Assets = Liabilities + Owners' Equity. For a corporation, the accounting equation is Assets = Liabilities + Stockholders' Equity. Business transactions affect financial position by decreasing or increasing assets, liabilities, or stockholders' equity in such a way that the accounting equation is always in balance.

LO6 Identify the four financial statements.

The four financial statements are the income statement, the statement of retained earnings, the balance sheet, and the statement of cash flows. They are the means by which accountants communicate the financial condition and activities of a business to those who have an interest in the business.

LO7 State the relationship of generally accepted accounting principles (GAAP) to financial statements and the independent CPA's report, and identify the organizations that influence GAAP.

Acceptable accounting practice consists of the conventions, rules, and procedures that make up generally accepted accounting principles at a particular time. GAAP are essential to the preparation and interpretation of financial statements and the independent CPA's report. Among the organizations that influence the formulation of GAAP are the Financial Accounting Standards Board, the American Institute of Certified Public Accountants, the Securities and Exchange Commission, and the Internal Revenue Service.

LO8 Define *ethics* and describe the ethical responsibilities of accountants.

All accountants are required to follow a code of professional ethics, the foundation of which is responsibility to the public. Accountants must act with integrity, objectivity, and independence, and they must exercise due care in all their activities.

Want more review? The student *Study Guide* provides a thorough review of each learning objective, a detailed outline, true/false and multiple-choice questions, and exercises. Answers are included. Ask for it at your bookstore.

REVIEW OF CONCEPTS AND TERMINOLOGY

Each chapter has a glossary of the key concepts and terms defined in the chapter. The LO next to each term indicates the section in which it is discussed.

The following concepts and terms were introduced in this chapter:

LO1 **Accounting:** An information system that measures, processes, and communicates financial information about an identifiable economic entity.

LO5 **Accounting equation:** Assets = Liabilities + Owners' Equity or, for corporations, Assets = Liabilities + Stockholders' Equity.

LO5 **Accounts:** The labels used by accountants to accumulate the amounts produced from similar transactions.

LO7 **American Institute of Certified Public Accuntants (AICPA):** The professional association of certified public accountants.

LO4 **Articles of incorporation:** An official document filed with and approved by a state that authorizes the incorporators to do business as a corporation.

LO5 **Assets:** Economic resources owned by a business that are expected to benefit future operations.

LO7 **Audit:** An examination of a company's financial statements in order to render an independent professional opinion that they have been presented fairly, in all material respects, in conformity with generally accepted accounting principles.

LO4 **Audit committee:** A subgroup of the board of directors of a corporation that is charged with ensuring that the board will be objective in reviewing management's performance; it engages the company's independent auditors and reviews their work.

LO6 **Balance sheet:** The financial statement that shows the assets, liabilities, and stockholders' equity of a business at a point in time. Also called a *statement of financial position*.

LO1 **Bookkeeping:** The process of recording financial transactions and keeping financial records.

LO1 **Business:** An economic unit that aims to sell goods and services to customers at prices that will provide an adequate return to its owners.

LO3 **Business transactions:** Economic events that affect the financial position of a business entity.

LO6 **Cash flows:** The inflows and outflows of cash into and out of a business.

LO7 **Certified public accountants (CPAs):** Public accountants who have met the stringent state licensing requirements.

LO1   **Computer:** An electronic tool for the rapid collection, organization, and communication of large amounts of information.

LO5   **Contributed capital:** The part of stockholders' equity that represents the amount invested in the business by the owners (stockholders).

LO4   **Corporation:** A business unit granted a state charter recognizing it as a separate legal entity having its own rights, privileges, and liabilities distinct from those of its owners.

LO5   **Dividends:** Distributions to stockholders of assets (usually cash) generated by past earnings.

LO8   **Due care:** Competence and diligence in carrying out professional responsibilities.

LO8   **Ethics:** A code of conduct that addresses whether everyday actions are right or wrong.

LO3   **Exchange rate:** The value of one currency in terms of another.

LO5   **Expenses:** Decreases in stockholders' equity that result from operating a business.

LO1   **Financial accounting:** The process of generating and communicating accounting information in the form of financial statements to those outside the organization.

LO7   **Financial Accounting Standards Board (FASB):** The most important body for developing and issuing rules on accounting practice, called *Statements of Financial Accounting Standards.*

LO5   **Financial position:** The economic resources that belong to a company and the claims (equities) against those resources at a point in time.

LO1   **Financial statements:** The primary means of communicating important accounting information to users. They include the income statement, statement of retained earnings, balance sheet, and statement of cash flows.

LO1   **Financing activities:** Activities undertaken by management to obtain adequate funds to begin and to continue operating a business.

LO7   **Generally accepted accounting principles (GAAP):** The conventions, rules, and procedures that define accepted accounting practice at a particular time.

LO7   **Governmental Accounting Standards Board (GASB):** The board responsible for issuing accounting standards for state and local governments.

LO6   **Income statement:** The financial statement that summarizes the revenues earned and expenses incurred by a business over a period of time.

LO8   **Independence:** The avoidance of all relationships that impair or appear to impair an accountant's objectivity.

LO8   **Institute of Management Accountants (IMA):** A professional organization made up primarily of management accountants.

LO8   **Integrity:** Honesty, candidness, and the subordination of personal gain to service and the public trust.

LO7   **Internal Revenue Service (IRS):** The federal agency that interprets and enforces the tax laws governing the assessment and collection of revenue for operating the national government.

LO7   **International Accounting Standards Board (IASB):** The organization that encourages worldwide cooperation in the development of accounting principles; it has approved more than 30 international standards of accounting.

LO1   **Investing activities:** Activities undertaken by management to spend capital in ways that are productive and will help a business achieve its objectives.

LO5   **Liabilities:** Present obligations of a business to pay cash, transfer assets, or provide services to other entities in the future.

LO1   **Liquidity:** Having enough cash available to pay debts when they are due.

LO2   **Management:** The people who have overall responsibility for operating a business and meeting its goals.

LO1   **Management accounting:** The process of producing accounting information for the internal use of a company's management.

LO1   **Management information system (MIS):** The interconnected subsystems that provide the information needed to run a business.

LO3   **Money measure:** The recording of all business transactions in terms of money.

LO5   **Net assets:** Assets minus liabilities; owners' equity or stockholders' equity.

LO5   **Net income:** The difference between revenues and expenses when revenues exceed expenses.

LO5   **Net loss:** The difference between expenses and revenues when expenses exceed revenues.

LO8   **Objectivity:** Impartiality and intellectual honesty.

LO1   **Operating activities:** Activities undertaken by management in the course of running the business.

LO5   **Owners' equity:** The residual interest in the assets of a business entity that remains after deducting the entity's liabilities. Also called *residual equity* or, for corporations, *stockholders' equity*.

LO4   **Partnership:** A business that is owned by two or more people and is not incorporated.

LO1   **Performance measures:** Indicators of whether managers are achieving business goals and whether the business activities are well managed.

LO8   **Professional ethics:** A code of conduct that applies to the practice of a profession.

LO1   **Profitability:** The ability to earn enough income to attract and hold investment capital.

LO5   **Retained earnings:** The equity of the stockholders generated from the income-producing activities of the business and kept for use in the business.

LO5   **Revenues:** Increases in stockholders' equity that result from operating a business.

LO2   **Securities and Exchange Commission (SEC):** An agency of the U.S. government set up by Congress to protect the public by regulating the issuing, buying, and selling of stocks. It has the legal power to set and enforce accounting practices for firms whose securities are sold to the general public.

LO3   **Separate entity:** A business that is treated as distinct from its creditors, customers, and owners.

LO4   **Share of stock:** A unit of ownership in a corporation.

LO4   **Sole proprietorship:** A business that is owned by one person and is not incorporated.

LO6   **Statement of cash flows:** The financial statement that shows the inflows and outflows of cash from operating activities, investing activities, and financing activities over a period of time.

LO6   **Statement of retained earnings:** The financial statement that shows the changes in retained earnings over a period of time.

LO6   **Statement of stockholders' equity:** A financial statement that summarizes changes in the components of stockholders' equity. Also called *statement of shareholders' equity*.

LO5   **Stockholders' equity:** The owners' equity of a corporation, consisting of contributed capital and retained earnings.

Not sure you understood the techniques and calculations, or want to check if you are ready for a chapter test? The Review Problem models main computations or analysis presented in the chapter and other problem assignments. The answer is provided for immediate feedback.

REVIEW PROBLEM

The Effect of Transactions on the Accounting Equation

LO5   Charlene Rudek finished law school in June and immediately set up her own law practice. During the first month of operation, she completed the following transactions:

a. Began the law practice by exchanging $2,000 for 1,000 shares of $2 par value common stock of the corporation.
b. Purchased a law library for $900 cash.
c. Purchased office supplies for $400 on credit.

d. Accepted $500 in cash for completing a contract.
e. Billed clients $1,950 for services rendered during the month.
f. Paid $200 of the amount owed for office supplies.
g. Received $1,250 in cash from one client who had been billed previously for services rendered.
h. Paid rent expense for the month in the amount of $1,200.
i. Declared and paid a dividend of $400.

REQUIRED ▶

1. Show the effect of each of these transactions on the accounting equation by completing a table similar to Exhibit 1. Identify each stockholders' equity transaction.
2. Contrast the effects on cash flows of transactions **c** and **f** with transaction **b** and of transactions **e** and **g** with transaction **d**.

ANSWER TO REVIEW PROBLEM

1. Table of effects of transactions on the accounting equation

		Assets			=	Liabilities	+	Stockholders' Equity		
	Cash	Accounts Receivable	Office Supplies	Law Library		Accounts Payable	Common Stock	Retained Earnings	Type of SE Transaction
a.	$2,000						$2,000		Stockholders' Investment
b.	−900			+$900					
bal.	$1,100			$900			$2,000		
c.			+$400			+$400			
bal.	$1,100		$400	$900		400	$2,000		
d.	+500							+$ 500	Legal Fees Earned
bal.	$1,600		$400	$900		$400	$2,000	$ 500	
e.		+$1,950						+1,950	Legal Fees Earned
bal.	$1,600	$1,950	$400	4900		$400	$2,000	$2,450	
f.	−200					−200			
bal.	$1,400	$1,950	$400	$900		$200	$2,000	$2,450	
g.	+1,250	−1,250							
bal.	$2,650	$ 700	$400	$900		$200	$2,000	$2,450	
h.	−1,200							−1,200	Rent Expense
bal.	$1,450	$ 700	$400	$900		$200	$2,000	$1,250	
i.	−400							−400	Dividends
bal.	$1,050	$ 700	$400	$900		$200	$2,000	$ 850	

$3,050 $3,050

2. Transaction **c**, a purchase on credit, enables the company to use the asset immediately and defer payment of cash until later. Cash is expended to partially pay for the asset in transaction **f**. The remainder is to be paid subsequently. This series of transactions contrasts with transaction **b**, in which cash is expended immediately for the asset. In each case, an asset is purchased, but the effects on cash flows are different.

Transaction **e**, a sale on credit, allows the customer to pay later for services provided. This payment is partially received in transaction **g**, and the remainder is to be received later. These transactions contrast with transaction **d**, in which payment is received immediately for the services performed. In each case, the revenue is earned initially, but the effect on cash flows is different.

Chapter Assignments

BUILDING YOUR KNOWLEDGE FOUNDATION

Questions review key concepts, terminology, and topics of the chapter.

QUESTIONS

1. Why is accounting considered an information system?
2. What is the role of accounting in the decision-making process, and what broad business goals and activities does it help management achieve and manage?
3. Distinguish between management accounting and financial accounting.
4. Distinguish among these terms: *accounting*, *bookkeeping*, and *management information systems*.
5. Which decision makers use accounting information?
6. A business is an economic unit whose goal is to sell goods and services to customers at prices that will provide an adequate return to the business's owners. What functions must management perform to achieve that goal?
7. Why are investors and creditors interested in reviewing the financial statements of a company?
8. Among those who use accounting information are people and organizations that have an indirect interest in the business entity. Briefly describe these people and organizations.
9. Why has society as a whole become one of the largest users of accounting information?
10. Use the terms *business transactions*, *money measure*, and *separate entity* in a single sentence that demonstrates their relevance to financial accounting.
11. How do sole proprietorships, partnerships, and corporations differ?
12. In a corporation, what are the functions of stockholders, the board of directors, and management?
13. Define *assets*, *liabilities*, and *stockholders' equity*.
14. Arnold Smith's corporation has assets of $22,000 and liabilities of $10,000. What is the amount of the stockholders' equity?
15. What three elements affect retained earnings? How?
16. Give examples of the types of transactions that (a) increase assets and (b) increase liabilities.
17. What is the function of the statement of retained earnings?
18. Why is the balance sheet sometimes called the statement of financial position?
19. Contrast the purpose of the balance sheet with that of the income statement.
20. A statement for an accounting period that ends in June can be headed "June 30, 20xx" or "For the Year Ended June 30, 20xx." Which heading is appropriate for (a) a balance sheet and (b) an income statement?
21. How does the income statement differ from the statement of cash flows?
22. What are GAAP? Why are they important to the readers of financial statements?
23. What do auditors mean by the phrase *in all material respects* when they state that financial statements "present fairly, in all material respects . . . in conformity with generally accepted accounting principles"?
24. What organization has the most influence on GAAP?
25. Discuss the importance of professional ethics in the accounting profession.

Short exercises are simple applications of chapter material for a single learning objective. If you need help locating the related text discussions, refer to the LO numbers in the margin.

SHORT EXERCISES

LO3   Accounting Concepts

SE 1.   Tell whether each of the following words or phrases relates most closely to (a) a business transaction, (b) a separate entity, or (c) a money measure:

1. Partnership   4. Corporation
2. U.S. dollar   5. Sale of an asset
3. Payment of an expense

SE 2.
LO4 Forms of Business Enterprises

Match the descriptions on the left with the forms of business enterprise on the right:

_____ 1. Most numerous

_____ 2. Commands most revenues

_____ 3. Two or more co-owners

_____ 4. Has stockholders

_____ 5. Owned by one person

_____ 6. Has a board of directors

a. Sole proprietorship
b. Partnership
c. Corporation

SE 3.
LO5 The Accounting Equation

Determine the amount missing from each accounting equation below.

	Assets	=	Liabilities	+	Stockholders' Equity
1.	?		$25,000		$35,000
2.	$ 78,000		$42,000		?
3.	$146,000		?		$96,000

SE 4.
LO5 The Accounting Equation

Use the accounting equation to answer each question below.

1. The assets of Sully Company are $480,000, and the liabilities are $360,000. What is the amount of the stockholders' equity?
2. The liabilities of Eva Company equal one-fifth of the total assets. The stockholders' equity is $80,000. What is the amount of the liabilities?

SE 5.
LO5 The Accounting Equation

Use the accounting equation to answer each question below.

1. At the beginning of the year, Lanier Company's assets were $180,000, and its stockholders' equity was $100,000. During the year, assets increased by $60,000 and liabilities increased by $10,000. What was the stockholders' equity at the end of the year?
2. At the beginning of the year, Fanto Company had liabilities of $50,000 and stockholders' equity of $48,000. If assets increased by $20,000 and liabilities decreased by $15,000, what was the stockholders' equity at the end of the year?

SE 6.
LO5 The Accounting Equation and Net Income

Use the following information and the accounting equation to determine the net income for the year for each alternative below.

	Assets	Liabilities
Beginning of the year	$ 70,000	$30,000
End of the year	100,000	50,000

1. No investments were made in the business, and no dividends were paid during the year.
2. Investments of $10,000 were made in the business, but no dividends were paid during the year.
3. No investments were made in the business, but dividends of $2,000 were paid during the year.

SE 7.
LO5 The Accounting Equation and Net Income

Meader Company had assets of $140,000 and liabilities of $60,000 at the beginning of the year, and assets of $200,000 and liabilities of $70,000 at the end of the year. During the year, there was an investment of $20,000 in the business, and dividends of $24,000 were paid. What amount of net income was earned during the year?

SE 8.
LO5 Effect of Transactions on the Accounting Equation

On a sheet of paper, list the numbers 1 through 6, with columns labeled Assets, Liabilities, and Stockholders' Equity. In the columns, indicate whether each transaction that follows caused an increase (+), a decrease (−), or no change (NC) in assets, liabilities, and stockholders' equity.

1. Purchased equipment on credit.
2. Purchased equipment for cash.
3. Billed customers for services performed.
4. Received and immediately paid a utility bill.
5. Received payment from a previously billed customer.
6. Received an additional investment from a stockholder.

SE 9.

LO5   Effect of Transactions on the Accounting Equation

On a sheet of paper, list the numbers 1 through 6, with columns labeled Assets, Liabilities, and Stockholders' Equity. In the columns, indicate whether each transaction below caused an increase (+), a decrease (−), or no change (NC) in assets, liabilities, and stockholders' equity.

1. Purchased supplies on credit.
2. Paid for previously purchased supplies.
3. Paid employee's weekly wages.
4. Paid a dividend to stockholders.
5. Purchased a truck with cash.
6. Received a telephone bill to be paid next month.

SE 10.

LO6   Preparation and Completion of a Balance Sheet

Use the following accounts and balances to prepare a balance sheet for Anatole Company at June 30, 20x1, using Exhibit 2 as a model:

Accounts Receivable	$ 800
Wages Payable	250
Retained Earnings	1,750
Common Stock	12,000
Building	10,000
Cash	?

Exercises are richer applications of all chapter material referenced by LOs. →

EXERCISES

E 1.

LO1   The Nature of Accounting
LO2
LO7

Match the terms on the left with the descriptions on the right:

_____ 1. Bookkeeping

_____ 2. Creditors

_____ 3. Measurement

_____ 4. Financial Accounting Standards Board (FASB)

_____ 5. Tax authorities

_____ 6. Computer

_____ 7. Communication

_____ 8. Securities and Exchange Commission (SEC)

_____ 9. Investors

_____ 10. Processing

_____ 11. Management

_____ 12. Management information system

a. Function of accounting
b. Often confused with accounting
c. User(s) of accounting information
d. Organization that influences current practice
e. Tool that facilitates the practice of accounting

E 2.

LO2   Users of Accounting
LO4   Information and Forms of Business Enterprise

Vylex Pharmaceuticals has recently been formed to develop a new type of drug treatment for cancer. Previously a partnership, Vylex has now become a corporation. Describe the various groups that will have an interest in the financial statements of Vylex. What is the difference between a partnership and a corporation, and what advantages does the corporate form have over the partnership?

E 3.

LO3   Business Transactions

Edgar owns and operates a minimart. State which of the actions below are business transactions. Explain why any other actions are not regarded as transactions.

1. Edgar reduces the price of a gallon of milk in order to match the price offered by a competitor.
2. Edgar pays a high school student cash for cleaning up the driveway behind the market.
3. Edgar fills his son's car with gasoline in payment for restocking the vending machines and the snack food shelves.
4. Edgar pays interest to himself on a loan he made to the business three years ago.

E 4.

LO3   Accounting Concepts
LO4

Financial accounting uses money measures to gauge the impact of business transactions on a separate business entity. Tell whether each of the following words or phrases relates most closely to (a) a business transaction, (b) a separate entity, or (c) a money measure:

1. Corporation *B*   6. U.S. dollar *C*
2. Euro *c*   7. Partnership *B*
3. Sales of products *A*   8. Stockholders' investments *I*
4. Receipt of cash *A*   9. Japanese yen *C*
5. Sole proprietorship *B*   10. Purchase of supplies *A*

LO3 Money Measure

E 5. You have been asked to compare the sales and assets of four companies that make computer chips and to determine which company is the largest in each category. You have gathered the following data, but they cannot be used for direct comparison because each company's sales and assets are in its own currency:

Company (Currency)	Sales	Assets
Inchip (U.S. dollar)	20,000,000	13,000,000
Chan (Hong Kong dollar)	50,000,000	24,000,000
Ito (Japanese yen)	3,500,000,000	2,500,000,000
Works (Euro)	30,000,000	39,000,000

Assuming that the exchange rates in Table 1 are current and appropriate, convert all the figures to U.S. dollars and determine which company is the largest in sales and which is the largest in assets.

LO5 The Accounting Equation

E 6. Use the accounting equation to answer each question that follows. Show any calculations you make.

1. The assets of Caton Corporation are $800,000, and the stockholders' equity is $310,000. What is the amount of the liabilities?
2. The liabilities and stockholders' equity of Sung Corporation are $72,000 and $53,000, respectively. What is the amount of the assets?
3. The liabilities of Plumb Corp. equal one-third of the total assets, and stockholders' equity is $240,000. What is the amount of the liabilities?
4. At the beginning of the year, Wilde Corporation's assets were $220,000 and its stockholders' equity was $120,000. During the year, assets increased $60,000, and liabilities decreased $18,000. What is the stockholders' equity at the end of the year?

LO5 Stockholders' Equity Transactions

E 7. Identify the following transactions by marking each as a stockholders' investment (I), dividend (D), revenue (R), expense (E), or not a stockholders' equity transaction (NSE):

a. Received cash for providing a service.
b. Took assets out of the business for personal use.
c. Received cash from a customer previously billed for a service.
d. Transferred assets to the business from a personal account.
e. Paid a service station for gasoline for a business vehicle.
f. Performed a service and received a promise of payment.
g. Paid cash to purchase equipment.
h. Paid cash to an employee for services performed.

LO5 Effect of Transactions on the Accounting Equation

E 8. During the month of April, Cosmos Corporation had the following transactions:

a. Paid salaries for April, $1,800.
b. Purchased equipment on credit, $3,000.
c. Purchased supplies with cash, $100.
d. Additional investment by stockholders, $4,000.
e. Received payment for services performed, $600.
f. Made partial payment on equipment purchased in transaction b, $1,000.
g. Billed customers for services performed, $1,600.
h. Received payment from customers billed in transaction g, $300.
i. Received utility bill, $70.
j. Declared and paid dividends of $1,500.

On a sheet of paper, list the letters a through j, with columns labeled Assets, Liabilities, and Stockholders' Equity. In the columns, indicate whether each transaction caused an increase (+), a decrease (−), or no change (NC) in assets, liabilities, and stockholders' equity.

LO5 Examples of Transactions

E 9. For each of the categories below, describe a transaction that would have the required effect on the elements of the accounting equation.

1. Increase one asset and decrease another asset.
2. Decrease an asset and decrease a liability.
3. Increase an asset and increase a liability.

4. Increase an asset and increase stockholders' equity.

5. Decrease an asset and decrease stockholders' equity.

E 10.
LO5 Effect of Transactions on the Accounting Equation

The total assets and liabilities at the beginning and end of the year for Flag Company are listed below.

	Assets	Liabilities
Beginning of the year	$140,000	$ 55,000
End of the year	220,000	130,000

Determine Flag Company's net income or loss for the year under each of the following alternatives:

1. The stockholders made no investments in the business, and no dividends were paid during the year. *5,000*

2. The stockholders made no investments in the business, but dividends of $22,000 were paid during the year. *27,000*

3. The stockholders invested $13,000 in the business, but no dividends were paid during the year. *8,000*

4. The stockholders invested $10,000 in the business, and dividends of $22,000 were paid during the year. *17,000*

E 11.
LO5 Identification of Accounts
LO6

1. Indicate whether each of the following accounts is an asset (A), a liability (L), or a part of stockholders' equity (SE):

a. Cash *A*   e. Land *A*
b. Salaries Payable *L*   f. Accounts Payable *(L)*
c. Accounts Receivable *A*   g. Supplies *(A)*
d. Common Stock *SE*

2. Indicate whether each account below would be shown on the income statement (IS), the statement of retained earnings (RE), or the balance sheet (BS).

IS a. Repair Revenue   *IS* e. Rent Expense
BS b. Automobile   *BS* f. Accounts Payable
IS c. Fuel Expense   *RE* g. Dividends
BS d. Cash

E 12.
LO6 Preparation of a Balance Sheet

Listed in random order below are the balance sheet figures for the Solos Company as of December 31, 20xx.

Accounts Payable	$ 40,000	Accounts Receivable	$50,000
Building	90,000	Cash	20,000
Common Stock	100,000	Equipment	40,000
Supplies	10,000	Retained Earnings	70,000

Sort the balances and prepare a balance sheet similar to the one in Exhibit 2.

E 13.
LO6 Completion of Financial Statements

Complete the following independent sets of financial statements by determining the amounts that correspond to the letters. (Assume no new investments by the stockholders.)

Income Statement	Set A	Set B	Set C
Revenues	$ 550	$ g *3400*	$120
Expenses	a *400*	2,600	m *80*
Net income	$ b *150*	$ h *800*	$ 40
Statement of Retained Earnings			
Beginning balance	$1,450	$ 7,700	$100
Net income	c *150*	800	n *40*
Less dividends	100	i *500*	o *0*
Ending balance	$1,500	$ j *8000*	$p *140*
Balance Sheet			
Total assets	$ d *3300*	$15,500	$q *290*
Liabilities	$ 800	$ 2,500	$r *100*
Stockholders' equity			
Common stock	1,000	5,000	50
Retained earnings	e *1500*	k *8000*	140
Total liabilities and stockholders' equity	$ f *3300*	$ l	$290

LO6 Preparation of Financial Statements

E 14. Ridge Corporation engaged in the following activities during the year: Service Revenue, $26,400; Rent Expense, $2,400; Wages Expense, $16,540; Advertising Expense, $2,700; Utilities Expense, $1,800; and Dividends, $1,400. In addition, the year-end balances of selected accounts were as follows: Cash, $3,100; Accounts Receivable, $1,500; Supplies, $200; Land, $2,000; Accounts Payable, $900; and Common Stock, $2,000.

In proper format, prepare the income statement, statement of retained earnings, and balance sheet for Ridge Corporation (assume the year ends on December 31, 20x3). (**Hint:** You must solve for the beginning and ending balances of retained earnings for 20x3.)

LO6 Statement of Cash Flows

E 15. Waters Corporation began the year 20x1 with cash of $43,000. In addition to earning a net income of $25,000 and paying a cash dividend of $15,000, Waters borrowed $60,000 from the bank and purchased equipment for $90,000 with cash. Also, Accounts Receivable increased by $6,000, and Accounts Payable increased by $9,000.

Determine the amount of cash on hand at December 31, 20x1, by preparing a statement of cash flows similar to the one in Exhibit 2.

LO7 Accounting Abbreviations

E 16. Identify the accounting meaning of each of the following abbreviations: AICPA, SEC, GAAP, FASB, IRS, GASB, IASB, IMA, and CPA.

Problems are comprehensive applications of chapter material, often covering multiple learning objectives.

PROBLEMS

LO5 Effect of Transactions on the Accounting Equation

P 1. After receiving her degree in computer science, Carmen Vega started her own business, Custom Systems Corporation. The company completed the following transactions:

a. Invested $9,000 in cash and a systems library valued at $920 in exchange for 992 shares of $10 par value common stock in the corporation.
b. Paid current month's rent on an office, $360.
c. Purchased a minicomputer for cash, $7,000.
d. Purchased computer supplies on credit, $600.
e. Received payment from a client for programming done, $800.
f. Billed a client on completion of a short programming project, $710.
g. Paid expenses, $400.
h. Received a partial payment from the client billed in transaction **f**, $80.
i. Made a partial payment on the computer supplies purchased in transaction **d**, $200.
j. Declared and paid dividends of $250.

REQUIRED ▶
1. Arrange the asset, liability, and stockholders' equity accounts in an equation similar to that in Exhibit 1, using the following account titles: Cash, Accounts Receivable, Computer Supplies, Equipment, Systems Library, Accounts Payable, Common Stock, and Retained Earnings.
2. Show by addition and subtraction, as in Exhibit 1, the effects of the transactions on the accounting equation. Show new balances after each transaction, and identify each stockholders' equity transaction by type.
3. Contrast the effects on cash flows of transactions **d** and **i** with transaction **c** and of transactions **f** and **h** with transaction **e**.

Curious if you got the right answer? Look at the Check Figures section before Chapter 1.

LO5 Effect of Transactions on the Accounting Equation

P 2. On June 1, Henry Redmond started a new business, the Redmond Transport Corporation. During the month of June, the firm completed the following transactions:

a. Invested $66,000 in cash in exchange for 6,600 shares of $10 par value common stock of the corporation.
b. Purchased a truck for cash, $43,000.
c. Purchased equipment on credit, $9,000.
d. Billed a customer for hauling goods, $1,200.
e. Received cash for hauling goods, $2,300.
f. Received cash payment from the customer billed in transaction **d**, $600.
g. Made a payment on the equipment purchased in transaction **c**, $5,000.
h. Paid wages expense in cash, $1,700.
i. Declared and paid dividends of $1,200.

REQUIRED ▶
1. Arrange the asset, liability, and stockholders' equity accounts in an equation similar to that in Exhibit 1, using the following account titles: Cash, Accounts Receivable, Trucks, Equipment, Accounts Payable, Common Stock, and Retained Earnings.

2. Show by addition and subtraction, as in Exhibit 1, the effects of the transactions on the accounting equation. Show new balances after each transaction, and identify each stockholders' equity transaction by type.

P 3.

LO5   Effect of Transactions on the Accounting Equation

After completing his M.B.A., Sol Lindberg set up a consulting practice. At the end of his first month of operation, he had the following account balances: Cash, $4,760; Accounts Receivable, $2,800; Office Supplies, $540; Office Equipment, $8,400; Accounts Payable, $3,800; Common Stock, $11,000; and Retained Earnings, $1,700. Soon thereafter, the following transactions were completed:

a. Paid current month's rent, $700.
b. Made payment toward accounts payable, $900.
c. Billed clients for services performed, $1,600.
d. Received payment from clients billed last month, $2,000.
e. Purchased office supplies for cash, $160.
f. Paid secretary's salary, $1,700.
g. Paid utilities expense, $180.
h. Paid telephone expense, $100.
i. Purchased additional office equipment for cash, $800.
j. Received cash from clients for services performed, $2,400.
k. Declared and paid dividends of $1,000.

REQUIRED ▶

1. Arrange the following asset, liability, and stockholders' equity accounts in an equation similar to that in Exhibit 1: Cash, Accounts Receivable, Office Supplies, Office Equipment, Accounts Payable, Common Stock, and Retained Earnings.
2. Enter the beginning balances of the assets, liabilities, and stockholders' equity.
3. Show by addition and subtraction, as in Exhibit 1, the effects of the transactions on the accounting equation. Show new balances after each transaction, and identify each stockholders' equity transaction by type.

P 4.

LO1   Preparation of Financial
LO6   Statements

At the end of October 20xx, the Common Stock account of Sunnydale Riding Club, Inc., had a balance of $30,000, and Retained Earnings had a balance of $7,300. After operating during November, the club had the following account balances:

Cash	$ 8,700	Building	$30,000
Accounts Receivable	1,200	Horses	10,000
Supplies	1,000	Accounts Payable	17,800
Land	21,000		

In addition, the following transactions affected stockholders' equity during November:

Stockholders' investment in common stock	$16,000
Riding lesson revenue	6,200
Locker rental revenue	1,700
Salaries expense	2,300
Feed expense	1,000
Utilities expense	600
Dividends	3,200

REQUIRED ▶

1. Using Exhibit 2 as a model, prepare an income statement, a statement of retained earnings, and a balance sheet for Sunnydale Riding Club, Inc. (**Hint:** The final total of Stockholders' Equity is $54,100.)
2. Identify the links among the financial statements in requirement 1.
3. Which of these statements are most closely associated with the goals of profitability and liquidity? Explain your answer. What other financial statement is helpful in evaluating liquidity?

P 5.

LO5   Effect of Transactions
LO6   on the Accounting Equation and Preparation of Financial Statements

Royal Copying Service, Inc., began operations and engaged in the following transactions during July 20xx:

a. Linda Friedman deposited $5,000 in cash in the name of the corporation in exchange for 500 shares of $10 par value common stock of the corporation.
b. Paid current month's rent, $450.
c. Purchased copier for cash, $2,500.
d. Paid cash for paper and other copier supplies, $190.
e. Copying job payments received in cash, $890.
f. Copying job billed to major customer, $680.
g. Paid wages to part-time employees, $280.
h. Purchased additional copier supplies on credit, $140.

i. Received partial payment from customer in transaction **f,** $300.
j. Paid current month's utilities bill, $90.
k. Made partial payment on supplies purchased in transaction **h,** $70.
l. Declared and paid dividends of $700.

REQUIRED ▶   1. Arrange the asset, liability, and stockholders' equity accounts in an equation similar to that in Exhibit 1, using these account titles: Cash, Accounts Receivable, Supplies, Copier, Accounts Payable, Common Stock, and Retained Earnings.
2. Show by addition and subtraction, as in Exhibit 1, the effects of the transactions on the accounting equation. Show new balances after each transaction, and identify each stockholders' equity transaction by type.
3. Using Exhibit 2 as a guide, prepare an income statement, a statement of retained earnings, and a balance sheet for Royal Copying Service, Inc. (Optional: Also prepare a statement of cash flows.)

Looking for more practice? Alternate problems have the same format and learning objectives as problems that appear earlier in the chapter. ——▶ **ALTERNATE PROBLEMS**

P 6.
LO5   Effect of Transactions on the Accounting Equation

Brenda Kuzma started Frame-It Center, Inc., in a small shopping center. In the first weeks of operation, the firm completed the following transactions:

a. Deposited $7,000 in an account in the name of the corporation, in exchange for 700 shares of $10 par value common stock of the corporation.
b. Paid the current month's rent, $500.
c. Purchased store equipment on credit, $3,600.
d. Purchased framing supplies for cash, $1,700.
e. Received framing revenue, $800.
f. Billed customers for services, $700.
g. Paid utilities expense, $250.
h. Received payment from customers in transaction **f,** $200.
i. Made payment on store equipment purchased in transaction **c,** $1,800.
j. Declared and paid dividends of $400.

REQUIRED ▶   1. Arrange the following asset, liability, and stockholders' equity accounts in an equation similar to that in Exhibit 1: Cash, Accounts Receivable, Framing Supplies, Store Equipment, Accounts Payable, Common Stock, and Retained Earnings.
2. Show by addition and subtraction, as in Exhibit 1, the effects of the transactions on the accounting equation. Show new balances after each transaction, and identify each stockholders' equity transaction by type.
3. Contrast the effects on cash flows of transactions **c** and **i** with transaction **d** and of transactions **f** and **h** with transaction **e.**

P 7.
LO1   Preparation of Financial
LO6   Statements

At the end of October 20xx, the Common Stock account of the Sioux City Landscaping Service, Inc., had a balance of $60,000, and Retained Earnings had a balance of $14,600. After operating during November, the company had the following account balances:

Cash	$17,400	Building	60,000
Accounts Receivable	2,400	Lawn Equipment	20,000
Supplies	2,000	Accounts Payable	35,600
Land	42,000		

In addition, the following transactions affected stockholders' equity during November:

Stockholders' investment in common stock	$32,000
Lawn care revenue	12,400
Spraying revenue	3,400
Salaries expense	4,600
Supplies expense	2,000
Utilities expense	1,200
Dividends	6,400

REQUIRED ▶   1. Using Exhibit 2 as a model, prepare an income statement, a statement of retained earnings, and a balance sheet for Sioux City Landscaping Service, Inc. (**Hint:** The final total of Stockholders' Equity is $108,200.)
2. Identify the links among the financial statements in **1.**
3. Which financial statement is most closely associated with the goal of liquidity? Which with the goal of profitability? Explain your answers. What other statement is helpful in evaluating liquidity?

LO5 Effect of Transactions
LO6 on the Accounting Equation and Preparation of Financial Statements

P 8. On April 1, 20xx, Dependable Taxi Service, Inc., began operation. The company engaged in the following transactions during April:

a. Madeline Curry deposited $42,000 in a bank account in the name of the corporation in exchange for 4,200 shares of $10 par value stock in the corporation.

b. Purchased taxi for cash, $19,000.

c. Purchased auto supplies on credit, $400.

d. Received taxi fares in cash, $3,200.

e. Paid wages to part-time drivers, $500.

f. Purchased gasoline during month for cash, $800.

g. Purchased car washes during month on credit, $120.

h. Owner made a further investment in 500 shares, $5,000.

i. Paid part of the amount owed for the auto supplies purchased in transaction c, $200.

j. Billed major client for fares, $900.

k. Paid for automobile repairs, $250.

l. Declared and paid dividends of $1,000.

REQUIRED ▶

1. Arrange the asset, liability, and stockholders' equity accounts in an equation similar to that in Exhibit 1, using the following account titles: Cash, Accounts Receivable, Auto Supplies, Taxi, Accounts Payable, Common Stock, and Retained Earnings.

2. Show by addition and subtraction, as in Exhibit 1, the effects of the transactions on the accounting equation. Show new balances after each transaction, and identify each stockholders' equity transaction by type.

3. Using Exhibit 2 as a guide, prepare an income statement, a statement of retained earnings, and a balance sheet for Dependable Taxi Service, Inc. (Optional: Also prepare a statement of cash flows.)

SKILLS DEVELOPMENT CASES

Conceptual Analysis ◀── These cases focus on conceptual accounting issues based on real companies and situations.

LO1 Business Activities and
LO2 Management Functions

SD 1. J.C. Penney Company, Inc., <www.jcpenney.com> is America's largest department store company. According to its letter to stockholders, financial results didn't meet company expectations.

> J.C. Penney is implementing a number of strategic initiatives to ensure our competitiveness, to meet our growth objectives, and to provide a strong return on our stockholders' investment. These initiatives include: accelerated growth in our top 10 markets; expand our women's apparel and accessories business; speed merchandise to market; reduce our cost structure and enhance customer service.[11]

To achieve its strategy, J.C. Penney must organize its management into functions that relate to the principal activities of a business. Discuss the three basic activities J.C. Penney will engage in to achieve its goals, and suggest some examples of each. What is the role of J.C. Penney's management, and what functions must its management perform to accomplish these activities?

LO 2 Users of Accounting
LO 7 Information

SD 2. Public companies report quarterly and annually on their success or failure in making a net income. The following item appeared in *The Wall Street Journal*: "Coca-Cola Co.'s <www.coca-cola.com> fourth-quarter net income plunged 27%, a dismal end to a disappointing year, as economic weakness in several overseas markets hurt sales of soft drinks."[12]

Discuss why each of the following individuals or groups might be interested in seeing the accounting reports that support this statement:

1. The management of Coca-Cola

2. The stockholders of Coca-Cola

3. The creditors of Coca-Cola

4. Potential stockholders of Coca-Cola

5. The Internal Revenue Service

6. The Securities and Exchange Commission

7. The Teamsters' union

8. A consumers' group called Public Cause
9. An economic adviser to the president of the United States

The financial statements of Coca-Cola are audited by a CPA firm. Why is the report of these independent auditors important to the users of Coca-Cola's financial statements?

 Group Activity: Assign each of these users to a different group. Ask each group to discuss and present why its user needs accounting information.

LO 3 Concept of an Asset

Ethical dilemmas provide practice in dealing with the tough choices people often face. ————————→

SD 3. Southwest Airlines Co. <www.southwest.com> is one of the most successful airlines in the United States. Its annual report contains this statement: "We are a company of People, not Planes. That is what distinguishes us from other airlines and other companies. At Southwest Airlines, People are our most important asset."[13] Are employees considered assets in the financial statements? Discuss in what sense Southwest considers its employees to be assets.

Ethical Dilemma

LO 8 Professional Ethics

SD 4. Discuss the ethical choices in the situations below. In each instance, describe the ethical dilemma, determine the alternative courses of action, and tell what you would do.

1. You are the payroll accountant for a small business. A friend asks you how much another employee is paid per hour.
2. As an accountant for the branch office of a wholesale supplier, you discover that several of the receipts the branch manager has submitted for reimbursement as selling expense actually stem from nights out with his spouse.
3. You are an accountant in the purchasing department of a construction company. When you arrive home from work on December 22, you find a large ham in a box marked "Happy Holidays—It's a pleasure to work with you." The gift is from a supplier who has bid on a contract your employer plans to award next week.
4. As an auditor with one year's experience at a local CPA firm, you are expected to complete a certain part of an audit in 20 hours. Because of your lack of experience, you know you cannot finish the job within that time. Rather than admit this, you are thinking about working late to finish the job and not telling anyone.
5. You are a tax accountant at a local CPA firm. You help your neighbor fill out her tax return, and she pays you $200 in cash. Because there is no record of this transaction, you are considering not reporting it on your tax return.
6. The accounting firm for which you work as a CPA has just won a new client, a firm in which you own 200 shares of stock that you received as an inheritance from your grandmother. Because it is only a small number of shares and you think the company will be very successful, you are considering not disclosing the investment.

Group Activity. Assign each case to a different group to resolve and report.

You are asked to gather information from the Internet or business publications and apply it to the accounting concepts in the chapter. ————————→

Research Activity

LO1 Need for Knowledge
LO2 of Accounting

SD 5. Locate an article about a company from one of the following sources: the business section of your local paper or a nearby metropolitan daily, *The Wall Street Journal, Business Week, Forbes,* or the Needles Accounting Resource Center Web Site at http://accounting.college.hmco.com/students. List all the financial and accounting terms used in the article. Bring the article to class and be prepared to discuss how a knowledge of accounting would help a reader understand the content of the article.

What are the relevant numbers, and what do they mean? Practice making business decisions based on accounting information. ————————→

Decision-Making Practice

LO5 Effect of Transactions
LO6 on the Balance Sheet

SD 6. Instead of hunting for a summer job after finishing her junior year in college, Beth Murphy started a lawn service business in her neighborhood. On June 1, she deposited $2,700 in a new bank account in the name of her corporation. The $2,700 consisted of a $1,000 loan from her father and $1,700 of her own money. In return for her investment, Murphy issued 1,700 shares of $1 par value common stock to herself.

Using the money in this checking account, Murphy rented lawn equipment, purchased supplies, and hired neighborhood high school students to mow and trim the lawns of neighbors who had agreed to pay her for the service. At the end of each month, she mailed bills to her customers.

On August 31, Murphy was ready to dissolve her business and go back to school for the fall term. Because she had been so busy, she had not kept any records other than her checkbook and a list of amounts owed by customers.

Her checkbook had a balance of $3,520, and her customers owed her $875. She expected these customers to pay her during September. She planned to return unused supplies to the Lawn Care Center for a full credit of $50. When she brought back the rented lawn equipment, the Lawn Care Center also would return a deposit of $200 she had made in June. She owed the Lawn Care Center $525 for equipment rentals and supplies. In addition, she owed the students who had worked for her $100, and she still owed her father $700. Although Murphy feels she did quite well, she is not sure just how successful she was. You have agreed to help her find out.

1. Prepare one balance sheet dated June 1 and another dated August 31 for Murphy Lawn Services, Inc.
2. Using information that can be inferred from comparing the balance sheets, write a memorandum to Murphy commenting on her company's performance in achieving profitability and liquidity. (Assume that she used none of the company's assets for personal purposes.) Also, mention the other two financial statements that would be helpful to her in evaluating these business goals.

Using excerpts from business articles or annual reports of well-known companies, FRA cases ask you to extract relevant data, make computations, and interpret your results.

FINANCIAL REPORTING AND ANALYSIS CASES

Interpreting Financial Reports

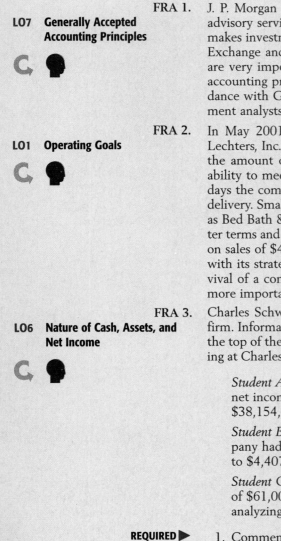

FRA 1.

LO7 Generally Accepted Accounting Principles

J. P. Morgan Investment Management Inc. <www.jpmorgan.com> is the investment advisory service of the well-known investment bank J.P. Morgan Chase & Company. It makes investments worth billions of dollars in companies listed on the New York Stock Exchange and other stock markets. Generally accepted accounting principles (GAAP) are very important for J.P. Morgan's investment analysts. What are generally accepted accounting principles? Why are financial statements that have been prepared in accordance with GAAP and audited by an independent CPA useful for J.P. Morgan's investment analysts? What organizations influence GAAP? Explain how they do so.

FRA 2.

LO1 Operating Goals

In May 2001, unable to get credit from enough of its lenders, housewares retailer Lechters, Inc., filed for Chapter 11 bankruptcy. It then secured new bank financing in the amount of $86 million. Suppliers, however, remained concerned about Lechters' ability to meet future obligations. Many retracted their term of sale, or the number of days the company had to pay for its merchandise, and asked for cash in advance or on delivery. Smaller home-furnishing retailers like Lechters struggle against big rivals, such as Bed Bath & Beyond, which are more valuable to suppliers and thus can demand better terms and pricing. In spite of these problems and an annual net loss of $101.8 million on sales of $405 million, management believed the company could eventually succeed with its strategy under the bankruptcy.[14] Which is more critical to the short-term survival of a company faced with Lechters' problems: liquidity or profitability? Which is more important in the long term? Explain your answers.

FRA 3.

LO6 Nature of Cash, Assets, and Net Income

Charles Schwab Corporation <www.schwab.com> is a well-known financial services firm. Information for 2001 and 2000 from the company's annual report is presented at the top of the next page.[15] (All numbers are in millions.) Three students who were looking at Charles Schwab's annual report were overheard to make the following comments:

Student A: What a great year Charles Schwab had in 2001! The company earned net income of $2,310,000,000 because its total assets increased from $38,154,000,000 to $40,464,000,000.

Student B: But the change in total assets isn't the same as net income! The company had a net loss of $469,000,000 because cash decreased from $4,876,000,000 to $4,407,000,000.

Student C: I see from the annual report that Charles Schwab paid cash dividends of $61,000,000 in 2001. Don't you have to take that into consideration when analyzing the company's performance?

REQUIRED ▶

1. Comment on the interpretations of Students A and B, and then answer Student C's question.

Charles Schwab Corporation
Condensed Balance Sheets
December 31, 2001 and 2000
(In millions)

	2001	2000
Assets		
Cash	$ 4,407	$ 4,876
Other assets	36,057	33,278
Total assets	$40,464	$38,154
Liabilities		
Total liabilities	$36,301	$33,924
Stockholders' Equity		
Common stock	$ 1,369	$ 1,517
Retained earnings	2,794	2,713
Total liabilities and stockholders' equity	$40,464	$38,154

2. Calculate Charles Schwab's net income for 2001. (**Hint:** Reconstruct the statement of retained earnings.)

 Group Activity: After groups discuss **1**, have them compete to see which one can come up with the answer to **2** first.

Explore accounting issues facing international companies. ——————▶ ***International Company***

FRA 4.
LO1   The Goal of Profitability

In 1998, the celebrated Danish toy company Lego Group <www.lego.com> reported its first loss since the 1930s. In subsequent years, Lego's performance continued to be erratic with profits in 1999, but with a loss in 2000. While its bright plastic bricks were still famous around the globe, Lego was rapidly losing market share to computer and video games. The company's president said, "The Lego Group is not in critical condition, but action is needed. . . . We have to acknowledge that growth and innovation are not enough. We also have to be a profitable business."[16] Discuss the meaning of *profitability*. What other goal must a business achieve? Why is the goal of profitability important to Lego's president? What is the accounting measure of profitability, and on which statement is it determined?

Every chapter has a case on Toys "R" Us; the complete Toys "R" Us Annual Report for a recent year follows this chapter. ——————▶ ***Toys "R" Us Annual Report***

FRA 5.
LO6   The Four Basic Financial Statements

Refer to the Toys "R" Us <www.tru.com> annual report in the Supplement to Chapter 1 to answer the questions below. Keep in mind that every company, while following basic principles, adapts financial statements and terminology to its own special needs. Therefore, the complexity of the financial statements and the terminology in the Toys "R" Us statements will sometimes differ from those in the text. (Note that 2002 refers to the year ended February 2, 2002, and 2001 refers to the year ended February 3, 2001.)

1. What names does Toys "R" Us give its four basic financial statements? (Note that the word *consolidated* in the names of the financial statements means that these statements combine those of several companies owned by Toys "R" Us.)
2. Prove that the accounting equation works for Toys "R" Us on February 2, 2002, by finding the amounts for the following equation: Assets = Liabilities + Stockholders' Equity.

3. What were the total revenues of Toys "R" Us for the year ended February 2, 2002?
4. Was Toys "R" Us profitable in the year ended February 2, 2002? How much was net income (loss) in that year, and did it increase or decrease from the year ended February 3, 2001?
5. Did the company's cash and cash equivalents increase from February 3, 2001, to February 2, 2002? By how much? In what two places in the statements can this number be found or computed?
6. Did cash flows from operating activities, cash flows from investing activities, and cash flows from financing activities increase or decrease from 2001 to 2002?

Group Activity: Assign the above questions to in-class groups of three or four students. Set a time limit. The first group to answer all questions correctly wins.

Comparison cases ask you to read the financial statements of Toys "R" Us and Walgreens in the supplement to Chapter 1 and to compare these companies on key financial performance measures and financial disclosures.

Comparison Case: Toys "R" Us and Walgreens

FRA 6.

LO1   Performance Measures
LO5   and Financial Statements
LO7

Refer to the Toys "R" Us <www.tru.com> annual report and the financial statements of Walgreens <www.walgreens.com> in the supplement to this chapter to answer these questions:

1. Which company is larger in terms of assets and in terms of revenues? What do you think is the best way to measure the size of a company?
2. Which company is more profitable in terms of net income? What is the trend of profitability over the past three years for both companies?
3. Which company has more cash? Which increased cash most in the last year? Which has more liquidity as measured by cash flows from operating activities?
4. Who is the auditor for each company? Why is the auditor's report that accompanies the financial statements important?

Use the professional software Fingraph® to analyze financial data.

Fingraph® Financial Analyst™

FRA 7.

LO1   Financial Statements,
LO6   Business Activities, and Goals

Choose a company from the list of Fingraph companies on the Needles Accounting Resource Center Web Site at http://accounting.college.hmco.com/students. Click on the company you selected to access the Microsoft Excel spreadsheet for that company. You will find the company's URL (Internet address) in the heading of the spreadsheet. Click on the URL for a link to the company's web site and annual report.

1. In the company's annual report, find a description of the business. What business is the company in? How would you describe its operating activities?
2. Find and identify the company's four basic financial statements. Which statement shows the resources of the business and the various claims to those resources? From the balance sheet, prove the accounting equation by showing that the company's assets equal its liabilities plus stockholders' equity. What is the company's largest category of assets? Which statement shows changes in all or part of the company's stockholders' equity during the year? Did the company pay any dividends in the last year?
3. Which statement is most closely associated with the company's profitability goal? How much net income did the company earn in the last year? Which statement is most closely associated with the company's liquidity goal? Did cash (and cash equivalents) increase in the last year? Which provided the most positive cash flows in the last year: operating, investing, or financing activities?
4. Prepare a one-page "executive summary" that highlights what you have learned from steps 1, 2, and 3. An executive summary is a short, easy-to-read report that emphasizes important data and conclusions by putting them in numbered paragraphs or bulleted lists.

Internet cases are accounting cases tailored to the Internet, based on concepts and applications from the chapter.

Internet Case

FRA 8.

LO1   Financial Performance
LO5   Comparison of Two
**   High-Tech Companies**

Microsoft <www.microsoft.com> and Intel <www.intel.com> are two very successful high-tech corporations. Access their web sites using the URLs listed here or go to the Needles Accounting Resource Center Web Site at http://accounting.college. hmco.com/students for a link to their web sites. Access each company's annual report and locate the consolidated balance sheet and consolidated statement of income. Find the amount of total assets, revenues, and net income for the most recent year shown. Then compute net income to revenues and net income to total assets for both companies. Which company is larger? Which is more profitable?

Supplement to Chapter 1
How to Read an Annual Report

More than 4 million corporations are chartered in the United States. Most of these are small, family-owned businesses. They are called *private* or *closely held corporations* because their common stock is held by only a few people and is not available for sale to the public. Larger companies usually find it desirable to raise investment funds from many investors by issuing common stock to the public. These companies are called *public companies*. Although they are fewer in number than private companies, their total economic impact is much greater.

Public companies must register their common stock with the Securities and Exchange Commission (SEC), which regulates the issuance and subsequent trading of the stock of public companies. One important responsibility of the management of public companies under SEC rules is to report each year to the company's stockholders on the financial performance of the company. This report, called an *annual report*, contains the annual financial statements and other information about the company. Annual reports, which are a primary source of financial information about public companies, are distributed to all the company's stockholders and filed with the SEC. When filed with the SEC, the annual report is called the 10-K because a Form 10-K is used to file the report. The general public may obtain an annual report by calling or writing the company or accessing it online at the company's web site. If a company has filed its 10-K electronically with the SEC, it may be accessed at **http://www.sec.gov/edgar.shtml**. Many libraries also maintain files of annual reports or have them available on electronic media, such as *Compact Disclosure*.

This supplement describes the major sections of the typical annual report and contains the annual report of one of the most successful retailers of this generation, Toys "R" Us, Inc. In addition to operating stores that sell toys and other items for children, the company has a chain of stores that sell children's clothes, called Kids "R" Us and a chain of stores devoted exclusively to babies, called Babies "R" Us. The Toys "R" Us annual report should be referred to in completing the case assignments related to the company in each chapter. For purposes of comparison, the supplement also includes the financial statements and notes to the financial statements of Walgreens, one of the largest drugstore chains in the United States.

THE COMPONENTS OF AN ANNUAL REPORT

In addition to listing the corporation's directors and officers, an annual report contains a letter to the stockholders, a multiyear summary of financial highlights, a description of the company, the financial statements, notes to the financial statements, a report of management's responsibilities, management's discussion of operating results and financial conditions, and the auditors' report.

LETTER TO THE STOCKHOLDERS

Traditionally, an annual report begins with a letter in which the top officers of the corporation tell stockholders about the performance and prospects of the company. In its 2001 annual report, the president and chief executive officer of Toys "R" Us wrote to the stockholders about the highlights of the past year, the key priorities for the new year, store format and redeployment plans, corporate citizenship, and other aspects of the business. He reported on future prospects as follows:

> This past year was a tumultuous one for our company, along with many top retailers. Challenging economic conditions, coupled with the tragic and

unprecedented events of September 11, had a significant negative impact on our fiscal 2001 results.

We were not pleased with our sales performance nor with our earnings performance in 2001. While we can't change it, I want to assure you that we're committed to deliver a solid 2002. We believe that's an achievable goal.

FINANCIAL HIGHLIGHTS

The financial highlights section of an annual report presents key statistics for a ten-year period and is often accompanied by graphs. The Toys "R" Us annual report, for example, gives key figures for operations, financial position, and number of stores at year end. Note that the financial highlights section often includes nonfinancial data, such as the number of stores.

DESCRIPTION OF THE COMPANY

An annual report contains a detailed description of the products and divisions of the company. Some analysts tend to scoff at this section of the annual report because it often contains glossy photographs and other image-building material, but it should not be overlooked because it may provide useful information about past results and future plans.

FINANCIAL STATEMENTS

All companies present four basic financial statements in their annual reports. As you can see in the annual report included with this supplement, Toys "R" Us presents statements of earnings (income statements), balance sheets, statements of cash flows, and statements of stockholders' equity (retained earnings).

The headings of all Toys "R" Us financial statements are preceded by the word *consolidated*. A corporation issues *consolidated* financial statements when it consists of more than one company and has combined their data for reporting purposes. For example, Toys "R" Us has combined the financial data of Kids "R" Us with those of the Toys "R" Us stores.

Toys "R" Us provides several years of data for each financial statement: two years for the balance sheet and three years for the others. Financial statements presented in this fashion are called *comparative financial statements*. Such statements are in accordance with generally accepted accounting principles and help readers assess the company's performance over several years.

You may notice that the fiscal year for Toys "R" Us ends on the Saturday nearest the end of January, rather than on the same date each year. The reason is that Toys "R" Us is a retail company. It is common for retailers to end their fiscal years at a slow period after the busiest time of year.

In a note at the bottom of each page of the financial statements, Toys "R" Us reminds the reader that the accompanying notes are an integral part of the statements and must be consulted in interpreting the data.

■ **STATEMENTS OF EARNINGS**   Toys "R" Us uses a multistep form of the income statement that shows gross margin as the difference between net sales and cost of sales (goods sold). Total operating expenses are deducted from gross margin to arrive at operating earnings (income). Interest expense is shown separately, and income taxes are deducted in another step. *Net earnings* is an alternative name for *net income*. The company also discloses the earnings per share, which is the net earnings divided by the weighted average number of shares of common stock held by stockholders during the year.

■ **BALANCE SHEETS**   Toys "R" Us has a typical balance sheet for a merchandising company. In the assets and liabilities sections, the company separates out the current assets and the current liabilities. Current assets will become available as cash or be used up in the next year; current liabilities will have to be paid or satisfied in the next year. These groupings help in understanding the company's liquidity.

Several items in the stockholders' equity section need additional explanation. Common stock represents the number of shares outstanding at par value. Additional paid-in capital represents amounts invested by stockholders in excess of the par value of the common stock. Treasury shares is a deduction from stockholders' equity that represents the cost of previously issued shares that have been bought back and held by the company.

■ **STATEMENTS OF CASH FLOWS**   Whereas the income statement reflects a company's profitability, the statement of cash flows reflects its liquidity. This statement provides information about a company's cash receipts, cash payments, and investing and financing activities during an accounting period.

Refer to the consolidated statements of cash flows in the Toys "R" Us annual report. The first major section shows cash flows from operating activities. It begins with the net earnings (income) from the consolidated statements of earnings and adjusts that figure to a figure that represents the net cash from operating activities. Among the adjustments are increases for depreciation and amortization, which are expenses that do not require the use of cash, and increases and decreases for the changes in the working capital accounts. In the year ended February 2, 2002, Toys "R" Us had net earnings of $67,000,000, and its net cash from operating activities was $504,000,000. Added to net income are such expenses as depreciation and amortization. Several small negative items were mostly offset by a positive amount associated with restructuring and other charges of $109 million. Decreases in accounts and other receivables, merchandise inventories, prepaid expenses, and other operating assets contributed to improvements in cash, as did an increase in income taxes payable. A large decrease of $241 million in accounts payable, accrued expenses, and other liabilities was a significant use of cash.

The second major section of the consolidated statements of cash flows is cash flows from investing activities. The main item in this category is capital expenditures, net, of $705,000,000. This figure demonstrates that Toys "R" Us is a growing company.

The third major section of the consolidated statements of cash flows is cash flows from financing activities. You can see here that the sources of cash from financing are long-term borrowings of $1,214,000,000, and exercise of stock options of $19,000,000, which were helpful in making short-term debt repayments of $588,000,000 and long-term debt repayments of $410,000,000, and share repurchases of $44,000,000. In total, the company received $191,000,000 in cash from financing activities during the year.

At the bottom of the consolidated statements of cash flows, the net effect of the operating, investing, and financing activities on the cash balance may be seen. Toys "R" Us had an increase in cash and cash equivalents during the year of $8,000,000 and ended the year with $283,000,000 of cash and cash equivalents on hand.

The supplemental disclosures of cash flow information show income tax and interest payments for the last three years.

■ **STATEMENTS OF STOCKHOLDERS' EQUITY**   Instead of a simple statement of retained earnings, Toys "R" Us presents a *statement of stockholders' equity*. This statement explains the changes in five components of stockholders' equity.

NOTES TO FINANCIAL STATEMENTS

To meet the requirements of full disclosure, a company must add *notes to the financial statements* to help users interpret some of the more complex items. The notes are considered an integral part of the financial statements. In recent years, the need for explanation and further details has become so great that the notes often take more space than the statements themselves. The notes to the financial statements can be put into three broad groups: summary of significant accounting policies, explanatory notes, and supplementary information notes.

■ **SUMMARY OF SIGNIFICANT ACCOUNTING POLICIES** Generally accepted accounting principles require that the financial statements include a *Summary of Significant Accounting Policies.* In most cases, this summary is presented in the first note to the financial statements or as a separate section just before the notes. In this summary, the company tells which generally accepted accounting principles it has followed in preparing the statements. For example, in the Toys "R" Us report, the company states the principles followed for property and equipment:

> Property and equipment are recorded at cost. Depreciation and amortization are provided using the straight-line method over the estimated useful lives of the assets or, where applicable, the terms of the respective leases, whichever is shorter.

Other important accounting policies listed by Toys "R" Us deal with fiscal year, reclassification, principles of consolidation, uses of estimates, revenue recognition, advertising costs, cash and cash equivalents, merchandise inventories, and financial instruments.

■ **EXPLANATORY NOTES** Other notes explain some of the items in the financial statements. For example, Toys "R" Us showed the details of its Property and Equipment account, which is reproduced below. Other notes had to do with seasonal financing and long-term debt, derivative instruments and hedging activities, leases, stockholders' equity, earnings per share, stock purchase warrants, investment in Toys—Japan, taxes on income, stock options, the profit-sharing plan, Toysrus.com, segments, restructuring and other charges, subsequent events, and other matters.

Property and Equipment			
	Useful Life (in years)	February 2, 2002	February 3, 2001
Land		$ 811	$ 810
Buildings	45–50	1,980	1,849
Furniture and equipment	5–20	1,927	2,218
Leaseholds and leasehold improvements	12½–35	1,542	1,291
Construction in progress		41	97
Leased property under capital lease		53	56
		6,354	6,321
Less accumulated depreciation and amortization		1,810	2,064
		$4,544	$4,257

■ **SUPPLEMENTARY INFORMATION NOTES** In recent years, the FASB and the SEC have ruled that certain supplemental information must be presented with financial statements. Examples are the quarterly reports that most companies present to their stockholders and to the SEC. These quarterly reports, called *interim financial statements,* are in most cases reviewed but not audited by the company's independent CPA firm. In its annual report, Toys "R" Us presented unaudited quarterly financial data from its 2001 quarterly statements, which are shown in the following table (for the year ended January 31, 2001; dollars in millions, except per share amounts):

	First Quarter	Second Quarter	Third Quarter	Fourth Quarter
2001				
Net sales	$2,061	$2,021	$2,178	$4,759
Gross margin	665	661	710	1,379
Net earnings	(18)	(29)	(44)	158[a]
Basic earnings per share/(loss)	$(0.09)	$(0.15)	$(0.22)	$0.80[a]
Diluted earnings per share	$(0.09)	$(0.15)	$(0.22)	$0.78[a]

(a) Includes restructuring and other charges of $213 ($126 net of tax, or $0.61 per share).

Interim data were presented for the prior year as well. Toys "R" Us also provides supplemental information on the market price of its common stock during the years and data on its store locations.

REPORT OF MANAGEMENT'S RESPONSIBILITIES

A statement of management's responsibility for the financial statements and the internal control structure may accompany the financial statements. The management report of Toys "R" Us acknowledges management's responsibility for the integrity and objectivity of the financial information and for the system of internal controls. It mentions the company's internal audit program and its distribution of company policies to employees. It also states that the company's financial statements have been audited.

MANAGEMENT'S DISCUSSION AND ANALYSIS

Management also presents a discussion and analysis of financial condition and results of operations. In this section, management explains the difference from one year to the next. For example, the management of Toys "R" Us describes the company's gross margin in the following way:

> Our consolidated gross margin, as a percentage of sales, improved by 10 basis points to 31.2%. This increase was primarily driven by our Babies "R" Us division which reported a 1.2% improvement in gross margin to 35%, primarily due to a favorable sales shift to higher margin juvenile import and proprietary product. Gross margin for the U.S. toy store division remained constant at 30.3%, reflecting our continued emphasis on higher margin exclusive product, which was offset by the impact of lower margin video product. Our International toy store business contributed to the improvement of our consolidated gross margin, reporting a 20 basis point increase to 31.9%, primarily due to our continued emphasis on exclusive products.

 Its management of cash flows is described as follows:

> The seasonal nature of the business typically causes cash balances to decline from the beginning of the year through October as inventory increases for the Holiday selling season and funds are used for construction of new stores, remodeling and other initiatives that normally occur in this period. The fourth

quarter, including the Holiday season, accounts for more than 40% of our net sales and a significant portion of our operating earnings.

REPORT OF CERTIFIED PUBLIC ACCOUNTANTS

The *independent auditors' report* deals with the credibility of the financial statements. This report by independent certified public accountants gives the accountants' opinion about how fairly these statements have been presented. Using financial statements prepared by managers without an independent audit would be like having a judge hear a case in which he or she was personally involved. Management, through its internal accounting system, is logically responsible for recordkeeping because it needs similar information for its own use in operating the business. The certified public accountants, acting independently, add the necessary credibility to management's figures for interested third parties. They report to the board of directors and the stockholders rather than to management.

In form and language, most auditors' reports are like the one shown in Figure 8. Usually such a report is short, but its language is very important. The report is divided into three parts.

1. The first paragraph identifies the financial statements subject to the auditors' report. This paragraph also identifies responsibilities. Company management is responsible for the financial statements, and the auditor is responsible for expressing an opinion on the financial statements based on the audit.

2. The second paragraph, or *scope section*, states that the examination was made in accordance with generally accepted auditing standards. These standards call for an acceptable level of quality in ten areas established by the American Institute of Certified Public Accountants. This paragraph also contains a brief description of the objectives and nature of the audit.

FIGURE 8
Auditors' Report for Toys "R" Us, Inc.

REPORT OF INDEPENDENT AUDITORS

To the Board of Directors and Stockholders
Toys"R"Us, Inc.

(1) We have audited the accompanying consolidated balance sheets of Toys"R"Us, Inc. and subsidiaries as of February 2, 2002 and February 3, 2001, and the related consolidated statements of earnings, stockholders' equity and cash flows for each of the three years in the period ended February 2, 2002. These financial statements are the responsibility of the Company's management. Our responsibility is to express an opinion on these financial statements based on our audits.

(2) We conducted our audits in accordance with auditing standards generally accepted in the United States. Those standards require that we plan and perform the audit to obtain reasonable assurance about whether the financial statements are free of material misstatement. An audit includes examining, on a test basis, evidence supporting the amounts and disclosures in the financial statements. An audit also includes assessing the accounting principles used and significant estimates made by management,

as well as evaluating the overall financial statement presentation. We believe that our audits provide a reasonable basis for our opinion.

(3) In our opinion, the financial statements referred to above present fairly, in all material respects, the consolidated financial position of Toys"R"Us, Inc. and subsidiaries at February 2, 2002 and February 3, 2001, and the consolidated results of their operations and their cash flows for each of the three years in the period ended February 2, 2002, in conformity with accounting principles generally accepted in the United States.

Ernst & Young LLP

New York, New York
March 14, 2002

Source: Reprinted by permission of Toys "R" Us. The notes to the financial statement, which are an integral part of the report, are not included.

3. The third paragraph, or *opinion section*, states the results of the auditors' examination. The use of the word *opinion* is very important because the auditor does not certify or guarantee that the statements are absolutely correct. To do so would go beyond the truth, since many items, such as depreciation, are based on estimates. Instead, the auditors simply give an opinion about whether, overall, the financial statements "present fairly," in all material respects, the financial position, results of operations, and cash flows. This means that the statements are prepared in accordance with generally accepted accounting principles. If, in the auditors' opinion, the statements do not meet accepted standards, the auditors must explain why and to what extent.

The Annual Report Project

Many instructors assign a term project that requires reading and analyzing a real annual report. The Annual Report Project described here has proved successful in the authors' classes. It may be used with the annual report of any company, including the Toys "R" Us annual report and the financial statements from the Walgreen Co. annual report that are provided with this supplement.

The extent to which financial analysis is required depends on the point in the course at which the Annual Report Project is assigned. Several options are provided in Instruction 3E, below.

INSTRUCTIONS:

1. Select any company from the list of Fingraph companies on the Needles Accounting Resource Center Web Site at **http://accounting.college. hmco.com/students**. Click on the company to access the Microsoft Excel spreadsheet for that company. Then click on the URL in the heading of the spreadsheet for a link to the company's web site and annual report. You may also obtain the annual report of a company of your own choice and access the company's annual report online or obtain it through your library or another source.

2. Library and Internet Research

   Go to the library or the Needles Accounting Resource Center Web Site (**http://accounting.college.hmco.com/students**) to learn about the company you have chosen and the industry in which it operates. Find at least two articles or other references to the industry and the company and summarize your findings.

   Also, access the company's Internet home page directly or through the Needles Accounting Resource Center. Review the company's products and services and find its financial information. Summarize what you have learned.

3. Your term project should consist of five or six double-spaced pages organized according to the following outline:

   A. **Introduction**
      Identify your company by writing a summary that includes the following elements:
      - Name of the chief executive officer
      - Location of the home office
      - Ending date of latest fiscal year
      - Description of the principal products or services that the company provides
      - Main geographic area of activity
      - Name of the company's independent accountants (auditors). In your own words, explain what the accountants said about the company's financial statements.
      - The most recent price of the company's stock and its dividend per share. Be sure to provide the date for this information.

   B. **Industry Situation and Company Plans**
      Describe the industry and its outlook; then summarize the company's future plans based on your library research and on reading the annual report. Be sure to read the letter to the stockholders. Include relevant information about the company's plans from that discussion.

C. **Financial Statements**

Income Statement: Is the format most like a single-step or multistep format? Determine gross profit, income from operations, and net income for the last two years; comment on the increases or decreases in these amounts.

Balance Sheet: Show that Assets = Liabilities + Stockholders' Equity for the past two years.

Statement of Cash Flows: Are cash flows from operations more or less than net income for the past two years? Is the company expanding through investing activities? What is the company's most important source of financing? Overall, has cash increased or decreased over the past two years?

D. **Accounting Policies**

What are the significant accounting policies, if any, relating to revenue recognition, cash, short-term investments, merchandise inventories, and property and equipment?

What are the topics of the notes to the financial statements?

E. **Financial Analysis**

For the past two years, calculate and discuss the significance of the following ratios:

Option (a): Basic (After Completing Chapter 5)

Liquidity Ratios
   Working capital
   Current ratio

Profitability Ratios
   Profit margin
   Asset turnover
   Return on assets
   Debt to equity
   Return on equity

Option (b): Basic with Enhanced Liquidity Analysis (After Completing Chapter 7)

Liquidity Ratios
   Working capital
   Current ratio
   Receivable turnover
   Average days' sales uncollected
   Inventory turnover
   Average days' inventory on hand
   Operating cycle

Profitability Ratios
   Profit margin
   Asset turnover
   Return on assets
   Debt to equity
   Return on equity

Option (c): Comprehensive (After Completing Chapter 15)

Liquidity Ratios
   Working capital
   Current ratio
   Receivable turnover
   Average days' sales uncollected
   Inventory turnover

Average days' inventory on hand
Payables turnover
Average days' payable
Operating cycle
Financing period

Profitability Ratios
Profit margin
Asset turnover
Return on assets
Return on equity

Long-Term Solvency Ratios
Debt to equity
Interest coverage

Cash Flow Adequacy
Cash flow yield
Cash flows to sales
Cash flows to assets
Free cash flow

Market Strength Ratios
Price/earnings per share
Dividends yield

***Option (d): Comprehensive Using Fingraph® Financial Analyst™
Software on the CD-ROM That Accompanies This Text***

ANNUAL REPORT 2001

This annual report is for the year ended February 2, 2002. Pages 1–7 and 22–44 reprinted by permission of Toys "R" Us, Inc.

company profile

TOYS"R"US, INC. — The world's leading
resource for kids, families and fun —
currently operates 1,599 stores;
701 TOYS"R"US stores in the United
States and 507 international toy stores,
including franchise stores; 184 KIDS"R"US
stores, 165 BABIES"R"US stores and
42 IMAGINARIUM stores. Visit
www.toysrus.com, www.babiesrus.com
and www.imaginarium.com.

TOYS"R"US

**TOYS"R"US
INTERNATIONAL**

KIDS"R"US

BABIES"R"US

IMAGINARIUM

TOYSRUS.COM

financial highlights

Toys"R"Us, Inc. and Subsidiaries

(Dollars in millions, except per share data)   Fiscal Year Ended

	Feb. 2, 2002	Feb. 3, 2001	Jan. 29, 2000	Jan. 30, 1999	Jan. 31, 1998	Feb. 1, 1997	Feb. 3, 1996	Jan. 28, 1995	Jan. 29, 1994	Jan. 30, 1993
Operations										
Total Enterprise Sales*	**$12,630**	$12,774	$12,118	$11,459	$11,315	$10,113	$9,498	$8,819	$8,018	$7,232
Net Sales	**11,019**	11,332	11,862	11,170	11,038	9,932	9,427	8,746	7,946	7,169
Net Earnings/(Loss)	**67**	404	279	(132)	490	427	148	532	483	438
Basic Earnings/(Loss) Per Share	**0.34**	1.92	1.14	(0.50)	1.72	1.56	0.54	1.88	1.66	1.51
Diluted Earnings/(Loss) Per Share	**0.33**	1.88	1.14	(0.50)	1.70	1.54	0.53	1.85	1.63	1.47
Financial Position at Year End										
Working Capital	**$ 631**	$ 556	$ 35	$ 106	$ 579	$ 619	$ 326	$ 484	$ 633	$ 797
Real Estate - Net	**2,313**	2,348	2,342	2,354	2,435	2,411	2,336	2,271	2,036	1,877
Total Assets	**8,076**	8,003	8,353	7,899	7,963	8,023	6,738	6,571	6,150	5,323
Long-Term Debt	**1,816**	1,567	1,230	1,222	851	909	827	785	724	671
Stockholders' Equity	**3,414**	3,418	3,680	3,624	4,428	4,191	3,432	3,429	3,148	2,889
Common Shares Outstanding	**196.7**	197.5	239.3	250.6	282.4	287.8	273.1	279.8	289.5	293.1
Number of Stores at Year End										
Toys"R"Us – U.S.	**701**	710	710	704	700	682	653	618	581	540
Toys"R"Us – International	**507**	491	462	452	441	396	337	293	234	167
Kids"R"Us – U.S.	**184**	198	205	212	215	212	213	204	217	211
Babies"R"Us – U.S.	**165**	145	131	113	98	82	–	–	–	–
Imaginarium – U.S.	**42**	37	40	–	–	–	–	–	–	–
Total Stores	**1,599**	1,581	1,548	1,481	1,454	1,372	1,203	1,115	1,032	918

*Total enterprise sales include sales by all stores, whether operated by the company, by licensees, franchisees or under joint-venture agreements.

contents

on the **move**

Message to our shareholders

This past year was a tumultuous one for our company, along with many top retailers. Challenging economic conditions, coupled with the tragic and unprecedented events of September 11, had a significant negative impact on our fiscal 2001 results.

We were not pleased with our sales performance nor with our earnings performance in 2001. While we can't change it, I want to assure you that we're committed to delivering a solid 2002. We believe that's an achievable goal.

It's important to note that despite the difficult retail climate post-9/11, the successful execution of our strategies resulted in a solid fourth quarter performance. We were able to increase net earnings before restructuring and other charges in that quarter by 13 percent to $284 million or $1.39 per share, compared to $251 million or $1.23 per share in last year's fourth quarter. In addition, our inventory discipline was excellent, and we ended the year with comparable store inventories down in every division. In our U.S. toy store division, comparable store inventories were down approximately $200 million, a 13 percent decrease. Total company inventory was down $266 million or 12 percent.

John Eyler, Chairman and Chief Executive Officer, Toys"R"Us, Inc.

While we saw a number of positive developments in the fourth quarter, we could not overcome the weakness exhibited during the prior three quarters. Thus, for the full year, our total sales of $11 billion were essentially flat with the prior year excluding the sales of Toys"R"Us–Japan, and our net earnings, before the impact of the restructuring and other charges, were $193 million or $0.94 per share, compared to net earnings of $264 million or $1.23 per share in 2000, excluding the gain from the IPO of Toys"R"Us–Japan and the Amazon.com alliance non-recurring charges.

Nonetheless, fueled by the momentum of our customer-focused strategic growth plan, Toys"R"Us reached several milestones for building brand equity, unique content and guest satisfaction. From the opening of our international flagship store in Times Square to our new marketing campaign featuring Geoffrey the Giraffe, to improving vendor relationships, to our solid holiday performance in a very tenuous climate, all indications are that we are still very much on track for fulfilling the strategic repositioning we set out to accomplish two years ago.

Responding from the heart

We were hard at work executing our strategies last year, and then came September 11. The most difficult times reveal the true nature of a company and its people. Throughout the days and weeks after September 11, the "R"Us family responded with extraordinary kindness and generosity. We took care of each other and we helped many in our communities.

/ shareholder letter /

We mobilized to create various fundraising efforts including in-store point of purchase programs, a create a flag program, and other initiatives, all of which benefited organizations in support of the children and families affected by the tragic events on September 11. The Toys"R"Us Children's Fund, Inc.'s "9/11 Emergency Relief Fund" has to-date donated approximately $2 million to local and national organizations supporting groups that were affected by 9/11. In addition, we made available a workbook titled, "First Aid for Feelings," authored by childhood grief expert, Denise Daniels, to guests in all of our Toys"R"Us and Kids"R"Us stores nationwide, free of charge. I was extremely proud of the way our company responded throughout an unimaginable time, and I believe our shareholders should be proud, too.

Moving forward, reenergizing stores

Despite the turmoil and stress of the past year, we remained focused on our business. By the end of 2001, 433 of our U.S. toy stores had been converted to the new Mission Possible format highlighting unique content, a fun and easy to shop environment and improved service for our guests. We believe in the long-term value of meeting the needs of our guests through unique shopping destinations that sell concepts, ideas and exciting products with services that help each guest select the perfect gift — and the Mission Possible stores achieve that goal.

Validating the underlying vitality of this strategy was a store-for-store increase of more than 8 percent for the last five-week period of the holiday selling season among the entire portfolio of newly renovated stores completed in 2001 — the best Toys"R"Us U.S. December results in nearly a decade. We will complete the conversion of the balance of our stores to our new format by holiday 2002.

Celebrating the brand

Our award winning flagship store in Times Square opened in November to great fanfare, terrific public response, tremendous media coverage and sales that exceeded our plans. Called a "unique entertainment experience for the young and young-at-heart," our flagship store continues to be an ongoing celebration of the "R"Us brand as well as a landmark destination that sets us apart from other toy retailers.

This store also exemplifies our strong relationship with our key resources, and is an excellent example of partnership at work. The flagship serves as a platform to support product introductions and exclusive licensing programs, and enhances our brand as well as the brands of our most valuable resources.

Also in 2001, our marketing campaign featuring Geoffrey the Giraffe garnered rave reviews from customers and was recognized by *USA Today* as one of the most effective advertising campaigns in 2001 in reaching its target audiences, according to their proprietary research. In addition, our independent consumer research showed that in the top 21 markets we had the highest advertising awareness of any of our largest competitors at the holiday season, confirming that our campaign truly resonates with customers.

Geoffrey has come to life as our lovable, wise-cracking spokes-animal.

Our strategic partnerships, licenses and alliances with exceptional brands and companies infused exciting products and events into our stores. Our own private brand business, which provides higher margins to fuel the revitalization and rebuilding of the "R"Us family of brands, reached an unprecedented $1 billion in sales in the U.S., a fourfold increase in just a few short years.

While we continue to focus on taking aggressive steps to separate and distinguish our stores and shopping experience from the competition, it is important that we listen to the consumer. And, we are pleased by what we are seeing...and hearing. We have conducted independent research for many years to track how our guests feel about Toys"R"Us. We are encouraged that our research shows that the population at large understands what we're trying to accomplish through our strategies. Consumer ratings show improvement in how guests feel about the content in our stores, our better in stock position, overall store experience, and particularly the enhancement of guest service. This became increasingly evident during the highly competitive holiday selling season where our traffic volume and purchasing records showed that we made significant inroads and gained market share in key strategic markets.

Growing the "R"Us family

Babies"R"Us, often our first relationship experience with young families, continues to be a high performer, opening 20 new stores as planned in 2001 and posting a 15 percent increase in operating earnings for the full year. We will continue to invest in Babies"R"Us by building 20 more new stores in 2002. The combination of authoritative merchandise assortments, easy-to-shop appealing stores and excellent guest service define the Babies"R"Us experience and represent the same strategic principals being implemented in all divisions.

We began the repositioning of Kids"R"Us this past year. Despite the effects of September 11, combined with an unseasonably mild winter, the results of that repositioning were reflected in improvement of our sales trend in the fall season. A major highlight was the performance by 11 prototype stores that generated solid double-digit increases. We plan to convert 30 more stores to the new prototype this year, continuing to position Kids"R"Us as the best source for "fashions that are trend-right at prices families can afford."

In the International division, operating earnings, excluding earnings from Toys"R"Us–Japan for all periods, reached an all-time high with an increase of 6 percent for the year. Our International business is working to reduce expenses and increase efficiencies throughout its global operations. International continues to execute many of the same strategies as the U.S. divisions, including the addition of Universe of Imagination — known in the U.S. as Imaginarium — and Animal Alley departments in all Toys"R"Us stores worldwide.

The Toysrus.com subsidiary emerged as the strongest player in its category, the #1 most visited site for toys, video games and baby products. Sales increased by 54 percent for the year versus the 2000 fiscal year. Fiscal 2001 operating losses at Toysrus.com were reduced by $42 million for the fiscal year, versus the same period in 2000, after excluding non-recurring charges related to the alliance with Amazon.com, which were recorded in the third quarter of 2000. Toysrus.com launched Babiesrus.com and Imaginarium.com web sites on the Amazon.com platform this year and had a very successful holiday season with a high level of guest delight.

An effective combination of thoughtful strategy and innovative vision is inherent throughout all divisions.

/ shareholder letter /

Through unique, high quality products and excellent customer service, Imaginarium continues to secure a leading position for Toys"R"Us and its divisions in the profitable specialty educational toy market, all from a winning combination of learning and play. By October of 2002, virtually all Toys"R"Us stores in the United States will have an Imaginarium presentation within the larger store.

Transforming our business and strengthening our financial position

Over the last two years, we have thoroughly assessed our business to determine how best to reposition Toys"R"Us and its divisions for growth and profitability. We have made solid progress, and in January we announced a restructuring which will enable us to concentrate our financial resources on those formats and stores that are most productive. The announcement detailed the closing of 64 stores and the related elimination of approximately 1,900 staff positions in our stores and headquarters.

We are closing 27 Toys"R"Us stores that, while cash-flow positive, do not meet our return-on-investment objectives. In addition, we announced the closing of 37 Kids"R"Us stores. In almost all of these locations, the nearest Toys"R"Us store will be converted to a combo store, a Toys"R"Us store with a Kids"R"Us store inside. Toys"R"Us currently operates 273 combo stores which are performing very well, and by the end of 2002 we expect to have approximately 375 combo stores in our portfolio.

Improved service for our guests isn't just about Mom & Dad... it's about making our store kid-friendly, too.

The restructuring also includes consolidating our five separate store support facilities throughout New Jersey into one central location in Wayne, New Jersey. By moving to a shared services model across a variety of corporate support functions such as finance and human resources, we believe we will significantly improve the effectiveness and efficiency of our company while materially lowering SG&A expenses.

In this period of economic uncertainty, we believe it is important to strengthen our balance sheet and enhance our liquidity. Therefore, in 2001, we sold $466 million of 3-year Eurobonds, $250 million of 5-year U.S. bonds and $500 million of 10-year U.S. bonds. We have also filed registration statements with the Securities and Exchange Commission to issue $550 million of equity and equity linked securities in the form of $350 million of equity security units and $200 million of Toys"R"Us common stock.

Looking forward with excitement and energy

We are optimistic about 2002, not only because we believe that our strategies will be successful, but also because our industry is becoming vibrant again. We are more enthusiastic than ever about the exciting product lines our stores will be offering, and we will continue to execute our strategies with all the energy and discipline at our command.

To that end, after a thorough review of our 2001 performance, we've concluded that the "R"Us organization must focus all its resources and efforts on four priorities that will provide our shareholders the greatest return on investment and position us solidly for success in 2002.

First and foremost, we must complete the repositioning of Toys"R"Us U.S. and deliver significant earnings improvement. We are committed to driving sales growth in the core toy business, with disciplined expense and inventory control essential to achieving meaningful earnings improvement. Nothing we do will impact our company more positively than showing substantial improvement in Toys"R"Us U.S., and therefore this is our most important priority.

Second, we will focus on sales and earnings growth in all other divisions. We have solid plans in place to grow sales and earnings across all divisions, and we must aggressively execute those plans. It's our job to make sure that we increase sales and earnings every quarter of the fiscal year.

Exceptional guest service is a top priority in all of our divisions.

We must continue to find ways to drive costs out of our business when they don't increase sales or earnings. For that reason, expense reduction is our third priority. We've already taken a significant step in that effort by consolidating all non-merchandise purchasing so that it can be managed effectively while leveraging our purchasing power and creating efficiencies. This builds on the solid expense management we achieved in 2001 as well as the reductions in SG&A inherent in our recently announced restructuring.

And finally, our fourth priority is to continue to build a world-class organization by developing our existing staff and by adding talented individuals to strengthen our capability. We will pursue our efforts to build upon our shared services model. We are also committed to developing training programs in support of building skills at all levels, and we will continue to implement programs that will recognize and reward superior results.

We are encouraged by the results of our strategic initiatives, and we sincerely appreciate the patience of our shareholders as we continue to move forward in unlocking the potential in the "R"Us business. While our overall performance improvement has been slower than we had hoped, caused, in some part, by circumstances that were unforeseen, we are clearly on the right track. We have developed our plans and our expense structures conservatively, and we expect that in 2002 we will generate meaningful earnings improvement and demonstrate that we are moving solidly ahead to a stronger, brighter future for our shareholders.

John H. Eyler

John H. Eyler, Jr.
Chairman and Chief Executive Officer
March 26, 2002

Management's Discussion and Analysis
of Results of Operations and Financial Condition

RESULTS OF OPERATIONS

Comparison of Fiscal Year 2001 to 2000

We reported net sales of $11.0 billion for the 52 week fiscal year ended February 2, 2002 and $11.3 billion for the 53 week fiscal year ended February 3, 2001. Net sales of Toys"R"Us – Japan, Ltd. ("Toys – Japan"), which has been accounted for on the "equity method" since its initial public offering, are included in our net sales in the first quarter of 2000 and excluded from our net sales thereafter. Our net sales were $11.0 billion for both fiscal 2001 and fiscal 2000, after excluding sales of Toys – Japan. Currency translation did not have a significant impact on our net sales for fiscal 2001. Our total enterprise sales, which include the net sales of all our brand stores, whether operated by us, by licensees, franchisees or under joint-venture agreements, were $12.6 billion versus $12.8 billion.

Our consolidated comparable store sales, in local currencies, declined 1%. Comparable store sales for our U.S. toy store division declined 1% for the fiscal year and increased 2% for the fourth quarter. Video sales, due to the introduction of XBox, Gamecube and Gameboy Advance in the latter half of the year, were the primary drivers of the fourth quarter increase. Video accounted for approximately 22% of our U.S. toy store sales in the fourth quarter of 2001 as compared to 18% in the fourth quarter of the prior year. We had 433 stores in the Mission Possible format by the start of the 2001 Holiday season, which also contributed to the comparable store sales increase in the fourth quarter. This gain partially offset the negative impact of 268 stores under construction during the first nine months of 2001, which were being retrofitted to the Mission Possible format, as well as the negative impact resulting from the events of the September 11th terrorist attacks. Our International division reported comparable toy store sales increases of 5%, in local currencies, primarily driven by the performance of our toy stores in the United Kingdom, which reported double-digit comparable store sales growth. Our Babies"R"Us division reported 8% net sales growth, primarily driven by the opening of 20 new Babies"R"Us stores in the United States this year, as well as a 2% comparable store sales increase. Toysrus.com reported net sales increases of 54% for the full year and 24% for the fourth quarter, which continues to reflect increases in its market share and the impact of the Toysrus.com alliance with Amazon.com that began in 2000.

In the fourth quarter of 2001, we recorded restructuring and other charges of $213 million (pre-tax) which are discussed in further detail in the section "Restructuring and Other Charges" in this report. In addition, our fiscal 2000 results include the impact of the initial public offering of Toys – Japan and the non-recurring costs and charges relating to the Toysrus.com/Amazon.com alliance, both of which are discussed in further detail in the section "Other Matters" in this report. For comparability purposes, the remaining discussion of our results of operations for 2001, 2000 and 1999 excludes the impact of these items, unless otherwise noted.

Our consolidated gross margin, as a percentage of sales, improved by 10 basis points to 31.2%. This increase was primarily driven by our Babies"R"Us division which reported a 1.2% improvement in gross margin to 35%, primarily due to a favorable sales shift to higher margin juvenile import and proprietary product. Gross margin for the U.S. toy store division remained constant at 30.3%, reflecting our continued emphasis on higher margin exclusive product, which was offset by the impact of lower margin video product. Our International toy store business contributed to the improvement of our consolidated gross margin, reporting a 20 basis point increase to 31.9%, primarily due to our continued emphasis on exclusive products.

Our consolidated SG&A, as a percentage of sales, increased 70 basis points to 25.0%. SG&A for our U.S. toy store division, increased 110 basis points to 22.6%, reflecting the strategic investments we are making in our business including the renovation of our U.S. toy stores to the Mission Possible format and certain guest focused initiatives, as well as additional SG&A expenses resulting from the September 11th events. SG&A for our international toy store business increased 10 basis points to 22.8%. SG&A for the Babies"R"Us division increased 40 basis points to 23.8%, primarily attributable to increased payroll costs to support our emphasis on guest focused initiatives.

Depreciation and amortization increased by $18 million, primarily due to the Mission Possible store remodeling program, continued new store expansion and strategic investments to improve our management information systems.

Interest expense decreased by $10 million, primarily due to lower interest rates, partially offset by the impact of higher average total debt outstanding during the year. Interest and other income decreased by $15 million, primarily due to lower average investments outstanding, as well as lower interest rates.

Our effective tax rate before restructuring and other charges remained unchanged at 36.5%. However, the impact of the 2001 restructuring and other charges reduced our tax rate to 26.9%.

Neither foreign currency exchange nor inflation had a significant impact on our consolidated net earnings.

management's discussion and analysis

Comparison of Fiscal Year 2000 to 1999

We reported net sales of $11.3 billion and $11.9 billion. Excluding the impact of Toys – Japan in both periods, our net sales increased 4% to $11.0 billion from $10.7 billion. Further, excluding the negative impact of currency translation of $172 million, our net sales increased 5%. The net sales growth was primarily driven by a 2% increase in comparable store sales, as well as new store growth in the Babies"R"Us division. Comparable store sales for the U.S. toy store division increased 1%, reflecting the strength of its core merchandise, improved guest service and instock inventory position, despite acute shortages in video product. Comparable store sales for the International toy store division, on a local currency basis, increased 6% mainly due to the implementation of strategies similar to those being implemented in the U.S., along with adding/improving Babies"R"Us shops within its toy stores. Net sales for the Babies"R"Us division increased 26% and comparable store sales grew at a double-digit rate. These increases were driven by strong sales in most merchandise categories and continued guest acceptance of the Babies"R"Us brand. Toysrus.com reported net sales of $180 million, up from $49 million in 1999, reflecting increased market share and the benefits from its strategic alliance with Amazon.com, which combined the two companies' expertise to create a compelling online shopping experience.

Our consolidated gross margin, as a percentage of sales, improved to 31.1% from 29.9%. This increase was primarily attributable to shifts in the merchandise mix and growth in higher margin categories, primarily exclusive product offerings, as well as the implementation of a new strategic pricing system. Gross margin for the U.S. toy store division increased to 30.3% from 28.4%, while gross margin for the Babies"R"Us division grew to 33.8% from 32.8%. The International toy store division reported gross margin of 31.7% versus 30.8%.

Our consolidated SG&A, as a percentage of sales, increased to 24.3% from 23.1%. SG&A for the U.S. toy store division increased to 21.5% from 19.8%. This increase is primarily due to increased payroll costs related to the implementation of our new guest-focused initiatives, higher distribution center costs due to changes in the handling and amount of inventory, costs associated with actions being taken to improve store ambiance, and systems enhancements. SG&A for the International toy store division decreased to 22.7% from 23.4%. This improvement was primarily a result of the strategic store closures in Central Europe and France, which have improved the overall profitability of this division. The Babies"R"Us division reported SG&A of 23.4% versus 24.0%. This improvement was primarily due to leveraging against sales growth.

Depreciation and amortization increased to $290 million from $278 million. This increase is primarily due to our continued store expansion, remodels and front end conversions, strategic investments to improve management information systems and amortization of goodwill related to our acquisition of Imaginarium Toy Centers, Inc. in the second half of 1999.

Interest expense – net, increased to $104 million from $80 million. This increase is mainly attributable to the funding of our stock repurchase program, higher interest rates, and the funding of Toysrus.com.

International operating earnings were unfavorably impacted by the translation of local currency into U.S. dollars by approximately $14 million in 2000. The effect of inflation had no material effect on our operating results for 2000.

Our effective tax rate remained unchanged at 36.5%.

Restructuring and Other Charges

On January 28, 2002, we announced a series of steps designed to enhance our future cash flows and operating earnings and to continue to allow us to concentrate our financial resources on those stores and store formats that we believe are most productive. We are closing 37 Kids"R"Us stores and, in almost all of these locations, we are converting the nearest Toys"R"Us stores into Toys"R"Us/Kids"R"Us combo stores in tandem with the Kids"R"Us store closings. We are also closing 27 non-Mission Possible format Toys"R"Us stores, eliminating approximately 1,900 staff positions at stores and headquarters, and consolidating our store support center facilities into our new headquarters in Wayne, New Jersey, which we intend to fully occupy by the summer of 2003.

The costs associated with facilities consolidation, elimination of positions, and other actions designed to improve efficiency in our support functions were $79 million, of which $15 million related to severance. The costs associated with store closings are $73 million for Kids"R"Us and $85 million for Toys"R"Us, of which $27 million was recorded in cost of sales. We are currently marketing all of the stores and store support center facilities included in this plan and will close all stores included in this plan by the end of 2002. We also reversed $24 million of previously accrued charges ($11 million from the 1998 program and $13 million from the 1995 program) that have been deemed no longer needed. See below for further details regarding the reversal of these reserves.

These actions are expected to increase free cash flow in 2002 and beyond and to yield improvements to pre-tax earnings of approximately $25 million in 2002, and approximately $45 million annually beginning in 2003. Payroll savings associated with changes in support functions are expected to account for $30 million of the $45 million annual savings.

management's discussion and analysis

Accordingly, based on all of these actions, we recorded $213 million of pre-tax ($126 million after-tax) restructuring and other charges in the fourth quarter of our fiscal year ended February 2, 2002. Details on the components of the charges are as follows:

Description	Initial charge	Utilized in 2001	Reserve balance 2/02/02
Store Closings:			
Lease commitments	$ 52	$ –	$ 52
Severance	4	–	4
Write-down of property and equipment	75	75	–
Markdowns	27	–	27
Store Support Center Consolidation:			
Lease commitments	28	–	28
Severance	15	–	15
Write-down of property and equipment	29	29	–
Other	7	7	–
Total restructuring and other charges	$ 237	$ 111	$ 126

During 1998, we announced strategic initiatives to reposition our business and other charges including the guest-focused reformatting of our toy stores into our new store format, as well as a restructuring of our international operations, all of which resulted in a charge of $353 million. Details on the components of the charges are described in the notes to the consolidated financial statements and are as follows:

Description	Initial charge	Reserve balance 1/29/00	Utilized/ reversed in 2000	Reserve balance 2/03/01	Utilized/ reversed in 2001	Reserve balance 2/02/02
Store Closings:						
Lease commitments	$ 81	$ 62	$ 13	$ 49	$ 24	$ 25
Severance and other closing costs	29	14	6	8	2	6
Write-down of property and equipment	155	–	–	–	–	–
Other	29	11	11	–	–	–
Total restructuring	$ 294	$ 87	$ 30	$ 57	$ 26	$ 31
Provisions for legal settlements	$ 59	$ 30	$ 19	$ 11	$ 11	$ –

In the fourth quarter of 2001, we determined that $11 million of unused reserves for the closing of under-performing stores in central Europe would no longer be needed and accordingly, reversed these reserves. In the third quarter of 2001, we completed the satisfaction of certain legal obligations and accordingly, reversed the remaining unused reserve of $5 million. In the third quarter of 2000, we determined that an $11 million unused reserve would no longer be needed and accordingly, reversed this reserve. Remaining reserves at February 2, 2002, primarily long-term lease commitment reserves, will be utilized during 2002 and thereafter.

In 1998, we also recorded markdowns and other charges of $345 million, which included $253 million for markdowns required to clear excess inventory from stores, $29 million for markdowns related to store closings and $63 million for charges to cost of sales for inventory system refinements and changes in accounting estimates.

In 1995, we announced certain initiatives to restructure our worldwide business. In the fourth quarter of 2001, we determined that unused reserves of $13 million for the restructuring of our international business would no longer be needed and accordingly, reversed these reserves. We have substantially completed the remainder of this program, with the exception of long-term lease commitment reserves that will be utilized during 2002 and thereafter.

We believe that unused reserves remaining at February 2, 2002 are reasonable estimates of what is required to complete all remaining initiatives.

Liquidity and Capital Resources

We have a $975 million unsecured committed revolving credit facility from a syndicate of financial institutions. The credit facility includes a $650 million 5-year facility expiring in September 2006 and a $325 million 364-day facility expiring in September 2002. This facility is available for seasonal borrowings and to support our domestic commercial paper borrowings. There were no outstanding balances under any of these committed revolvers at the end of fiscal 2001, 2000 or 1999. Additionally, we have lines of credit with various banks to meet short-term financing needs of our foreign subsidiaries. Cash requirements for operations, capital expenditures and lease commitments will be met primarily through operating activities and issuance of equity and/or debt.

On March 13, 2002, Moody's revised our long-term debt and commercial paper rating to "Baa3/P-3," with a stable outlook. Our long-term debt and commercial paper is currently rated "BBB+/A-2" by Standard & Poor's. However, Standard & Poor's has placed our long-term debt on watch for possible downgrade. We continue to be confident in our ability to refinance maturing debt, as well as to provide for new capital.

The seasonal nature of our business typically causes cash balances to decline from the beginning of the year through October as inventory increases for the Holiday selling season and funds are used for construction of new stores, remodeling and other initiatives that normally occur in this period. The fourth quarter, including the Holiday season, accounts for more than 40% of our net sales and a significant portion of our operating earnings.

management's discussion and analysis

Operating Activities

Net cash provided by operating activities was $504 million in 2001, which was primarily driven by net income adjusted for non-cash items, as well as an increase in income taxes payable. Net cash used in operations was $151 million in 2000, primarily due to an increase in merchandise inventories, which more than offset net earnings adjusted for non-cash items. Net cash provided by operations was $865 million in 1999, which was primarily driven by net income adjusted for non-cash items, as well as an increase in accounts payable and accrued expenses.

Investing Activities

Capital expenditures – net of dispositions, were $705 million in 2001, $402 million in 2000 and $533 million in 1999. Capital expenditures during these periods include investments: to open new stores, to reformat certain of our existing store base to new store formats and combo stores, and to improve and enhance our management information systems. We reformatted 268 existing U.S. toy stores to the Mission Possible format, and converted another 94 existing U.S. toy stores to Toys"R"Us/Kids"R"Us combo stores in 2001. In addition, we converted 10 Kids"R"Us stores to our new store prototype. Also, in 2001, we opened 39 new stores worldwide, opened our new Flagship store in the center of Times Square, New York City, and opened our new state of the art distribution center in Texas. The significant decrease in capital expenditures, net, from 1999 to 2000 was primarily due to the disposal of distribution centers and other facilities in 2000. During 2002, we plan on investing approximately $475 million in capital to open approximately 30 new stores, primarily Babies"R"Us and International stores, to convert the remainder of our U.S. toy store chain to the Mission Possible format (approximately 240 stores), to convert approximately 102 existing U.S. toy stores to combo stores and to convert approximately 30 existing Kids"R"Us stores into our new store prototype.

Investing activities for 2000 included $267 million of cash proceeds related to the initial public offering of shares of Toys – Japan, which is discussed in the section "Other Matters" in this report. Investing activities for 1999 included net cash expended to acquire all of the outstanding common stock of Imaginarium Toy Centers, Inc, which is also described further in the section "Other Matters" in this report.

Financing Activities

Net cash from financing activities was $191 million in 2001, primarily as a result of net borrowings of $216 million during the year. On July 19, 2001, we issued and sold $500 million of notes bearing interest at 7.625% per annum maturing on August 1, 2011, and also borrowed $250 million of notes bearing interest at 6.875% per annum maturing on August 1, 2006. Simultaneously, we entered into interest rate swap agreements. As a result of the interest rate swap agreements, interest on the $500 million notes will accrue at the rate of LIBOR plus 1.5120% and interest on the $250 million notes will accrue at the rate of LIBOR plus 1.1515%. Interest is payable on both notes semi-annually on February 1 and August 1 of each year, commencing on February 1, 2002. On February 13, 2001, we borrowed 500 million EURO through the public issuance of a EURO bond bearing interest at 6.375% per annum. The obligation was swapped into a $466 million fixed rate obligation with an effective rate of 7.43% per annum with interest payments due annually and principal due February 13, 2004. The proceeds were used to reduce outstanding commercial paper obligations. Accordingly, we have reclassified $466 million from short-term borrowings to long-term debt at February 3, 2001.

Net cash used for financing activities was $2 million for 2000. Net borrowings for 2000 were $521 million, primarily driven by the repurchase of 42 million shares of our common stock, increased inventory levels and the funding of Toysrus.com. In 2000, we received a total of $97 million from SOFTBANK Venture Capital and affiliates ("SOFTBANK") relating to our 20% minority interest in Toysrus.com, which is discussed in further detail in the section "Other Matters" in this report.

Net cash used for financing activities were $102 million for 1999, which was principally driven by the repurchase of 12 million shares of our common stock, partially offset by net borrowings of $84 million.

/ management's discussion and analysis /

Other Matters

On March 19, 2002, we refinanced our note payable originally due 2005 and increased the amount outstanding to $160 million from $100 million. This borrowing is repayable in semi-annual installments, with the final installment due on February 20, 2008. The effective cost of this borrowing is 2.23% and is secured by expected future cash flows from license fees due from Toys – Japan.

On March 13, 2002, we filed registration statements with the Securities and Exchange Commission indicating our intention to issue $550 million of equity and equity-linked securities. These securities take the form of $350 million of equity security units and $200 million of Toys"R"Us common stock. We plan to issue these securities promptly after the registration statements are declared effective. We will use the net proceeds from these offerings as an alternative to short-term borrowings and for other general corporate purposes.

On February 24, 2000, we entered into an agreement with SOFTBANK, which included an investment by SOFTBANK of $60 million in Toysrus.com for a 20% ownership interest. Accordingly, we have recorded a 20% minority interest in the net losses of Toysrus.com in selling, general and administrative expenses. In addition, Toysrus.com received additional capital contributions of $37 million from SOFTBANK representing its proportionate share of funding required for the operation of Toysrus.com.

In connection with the agreement with SOFTBANK, we issued 1.2 million stock purchase warrants for $8.33 per warrant. Each warrant gives the holder thereof the right to purchase one share of Toys"R"Us common stock at an exercise price of $13 per share, until the expiration date of February 24, 2010. These warrants have not been exercised.

In August 2000, Toysrus.com entered into a 10-year strategic alliance with Amazon.com to operate a co-branded toy and video game on-line store, which was launched in the third quarter of 2000. In addition, a co-branded baby products on-line store was launched in May 2001 and a co-branded creative and learning products on-line store was launched in July 2001. Under this alliance, Toysrus.com and Amazon.com are responsible for specific aspects of the on-line stores. Toysrus.com is responsible for merchandising and content for the co-branded store. Toysrus.com also identifies, buys, owns and manages the inventory. Amazon.com handles web-site development, order fulfillment, guest service, and the housing of Toysrus.com's inventory in Amazon.com's U.S. distribution centers. Also in August 2000, Amazon.com was granted a warrant entitling it to acquire up to 5% (subject to dilution under certain circumstances) of the capital of Toysrus.com at the then market value. This warrant has not been exercised.

In the third quarter of 2000, Toysrus.com recorded $118 million in non-recurring costs and charges as a result of the transition to the co-branded site, of which, $10 million were included in cost of sales and $108 million were included in selling, general and administrative expenses. These costs and charges related primarily to the closure of three distribution centers and web-site asset write-offs, as well as other costs associated with migrating data and merchandise to the new site and facilities. At the end of 2001, Toysrus.com had remaining

reserves of approximately $42 million, primarily for the exit of its Memphis Tennessee distribution center, which is being actively marketed. We believe that these remaining reserves are adequate to complete all remaining action plans.

We recorded a non-operating gain of $315 million ($200 million net of taxes) resulting from the initial public offering of shares of Toys – Japan, which was completed in April 2000. Of this gain, $91 million resulted from an adjustment to the basis of our investment in Toys – Japan and $224 million related to the sale of a portion of company-owned common stock of Toys – Japan. In connection with this transaction, we also received net cash proceeds of $267 million and recorded a provision for current income taxes of $82 million and a provision for deferred income taxes of $33 million. As a result of this transaction, our ownership percentage in the common stock of Toys – Japan was reduced from 80% to 48%. Toys – Japan is a licensee.

In August 1999, we acquired all of the capital stock of Imaginarium Toy Centers, Inc. for approximately $43 million in cash and the assumption of certain liabilities. In addition to currently operating 42 Imaginarium toy stores throughout the U.S., we have incorporated the Imaginarium learning center concept in our Mission Possible store format. The operating results of Imaginarium were not material to our overall results or financial condition.

In August 1999, Robert C. Nakasone resigned as our Chief Executive Officer and as a director. We entered into a Separation and Release Agreement with Mr. Nakasone providing for cash payments, the immediate vesting of all unvested options and unvested profit shares held by Mr. Nakasone, as well as the prorated vesting of other unvested equity based awards on the second anniversary of the termination date. We accrued all costs related to this matter as of January 29, 2000. These amounts were not material to our overall results or financial condition.

Quantitative and Qualitative Disclosures About Market Risks

We are exposed to market risk from potential changes in interest rates and foreign exchange rates. We regularly evaluate these risks and have taken the following measures to mitigate these risks: the countries in which we own assets and operate stores are politically stable; our foreign exchange risk management objectives are to stabilize cash flow from the effects of foreign currency fluctuations; we do not participate in speculative hedges; and we will, whenever practical, offset local investments in foreign currencies with borrowings denominated in the same currencies. We also enter into derivative financial instruments to hedge a variety of risk exposures including interest rate and currency risks.

Our foreign currency exposure is primarily concentrated in the United Kingdom, Europe, Canada, and Australia. We face currency exposures that arise from translating the results of our worldwide operations into U.S. dollars from exchange rates that have fluctuated from the beginning of the period. We also face transactional currency exposures relating to merchandise that we purchase in foreign currencies. We enter into forward exchange contracts to minimize and manage the currency risks associated with these transactions. The counter-parties to these contracts are highly rated financial institutions and we do not have significant exposure to any counter-party. Gains or losses on these derivative instruments are largely offset by the gains or losses on the underlying hedged transactions. For foreign currency derivative instruments, market risk is determined by calculating the impact on fair value of an assumed one-time change in foreign rates relative to the U.S. dollar. Fair values were estimated based on market prices where available, or dealer quotes. With respect to derivative instruments outstanding at February 2, 2002, a 10% appreciation of the U.S. dollar would have increased pre-tax earnings by $13 million, while a 10% depreciation of the U.S. dollar would have decreased pre-tax earnings by $13 million. Comparatively, considering our derivative instruments outstanding at February 3, 2001, a 10% appreciation of the U.S. dollar would have increased pre-tax earnings by $9 million, while a 10% depreciation of the U.S. dollar would have decreased pre-tax earnings by $10 million.

We are faced with interest rate risks resulting from interest rate fluctuations. We have a variety of fixed and variable rate debt instruments. In an effort to manage interest rate exposures, we strive to achieve an acceptable balance between fixed and variable rate debt and have entered into interest rate swaps to maintain that balance. For interest rate derivative instruments, market risk is determined by calculating the impact to fair value of an assumed one-time change in interest rates across all maturities. Fair values were estimated based on market prices where available, or dealer quotes. A change in interest rates on variable rate debt is assumed to impact earnings and cash flow, but not fair value of debt. A change in interest rates on fixed rate debt is assumed to impact the fair value of debt, but not earnings and cash flow. Based on our overall interest rate exposure at February 2, 2002 and February 3, 2001, a 100 basis point change in interest rates would not have a material effect on our earnings or cash flows over a one-year period. A 100 basis point increase in interest rates would decrease the fair value of our long-term debt at February 2, 2002 and February 3, 2001 by approximately $79 million and $29 million, respectively. A 100 basis point decrease in interest rates would increase the fair value of our long-term debt at February 2, 2002 and February 3, 2001 by approximately $87 million and $34 million, respectively.

See the notes to the consolidated financial statements for additional discussion of our outstanding derivative financial instruments at February 2, 2002.

Critical Accounting Policies

Our discussion and analysis of our financial condition and results of our operations is based upon the consolidated financial statements, which have been prepared in accordance with accounting principles generally accepted in the United States. The preparation of these financial statements requires us to make certain estimates and assumptions that affect the reported amounts of assets, liabilities, revenues and expenses, and the related disclosure of contingent assets and liabilities as of the date of the financial statements and during the applicable periods. We base these estimates on historical experience and on various other assumptions that we believe to be reasonable under the circumstances. Actual results may differ materially from these estimates under different assumptions or conditions.

We believe the following critical accounting policies affect our more significant judgments and estimates used in the preparation of our consolidated financial statements.

Inventories:

Merchandise inventories for the U.S. toy store division, which represent approximately 70% of total merchandise inventories, are stated at the lower of LIFO (last-in, first-out) cost or market value, as determined by the retail inventory method. All other merchandise inventories are stated at the lower of FIFO (first-in, first-out) cost or market as determined by the retail inventory method. We record adjustments to the value of inventory based upon forecasted plans and marketing events to sell merchandise inventories. These adjustments are estimates which could vary significantly, either favorably or unfavorably, from actual results if future economic conditions, consumer preference trends or competitive conditions differ from our expectations.

We receive various types of merchandise allowances from our vendors, which are based primarily on negotiated terms. We use estimates at interim periods to record our provisions for inventory shortage and to record vendor funded merchandise allowances. These estimates are based on historical and current available data and other factors and are adjusted to actual amounts at the completion of our physical inventories and finalization of all vendor allowances. Although we believe that these estimates are adequate and proper, the actual amounts could vary.

Deferred Tax Assets:

As part of the process of preparing our consolidated financial statements, we are required to estimate our income taxes in each of the jurisdictions in which we operate. This process involves estimating our actual current tax exposure, together with assessing temporary differences resulting from differing treatment of items for tax and accounting purposes. These differences result in deferred tax assets and liabilities, which are included within our consolidated balance sheet. The measurement of deferred tax assets is adjusted by a valuation allowance to recognize the extent to which, more likely than not, the future tax benefits will be recognized.

At February 2, 2002, we have recorded deferred tax assets, net of valuation allowances, of $289 million. We believe it is more likely than not that we will be able to realize these assets through reduction of future taxable income. We base this belief upon the levels of taxable income historically generated by our business, as well as projections of future taxable income. If future levels of taxable income are not consistent with our expectations, we may be required to record an additional valuation allowance, which could reduce our net income by a material amount.

Derivatives and Hedging Activities:

We enter into derivative financial arrangements to hedge a variety of risk exposures, including interest rate and currency risks associated with our long-term debt, as well as foreign currency risk relating to import merchandise purchases. We account for these hedges in accordance with SFAS No. 133, "Accounting for Derivatives Instruments and Hedging Activities," and we record the fair value of these instruments within our consolidated balance sheet. Gains and losses from derivative financial instruments are largely offset by gains and losses on the underlying transactions. At February 2, 2002, we have reduced the carrying amount of our long-term debt by $84 million, representing the carrying amount of the debt in excess of fair value on that date. Also at February 2, 2002, we have recorded derivative assets of $42 million and derivative liabilities of $122 million. While we intend to continue to meet the conditions for hedge accounting, if hedges were not to be highly effective in achieving offsetting cash flows attributable to the hedged risk, the changes in the fair value of the derivatives used as hedges could have a material effect on our financial position or results of operations.

Insurance Risks:
We insure a substantial portion of our general liability and workers compensation risks through a wholly-owned insurance subsidiary. Provisions for losses related to these risks are based upon independent actuarially determined estimates. While we believe these provisions for losses to be adequate, the ultimate liabilities may be in excess of, or less than, the amounts recorded.

Synthetic Lease:
Our new corporate headquarters facility, located in Wayne, New Jersey, which we intend to fully occupy by the summer of 2003, is being financed under a lease arrangement commonly referred to as a "synthetic lease." Under this lease, unrelated third parties, arranged by Wachovia Development Corporation, a multi-purpose real estate investment company, will fund up to $125 million for the acquisition and construction of the facility. Upon completion of the construction, which is expected to be in 2003, we will begin paying rent on the facility until the lease expires in 2011. The rent will be based on a mix of fixed and variable interest rates which will be applied against the final amount funded. Upon expiration of the lease, we would expect to either: renew the lease arrangement; purchase the facility from the lessor; or remarket the property on behalf of the owner. Under accounting principles generally accepted in the United States, this arrangement is required to be treated as an operating lease for accounting purposes and will be treated as a financing for tax purposes.

Recent Accounting Pronouncements
In August 2001, the Financial Accounting Standards Board issued SFAS No. 144, "Accounting for the Impairment or Disposal of Long-Lived Assets," which addresses financial accounting and reporting for the impairment or disposal of long-lived assets and supersedes SFAS No. 121, "Accounting for the Impairment of Long-Lived Assets and for Long-Lived Assets to be Disposed Of." SFAS No. 144 is effective for fiscal years beginning after December 15, 2001. We have adopted SFAS No. 144 as of February 3, 2002 and we do not expect that this adoption will have a significant effect on our consolidated financial condition, results of operations or cash flow.

In July 2001, the Financial Accounting Standards Board issued SFAS No. 142, "Goodwill and Other Intangible Assets," which is effective for fiscal years beginning after December 15, 2001. SFAS No. 142

changes the accounting for goodwill from an amortization method to an impairment only approach. We have adopted this pronouncement on February 3, 2002. As a result of this adoption, $348 million of unamortized goodwill, which was to be amortized ratably through 2037, will no longer be amortized. Application of the non-amortization provisions of SFAS No. 142 is expected to result in an increase in net income of approximately $8 million per year.

SFAS No. 142 also requires that goodwill be tested annually for impairment. Intangible assets deemed to have an indefinite life will be tested for impairment using a one-step process which compares the fair value to the carrying amount of the asset as of the beginning of the fiscal year. Our unamortized goodwill at February 2, 2002 relates to the acquisition of Baby Super Stores, Inc. in 1997 ($319 million), which is now part of our Babies"R"Us division, and the acquisition of Imaginarium Toy Centers, Inc. in 1999 ($29 million), which is now part of our U.S. toy store division. Based on the historical and projected operating results of these reporting units, we have determined that no impairment of our goodwill exists. Therefore, the adoption of this SFAS No. 142 is not anticipated to have a material impact on our consolidated financial condition, results of operations or cash flows.

Forward Looking Statements
This annual report contains "forward looking" statements within the meaning of Section 27A of the Securities Act of 1933, as amended, and Section 21E of the Securities Exchange Act of 1934, which are intended to be covered by the safe harbors created thereby. All statements that are not historical facts, including statements about our beliefs or expectations, are forward-looking statements. We generally identify these statements by words or phrases such as "anticipate," "estimate," "plan," "expect," "believe," "intend," "forsee," "will," "may," and similar words or phrases. These statements discuss, among other things, expected growth, strategy, store openings and renovations, future performance and anticipated cost savings and results of our 2001 restructuring. Such statements involve risks and uncertainties that exist in our operations and business environment that could render actual outcomes and results materially different than predicted. Our forward-looking statements are based on assumptions about many factors, including, but not limited to, ongoing competitive pressures in the retail industry, changes in consumer spending and consumer preferences, general economic conditions in the United States and other jurisdictions in which we conduct business (such as interest rates, currency exchange rates and consumer confidence) and normal business uncertainty. While we believe that our assumptions are reasonable at the time forward-looking statements were made, we caution that it is impossible to predict the actual outcome of numerous factors and, therefore, readers should not place undue reliance on such statements. Forward-looking statements speak only as of the date they are made, and we undertake no obligation to update such statements in light of new information or future events that involve inherent risks and uncertainties. Actual results may differ materially from those contained in any forward-looking statement.

consolidated financial statements

Consolidated Statements of Earnings
Toys"R"Us, Inc. and Subsidiaries

(In millions, except per share data)	February 2, 2002	February 3, 2001	Year Ended January 29, 2000
Net sales	$ 11,019	$ 11,332	$ 11,862
Cost of sales	7,604	7,815	8,321
Gross Margin	3,415	3,517	3,541
Selling, general and administrative expenses	2,750	2,832	2,743
Depreciation and amortization	308	290	278
Equity in net earnings of Toys – Japan	(29)	(31)	–
Restructuring and other charges	186	–	–
Total Operating Expenses	3,215	3,091	3,021
Operating Earnings	200	426	520
Other income (expense):			
Interest expense	(117)	(127)	(91)
Interest and other income	8	23	11
Gain from IPO of Toys – Japan	–	315	–
Earnings before income taxes	91	637	440
Income taxes	24	233	161
Net earnings	$ 67	$ 404	$ 279
Basic earnings per share	$ 0.34	$ 1.92	$ 1.14
Diluted earnings per share	$ 0.33	$ 1.88	$ 1.14

See notes to consolidated financial statements.

Consolidated Balance Sheets

Toys"R"Us, Inc. and Subsidiaries

(In millions)	February 2, 2002	February 3, 2001
Assets		
Current Assets:		
Cash and cash equivalents	$ 283	$ 275
Accounts and other receivables	210	225
Merchandise inventories	2,041	2,307
Prepaid expenses and other current assets	97	100
Total current assets	2,631	2,907
Property and Equipment:		
Real estate, net	2,313	2,348
Other, net	2,231	1,909
Total property and equipment	4,544	4,257
Investment in Toys – Japan	123	108
Goodwill, net	348	361
Derivative assets	42	–
Other assets	388	370
	$ 8,076	$ 8,003
Liabilities and Stockholders' Equity		
Current Liabilities:		
Short-term borrowings	$ –	$ 121
Accounts payable	878	1,152
Accrued expenses and other current liabilities	777	837
Income taxes payable	345	241
Total current liabilities	2,000	2,351
Long-term debt	1,816	1,567
Deferred income taxes	395	402
Derivative liabilities	122	–
Other liabilities	276	195
Minority interest in Toysrus.com	53	70
Stockholders' Equity:		
Common stock	30	30
Additional paid-in capital	444	439
Retained earnings	5,228	5,161
Accumulated other comprehensive loss	(267)	(211)
Treasury shares, at cost	(2,021)	(2,001)
Total stockholders' equity	3,414	3,418
	$ 8,076	$ 8,003

See notes to consolidated financial statements.

Consolidated Statements of Cash Flows

Toys"R"Us, Inc. and Subsidiaries

(In millions)	February 2, 2002	February 3, 2001	Year Ended January 29, 2000
Cash Flows from Operating Activities			
Net earnings	$ 67	$ 404	$ 279
Adjustments to reconcile net earnings to net cash from operating activities:			
Depreciation and amortization	308	290	278
Deferred income taxes	(58)	67	156
Minority interest in Toysrus.com	(24)	(33)	–
Equity in net earnings of Toys – Japan	(29)	(31)	–
Restructuring and other charges	109	–	–
Gain from initial public offering of Toys – Japan	–	(315)	–
Toysrus.com related non-cash costs and charges	–	81	–
Changes in operating assets and liabilities:			
Accounts and other receivables	15	(69)	35
Merchandise inventories	217	(486)	(192)
Prepaid expenses and other operating assets	36	(54)	(69)
Accounts payable, accrued expenses and other liabilities	(241)	(178)	497
Income taxes payable	104	173	(119)
Net cash from operating activities	504	(151)	865
Cash Flows from Investing Activities			
Capital expenditures, net	(705)	(402)	(533)
Net proceeds from sale of Toys – Japan common stock	–	267	–
Reduction in cash due to deconsolidation of Toys – Japan	–	(15)	–
Purchase of Imaginarium, net of cash acquired	–	–	(43)
Other assets	–	–	(28)
Net cash from investing activities	(705)	(150)	(604)
Cash Flows from Financing Activities			
Short-term borrowings, net	(588)	419	95
Long-term borrowings	1,214	147	593
Long-term debt repayments	(410)	(45)	(604)
Exercise of stock options	19	2	14
Share repurchase program	(44)	(632)	(200)
Proceeds received from investors in Toysrus.com	–	97	–
Issuance of stock warrants	–	10	–
Net cash from financing activities	191	(2)	(102)
Effect of exchange rate changes on cash and cash equivalents	18	(6)	15
Cash and Cash Equivalents			
Increase/(decrease) during year	8	(309)	174
Beginning of year	275	584	410
End of year	$ 283	$ 275	$ 584
Supplemental Disclosures of Cash Flow Information			
Income tax (refunds) payments, net	$ (22)	$ (2)	$ 126
Interest payments	$ 85	$ 128	$ 92

See notes to consolidated financial statements.

Consolidated Statements of Stockholders' Equity

Toys"R"Us, Inc. and Subsidiaries

| (In millions) | Common Stock | | | | Additional paid-in capital | Accumulated other comprehensive loss | Retained earnings | Total stockholders' equity |
| | Issued | | In Treasury | | | | | |
	Shares	Amount	Shares	Amount				
Balance, January 30, 1999	300.4	$ 30	(49.8)	$ (1,243)	$ 459	$ (100)	$ 4,478	$ 3,624
Net earnings for the year	–	–	–	–	–	–	279	279
Foreign currency translation adjustments	–	–	–	–	–	(37)	–	(37)
Comprehensive income								242
Share repurchase program	–	–	(12.0)	(200)	–	–	–	(200)
Issuance of restricted stock, net	–	–	–	3	(4)	–	–	(1)
Exercise of stock options, net	–	–	0.7	17	(2)	–	–	15
Balance, January 29, 2000	300.4	$ 30	(61.1)	$ (1,423)	$ 453	$ (137)	$ 4,757	$ 3,680
Net earnings for the year	–	–	–	–	–	–	404	404
Foreign currency translation adjustments	–	–	–	–	–	(74)	–	(74)
Comprehensive income								330
Share repurchase program	–	–	(42.1)	(632)	–	–	–	(632)
Issuance of restricted stock, net	–	–	–	50	(21)	–	–	29
Exercise of stock options, net	–	–	0.3	4	(3)	–	–	1
Issuance of stock warrants	–	–	–	–	10	–	–	10
Balance, February 3, 2001	300.4	$ 30	(102.9)	$ (2,001)	$ 439	$ (211)	$ 5,161	$ 3,418
Net earnings for the year	–	–	–	–	–	–	67	67
Foreign currency translation adjustments	–	–	–	–	–	(55)	–	(55)
Unrealized loss on hedged transactions	–	–	–	–	–	(1)	–	(1)
Comprehensive income								11
Share repurchase program	–	–	(2.1)	(44)	–	–	–	(44)
Issuance of restricted stock, net	–	–	0.5	5	4	–	–	9
Exercise of stock options, net	–	–	0.8	19	1	–	–	20
Balance, February 2, 2002	300.4	$ 30	(103.7)	$(2,021)	$ 444	$ (267)	$ 5,228	$ 3,414

See notes to consolidated financial statements.

Notes to Consolidated Financial Statements

Toys"R"Us, Inc. and Subsidiaries

(Amounts in millions, except per share data)

SUMMARY OF SIGNIFICANT ACCOUNTING POLICIES

Fiscal Year

The company's fiscal year ends on the Saturday nearest to January 31. References to 2001, 2000, and 1999 are for the 52 weeks ended February 2, 2002, the 53 weeks ended February 3, 2001 and the 52 weeks ended January 29, 2000, respectively.

Reclassification

Certain amounts in 2000 and 1999 have been reclassified to conform to the 2001 presentation.

Principles of Consolidation

The consolidated financial statements include the accounts of the company and its subsidiaries. All material intercompany balances and transactions have been eliminated. Assets and liabilities of foreign operations are translated at current rates of exchange at the balance sheet date while results of operations are translated at average rates in effect for the period. Unrealized translation gains or losses are shown as a component of accumulated other comprehensive loss within stockholders' equity.

Use of Estimates

The preparation of financial statements in conformity with accounting principles generally accepted in the United States requires management to make estimates and assumptions that affect the amounts reported in the consolidated financial statements and accompanying notes. Actual results could differ from those estimates.

Revenue Recognition

The company recognizes retail sales at the time the guest takes possession of merchandise or the point of sale. Revenues from the sale of gift cards and issuance of store credits are recognized when they are utilized or redeemed.

Advertising Costs

Net advertising costs are included in selling, general and administrative expenses and are expensed at the point of first broadcast or distribution. Net advertising costs were $166, $135, and $125 for 2001, 2000 and 1999, respectively.

Cash and Cash Equivalents

The company considers its highly liquid investments with original maturities of less than three months to be cash equivalents.

Merchandise Inventories

Merchandise inventories for the U.S. toy store division, which represent approximately 70% of total inventories, are stated at the lower of LIFO (last-in, first-out) cost or market, as determined by the retail inventory method. If inventories had been valued at the lower of FIFO (first-in, first-out) cost or market, inventories would show no change at February 2, 2002 or February 3, 2001. All other merchandise inventories are stated at the lower of FIFO cost or market as determined by the retail inventory method.

Property and Equipment

Property and equipment are recorded at cost. Depreciation and amortization are provided using the straight-line method over the estimated useful lives of the assets or, where applicable, the terms of the respective leases, whichever is shorter. The company evaluates the need to recognize impairment losses relating to long-lived assets based on several factors including, but not limited to, management's plans for future operations, recent operating results and projected cash flows.

Financial Instruments

The company adopted the provisions of Statement of Financial Accounting Standards ("SFAS") No. 133, "Accounting for Derivative Instruments and Hedging Activities," as amended, effective February 4, 2001, as discussed in the footnote "Derivative Instruments and Hedging Activities." This statement requires that all derivatives be recorded on the balance sheet at fair value and that changes in fair value be recognized currently in earnings unless specific hedge accounting criteria is met.

The company enters into forward foreign exchange contracts to minimize the risk associated with currency movement relating to its short-term intercompany loan program with foreign subsidiaries. Gains and losses, which offset the movement in the underlying transactions, are recognized as part of such transactions. Gross deferred unrealized gains and losses on the forward contracts were not material at either February 2, 2002 or February 3, 2001. The related receivable, payable and deferred gain or loss are included on a net basis in the balance sheet. The company had $158 and $95 of short-term outstanding forward contracts at February 2, 2002 and February 3, 2001, maturing in 2002 and 2001, respectively. These contracts are entered into with counter-parties that have high credit ratings and with which the company has the contractual right to net forward currency settlements.

PROPERTY AND EQUIPMENT

	Useful Life (in years)	February 2, 2002	February 3, 2001
Land		$ 811	$ 810
Buildings	45-50	1,980	1,849
Furniture and equipment	5-20	1,927	2,218
Leaseholds and leasehold improvements	12½-35	1,542	1,291
Construction in progress		41	97
Leased property and equipment under capital lease		53	56
		6,354	6,321
Less accumulated depreciation and amortization		1,810	2,064
		$ 4,544	$ 4,257

Included in accumulated depreciation and amortization is approximately $26 and $24 related to assets under capital lease at February 2, 2002 and February 3, 2001, respectively.

notes to consolidated financial statements

SEASONAL FINANCING AND LONG-TERM DEBT

	February 2, 2002	February 3, 2001
7.625% notes, due fiscal 2011	$ 500	$ –
6.875% notes, due fiscal 2006	250	–
500 Euro Bond, due fiscal 2004	466	–
475 Swiss franc note payable, due fiscal 2003[a]	342	342
8³/₄% debentures, due fiscal 2021, net of expenses[b]	198	198
Note payable at an effective cost of 2.32% due in semi-annual installments through fiscal 2005[c]	119	147
Industrial revenue bonds, net of expenses[d]	34	41
Obligation under capital leases	21	32
Mortgage notes payable at annual interest rates from 10.16% to 11.00%[e]	9	9
Commercial paper, interest rates from 6.37% to 6.75% for 2000[f]	–	834
Fair value hedging adjustment	(84)	–
	1,855	1,603
Less current portion[g]	39	36
	$ 1,816	$ 1,567

(a) Supported by a 406 Swiss franc bank letter of credit. This note has been converted by an interest rate and currency swap to a floating rate, US dollar obligation at 3 month LIBOR less approximately 121 basis points.

(b) Fair value was $204 and $209 at February 2, 2002 and February 3, 2001. The fair market value was estimated using quoted market rates for publicly traded debt and estimated interest rates for non-public debt.

(c) Amortizing note, secured by the expected future yen cash flows from license fees due from Toys – Japan.

(d) Bank letters of credit of $14, expiring in 2003, support certain of these industrial revenue bonds. The bonds have fixed or variable interest rates with an average rate of 1.5% and 5.5% at February 2, 2002 and February 3, 2001, respectively.

(e) Collateralized by property and equipment with an aggregate carrying value of $6 and $9 at February 2, 2002 and February 3, 2001, respectively.

(f) Included in this amount is the EURO equivalent of $466 used to refinance outstanding commercial paper obligations.

(g) Included in accrued expenses and other current liabilities on the consolidated balance sheets.

On February 13, 2001, the company issued and sold 500 EURO through the public issuance of a EURO bond bearing interest at 6.375% per annum. Through the use of derivative instruments, this obligation was swapped into a $466 fixed rate obligation at an effective rate of 7.43% per annum with interest payments due annually and principal due on February 13, 2004. Accordingly, the company reclassified $466 from short-term borrowings to long-term debt at February 3, 2001.

On July 19, 2001, the company issued and sold $500 of notes bearing interest at 7.625% per annum maturing on August 1, 2011 and $250 of notes bearing interest at 6.875% per annum maturing on August 1, 2006. Simultaneously, the company entered into interest rate swap agreements. As a result of the interest rate swap agreements, interest on the $500 notes will accrue at the rate of LIBOR plus 1.5120% per annum and interest on the $250 notes

will accrue at the rate of LIBOR plus 1.1515% per annum. Interest is payable on both notes semi-annually on February 1 and August 1 of each year, commencing on February 1, 2002.

Long-term debt balances as of February 2, 2002 have been impacted by currency and interest rate swaps entered into during fiscal 2001, as discussed in the footnote "Derivative Instruments and Hedging Activities."

The company has a $975 unsecured committed revolving credit facility from a syndicate of financial institutions. The credit facility includes a $650 5-Year facility expiring in September 2006 and a $325 364-Day facility expiring in September 2002. This facility is available for seasonal borrowings and to support the company's domestic commercial paper borrowings. There were no outstanding balances under any of these committed revolvers at the end of fiscal 2001, 2000 or 1999. Additionally, the company has lines of credit with various banks to meet short-term financing needs of its foreign subsidiaries. Cash requirements for operations, capital expenditures and lease commitments will be met primarily through operating activities and issuance of equity and/or debt.

During 2000, the company classified $368 of commercial paper as long-term debt, as the company maintained long-term committed credit agreements, as described above, to support these borrowings and intended to refinance them on a long-term basis. This amount was repaid out of the proceeds of the 7.625% notes discussed above.

The weighted-average interest rate on short-term borrowings outstanding at February 3, 2001 was 6.6%. There were no short-term borrowings outstanding at February 2, 2002.

The annual maturities of long-term debt at February 2, 2002 are as follows:

2002	$ 39
2003	378
2004	503
2005	54
2006	252
2007 and subsequent	713
Fair value hedging adjustment	(84)
	$ 1,855

DERIVATIVE INSTRUMENTS AND HEDGING ACTIVITIES

The company is exposed to market risk from potential changes in interest rates and foreign exchange rates. The company regularly evaluates these risks and has taken the following measures to mitigate these risks: the countries in which the company owns assets and operates stores are politically stable; the company's foreign exchange risk management objectives are to stabilize cash flow from the effects of foreign currency fluctuations; the company does not participate in speculative hedges; and the company will, whenever practical, offset local investments in foreign currencies with borrowings denominated in the same currencies. The company also enters into derivative financial instruments to hedge a variety of risk exposures including interest rate and currency risks.

/ notes to consolidated financial statements /

The company purchases forward exchange contracts to minimize and manage the foreign currency risks related to its import merchandise purchase program. The counter-parties to these contracts are highly rated financial institutions and the company does not have significant exposure to any counter-party. These forward exchange contracts are designated as dual purpose hedges, as defined by SFAS No. 133, and are effective as hedges. The forward exchange contracts are designated as cash flow hedges from the inception of the forward exchange contract until the import merchandise is received and the related accounts payable is recorded. Accordingly, changes in the effective portion of the fair value of these forward exchange contracts during this period are included in other comprehensive income. Once merchandise is received, these forward exchange contracts are then designated as fair value hedges until the settlement of the import merchandise accounts payable. Accordingly, related gains and losses on these forward contracts offset the foreign currency gains and losses on the underlying transactions. Once the hedged transactions are completed, or when merchandise is sold, the unrealized gains and losses on the forward contracts are reclassified from accumulated other comprehensive income to earnings. The company did not realize any material gain or loss related to these transactions in 2001. The unrealized loss recorded in other comprehensive income at February 2, 2002 was not material to the company's consolidated financial condition.

The company is faced with interest rate risks resulting from interest rate fluctuations. The company has a variety of fixed and variable rate debt instruments. In an effort to manage interest rate exposures, the company strives to achieve an acceptable balance between fixed and variable rate debt and has entered into interest rate swaps to maintain that balance.

In July 2001, the company entered into interest rate swap agreements on its 7.625% $500 notes, due August 1, 2011, and its 6.875% $250 notes, due August 1, 2006. Under these agreements, the company will pay interest at a variable rate in exchange for fixed rate payments, effectively transforming the debentures to floating rate obligations. This swap is designated as a highly effective fair value hedge, as defined by SFAS No. 133. Changes in the fair value of the interest rate swap perfectly offset changes in the fair value of the fixed rate debt due to changes in market interest rates. As such, there was no ineffective hedge portion recognized in earnings during 2001.

On February 13, 2001, the company issued and sold 500 EURO through the public issuance of a EURO bond bearing interest at 6.375% per annum. The obligation was swapped into a $466 fixed rate obligation with an effective rate of 7.43% per annum with interest payments due annually and principal due February 13, 2004. This cross currency swap is designated as a cash flow hedge, as defined by SFAS No. 133, and is effective as a hedge. The portion of the fair value of the swap attributable to changes in the spot rate is matched in earnings against changes in the fair value of debt.

The company entered into a Swiss franc floating rate loan with a financial institution in January 1999, due January 2004. The company also entered into a contract to swap U.S. dollars to Swiss francs, within exact terms of the loan. This cross currency swap has been designated as a foreign currency fair value hedge, as defined by SFAS No. 133, and is effective as a hedge.

The company entered into a note payable for $147 with a syndicate of financial institutions in July 2000, repayable in semi-annual installments, with the final installment due August 2005. The company also entered into a contract to swap yen to U.S. dollars, within exact terms of the loan. This cross currency swap has been designated as a foreign currency cash flow hedge, as defined by SFAS No. 133, and is effective as a hedge.

The company has reduced the carrying amount of its long-term debt by $84 at February 2, 2002, representing the carrying amount of the debt in excess of fair value on that date. Also at February 2, 2002, the company has recorded derivative assets of $42 and derivative liabilities of $122, representing the fair value of these derivatives at that date.

These transactions did not have a material impact on the company's results of operations or cash flows.

LEASES

The company leases a portion of the real estate used in its operations. Most leases require the company to pay real estate taxes and other expenses; some require additional amounts based on percentages of sales.

Minimum rental commitments under noncancelable operating leases having a term of more than one year as of February 2, 2002 are as follows:

	Gross minimum rentals	Sublease income	Net minimum rentals
2002	$ 286	$ 24	$ 262
2003	286	20	266
2004	280	17	263
2005	268	14	254
2006	255	13	242
2007 and subsequent	1,960	62	1,898
	$ 3,335	$ 150	$ 3,185

Total rent expense, net of sublease income, was $261, $291 and $350 in 2001, 2000 and 1999, respectively.

The company's new corporate headquarters facility, located in Wayne, New Jersey, which the company intends to fully occupy by the summer of 2003, is being financed under a lease arrangement commonly referred to as a "synthetic lease." Under this lease, unrelated third parties, arranged by Wachovia Development Corporation, a multi-purpose real estate investment company, will fund up to $125 for the acquisition and construction of the facility. Upon completion of the construction, which is expected to be in 2003, the company will begin paying rent on the facility until the lease expires in 2011. The rent will be based on a mix of fixed and variable interest rates which will be applied against the final amount funded. Upon expiration of the lease, the company would expect to either: renew the lease arrangement; purchase the facility from the lessor; or remarket the property on behalf of the owner. Under accounting principles generally accepted in the United States, this arrangement is required to be treated as an operating lease for accounting purposes and will be treated as a financing for tax purposes.

notes to consolidated financial statements

STOCKHOLDERS' EQUITY

The common shares of the company, par value $0.10 per share, were as follows:

	February 2, 2002	February 3, 2001
Authorized shares	650.0	650.0
Issued shares	300.4	300.4
Treasury shares	103.7	102.9
Issued and outstanding shares	196.7	197.5

EARNINGS PER SHARE

The following table sets forth the computation of basic and diluted earnings per share:

	2001	2000	1999
Numerator:			
Net earnings available to common stockholders	$ 67	$ 404	$ 279
Denominator for basic earnings per share – weighted average shares	197.6	210.9	244.8
Effect of dilutive securities: Stock options, etc.	8.4	4.1	0.6
Denominator for diluted earnings per share – weighted average shares	206.0	215.0	245.4
Basic earnings per share	$ 0.34	$ 1.92	$ 1.14
Diluted earnings per share	$ 0.33	$ 1.88	$ 1.14

Options to purchase approximately 10.3, 3.0 and 38.7 shares of common stock were outstanding during 2001, 2000 and 1999, respectively, but were not included in the computation of diluted earnings per share because the option exercise prices were greater than the average market price of the common shares.

STOCK PURCHASE WARRANTS

The company issued 1.2 stock purchase warrants to SOFTBANK Venture Capital and affiliates ("SOFTBANK") for $8.33 per warrant. Each warrant gives the holder thereof the right to purchase one share of Toys"R"Us common stock at an exercise price of $13 per share, until the expiration date of February 24, 2010. As of February 2, 2002, these warrants have not been exercised. In addition, the company granted a warrant on August 9, 2000 entitling Amazon.com to acquire up to 5% (subject to dilution under certain circumstances) of the capital of Toysrus.com at the then market value. As of February 2, 2002, this warrant has not been exercised.

INVESTMENT IN TOYS – JAPAN

The company accounts for its investment in the common stock of Toys – Japan under the "equity method" of accounting since the initial public offering on April 24, 2000. The quoted market value of the company's investment in Toys – Japan was $283 at February 2, 2002. The valuation represents a mathematical calculation based on the closing quotation published by the Tokyo over-the-counter market and is not necessarily indicative of the amount that could be realized upon sale.

TAXES ON INCOME

The provisions for income taxes consist of the following:

	2001	2000	1999
Current:			
Federal	$ 63	$ 120	$ (12)
Foreign	10	36	17
State	9	10	–
	82	166	5
Deferred:			
Federal	(60)	50	31
Foreign	16	13	124
State	(14)	4	1
	(58)	67	156
Total tax provision	$ 24	$ 233	$ 161

At February 2, 2002 and February 3, 2001, the company had gross deferred tax assets, before valuation allowances, of $576 and $486, respectively, and gross deferred tax liabilities of $484 and $461, respectively. Deferred tax assets of $45 were included in "Prepaid expenses and other current assets" at February 2, 2002 and February 3, 2001. Deferred tax assets, net of valuation allowances of $244 and $175 were included in "Other assets" at February 2, 2002 and February 3, 2001. Deferred tax liabilities of $36 and $59 were included in "Accrued expenses and other current liabilities" at February 2, 2002 and February 3, 2001. The tax effects of temporary differences and carryforwards that give rise to significant portions of deferred tax assets and liabilities consist of the following:

	February 2, 2002	February 3, 2001
Net deferred tax assets/(liabilities):		
Foreign loss carryforwards	$ 296	$ 290
Valuation allowances, primarily related to foreign loss carryforwards	(287)	(266)
Restructuring	131	42
Property, plant and equipment	(322)	(316)
LIFO inventory	3	(16)
Other	(16)	25
Net deferred tax liability	$ (195)	$ (241)

On February 2, 2002, the company had $772 of foreign loss carryforwards of which $224 must be utilized within the next seven years and $548 over an indefinite period.

A reconciliation of the federal statutory tax rate with the effective tax rate follows:

	2001	2000	1999
Statutory tax rate	35.0%	35.0%	35.0%
State income taxes, net of federal income tax benefit	1.8	1.4	0.6
Foreign taxes, net of valuation allowance	(9.4)	(1.2)	25.8
Reversal of deferred tax asset	(6.5)	–	–
Tax benefit of branch election	–	(1.4)	(22.5)
Subpart F income	5.4	0.6	1.0
Tax on previously unremitted earnings	–	3.7	–
Amortization of goodwill	3.5	0.5	0.7
Other, net	(2.9)	(2.1)	(4.1)
Effective tax rate	26.9%	36.5%	36.5%

/ notes to consolidated financial statements /

Deferred income taxes are not provided on unremitted earnings of foreign subsidiaries that are intended to be indefinitely invested. Exclusive of amounts that, if remitted, would result in little or no tax under current U.S. tax laws, unremitted earnings were approximately $506 at February 2, 2002. Net income taxes of approximately $108 would be due if these earnings were remitted.

In 2000, the company elected to treat one of its foreign subsidiaries as a U.S. branch, claimed deductions for its investment in this subsidiary, and reduced its current tax expense. In 1999, the company also elected to treat two of its other foreign subsidiaries as U.S. branches. Income earned by these foreign subsidiaries can be offset by foreign loss carryforwards but will be subject to current U.S. income tax.

STOCK OPTIONS

The company has stock option plans (the "Plans") which provide for the granting of options to purchase the company's common stock. The Plans cover substantially all employees and directors of the company and provide for the issuance of non-qualified options, incentive stock options, performance share options, performance units, stock appreciation rights, restricted shares, restricted units and unrestricted shares. The Plans provide for a variety of vesting dates with the majority of the options vesting approximately three years from the date of grant, 50% over the first two years and the remaining 50% over three years. Prior to June 10, 1999, options granted to directors are exercisable 20% each year on a cumulative basis commencing one year from the date of grant. Effective June 10, 1999, the options granted to directors are exercisable one-third on a cumulative basis commencing on the third, fourth and fifth anniversaries from the date of grant.

The exercise price per share of all options granted has been the average of the high and low market price of the company's common stock on the date of grant. All options must be exercised within ten years from the date of grant.

At February 2, 2002, an aggregate of 48.9 shares of authorized common stock were reserved for all of the Plans noted above, including 5.0 shares reserved for the issuance of restricted shares, restricted units, performance units, and unrestricted shares. Of these amounts, 15.4 were available for future grants. All outstanding options expire at dates ranging from November 2, 2002 to December 31, 2011.

Stock option transactions are summarized as follows:

	Shares	Exercise Price Per Share	Weighted-Average Exercise Price
Outstanding at January 30, 1999	36.8	$ 14.78 - $ 40.94	$ 26.02
Granted	9.7	11.69 - 24.22	18.63
Exercised	(1.3)	18.16 - 25.44	17.71
Canceled	(5.4)	18.16 - 39.88	25.34
Outstanding at January 29, 2000	39.8	$ 11.69 - $ 40.94	$ 24.59
Granted	7.5	10.25 - 26.25	15.29
Exercised	(0.4)	14.78 - 22.06	18.96
Canceled	(22.2)	14.63 - 40.94	28.60
Outstanding at February 3, 2001	24.7	$ 10.25 - $ 40.94	$ 18.36
Granted	8.6	15.53 - 38.36	28.03
Exercised	(1.1)	14.63 - 25.44	16.21
Canceled	(1.6)	11.50 - 39.88	24.26
Outstanding at February 2, 2002	**30.6**	**$ 10.25 - $ 40.94**	**$ 20.39**

Options exercisable and the weighted-average exercise prices were 20.7 and $23.94 at January 29, 2000, and 11.3 and $19.60 at February 3, 2001 and 16.1 and $20.74 at February 2, 2002, respectively.

At February 2, 2002 and February 3, 2001, the company's Toysrus.com internet subsidiary had approximately 11.3 and 15.0 stock options outstanding to both employees and non-employees of the company, representing approximately 12% and 15% of the authorized common stock of Toysrus.com at February 2, 2002 and February 3, 2001, respectively. These outstanding options, with exercise prices ranging between $0.30 and $2.25 per share, entitle each option holder the right to purchase one share of the common stock of Toysrus.com.

The company utilizes a restoration feature to encourage the early exercise of certain options and retention of shares, thereby promoting increased employee ownership. This feature provides for the grant of new options when previously owned shares of company stock are used to exercise existing options. Restoration option grants are non-dilutive as they do not increase the combined number of shares of company stock and options held by an employee prior to exercise. The new options are granted at a price equal to the fair market value on the date of the new grant, and generally expire on the same date as the original options that were exercised.

The company has adopted the disclosure only provisions of SFAS No. 123, "Accounting for Stock-Based Compensation," issued in October 1995. In accordance with the provisions of SFAS No. 123, the company applies APB Opinion No. 25 and related interpretations in accounting for its stock option plans and, accordingly, does not recognize compensation cost. If the company had elected to recognize compensation cost based on the fair value of the options granted at grant date as prescribed by SFAS No. 123, net earnings and earnings per share would have been reduced to the pro forma amounts indicated in the table below:

/ notes to consolidated financial statements /

	2001	2000	1999
Net earnings – as reported	**$ 67**	$ 404	$ 279
Net earnings – pro forma	**28**	385	232
Basic earnings per share – reported	**0.34**	1.92	1.14
Basic earnings per share – pro forma	**0.14**	1.83	0.95
Diluted earnings per share – as reported	**0.33**	1.88	1.14
Diluted earnings per share – pro forma	**0.14**	1.79	0.95

The weighted-average fair value at date of grant for options granted in 2001, 2000 and 1999 was $9.16, $5.88 and $6.26, respectively. The fair value of each option grant is estimated on the date of grant using the Black-Scholes option pricing model. As there were a number of options granted during the years of 1999 through 2001, a range of assumptions are provided below:

	2001	2000	1999
Expected stock price volatility	**.407 - .567**	.434 - .585	.351 - .568
Risk-free interest rate	**3.6% - 5.1%**	5.0% - 6.8%	4.7% - 6.7%
Weighted average expected life of options	**5 years**	5 years	6 years

The effects of applying SFAS No. 123 and the results obtained through the use of the Black-Scholes option pricing model are not necessarily indicative of future values.

REPLACEMENT OF CERTAIN STOCK OPTION GRANTS WITH RESTRICTED STOCK

In 2000, the company authorized the exchange of certain stock options, having an exercise price above $22 per share, for an economically equivalent grant of restricted stock. The exchange, which was voluntary, replaced approximately 14.4 options with approximately 1.7 restricted shares. Shares of restricted stock resulting from the exchange vest over a period of three years, with one-half of the grant vesting on April 1, 2002 and the remainder vesting on April 1, 2003. Accordingly, the company recognizes compensation expense throughout the vesting period of the restricted stock. The company recorded $8 in compensation expense related to this restricted stock in both 2002 and 2001.

PROFIT SHARING PLAN

The company has a profit sharing plan with a 401(k) salary deferral feature for eligible domestic employees. The terms of the plan call for annual contributions by the company as determined by the Board of Directors, subject to certain limitations. The profit sharing plan may be terminated at the company's discretion. Provisions of $46, $50 and $48 have been charged to earnings in 2001, 2000 and 1999, respectively.

TOYSRUS.COM

The company entered into an agreement with SOFTBANK which included an investment by SOFTBANK of $60 in Toysrus.com for a 20% ownership interest. Accordingly, the company has recorded a 20% minority interest in the net losses of Toysrus.com in selling, general and administrative expenses. Toysrus.com received additional capital contributions of $37 from SOFTBANK representing its proportionate share of funding required for the operations of Toysrus.com. In connection with the agreement with SOFTBANK, the company issued 1.2 stock purchase warrants for $8.33 per warrant. Each warrant gives the holder thereof the right to purchase one share of Toys"R"Us common stock at an exercise price of $13 per share, until the expiration date of February 24, 2010. As of February 2, 2002, none of these warrants have been exercised.

Toysrus.com entered into a 10-year strategic alliance with Amazon.com to create a co-branded toy and video game on-line store, which was launched in the third quarter 2000. In addition, a co-branded baby products on-line store was launched in May 2001 and a co-branded creative and learning products on-line store launched in July 2001. Under this alliance, Toysrus.com and Amazon.com are responsible for specific aspects of the on-line stores. Toysrus.com is responsible for merchandising and content for the co-branded stores. Toysrus.com also identifies, buys, owns and manages the inventory. Amazon.com handles web-site development, order fulfillment, guest services, and the housing of Toysrus.com's inventory in Amazon.com's U.S. distribution centers. Also in August 2000, Amazon.com was granted a warrant entitling it to acquire up to 5% (subject to dilution under certain circumstances) of the capital of Toysrus.com at the then market value. As of February 2, 2002, this warrant has not been exercised.

In the third quarter of 2000, Toysrus.com recorded $118 in non-recurring costs and charges as a result of the transition to the co-branded site, of which, $10 were included in cost of sales and $108 were included in selling, general and administrative expenses. These costs and charges related primarily to the closure of three distribution centers and web-site asset write-offs, as well as other costs associated with migrating data and merchandise to the new site and facilities. At the end of 2001, Toysrus.com had remaining reserves of approximately $42, primarily for the exit of its Memphis Tennessee distribution center, which is being actively marketed. The company believes that these remaining reserves are adequate to complete all remaining action plans.

SEGMENTS

The company's reportable segments are Toys"R"Us – U.S., which operates toy stores in 49 states and Puerto Rico, Toys"R"Us – International, which operates, licenses or franchises toy stores in 28 countries outside the United States, Babies"R"Us, which operates stores in 34 states, and Toysrus.com, the company's internet subsidiary.

/ notes to consolidated financial statements /

Information on segments and reconciliation to earnings before income taxes, are as follows:

	February 2, 2002	February 3, 2001	January 29, 2000
Net sales			
Toys"R"Us – U.S.	$ 6,877	$ 7,073	$ 6,911
Toys"R"Us – International	1,889	1,872	1,990
Babies"R"Us	1,421	1,310	1,036
Toysrus.com	277	180	49
Other[a]	555	897	1,876
Total	$11,019	$11,332	$11,862
Operating earnings			
Toys"R"Us – U.S.[b]	$ 308	$ 431	$ 432
Toys"R"Us – International	131	124	102
Babies"R"Us	138	120	78
Toysrus.com, net of minority interest	(76)	(212)	(86)
Other[b],[c]	(115)	(37)	(6)
Restructuring and other charges	(186)	–	–
Operating earnings	$ 200	$ 426	$ 520
Interest expense, net	(109)	(104)	(80)
Gain from IPO of Toys – Japan	–	315	–
Earning before income taxes	$ 91	$ 637	$ 440
Identifiable assets			
Toys"R"Us – U.S.	$ 5,412	$ 5,384	$ 4,801
Toys"R"Us – International	1,146	1,235	1,274
Babies"R"Us	574	486	389
Toysrus.com	84	141	65
Other	860	757	1,824
Total	$ 8,076	$ 8,003	$ 8,353
Depreciation and amortization			
Toys"R"Us – U.S.	$ 212	$ 193	$ 172
Toys"R"Us – International	41	42	47
Babies"R"Us	29	26	22
Toysrus.com	6	6	2
Other	20	23	35
Total	$ 308	$ 290	$ 278

(a) Includes the net sales of Kids"R"Us division and the Toys – Japan division prior to its initial public offering on April 24, 2000.

(b) Includes markdowns related to the store closings announced as part of restructuring.

(c) Includes the results of the Kids"R"Us division and the company's share of the net earnings of Toys – Japan, as well as other corporate related items.

RESTRUCTURING AND OTHER CHARGES

On January 28, 2002, the company announced a series of steps designed to enhance its future cash flow and operating earnings and to allow the company to continue to concentrate its financial resources on those stores and store formats that are most productive. The company is closing 37 Kids"R"Us stores and, in almost all of these locations, is converting the nearest Toys"R"Us store into a Toys"R"Us/Kids"R"Us combo store in tandem with the Kids"R"Us store closings. The company is also closing 27 non-Mission Possible format Toys"R"Us stores, eliminating approximately 1,900 staff positions at stores and headquarters, and consolidating its

store support center facilities for its intended move into its new headquarters in Wayne, New Jersey, which the company intends to fully occupy by the summer of 2003. The five New Jersey facilities to be consolidated into the new headquarters in Wayne, New Jersey, include two locations in Montvale, and one facility each in Paramus, East Hanover, and Fort Lee.

The costs associated with facilities consolidation, elimination of positions, and other actions designed to improve efficiency in support functions were $79, of which $15 related to severance. The costs associated with store closings were $73 for Kids"R"Us and $85 for Toys"R"Us, of which $27 was recorded in cost of sales. The fair values of facilities to be consolidated and store closings were obtained from third party appraisals. The company also reversed $24 million of previously accrued charges ($11 from the 1998 charge and $13 from the 1995 charge) that have been deemed no longer needed. See below for further details regarding the reversal of these reserves. Accordingly, based on all of these actions, the company recorded $213 million of pre-tax ($126 million after-tax) restructuring and other charges in the fourth quarter of its fiscal year ending February 2, 2002. Details on the components of the charges are as follows:

Description	Initial Charge	Utilized In 2001	Reserve Balance 2/02/02
Store Closings:			
Lease commitments	$ 52	$ –	$ 52
Severance	4	–	4
Write-down of property and equipment	75	75	–
Markdowns	27	–	27
Store Support Center Consolidation:			
Lease commitments	28	–	28
Write-down of property and equipment	29	29	–
Severance	15	–	15
Other	7	7	–
Total restructuring and other charges	$ 237	$ 111	$ 126

In 1998, the company announced strategic initiatives to reposition its worldwide business, and recorded restructuring and other charges of $353, including a restructuring charge of $294 to close and/or downsize stores, distribution centers and administrative functions. This worldwide plan included the closing of 50 toy stores in the International division, predominantly in continental Europe, and 9 in the United States and the closing of 31 Kids"R"Us stores and conversion of 28 nearby U.S. toy stores into Toys"R"Us/Kids"R"Us combo stores. Other charges consisted primarily of changes in accounting estimates and provisions for legal settlements of $59 recorded in selling, general and administrative expenses. The remaining reserves related to these charges were $31 at the end of 2001.

In the fourth quarter of 2001, the company determined that $11 of unused reserves for the closing of under-performing stores in central Europe would no longer be needed and reversed these reserves. In the third quarter of 2001, the company completed the satisfaction of certain legal obligations and reversed the remaining unused reserve of $5 million. In the third quarter of 2000, the company determined

notes to consolidated financial statements

that an $11 million reserve would no longer be needed and reversed this reserve. These remaining reserves, primarily for long-term lease commitments, will be utilized during 2002 and thereafter.

In 1998, the company also recorded markdowns and other charges of $345, which included $253 for markdowns required to clear excess inventory from stores, $29 for markdowns related to the store closings and $63 for charges to cost of sales for inventory system refinements and changes in accounting estimates.

In 1995, the company announced certain initiatives to restructure its world-wide business. In the fourth quarter of 2001, the company determined that unused reserves of $13 for the restructuring of its international business would no longer be needed and accordingly, reversed these reserves. The company has substantially completed the remainder of this program, with the exception of long-term lease commitment reserves that will be utilized throughout 2002 and thereafter.

The company believes that unused reserves existing at February 2, 2002 are reasonable estimates of what is required to complete all remaining initiatives.

GAIN FROM INITIAL PUBLIC OFFERING OF TOYS–JAPAN

The company recorded a pre-tax non-operating gain of $315 ($200 net of taxes) in the first quarter of fiscal 2000 resulting from the initial public offering of shares of Toys – Japan. Of this gain, $91 resulted from an adjustment to the basis of the company's investment in Toys – Japan and $224 related to the sale of a portion of company-owned common stock of Toys – Japan. In connection with this transaction the company also received net cash proceeds of $267 and recorded a provision for current income taxes of $82 and a provision for deferred income taxes of $33, respectively. As a result of this transaction, the company's ownership percentage in the common stock of Toys – Japan was reduced from 80% to 48%. Toys – Japan is a licensee of the company.

SUBSEQUENT EVENTS

On March 19, 2002, the company refinanced its note payable originally repayable through fiscal 2005 and increased the amount outstanding to $160 from $100. This borrowing is repayable in semi-annual installments, with the final installment due on February 20, 2008. The effective cost of this borrowing is 2.23% and is secured by expected future cash flows from license fees due from Toys-Japan.

On March 13, 2002, the company filed registration statements with the Securities and Exchange Commission indicating the company's intention to issue $550 of Toys"R"Us equity and equity-linked securities. These securities take the form of $350 of equity security units and $200 of Toys"R"Us common stock. The company plans to issue these securities promptly after the registration statements are declared effective. The net proceeds from these offerings will be utilized as an alternative to short-term borrowings and other general corporate purposes.

OTHER MATTERS

In August 2000, eleven purported class action lawsuits were filed (six in the United States District Court for the District of New Jersey, three in the United States District Court for the Northern District of California, one in the United States District Court for the Western District of Texas and one in the Superior Court of the State of California, County of San Bernadino), against the company and its affiliates Toysrus.com, Inc. and Toysrus.com, LLC. In September 2000, three additional purported class action lawsuits were filed (two in the United States District Court for the District of New Jersey and one in the United States District Court for the Western District of Texas). These actions generally purport to bring claims on behalf of all persons who have visited one or more of the company's web sites and either made an online purchase or allegedly had information about them unlawfully "intercepted," "monitored," "transmitted," or "used." All the suits (except one filed in the United States District Court for the District of New Jersey) also named Coremetrics, Inc. ("Coremetrics"), an internet marketing company, as a defendant.

These lawsuits assert various claims under the federal privacy and computer fraud statutes, as well as under state statutory and common law, arising out of an agreement between the company and Coremetrics, alleging that the company tracks its web site users' activities online and shares that information with third parties in violation of the law. These suits seek damages in unspecified amounts and other relief under state and federal law.

The company and Coremetrics filed a joint application with the Multidistrict litigation panel to have all of the federal actions consolidated and transferred to the United States District Court for the Northern District of California. A hearing on that application was held on November 17, 2000, and all matters have now been consolidated in the United States District Court for the Northern District of California.

The company moved for a stay of the action in the Superior Court of the State of California, County of San Bernadino pending resolution of the actions filed in federal court. The court granted the company's motion for stay on May 22, 2001. Plaintiffs subsequently voluntarily dismissed the action without prejudice.

The company filed a motion to dismiss plaintiffs' federal causes of action on August 3, 2001. On October 9, 2001, the United States District Court, Northern California District, granted in part and denied in part the company's motion to dismiss. The court's order dismissed one cause of action without leave to amend, dismissed a second cause of action with leave to amend and denied the company's motion as to the third cause of action. On October 16, 2001, plaintiffs filed an amended complaint to remedy the defects in the cause of action previously dismissed with leave to amend.

The company believes that it has substantial defenses to these claims and plans to vigorously defend these lawsuits.

The company is party to certain other litigation which, in management's judgement, based in part on the opinion of legal counsel, will not have a material adverse effect on the company's financial position.

reports

Report of Management

Responsibility for the integrity and objectivity of the financial information presented in this Annual Report rests with the management of Toys"R"Us. The accompanying financial statements have been prepared from accounting records which management believes fairly and accurately reflect the operations and financial position of the company. Management has established a system of internal controls to provide reasonable assurance that assets are maintained and accounted for in accordance with its policies and that transactions are recorded accurately on the company's books and records.

The company's comprehensive internal audit program provides for constant evaluation of the adequacy of the adherence to management's established policies and procedures. The company has distributed to key employees its policies for conducting business affairs in a lawful and ethical manner.

The Audit Committee of the Board of Directors, which is comprised solely of outside directors, provides oversight to the financial reporting process through periodic meetings with our independent auditors, internal auditors and management.

The financial statements of the company have been audited by Ernst & Young LLP, independent auditors, in accordance with auditing standards generally accepted in the United States, including a review of financial reporting matters and internal controls to the extent necessary to express an opinion on the consolidated financial statements.

John H. Eyler, Jr.
Chairman and
Chief Executive Officer

Louis Lipschitz
Executive Vice President
and Chief Financial Officer

Report of Independent Auditors

The Board of Directors and Stockholders
Toys"R"Us, Inc.

We have audited the accompanying consolidated balance sheets of Toys"R"Us, Inc. and subsidiaries as of February 2, 2002 and February 3, 2001, and the related consolidated statements of earnings, stockholders' equity and cash flows for each of the three years in the period ended February 2, 2002. These financial statements are the responsibility of the company's management. Our responsibility is to express an opinion on these financial statements based on our audits.

We conducted our audits in accordance with auditing standards generally accepted in the United States. Those standards require that we plan and perform the audit to obtain reasonable assurance about whether the financial statements are free of material misstatement. An audit includes examining, on a test basis, evidence supporting the amounts and disclosures in the financial statements. An audit also includes assessing the accounting principles used and significant estimates made by management, as well as evaluating the overall financial statement presentation. We believe that our audits provide a reasonable basis for our opinion.

In our opinion, the financial statements referred to above present fairly, in all material respects, the consolidated financial position of Toys"R"Us, Inc. and subsidiaries at February 2, 2002 and February 3, 2001, and the consolidated results of their operations and their cash flows for each of the three years in the period ended February 2, 2002, in conformity with accounting principles generally accepted in the United States.

Ernst & Young LLP

New York, New York
March 14, 2002

/ directors and officers /

Directors

Charles Lazarus
Chairman Emeritus of the company

John H. Eyler, Jr.
*Chairman and
Chief Executive Officer
of the company*

RoAnn Costin
*President, Reservoir Capital
Management, Inc.*

Roger N. Farah
*President and
Chief Operating Officer,
Polo Ralph Lauren*

Peter A. Georgescu
*Chairman Emeritus,
Young & Rubicam, Inc.*

Michael Goldstein
*Chairman, The Toys"R"Us
Children's Fund, Inc.*

Calvin Hill
Consultant

Nancy Karch
*Retired Senior Partner,
McKinsey & Company*

Shirley Strum Kenny
*President, State University
of New York at Stony Brook*

Norman S. Matthews
*Consultant and former
Vice Chairman of the Board
and President of Federated
Department Stores*

Arthur B. Newman
*Senior Managing Director,
Blackstone Group*

Corporate and Administrative Officers

John H. Eyler, Jr.
Chairman and Chief Executive Officer

Francesca L. Brockett
*Executive Vice President – Strategic
Planning/Business Development*

Michael D'Ambrose
*Executive Vice President –
Human Resources*

Christopher K. Kay
*Executive Vice President –
Operations and General Counsel,
Corporate Secretary*

Warren F. Kornblum
*Executive Vice President –
Chief Marketing Officer*

Louis Lipschitz
*Executive Vice President –
Chief Financial Officer*

John Holohan
*Senior Vice President –
Chief Information Officer*

Jon W. Kimmins
*Senior Vice President –
Treasurer*

Dorvin D. Lively
*Senior Vice President –
Corporate Controller*

Peter W. Weiss
Senior Vice President – Taxes

Rebecca A. Caruso
*Vice President –
Corporate Communications*

Ursula H. Moran
*Vice President –
Investor Relations*

Divisional Officers

Raymond L. Arthur
President – Toysrus.com

John Barbour
*President –
Toys"R"Us International*

Janet L. Emerson
*President – Kids"R"Us
and Imaginarium*

James E. Feldt
*President – Merchandising
and Marketing, Toys"R"Us U.S.*

Richard L. Markee
*President – Specialty Businesses
and International Operations*

Gregory R. Staley
President – Toys"R"Us U.S.

James R. Bodemuller
*Senior Vice President –
Planning and Allocation,
Toys"R"Us U.S.*

Joan W. Donovan
*Senior Vice President –
General Merchandise Manager,
Toys"R"Us International*

Martin E. Fogelman
*Senior Vice President –
General Merchandise Manager,
Juvenile Babies"R"Us*

Jonathan M. Friedman
*Senior Vice President –
Chief Financial Officer,
Toys"R"Us U.S.*

Andrew R. Gatto
*Senior Vice President –
Product Development,
Toys"R"Us U.S.*

Steven J. Krajewski
*Senior Vice President –
Operations, Toys"R"Us U.S.*

James G. Parros
*Senior Vice President –
Stores and Distribution Center
Operations, Kids"R"Us*

David E. Schoenbeck
*Senior Vice President –
Operations, Babies"R"Us*

Ernest V. Speranza
*Senior Vice President –
Marketing, Toys"R"Us International*

Pamela B. Wallack
*Senior Vice President –
General Merchandise Manager,
Kids"R"Us*

International Country Presidents and Managing Directors

David Rurka
*Managing Director –
Toys"R"Us United Kingdom
and Chairman of the
European Management Board*

Jacques LeFoll
President – Toys"R"Us France

Monika Merz
President – Toys"R"Us Canada

John Schryver
*Managing Director –
Toys"R"Us Australia*

Michael C. Taylor
*Acting President –
Toys"R"Us Central Europe*

Antonio Urcelay
*Managing Director –
Toys"R"Us Iberia*

financial data

Quarterly Financial Data and Market Information

Toys"R"Us, Inc. and Subsidiaries

Quarterly Financial Data

(In millions except per share data)

The following table sets forth certain unaudited quarterly financial information:

	First Quarter	Second Quarter	Third Quarter	Fourth Quarter
2001				
Net Sales	$ 2,061	$ 2,021	$ 2,178	$ 4,759
Gross Margin	665	661	710	1,379
Net Earnings/(loss)	(18)	(29)	(44)	158[a]
Basic Earnings per Share/(loss)	$ (0.09)	$ (0.15)	$ (0.22)	$ 0.80[a]
Diluted Earnings per Share/(loss)	$ (0.09)	$ (0.15)	$ (0.22)	$ 0.78[a]
2000				
Net Sales	$ 2,319	$ 1,994	$ 2,220	$ 4,799
Gross Margin	718	636	698	1,465
Net Earnings/(Loss)	215[b]	3	(65)[c]	251
Basic Earnings/(Loss) per Share	$ 0.93[b]	$ 0.01	$ (0.32)[c]	$ 1.27
Diluted Earnings/(Loss) per Share	$ 0.93[b]	$ 0.01	$ (0.32)[c]	$ 1.23

(a) Includes restructuring and other charges of $213 ($126 net of tax, or $0.61 per share).

(b) Includes a non-operating gain from the initial public offering of Toys – Japan of $315 ($200 net of tax, or $0.87 per share).

(c) Includes Toysrus.com/Amazon.com alliance non-recurring charges of $94 ($60 net of tax, or $0.30 per share).

Market Information

The company's common stock is listed on the New York Stock Exchange. The following table reflects the high and low prices (rounded to the nearest hundredth) based on New York Stock Exchange trading since January 29, 2000.

The company has not paid any cash dividends, however, the Board of Directors of the company periodically reviews this policy.

The company had approximately 30,269 Stockholders of Record on March 13, 2002.

			High	Low
2000	1st	Quarter	$ 15.50	$ 10.06
	2nd	Quarter	18.00	13.44
	3rd	Quarter	19.25	14.88
	4th	Quarter	26.69	14.50
2001	1st	Quarter	$ 26.52	$ 23.00
	2nd	Quarter	31.00	22.30
	3rd	Quarter	25.10	16.81
	4th	Quarter	24.00	18.25

WALGREENS 2001 ANNUAL REPORT

Our Corner Walgreens

This annual report is for the year ended August 31, 2001. Page 1 and pages 20–31 are reprinted with permission from Walgreen Co., Deerfield, IL.

WALGREEN CO.

More than a century old–somehow that doesn't bring to mind the vision of an agile and fast-growing retailer like Walgreens. We're the oldest major U.S. drugstore chain... with the youngest, most innovative stores. And we lead the industry in sales, profits and store growth. We place a high value on our history as we move ahead with plans to reaffirm–every day–our position as America's most convenient and technologically advanced healthcare retailer.

Sales in 2001 reached $24.6 billion, generated by 3,520 stores in 43 states and Puerto Rico. We filled 323 million prescriptions–11 percent of the U.S. retail market and more per store than all major competitors.

Walgreens has 130,000 employees and over one-half million shareholders. Our stores serve three million customers daily and average $6.8 million in annual sales. That's $628 per square foot, among the highest in the chain drugstore industry.

Walgreens has paid dividends in every quarter since 1933 and has raised them in each of the past 25 years. Since 1980, we've had seven two-for-one stock splits. With a market capitalization of $35 billion as of August 31, 2001, Walgreens ranks third among U.S. retailers and fifth in the world.

ABOUT THE COVER
Amy Hegi and her daughter Kate, loyal Walgreen customers in Dallas, rely on employees like pharmacist Sreedhar Vasireddy in Dallas (top) and photo specialist Artayvier Miller in Atlanta (left) to provide services at convenient stores like the one in Cheyenne, Wyoming (bottom).

Financial Highlights

For the Years Ended August 31, 2001 and 2000

(In Millions, except per share data)	*2001*	*2000*	*Increase*
Net Sales	$24,623.0	$21,206.9	16.1%
Net Earnings	$ 885.6	$ 776.9	14.0%
Net Earnings per Common Share (diluted)	$ .86	$ .76	13.2%
Shareholders' Equity	$ 5,207.2	$ 4,234.0	23.0%
Return on Average Shareholders' Equity	18.8%	20.1%	
Closing Stock Price per Common Share	$ 34.35	$ 32.88	
Total Market Value of Common Stock	$ 35,017	$ 33,231	5.4%
Dividends Declared per Common Share	$ .14	$ .135	3.7%
Average Shares Outstanding (diluted)	1,028.9	1,019.9	

Earnings
Millions of Dollars

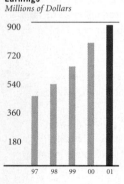

Earnings per Share (diluted)
Dollars

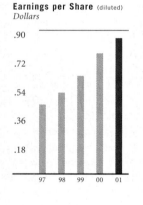

Sales
Billions of Dollars

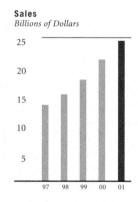

Shareholders' Equity
Dollars per Share

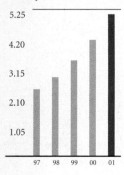

Stock Performance
Closing Price per Share*

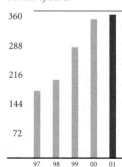

Net Store Growth
Number of Stores

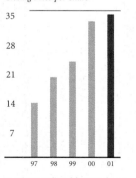

* *Prices are adjusted for a two-for-one stock split in 1999.*

WALGREEN STOCK PERFORMANCE

10 YEARS

On August 31, 1991, 100 shares of Walgreen stock sold for $3,438. Ten years later, on August 31, 2001, those 100 shares, having split three times, were 800 shares worth $27,480, for a gain of 700 percent.

20 YEARS

On August 31, 1981, 100 shares of Walgreen stock sold for $4,438. Twenty years later, those 100 shares, having split seven times, were 12,800 shares worth $439,680, for a gain of 9,807 percent.

Don Lockett, Customer
Chicago, Illinois

Management's Discussion and Analysis of Results of Operations and Financial Condition

Results of Operations

Fiscal 2001 was the 27th consecutive year of record sales and earnings. Net earnings were $885.6 million or $.86 per share (diluted), an increase of 14.0% from last year's earnings of $776.9 million or $.76 per share. Included in this year's results was a $22.1 million pre-tax gain ($.01 per share) for a partial payment of the company's share of the brand name prescription drugs antitrust litigation settlement. Last year's results included a $33.5 million ($.02 per share) comparable payment. Excluding these gains, fiscal year earnings rose 15.3%.

Total net sales increased by 16.1% to $24.6 billion in fiscal 2001 compared to increases of 18.9% in 2000 and 16.5% in 1999. Drugstore sales increases resulted from sales gains in existing stores and added sales from new stores, each of which include an indeterminate amount of market-driven price changes. Comparable drugstore (those open at least one year) sales were up 10.5% in 2001, 11.7% in 2000 and 11.2% in 1999. New store openings accounted for 11.3% of the sales gains in 2001, 10.6% in 2000 and 10.0% in 1999. The company operated 3,520 drugstores as of August 31, 2001, compared to 3,165 a year earlier.

Prescription sales increased 20.9% in 2001, 25.3% in 2000 and 23.3% in 1999. Comparable drugstore prescription sales were up 17.6% in 2001, 19.0% in 2000 and 19.4% in 1999. Prescription sales were 57.5% of total sales for fiscal 2001 compared to 55.2% in 2000 and 52.4% in 1999. Third party sales, where reimbursement is received from managed care organizations and government and private insurance, were 88.4% of pharmacy sales in 2001, 86.1% in 2000 and 83.5% in 1999. Pharmacy sales trends are expected to continue primarily because of increased penetration in existing markets, availability of new drugs and demographic changes such as the aging population.

SG&A Expense
(as a percent to sales)

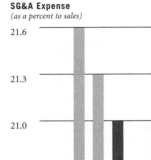

21.6 — 21.3 — 21.0

99   00   01

Gross margins as a percent of sales were 26.7% in 2001, 27.1% in 2000 and 27.2% in 1999. Contributing to the decline in gross margin was the continuing shift in sales mix toward pharmacy, which carries lower margins than the rest of the store. Within pharmacy, third party prescription sales, which typically have lower profit margins than cash prescriptions, continue to trend upward. Non-pharmacy margins also declined as a result of aggressive sale pricing and reduced prices in the cosmetic area, which were designed to increase customer count.

The company uses the last-in, first-out (LIFO) method of inventory valuation. The effective LIFO inflation rates were 1.93% in 2001, 1.36% in 2000 and 1.84% in 1999, which resulted in charges to cost of sales of $62.8 million in 2001, $38.8 million in 2000 and $45.2 million in 1999. Inflation on prescription inventory was 4.9% in 2001, 3.5% in 2000 and 5.2% in 1999.

Selling, occupancy and administration expenses were 21.0% of sales in fiscal 2001, 21.3% of sales in fiscal 2000 and 21.6% of sales in fiscal 1999. The decrease in fiscal 2001, as a percent to sales, was caused by lower advertising and headquarters expenses as well as other fixed costs which are being spread over a larger base of stores.

Interest income decreased in 2001 principally due to lower investment levels. Average net investment levels were approximately $31 million in 2001, $64 million in 2000 and $220 million in 1999.

The effective tax rate decreased to 37.75% this fiscal year compared to 38.50% in fiscal 2000 and 39.25% in fiscal 1999. These decreases were principally the result of lower state income taxes and the settlement of various IRS matters.

Laura Zadravecz, Store Manager
West Palm Beach, Florida

Financial Condition

Cash and cash equivalents were $16.9 million at August 31, 2001, compared to $12.8 million at August 31, 2000. Short-term investment objectives are to maximize yields while minimizing risk and maintaining liquidity. To attain these objectives, investment limits are placed on the amount, type and issuer of securities.

Net cash provided by operating activities for fiscal 2001 was $719.2 million compared to $971.7 million a year ago. The change between periods was principally due to increased inventory levels which increased, in part, due to the opening of 355 net new stores from a year ago. The company's profitability is the principal source for providing funds for expansion and remodeling programs, dividends to shareholders and funding for various technological improvements.

Net cash used for investing activities was $1.1 billion in fiscal 2001 and $1.0 billion in 2000. Additions to property and equipment were $1.2 billion compared to $1.1 billion last year. During the year, 474 new or relocated drugstores were opened. This compares to 462 new or relocated drugstores opened in the same period last year. New stores are owned or leased. There were 245 owned locations opened during the year or under construction at August 31, 2001, versus 253 for the same period last year.

Capital expenditures for fiscal 2002 are expected to be approximately $1.3 billion. The company expects to open 475 new stores in fiscal 2002 and have a total of 6,000 drugstores by the year 2010. The company is continuing to relocate stores to more convenient and profitable freestanding locations. In addition to new stores, a significant portion of the expenditures will be made for technology and distribution centers. Three new distribution centers are under construction in West Palm Beach, Florida, Ohio and the Dallas metropolitan area. Another is planned in Southern California. An existing center in Woodland, California, is being expanded.

Net cash provided by financing activities was $419.4 million compared to $63.3 million used a year ago. The change was principally due to increases in short-term commercial paper borrowings. These were needed to support the company's store and distribution

Capital Expenditures —
Fiscal Year 2002
We plan to spend $1.3 billion.

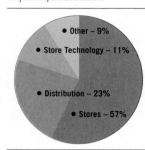

- Other – 9%
- Store Technology – 11%
- Distribution – 23%
- Stores – 57%

center growth, which includes purchases of new store property, equipment and inventory. Based on the company's credit rating, additional short-term borrowings are readily available to support this growth. At August 31, 2001, the company had approximately $152 million in unused bank lines of credit and $100 million of unissued authorized debt securities, previously filed with the Securities and Exchange Commission.

In June 2001, Financial Accounting Standards Board Statement No. 142, "Goodwill and Other Intangible Assets," was issued. Under this pronouncement, which the company intends to adopt in fiscal 2002, goodwill will no longer be amortized but periodically tested for impairment. The adoption of this pronouncement is not expected to have a material impact on the company's consolidated financial position or results of operations.

Also issued during the year were SFAS No. 141, "Business Combinations," and SFAS No. 143, "Accounting for Asset Retirement Obligations," neither of which are expected to impact the company's consolidated financial position or results of operations. SFAS No. 141 requires business combinations to be accounted for by the purchase method of accounting as opposed to pooling of interest. SFAS No. 143 defines the timing and valuation of legal obligations associated with the retirement of long-term assets.

Cautionary Note Regarding Forward-Looking Statements

Certain statements and projections of future results made in this report constitute forward-looking information that is based on current market, competitive and regulatory expectations that involve risks and uncertainties. Those risks and uncertainties include changes in economic conditions generally or in the markets served by the company; consumer preferences and spending patterns; changes in state or federal legislation or regulations; the availability and cost of real estate and construction; competition; and risks of new business areas. Please see Walgreen Co.'s Form 10-K for the period ended August 31, 2001, for a discussion of certain other important factors as they relate to forward-looking statements. Actual results could differ materially.

Zahira Gonzalez,
Pharmacy Technician
Mayaguez, Puerto Rico

Consolidated Statements of Earnings and Shareholders' Equity

Walgreen Co. and Subsidiaries for the Years Ended August 31, 2001, 2000 and 1999 (Dollars in Millions, except per share data)

	Earnings	2001	2000	1999
Net Sales		$24,623.0	$21,206.9	$17,838.8
Costs and Deductions	Cost of sales	18,048.9	15,465.9	12,978.6
	Selling, occupancy and administration	5,175.8	4,516.9	3,844.8
		23,224.7	19,982.8	16,823.4
Other (Income) Expense	Interest income	(5.4)	(6.1)	(12.3)
	Interest expense	3.1	.4	.4
	Other income	(22.1)	(33.5)	–
		(24.4)	(39.2)	(11.9)
Earnings	Earnings before income tax provision	1,422.7	1,263.3	1,027.3
	Income tax provision	537.1	486.4	403.2
	Net Earnings	$ 885.6	$ 776.9	$ 624.1
Net Earnings	Basic	$ .87	$ .77	$ .62
per Common Share	Diluted	$ .86	$ .76	$ .62
	Average shares outstanding	1,016,197,785	1,007,393,572	1,000,363,234
	Dilutive effect of stock options	12,748,828	12,495,236	13,918,481
	Average shares outstanding assuming dilution	1,028,946,613	1,019,888,808	1,014,281,715

		Common Stock		Paid-in	Retained
	Shareholders' Equity	Shares	Amount	Capital	Earnings
	Balance, August 31, 1998	996,487,044	$77.8	$118.1	$2,653.0
	Net earnings	–	–	–	624.1
	Cash dividends declared ($.13 per share)	–	–	–	(130.1)
	Employee stock purchase and option plans	7,535,214	.6	140.8	–
	Balance, August 31, 1999	1,004,022,258	78.4	258.9	3,147.0
	Net earnings	–	–	–	776.9
	Cash dividends declared ($.135 per share)	–	–	–	(136.1)
	Employee stock purchase and option plans	6,796,632	.6	108.3	–
	Balance, August 31, 2000	1,010,818,890	79.0	367.2	3,787.8
	Net earnings	–	–	–	885.6
	Cash dividends declared ($.14 per share)	–	–	–	(142.5)
	Employee stock purchase and option plans	8,606,162	.6	229.5	–
	Balance, August 31, 2001	1,019,425,052	$79.6	$596.7	$4,530.9

The accompanying Statement of Major Accounting Policies and the Notes to Consolidated Financial Statements are integral parts of these statements.

Richard Drew,
Distribution Employee
Mt. Vernon, Illinois

Consolidated Balance Sheets

Walgreen Co. and Subsidiaries at August 31, 2001 and 2000 (Dollars in Millions)

	Assets	2001	2000
Current Assets	Cash and cash equivalents	$ 16.9	$ 12.8
	Accounts receivable, net	798.3	614.5
	Inventories	3,482.4	2,830.8
	Other current assets	96.3	92.0
	Total Current Assets	4,393.9	3,550.1
Non-Current Assets	Property and equipment, at cost, less accumulated depreciation and amortization	4,345.3	3,428.2
	Other non-current assets	94.6	125.4
	Total Assets	$8,833.8	$7,103.7
	Liabilities and Shareholders' Equity		
Current Liabilities	Short-term borrowings	$ 440.7	$ —
	Trade accounts payable	1,546.8	1,364.0
	Accrued expenses and other liabilities	937.5	847.7
	Income taxes	86.6	92.0
	Total Current Liabilities	3,011.6	2,303.7
Non-Current Liabilities	Deferred income taxes	137.0	101.6
	Other non-current liabilities	478.0	464.4
	Total Non-Current Liabilities	615.0	566.0
Shareholders' Equity	Preferred stock, $.0625 par value; authorized 32 million shares; none issued	—	—
	Common stock, $.078125 par value; authorized 3.2 billion shares; issued and outstanding 1,019,425,052 in 2001 and 1,010,818,890 in 2000	79.6	79.0
	Paid-in capital	596.7	367.2
	Retained earnings	4,530.9	3,787.8
	Total Shareholders' Equity	5,207.2	4,234.0
	Total Liabilities and Shareholders' Equity	$8,833.8	$7,103.7

The accompanying Statement of Major Accounting Policies and the Notes to Consolidated Financial Statements are integral parts of these statements.

Sean LeBreque,
Store Manager
Oxnard, California

Consolidated Statements of Cash Flows

Walgreen Co. and Subsidiaries for the Years Ended August 31, 2001, 2000 and 1999 (In Millions)

Fiscal Year		2001	2000	1999
Cash Flows from	Net earnings	$ 885.6	$ 776.9	$ 624.1
Operating Activities	Adjustments to reconcile net earnings to net			
	cash provided by operating activities –			
	Depreciation and amortization	269.2	230.1	210.1
	Deferred income taxes	46.9	21.0	(9.4)
	Income tax savings from employee stock plans	67.3	38.5	26.8
	Other	2.1	13.6	12.2
	Changes in operating assets and liabilities –			
	Inventories	(651.6)	(368.2)	(435.7)
	Trade accounts payable	182.8	233.7	223.4
	Accounts receivable, net	(177.3)	(135.4)	(106.0)
	Accrued expenses and other liabilities	82.2	101.2	103.7
	Income taxes	(5.4)	28.6	8.6
	Other	17.4	31.7	(5.8)
	Net cash provided by operating activities	719.2	971.7	652.0
Cash Flows from	Additions to property and equipment	(1,237.0)	(1,119.1)	(696.3)
Investing Activities	Disposition of property and equipment	43.5	22.9	41.7
	Net proceeds from corporate-owned life insurance	59.0	58.8	9.1
	Net cash used for investing activities	(1,134.5)	(1,037.4)	(645.5)
Cash Flows from	Proceeds from short-term borrowings	440.7	–	–
Financing Activities	Cash dividends paid	(140.9)	(134.6)	(128.6)
	Proceeds from employee stock plans	126.1	79.2	105.0
	Other	(6.5)	(7.9)	14.5
	Net cash provided by (used for) financing activities	419.4	(63.3)	(9.1)
Changes in Cash and	Net increase (decrease) in cash and cash equivalents	4.1	(129.0)	(2.6)
Cash Equivalents	Cash and cash equivalents at beginning of year	12.8	141.8	144.4
	Cash and cash equivalents at end of year	$ 16.9	$ 12.8	$ 141.8

The accompanying Statement of Major Accounting Policies and the Notes to Consolidated Financial Statements are integral parts of these statements.

Bambi Poulan,
Service Clerk
Tampa, Florida

Statement of Major Accounting Policies

Description of Business

The company is principally in the retail drugstore business and its operations are within one reportable segment. Stores are located in 43 states and Puerto Rico. At August 31, 2001, there were 3,517 retail drugstores and three mail service facilities. Prescription sales were 57.5% of total sales for fiscal 2001 compared to 55.2% in 2000 and 52.4% in 1999.

Basis of Presentation

The consolidated statements include the accounts of the company and its subsidiaries. All significant intercompany transactions have been eliminated. The financial statements are prepared in accordance with generally accepted accounting principles and include amounts based on management's prudent judgments and estimates. Actual results may differ from these estimates.

Cash and Cash Equivalents

Cash and cash equivalents include cash on hand and all highly liquid investments with an original maturity of three months or less. The company's cash management policy provides for the bank disbursement accounts to be reimbursed on a daily basis. Checks issued but not presented to the banks for payment of $233 million and $211 million at August 31, 2001 and 2000, respectively, are included in cash and cash equivalents as reductions of other cash balances.

Financial Instruments

The company had approximately $53 million and $89 million of outstanding letters of credit at August 31, 2001 and 2000, respectively, which guaranteed foreign trade purchases. Additional outstanding letters of credit of $71 million and $62 million at August 31, 2001 and 2000, respectively, guaranteed payments of casualty claims. The casualty claim letters of credit are annually renewable and will remain in place until the casualty claims are paid in full. The company pays a nominal facility fee to the financing bank to keep this line of credit facility active. The company also had purchase commitments of approximately $162 million and $525 million at August 31, 2001 and 2000, respectively, related to the purchase of store locations. There were no investments in derivative financial instruments during fiscal 2001 and 2000.

Inventories

Inventories are valued on a lower of last-in, first-out (LIFO) cost or market basis. At August 31, 2001 and 2000, inventories would have been greater by $637.6 million and $574.8 million, respectively, if they had been valued on a lower of first-in, first-out (FIFO) cost or market basis. Cost of sales is primarily derived from an estimate based upon point-of-sale scanning information and adjusted based on periodic inventories.

Property and Equipment

Depreciation is provided on a straight-line basis over the estimated useful lives of owned assets. Leasehold improvements and leased properties under capital leases are amortized over the estimated physical life of the property or over the term of the lease, whichever is shorter. Estimated useful lives range from 12½ to 39 years for land improvements, buildings and building improvements and 5 to 12½ years for equipment. Major repairs, which extend the useful life of an asset, are capitalized in the property and equipment accounts. Routine maintenance and repairs are charged against earnings. The composite method of depreciation is used for equipment; therefore, gains and losses on retirement or other disposition of such assets are included in earnings only when an operating

location is closed, completely remodeled or impaired resulting in the carrying amount not being recoverable. Impaired assets write-offs are measured by comparing the present value of the estimated future cash flows to the carrying value of the assets. The present value of future lease costs is charged against earnings when a commitment makes it probable that the location will close before the end of the lease term. Fully depreciated property and equipment are removed from the cost and related accumulated depreciation and amortization accounts.

Property and equipment consists of *(In Millions)*:

	2001	2000
Land and land improvements		
Owned stores	$1,109.2	$ 821.8
Distribution centers	38.7	33.3
Other locations	18.6	14.9
Buildings and building improvements		
Owned stores	1,156.6	870.4
Leased stores		
(leasehold improvements only)	411.1	354.4
Distribution centers	309.1	203.4
Other locations	70.6	61.4
Equipment		
Stores	1,440.3	1,266.8
Distribution centers	350.2	219.6
Other locations	462.7	452.8
Capitalized system development costs	117.4	99.8
Capital lease properties	18.8	21.1
	5,503.3	4,419.7
Less: accumulated depreciation and amortization	1,158.0	991.5
	$4,345.3	$3,428.2

The company capitalizes costs that primarily relate to the application development stage of significant internally developed software. These costs principally relate to Intercom Plus, a pharmacy computer and workflow system. These costs are amortized over a five-year period. Amortization of these costs was $20.8 million in 2001, $13.1 million in 2000 and $15.6 million in 1999. Unamortized costs as of August 31, 2001 and 2000, were $66.1 million and $65.2 million, respectively.

Income Taxes

The company provides for federal and state income taxes on items included in the Consolidated Statements of Earnings regardless of the period when such taxes are payable. Deferred taxes are recognized for temporary differences between financial and income tax reporting based on enacted tax laws and rates.

Insurance

The company obtains insurance coverage for catastrophic exposures as well as those risks required to be insured by law. It is the company's policy to retain a significant portion of certain losses related to worker's compensation, property losses, business interruptions relating from such losses and comprehensive general, pharmacist and vehicle liability. Provisions for these losses are recorded based upon the company's estimates for claims incurred. Such estimates use certain assumptions followed in the insurance industry.

Carol Cantrell, Customer
Dallas, Texas

Statement of Major Accounting Policies
(continued)

Pre-Opening Expenses

Non-capital expenditures incurred prior to the opening of a new or remodeled store are charged against earnings when they are incurred.

Advertising Costs

Advertising costs are expensed as incurred, and were $54.1 million in 2001, $76.7 million in 2000 and $58.7 million in 1999.

Notes to Consolidated Financial Statements

Interest Expense

The company capitalized $15.6 million, $4.0 million and $2.6 million of interest expense as part of significant construction projects during fiscal 2001, 2000 and 1999. Interest paid, net of amounts capitalized, was $3.4 million in 2001, $.2 million in 2000 and $.4 million in 1999.

Other Income

In February 2001 and July 2000, the company received partial payments of the brand name prescription drugs antitrust litigation settlement for pre-tax income of $22.1 million ($13.6 million after-tax or $.01 per share) and $33.5 million ($20.5 million after-tax or $.02 per share), respectively. The company was involved in the pharmacy class action against drug manufacturers, which resulted in a $700 million settlement for all recipients. The final payment was received in the first quarter of fiscal 2002 for pre-tax income of $5.5 million ($3.4 million after-tax).

Leases

Although some locations are owned, the company generally operates in leased premises. Original non-cancelable lease terms typically are 20 years and may contain escalation clauses, along with options that permit renewals for additional periods. The total amount of the minimum rent is expensed on a straight-line basis over the term of the lease. In addition to minimum fixed rentals, most leases provide for contingent rentals based upon sales.

Minimum rental commitments at August 31, 2001, under all leases having an initial or remaining non-cancelable term of more than one year are shown below *(In Millions)*:

Year	
2002	$ 782.7
2003	826.3
2004	817.0
2005	804.7
2006	785.4
Later	9,010.2
Total minimum lease payments	$13,026.3

The above minimum lease payments include minimum rental commitments related to capital leases amounting to $13.3 million at August 31, 2001. The present value of net minimum capital lease payments, due after 2002, is reflected in the accompanying Consolidated Balance Sheets as part of other non-current liabilities. Total minimum lease payments have not been reduced by minimum sublease rentals of approximately $42.6 million on leases due in the future under non-cancelable subleases.

Rental expense was as follows *(In Millions)*:

	2001	2000	1999
Minimum rentals	$730.1	$605.7	$482.0
Contingent rentals	26.2	31.4	34.8
Less: Sublease rental income	(10.4)	(7.6)	(5.4)
	$745.9	$629.5	$511.4

Income Taxes

The provision for income taxes consists of the following *(In Millions)*:

	2001	2000	1999
Current provision – Federal	$417.1	$400.9	$350.5
– State	73.1	64.5	62.1
	490.2	465.4	412.6
Deferred provision – Federal	47.1	17.7	(8.0)
– State	(.2)	3.3	(1.4)
	46.9	21.0	(9.4)
	$537.1	$486.4	$403.2

The components of the deferred provision were *(In Millions)*:

	2001	2000	1999
Accelerated depreciation	$ 49.7	$ 51.5	$ 9.7
Inventory	18.6	(2.3)	11.1
Insurance	(15.7)	(11.0)	(2.7)
Employee benefit plans	(11.1)	(17.7)	(12.2)
Accrued rent	2.2	(5.2)	(8.7)
Other	3.2	5.7	(6.6)
	$ 46.9	$ 21.0	$ (9.4)

The deferred tax assets and liabilities included in the Consolidated Balance Sheets consist of the following *(In Millions)*:

	2001	2000
Deferred tax assets –		
Employee benefit plans	$146.3	$135.4
Accrued rent	52.7	54.9
Insurance	68.3	52.6
Inventory	28.1	23.6
Other	39.0	38.9
	334.4	305.4
Deferred tax liabilities –		
Accelerated depreciation	341.7	292.0
Inventory	92.9	69.8
Other	16.1	13.0
	450.7	374.8
Net deferred tax liabilities	$116.3	$ 69.4

Shawn Horst, Store Manager
Cheyenne, Wyoming

Notes to Consolidated Financial Statements

(continued)

Income taxes paid were $432.1 million, $398.4 million and $377.3 million during the fiscal years ended August 31, 2001, 2000 and 1999, respectively. The difference between the statutory income tax rate and the effective tax rate is principally due to state income tax provisions.

Short-Term Borrowings

The company obtained funds through the placement of commercial paper, as follows *(Dollars in Millions)*:

	2001	2000	1999
Average outstanding during the year	$304.9	$14.0	$ 9.6
Largest month-end balance	461.2	98.0	100.0
	(Nov)	*(Nov)*	*(Nov)*
Weighted-average interest rate	5.2%	5.9%	5.1%

At August 31, 2001, the company had approximately $152 million of available bank lines of credit. The credit lines are renewable annually at various dates and provide for loans of varying maturities at the prime rate. There are no compensating balance arrangements.

Contingencies

The company is involved in various legal proceedings incidental to the normal course of business. Company management is of the opinion, based upon the advice of General Counsel, that although the outcome of such litigation cannot be forecast with certainty, the final disposition should not have a material adverse effect on the company's consolidated financial position or results of operations.

Capital Stock

The company's common stock is subject to a Rights Agreement under which each share has attached to it a Right to purchase one one-hundredth of a share of a new series of Preferred Stock, at a price of $37.50 per Right. In the event an entity acquires or attempts to acquire 15% of the then outstanding shares, each Right, except those of an acquiring entity, would entitle the holder to purchase a number of shares of common stock pursuant to a formula contained in the Agreement. These non-voting Rights will expire on August 21, 2006, but may be redeemed at a price of $.0025 per Right at any time prior to a public announcement that the above event has occurred.

As of August 31, 2001, 92,321,616 shares of common stock were reserved for future stock issuances under the company's various employee benefit plans. Preferred stock of 10,194,251 shares have been reserved for issuance upon the exercise of Preferred Share Purchase Rights.

Stock Compensation Plans

The Walgreen Co. Executive Stock Option Plan provides for the granting to key employees of options to purchase company common stock over a 10-year period, at a price not less than the fair market value on the date of the grant. Under this Plan, options may be granted until October 9, 2006, for an aggregate of 38,400,000 shares of common stock of the company. Compensation expense related to the plan was $1.4 million in fiscal 2001 and less than $1 million in fiscal 2000 and 1999. The options granted during fiscal 2001, 2000 and 1999 have a minimum three-year holding period.

The Walgreen Co. Stock Purchase/Option Plan (Share Walgreens) provides for the granting of options to purchase company common stock over a period of 10 years to eligible employees upon the purchase of company shares subject to certain restrictions. Under the terms of the Plan, the option price cannot be less than 85% of the fair market value at the date of grant. Compensation expense related to the Plan was $9.6 million in fiscal 2001 and less than $1 million in fiscal 2000 and 1999. Options may be granted under this Plan until September 30, 2002, for an aggregate of 40,000,000 shares of common stock of the company. This Plan was amended on July 11, 2001. Effective October 1, 2002, options may be granted under this Plan until September 30, 2012, for an aggregate of 42,000,000 shares of common stock of the company. The options granted during fiscal 2001, 2000 and 1999 have a two-year holding period.

On May 11, 2000, substantially all employees, in conjunction with opening the company's 3,000th store, were granted a stock option award to purchase from 75 to 500 shares, based on years of service. The stock option award, issued at fair market value on the date of the grant, represents a total of 14,859,275 shares of Walgreen Co. common stock. The options vest after three years and are exercisable up to 10 years after the grant date.

A summary of information relative to the company's stock option plans follows:

	Options Outstanding		Options Exercisable	
	Shares	Weighted-Average Exercise Price	Shares	Weighted-Average Exercise Price
August 31, 1998	29,605,956	$ 6.59		
Granted	2,606,350	19.70		
Exercised	(3,644,250)	5.71		
Canceled/Forfeited	(88,818)	9.81		
August 31, 1999	28,479,238	$ 7.89	21,821,426	$5.91
Granted	17,040,383	28.43		
Exercised	(5,055,842)	5.59		
Canceled/Forfeited	(1,086,118)	27.39		
August 31, 2000	39,377,661	$16.55	19,267,211	$6.45
Granted	5,354,388	36.68		
Exercised	(5,532,895)	5.75		
Canceled/Forfeited	(2,943,030)	28.02		
August 31, 2001	36,256,124	$20.24	14,824,227	$7.40

Vianney Bolaños,
Store Manager
Dallas, Texas

Notes to Consolidated Financial Statements

(continued)

The following table summarizes information concerning currently outstanding and exercisable options:

	Options Outstanding			Options Exercisable	
Range of Exercise Prices	Number Outstanding at 08/31/01	Weighted-Average Remaining Contractual Life	Weighted-Average Exercise Price	Number Exercisable at 8/31/01	Weighted-Average Exercise Price
$ 4 to 14	14,685,847	3.76 yrs.	$ 7.26	14,672,859	$ 7.25
15 to 30	16,318,488	8.31	26.66	143,750	20.88
31 to 46	5,251,789	9.15	36.62	7,618	38.78
$ 4 to 46	36,256,124	6.58 yrs.	$20.24	14,824,227	$ 7.40

Under the Walgreen Co. 1982 Employees Stock Purchase Plan, eligible employees may purchase company stock at 90% of the fair market value at the date of purchase. Employees may purchase shares through cash purchases, loans or payroll deductions up to certain limits. The aggregate number of shares for which all participants have the right to purchase under this Plan is 64,000,000.

The Walgreen Co. Restricted Performance Share Plan provides for the granting of up to 32,000,000 shares of common stock to certain key employees, subject to restrictions as to continuous employment except in the case of death, normal retirement and total and permanent disability. Restrictions generally lapse over a four-year period from the date of grant. Compensation expense is recognized in the year of grant. Compensation expense related to the Plan was $3.6 million in fiscal 2001, $5.1 million in fiscal 2000 and $3.7 million in fiscal 1999. The number of shares granted was 61,136 in 2001, 84,746 in 2000 and 95,038 in 1999.

The company applies Accounting Principles Board (APB) Opinion No. 25 and related interpretations in accounting for its plans. Accordingly, no compensation expense has been recognized based on the fair value of its grants under these plans. Had compensation costs been determined consistent with the method of FASB Statement No. 123 for options granted in fiscal 2001, 2000 and 1999, pro forma net earnings and net earnings per common share would have been as follows *(In Millions, except per share data)*:

	2001	2000	1999
Net earnings			
As reported	$885.6	$776.9	$624.1
Pro forma	833.3	754.3	605.3
Net earnings per common share – Basic			
As reported	.87	.77	.62
Pro forma	.82	.75	.61
Net earnings per common share – Diluted			
As reported	.86	.76	.62
Pro forma	.81	.74	.60

The weighted-average fair value and exercise price of options granted for fiscal 2001, 2000 and 1999 were as follows:

	2001	2000	1999
Granted at market price –			
Weighted-average fair value	$14.28	$12.17	$ 6.99
Weighted-average exercise price	32.88	28.44	19.61
Granted below market price –			
Weighted-average fair value	20.78	10.56	9.45
Weighted-average exercise price	38.78	24.12	20.89

The fair value of each option grant used in the pro forma net earnings and net earnings per share was determined using the Black-Scholes option pricing model with weighted-average assumptions used for grants in fiscal 2001, 2000 and 1999:

	2001	2000	1999
Risk-free interest rate	6.16%	6.64%	5.11%
Average life of option (years)	7	7	7
Volatility	25.95%	25.86%	21.78%
Dividend yield	.16%	.27%	.32%

Retirement Benefits

The principal retirement plan for employees is the Walgreen Profit-Sharing Retirement Trust to which both the company and the employees contribute. The company's contribution, which is determined annually at the discretion of the Board of Directors, has historically related to pre-tax income. The profit-sharing provision was $126.6 million in 2001, $112.4 million in 2000 and $91.4 million in 1999.

The company provides certain health and life insurance benefits for retired employees who meet eligibility requirements, including age and years of service. The costs of these benefits are accrued over the period earned. In fiscal 2001 several changes were made prospectively to retiree medical and prescription drug coverage. Employees hired after December 31, 2001, will not be eligible for the Walgreen Medical Plan for Retirees. In addition, for retirements occurring on or after January 1, 2017, retirees will contribute more toward the cost of their prescription coverage. At August 31, 2001, the unrecognized actuarial loss was $27.9 million, compared to a $5.1 million loss at August 31, 2000. The actuarial loss is amortized over the future service period of employees, which approximates 20 years. The company's postretirement health and life benefit plans currently are not funded.

Components of net periodic benefit costs *(In Millions)*:

	2001	2000	1999
Service cost	$ 4.8	$ 4.7	$ 5.2
Interest cost	8.7	7.7	7.3
Amortization of actuarial loss	.3	–	.4
Total postretirement healthcare benefits costs	$13.8	$12.4	$12.9

*SolMarie Comacho, Bookkeeper,
with daughter Alondra
San German, Puerto Rico*

Notes to Consolidated Financial Statements
(continued)

Change in benefit obligation *(In Millions)*:

	2001	2000
Benefit obligation at September 1	$118.6	$104.6
Service cost	4.8	4.7
Interest cost	8.7	7.7
Amendments	(7.1)	–
Actuarial loss (gain)	23.1	5.7
Benefit payments	(6.3)	(4.9)
Participants contributions	.9	.8
Benefit obligation at August 31	$142.7	$118.6

The discount rate assumptions used to compute the postretirement benefit obligation at year-end were 7.5% for 2001 and 2000.

Future benefit costs were estimated assuming medical costs would increase at a 6.5% annual rate decreasing to 5% over the next 4 years and then remaining at a 5% annual growth rate thereafter. A one percentage point change in the assumed medical cost trend rate would have the following effects *(In Millions)*:

	1% Increase	1% Decrease
Effect on service and interest cost	$ 4.0	$ (3.0)
Effect on postretirement obligation	28.2	(21.6)

Supplementary Financial Information

Included in the Consolidated Balance Sheets captions are the following assets and liabilities *(In Millions)*:

	2001	2000
Accounts receivable –		
Accounts receivable	$819.2	$631.4
Allowances for doubtful accounts	(20.9)	(16.9)
	$798.3	$614.5
Accrued expenses and other liabilities –		
Accrued salaries	$272.7	$266.4
Taxes other than income taxes	155.5	125.4
Profit sharing	122.1	110.7
Other	387.2	345.2
	$937.5	$847.7

Summary of Quarterly Results *(Unaudited)*

(Dollars in Millions, except per share data)

		November	February	May	August	Fiscal Year
Fiscal 2001	Net sales	$5,614.2	$6,429.0	$6,296.2	$6,283.6	$24,623.0
	Gross profit	1,488.1	1,770.8	1,651.6	1,663.6	6,574.1
	Net earnings	158.4	296.9	213.4	216.9	885.6
	Per Common Share – Basic	$ .16	$ .29	$ .21	$ .21	$ .87
	– Diluted	.15	.29	.21	.21	.86
Fiscal 2000	Net sales	$4,823.2	$5,608.8	$5,394.1	$5,380.8	$21,206.9
	Gross profit	1,272.2	1,543.5	1,451.0	1,474.3	5,741.0
	Net earnings	127.8	238.9	193.6	216.6	776.9
	Per Common Share – Basic	$ .13	$ .23	$ .20	$ .21	$ .77
	– Diluted	.13	.23	.19	.21	.76

Comments on Quarterly Results: In further explanation of and supplemental to the quarterly results, the 2001 fourth quarter LIFO adjustment was a charge of $2.8 million compared to a 2000 credit of $8.7 million. If the 2001 interim results were adjusted to reflect the actual inventory inflation rates and inventory levels as computed at August 31, 2001, earnings per share would have been higher in the second quarter by $.01 and lower in the fourth quarter by $.01. Similar adjustments in 2000 would have increased earnings per share in the first quarter by $.01 and decreased the fourth quarter by $.01.

The quarter ended February 28, 2001, includes the pre-tax income of $22.1 million ($13.6 million after-tax or $.01 per share) from the partial payment of the brand name prescription drugs litigation settlement. The quarter ended August 31, 2000, includes the pre-tax income of $33.5 million ($20.5 million after-tax or $.02 per share) from the initial payment.

Common Stock Prices

Below are the New York Stock Exchange high and low for each quarter of fiscal 2001 and 2000.

		November	February	May	August	Fiscal Year
Fiscal 2001	High	$45.63	$44.32	$45.27	$41.85	$45.63
	Low	33.44	36.88	39.12	31.43	31.43
Fiscal 2000	High	$29.94	$32.75	$29.19	$35.25	$35.25
	Low	23.56	25.81	22.75	27.56	22.75

Jerry Lizalek, Photo Technician
Scottsdale, Arizona

Report of Independent Public Accountants

To the Board of Directors and Shareholders of Walgreen Co.:
We have audited the accompanying consolidated balance sheets of Walgreen Co. (an Illinois corporation) and Subsidiaries as of August 31, 2001 and 2000, and the related consolidated statements of earnings, shareholders' equity and cash flows for each of the three years in the period ended August 31, 2001. These financial statements are the responsibility of the company's management. Our responsibility is to express an opinion on these financial statements based on our audits.

We conducted our audits in accordance with auditing standards generally accepted in the United States. Those standards require that we plan and perform the audit to obtain reasonable assurance about whether the financial statements are free of material misstatement. An audit includes examining, on a test basis, evidence supporting the amounts and disclosures in the financial statements. An audit also includes assessing the accounting principles used and significant estimates made by management, as well as evaluating the overall financial statement presentation. We believe that our audits provide a reasonable basis for our opinion.

In our opinion, the financial statements referred to above present fairly, in all material respects, the financial position of Walgreen Co. and Subsidiaries as of August 31, 2001 and 2000 and the results of their operations and their cash flows for each of the three years in the period ended August 31, 2001 in conformity with accounting principles generally accepted in the United States.

Arthur Andersen LLP

Chicago, Illinois,
 September 28, 2001

Management's Report

The primary responsibility for the integrity and objectivity of the consolidated financial statements and related financial data rests with the management of Walgreen Co. The financial statements were prepared in conformity with generally accepted accounting principles appropriate in the circumstances and included amounts that were based on management's most prudent judgments and estimates relating to matters not concluded by fiscal year-end. Management believes that all material uncertainties have been either appropriately accounted for or disclosed. All other financial information included in this annual report is consistent with the financial statements.

The firm of Arthur Andersen LLP, independent public accountants, was engaged to render a professional opinion on Walgreen Co.'s consolidated financial statements. Their report contains an opinion based on their audit, which was made in accordance with generally accepted auditing standards and procedures, which they believed were sufficient to provide reasonable assurance that the consolidated financial statements, considered in their entirety, are not misleading and do not contain material errors.

Four outside members of the Board of Directors constitute the company's Audit Committee, which meets at least quarterly and is responsible for reviewing and monitoring the company's financial and accounting practices. Arthur Andersen LLP and the company's General Auditor meet alone with the Audit Committee, which also meets with the company's management to discuss financial matters, auditing and internal accounting controls.

The company's systems are designed to provide an effective system of internal accounting controls to obtain reasonable assurance at reasonable cost that assets are safeguarded from material loss or unauthorized use and transactions are executed in accordance with management's authorization and properly recorded. To this end, management maintains an internal control environment which is shaped by established operating policies and procedures, an appropriate division of responsibility at all organizational levels, and a corporate ethics policy which is monitored annually. The company also has an Internal Control Evaluation Committee, composed primarily of senior management from the Accounting and Auditing Departments, which oversees the evaluation of internal controls on a company-wide basis. Management believes it has appropriately responded to the internal auditors' and independent public accountants' recommendations concerning the company's internal control system.

L. Daniel Jorndt
Chairman of the Board
and Chief Executive Officer

William M. Rudolphsen
Controller
and Chief Accounting Officer

Roger L. Polark
Senior Vice President
and Chief Financial Officer

Board of Directors

Officers
As of October 31, 2001

Directors

L. Daniel Jorndt*
Chairman and
Chief Executive Officer
Elected 1990

David W. Bernauer*
President and
Chief Operating Officer
Elected 1999

William C. Foote
Chairman of the Board,
Chief Executive Officer
and President
USG Corporation
Elected 1997

James J. Howard
Chairman Emeritus
Xcel Energy, Inc.
Elected 1986

Alan G. McNally
Chairman and
Chief Executive Officer
Harris Bankcorp Inc.
Elected 1999

Cordell Reed
Former Senior Vice President
Commonwealth Edison Co.
Elected 1994

David Y. Schwartz
Former Partner
Arthur Andersen LLP
Elected 2000

John B. Schwemm
Former Chairman and
Chief Executive Officer
R.R. Donnelley & Sons Co.
Elected 1985

Marilou M. von Ferstel
Former Executive Vice President
and General Manager
Ogilvy Adams & Rinehart
Elected 1987

Charles R. Walgreen III
Chairman Emeritus
Elected 1963

Committees

Executive Committee
L. Daniel Jorndt,
    Chairman
David W. Bernauer
Cordell Reed
John B. Schwemm

Audit Committee
John B. Schwemm,
    Chairman
William C. Foote
David Y. Schwartz
Marilou M. von Ferstel

Compensation Committee
Cordell Reed,
    Chairman
James J. Howard
John B. Schwemm

Finance Committee
David Y. Schwartz,
    Chairman
David W. Bernauer
L. Daniel Jorndt
Alan G. McNally
Cordell Reed
Charles R. Walgreen III

**Nominating and
Governance Committee**
William C. Foote,
    Chairman
James J. Howard
John B. Schwemm
Marilou M. von Ferstel

Corporate

Chairman
L. Daniel Jorndt*
    Chief Executive Officer

President
David W. Bernauer*
    Chief Operating Officer

Executive Vice Presidents
Jerome B. Karlin
    Store Operations
Jeffrey A. Rein
    Marketing

Senior Vice Presidents
R. Bruce Bryant
    Western Store Operations
W. Lynn Earnest
    Central Store Operations
George C. Eilers
    Eastern Store Operations
J. Randolph Lewis
    Distribution & Logistics
Julian A. Oettinger
    General Counsel and
    Corporate Secretary
Roger L. Polark
    Chief Financial Officer
William A. Shiel
    Facilities Development

Vice Presidents
John W. Gleeson
    Corporate Strategy
Dana I. Green
    Human Resources
Robert H. Halaska
    President
    Walgreens Health Initiatives
Dennis R. O'Dell
    Health Services
Robert E. Sgarlata
    Retail Marketing
Trent E. Taylor
    Chief Information Officer
Mark A. Wagner
    Treasurer
Gregory D. Wasson
    Executive Vice President
    Walgreens Health Initiatives

Operational and Divisional

Store Operations Vice Presidents
James F. Cnota
Kermit R. Crawford
David L. Gloudemans
Frank C. Grilli
William M. Handal
Patrick E. Hanifen
Don R. Holman
Robert M. Kral
Barry L. Markl
Richard Robinson
Michael D. Tovian
Bill J. Vernon
Kevin P. Walgreen
Christine D. Whelan
Edward E. Williams
Bruce C. Zarkowsky

Divisional Vice Presidents
Thomas Bergseth
    Facilities Planning and Design
Thomas J. Connolly
    Real Estate
Laurie L. Meyer
    Corporate Communications
Allan M. Resnick
    Law
Robert E. Rogan
    Distribution Centers
Jerry A. Rubin
    Real Estate
William M. Rudolphsen
    Controller
James M. Schultz
    Performance Development
Craig M. Sinclair
    Advertising
Terry R. Watkins
    Distribution Centers
Kenneth R. Weigand
    Employee Relations
Chester G. Young
    General Auditor
Robert G. Zimmerman
    Vice President – Administration
    Walgreens Health Initiatives

** David W. Bernauer will become
Chief Executive Officer in January 2002.
L. Daniel Jorndt will retain the
position of Chairman.*

2

Chapter 2 continues the exploration of accounting measurement by focusing on the problems of recognition, valuation, and classification and how they are solved in the measuring and recording of business transactions.

Measuring Business Transactions

LEARNING OBJECTIVES

LO1 Explain, in simple terms, the generally accepted ways of solving the measurement issues of recognition, valuation, and classification.

LO2 Describe the chart of accounts and recognize commonly used accounts.

LO3 Define *double-entry system* and state the rules for double entry.

LO4 Apply the steps for transaction analysis and processing to simple transactions.

LO5 Prepare a trial balance and describe its value and limitations.

SUPPLEMENTAL OBJECTIVE

SO6 Record transactions in the general journal and post transactions from the general journal to the ledger.

DECISION POINT

A USER'S FOCUS

Continental Airlines, Inc. <www.continental.com> & The Boeing Co. <www.boeing.com> In October 2000, Continental Airlines, Inc., announced that it had ordered 15 Boeing 757-300 jetliners.[1] The $1.2 billion order was part of an exclusive agreement Boeing negotiated with Continental. This exclusive 20-year agreement to purchase only Boeing aircraft was Boeing's fourth such agreement with a major airline and positioned the company favorably against Airbus, its European competitor. How should this important order have been recorded, if at all, in the records of Continental and Boeing? When should the purchase and sale that result from this order be recorded in the companies' records?

The order obviously was an important event, one with long-term consequences for both companies. But, as you will see in this chapter, it was not recorded in the accounting records of either company. At the time the order was placed, the aircraft were yet to be manufactured, and the first of them would not be delivered for several years. Even for "firm" orders, Boeing has cautioned that "an economic downturn could result in airline equipment requirements less than currently anticipated resulting in requests to negotiate the rescheduling or possible cancellation of firm orders."[2] The aircraft were not assets of Continental, and the company had not incurred a liability. No aircraft had been delivered or even built, so Continental was not obligated to pay at that point. And Boeing could not record any revenue until it manufactured and delivered the aircraft to Continental, and title to them shifted from Boeing to Continental.

When does Continental record the purchase of a new aircraft it orders from Boeing? When does Boeing record the revenue from the sale?

In fact, Boeing later experienced cancellation or extension of large, previously firm orders from China because of the economic slowdown in Asia.[3] The further slowdown in air traffic following the events of September 11, 2001 led to more cancellations of aircraft orders.

To understand and effectively use financial statements, it is important to know how to analyze events in order to determine the extent of their impact on those statements.

MEASUREMENT ISSUES

LO1 Explain, in simple terms, the generally accepted ways of solving the measurement issues of recognition, valuation, and classification.

RELATED TEXT ASSIGNMENTS
Q: 1, 2, 3, 4, 5
SE: 1, 2
E: 1, 2
P: 3, 4, 7
SD: 1, 2, 3
FRA: 4, 5

Business transactions are economic events that affect the financial position of a business entity. To measure a business transaction, the accountant must decide when the transaction occurred (the recognition issue), what value to place on the transaction (the valuation issue), and how the components of the transaction should be categorized (the classification issue).

These three issues—recognition, valuation, and classification—underlie almost every major decision in financial accounting today. They lie at the heart of accounting for pension plans, for mergers of giant companies, and for international transactions. In discussing the three basic issues, we follow generally accepted accounting principles and use an approach that promotes an understanding of the basic ideas of accounting. Keep in mind, however, that controversy does exist, and that solutions to some problems are not as cut-and-dried as they appear.

THE RECOGNITION ISSUE

TERMINOLOGY NOTE: In accounting, *recognize* means to record a transaction or event.

The **recognition** issue refers to the difficulty of deciding when a business transaction should be recorded. Often the facts of a situation are known, but there is disagreement about *when* the event should be recorded. Suppose, for instance, that a company orders, receives, and pays for an office desk. Which of the following actions constitutes a recordable event?

KEY POINT: A purchase should not be recognized (recorded) before title is transferred because until that point, the vendor has not fulfilled its contractual obligation and the buyer has no liability.

1. An employee sends a purchase requisition to the purchasing department.
2. The purchasing department sends a purchase order to the supplier.
3. The supplier ships the desk.
4. The company receives the desk.
5. The company receives the bill from the supplier.
6. The company pays the bill.

The answer to this question is important because the date on which a purchase is recorded affects amounts in the financial statements. According to accounting tradition, the transaction is recorded when title to the desk passes from the supplier to the purchaser, creating an obligation to pay. Thus, depending on the details of the shipping agreement, the transaction is recognized (recorded) at the time of either action **3** or action **4**. This is the guideline that we generally use in this book. However, in many small businesses that have simple accounting systems, the transaction is not recorded until the bill is received (action **5**) or paid (action **6**) because these are the implied points of title transfer. The predetermined time at which a transaction should be recorded is the **recognition point**.

The recognition issue is not always easy to resolve. Consider an advertising agency that prepares a major advertising campaign for a client. Employees may work on the campaign several hours a day for a number of weeks. They add value to the plan as they develop it. Should this added value be recognized as the campaign is being produced or at the time it is completed? Normally, the increase in value is recorded at the time the plan is finished and the client is billed for it. However, if a plan is going to take a long period to develop, the agency and the client may agree

FOCUS ON BUSINESS PRACTICE

Accounting Policies: Where Do You Find Them?

As noted in the Decision Point at the beginning of this chapter, Continental Airlines' <www.continental.com> order of jetliners from Boeing <www.boeing.com> was not an event that either company should have recorded as a transaction. But when do companies record such events as sales or purchase transactions? The answer to this question and others about a company's accounting policies may be found in the Summary of Significant Accounting Policies in the company's annual report. For example, under the heading "Sales and Other Operating Expenses," Boeing's Summary of Significant Accounting Policies states that "commercial aircraft sales are recorded as deliveries are made."[4]

that the client will be billed at key points during its development. A transaction is recorded at each billing.

Here are some more examples of the distinction between business events and transactions:

Business Events That Are *Not* Transactions	Business Events That *Are* Transactions
A customer inquires about the availability of a service.	A customer buys a service.
A company orders a product from a supplier.	A company receives a product previously ordered.
A company hires a new employee.	A company pays an employee for work performed.

THE VALUATION ISSUE

ENRICHMENT NOTE: The value of a transaction usually is based on a business document—a canceled check or an invoice. In general, appraisals or other subjective amounts are not recorded.

Valuation is perhaps the most controversial issue in accounting. The **valuation** issue focuses on assigning a monetary value to a business transaction. Generally accepted accounting principles state that the original cost (often called *historical cost*) is the appropriate value to assign to all business transactions—and therefore to all assets, liabilities, and components of stockholders' equity, including revenues and expenses, recorded by a business.

Cost is defined here as the exchange price associated with a business transaction at the point of recognition. According to this guideline, the purpose of accounting is not to account for value in terms of worth, which can change after a transaction occurs, but to account for value in terms of cost at the time of the transaction. For example, the cost of an asset is recorded when the asset is acquired, and the value is held at that level until the asset is sold, expires, or is consumed. In this context, *value* means the cost at the time of the transaction. The practice of recording transactions at cost is referred to as the **cost principle**.

Stop and Think!
Which is the most important issue in recording a transaction: recognition, valuation, or classification?
No issue is more important than another. Each must be resolved satisfactorily for a transaction to be recorded correctly. ■

Suppose that a person offers a building for sale at $120,000. It may be valued for real estate taxes at $75,000, and it may be insured for $90,000. One prospective buyer may offer $100,000 for the building, and another may offer $105,000. At this point, several different, unverifiable opinions of value have been expressed. Finally, suppose the seller and a buyer settle on a price and complete the sale for $110,000. All these figures are values of one kind or another, but only the last is sufficiently reliable to be used in the records. The market value of the building may vary over the years, but the building will remain on the new buyer's records at $110,000 until it is sold again. At that point, the accountant will record the new transaction at the new exchange price, and a profit or loss will be recognized.

FOCUS ON INTERNATIONAL BUSINESS

No Dollar Amount: How Can That Be?

Determining the valuation of a sale or purchase transaction is often not difficult because it equals the amount of cash, or dollar amount, that changes hands. However, in some areas of the world, valuation is not so easy to determine. In a country where the currency is declining in value and inflation is high, companies often are forced to resort to barter transactions, in which one good or service is traded for another. In Russia, for example, perhaps as many as two-thirds of all transactions are barters. It is not uncommon for Russian companies to end up with piles of goods stacked around their offices and warehouses. In one case, an electric utility company provided a textile-machinery plant with electricity in exchange for wool blankets, which the plant had received in exchange for equipment sold to another company. Determining the value can be difficult in such cases because it becomes a matter of determining the fair value of the goods being traded.[5]

FOCUS ON BUSINESS PRACTICE

Is It Always Cost?

There are sometimes exceptions to the general rules of accounting. For instance, the cost principle is not followed in all parts of the financial statements. Investments, for example, are often accounted for at fair or market value because these investments are available for sale. The fair or market value is the best measure of the potential benefit to the company. Intel Corp. <www.intel.com>, the large microprocessor company, states in its annual report:

A substantial majority of the company's marketable investments are classified as available-for-sale as of the balance sheet date and are reported at fair value.[6]

KEY POINT: Assets, liabilities, and the components of owners' equity are not accounts, but account *classifications*. For example, Cash is a type of asset account, and Accounts Payable is a type of liability account.

The cost principle is used because the cost is verifiable. It results from the actions of independent buyers and sellers who come to an agreement on price. An exchange price is an objective price that can be verified by evidence created at the time of the transaction. It is this final price, verified by agreement of the two parties, at which the transaction is recorded.

THE CLASSIFICATION ISSUE

The **classification** issue has to do with assigning all the transactions in which a business engages to appropriate categories, or accounts. Classification of debts can affect a company's ability to borrow money. And classification of purchases can affect its income; for example, purchases of tools may be considered repair expenses (a component of stockholders' equity) or equipment (assets).

Proper classification depends not only on correctly analyzing the effect of each transaction on the business, but also on maintaining a system of accounts that reflects that effect. The rest of this chapter explains the classification of accounts and the analysis and recording of transactions.

✓ Check out ACE for a Review Quiz at http://accounting.college.hmco.com/students.

ACCOUNTS AND THE CHART OF ACCOUNTS

LO2 Describe the chart of accounts and recognize commonly used accounts.

RELATED TEXT ASSIGNMENTS
Q: 6, 7, 8, 23
SE: 3
E: 3
FRA: 1, 6

KEY POINT: A chart of accounts is a table of contents for the ledger. Typically, it lists accounts in the order they appear in the ledger, which is usually the order in which they appear on the financial statements, and the numbering scheme allows for some flexibility.

Measuring business transactions often involves gathering large amounts of data. These data require a method of storage that allows businesspeople to retrieve transaction data quickly and in usable form—in other words, a filing system that classifies all transactions according to accounts. Recall that accounts are the basic storage units for accounting data and are used to accumulate amounts from similar transactions. An accounting system has a separate account for each asset, each liability, and each component of stockholders' equity, including revenues and expenses. Whether a company keeps records by hand or by computer, management must be able to refer to accounts so that it can study the company's financial history and plan for the future. A very small company may need only a few dozen accounts; a multinational corporation may need thousands.

In a manual accounting system, each account is kept on a separate page or card. These pages or cards are placed together in a book or file called the **general ledger**. In the computerized systems that most companies have today, accounts are maintained on magnetic tapes or disks. However, as a matter of convenience, accountants still refer to the group of company accounts as the *general ledger*, or simply the *ledger*.

To help identify accounts in the ledger and to make them easy to find, the accountant often numbers them. A list of these numbers with the corresponding account names is called a **chart of accounts**. A very simple chart of accounts appears in Exhibit 1. Notice that the first digit refers to the major financial statement classification. An account number that begins with the digit 1 represents an asset, an account number that begins with a 2 represents a liability, and so forth. The second and third digits refer to individual accounts. Also notice the gaps in the sequence of numbers. These gaps allow the accountant to expand the number of accounts.

In this chapter and in the next two, we refer to the accounts listed in Exhibit 1 as we discuss the sample case of the Joan Miller Advertising Agency, Inc.

EXHIBIT 1
Chart of Accounts for a Small Business

Account Number	Account Name	Description
		Assets
111	Cash	Money and any medium of exchange, including coins, currency, checks, postal and express money orders, and money on deposit in a bank
112	Notes Receivable	Amounts due from others in the form of promissory notes (written promises to pay definite sums of money at fixed future dates)
113	Accounts Receivable	Amounts due from others for revenues or sale on credit (sales on account)
115	Art Supplies	Prepaid expense; art supplies purchased and not used
116	Office Supplies	Prepaid expense; office supplies purchased and not used
117	Prepaid Rent	Prepaid expense; rent paid in advance and not used
118	Prepaid Insurance	Prepaid expense; insurance purchased and not expired; unexpired insurance
141	Land	Property owned for use in the business
142	Buildings	Structures owned for use in the business
143	Accumulated Depreciation, Buildings	Sum of the periodic allocation of the cost of buildings to expense
144	Art Equipment	Art equipment owned for use in the business
145	Accumulated Depreciation, Art Equipment	Sum of the periodic allocation of the cost of art equipment to expense
146	Office Equipment	Office equipment owned for use in the business
147	Accumulated Depreciation, Office Equipment	Sum of the periodic allocation of the cost of office equipment to expense
		Liabilities
211	Notes Payable	Amounts due to others in the form of promissory notes
212	Accounts Payable	Amounts due to others for purchases on credit
213	Unearned Art Fees	Unearned revenue; advance deposits for artwork to be provided in the future
214	Wages Payable	Amounts due to employees for wages earned and not paid
215	Income Taxes Payable	Amounts due to government for income taxes owed and not paid
221	Mortgage Payable	Amounts due on loans that are backed by the company's property and buildings
		Stockholders' Equity
311	Common Stock	Stockholders' investments in a corporation for which they receive shares of capital stock
312	Retained Earnings	Stockholders' claims against company assets derived from profitable operations
313	Dividends	Distributions of assets (usually cash) that reduce retained earnings
314	Income Summary	Temporary account used at the end of the accounting period to summarize the revenues and expenses for the period
		Revenues
411	Advertising Fees Earned	Revenues derived from performing advertising services
412	Art Fees Earned	Revenues derived from performing art services

(continued)

EXHIBIT 1
Chart of Accounts for a Small Business *(continued)*

Account Number	Account Name	Description
		Expenses
511	Wages Expense	Amounts earned by employees
512	Utilities Expense	Amounts of utilities, such as water, electricity, and gas, used
513	Telephone Expense	Amounts of telephone services used
514	Rent Expense	Amounts of rent on property and buildings used
515	Insurance Expense	Amounts for insurance expired
516	Art Supplies Expense	Amounts for art supplies used
517	Office Supplies Expense	Amounts for office supplies used
518	Depreciation Expense, Buildings	Amount of buildings' cost allocated to expense
519	Depreciation Expense, Art Equipment	Amount of art equipment cost allocated to expense
520	Depreciation Expense, Office Equipment	Amount of office equipment cost allocated to expense
521	Income Tax Expense	Amount of tax on income

◆**STOP AND THINK!**

How would the asset accounts in the chart of accounts for Joan Miller Advertising Agency, Inc., differ if it were a retail company that sold advertising products instead of a service company?

If it were a retail company, it would have an account for inventory.■

KEY POINT: Although dividends are a component of stockholders' equity, they normally appear only in the statement of retained earnings, not in the stockholders' equity section of the balance sheet. In addition, they do not appear as an expense on the income statement.

STOCKHOLDERS' EQUITY ACCOUNTS

In the chart of accounts shown in Exhibit 1, the revenue and expense accounts are separated from the stockholders' equity accounts. Figure 1 illustrates the relationships of these accounts to each other and to the financial statements. The distinctions among them are important for legal and financial reporting purposes.

First, the stockholders' equity accounts represent legal claims by the stockholders against the assets of the company. Common Stock is a capital stock account (corporations may have more than one type of capital stock) that represents stockholders' claims arising from their investments in the company, and Retained Earnings represents stockholders' claims arising from profitable operations. Both are claims against the general assets of the company, not against specific assets. They do not represent pools of funds that have been set aside. Dividends are included among the stockholders' equity accounts because they are distributions of assets that reduce stockholders' claims on retained earnings and are shown on the statement of retained earnings.

Second, by law, capital investments and dividends must be separated from revenues and expenses for income tax and financial reporting and other purposes.

Third, management needs a detailed breakdown of revenues and expenses for budgeting and operating purposes. From these accounts, which are included on the income statement, management can identify the sources of all revenues and the nature of all expenses. In this way, accounting gives management information about whether it has achieved its primary goal of earning a net income.

ACCOUNT TITLES

The names of accounts often confuse beginning accounting students because some words are new or have technical meanings. Also, the same asset, liability, or stockholders' equity account can have different names in different companies. (Actually, this is not so strange. People, too, often are called different names by their friends, families, and associates.) For example, Fixed Assets, Plant and Equipment, Capital Assets, and Long-Lived Assets are all names for long-term asset accounts. Even the

FIGURE 1
**Relationships of Stockholders'
Equity Accounts**

KEY POINT: Although revenues and expenses are components of stockholders' equity, they appear on the income statement, *not* on the stockholders' equity section of the balance sheet. Figure 1 illustrates this point.

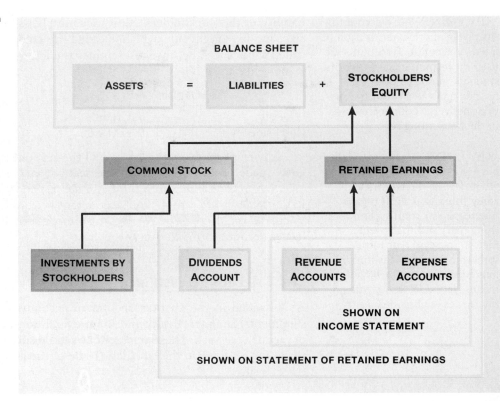

KEY POINT: Account names must be both concise and descriptive. Although some account names, such as Cash and Land, generally are fixed, others are not.

most acceptable names change over time, but out of habit, some companies continue to use names that are out of date.

In general, an account title should describe what is recorded in the account. When you come across an account title that you do not recognize, examine the context of the name—whether it is classified as an asset, liability, or stockholders' equity component, including revenue or expense, on the financial statements—and look for the kind of transaction that gave rise to the account.

 Check out ACE for Review Quiz at http://accounting.college.hmco.com/students.

THE DOUBLE-ENTRY SYSTEM: THE BASIC METHOD OF ACCOUNTING

LO3 Define *double-entry system* and state the rules for double entry.
RELATED TEXT ASSIGNMENTS
Q: 9, 10, 11, 12, 13
SE: 2
FRA: 5

KEY POINT: Each transaction must include at least one debit and one credit, and the debit totals must equal the credit totals.

The double-entry system, the backbone of accounting, evolved during the Renaissance. The first systematic description of double-entry bookkeeping appeared in 1494, two years after Columbus discovered America, in a mathematics book by Fra Luca Pacioli. Goethe, the famous German poet and dramatist, referred to double-entry bookkeeping as "one of the finest discoveries of the human intellect." Werner Sombart, an eminent economist-sociologist, believed that "double-entry bookkeeping is born of the same spirit as the system of Galileo and Newton."

What is the significance of the double-entry system? The system is based on the *principle of duality*, which means that every economic event has two aspects—effort and reward, sacrifice and benefit, source and use—that offset or balance each other. In the **double-entry system**, each transaction must be recorded with at least one debit and one credit, so that the total dollar amount of debits and the total dollar amount of credits equal each other. Because of the way it is designed, the whole system is always in balance. All accounting systems, no matter how sophisticated, are based on the principle of duality.

THE T ACCOUNT

The T account is a good place to begin the study of the double-entry system. In its simplest form, an account has three parts: (1) a title, which describes the asset, the

KEY POINT: A T account is simply an abbreviated version of a ledger account. T accounts are used by accountants, instructors, students, and textbooks to quickly analyze a set of transactions; ledger accounts are used in the accounting records.

KEY POINT: Many students have preconceived ideas about what *debit* and *credit* mean. They think that *debit* means "decrease" (or implies something bad) and that *credit* means "increase" (or implies something good). It is important to realize that *debit* simply means "left side" and *credit* simply means "right side."

liability, or the stockholders' equity account; (2) a left side, which is called the **debit** side; and (3) a right side, which is called the **credit** side. This form of an account, called a **T account** because it resembles the letter *T*, is used to analyze transactions. It looks like this:

Title of Account	
Debit (left) side	Credit (right) side

Any entry made on the left side of the account is a debit, or debit entry, and any entry made on the right side of the account is a credit, or credit entry. The terms *debit* (abbreviated Dr., from the Latin *debere*) and *credit* (abbreviated Cr., from the Latin *credere*) are simply the accountant's words for "left" and "right" (not for "increase" or "decrease"). We present a more formal version of the T account, the ledger account form, later in this chapter.

THE T ACCOUNT ILLUSTRATED

As discussed in the chapter on uses of accounting information and the financial statements, Shannon Realty, Inc., had several transactions that involved the receipt or payment of cash. These transactions can be summarized in the Cash account by recording receipts on the left (debit) side of the account and payments on the right (credit) side:

		Cash			
(1)	50,000		(2)	35,000
(5)	1,500		(4)	200
(7)	1,000		(8)	1,000
			(9)	400
			(11)	600
	52,500			37,200
Bal.	15,300			

Footings →

The cash receipts on the left total $52,500. (The total is written in small figures so that it cannot be confused with an actual debit entry.) The cash payments on the right side total $37,200. These totals are simply working totals, or **footings**. Footings, which are calculated at the end of each month, are an easy way to determine cash on hand. The difference in dollars between the total debit footing and the total credit footing is called the **balance**, or *account balance*. If the balance is a debit, it is written on the left side. If it is a credit, it is written on the right side. Notice that Shannon Realty's Cash account has a debit balance of $15,300 ($52,500 − $37,200). This is the amount of cash the business has on hand at the end of the month.

ANALYZING AND PROCESSING TRANSACTIONS

The two rules of double-entry bookkeeping are that every transaction affects at least two accounts and that total debits must equal total credits. In other words, for every transaction, one or more accounts must be debited and one or more accounts must be credited, and the total dollar amount of the debits must equal the total dollar amount of the credits.

Look again at the accounting equation:

$$\text{Assets} = \text{Liabilities} + \text{Stockholders' Equity}$$

You can see that if a debit increases assets, then a credit must be used to increase liabilities or stockholders' equity because they are on opposite sides of the equal sign. Likewise, if a credit decreases assets, then a debit must be used to decrease liabilities or stockholders' equity. These rules can be shown as follows:

Assets			=	Liabilities		+	Stockholders' Equity	
Debit for increases (+)	Credit for decreases (−)			Debit for decreases (−)	Credit for increases (+)		Debit for decreases (−)	Credit for increases (+)

◆STOP AND THINK!

How are assets and expenses related, and why are the debit and credit effects for assets and expenses the same?

Assets and expenses are closely related because many assets are expenses that have not yet been used. Examples are prepaid assets and plant and equipment. As a result, debits increase assets and expenses, and credits decrease assets and expenses. They appear on opposite sides of the accounting equation. ■

1. Increases in assets are debited to asset accounts. Decreases in assets are credited to asset accounts.

2. Increases in liabilities and stockholders' equity are credited to liability and stockholders' equity accounts. Decreases in liabilities and stockholders' equity are debited to liability and stockholders' equity accounts.

One of the more difficult points to understand is the application of double-entry rules to the stockholders' equity components. The key is to remember that dividends and expenses are deductions from stockholders' equity. Thus, transactions that *increase* dividends or expenses *decrease* stockholders' equity. Consider this expanded version of the accounting equation:

$$\text{Assets} = \text{Liabilities} + \underbrace{\text{Common} + \text{Retained} - \text{Dividends} + \text{Revenues} - \text{Expenses}}_{\text{Stockholders' Equity}}$$
$$\text{Stock} \qquad \text{Earnings}$$

This equation may be rearranged by shifting dividends and expenses to the left side, as follows:

Assets		+	Dividends		+	Expenses		=	Liabilities		+	Common Stock		+	Retained Earnings		+	Revenues	
+ (debits)	− (credits)		+ (debits)	− (credits)		+ (debits)	− (credits)		− (debits)	+ (credits)		− (debits)	+ (credits)		− (debits)	+ (credits)		− (debits)	+ (credits)

Note that the rules for double entry for all the accounts on the left of the equal sign are just the opposite of the rules for all the accounts on the right of the equal sign. Assets, dividends, and expenses are increased by debits and decreased by credits. Liabilities, common stock, retained earnings, and revenues are increased by credits and decreased by debits.

With this basic information about double entry, it is possible to analyze and process transactions by following the five steps illustrated in Figure 2. To show how the steps are applied, assume that on June 1, Koenig Art Supplies borrows $100,000 from its bank on a promissory note. The list that follows describes how this transaction is analyzed and processed.

FIGURE 2
Analyzing and Processing Transactions

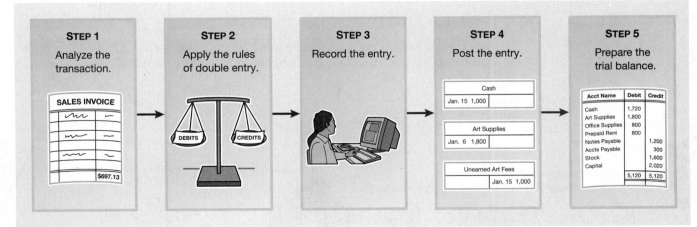

1. *Analyze the transaction to determine its effect on assets, liabilities, and stockholders' equity.* In this case, both an asset (Cash) and a liability (Notes Payable) increase. A transaction is usually supported by some kind of **source document**—an invoice, receipt, check, or contract; here, it would be a copy of the signed note.

2. *Apply the rules of double entry.* Increases in assets are recorded by debits. Increases in liabilities are recorded by credits.

3. *Record the entry.* Transactions are recorded in chronological order in a journal. In one form of journal, which is explained in more detail later in this chapter, the date, debit account, and debit amount are recorded on one line and the credit account and credit amount, indented, on the next line, as follows:

A = L + OE
+   +

		Dr.	Cr.
June 1	Cash	100,000	
	Notes Payable		100,000

This form is called **journal form.** An explanation appears right after the entry. If more than one account is debited or credited, more lines are used.

4. *Post the entry.* The entry is posted to the general ledger by transferring the date and amounts to the proper accounts. The T account is one form of ledger account.

Cash	
June 1	100,000

Notes Payable	
	June 1 100,000

In formal records, step **3** is never omitted. However, for purposes of analysis, accountants often bypass step **3** and record entries directly in T accounts because doing so clearly and quickly shows the effects of transactions on the accounts. Some of the assignments in this chapter use the same approach to emphasize the analytical aspects of double entry.

5. *Prepare the trial balance to confirm the balance of the accounts.* Periodically, accountants prepare a trial balance to confirm that the accounts are still in balance after the recording and posting of transactions. Preparation of the trial balance is explained later in this chapter.

✔ Check out ACE for a Review Quiz at http://accounting.college.hmco.com/students.

(handwritten margin note: Journal entries are done first.)

(handwritten margin note: go over for next class)

TRANSACTION ANALYSIS ILLUSTRATED

LO4 Apply the steps for transaction analysis and processing to simple transactions.

RELATED TEXT ASSIGNMENTS
Q: 14, 15, 16, 20, 24
SE: 5, 6
E: 4, 5, 7, 12
P: 1, 2, 3, 4, 5, 6, 7, 8
SD: 2, 4, 5
FRA: 1, 2, 3, 5, 6

KEY POINT: For this transaction, many students incorrectly credit Stockholders' Equity rather than Common Stock. Stockholders' equity is an account *classification*, not an account title.

In the next few pages, we examine the transactions for Joan Miller Advertising Agency, Inc., during the month of July. In the discussion, we illustrate the principle of duality and show how transactions are recorded in the accounts.

July 1: Joan Miller obtains a charter from the state and invests $20,000 in her own advertising agency in exchange for 20,000 shares of $1 par value common stock.

A = L + OE
+   +

		Dr.	Cr.
July 1	Cash	20,000	
	Common Stock		20,000

Cash	
July 1	20,000

Common Stock	
	July 1 20,000

Transaction: Investment in business.
Analysis: Assets increase. Stockholders' equity increases.
Rules: Increases in assets are recorded by debits. Increases in stockholders' equity are recorded by credits.
Entry: The increase in assets is recorded by a debit to Cash. The increase in stockholders' equity is recorded by a credit to Common Stock.

Analysis: If Joan Miller had invested assets other than cash in the business, the appropriate asset accounts would be debited.

July 2: Rents an office, paying two months' rent, $1,600, in advance.

A = L + OE
+
−

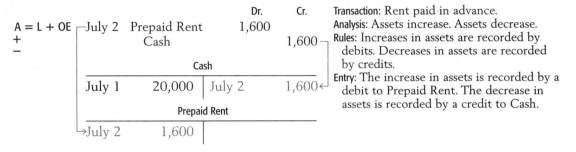

		Dr.	Cr.
July 2	Prepaid Rent	1,600	
	Cash		1,600

Cash

July 1	20,000	July 2	1,600

Prepaid Rent

July 2	1,600	

Transaction: Rent paid in advance.
Analysis: Assets increase. Assets decrease.
Rules: Increases in assets are recorded by debits. Decreases in assets are recorded by credits.
Entry: The increase in assets is recorded by a debit to Prepaid Rent. The decrease in assets is recorded by a credit to Cash.

July 3: Purchases art equipment, $4,200, with cash.

A = L + OE
+
−

		Dr.	Cr.
July 3	Art Equipment	4,200	
	Cash		4,200

Cash

July 1	20,000	July 2	1,600
		3	4,200

Art Equipment

July 3	4,200	

KEY POINT: Terms such as *Cash Paid* and *Art Equipment Purchased* are not acceptable account names. *Cash* and *Art Equipment* are the correct account names.

Transaction: Purchase of equipment.
Analysis: Assets increase. Assets decrease.
Rules: Increases in assets are recorded by debits. Decreases in assets are recorded by credits.
Entry: The increase in assets is recorded by a debit to Art Equipment. The decrease in assets is recorded by a credit to Cash.

July 4: Orders art supplies, $1,800, and office supplies, $800.

Analysis: No entry is made because no transaction has occurred. According to the recognition issue, there is no liability until the supplies are shipped or received and there is an obligation to pay for them.

July 5: Purchases office equipment, $3,000, from Morgan Equipment; pays $1,500 in cash and agrees to pay the rest next month.

A = L + OE
+   +
−

		Dr.	Cr.
July 5	Office Equipment	3,000	
	Cash		1,500
	Accounts Payable		1,500

Cash

July 1	20,000	July 2	1,600
		3	4,200
		5	1,500

Office Equipment

July 5	3,000	

Accounts Payable

		July 5	1,500

KEY POINT: Office equipment is recorded at the full $3,000, even though only half of it has been paid for.

Transaction: Purchase of equipment and partial payment.
Analysis: Assets increase. Assets decrease. Liabilities increase.
Rules: Increases in assets are recorded by debits. Decreases in assets are recorded by credits. Increases in liabilities are recorded by credits.
Entry: The increase in assets is recorded by a debit to Office Equipment. The decrease in assets is recorded by a credit to Cash. The increase in liabilities is recorded by a credit to Accounts Payable.

FOCUS ON BUSINESS ETHICS

Are Financial Statements Always Truthful?

The accounting solutions related to recognition (when a transaction occurred), valuation (what value to place on the transaction), and classification (how the components of the transaction should be categorized) are not only important for good financial reporting; they are also designed to help a company's management fulfill its responsibilities to the owners and the public.

A prime example of this responsibility was recently demonstrated at Lucent Technologies <www.lucent.com>, a major telecommunications equipment manufacturer. After years of excellent results, Lucent surprised its investors by admitting

that because of returns of equipment that distributors had been unable to sell, it was going to have to erase $452 million in equipment sales from the $679 million it had reported for the year.

The problem related to how and when Lucent recognizes proceeds from sales. The company's chief executive officer explained that to meet short-term growth targets, "We mortgaged future sales and revenue in a way we are paying for now."[7] In the aftermath, the company's stock dropped from $80 per share to less than $5 per share, and more than 10,000 employees were laid off.

July 6: Purchases art supplies, $1,800, and office supplies, $800, from Taylor Supply Company, on credit.

		Dr.	Cr.
A = L + OE July 6	Art Supplies	1,800	
+ +	Office Supplies	800	
+	Accounts Payable		2,600

Transaction: Purchase of supplies on credit.
Analysis: Assets increase. Liabilities increase.
Rules: Increases in assets are recorded by debits. Increases in liabilities are recorded by credits.
Entry: The increase in assets is recorded by debits to Art Supplies and Office Supplies. The increase in liabilities is recorded by a credit to Accounts Payable.

KEY POINT: Accounts Payable is used when there is a delay between purchase and payment.

Art Supplies

July 6	1,800	

Office Supplies

July 6	800	

Accounts Payable

	July 5	1,500
	6	2,600

July 8: Pays for a one-year life insurance policy, $960, with coverage effective July 1.

		Dr.	Cr.
A = L + OE July 8	Prepaid Insurance	960	
+	Cash		960
−			

Transaction: Insurance purchased in advance.
Analysis: Assets increase. Assets decrease.
Rules: Increases in assets are recorded by debits. Decreases in assets are recorded by credits.
Entry: The increase in assets is recorded by a debit to Prepaid Insurance. The decrease in assets is recorded by a credit to Cash.

Cash

July 1	20,000	July 2	1,600
		3	4,200
		5	1,500
		8	960

Prepaid Insurance

July 8	960	

July 9: Pays Taylor Supply Company $1,000 of the amount owed.

	Dr.	Cr.
July 9 Accounts Payable	1,000	
Cash		1,000

A = L + OE
–   –

KEY POINT: Accounts Payable, not Art Supplies or Office Supplies, is debited. Also, a liability usually is credited before it can be debited.

Cash

July 1	20,000	July 2	1,600
		3	4,200
		5	1,500
		8	960
		9	1,000

Accounts Payable

July 9	1,000	July 5	1,500
		6	2,600

Transaction: Partial payment on a liability.
Analysis: Assets decrease. Liabilities decrease.
Rules: Decreases in liabilities are recorded by debits. Decreases in assets are recorded by credits.
Entry: The decrease in liabilities is recorded by a debit to Accounts Payable. The decrease in assets is recorded by a credit to Cash.

July 10: Performs a service for an automobile dealer by placing advertisements in a newspaper and collects a fee, $1,400.

A = L + OE
+   +

	Dr.	Cr.
July 10 Cash	1,400	
Advertising Fees Earned		1,400

Cash

July 1	20,000	July 2	1,600
10	1,400	3	4,200
		5	1,500
		8	960
		9	1,000

Advertising Fees Earned

		July 10	1,400

Transaction: Revenue earned and cash collected.
Analysis: Assets increase. Stockholders' equity increases.
Rules: Increases in assets are recorded by debits. Increases in stockholders' equity are recorded by credits.
Entry: The increase in assets is recorded by a debit to Cash. The increase in stockholders' equity is recorded by a credit to Advertising Fees Earned.

July 12: Pays the secretary two weeks' wages, $1,200.

A = L + OE
–   –

	Dr.	Cr.
July 12 Wages Expense	1,200	
Cash		1,200

Cash

July 1	20,000	July 2	1,600
10	1,400	3	4,200
		5	1,500
		8	960
		9	1,000
		12	1,200

Wages Expense

July 12	1,200		

Transaction: Payment of wages expense.
Analysis: Assets decrease. Stockholders' equity decreases.
Rules: Decreases in stockholders' equity are recorded by debits. Decreases in assets are recorded by credits.
Entry: The decrease in stockholders' equity is recorded by a debit to Wages Expense. The decrease in assets is recorded by a credit to Cash.

July 15: Accepts an advance fee, $1,000, for artwork to be done for another agency.

A = L + OE
+   +

		Dr.	Cr.
July 15	Cash	1,000	
	Unearned Art Fees		1,000

Cash

July	1	20,000	July	2	1,600
	10	1,400		3	4,200
	15	1,000		5	1,500
				8	960
				9	1,000
				12	1,200

Unearned Art Fees

		July 15	1,000

Transaction: Payment received for future services.

Analysis: Assets increase. Liabilities increase.

Rules: Increases in assets are recorded by debits. Increases in liabilities are recorded by credits.

Entry: The increase in assets is recorded by a debit to Cash. The increase in liabilities is recorded by a credit to Unearned Art Fees.

◆**STOP AND THINK!**

In what way are unearned revenues the opposite of prepaid expenses?

With unearned revenues (a liability), cash is received in advance for a service to be performed later. With prepaid expenses (an asset), cash is paid in advance of receiving a service. ■

July 19: Performs a service by placing several major advertisements for Ward Department Stores. The fee, $4,800, is billed now but will be collected next month.

A = L + OE
+   +

		Dr.	Cr.
July 19	Accounts Receivable	4,800	
	Advertising Fees Earned		4,800

Accounts Receivable

July 19	4,800	

Advertising Fees Earned

		July 10	1,400
		19	4,800

Transaction: Revenue earned, to be received later.

Analysis: Assets increase. Stockholders' equity increases.

Rules: Increases in assets are recorded by debits. Increases in stockholders' equity are recorded by credits.

Entry: The increase in assets is recorded by a debit to Accounts Receivable. The increase in stockholders' equity is recorded by a credit to Advertising Fees Earned.

KEY POINT: Revenue is recognized even though payment has not been received yet. Accounts Receivable is used when there is a delay between the sale of services or merchandise and payment.

July 26: Pays the secretary two more weeks' wages, $1,200.

A = L + OE
–   –

		Dr.	Cr.
July 26	Wages Expense	1,200	
	Cash		1,200

Cash

July	1	20,000	July	2	1,600
	10	1,400		3	4,200
	15	1,000		5	1,500
				8	960
				9	1,000
				12	1,200
				26	1,200

Wages Expense

July 12	1,200	
26	1,200	

Transaction: Payment of wages expense.

Analysis: Assets decrease. Stockholders' equity decreases.

Rules: Decreases in stockholders' equity are recorded by debits. Decreases in assets are recorded by credits.

Entry: The decrease in stockholders' equity is recorded by a debit to Wages Expense. The decrease in assets is recorded by a credit to Cash.

July 29: Receives and pays the utility bill, $200.

A = L + OE
−   −

		Dr.	Cr.
July 29	Utilities Expense	200	
	Cash		200

Cash

July 1	20,000	July 2	1,600
10	1,400	3	4,200
15	1,000	5	1,500
		8	960
		9	1,000
		12	1,200
		26	1,200
		29	200←

Utilities Expense

July 29	200	

Transaction: Payment of utilities expense.
Analysis: Assets decrease. Stockholders' equity decreases.
Rules: Decreases in stockholders' equity are recorded by debits. Decreases in assets are recorded by credits.
Entry: The decrease in stockholders' equity is recorded by a debit to Utilities Expense. The decrease in assets is recorded by a credit to Cash.

July 30: Receives (but does not pay) the telephone bill, $140.

A = L + OE
+   −

		Dr.	Cr.
July 30	Telephone Expense	140	
	Accounts Payable		140

Accounts Payable

July 9	1,000	July 5	1,500
		6	2,600
		30	140←

Telephone Expense

July 30	140	

KEY POINT: The expense and liability are recognized at this point, even though payment has not yet been made, because an expense has been incurred. Telephone services have been used, and the obligation to pay exists.

Transaction: Expense incurred, to be paid later.
Analysis: Liabilities increase. Stockholders' equity decreases.
Rules: Decreases in stockholders' equity are recorded by debits. Increases in liabilities are recorded by credits.
Entry: The decrease in stockholders' equity is recorded by a debit to Telephone Expense. The increase in liabilities is recorded by a credit to Accounts Payable.

July 31: Declared and paid a dividend of $1,400.

A = L + OE
−   −

		Dr.	Cr.
July 31	Dividends	1,400	
	Cash		1,400

Cash

July 1	20,000	July 2	1,600
10	1,400	3	4,200
15	1,000	5	1,500
		8	960
		9	1,000
		12	1,200
		26	1,200
		29	200
		31	1,400←

Dividends

July 31	1,400	

KEY POINT: Dividends are not considered expenses. Expenses are costs of operating a business, but dividends are assets distributed to the stockholders of the business.

Transaction: Declaration and payment of dividends.
Analysis: Assets decrease. Stockholders' equity decreases.
Rules: Decreases in stockholders' equity are recorded by debits. Decreases in assets are recorded by credits.
Entry: The decrease in stockholders' equity is recorded by a debit to Dividends. The decrease in assets is recorded by a credit to Cash.

EXHIBIT 2
Summary of Transactions for Joan Miller Advertising Agency, Inc.

	Assets	=	Liabilities	+	Stockholders' Equity

Cash

July	1	20,000	July	2	1,600
	10	1,400		3	4,200
	15	1,000		5	1,500
				8	960
				9	1,000
				12	1,200
				26	1,200
				29	200
				31	1,400
		22,400			13,260
Bal.		9,140			

Accounts Payable

July 9	1,000	July 5	1,500
		6	2,600
		30	140
1,000			4,240
		Bal.	3,240

Unearned Art Fees

	July 15	1,000

Common Stock

	July 1	20,000

Dividends

July 31	1,400	

Advertising Fees Earned

	July 10	1,400
	19	4,800
Bal.		6,200

Accounts Receivable

July 19	4,800	

Art Supplies

July 6	1,800	

Office Supplies

July 6	800	

Prepaid Rent

July 2	1,600	

Prepaid Insurance

July 8	960	

Art Equipment

July 3	4,200	

Office Equipment

July 5	3,000	

Wages Expense

July 12	1,200	
26	1,200	
Bal.	2,400	

Utilities Expense

July 29	200	

Telephone Expense

July 30	140	

This account links to the statement of cash flows.

These accounts link to the income statement.

Exhibit 2 shows the transactions for July in their accounts and in relation to the accounting equation. Note that all transactions have been recorded on the date they are recognized. Most of these transactions involve either the receipt or payment of cash, as reflected in the Cash account. There are important exceptions, however. For instance, on July 19 Advertising Fees were earned, but receipt of cash for these fees will come later. Also, on July 5, 6, and 30 there were transactions recognized that totaled $4,240 in Accounts Payable. This means the company can wait to pay. At the end of the month, only the $1,000 recorded on July 9 had been paid. These lags between recognition of transactions and the subsequent cash inflows or outflows have an impact on achieving the goal of liquidity.

 Check out ACE for a Review Quiz at http://accounting.college.hmco.com/students.

THE TRIAL BALANCE

LO5 Prepare a trial balance and describe its value and limitations.

RELATED TEXT ASSIGNMENTS
Q: 17, 18, 19, 24
SE: 4, 7, 8
E: 3, 6, 8, 9, 10, 11
P: 2, 3, 4, 5, 7, 8
SD: 5

KEY POINT: The trial balance is prepared at the end of the accounting period. It is an initial check that the ledger is in balance.

For every amount debited, an equal amount must be credited. This means that the total of debits and credits in the T accounts must be equal. To test this, the accountant periodically prepares a **trial balance**. Exhibit 3 shows a trial balance for Joan Miller Advertising Agency, Inc. It was prepared from the accounts in Exhibit 2.

A trial balance may be prepared at any time but is usually prepared on the last day of the month. Here are the steps in preparing a trial balance:

1. List each T account that has a balance, with debit balances in the left column and credit balances in the right column. Accounts are listed in the order in which they appear in the ledger.

2. Add each column.

3. Compare the totals of the columns.

In accounts in which increases are recorded by debits, the **normal balance** (the usual balance) is a debit balance; in accounts in which increases are recorded by credits, the normal balance is a credit balance. Table 1 summarizes the normal account balances of the major account categories. According to the table, the T account Accounts Payable (a liability) typically has a credit balance and is copied into the trial balance as a credit balance.

EXHIBIT 3
Trial Balance

KEY POINT: The accounts are listed in the same order as in the ledger. At this point, the Retained Earnings account does not reflect any revenues, expenses, or dividends for the period.

Joan Miller Advertising Agency, Inc.
Trial Balance
July 31, 20xx

Cash	$ 9,140	
Accounts Receivable	4,800	
Art Supplies	1,800	
Office Supplies	800	
Prepaid Rent	1,600	
Prepaid Insurance	960	
Art Equipment	4,200	
Office Equipment	3,000	
Accounts Payable		$ 3,240
Unearned Art Fees		1,000
Common Stock		20,000
Dividends	1,400	
Advertising Fees Earned		6,200
Wages Expense	2,400	
Utilities Expense	200	
Telephone Expense	140	
	$30,440	$30,440

√(ChartT)√ *(handwritten)*

Know Chart *(handwritten)*

● **STOP AND THINK!**

Which account category would be most likely to have an account balance that is not normal?

Retained Earnings is the most likely account to have an abnormal balance (debit) because of situations in which expenses exceed revenues (net loss). It is unusual for any of the other accounts to have abnormal balances. ■

TABLE 1.   Normal Account Balances of Major Account Categories

Account Category	Increases Recorded by		Normal Balance	
	Debit	Credit	Debit	Credit
Assets	X		X	
Liabilities		X		X
Stockholders' equity:				
Common stock		X		X
Retained earnings		X		X
Dividends	X		X	
Revenues		X		X
Expenses	X		X	

Once in a while, a transaction leaves an account with a balance that is not "normal." For example, when a company overdraws its account at the bank, its Cash account (an asset) will show a credit balance instead of a debit balance. The "abnormal" balance should be copied into the trial balance columns as it stands, as a debit or a credit.

The trial balance proves whether or not the ledger is in balance. *In balance* means that the total of all debits recorded equals the total of all credits recorded. But the trial balance does not prove that the transactions were analyzed correctly or recorded in the proper accounts. For example, there is no way of determining from the trial balance that a debit should have been made in the Art Equipment account rather than the Office Equipment account. And the trial balance does not detect whether transactions have been omitted, because equal debits and credits will have been omitted. Also, if an error of the same amount is made in both a debit and a credit, it will not be discovered by the trial balance. The trial balance proves only that the debits and credits in the accounts are in balance.

If the debit and credit columns of the trial balance are not equal, look for one or more of the following errors: (1) a debit was entered in an account as a credit, or vice versa; (2) the balance of an account was computed incorrectly; (3) an error was made in carrying the account balance to the trial balance; or (4) the trial balance was summed incorrectly.

Other than simply adding the columns incorrectly, the two most common mistakes in preparing a trial balance are (1) recording an account with a debit balance as a credit, or vice versa, and (2) transposing two numbers when transferring an amount to the trial balance (for example, entering $23,459 as $23,549). The first of these mistakes causes the trial balance to be out of balance by an amount divisible by 2. The second causes the trial balance to be out of balance by a number divisible by 9. Thus, if a trial balance is out of balance and the addition has been verified, determine the amount by which the trial balance is out of balance and divide it first by 2 and then by 9. If the amount is divisible by 2, look in the trial balance for an amount that is equal to the quotient. If you find such an amount, it is probably in the wrong column. If the amount is divisible by 9, trace each amount to the ledger account balance, checking carefully for a transposition error. If neither of these techniques identifies the error, first recompute the balance of each account in the ledger.

FOCUS ON BUSINESS TECHNOLOGY

Are All Trial Balances Created Equal?

In computerized accounting systems, posting is done automatically, and the trial balance can be easily prepared as often as needed. Any accounts with abnormal balances are highlighted for investigation. Some general ledger software packages for small businesses list the trial balance amounts in a single column, with credit balances shown as minuses. In such cases, the trial balance is in balance if the total is zero.

Then, if you still have not found the error, retrace each posting from the journal to the ledger.

✓ Check out ACE for a Review Quiz at http://accounting.college.hmco.com/students.

RECORDING AND POSTING TRANSACTIONS

SO6 Record transactions in the general journal and post transactions from the general journal to the ledger.

RELATED TEXT ASSIGNMENTS
Q: 20, 21, 22, 23, 24
SE: 9, 10
E: 12, 13
P: 5, 8

KEY POINT: The journal is a chronological record of events. Only the general journal is discussed in this chapter.

Let us now take a look at the formal process of recording transactions in the general journal and posting them to the ledger.

THE GENERAL JOURNAL

As you have seen, transactions can be entered directly into the accounts. But this method makes identifying individual transactions or finding errors very difficult because the debit is recorded in one account and the credit in another. The solution is to record all transactions chronologically in a **journal**. The journal is sometimes called the *book of original entry* because it is where transactions first enter the accounting records. Later, the debit and credit portions of each transaction can be transferred to the appropriate accounts in the ledger. A separate **journal entry** is used to record each transaction, and the process of recording transactions is called **journalizing**.

Most businesses have more than one kind of journal. Several types of journals are discussed in the appendix on special-purpose journals. The simplest and most flexible type is the **general journal**, the one we focus on in this chapter. Entries in the general journal include the following information about each transaction:

1. The date
2. The names of the accounts debited and the dollar amounts on the same lines in the debit column
3. The names of the accounts credited and the dollar amounts on the same lines in the credit column
4. An explanation of the transaction
5. The account identification numbers, if appropriate

Exhibit 4 displays two of the transactions for Joan Miller Advertising Agency, Inc., that we discussed earlier. The procedure for recording transactions in the general journal is as follows:

1. Record the date by writing the year in small figures on the first line at the top of the first column, the month on the next line of the first column, and the day in the second column opposite the month. For subsequent entries on the same page for the same month and year, the month and year can be omitted.

2. Write the exact names of the accounts debited and credited in the Description column. Starting on the same line as the date, write the name(s) of the account(s) debited next to the left margin and indent the name(s) of the account(s) credited. The explanation is placed on the next line and is further indented. The explanation should be brief but sufficient to explain and identify the transaction. A transaction can have more than one debit or credit entry; this is called a **compound entry**. In a compound entry, all debit accounts are listed before any credit accounts. (The July 6 transaction of Joan Miller Advertising Agency, Inc., in Exhibit 4 is an example of a compound entry.)

3. Write the debit amounts in the Debit column opposite the accounts to be debited, and write the credit amounts in the Credit column opposite the accounts to be credited.

EXHIBIT 4
The General Journal

A = L + OE
+   +
+

A = L + OE
+
–

Date		Description	Post. Ref.	Debit	Credit
20xx July	6	Art Supplies		1,800	
		Office Supplies		800	
		Accounts Payable			2,600
		Purchase of art and office supplies on credit			
	8	Prepaid Insurance		960	
		Cash			960
		Paid one-year life insurance premium			

General Journal — Page 1

4. At the time the transactions are recorded, nothing is placed in the Post. Ref. (posting reference) column. (This column is sometimes called *LP* or *Folio.*) Later, if the company uses account numbers to identify accounts in the ledger, fill in the account numbers to provide a convenient cross-reference from the general journal to the ledger and to indicate that the entry has been posted to the ledger. If the accounts are not numbered, use a checkmark (✔).

5. It is customary to skip a line after each journal entry.

THE GENERAL LEDGER

The general journal is used to record the details of each transaction. The general ledger is used to update each account.

■ **THE LEDGER ACCOUNT FORM**   The T account is a simple, direct means of recording transactions. In practice, a somewhat more complicated form of the account is needed in order to record more information. The **ledger account form**, which contains four columns for dollar amounts, is illustrated in Exhibit 5.

The account title and number appear at the top of the account form. As in the journal, the transaction date appears in the first two columns. The Item column is

EXHIBIT 5
Accounts Payable in the General Ledger

General Ledger

Accounts Payable   Account No. 212

Date		Item	Post. Ref.	Debit	Credit	Balance Debit	Balance Credit
20xx July	5		J1		1,500		1,500
	6		J1		2,600		4,100
	9		J1	1,000			3,100
	30		J2		140		3,240

EXHIBIT 6
Posting from the General Journal to the Ledger

A = L + OE
    +   −

General Journal   ② Page 2

Date		Description	Post. Ref.	Debit	Credit
20xx	②	①	⑤	③	
July	30	Telephone Expense	513	140	
		Accounts Payable	212		140
		Received bill for			
		telephone expense			

General Ledger

Accounts Payable   Account No. 212

Date		Item	Post. Ref.	Debit	Credit	Balance Debit	Balance Credit
20xx							
July	5		J1		1,500		1,500
	6		J1		2,600		4,100
	9		J1	1,000			3,100
	30		J2		140		3,240

General Ledger

Telephone Expense   Account No. 513

Date		Item	Post. Ref.	Debit	Credit	Balance Debit	Balance Credit
20xx						④	
July	30		J2	140		140	

rarely used to identify transactions, because explanations already appear in the journal. The Post. Ref. column is used to note the journal page where the original entry for the transaction can be found. The dollar amount is entered in the appropriate Debit or Credit column, and a new account balance is computed in the final two columns after each entry. The advantage of this account form over the T account is that the current balance of the account is readily available.

■ **POSTING TO THE LEDGER**   After transactions have been entered in the journal, they must be transferred to the ledger. The process of transferring journal entry information from the journal to the ledger is called **posting**. Posting is usually done after several entries have been made—for example, at the end of each day or less frequently, depending on the number of transactions. As shown in Exhibit 6, through posting, each amount in the Debit column of the journal is transferred into the Debit column of the appropriate account in the ledger, and each amount in the

Credit column of the journal is transferred into the Credit column of the appropriate account in the ledger. The steps in the posting process are as follows:

1. In the ledger, locate the debit account named in the journal entry.
2. Enter the date of the transaction and, in the Post. Ref. column of the ledger, the journal page number from which the entry comes.
3. Enter in the Debit column of the ledger account the amount of the debit as it appears in the journal.
4. Calculate the account balance and enter it in the appropriate Balance column.
5. Enter in the Post. Ref. column of the journal the account number to which the amount has been posted.
6. Repeat the same five steps for the credit side of the journal entry.

Notice that step **5** is the last step in the posting process for each debit and credit. In addition to serving as an easy reference between the journal entry and the ledger account, this entry in the Post. Ref. column of the journal indicates that all steps for the transaction have been completed. This allows accountants who have been called away from their work to easily find where they were before they were interrupted.

SOME NOTES ON PRESENTATION

A ruled line appears in financial reports before each subtotal or total to indicate that the amounts above are added or subtracted. It is common practice to use a double line under a final total to show that it has been checked, or verified.

Dollar signs ($) are required in all financial statements, including the balance sheet and income statement, and in the trial balance and other schedules. On these statements, a dollar sign should be placed before the first amount in each column and before the first amount in a column following a ruled line. Dollar signs in the same column are aligned. Dollar signs are not used in journals and ledgers.

On unruled paper, commas and decimal points are used in dollar amounts. On paper with ruled columns—like the paper in journals and ledgers—commas and decimal points are not needed. In this book, because most problems and illustrations are in whole dollar amounts, the cents column usually is omitted. When accountants deal with whole dollars, they often use a dash in the cents column to indicate whole dollars rather than taking the time to write zeros.

 Check out ACE for a Review Quiz at http://accounting.college.hmco.com/students.

Chapter Review

REVIEW OF LEARNING OBJECTIVES

LO1 Explain, in simple terms, the generally accepted ways of solving the measurement issues of recognition, valuation, and classification.

To measure a business transaction, the accountant determines when the transaction occurred (the recognition issue), what value should be placed on the transaction (the valuation issue), and how the components of the transaction should be categorized (the classification issue). In general, recognition occurs when title passes, and a transaction is valued at the exchange price, the cost at the time the transaction is recognized. Classification refers to the categorizing of transactions according to a system of accounts.

LO2 Describe the chart of accounts and recognize commonly used accounts.

An account is a device for storing data from transactions. There is one account for each asset, liability, and component of stockholders' equity, including revenues and expenses. The ledger is a book or file containing all of a company's accounts, arranged according to a chart of accounts. Commonly used asset accounts are Cash, Notes Receivable,

Accounts Receivable, Prepaid Expenses, Land, Buildings, and Equipment. Common liability accounts are Notes Payable, Accounts Payable, Wages Payable, and Mortgage Payable. Common stockholders' equity accounts are Common Stock, Retained Earnings, Dividends, and revenue and expense accounts.

LO3 Define *double-entry system* and state the rules for double entry.

In the double-entry system, each transaction must be recorded with at least one debit and one credit, so that the total dollar amount of the debits equals the total dollar amount of the credits. The rules for double entry are (1) increases in assets are debited to asset accounts; decreases in assets are credited to asset accounts; and (2) increases in liabilities and stockholders' equity are credited to those accounts; decreases in liabilities and stockholders' equity are debited to those accounts.

LO4 Apply the steps for transaction analysis and processing to simple transactions.

The procedure for analyzing transactions is (1) analyze the effect of the transaction on assets, liabilities, and stockholders' equity; (2) apply the appropriate double-entry rule; (3) record the entry; (4) post the entry; and (5) prepare a trial balance.

LO5 Prepare a trial balance and describe its value and limitations.

A trial balance is used to check that the debit and credit balances are equal. It is prepared by listing each account with its balance in the Debit or Credit column. Then the two columns are added and the totals compared to test the balances. The major limitation of the trial balance is that even if debit and credit balances are equal, this does not guarantee that the transactions were analyzed correctly or recorded in the proper accounts.

SUPPLEMENTAL OBJECTIVE

SO6 Record transactions in the general journal and post transactions from the general journal to the ledger.

The general journal is a chronological record of all transactions. That record contains the date of each transaction, the names of the accounts and the dollar amounts debited and credited, an explanation of each entry, and the account numbers to which postings have been made. After transactions have been entered in the general journal, they are posted to the ledger. Posting is done by transferring each amount in the Debit column of the general journal to the Debit column of the appropriate account in the ledger, and transferring each amount in the Credit column of the general journal to the Credit column of the appropriate account in the ledger. After each entry is posted, a new balance is entered in the appropriate Balance column.

REVIEW OF CONCEPTS AND TERMINOLOGY

The following concepts and terms were introduced in this chapter:

LO3 **Balance:** The difference in dollars between the total debit footing and the total credit footing of an account. Also called *account balance*.

LO2 **Chart of accounts:** A scheme that assigns a unique number to each account to facilitate finding the account in the ledger; also, the list of account numbers and titles.

LO1 **Classification:** The process of assigning transactions to the appropriate accounts.

SO6 **Compound entry:** An entry that has more than one debit or credit entry.

LO1 **Cost:** The exchange price associated with a business transaction at the point of recognition.

LO1 **Cost principle:** The practice of recording transactions at cost.

LO3 **Credit:** The right side of an account.

LO3 **Debit:** The left side of an account.

LO3 **Double-entry system:** The accounting system in which each transaction is recorded with at least one debit and one credit, so that the total dollar amount of debits and the total dollar amount of credits equal each other.

LO3 **Footings:** Working totals of columns of numbers. *To foot* means to total a column of numbers.

SO6   **General journal:** The simplest and most flexible type of journal.

LO2   **General ledger:** The book or file that contains all of the company's accounts, arranged in the order of the chart of accounts. Also called *ledger*.

SO6   **Journal:** A chronological record of all transactions; the place where transactions first enter the accounting records. Also called *book of original entry*.

SO6   **Journal entry:** Journal notations that record a single transaction.

LO3   **Journal form:** A form of journal in which the date, the debit account, and the debit amount of a transaction are recorded on one line and the credit account and credit amount on the next line.

SO6   **Journalizing:** The process of recording transactions in a journal.

SO6   **Ledger account form:** The form of account that has four dollar amount columns: one column for debit entries, one column for credit entries, and two columns (debit and credit) for showing the balance of the account.

LO5   **Normal balance:** The usual balance of an account; also the side (debit or credit) that increases the account.

SO6   **Posting:** The process of transferring journal entry information from the journal to the ledger.

LO1   **Recognition:** The determination of when a business transaction should be recorded.

LO1   **Recognition point:** The predetermined time at which a transaction should be recorded; usually, the point at which title passes to the buyer.

LO3   **Source document:** An invoice, check, receipt, or other document that supports a transaction.

LO3   **T account:** The simplest form of an account, used to analyze transactions.

LO5   **Trial balance:** A comparison of the total of debit and credit balances in the accounts to check that they are equal.

LO1   **Valuation:** The process of assigning a monetary value to a business transaction.

REVIEW PROBLEM

Transaction Analysis, Journalizing, T Accounts, and Trial Balance

LO4
LO5   After graduation from veterinary school, Laura Cox entered private practice. The transactions of the business through May 27 are as follows:

20xx

May   1   Laura Cox invested $2,000 in 2,000 shares of $1 par value common stock of her newly chartered company, Pet Clinic, Inc.
      3   Paid $300 for two months' rent in advance for an office.
      9   Purchased medical supplies for $200 in cash.
      12   Purchased $400 of equipment on credit, making a 25 percent down payment.
      15   Delivered a calf for a fee of $35 on credit.
      18   Made a partial payment of $50 on the equipment purchased May 12.
      27   Paid a utility bill of $40.

REQUIRED ▶   1. Record these transactions in journal form.
              2. Post the transactions to the following T accounts: Cash; Accounts Receivable; Medical Supplies; Prepaid Rent; Equipment; Accounts Payable; Common Stock; Veterinary Fees Earned; and Utilities Expense.
              3. Prepare a trial balance as of May 31.

4. How does the transaction of May 15 relate to recognition and cash flows? Also compare the transactions of May 9 and May 27 with regard to classification.

ANSWER TO REVIEW PROBLEM

1. Transactions recorded in journal form

May	1	Cash	2,000	
		Common Stock		2,000
		Invested $2,000 in 2,000 shares of $1 par value common stock		
	3	Prepaid Rent	300	
		Cash		300
		Paid two months' rent in advance for an office		
	9	Medical Supplies	200	
		Cash		200
		Purchased medical supplies for cash		
	12	Equipment	400	
		Accounts Payable		300
		Cash		100
		Purchased equipment on credit, paying 25 percent down		
	15	Accounts Receivable	35	
		Veterinary Fees Earned		35
		Fee on credit for delivery of a calf		
	18	Accounts Payable	50	
		Cash		50
		Partial payment for equipment purchased May 12		
	27	Utilities Expense	40	
		Cash		40
		Paid utility bill		

2. Transactions posted to T accounts

Cash

May 1	2,000	May 3	300
		9	200
		12	100
		18	50
		27	40
	2,000		690
Bal.	1,310		

Accounts Receivable

May 15	35	

Medical Supplies

May 9	200	

Prepaid Rent

May 3	300	

Equipment

May 12	400	

Accounts Payable

May 18	50	May 12	300
		Bal.	250

Common Stock

		May 1	2,000

Veterinary Fees Earned

		May 15	35

Utilities Expense

May 27	40	

3. Trial balance prepared

Pet Clinic, Inc. Trial Balance May 31, 20xx		
Cash	$1,310	
Accounts Receivable	35	
Medical Supplies	200	
Prepaid Rent	300	
Equipment	400	
Accounts Payable		$ 250
Common Stock		2,000
Veterinary Fees Earned		35
Utilities Expense	40	
	$2,285	$2,285

4. The transaction is recorded, or recognized, on May 15, even though no cash is received. The revenue is earned because the service was provided to and accepted by the buyer. The customer now has an obligation to pay the seller. It is recorded as an accounts receivable because the customer has been allowed to pay later. The transaction on May 9 is classified as an asset, Medical Supplies, because these supplies will benefit the company in the future. The transaction on May 27 is classified as an expense, Utilities Expense, because the utilities have already been used and will not benefit the company in the future.

Chapter Assignments

BUILDING YOUR KNOWLEDGE FOUNDATION

QUESTIONS

1. What three issues underlie most accounting measurement decisions?

2. Why is recognition an issue for accountants?

3. A customer asks the owner of a store to save an item for him and says that he will pick it up and pay for it next week. The owner agrees to hold it. Should this transaction be recorded as a sale? Explain your answer.

4. Why is it practical for accountants to rely on original cost for valuation purposes?

5. Under the cost principle, changes in value after a transaction is recorded are not usually recognized in the accounts. Comment on this possible limitation of using original cost in accounting measurements.

6. What is an account, and how is it related to the ledger?

7. Tell whether each of the following accounts is an asset account, a liability account, or a stockholders' equity account:

   a. Notes Receivable
   b. Land
   c. Dividends
   d. Mortgage Payable
   e. Prepaid Rent
   f. Insurance Expense
   g. Service Revenue

8. In the stockholders' equity accounts, why do accountants maintain separate accounts for revenues and expenses rather than using the Retained Earnings account?

9. Why is the system of recording entries called the double-entry system? What is significant about this system?

10. "Double-entry accounting refers to entering a transaction in both the journal and the ledger." Comment on this statement.

11. "Debits are bad; credits are good." Comment on this statement.

12. What are the rules of double entry for (a) assets, (b) liabilities, and (c) stockholders' equity?

13. Why are the rules of double entry the same for liabilities and stockholders' equity?

14. What is the meaning of the statement, "The Cash account has a debit balance of $500"?

15. Explain why debits, which decrease stockholders' equity, also increase expenses, which are a component of stockholders' equity.

16. What are the five steps in analyzing and processing a transaction?

17. What does a trial balance prove?

18. What is the normal balance of Accounts Payable? Under what conditions could Accounts Payable have a debit balance?

19. Is it possible for errors to be present even though a trial balance balances? Explain your answer.

20. Is it a good idea to forgo the journal and enter a transaction directly into the ledger? Explain your answer.

21. In recording entries in a journal, which is written first, the debit or the credit? How is indentation used in the journal?

22. What is the relationship between the journal and the ledger?

23. Describe each of the following:

    a. Account
    b. Journal
    c. Ledger
    d. Book of original entry
    e. Post. Ref. column
    f. Journalizing
    g. Posting
    h. Footings
    i. Compound entry

24. List the following six items in sequence to illustrate the flow of events through the accounting system:

    a. Analysis of the transaction
    b. Debits and credits posted from the journal to the ledger
    c. Occurrence of the business transaction
    d. Preparation of the financial statements
    e. Entry made in the journal
    f. Preparation of the trial balance

SHORT EXERCISES

LO1 Recognition

SE 1. Which of the following events would be recognized and entered in the accounting records of Thorpe Corporation? Why?

Jan. 10   Thorpe Corporation places an order for office supplies.
Feb. 15   Thorpe Corporation receives the office supplies and a bill for them.
Mar. 1   Thorpe Corporation pays for the office supplies.

LO1   Recognition, Valuation,
LO3   and Classification

SE 2.   Tell how the concepts of recognition, valuation, and classification apply to this transaction:

Cash			Supplies		
June 1	250		June 1	250	

LO2   Classification of Accounts

SE 3.   Tell whether each of the following accounts is an asset, a liability, a revenue, an expense, or none of these:

a. Accounts Payable L
b. Supplies A
c. Dividends
d. Fees Earned r
e. Supplies Expense e
f. Accounts Receivable A
g. Unearned Revenue L
h. Equipment

LO5   Normal Balances

SE 4.   Tell whether the normal balance of each account in SE 3 is a debit or a credit.

LO4   Transaction Analysis

SE 5.   For each transaction below, tell which account is debited and which account is credited.

May   2   Han Kim started a computer programming business, Kim's Programming Service, Inc., by investing $5,000 in exchange for common stock.
    5   Purchased a computer for $2,500 in cash.
    7   Purchased supplies on credit for $300.
   19   Received cash for programming services performed, $500.
   22   Received cash for programming services to be performed, $600.
   25   Paid the rent for May, $650.
   31   Billed a customer for programming services performed, $250.

LO4   Recording Transactions in
**   T Accounts**

SE 6.   Set up T accounts and record each transaction in SE 5. Determine the balance of each account.

LO5   Preparing a Trial Balance

SE 7.   From the T accounts created in SE 6, prepare a trial balance dated May 31, 20x4.

LO5   Correcting Errors in a Trial
**   Balance**

SE 8.   The trial balance that follows is out of balance. Assuming all balances are normal, place the accounts in proper order and correct the trial balance so that debits equal credits.

Serowik Boating Service, Inc.
Trial Balance
January 31, 20x4

Cash	$2,000	
Accounts Payable	400	
Fuel Expense	800	
Unearned Service Revenue	250	
Accounts Receivable		$1,300
Prepaid Rent		150
Common Stock		1,500
Service Revenue	1,750	
Wages Expense		300
Retained Earnings	650	
	$5,850	$3,250

SE 9.
SO6 Recording Transactions in the General Journal

Prepare a general journal form like the one in Exhibit 4 and label it Page 4. Record the following transactions in the journal:

Sept. 6   Billed a customer for services performed, $1,900.
16   Received partial payment from the customer billed on Sept. 6, $900.

SE 10.
SO6 Posting to the Ledger Accounts

Prepare ledger account forms like the ones in Exhibit 5 for the following accounts: Cash (111), Accounts Receivable (113), and Service Revenue (411). Post the transactions that are recorded in **SE 9** to the ledger accounts, at the same time making the proper posting references.

EXERCISES

E 1.
LO1 Recognition

Which of the following events would be recognized and recorded in the accounting records of the Friese Corporation on the date indicated?

Jan.   15   Friese Corporation offers to purchase a tract of land for $140,000. There is a high likelihood that the offer will be accepted. *no*

Feb.   2   Friese Corporation receives notice that its rent will be increased from $500 per month to $600 per month effective March 1. *no*

Mar.   29   Friese Corporation receives its utility bill for the month of March. The bill is not due until April 9. *yes*

June   10   Friese Corporation places a firm order for new office equipment costing $21,000. *no*

July   6   The office equipment ordered on June 10 arrives. Payment is not due until August 1. *yes*

E 2.
LO1 Application of Recognition Point

Dempsey's Parts Shop, Inc., uses a large amount of supplies in its business. The following table summarizes selected transaction data for supplies that Dempsey's Parts Shop purchased:

Order	Date Shipped	Date Received	Amount
a	June 26	July 5	$ 600
b	July 10	15	1,500
c	16	22	800
d	23	30	1,200
e	27	Aug. 1	1,500
f	Aug. 3	7	1,000

Determine the total purchases of supplies for July alone under each of the following assumptions:

1. Dempsey's Parts Shop, Inc., recognizes purchases when orders are shipped. *5000*
2. Dempsey's Parts Shop, Inc., recognizes purchases when orders are received. *4100*

E 3.
LO2 Classification of Accounts
LO5

The following ledger accounts are for the Arif Service Corporation:

a. Cash   n. Utilities Expense
b. Wages Expense   o. Fees Earned
c. Accounts Receivable   p. Dividends
d. Common Stock   q. Wages Payable
e. Service Revenue   r. Unearned Revenue
f. Prepaid Rent   s. Office Equipment
g. Accounts Payable   t. Rent Payable
h. Investments in Securities u. Notes Receivable
i. Income Taxes Payable   v. Interest Expense
j. Income Taxes Expense   w. Notes Payable
k. Land   x. Supplies
l. Supplies Expense   y. Interest Receivable
m. Prepaid Insurance   z. Rent Expense

Complete the table that appears at the top of the next page, using Xs to indicate each account's classification and normal balance (whether a debit or a credit increases the account).

				Type of Account				
				Stockholders' Equity			Normal Balance (increases balance)	
			Common Stock		Retained Earnings			
Item	Asset	Liability		Dividends	Revenue	Expense	Debit	Credit
a.	X						X	

LO4 Transaction Analysis

E 4. Analyze transactions **a–g,** following the example below.

    a. Harry Boka established Whiskers Barber Shop, Inc., by incorporating and investing $1,200 in exchange for 120 shares of $10 par value common stock.

    b. Paid two months' rent in advance, $840.

    c. Purchased supplies on credit, $60.

    d. Received cash for barbering services, $300.

    e. Paid for supplies purchased in **c.**

    f. Paid utility bill, $36.

    g. Declared and paid a dividend of $50.

Example:

    a. The asset Cash was increased. Increases in assets are recorded by debits. Debit Cash $1,200. A component of stockholders' equity, Common Stock, was increased. Increases in stockholders' equity are recorded by credits. Credit Common Stock $1,200.

LO4 Recording Transactions in T Accounts

E 5. Open the following T accounts: Cash; Repair Supplies; Repair Equipment; Accounts Payable; Common Stock; Dividends; Repair Fees Earned; Salaries Expense; and Rent Expense. Record the following transactions for the month of June directly in the T accounts; use the letters to identify the transactions in your T accounts. Determine the balance in each account.

    a. Ella Clunie opened Ceramics Repair Service, Inc., by investing $4,300 in cash and $1,600 in repair equipment in return for 5,900 shares of the company's $1 par value common stock.

    b. Paid $400 for the current month's rent.

    c. Purchased repair supplies on credit, $500.

    d. Purchased additional repair equipment for cash, $300.

    e. Paid salary to a helper, $450.

    f. Paid $200 of amount purchased on credit in **c.**

    g. Accepted cash for repairs completed, $1,860.

    h. Declared and paid a dividend of $600.

LO5 Trial Balance

E 6. After recording the transactions in **E 5,** prepare a trial balance in proper sequence for Ceramics Repair Service, Inc., as of June 30, 20xx.

LO4 Analysis of Transactions

E 7. Explain each transaction **(a–h)** entered in the following T accounts:

Cash				Accounts Receivable				Equipment			
a.	60,000	b.	15,000	c.	6,000	g.	1,500	b.	15,000	h.	900
g.	1,500	e.	3,000					d.	9,000		
h.	900	f.	4,500								

Accounts Payable				Common Stock				Service Revenue			
f.	4,500	d.	9,000			a.	60,000			c.	6,000

Wages Expense			
e.	3,000		

LO5 Preparing a Trial Balance

E 8. The list that follows presents the accounts of the Gobi Metal Corporation as of March 31, 20xx, in alphabetical order. The list does not include the amount of Accounts Payable.

Accounts Payable	?
Accounts Receivable	$ 3,000
Building	34,000
Cash	9,000
Common Stock	20,000
Equipment	12,000
Land	5,200
Notes Payable	20,000
Prepaid Insurance	1,100
Retained Earnings	11,450

Prepare a trial balance with the proper heading (see Exhibit 3) and with the accounts listed in the chart of accounts sequence (see Exhibit 1). Compute the balance of Accounts Payable.

E 9.

LO5 Effects of Errors on a Trial Balance

Which of the following errors would cause a trial balance to have unequal totals? Explain your answers.

a. A payment to a creditor was recorded as a debit to Accounts Payable for $86 and as a credit to Cash for $68.

b. A payment of $100 to a creditor for an account payable was debited to Accounts Receivable and credited to Cash.

c. A purchase of office supplies of $280 was recorded as a debit to Office Supplies for $28 and as a credit to Cash for $28.

d. A purchase of equipment for $300 was recorded as a debit to Supplies for $300 and as a credit to Cash for $300.

E 10.

LO5 Correcting Errors in a Trial Balance

This was the trial balance for Maxx Services, Inc., at the end of July:

Maxx Services, Inc.
Trial Balance
July 31, 20xx

Cash	$ 1,920	
Accounts Receivable	2,830	
Supplies	60	
Prepaid Insurance	90	
Equipment	4,200	
Accounts Payable		$ 2,270
Common Stock		2,000
Retained Earnings		3,780
Dividends		350
Revenues		2,960
Salaries Expense	1,300	
Rent Expense	300	
Advertising Expense	170	
Utilities Expense	13	
	$10,883	$11,360

The trial balance does not balance because of a number of errors. Maxx's accountant compared the amounts in the trial balance with the ledger, recomputed the account balances, and compared the postings. He found the following errors:

a. The balance of Cash was understated by $200.

b. A cash payment of $210 was credited to Cash for $120.

c. A debit of $60 to Accounts Receivable was not posted.

d. Supplies purchased for $30 were posted as a credit to Supplies.

e. A debit of $90 to Prepaid Insurance was not posted.

f. The Accounts Payable account had debits of $2,660 and credits of $4,590.

g. The Notes Payable account, with a credit balance of $1,200, was not included on the trial balance.

h. The debit balance of Dividends was listed in the trial balance as a credit.

i. A $100 debit to Dividends was posted as a credit.

j. The actual balance of Utilities Expense, $130, was listed as $13 in the trial balance.

Prepare a corrected trial balance.

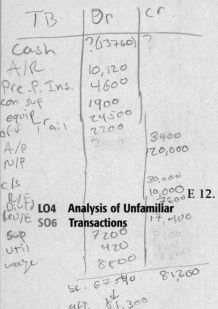

E 11.
LO5 Preparing a Trial Balance

The Loreau Construction Corporation builds foundations for buildings and parking lots. The following alphabetical list shows Loreau Construction's account balances as of April 30, 20xx:

Accounts Payable	$ 3,900	Office Trailer	$ 2,200
Accounts Receivable	10,120	Prepaid Insurance	4,600
Cash	?	Retained Earnings	10,000
Common Stock	30,000	Supplies Expense	7,200
Construction Supplies	1,900	Revenue Earned	17,400
Dividends	7,800	Utilities Expense	420
Equipment	24,500	Wages Expense	8,800
Notes Payable	20,000		

Prepare a trial balance for the company with the proper heading and with the accounts in balance sheet sequence. Determine the correct balance for the Cash account on April 30, 20xx.

E 12.
LO4 Analysis of Unfamiliar
SO6 Transactions

Managers and accountants often encounter transactions with which they are unfamiliar. Use your analytical skills to analyze and record in journal form the transactions that follow, which have not yet been discussed in the text.

May 1 Purchased merchandise inventory on account, $2,400.

2 Purchased marketable securities for cash, $5,600.

3 Returned part of merchandise inventory purchased in a for full credit, $500.

4 Sold merchandise inventory on account, $1,600 (record sale only).

5 Purchased land and a building for $600,000. Payment is $120,000 cash, and there is a thirty-year mortgage for the remainder. The purchase price is allocated as follows: $200,000 to the land and $400,000 to the building.

6 Received an order for $24,000 in services to be provided. With the order was a deposit of $8,000.

E 13.
SO6 Recording Transactions in the General Journal and Posting to the Ledger Accounts

Open a general journal form like the one in Exhibit 4, and label it Page 10. After opening the form, record the following transactions in the journal:

Dec. 14 Purchased an item of equipment for $6,000, paying $2,000 as a cash down payment.

28 Paid $3,000 of the amount owed on the equipment.

Prepare three ledger account forms like the one shown in Exhibit 5. Use the following account numbers: Cash, 111; Equipment, 144; and Accounts Payable, 212. Then post the two transactions from the general journal to the ledger accounts, being sure to make proper posting references.

Assume that the Cash account has a debit balance of $8,000 on the day prior to the first transaction.

PROBLEMS

P 1.
LO4 Transaction Analysis

The following accounts are applicable to Walter's Chimney Sweeps, Inc.:

1. Cash
2. Accounts Receivable
3. Supplies
4. Prepaid Insurance
5. Equipment

6. Notes Payable
7. Accounts Payable
8. Common Stock
9. Retained Earnings
10. Dividends
11. Service Revenue-To be pd.
12. Rent Expense
13. Repair Expense

Walter's Chimney Sweeps, Inc., completed the following transactions:

	Debit	Credit
a. Paid for supplies purchased on credit last month.	7	1
b. Billed customers for services performed.	2	11
c. Paid the current month's rent.	12	1
d. Purchased supplies on credit.	3	7
e. Received cash from customers for services performed but not yet billed.	1	11
f. Purchased equipment on account.	5	7
g. Received a bill for repairs.	13	7
h. Returned part of the equipment purchased in f for a credit.	7	5
i. Received payments from customers previously billed.	1	2
j. Paid the bill received in g.	7	1
k. Received an order for services to be performed.	none	none
l. Paid for repairs with cash.	13	1
m. Made a payment to reduce the principal of the note payable.	6	1
n. Declared and paid a dividend.	10	1

REQUIRED ▶ Analyze each transaction and show the accounts affected by entering the corresponding numbers in the appropriate debit or credit column as shown in transaction a. Indicate no entry, if appropriate.

P 2. Bob Lutz opened a secretarial school called Best Secretarial Training, Inc.

**LO4 Transaction Analysis,
LO5 T Accounts, and Trial
Balance**

a. He contributed the following assets to the business in exchange for 13,600 shares of $1 par value common stock:

Cash $5,700
Computers   4,300
Office Equipment 3,600

b. Found a location for his business and paid the first month's rent, $260.
c. Paid for an advertisement announcing the opening of the school, $190.
d. Received applications from three students for a four-week secretarial program and two students for a ten-day keyboarding course. The students will be billed a total of $1,300.
e. Purchased supplies on credit, $330.
f. Billed the enrolled students, $1,300.
g. Paid an assistant one week's salary, $220.
h. Purchased a second-hand computer, $480, and office equipment, $380, on credit.
i. Paid for the supplies purchased on credit in e, $330.
j. Paid cash to repair a broken computer, $40.
k. Billed new students who enrolled late in the course, $440.
l. Received partial payment from students previously billed, $1,080.
m. Paid the utility bill for the current month, $90.
n. Paid an assistant one week's salary, $220.
o. Received cash revenue from another new student, $250.
p. Declared and paid a dividend of $300.

REQUIRED ▶ 1. Set up the following T accounts: Cash; Accounts Receivable; Supplies; Computers; Office Equipment; Accounts Payable; Common Stock; Dividends; Tuition Revenue; Salaries Expense; Utilities Expense; Rent Expense; Repair Expense; and Advertising Expense.
2. Record the transactions directly in the T accounts, using the transaction letter to identify each debit and credit.
3. Prepare a trial balance using today's date.

LO1   Transaction Analysis, T
LO4   Accounts, and Trial
LO5   Balance

P 3.   Hiroshi Tanaka began an upholstery-cleaning business on October 1 and engaged in the following transactions during the month:

Oct.   1   Began business by depositing $6,000 in a bank account in the name of the corporation in exchange for 6,000 shares of $1 par value common stock.
        2   Ordered cleaning supplies, $500.
        3   Purchased cleaning equipment for cash, $1,400.
        4   Leased a van by making two months' lease payment in advance, $600.
        7   Received the cleaning supplies ordered on October 2 and agreed to pay half the amount in ten days and the rest in thirty days.
        9   Paid for repairs on the van with cash, $40.
        12   Received cash for cleaning upholstery, $480.
        17   Paid half the amount owed on supplies purchased on October 7, $250.
        21   Billed customers for cleaning upholstery, $670.
        24   Paid cash for additional repairs on the van, $40.
        27   Received $300 from the customers billed on October 21.
        31   Declared and paid a dividend of $350.

REQUIRED ▶   1. Set up the following T accounts: Cash; Accounts Receivable; Cleaning Supplies; Prepaid Lease; Cleaning Equipment; Accounts Payable; Common Stock; Dividends; Cleaning Revenue; and Repair Expense.
2. Record transactions directly in the T accounts. Identify each entry by date.
3. Prepare a trial balance for Tanaka Upholstery-Cleaning, Inc., as of October 31, 20xx.
4. Compare and contrast how the issue of recognition, valuation, and classification are settled in the transactions of October 7 and 9.

LO1   Transaction Analysis,
LO4   Journal Form, T Accounts,
LO5   and Trial Balance

P 4.   Sonny Hales is a house painter. During the month of April, he completed the following transactions:

Apr.   2   Began his business by contributing equipment valued at $1,230 and depositing $7,100 in a checking account in the name of the corporation in exchange for 833 shares of $10 par value common stock of the corporation.
        3   Purchased a used truck costing $1,900. Paid $500 cash and signed a note for the balance.
        4   Purchased supplies on account for $320.
        5   Completed a painting job and billed the customer $480.
        7   Received $150 in cash for painting two rooms.
        8   Hired an assistant at $6 per hour.
        10   Purchased supplies for $160 in cash.
        11   Received a $480 check from the customer billed on April 5.
        12   Paid $400 for an insurance policy for eighteen months' coverage.
        13   Billed a customer $620 for a painting job.
        14   Paid the assistant $150 for twenty-five hours' work.
        15   Paid $40 for a tune-up for the truck.
        18   Paid for the supplies purchased on April 4.
        20   Purchased a new ladder (equipment) for $60 and supplies for $290, on account.
        22   Received a telephone bill for $60, due next month.
        23   Received $330 in cash from the customer billed on April 13.
        25   Received $360 in cash for painting a five-room apartment.
        27   Paid $200 on the note signed for the truck.
        29   Paid the assistant $180 for thirty hours' work.
        30   Declared and paid a dividend of $300.

REQUIRED ▶   1. Prepare entries to record these transactions in journal form.
2. Set up the following T accounts and post all the journal entries: Cash; Accounts Receivable; Supplies; Prepaid Insurance; Equipment; Truck; Notes Payable; Accounts Payable; Common Stock; Dividends; Painting Fees Earned; Wages Expense; Telephone Expense; and Repair Expense.
3. Prepare a trial balance for Hales Painting Service, Inc., as of April 30, 20xx.
4. Compare how recognition applies to the transactions of April 5 and 7 and their effects on cash flow and how classification applies to the transactions of April 12 and 14.

P 5. The Acorn Nursery School Corporation provides baby-sitting and child-care programs. On January 31, 20xx, the company had the following trial balance:

Acorn Nursery School Corporation
Trial Balance
January 31, 20xx

Cash (111)	$ 1,870	
Accounts Receivable (113)	1,700	
Equipment (141)	1,040	
Buses (143)	17,400	
Notes Payable (211)		$15,000
Accounts Payable (212)		1,640
Common Stock (311)		4,000
Retained Earnings (312)		1,370
	$22,010	$22,010

During the month of February, the company completed the following transactions:

Feb.	2	Paid this month's rent, $270.
	3	Received fees for this month's services, $650.
	4	Purchased supplies on account, $85.
	5	Reimbursed the bus driver for gas expenses, $40.
	6	Ordered playground equipment, $1,000.
	8	Made a payment on account, $170.
	9	Received payments from customers on account, $1,200.
	10	Billed customers who had not yet paid for this month's services, $700.
	11	Paid for the supplies purchased on February 4.
	12	Paid part-time assistants for two weeks' services, $230.
	13	Purchased playground equipment for cash, $1,000.
	17	Purchased equipment on account, $290.
	19	Paid this month's utility bill, $145.
	22	Received payment for one month's services from customers previously billed, $500.
	26	Paid part-time assistants for two weeks' services, $230.
	27	Purchased gas and oil for the bus on account, $35.
	28	Paid for a one-year insurance policy, $290.
	28	Declared and paid a dividend of $110.

REQUIRED ▶

1. Open accounts in the ledger for the accounts in the trial balance plus the following ones: Supplies (115); Prepaid Insurance (116); Dividends (313); Service Revenue (411); Rent Expense (511); Gas and Oil Expense (512); Wages Expense (513); and Utilities Expense (514).
2. Enter the January 31, 20xx, account balances from the trial balance.
3. Enter the above transactions in the general journal (Pages 17, 18, and 19).
4. Post the entries to the ledger accounts. Be sure to make the appropriate posting references in the journal and ledger as you post.
5. Prepare a trial balance as of February 28, 20xx.

ALTERNATE PROBLEMS

P 6. The following accounts are applicable to Dale's Lawn Service, Inc., a company that maintains condominium grounds:

1. Cash
2. Accounts Receivable

3. Supplies
4. Prepaid Insurance
5. Equipment
6. Accounts Payable
7. Common Stock
8. Retained Earnings
9. Dividends
10. Lawn Services Revenue
11. Wages Expense
12. Rent Expense
13. Utilities Expense

Dale's Lawn Service, Inc., completed the following transactions:

	Debit	Credit
a. Received cash from customers billed last month.	1	2
b. Made a payment on accounts payable.	6	1
c. Purchased a new one-year insurance policy in advance.	4	1
d. Purchased supplies on credit.	3	6
e. Billed a client for lawn services.	2	10
f. Made a rent payment for the current month.	12	1
g. Received cash from customers for lawn services.	1	10
h. Paid wages for the staff.	11	1
i. Ordered equipment.	none	none
j. Paid the current month's utility bill.	13	1
k. Received and paid for the equipment ordered in i.	5	1
l. Returned for full credit some of the supplies purchased in d because they were defective.	6	3
m. Paid for supplies purchased in d, less the return in l.	6	1
n. Declared and paid a dividend.	9	1

REQUIRED ▶ Analyze each transaction and show the accounts affected by entering the corresponding numbers in the appropriate debit or credit columns as shown in transaction **a**. Indicate no entry, if appropriate.

P 7.

LO1 Transaction Analysis,
LO4 Journal Form, T Accounts,
LO5 and Trial Balance

Nomar Parra won a concession to rent bicycles in the local park during the summer. During the month of June, Parra completed the following transactions for his bicycle rental business:

June   2   Began business by placing $7,200 in a business checking account in the name of the corporation in exchange for 7,200 shares of $1 par value common stock.

3   Purchased supplies on account for $150.

4   Purchased ten bicycles for $2,500, paying $1,200 down and agreeing to pay the rest in thirty days.

5   Paid $2,900 in cash for a small shed to store the bicycles and to use for other operations.

6   Received $470 in cash for rentals during the first week of operation.

8   Paid $400 in cash for shipping and installation costs (considered an addition to the cost of the shed) to place the shed at the park entrance.

9   Hired a part-time assistant to help out on weekends at $7 per hour.

10   Paid a maintenance person $75 to clean the grounds.

13   Received $500 in cash for rentals during the second week of operation.

15   Paid the assistant $80 for a weekend's work.

17   Paid $150 for the supplies purchased on June 3.

18   Paid a $55 repair bill on bicycles.

20   Received $550 in cash for rentals during the third week of operation.

22   Paid the assistant $80 for a weekend's work.

23   Billed a company $110 for bicycle rentals for an employee outing.

25   Paid the $100 fee for June to the Park District for the right to the bicycle concession.

27   Received $410 in cash for rentals during the week.

29   Paid the assistant $80 for a weekend's work.

30   Declared and paid a dividend of $500.

REQUIRED ▶
1. Prepare entries to record these transactions in journal form.
2. Set up the following T accounts and post all the journal entries: Cash; Accounts Receivable; Supplies; Shed; Bicycles; Accounts Payable; Common Stock; Dividends; Rental Revenue; Wages Expense; Maintenance Expense; Repair Expense; and Concession Fee Expense.
3. Prepare a trial balance for Parra Rentals, Inc., as of June 30, 20xx.
4. Compare and contrast how the issues of recognition, valuation, and classification are settled in the transactions of June 3 and 10.

P 8.

LO4 Transaction Analysis,
LO5 General Journal, Ledger
SO6 Accounts, and Trial Balance

Yury Wagoner Corporation is a marketing firm. On July 31, 20xx, the company's trial balance was as follows:

Yury Wagoner Corporation
Trial Balance
July 31, 20xx

Cash (111)	$10,200	
Accounts Receivable (113)	5,500	
Supplies (115)	610	
Office Equipment (141)	4,200	
Accounts Payable (212)		$ 2,600
Common Stock (311)		12,000
Retained Earnings (312)		5,910
	$20,510	$20,510

During the month of August, the company completed the following transactions:

Aug. 2 Paid rent for August, $650.
3 Received cash from customers on account, $2,300.
7 Ordered supplies, $380.
10 Billed customers for services provided, $2,800.
12 Made a payment on accounts payable, $1,100.
14 Received the supplies ordered on August 7 and agreed to pay for them in 30 days, $380.
15 Paid salaries for the first half of August, $1,900.
17 Discovered some of the supplies were not as ordered and returned them for full credit, $80.
19 Received cash from a customer for services provided, $4,800.
24 Paid the utility bill for August, $160.
25 Paid the telephone bill for August, $120.
26 Received a bill, to be paid in September, for advertisements placed in the local newspaper during the month of August to promote Yury Wagoner Corporation, $700.
29 Billed a customer for services provided, $2,700.
30 Paid salaries for the last half of August, $1,900.
31 Declared and paid a dividend of $1,200.

REQUIRED ▶
1. Open accounts in the ledger for the accounts in the trial balance plus the following accounts: Dividends (313); Public Relations Fees (411); Salaries Expense (511); Rent Expense (512); Utilities Expense (513); Telephone Expense (514); and Advertising Expense (515).
2. Enter the July 31, 20xx, account balances from the trial balance.
3. Enter the above transactions in the general journal (Pages 22 and 23).
4. Post the journal entries to the ledger accounts. Be sure to make the appropriate posting references in the journal and ledger as you post.
5. Prepare a trial balance as of August 31, 20xx.

SKILLS DEVELOPMENT CASES

Conceptual Analysis

LO1   **Valuation Issue**

SD 1.   Nike, Inc., <www.nike.com> manufactures athletic shoes and related products. In one of its annual reports, Nike made this statement: "Property, plant, and equipment are recorded at cost."[8] Given that the property, plant, and equipment undoubtedly were purchased over several years and that the current value of those assets was likely to be very different from their original cost, tell what authoritative basis there is for carrying the assets at cost. Does accounting generally recognize changes in value after the purchase of property, plant, and equipment? Assume you are a Nike accountant. Write a memo to management explaining the rationale underlying Nike's approach.

LO1   **Valuation and Classification**
LO4   **Issues for Dot-Coms**

SD 2.   The dot-com business has raised many issues about accounting practices, some of which are of great concern to both the SEC and the FASB. Important ones relate to the valuation and classification of revenue transactions. Many dot-com companies seek to report as much revenue as possible because revenue growth is seen as a key performance measure for these companies. Amazon.com is a good example. Consider the following situations:

a. An Amazon.com <www.amazon.com> customer orders and pays $28 for a Gameboy® electronic game on the Internet. Amazon sends an email to the company that makes the product, which sends the Gameboy to the customer. Amazon collects $28 from the customer and pays $24 to the other company. Amazon never owns the Gameboy.

b. Amazon agrees to place a banner advertisement on its web site for another dot-com company. Instead of paying cash for the advertisement, the other company agrees to let Amazon advertise on its web site.

c. Assume the same facts as in situation **b** except that Amazon agrees to accept the other company's common stock in this barter transaction. Over the next six months, the price of the stock received goes down.

Discuss the valuation and classification issues that arise in each of these situations, including how Amazon should account for each transaction.

 Group Activity: Divide the class into groups. Assign each group one of the above cases so that one-third of the groups have each case. Debrief and discuss.

Ethical Dilemma

LO1   **Recognition Point and Ethical**
     Considerations

SD 3.   Jerry Hasbrow, a sales representative for Penn Office Supplies Corporation, is compensated on a commission basis and receives a substantial bonus for meeting his annual sales goal. The company's recognition point for sales is the day of shipment. On December 31, Hasbrow realizes he needs sales of $2,000 to reach his sales goal and receive the bonus. He calls a purchaser for a local insurance company, whom he knows well, and asks him to buy $2,000 worth of copier paper today. The purchaser says, "But Jerry, that's more than a year's supply for us." Hasbrow says, "Buy it today. If you decide it's too much, you can return however much you want for full credit next month." The purchaser says, "Okay, ship it." The paper is shipped on December 31 and recorded as a sale. On January 15, the purchaser returns $1,750 worth of paper for full credit (approved by Hasbrow) against the bill. Should the shipment on December 31 be recorded as a sale? Discuss the ethics of Hasbrow's action.

Group Activity: Divide the class into informal groups to discuss and report on the ethical issues of this case.

Research Activity

LO4   **Transactions in a Business**
     Article

SD 4.   Locate an article on a company you recognize or on a company in a business that interests you in one of the following sources: a recent issue of a business publication (such as *Barron's, Fortune, The Wall Street Journal, BusinessWeek,* or *Forbes*) or the Needles Accounting Resource Center Web Site at http://accounting.college.hmco.com/students.

Read the article carefully, noting any references to transactions in which the company engages. These may be normal transactions (such as sales or purchases) or unusual transactions (such as a merger or the purchase of another company). Bring a copy of the article to class and be prepared to describe how you would analyze and record the transactions you have noted.

Decision-Making Practice

SD 5.

LO4 Transaction Analysis
LO5 and Evaluation of a Trial Balance

Luis Ruiz hired an attorney to help him start Ruiz Repair Service Corporation. On March 1, Ruiz deposited $11,500 cash in a bank account in the name of the corporation in exchange for 1,150 shares of $10 par value common stock. When he paid the attorney's bill of $700, the attorney advised him to hire an accountant to keep his records. Ruiz was so busy that it was March 31 before he asked you to straighten out his records. Your first task is to develop a trial balance based on the March transactions, which are described in the next two paragraphs.

After investing in his business and paying his attorney, Ruiz borrowed $5,000 from the bank. He later paid $260, including interest of $60, on this loan. He also purchased a used pickup truck in the company's name, paying $2,500 down and financing $7,400. The first payment on the truck is due April 15. Ruiz then rented an office and paid three months' rent, $900, in advance. Credit purchases of office equipment of $800 and repair tools of $500 must be paid by April 10.

In March, Ruiz Repair Service completed repairs of $1,300, of which $400 were cash transactions. Of the credit transactions, $300 were collected during March, and $600 remained to be collected at the end of March. Wages of $450 were paid to employees. On March 31, the company received a $75 bill for the March utilities expense and a $50 check from a customer for work to be completed in April.

1. Record all of the transactions for March in journal form. Label each of the entries alphabetically.
2. Set up T accounts. Then post the entries to the T accounts. Identify each posting with the letter corresponding to the transaction.
3. Determine the balance of each account.
4. Prepare a trial balance for Ruiz Repair Service Corporation as of March 31.
5. Luis Ruiz is unsure how to evaluate the trial balance. His Cash account balance is $12,440, which exceeds his original investment of $11,500 by $940. Did he make a profit of $940? Explain why the Cash account is not an indicator of business earnings. Cite specific examples to show why it is difficult to determine net income by looking solely at figures in the trial balance.

FINANCIAL REPORTING AND ANALYSIS CASES

Interpreting Financial Reports

FRA 1.

LO2 Interpreting a Bank's
LO4 Financial Statements

Mellon Bank <www.mellon.com> is a large bank holding company. Selected accounts from the company's 2000 annual report are as follows (in millions):[9]

| Cash and Due from Banks | $ 3,506 | Securities Available for Sale | $ 7,910 |
| Loans to Customers | 26,369 | Deposits by Customers | 36,890 |

REQUIRED ▶

1. Indicate whether each of the accounts just listed is an asset, a liability, or a component of stockholders' equity on Mellon Bank's balance sheet.
2. Assume that you are in a position to do business with this large company. Prepare the entry on Mellon Bank's books in journal form to record each of the following transactions:
   a. You sell securities in the amount of $2,000 to the bank.
   b. You deposit the $2,000 received in step **a** in the bank.
   c. You borrow $5,000 from the bank.

International Company

FRA 2.

LO4   Transaction Analysis

Ajinomoto Company <www.ajinomoto.com>, a Japanese company with operations in 22 countries, is primarily engaged in the manufacture and sale of food products. The following selected aggregate cash transactions were reported in the statement of cash flows in Ajinomoto's annual report (amounts in millions of yen):[10]

Dividends paid	¥ 7,793
Purchase of property, plant, and equipment	46,381
Proceeds from issuance of long-term debt	10,357
Repayment of long-term debt	11,485

REQUIRED ▶   Prepare entries in journal form to record the above transactions.

Toys "R" Us Annual Report

FRA 3.

LO4   Transaction Analysis

Refer to the balance sheet in the Toys "R" Us <www.tru.com> annual report in the Supplement to Chapter 1. Prepare T accounts for the accounts Cash and Cash Equivalents, Accounts and Other Receivables, Prepaid Expenses and Other Current Assets, Accounts Payable, and Income Taxes Payable. Properly place the balance of the account at February 2, 2002, in the T accounts. Below are some typical transactions in which Toys "R" Us would engage. Analyze each transaction, enter it in the T accounts, and determine the balance of each account. Assume all entries are in thousands.

a. Paid cash in advance for certain expenses, $20,000.
b. Received cash from customers billed previously, $35,000.
c. Paid cash for income taxes previously owed, $70,000.
d. Paid cash to suppliers for amounts owed, $120,000.

Comparison Case: Toys "R" Us and Walgreen Co.

FRA 4.

LO1   Recognition, Valuation, and Classification

Refer to the Summary of Significant Accounting Policies in the notes to the financial statements in the Toys "R" Us <www.tru.com> annual report and to the financial statements of Walgreens <www.walgreens.com> to answer these questions:

1. How does the concept of recognition apply to advertising costs for both Toys "R" Us and Walgreens?
2. How does the concept of valuation apply to property and equipment for both companies?
3. How does the concept of classification apply to cash and cash equivalents for both companies?

Discuss any differences that you may observe.

Fingraph® Financial Analyst™

FRA 5.

LO1   Transaction Identification
LO3
LO4

Choose a company from the list of Fingraph companies on the Needles Accounting Resource Center Web Site at http://accounting.college.hmco.com/students. Click on the company you selected to access the Microsoft Excel spreadsheet for that company. You will find the company's URL (Internet address) in the heading of the spreadsheet. Click on the URL for a link to the company's web site and annual report.

1. From the company's annual report, determine the industry(ies) in which the company operates.
2. Find the summary of significant accounting policies that follows the financial statements. In these policies, find examples of the application of recognition, valuation, and classification.
3. Identify six types of transactions the company would commonly engage in. Are any of these transactions more common in the industry in which the company operates than in other industries? For each transaction, tell what account would typically be debited and what account would be credited.
4. Prepare a one-page executive summary that highlights what you have learned from steps **1**, **2**, and **3**.

Internet Case

FRA 6.

LO2 Comparison of
LO4 Contrasting Companies

Sun Microsystems <www.sun.com> and Oracle Corporation <www.oracle.com> are leading computer and software companies. Go to their web sites directly using the URLs shown here, or go to the Needles Accounting Resource Center Web Site at http://accounting.college.hmco.com/students for a link to their web sites. Access each company's annual report and find its balance sheet.

1. What differences and similarities do you find in the account titles used by Sun Microsystems and those used by Oracle? What differences and similarities do you find in the account titles used by the two companies and those used in this text?

2. Although the companies are in the same general industry, their businesses differ. How are these differences reflected on the balance sheets? What types of transactions resulted in the differences?

3

Chapter 3 defines the accounting concept of business income, discusses the role of adjusting entries in the measurement of income, and demonstrates the preparation of financial statements.

Measuring Business Income

LEARNING OBJECTIVES

LO1 Define *net income* and its two major components, *revenues* and *expenses.*

LO2 Explain how the income measurement issues of accounting period, continuity, and matching are resolved.

LO3 Define *accrual accounting* and explain three broad ways of accomplishing it.

LO4 State four principal situations that require adjusting entries and prepare typical adjusting entries.

LO5 Prepare financial statements from an adjusted trial balance.

SUPPLEMENTAL OBJECTIVE

SO6 Analyze cash flows from accrual-based information.

DECISION POINT
A USER'S FOCUS

Kelly Services <www.kellyservices.com> Kelly Services is one of the most successful temporary employment agencies. During any given year, Kelly incurs various operating expenses that are recorded as expenses when they are paid. However, at the end of the year, some expenses—including, for example, the wages of employees during the last days before the end of the year—will have been incurred but will not be paid until the next year. If these expenses are not accounted for correctly, they will appear in the wrong year—the year in which they are paid instead of the year in which Kelly benefited from them. The result is a misstatement of the company's income, a key profitability performance measure. How is this problem avoided?

According to the concepts of accrual accounting and the matching rule, which you will learn in this chapter, the amount of expenses that have been incurred but not paid must be determined and then recorded as expenses of the current year with corresponding liabilities to be paid the next year. The accompanying figure shows the liabilities, called *accrued liabilities,* that resulted from this process at Kelly Services.[1] Total accrued liabilities for payroll and related expenses, accrued insurance, and income and other taxes were $330,592,000 in 1999 and $338,893,000 in 2000. If these items had not been recorded in their respective years, income would have been misstated by a significant amount.

How does Kelly Services record wages that have been incurred in December but won't be paid until January?

Financial Highlights: Notes to the Financial Statements

3. ACCRUED LIABILITIES
(In thousands)

	2000	1999
Payroll and related expenses	$234,807	$215,706
Accrued insurance	55,272	65,881
Income and other taxes	48,814	49,005
Total accrued liabilities	$338,893	$330,592

PROFITABILITY MEASUREMENT: THE ROLE OF BUSINESS INCOME

LO1 Define *net income* and its two major components, *revenues* and *expenses*.

RELATED TEXT ASSIGNMENTS
Q: 1
SD: 5
FRA: 6

KEY POINT: Accounting measures and reports a business's profitability. The extent of the reported profit or loss communicates the company's success or failure in meeting this business goal.

⬢ **STOP AND THINK!**
When a company has net income, what happens to assets and/or liabilities?
Stockholders' equity increases, but there is also an increase in assets and/or a decrease in liabilities. ■

Profitability is one of the two major goals of a business (the other being liquidity). For a business to succeed, or even to survive, it must earn a profit. The word **profit**, though, has many meanings. One is the increase in stockholders' equity that results from business operations. However, even this definition can be interpreted differently by economists, lawyers, businesspeople, and the public. Because the word *profit* has more than one meaning, accountants prefer to use the term *net income*, which can be precisely defined from an accounting point of view. Net income is reported on the income statement and is a performance measure used by management, stockholders, and others to monitor a business's progress in meeting the goal of profitability. Readers of income statements need to understand how the accountant defines net income and to be aware of its strengths and weaknesses as a measure of company performance.

NET INCOME

Net income is the net increase in stockholders' equity that results from the operations of a company and is accumulated in the Retained Earnings account. Net income, in its simplest form, is measured by the difference between revenues and expenses when revenues exceed expenses:

$$\text{Net Income} = \text{Revenues} - \text{Expenses}$$

When expenses exceed revenues, a **net loss** occurs.

REVENUES

KEY POINT: The essence of revenue is that something has been *earned* through the sale of goods or services. That is why cash received through a loan does not constitute revenue.

Revenues are increases in stockholders' equity resulting from selling goods, rendering services, or performing other business activities. In the simplest case, revenues equal the price of goods sold or services rendered over a specific period of time. When a business delivers a product or provides a service to a customer, it usually receives either cash or a promise to pay cash in the near future. The promise to pay is recorded in either Accounts Receivable or Notes Receivable. The revenue for a given period equals the total of cash and receivables from goods and services provided to customers during that period.

Liabilities generally are not affected by revenues, and some transactions that increase cash and other assets are not revenues. For example, a bank loan increases liabilities and cash but does not produce revenue. The collection of accounts receivable, which increases cash and decreases accounts receivable, does not produce revenue either. Remember that when a sale on credit takes place, the asset account Accounts Receivable increases; at the same time, a stockholders' equity revenue account increases. So counting the collection of the receivable as revenue later would be counting the same sale twice.

Not all increases in stockholders' equity arise from revenues. Stockholders' investments increase stockholders' equity but are not revenue.

EXPENSES

KEY POINT: The primary purpose of an expense is to generate revenue.

Expenses are decreases in stockholders' equity resulting from the costs of selling goods, rendering services, or performing other business activities. In other words, expenses are the costs of the goods and services used up in the course of earning revenues. Often called the *cost of doing business*, expenses include the costs of goods sold, the costs of activities necessary to carry on a business, and the costs of attracting and serving customers. Examples of expenses are salaries, rent, advertising, telephone service, and depreciation (allocation of cost) of a building or office equipment.

Income measurement is difficult in many industries because of the uncertainties associated with their revenues and expenses. For example, construction companies must estimate their revenues based on a project's percentage of completion.

Just as not all cash receipts are revenues, not all cash payments are expenses. A cash payment to reduce a liability does not result in an expense. The liability, however, may have come from incurring a previous expense, such as advertising, that is to be paid later. There may also be two steps before an expenditure of cash becomes an expense. For example, prepaid expenses and plant assets (such as machinery and equipment) are recorded as assets when they are acquired. Later, as their usefulness expires in the operation of the business, their cost is allocated to expenses. In fact, expenses sometimes are called *expired costs*.

Not all decreases in stockholders' equity arise from expenses. Dividends decrease stockholders' equity, but they are not expenses.

✔ Check out ACE for a Review Quiz at http://accounting.college.hmco.com/students.

INCOME MEASUREMENT ISSUES

LO2 Explain how the income measurement issues of accounting period, continuity, and matching are resolved.

RELATED TEXT ASSIGNMENTS
Q: 2, 3, 4
SE: 1
E: 1
SD: 1, 3
FRA: 1, 3, 5, 6

KEY POINT: Accounting periods must be of equal length so that one period can be compared with the next.

Several issues must be addressed in the measurement of income. These include the accounting period issue, the continuity issue, and the matching issue.

THE ACCOUNTING PERIOD ISSUE

The **accounting period issue** addresses the difficulty of assigning revenues and expenses to a short period of time, such as a month or a year. Not all transactions can be easily assigned to specific time periods. Purchases of buildings and equipment, for example, have effects that extend over many years. Accountants solve this problem by estimating the number of years the buildings or equipment will be in use and the cost that should be assigned to each year. In the process, they make an assumption about **periodicity**: that the net income for any period of time less than the life of the business, although tentative, is still a useful estimate of the entity's profitability for the period.

Generally, to make comparisons easier, the time periods are of equal length. Financial statements may be prepared for any time period. Accounting periods of less than one year—for example, a month or a quarter—are called *interim periods*. The 12-month accounting period used by an organization is called its **fiscal year**. Many organizations use the calendar year, January 1 to December 31, for their fiscal year. Others find it convenient to choose a fiscal year that ends during a slack season rather than a peak season. In this case, the fiscal year corresponds to the yearly cycle of business activity. The time period should always be noted in the financial statements.

FOCUS ON BUSINESS PRACTICE

Fiscal Year-Ends Vary.

The table below shows the diverse fiscal years used by some well-known companies. Many governmental and educational units use fiscal years that end June 30 or September 30.

Company	Last Month of Fiscal Year
Caesars World Inc. <www.caesarsworld.com>	July
The Walt Disney Company <www.disney.go.com>	September
Fleetwood Enterprises, Inc. <www.fleetwood.com>	April
H.J. Heinz, Inc. <www.heinz.com>	March
Kelly Services <www.kellyservices.com>	December
MGM-UA Communications Co. <www.mgm.com>	August
Toys "R" Us <www.tru.com>	January

THE CONTINUITY ISSUE

The process of measuring business income requires that certain expense and revenue transactions be allocated over several accounting periods. The number of accounting periods raises the **continuity issue**. How long will the business entity last? Many businesses last less than five years; in any given year, thousands of businesses go bankrupt. To prepare financial statements for an accounting period, the accountant must make an assumption about the ability of the business to survive. Specifically, unless there is evidence to the contrary, the accountant assumes that the business will continue to operate indefinitely—that it is a **going concern**. Justification for all the techniques of income measurement rests on the assumption of

BUSINESS-WORLD EXAMPLE: The continuity assumption is set aside when an organization is formed for a limited venture, such as a World's Fair or the Olympics.

continuity. For example, this assumption allows the cost of certain assets to be held on the balance sheet until a future year, when it will become an expense on the income statement.

Another example has to do with the value of assets on the balance sheet. The accountant records assets at cost and does not record subsequent changes in their value. But the value of assets to a going concern is much higher than the value of assets to a firm facing bankruptcy. In the latter case, the accountant may be asked to set aside the assumption of continuity and to prepare financial statements based on the assumption that the firm will go out of business and sell all of its assets at liquidation value—that is, for what they will bring in cash.

THE MATCHING ISSUE

KEY POINT: Although the cash basis often is used for tax purposes, it seldom produces an accurate measurement of a business's performance for financial reporting purposes.

Revenues and expenses can be accounted for on a cash received and cash paid basis. This practice is known as the **cash basis of accounting**. Individuals and some businesses may use the cash basis of accounting for income tax purposes. Under this method, revenues are reported in the period in which cash is received, and expenses are reported in the period in which cash is paid. Taxable income, therefore, is calculated as the difference between cash receipts from revenues and cash payments for expenses.

Although the cash basis of accounting works well for some small businesses and many individuals, it does not meet the needs of most businesses. As explained above, revenues can be earned in a period other than the one in which cash is received, and expenses can be incurred in a period other than the one in which cash is paid. To measure net income adequately, revenues and expenses must be assigned to the appropriate accounting period. The accountant solves this problem by applying the **matching rule**:

● **STOP AND THINK!**
Why must a company that gives a guaranty or warranty with its product or service show an expense in the year of sale rather than in a later year when a repair or replacement is made?

To measure a company's performance (net income) accurately, each expense (in this case, guaranty or warranty expense) must be matched with the related revenue in the year in which the product or service was sold. Otherwise, net income will be overstated, and the related liability will be understated. ■

Revenues must be assigned to the accounting period in which the goods are sold or the services performed, and expenses must be assigned to the accounting period in which they are used to produce revenue.

Direct cause-and-effect relationships seldom can be demonstrated for certain, but many costs appear to be related to particular revenues. The accountant recognizes these expenses and the related revenues in the same accounting period. Examples are the costs of goods sold and sales commissions. When there is no direct means of connecting expenses and revenues, the accountant tries to allocate costs in a systematic way among the accounting periods that benefit from the costs. For example, a building is converted from an asset to an expense by allocating its cost over the years that the company benefits from its use.

 Check out ACE for a Review Quiz at http://accounting.college.hmco.com/students.

ACCRUAL ACCOUNTING

LO3 Define *accrual accounting* and explain three broad ways of accomplishing it.

RELATED TEXT ASSIGNMENTS
Q: 5, 6, 7, 8
SE: 1
E: 1, 2
P: 2, 7
SD: 1, 2, 3
FRA: 3

To apply the matching rule, accountants have developed accrual accounting. **Accrual accounting** "attempts to record the financial effects on an enterprise of transactions and other events and circumstances . . . in the periods in which those transactions, events, and circumstances occur rather than only in the periods in which cash is received or paid by the enterprise."[2] That is, accrual accounting consists of all the techniques developed by accountants to apply the matching rule. It is done in the following general ways: (1) by recording revenues when earned, (2) by recording expenses when incurred, and (3) by adjusting the accounts.

RECOGNIZING REVENUES WHEN EARNED

The process of determining when revenue is earned, and consequently when it should be recorded, is called **revenue recognition**. The Securities and Exchange

Commission has said that all the following conditions must exist before revenue is recognized:

- Persuasive evidence of an arrangement exists.
- Delivery has occurred or services have been rendered.
- The seller's price to the buyer is fixed or determinable.
- Collectibility is reasonably assured.[3]

For example, when Joan Miller Advertising Agency, Inc., bills a customer for placing an advertisement, it is recorded as revenue because the transaction meets these four criteria. It is agreed that the customer owes for the service, the service has been rendered, the parties understand the price, and there is a reasonable expectation that the customer will pay the bill. Revenue is recorded by debiting Accounts Receivable and crediting Advertising Fees Earned. Note that it is not necessary for cash to be collected for revenue to be recorded. There only needs to be a reasonable expectation that it will be paid.

RECOGNIZING EXPENSES WHEN INCURRED

Expenses are recorded when there is an agreement to purchase goods or services, the goods have been delivered or the services rendered, a price is established or can be determined, and the goods or services have been used to produce revenue. For example, when Joan Miller Advertising Agency receives its telephone bill, the expense is recognized both as having been incurred and as helping to produce revenue. The transaction is recorded by debiting Telephone Expense and crediting Accounts Payable. Until the bill is paid, Accounts Payable serves as a holding account. Notice that recognition of the expense does not depend on the payment of cash.

ADJUSTING THE ACCOUNTS

ENRICHMENT NOTE: The accountant waits until the end of an accounting period to update certain revenues and expenses even though the revenues and expenses theoretically have changed during the period. There usually is no need to adjust them until the end of the period, when the financial statements are prepared. In fact, it would be impractical, even impossible, to adjust the accounts each time they are affected.

A third application of accrual accounting is adjusting the accounts. Adjustments are necessary because the accounting period, by definition, ends on a particular day. The balance sheet must list all assets and liabilities as of the end of that day, and the income statement must contain all revenues and expenses applicable to the period ending on that day. Although operating a business is a continuous process, there must be a cutoff point for the periodic reports. Some transactions invariably span the cutoff point; thus, some accounts need adjustment.

For example, some of the accounts in the end-of-the-period trial balance for Joan Miller Advertising Agency (Exhibit 1) do not show the correct balances for

FOCUS ON BUSINESS ETHICS

Aggressive Accounting or Deception? You Judge.

Accounting principles, such as revenue recognition and the matching rule, should not be applied in a way that will distort or obscure financial information. Accounting practices are meant to inform readers of financial statements, not to deceive them. In recent years, the Securities and Exchange Commission <www.sec.gov> has been waging a public campaign against corporate accounting practices that manage or manipulate earnings to meet the expectations of Wall Street analysts.[4] Corporations engage in such practices in the hope of avoiding shortfalls that might cause serious declines in their stock price. The following describes a few of the corporate accounting practices that the SEC has challenged:

- Lucent Technologies <www.lucent.com> sold telecommunications equipment to companies from which there was no reasonable expectation of payment because of the companies' poor financial condition.
- America Online (AOL) <www.aol.com> recorded advertising as an asset rather than as an expense.
- Eclipsys <www.eclipsys.com> recorded software contracts as revenue even though it had not yet rendered the services.
- KnowledgeWare <knowledgeware.itil.com> recorded revenue from sales of software even though it told customers they did not have to pay until they had the software.

EXHIBIT 1
Trial Balance for Joan Miller Advertising Agency, Inc.

Joan Miller Advertising Agency, Inc.
Trial Balance
July 31, 20xx

Cash	$ 9,140	
Accounts Receivable	4,800	
Art Supplies	1,800	
Office Supplies	800	
Prepaid Rent	1,600	
Prepaid Insurance	960	
Art Equipment	4,200	
Office Equipment	3,000	
Accounts Payable		$ 3,240
Unearned Art Fees		1,000
Common Stock		20,000
Dividends	1,400	
Advertising Fees Earned		6,200
Wages Expense	2,400	
Utilities Expense	200	
Telephone Expense	140	
	$30,440	$30,440

preparing the financial statements. The July 31 trial balance lists prepaid rent of $1,600. At $800 per month, this represents rent for the months of July and August. So on July 31, one-half of the $1,600, or $800, represents rent expense for July; the remaining $800 represents an asset that will be used in August. An adjustment is needed to reflect the $800 balance in the Prepaid Rent account on the balance sheet and the $800 rent expense on the income statement. As you will see on the following pages, several other accounts in the Joan Miller Advertising Agency trial balance do not reflect their correct balances. Like the Prepaid Rent account, they need to be adjusted.

ACCRUAL ACCOUNTING AND PERFORMANCE MEASURES

Accrual accounting can be difficult to understand. The related adjustments take time to calculate and enter in the records. Also, adjusting entries do not affect cash flows in the current period because they never involve the Cash account. You might ask, "Why go to all the trouble of making them? Why worry about them?" The Securities and Exchange Commission, in fact, has identified issues related to accrual accounting and adjustments as an area of utmost importance because of the potential for abuse and misrepresentation.[5]

All adjustments are important because they are necessary to measure key profitability performance measures. Adjusting entries affect net income on the income statement, and they affect profitability comparisons from one accounting period to the next. They also affect assets and liabilities on the balance sheet and thus provide information about a company's *future* cash inflows and outflows. This information is needed to assess management's short-term goal of achieving sufficient liquidity to meet its need for cash to pay ongoing obligations. The potential for abuse arises because considerable judgment underlies the application of adjusting entries. Misuse of this judgment can result in misleading measures of performance.

 Check out ACE for a Review Quiz at http://accounting.college.hmco.com/students.

◆ **STOP AND THINK!**

Is accrual accounting more closely related to a company's goal of profitability or liquidity?

It is more closely related to profitability because the purpose of accrual accounting is to measure net income. Cash accounting is more closely related to the goal of liquidity. ■

THE ADJUSTMENT PROCESS

LO4 State four principal situations that require adjusting entries and prepare typical adjusting entries.

RELATED TEXT ASSIGNMENTS
Q: 9, 10, 11, 12, 13, 14, 15,
     16, 17, 18, 19
SE: 2, 3, 4, 5, 6
E: 1, 3, 4, 5, 6, 7, 8, 9
P: 1, 2, 3, 4, 5, 6, 7, 8
SD: 1, 2, 3, 4, 5
FRA: 1, 2, 4, 5, 6, 7

KEY POINT: Each adjusting entry must include at least one balance sheet account and one income statement account. By definition, it cannot include a debit or a credit to Cash. Because adjusting entries never involve the cash account, they never affect cash flows.

Accountants use **adjusting entries** to apply accrual accounting to transactions that span more than one accounting period. There are four situations in which adjusting entries are required, as illustrated in Figure 1. As shown, each situation affects one balance sheet account and one income statement account. Adjusting entries never involve the Cash account. The four types of adjusting entries may be stated as follows:

1. Costs have been recorded that must be allocated between two or more accounting periods. Examples are prepaid rent, prepaid insurance, supplies, and costs of a building. The adjusting entry in this case involves an asset account and an expense account.

2. Expenses have been incurred but are not yet recorded. Examples are the wages earned by employees in the current accounting period but after the last pay period. The adjusting entry involves an expense account and a liability account.

3. Revenues have been recorded that must be allocated between two or more accounting periods. An example is payments collected for services yet to be rendered. The adjusting entry involves a liability account and a revenue account.

4. Revenues have been earned but are not yet recorded. An example is fees earned but not yet collected or billed to customers. The adjusting entry involves an asset account and a revenue account.

Accountants often refer to adjusting entries as deferrals or accruals. A **deferral** is the postponement of the recognition of an expense already paid (Type 1 adjustment) or of a revenue received in advance (Type 3 adjustment). Recording of the receipt or payment of cash precedes the adjusting entry. An **accrual** is the recognition of a revenue (Type 4 adjustment) or expense (Type 2 adjustment) that has arisen but has not yet been recorded. No cash was received or paid prior to the adjusting entry; this will occur in a future accounting period. Once again, we use Joan Miller Advertising Agency, Inc., to illustrate the kinds of adjusting entries that most businesses make.

TYPE 1: ALLOCATING RECORDED COSTS BETWEEN TWO OR MORE ACCOUNTING PERIODS (DEFERRED EXPENSES)

Companies often make expenditures that benefit more than one period. These expenditures are usually debited to an asset account. At the end of the accounting period, the amount that has been used is transferred from the asset account to an

FIGURE 1
The Four Types of Adjustments

		BALANCE SHEET	
		Asset	**Liability**
INCOME STATEMENT	**Expense**	1. Recorded costs are allocated between two or more accounting periods.	2. Expenses are incurred but not yet recorded.
	Revenue	4. Revenues are earned but not yet recorded.	3. Recorded unearned revenues are allocated between two or more accounting periods.

FIGURE 2
Adjustment for Prepaid (Deferred) Expenses

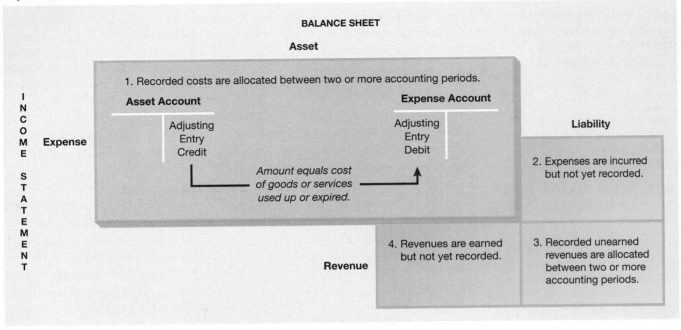

expense account. Two of the more important kinds of adjustments are those for prepaid expenses and the depreciation of plant and equipment.

■ **PREPAID EXPENSES**   Soqme expenses customarily are paid in advance. These expenditures are called **prepaid expenses**. Among them are rent, insurance, and supplies. At the end of an accounting period, a portion (or all) of these goods or services will have been used up or will have expired. An adjusting entry reducing the asset and increasing the expense, as shown in Figure 2, is always required. The amount of the adjustment equals the cost of the goods or services used up or expired. If adjusting entries for prepaid expenses are not made at the end of the period, both the balance sheet and the income statement will present incorrect information; the assets of the company will be overstated, and the expenses of the company will be understated. This means that stockholders' equity on the balance sheet and net income on the income statement will be overstated.

At the beginning of the month, Joan Miller Advertising Agency paid two months' rent in advance. This expenditure resulted in an asset consisting of the right to occupy the office for two months. As each day in the month passed, part of the asset's cost expired and became an expense. By July 31, one-half of the asset's cost had expired and should be treated as an expense. Here is the analysis of this economic event:

KEY POINT: The expired portion of a prepayment is converted to an expense; the unexpired portion remains an asset.

Prepaid Rent (Adjustment a)

		Dr.	Cr.
A = L + OE ⌐July 31	Rent Expense	800	
— —	Prepaid Rent		800⌐

Prepaid Rent

July 2	1,600	July 31	800←

Rent Expense

↳July 31	800	

Transaction: Expiration of one month's rent.
Analysis: Assets decrease. Stockholders' equity decreases.
Rules: Decreases in stockholders' equity are recorded by debits. Decreases in assets are recorded by credits.
Entries: The decrease in stockholders' equity is recorded by a debit to Rent Expense. The decrease in assets is recorded by a credit to Prepaid Rent.

The Prepaid Rent account now has a balance of $800, which represents one month's rent paid in advance. The Rent Expense account reflects the $800 expense for the month of July.

Besides rent, Joan Miller Advertising Agency prepaid expenses for insurance, art supplies, and office supplies, all of which call for adjusting entries.

On July 8, the agency purchased a one-year life insurance policy, paying for it in advance. Like prepaid rent, prepaid insurance offers benefits (in this case, protection) that expire day by day. By the end of the month, one-twelfth of the protection had expired. The adjustment is analyzed and recorded like this:

Prepaid Insurance (Adjustment b)

		Dr.	Cr.	
A = L + OE	July 31 Insurance Expense	80		Transaction: Expiration of one month's life insurance.
− −	Prepaid Insurance		80	Analysis: Assets decrease. Stockholders' equity decreases.

Prepaid Insurance

July 8	960	Jan. 31	80

Insurance Expense

July 31	80	

Rules: Decreases in stockholders' equity are recorded by debits. Decreases in assets are recorded by credits.

Entries: The decrease in stockholders' equity is recorded by a debit to Insurance Expense. The decrease in assets is recorded by a credit to Prepaid Insurance.

The Prepaid Insurance account now shows the correct balance, $880, and Insurance Expense reflects the expired cost, $80 for the month of July.

Early in the month, Joan Miller Advertising Agency purchased art supplies and office supplies. As Joan Miller prepared advertising designs for various clients, art supplies were consumed, and her secretary used office supplies. There is no need to account for these supplies every day because the financial statements are not prepared until the end of the month and the recordkeeping would involve too much work. Instead, Joan Miller makes a careful inventory of the art and office supplies at the end of the month. This inventory records the number and cost of those supplies that are still assets of the company—that are yet to be consumed.

KEY POINT: Notice that the cost of supplies consumed is inferred, not observed.

Suppose the inventory shows that art supplies costing $1,300 and office supplies costing $600 are still on hand. This means that of the $1,800 of art supplies originally purchased, $500 worth were used up (became an expense) in July. Of the original $800 of office supplies, $200 worth were consumed. These transactions are analyzed and recorded as follows:

Art Supplies and Office Supplies (Adjustments c and d)

		Dr.	Cr.	
A = L + OE	July 31 Art Supplies			Transaction: Consumption of supplies.
− −	Expense	500		Analysis: Assets decrease. Stockholders' equity decreases.
	Art Supplies		500	Rules: Decreases in stockholders' equity are recorded by debits. Decreases in assets are recorded by credits.
A = L + OE	July 31 Office Supplies			
− −	Expense	200		Entries: The decreases in stockholders' equity are recorded by debits to Art Supplies Expense and Office Supplies Expense. The
	Office Supplies		200	decreases in assets are recorded by credits to Art Supplies and Office Supplies.

Art Supplies

July 6	1,800	July 31	500

Art Supplies Expense

July 31	500	

Office Supplies

July 6	800	July 31	200

Office Supplies Expense

July 31	200	

The asset accounts Art Supplies and Office Supplies now reflect the correct balances, $1,300 and $600, respectively, of supplies that are yet to be consumed. In addition, the amount of art supplies used up during the month of July is shown as $500, and the amount of office supplies used up is shown as $200.

KEY POINT: In accounting, depreciation refers only to the *allocation* of an asset's cost, not to the decline in its value.

■ **DEPRECIATION OF PLANT AND EQUIPMENT** When a company buys a long-term asset—a building, trucks, computers, store fixtures, or furniture—it is, in effect, prepaying for the usefulness of that asset for as long as it benefits the company. Because a long-term asset is a deferral of an expense, the accountant must allocate the cost of the asset over its estimated useful life. The amount allocated to any one accounting period is called **depreciation** or *depreciation expense*. Depreciation, like other expenses, is incurred during an accounting period to produce revenue.

KEY POINT: The difficulty in estimating an asset's useful life is further evidence that the bottom-line figure is, at best, an estimate.

It is often impossible to tell how long an asset will last or how much of the asset is used in any one period. For this reason, depreciation must be estimated. Accountants have developed a number of methods for estimating depreciation and for dealing with the related complex problems. Here we look at the simplest case, depreciation on the art and office equipment for Joan Miller Advertising Agency.

Art Equipment and Office Equipment (Adjustments e and f)

	Dr.	Cr.
A = L + OE July 31 Depreciation Expense, Art Equipment	70	
Accumulated Depreciation, Art Equipment		70
A = L + OE July 31 Depreciation Expense, Office Equipment	50	
Accumulated Depreciation, Office Equipment		50

Transaction: Recording depreciation expense.
Analysis: Assets decrease. Stockholders' equity decreases.
Rules: Decreases in stockholders' equity are recorded by debits. Decreases in assets are recorded by credits.
Entries: The stockholders' equity is decreased by debits to Depreciation Expense, Art Equipment and Depreciation Expense, Office Equipment. The assets are decreased by credits to Accumulated Depreciation, Art Equipment and Accumulated Depreciation, Office Equipment.

Art Equipment	
July 3 4,200	

Accumulated Depreciation, Art Equipment	
	July 31 70

Office Equipment	
July 5 3,000	

Accumulated Depreciation, Office Equipment	
	July 31 50

Depreciation Expense, Art Equipment	
July 31 70	

Depreciation Expense, Office Equipment	
July 31 50	

Suppose, for example, that Joan Miller estimates that the art equipment and office equipment for which she paid $4,200 and $3,000, respectively, will last five years (60 months) and will have zero value at the end of that time. The monthly

FIGURE 3
Adjustment for Depreciation

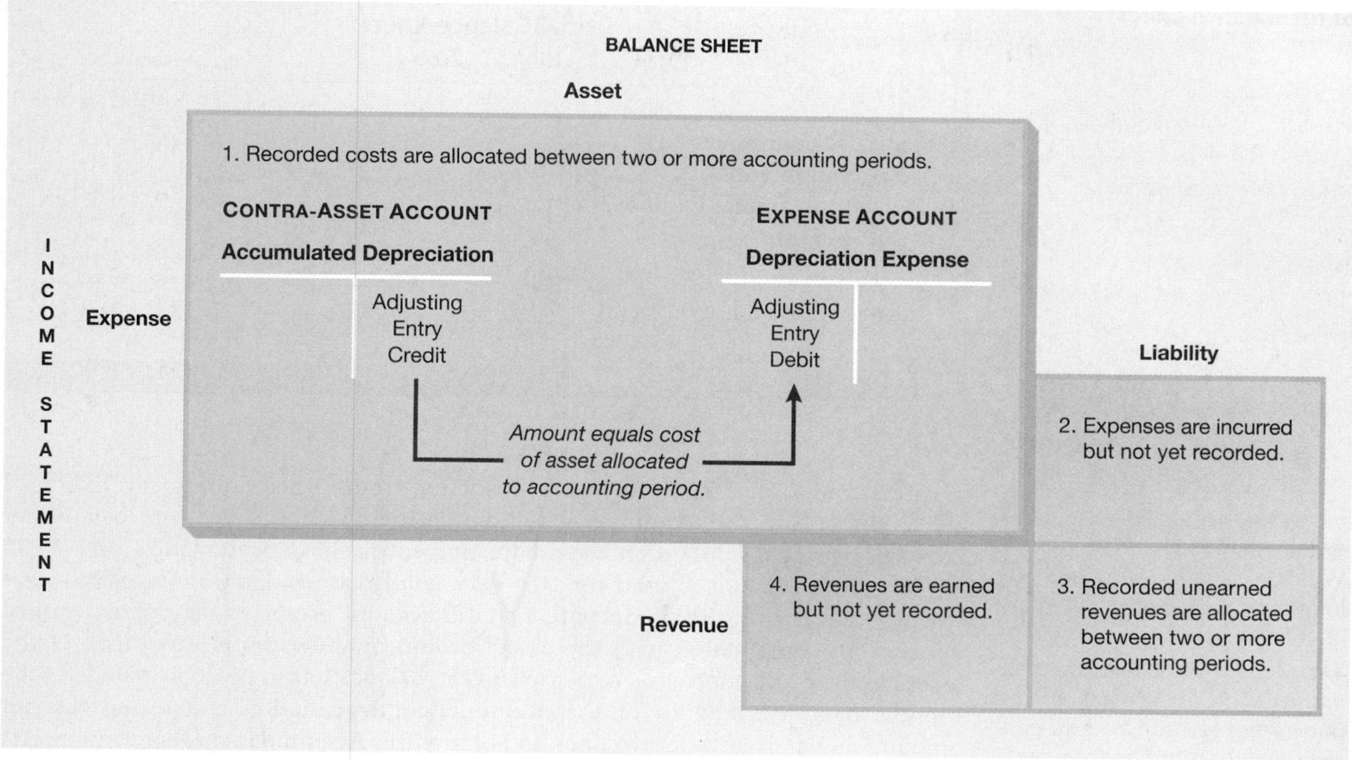
BALANCE SHEET
Asset
1. Recorded costs are allocated between two or more accounting periods.
CONTRA-ASSET ACCOUNT
Accumulated Depreciation
Adjusting Entry Credit
EXPENSE ACCOUNT
Depreciation Expense
Adjusting Entry Debit
Amount equals cost of asset allocated to accounting period.
INCOME STATEMENT
Expense
Liability
2. Expenses are incurred but not yet recorded.
Revenue
4. Revenues are earned but not yet recorded.
3. Recorded unearned revenues are allocated between two or more accounting periods.

depreciation of art equipment and office equipment is $70 ($4,200 ÷ 60 months) and $50 ($3,000 ÷ 60 months), respectively. These amounts represent the costs allocated to July, and they are the amounts by which the asset accounts must be reduced and the expense accounts increased (reducing stockholders' equity).

■ **ACCUMULATED DEPRECIATION—A CONTRA ACCOUNT** Notice that in the previous analysis, the asset accounts are not credited directly. Instead, as shown in Figure 3, new accounts—Accumulated Depreciation, Art Equipment; and Accumulated Depreciation, Office Equipment—are credited. These **accumulated depreciation accounts** are contra-asset accounts used to total the past depreciation expense on specific long-term assets. A **contra account** is a separate account that is paired with a related account—in this case an asset account. The balance of the contra account is shown on the financial statement as a deduction from the related account.

There are several types of contra accounts. In this case, the balance of Accumulated Depreciation, Art Equipment is shown on the balance sheet as a deduction from the associated account Art Equipment. Likewise, Accumulated

FOCUS ON INTERNATIONAL BUSINESS

Who Needs Accounting Knowledge?

The privatization of businesses in Eastern Europe and the republics of the former Soviet Union has created a great need for Western accounting knowledge. Many managers from these countries are anxious to study accounting. Under the old governmental systems, the concept of net income as Westerners know it did not exist because the state owned everything and there was no such thing as income.

The new businesses, because they are private, require accounting systems that recognize the importance of net income. In these new systems, it is necessary to make adjusting entries to record such things as depreciation and accrued expenses. Many Eastern European businesses have been suffering losses for years without knowing it and, as a result, are now in poor financial condition.

EXHIBIT 2
Plant and Equipment Section of the Balance Sheet

Joan Miller Advertising Agency, Inc.
Partial Balance Sheet
July 31, 20xx

Plant and equipment		
Art equipment	$4,200	
Less accumulated depreciation	70	$4,130
Office equipment	$3,000	
Less accumulated depreciation	50	2,950
Total plant and equipment		$7,080

STOP AND THINK!

Will the carrying value of a long-term asset normally equal its market value?

The carrying value will equal the market value of the asset only by coincidence because the goal of recording depreciation is to allocate the cost of the asset over its life, not to determine its market value. ■

Depreciation, Office Equipment is a deduction from Office Equipment. Exhibit 2 shows the plant and equipment section of the balance sheet for Joan Miller Advertising Agency, Inc., after these adjusting entries have been made.

A contra account is used for two very good reasons. First, it recognizes that depreciation is an estimate. Second, a contra account preserves the original cost of an asset. In combination with the asset account, it shows both how much of the asset has been allocated as an expense and the balance left to be depreciated. As the months pass, the amount of the accumulated depreciation grows, and the net amount shown as an asset declines. In six months, Accumulated Depreciation, Art Equipment will show a balance of $420; when this amount is subtracted from Art Equipment, a net amount of $3,780 will remain. The net amount is called the **carrying value**, or *book value*, of the asset.

TYPE 2: RECOGNIZING UNRECORDED EXPENSES (ACCRUED EXPENSES)

At the end of an accounting period, there usually are expenses that have been incurred but not recorded in the accounts. These expenses require adjusting entries. One such case is interest on borrowed money. Each day, interest accumulates on the debt. As shown in Figure 4, at the end of the accounting period, an adjusting entry is made to record this accumulated interest, which is an expense of the period, and the corresponding liability to pay the interest. Other common unrecorded expenses are taxes, wages, and utilities. As the expense and the corresponding liability accumulate, they are said to *accrue*—hence the term **accrued expenses**.

■ **ACCRUED WAGES** Suppose the calendar for the month of July looks like the calendar that follows.

July

Su	M	T	W	Th	F	Sa
	1	2	3	4	5	6
7	8	9	10	11	12	13
14	15	16	17	18	19	20
21	22	23	24	25	26	27
28	29	30	31			

By the end of business on July 31, the secretary at Joan Miller Advertising Agency will have worked three days (Monday, Tuesday, and Wednesday) beyond the last

FIGURE 4
Adjustment for Unrecorded (Accrued) Expenses

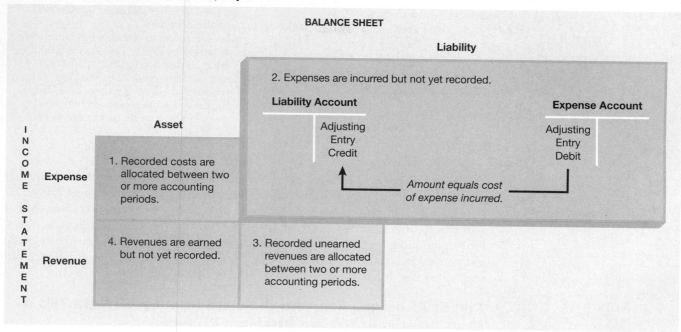

biweekly pay period, which ended on July 26. The employee has earned the wages for these days, but she will not be paid until the regular payday in August. The wages for these three days are rightfully an expense for July, and the liabilities should reflect that the company owes the secretary for those days. Because the secretary's wage rate is $1,200 every two weeks, or $120 per day ($1,200 ÷ 10 working days), the expense is $360 ($120 × 3 days).

Accrued Wages (Adjustment g)

KEY POINT: Remember that an expense must be recorded in the period in which it is incurred, regardless of when payment is made.

		Dr.	Cr.
July 31	Wages Expense	360	
	Wages Payable		360

A = L + OE
  +   −

Wages Payable

| July 31 | 360 |

Wages Expense

July 12	1,200
26	1,200
31	360

Transaction: Accrual of unrecorded expense.
Analysis: Liabilities increase. Stockholders' equity decreases.
Rules: Decreases in stockholders' equity are recorded by debits. Increases in liabilities are recorded by credits.
Entries: The decrease in stockholders' equity is recorded by a debit to Wages Expense. The increase in liabilities is recorded by a credit to Wages Payable.

The liability of $360 is now reflected correctly in the Wages Payable account. The actual expense incurred for wages during July, $2,760, is also correct.

■ **ESTIMATED INCOME TAXES** As a corporation, Joan Miller Advertising Agency is subject to federal income taxes. Although the actual amount owed cannot be determined until after net income is computed at the end of the fiscal year, each month should bear its part of the total year's expense, in accordance with the matching rule. Therefore, the amount of income taxes expense for the current month must be estimated. Assume that after analyzing the first month's operations and conferring with her CPA, Joan Miller estimates July's share of federal income taxes for the year to be $400. This estimated expense can be analyzed and recorded as shown next.

Estimated Income Taxes (Adjustment h)

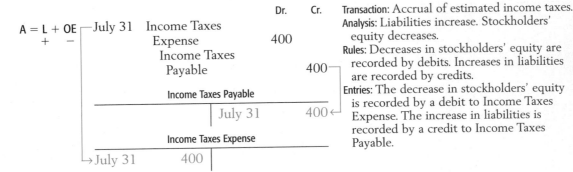

		Dr.	Cr.
A = L + OE	July 31 Income Taxes		
+ −	Expense	400	
	Income Taxes		
	Payable		400

Income Taxes Payable

| | July 31 | 400 |

Income Taxes Expense

| July 31 | 400 | |

Transaction: Accrual of estimated income taxes.
Analysis: Liabilities increase. Stockholders' equity decreases.
Rules: Decreases in stockholders' equity are recorded by debits. Increases in liabilities are recorded by credits.
Entries: The decrease in stockholders' equity is recorded by a debit to Income Taxes Expense. The increase in liabilities is recorded by a credit to Income Taxes Payable.

Expenses for July will now reflect the estimated income taxes attributable to that month, and the liability for these taxes will appear on the balance sheet.

www.kellyservices.com

As noted in this chapter's Decision Point, Kelly Services, like Joan Miller Advertising Agency, has accrued liabilities for payroll and for income taxes. However, unlike Joan Miller Advertising Agency, which has *prepaid* insurance, Kelly has *accrued* insurance. This means Kelly does not pay for insurance in advance but recognizes that it has an expense for insurance that it will have to pay later.

TYPE 3: ALLOCATING RECORDED UNEARNED REVENUES BETWEEN TWO OR MORE ACCOUNTING PERIODS (DEFERRED REVENUES)

KEY POINT: Unearned Revenue is a liability because there is an obligation to deliver goods or perform a service, or to return the payment. Once the goods have been delivered or the service performed, the liability is converted into revenue.

Just as expenses can be paid before they are used, revenues can be received before they are earned. When revenues are received in advance, the company has an obligation to deliver goods or perform services. Therefore, **unearned revenues** are shown in a liability account. For example, publishing companies usually receive payment in advance for magazine subscriptions. These receipts are recorded in a liability account. If the company fails to deliver the magazines, subscribers are entitled to their money back. As the company delivers each issue of the magazine, it earns a part of the advance payments. This earned portion must be transferred from the

FIGURE 5
Adjustment for Unearned (Deferred) Revenues

BALANCE SHEET

		Asset	Liability
I N C O M E	**Expense**	1. Recorded costs are allocated between two or more accounting periods.	2. Expenses are incurred but not yet recorded.
S T A T E M E N T	**Revenue**	4. Revenues are earned but not yet recorded.	3. Recorded unearned revenues are allocated between two or more accounting periods.

Liability Account

Adjusting Entry Debit

Revenue Account

Adjusting Entry Credit

Amount equals price of services performed or goods delivered.

Unearned Subscriptions (liability) account to the Subscription Revenue account, as shown in Figure 5.

During the month of July, Joan Miller Advertising Agency received $1,000 as an advance payment for advertising designs to be prepared for another agency. Assume that by the end of the month, $400 of the design was completed and accepted by the other agency. Here is the transaction analysis:

Unearned Art Fees (Adjustment i)

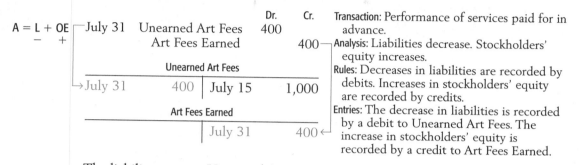

			Dr.	Cr.
A = L + OE	July 31	Unearned Art Fees	400	
− +		Art Fees Earned		400

Unearned Art Fees

July 31	400	July 15	1,000

Art Fees Earned

	July 31	400

Transaction: Performance of services paid for in advance.

Analysis: Liabilities decrease. Stockholders' equity increases.

Rules: Decreases in liabilities are recorded by debits. Increases in stockholders' equity are recorded by credits.

Entries: The decrease in liabilities is recorded by a debit to Unearned Art Fees. The increase in stockholders' equity is recorded by a credit to Art Fees Earned.

The liability account Unearned Art Fees now reflects the amount of work still to be performed, $600. The revenue account Art Fees Earned reflects the services performed and the revenue earned for them during July, $400.

TYPE 4: RECOGNIZING UNRECORDED REVENUES (ACCRUED REVENUES)

Accrued revenues are revenues for which a service has been performed or goods delivered but for which no entry has been recorded. Any revenues earned but not recorded during the accounting period call for an adjusting entry that debits an asset account and credits a revenue account, as shown in Figure 6. For example, the interest on a note receivable is earned day by day but may not be received until another accounting period. Interest Receivable should be debited and Interest Income should be credited for the interest accrued at the end of the current period.

FIGURE 6
Adjustment for Unrecorded (Accrued) Revenues

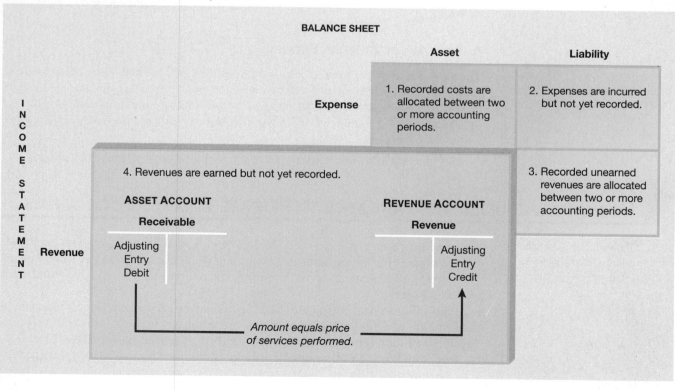

Suppose that Joan Miller Advertising Agency has agreed to place a series of advertisements for Marsh Tire Company and that the first appears on July 31, the last day of the month. The fee of $200 for this advertisement, which has been earned but not recorded, should be recorded this way:

Accrued Advertising Fees (Adjustment j)

		Dr.	Cr.
A = L + OE ⌐ July 31	Accounts Receivable	200	
+ +	Advertising Fees Earned		200 ⌐

Accounts Receivable

July 19	4,800	
↳ 31	200	

Advertising Fees Earned

	July 10	1,400
	19	4,800
	31	200 ←

Transaction: Accrual of unrecorded revenue.
Analysis: Assets increase. Stockholders' equity increases.
Rules: Increases in assets are recorded by debits. Increases in stockholders' equity are recorded by credits.
Entries: The increase in assets is recorded by a debit to Accounts Receivable. The increase in stockholders' equity is recorded by a credit to Advertising Fees Earned.

Now both the asset and the revenue accounts show the correct balance: The $5,000 in Accounts Receivable is owed to the company, and the $6,400 in Advertising Fees Earned has been earned by the company during July. Marsh Tire Company will be billed for the series of advertisements when they are completed.

A NOTE ABOUT JOURNAL ENTRIES

Thus far, we have presented a full analysis of each journal entry. The analyses showed you the thought process behind each entry. By now, you should be fully aware of the effects of transactions on the accounting equation and the rules of debit and credit. For this reason, in the rest of the book, we present journal entries without full analysis.

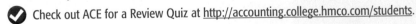

✓ Check out ACE for a Review Quiz at http://accounting.college.hmco.com/students.

USING THE ADJUSTED TRIAL BALANCE TO PREPARE FINANCIAL STATEMENTS

LO5 Prepare financial statements from an adjusted trial balance.

RELATED TEXT ASSIGNMENTS
Q: 20, 21
SE: 7, 8
E: 10
P: 4, 5

After adjusting entries have been recorded and posted, an **adjusted trial balance** is prepared by listing all accounts and their balances. If the adjusting entries have been posted to the accounts correctly, the adjusted trial balance should have equal debit and credit totals.

The adjusted trial balance for Joan Miller Advertising Agency, Inc., is shown on the left side of Exhibit 3. Notice that some accounts, such as Cash and Accounts Payable, have the same balances as they have in the trial balance (see Exhibit 1) because no adjusting entries affected them. Some new accounts, such as depreciation accounts and Wages Payable, appear in the adjusted trial balance, and other

EXHIBIT 3
Relationship of Adjusted Trial Balance to Income Statement

Joan Miller Advertising Agency, Inc.
Adjusted Trial Balance
July 31, 20xx

Cash	$ 9,140	
Accounts Receivable	5,000	
Art Supplies	1,300	
Office Supplies	600	
Prepaid Rent	800	
Prepaid Insurance	880	
Art Equipment	4,200	
Accumulated Depreciation, Art Equipment		$ 70
Office Equipment	3,000	
Accumulated Depreciation, Office Equipment		50
Accounts Payable		3,240
Unearned Art Fees		600
Wages Payable		360
Income Taxes Payable		400
Common Stock		20,000
Dividends	1,400	
Advertising Fees Earned		6,400
Art Fees Earned		400
Wages Expense	2,760	
Utilities Expense	200	
Telephone Expense	140	
Rent Expense	800	
Insurance Expense	80	
Art Supplies Expense	500	
Office Supplies Expense	200	
Depreciation Expense, Art Equipment	70	
Depreciation Expense, Office Equipment	50	
Income Taxes Expense	400	
	$31,520	$31,520

Joan Miller Advertising Agency, Inc.
Income Statement
For the Month Ended July 31, 20xx

Revenues

Advertising fees earned		$6,400
Art fees earned		400
Total revenues		$6,800

Expenses

Wages expense	$2,760	
Utilities expense	200	
Telephone expense	140	
Rent expense	800	
Insurance expense	80	
Art supplies expense	500	
Office supplies expense	200	
Depreciation expense, Art equipment	70	
Depreciation expense, Office equipment	50	
Income taxes expense	400	
Total expenses		5,200
Net income		$1,600

KEY POINT: The net income figure from the income statement is needed to prepare the statement of retained earnings, and the bottom-line figure of that statement is needed to prepare the balance sheet. Thus, the income statement is prepared before the statement of retained earnings, and that statement is prepared before the balance sheet.

⬢ STOP AND THINK!
Why is Retained Earnings not listed on the trial balance for Joan Miller Advertising Agency, Inc., in Exhibits 3 and 4?
It is not listed because it begins with a zero balance in Joan Miller's first month of operation. It does not yet reflect the amounts of revenues, expenses, and dividends for the year, which are listed in the adjusted trial balance. ■

accounts, such as Art Supplies, Office Supplies, Prepaid Rent, and Prepaid Insurance, have balances that differ from those in the trial balance because adjusting entries did affect them.

Using the adjusted trial balance, the financial statements can be easily prepared. The income statement is prepared from the revenue and expense accounts, as shown in Exhibit 3. Then, as shown in Exhibit 4, the statement of retained earnings and the balance sheet are prepared. Notice that the net income from the income statement is combined with dividends on the statement of retained earnings to give the net change in Joan Miller Advertising Agency's Retained Earnings account. The resulting balance of Retained Earnings at July 31 is used on the balance sheet, as are the asset and liability accounts.

Exhibit 4
Relationship of Adjusted Trial Balance to Balance Sheet and Statement of Retained Earnings

Joan Miller Advertising Agency, Inc.
Adjusted Trial Balance
July 31, 20xx

Cash	$ 9,140	
Accounts Receivable	5,000	
Art Supplies	1,300	
Office Supplies	600	
Prepaid Rent	800	
Prepaid Insurance	880	
Art Equipment	4,200	
Accumulated Depreciation, Art Equipment		$ 70
Office Equipment	3,000	
Accumulated Depreciation, Office Equipment		50
Accounts Payable		3,240
Unearned Art Fees		600
Wages Payable		360
Income Taxes Payable		400
Common Stock		20,000
Dividends	1,400	
Advertising Fees Earned		6,400
Art Fees Earned		400
Wages Expense	2,760	
Utilities Expense	200	
Telephone Expense	140	
Rent Expense	800	
Insurance Expense	80	
Art Supplies Expense	500	
Office Supplies Expense	200	
Depreciation Expense, Art Equipment	70	
Depreciation Expense, Office Equipment	50	
Income Taxes Expense	400	
	$31,520	$31,520

Joan Miller Advertising Agency, Inc.
Balance Sheet
July 31, 20xx

Assets

Cash		$ 9,140
Accounts receivable		5,000
Art supplies		1,300
Office supplies		600
Prepaid rent		800
Prepaid insurance		880
Art equipment	$ 4,200	
Less accumulated depreciation	70	4,130
Office equipment	$ 3,000	
Less accumulated depreciation	50	2,950
Total assets		$24,800

Liabilities

Accounts payable		$ 3,240
Unearned art fees		600
Wages payable		360
Income taxes payable		400
Total liabilities		$ 4,600

Stockholders' Equity

Common stock	$20,000	
Retained earnings	200	
Total stockholders' equity		20,200
Total liabilities and stockholders' equity		$24,800

KEY POINT: Notice that the figure for Retained Earnings does not appear on the adjusted trial balance. The balance is updated when the closing entries are prepared.

From Income Statement in Exhibit 3

KEY POINT: The adjusted trial balance is a second check that the ledger is still in balance. Because it reflects updated information from the adjusting entries, it may be used to prepare the formal statements.

Joan Miller Advertising Agency, Inc.
Statement of Retained Earnings
For the Month Ended July 31, 20xx

Retained earnings, July 1, 20xx	—
Net income	$1,600
Subtotal	$1,600
Less dividends	$1,400
Retained earnings, July 31, 20xx	$ 200

FOCUS ON BUSINESS TECHNOLOGY

Entering Adjustments With the Touch of a Button

In a computerized accounting system, adjusting entries can be entered just like any other transactions. However, when the adjusting entries are similar for each accounting period, such as those for insurance expense and depreciation expense, or when they always involve the same accounts, such as those for accrued wages, the computer can be programmed to display them automatically. All the accountant has to do is verify the amounts or enter the correct amounts. The adjusting entries are then entered and posted, and the adjusted trial balance is prepared with the touch of a button.

✓ Check out ACE for a Review Quiz at http://accounting.college.hmco.com/students.

CASH FLOWS FROM ACCRUAL-BASED INFORMATION —Not necessary for test

SO6 Analyze cash flows from accrual-based information.

RELATED TEXT ASSIGNMENTS
Q: 22
SE: 9, 10
E: 11, 12

Management has the short-range goal of achieving sufficient liquidity to meet its needs for cash to pay its ongoing obligations. It is important for managers to be able to use accrual-based financial information to analyze cash flows in order to plan payments to creditors and assess the need for short-term borrowing.

Every revenue or expense account on the income statement has one or more related accounts on the balance sheet. For instance, Supplies Expense is related to Supplies, Wages Expense is related to Wages Payable, and Art Fees Earned is related to Unearned Art Fees. As we have shown, these accounts are related through adjusting entries whose purpose is to apply the matching rule in the measurement of net income. The cash flows generated or paid by company operations may also be determined by analyzing these relationships. For example, suppose that after receiving the financial statements in Exhibits 3 and 4, management wants to know how much cash was expended for art supplies. On the income statement, Art Supplies Expense is $500, and on the balance sheet, Art Supplies is $1,300. Because July was the company's first month of operation, there was no prior balance of art supplies, so the amount of cash expended for art supplies during the month was $1,800. The cash flow used to purchase art supplies ($1,800) was much greater than the amount expensed in determining income ($500). In planning for August, management can anticipate that the cash needed may be less than the amount expensed because, given the large inventory of art supplies, it will probably not be necessary to buy art supplies for more than a month. Understanding these cash flow effects enables management to better predict the business's need for cash in August.

The general rule for determining the cash flow received from any revenue or paid for any expense (except depreciation, which is a special case not covered here) is to determine the potential cash payments or cash receipts and deduct the amount not paid or received. The application of the general rule varies with the type of asset or liability account, which is shown as follows:

Type of Account	Potential Payment or Receipt	Not Paid or Received	Result
Prepaid Expense	Ending Balance + Expense for the Period	− Beginning Balance =	Cash Payments for Expenses
Unearned Revenue	Ending Balance + Revenue for the Period	− Beginning Balance =	Cash Receipts from Revenues
Accrued Payable	Beginning Balance + Expense for the Period	− Ending Balance =	Cash Payments for Expenses
Accrued Receivable	Beginning Balance + Revenue for the Period	− Ending Balance =	Cash Receipts from Revenues

For instance, assume that on May 31 a company had a balance of $480 in Prepaid Insurance and that on June 30 the balance was $670. If the insurance expense during June was $120, the amount of cash expended on insurance during June can be computed as follows:

Prepaid Insurance at June 30	$670
Insurance Expense during June	120
Potential cash payments for insurance	$790
Less Prepaid Insurance at May 31	480
Cash payments for insurance during June	$310

The beginning balance is deducted because it was paid in a prior accounting period. Note that the cash payments equal the expense plus the increase in the balance of the Prepaid Insurance account [$120 + ($670 − $480) = $310]. In this case, the cash paid was almost three times the amount of insurance expense. In future months, cash payments are likely to be less than the expense.

✓ Check out ACE for a Review Quiz at http://accounting.college.hmco.com/students.

Chapter Review

REVIEW OF LEARNING OBJECTIVES

LO1 Define *net income* and its two major components, *revenues* and *expenses.*

Net income is the net increase in stockholders' equity that results from the operations of a company. Net income equals revenues minus expenses, unless expenses exceed revenues, in which case a net loss results. Revenues equal the price of goods sold and services rendered during a specific period. Expenses are the costs of goods and services used up in the process of producing revenues.

LO2 Explain how the income measurement issues of accounting period, continuity, and matching are resolved.

The accounting period issue recognizes that net income measurements for short periods of time are necessarily tentative. The continuity issue recognizes that even though businesses face an uncertain future, without evidence to the contrary, accountants must assume that a business will continue indefinitely. The matching issue has to do with the difficulty of assigning revenues and expenses to a period of time. It is addressed by applying the matching rule: Revenues must be assigned to the accounting period in which the goods are sold or the services performed, and expenses must be assigned to the accounting period in which they are used to produce revenue.

LO3 Define *accrual accounting* and explain three broad ways of accomplishing it.

Accrual accounting consists of all the techniques developed by accountants to apply the matching rule. Three broad ways of accomplishing it are by recognizing revenues when earned, recognizing expenses when incurred, and adjusting the accounts.

LO4 State four principal situations that require adjusting entries and prepare typical adjusting entries.

Adjusting entries are required when (1) recorded costs have to be allocated between two or more accounting periods, (2) unrecorded expenses exist, (3) recorded unearned revenues must be allocated between two or more accounting periods, and (4) unrecorded revenues exist. The preparation of adjusting entries is summarized as follows:

Type of Adjusting Entry	Type of Account		Balance Sheet Account Examples
	Debited	Credited	
1. Allocating recorded costs (previously paid, expired)	Expense	Asset (or contra-asset)	Prepaid Rent Prepaid Insurance Supplies Accumulated Depreciation, Buildings Accumulated Depreciation, Equipment
2. Accrued expenses (incurred, not paid)	Expense	Liability	Wages Payable Income Taxes Payable
3. Allocating recorded unearned revenues (previously received, earned)	Liability	Revenue	Unearned Art Fees
4. Accrued revenues (earned, not received)	Asset	Revenue	Accounts Receivable Interest Receivable

LO5 Prepare financial statements from an adjusted trial balance.

An adjusted trial balance is prepared after adjusting entries have been posted to the accounts. Its purpose is to test whether the adjusting entries are posted correctly before the financial statements are prepared. The income statement is prepared from the revenue and expense accounts in the adjusted trial balance. The balance sheet is prepared from the asset and liability accounts in the adjusted trial balance and from the statement of retained earnings.

SUPPLEMENTAL OBJECTIVE

SO6 Analyze cash flows from accrual-based information.

Cash flow information relates to management's liquidity goal. The general rule for determining the cash flow effect of any revenue or expense (except depreciation, which is a special case not covered here) is to determine the potential cash payments or cash receipts and deduct the amount not paid or received.

REVIEW OF CONCEPTS AND TERMINOLOGY

The following concepts and terms were introduced in this chapter:

LO2 **Accounting period issue:** The difficulty of assigning revenues and expenses to a short period of time.

LO4 **Accrual:** The recognition of an expense or revenue that has arisen but has not yet been recorded.

LO3 **Accrual accounting:** The attempt to record the financial effects of transactions and other events in the periods in which those transactions or events occur, rather than only in the periods in which cash is received or paid by the business; all the techniques developed by accountants to apply the matching rule.

LO4 **Accrued expenses:** Expenses incurred but not recognized in the accounts; unrecorded expenses.

LO4 **Accrued revenues:** Revenues for which a service has been performed or goods delivered but for which no entry has been made; unrecorded revenues.

LO4 **Accumulated depreciation accounts:** Contra-asset accounts used to accumulate the depreciation expense of specific long-lived assets.

LO5 **Adjusted trial balance:** A trial balance prepared after all adjusting entries have been recorded and posted to the accounts.

LO4 **Adjusting entries:** Entries made to apply accrual accounting to transactions that span more than one accounting period.

LO4 **Carrying value:** The unexpired portion of the cost of an asset. Also called *book value*.

LO2 **Cash basis of accounting:** Accounting for revenues and expenses on a cash received and cash paid basis.

LO2 **Continuity issue:** The difficulty associated with not knowing how long a business entity will survive.

LO4 **Contra account:** An account whose balance is subtracted from an associated account in the financial statements.

LO4 **Deferral:** The postponement of the recognition of an expense that already has been paid or of a revenue that already has been received.

LO4 **Depreciation:** The portion of the cost of a tangible long-term asset allocated to any one accounting period. Also called *depreciation expense*.

LO1 **Expenses:** Decreases in stockholders' equity resulting from the costs of goods and services used up in the course of earning revenues. Also called *cost of doing business* or *expired costs*.

LO2 **Fiscal year:** Any 12-month accounting period used by an economic entity.

LO2 **Going concern:** The assumption, unless there is evidence to the contrary, that a business entity will continue to operate indefinitely.

LO2   Matching rule: Revenues must be assigned to the accounting period in which the goods are sold or the services performed, and expenses must be assigned to the accounting period in which they are used to produce revenue.

LO1   Net income: The net increase in stockholders' equity that results from business operations and is accumulated in the Retained Earnings account; revenues less expenses when revenues exceed expenses.

LO1   Net loss: The net decrease in stockholders' equity that results from business operations when expenses exceed revenues. It is accumulated in the Retained Earnings account.

LO2   Periodicity: The recognition that net income for any period less than the life of the business, although tentative, is still a useful measure.

LO4   Prepaid expenses: Expenses paid in advance that have not yet expired; an asset account.

LO1   Profit: The increase in stockholders' equity that results from business operations.

LO3   Revenue recognition: In accrual accounting, the process of determining when revenue is earned.

LO1   Revenues: Increases in stockholders' equity resulting from selling goods, rendering services, or performing other business activities.

LO4   Unearned revenues: Revenues received in advance for which the goods have not yet been delivered or the services performed; a liability account.

REVIEW PROBLEM

Determining Adjusting Entries, Posting to T Accounts, Preparing Adjusted Trial Balance, and Preparing Financial Statements

LO4
LO5 The following is the unadjusted trial balance for Certified Answering Service, Inc., on December 31, 20x2:

Certified Answering Service, Inc.
Trial Balance
December 31, 20x2

Cash	$2,160	
Accounts Receivable	1,250	
Office Supplies	180	
Prepaid Insurance	240	
Office Equipment	3,400	
Accumulated Depreciation, Office Equipment		$ 600
Accounts Payable		700
Unearned Revenue		460
Common Stock		2,000
Retained Earnings		2,870
Dividends	400	
Answering Service Revenue		2,900
Wages Expense	1,500	
Rent Expense	400	
	$9,530	$9,530

The following information is also available:

a. Insurance that expired during December amounted to $40.
b. Office supplies on hand at the end of December totaled $75.

c. Depreciation for the month of December totaled $100.
d. Accrued wages at the end of December totaled $120.
e. Revenues earned for services performed in December but not yet billed on December 31 totaled $300.
f. Revenues earned in December for services performed that were paid in advance totaled $160.
g. Income taxes for December are estimated to be $250.

REQUIRED ▶
1. Prepare T accounts for the accounts in the trial balance and enter the balances.
2. Determine the required adjusting entries and record them directly to the T accounts. Open new T accounts as needed.
3. Prepare an adjusted trial balance.
4. Prepare an income statement, a statement of retained earnings, and a balance sheet for the month ended December 31, 20x2.

ANSWER TO REVIEW PROBLEM

1. T accounts set up and amounts from trial balance entered
2. Adjusting entries recorded

Cash
Bal. 2,160	

Accounts Receivable
Bal. 1,250	
(e) 300	
Bal. 1,550	

Office Supplies
Bal. 180	(b) 105
Bal. 75	

Prepaid Insurance
Bal. 240	(a) 40
Bal. 200	

Office Equipment
Bal. 3,400	

Accumulated Depreciation, Office Equipment
	Bal. 600
	(c) 100
	Bal. 700

Accounts Payable
	Bal. 700

Unearned Revenue
(f) 160	Bal. 460
	Bal. 300

Wages Payable
	(d) 120

Income Taxes Payable
	(g) 250

Common Stock
	Bal. 2,000

Retained Earnings
	Bal. 2,870

Dividends
Bal. 400	

Answering Service Revenue
	Bal. 2,900
	(e) 300
	(f) 160
	Bal. 3,360

Wages Expense
Bal. 1,500	
(d) 120	
Bal. 1,620	

Rent Expense
Bal. 400	

Insurance Expense
(a) 40	

Office Supplies Expense
(b) 105	

Depreciation Expense, Office Equipment
(c) 100	

Income Taxes Expense
(g) 250	

3. Adjusted trial balance prepared

Certified Answering Service, Inc.
Adjusted Trial Balance
December 31, 20x2

Cash	$ 2,160	
Accounts Receivable	1,550	
Office Supplies	75	
Prepaid Insurance	200	
Office Equipment	3,400	
Accumulated Depreciation, Office Equipment		$ 700
Accounts Payable		700
Unearned Revenue		300
Wages Payable		120
Income Taxes Payable		250
Common Stock		2,000
Retained Earnings		2,870
Dividends	400	
Answering Service Revenue		3,360
Wages Expense	1,620	
Rent Expense	400	
Insurance Expense	40	
Office Supplies Expense	105	
Depreciation Expense, Office Equipment	100	
Income Taxes Expense	250	
	$10,300	$10,300

4. Financial statements prepared

Certified Answering Service, Inc.
Income Statement
For the Month Ended December 31, 20x2

Revenues		
Answering service revenue		$3,360
Expenses		
Wages expense	$1,620	
Rent expense	400	
Insurance expense	40	
Office supplies expense	105	
Depreciation expense, office equipment	100	
Income taxes expense	250	
Total expenses		2,515
Net income		$ 845

Financial statements prepared (*continued*)

Certified Answering Service, Inc.
Statement of Retained Earnings
For the Month Ended December 31, 20x2

Retained earnings, November 30, 20x2	$2,870
Net income	845
Subtotal	$3,715
Less dividends	400
Retained earnings, December 31, 20x2	$3,315

Financial statements prepared (*continued*)

Certified Answering Service, Inc.
Balance Sheet
December 31, 20x2

Assets

Cash		$2,160
Accounts receivable		1,550
Office supplies		75
Prepaid insurance		200
Office equipment	$3,400	
Less accumulated depreciation	700	2,700
Total assets		$6,685

Liabilities

Accounts payable	$ 700
Unearned revenue	300
Wages payable	120
Income taxes payable	250
Total liabilities	$1,370

Stockholders' Equity

Common stock	$2,000	
Retained earnings	3,315	
Total stockholders' equity		5,315
Total liabilities and stockholders' equity		$6,685

Chapter Assignments

BUILDING YOUR KNOWLEDGE FOUNDATION

QUESTIONS

1. Why does the accountant use the term *net income* instead of *profit*?
2. Why does the need for an accounting period cause problems?
3. What is the significance of the continuity assumption?
4. "The matching rule is the most significant concept in accounting." Do you agree with this statement? Explain your answer.
5. What are the conditions for recognizing revenue?
6. What is the difference between the cash basis and the accrual basis of accounting?
7. In what three ways is accrual accounting accomplished?
8. Why are adjusting entries necessary?
9. What are the four situations that require adjusting entries? Give an example of each.
10. "Some assets are expenses that have not expired." Explain this statement.
11. What do plant and equipment, office supplies, and prepaid insurance have in common?
12. What is the difference between accumulated depreciation and depreciation expense?
13. What is a contra account? Give an example.
14. Why are contra accounts used to record depreciation?
15. How does unearned revenue arise? Give an example.
16. Where does unearned revenue appear in the financial statements?
17. What accounting problem does a magazine publisher who sells three-year subscriptions have?
18. Under what circumstances does a company have accrued revenues? Give an example. What asset arises when the adjustment is made?
19. What is an accrued expense? Give two examples.
20. "Why worry about adjustments? Doesn't it all come out in the wash?" Discuss these questions.
21. Why is the income statement usually the first statement prepared from the adjusted trial balance?
22. To what management goals do the measurements of net income and cash flow relate?

SHORT EXERCISES

SE 1.

LO2 **Accrual Accounting Concepts**
LO3

Match the concepts of accrual accounting on the right with the assumptions or actions on the left:

1. Assumes expenses can be assigned to the accounting period in which they are used to produce revenues
2. Assumes a business will last indefinitely
3. Assumes revenues are earned at a point in time
4. Assumes net income measured for a short period of time, such as one quarter, is a useful measure

a. Periodicity
b. Going concern
c. Matching rule
d. Revenue recognition

SE 2.

LO4 **Adjustment for Prepaid Insurance**

The Prepaid Insurance account began the year with a balance of $230. During the year, insurance in the amount of $570 was purchased. At the end of the year (December 31), the amount of insurance still unexpired was $350. Make the year-end entry in journal form to record the adjustment for insurance expense for the year.

SE 3.

LO4 Adjustment for Supplies

The Supplies account began the year with a balance of $190. During the year, supplies in the amount of $490 were purchased. At the end of the year (December 31), the inventory of supplies on hand was $220. Make the year-end entry in journal form to record the adjustment for supplies expense for the year.

SE 4.

LO4 Adjustment for Depreciation

The depreciation expense on office equipment for the month of March is $50. This is the third month that the office equipment, which cost $950, has been owned. Prepare the adjusting entry in journal form to record depreciation for March and show the balance sheet presentation for office equipment and related accounts after the adjustment.

SE 5.

LO4 Adjustment for Accrued Wages

Wages are paid each Saturday for a six-day work week. Wages are currently running $690 per week. Make the adjusting entry required on June 30, assuming July 1 falls on a Tuesday.

SE 6.

LO4 Adjustment for Unearned Revenue

During the month of August, deposits in the amount of $550 were received for services to be performed. By the end of the month, services in the amount of $380 had been performed. Prepare the necessary adjustment for Service Revenue at the end of the month.

SE 7.

LO5 Preparation of an Income Statement from an Adjusted Trial Balance

The adjusted trial balance for Reingold Company on December 31, 20x3, contains the following accounts and balances: Retained Earnings, $4,300; Dividends, $350; Service Revenue, $2,600; Rent Expense, $400; Wages Expense, $900; Utilities Expense, $200; Telephone Expense, $50; and Income Taxes Expense, $350. Prepare an income statement in proper form for the month of December.

SE 8.

LO5 Preparation of a Statement of Retained Earnings

Using the data in **SE 7,** prepare a statement of retained earnings for Reingold Company.

SE 9.

SO6 Determination of Cash Flows

Wages Payable was $590 at the end of May and $920 at the end of June. Wages Expense for June was $2,300. How much cash was paid for wages during June?

SE 10.

SO6 Determination of Cash Flows

Unearned Revenue was $1,300 at the end of November and $900 at the end of December. Service Revenue was $5,100 for the month of December. How much cash was received for services provided during December?

EXERCISES

E 1.

LO2 Applications of Accounting
LO3 Concepts Related to Accrual
LO4 Accounting

The accountant for Ampere Company makes the assumptions or performs the activities listed below. Tell which of the following concepts of accrual accounting most directly relates to each assumption or action: (a) periodicity, (b) going concern, (c) matching rule, (d) revenue recognition, (e) deferral, and (f) accrual.

1. In estimating the life of a building, assumes that the business will last indefinitely
2. Records a sale when the customer is billed
3. Postpones the recognition of a one-year insurance policy as an expense by initially recording the expenditure as an asset
4. Recognizes the usefulness of financial statements prepared on a monthly basis even though they are based on estimates
5. Recognizes, by making an adjusting entry, wages expense that has been incurred but not yet recorded
6. Prepares an income statement that shows the revenues earned and the expenses incurred during the accounting period

E 2.

LO3 Application of Conditions for Revenue Recognition

Four conditions must be met before revenue should be recognized. In each of the following cases, tell which condition has *not* been met:

a. Company A accepts a contract to perform services in the future for $1,000.
b. Company B ships products to another company worth $1,500 without an order from the other company but tells the company that it can return the products if it does not sell them.
c. Company C performs services for $5,000 for a company that is in financial difficulty.
d. Company D agrees to work out a price later for services that it performs for another company.

E 3.

LO4 Adjusting Entry for Unearned Revenue

City Fun Company of Canton, Ohio, publishes a monthly magazine featuring local restaurant reviews and upcoming social, cultural, and sporting events. Subscribers pay for subscriptions either one year or two years in advance. Cash received from subscribers is credited to an account called Magazine Subscriptions Received in Advance. On

December 31, 20x3, the end of the company's fiscal year, the balance of this account was $1,000,000. Expiration of subscriptions revenue is as follows:

During 20x3 $200,000
During 20x4   500,000
During 20x5   300,000

Prepare the adjusting entry in journal form for December 31, 20x3.

E 4.
LO4 Adjusting Entries for Prepaid Insurance

An examination of the Prepaid Insurance account shows a balance of $4,112 at the end of an accounting period, before adjustment. Prepare entries in journal form to record the insurance expense for the period under the following independent assumptions:

1. An examination of the insurance policies shows unexpired insurance that cost $1,974 at the end of the period.
2. An examination of the insurance policies shows that insurance that cost $694 has expired during the period.

E 5.
LO4 Supplies Account: Missing Data

Each of the following columns represents a Supplies account:

	a	b	c	d
Supplies on hand at July 1	$132	$217	$98	$?
Supplies purchased during the month	26	?	87	964
Supplies consumed during the month	97	486	?	816
Supplies on hand at July 31	?	218	28	594

1. Determine the amounts indicated by the question marks.
2. Make the adjusting entry for column **a,** assuming supplies purchased are debited to an asset account.

E 6.
LO4 Adjusting Entry for Accrued Salaries

Oland has a five-day work week and pays salaries of $35,000 each Friday.

1. Make the adjusting entry required on May 31, assuming that June 1 falls on a Wednesday.
2. Make the entry to pay the salaries on June 3.

E 7.
LO4 Revenue and Expense Recognition

Remini Company produces computer software that is sold by Elton Comp, Inc. Remini receives a royalty of 15 percent of sales. Royalties are paid by Elton Comp and received by Remini semiannually on May 1 for sales made in July through December of the previous year and on November 1 for sales made in January through June of the current year. Royalty expense for Elton Comp and royalty income for Remini in the amount of $12,000 were accrued on December 31, 20x2. Cash in the amounts of $12,000 and $20,000 was paid and received on May 1 and November 1, 20x3, respectively. Software sales during the July to December 20x3 period totaled $300,000.

1. Calculate the amount of royalty expense for Elton Comp and royalty income for Remini during 20x3.
2. Record the adjusting entry made by each company on December 31, 20x3.

E 8.
LO4 Adjusting Entries

Prepare year-end adjusting entries for each of the following:

1. Office Supplies had a balance of $84 on January 1. Purchases debited to Office Supplies during the year amount to $415. A year-end inventory reveals supplies of $285 on hand.
2. Depreciation of office equipment is estimated to be $2,130 for the year.
3. Property taxes for six months, estimated at $875, have accrued but have not been recorded.
4. Unrecorded interest receivable on U.S. government bonds is $850.
5. Unearned Revenue has a balance of $900. Services for $300 received in advance have now been performed.
6. Services totaling $200 have been performed; the customer has not yet been billed.

E 9.
LO4 Accounting for Revenue Received in Advance

Olaf Bjorn, a lawyer, was paid $24,000 on October 1 to represent a client in real estate negotiations over the next 12 months.

1. Record the entries required in Bjorn's records on October 1 and at the end of the fiscal year, December 31.
2. How would this transaction be reflected on the income statement and balance sheet on December 31?

E 10.
LO5 Preparation of Financial Statements

Prepare the monthly income statement, statement of retained earnings, and balance sheet for Totally Clean, Inc., from the data provided in the following adjusted trial balance:

Totally Clean, Inc.
Adjusted Trial Balance
August 31, 20xx

Cash	$ 2,295	
Accounts Receivable	1,296	
Prepaid Insurance	190	
Prepaid Rent	100	
Cleaning Supplies	76	
Cleaning Equipment	1,600	
Accumulated Depreciation, Cleaning Equipment		$ 160
Truck	3,600	
Accumulated Depreciation, Truck		360
Accounts Payable		210
Wages Payable		40
Unearned Janitorial Revenue		460
Income Taxes Payable		400
Common Stock		2,000
Retained Earnings		5,517
Dividends	1,000	
Janitorial Revenue		7,310
Wages Expense	2,840	
Rent Expense	600	
Gas, Oil, and Other Truck Expenses	290	
Insurance Expense	190	
Supplies Expense	1,460	
Depreciation Expense, Cleaning Equipment	160	
Depreciation Expense, Truck	360	
Income Taxes Expense	400	
	$16,457	$16,457

E 11.

SO6 Determination of Cash Flows

After adjusting entries had been made, the balance sheets of Yun Company showed the following asset and liability amounts at the end of 20x3 and 20x4:

	20x4	20x3
Prepaid insurance	$2,400	$2,900
Wages payable	1,200	2,200
Unearned fees	4,200	1,900

The following amounts were taken from the 20x4 income statement:

Insurance expense	$ 3,800
Wages expense	19,500
Fees earned	8,900

Calculate the amount of cash paid for insurance and wages and the amount of cash received for fees during 20x4.

E 12.

SO6 Relationship of Expenses to Cash Paid

The income statement for Libra Company included the following expenses for 20xx:

Rent expense	$ 2,600
Interest expense	3,900
Salaries expense	41,500

Listed below are the related balance sheet account balances at year end for last year and this year.

	Last Year	This Year
Prepaid rent	—	$ 450
Interest payable	$ 600	—
Salaries payable	2,500	4,800

1. Compute the cash paid for rent during the year.
2. Compute the cash paid for interest during the year.
3. Compute the cash paid for salaries during the year.

PROBLEMS

P 1.

LO4   Determining Adjustments

At the end of its fiscal year, the trial balance for Roosevelt Cleaners, Inc., appears as follows:

Roosevelt Cleaners, Inc.
Trial Balance
September 30, 20x4

Cash	$ 11,788	
Accounts Receivable	26,494	
Prepaid Insurance	3,400	
Cleaning Supplies	7,374	
Land	18,000	
Building	185,000	
Accumulated Depreciation, Building		$ 45,600
Accounts Payable		20,400
Unearned Dry Cleaning Revenue		1,600
Mortgage Payable		110,000
Common Stock		40,000
Retained Earnings		16,560
Dividends	10,000	
Dry Cleaning Revenue		120,334
Laundry Revenue		37,300
Wages Expense	101,330	
Cleaning Equipment Rent Expense	6,000	
Delivery Truck Expense	4,374	
Interest Expense	11,000	
Other Expenses	7,034	
	$391,794	$391,794

The following information is also available:

a. A study of the company's insurance policies shows that $680 is unexpired at the end of the year.
b. An inventory of cleaning supplies shows $1,244 on hand.
c. Estimated depreciation on the building for the year is $12,800.
d. Accrued interest on the mortgage payable amounts to $1,000.
e. On September 1, the company signed a contract, effective immediately, with Kings County Hospital to dry clean, for a fixed monthly charge of $400, the uniforms used by doctors in surgery. The hospital paid for four months' service in advance.
f. Sales and delivery wages are paid on Saturday. The weekly payroll is $2,520. September 30 falls on a Thursday and the company has a six-day pay week.
g. Federal income taxes for the period are estimated to be $2,000.

REQUIRED ▶   All adjustments affect one balance sheet account and one income statement account. For each of the above situations, show the accounts affected, the amount of the adjustment (using a + or − to indicate an increase or decrease), and the balance of the account after the adjustment in the following format:

Balance Sheet Account	Amount of Adjustment (+ or −)	Balance after Adjustment	Income Statement Account	Amount of Adjustment (+ or −)	Balance after Adjustment

P 2.

On June 30, the end of the current fiscal year, the following information was available to aid the Sterling Company's accountants in making adjusting entries:

a. Among the liabilities of the company is a mortgage payable in the amount of $240,000. On June 30, the accrued interest on this mortgage amounted to $12,000.

b. On Friday, July 2, the company, which is on a five-day workweek and pays employees weekly, will pay its regular salaried employees $19,200.

c. On June 29, the company completed negotiations and signed a contract to provide services to a new client at an annual rate of $3,600.

d. The Supplies account showed a beginning balance of $1,615 and purchases during the year of $3,766. The end-of-year inventory revealed supplies on hand of $1,186.

e. The Prepaid Insurance account showed the following entries on June 30:

Beginning Balance $1,530
January 1   2,900
May 1   3,366

The beginning balance represents the unexpired portion of a one-year policy purchased the previous year. The January 1 entry represents a new one-year policy, and the May 1 entry represents the additional coverage of a three-year policy.

f. The following table contains the cost and annual depreciation for buildings and equipment, all of which were purchased before the current year:

Account	Cost	Annual Depreciation
Buildings	$185,000	$ 7,300
Equipment	218,000	21,800

g. On June 1, the company completed negotiations with another client and accepted a payment of $21,000, representing one year's services paid in advance. The $21,000 was credited to Services Collected in Advance.

h. The company calculated that as of June 30 it had earned $3,500 on a $7,500 contract that would be completed and billed in August.

i. Federal income taxes for the year are estimated to be $7,500.

REQUIRED ▶

1. Prepare adjusting entries for each item listed above.
2. Explain how the conditions for revenue recognition are applied to transactions **c** and **h.**

P 3.

The trial balance for Financial Strategies Service, Inc., on December 31 is presented below.

Financial Strategies Service, Inc.
Trial Balance
December 31, 20xx

Cash	$ 16,500	
Accounts Receivable	8,250	
Office Supplies	2,662	
Prepaid Rent	1,320	
Office Equipment	9,240	
Accumulated Depreciation, Office Equipment		$ 1,540
Accounts Payable		5,940
Notes Payable		11,000
Unearned Service Revenue		2,970
Common Stock		10,000
Retained Earnings		14,002
Dividends	22,000	
Service Revenue		72,600
Salaries Expense	49,400	
Rent Expense	4,400	
Utilities Expense	4,280	
	$118,052	$118,052

The following information is also available:

a. Ending inventory of office supplies, $264.
b. Prepaid rent expired, $440.
c. Depreciation of office equipment for the period, $660.
d. Accrued interest expense at the end of the period, $550.
e. Accrued salaries at the end of the period, $330.
f. Service revenue still unearned at the end of the period, $1,166.
g. Service revenue earned but unrecorded, $2,200.
h. Management estimates income taxes for the period to be $4,000.

REQUIRED ▶

1. Open T accounts for the accounts in the trial balance plus the following: Interest Payable; Salaries Payable; Income Taxes Payable; Office Supplies Expense; Depreciation Expense, Office Equipment; Interest Expense; and Income Taxes Expense. Enter the balances shown on the trial balance.
2. Determine the adjusting entries and post them directly to the T accounts.
3. Prepare an adjusted trial balance.

P 4.

LO4   Determining Adjusting Entries
LO5   and Tracing Their Effects to
        Financial Statements

Having graduated from college with a degree in accounting, Joyce Ozaki opened a small tax-preparation service. At the end of its second year of operation, Ozaki Tax Service, Inc., had the trial balance shown below.

Ozaki Tax Service, Inc.
Trial Balance
December 31, 20x4

Cash	$ 2,268	
Accounts Receivable	1,031	
Prepaid Insurance	240	
Office Supplies	782	
Office Equipment	4,100	
Accumulated Depreciation, Office Equipment		$ 410
Copier	3,000	
Accumulated Depreciation, Copier		360
Accounts Payable		635
Unearned Tax Fees		219
Common Stock		2,000
Retained Earnings		3,439
Dividends	6,000	
Tax Fees Revenue		21,926
Office Salaries Expense	8,300	
Advertising Expense	650	
Rent Expense	2,400	
Telephone Expense	218	
	$28,989	$28,989

The following information was also available:

a. Office supplies on hand, December 31, 20x4, were $227.
b. Insurance still unexpired amounted to $120.
c. Estimated depreciation of office equipment was $410.
d. Estimated depreciation of the copier was $360.
e. The telephone expense for December was $19. Bill was received but not recorded.
f. The services for all unearned tax fees had been performed by the end of the year.
g. Federal income taxes for the year were estimated to be $1,800.

REQUIRED ▶

1. Open T accounts for the accounts in the trial balance plus the following: Income Taxes Payable; Insurance Expense; Office Supplies Expense; Depreciation Expense, Office Equipment; Depreciation Expense, Copier; and Income Taxes Expense. Record the balances shown in the trial balance.

2. Determine the adjusting entries and post them directly to the T accounts.
3. Prepare an adjusted trial balance, an income statement, a statement of retained earnings, and a balance sheet.

P 5.
LO4 Determining Adjusting Entries
LO5 and Tracing Their Effects to
Financial Statements

The Elite Livery Service, Inc., was organized to provide limousine service between the airport and various suburban locations. It has just completed its second year of business. Its trial balance appears below.

Elite Livery Service, Inc.
Trial Balance
June 30, 20x4

Cash (111)	$ 9,812	
Accounts Receivable (112)	14,227	
Prepaid Rent (117)	12,000	
Prepaid Insurance (118)	4,900	
Prepaid Maintenance (119)	12,000	
Spare Parts (141)	11,310	
Limousines (142)	200,000	
Accumulated Depreciation, Limousines (143)		$ 25,000
Notes Payable (211)		45,000
Unearned Passenger Service Revenue (212)		30,000
Common Stock (311)		30,000
Retained Earnings (312)		48,211
Dividends (313)	20,000	
Passenger Service Revenue (411)		428,498
Gas and Oil Expense (511)	89,300	
Salaries Expense (512)	206,360	
Advertising Expense (513)	26,800	
	$606,709	$606,709

The following information is also available:

a. To obtain space at the airport, Elite paid two years' rent in advance when it began the business.
b. An examination of insurance policies reveals that $2,800 expired during the year.
c. To provide regular maintenance for the vehicles, a deposit of $12,000 was made with a local garage. Examination of maintenance invoices reveals that there are $10,944 in charges against the deposit.
d. An inventory of spare parts shows $1,902 on hand.
e. All of the Elite Livery Service's limousines are to be depreciated at the rate of 12.5 percent per year. There were no limousines purchased during the year.
f. A payment of $10,500 for one full year's interest on notes payable is now due.
g. Unearned Passenger Service Revenue on June 30 includes $17,815 in tickets that were purchased by employers for use by their executives and have not been redeemed.
h. Federal income taxes for the year are estimated to be $12,000.

REQUIRED ▶

1. Determine adjusting entries and enter them in the general journal (Page 14).
2. Open ledger accounts for the accounts in the trial balance plus the following: Interest Payable (213); Income Taxes Payable (214); Rent Expense (514); Insurance Expense (515); Spare Parts Expense (516); Depreciation Expense, Limousines (517); Maintenance Expense (518); Interest Expense (519); and Income Taxes Expense (520). Record the balances shown in the trial balance.
3. Post the adjusting entries from the general journal to the ledger accounts, showing proper references.
4. Prepare an adjusted trial balance, an income statement, a statement of retained earnings, and a balance sheet.

ALTERNATE PROBLEMS

LO4   Determining Adjustments

P 6. At the end of the first three months of operation, the trial balance of Metropolitan Answering Service, Inc., appears as shown below. Oscar Rienzo, the owner of Metropolitan, has hired an accountant to prepare financial statements to determine how well the company is doing after three months. Upon examining the accounting records, the accountant finds the following items of interest:

a. An inventory of office supplies reveals supplies on hand of $133.
b. The Prepaid Rent account includes the rent for the first three months plus a deposit for April's rent.
c. Depreciation on the equipment for the first three months is $208.
d. The balance of the Unearned Answering Service Revenue account represents a 12-month service contract paid in advance on February 1.
e. On March 31, accrued wages total $80.
f. Federal income taxes for the three months are estimated to be $1,500.

Metropolitan Answering Service, Inc.
Trial Balance
March 31, 20x2

Cash	$ 3,482	
Accounts Receivable	4,236	
Office Supplies	903	
Prepaid Rent	800	
Equipment	4,700	
Accounts Payable		$ 2,673
Unearned Answering Service Revenue		888
Common Stock		5,933
Dividends	2,130	
Answering Service Revenue		9,002
Wages Expense	1,900	
Office Cleaning Expense	345	
	$18,496	$18,496

REQUIRED ▶ All adjustments affect one balance sheet account and one income statement account. For each of the above situations, show the accounts affected, the amount of the adjustment (using a + or − to indicate an increase or decrease), and the balance of the account after the adjustment in the following format.

Balance Sheet Account	Amount of Adjustment (+ or −)	Balance after Adjustment	Income Statement Account	Amount of Adjustment (+ or −)	Balance after Adjustment

LO3   Preparing Adjusting Entries
LO4

P 7. On November 30, the end of the current fiscal year, the following information was available to assist Pinder Corporation's accountants in making adjusting entries:

a. Pinder Corporation's Supplies account showed a beginning balance of $2,174. Purchases during the year were $4,526. The end-of-year inventory revealed supplies on hand of $1,397.
b. The Prepaid Insurance account showed the following on November 30:

Beginning Balance	$3,580
July 1	4,200
October 1	7,272

The beginning balance represents the unexpired portion of a one-year policy purchased the previous year. The July 1 entry represents a new one-year policy, and the October 1 entry represents additional coverage in the form of a three-year policy.

c. The following table contains the cost and annual depreciation for buildings and equipment, all of which were purchased before the current year:

Account	Cost	Annual Depreciation
Buildings	$286,000	$14,500
Equipment	374,000	35,400

d. On September 1, the company completed negotiations with a client and accepted a payment of $16,800, which represented one year's services paid in advance. The $16,800 was credited to Unearned Services Revenue.

e. The company calculated that as of November 30, it had earned $4,000 on an $11,000 contract that would be completed and billed in January.

f. Among the liabilities of the company is a note payable in the amount of $300,000. On November 30, the accrued interest on this note amounted to $15,000.

g. On Saturday, December 2, the company, which is on a six-day workweek, will pay its regular salaried employees $12,300.

h. On November 29, the company completed negotiations and signed a contract to pro-vide services to a new client at an annual rate of $17,500. *No entry required*

i. Management estimates income taxes for the year to be $25,000.

REQUIRED ▶

1. Prepare adjusting entries for each item listed above.
2. Explain how the conditions for revenue recognition are applied to transactions e and h.

P 8.

LO4 Determining Adjusting Entries, Posting to T Accounts, and Preparing an Adjusted Trial Balance

The schedule below presents the trial balance for the Sigma Consultants Corporation on December 31, 20x4.

Sigma Consultants Corporation
Trial Balance
December 31, 20x4

Cash	$ 12,786	
Accounts Receivable	24,840	
Office Supplies	991	
Prepaid Rent	1,400	
Office Equipment	6,700	
Accumulated Depreciation, Office Equipment		$ 1,600
Accounts Payable		1,820
Notes Payable		10,000
Unearned Service Revenue		2,860
Common Stock		10,000
Retained Earnings		19,387
Dividends	15,000	
Service Revenue		58,500
Salaries Expense	33,000	
Utilities Expense	1,750	
Rent Expense	7,700	
	$104,167	$104,167

The following information is also available:

a. Ending inventory of office supplies, $86.
b. Prepaid rent expired, $700.
c. Depreciation of office equipment for the period, $600.
d. Interest accrued on the note payable, $600.
e. Salaries accrued at the end of the period, $200.
f. Service revenue still unearned at the end of the period, $1,410.
g. Service revenue earned but not billed, $600.
h. Estimated federal income taxes for the period, $3,000.

REQUIRED ▶ 1. Open T accounts for the accounts in the trial balance plus the following: Interest Payable; Salaries Payable; Income Taxes Payable; Office Supplies Expense; Depreciation Expense, Office Equipment; Interest Expense; and Income Taxes Expense. Enter the account balances.
2. Determine the adjusting entries and post them directly to the T accounts.
3. Prepare an adjusted trial balance.

SKILLS DEVELOPMENT CASES

Conceptual Analysis

SD 1.

LO2 **Importance of Adjustments**
LO3
LO4

Never Flake Company, which operated in the northeastern part of the United States, provided a rust-prevention coating for the underside of new automobiles. The company advertised widely and offered its services through new car dealers. When a dealer sold a new car, the salesperson attempted to sell the rust-prevention coating as an option. The protective coating was supposed to make cars last longer in the severe northeastern winters. A key selling point was Never Flake's warranty, which stated that it would repair any damage due to rust at no charge for as long as the buyer owned the car.

During the 1990s, Never Flake was very successful in generating enough cash to continue operations. But in 2001 the company suddenly declared bankruptcy. Company officials said that the firm had only $5.5 million in assets against liabilities of $32.9 million. Most of the liabilities represented potential claims under the company's lifetime warranty. It seemed that owners were keeping their cars longer now than previously. Therefore, more damage was being attributed to rust. Discuss what accounting decisions could have helped Never Flake to survive under these circumstances.

Group Activity: Divide the class into groups to discuss this case. Then debrief as a class by asking a person from each group to comment.

SD 2.

LO3 **Application of Accrual**
LO4 **Accounting**

The Lyric Opera of Chicago <www.lyricopera.com> is one of the largest and best-managed opera companies in the United States. Managing opera productions requires advance planning, including the development of scenery, costumes, and stage properties and the sale of tickets. To measure how well the company is operating in any given year, accrual accounting must be applied to these and other transactions. At year end, April 30, 2001, Lyric Opera's balance sheet showed Deferred Production Costs of $1,639,949 and Deferred Ticket Revenue of $19,100,781.[7] Be prepared to discuss what accounting policies and adjusting entries are applicable to these accounts. Why are they important to Lyric Opera's management?

Ethical Dilemma

SD 3.

LO2 **Importance of Adjustments**
LO3
LO4

Central Appliance Service Co., Inc., has achieved fast growth in the St. Louis area by selling service contracts on large appliances, such as washers, dryers, and refrigerators. For a fee, Central Appliance agrees to provide all parts and labor on an appliance after the regular warranty runs out. For example, by paying a fee of $200, a person who buys a dishwasher can add two years (years 2 and 3) to the regular one-year (year 1) warranty on the appliance. In 2002, the company sold service contracts in the amount of $1.8 million, all of which applied to future years. Management wanted all the sales recorded as revenues in 2002, contending that the amount of the contracts could be determined and the cash had been received. Discuss whether you agree with this logic. How would you record the cash receipts? What assumptions do you think should be made? Would you consider it unethical to follow management's recommendation? Who might be hurt or helped by this action?

Research Activity

SD 4.

LO4 **Real-World Observation of**
     Business Activities

Choose a company with which you are familiar. Visit the company and observe its operations. For example, it can be where you work, where you eat, or where you buy things. Identify at least two sources of revenue for the company and six types of expenses. For each type of revenue and each type of expense, determine whether it is probable that an adjusting entry is required at the end of the accounting period and specify the adjusting entry as a deferred revenue, deferred expense, accrued revenue, or accrued expense.

Decision-Making Practice

SD 5.
LO 1 Adjusting Entries, Divided
LO 4 Performance Evaluation, and
Dividend Policy

Karen Jamison, the owner of a newsletter for managers of hotels and restaurants, has prepared the following condensed amounts from her company's financial statements for 20x3:

Revenues	$346,000
Expenses	282,000
Net income	$ 64,000
Total assets	$172,000
Liabilities	$ 48,000
Stockholders' equity	124,000
Total liabilities and stockholders' equity	$172,000

Given these figures, Jamison is planning a cash dividend of $50,000. However, Jamison's accountant has found that the following items were overlooked:

a. Although the balance of the Printing Supplies account is $32,000, only $14,000 in supplies is on hand at the end of the year.
b. Depreciation of $20,000 on equipment has not been recorded.
c. Wages of $9,400 have been earned by Jamison's employees but not recognized in the accounts.
d. No provision has been made for estimated income taxes payable of $10,800.
e. A liability account called Unearned Subscriptions has a balance of $16,200, although it has been determined that one-third of these subscriptions have been mailed to subscribers.

1. Prepare the necessary adjusting entries.
2. Recast the condensed financial statement figures after you have made the necessary adjustments.
3. Discuss the performance of Jamison's business after the adjustments have been made. (**Hint:** Compare net income to revenues and total assets before and after the adjustments.) Do you think that paying the dividend is advisable?

FINANCIAL REPORTING AND ANALYSIS CASES

Interpreting Financial Reports

FRA 1.
LO2 Analysis of an Asset Account
LO4

The Walt Disney Company <www.disney.go.com> is engaged in the financing, production, and distribution of motion pictures and television programming. In Disney's annual report, the balance sheet contains an asset called Film and Television Costs. Film and Television Costs, which consist of the cost associated with producing films and television programs less the amount expensed, were $3,606,000,000. The statement of cash flows reveals that the amount of film and television costs expensed (amortized) during the year was $2,469,000,000. The amount spent for new film productions was $2,679,000,000.[8]

REQUIRED ▶

1. What are Film and Television Costs, and why would they be classified as an asset?
2. Prepare an entry in T account form to record the amount the company spent on new film and television production during the year (assume all expenditures are paid for in cash).
3. Prepare an adjusting entry in T account form to record the expense for film and television productions.
4. Can you suggest a method by which The Walt Disney Company might have determined the amount of the expense in **3** in accordance with the matching rule?

FRA 2.

LO4   Identification of Accruals

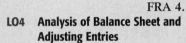

H.J. Heinz Company, <www.heinz.com>, a major food company, had a net income in 2001 of $478,012,000 and the following current liabilities at the end of 2001:[9]

Current Liabilities (in thousands):	2001
Short-term debt	$1,555,869
Portion of long-term debt due within one year	314,965
Accounts payable	962,497
Salaries and wages	54,036
Accrued marketing	146,138
Accrued restructuring costs	134,550
Other accrued liabilities	388,582
Income taxes	98,460
Total current liabilities	$3,655,097

REQUIRED ▶

1. Which of the current liabilities definitely arose as the result of an adjusting entry at the end of the year? Which ones may partially have arisen from an adjusting entry? Which ones probably did not arise from an adjusting entry?
2. What effect do adjustments that create new liabilities have on net income or loss? Based on your answer in **1,** what percentage of current liabilities was definitely the result of an adjusting entry? Assuming the adjusting entries for these items had not been performed, what would Heinz's net income or loss have been?

International Company

FRA 3.

LO2   Account Identification and
LO3   Accrual Accounting

Takashimaya Company, Ltd. <www.takashimaya.co.jp> is Japan's largest department store chain. An account on Takashimaya's balance sheet called Gift Certificates contains ¥41,657 million ($404 million).[10] Is this account an asset or a liability? What transaction gives rise to the account? How is this account an example of the application of accrual accounting? Explain the conceptual issues that must be resolved for an adjusting entry to be valid.

Toys "R" Us Annual Report

FRA 4.

LO4   Analysis of Balance Sheet and
Adjusting Entries

Refer to the balance sheet in the Toys "R" Us <www.tru.com> annual report. Examine the accounts listed in the current assets, property and equipment, and current liabilities sections. Which accounts are most likely to have had year-end adjusting entries? Describe the nature of the adjusting entries. For more information about the property and equipment section, refer to the notes to the consolidated financial statements.

Comparison Case: Toys "R" Us and Walgreen Co.

FRA 5.

LO2   Depreciation Expense and
LO4   Estimates

Depreciation expense is recorded by an adjusting entry and is one of the most important expenses for many companies. In the supplement to Chapter 1, refer to the Summary of Significant Accounting Policies in the notes to the financial statements in the Toys "R" Us <www.tru.com> annual report and to Walgreens' <www.walgreens.com> financial statements to answer these questions:

1. Where is depreciation (and amortization) expense disclosed on the financial statements for each company? Note that depreciation expense is not listed on Walgreens' income statement. Does this mean it is not a factor in computing net income for the company? (Also, note that amortization expense is similar to depreciation expense and is often included with it.)
2. Determine the importance of depreciation to each company by computing the ratio of depreciation to net sales. Why do you think the percentages are small?
3. Each company has a statement on the "Use of Estimates" in its Summary of Significant Accounting Policies. Read these statements and tell how important estimates are to the determination of depreciation expense. What assumptions do accountants make that allow these estimates to be made?

Fingraph® Financial Analyst™

FRA 6.

LO1 Income Measurement and
LO2 Adjustments
LO4

Choose a company from the list of Fingraph companies on the Needles Accounting Resource Center Web Site at http://accounting.college.hmco.com/students. Click on the company you selected to access the Microsoft Excel spreadsheet for that company. You will find the company's URL (Internet address) in the heading of the spreadsheet. Click on the URL for a link to the company's web site and annual report.

1. Identify the type of fiscal year that the company uses. Do you think the year end corresponds to the company's natural business year?
2. Find the company's balance sheet. From the asset accounts and liability accounts, find four examples of accounts that might have been related to an adjusting entry at the end of the year. For each example, tell whether it is a deferral or an accrual and suggest an income statement account that might be associated with it.
3. Find the summary of significant accounting policies that appears following the financial statements. In these policies, find examples of the application of going concern and accrual accounting. Explain your choices of examples.
4. Prepare a one-page executive summary that highlights what you have learned from parts 1, 2, and 3.

Internet Case

FRA 7.

LO4 Comparison of Accrued
Expenses

How important are accrued expenses? Randomly choose four different companies from the Needles Accounting Resource Center Web Site at http://accounting.college. hmco.com/students. Use the links to get to each company's web site and annual report. For each company, find the section of the balance sheet labeled "Current Liabilities" and identify the current liabilities that are accrued expenses (sometimes called *accrued liabilities*). More than one account may be involved. On a pad, write the information you find in four columns: name of company, total current liabilities, total accrued liabilities, and total accrued liabilities as a percentage of total current liabilities. Write a memorandum to your instructor listing the companies you chose, telling how you obtained their reports, reporting the data you have gathered in the form of a table, and stating a conclusion, with reasons, as to the importance of accrued expenses to the companies you studied. (**Hint:** Compute the average percentage of total accrued expenses for the four companies.)

4

Chapter 4 focuses on the principles of designing accounting information systems and on the preparation of closing entries and the completion of the accounting cycle.

Accounting Information Systems

DECISION POINT

A USER'S FOCUS

Hershey Foods Corp. <www.hersheys.com> is a large multinational company well known for its chocolate products. As a company whose shares are traded on the New York Stock Exchange, Hershey must prepare both annual and quarterly financial statements for its stockholders and file them with the Securities and Exchange Commission. Note the interim income statement from Hershey's quarterly report that appears on the opposite page.[1] This statement shows that Hershey's net sales for the third quarter ended September 30, 2001, were greater than those for the same period of the preceding year and that net income increased by approximately 12.4 percent, from $107,405,000 to $120,762,000, for the same period.

Whether required by law or not, the preparation of *interim financial statements* every quarter, or even every month, is a good idea for all businesses because such reports give management an ongoing view of a company's financial performance. What are the costs and time involved in preparing interim financial statements?

The preparation of interim financial statements throughout the year requires more effort than the preparation of a single set of financial statements for the entire year. Each time the financial statements are prepared, adjusting entries must be determined, prepared, and recorded. Also, the ledger accounts must be prepared to begin the next accounting period. These procedures are time-consuming and costly. However, the advantages of preparing interim finan-

188

Why is it important for Hershey Foods to prepare interim financial statements throughout the year?

cial statements, even when they are not required, usually outweigh the costs, because such statements give management timely information for making decisions that will improve operations. This chapter explains the accounting information systems used to process data and prepare financial statements at the end of an accounting period, whether that period is a month, a quarter, or a year.

Financial Highlights: Interim Income Statement
(Unaudited—in thousands)

| | Third Quarter | |
	2001	2000
Net Sales	$1,304,184	$1,196,755
Costs and Expenses:		
Cost of sales	752,575	696,431
Selling, marketing and administrative	342,622	303,688
Gain on sale of business	(19,237)	—
Total costs and expenses	1,075,960	1,000,119
Income before Interest and Income Taxes	228,224	196,636
Interest expense, net	18,147	21,152
Income before Income Taxes	210,077	175,484
Provision for income taxes	89,315	68,079
Net Income	$ 120,762	$ 107,405

ACCOUNTING INFORMATION SYSTEMS: PRINCIPLES OF DESIGN

LO1 Identify the principles of designing accounting information systems.

RELATED TEXT ASSIGNMENTS
Q: 1, 2
SE: 1
FRA: 6

www.sap.com
www.peoplesoft.com
www.baan.pl

⬢ STOP AND THINK!

Certainly, it is important to make right decisions and avoid wrong decisions, but what is the cost of making no decisions?

The cost can be high. For example, assume a product suddenly becomes so popular that it will soon be sold out. If the retailer's accounting information system is not set up to provide this information to the sales manager quickly, the sales manager's failure to make the decision to reorder could cause the company to lose valuable sales. ■

KEY POINT: The cost of making a wrong decision is an intangible cost that can easily be overlooked in designing an accounting system. It is the systems analyst's job to strike the optimal balance between expected benefits and costs.

KEY POINT: An accounting information system should help protect the company's assets and provide reliable data.

Accounting information systems summarize financial data about a business and organize the data into useful forms. Accountants communicate the results to management. The means by which an accounting system accomplishes these objectives is called **data processing**. Management uses the resulting information to make a variety of business decisions.

As businesses have grown larger and more complex, the role of accounting information systems has grown. Today, many organizations use comprehensive, computerized information systems that integrate financial and nonfinancial information about customers, operations, and suppliers in a single database. Though integrated with a wide variety of other information, accounting information serves as the base for these integrated information systems, which are known as **enterprise resource planning (ERP) systems**. Three companies that specialize in ERP software are the German-based company SAP and the U.S.-based companies PeopleSoft and iBAAN.

ERP systems are most often set up, monitored, and operated by accountants. The primary purpose of these systems is to integrate all functions of a company to provide timely information to decision makers throughout the organization. For this reason, accountants must understand all phases of their company's operations as well as the latest developments in systems design and technology. Additionally, while a computerized accounting system may automate many or all bookkeeping functions, it does not eliminate the need to understand the accounting process. In fact, it is impossible to use any accounting information system, manual or computerized, without a basic knowledge of accounting.

The design of an accounting information system involves four general principles: (1) the cost-benefit principle, (2) the control principle, (3) the compatibility principle, and (4) the flexibility principle.

COST-BENEFIT PRINCIPLE

The most important systems principle, the **cost-benefit principle**, holds that the benefits derived from an accounting information system must be equal to or greater than the system's cost. In addition to performing certain routine tasks—preparing payroll and tax reports and financial statements, and maintaining internal control—the accounting system may be called upon to provide other information that management wants or needs. The benefits from that information must be weighed against both the tangible and the intangible costs of gathering it.

Among the tangible costs are those for personnel, forms, and equipment. One of the intangible costs is the cost of wrong decisions stemming from the lack of good information. For instance, wrong decisions can lead to loss of sales, production stoppages, or inventory losses. Some companies have spent thousands of dollars on computerized systems that do not offer enough benefits. On the other hand, some have failed to realize the important benefits that could be gained from investing in more advanced systems. It is the job of the accountant and the systems designer or analyst to weigh the costs and benefits.

CONTROL PRINCIPLE

The **control principle** requires that an accounting information system provide all the features of internal control needed to protect a firm's assets and to ensure that data are reliable. For example, before expenditures are made, a responsible member of management should approve them.

FOCUS ON BUSINESS PRACTICE

How Much Is a Used Computerized Accounting System Worth?

Apparently, a second-hand computerized accounting system has value in the marketplace, if it's a good one. When it declared bankruptcy, the old-line retailer Montgomery Ward had many problems, but accounting, inventory, and sales software wasn't one of them. When the company auctioned off its custom-designed software system, bids started at $100 million.[2]

COMPATIBILITY PRINCIPLE

The **compatibility principle** holds that the design of an accounting information system must be in harmony with the organizational and human factors of the business. The organizational factors have to do with the nature of a company's business and the formal roles its units play in meeting business objectives. For example, a company can organize its marketing efforts by region or by product. If a company is organized by region, its accounting information system should report revenues and expenses by region. If a company is organized by product, its system should report revenues and expenses first by product and then by region.

The human factors of business have to do with the people within the organization and their abilities, behaviors, and personalities. The interest, support, and competence of a company's employees are very important to the success or failure of systems design. In changing systems or installing new ones, the accountant must deal with the people who are carrying out or supervising existing procedures. Such people must understand, accept, and, in many cases, be trained in the new procedures. The new system cannot succeed unless the system and the people in the organization are compatible.

KEY POINT: A systems analyst must carefully consider a business's activities, objectives, and performance measures as well as the behavioral characteristics of its employees.

FLEXIBILITY PRINCIPLE

The **flexibility principle** holds that an accounting information system must be flexible enough to allow for growth in the volume of transactions and for organizational changes. Businesses do not stay the same. They grow, they offer new products, they add new branch offices, they sell existing divisions, or they make other changes that require adjustments in the accounting system. A carefully designed accounting system allows a business to grow and change without having to make major alterations in the system. For example, the chart of accounts should be designed to accommodate the addition of new asset, liability, stockholders' equity, revenue, and expense accounts.

KEY POINT: To work effectively with a computerized accounting system, students must understand how a manual accounting system works. A computerized system functions exactly like a manual system, except that it processes information at lightning speed.

 Check out ACE for a Review Quiz at http://accounting.college.hmco.com/students.

OVERVIEW OF THE ACCOUNTING CYCLE

LO2 State all the steps in the accounting cycle.

RELATED TEXT ASSIGNMENTS
Q: 3
SE: 2
P: 3
SD: 1, 3, 4, 5
FRA: 3, 4

◆ **STOP AND THINK!**
Why is the accounting cycle called a "cycle"?

It is so called because its steps are repeated each accounting period. Step 1 of one period follows step 6 of the prior period. ■

The **accounting cycle** is a series of steps in the accounting information system whose purpose is to measure business activities in the form of transactions and to transform these transactions into financial statements that will communicate useful information to decision makers. The steps in the accounting cycle, illustrated in Figure 1, are as follows:

1. *Analyze* business transactions from source documents.
2. *Record* the entries in the journal.
3. *Post* the entries to the ledger and prepare a trial balance.
4. *Adjust* the accounts and prepare an adjusted trial balance.
5. *Close* the accounts and prepare a post-closing trial balance.
6. *Prepare* financial statements.

You are already familiar with steps 1 through 4 and 6. Step 5 is covered in this chapter. The order of these steps can vary to some extent depending on the system

FIGURE 1
Overview of the Accounting Cycle

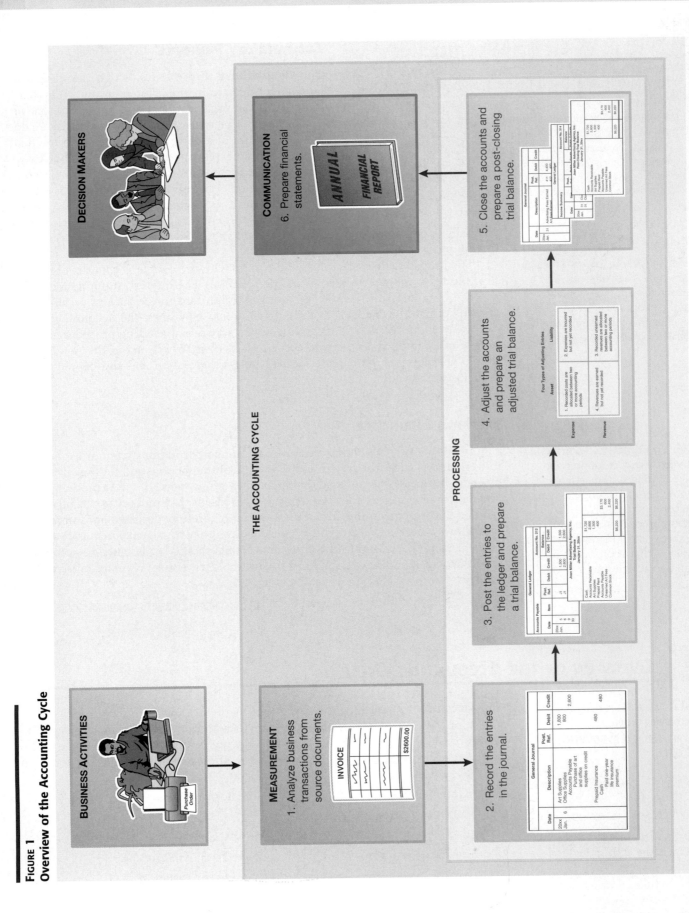

KEY POINT: Steps 1 through 3 are carried out throughout the period, whereas steps 4 through 6 are carried out at the end of the period only.

in place. For instance, the financial statements (step 6) may be completed before the closing entries are prepared (step 5). In fact, in a computerized system, step 6 usually must be performed before step 5. The point is that all these steps must be accomplished to complete the accounting cycle. At key points in the accounting cycle, trial balances are prepared to ensure that the ledger remains in balance.

✓ Check out ACE for a Review Quiz at http://accounting.college.hmco.com/students.

COMPUTERIZED ACCOUNTING INFORMATION SYSTEMS

LO3 Describe the use and structure of spreadsheet software and general ledger systems in computerized accounting information systems.

RELATED TEXT ASSIGNMENTS
Q: 4, 5, 6
SE: 3
FRA: 2, 6

Businesses use computerized systems for accounting and many other purposes. Large, multinational companies have vast computer resources and use very powerful computers that are linked together to provide communication and data transfer around the world. However, even in these large companies and in most small companies, the microcomputer, or PC, is a critical element in the processing of information. It has become even more critical as companies have expanded their use of the Internet to communicate and transact business directly with vendors, suppliers, and clients. Two kinds of microcomputer programs on which accountants rely heavily are spreadsheet software and general ledger systems.

SPREADSHEET SOFTWARE

Spreadsheet software is used to analyze data. A **spreadsheet** is a computerized grid of columns and rows into which the user places data or formulas related to financial planning, cost estimating, and other accounting tasks. Windows® Excel and Lotus are popular commercial spreadsheet programs used for financial analysis and other purposes.

GENERAL LEDGER SYSTEMS

KEY POINT: Five kinds of transactions—credit sales, credit purchases, cash receipts, cash payments, and miscellaneous—are common in the typical business. In a manual system, a separate journal should be used for each type of transaction, and a general journal should be used for all other transactions. In a computerized system, a separate function is chosen for each type.

General ledger systems is the terminology commonly used to identify the group of integrated software programs that accountants use to perform major functions, such as accounting for sales and accounts receivable, purchases and accounts payable, cash receipts and disbursements, and payroll.

Today, most general ledger systems are written using the Windows® operating system, which has a **graphical user interface (GUI)**. A graphical user interface employs symbols, called **icons**, to represent operations. Examples of icons include a file folder, eraser, hourglass, and magnifying glass. The keyboard can be used in the traditional way, or a *mouse* or *trackball* may be used. When a program uses Windows as its graphical user interface, the program is termed *Windows-compatible*. The visual format and the ability to use a mouse or trackball make Windows-compatible software easy to use.

FOCUS ON BUSINESS TECHNOLOGY

Networking: How to Get It Done

Many businesses achieve the computing power of mainframes (large computers) by linking many microcomputers in a network. In a daisy chain network, the microcomputers are linked in a type of circle, or daisy chain. With this network, a person may have to go through several other microcomputers to reach a file or communicate with a person at another computer. In a home base, or star, network, all microcomputers are linked to a central switching point, or home base. A separate microcomputer called a *server* contains all the common data files, such as the accounting records. The server is also connected to the home base. All users can access accounting records and other data files by going through the home base. This type of network is faster and more efficient than the daisy chain network.

FIGURE 2
Graphical User Interface

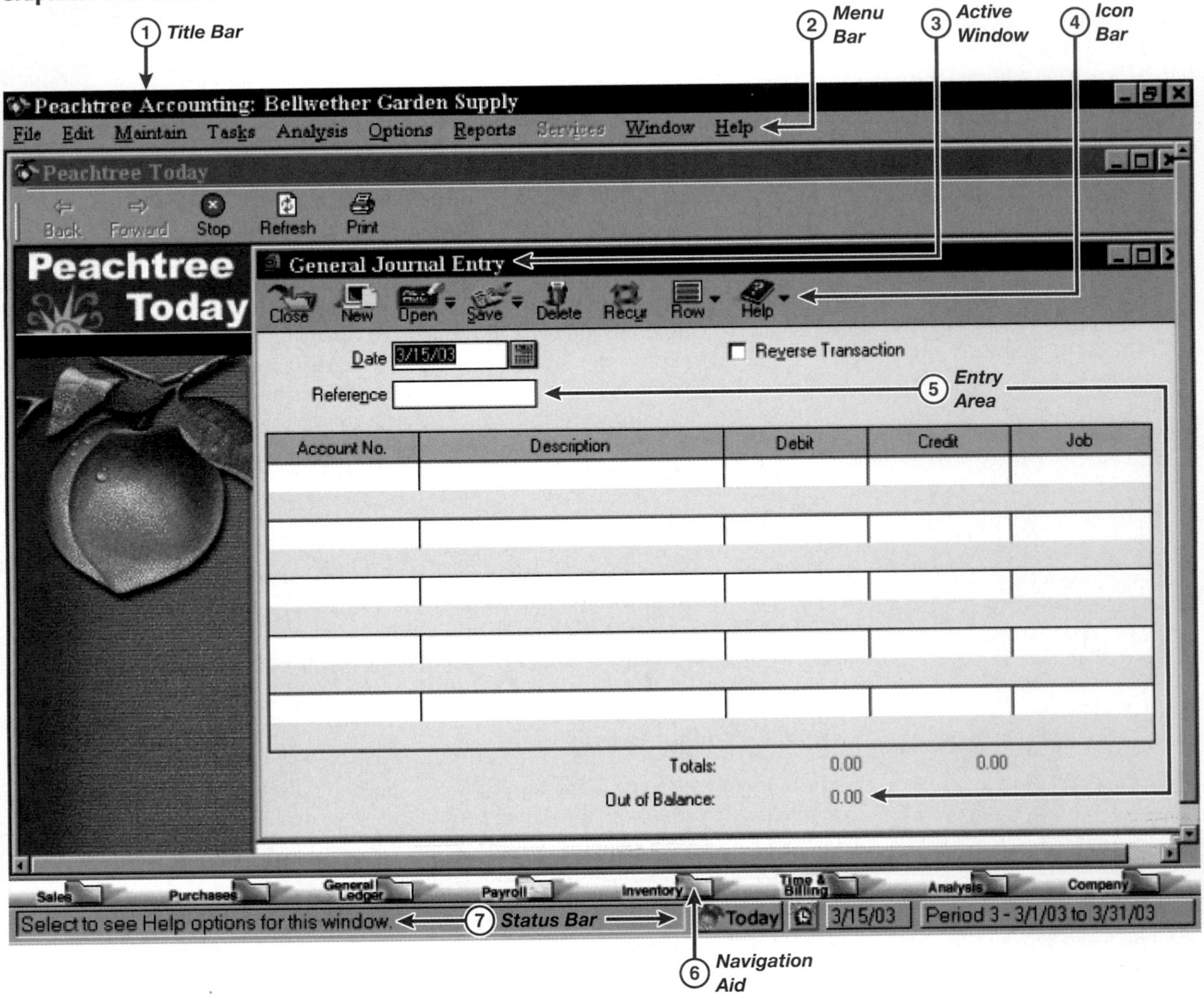

1 **Title Bar:** The title bar at the top of the screen identifies the program and the company under consideration.

2 **Menu Bar:** When you click on one of the menu bar headings, a submenu of options opens. You select an option with a mouse or by holding down the <Alt> key and pressing the letter underlined in the desired option.

3 **Active Window:** This bar shows what window is open, or "active." Here, the "General Journal Entry" window is active.

4 **Icon Bar:** The icon bar shows visual images that pertain to the window. Some icons are common to all windows, whereas others are specific to a particular window. You click on an icon to perform the associated function.

5 **Entry Area:** This part of the screen is where you enter information for the journal entry.

6 **Navigation Aid:** The navigation aid offers a graphical supplement to the menu bar. The major functions of the program are represented as icons or pictures that show you how tasks flow through the system.

7 **Status Bar:** The gray bar (screen colors may vary) at the bottom of the window shows the current date and the current accounting period.

Source: "Graphical User Interface" from *Peachtree Complete Accounting™ for Windows®*. Reprinted by permission of Peachtree Software.

Read

◆ STOP AND THINK!
Why is knowledge of accounting necessary when a computerized general ledger system will do the steps in the accounting cycle automatically?
Knowledge of accounting is necessary for two reasons. First, transactions must be entered in the proper way and in the proper accounts. Second, an understanding of the financial statements that the system produces is a necessary component in making business decisions. ■

KEY POINT: At least one source document should support each business transaction entered in the records. The accounting system should provide easy reference to the source documents to facilitate subsequent examination (e.g., by an auditor). For instance, canceled checks should be filed by check number.

Figure 2 shows how Peachtree Complete Accounting™ for Windows (PCW) uses a combination of text and icons. It is an example of what a graphical user interface looks like on your computer.

One of the benefits of Windows-compatible programs is that they use standardized terms and operations. Once you have mastered one Windows-compatible program, such as Peachtree Complete, you will be able to use other Windows-compatible applications.

Three software programs available for this book are (1) General Ledger Software, (2) Peachtree Complete Accounting for Windows, and (3) Quickbooks®. General Ledger Software is used to work end-of-chapter problems. It is designed for educational use and cannot be purchased commercially. Peachtree Complete and Quickbooks can be purchased through retail stores. They, too, can be used with selected end-of-chapter problems.

STRUCTURE OF GENERAL LEDGER SYSTEMS

Most general ledger systems are organized so that each module performs a major task of the accounting information system. Figure 3 shows a typical configuration of general ledger systems. Note that there is a software module for each major accounting function: sales/accounts receivable, purchases/accounts payable, cash receipts, cash disbursements, payroll, and general journal. When these features interact with one another, the software is called an *integrated program*.

Source documents, or written evidence, should support each transaction entered into the accounting system. Source documents verify that a transaction occurred and provide the details of the transaction. For example, a customer's invoice should support each sale on account, and a vendor's invoice should support each purchase. Even though the transactions are recorded in a computer file

FIGURE 3
Microcomputer Accounting Information System Using a General Ledger System

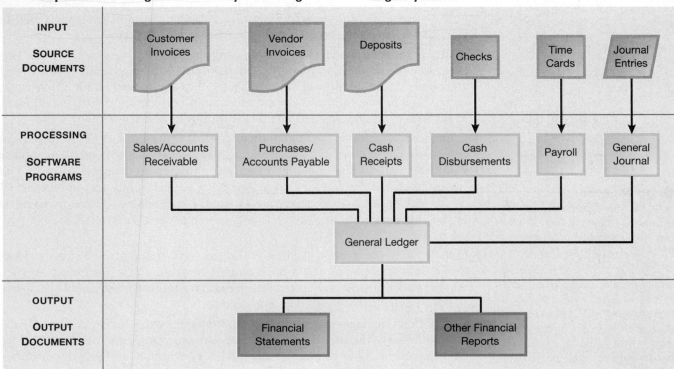

(on floppy disks or hard disks), the original documents should be stored so that they can be examined at a later date if a question arises about the accuracy of the accounting records.

After transactions are processed in a general ledger system, there is a procedure for posting them, updating the ledgers, and preparing the trial balance. Finally, the financial statements and other accounting reports are printed.

Peachtree Complete Accounting for Windows allows either *batch* posting or *real-time* posting. In a batch posting system, source documents are recorded in the appropriate journal and saved; posting is done at the end of the day, week, or month. In a real-time posting system, documents are posted as they are recorded in the journal. The basic goal of a general ledger system is to make accounting tasks less time-consuming and more accurate and dependable. However, it is important to understand just what the computer is accomplishing. Knowledge of the underlying accounting process helps ensure that the accounting records are accurate and that the assets of the business are protected.

✓ Check out ACE for a Review Quiz at http://accounting.college.hmco.com/students.

ACCOUNTANTS AND THE INTERNET

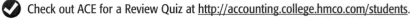

LO4 Explain how accountants and businesses use the Internet.

RELATED TEXT ASSIGNMENTS
Q: 7
SE: 4

The **Internet** is the world's largest computer network. The Internet allows any computer on the network to communicate with any other computer on the network. To access the Internet, a computer needs a modem that connects it to a phone line.

Most people are well aware of the Internet's ability to provide access to the World Wide Web (WWW), electronic mail (email), and electronic bulletin boards. Recent research shows that even businesses with fewer than ten employees are users of the Internet. More than 50 percent of these small businesses have Internet access, and more than 20 percent have their own web sites.[3] Among the ways in which accountants and businesses of all sizes use the Internet are the following:

www.sec.gov/edgar.shtml

- **Financial reporting.** Companies today commonly make their financial statements available on the Internet. Large companies are required to file their financial information electronically with the SEC, and it is available on Edgar, the SEC's online warehouse of financial information. Additionally, most companies publish electronic versions of their annual reports on their web sites.

- **XBRL. Extensible Business Reporting Language (XBRL)** is a new computer language developed by accountants and others for the express purpose of identifying and communicating financial information. It allows businesses to post information on the Web in a uniform way so that users can access the information, summarize it, perform computations, and format the output in any manner they wish.

- **Ecommerce. Electronic commerce (ecommerce)** is the conduct of business transactions on computer networks, including the Internet. Most people are familiar with the buying and selling of products from business to consumers (B to C) on the Internet, but the Internet is used far more widely in business-to-business (B to B) and business to government (B to G) transactions. These transactions include buying and selling products and services, collecting receivables, and paying bills.

● **STOP AND THINK!**
Why do you think small businesses may be reluctant to establish their own web sites?

There are several possible reasons. A web site is costly to set up and maintain; management may lack knowledge or expertise about web sites and may fail to see their benefits; or the business may be of a type that would not benefit from the principal features of a web site. ■

- **EDI.** Ecommerce is often facilitated through private links, referred to as **Electronic Data Interchange (EDI).** For example, companies in many industries, such as retail chemicals, oil, and automobile parts, have formed private networks to use EDI for buying and selling goods and services.

- **Supply-chain management. Supply-chain management** is a system that uses the Internet to track the supplies and materials a manufacturer will need on a day-to-day—sometimes hour-to-hour—basis. Such a system may also link the manufacturer to its customers.

FOCUS ON BUSINESS PRACTICE

B to B and EDI: How Much Can They Save?

An officer of Target Corporation <www.target.com>, the large discount retailer, is quoted as saying, B to B is "real, and it's big, and it's growing. In five years all of our purchasing activity will be done over the Internet." Most executives agree with this statement. Sales and purchases that in the past would have been made by telephone or fax are now transacted by electronic data interchange (EDI). For example, Target participates in a worldwide Retail Exchange, an electronic marketplace formed by over 50 large retailers, including J.C. Penney

<www.jcpenney.com> and Safeway Inc. <www.safeway.com>. The purpose of the Retail Exchange is to provide a market for online sales and purchases. When Target wants to purchase something—for instance, fax paper, cleaning products, or jeans—it posts its needs, and other companies bid on the business. Retailers participating in the exchange have seen a 12 to 15 percent reduction in purchasing costs. Even greater reductions are likely because at present only about 50 percent of purchases are made this way.[4]

- **E2K. Event-to-knowledge (E2K) management** means that the Internet is used to get information to users within and outside a company in the quickest possible way after an event like a sale or a purchase has occurred.

- **Document-less transactions.** One of the limitations on the growth of electronic commerce is that although the transactions are conducted electronically, source documents, such as those used in general ledger systems, are still often needed to back up the transactions. For example, a purchase is made on the Internet, but a confirmation is emailed, faxed, or mailed to provide documentation of the transaction. Gradually, methods that eliminate the need for source documents are being developed.

 Check out ACE for a Review Quiz at http://accounting.college.hmco.com/students.

CLOSING ENTRIES

LO5 Explain the purposes of closing entries and prepare required closing entries.

RELATED TEXT ASSIGNMENTS
Q: 8, 9, 10, 11
SE: 5, 6, 7, 8, 10
E: 1, 8
P: 1, 2, 3, 4, 5, 6, 7, 8
SD: 4
FRA: 1, 3, 5

Balance sheet accounts are considered **permanent accounts**, or *real accounts*, because they carry their end-of-period balances into the next accounting period. On the other hand, revenue and expense accounts are considered **temporary accounts**, or *nominal accounts*, because they begin each accounting period with a zero balance, accumulate a balance during the period, and are then cleared by means of closing entries.

Closing entries are journal entries made at the end of an accounting period. They have two purposes. First, closing entries set the stage for the next accounting period by clearing revenue, expense, and Dividends accounts of their balances. Remember that the income statement reports net income (or loss) for a single accounting period and shows revenues and expenses for that period only. For the income statement to present the activity of a single accounting period, the revenue

FOCUS ON BUSINESS TECHNOLOGY

E2K: How Much Time Can It Save?

E2K, or event-to-knowledge, is the concept of the time it takes to turn the results of a transaction, such as a sale or a purchase, into useful information for managers. It involves the application of the just-in-time management philosophy to accounting. The goal of just-in-time accounting (JITA) is to reduce the time it takes to produce and distribute financial reports from days or weeks to a single business day so that

managers receive them when they need them, or "just in time." Cisco Systems <www.cisco.com>, the large software company, believes it has achieved a breakthrough with a "virtual close" program that gives managers the financial results of one day by 2 P.M. the next day. A reduction in E2K time means that managers have more time to consider the information and can thus make better decisions.[5]

FIGURE 4
Overview of the Closing Process

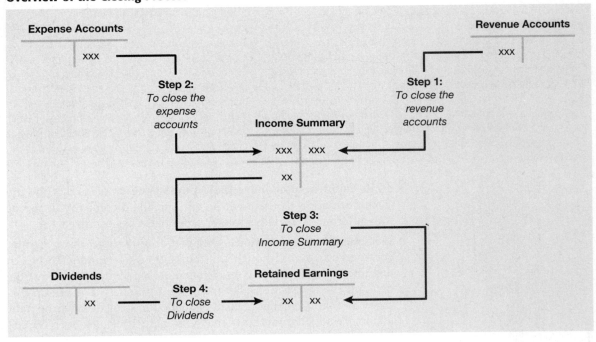

and expense accounts must begin each new period with zero balances. The zero balances are obtained by using closing entries to clear the balances in the revenue and expense accounts at the end of each accounting period. The Dividends account is closed in a similar manner.

Second, closing entries summarize a period's revenues and expenses. This is done by transferring the balances of revenue and expense accounts to the **Income Summary** account. This temporary account, which appears in the chart of accounts between the Dividends account and the first revenue account, provides a place to summarize all revenues and expenses. It is used only in the closing process and never appears in the financial statements.

The balance of the Income Summary account equals the net income or loss reported on the income statement. The net income or loss is then transferred to the Retained Earnings account. This is done because even though revenues and expenses are recorded in revenue and expense accounts, they actually represent increases and decreases in stockholders' equity. Closing entries transfer the net effect of increases (revenues) and decreases (expenses) to stockholders' equity. An overview of the closing process is illustrated in Figure 4.

Closing entries are required at the end of any period for which financial statements are prepared. As noted in the Decision Point at the beginning of the chapter, Hershey Foods prepares financial statements each quarter; when it does so, it must close its books. Such interim information is helpful to investors and creditors in assessing the ongoing financial performance of a company. Many companies, including Hershey, also close their books monthly to give management a more timely view of ongoing operations.

REQUIRED CLOSING ENTRIES

There are four important steps in closing the accounts:

1. Closing the credit balances from income statement accounts to the Income Summary account

---

⬢ **STOP AND THINK!**

Could closing entries be done without using the Income Summary account?

Since the Income Summary account is used to accumulate a balance (steps 1 and 2) that is subsequently transferred to Retained Earnings (step 3), it would be possible to eliminate the use of the Income Summary account by closing the accounts in steps 1 and 2 directly to the Retained Earnings account and eliminating step 3. ■

www.hersheys.com

EXHIBIT 1
Preparing Closing Entries from the Adjusted Trial Balance

Joan Miller Advertising Agency, Inc.
Adjusted Trial Balance
July 31, 20xx

Cash	$ 9,140	
Accounts Receivable	5,000	
Art Supplies	1,300	
Office Supplies	600	
Prepaid Rent	800	
Prepaid Insurance	880	
Art Equipment	4,200	
Accumulated Depreciation, Art Equipment		$ 70
Office Equipment	3,000	
Accumulated Depreciation, Office Equipment		50
Accounts Payable		3,240
Unearned Art Fees		600
Wages Payable		360
Income Taxes Payable		400
Common Stock		20,000
Dividends	1,400	
Advertising Fees Earned		6,400
Art Fees Earned		400
Wages Expense	2,760	
Utilities Expense	200	
Telephone Expense	140	
Rent Expense	800	
Insurance Expense	80	
Art Supplies Expense	500	
Office Supplies Expense	200	
Depreciation Expense, Art Equipment	70	
Depreciation Expense, Office Equipment	50	
Income Taxes Expense	400	
	$31,520	$31,520

Entry 1:

July 31	Advertising Fees Earned	411	6,400	
	Art Fees Earned	412	400	
	Income Summary	314		6,800
	To close the revenue accounts			

Entry 2:

July 31	Income Summary	314	5,200	
	Wages Expense	511		2,760
	Utilities Expense	512		200
	Telephone Expense	513		140
	Rent Expense	514		800
	Insurance Expense	515		80
	Art Supplies Expense	516		500
	Office Supplies Expense	517		200
	Depreciation Expense, Art Equipment	519		70
	Depreciation Expense, Office Equipment	520		50
	Income Taxes Expense	521		400
	To close the expense accounts			

Income Summary

July 31	5,200	July 31	6,800	
July 31	1,600			
		Bal.	—	

Entry 3:

July 31	Income Summary	314	1,600	
	Retained Earnings	312		1,600
	To close the Income Summary account			

Entry 4:

July 31	Retained Earnings	312	1,400	
	Dividends	313		1,400
	To close the Dividends account			

ENRICHMENT NOTE: It is not absolutely necessary to use the Income Summary account when preparing closing entries. However, it does simplify the procedure. The Income Summary account is opened and closed with the preparation of closing entries.

2. Closing the debit balances from income statement accounts to the Income Summary account

3. Closing the Income Summary account balance to the Retained Earnings account

4. Closing the Dividends account balance to the Retained Earnings account

Each step is accomplished by a closing entry. All the data needed to record the closing entries are found in the adjusted trial balance. The relationships of the four kinds of entries to the adjusted trial balance are shown in Exhibit 1.

EXHIBIT 2
Posting the Closing Entry of the Credit Balances from the
Income Statement Accounts to the Income Summary Account

Advertising Fees Earned — Account No. 411

Date	Item	Post. Ref.	Debit	Credit	Balance Debit	Balance Credit
July 10		J2		1,400		1,400
19		J2		4,800		6,200
31	Adj. (j)	J3		200		6,400
31	Closing	J4	6,400			—

Art Fees Earned — Account No. 412

Date	Item	Post. Ref.	Debit	Credit	Balance Debit	Balance Credit
July 31	Adj. (i)	J3		400		400
31	Closing	J4	400			—

6,400
400
6,800

Income Summary — Account No. 314

Date	Item	Post. Ref.	Debit	Credit	Balance Debit	Balance Credit
July 31	Closing	J4		6,800		6,800

■ **STEP 1: CLOSING THE CREDIT BALANCES FROM INCOME STATEMENT ACCOUNTS TO THE INCOME SUMMARY ACCOUNT**   On the credit side of the adjusted trial balance in Exhibit 1, two revenue accounts show balances: Advertising Fees Earned and Art Fees Earned. To close these two accounts, a journal entry must be made debiting each account in the amount of its balance and crediting the total to the Income Summary account. The effect of posting the entry is illustrated in Exhibit 2. Notice that the entry (1) sets the balances of the revenue accounts to zero and (2) transfers the total revenues to the credit side of the Income Summary account.

KEY POINT: The Income Summary account now reflects the account balances that the revenue accounts contained before they were closed.

■ **STEP 2: CLOSING THE DEBIT BALANCES FROM INCOME STATEMENT ACCOUNTS TO THE INCOME SUMMARY ACCOUNT**   Several expense accounts show balances on the debit side of the adjusted trial balance in Exhibit 1. A compound entry is needed to credit each of these expense accounts for its balance and to debit the Income Summary account for the total. The effect of posting the closing entry is shown in Exhibit 3.

EXHIBIT 3
Posting the Closing Entry of the Debit Balances from the Income Statement Accounts to the Income Summary Account

Wages Expense — Account No. 511

Date	Item	Post. Ref.	Debit	Credit	Balance Debit	Balance Credit
July 12		J2	1,200		1,200	
26		J2	1,200		2,400	
31	Adj. (g)	J3	360		2,760	
31	Closing	J4		2,760	—	

Income Summary — Account No. 314

Date	Item	Post. Ref.	Debit	Credit	Balance Debit	Balance Credit
July 31	Closing	J4		6,800		6,800
31	Closing	J4	5,200			1,600

Utilities Expense — Account No. 512

Date	Item	Post. Ref.	Debit	Credit	Balance Debit	Balance Credit
July 29		J2	200		200	
31	Closing	J4		200	—	

Telephone Expense — Account No. 513

Date	Item	Post. Ref.	Debit	Credit	Balance Debit	Balance Credit
July 30		J2	140		140	
31	Closing	J4		140	—	

Income Summary detail list: 2,760 / 200 / 140 / 800 / 80 / 500 / 200 / 400 / 50 / 70 / 5,200

Rent Expense — Account No. 514

Date	Item	Post. Ref.	Debit	Credit	Balance Debit	Balance Credit
July 31	Adj. (a)	J3	800		800	
31	Closing	J4		800	—	

Insurance Expense — Account No. 515

Date	Item	Post. Ref.	Debit	Credit	Balance Debit	Balance Credit
July 31	Adj. (b)	J3	80		80	
31	Closing	J4		80	—	

Depreciation Expense, Art Equipment — Account No. 519

Date	Item	Post. Ref.	Debit	Credit	Balance Debit	Balance Credit
July 31	Adj. (e)	J3	70		70	
31	Closing	J4		70	—	

Art Supplies Expense — Account No. 516

Date	Item	Post. Ref.	Debit	Credit	Balance Debit	Balance Credit
July 31	Adj. (c)	J3	500		500	
31	Closing	J4		500	—	

Depreciation Expense, Office Equipment — Account No. 520

Date	Item	Post. Ref.	Debit	Credit	Balance Debit	Balance Credit
July 31	Adj. (f)	J3	50		50	
31	Closing	J4		50	—	

Office Supplies Expense — Account No. 517

Date	Item	Post. Ref.	Debit	Credit	Balance Debit	Balance Credit
July 31	Adj. (d)	J3	200		200	
31	Closing	J4		200	—	

Income Taxes Expense — Account No. 521

Date	Item	Post. Ref.	Debit	Credit	Balance Debit	Balance Credit
July 31	Adj. (h)	J3	400		400	
31	Closing	J4		400	—	

KEY POINT: The credit balance of the Income Summary account at this point ($1,600) represents the key performance measure of net income.

Notice how the entry (1) reduces the expense account balances to zero and (2) transfers the total of the account balances to the debit side of the Income Summary account.

■ **STEP 3: CLOSING THE INCOME SUMMARY ACCOUNT BALANCE TO THE RETAINED EARNINGS ACCOUNT** After the entries closing the revenue and expense accounts have been posted, the balance of the Income Summary account equals the net

EXHIBIT 4
Posting the Closing Entry of the Income Summary Account
Balance to the Retained Earnings Account

Income Summary						Account No. 314		Retained Earnings						Account No. 312
		Post.			Balance					Post.			Balance	
Date	Item	Ref.	Debit	Credit	Debit	Credit		Date	Item	Ref.	Debit	Credit	Debit	Credit
July 31	Closing	J4		6,800		6,800		July 31	Closing	J4		1,600		1,600
31	Closing	J4	5,200			1,600								
31	Closing	J4	1,600			—								

KEY POINT: In a net loss situation, debit the Retained Earnings account (to reduce it) and credit Income Summary (to close it).

income or loss for the period. Since revenues are represented by the credit to Income Summary and expenses are represented by the debit to Income Summary, a net income is indicated by a credit balance (where revenues exceed expenses) and a net loss by a debit balance (where expenses exceed revenues). At this point, the Income Summary account balance, whatever its nature, must be closed to the Retained Earnings account, as shown in Exhibit 1. The effect of posting the closing entry when the company has a net income is shown in Exhibit 4. Notice the dual effect of (1) closing the Income Summary account and (2) transferring the balance, net income in this case, to Retained Earnings.

KEY POINT: Notice that the Dividends account is closed to the Retained Earnings account, not to the Income Summary account.

■ **STEP 4: CLOSING THE DIVIDENDS ACCOUNT BALANCE TO THE RETAINED EARNINGS ACCOUNT** The Dividends account shows the amount by which retained earnings are reduced during the accounting period by cash dividends. The debit balance of the Dividends account is closed to the Retained Earnings account, as illustrated in Exhibit 1. The effect of this closing entry, as shown in Exhibit 5, is to (1) close the Dividends account and (2) transfer the balance to the Retained Earnings account.

THE ACCOUNTS AFTER CLOSING

After all the steps in the closing process have been completed and all closing entries have been posted to the accounts, everything is ready for the next accounting period. The ledger accounts of Joan Miller Advertising Agency, Inc., as they appear at this point, are shown in Exhibit 6. The revenue, expense, and Dividends accounts

EXHIBIT 5
Posting the Closing Entry of the Dividends
Account Balance to the Retained Earnings Account

Dividends						Account No. 313		Retained Earnings						Account No. 312
		Post.			Balance					Post.			Balance	
Date	Item	Ref.	Debit	Credit	Debit	Credit		Date	Item	Ref.	Debit	Credit	Debit	Credit
July 31		J2	1,400		1,400			July 31	Closing	J4		1,600		1,600
31	Closing	J4		1,400	—			31	Closing	J4	1,400			200

EXHIBIT 6
The Accounts After Closing Entries Are Posted

Cash Account No. 111

Date	Item	Post. Ref.	Debit	Credit	Balance Debit	Balance Credit
July 1		J1	20,000		20,000	
2		J1		1,600	18,400	
3		J1		4,200	14,200	
5		J1		1,500	12,700	
8		J1		960	11,740	
9		J1		1,000	10,740	
10		J2	1,400		12,140	
12		J2		1,200	10,940	
15		J2	1,000		11,940	
26		J2		1,200	10,740	
29		J2		200	10,540	
31		J2		1,400	9,140	

Accounts Receivable Account No. 113

Date	Item	Post. Ref.	Debit	Credit	Balance Debit	Balance Credit
July 19		J2	4,800		4,800	
31	Adj. (j)	J3	200		5,000	

Art Supplies Account No. 115

Date	Item	Post. Ref.	Debit	Credit	Balance Debit	Balance Credit
July 6		J1	1,800		1,800	
31	Adj. (c)	J3		500	1,300	

Office Supplies Account No. 116

Date	Item	Post. Ref.	Debit	Credit	Balance Debit	Balance Credit
July 6		J1	800		800	
31	Adj. (d)	J3		200	600	

Prepaid Rent Account No. 117

Date	Item	Post. Ref.	Debit	Credit	Balance Debit	Balance Credit
July 2		J1	1,600		1,600	
31	Adj. (a)	J3		800	800	

Prepaid Insurance Account No. 118

Date	Item	Post. Ref.	Debit	Credit	Balance Debit	Balance Credit
July 8		J1	960		960	
31	Adj. (b)	J3		80	880	

Art Equipment Account No. 144

Date	Item	Post. Ref.	Debit	Credit	Balance Debit	Balance Credit
July 3		J1	4,200		4,200	

Accumulated Depreciation, Art Equipment Account No. 145

Date	Item	Post. Ref.	Debit	Credit	Balance Debit	Balance Credit
July 31	Adj. (e)	J3		70		70

Office Equipment Account No. 146

Date	Item	Post. Ref.	Debit	Credit	Balance Debit	Balance Credit
July 5		J1	3,000		3,000	

Accumulated Depreciation, Office Equipment Account No. 147

Date	Item	Post. Ref.	Debit	Credit	Balance Debit	Balance Credit
July 31	Adj. (f)	J3		50		50

Accounts Payable Account No. 212

Date	Item	Post. Ref.	Debit	Credit	Balance Debit	Balance Credit
July 5		J1		1,500		1,500
6		J1		2,600		4,100
9		J1	1,000			3,100
30		J2		140		3,240

Unearned Art Fees Account No. 213

Date	Item	Post. Ref.	Debit	Credit	Balance Debit	Balance Credit
July 15		J2		1,000		1,000
31	Adj. (i)	J3	400			600

Wages Payable Account No. 214

Date	Item	Post. Ref.	Debit	Credit	Balance Debit	Balance Credit
July 31	Adj. (g)	J3		360		360

Income Taxes Payable Account No. 215

Date	Item	Post. Ref.	Debit	Credit	Balance Debit	Balance Credit
July 31	Adj. (h)	J3		400		400

Common Stock Account No. 311

Date	Item	Post. Ref.	Debit	Credit	Balance Debit	Balance Credit
July 1		J1		20,000		20,000

(continued)

EXHIBIT 6
The Accounts After Closing Entries Are Posted (continued)

Retained Earnings — Account No. 312

Date	Item	Post. Ref.	Debit	Credit	Balance Debit	Balance Credit
July 31	Closing	J4		1,600		1,600
31	Closing	J4	1,400			200

Telephone Expense — Account No. 513

Date	Item	Post. Ref.	Debit	Credit	Balance Debit	Balance Credit
July 30		J2	140		140	
31	Closing	J4		140	—	

Dividends — Account No. 313

Date	Item	Post. Ref.	Debit	Credit	Balance Debit	Balance Credit
July 31		J2	1,400		1,400	
31	Closing	J4		1,400	—	

Rent Expense — Account No. 514

Date	Item	Post. Ref.	Debit	Credit	Balance Debit	Balance Credit
July 31	Adj. (a)	J3	800		800	
31	Closing	J4		800	—	

Income Summary — Account No. 314

Date	Item	Post. Ref.	Debit	Credit	Balance Debit	Balance Credit
July 31	Closing	J4		6,800		6,800
31	Closing	J4	5,200			1,600
31	Closing	J4	1,600			—

Insurance Expense — Account No. 515

Date	Item	Post. Ref.	Debit	Credit	Balance Debit	Balance Credit
July 31	Adj. (b)	J3	80		80	
31	Closing	J4		80	—	

Advertising Fees Earned — Account No. 411

Date	Item	Post. Ref.	Debit	Credit	Balance Debit	Balance Credit
July 10		J2		1,400		1,400
19		J2		4,800		6,200
31	Adj. (j)	J3		200		6,400
31	Closing	J4	6,400			

Art Supplies Expense — Account No. 516

Date	Item	Post. Ref.	Debit	Credit	Balance Debit	Balance Credit
July 31	Adj. (c)	J3	500		500	
31	Closing	J4		500	—	

Art Fees Earned — Account No. 412

Date	Item	Post. Ref.	Debit	Credit	Balance Debit	Balance Credit
July 31	Adj. (i)	J3		400		400
31	Closing	J4	400			—

Office Supplies Expense — Account No. 517

Date	Item	Post. Ref.	Debit	Credit	Balance Debit	Balance Credit
July 31	Adj. (d)	J3	200		200	
31	Closing	J4		200	—	

Wages Expense — Account No. 511

Date	Item	Post. Ref.	Debit	Credit	Balance Debit	Balance Credit
July 12		J2	1,200		1,200	
26		J2	1,200		2,400	
31	Adj. (g)	J3	360		2,760	
31	Closing	J4		2,760	—	

Depreciation Expense, Art Equipment — Account No. 519

Date	Item	Post. Ref.	Debit	Credit	Balance Debit	Balance Credit
July 31	Adj. (e)	J3	70		70	
31	Closing	J4		70	—	

Depreciation Expense, Office Equipment — Account No. 520

Date	Item	Post. Ref.	Debit	Credit	Balance Debit	Balance Credit
July 31	Adj. (f)	J3	50		50	
31	Closing	J4		50	—	

Utilities Expense — Account No. 512

Date	Item	Post. Ref.	Debit	Credit	Balance Debit	Balance Credit
July 29		J2	200		200	
31	Closing	J4		200	—	

Income Taxes Expense — Account No. 521

Date	Item	Post. Ref.	Debit	Credit	Balance Debit	Balance Credit
July 31	Adj. (h)	J3	400		400	
31	Closing	J4		400	—	

(temporary accounts) have zero balances. Retained Earnings has been increased to reflect the agency's net income and decreased for dividends. The balance sheet accounts (permanent accounts) show the correct balances, which are carried forward to the next period.

 Check out ACE for a Review Quiz at http://accounting.college.hmco.com/students.

FOCUS ON INTERNATIONAL BUSINESS

Closing Doesn't Have to Be Such a Headache.

For companies with extensive international operations, like Caterpillar Inc. <www.caterpillar.com>, Dow Chemical <www.dow.com>, Phillips Petroleum <www.phillips66.com>, Gillette <www.gillette.com>, and Bristol-Myers Squibb <www.bms.com>, closing the records and preparing financial statements on a timely basis used to be a problem. It was common practice for foreign divisions of companies like these to end their fiscal year one month before the end of the fiscal year of their counterparts in the United States. This gave them the extra time they needed to perform closing procedures and mail the results back to U.S. headquarters to be used in preparation of the company's overall financial statements. This setup is usually unnecessary today because high-speed computers and electronic communications enable companies to close records and prepare financial statements for both foreign and domestic operations in less than a week.

THE POST-CLOSING TRIAL BALANCE

LO6 Prepare the post-closing trial balance.

RELATED TEXT ASSIGNMENTS
Q: 12, 13
P: 3
SD: 4

Because it is possible to make errors in posting the closing entries to the ledger accounts, it is necessary to determine that all temporary accounts have zero balances and to double-check that total debits equal total credits by preparing a new trial balance. This final trial balance, called the **post-closing trial balance**, is shown in Exhibit 7 for Joan Miller Advertising Agency, Inc. Notice that only the balance sheet accounts show balances because the income statement accounts and the Dividends account have all been closed. Also, notice that Retained Earnings is shown on the post-closing trial balance but was not shown on the adjusted trial balance in Exhibit 1. This is because it is the company's first month of operation and the account had a zero beginning balance. At the end of the month, after income and dividends are posted, Retained Earnings has a balance of $200.

EXHIBIT 7
Post-Closing Trial Balance

⬢ **STOP AND THINK!**
Why does the post-closing trial balance contain only balance sheet accounts?
All the income statement, or temporary, accounts have been closed, thus leaving only the balance sheet, or permanent, accounts to carry over to the next accounting period. ▪

KEY POINT: Notice that Retained Earnings now reflects the correct month-end balance, $200.

Joan Miller Advertising Agency, Inc.
Post-Closing Trial Balance
July 31, 20xx

Cash	$ 9,140	
Accounts Receivable	5,000	
Art Supplies	1,300	
Office Supplies	600	
Prepaid Rent	800	
Prepaid Insurance	880	
Art Equipment	4,200	
Accumulated Depreciation, Art Equipment		$ 70
Office Equipment	3,000	
Accumulated Depreciation, Office Equipment		50
Accounts Payable		3,240
Unearned Art Fees		600
Wages Payable		360
Income Taxes Payable		400
Common Stock		20,000
Retained Earnings		200
	$24,920	$24,920

✓ Check out ACE for a Review Quiz at http://accounting.college.hmco.com/students.

REVERSING ENTRIES: THE OPTIONAL FIRST STEP IN THE NEXT ACCOUNTING PERIOD

SO7 Prepare reversing entries as appropriate.

RELATED TEXT ASSIGNMENTS
Q: 14, 15
SE: 9
E: 3, 7
P: 4, 5, 8
SD: 2, 4

At the end of each accounting period, adjusting entries are made to bring revenues and expenses into conformity with the matching rule. A **reversing entry** is a general journal entry made on the first day of a new accounting period; it is the exact reverse of an adjusting entry made at the end of the previous accounting period. Reversing entries are optional. They simplify the bookkeeping process for transactions involving certain types of adjustments. Not all adjusting entries can be reversed. Under the recording system used in this book, only adjustments for accruals (accrued revenues and accrued expenses) can be reversed. Deferrals cannot be reversed because such reversals would not simplify the bookkeeping process in future accounting periods.

To see how reversing entries can be helpful, consider the adjusting entry made in the records of Joan Miller Advertising Agency, Inc., to accrue wages expense:

A = L + OE
    + −

July 31	Wages Expense	360	
	Wages Payable		360
	To accrue unrecorded wages		

When the secretary is paid on the next regular payday, the accountant would make this entry:

A = L + OE
−   −   −

Aug. 9	Wages Payable	360	
	Wages Expense	840	
	Cash		1,200
	Payment of two weeks' wages to secretary, $360 of which accrued in the previous period		

KEY POINT: Reversing entries are the opposite of adjusting entries and are dated the first day of the new period. They apply only to certain adjusting entries and are never required.

Notice that when the payment is made, if there is no reversing entry, the accountant must look in the records to find out how much of the $1,200 applies to the current accounting period and how much is applicable to the previous period. This may seem easy in our example, but think how difficult and time-consuming it would be if a company had hundreds of employees working on different schedules. A reversing entry helps solve the problem of applying revenues and expenses to the correct accounting period. It is exactly what its name implies: a reversal made by debiting the credits and crediting the debits of a previously made adjusting entry.

For example, notice the following sequence of entries and their effects on the ledger account Wages Expense:

1. Adjusting Entry

| July 31 | Wages Expense | 360 | |
| | Wages Payable | | 360 |

2. Closing Entry

| July 31 | Income Summary | 2,760 | |
| | Wages Expense | | 2,760 |

3. Reversing Entry

| Aug. 1 | Wages Payable | 360 | |
| | Wages Expense | | 360 |

4. Payment Entry

| Aug. 9 | Wages Expense | 1,200 | |
| | Cash | | 1,200 |

Wages Expense   Account No. 511

Date	Post. Ref.	Debit	Credit	Balance Debit	Balance Credit
July 12	J2	1,200		1,200	
26	J2	1,200		2,400	
31	J3	360		2,760	
31	J4		2,760	—	
Aug. 1	J5		360		360
9	J6	1,200		840	

Entry 1 adjusted Wages Expense to accrue $360 in the July accounting period.

Entry 2 closed the $2,760 in Wages Expense for July to Income Summary, leaving a zero balance.

KEY POINT: Notice the abnormal credit balance as of August 1. This situation is "corrected" with the August 9 entry, an entry the bookkeeper can easily make.

Entry 3, the reversing entry, set up a credit balance of $360 on August 1 in Wages Expense, which is the expense recognized through the adjusting entry in July (and also reduced the liability account Wages Payable to a zero balance). The reversing entry always sets up an abnormal balance in the income statement account and produces a zero balance in the balance sheet account.

Entry 4 recorded the $1,200 payment of two weeks' wages as a debit to Wages Expense, automatically leaving a balance of $840, which represents the correct wages expense to date in August.

The reversing entry simplified the process of making the payment entry on August 9.

Reversing entries apply to any accrued expenses or revenues. In the case of Joan Miller Advertising Agency, Inc., Income Taxes Expense is also an accrued expense that can be reversed. The adjusting entry for accrued revenue (advertising fees earned) can be reversed as well. The two additional reversing entries are as follows:

A = L + OE − +	Aug. 1	Income Taxes Payable	400
		Income Taxes Expense		400
		To reverse adjusting entry for estimated income taxes		
A = L + OE − −	1	Advertising Fees Earned	200
		Accounts Receivable		200
		To reverse adjusting entry for accrued fees earned		

When the series of advertisements is finished, the company can credit all the proceeds to Advertising Fees Earned without regard to the amount accrued in the previous period. The credit will automatically be reduced to the amount earned during August by the $200 debit in the account.

As noted earlier, under our system of recording, reversing entries apply only to accruals. They do not apply to deferrals, such as the entries that involve supplies, prepaid rent, prepaid insurance, depreciation, and unearned art fees.

✓ Check out ACE for a Review Quiz at http://accounting.college.hmco.com/students.

THE WORK SHEET: AN ACCOUNTANT'S TOOL

SO8 Prepare and use a work sheet.

RELATED TEXT ASSIGNMENTS
Q: 16, 17, 18, 19, 20, 21, 22, 23, 24, 25
SE: 10
E: 2, 4, 5, 6, 7, 8
P: 4, 5, 8
SD: 4

Accountants must collect relevant data to determine what should be included in financial reports. For example, they must examine insurance policies to see how much prepaid insurance has expired, examine plant and equipment records to determine depreciation, take an inventory of supplies on hand, and calculate the amount of accrued wages. These calculations, along with other computations, analyses, and preliminary drafts of statements, make up the accountants' **working papers**. Working papers are important for two reasons. First, they help accountants organize their work and thus avoid omitting important data or steps that affect the financial statements. Second, they provide evidence of past work so that accountants or auditors can retrace their steps and support the information in the financial statements.

KEY POINT: The work sheet is extremely useful when an accountant must prepare numerous adjustments. It is not a financial statement, it is not required, and it is not made public.

The **work sheet** is a special kind of working paper. It is often used as a preliminary step in the preparation of financial statements. Using a work sheet lessens the possibility of leaving out an adjustment, helps the accountant check the arithmetical accuracy of the accounts, and facilitates the preparation of financial statements. The work sheet is never published and is rarely seen by management. It is a tool for the accountant. Because preparing a work sheet is a very mechanical process, many accountants use a microcomputer for this purpose. In some cases, accountants use

EXHIBIT 8
Entering the Account Balances in the Trial Balance Columns

Joan Miller Advertising Agency, Inc.
Work Sheet
For the Month Ended July 31, 20xx

Account Name	Trial Balance		Adjustments		Adjusted Trial Balance		Income Statement		Balance Sheet	
	Debit	Credit	Debit	Credit	Debit	Credit	Debit	Credit	Debit	Credit
Cash	9,140									
Accounts Receivable	4,800									
Art Supplies	1,800									
Office Supplies	800									
Prepaid Rent	1,600									
Prepaid Insurance	960									
Art Equipment	4,200									
Accumulated Depreciation, Art Equipment										
Office Equipment	3,000									
Accumulated Depreciation, Office Equipment										
Accounts Payable		3,240								
Unearned Art Fees		1,000								
Common Stock		20,000								
Dividends	1,400									
Advertising Fees Earned		6,200								
Wages Expense	2,400									
Utilities Expense	200									
Telephone Expense	140									
	30,440	30,440								

a spreadsheet program to prepare the work sheet. In other cases, they use a general ledger system to prepare financial statements from the adjusted trial balance.

PREPARING THE WORK SHEET

So far, adjusting entries for Joan Miller Advertising Agency, Inc., have been entered directly in the journal and posted to the ledger, and the financial statements have been prepared from the adjusted trial balance. The process has been relatively simple because of the small size of the company. For larger companies, which may require many adjusting entries, a work sheet is essential. To illustrate the preparation of the work sheet, we continue with the Joan Miller Advertising Agency example.

A common form of work sheet has one column for account names and/or numbers and ten more columns with the headings shown in Exhibit 8. Notice that the work sheet is identified by a heading that consists of the name of the company, the title "Work Sheet," and the period of time covered (as on the income statement).

Preparation of a work sheet involves the following five steps:

KEY POINT: The work sheet Trial Balance columns take the place of the "traditional" trial balance.

1. **Enter and total the account balances in the Trial Balance columns.** The titles and balances of the accounts as of July 31 are copied directly from the ledger into the Trial Balance columns, as shown in Exhibit 8. When accountants use a work sheet, they do not have to prepare a separate trial balance.

EXHIBIT 9
Entries in the Adjustments Columns

Joan Miller Advertising Agency, Inc.
Work Sheet
For the Month Ended July 31, 20xx

Account Name	Trial Balance Debit	Trial Balance Credit	Adjustments Debit	Adjustments Credit	Adjusted Trial Balance Debit	Adjusted Trial Balance Credit	Income Statement Debit	Income Statement Credit	Balance Sheet Debit	Balance Sheet Credit
Cash	9,140									
Accounts Receivable	4,800		(j) 200							
Art Supplies	1,800			(c) 500						
Office Supplies	800			(d) 200						
Prepaid Rent	1,600			(a) 800						
Prepaid Insurance	960			(b) 80						
Art Equipment	4,200									
Accumulated Depreciation, Art Equipment				(e) 70						
Office Equipment	3,000									
Accumulated Depreciation, Office Equipment				(f) 50						
Accounts Payable		3,240								
Unearned Art Fees		1,000	(i) 400							
Common Stock		20,000								
Dividends	1,400									
Advertising Fees Earned		6,200		(j) 200						
Wages Expense	2,400		(g) 360							
Utilities Expense	200									
Telephone Expense	140									
	30,440	30,440								
Rent Expense			(a) 800							
Insurance Expense			(b) 80							
Art Supplies Expense			(c) 500							
Office Supplies Expense			(d) 200							
Depreciation Expense, Art Equipment			(e) 70							
Depreciation Expense, Office Equipment			(f) 50							
Wages Payable				(g) 360						
Income Taxes Expense			(h) 400							
Income Taxes Payable				(h) 400						
Art Fees Earned				(i) 400						
			3,060	3,060						

2. **Enter and total the adjustments in the Adjustments columns.** The required adjustments are entered in the Adjustments columns of the work sheet, as shown in Exhibit 9. As each adjustment is entered, a letter is used to identify its debit and credit parts. The first adjustment, identified by the letter **a,** is to recognize rent expense, which results in a debit to Rent Expense and a credit to

Prepaid Rent. In practice, this letter may be used to reference supporting computations or documentation underlying the adjusting entry and may simplify the recording of adjusting entries in the general journal.

If an adjustment calls for an account that has not been used in the trial balance, the new account is added below the accounts listed in the trial balance. The trial balance includes only those accounts that have balances. For example, Rent Expense has been added in Exhibit 9. The only exception to this rule is the Accumulated Depreciation accounts, which have a zero balance only in the initial period of operation. Accumulated Depreciation accounts are listed immediately after their associated asset accounts.

When all the adjustments have been made, the two Adjustments columns must be totaled. This procedure proves that the debits and credits of the adjustments are equal, and it generally reduces errors in the preparation of the work sheet.

3. **Enter and total the adjusted account balances in the Adjusted Trial Balance columns.** Exhibit 10 shows the adjusted trial balance. It is prepared by combining the amount of each account in the original Trial Balance columns with the corresponding amount in the Adjustments columns and entering each result in the Adjusted Trial Balance columns.

Exhibit 10 contains examples of **crossfooting**, or adding and subtracting a group of numbers horizontally. The first line shows Cash with a debit balance of $9,140. Because there are no adjustments to the Cash account, $9,140 is entered in the debit column of the Adjusted Trial Balance columns. On the second line, Accounts Receivable shows a debit of $4,800 in the Trial Balance columns. Since there is a debit of $200 from Adjustment j in the Adjustments column, it is added to the $4,800 and carried over to the debit column of the Adjusted Trial Balance columns at $5,000. On the next line, Art Supplies shows a debit of $1,800 in the Trial Balance columns and a credit of $500 from adjustment c in the Adjustments columns. Subtracting $500 from $1,800 results in a $1,300 debit balance in the Adjusted Trial Balance columns. This process is followed for all the accounts, including those added below the trial balance totals. The Adjusted Trial Balance columns are then footed (totaled) to check the accuracy of the crossfooting.

4. **Extend the account balances from the Adjusted Trial Balance columns to the Income Statement columns or the Balance Sheet columns.** Every account in the adjusted trial balance is either a balance sheet account or an income statement account. Each account is extended to its proper place as a debit or credit in either the Income Statement columns or the Balance Sheet columns. The result of extending the accounts is shown in Exhibit 11. Revenue and expense accounts are copied to the Income Statement columns. Assets, liabilities, and the Common Stock and Dividends accounts are extended to the Balance Sheet columns. To avoid overlooking an account, the accounts are extended line by line, beginning with the first line (which is Cash) and not omitting any subsequent lines. For instance, the Cash debit balance of $9,140 is extended to the debit column of the Balance Sheet columns; the Accounts Receivable debit balance of $5,000 is extended to the same debit column, and so forth. Each amount is carried across to only one column.

5. **Total the Income Statement columns and the Balance Sheet columns. Enter the net income or net loss in both pairs of columns as a balancing figure, and recompute the column totals.** This last step, shown in Exhibit 12, is necessary in order to compute net income or net loss and to prove the arithmetical accuracy of the work sheet.

EXHIBIT 10
Entries in the Adjusted Trial Balance Columns

Joan Miller Advertising Agency, Inc.
Work Sheet
For the Month Ended July 31, 20xx

Account Name	Trial Balance Debit	Trial Balance Credit	Adjustments Debit	Adjustments Credit	Adjusted Trial Balance Debit	Adjusted Trial Balance Credit	Income Statement Debit	Income Statement Credit	Balance Sheet Debit	Balance Sheet Credit
Cash	9,140				9,140					
Accounts Receivable	4,800		(j) 200		5,000					
Art Supplies	1,800			(c) 500	1,300					
Office Supplies	800			(d) 200	600					
Prepaid Rent	1,600			(a) 800	800					
Prepaid Insurance	960			(b) 80	880					
Art Equipment	4,200				4,200					
Accumulated Depreciation, Art Equipment				(e) 70		70				
Office Equipment	3,000				3,000					
Accumulated Depreciation, Office Equipment				(f) 50		50				
Accounts Payable		3,240				3,240				
Unearned Art Fees		1,000	(i) 400			600				
Common Stock		20,000				20,000				
Dividends	1,400				1,400					
Advertising Fees Earned		6,200		(j) 200		6,400				
Wages Expense	2,400		(g) 360		2,760					
Utilities Expense	200				200					
Telephone Expense	140				140					
	30,440	30,440								
Rent Expense			(a) 800		800					
Insurance Expense			(b) 80		80					
Art Supplies Expense			(c) 500		500					
Office Supplies Expense			(d) 200		200					
Depreciation Expense, Art Equipment			(e) 70		70					
Depreciation Expense, Office Equipment			(f) 50		50					
Wages Payable				(g) 360		360				
Income Taxes Expense			(h) 400		400					
Income Taxes Payable				(h) 400		400				
Art Fees Earned				(i) 400		400				
			3,060	3,060	31,520	31,520				

EXHIBIT 11
Extensions to the Income Statement and Balance Sheet Columns

Joan Miller Advertising Agency, Inc.
Work Sheet
For the Month Ended July 31, 20xx

Account Name	Trial Balance Debit	Trial Balance Credit	Adjustments Debit	Adjustments Credit	Adjusted Trial Balance Debit	Adjusted Trial Balance Credit	Income Statement Debit	Income Statement Credit	Balance Sheet Debit	Balance Sheet Credit
Cash	9,140				9,140				9,140	
Accounts Receivable	4,800		(j) 200		5,000				5,000	
Art Supplies	1,800			(c) 500	1,300				1,300	
Office Supplies	800			(d) 200	600				600	
Prepaid Rent	1,600			(a) 800	800				800	
Prepaid Insurance	960			(b) 80	880				880	
Art Equipment	4,200				4,200				4,200	
Accumulated Depreciation, Art Equipment				(e) 70		70				70
Office Equipment	3,000				3,000				3,000	
Accumulated Depreciation, Office Equipment				(f) 50		50				50
Accounts Payable		3,240				3,240				3,240
Unearned Art Fees		1,000	(i) 400			600				600
Common Stock		20,000				20,000				20,000
Dividends	1,400				1,400				1,400	
Advertising Fees Earned		6,200		(j) 200		6,400		6,400		
Wages Expense	2,400		(g) 360		2,760		2,760			
Utilities Expense	200				200		200			
Telephone Expense	140				140		140			
	30,440	30,440								
Rent Expense			(a) 800		800		800			
Insurance Expense			(b) 80		80		80			
Art Supplies Expense			(c) 500		500		500			
Office Supplies Expense			(d) 200		200		200			
Depreciation Expense, Art Equipment			(e) 70		70		70			
Depreciation Expense, Office Equipment			(f) 50		50		50			
Wages Payable				(g) 360		360				360
Income Taxes Expense			(h) 400		400		400			
Income Taxes Payable				(h) 400		400				400
Art Fees Earned				(i) 400		400		400		
			3,060	3,060	31,520	31,520				

EXHIBIT 12
Totals of the Income Statement and Balance Sheet Columns and Net Income

Joan Miller Advertising Agency, Inc.
Work Sheet
For the Month Ended July 31, 20xx

Account Name	Trial Balance Debit	Trial Balance Credit	Adjustments Debit	Adjustments Credit	Adjusted Trial Balance Debit	Adjusted Trial Balance Credit	Income Statement Debit	Income Statement Credit	Balance Sheet Debit	Balance Sheet Credit
Cash	9,140				9,140				9,140	
Accounts Receivable	4,800		(j) 200		5,000				5,000	
Art Supplies	1,800			(c) 500	1,300				1,300	
Office Supplies	800			(d) 200	600				600	
Prepaid Rent	1,600			(a) 800	800				800	
Prepaid Insurance	960			(b) 80	880				880	
Art Equipment	4,200				4,200				4,200	
Accumulated Depreciation, Art Equipment				(e) 70		70				70
Office Equipment	3,000				3,000				3,000	
Accumulated Depreciation, Office Equipment				(f) 50		50				50
Accounts Payable		3,240				3,240				3,240
Unearned Art Fees		1,000	(i) 400			600				600
Common Stock		20,000				20,000				20,000
Dividends	1,400				1,400				1,400	
Advertising Fees Earned		6,200		(j) 200		6,400		6,400		
Wages Expense	2,400		(g) 360		2,760		2,760			
Utilities Expense	200				200		200			
Telephone Expense	140				140		140			
	30,440	30,440								
Rent Expense			(a) 800		800		800			
Insurance Expense			(b) 80		80		80			
Art Supplies Expense			(c) 500		500		500			
Office Supplies Expense			(d) 200		200		200			
Depreciation Expense, Art Equipment			(e) 70		70		70			
Depreciation Expense, Office Equipment			(f) 50		50		50			
Wages Payable				(g) 360		360				360
Income Taxes Expense			(h) 400		400		400			
Income Taxes Payable				(h) 400		400				400
Art Fees Earned				(i) 400		400		400		
Net Income			3,060	3,060	31,520	31,520	5,200	6,800	26,320	24,720
							1,600			1,600
							6,800	6,800	26,320	26,320

Net income (or net loss) is equal to the difference between the total debits and credits of the Income Statement columns. It also equals the difference between the total debits and credits of the Balance Sheet columns:

Revenues (Income Statement credit column total)	$6,800
Expenses (Income Statement debit column total)	(5,200)
Net Income	$1,600

In this case, revenues (credit column) exceed expenses (debit column). Thus, the company has a net income of $1,600. The same difference is shown between the total debits and credits of the Balance Sheet columns.

The $1,600 is entered in the debit side of the Income Statement columns to balance the columns, and it is entered in the credit side of the Balance Sheet columns to balance the columns. Remember that the excess of revenues over expenses (net income) increases stockholders' equity and that increases in stockholders' equity are recorded by credits.

When a net loss occurs, the opposite rule applies. The excess of expenses over revenues—net loss—is placed in the credit side of the Income Statement columns as a balancing figure. It is then placed in the debit side of the Balance Sheet columns because a net loss decreases stockholders' equity, and decreases in stockholders' equity are recorded by debits.

As a final check, the four columns are totaled again. If the Income Statement columns and the Balance Sheet columns do not balance, an account may have been extended or sorted to the wrong column, or an error may have been made in adding the columns. Of course, equal totals in the two pairs of columns are not absolute proof of accuracy. If an asset has been carried to the Income Statement debit column (or an expense has been carried to the Balance Sheet debit column) or a similar error with revenues or liabilities has been made, the work sheet will still balance, but the net income figure will be wrong.

USING THE WORK SHEET

The completed work sheet assists the accountant in three principal tasks: (1) recording the adjusting entries, (2) recording the closing entries in the general journal to prepare the records for the beginning of the next period, and (3) preparing the financial statements.

STUDY NOTE:
Theoretically, the adjusting entries can be recorded in the accounting records before the financial statements are prepared, or even before the work sheet itself is completed. However, they always precede the preparation of formal closing entries. It is in the preparation of formal adjusting entries that the value of identification letters becomes apparent.

■ **RECORDING THE ADJUSTING ENTRIES** For Joan Miller Advertising Agency, Inc., the adjustments were determined while completing the work sheet because they are essential to the preparation of the financial statements. The adjusting entries could have been recorded in the general journal at that point. However, in a manual system it is often convenient to delay recording the adjusting entries until after the work sheet and the financial statements have been prepared because this task can be accomplished at the same time the closing entries are recorded, a process described earlier in this chapter.

Recording the adjusting entries with appropriate explanations in the general journal, shown in Exhibit 13, is an easy step. The information can be copied from the work sheet. Adjusting entries are then posted to the general ledger.

■ **RECORDING THE CLOSING ENTRIES** The four closing entries for Joan Miller Advertising Agency, Inc., are entered in the journal and posted to the ledger, as illustrated in Exhibits 1 through 5. All accounts that need to be closed, except for the Dividends account, may be found in the Income Statement columns of the work sheet.

EXHIBIT 13
Adjustments from Work Sheet Entered in the General Journal

		General Journal			Page 3
Date		Description	Post. Ref.	Debit	Credit
20xx July	31	Rent Expense	514	800	
		Prepaid Rent	117		800
		To recognize expiration of one month's rent			
	31	Insurance Expense	515	80	
		Prepaid Insurance	118		80
		To recognize expiration of one month's insurance			
	31	Art Supplies Expense	516	500	
		Art Supplies	115		500
		To recognize art supplies used during the month			
	31	Office Supplies Expense	517	200	
		Office Supplies	116		200
		To recognize office supplies used during the month			
	31	Depreciation Expense, Art Equipment	519	70	
		Accumulated Depreciation, Art Equipment	145		70
		To record depreciation of art equipment for a month			
	31	Depreciation Expense, Office Equipment	520	50	
		Accumulated Depreciation, Office Equipment	147		50
		To record depreciation of office equipment for a month			
	31	Wages Expense	511	360	
		Wages Payable	214		360
		To accrue unrecorded wages			
	31	Income Taxes Expense	521	400	
		Income Taxes Payable	215		400
		To accrue estimated income taxes			
	31	Unearned Art Fees	213	400	
		Art Fees Earned	412		400
		To recognize performance of services paid for in advance			
	31	Accounts Receivable	113	200	
		Advertising Fees Earned	411		200
		To accrue advertising fees earned but unrecorded			

■ **PREPARING THE FINANCIAL STATEMENTS** Once the work sheet has been completed, preparing the financial statements is simple because the account balances have been sorted into Income Statement and Balance Sheet columns. The income statement in Exhibit 14 was prepared from the account balances in the Income Statement columns of Exhibit 12. The account balances for the statement of retained earnings and the balance sheet in Exhibits 15 and 16 were drawn from the Balance Sheet columns of the work sheet in Exhibit 12. Notice that the total assets and the total liabilities and

EXHIBIT 14
Income Statement for Joan Miller Advertising Agency, Inc.

Joan Miller Advertising Agency, Inc.
Income Statement
For the Month Ended July 31, 20xx

Revenues

Advertising fees earned		$6,400
Art fees earned		400
Total revenues		$6,800

Expenses

Wages expense	$2,760	
Utilities expense	200	
Telephone expense	140	
Rent expense	800	
Insurance expense	80	
Art supplies expense	500	
Office supplies expense	200	
Depreciation expense, art equipment	70	
Depreciation expense, office equipment	50	
Income taxes expense	400	
Total expenses		5,200
Net income		$1,600

stockholders' equity in the balance sheet are not the same as the totals of the Balance Sheet columns in the work sheet. The reason is that the Accumulated Depreciation and Dividends accounts have normal balances that appear in different columns from their associated accounts on the balance sheet. In addition, the Retained Earnings account on the balance sheet is the amount determined on the statement of retained earnings. At this point, the financial statements have been prepared from the work sheet, not from the ledger accounts. For the ledger accounts to show the correct balances, the adjusting entries must be journalized and posted to the ledger.

EXHIBIT 15
Statement of Retained Earnings for Joan Miller Advertising Agency, Inc.

Joan Miller Advertising Agency, Inc.
Statement of Retained Earnings
For the Month Ended July 31, 20xx

Retained earnings, July 1, 20xx	$ —
Net income	1,600
Subtotal	$1,600
Less dividends	1,400
Retained earnings, July 31, 20xx	$ 200

EXHIBIT 16
Balance Sheet for Joan Miller Advertising Agency, Inc.

Joan Miller Advertising Agency, Inc.
Balance Sheet
July 31, 20xx

Assets

Cash		$ 9,140
Accounts receivable		5,000
Art supplies		1,300
Office supplies		600
Prepaid rent		800
Prepaid insurance		880
Art equipment	$ 4,200	
Less accumulated depreciation	70	4,130
Office equipment	$ 3,000	
Less accumulated depreciation	50	2,950
Total assets		$24,800

Liabilities

Accounts payable	$ 3,240	
Unearned art fees	600	
Wages payable	360	
Income taxes payable	400	
Total liabilities		$4,600

Stockholders' Equity

Common stock	$20,000	
Retained earnings	200	
Total stockholders' equity		20,200
Total liabilities and stockholders' equity		$24,800

✓ Check out ACE for a Review Quiz at http://accounting.college.hmco.com/students.

Chapter Review

REVIEW OF LEARNING OBJECTIVES

LO1 Identify the principles of designing accounting information systems.

The developers of an accounting system must keep in mind the four principles of systems design: the cost-benefit principle, the control principle, the compatibility principle, and the flexibility principle.

LO2 State all the steps in the accounting cycle.

The steps in the accounting cycle are (1) analyze business transactions from source documents, (2) record the entries in the journal, (3) post the entries to the ledger and prepare a trial balance, (4) adjust the accounts and prepare an adjusted trial balance, (5) close the accounts and prepare a post-closing trial balance, and (6) prepare the financial statements.

LO3 Describe the use and structure of spreadsheet software and general ledger systems in computerized accounting information systems.

Most companies today have computerized accounting information systems that use spreadsheet software and general ledger systems. Spreadsheet software is used widely by accountants for analysis of data. General ledger systems are a group of integrated software programs that perform major accounting functions, such as accounting for purchases and accounts payable, sales and accounts receivable, and payroll. Some software uses icons in a graphical user interface to guide the accountant through the tasks.

LO4 Explain how accountants and businesses use the Internet.

In addition to using the Internet for access to the Web, email, and electronic bulletin boards, accountants and businesses use it for financial reporting, Extensible Business Reporting Language (XBRL), electronic commerce (ecommerce), electronic data interchange (EDI), supply-chain management, event-to-knowledge management (E2K), and document-less transactions.

LO5 Explain the purposes of closing entries and prepare required closing entries.

Closing entries have two purposes. First, they clear the balances of all temporary accounts (revenue, expense, and Dividends accounts) so that they have zero balances at the beginning of the next accounting period. Second, they summarize a period's revenues and expenses in the Income Summary account so that the net income or loss for the period can be transferred as a total to Retained Earnings. In preparing closing entries, first the revenue and expense account balances are transferred to the Income Summary account. Then the balance of the Income Summary account is transferred to the Retained Earnings account. And, finally, the balance of the Dividends account is transferred to the Retained Earnings account.

LO6 Prepare the post-closing trial balance.

As a final check on the balance of the ledger and to ensure that all temporary (nominal) accounts have been closed, a post-closing trial balance is prepared after the closing entries are posted to the ledger accounts.

SUPPLEMENTAL OBJECTIVES

SO7 Prepare reversing entries as appropriate.

Reversing entries are optional entries made on the first day of a new accounting period in order to simplify routine bookkeeping procedures. They reverse certain adjusting entries made in the previous period. Under the system used in this text, they apply only to accruals.

SO8 Prepare and use a work sheet.

There are five steps in the preparation of a work sheet: (1) Enter and total the account balances in the Trial Balance columns; (2) enter and total the adjustments in the Adjustments columns; (3) enter and total the adjusted account balances in the Adjusted Trial Balance columns; (4) extend the account balances from the Adjusted Trial Balance columns to the Income Statement or Balance Sheet columns; and (5) total the Income Statement and Balance Sheet columns, enter the net income or net loss in both pairs of columns as a balancing figure, and recompute the column totals. A work sheet is useful in (1) recording the adjusting entries, (2) recording the closing entries, and (3) preparing the financial statements. Adjusting entries can be recorded in the general journal directly from the Adjustments columns of the work sheet. Closing entries may be prepared from the Income Statement columns, except for Dividends, which is found in the Balance Sheet columns. The balance sheet and income statement can be prepared directly from the Balance Sheet and Income Statement columns of the completed work sheet. The statement of retained earnings is prepared using Dividends, net income, and the beginning balance of Retained Earnings. Notice that the ending balance of Retained Earnings does not appear on the work sheet.

REVIEW OF CONCEPTS AND TERMINOLOGY

The following concepts and terms were introduced in this chapter:

LO2 **Accounting cycle:** The sequence of steps followed in the accounting system to measure business transactions and transform them into financial statements; it includes analyzing and recording transactions, posting entries, adjusting and closing the accounts, and preparing financial statements.

LO1 **Accounting information systems:** The processes that gather data, put them into useful form, and communicate the results to management.

LO5   **Closing entries:** Journal entries made at the end of an accounting period that set the stage for the next accounting period by clearing the temporary accounts of their balances and transferring them to Retained Earnings; they summarize a period's revenues and expenses.

LO1   **Compatibility principle:** The principle that holds that the design of an accounting information system must be in harmony with the organizational and human factors of the business.

LO1   **Control principle:** The principle that holds that an accounting information system must provide all the features of internal control needed to protect the firm's assets and ensure that data are reliable.

LO1   **Cost-benefit principle:** The principle that holds that the benefits derived from an accounting information system must be equal to or greater than its cost.

SO8   **Crossfooting:** Adding and subtracting numbers across a row.

LO1   **Data processing:** The means by which an accounting information system gathers data, organizes them into useful forms, and issues the resulting information to users.

LO4   **Electronic commerce (ecommerce):** The conduct of business transactions on computer networks, including the Internet.

LO4   **Electronic Data Interchange (EDI):** Private links for conducting electronic commerce.

LO1   **Enterprise resource planning (ERP) systems:** Comprehensive, computerized information systems that integrate financial and nonfinancial information about customers, operations, and suppliers in a single database.

LO4   **Event-to-knowledge (E2K) management:** A system that uses the Internet to get information to users within and outside a company in the quickest possible way after an event like a sale or a purchase has occurred.

LO4   **Extensible Business Reporting Language (XBRL):** A new computer language developed by accountants and others for the express purpose of identifying and communicating financial information.

LO1   **Flexibility principle:** The principle that holds that an accounting information system must be flexible enough to allow for growth in the volume of transactions and for organizational changes.

LO3   **General ledger systems:** A group of integrated software programs that accountants use to perform the major accounting functions.

LO3   **Graphical user interface (GUI):** The employment of symbols, called *icons*, to represent operations, which makes software easier to use.

LO3   **Icons:** Symbols representing operations that appear on a computer screen as part of a graphical user interface.

LO5   **Income Summary:** A temporary account used during the closing process that holds a summary of all revenues and expenses before the net income or loss is transferred to the Retained Earnings account.

LO4   **Internet:** The world's largest computer network.

LO5   **Permanent accounts:** Balance sheet accounts; accounts whose balances can extend past the end of an accounting period. Also called *real accounts*.

LO6   **Post-closing trial balance:** A trial balance prepared at the end of the accounting period after all adjusting and closing entries have been posted; a final check on the balance of the ledger to ensure that all temporary accounts have zero balances and that total debits equal total credits.

SO7   **Reversing entry:** A journal entry made on the first day of a new accounting period that is the exact opposite of an adjusting entry made on the last day of the previous accounting period.

LO3   **Source documents:** The written evidence that supports each accounting transaction for each major accounting function.

LO3   **Spreadsheet:** A computerized grid of columns and rows into which the user places data or formulas related to cost estimating and other accounting tasks.

LO4   **Supply-chain management:** A system that uses the Internet to track the supplies and materials a manufacturer will need on a day-to-day basis.

LO5   **Temporary accounts:** Accounts that show the accumulation of revenues and expenses over one accounting period; at the end of the accounting period, these account balances are transferred to stockholders' equity. Also called *nominal accounts*.

SO8   **Working papers:** Documents used by accountants to organize their work and to support the information in the financial statements.

SO8   **Work sheet:** A type of working paper used as a preliminary step in recording adjusting and closing entries and in the preparation of financial statements.

REVIEW PROBLEM

Preparation of Closing Entries

LO5   At the end of the current fiscal year, the adjusted trial balance for Westwood Movers, Inc., is as follows:

Westwood Movers, Inc.		
Adjusted Trial Balance		
June 30, 20xx		
Cash	$ 14,200	
Accounts Receivable	18,600	
Packing Supplies	4,200	
Prepaid Insurance	7,900	
Land	4,000	
Building	80,000	
Accumulated Depreciation, Building		$ 7,500
Trucks	106,000	
Accumulated Depreciation, Trucks		27,500
Accounts Payable		7,650
Unearned Storage Fees		5,400
Income Taxes Payable		9,000
Mortgage Payable		70,000
Common Stock		80,000
Retained Earnings		24,740
Dividends	18,000	
Moving Services Earned		159,000
Storage Fees Earned		26,400
Driver Wages Expense	88,900	
Fuel Expense	19,000	
Wages Expense	14,400	
Packing Supplies Expense	6,200	
Office Equipment Rental Expense	3,000	
Utilities Expense	4,450	
Insurance Expense	4,200	
Interest Expense	5,100	
Depreciation Expense, Building	4,000	
Depreciation Expense, Trucks	6,040	
Income Taxes Expense	9,000	
	$417,190	$417,190

REQUIRED ▶   Prepare the necessary closing entries.

ANSWER TO REVIEW PROBLEM

Closing entries prepared

June 30	Moving Services Earned	159,000	
	Storage Fees Earned	26,400	
	Income Summary		185,400
	To close the revenue accounts		

30	Income Summary	164,290	
	Driver Wages Expense		88,900
	Fuel Expense		19,000
	Wages Expense		14,400
	Packing Supplies Expense		6,200
	Office Equipment Rental Expense		3,000
	Utilities Expense		4,450
	Insurance Expense		4,200
	Interest Expense		5,100
	Depreciation Expense, Building		4,000
	Depreciation Expense, Trucks		6,040
	Income Taxes Expense		9,000
	To close the expense accounts		

30	Income Summary	21,110	
	Retained Earnings		21,110
	To close the Income Summary account		

30	Retained Earnings	18,000	
	Dividends		18,000
	To close the Dividends account		

Chapter Assignments

BUILDING YOUR KNOWLEDGE FOUNDATION

QUESTIONS

1. What is the relationship of accounting information systems to data processing?
2. Describe the four principles of accounting information systems design.
3. Resequence the following activities **a** through **f** to indicate the correct order of the accounting cycle:

   a. The transactions are entered in the journal.
   b. The financial statements are prepared.
   c. The transactions are analyzed from the source documents.
   d. The adjusting entries are prepared.
   e. The closing entries are prepared.
   f. The transactions are posted to the ledger.

4. Why is a graphical user interface important to the successful use of general ledger systems?
5. Data are the raw material of a computer system. Trace the flow of data through the different parts of a computerized accounting information system.
6. How does a computerized accounting information system using a general ledger system relate to the major accounting functions?
7. In what ways can the Internet assist businesses in their operations?
8. What are the two purposes of closing entries?
9. What is the difference between adjusting entries and closing entries?
10. What is the purpose of the Income Summary account?

11. Which of the following accounts do not show a balance after the closing entries are prepared and posted?

a. Insurance Expense   e. Dividends
b. Accounts Receivable   f. Supplies
c. Commission Revenue   g. Supplies Expense
d. Prepaid Insurance   h. Retained Earnings

12. What is the significance of the post-closing trial balance?

13. Which of the following accounts would you expect to find in the post-closing trial balance?

a. Insurance Expense   e. Dividends
b. Accounts Receivable   f. Supplies
c. Commission Revenue   g. Supplies Expense
d. Prepaid Insurance   h. Retained Earnings

14. How do reversing entries simplify the bookkeeping process?

15. To what types of adjustments do reversing entries apply? To what types do they not apply?

16. Why are working papers important to accountants?

17. Why are work sheets never published and rarely seen by management?

18. Can the work sheet be used as a substitute for the financial statements? Explain your answer.

19. What is the normal balance (debit or credit) of the following accounts?

a. Cash   f. Dividends
b. Accounts Payable   g. Rent Expense
c. Prepaid Rent   h. Accumulated Depreciation, Office Equipment
d. Common Stock   i. Office Equipment
e. Commission Revenue

20. Why should the Adjusted Trial Balance columns of the work sheet be totaled before the adjusted amounts are carried to the Income Statement and Balance Sheet columns?

21. What sequence should be followed in extending the amounts in the Adjusted Trial Balance columns to the Income Statement and Balance Sheet columns? Discuss your answer.

22. Do the Income Statement columns and the Balance Sheet columns of the work sheet balance after the amounts from the Adjusted Trial Balance columns are extended?

23. Do the totals of the Balance Sheet columns of the work sheet agree with the totals on the balance sheet? Explain your answer.

24. Should adjusting entries be posted to the ledger accounts before or after the closing entries? Explain your answer.

25. At the end of the accounting period, does the posting of adjusting entries to the ledger precede or follow the preparation of the work sheet?

Short Exercises

SE 1.

LO1 Principles of Accounting Information System Design

Indicate whether each of the following statements concerning a newly installed accounting information system is most closely related to the (a) cost-benefit principle, (b) control principle, (c) compatibility principle, or (d) flexibility principle:

1. Procedures are in place to ensure that the data entered into the accounting information system are reliable.
2. The system allows for growth in the number and types of transactions entered into by the company.
3. The system was installed after its costs were carefully weighed against the improved decision making that will result.
4. The system takes into account the various operations of the business and the capabilities of the people who will interact with the system.

LO2 Accounting Cycle

SE 2. Resequence the following activities to indicate the usual order of the accounting cycle:

  a. Close the accounts. 7
  b. Analyze the transactions. 1
  c. Post the entries to the ledger. 3
  d. Prepare the financial statements. 8
  e. Adjust the accounts. 5
  f. Record the transactions in the journal. 2
  g. Prepare the post-closing trial balance. 9
  h. Prepare the initial trial balance. 4
  i. Prepare the adjusted trial balance. 6

LO3 Microcomputer Accounting Information System

SE 3. Assuming that a company uses a general ledger package for its microcomputer accounting information system, indicate whether each of the following source documents would provide input to (a) sales/accounts receivable, (b) purchases/accounts payable, (c) cash receipts, (d) cash disbursements, (e) payroll, or (f) the general journal:

  1. Deposit slips c
  2. Time cards e
  3. Vendor invoices b
  4. Checks issued d
  5. Customer invoices a
  6. Documents for other journal entries f

LO4 Use of the Internet

SE 4. Define and contrast the following uses of the Internet:

  1. Electronic commerce (ecommerce) i business
  2. Electronic Data Interchange (EDI) ecomerce
  3. Supply-chain management

LO5 Closing Revenue and Expense Accounts

SE 5. Assume that at the end of the accounting period there are credit balances of $3,400 in Patient Services Revenues and $1,800 in Laboratory Fees Revenues and debit balances of $1,400 in Rent Expense, $1,100 in Wages Expense, and $500 in Other Expenses. Prepare the required entries to close the revenue and expense accounts. The accounting period ends December 31.

LO5 Closing the Income Summary Account

SE 6. Assuming that total revenues were $5,200 and total expenses were $3,000, prepare the entry in journal form to close the Income Summary account. The accounting period ends December 31. 2200

LO5 Closing the Dividends Account

SE 7. Assuming that dividends during the accounting period were $800, prepare the entry in journal form to close the Dividends account. The accounting period ends December 31.

LO5 Posting Closing Entries

SE 8. Show the effects of the transactions in SE 5, SE 6, and SE 7 by entering beginning balances in appropriate T accounts and recording the transactions. Assume that Retained Earnings has a beginning balance of $1,300.

SO7 Preparation of Reversing Entries

SE 9. Below, indicated by letters, are the adjusting entries at the end of March.

Account Name	Debit	Credit
Prepaid Insurance		(a) 180
Accumulated Depreciation, Office Equipment		(b) 1,050
Salaries Expense	(c) 360	
Insurance Expense	(a) 180	
Depreciation Expense, Office Equipment	(b) 1,050	
Salaries Payable		(c) 360
Income Taxes Expense	(d) 470	
Income Taxes Payable		(d) 470
	2,060	2,060

Prepare the required reversing entries.

SE 10.

LO5 Preparing Closing Entries from
SO8 a Work Sheet

Prepare the required closing entries for the year ended December 31, using the following items from the Income Statement columns of a work sheet and assuming that dividends were $6,000:

	Income Statement	
Account Name	Debit	Credit
Repair Revenue		36,860
Wages Expense	12,260	
Rent Expense	1,800	
Supplies Expense	6,390	
Insurance Expense	1,370	
Depreciation Expense, Repair Equipment	2,020	
Income Taxes Expense	4,000	
	27,840	36,860
Net Income	9,020	
	36,860	36,860

EXERCISES

E 1.

LO5 Preparation of Closing Entries

The adjusted trial balance for the Phoenix Consultant Corporation at the end of its fiscal year is shown below. Prepare the required closing entries.

Phoenix Consultant Corporation
Adjusted Trial Balance
December 31, 20xx

Cash	$ 7,275	
Accounts Receivable	2,325	
Prepaid Insurance	585	
Office Supplies	440	
Office Equipment	6,300	
Accumulated Depreciation, Office Equipment		$ 765
Automobile	6,750	
Accumulated Depreciation, Automobile		750
Accounts Payable		1,700
Unearned Consulting Fees		1,500
Income Taxes Payable		3,000
Common Stock		10,000
Retained Earnings		4,535
Dividends	7,000	
Consulting Fees Earned		31,700
Office Salaries Expense	13,500	
Advertising Expense	2,525	
Rent Expense	2,650	
Telephone Expense	1,600	
Income Taxes Expense	3,000	
	$53,950	$53,950

E 2.

SO8 **Preparation of a Statement of Retained Earnings**

The Retained Earnings, Dividends, and Income Summary accounts for Lou's Hair Salon, Inc., are shown in T account form below. The closing entries have been recorded for the year ended December 31, 20x3.

Retained Earnings					Income Summary			
12/31/x3	9,000	12/31/x2	26,000		12/31/x3	43,000	12/31/x3	62,000
		12/31/x3	19,000		12/31/x3	19,000		
		Bal.	36,000		Bal.	—		

Dividends			
4/1/x3	3,000	12/31/x3	9,000
7/1/x3	3,000		
10/1/x3	3,000		
Bal.	—		

Prepare a statement of retained earnings for Lou's Hair Salon, Inc.

E 3.

SO7 **Reversing Entries**

Selected T accounts for Pilar Corporation are presented below.

Supplies					Supplies Expense			
12/1 Bal.	430	12/31 Adjust.	640		12/31 Adjust.	640	12/31 Closing	640
Dec. purchases	470				Bal.	—		
Bal.	260							

Wages Payable					Wages Expense			
		12/31 Adjust.	320		Dec. wages	1,970	12/31 Closing	2,290
		Bal.	320		12/31 Adjust.	320		
					Bal.	—		

1. In which of the accounts would a reversing entry be helpful? Why?
2. Prepare the appropriate reversing entry.
3. Prepare the entry to record a payment on January 5 for wages totaling $1,570. How much of this amount represents wages expense for January?

E 4.

SO8 **Preparation of a Trial Balance**

The following alphabetical list presents the accounts and balances for Results Realty, Inc., on December 31, 20xx. All the accounts have normal balances.

Accounts Payable	$ 5,140
Accounts Receivable	2,550
Accumulated Depreciation, Office Equipment	450
Advertising Expense	600
Cash	2,545
Common Stock	5,000
Dividends	9,000
Office Equipment	5,170
Prepaid Insurance	560
Rent Expense	2,400
Retained Earnings	5,210
Revenue from Commissions	19,300
Supplies	275
Wages Expense	12,000

Prepare the trial balance by listing the accounts in the correct order for work sheet preparation, with the balances in the appropriate debit or credit column.

E 5.

SO8 **Completion of a Work Sheet**

The following is a highly simplified alphabetical list of trial balance accounts and their normal balances for the month ended October 31, 20xx:

Trial Balance Accounts and Balances

Accounts Payable	$ 4	Prepaid Insurance	$ 2
Accounts Receivable	7	Retained Earnings	7
Accumulated Depreciation,		Service Revenue	23
Office Equipment	1	Supplies	4
Cash	4	Unearned Revenues	3
Common Stock	5	Utilities Expense	2
Dividends	6	Wages Expense	10
Office Equipment	8		

1. Prepare a work sheet, entering the trial balance accounts in the order in which they would normally appear and entering the balances in the correct debit or credit column.
2. Complete the work sheet using the following information:

   a. Expired insurance, $1.
   b. Of the unearned revenues balance, $2 has been earned by the end of the month.
   c. Estimated depreciation on office equipment, $1.
   d. Accrued wages, $1.
   e. Unused supplies on hand, $1.
   f. Estimated federal income taxes, $1.

E 6.

SO8 **Derivation of Adjusting Entries and Preparation of a Balance Sheet**

Below is a partial work sheet of Song Corporation at June 30, 20x3, in which the Trial Balance and Income Statement columns have been completed. All amounts shown are in dollars.

Account Name	Trial Balance Debit	Trial Balance Credit	Income Statement Debit	Income Statement Credit
Cash	8			
Accounts Receivable	12			
Supplies	11			
Prepaid Insurance	8			
Building	25			
Accumulated Depreciation, Building		8		
Accounts Payable		4		
Unearned Revenues		2		
Common Stock		20		
Retained Earnings		12		
Revenues		45		47
Wages Expense	27		30	
	91	91		
Insurance Expense			4	
Supplies Expense			8	
Depreciation Expense, Building			2	
Wages Payable				
Income Taxes Expense			1	
Income Taxes Payable				
			45	47
Net Income			2	
			47	47

1. Show the adjustments that have been made in journal form without explanation.
2. Prepare a balance sheet.

E 7.

SO7 **Preparation of Adjusting and**
SO8 **Reversing Entries from Work Sheet Columns**

The items that appears below are from the Adjustments columns of a work sheet dated June 30, 20xx.

Account Name	Adjustments	
	Debit	Credit
Prepaid Insurance		(a) 120
Office Supplies		(b) 315
Accumulated Depreciation, Office Equipment		(c) 700
Accumulated Depreciation, Store Equipment		(d) 1,100
Office Salaries Expense	(e) 120	
Store Salaries Expense	(e) 240	
Insurance Expense	(a) 120	
Office Supplies Expense	(b) 315	
Depreciation Expense, Office Equipment	(c) 700	
Depreciation Expense, Store Equipment	(d) 1,100	
Salaries Payable		(e) 360
Income Taxes Expense	(f) 400	
Income Taxes Payable		(f) 400
	2,995	2,995

1. Prepare the adjusting entries.
2. Where required, prepare appropriate reversing entries

E 8.

LO5 **Preparation of Closing Entries**
SO8 **from the Work Sheet**

The items below are from the Income Statement columns of the work sheet for Best Repair Shop, Inc., for the year ended December 31, 20xx.

Account Name	Income Statement	
	Debit	Credit
Repair Revenue		25,620
Wages Expense	8,110	
Rent Expense	1,200	
Supplies Expense	4,260	
Insurance Expense	915	
Depreciation Expense, Repair Equipment	1,345	
Income Taxes Expense	1,000	
	16,830	25,620
Net Income	8,790	
	25,620	25,620

Prepare entries to close the revenue, expense, Income Summary, and Dividends accounts. Dividends of $5,000 were paid during the year.

PROBLEMS

P 1.

LO5   Closing Entries Using T Accounts and Preparation of Financial Statements

The adjusted trial balance for Salonga Tennis Club, Inc., at the end of the company's fiscal year appears below.

Salonga Tennis Club, Inc.
Adjusted Trial Balance
June 30, 20x5

Cash	$ 26,200	
Prepaid Advertising	9,600	
Supplies	1,200	
Land	100,000	
Building	645,200	
Accumulated Depreciation, Building		$ 260,000
Equipment	156,000	
Accumulated Depreciation, Equipment		50,400
Accounts Payable		73,000
Wages Payable		9,000
Property Taxes Payable		22,500
Unearned Revenues, Locker Fees		3,000
Income Taxes Payable		20,000
Common Stock		200,000
Retained Earnings		271,150
Dividends	54,000	
Revenues from Court Fees		678,100
Revenues from Locker Fees		9,600
Wages Expense	351,000	
Maintenance Expense	51,600	
Advertising Expense	39,750	
Utilities Expense	64,800	
Supplies Expense	6,000	
Depreciation Expense, Building	30,000	
Depreciation Expense, Equipment	12,000	
Property Taxes Expense	22,500	
Miscellaneous Expense	6,900	
Income Taxes Expense	20,000	
	$1,596,750	$1,596,750

REQUIRED ▶

1. Prepare T accounts and enter the balances for Retained Earnings, Dividends, Income Summary, and all revenue and expense accounts.
2. Enter the four required closing entries in the T accounts, labeling the components *a*, *b*, *c*, and *d*, as appropriate.
3. Prepare an income statement, a statement of retained earnings, and a balance sheet for Salonga Tennis Club, Inc.
4. Explain why closing entries are necessary at the end of the accounting period.

P 2.

LO5   Closing Entries Using Journal Form and Preparation of Financial Statements

Mountain Campgrounds, Inc., rents out campsites in a wooded park. The adjusted trial balance for Mountain Campgrounds on March 31, 20x5, the end of the current fiscal year, appears at the top of the next page:

REQUIRED ▶

1. Record the closing entries in journal form.
2. From the information given, prepare an income statement, a statement of retained earnings, and a balance sheet.

Mountain Campgrounds, Inc.
Adjusted Trial Balance
March 31, 20x5

Cash	$ 4,080	
Accounts Receivable	7,320	
Supplies	228	
Prepaid Insurance	1,188	
Land	30,000	
Building	91,800	
Accumulated Depreciation, Building		$ 21,000
Accounts Payable		3,450
Wages Payable		1,650
Income Taxes Payable		10,000
Common Stock		40,000
Retained Earnings		53,070
Dividends	36,000	
Campsite Rentals		88,200
Wages Expense	23,850	
Insurance Expense	3,784	
Utilities Expense	1,800	
Supplies Expense	1,320	
Depreciation Expense, Building	6,000	
Income Taxes Expense	10,000	
	$217,370	$217,370

P 3.

LO2 The Complete Accounting
LO5 Cycle Without a Work Sheet:
LO6 Two Months (second month optional)

On May 1, 20xx, Julio Mineta opened Julio's Repair Service, Inc. During the month, he completed the following transactions for the company:

May 1 Began business by depositing $5,000 in a bank account in the name of the company in exchange for 500 shares of $10 par value common stock.
1 Paid the rent for a store for current month, $425.
1 Paid the premium on a one-year insurance policy, $480.
2 Purchased repair equipment from Doone Company, $4,200. Terms were $600 down and $300 per month for one year. First payment is due June 1.
5 Purchased repair supplies from BXE Company on credit, $468.
8 Paid cash for an advertisement in a local newspaper, $60.
15 Received cash repair revenue for the first half of the month, $400.
21 Paid BXE Company on account, $225.
31 Received cash repair revenue for the second half of May, $975.
31 Declared and paid a cash dividend, $300.

REQUIRED FOR MAY ▶

1. Prepare journal entries to record the May transactions.
2. Open the following accounts: Cash (111); Prepaid Insurance (117); Repair Supplies (119); Repair Equipment (144); Accumulated Depreciation, Repair Equipment (145); Accounts Payable (212); Income Taxes Payable (213); Common Stock (311); Retained Earnings (312); Dividends (313); Income Summary (314); Repair Revenue (411); Store Rent Expense (511); Advertising Expense (512); Insurance Expense (513); Repair Supplies Expense (514); Depreciation Expense, Repair Equipment (515); and Income Taxes Expense (516). Post the May journal entries to the ledger accounts.
3. Using the following information, record adjusting entries in the general journal and post to the ledger accounts:
   a. One month's insurance has expired.
   b. The remaining inventory of unused repair supplies is $169.
   c. The estimated depreciation on repair equipment is $70.
   d. Estimated income taxes are $50.
4. From the accounts in the ledger, prepare an adjusted trial balance. (*Note:* Normally a trial balance is prepared before adjustments but is omitted here to save time.)

5. From the adjusted trial balance, prepare an income statement, a statement of retained earnings, and a balance sheet for May.
6. Prepare and post closing entries.
7. Prepare a post-closing trial balance.

(Optional) During June, Julio Mineta completed these transactions for Julio's Repair Service, Inc.:

June 1 Paid the monthly rent, $425.
   1 Made the monthly payment to Doone Company, $300.
   6 Purchased additional repair supplies on credit from BXE Company, $863.
  15 Received cash repair revenue for the first half of the month, $914.
  20 Paid cash for an advertisement in the local newspaper, $60.
  23 Paid BXE Company on account, $600.
  30 Received cash repair revenue for the last half of the month, $817.
  30 Declared and paid a cash dividend, $300.

REQUIRED FOR JUNE ▶

8. Prepare and post journal entries to record the June transactions.
9. Using the following information, record adjusting entries in the general journal and post to the ledger accounts:
   a. One month's insurance has expired.
   b. The inventory of unused repair supplies is $413.
   c. The estimated depreciation on repair equipment is $70.
   d. Estimated income taxes are $50.
10. From the accounts in the ledger, prepare an adjusted trial balance.
11. From the adjusted trial balance, prepare the June income statement, statement of retained earnings, and balance sheet.
12. Prepare and post closing entries.
13. Prepare a post-closing trial balance.

P 4.

LO5   Preparation of a Work Sheet,
SO7   Financial Statements, and
SO8   Adjusting, Closing, and
Reversing Entries

This was Berensonia Theater Corporation's trial balance at the end of its current fiscal year:

Berensonia Theater Corporation Trial Balance June 30, 20x4		
Cash	$ 31,800	
Accounts Receivable	18,544	
Prepaid Insurance	19,600	
Office Supplies	780	
Cleaning Supplies	3,590	
Land	20,000	
Building	400,000	
Accumulated Depreciation, Building		$ 39,400
Theater Furnishings	370,000	
Accumulated Depreciation, Theater Furnishings		65,000
Office Equipment	31,600	
Accumulated Depreciation, Office Equipment		15,560
Accounts Payable		45,506
Gift Books Liability		41,900
Mortgage Payable		300,000
Common Stock		200,000
Retained Earnings		112,648
Dividends	60,000	
Ticket Sales Revenue		411,400
Theater Rental Revenue		45,200
Usher Wages Expense	157,000	
Office Wages Expense	24,000	
Utilities Expense	112,700	
Interest Expense	27,000	
	$1,276,614	$1,276,614

REQUIRED ▶ 1. Enter the trial balance amounts in the Trial Balance columns of a work sheet and complete the work sheet using the following information:

    a. Expired insurance, $17,400.
    b. Inventory of unused office supplies, $244.
    c. Inventory of unused cleaning supplies, $468.
    d. Estimated depreciation on the building, $14,000.
    e. Estimated depreciation on the theater furnishings, $36,000.
    f. Estimated depreciation on the office equipment, $3,160.
    g. The company credits all gift books sold during the year to the Gift Books Liability account. A gift book is a booklet of ticket coupons that is purchased in advance as a gift. The recipient redeems the coupons at some point in the future. On June 30 it was estimated that $37,800 worth of the gift books had been redeemed.
    h. Accrued but unpaid usher wages at the end of the accounting period, $860.
    i. Estimated federal income taxes, $20,000.

2. Prepare an income statement, a statement of retained earnings, and a balance sheet.
3. Prepare adjusting, closing, and, if required, reversing entries.

P 5.

LO5 Preparation of a Work Sheet,
SO7 Financial Statements, and
SO8 Adjusting, Closing, and Reversing Entries

The following trial balance was taken from the ledger of Wicker Package Delivery Corporation on August 31, 20x4, the end of the company's fiscal year:

Wicker Package Delivery Corporation
Trial Balance
August 31, 20x4

Cash	$ 5,036	
Accounts Receivable	14,657	
Prepaid Insurance	2,670	
Delivery Supplies	7,350	
Office Supplies	1,230	
Land	7,500	
Building	98,000	
Accumulated Depreciation, Building		$ 26,700
Trucks	51,900	
Accumulated Depreciation, Trucks		15,450
Office Equipment	7,950	
Accumulated Depreciation, Office Equipment		5,400
Accounts Payable		4,698
Unearned Lockbox Fees		4,170
Mortgage Payable		36,000
Common Stock		20,000
Retained Earnings		44,365
Dividends	15,000	
Delivery Services Revenue		141,735
Lockbox Fees Earned		14,400
Truck Drivers' Wages Expense	63,900	
Office Salaries Expense	22,200	
Gas, Oil, and Truck Repairs Expense	15,525	
	$312,918	$312,918

REQUIRED ▶ 1. Enter the trial balance amounts in the Trial Balance columns of a work sheet and complete the work sheet using the following information:

    a. Expired insurance, $1,530.
    b. Inventory of unused delivery supplies, $715.
    c. Inventory of unused office supplies, $93.
    d. Estimated depreciation, building, $7,200.
    e. Estimated depreciation, trucks, $7,725.
    f. Estimated depreciation, office equipment, $1,350.

g. The company credits the lockbox fees of customers who pay in advance to the Unearned Lockbox Fees account. Of the amount credited to this account during the year, $2,815 had been earned by August 31.

h. Lockbox fees earned but unrecorded and uncollected at the end of the accounting period, $408.

i. Accrued but unpaid truck drivers' wages at the end of the year, $960.

j. Management estimates federal income taxes to be $6,000.

2. Prepare an income statement, a statement of retained earnings, and a balance sheet.

3. Prepare adjusting, closing, and, if required, reversing entries.

ALTERNATE PROBLEMS

P 6.

LO5   Closing Entries Using T Accounts and Preparation of Financial Statements

The adjusted trial balance for Eagle Bowling Lanes, Inc., at the end of the company's fiscal year is as follows:

Eagle Bowling Lanes, Inc.
Adjusted Trial Balance
December 31, 20x4

Cash	$ 16,214	
Accounts Receivable	7,388	
Supplies	156	
Prepaid Insurance	300	
Land	5,000	
Building	100,000	
Accumulated Depreciation, Building		$ 27,200
Equipment	125,000	
Accumulated Depreciation, Equipment		33,000
Accounts Payable		15,044
Notes Payable		70,000
Unearned Revenues		300
Wages Payable		3,962
Property Taxes Payable		10,000
Income Taxes Payable		15,000
Common Stock		20,000
Retained Earnings		40,813
Dividends	24,000	
Revenues		618,263
Wages Expense	381,076	
Advertising Expense	15,200	
Maintenance Expense	84,100	
Supplies Expense	1,148	
Insurance Expense	1,500	
Depreciation Expense, Building	4,800	
Depreciation Expense, Equipment	11,000	
Utilities Expense	42,200	
Miscellaneous Expense	9,500	
Property Taxes Expense	10,000	
Income Taxes Expense	15,000	
	$853,582	$853,582

REQUIRED ▶

1. Prepare T accounts and enter the balances for Retained Earnings, Dividends, Income Summary, and all revenue and expense accounts.

2. Enter in the T accounts the four required closing entries, labeling the components *a*, *b*, *c*, and *d* as appropriate.

3. Prepare an income statement, a statement of retained earnings, and a balance sheet.

4. Explain why closing entries are necessary at the end of the accounting period.

P 7.

LO5 Closing Entries Using Journal Form and Preparation of Financial Statements

Your Move Trailer Rental, Inc., owns 30 small trailers that it rents by the day for local moving jobs. This is its adjusted trial balance at the end of the current fiscal year:

Your Move Trailer Rental, Inc.
Adjusted Trial Balance
June 30, 20x4

Cash	$ 692	
Accounts Receivable	972	
Supplies	119	
Prepaid Insurance	360	
Trailers	12,000	
Accumulated Depreciation, Trailers		$ 7,200
Accounts Payable		271
Wages Payable		200
Income Taxes Payable		2,000
Common Stock		1,000
Retained Earnings		4,694
Dividends	7,200	
Trailer Rentals Revenue		45,546
Wages Expense	23,400	
Insurance Expense	720	
Supplies Expense	266	
Depreciation Expense, Trailers	2,400	
Other Expenses	10,782	
Income Taxes Expense	2,000	
	$60,911	$60,911

REQUIRED ▶

1. From the information given, record closing entries in journal form.
2. Prepare an income statement, a statement of retained earnings, and a balance sheet.

P 8.

LO5 Preparation of a Work Sheet,
SO7 Financial Statements, and
SO8 Adjusting, Closing, and Reversing Entries

Kayla Sharpe began her consulting practice just after earning her MBA. To help her get started, several clients paid her retainers (payments in advance) for future services. Others paid when service was provided. Here is the firm's trial balance after one year:

Kayla Sharpe Consultant, Inc.
Trial Balance
June 30, 20x3

Cash	$ 9,750	
Accounts Receivable	8,127	
Office Supplies	1,146	
Office Equipment	11,265	
Accounts Payable		$ 3,888
Unearned Retainers		15,000
Common Stock		12,000
Dividends	18,000	
Consulting Fees		54,525
Rent Expense	5,400	
Utilities Expense	2,151	
Wages Expense	29,574	
	$85,413	$85,413

REQUIRED ▶ 1. Enter the trial balance amounts in the Trial Balance columns of a work sheet. Remember that accumulated depreciation is listed with its asset account. Complete the work sheet using the following information:

    a. Inventory of unused office supplies, $174.
    b. Estimated depreciation on office equipment, $1,800.
    c. Services rendered during the month but not yet billed, $2,175.
    d. Services rendered that should be applied against unearned retainers, $9,450.
    e. Wages earned by employees but not yet paid, $360.
    f. Estimated income taxes for the year, $3,000.

2. Prepare an income statement, a statement of retained earnings, and a balance sheet.
3. Prepare adjusting, closing, and, if required, reversing entries.
4. How would you evaluate Kayla Sharpe's first year in practice?

SKILLS DEVELOPMENT CASES

Conceptual Analysis

SD 1.
LO2 Interim Financial Statements

Ocean Oil Services Corporation provides services for drilling operations off the coast of Louisiana. The company has a significant amount of debt to River National Bank in Baton Rouge. The bank requires the company to provide it with quarterly financial statements. Explain what is involved in preparing financial statements every quarter.

SD 2.
SO7 Accounting Efficiency

Way Heaters, Inc., located just outside Milwaukee, Wisconsin, is a small, successful manufacturer of industrial heaters, which candy manufacturers use to heat chocolate. The company sells its heaters to some of its customers on credit with generous terms. The terms usually specify payment six months after purchase and an interest rate based on current bank rates. Because the interest on the loans accrues a little bit every day but is not paid until the due date of the note, it is necessary to make an adjusting entry at the end of each accounting period to debit Interest Receivable and credit Interest Income for the amount of the interest accrued but not paid to date. The company prepares financial statements every month. Keeping track of what has been accrued in the past is time-consuming because the notes carry different dates and interest rates. Discuss what the accountant can do to simplify the process of making the adjusting entry for accrued interest each month.

Ethical Dilemma

SD 3.
LO2 Ethics and Time Pressure

Jay Wheeler, an accountant for WB, Inc., has made adjusting entries and is preparing the adjusted trial balance for the first six months of the year. Financial statements must be delivered to the bank by 5 P.M. to support a critical loan agreement. By noon, Wheeler has been unable to balance the adjusted trial balance. The figures are off by $1,320, so he increases the balance of the Retained Earnings account by $1,320. He closes the accounts, prepares the statements, and sends them to the bank on time. Wheeler hopes that no one will notice the problem and believes that he can find the error and correct it by the end of next month. Are Wheeler's actions ethical? Why or why not? Did he have other alternatives?

Research Activity

SD 4.
LO2 Interview of a Local
LO5 Businessperson
LO6
SO7
SO8

Arrange to spend about an hour interviewing the owner, manager, or accountant of a local service or retail business. Your goal is to learn as much as you can about the accounting cycle of the person's business. Ask the interviewee to show you his or her accounting records and to tell you how such transactions as sales, purchases, payments, and payroll are handled. Examine the documents used to support the transactions. Look at any journals, ledgers, or work sheets. Does the business use a computer? Does it use its own accounting system, or does it use an outside or centralized service? Does it use the cash or the accrual basis of accounting? When does it prepare adjusting entries? When does it prepare closing entries? How often does it prepare financial statements? Does it prepare reversing entries? How do its procedures differ from those described in the text? When the interview is finished, organize and write up your findings and be prepared to present them in class.

 Group Activity: Divide the class into groups and have each group investigate a different type of business, such as a shoe store, grocery store, hardware store, and fast-food restaurant. Have the groups give presentations in class.

Decision-Making Practice

SD 5.

LO2 Conversion from Accrual to Cash Statement

Adele's Secretarial Service, Inc., provides word processing services for students at the local university. Adele's accountant prepared the income statement that appears below for the year ended June 30, 20x4.

Adele's Secretarial Service, Inc.
Income Statement
For the Year Ended June 30, 20x4

Revenues		
Word processing services		$20,980
Expenses		
Rent expense	$2,400	
Depreciation expense, office equipment	2,200	
Supplies expense	960	
Other expenses	1,240	
Total expenses		6,800
Net income		$14,180

In reviewing this statement, Adele is puzzled. She knows the company paid cash dividends of $15,600 to her, the sole stockholder, yet the cash balance in the company's bank account increased from $460 to $3,100 from last June 30 to this June 30. She wants to know how her net income could be less than the cash dividends she took out of the business if there is an increase in the cash balance.

Her accountant has completed the closing entries and shows her the balance sheets for June 30, 20x4, and June 30, 20x3. The accountant explains that besides the change in the cash balance, Accounts Receivable decreased by $1,480 and Accounts Payable increased by $380 (supplies are the only items Adele buys on credit). The only other asset or liability account that changed during the year was Accumulated Depreciation, Office Equipment, which increased by $2,200.

1. Verify the cash balance increase by preparing a statement that lists the receipts of cash and the expenditures of cash during the year.
2. Write a memorandum to Adele explaining why the accountant is pointing out year-to-year changes in the balance sheet. Include an explanation of your treatment of depreciation expense, giving your reasons for the treatment.

FINANCIAL REPORTING AND ANALYSIS CASES

Interpreting Financial Reports

FRA 1.

LO5 Closing Entries

H&R Block, Inc., <www.hrblock.com> is the world's largest tax preparation service firm. Adapted information from the statement of earnings (in thousands, without earnings per share information) in its annual report for the year ended April 30, 2000, is shown on the next page.[6]

Revenues	
Service revenues	$2,451,943
Other revenues	10,178
Total revenues	$2,462,121
Expenses	
Employee compensation and benefits	$ 963,536
Occupancy and equipment expense	253,171
Depreciation expense	147,218
Marketing and advertising expense	140,683
Supplies, freight, and postage expense	64,599
Interest expense	155,027
Other operating expenses	325,621
Total expenses	$2,049,855
Earnings before income taxes	$ 412,266
Income taxes	160,371
Net earnings	$ 251,895

In its statement of retained earnings, the company reported cash dividends in the amount of $108,374,000 to the owners in 2000.

REQUIRED ▶

1. Prepare, in journal form, the closing entries that H&R Block would have made on April 30, 2000.
2. Based on the way you handled expenses and cash distributions in step 1 and their ultimate effect on stockholders' equity, what theoretical reason can you give for not including expenses and cash distributions in the same closing entry?

FRA 2.
LO4   Uses of the Internet

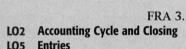

Baxter International <www.baxter.com> is one of the largest and most successful pharmaceutical companies in the world. Its annual sales are more than $8 billion. One of the company's goals is to use the Internet as much as possible to improve the efficiency of its operations. In what ways do you think Baxter International may be using the Internet in its operations?

International Company

FRA 3.
LO2   Accounting Cycle and Closing
LO5   Entries

Nestlé S.A. <www.nestle.com>, maker of such well-known products as Nescafé, Lean Cuisine, and Perrier, is one of the largest and most internationally diverse companies in the world. Only 2 percent of its $81.4 billion in revenues comes from its home country of Switzerland; the rest comes from sales in almost every other country of the world. Nestlé has over 224,000 employees in 70 countries and is highly decentralized; that is, many of its divisions operate as separate companies.[7] Managing the accounting operations of such a vast empire is a tremendous challenge. In what ways do you think the accounting cycle, including the closing process, would be the same for Nestlé as it is for Joan Miller Advertising Agency, Inc., and in what ways would it be different?

Toys "R" Us Annual Report

FRA 4.
LO2   Fiscal Year, Closing Process,
and Interim Reports

Refer to the notes to the financial statements in the Toys "R" Us <www.tru.com> annual report. When does Toys "R" Us end its fiscal year? What reasons can you give for the company's having chosen this date? From the standpoint of completing the accounting cycle, what advantages does this date have? Does Toys "R" Us prepare interim financial statements? What are the implications of interim financial statements for the accounting cycle?

Comparison Case: Toys "R" Us and Walgreen Co.

FRA 5.

LO5   Interim Financial Reporting and Seasonality

As does Hershey Foods <www.hersheys.com> in the opening Decision Point, both Walgreens <www.walgreens.com> and Toys "R" Us <www.tru.com> provide quarterly financial information at the end of their notes to the financial statements. Quarterly financial reports provide important information about the "seasonality" of a company's operations. *Seasonality* refers to how dependent a company is on sales during one season of the year, such as the Christmas season, and it affects a company's need to plan for cash flows and inventory. From the quarterly financial information for Walgreens and for Toys "R" Us in the Supplement to Chapter 1, determine which company has more seasonal sales and income by calculating for the most recent year the percentage of annual totals of net sales and net earnings. Discuss the results.

Fingraph® Financial Analyst™

This activity is not applicable to this chapter.

Internet Case

FRA 6.

LO1   Enterprise Resource Planning
LO3   (ERP) Systems

We defined enterprise resource planning (ERP) systems as comprehensive, computerized information systems that integrate financial and nonfinancial information about customers, operations, and suppliers in a single database." Explore further what this concept means by visiting the web site of a company that produces ERP software, such as SAP <www.sap.com>, PeopleSoft <www.peoplesoft.com>, or iBAAN <www.baan.pl>. After accessing one of these web sites, find out what products the company offers and explain how these products relate to the definition of ERP. In addition to financial systems, what other business functions are included in ERP? Take notes and be prepared to discuss your findings in class.

5

Chapter 5 introduces the objectives and qualitative aspects of financial information and demonstrates how much more useful classified financial statements are than simple financial statements in presenting information to statement users.

Financial Reporting and Analysis

LEARNING OBJECTIVES

LO1 State the objectives of financial reporting.

LO2 State the qualitative characteristics of accounting information and describe their interrelationships.

LO3 Define and describe the conventions of *comparability* and *consistency, materiality, conservatism, full disclosure,* and *cost-benefit.*

LO4 Explain management's responsibility for ethical financial reporting and define *fraudulent financial reporting.*

LO5 Identify and describe the basic components of a classified balance sheet.

LO6 Prepare multistep and single-step classified income statements.

LO7 Evaluate liquidity and profitability using classified financial statements.

DECISION POINT
A USER'S FOCUS

General Mills, Inc. <www.generalmills.com> The management of a corporation is judged by the company's financial performance. Financial performance is reported to stockholders and others outside the business in the company's annual report, which includes the financial statements and other relevant information. Performance measures are usually based on the relationships of key data in the financial statements. For large companies, this often means condensing a tremendous amount of information to a few numbers that management considers important. For example, what key measures does the management of General Mills, Inc., a successful food products company that recently acquired its long-time rival Pillsbury and offers such well-known brands as Cheerios, Wheaties, Hamburger Helper, and Progresso Soups, choose to focus on as its goals?

In its letter to shareholders, General Mills states its financial goals as follows:

> Our target is 7 percent compound annual sales growth between now and 2010. With this faster topline growth, ... our Earnings Per Share (EPS) growth should accelerate, too. Our target is to deliver 11 to 15 percent annual earnings per share growth over the balance of this decade. We believe achieving these goals will represent superior performance when benchmarked against major consumer products companies.[1]

General Mills' management has thus set forth measurable performance goals by which it can be evaluated. The graph on the opposite page shows that the company reached its growth in sales target in only

What key performance measures does the management of General Mills choose to focus on as its goals?

one of the past three years. However, it reached its growth in EPS in all three years.

Of course, investors and creditors will want to do their own analysis of General Mills. This will require reading and interpreting the financial statements and calculating other ratios. However, the analysis will be meaningless unless the reader understands financial statements and generally accepted accounting principles, on which the statements are based. Also important to learning how to read and interpret financial statements is a comprehension of the categories and classifications used in balance sheets and income statements. Key financial ratios used in financial statement analysis are based on those categories. This chapter begins by describing the objectives, characteristics, and conventions that underlie the preparation of financial statements.

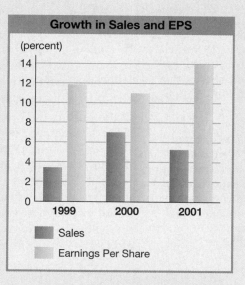

OBJECTIVES OF FINANCIAL INFORMATION

LO1 State the objectives of financial reporting.

RELATED TEXT ASSIGNMENTS
Q: 1
SE: 1
E: 1

The United States has a highly developed exchange economy. In this kind of economy, most goods and services are exchanged for money or claims to money instead of being used or bartered by their producers. Most business is carried on through corporations, including many extremely large firms that buy, sell, and obtain financing in U.S. and world markets.

By issuing stocks and bonds that are traded in financial markets, businesses can raise capital for production and marketing activities. Investors are interested mainly in returns from dividends and increases in the market price of their investments. Creditors want to know if the business can repay a loan plus interest in accordance with required terms. Thus, both investors and creditors need to know if a company can generate adequate cash flows. Financial statements are important to both groups in making that judgment. They offer valuable information that helps investors and creditors judge a company's ability to pay dividends and repay debts with interest. In this way, the market puts scarce resources to work in the companies that can use them most efficiently.

The information needs of users and the general business environment are the basis for the three objectives of financial reporting established by the Financial Accounting Standards Board (FASB):[2]

KEY POINT: Although reading financial reports requires some understanding of business, it does not require the skills of a CPA.

1. *To furnish information that is useful in making investment and credit decisions.* Financial reporting should offer information that can help current and potential investors and creditors make rational investment and credit decisions. The reports should be in a form that makes sense to those who have some understanding of business and are willing to study the information carefully.

2. *To provide information useful in assessing cash flow prospects.* Financial reporting should supply information to help current and potential investors and creditors judge the amounts, timing, and risk of expected cash receipts from dividends or interest and the proceeds from the sale, redemption, or maturity of stocks or loans.

◆ **STOP AND THINK!**
How do the four basic financial statements meet the third objective of financial reporting?
The balance sheet provides information about a company's resources (assets) and claims to those resources (liabilities and owners' equity). The income statement, statement of cash flows, and statement of retained earnings provide information about changes in resources and claims to them. ■

3. *To provide information about business resources, claims to those resources, and changes in them.* Financial reporting should give information about the company's assets, liabilities, and stockholders' equity, and the effects of transactions on the company's assets, liabilities, and stockholders' equity.

Financial statements are the most important way of periodically presenting to parties outside the business the information that has been gathered and processed in the accounting system. For this reason, the financial statements—the balance sheet, the income statement, the statement of retained earnings, and the statement of cash flows—are the most important output of the accounting system. These financial statements are "general purpose" because of their wide audience. They are "external" because their users are outside the business. Because of a potential conflict of interest between managers, who must prepare the statements, and investors or creditors, who invest in or lend money to the business, these statements often are audited by outside accountants to increase confidence in their reliability.

 Check out ACE for a Review Quiz at http://accounting.college.hmco.com/students.

QUALITATIVE CHARACTERISTICS OF ACCOUNTING INFORMATION

LO2 State the qualitative characteristics of accounting information and describe their interrelationships.

RELATED TEXT ASSIGNMENTS
Q: 2
SE: 1
E: 1

It is easy for students in their first accounting course to get the idea that accounting is 100 percent accurate. This idea is reinforced by the fact that all the problems in this and other introductory books can be solved. The numbers all add up; what is supposed to equal something else does. Accounting seems very much like mathematics in its precision. In this book, the basics of accounting are presented in a simple form to help you understand them. In practice, however, accounting information

FIGURE 1
Qualitative Characteristics and the Conventions of Accounting Information

look over

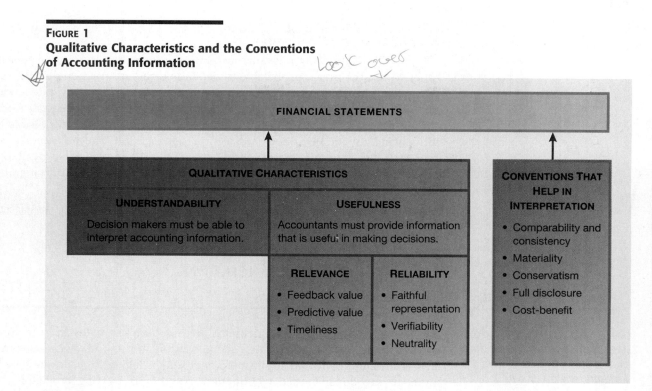

is neither simple nor precise, and it rarely satisfies all criteria. The FASB emphasizes this fact in the following statement:

> The information provided by financial reporting often results from approximate, rather than exact, measures. The measures commonly involve numerous estimates, classifications, summarizations, judgments and allocations. The outcome of economic activity in a dynamic economy is uncertain and results from combinations of many factors. Thus, despite the aura of precision that may seem to surround financial reporting in general and financial statements in particular, with few exceptions the measures are approximations, which may be based on rules and conventions, rather than exact amounts.[3]

The goal of accounting information—to provide the basic data that different users need to make informed decisions—is an ideal. The gap between the ideal and the actual provides much of the interest and controversy in accounting. To facilitate interpretation, the FASB has described the **qualitative characteristics** of accounting information, which are standards for judging that information. In addition, there are generally accepted conventions for recording and reporting that simplify interpretation. The relationships among these concepts are shown in Figure 1.

The most important qualitative characteristics are understandability and usefulness. **Understandability** depends on both the accountant and the decision maker. The accountant prepares the financial statements in accordance with accepted practices, generating important information that is believed to be understandable. But the decision maker must interpret the information and use it in making decisions. The decision maker must judge what information to use, how to use it, and what it means.

For accounting information to meet the standard of **usefulness**, it must have two major qualitative characteristics: relevance and reliability. **Relevance** means that the information can affect the outcome of a decision. In other words, a different decision would be made if the relevant information were not available. To be relevant, information must provide feedback, help predict future conditions, and be timely. For example, the income statement provides information about how a company performed over the past year (feedback), and it helps in planning for the next year (prediction). To be useful, however, it also must be communicated soon

● **STOP AND THINK!**
What are some areas that require estimates to record transactions under the matching rule?

To record depreciation expense, it is necessary to estimate the useful life of the asset. To record the amount of unearned revenue that is now earned or the amount of accrued revenue on a project in process, it is necessary to estimate the amount of revenue earned. ■

KEY POINT: Financial statements should be free of material misstatements.

enough after the end of the accounting period to enable the reader to make decisions (timeliness).

In addition to being relevant, accounting information must have **reliability**. In other words, the user must be able to depend on the information. It must represent what it is meant to represent. It must be credible and verifiable by independent parties using the same methods of measuring. It also must be neutral. Accounting should convey information about business activity as faithfully as possible without influencing anyone in a specific direction. For example, the balance sheet should represent the economic resources, obligations, and stockholders' equity of a business as faithfully as possible in accordance with generally accepted accounting principles, and it should be verifiable by an auditor.

✓ Check out ACE for a Review Quiz at http://accounting.college.hmco.com/students.

CONVENTIONS THAT HELP IN THE INTERPRETATION OF FINANCIAL INFORMATION

LO3 Define and describe the conventions of *comparability* and *consistency, materiality, conservatism, full disclosure,* and *cost-benefit.*

RELATED TEXT ASSIGNMENTS
Q: 3
SE: 2
E: 1, 2
P: 1, 6
SD: 1, 2

To a large extent, financial statements are based on estimates and the application of accounting rules for recognition and allocation. In this book, we point out a number of difficulties with financial statements. One is failing to recognize the changing value of the dollar caused by inflation. Another is treating intangibles, such as research and development costs, as assets if they are purchased outside the company and as expenses if they are developed within the company. Such problems do not mean that financial statements are useless; they are essential. However, users must know how to interpret them. To help in this interpretation, accountants depend on five **conventions**, or rules of thumb, in recording transactions and preparing financial statements: (1) comparability and consistency, (2) materiality, (3) conservatism, (4) full disclosure, and (5) cost-benefit.

COMPARABILITY AND CONSISTENCY

A characteristic that increases the usefulness of accounting information is comparability. Information about a company is more useful if it can be compared with similar facts about the same company over several time periods or about another company for the same time period. **Comparability** means that the information is presented in such a way that a decision maker can recognize similarities, differences, and trends over different time periods or between different companies.

Consistent use of accounting measures and procedures is important in achieving comparability. The **consistency** convention requires that once an accounting procedure is adopted by a company, it remain in use from one period to the next unless users of the financial statements are informed of the change. Thus, without a note to the contrary, the users can assume that there has been no change in the treatment of a particular transaction, account, or item that would affect the interpretation of the statements.

If management decides that a certain procedure is no longer appropriate and should be changed, generally accepted accounting principles require that the change and its dollar effect be described in the notes to the financial statements:

> The nature of and justification for a change in accounting principle and its effect on income should be disclosed in the financial statements of the period in which the change is made. The justification for the change should explain clearly why the newly adopted accounting principle is preferable.[4]

⬢ **STOP AND THINK!**

How can financial information be consistent but not comparable?

Consistency in accounting applies only to the use of the accounting principles for presenting the financial information. It does not apply to the conditions that are represented in the financial statements. For example, changes in business operations or the economy may make financial information incomparable from year to year, even though the same accounting policies have been followed. ■

www.goodyeartires.com

For example, Goodyear Tire & Rubber Co. recently reported that it changed its method of accounting for inventories because management felt the new method improved the matching of revenues and costs.

FOCUS ON BUSINESS PRACTICE

How Much Is Material? It's Not Only a Matter of Numbers.

The materiality issue has been a pet peeve of the SEC <www.sec.gov>, which contends that companies have increasingly abused the convention to protect their stocks from taking a pounding when earnings do not reach their targets. Over the years, companies have excluded from earnings any losses that they deem so small as to have virtually no effect on net income. Accountants and companies have typically used a rule of thumb of 5 percent of net income. The SEC has issued a new rule that puts stricter requirements on the use of materiality in that it calls for qualitative considerations in addition to quantitative guides. The percentage assessment is acceptable as an initial screening, but now companies cannot decline to book items in order to meet earnings estimates, preserve a growing earnings trend, convert a loss to a profit, increase management compensation, or hide an illegal transaction, such as a bribe.[5]

MATERIALITY

BUSINESS-WORLD EXAMPLE: By definition, a $10 stapler is a long-term asset that, theoretically, should be capitalized and depreciated over its useful life. However, the convention of materiality allows the stapler to be expensed entirely in the year of purchase because its cost is small and writing it off in one year has no effect on anyone's decision making.

KEY POINT: Illegal acts involving even small dollar amounts should be investigated.

Materiality refers to the relative importance of an item or event. If an item or event is material, it is probably relevant to users of the financial statements. In other words, an item is material if users would have done something differently if they had not known about the item. The accountant is often faced with decisions about small items or events that make little difference to users no matter how they are handled. For example, a large company may decide that expenditures for durable items of less than $500 should be charged as expenses rather than recorded as long-term assets and depreciated.

In general, an item is material if there is a reasonable expectation that knowing about it would influence the decisions of users of financial statements. The materiality of an item normally is determined by relating its dollar value to an element of the financial statements, such as net income or total assets. Some accountants feel that when an item is 5 percent or more of net income, it is material. However, materiality also depends on the nature of the item, not just its value. For example, in a multimillion-dollar company, a mistake of $5,000 in recording an item may not be important, but the discovery of a $5,000 bribe or theft can be very important. Also, many small errors can combine into a material amount. Accountants judge the materiality of many things, and the users of financial statements depend on their judgments being fair and accurate. The SEC has recently questioned whether a desire to avoid showing certain items in the financial statements has influenced some companies' judgment about materiality.

CONSERVATISM

KEY POINT: The purpose of conservatism is not to produce the lowest net income and lowest asset value. It is a guideline for choosing among GAAP alternatives, and it should be used with care.

Accountants try to base their decisions on logic and evidence that lead to the fairest report of what happened. In judging and estimating, however, accountants often are faced with uncertainties. In these cases, they look to the convention of **conservatism**. This convention means that when accountants face major uncertainties about which accounting procedure to use, they generally choose the one that is least likely to overstate assets and income.

One of the most common applications of the conservatism convention is the use of the lower-of-cost-or-market method in accounting for inventories. Under this method, if an item's market value is greater than its cost, the more conservative cost figure is used. If the market value falls below the cost, the more conservative market value is used. The latter situation often occurs in the computer industry.

KEY POINT: Expensing a long-term asset in the period of purchase is not a GAAP alternative.

Conservatism can be a useful tool in doubtful cases, but its abuse leads to incorrect and misleading financial statements. Suppose that someone incorrectly applies the conservatism convention by expensing a long-term asset of material cost in the period of purchase. In this case, there is no uncertainty. Income and assets for the current period would be understated, and income in future periods would be overstated. For this reason, accountants depend on the conservatism convention only when there is uncertainty about which accounting procedure to use.

FOCUS ON BUSINESS PRACTICE

When Is "Full Disclosure" Too Much? It's a Matter of Cost and Benefits.

The large accounting firm of Ernst & Young <www.ey.com> reports that over a 20-year period, the total number of pages in the annual reports of 25 large, well-known companies has increased an average of 84 percent and the number of pages of notes has increased 325 percent—from 4 to 17 pages. Management's discussion and analysis increased 300 percent, from 3 pages to 12.[6] Because some people feel that "these documents are so daunting that people don't read them at all," the SEC allows companies to issue to the public "summary reports" in which the bulk of the notes can be reduced.

Although more accessible and less costly, summary reports are controversial because many analysts feel that it is in the notes that one gets the detailed information necessary to understand complex business operations. One analyst remarked, "To banish the notes for fear they will turn off readers would be like eliminating fractions from math books on the theory that the average student prefers to work with whole numbers."[7] Where this controversy will end, nobody knows. Detailed reports still must be filed with the SEC, but more and more companies are providing summary reports to the public.

FULL DISCLOSURE

The convention of **full disclosure** requires that financial statements and their notes present all information that is relevant to the users' understanding of the statements. That is, the statements should offer any explanation needed to keep them from being misleading. Explanatory notes are considered an integral part of the financial statements. For instance, a change from one accounting procedure to another should be reported. In general, the form of the financial statements can affect their usefulness in making certain decisions—for example, the categories used to group accounts in the statements convey information about the accounts. Also, certain items, such as the amount of depreciation expense on the income statement and the accumulated depreciation on the balance sheet, are essential to the readers of financial statements.

Other examples of disclosures required by the FASB and other official bodies are the accounting procedures used in preparing the statements, important terms of the company's debt, commitments and contingencies, and important events taking place after the date of the statements. However, the statements can become so cluttered with notes that they impede rather than help understanding. Beyond required disclosures, the application of the full-disclosure convention is based on the judgment of management and of the accountants who prepare the financial statements.

In recent years, the principle of full disclosure also has been influenced by investors and creditors. To protect them, independent auditors, the stock exchanges, and the SEC have made more demands for disclosure by publicly owned companies. The SEC has been pushing especially hard for the enforcement of full disclosure. As a result, more and better information about corporations is available to the public today than ever before.

COST-BENEFIT

The **cost-benefit** convention underlies all the qualitative characteristics and conventions. It holds that the benefits to be gained from providing accounting information should be greater than the costs of providing it. Of course, minimum levels of relevance and reliability must be reached if accounting information is to be useful. Beyond the minimum levels, however, it is up to the FASB and the SEC, which require the information, and the accountant, who provides the information, to judge the costs and benefits in each case. Most of the costs of providing information fall at first on the preparers; the benefits are reaped by both preparers and users. Finally, both the costs and the benefits are passed on to society in the form of prices and social benefits from more efficient allocation of resources.

The costs and benefits of a particular requirement for accounting disclosure are both direct and indirect, immediate and deferred. For example, it is hard to judge the final costs and benefits of a far-reaching and costly regulation. The FASB, for instance, allows certain large companies to make a supplemental disclosure in their financial statements of the effects of changes in current costs. Most companies choose not to present this information because they believe the costs of producing and providing it exceed its benefits to the readers of their financial statements. Cost-benefit is a question faced by all regulators, including the FASB and the SEC. Even though there are no definitive ways of measuring costs and benefits, much of an accountant's work deals with these concepts.

 Check out ACE for a Review Quiz at http://accounting.college.hmco.com/students.

MANAGEMENT'S RESPONSIBILITY FOR ETHICAL REPORTING

LO4 Explain management's responsibility for ethical financial reporting and define *fraudulent financial reporting.*

RELATED TEXT ASSIGNMENTS
Q: 4
SD: 3, 4, 5

www.generalmills.com

The users of financial statements depend on the good faith of those who prepare these statements. This dependence places a duty on a company's management and its accountants to act ethically in the reporting process. That duty is often expressed in the report of management that accompanies financial statements. For example, the report of the management of General Mills, Inc., a company known for strong financial reporting and controls, states:

> The management . . . is responsible for the fairness and accuracy of the consolidated financial statements. The consolidated financial statements have been prepared in accordance with accounting principles that are generally accepted in the United States, using management's best estimates and judgments where appropriate.[8]

General Mills' management also tells how it meets this responsibility:

> Management has established a system of internal controls that provides reasonable assurance that assets are adequately safeguarded and transactions are recorded accurately in all material respects, in accordance with management's authorization. We maintain a strong audit program that independently evaluates the adequacy and effectiveness of internal controls.[9]

● **STOP AND THINK!**
What is the difference between aggressive accounting and fraudulent financial reporting?

There is often a fine line between aggressive accounting, which is the use of legitimate accounting methods to achieve business purposes, and fraudulent financial reporting, which is the intentional misrepresentation of financial information. The former is acceptable, whereas the latter is unethical and sometimes illegal. ■

The intentional preparation of misleading financial statements is called **fraudulent financial reporting**.[10] It can result from the distortion of records (e.g., the manipulation of inventory records), falsified transactions (e.g., fictitious sales), or the misapplication of accounting principles (e.g., treating as an asset an item that should be expensed). There are a number of possible motives for fraudulent reporting—for instance, to obtain a higher price when a company is sold, to meet the expectations of stockholders, or to obtain a loan. Sometimes, the incentive is personal gain, such as additional compensation, promotion, or avoidance of penalties for poor performance. The personal costs of such actions can be high. Individuals who authorize or prepare fraudulent financial statements may face prison sentences

FOCUS ON BUSINESS ETHICS

Questionable Accounting Practices Are Under Scrutiny.

There is a difference between management's choosing to follow accounting principles that are favorable to its actions and fraudulent financial reporting. Because of recent, highly visible accounting misstatements by such companies as WorldCom <www.worldcom.com>, Enron <www.enron.com>, Sunbeam Corporation <www.sunbeam.com>, and many others attempting to meet the earnings expectations of stock analysts, the SEC is cracking down on what it sees as the main abuses, which the chairman of the SEC has called "accounting hocus-pocus." These are cases in which real transactions are accounted for in

such a way as to distort reality. Examples include one-time "big bath" restructuring charges that overstate current expenses to benefit future periods, creative acquisition accounting in mergers, writing off purchased research and development inappropriately, miscellaneous "cookie jar reserves" involving unrealistic assumptions about such items as sales returns and warranty costs, and the abuse of the materiality convention.[11] The SEC brings about 100 accounting actions each year. In recent times, executives at WorldCom and Sunbeam have been indicted. Executives at Enron are under investigation.[12]

and fines. A company's investors and lenders, employees, and customers suffer from fraudulent financial reporting as well.

www.worldcom.com
www.enron.com

Due to recent abuses in financial reporting that have come to light in companies like WorldCom and Enron, Congress passed the Sarbanes-Oxley Act. This legislation orders the SEC to draw up rules requiring chief executives and chief financial officers of all 15,000 publicly traded companies to file statements each quarter swearing that, based on their knowledge, their company's quarterly and annual statements are accurate and complete. Violation can result in criminal penalties. To comply with this law and meet ethical reporting requirements, a company's accountants and auditors must apply financial accounting concepts in such a way as to present a fair view of the company's operations and financial position and to avoid misleading readers of the financial statements.

✔ Check out ACE for a Review Quiz at http://accounting.college.hmco.com/students.

CLASSIFIED BALANCE SHEET

LO5   Identify and describe the basic components of a classified balance sheet.

RELATED TEXT ASSIGNMENTS
Q: 5, 6, 7, 8, 9, 10, 11, 12
SE: 3, 4
E: 3, 4
P: 3, 5
FRA: 4, 5

The balance sheets you have seen in the chapters thus far categorize accounts as assets, liabilities, and stockholders' equity. Because even a fairly small company can have hundreds of accounts, simply listing accounts in these broad categories is not particularly helpful to a statement user. Setting up subcategories within the major categories often makes financial statements much more useful. Investors and creditors study and evaluate the relationships among the subcategories. General-purpose external financial statements that are divided into subcategories are called **classified financial statements**.

The balance sheet presents the financial position of a company at a particular time. The subdivisions of the classified balance sheet shown in Exhibit 1 are typical of those used by most companies in the United States. The subdivisions under owners' or stockholders' equity depend, of course, on the form of business.

ASSETS

A company's assets are often divided into four categories: (1) current assets; (2) investments; (3) property, plant, and equipment; and (4) intangible assets. These categories are listed in the order of their presumed ease of conversion into cash. For example, current assets are usually more easily converted to cash than are property, plant, and equipment. For simplicity, some companies group investments, intangible assets, and other miscellaneous assets into a category called "**other assets**."

■ **CURRENT ASSETS**   **Current assets** are cash and other assets that are reasonably expected to be converted to cash, sold, or consumed within one year or within the normal operating cycle of the business, whichever is longer. The normal operating cycle of a company is the average time needed to go from cash to cash. For example, cash is used to buy merchandise inventory, which is sold for cash or for a promise of cash if the sale is made on account. If a sale is made on account, the resulting receivable must be collected before the cycle is completed.

KEY POINT: Use one year as the current period unless the normal operating cycle happens to be longer.

The normal operating cycle for most companies is less than one year, but there are exceptions. Tobacco companies, for example, must age their tobacco for two or three years before it can be sold. The tobacco inventory is nonetheless considered a current asset because it will be sold within the normal operating cycle. Another example is a company that sells on the installment basis. The payments for a television set or a refrigerator can be extended over 24 or 36 months, but these receivables are still considered current assets.

Cash is obviously a current asset. Short-term investments, notes and accounts receivable, and inventory are also current assets because they are expected to be converted to cash within the next year or during the normal operating cycle. On the balance sheet, they are listed in the order of their ease of conversion into cash.

EXHIBIT 1
Classified Balance Sheet for Shafer Auto Parts Corporation

Shafer Auto Parts Corporation
Balance Sheet
December 31, 20x2

Assets

Current assets

Cash	$10,360	
Short-term investments	2,000	
Notes receivable	8,000	
Accounts receivable	35,300	
Merchandise inventory	60,400	
Prepaid insurance	6,600	
Store supplies	1,060	
Office supplies	636	
Total current assets		$124,356

Investments

Land held for future use	5,000

Property, plant, and equipment

Land		$ 4,500	
Building	$20,650		
Less accumulated depreciation	8,640	12,010	
Delivery equipment	$18,400		
Less accumulated depreciation	9,450	8,950	
Office equipment	$ 8,600		
Less accumulated depreciation	5,000	3,600	
Total property, plant, and equipment			29,060

Intangible assets

Trademark	500
Total assets	$158,916

Liabilities

Current liabilities

Notes payable	$15,000	
Accounts payable	25,683	
Salaries payable	2,000	
Total current liabilities		$ 42,683

Long-term liabilities

Mortgage payable	17,800
Total liabilities	$ 60,483

Stockholders' Equity

Contributed capital

Common stock, $10 par value, 5,000 shares authorized, issued, and outstanding	$50,000	
Additional paid-in capital	10,000	
Total contributed capital	$60,000	
Retained earnings	38,433	
Total stockholders' equity		98,433
Total liabilities and stockholders' equity		$158,916

Prepaid expenses, such as rent and insurance paid in advance, and inventories of supplies bought for use rather than for sale also should be classified as current assets. Such assets are current in the sense that if they had not been bought earlier, a current outlay of cash would be needed to obtain them.[13]

In deciding whether an asset is current or noncurrent, the idea of "reasonable expectation" is important. For example, Short-Term Investments, also called "Marketable Securities," is an account used for temporary investments of "idle" cash—that is, cash not immediately required for operating purposes. Management can reasonably expect to sell these securities as cash needs arise over the next year or operating cycle. Investments in securities that management does not expect to sell within the next year and that do not involve the temporary use of idle cash should be shown in the investments category of a classified balance sheet.

KEY POINT: For an investment to be classified as current, management must intend to sell it within the next year or the current operating cycle, and it must be readily marketable.

■ **INVESTMENTS** The **investments** category includes assets, usually long term, that are not used in the normal operation of the business and that management does not plan to convert to cash within the next year. Items in this category are securities held for long-term investment, long-term notes receivable, land held for future use, plant or equipment not used in the business, and special funds established to pay off a debt or buy a building. Also included are large permanent investments in another company for the purpose of controlling that company.

◆ **STOP AND THINK!**
Why is it that land held for future use and equipment not currently used in the business are classified as investments rather than as property, plant, and equipment?

They are classified as investments because doing so helps users of financial statements assess the performance of the company using such measures as return on assets. Also, the investment category gives users some idea of resources the company may be able to draw on without disturbing the current business operations. ■

■ **PROPERTY, PLANT, AND EQUIPMENT** **Property, plant, and equipment** are tangible long-term assets used in the continuing operation of the business. They represent a place to operate (land and buildings) and the equipment to produce, sell, deliver, and service the company's goods. They are therefore also called *operating assets* or, sometimes, *fixed assets, tangible assets, long-lived assets,* or *plant assets.* Through depreciation, the costs of these assets (except land) are spread over the periods they benefit. Past depreciation is recorded in the Accumulated Depreciation accounts. The order in which property, plant, and equipment are listed on the balance sheet is not the same everywhere. In practice, accounts are often combined to make the financial statements less cluttered. For example:

Property, Plant, and Equipment

Land		$ 4,500
Buildings and equipment	$47,650	
Less accumulated depreciation	23,090	24,560
Total property, plant, and equipment		$29,060

Many companies simply show a single line with a total for property, plant, and equipment and provide the details in a note to the financial statements.

The property, plant, and equipment category also includes natural resources owned by the company, such as forest lands, oil and gas properties, and coal mines, if they are used in the regular course of business. If they are not, they are listed in the investments category, as noted above.

■ **INTANGIBLE ASSETS** **Intangible assets** are long-term assets with no physical substance whose value stems from the rights or privileges they extend to their owners. Examples are patents, copyrights, goodwill, franchises, and trademarks. These assets are recorded at cost, which is spread over the expected life of the right or privilege.

LIABILITIES

Liabilities are divided into two categories, based on when the liabilities fall due: current liabilities and long-term liabilities.

■ **CURRENT LIABILITIES** The category of **current liabilities** consists of obligations due to be paid or performed within one year or within the normal operating cycle of the business, whichever is longer. Current liabilities are typically paid from

BUSINESS-WORLD
EXAMPLE: The portion of a
mortgage paid monthly for 120
months that is due during the
next year or the current operating cycle would be classified as a
current liability; the portion due
after the next year or the current operating cycle would be
classified as a long-term liability.

current assets or by incurring new short-term liabilities. They include notes payable, accounts payable, the current portion of long-term debt, salaries and wages payable, taxes payable, and customer advances (unearned revenues).

■ **LONG-TERM LIABILITIES**   The debts of a business that fall due more than one year in the future or beyond the normal operating cycle, which will be paid out of noncurrent assets, are **long-term liabilities**. Mortgages payable, long-term notes, bonds payable, employee pension obligations, and long-term lease liabilities generally fall into the category of long-term liabilities. Deferred income taxes are often disclosed as a separate category in the long-term liability section of the balance sheet of publicly held corporations. This liability arises because the rules for measuring income for tax purposes differ from those for financial reporting. The cumulative annual difference between the income taxes payable to governments and the income taxes expense reported on the income statement is included in the account Deferred Income Taxes.

STOCKHOLDERS' EQUITY

The stockholders' equity section for a corporation would appear as shown in the balance sheet for Shafer Auto Parts Corporation (see Exhibit 1). As you learned ear-lier, corporations are separate legal entities owned by their stockholders. The stock-holders' equity section of a balance sheet has two parts: contributed capital and retained earnings. Generally, contributed capital is shown on corporate balance sheets as two amounts: the par value of the issued stock, and the paid-in capital in excess of the par value per share.

OTHER FORMS OF BUSINESS ORGANIZATION

Although the form of business organization does not usually affect the accounting treatment of assets and liabilities, the equity section of the balance sheet for a sole proprietorship or partnership is very different from the equity section of a corpora-tion's balance sheet.

■ **SOLE PROPRIETORSHIP**   The equity section for a sole proprietorship simply shows the capital in the owner's name at an amount equal to the net assets of the company. It might appear as follows:

Owner's Equity

Hershell Serton, capital $57,390

Because there is no legal separation between an owner and his or her sole propri-etorship, there is no need for contributed capital to be separated from earnings retained for use in a business. This capital account is increased by both the owner's investments and net income. It is decreased by net losses and withdrawals of assets from the business for personal use by the owner. In this kind of business, the for-mality of declaring and paying dividends is not required.

In fact, the terms *owner's equity, proprietorship, capital,* and *net worth* are used interchangeably. They all stand for the owner's interest in the company. The first three terms are preferred to *net worth* because most assets are recorded at original cost rather than at current value. For this reason, the ownership section will not rep-resent "worth." It is really a claim against the assets of the company.

KEY POINT: The only difference in equity between a
sole proprietorship and a partnership is in the number of
capital accounts.

■ **PARTNERSHIP**   The equity section of the balance sheet for a partnership is called *partners' equity* and is much like that for the sole proprietorship. It might appear as follows:

Partners' Equity

A. J. Martin, capital	$21,666	
R. C. Moore, capital	35,724	
Total partners' equity		$57,390

EXHIBIT 2
Balance Sheet for Dell Computer Corporation

Dell Computer Corporation
Consolidated Statement of Financial Position
(in millions)

	February 1, 2002	February 2, 2001
ASSETS		
Current assets:		
Cash and cash equivalents	$ 3,641	$ 4,910
Short-term investments	273	525
Accounts receivable, net	2,269	2,424
Inventories	278	400
Other	1,416	1,467
Total current assets	7,877	9,726
Property, plant and equipment, net	826	996
Investments	4,373	2,418
Other non-current assets	459	530
Total assets	$13,535	$13,670
LIABILITIES AND STOCKHOLDERS' EQUITY		
Current liabilities:		
Accounts payable	$ 5,075	$ 4,286
Accrued and other	2,444	2,492
Total current liabilities	7,519	6,778
Long-term debt	520	509
Other liabilities	802	761
Total liabilities	8,841	8,048
Stockholders' equity:		
Common stock and capital in excess of $.01 par value; shares authorized: 7,000; shares issued: 2,654 and 2,601, respectively	5,605	4,795
Treasury stock, at cost; 52 shares and no shares, respectively	(2,249)	—
Retained earnings	1,364	839
Other comprehensive income	38	62
Other	(64)	(74)
Total stockholders' equity	4,694	5,622
Total liabilities and stockholders' equity	$13,535	$13,670

Source: Dell Computer Corporation, *Annual Report,* 2001.

READING AND GRAPHING REAL COMPANY BALANCE SHEETS

www.dell.com

Although financial statements usually follow the same general form as illustrated for Shafer Auto Parts Corporation, no two companies have statements that are exactly alike. The balance sheet of Dell Computer Corporation, the world's leading direct seller of computer systems, is a good example of some of the variations. As shown in Exhibit 2, it provides data for two years so that the change from one year to the next can be evaluated. Note that its major classifications are similar but not identical to Shafer's. For instance, Shafer's assets include investments and intangible assets categories, whereas Dell has an asset category called "other non-current

FIGURE 2
Graphic Presentation of Dell Computer Corporation's Balance Sheet

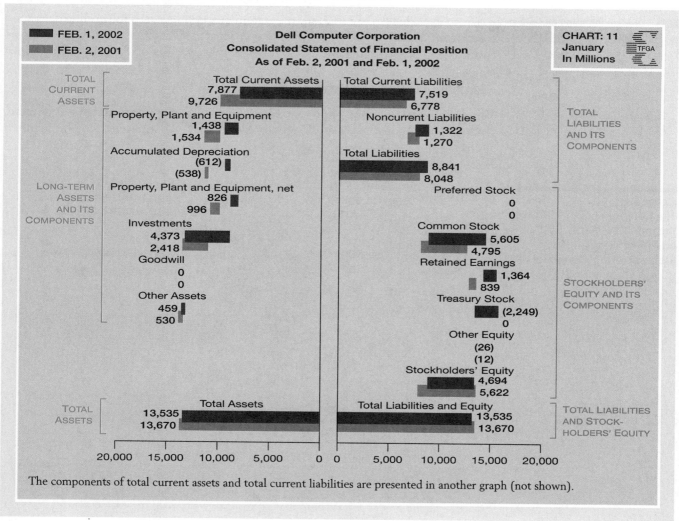

The components of total current assets and total current liabilities are presented in another graph (not shown).

assets," which is a small amount of its total assets. Also note that Dell has a category called "other liabilities." Because this category appears after long-term debt, it represents longer-term liabilities, due more than one year from the balance sheet dates.

Dell's stockholders' equity section also differs from that of Shafer Auto Parts in that it subtracts a category called "other" from common stock, retained earnings, and other comprehensive income. However, it is possible to look at the total stockholders' equity and know that this amount relates to the stockholders' claims on the company.

When we look at columns of numbers, it is sometimes difficult to see the patterns. Graphic presentation of the numbers can be helpful in visualizing the changes taking place in a company's financial position. Figure 2, which was prepared with the Fingraph® Financial Analyst™ CD-ROM software that accompanies this text, is a graphic presentation of a portion of the balance sheet shown in Exhibit 2. Total assets and its components are graphed on the left side, and total liabilities and its components, together with total stockholders' equity, are on the right. The composition of the assets and liabilities, their relation to stockholders' equity, and the changes in them from 2001 to 2002 are easily seen. These graphs show that overall Dell was relatively stable in both totals and components from 2001 to 2002. Also note that the graphic presentation of the balance sheet reduces the detailed clutter of the statement. For instance, all current assets are combined and represented by a single component line.

✓ Check out ACE for a Review Quiz at http://accounting.college.hmco.com/students.

FORMS OF THE INCOME STATEMENT

LO6 Prepare multistep and single-step classified income statements.

RELATED TEXT ASSIGNMENTS
Q: 13, 14, 15, 16, 17, 18, 19, 20
SE: 5, 6, 7
E: 5, 6, 7
P: 2, 5, 7
FRA: 5

Thus far, we have presented income statements in single-step form: all expenses are deducted from revenue in one step to arrive at net income. Here, we look at the multistep income statement and a more complex version of the single-step form.

MULTISTEP INCOME STATEMENT

In practice, many companies use some form of a **multistep income statement**, which goes through a series of steps, or subtotals, to arrive at net income. Figure 3

FIGURE 3
The Components of Multistep Income Statements for Service and Merchandising or Manufacturing Companies

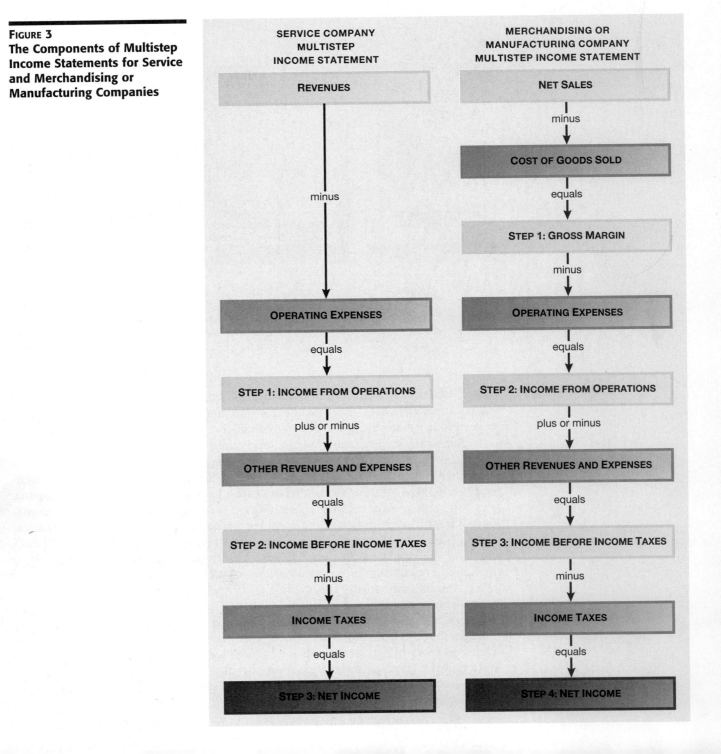

EXHIBIT 3
Multistep Income Statement for Shafer Auto Parts Corporation

Shafer Auto Parts Corporation
Income Statement
For the Year Ended December 31, 20x2

Net sales		$289,656
Cost of goods sold		181,260
Step 1: Gross margin		$108,396
Operating expenses		
Selling expenses	$54,780	
General and administrative expenses	34,504	
Total operating expenses		89,284
Step 2: Income from operations		$ 19,112
Other revenues and expenses		
Interest income	$ 1,400	
Less interest expense	2,631	
Excess of other expenses over other revenues		1,231
Step 3: Income before income taxes		$ 17,881
Income taxes		3,381
Step 4: Net income		$ 14,500
Earnings per share		$ 2.90

BUSINESS-WORLD EXAMPLE: The multistep income statement is a valuable analytical tool that is often overlooked. Analysts frequently convert a single-step statement into a multistep one because the latter separates operating sources of net income from nonoperating ones. Investors want net income to result primarily from operations, not from one-time gains or losses.

compares the multistep income statement for service companies with that for **merchandising companies**, which buy and sell products, and **manufacturing companies**, which make and sell products. Note that in the multistep income statement for service companies, the operating expenses are deducted from revenues in a single step to arrive at income from operations. In contrast, because manufacturing and merchandising companies make or buy goods for sale, they must include an additional step in the multistep income statement for the cost of these goods that are sold. In the following discussion of these components, the income statement presented in Exhibit 3 for Shafer Auto Parts Corporation, a merchandising company, will serve as an example of a multistep income statement.

■ **NET SALES**   The first major part of the multistep income statement for a merchandising or manufacturing company is **net sales**, often simply called *sales*. Net sales consist of the gross proceeds from sales of merchandise, or gross sales, less sales returns and allowances and any discounts allowed. **Gross sales** consist of total cash sales and total credit sales during an accounting period. Even though the cash may not be collected until the following accounting period, under the revenue recognition rule, revenue is recorded as earned when title for merchandise passes from seller to buyer at the time of sale. Sales returns and allowances are cash refunds, credits on account, and allowances off selling prices made to customers who have received defective products or products that are otherwise unsatisfactory. If other discounts or allowances are given to customers, they also should be deducted from gross sales.

Management, investors, and others often use the amount of sales and trends suggested by sales as indicators of a firm's progress. Increasing sales suggest growth; decreasing sales indicate the possibility of decreased future earnings and other financial problems. To detect trends, comparisons are frequently made between the net sales of different accounting periods.

KEY POINT: The matching rule precludes the cost of inventory from being expensed until the inventory has been sold.

KEY POINT: For a merchandiser or manufacturer, net income equals gross margin less operating expenses plus or minus other revenue or expenses and income taxes.

KEY POINT: Gross margin is an important measure of profitability. When it is less than operating expenses, the company has suffered a net loss from operations.

www.samsclub.com
www.costco.com

www.neimanmarcus.com
www.tiffany.com

BUSINESS-WORLD EXAMPLE: Companies that are restructuring their operations often focus on reducing operating expenses.

KEY POINT: The most common types of operating expenses are selling expenses and general and administrative expenses. They are deducted from gross margin on the income statement.

KEY POINT: Financial analysts often focus on income from operations as a key profitability measure.

■ **COST OF GOODS SOLD**   The second part of the multistep income statement for a merchandiser or manufacturer is **cost of goods sold**, or simply *cost of sales.* Cost of goods sold (an expense) is the amount a merchandiser paid for the merchandise it sold during an accounting period or the cost to a manufacturer of making the products it sold during an accounting period.

■ **GROSS MARGIN**   The third major part of the multistep income statement for a merchandiser or manufacturer is **gross margin**, or *gross profit*, which is the difference between net sales and cost of goods sold (Step 1 in Exhibit 3). To be successful, companies must achieve a gross margin that is sufficient to cover operating expenses and provide an adequate after-tax income.

Management is interested in both the amount and the percentage of gross margin. The percentage of gross margin is computed by dividing the amount of gross margin by net sales. In the case of Shafer Auto Parts Corporation, the amount of gross margin is $108,396 and the percentage of gross margin is 37.4 percent ($108,396 ÷ $289,656). This information is useful in planning business operations. For instance, management may try to increase total sales dollars by reducing the selling price. This strategy reduces the percentage of gross margin, but it will work if the total of items sold increases enough to raise the absolute amount of gross margin. This is the strategy followed by discount warehouse stores like Sam's Clubs and Costco Wholesale Corporation. On the other hand, management may decide to keep a high gross margin from sales and attempt to increase sales and the amount of gross margin by increasing operating expenses, such as advertising. This is the strategy followed by upscale specialty stores like Neiman Marcus and Tiffany & Co. Other strategies to increase gross margin from sales include reducing cost of goods sold by using better purchasing methods.

■ **OPERATING EXPENSES**   The next major area of the multistep income statement consists of **operating expenses**, which are the expenses other than cost of goods sold that are incurred in running a business. It is customary to group operating expenses into categories, such as selling expenses and general and administrative expenses. Selling expenses include the costs of storing goods and preparing them for sale; preparing displays, advertising, and otherwise promoting sales; making sales; and delivering goods to the buyer, if the seller pays the cost of delivery. The latter cost is often called **freight out expense**, or *delivery expense.* Among general and administrative expenses are general office expenses, which include expenses for accounting, personnel, and credit and collections, and any other expenses that apply to overall operations. Although general occupancy expenses, such as rent expense, insurance expense, and utilities expense, are often classified as general and administrative expenses, they may also be allocated between the selling and the general and administrative categories. Careful planning and control of operating expenses can improve a company's profitability.

■ **INCOME FROM OPERATIONS**   **Income from operations**, or simply *operating income*, is the difference between gross margin and operating expenses (Step 2 in Exhibit 3). It represents the income from a company's normal, or main, business. Because companies may have significant other revenues and expenses and different income tax rates, income from operations is often used to compare the profitability of two or more companies or divisions within a company.

■ **OTHER REVENUES AND EXPENSES**   **Other revenues and expenses**, or *nonoperating revenues and expenses*, are not part of a company's operating activities. This section of the multistep income statement includes revenues from investments (such as dividends and interest on stocks, bonds, and savings accounts) and interest earned on credit or notes extended to customers. It also includes interest expense and other expenses that result from borrowing money or from credit extended to the company. If the company has yet other kinds of revenues and expenses not related to the company's normal business operations, they, too, are included in this part of the income statement. An analyst who wants to compare two companies independent of their financing methods—that is, before considering other revenues and expenses—would focus on income from operations.

■ **INCOME BEFORE INCOME TAXES**   **Income before income taxes** is the amount a company has earned from all activities—operating and nonoperating—before taking into account the amount of income taxes it incurred (Step 3 in Exhibit 3). Because companies may be subject to different income tax rates, income before income taxes is often used to compare the profitability of two or more companies or divisions within a company.

■ **INCOME TAXES**   **Income taxes**, also called *provision for income taxes*, represent the expense for federal, state, and local taxes on corporate income. Income taxes are shown as a separate item on the income statement. Usually the word *expense* is not used. Income taxes do not appear on the income statements of sole proprietorships and partnerships because they are not tax-paying units. The individuals who own these businesses are the tax-paying units, and they pay income taxes on their share of the business income. Corporations, however, must report and pay income taxes on earnings. Because federal, state, and local income taxes for corporations are substantial, they have a significant effect on business decisions. Current federal income tax rates for corporations vary from 15 percent to 38 percent, depending on the amount of income before income taxes and other factors. Most other taxes, such as property and employment taxes, are included in the operating expenses.

■ **NET INCOME**   **Net income**, the final figure, or "bottom line," of the income statement, is what remains of the gross margin after operating expenses are deducted, other revenues and expenses are added or deducted, and income taxes are deducted (Step 4 in Exhibit 3). It is an important performance measure because it represents the amount of business earnings that accrue to stockholders. It is the amount that is transferred to retained earnings from all the income-generating activities during the year. Both management and investors often use net income to measure whether a business has operated successfully during the past accounting period.

■ **EARNINGS PER SHARE**   **Earnings per share**, often called *net income per share*, is the net income earned on each share of common stock. It is unique to corporate reporting. Ownership in corporations is represented by shares of stock, and the net income per share is reported immediately below net income on the income statement. In the simplest case, it is computed by dividing the net income by the average number of shares of common stock outstanding during the year. For example, Shafer's earnings per share of $2.90 was computed by dividing the net income of $14,500 by the 5,000 shares of common stock outstanding (see the stockholders' equity section of the balance sheet in Exhibit 1). Investors find the figure useful as a quick way of assessing both a company's profit-earning success and its earnings in relation to the market price of its stock.

READING AND GRAPHING REAL COMPANY INCOME STATEMENTS

Income statements, like balance sheets, vary among companies. You will rarely, if ever, find an income statement exactly like the one for Shafer Auto Parts Corporation. You will encounter terms and structure that differ, such as those on the multistep income statement for Dell Computer Corporation in Exhibit 4, in which management provides three years of data for comparison purposes. You may also encounter components that are not covered in this chapter. If this occurs, refer to the index at the end of the book to find the topic and read about it.

◆ **STOP AND THINK!**
Which is the better measure of a company's performance: income from operations or net income?
Neither measure is better than the other. Both measure different aspects of profitability. Income from operations measures the income from a company's ongoing operations before considering issues of financing (interest expense), nonoperating revenues, and income taxes. Net income measures whether a business has been operating successfully. ■

ENRICHMENT NOTE:
Earnings per share is the most commonly cited performance measure in the business press because it is a shorthand measure of profitability.

www.dell.com

EXHIBIT 4
Income Statement for Dell Computer Corporation

Dell Computer Corporation
Consolidated Statement of Income
(in millions, except per share amounts)

	Fiscal Year Ended		
	February 1, 2002	February 2, 2001	January 28, 2000
Net revenue	$31,168	$31,888	$25,265
Cost of revenue	25,661	25,445	20,047
Gross margin	5,507	6,443	5,218
Operating expenses:			
Selling, general and administrative	2,784	3,193	2,387
Research, development and engineering	452	482	374
Special charges	482	105	194
Total operating expenses	3,718	3,780	2,955
Operating income	1,789	2,663	2,263
Investment and other income (loss), net	(58)	531	188
Income before income taxes and cumulative effect of change in accounting principle	1,731	3,194	2,451
Provision for income taxes	485	958	785
Income before cumulative effect of change in accounting principle	1,246	2,236	1,666
Cumulative effect of change in accounting principle, net	—	59	—
Net income	$ 1,246	$ 2,177	$ 1,666

Source: Dell Computer Corporation, *Annual Report,* 2001.

Figure 4, which was prepared with the Fingraph® Financial Analyst™ CD-ROM software that is available with this text, is a graphic presentation of a portion of Dell's income statement. It helps show the company's progress in meeting its profitability objectives. On the left side of the graph are the components of income from operations, beginning with net revenues at the top and ending with income from operations at the bottom. The right side graphs the percentage changes in the components. Increases are shown on the right of the vertical column, and decreases are shown on the left. Except for other charges, there was little change in the components from 2001 to 2002.

No ⇒ ## SINGLE-STEP INCOME STATEMENT

The **single-step income statement**, illustrated for Shafer Auto Parts Corporation in Exhibit 5, derives income before income taxes in a single step by putting the major categories of revenues in the first part of the statement and the major categories of costs and expenses in the second part. Income taxes are shown as a separate item, as on the multistep income statement. Both the multistep form and the single-step form have advantages: the multistep form shows the components used in deriving net income, and the single-step form has the advantage of simplicity.

www.nike.com   Exhibit 6 shows the single-step income statement used by Nike, Inc., the footwear company. When a company uses the single-step form, most analysts will

FIGURE 4
Graphic Presentation of a Portion of Dell Computer Corporation's Income Statement

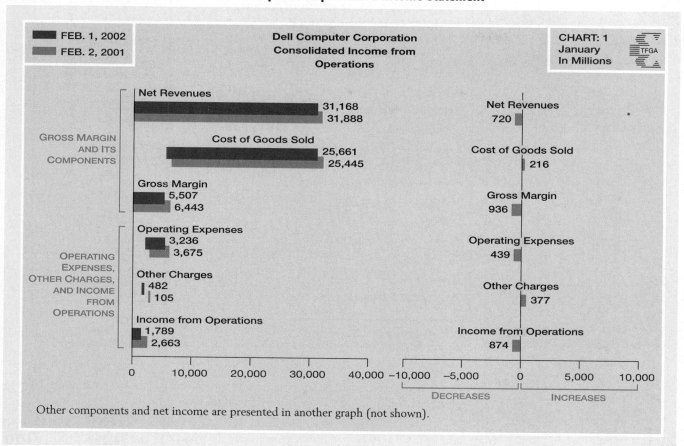

Other components and net income are presented in another graph (not shown).

EXHIBIT 5
Single-Step Income Statement for Shafer Auto Parts Corporation

Shafer Auto Parts Corporation
Income Statement
For the Year Ended December 31, 20x2

Revenues		
Net sales		$289,656
Interest income		1,400
Total revenues		$291,056
Costs and expenses		
Cost of goods sold	$181,260	
Selling expenses	54,780	
General and administrative expenses	34,504	
Interest expense	2,631	
Total costs and expenses		273,175
Income before income taxes		$ 17,881
Income taxes		3,381
Net income		$ 14,500
Earnings per share		$ 2.90

EXHIBIT 6
Single-Step Income Statement for Nike, Inc.

Nike, Inc.
Consolidated Statements of Income
(In millions, except per share data)

	Year Ended May 31,		
	2001	2000	1999
Revenues	$9,488.8	$8,995.1	$8,776.9
Costs and expenses:			
Costs of sales	5,784.9	5,403.8	5,493.5
Selling and administrative	2,689.7	2,606.4	2,426.6
Interest expense	58.7	45.0	44.1
Other income/expense, net	34.2	23.2	21.5
Restructuring charge, net	(.1)	(2.5)	45.1
Total costs and expenses	8,567.4	8,075.9	8,030.8
Income before income taxes	921.4	919.2	746.1
Income taxes	331.7	340.1	294.7
Net income	$ 589.7	$ 579.1	$ 451.4
Basic income per common share	$ 2.18	$ 2.10	$ 1.59

Source: Nike, Inc., *Annual Report,* 2001.
The accompanying notes to consolidated financial statements are an integral part of this statement.

still calculate gross margin, income from operations, and each component's percentage of revenues. Such calculations for Nike would be as follows:

	2001	Percent	2000	Percent
Revenues	$9,488.8	100.0	$8,995.1	100.0
Cost of sales	5,784.9	61.0	5,403.8	60.1
Gross margin	$3,703.9	39.0	$3,591.3	39.9
Selling and administrative expenses	2,689.7	28.3	2,606.4	29.0
Income from operations	$1,014.2	10.7	$ 984.9	10.9

This analysis shows that Nike's income from operations decreased slightly, from 10.9 to 10.7 percent. The difference of 0.2 percent may not seem like a lot, but on revenues of $9,488.8 million, it amounts to almost $1.9 million. The company improved its efficiency by decreasing its selling and administrative expenses by 0.7 percent (29.0 minus 28.3), but this was more than offset by the increase in cost of sales by 0.9 percent (61.0 minus 60.1).

✓ Check out ACE for a Review Quiz at http://accounting.college.hmco.com/students.

USING CLASSIFIED FINANCIAL STATEMENTS

LO7 Evaluate liquidity and profitability using classified financial statements.

RELATED TEXT ASSIGNMENTS
Q: 21, 22, 23, 24, 25
SE: 8, 9, 10
E: 8, 9, 10
P: 4, 5, 8
SD: 6
FRA: 1, 2, 3, 4, 5, 6, 7, 8

Earlier in this chapter, you learned that the objectives of financial reporting established by the Financial Accounting Standards Board are to provide information that is useful in making investment and credit decisions, in judging cash flow prospects, and in understanding business resources, claims to those resources, and changes in them. These objectives are related to two important goals of management: maintaining adequate liquidity and achieving satisfactory profitability. Investors and creditors base their decisions largely on their assessment of a company's potential liquidity and profitability. The following analysis shows how ratios make use of the components in classified financial statements to reflect a company's performance with respect to these important goals.

EVALUATION OF LIQUIDITY

Liquidity means having enough money on hand to pay bills when they are due and to take care of unexpected needs for cash. Two measures of liquidity are working capital and the current ratio.

■ **WORKING CAPITAL**   The first measure, **working capital**, is the amount by which total current assets exceed total current liabilities. This is an important measure of liquidity because current liabilities are debts that must be paid or obligations that must be performed within one year, and current assets are assets that will be realized in cash or used up within one year or one operating cycle, whichever is longer. By definition, current liabilities are paid out of current assets. So the excess of current assets over current liabilities is the net current assets, or working capital, on hand to continue business operations. Working capital can be used to buy inventory, obtain credit, and finance expanded sales. Lack of working capital can lead to a company's failure.

For Shafer Auto Parts Corporation, working capital is computed as follows:

Current assets	$124,356
Less current liabilities	42,683
Working capital	$ 81,673

■ **CURRENT RATIO**   The second measure of liquidity, the current ratio, is closely related to working capital and is believed by many bankers and other creditors to be a good indicator of a company's ability to pay its bills and to repay outstanding loans. The **current ratio** is the ratio of current assets to current liabilities. For Shafer Auto Parts Corporation, it would be computed like this:

$$\text{Current Ratio} = \frac{\text{Current Assets}}{\text{Current Liabilities}} = \frac{\$124,356}{\$42,683} = 2.9$$

Thus, Shafer has $2.90 of current assets for each $1.00 of current liabilities. Is that good or bad? The answer requires the comparison of this year's ratio with ratios for earlier years and with similar measures for successful companies in the same industry. The average current ratio varies widely from industry to industry, as shown in Figure 5. For the advertising industry, which has no merchandise inventory, the current ratio is 1.4. In contrast, auto and home supply, which carries large merchandise inventories, has an average current ratio of 2.2. The current ratio for Shafer Auto Parts Corporation, 2.9, exceeds the average for its industry. A very low current ratio, of course, can be unfavorable, but so can a very high one. The latter may indicate that the company is not using its assets effectively.

FIGURE 5
Average Current Ratio for Selected Industries

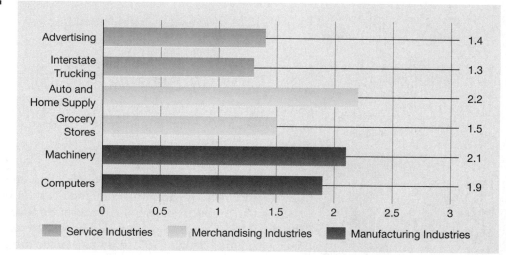

Source: Data from Dun & Bradstreet, *Industry Norms and Key Business Ratios*, 2000–2001.

FOCUS ON BUSINESS PRACTICE

Who Is Right: The Credit-Worthiness Analyst or the Profitability Analyst?

The answer depends on your point of view. For example, the future of Amazon.com, the online retailer, has sparked controversy in the big investment company of Lehman Brothers Inc. <www.lehman.com>. One Lehman analyst, who focuses on debt and credit worthiness, has provided a very bearish prediction of the future of Amazon.com because of the company's high level of debt and lack of cash flows to make debt payments. Another Lehman analyst, who focuses on growth and future profitability, is bullish on Amazon.com because the company is growing fast and reducing costs, which should lead to future profitability. Credit analysts tend to look at the downside of future prospects, whereas profitability analysts look at the upside. Which view of Amazon.com's future will prevail? Only time will tell.[14]

EVALUATION OF PROFITABILITY

Just as important as paying bills on time is **profitability**—the ability to earn a satisfactory income. As a goal, profitability competes with liquidity for managerial attention because liquid assets, although important, are not the best profit-producing resources. Cash, for example, means purchasing power, but a satisfactory profit can be made only if purchasing power is used to buy profit-producing (and less liquid) assets, such as inventory and long-term assets.

Among the common measures of a company's ability to earn income are (1) profit margin, (2) asset turnover, (3) return on assets, (4) debt to equity ratio, and (5) return on equity. To evaluate a company meaningfully, one must relate its profit performance to its past performance and prospects for the future as well as to the averages for other companies in the same industry.

■ **PROFIT MARGIN** The **profit margin** shows the percentage of each sales dollar that results in net income. It is figured by dividing net income by net sales. It should not be confused with gross margin, which is not a ratio but rather the amount by which revenues exceed the cost of goods sold.

Shafer Auto Parts Corporation has a profit margin of 5.0 percent:

$$\text{Profit Margin} = \frac{\text{Net Income}}{\text{Net Sales}} = \frac{\$14,500}{\$289,656} = .050 \ (5.0\%)$$

On each dollar of net sales, Shafer made 5.0 cents. A difference of 1 or 2 percent in a company's profit margin can mean the difference between a fair year and a very profitable one.

■ **ASSET TURNOVER** **Asset turnover** measures how efficiently assets are used to produce sales. Computed by dividing net sales by average total assets, it shows how many dollars of sales were generated by each dollar of assets. A company with a higher asset turnover uses its assets more productively than one with a lower asset turnover. Average total assets is computed by adding total assets at the beginning of the year to total assets at the end of the year and dividing by 2.

Assuming that total assets for Shafer Auto Parts Corporation were $148,620 at the beginning of the year, its asset turnover is computed as follows:

> **KEY POINT:** Average total assets equals assets at the beginning of the year plus assets at the end of the year, divided by 2.

$$\text{Asset Turnover} = \frac{\text{Net Sales}}{\text{Average Total Assets}}$$

$$= \frac{\$289,656}{(\$158,916 + \$148,620) \div 2} = \frac{\$289,656}{\$153,768} = 1.9 \text{ times}$$

Shafer produces $1.90 in sales for each $1.00 invested in average total assets. This ratio shows a meaningful relationship between an income statement figure and a balance sheet figure.

■ **RETURN ON ASSETS** Both the profit margin and the asset turnover ratios have some limitations. The profit margin ratio does not take into consideration the assets necessary to produce income, and the asset turnover ratio does not take into account the amount of income produced. The **return on assets** ratio overcomes these deficiencies by relating net income to average total assets. For Shafer Auto Parts, it is computed like this:

FIGURE 6
Average Profit Margin for Selected Industries

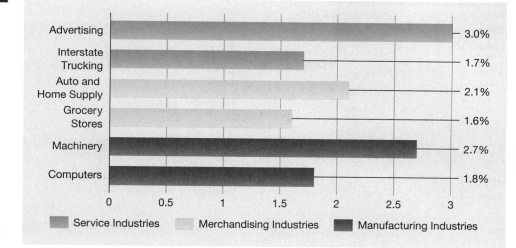

Source: Data from Dun & Bradstreet, *Industry Norms and Key Business Ratios,* 2000–2001.

$$\text{Return on Assets} = \frac{\text{Net Income}}{\text{Average Total Assets}}$$

$$= \frac{\$14,500}{(\$158,916 + \$148,620) \div 2} = \frac{\$14,500}{\$153,768} = .094 \ (9.4\%)$$

KEY POINT: Return on assets is one of the most widely used measures of profitability because it reflects both the profit margin and asset turnover.

For each dollar invested, Shafer's assets generated 9.4 cents of net income. This ratio indicates the income-generating strength (profit margin) of the company's resources and how efficiently the company is using all its assets (asset turnover).

Return on assets, then, combines profit margin and asset turnover:

$$\frac{\text{Net Income}}{\text{Net Sales}} \times \frac{\text{Net Sales}}{\text{Average Total Assets}} = \frac{\text{Net Income}}{\text{Average Total Assets}}$$

$$\text{Profit Margin} \times \quad \text{Asset Turnover} \quad = \quad \text{Return on Assets}$$

$$5.0\% \quad \times \quad 1.9 \text{ times} \quad = \quad 9.5\%*$$

*The slight difference between 9.4 and 9.5 is due to rounding.

Thus, a company's management can improve overall profitability by increasing the profit margin, the asset turnover, or both. Similarly, in evaluating a company's overall profitability, the financial statement user must consider the interaction of both ratios to produce return on assets.

Careful study of Figures 6, 7, and 8 shows the different ways in which the selected industries combine profit margin and asset turnover to produce return on

FIGURE 7
Asset Turnover for Selected Industries

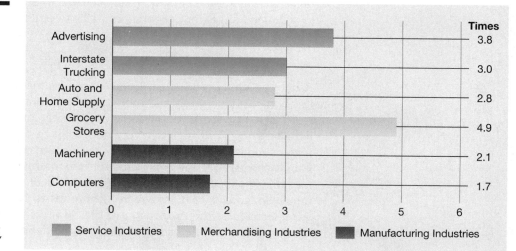

Source: Data from Dun & Bradstreet, *Industry Norms and Key Business Ratios,* 2000–2001.

FIGURE 8
Return on Assets for Selected Industries

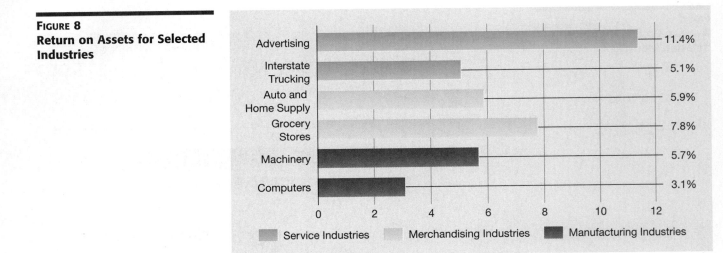

Source: Data from Dun & Bradstreet, *Industry Norms and Key Business Ratios,* 2000–2001.

● **STOP AND THINK!**

Why is it important to compare a company's financial performance with industry averages?

When calculating ratios to measure performance, analysts need benchmarks to measure whether the performance was good or bad. Past performance of the company is one measure, but a better measure is the financial performance of similar companies. This is done by examining industry averages. ■

KEY POINT: A company with a low debt to equity ratio has a better chance of surviving in rough times. Debt requires additional expenses (interest) that must be paid.

assets. For instance, by comparing the return on assets for grocery stores and machinery manufacturers, you can see how they achieve it in very different ways. The grocery store industry has a profit margin of 1.6 percent, which when multiplied by an asset turnover of 4.9 times, gives a return on assets of 7.8 percent. The machinery industry, on the other hand, has a higher profit margin, 2.7 percent, and a lower asset turnover, 2.1 times, and produces a return on assets of 5.7 percent.

Shafer's profit margin of 5.0 percent is well above the auto and home supply industry average of 2.1 percent, but its asset turnover of 1.9 times lags behind the industry average of 2.8 times. Shafer is sacrificing asset turnover to achieve a higher profit margin. It is clear that this strategy is working, because Shafer's return on assets of 9.4 percent exceeds the industry average of 5.9 percent.

■ **DEBT TO EQUITY RATIO**   Another useful measure of profitability is the **debt to equity ratio**, which shows the proportion of the company financed by creditors in comparison with that financed by stockholders. This ratio is computed by dividing total liabilities by stockholders' equity. Since the balance sheets of most public companies do not show total liabilities, a short way of determining total liabilities is to deduct the total stockholders' equity from total assets. A debt to equity ratio of 1.0 means that total liabilities equal stockholders' equity—that half of the company's assets are financed by creditors. A ratio of .5 means that one-third of the assets are financed by creditors. A company with a high debt to equity ratio is at risk in poor economic times because it must continue to repay creditors. Stockholders' investments, on the other hand, do not have to be repaid, and dividends can be deferred when the company suffers because of a poor economy.

Shafer Auto Parts Corporation's debt to equity ratio is computed as follows:

$$\text{Debt to Equity} = \frac{\text{Total Liabilities}}{\text{Stockholders' Equity}} = \frac{\$60,483}{\$98,433} = .614 \ (61.4\%)$$

A debt to equity ratio of 61.4 percent means that Shafer receives less than half its financing from creditors and more than half from its investors.

The debt to equity ratio does not fit neatly into either the liquidity or the profitability category. It is clearly very important to liquidity analysis because it relates to debt and its repayment. However, the debt to equity ratio is also relevant to profitability for two reasons. First, creditors are interested in the proportion of the business that is debt-financed because the more debt a company has, the more profit it must earn to ensure the payment of interest to its creditors. Second, stockholders are interested in the proportion of the business that is debt-financed because the amount of interest that must be paid on the debt affects the amount of profit that

FIGURE 9
Average Debt to Equity Ratio for Selected Industries

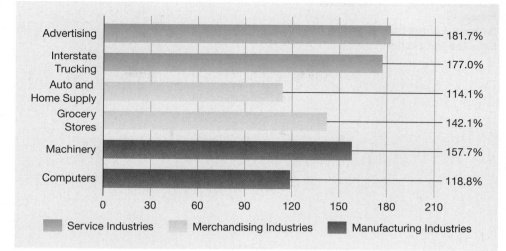

Source: Data from Dun & Bradstreet, *Industry Norms and Key Business Ratios,* 2000–2001.

is left to provide a return on stockholders' investments. The debt to equity ratio also shows how much expansion is possible by borrowing additional long-term funds. Figure 9 shows that the debt to equity ratio in our selected industries varies from a low of 114.1 percent in the auto and home supply industry to a high of 181.7 percent in the advertising industry.

■ **RETURN ON EQUITY** Of course, stockholders are interested in how much they have earned on their investment in the business. Their **return on equity** is measured by the ratio of net income to average stockholders' equity. Taking the ending stockholders' equity from the balance sheet and assuming that beginning stockholders' equity is $100,553, Shafer's return on equity is computed as follows:

$$\text{Return on Equity} = \frac{\text{Net Income}}{\text{Average Stockholders' Equity}}$$

$$= \frac{\$14,500}{(\$98,433 + \$100,553) \div 2} = \frac{\$14,500}{\$99,493} = .146 \ (14.6\%)$$

In 20x2, Shafer earned 14.6 cents for every dollar invested by stockholders.

Whether this is an acceptable return depends on several factors, such as how much the company earned in previous years and how much other companies in the same industry earned. As measured by return on equity (Figure 10), the advertising industry is the most profitable of our sample industries, with a return on equity of

FOCUS ON BUSINESS PRACTICE

To What Level of Profitability Should a Company Aspire?

At one time, a company earning a 20 percent return on equity ranked among the elite. Only Disney <www.disney.go.com>, Wal-Mart <www.walmart.com>, Coca-Cola <www.coca-cola.com>, and a few other companies were able to achieve this level of profitability. However, in the first quarter of 1995, for the first time, the average company of the Standard & Poor's 500 companies made a return on equity of 20.12 percent. *The Wall Street Journal* described this performance as "akin to the average ball player hitting .350."[15] This meant that stockholders' equity would double every four years.

Why did this happen? First, a good business environment and cost cutting led to more profitable operations. Second, special charges and other accounting transactions reduced stockholders' equity for many companies. In this way, the denominator of the ratio is reduced, thus increasing the ratio.

Until 2000, the number of companies with a return on equity of more than 20 percent continued to increase, but during the recession of 2001 and 2002, this number declined. When earnings are declining, companies tend to emphasize measures of performance other than profitability.

FIGURE 10
Average Return on Equity for Selected Industries

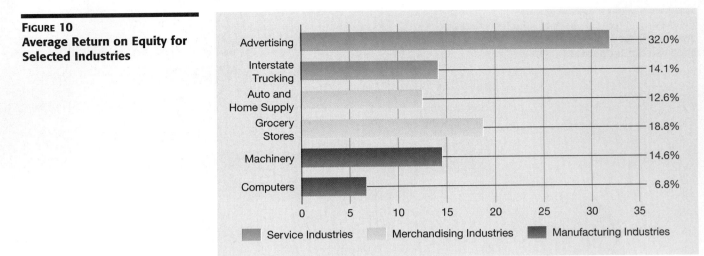

Source: Data from Dun & Bradstreet, *Industry Norms and Key Business Ratios,* 2000–2001.

32.0 percent. Shafer Auto Parts Corporation's average return on equity of 14.6 percent is more than the average of 12.6 percent for the auto and home supply industry.

■ **GRAPHING RATIO ANALYSIS**   Figure 11, prepared with the Fingraph® Financial Analyst™ software that is available with this text, graphically presents Dell Computer Corporation's profitability ratios involving net income. It helps us

www.dell.com

FIGURE 11
Graphic Presentation of Dell Computer Corporation's Profitability Ratios

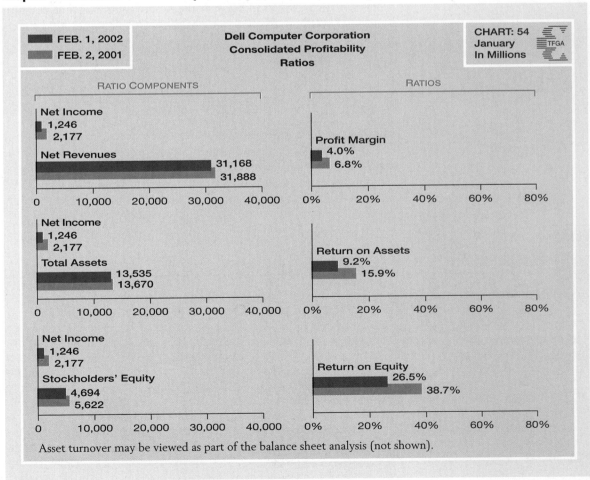

Asset turnover may be viewed as part of the balance sheet analysis (not shown).

visualize the progress of the company in meeting its profitability objectives. On the left of the figure are the components of the ratios. On the right are the ratios for the past two years. Notice that the changes in return on equity and return on assets are linked to changes in profit margin or asset turnover. The Fingraph Financial Analyst CD-ROM software graphs all the ratios used in this book and provides narrative analysis. The asset turnover ratio is shown graphically with the Fingraph balance sheet analysis.

✔ Check out ACE for a Review Quiz at http://accounting.college.hmco.com/students.

Chapter Review

REVIEW OF LEARNING OBJECTIVES

LO1 State the objectives of financial reporting.

The objectives of financial reporting are (1) to furnish information that is useful in making investment and credit decisions, (2) to provide information that can be used to assess cash flow prospects, and (3) to provide information about business resources, claims to those resources, and changes in them.

LO2 State the qualitative characteristics of accounting information and describe their interrelationships.

Understandability depends on the knowledge of the user and the ability of the accountant to provide useful information. Usefulness is a function of two primary characteristics, relevance and reliability. Information is relevant when it affects the outcome of a decision. Information that is relevant has feedback value and predictive value, and is timely. To be reliable, information must represent what it is supposed to represent and be verifiable and neutral.

LO3 Define and describe the conventions of *comparability* and *consistency, materiality, conservatism, full disclosure,* and *cost-benefit.*

Because accountants' measurements are not exact, certain conventions are applied in current practice to help users interpret financial statements. The first of these conventions is comparability and consistency. Consistency requires the use of the same accounting procedures from period to period and enhances the comparability of financial statements. The second is materiality, which has to do with the relative importance of an item. The third is conservatism, which entails using the procedure that is least likely to overstate assets and income. The fourth is full disclosure, which means including all relevant information in the financial statements. The fifth is cost-benefit, which suggests that above a minimum level of information, additional information should be provided only if the benefits derived from the information exceed the costs of providing it.

LO4 Explain management's responsibility for ethical financial reporting and define *fraudulent financial reporting.*

Management is responsible for the preparation of financial statements in accordance with generally accepted accounting principles and for the internal controls that provide assurance that this objective is achieved. Fraudulent financial reporting is the intentional preparation of misleading financial statements.

LO5 Identify and describe the basic components of a classified balance sheet.

The classified balance sheet is subdivided as follows:

Assets	Liabilities
Current assets	Current liabilities
Investments	Long-term liabilities
Property, plant, and equipment	**Stockholders' Equity**
Intangible assets	Contributed capital
(Other assets)	Retained earnings

A current asset is an asset that can reasonably be expected to be realized in cash or consumed during the next year or the normal operating cycle, whichever is longer. Investments are assets, usually long term, that are not used in the normal operation of a business. Property, plant, and equipment are tangible long-term assets used in day-to-day operations. Intangible assets are long-term assets with no physical substance whose value stems from the rights or privileges they extend to stockholders. A current liability is an obligation that can reasonably be expected to be paid or performed during the next year or the normal operating cycle, whichever is longer. Long-term liabilities are debts that fall due more than one year in the future or beyond the normal operating cycle. The equity section of the balance sheet for a corporation differs from that for a proprietorship or partnership in that it has subdivisions of contributed capital (the value of assets invested by stockholders) and retained earnings (stockholders' claim to assets earned from operations and reinvested in operations).

LO6 Prepare multistep and single-step classified income statements.

Classified income statements for external reporting can be in multistep or single-step form. The multistep form arrives at income before income taxes through a series of steps; the single-step form arrives at income before income taxes in a single step. There is usually a separate section in the multistep form for other revenues and expenses.

LO7 Evaluate liquidity and profitability using classified financial statements.

One important use of classified financial statements is to evaluate a company's liquidity and profitability. Two measures of liquidity are working capital and the current ratio. Five measures of profitability are profit margin, asset turnover, return on assets, debt to equity ratio, and return on equity. Referring to industry averages aids interpretation of these ratios.

REVIEW OF CONCEPTS AND TERMINOLOGY

The following concepts and terms were introduced in this chapter:

LO7 **Asset turnover:** A measure of profitability that shows how efficiently assets are used to produce sales; net sales divided by average total assets.

LO5 **Classified financial statements:** General-purpose external financial statements that are divided into subcategories.

LO3 **Comparability:** The convention of presenting information in a way that enables decision makers to recognize similarities, differences, and trends over different time periods or between different companies.

LO3 **Conservatism:** The convention that when faced with two equally acceptable alternatives, the accountant must choose the one least likely to overstate assets and income.

LO3 **Consistency:** The convention requiring that once an accounting procedure is adopted, it not be changed from one period to the next unless users of the financial statements are informed of the change.

LO3 **Conventions:** Rules of thumb, or general principles, for recording transactions and preparing financial statements.

LO3 **Cost-benefit:** The convention that the benefits gained from providing accounting information should be greater than the costs of providing that information.

LO6 **Cost of goods sold:** The amount a merchandiser paid for the merchandise it sold during an accounting period or the cost to a manufacturer of making the products it sold during an accounting period. Also called *cost of sales*.

LO5 **Current assets:** Cash and other assets that are reasonably expected to be converted to cash, sold, or consumed within one year or within a normal operating cycle, whichever is longer.

LO5 **Current liabilities:** Obligations due to be paid or performed within one year or within the normal operating cycle, whichever is longer.

LO7 **Current ratio:** A measure of liquidity; current assets divided by current liabilities.

LO7 **Debt to equity ratio:** A measure of profitability that shows the relationship of assets financed by creditors to those financed by stockholders; total liabilities divided by stockholders' equity.

LO6 **Earnings per share:** Net income earned on each share of common stock; net income divided by the average number of common shares outstanding during the year. Also called *net income per share*.

LO4 **Fraudulent financial reporting:** The intentional preparation of misleading financial statements.

LO6 **Freight out expense:** The cost to the seller of shipping goods to the buyer. Also called *delivery expense*.

LO3   Full disclosure: The convention requiring that a company's financial statements and their notes present all information relevant to the users' understanding of the statements.

LO6   Gross margin: The difference between net sales and cost of goods sold. Also called *gross profit.*

LO6   Gross sales: Total sales for cash and on credit during an accounting period.

LO6   Income before income taxes: The amount a company has earned from all activities—operating and nonoperating—before taking into account the amount of income taxes incurred.

LO6   Income from operations: Gross margin less operating expenses. Also called *operating income.*

LO6   Income taxes: A category for the expense of federal, state, and local taxes that appears only on income statements of corporations. Also called *provision for income taxes.*

LO5   Intangible assets: Long-term assets with no physical substance whose value stems from the rights or privileges they extend to their owners.

LO5   Investments: Assets, usually long term, that are not used in the normal operation of a business and that management does not intend to convert to cash within the next year.

LO7   Liquidity: Having enough money on hand to pay bills when they are due and to take care of unexpected needs for cash.

LO5   Long-term liabilities: Debts that fall due more than one year in the future or beyond the normal operating cycle.

LO6   Manufacturing companies: Companies that make and sell products.

LO3   Materiality: The convention that refers to the relative importance of an item or event in a financial statement and its influence on the decisions of the users of financial statements.

LO6   Merchandising companies: Companies, including both wholesalers and retailers, that buy and sell products.

LO6   Multistep income statement: An income statement that goes through a series of steps to arrive at income before income taxes.

LO6   Net income: What remains of gross margin after operating expenses are deducted, other revenues and expenses are added or deducted, and income taxes are deducted. Also referred to as the "bottom line."

LO6   Net sales: The gross proceeds from sales of merchandise, or gross sales, less sales returns and allowances and any discounts allowed. Often simply called *sales.*

LO6   Operating expenses: Expenses other than cost of goods sold that are incurred in running a business.

LO5   Other assets: A balance sheet category that some companies use to group all assets other than current assets and property, plant, and equipment.

LO6   Other revenues and expenses: The section of a multistep income statement that includes revenues and expenses not related to business operations. Also called *nonoperating revenues and expenses.*

 LO7   Profitability: The ability of a business to earn a satisfactory income.

LO7   Profit margin: A measure of profitability that shows the percentage of each sales dollar that results in net income; net income divided by net sales.

LO5   Property, plant, and equipment: Tangible long-term assets used in the continuing operation of a business. Also called *operating assets, fixed assets, tangible assets, long-lived assets,* or *plant assets.*

LO2   Qualitative characteristics: Standards for judging the information that accountants give to decision makers.

LO2 **Relevance:** The qualitative characteristic of information that bears directly on the outcome of a decision.

LO2 **Reliability:** The qualitative characteristic of information that represents what it is supposed to represent and is verifiable and neutral.

LO7 **Return on assets:** A measure of profitability that shows how efficiently a company uses its assets to produce income; net income divided by average total assets.

LO7 **Return on equity:** A measure of profitability that relates the amount earned by a business to the stockholders' investment in the business; net income divided by average stockholders' equity.

LO6 **Single-step income statement:** An income statement that arrives at income before income taxes in a single step.

LO2 **Understandability:** The qualitative characteristic of information that communicates an intended meaning.

LO2 **Usefulness:** The qualitative characteristic of information that is relevant and reliable.

LO7 **Working capital:** A measure of liquidity that shows the net current assets on hand to continue business operations; total current assets minus total current liabilities.

REVIEW PROBLEM

Analyzing Liquidity and Profitability Using Ratios

LO7 Flavin Shirt Company has faced increased competition from overseas shirtmakers in recent years. Presented below is summary information for the last two years:

	20x2	20x1
Current Assets	$ 200,000	$ 170,000
Total Assets	880,000	710,000
Current Liabilities	90,000	50,000
Long-Term Liabilities	150,000	50,000
Stockholders' Equity	640,000	610,000
Sales	1,200,000	1,050,000
Net Income	60,000	80,000

Total assets and stockholders' equity at the beginning of 20x1 were $690,000 and $590,000, respectively.

REQUIRED ▶ Use (1) liquidity analysis and (2) profitability analysis to document the declining financial position of Flavin Shirt Company.

ANSWER TO REVIEW PROBLEM

1. Liquidity analysis

	Current Assets	Current Liabilities	Working Capital	Current Ratio
20x1	$170,000	$50,000	$120,000	3.40
20x2	200,000	90,000	110,000	2.22
Decrease in working capital			$ 10,000	
Decrease in current ratio				1.18

Both working capital and the current ratio declined from 20x1 to 20x2 because the $40,000 increase in liabilities ($90,000 − $50,000) was greater than the $30,000 increase in currents assets.

2. Profitability analysis

	Net Income	Sales	Profit Margin	Average Total Assets	Asset Turnover	Return on Assets	Average Stock-holders' Equity	Return on Equity
20x1	$80,000	$1,050,000	7.6%	$700,000[1]	1.50	11.4%	$600,000[3]	13.3%
20x2	60,000	1,200,000	5.0	795,000[2]	1.51	7.5	625,000[4]	9.6
Increase (decrease)	($20,000)	$ 150,000	(2.6)%	$ 95,000	0.01	(3.9)%	$ 25,000	(3.7)%

[1]($710,000 + $690,000) ÷ 2   [3]($610,000 + $590,000) ÷ 2
[2]($880,000 + $710,000) ÷ 2   [4]($640,000 + $610,000) ÷ 2

Net income decreased by $20,000 despite an increase in sales of $150,000 and an increase in average total assets of $95,000. The results were decreases in profit margin from 7.6 percent to 5.0 percent and in return on assets from 11.4 percent to 7.5 percent. Asset turnover showed almost no change and so did not contribute to the decline in profitability. The decrease in return on equity, from 13.3 percent to 9.6 percent, was not as great as the decrease in return on assets because the growth in total assets was financed mainly by debt instead of by stockholders' equity, as shown by the capital structure analysis below.

	Total Liabilities	Stockholders' Equity	Debt to Equity Ratio
20x1	$100,000	$610,000	16.4%
20x2	240,000	640,000	37.5
Increase	$140,000	$ 30,000	21.1%

Total liabilities increased by $140,000, while stockholders' equity increased by $30,000. As a result, the amount of the business financed by debt in relation to the amount of the business financed by stockholders' equity increased from 20x1 to 20x2.

Chapter Assignments

BUILDING YOUR KNOWLEDGE FOUNDATION

QUESTIONS

1. What are the three objectives of financial reporting?
2. What are the qualitative characteristics of accounting information, and what is their significance?
3. What are the accounting conventions? How does each help in the interpretation of financial information?

4. Who is responsible for the preparation of reliable financial statements, and what is a principal way of achieving this objective?

5. What is the purpose of classified financial statements?

6. What are four common categories of assets?

7. What criteria must an asset meet to be classified as current? Under what condition is an asset considered current even though it will not be realized as cash within a year? What are two examples of assets that fall into this category?

8. In what order should current assets be listed?

9. What is the difference between a short-term investment in the current assets section of the balance sheet and a security in the investments section?

10. What is an intangible asset? Give at least three examples.

11. Name the two major categories of liabilities.

12. What are the primary differences between the equity section of the balance sheet for a sole proprietorship or partnership and the corresponding section for a corporation?

13. What is the primary difference between the operations of a merchandising business and those of a service business? How is this difference reflected on the income statement?

14. Define *gross margin*. Why is it important?

15. During its first year in operation, Kumler Nursery had a cost of goods sold of $64,000 and a gross margin equal to 40 percent of sales. What was the dollar amount of the company's sales?

16. Could Kumler Nursery (in Question 15) have a net loss for the year? Explain your answer.

17. Explain how the multistep form of income statement differs from the single-step form. What are the relative merits of each?

18. Why are other revenues and expenses separated from operating revenues and expenses in the multistep income statement?

19. What are some of the differences between the income statement for a sole proprietorship and that for a corporation?

20. Explain earnings per share and indicate how this figure appears on the income statement.

21. Define *liquidity* and name two measures of liquidity.

22. How is the current ratio computed, and why is it important?

23. Which is the more important goal, liquidity or profitability? Explain your answer.

24. Name five measures of profitability.

25. "Return on assets is a better measure of profitability than profit margin." Evaluate this statement.

SHORT EXERCISES

SE 1.

LO1 Objectives and Qualitative
LO2 Characteristics

Identify each of the following statements as either an objective (O) of financial information or a qualitative (Q) characteristic of accounting information:

1. Information about business resources, claims to those resources, and changes in them should be provided.
2. Decision makers must be able to interpret accounting information.
3. Information that is useful in making investment and credit decisions should be furnished.
4. Accounting information must be relevant and reliable.
5. Information useful in assessing cash flow prospects should be provided.

SE 2.

LO3 Accounting Conventions

State which of the accounting conventions—comparability and consistency, materiality, conservatism, full disclosure, or cost-benefit—is being followed in each of the cases listed below.

1. Management provides detailed information about the company's long-term debt in the notes to the financial statements.

2. A company does not account separately for discounts received for prompt payment of accounts payable because few of these transactions occur and the total amount of the discounts is small. m

3. Management eliminates a weekly report on property, plant, and equipment acquisitions and disposals because no one finds it useful. Co

4. A company follows the policy of recognizing a loss on inventory when the market value of an item falls below its cost but does nothing if the market value rises. c

5. When several accounting methods are acceptable, management chooses a single method and follows that method from year to year. com, tc

LO5 Classification of Accounts: Balance Sheet

SE 3. Tell whether each of the following accounts is a current asset; an investment; property, plant, and equipment; an intangible asset; a current liability; a long-term liability; stockholders' equity; or not on the balance sheet:

1. Delivery Trucks
2. Accounts Payable CL
3. Note Payable (due in 90 days) CL
4. Delivery Expense no
5. Common Stock

6. Prepaid Insurance CA
7. Trademark Ia
8. Investment to Be Held Six Months cA
9. Income Taxes Payable CL
10. Factory Not Used in Business L

LO5 Classified Balance Sheet

SE 4. Using the following accounts, prepare a classified balance sheet at year end, May 31, 20xx: Accounts Payable, $400; Accounts Receivable, $550; Accumulated Depreciation, Equipment, $350; Cash, $100; Common Stock, $500; Equipment, $2,000; Franchise, $100; Investments (long-term), $250; Merchandise Inventory, $300; Notes Payable (long-term), $200; Retained Earnings, ?; Wages Payable, $50.

LO6 Classification of Accounts: Income Statement

SE 5. Tell whether each of the following accounts is part of net sales, cost of goods sold, operating expenses, or other revenues and expenses, or is not on the income statement:

1. Delivery Expense oe
2. Interest Expense
3. Unearned Revenue
4. Sales Returns and Allowances

5. Cost of Goods Sold
6. Depreciation Expense
7. Investment Income
8. Retained Earnings

LO6 Single-Step Income Statement

SE 6. Using the following accounts, prepare a single-step income statement at year end, May 31, 20xx: Cost of Goods Sold, $280; General Expenses, $150; Income Taxes, $35; Interest Expense, $70; Interest Income, $30; Net Sales, $800; Selling Expenses, $185. Ignore earnings per share.

LO6 Multistep Income Statement

SE 7. Using the accounts presented in SE 6, prepare a multistep income statement.

LO7 Liquidity Ratios

SE 8. Using the following accounts and balances taken from a year-end balance sheet, compute working capital and the current ratio:

Accounts Payable	$ 7,000
Accounts Receivable	10,000
Cash	4,000
Common Stock	20,000
Marketable Securities	2,000
Merchandise Inventory	12,000
Notes Payable in Three Years	13,000
Property, Plant, and Equipment	40,000
Retained Earnings	28,000

LO7 Profitability Ratios

SE 9. Using the following information from a balance sheet and an income statement, compute the (1) profit margin, (2) asset turnover, (3) return on assets, (4) debt to equity ratio, and (5) return on equity. (The previous year's total assets were $100,000 and stockholders' equity was $70,000.)

Total assets	$120,000
Total liabilities	30,000
Total stockholders' equity	90,000
Net sales	130,000
Cost of goods sold	70,000
Operating expenses	40,000
Income taxes	5,000

LO7 Relationship of Profitability Ratios

SE 10. Assume that a company has a profit margin of 6.0 percent, an asset turnover of 3.2 times, and a debt to equity ratio of 50 percent. What are the company's return on assets and return on equity?

EXERCISES

E 1.

LO1 Financial Accounting Concepts
LO2
LO3

The lettered items below represent a classification scheme for the concepts of financial accounting. Match each numbered term with the letter of the category in which it belongs.

a. Decision makers (users of accounting information)
b. Business activities or entities relevant to accounting measurement
c. Objectives of accounting information
d. Accounting measurement considerations
e. Accounting processing considerations
f. Qualitative characteristics
g. Accounting conventions
h. Financial statements

1. Conservatism
2. Verifiability
3. Statement of cash flows
4. Materiality
5. Reliability
6. Recognition
7. Cost-benefit
8. Understandability
9. Business transactions
10. Consistency
11. Full disclosure
12. Furnishing information that is useful to investors and creditors

13. Specific business entities
14. Classification
15. Management
16. Neutrality
17. Internal accounting control
18. Valuation
19. Investors
20. Timeliness
21. Relevance
22. Furnishing information that is useful in assessing cash flow prospects

E 2.

LO3 Accounting Concepts and Conventions

Each of the statements below violates a convention in accounting. State which of the following accounting conventions is violated: comparability and consistency, materiality, conservatism, full disclosure, or cost-benefit.

1. A series of reports that are time-consuming and expensive to prepare is presented to the board of directors each month even though the reports are never used.
2. A company changes its method of accounting for depreciation.
3. The company in 2 does not indicate in the financial statements that the method of depreciation was changed, nor does it specify the effect of the change on net income.
4. A new office building next to the factory is debited to the Factory account because it represents a fairly small dollar amount in relation to the factory.
5. The asset account for a pickup truck still used in the business is written down to what the truck could be sold for even though the carrying value under conventional depreciation methods is higher.

E 3.

LO5 Classification of Accounts: Balance Sheet

The lettered items below represent a classification scheme for a balance sheet, and the numbered items are account titles. Match each account with the letter of the category in which it belongs.

a. Current assets
b. Investments
c. Property, plant, and equipment
d. Intangible assets

e. Current liabilities
f. Long-term liabilities
g. Stockholders' equity
h. Not on balance sheet

1. Patent
2. Building Held for Sale
3. Prepaid Rent
4. Wages Payable
5. Note Payable in Five Years
6. Building Used in Operations
7. Fund Held to Pay Off Long-Term Debt
8. Inventory

9. Prepaid Insurance
10. Depreciation Expense
11. Accounts Receivable
12. Interest Expense
13. Unearned Revenue
14. Short-Term Investments
15. Accumulated Depreciation
16. Retained Earnings

E 4.

LO5 Classified Balance Sheet Preparation

The following data pertain to Mia, Inc.: Accounts Payable, $51,000; Accounts Receivable, $38,000; Accumulated Depreciation, Building, $14,000; Accumulated Depreciation, Equipment, $17,000; Bonds Payable, $60,000; Building, $70,000; Cash, $31,200; Common Stock, $10 par, 10,000 shares authorized, issued, and outstanding, $100,000;

Copyright, $6,200; Equipment, $152,000; Inventory, $40,000; Investment in Corporate Securities (long-term), $20,000; Investment in Six-Month Government Securities, $16,400; Land, $8,000; Paid-in Capital in Excess of Par Value, $50,000; Prepaid Rent, $1,200; Retained Earnings, $88,200; and Revenue Received in Advance, $2,800.

Prepare a classified balance sheet at December 31, 20xx.

E 5.

LO6   Classification of Accounts: Income Statement

Using the classification scheme below for a multistep income statement, match each account with the letter of the category in which it belongs.

a. Net sales
b. Cost of goods sold
c. Selling expenses
d. General and administrative expenses
e. Other revenues and expenses
f. Not on income statement

1. Sales Discounts
2. Cost of Goods Sold
3. Dividend Income
4. Advertising Expense
5. Office Salaries Expense
6. Freight Out Expense
7. Prepaid Insurance

8. Utilities Expense
9. Sales Salaries Expense
10. Rent Expense
11. Depreciation Expense, Delivery Equipment
12. Taxes Payable
13. Interest Expense

E 6.

LO6   Preparation of Income Statements

Homework

The following data pertain to a corporation: net sales, $810,000; cost of goods sold, $440,000; selling expenses, $180,000; general and administrative expenses, $120,000; income taxes, $15,000; interest expense, $8,000; interest income, $6,000; and common stock outstanding, 100,000 shares.

1. Prepare a single-step income statement.
2. Prepare a multistep income statement.

E 7.

LO6   Multistep Income Statement

A single-step income statement appears below. Present the information in a multistep income statement, and tell what insights can be obtained from the multistep form as opposed to the single-step form.

Skye Linens Corporation
Income Statement
For the Year Ended December 31, 20xx

Revenues		
Net sales		$598,566
Interest income		2,860
Total revenues		$601,426
Costs and expenses		
Cost of goods sold	$388,540	
Selling expenses	101,870	
General and administrative expenses	50,344	
Interest expense	6,780	
Total costs and expenses		547,534
Income before income taxes		$ 53,892
Income taxes		12,000
Net income		$ 41,892
Earnings per share		$ 4.19

E 8.

LO7   Liquidity Ratios

The accounts and balances that follow are from the general ledger of Lake Corporation. Compute the (1) working capital and (2) current ratio.

C.L.   ~ Accounts Payable $16,600
C.A   — Accounts Receivable   10,200
C.A. — Cash   1,500
C.L. ___ Current Portion of Long-Term Debt   10,000
        Long-Term Investments   10,400
Inv. — Marketable Securities   12,600
C.A.   Merchandise Inventory   25,400
E.L — Notes Payable, 90 days   15,000
        Notes Payable, 2 years   20,000
C.A. — Notes Receivable, 90 days   26,000
        Notes Receivable, 2 years   10,000
C.A. ~ Prepaid Insurance   400
      ~ Property, Plant, and Equipment   60,000
C.L ~ Property Taxes Payable   1,250
        Retained Earnings   28,300
C.L. Salaries Payable   850
C A. Supplies   350
      —Unearned Revenue   750

E 9.   The following end-of-year amounts are from the financial statements of Parto
        Corporation: total assets, $426,000; total liabilities, $172,000; stockholders' equity,
        $254,000; net sales, $782,000; cost of goods sold, $486,000; operating expenses,
        $178,000; income taxes, $24,000; and dividends, $40,000. During the past year, total
        assets increased by $75,000. Total stockholders' equity was affected only by net income
        and dividends. Compute the (1) profit margin, (2) asset turnover, (3) return on assets,
        (4) debt to equity ratio, and (5) return on equity.

LO7   Profitability Ratios

E 10.   The simplified balance sheet and income statement for a corporation appear below.

LO7   Computation of Ratios

Balance Sheet
December 31, 20xx

Assets		Liabilities	
Current assets	$100,000	Current liabilities	$ 40,000
Investments	20,000	Long-term liabilities	60,000
Property, plant, and		Total liabilities	$100,000
equipment	293,000		
Intangible assets	27,000	**Stockholders' Equity**	
		Common stock	$200,000
		Retained earnings	140,000
		Total stockholders'	
		equity	$340,000
		Total liabilities and	
Total assets	$440,000	stockholders' equity	$440,000

Income Statement
For the Year Ended December 31, 20xx

Net sales	$820,000
Cost of goods sold	500,000
Gross margin	$320,000
Operating expenses	260,000
Income before income taxes	$ 60,000
Income taxes	10,000
Net income	$ 50,000

Total assets and stockholders' equity at the beginning of 20xx were $360,000 and $280,000, respectively.

1. Compute the following liquidity measures: (a) working capital and (b) current ratio.
2. Compute the following profitability measures: (a) profit margin, (b) asset turnover, (c) return on assets, (d) debt to equity ratio, and (e) return on equity.

PROBLEMS

P 1.

LO3 Accounting Conventions

In each case below, accounting conventions *may* have been violated.

1. Arinno Manufacturing Company uses the cost method for computing the balance sheet amount of inventory unless the market value of the inventory is less than the cost, in which case the market value is used. At the end of the current year, the market value is $77,000, and the cost is $80,000. Arinno uses the $77,000 figure to compute current assets because management feels it is the more cautious approach.
2. Shuess Company has annual sales of $5,000,000. It follows the practice of charging any items costing less than $100 to expenses in the year purchased. During the current year, it purchased several chairs for the executive conference rooms at $97 each, including freight. Although the chairs were expected to last for at least ten years, they were charged as an expense in accordance with company policy.
3. Wong Company closed its books on December 31, 20x3, before preparing its annual report. A day later, a fire destroyed one of its two factories. Although Wong had fire insurance and would not suffer a loss on the building, it expected a significant decrease in sales in 20x4 because of the fire. It did not report the fire damage in its 20x3 financial statements because the fire did not affect that years's operations.
4. Duffy Drug Company spends a substantial portion of its profits on research and development. The company has been reporting its $2,500,000 expenditure for research and development as a lump sum, but management recently decided to begin classifying the expenditures by project even though the recordkeeping costs will increase.
5. During the current year, Himall Company changed from one generally accepted method of accounting for inventories to another method.

REQUIRED ▶ In each case, identify the convention that applies, state whether or not the treatment is in accord with the convention and GAAP, and briefly explain why.

P 2.

LO6 Forms of the Income Statement

Ivy Nursery Corporation's single-step income statements for 20x4 and 20x3 follow.

Ivy Nursery Corporation
Income Statements
For the Years Ended April 30, 20x4 and 20x3

	20x4	20x3
Revenues		
Net sales	$525,932	$475,264
Interest income	800	700
Total revenues	$526,732	$475,964
Costs and expenses		
Cost of goods sold	$234,948	$171,850
Selling expenses	161,692	150,700
General and administrative expenses	62,866	42,086
Interest expense	3,600	850
Total costs and expenses	$463,106	$365,486
Income before income taxes	$ 63,626	$110,478
Income taxes	15,000	27,600
Net income	$ 48,626	$ 82,878
Earnings per share	$ 2.43	$ 4.14

Ivy Nursery Corporation had 20,000 shares of common stock outstanding during both 20x4 and 20x3.

REQUIRED ▶

1. From the information provided, prepare multistep income statements for 20x3 and 20x4 showing percentages of net sales for each component.
2. Did income from operations increase or decrease from 20x3 to 20x4? Write a short explanation of why this change occurred.
3. What effect did other revenues and expenses have on the change in income before income taxes? What action by management probably caused this change?

P 3.

LO5   Classified Balance Sheet

The following information is from the June 30, 20x4, post-closing trial balance of Olcott Hardware Corporation.

Account Name	Debit	Credit
Cash	$ 24,000	
Short-Term Investments	13,150	
Notes Receivable	45,000	
Accounts Receivable	76,570	
Merchandise Inventory	156,750	
Prepaid Rent	2,000	
Prepaid Insurance	1,200	
Sales Supplies	426	
Office Supplies	97	
Land Held for Future Expansion	11,500	
Selling Fixtures	72,400	
Accumulated Depreciation, Selling Fixtures		$ 22,000
Office Equipment	24,100	
Accumulated Depreciation, Office Equipment		12,050
Trademark	4,000	
Accounts Payable		109,745
Salaries Payable		787
Interest Payable		600
Notes Payable (due in three years)		36,000
Common Stock, $1 par value, 20,000 shares authorized, issued, and outstanding		20,000
Paid-in Capital in Excess of Par Value		130,000
Retained Earnings		100,011

REQUIRED ▶   From the information provided, prepare a classified balance sheet.

P 4.

LO7   Ratio Analysis: Liquidity and Profitability

Ⓚ/Ⓡ

Below is a summary of data from the income statements and balance sheets for Gamber Construction Supply, Inc., for 20x4 and 20x3.

	20x4	20x3
Current assets	$ 183,000	$ 155,000
Total assets	1,160,000	870,000
Current liabilities	90,000	60,000
Long-term liabilities	300,000	200,000
Stockholders' equity	670,000	520,000
Net sales	2,300,000	1,740,000
Net income	150,000	102,000

Total assets and stockholders' equity at the beginning of 20x3 were $680,000 and $420,000, respectively.

REQUIRED ▶

1. Compute the following liquidity measures for 20x3 and 20x4: (a) working capital and (b) current ratio. Comment on the differences between the years.

2. Compute the following measures of profitability for 20x3 and 20x4: (a) profit margin, (b) asset turnover, (c) return on assets, (d) debt to equity ratio, and (e) return on equity. Comment on the change in performance from 20x3 to 20x4.

LO5 Classified Financial
LO6 Statement Preparation
LO7 and Evaluation

Ⓚ/Ⓡ

P 5. Sol Corporation is in the auto supply business. At the December 31, 20x6, year end, the following financial information was available from the income statement: administrative expenses, $161,600; cost of goods sold, $700,840; income taxes, $14,000; interest expense, $45,280; interest income, $5,600; net sales, $1,428,780; and selling expenses, $440,400.

The following information was available from the balance sheet (after closing entries were made): accounts payable, $65,200; accounts receivable, $209,600; accumulated depreciation, delivery equipment, $34,200; accumulated depreciation, store fixtures, $84,440; cash, $56,800; common stock, $1 par value, 20,000 shares authorized, issued, and outstanding, $20,000; delivery equipment, $177,000; inventory, $273,080; investment in securities (long-term), $112,000; investment in U.S. government securities (short-term), $79,200; long-term notes payable, $200,000; paid-in capital in excess of par value, $180,000; retained earnings, $518,600 (ending balance); notes payable (short-term), $100,000; prepaid expenses (short-term), $11,520; and store fixtures, $283,240.

Total assets and total stockholders' equity at December 31, 20x5, were $1,048,800 and $766,340, respectively, and dividends for the year were $120,000.

REQUIRED ▶

1. From the information above, prepare (a) an income statement in single-step form, (b) a statement of retained earnings, and (c) a classified balance sheet.
2. From the statements you have prepared, compute the following measures: (a) working capital and current ratio (for liquidity); and (b) profit margin, asset turnover, return on assets, debt to equity ratio, and return on equity (for profitability).
3. Using the industry averages for the auto and home supply business in Figures 5-10 in this chapter, determine whether Sol Corporation needs to improve its liquidity or its profitability. Explain your answer, making recommendations as to specific areas on which Sol Corporation should concentrate.

ALTERNATE PROBLEMS

LO3 Accounting Conventions

P 6. In each case below, accounting conventions *may* have been violated.

1. After careful study, Murphy Company, which has offices in forty states, has determined that in the future its method of depreciating office furniture should be changed. The new method is adopted for the current year, and the change is noted in the financial statements.
2. In the past, Bofti Corporation has recorded operating expenses in general accounts for each classification (e.g., Salaries Expense, Depreciation Expense, and Utilities Expense). Management has determined that despite the additional recordkeeping costs, the company's income statement should break down each operating expense into its components of selling expense and administrative expense.
3. Lilly Soo, the auditor of Norto Corporation, discovered that an official of the company had authorized the payment of a $1,000 bribe to a local government official. The management of Norto Corporation argued that because the item was so small in relation to the size of the company ($1,000,000 in sales), the illegal payment should not be disclosed.
4. Hayley's Bookstore built a small addition to its main building to house a new computer games section. Because no one could be sure that the computer games section would succeed, the accountant took a conservative approach and recorded the addition as an expense.
5. Since its origin ten years ago, Tor Company has used the same generally accepted inventory method. Because there has been no change in the inventory method, the company does not declare in its financial statements what inventory method it uses.

REQUIRED ▶ In each case, identify the convention that applies, state whether or not the treatment is in accord with the convention and generally accepted accounting principles, and briefly explain why.

P 7.   The income statements that follow are for Fitz Hardware Corporation.

Fitz Hardware Corporation
Income Statements
For the Years Ended July 31, 20x5 and 20x4

	20x5	20x4
Revenues		
Net sales	$464,200	$388,466
Interest income	420	500
Total revenues	$464,620	$388,966
Costs and expenses		
Cost of goods sold	$243,880	$198,788
Selling expenses	95,160	55,644
General and administrative expenses	90,840	49,286
Interest expense	5,600	1,100
Total costs and expenses	$435,480	$304,818
Income before income taxes	$ 29,140	$ 84,148
Income taxes	7,000	21,000
Net income	$ 22,140	$ 63,148
Earnings per share	$ 2.21	$ 6.31

REQUIRED ▶   1. From the information provided, prepare a multistep income statement for 20x4 and
20x5 showing percentages of net sales for each component.
2. Did income from operations increase or decrease from 20x4 to 20x5? Write a short
explanation of why this change occurred.
3. What effect did other revenues and expenses have on the change in income before
income taxes? What action by Fitz Hardware's management probably accounted for
this change?

P 8.   Murillo Products Corporation has had poor operating results for the past two years. As
the accountant for Murillo Products Corporation, you have the following information
available to you:

	20x4	20x3
Current assets	$ 90,000	$ 70,000
Total assets	290,000	220,000
Current liabilities	40,000	20,000
Long-term liabilities	40,000	—
Stockholders' equity	210,000	200,000
Net sales	524,000	400,000
Net income	32,000	22,000

Total assets and stockholders' equity at the beginning of 20x3 were $180,000 and
$160,000, respectively.

REQUIRED ▶   1. Compute the following measures of liquidity for 20x3 and 20x4: (a) working capital
and (b) current ratio. Comment on the differences between the years.

2. Compute the following measures of profitability for 20x3 and 20x4: (a) profit margin, (b) asset turnover, (c) return on assets, (d) debt to equity ratio, and (e) return on equity. Comment on the change in performance from 20x3 to 20x4.

SKILLS DEVELOPMENT CASES

Conceptual Analysis

LO3   Accounting Conventions

SD 1. Central Parking, which operates a seven-story parking building in downtown Chicago, has a calendar year end. It serves daily and hourly parkers, as well as monthly parkers who pay a fixed monthly rate in advance. The company traditionally has recorded all cash receipts as revenues when received. Most monthly parkers pay in full during the month prior to that in which they have the right to park. The company's auditors have said that beginning in 20x3, the company should consider recording the cash receipts from monthly parking on an accrual basis, crediting Unearned Revenues. Total cash receipts for 20x3 were $2,500,000, and the cash receipts received in 20x3 and applicable to January 20x4 were $125,000. Discuss the relevance of the accounting conventions of consistency, materiality, and full disclosure to the decision to record the monthly parking revenues on an accrual basis.

LO3   Materiality

SD 2. Sophia Electronics, Inc., operates a chain of consumer electronics stores in the Atlanta area. This year the company achieved annual sales of $50 million, on which it earned a net income of $2 million. At the beginning of the year, management implemented a new inventory system that enabled it to track all purchases and sales. At the end of the year, a physical inventory revealed that the actual inventory was $80,000 below what the new system indicated it should be. The inventory loss, which probably resulted from shoplifting, is reflected in a higher cost of goods sold. The problem concerns management but seems to be less important to the company's auditors. What is materiality? Why might the inventory loss concern management more than it does the auditors? Do you think the amount is material?

Ethical Dilemma

LO4   Ethics and Financial Reporting

SD 3. Sensor Software, located outside Boston, develops computer software and licenses it to financial institutions. The firm uses an aggressive accounting method that records revenues from the software it has developed on a percentage of completion basis. Consequently, revenue for partially completed projects is recognized based on the proportion of the project that is completed. If a project is 50 percent completed, then 50 percent of the contracted revenue is recognized. In 20x4, preliminary estimates for a $5 million project are that the project is 75 percent complete. Because the estimate of completion is a matter of judgment, management asks for a new report showing the project to be 90 percent complete. The change will enable senior managers to meet their financial goals for the year and thus receive substantial year-end bonuses. Do you think management's action is ethical? If you were the company controller and were asked to prepare the new report, would you do it? What action would you take?

 Group Activity: Use in-class groups to debate the ethics of the action.

LO4   Ethics and Financial Reporting

SD 4. The SEC is conducting an investigation into possible fraudulent accounting practices at Lucent Technologies, Inc. <www.lucent.com>. The probe focuses on whether Lucent improperly booked $679 million in revenue. The SEC is looking at how Lucent recognized revenue on sales to its distribution partners, who may not have sold the products or even may not have been able to sell the products. This practice is known as "stuffing the channels." In an adjustment, the company took back $452 million in revenue it had sent to its distribution partners but never actually sold to end customers. Normal accounting practice does not allow recording as revenue shipments to distributors on consignment—that is, with the right of return if not sold. It is not clear what rights of return exist in this case, but analysts have been critical of Lucent's aggressive practice. Lucent maintains the practice is legal.[16] What is the difference between aggressive accounting and fraudulent financial reporting? Can Lucent's revenue recognition practice be legal but also fraudulent?

Research Activity

SD 5.

LO4   Accounting and Fraud

Most university and public libraries have access to indexes of leading newspapers, such as *The Wall Street Journal* and *The New York Times*, on CD-ROM. Go to a library and do a search for a recent year using the key words "accounting and fraud," "accounting and restatement," or "accounting and irregularities." Choose one of the articles you find and read it. What company is involved, and how is accounting connected with the fraud, restatement, or irregularity? Describe the situation. Does it involve an apparently legal or illegal activity? Does it involve fraudulent financial reporting? Explain your answer and be prepared to discuss it in class.

Decision-Making Practice

SD 6.

LO7   Financial Analysis for Loan Decision

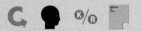

Steve Sulong was recently promoted to loan officer at First National Bank. He has authority to issue loans up to $50,000 without approval from a higher bank official. This week two small companies, Handy Harvey, Inc., and Sheila's Fashions, Inc., have each submitted a proposal for a six-month, $50,000 loan. To prepare financial analyses of the two companies, Sulong has obtained the information summarized below.

Handy Harvey, Inc., is a local lumber and home improvement company. Because sales have increased so much during the past two years, Handy Harvey has had to raise additional working capital, especially as represented by receivables and inventory. The $50,000 loan is needed to assure the company of enough working capital for the next year. Handy Harvey began the year with total assets of $740,000 and stockholders' equity of $260,000. During the past year, the company had a net income of $40,000 on net sales of $760,000. Handy Harvey's unclassified balance sheet as of the current date appears as follows:

Assets		Liabilities and Stockholders' Equity	
Cash	$ 30,000	Accounts payable	$200,000
Accounts receivable (net)	150,000	Notes payable	
Inventory	250,000	(short term)	100,000
Land	50,000	Notes payable	
Buildings (net)	250,000	(long term)	200,000
Equipment (net)	70,000	Common stock	250,000
		Retained earnings	50,000
		Total liabilities and	
Total assets	$800,000	stockholders' equity	$800,000

Sheila's Fashions, Inc., has for three years been a successful clothing store for young professional women. The leased store is located in the downtown financial district. Sheila's loan proposal asks for $50,000 to pay for stocking a new line of women's suits during the coming season. At the beginning of the year, the company had total assets of $200,000 and total stockholders' equity of $114,000. Over the past year, the company earned a net income of $36,000 on net sales of $480,000. The firm's unclassified balance sheet at the current date is as follows:

Assets		Liabilities and Stockholder's Equity	
Cash	$ 10,000	Accounts payable	$ 80,000
Accounts receivable (net)	50,000	Accrued liabilities	10,000
Inventory	135,000	Common stock	50,000
Prepaid expenses	5,000	Retained earnings	100,000
Equipment (net)	40,000		
		Total liabilities and	
Total assets	$240,000	stockholders' equity	$240,000

1. Prepare a financial analysis of each company's liquidity before and after receiving the proposed loan. Also compute profitability ratios before and after, as appropriate. Write a brief summary of the effect of the proposed loan on each company's financial position.
2. Assume you are Sulong and can make a loan to only one of these companies. Write a memorandum to the bank's vice president outlining your decision and naming the company to which you would lend $50,000. Be sure to state what positive and negative factors could affect each company's ability to pay back the loan in the next year. Also indicate what other information of a financial or nonfinancial nature would be helpful in making a final decision.

FINANCIAL REPORTING AND ANALYSIS CASES

Interpreting Financial Reports

FRA 1.
LO7 Comparison of Profitability

Two of the largest chains of grocery stores in the United States are Albertson's Inc. <www.albertsons.com> and the Great Atlantic & Pacific Tea Company (A&P) <www.aptea.com>. In a recent fiscal year, Albertson's had a net income of $765 million, and A&P had a net income of $14 million. It is difficult to judge which company is more profitable from those figures alone because they do not take into account the relative sales, sizes, and investments of the companies. Data (in millions) to complete a financial analysis of the two companies follow:[17]

	Albertson's	A&P
Net sales	$36,762	$10,151
Beginning total assets	15,719	3,335
Ending total assets	16,078	3,309
Beginning total liabilities	10,017	2,489
Ending total liabilities	10,394	2,512
Beginning stockholders' equity	5,702	846
Ending stockholders' equity	5,684	797

REQUIRED ▶

1. Determine which company was more profitable by computing profit margin, asset turnover, return on assets, debt to equity ratio, and return on equity for the two companies. Comment on the relative profitability of the two companies.
2. What do the ratios tell you about the factors that go into achieving an adequate return on assets in the grocery industry? For industry data, refer to Figures 6 through 10 in this chapter.
3. How would you characterize the use of debt financing in the grocery industry and the use of debt by the two companies?

Group Activity: Assign each ratio or company to a group and hold a class discussion.

FRA 2.
LO7 Evaluation of Profitability

Carla Cruz is the principal stockholder and president of Cruz Tapestries, Inc., which wholesales fine tapestries to retail stores. Because Cruz was not satisfied with the company earnings in 20x3, she raised prices in 20x4, increasing gross margin from sales from

30 percent in 20x3 to 35 percent in 20x4. Cruz is pleased that net income went up from 20x3 to 20x4, as shown in the following comparative income statements:

	20x4	20x3
Revenues		
Net sales	$611,300	$693,200
Costs and expenses		
Cost of goods sold	$397,345	$485,240
Selling and administrative expenses	154,199	152,504
Total costs and expenses	$551,544	$637,744
Income before income taxes	$ 59,756	$ 55,456
Income taxes	15,000	14,000
Net income	$ 44,756	$ 41,456

Total assets for Cruz Tapestries, Inc., at year end for 20x2, 20x3, and 20x4 were $623,390, $693,405, and $768,455, respectively.

Has Cruz Tapestries' profitability really improved? (**Hint:** Compute profit margin and return on assets, and comment.) What factors has Cruz overlooked in evaluating the profitability of the company? (**Hint:** Compute asset turnover and comment on the role it plays in profitability.)

FRA 3.
LO7   Financial Analysis with Industry Comparison

REQUIRED ▶

Exhibits 2 and 4 in this chapter contain the comparative balance sheet and income statement for Dell Computer Corporation <www.dell.com>. Assume you are the chief financial officer.

1. Compute liquidity ratios (working capital and current ratio) and profitability ratios (profit margin, asset turnover, return on assets, debt to equity ratio, and return on equity) for 2001 and 2002 and show the industry ratios (except working capital) from Figures 5 to 10 in this chapter. Use income from continuing operations and end-of-year assets and stockholders' equity to compute the ratios.
2. Write a memorandum to the board of directors in executive summary form describing changes in Dell's liquidity and profitability performance from 2001 to 2002 compared with the industry averages.

International Company

FRA 4.
LO5   Interpretation and Analysis
LO7   of British Financial Statements

REQUIRED ▶

Presented on the opposite page are the classified balance sheets for the British company GlaxoSmithKline PLC <www.gsk.com>, a pharmaceutical firm with marketing and manufacturing operations in 57 countries.[18]

In the United Kingdom, the format of classified financial statements usually differs from that used in the United States. To compare the financial statements of companies in different countries, it is important to know how to interpret a variety of formats.

1. For each line on GlaxoSmithKline's balance sheet, indicate the corresponding term that would be found on a U.S. balance sheet. (For this exercise, consider Provisions for liabilities and Charges to be long-term liabilities.) What is the focus or rationale behind the format of the U.K. balance sheet?
2. Assuming that GlaxoSmithKline earned a net income of £4,147 million and £2,543 million in 2000 and 1999, respectively, compute the current ratio, debt to equity

GlaxoSmithKline PLC and Subsidiaries
Consolidated Balance Sheets

	2000 £m	1999 £m
Goodwill	170	160
Intangible assets	966	926
Tangible assets	6,642	6,402
Investments	2,544	1,804
Fixed assets	10,322	9,292
Equity investments	171	52
Stocks	2,277	2,243
Debtors	5,399	4,828
Liquid investments	2,138	1,780
Cash at bank	1,283	579
Current assets	11,268	9,482
Loans and overdrafts	(2,281)	(2,819)
Other creditors	(6,803)	(5,629)
Creditors: amounts due within one year	(9,084)	(8,448)
Net current assets	2,184	1,034
Total assets less current liabilities	12,506	10,326
Loans	(1,751)	(1,897)
Other creditors	(143)	(147)
Creditors: amounts due after one year	(1,894)	(2,044)
Provisions for liabilities and charges	(1,657)	(1,675)
Net assets	8,955	6,607
Called up share capital	1,556	1,549
Share premium account	30	—
Other reserves	6,125	3,915
Equity shareholders' funds	7,711	5,464
Non-equity minority interest	1,039	961
Equity minority interests	205	182
Capital employed	8,955	6,607

ratio, return on assets, and return on equity for 2000 and 1999. (Use year-end amounts to compute ratios.)

Toys "R" Us Annual Report

FRA 5.

LO5   Reading and Analyzing an
LO6   Annual Report
LO7

Refer to the Toys "R" Us <www.tru.com> annual report in the Supplement to Chapter 1 to answer the following questions. (Note that 2001 refers to the year ended February 2, 2002, and 2000 refers to the year ended February 1, 2001.)

1. Consolidated balance sheets: (a) Did the amount of working capital increase or decrease from 2000 to 2001? By how much? (b) Did the current ratio improve from 2000 to 2001? (c) Does the company have long-term investments or intangible assets? (d) Did the debt to equity ratio of Toys "R" Us change from 2000 to 2001? (e) What is the contributed capital for 2001? How does contributed capital compare with retained earnings?
2. Consolidated statements of earnings: (a) Does Toys "R" Us use a multistep or single-step income statement? (b) Is it a comparative statement? (c) What is the trend of net earnings? (d) How significant are income taxes for Toys "R" Us? (e) Did the profit margin increase from 2000 to 2001? (f) Did asset turnover improve from 2000 to 2001? (g) Did the return on assets increase from 2000 to 2001? (h) Did the return on equity increase from 2000 to 2001? Total assets and total stockholders' equity for 1999 may be obtained from the financial highlights.
3. Multistep income statement: In the 1987 Toys "R" Us annual report, management stated that the company's "[operating] expense levels were among the best controlled in retailing [at] 18.8 percent. . . . We were able to operate with lower merchandise margins and still increase our earnings and return on sales."[19] Prepare a multistep income statement for Toys "R" Us down to income from operations for 2000 and 2001, excluding the equity in net earnings of Toys—Japan and restructuring and other charges, and compute the ratios of gross margin, operating expenses, and income from operations to net sales. Comment on whether the company continued, as of 2001, to maintain the level of performance indicated by management in 1987. In 1987, gross margin was 31.2 percent and income from operations was 12.4 percent of net sales.

Comparison Case: Toys "R" Us and Walgreen Co.

FRA 6.

LO7   Financial Analysis
Comparison: Toys "R" Us vs.
Walgreens

Compare the financial performance of Toys "R" Us <www.tru.com> and Walgreens <www.walgreens.com> on the basis of liquidity and profitability for 2002 and 2001. Use the following ratios: working capital, current ratio, debt to equity ratio, profit margin, asset turnover, return on assets, and return on equity. In 1999, Walgreens' total assets were $5,906,700,000, and total stockholders' equity was $3,484,300,000. Comment on the relative performance of the two companies. (If you have done **FRA 5,** use the computations you made in that solution for Toys "R" Us.) In general, how does Walgreens' performance compare to Toys "R" Us with respect to liquidity and profitability? What distinguishes Walgreens' profitability performance from that of Toys "R" Us?

Fingraph® Financial Analyst™

FRA 7.

LO7   Analysis of Dell Computer
Corporation or Toys "R" Us

Choose one or both of the following analyses:

1. *Alternative to FRA 3:* Analyze the balance sheet and income statement of Dell Computer Corporation <www.dell.com> using Fingraph Financial Analyst CD-ROM software. To do this assignment, you will need to enter the data from Dell's financial statements shown in this chapter. Complete part 1 of **FRA 3.** Prepare the memorandum required in part 2 of **FRA 3** separately.
2. *Alternative to FRA 5:* Refer to the Toys "R" Us <www.tru.com> annual report in the Supplement to Chapter 1. Analyze the Toys "R" Us balance sheet and income statement using Fingraph Financial Analyst CD-ROM software. Your instructor will specify which year to analyze. Complete requirements 1, 2, and 3 of **FRA 5.**

Internet Case

FRA 8.

LO7 Annual Reports and Financial Analysis

Select a large, well-known company and access its annual report online. Or, choose a company on the Needles Accounting Resource Center Web Site at http://accounting.college.hmco.com/students and use the links provided there to access the company's web site and its annual report. In the annual report of the company you have chosen, identify the four basic financial statements and the notes to the financial statements. Perform a liquidity analysis, including the calculation of working capital and the current ratio. Perform a profitability analysis, calculating profit margin, asset turnover, return on assets, debt to equity ratio, and return on equity. Be prepared to present your findings in class.

6

Chapter 6 introduces the operating cycle, the perpetual and periodic inventory systems, and internal control for merchandising businesses.

Merchandising Operations and Internal Control

LEARNING OBJECTIVES

LO1 Identify the management issues related to merchandising businesses.

LO2 Define and distinguish the terms of sale for merchandising transactions.

LO3 Prepare an income statement and record merchandising transactions under the perpetual inventory system.

LO4 Prepare an income statement and record merchandising transactions under the periodic inventory system.

LO5 Define *internal control* and its basic components, give examples of control activities, and describe the limitations of internal control.

LO6 Apply internal control activities to common merchandising transactions.

SUPPLEMENTAL OBJECTIVE

SO7 Apply sales and purchases discounts to merchandising transactions.

DECISION POINT

A USER'S FOCUS

Target Stores <www.target.com> Merchandising businesses have two key decisions to make: the price at which they sell merchandise and the level of service they provide. A department store may set the price of its merchandise at a relatively high level and provide a great deal of service. A discount store, on the other hand, may price its merchandise at a relatively low level and provide limited service. Target Stores, a division of Target Corp., is a successful discount retailer, as the figures in the table below show.[1] What decisions did Target Stores' management make about pricing and service to achieve this success?

Target distinguishes itself from other discounters by providing its customers with high-quality, name-brand merchandise, superior service, a convenient shopping experience, and competitive prices. Target's merchandise might be sold at full price in specialty stores; Target sells it at prices that are competitive with those of other discount stores that sell less well-known merchandise. Target's chief executive officer says, "Our performance in 2000 demonstrates the strength of our brands.... In a difficult environment, we achieved solid financial results.... By leveraging the power of our Target brand, we believe we can continue to deliver strong growth and financial success for years to come."[2]

What decisions did Target's management make about pricing and service that resulted in Target's becoming a leading discount retailer?

Financial Highlights

(In millions, except stores and square feet)

	2000	1999	1998
Revenues	$29,278	$26,080	$23,014
Operating profit	2,223	$2,022	$1,578
Stores	977	912	851
Retail square feet*	112,604	102,945	94,553

*In thousands, reflects total square feet, less office, warehouse, and vacant space.

MANAGEMENT ISSUES IN MERCHANDISING BUSINESSES

LO1 Identify the management issues related to merchandising businesses.

RELATED TEXT ASSIGNMENTS
Q: 1, 2, 3, 4
SE: 1
E: 1, 2
P: 1, 3, 7, 9
SD: 1, 2, 4, 5
FRA: 1, 2, 5, 6, 7, 8

KEY POINT: The operating cycle is average day's inventory on hand plus the average number of days to collect credit sales.

A **merchandising business** earns income by buying and selling goods. Such a company, whether wholesale or retail, uses the same basic accounting methods as service companies, but the buying and selling of goods adds to the complexity of the process. As a foundation for discussing the accounting issues of merchandising businesses, we must first identify the management issues involved in running such a business. It is also important to note that analyses, systems, and controls for merchandising businesses are equally relevant to manufacturing companies.

CASH FLOW MANAGEMENT

Cash flow management involves planning a company's receipts and payments of cash. If a company is not able to pay its bills when they are due, it may be forced out of business. This is particularly true for merchandising businesses, which differ from service businesses in that they must have goods on hand so that they are available for sale to customers. These goods are called **merchandise inventory**.

Merchandising businesses engage in a series of transactions called the **operating cycle**, which is illustrated in Figure 1. The transactions in the operating cycle consist of (1) purchase of merchandise inventory for cash or on credit, (2) payment for purchases made on credit, (3) sales of merchandise inventory for cash or on credit, and (4) collection of cash from credit sales. Purchases of merchandise are usually made on credit, so the merchandiser has a period of time before payment is due, but this period is generally less than the time it takes to sell the merchandise. To finance the inventory until it is sold and the resulting revenue is collected, management must plan for cash flows from within the company or from borrowing.

The need for cash flow management is demonstrated in Figure 2, which shows the financing period. Sometimes referred to as the *cash gap*, the **financing period** is the amount of time from the purchase of inventory until it is sold and payment is collected, less the amount of time creditors give the company to pay for the inventory. Thus, if it takes 60 days to sell inventory, 90 days to collect for the sale, and creditors' payment terms are 30 days, the financing period is 120 days. During the financing period, the company will be without cash from this series of transactions and will need either to have funds available internally or to borrow from a bank.

FIGURE 1
The Operating Cycle of Merchandising Businesses

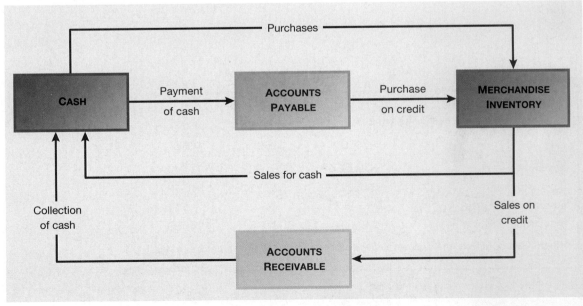

Claire's Stores, Inc. <www.clairestores.com>

OBJECTIVES

■ To become familiar with the nature of merchandising operations.

■ To identify the management issues associated with a merchandising business.

■ To show how gross margin and operating expenses affect the business goal of profitability.

BACKGROUND FOR THE CASE

Claire's Stores, Inc. is a leading international retailer offering value-priced costume jewelry, accessories, and cosmetics to fashion-aware teens and young adults. Claire's Accessories is the company's core business. In the 1980s, the company sold its capital-intensive manufacturing businesses to concentrate on the specialty retailing of women's fashion accessories. The company has grown steadily and now has about 2,200 stores throughout North America, Europe, and Japan. Claire's Accessories stores are approximately 1,000 square feet in size in North America and 600 square feet in Europe and Japan. Claire's expansion into Europe has been particularly successful, with high store traffic and sales per square foot at 250 percent of that in North America. Keys to the company's success are the merchandising and marketing practices that reinforce its position as the place for customers to find new accessories. Constant product testing, test placement of successful items in all departments, and an efficient distribution system all enable Claire's to make quick responses to "what's new." The company's North American distribution center receives and ships merchandise on the same day, and the retail outlets receive shipments three to five times per week.

For more information about Claire's Stores, Inc., visit the company's web site through the Needles Accounting Resource Center Web Site at **http://accounting.college. hmco.com/students.**

REQUIRED

View the video on Claire's Stores, Inc., that accompanies this book. As you are watching the video, take notes related to the following questions:

1. All merchandising companies have inventories. What is inventory, and why is it important to implement controls over it? Identify the types of products that Claire's Accessories stores typically have in inventory and some ways in which the company might control its inventory.

2. All merchandising companies have an operating cycle. Describe the operating cycle and explain how Claire's successfully manages its operating cycle.

3. All merchandising companies try to achieve the goal of profitability by producing a satisfactory gross margin and maintaining acceptable levels of operating expenses. Describe how Claire's operations affect gross margin and operating expenses in a way that enables the company to achieve superior profitability.

www.dillards.com

www.target.com

The financing period for a merchandising company can be less than 120 days. For example, Dillard Dept. Stores, Inc., a successful chain of U.S. department stores, has a financing period of 101 days. It consists of inventory on hand for an average of 102 days, plus an average of 42 days to collect its receivables, minus an average of 43 days to pay for its merchandise. Target, on the other hand, has a much shorter

FIGURE 2
The Financing Period

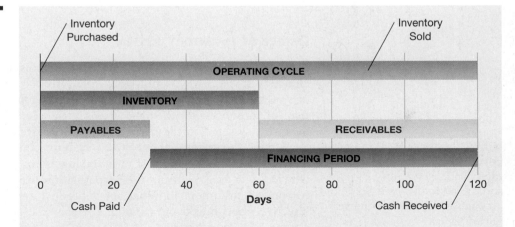

◆ **STOP AND THINK!**

Can a company have a "negative" financing period?

Yes, if its merchandise is held for a very short time, if its sales are made mostly for cash, or if it has long terms to pay its suppliers. For example, Dell makes its computers to order (resulting in small inventories), sells on credit cards (which reduces accounts receivable), and takes 30 days or more to pay its suppliers. ■

KEY POINT: A sale takes place when title to the goods transfers to the buyer.

KEY POINT: An operating budget is a financial plan for achieving the goal of profitability.

KEY POINT: Under the perpetual inventory system, the Merchandise Inventory account and the Cost of Goods Sold account are updated with every sale.

financing period, only 29 days. Its period consists of inventory on hand for an average of 61 days, plus an average of 20 days to collect its receivables, minus an average of 52 days to pay for its merchandise. Target derives its advantage from selling most of its merchandise for cash, which results in very low receivables.

As Target demonstrates, a company can help its cash flow by reducing its financing period. Many retailers, including Target, do this by selling as much as possible for cash. Cash sales include sales on bank credit cards, such as Visa or MasterCard, and on debit cards, which draw directly on the purchaser's bank account. They are considered cash sales because funds from them are available to the merchandiser immediately. In the case of credit sales, the company must wait a period of time before receiving the cash. Small retail stores may have mostly cash sales and very few credit sales, whereas large wholesale concerns may have almost all credit sales. Most merchandising concerns, however, have a combination of cash and credit sales.

PROFITABILITY MANAGEMENT

In addition to managing cash flow, management must achieve a satisfactory level of profitability. It must sell merchandise at a price that exceeds its cost by a sufficient margin to pay operating expenses and have enough left to provide sufficient income, or profitability. **Profitability management** is a complex activity that includes, first, achieving a satisfactory gross margin and, second, maintaining acceptable levels of operating expenses. Achieving a satisfactory gross margin depends on setting appropriate prices for merchandise and purchasing merchandise at favorable prices and terms. Maintaining acceptable levels of operating expenses depends on controlling expenses and operating efficiently.

One of the more effective ways of controlling expenses is to use operating budgets. An **operating budget** reflects management's operating plans and consists of detailed listings of projected selling expenses and general and administrative expenses. At key times during the year and at the end of the year, management should compare the budget with actual expenses and make adjustments to operations as appropriate. Exhibit 1 shows an operating budget for Fenwick Fashions Corporation, a merchandising company that we use as an example throughout this chapter. Fenwick's total selling expenses exceeded the budget by only $80, but four of its selling expense categories exceeded the budget by a total of $2,080. Management should investigate the possibility that underspending in advertising of $2,000 hid inefficiencies and waste in other areas. Also, sales may have been penalized by not spending the budgeted amount on advertising. Total general and administrative expenses exceeded the budget by $6,904. Management should determine why large differences occurred for office salaries expense, insurance expense, and office supplies expense. The amount of insurance expense is usually set by the insurance company; thus, an error in the initial budgeting of insurance expense may have caused the unfavorable result. The operating budget helps management focus on specific areas that need attention.

CHOICE OF INVENTORY SYSTEM

Another issue the management of a merchandising business must address is the choice of inventory system. Management must choose the system or combination of systems that is best for achieving the company's goals. There are two basic systems of accounting for the many items in the merchandise inventory: the perpetual inventory system and the periodic inventory system.

Under the **perpetual inventory system**, continuous records are kept of the quantity and, usually, the cost of individual items as they are bought and sold. The detailed data available from the perpetual inventory system enable management to respond to customers' inquiries about product availability, to order inventory more effectively and thus avoid running out of stock, and to control the financial costs associated with investments in inventory. Under this system, the cost of each item

EXHIBIT 1
An Example of an Operating Budget

Fenwick Fashions Corporation
Operating Budget
For the Year Ended December 31, 20x2

Operating Expenses	Budget	Actual	Difference Under (Over) Budget
Selling Expenses			
Sales Salaries Expense	$22,000	$22,500	($ 500)
Freight Out Expense	5,500	5,740	(240)
Advertising Expense	12,000	10,000	2,000
Insurance Expense, Selling	800	1,600	(800)
Store Supplies Expense	1,000	1,540	(540)
Total Selling Expenses	$41,300	$41,380	($ 80)
General and Administrative Expenses			
Office Salaries Expense	$23,000	$26,900	($3,900)
Insurance Expense, General	2,100	4,200	(2,100)
Office Supplies Expense	500	1,204	(704)
Depreciation Expense, Building	2,600	2,600	—
Depreciation Expense, Office Equipment	2,000	2,200	(200)
Total General and Administrative Expenses	$30,200	$37,104	($6,904)
Total Operating Expenses	$71,500	$78,484	($6,984)

KEY POINT: The valuation of ending inventory on the balance sheet is determined by multiplying the quantity of each inventory item by its unit cost.

is recorded in the Merchandise Inventory account when it is purchased. As merchandise is sold, its cost is transferred from the Merchandise Inventory account to the Cost of Goods Sold account. Thus, at all times the balance of the Merchandise Inventory account equals the cost of goods on hand, and the balance in Cost of Goods Sold equals the cost of merchandise sold to customers.

Under the **periodic inventory system**, the inventory not yet sold, or on hand, is counted periodically, usually at the end of the accounting period. No detailed records of the inventory on hand are maintained during the accounting period. The figure for inventory on hand is accurate only on the balance sheet date. As soon as any purchases or sales are made, the inventory figure becomes a historical amount, and it remains so until the new ending inventory amount is entered at the end of the next accounting period.

Some retail and wholesale businesses use the periodic inventory system because it reduces the amount of clerical work. If a business is fairly small, management can maintain control over its inventory simply through observation or by using an offline system of cards or computer records. But for larger businesses, the lack of detailed records may lead to lost sales or high operating costs.

FOCUS ON BUSINESS TECHNOLOGY

Bar Codes—How Have They Influenced Choice of Inventory Systems?

Many grocery stores, which traditionally used the periodic inventory system, now employ bar coding to update the physical inventory as items are sold. At the checkout counter, the cashier scans the electronic marking on each product, called a *bar code* or *universal product code* (UPC), into the cash register, which is linked to a computer that records the sale. Bar coding has become common in all types of retail companies, and in manufacturing firms and hospitals as well. It has also become a major factor in the increased use of the perpetual inventory system. Interestingly, some retail businesses now use the perpetual inventory system for keeping track of the physical flow of inventory and the periodic inventory system for preparing their financial statements.

Because of the difficulty and expense of accounting for the purchase and sale of each item, companies that sell items of low value in high volume have traditionally used the periodic inventory system. Examples of such companies are drugstores, automobile parts stores, department stores, and discount stores. In contrast, companies that sell items of high unit value, such as appliances or automobiles, have tended to use the perpetual inventory system. The distinction between high and low unit value for inventory systems has blurred considerably in recent years because of the widespread use of computers. Although the periodic inventory system is still widely used, use of the perpetual inventory system has increased greatly.

CONTROL OF MERCHANDISING OPERATIONS

Buying and selling, the principal transactions of merchandising businesses, involve assets—cash, accounts receivable, and merchandise inventory—that are vulnerable to theft and embezzlement. One reason for this vulnerability is that cash and inventory may be fairly easy to steal. Another is the difficulty of monitoring the large number of transactions (including cash receipts, receipts on account, payments for purchases, and receipts and shipments of inventory) in which these assets are usually involved. If a merchandising company does not take steps to protect its assets, it may suffer high losses of cash and inventory. Management's responsibility is to establish an environment, accounting systems, and control procedures that will protect the company's assets. These systems and procedures are called *internal controls*.

Maintaining control over merchandise inventory is facilitated by taking a **physical inventory**. This process involves an actual count of all merchandise on hand. It can be a difficult task because it is easy to accidentally omit items or to count them twice. A physical inventory must be taken under both the periodic and the perpetual inventory systems. Under the perpetual inventory system, the records need to be compared with the physical inventory to determine whether any inventory shortages exist.

Merchandise inventory includes all goods intended for sale that are owned by a business, regardless of where they are located—on shelves, in storerooms, in warehouses, or in trucks between warehouses and stores. It also includes goods in transit from suppliers if title to the goods has passed to the merchant. Ending inventory does not include merchandise that has been sold but not yet delivered to customers or goods that cannot be sold because they are damaged or obsolete. If the damaged or obsolete goods can be sold at a reduced price, however, they should be included in ending inventory at their reduced value.

The actual count is usually taken after the close of business on the last day of the fiscal year. To facilitate taking the physical inventory, many companies end their fiscal year in a slow season, when inventories are at relatively low levels. Retail department stores often end their fiscal year in January or February, for example. After hours, at night, or on the weekend, employees count all items and record the results on numbered inventory tickets or sheets, following procedures to ensure no items will be missed. Sometimes a store closes for all or part of a day for inventory taking. The use of bar coding to take inventory electronically has greatly facilitated the process in many companies.

Most companies experience losses of merchandise inventory from spoilage, shoplifting, and theft by employees. When such losses occur, the periodic inventory system provides no means of identifying them because the costs are automatically included in the cost of goods sold. For example, assume that a company has lost $1,250 in stolen merchandise during an accounting period. When the physical inventory is taken, the missing items are not in stock, so they cannot be counted. Because the ending inventory does not contain these items, the amount subtracted from goods available for sale is less than it would be if the goods were in stock. The cost of goods sold, then, is overstated by $1,250. In a sense, the cost of goods sold is inflated by the amount of merchandise that has been lost.

The perpetual inventory system makes it easier to identify such losses. Because the Merchandise Inventory account is continuously updated for sales, purchases, and returns, the loss will show up as the difference between the inventory records and the physical inventory taken at the end of the accounting period. Once the amount of the loss has been identified, the ending inventory is updated by crediting the Merchandise Inventory account. The offsetting debit is usually an increase in Cost of Goods Sold because the loss is considered a cost that reduces the company's gross margin.

✔ Check out ACE for a Review Quiz at http://accounting.college.hmco.com/students.

TERMS OF SALE

When goods are sold on credit, both parties should understand the amount and timing of payment as well as other terms of the purchase, such as who pays delivery charges and what warranties or rights of return apply. Sellers quote prices in different ways. Many merchants quote the price at which they expect to sell their goods. Others, particularly manufacturers and wholesalers, quote prices as a percentage (usually 30 percent or more) off their list or catalogue prices. Such a reduction is called a **trade discount**. For example, if an article is listed at $1,000 with a trade discount of 40 percent, or $400, the seller records the sale at $600 and the buyer records the purchase at $600. The seller may raise or lower the trade discount depending on the quantity purchased. The list or catalogue price and related trade discount are used only to arrive at the agreed-upon price; they do not appear in the accounting records.

The terms of sale are usually printed on the sales invoice and thus constitute part of the sales agreement. Customary terms differ from industry to industry. In some industries, payment is expected in a short period of time, such as 10 or 30 days. In these cases, the invoice is marked "n/10" ("net 10") or "n/30" ("net 30"), meaning that the amount of the invoice is due either 10 days or 30 days after the invoice date. If the invoice is due 10 days after the end of the month, it is marked "n/10 eom."

FOCUS ON BUSINESS TECHNOLOGY

How Are Web Sales Doing?

In spite of the well-publicized dot-com meltdown and the demise of "pure-play" Internet retailers like eToys.com and Pets.com, merchandise sales over the Internet are thriving. Internet sales amounted to $44.5 billion in 2001 and were expected to double in the next few years. As it has turned out, the most successful Internet retailing companies are established retailers that use the Internet to enhance their current operations. For example, mail-order catalogue companies like Lands' End <www.landsend.com> and L.L. Bean <www.llbean.com> have profitable Internet operations. Circuit City <www.circuitcity.com> allows customers to purchase online and pick up the products at stores near their homes. Office Depot <www.officedepot.com>, which focuses primarily on business-to-business Internet sales, has set up customized web pages for 37,000 corporate clients. These web sites allow customers to make online purchases or to check store inventories.[3] Although Internet transactions are recorded in the same way as on-site transactions, the technology adds a level of complexity to the transaction.

In some industries, it is customary to give a discount for early payment. This discount, called a **sales discount**, is intended to increase the seller's liquidity by reducing the amount of money tied up in accounts receivable. An invoice that offers a sales discount might be labeled "2/10, n/30," which means that the buyer either can pay the invoice within 10 days of the invoice date and take a 2 percent discount or can wait 30 days and pay the full amount of the invoice. It is almost always advantageous for a buyer to take the discount because the saving of 2 percent over a period of 20 days (from the eleventh day to the thirtieth day) represents an effective annual rate of 36.5 percent (365 days ÷ 20 days × 2% = 36.5%). Most companies would be better off borrowing money to take the discount. The practice of giving sales discounts has been declining because it is costly to the seller and because, from the buyer's viewpoint, the amount of the discount is usually very small in relation to the price of the purchase. Accounting for sales discounts is covered in supplemental objective 7.

In some industries, the seller usually pays transportation costs and charges a price that includes those

◆ **STOP AND THINK!**

Assume a large shipment of uninsured merchandise to your company was destroyed when the delivery truck had an accident and burned. Would you want the terms to be FOB shipping point or FOB destination?

You would want the terms to be FOB destination because the loss of merchandise would be the responsibility of the shipper. If the terms were FOB shipping point, the merchandise would belong to you when it left the shipper and would be your loss. ■

costs. In other industries, it is customary for the purchaser to pay transportation charges. Special terms designate whether the seller or the purchaser pays the freight charges. **FOB shipping point** means that the seller places the merchandise "free on board" at the point of origin and the buyer bears the shipping costs. The title to the merchandise passes to the buyer at that point. For example, when the sales agreement for the purchase of a car says "FOB factory," the buyer must pay the freight from where the car was made to wherever he or she is located, and the buyer owns the car from the time it leaves the factory.

On the other hand, **FOB destination** means that the seller bears the transportation costs to the place where the merchandise is delivered. The seller retains title until the merchandise reaches its destination and usually prepays the shipping costs, in which case the buyer makes no accounting entry for freight. The effects of these special shipping terms are summarized as follows:

Shipping Term	Where Title Passes	Who Pays the Cost of Transportation
FOB shipping point	At origin	Buyer
FOB destination	At destination	Seller

Many retailers allow customers to charge their purchases to a third-party company that the customer will pay later. These transactions are normally handled with credit cards. Five of the most widely used credit cards are American Express, Discover Card, Diners Club, MasterCard, and Visa. The customer establishes credit with the lender (the credit card issuer) and receives a plastic card to use in making charge purchases. If the seller accepts the card, an invoice is prepared and signed by the customer at the time of the sale. The sale is communicated to the seller's bank, resulting in a cash deposit in the seller's bank account. Thus, the seller does not have to establish the customer's credit, collect from the customer, or tie up money in accounts receivable. As payment, the lender, rather than paying the total amount of the credit card sales, takes a discount of 2 to 6 percent. The discount is a selling expense for the merchandiser. For example, assume that a restaurant made sales of $1,000 on Visa credit cards and that Visa takes a 4 percent discount on the sales. Assume also that the sales invoices are deposited in a special Visa bank account in the name of the company, in much the same way that checks from cash sales are deposited. The sales are recorded as follows:

$A = L + OE$	Cash	960	
$+$ $-$	Credit Card Discount Expense	40	
$+$	Sales		1,000
	Made sales on Visa cards		

✓ Check out ACE for a Review Quiz at http://accounting.college.hmco.com/students.

APPLYING THE PERPETUAL INVENTORY SYSTEM

LO3 Prepare an income statement and record merchandising transactions under the perpetual inventory system.

RELATED TEXT ASSIGNMENTS
Q: 7, 8, 9, 10, 14, 15
SE: 3
E: 4, 5, 6
P: 1, 2, 7, 8
SD: 4, 5
FRA: 1, 2, 7, 8

Exhibit 2 shows the income statement for Fenwick Fashions Corporation as it would appear if the company used the perpetual inventory system. The focal point of this income statement is cost of goods sold, which is deducted from net sales to arrive at gross margin. Under the perpetual inventory system, this account is continually updated during the accounting period as purchases, sales, and other inventory transactions take place. The Merchandise Inventory account on the balance sheet is updated at the same time.

TRANSACTIONS RELATED TO PURCHASES OF MERCHANDISE

The following sections illustrate the recording of typical transactions related to purchases of merchandise under the perpetual inventory system. Transactions related to sales made by Fenwick Fashions Corporation follow.

EXHIBIT 2
Income Statement Under the Perpetual Inventory System

Fenwick Fashions Corporation
Income Statement
For the Year Ended December 31, 20x2

Net sales		$239,325
Cost of goods sold*		131,360
Gross margin		$107,965
Operating Expenses		
Selling expenses	$41,380	
General and administrative expenses	37,104	
Total operating expenses		78,484
Income before income taxes		$ 29,481
Income taxes		5,000
Net income		$ 24,481

*Freight in has been included in cost of goods sold.

KEY POINT: The Merchandise Inventory account is increased when a purchase is made.

A = L + OE
+   +

● STOP AND THINK!
Under the perpetual inventory system, the Merchandise Inventory account is constantly updated. What would cause it to have the wrong balance?
The balance would be wrong if an error were made in updating the account or if merchandise had been lost or stolen. ■

A = L + OE
+   −

KEY POINT: Freight In appears within the cost of goods sold section of the income statement, and Freight Out Expense appears as an operating expense.

Purchases of Merchandise on Credit

Oct. 3   Received merchandise purchased on credit from Neebok Company, invoice dated October 1, terms n/10, FOB shipping point, $4,890.

Oct. 3   Merchandise Inventory   4,890
       Accounts Payable   4,890
         Purchased merchandise from
         Neebok Company, terms n/10, FOB
         shipping point, invoice dated Oct. 1

Under the perpetual inventory system, the cost of merchandise purchased is placed in the Merchandise Inventory account at the time of purchase.

Transportation Costs on Purchases

Oct. 4   Received bill from Transfer Freight Company for transportation costs on October 3 shipment, invoice dated October 1, terms n/10, $160.

Oct. 4   Freight In   160
       Accounts Payable   160
         Received transportation charges on
         Oct. 3 purchase, Transfer Freight
         Company, terms n/10,
         invoice dated Oct. 1

Freight in, also called *transportation in*, is the transportation cost of receiving merchandise. Transportation costs are accumulated in a Freight In account because most shipments contain multiple items. It is usually not practical to identify the specific cost of shipping each item of inventory. In Exhibit 2, freight in is included in cost of goods sold. Theoretically, freight in should be allocated between ending inventory and cost of goods sold, but most companies choose to include the cost of freight in with the cost of goods sold on the income statement because it is a relatively small amount.

In some cases, the seller pays the freight charges and bills them to the buyer as a separate item on the invoice. When this occurs, the entries are the same as in the October 3 example, except that an additional debit is made to Freight In for the amount of the freight charges and Accounts Payable is increased by a like amount.

Purchases Returns and Allowances

Oct. 6   Returned merchandise received from Neebok Company on October 3 for credit, $480.

A = L + OE   Oct. 6   Accounts Payable   480
$-$ $-$ Merchandise Inventory   480
                                   Returned merchandise from purchase of Oct. 3 to Neebok Company for full credit

If a seller sends the wrong product or one that is otherwise unsatisfactory, the buyer may be allowed to return the item for a cash refund or credit on account, or the buyer may be given an allowance off the sales price. Under the perpetual inventory system, the returned merchandise is removed from the Merchandise Inventory account.

Payments on Account

Oct. 10   Paid in full the amount due to Neebok Company for the purchase of October 3, part of which was returned on October 6.

A = L + OE   Oct. 10   Accounts Payable   4,410
$-$ $-$ Cash   4,410
                                   Made payment on account to Neebok Company
                                   $4,890 − $480 = $4,410

TRANSACTIONS RELATED TO SALES OF MERCHANDISE

KEY POINT: The Cost of Goods Sold account is increased and the Merchandise Inventory account is decreased when a sale is made.

Under the perpetual inventory system, at the time of a sale, the cost of the merchandise is transferred from the Merchandise Inventory account to the Cost of Goods Sold account. In the case of a return of sold merchandise, the cost of the merchandise is transferred from Cost of Goods Sold back to Merchandise Inventory. Transactions related to sales made by Fenwick Fashions follow.

Sales of Merchandise on Credit

Oct. 7   Sold merchandise on credit to Gonzales Distributors, terms n/30, FOB destination, $1,200; the cost of the merchandise was $720.

A = L + OE   Oct. 7   Accounts Receivable   1,200
$+$ $+$ Sales   1,200
                                   Sold merchandise to Gonzales Distributors, terms n/30, FOB destination

A = L + OE   Cost of Goods Sold   720
$-$ $-$ Merchandise Inventory   720
                                   Transferred cost of merchandise inventory sold to Cost of Goods Sold account

Under the perpetual inventory system, two entries are necessary. First, the sale is recorded. Second, Cost of Goods Sold is updated by a transfer from Merchandise Inventory. In the case of cash sales, Cash rather than Accounts Receivable is debited for the amount of the sale.

Payment of Delivery Costs

Oct. 8   Paid transportation costs for the sale on October 7, $78.

A = L + OE   Oct. 8   Freight Out Expense   78
$-$ $-$ Cash   78
                                   Paid delivery costs on Oct. 7 sale

FOCUS ON BUSINESS PRACTICE

Are Sales Returns Worth Accounting For?

Some industries routinely have a high percentage of sales returns. More than 6 percent of all nonfood items sold in stores are eventually returned to vendors. This amounts to more than $100 billion a year, or more than the gross national product of two-thirds of the world's nations.[4] Book publishers like Simon & Schuster <www.simonsays.com> often have returns as high as 30 to 50 percent of books shipped because to gain the attention of potential buyers, large numbers of copies must be distributed to various outlets. Magazine publishers like AOL Time Warner <www.aoltw.com> expect to sell no more than 35 to 38 percent of the magazines they send to newsstands and other outlets.[5] In all these businesses, it pays for management to scrutinize the Sales Returns and Allowances account for ways to reduce returns and increase profitability.

A seller will often absorb delivery or freight out costs in the belief that doing so will facilitate the sale of its products. These costs are accumulated in an account called **Freight Out Expense**, or *Delivery Expense*, which is shown as a selling expense on the income statement.

Returns of Merchandise Sold

Oct. 9   Return of merchandise sold on October 7 accepted from Gonzales Distributors for full credit and returned to merchandise inventory, $300; the cost of the merchandise was $180.

A = L + OE   Oct. 9   Sales Returns and Allowances   300
−   −   Accounts Receivable   300
                                    Accepted returns of merchandise from
                                    Gonzales Distributors

A = L + OE   Oct. 9   Merchandise Inventory   180
+   +   Cost of Goods Sold   180
                                    Transferred cost of merchandise
                                    returned to the Merchandise Inventory
                                    account

KEY POINT: Because the Sales account is established with a credit, its contra account, Sales Returns and Allowances, is established with a debit.

Returns and allowances to customers for wrong or unsatisfactory merchandise are often an indicator of customer dissatisfaction. Such amounts are accumulated in a **Sales Returns and Allowances** account, which gives management a readily available measure of unsatisfactory products and dissatisfied customers. This contra-revenue account has a normal debit balance and is deducted from sales on the income statement. Under the perpetual inventory system, the cost of the merchandise must also be transferred from the Cost of Goods Sold account back into the Merchandise Inventory account. If an allowance is made instead of accepting a return, or if the merchandise cannot be returned to inventory and resold, this transfer is not made.

Receipts on Account

Nov. 5   Received payment in full from Gonzales Distributors for sale of merchandise on October 7, less the return on October 9.

A = L + OE   Nov. 5   Cash   900
+   Accounts Receivable   900
−   Received on account from
                                    Gonzales Distributors
                                    $1,200 − $300 = $900

✓ Check out ACE for a Review Quiz at http://accounting.college.hmco.com/students.

APPLYING THE PERIODIC INVENTORY SYSTEM

LO4 Prepare an income statement and record merchandising transactions under the periodic inventory system.

RELATED TEXT ASSIGNMENTS
Q: 11, 12, 13, 14, 15
SE: 4, 5, 6
E: 7, 8, 9, 10
P: 3, 4, 6, 9, 10
SD: 4, 5
FRA: 1, 4

Exhibit 3 shows the income statement for Fenwick Fashions Corporation as it would appear if the company used the periodic inventory system. A major feature of this income statement is the computation of cost of goods sold. Cost of goods sold must be computed because it is not updated for purchases, sales, and other transactions during the accounting period, as it is under the perpetual inventory system. Figure 3 illustrates the components of cost of goods sold.

To calculate cost of goods sold, the **goods available for sale** must first be determined. The goods available for sale during the year is the sum of two factors, beginning inventory and the net cost of purchases during the year. In this case, the goods available for sale is $179,660 ($52,800 + $126,860).

If a company sold all the goods available for sale during an accounting period, the cost of goods sold would equal the goods available for sale. In most businesses, however, some merchandise remains unsold and on hand at the end of the period. This merchandise, or ending inventory, must be deducted from the goods available for sale to determine the cost of goods sold. In the case of Fenwick Fashions Corporation, the ending inventory on December 31, 20x2, is $48,300. Thus, the cost of goods sold is $131,360 ($179,660 − $48,300).

An important component of the cost of goods sold section is **net cost of purchases**, which consists of net purchases plus any freight charges on the purchases. **Net purchases** equal total purchases less any deductions, such as purchases returns

EXHIBIT 3
Income Statement Under the Periodic Inventory System

ENRICHMENT NOTE:
Most published financial statements are condensed, eliminating much of the detail shown here.

Fenwick Fashions Corporation
Income Statement
For the Year Ended December 31, 20x2

Net sales			$239,325
Cost of goods sold			
Merchandise inventory,			
December 31, 20x1		$ 52,800	
Purchases	$126,400		
Less purchases returns			
and allowances	7,776		
Net purchases	$118,624		
Freight in	8,236		
Net cost of purchases		126,860	
Goods available for sale		$179,660	
Less merchandise inventory,			
December 31, 20x2		48,300	
Cost of goods sold			131,360
Gross margin			$107,965
Operating expenses			
Selling expenses		$ 41,380	
General and administrative			
expenses		37,104	
Total operating expenses			78,484
Income before income taxes			$ 29,481
Income taxes			5,000
Net income			$ 24,481

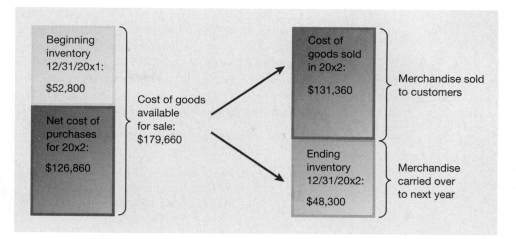

FIGURE 3
The Components of Cost of Goods Sold

Beginning inventory 12/31/20x1: $52,800

Net cost of purchases for 20x2: $126,860

Cost of goods available for sale: $179,660

Cost of goods sold in 20x2: $131,360 — Merchandise sold to customers

Ending inventory 12/31/20x2: $48,300 — Merchandise carried over to next year

● **STOP AND THINK!**
Why is a physical inventory needed under both the periodic and perpetual inventory systems?
Under the periodic inventory system, a physical inventory is needed to determine the cost of goods sold. Under the perpetual inventory system, a physical inventory is required to verify the inventory as shown in the accounting records. ∎

and allowances and any discounts allowed by suppliers for early payment (see supplemental objective 7). Because transportation charges, or freight in, are a necessary cost of receiving merchandise for sale, they are added to net purchases to arrive at the net cost of purchases, as shown in Exhibit 3.

TRANSACTIONS RELATED TO PURCHASES OF MERCHANDISE

The primary difference between the perpetual and periodic inventory systems is that in the perpetual inventory system, the Merchandise Inventory account is adjusted each time a purchase, sale, or other inventory transaction occurs, whereas in the periodic inventory system, the Merchandise Inventory account stays at its beginning balance until the physical inventory is recorded at the end of the period. In the periodic system, a Purchases account is used to accumulate the purchases of merchandise during the accounting period, and a Purchases Returns and Allowances account is used to accumulate returns of and allowances on purchases.

The following sections illustrate how purchase transactions made by Fenwick Fashions Corporation would be recorded under the periodic inventory system.

KEY POINT: The Purchases account is increased when a purchase is made under the periodic inventory system.

Purchases of Merchandise on Credit

Oct. 3   Received merchandise purchased on cedit from Neebok Company, invoice dated October 1, terms n/10, FOB shipping point, $4,890.

A = L + OE
   +   −

Oct. 3   Purchases   4,890
        Accounts Payable   4,890
                Purchased merchandise from Neebok Company, terms n/10, FOB shipping point, invoice dated Oct. 1

Purchases is a temporary account used under the periodic inventory system. Its sole purpose is to accumulate the total cost of merchandise purchased for resale during an accounting period. (Purchases of other assets, such as equipment, are recorded in the appropriate asset account, not in the Purchases account.) The Purchases account does not indicate whether merchandise has been sold or is still on hand.

Transportation Costs on Purchases

Oct. 4   Received bill from Transfer Freight Company for transportation costs on October 3 shipment, invoice dated October 1, terms n/10, $160.

A = L + OE
   +   −

Oct. 4   Freight In   160
        Accounts Payable   160
                Received transportation charges on Oct. 3 purchase, Transfer Freight Company, terms n/10, invoice dated Oct. 1

Transportation costs on purchases are usually accumulated in a Freight In account. In some cases, the seller pays the freight charges and bills them to the buyer as a separate item on the invoice. When this occurs, the entries are the same as in the October 3 example, except that an additional debit is made to Freight In for the amount of the freight charges and Accounts Payable is increased by a like amount.

Purchases Returns and Allowances

Oct. 6   Returned merchandise received from Neebok Company on October 3 for credit, $480.

ENRICHMENT NOTE:
Accounts such as Purchases and Purchases Returns and Allowances are used only in conjunction with a periodic inventory system.

A = L + OE
    −   +

Oct. 6	Accounts Payable	480
	Purchases Returns and Allowances	480
	Returned merchandise from purchase	
	of Oct. 3 to Neebok Company for	
	full credit	

KEY POINT: Because the Purchases account is established with a debit, its contra account, Purchases Returns and Allowances, is established with a credit.

If a seller sends the wrong product or one that is otherwise unsatisfactory, the buyer may be allowed to return the item for a cash refund or credit on account, or the buyer may be given an allowance off the sales price. Under the periodic inventory system, the amount of the return or allowance is recorded in the **Purchases Returns and Allowances** account. This account is a contra-purchases account with a normal credit balance, and it is deducted from purchases on the income statement.

Payments on Account

Oct. 10   Paid in full the amount due to Neebok Company for the purchase of October 3, part of which was returned on October 6.

A = L + OE
    −   −

Oct. 10	Accounts Payable	4,410
	Cash	4,410
	Made payment on account to	
	Neebok Company	
	$4,890 − $480 = $4,410	

TRANSACTIONS RELATED TO SALES OF MERCHANDISE

The Cost of Goods Sold account, which is updated for sales and returns under the perpetual inventory system, is not used under the periodic inventory system because the Merchandise Inventory account is not updated until the end of the accounting period. Transactions related to sales made by Fenwick Fashions Corporation follow.

Sales of Merchandise on Credit

Oct. 7   Sold merchandise on credit to Gonzales Distributors, terms n/30, FOB destination, $1,200; the cost of the merchandise was $720.

A = L + OE
  +   +

Oct. 7	Accounts Receivable	1,200
	Sales	1,200
	Sold merchandise to	
	Gonzales Distributors, terms n/30,	
	FOB destination	

In the case of cash sales, Cash rather than Accounts Receivable is debited for the amount of the sale.

Payment of Delivery Costs

Oct. 8   Paid transportation costs for the sale on October 7, $78.

A = L + OE
    −   −

Oct. 8	Freight Out Expense	78
	Cash	78
	Paid delivery costs on Oct. 7 sale	

Delivery costs are accumulated in the Freight Out Expense account. This account is shown as a selling expense on the income statement.

Returns of Merchandise Sold

Oct. 9   Return of Merchandise sold on October 7 accepted from Gonzales Distributors for full credit and returned to merchandise inventory, $300.

A = L + OE   Oct. 9   Sales Returns and Allowances *–Contra*   300
–   –
           Accounts Receivable *revenue*   300
              Accepted return of merchandise from *account*
              Gonzales Distributors

Returns and allowances to customers for wrong or unsatisfactory merchandise are accumulated in the Sales Returns and Allowances account. This account is a contra-revenue account with a normal debit balance and is deducted from sales on the income statement.

Receipts on Account

Nov. 5   Received payment in full from Gonzales Distributors for sale of merchandise on October 7, less the return on October 9.

A = L + OE   Nov. 5   Cash   900
+
–   Accounts Receivable   900
              Received on account from
              Gonzales Distributors
              $1,200 – $300 = $900

✓ Check out ACE for a Review Quiz at http://accounting.college.hmco.com/students.

INTERNAL CONTROL: BASIC COMPONENTS AND CONTROL ACTIVITIES

LO5 Define *internal control* and its basic components, give examples of control activities, and describe the limitations of internal control.

RELATED TEXT ASSIGNMENTS
Q: 17, 18, 19, 20
SE: 8, 9
E: 11, 12, 13
P: 5
SD: 4, 5
FRA: 3

www.circuitcity.com

A merchandising company can have inaccurate accounting records as well as high losses of cash and inventory if it does not take steps to protect its assets. The best way to do this is to set up and maintain a good system of internal control.

MANAGEMENT'S RESPONSIBILITY FOR INTERNAL CONTROL

Management is responsible for establishing a satisfactory system of internal control. **Internal control** is defined as all the policies and procedures management uses to ensure the reliability of financial reporting, compliance with laws and regulations, and the effectiveness and efficiency of operations. In other words, management must safeguard the firm's assets and have reliable accounting records. It must ensure that employees comply with legal requirements and operate the company in the best way possible.

    Management comments on its responsibility and effectiveness in achieving the goals of internal control in the "Report of Management" in the company's annual report to stockholders. A portion of this statement from the annual report of Circuit City Stores, Inc., follows:

> Management is responsible for maintaining an internal control structure designed to provide reasonable assurance that the books and records reflect the transactions of the Company and that the Company's established policies and procedures are carefully followed. Because of inherent limitations in any system, there can be no absolute assurance that errors or irregularities will not occur. Nevertheless, management believes that the internal control structure provides reasonable assurance that assets are safeguarded and that financial information is objective and reliable.[6]

COMPONENTS OF INTERNAL CONTROL

To accomplish the objectives of internal control, management must establish five interrelated components of internal control:[7]

1. *Control environment*   The **control environment** is created by the overall attitude, awareness, and actions of management. It includes management's integrity and ethics, philosophy and operating style, organizational structure, method of assigning authority and responsibility, and personnel policies and practices. Personnel should be qualified to handle responsibilities, which means that employees must be trained and informed. For example, the manager of a retail store should train employees to follow prescribed procedures for handling cash sales, credit card sales, and returns and refunds.

2. *Risk assessment*   **Risk assessment** is the identification of areas in which risks of loss of assets or inaccuracies in the accounting records are high so that adequate controls can be implemented. Among the greater risks in a retail store are that employees will take cash or that customers will shoplift merchandise.

3. *Information and communication*   **Information and communication** relates to the accounting system established by management to identify, assemble, analyze, classify, record, and report a company's tramsactions, and to the need for clear communication of individual responsibilities in performing the accounting functions.

4. *Control activities*   **Control activities** are the policies and procedures management puts in place to see that its directives are carried out. Control activities are discussed in more detail below.

5. *Monitoring*   **Monitoring** involves management's regular assessment of the quality of internal control, including periodic review of compliance with all policies and procedures. For example, large companies often have a staff of internal auditors who review the company's system of internal control to determine if it is working properly and if procedures are being followed. In smaller businesses, owners and managers conduct these reviews.

CONTROL ACTIVITIES

Control activities are a principal way in which internal control is implemented in an accounting information system. They safeguard a company's assets and ensure the reliability of accounting records. These control activities include the following:

1. *Authorization*   All transactions and activities should be properly authorized by management. In a retail store, for example, some transactions, such as normal cash sales, are authorized routinely; others, such as issuing a refund, may require a manager's approval.

2. *Recording transactions*   To facilitate preparation of financial statements and to establish accountability for assets, all transactions should be recorded. For example, in a retail store, the cash register records sales, refunds, and other transactions internally on a paper tape or computer disk so that the cashier can be held responsible for the cash received and the merchandise removed during his or her shift.

3. *Documents and records*   Using well-designed documents helps ensure the proper recording of transactions. For example, to ensure that all transactions are recorded, invoices and other documents should be prenumbered, and all numbers should be accounted for.

4. *Physical controls*   Physical controls permit access to assets only with management's authorization. For example, retail stores should use cash registers, and only the cashier responsible for the cash in a register should have access to it. Other employees should not be able to open the cash drawer if the cashier is not present. Likewise, warehouses and storerooms should be accessible only to

● **STOP AND THINK!**
Which of the following accounts would be assigned a higher level of risk: Buildings or Merchandise Inventory?
Merchandise Inventory would because there is a greater risk of human error in recording the large number of transactions involved and because there is a greater risk of theft. ■

FOCUS ON BUSINESS ETHICS

Which Frauds Are Most Common?

A survey of 5,000 large U.S. businesses disclosed that 21 percent suffered frauds in excess of $1 million. The most common were credit card frauds, check frauds, inventory theft, false invoices and phantom vendors, and expense account abuse. Major factors in allowing these frauds to take place were poor internal controls, management override of internal controls, and collusion. The most common methods of detection were notification by an employee, internal controls, internal auditor review, notification by a customer, and accidental discovery. Companies successful in preventing fraud have a good system of internal control and a formal code of ethics with a program to monitor compliance that includes a system for reporting incidents of fraud. These companies routinely communicate the existence of the program to their employees.[8]

authorized personnel. Access to accounting records, including those stored in company computers, should also be controlled.

5. *Periodic independent verification* The records should be periodically checked against the assets by someone other than the persons responsible for those records and assets. For example, at the end of each shift or day, the owner or store manager should count the cash in the cash drawer and compare the amount with the amount recorded on the tape or computer disk in the cash register. Other examples of independent verification are the monthly bank reconciliation and periodic counts of physical inventory.

6. *Separation of duties* The organizational plan should separate functional responsibilities. Within a department, no one person should be in charge of authorizing transactions, operating the department, handling assets, and keeping records of assets. For example, in a stereo store, each employee should oversee only a single part of a transaction. A sales employee takes the order and creates an invoice. Another employee receives the customer's cash or credit card payment and issues a receipt. Once the customer has a paid receipt, and only then, a third employee obtains the item from the warehouse and gives it to the customer. A person in the accounting department subsequently records the sales from the tape or disk in the cash register, comparing them with the sales invoices and updating the inventory in the records. The separation of duties means that a mistake, careless or not, cannot be made without being seen by at least one other person.

KEY POINT: No control procedure can guarantee the prevention of theft. However, the more procedures there are in place, the less likely it is that a theft will occur.

7. *Sound personnel procedures* Sound practices should be followed in managing the people who carry out the functions of each department. Among those practices are supervision, rotation of key people among different jobs, insistence that employees take vacations, and bonding of personnel who handle cash or inventories. **Bonding** is the process of carefully checking an employee's background and insuring the company against theft by that person. Bonding does not guarantee against theft, but it does prevent or reduce economic loss if theft occurs. Prudent personnel procedures help ensure that employees know their jobs, are honest, and will find it difficult to carry out and conceal embezzlement over time.

LIMITATIONS OF INTERNAL CONTROL

No system of internal control is without weaknesses. As long as control procedures are performed by people, the internal control system will be vulnerable to human error. Errors may arise from misunderstandings, mistakes in judgment, carelessness, distraction, or fatigue. Separation of duties can be defeated through collusion by employees who secretly agree to deceive the company. In addition, established procedures may be ineffective against employees' errors or dishonesty, and controls that were initially effective may become ineffective when conditions change.[9] In some cases, the costs of establishing and maintaining elaborate systems may exceed the benefits. In a small business, for example, active involvement by the owner can be a practical substitute for the separation of some duties.

 Check out ACE for a Review Quiz at http://accounting.college.hmco.com/students.

INTERNAL CONTROL OVER MERCHANDISING TRANSACTIONS

LO6 Apply internal control activities to common merchandising transactions.

RELATED TEXT ASSIGNMENTS
Q: 21, 22, 23
SE: 8
E: 12
P: 5
SD: 4

Sound internal control activities are needed in all aspects of a business, but particularly when assets are involved. Assets are especially vulnerable when they enter or leave a business. When sales are made, for example, cash or other assets enter the business, and goods or services leave the business. Activities must be set up to prevent theft during those transactions.

Likewise, purchases of assets and payments of liabilities must be controlled. The majority of those transactions can be safeguarded by adequate purchasing and payment systems. In addition, assets on hand, such as cash, investments, inventory, plant, and equipment, must be protected.

In this section, you will see how internal control activities are applied to such merchandising transactions as cash sales, receipts, purchases, and cash payments. Similar activities are applicable to service and manufacturing businesses.

INTERNAL CONTROL AND MANAGEMENT GOALS

When a system of internal control is applied effectively to merchandising transactions, it can achieve important management goals. For example, two key goals for the success of a merchandising business are:

1. To prevent losses of cash or inventory owing to theft or fraud
2. To provide accurate records of merchandising transactions and account balances

Three broader goals for management are:

1. To keep enough inventory on hand to sell to customers without overstocking
2. To keep enough cash on hand to pay for purchases in time to receive discounts
3. To keep credit losses as low as possible by making credit sales only to customers who are likely to pay on time

KEY POINT: Maintaining internal control is especially complex and difficult for a merchandiser. Management must not only establish controls for cash sales receipts, purchases, and cash payments, but also go to great lengths to manage and protect its inventory.

One control used in meeting broad management goals is the cash budget, which projects future cash receipts and disbursements. By maintaining adequate cash balances, a company is able to take advantage of discounts on purchases, prepare to borrow money when necessary, and avoid the damaging effects of being unable to pay bills when they are due. By investing excess cash, the company can earn interest until the cash is needed.

A more specific accounting control is the separation of duties that involve the handling of cash. Such separation makes theft without detection extremely unlikely, unless two or more employees conspire. The separation of duties is easier in large businesses than in small ones, where one person may have to carry out several duties. The effectiveness of internal control over cash varies, based on the size and nature of the company. Most firms, however, should use the following procedures:

1. Separate the functions of authorization, recordkeeping, and custodianship of cash.
2. Limit the number of people who have access to cash.
3. Designate specific people who are responsible for handling cash.
4. Use banking facilities as much as possible, and keep the amount of cash on hand to a minimum.
5. Bond all employees who have access to cash.

6. Physically protect cash on hand by using cash registers, cashiers' cages, and safes.

7. Have a person who does not handle or record cash make periodic independent verifications of the cash on hand.

8. Record all cash receipts promptly.

9. Deposit all cash receipts promptly.

10. Make payments by check rather than by currency.

11. Have a person who does not authorize, handle, or record cash transactions reconcile the Cash account.

Notice that each of the foregoing procedures helps safeguard cash by making it more difficult for any one individual who has access to cash to steal or misuse it without being detected.

CONTROL OF CASH SALES RECEIPTS

Cash payments for sales of goods and services can be received by mail or over the counter in the form of checks, credit or debit cards, or currency. Whatever the source of the payments, cash should be recorded immediately upon receipt. This is usually done by making an entry in a cash receipts journal. Such a journal establishes a written record of cash receipts that should prevent errors and make theft more difficult.

■ **CONTROL OF CASH RECEIVED THROUGH THE MAIL**   Payment by mail is increasing because of the expansion of mail-order sales. Cash receipts that arrive by mail are vulnerable to theft by the employees who handle them. To control mailed receipts, customers should be urged to pay by check or credit card instead of with currency.

Cash received through the mail should be handled by two or more employees. The employee who opens the mail should make a list in triplicate of the money received. The list should contain each payer's name, the purpose for which the money was sent, and the amount. One copy goes with the cash to the cashier, who deposits the money. The second copy goes to the accounting department for recording. The third copy is kept by the person who opens the mail. Errors can be easily caught because the amount deposited by the cashier must agree with the amount received and the amount recorded in the cash receipts journal.

■ **CONTROL OF CASH RECEIVED OVER THE COUNTER**   Two common tools for controlling cash sales receipts are cash registers and prenumbered sales tickets. The amount of a cash sale should be rung up on a cash register at the time of the sale. The cash register should be placed so that the customer can see the amount recorded. Each cash register should have a locked-in tape on which it prints the day's transactions. At the end of the day, the cashier counts the cash in the cash register and turns it in to the cashier's office. Another employee takes the tape out of the cash register and records the cash receipts for the day in the cash receipts journal. The amount of cash turned in and the amount recorded on the tape should agree; if not, any differences must be explained. Large retail chains commonly monitor cash receipts by having each cash register tied directly into a computer that records each transaction as it occurs. Whether the elements are performed manually or by computer, separating responsibility for cash receipts, cash deposits, and record-keeping is necessary to ensure good internal control.

In some stores, internal control is further strengthened by the use of prenumbered sales tickets and a central cash register or cashier's office, where all sales are rung up and collected by a person who does not participate in the sale. The salesperson completes a prenumbered sales ticket at the time of the sale, giving one copy to the customer and keeping a copy. At the end of the day, all sales tickets must be accounted for, and the sales total computed from the sales tickets should equal the total sales recorded on the cash register.

◆ **STOP AND THINK!**

Why is it important to write down the amount of cash received through the mail or over the counter?

It is important because until there is a written record of the cash, there is no accountability. This is why some stores offer a reward to customers who report making a purchase without receiving a receipt. ■

KEY POINT: The cashier should not be allowed to remove the cash register tape or to record the day's cash receipts.

FIGURE 4
Internal Control for Purchasing and Paying for Goods and Services

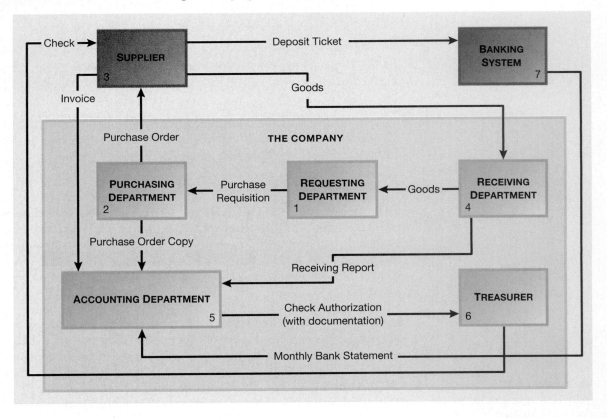

CONTROL OF PURCHASES AND CASH DISBURSEMENTS

 Cash disbursements are particularly vulnerable to fraud and embezzlement. In one case, the treasurer of one of the nation's largest jewelry retailers was charged with having stolen over $500,000 by systematically overpaying federal income taxes and keeping the refund checks as they came back to the company.

To avoid such theft, cash should be paid only after the receipt of specific authorization supported by documents that establish the validity and amount of the claim. In addition, maximum possible use should be made of the principle of separation of duties in the purchase of goods and services and the payment for them. The degree of separation of duties varies, depending on the size of the business. Figure 4 shows how separation of duties can be maximized in large companies. Five

FOCUS ON BUSINESS TECHNOLOGY

How Do Computers Influence Internal Controls?

One of the more difficult challenges facing computer programmers is to build good internal controls into computerized accounting programs. Such computer programs must include controls that prevent unintentional errors as well as unauthorized access and tampering. The programs prevent errors through reasonableness checks (such as not allowing any transactions over a specified amount), mathematical checks that verify the arithmetic of transactions, and sequence checks that require documents and transactions to be in proper order. They typically use passwords and questions about randomly selected personal data to prevent unauthorized access to computer records. They may also use firewalls, which are strong electronic barriers to unauthorized access, as well as data encryption. Data encryption is a way of coding data so that if they are stolen, they are useless to the thief.

internal units (the requesting department, the purchasing department, the accounting department, the receiving department, and the treasurer) and two external contacts (the supplier and the banking system) all play a role in the internal control plan. Notice that business documents are also crucial components of the plan.

As shown in Figure 5 (on the following pages), every action is documented and verified by at least one other person. Thus, the requesting department cannot work out a kickback scheme to make illegal payments to the supplier because the receiving department independently records receipts and the accounting department verifies prices. The receiving department cannot steal goods because the receiving report must equal the invoice. For the same reason, the supplier cannot bill for more goods than it ships. The accounting department's work is verified by the treasurer, and the treasurer ultimately is checked by the accounting department.

> **KEY POINT:** A purchase requisition is not the same as a purchase order. A purchase requisition is sent to the purchasing department; a purchase order is sent to the vendor.

Figure 5 illustrates the typical sequence of documents used in an internal control plan for purchases and cash disbursements. To begin, the credit office (requesting department) of Fenwick Fashions Corporation fills out a formal request for a purchase, or **purchase requisition**, for 20 boxes of fax paper rolls (item 1). The department head approves it and forwards it to the purchasing department. The people in the purchasing department prepare a **purchase order**, as shown in item 2. The purchase order is addressed to the vendor (seller) and contains a description of the items ordered; the expected price, terms, and shipping date; and other shipping instructions. Fenwick Fashions Corporation does not pay any bill that is not accompanied by a purchase order number.

> **KEY POINT:** *Invoice* is the business term for "bill." Every business document must have a number for purposes of reference.

After receiving the purchase order, the vendor, Henderson Supply Company, ships the goods and sends an **invoice** or bill (item 3) to Fenwick Fashions Corporation. The invoice gives the quantity and description of the goods delivered, the price, and the terms of payment. If goods cannot all be shipped immediately, the estimated date for shipment of the remainder is indicated.

When the goods reach the receiving department of Fenwick Fashions Corporation, an employee writes the description, quantity, and condition of the goods on a form called a **receiving report** (item 4). The receiving department does not receive a copy of the purchase order or the invoice, so its employees do not know what should be received or its value. Thus, they are not tempted to steal any excess that may be delivered.

The receiving report is sent to the accounting department, where it is compared with the purchase order and the invoice. If everything is correct, the accounting department completes a **check authorization** and attaches it to the three supporting documents. The check authorization form shown in item 5 has a space for each item to be checked off as it is examined. Notice that the accounting department has all the documentary evidence for the transaction but does not have access to the assets purchased. Nor does it write the check for payment. This means that the people performing the accounting function cannot gain by falsifying documents in an effort to conceal fraud.

Finally, the treasurer examines all the documents and issues an order to the bank for payment, called a **check** (item 6), for the amount of the invoice less any appropriate discount. In some systems, the accounting department fills out the check so that all the treasurer has to do is inspect and sign it. The check is then sent to the supplier, with a remittance advice that shows what the check is for. A supplier who is not paid the proper amount will complain, of course, thus providing a form of outside control over the payment. Using a deposit ticket, the supplier deposits the check in the bank, which returns the canceled check with Fenwick Fashions Corporation's next bank statement (item 7). If the treasurer has made the check out for the wrong amount (or altered a pre-filled-in check), the problem will show up in the bank reconciliation.

There are many variations of the system just described. This example is offered as a simple system that provides adequate internal control.

✓ Check out ACE for a Review Quiz at http://accounting.college.hmco.com/students.

FIGURE 5
Internal Control Plan for Purchases and Cash Disbursements

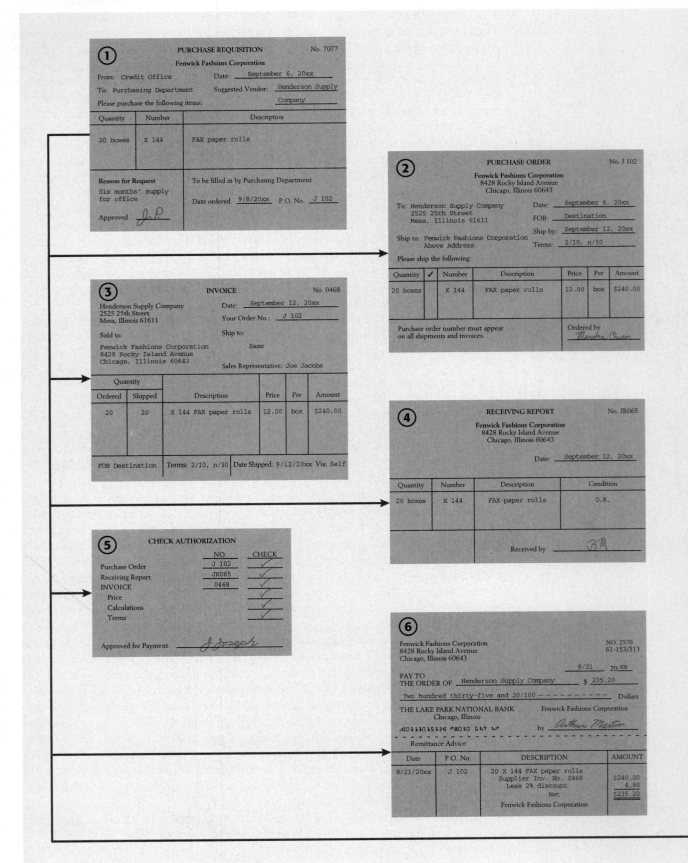

Business Document	Prepared by	Sent to	Verification and Related Procedures
① Purchase requisition	Requesting department	Purchasing department	Purchasing verifies authorization.
② Purchase order	Purchasing department	Supplier	Supplier sends goods or services in accordance with purchase order.
③ Invoice	Supplier	Accounting department	Accounting receives invoice from supplier.
④ Receiving report	Receiving department	Accounting department	Accounting compares invoice, purchase order, and receiving report. Accounting verifies prices.
⑤ Check authorization	Accounting department	Treasurer	Accounting attaches check authorization to invoice, purchase order, and receiving report.
⑥ Check	Treasurer	Supplier	Treasurer verifies all documents before preparing check.
⑦ Bank statement	Buyer's bank	Accounting department	Accounting compares amount and payee's name on returned check with check authorization.

⑦

Statement of Account with
THE LAKE PARK NATIONAL BANK
Chicago, Illinois

Fenwick Fashions Corporation
8428 Rocky Island Avenue
Chicago, Illinois 60643

Checking Acct No
8030-647-4
Period covered
Sept.30-Oct.31,20xx

Previous Balance	Checks/Debits—No.	Deposits/Credits—No.	S.C.	Current Balance
$2,645.78	$4,319.33 --16	$5,157.12 --7	$12.50	$3,471.07

CHECKS/DEBITS			DEPOSITS/CREDITS		DAILY BALANCES	
Posting Date	Check No.	Amount	Posting Date	Amount	Date	Amount
					09/30	2,645.78
10/01	2564	100.00	10/01	586.00	10/01	2,881.78
10/01	2565	250.00	10/05	1,500.00	10/04	2,825.60
10/04	2567	56.18	10/06	300.00	10/05	3,900.46
10/05	2566	425.14	10/16	1,845.50	10/06	4,183.34
10/06	2568	17.12	10/21	600.00	10/12	2,242.34
10/12	2569	1,705.80	10/24	300.00CM	10/16	3,687.84
10/12	2570	235.20	10/31	25.62IN	10/17	3,589.09
10/16	2571	400.00			10/21	4,189.09
10/17	2572	29.75			10/24	3,745.59
10/17	2573	69.00			10/25	3,586.09
10/24	2574	738.50			10/28	3,457.95
10/24		5.00DM			10/31	3,471.07
10/25	2575	7.50				
10/25	2577	152.00				
10/28		118.14NSF				
10/28		10.00DM				
10/31		12.50SC				

Explanation of Symbols:

CM – Credit Memo   SC – Service Charge   The last amount
DM – Debit Memo   EC – Error Correction   in this column
NSF – Non-Sufficient Funds OD – Overdraft   is your balance.
                          IN – Interest on Average Balance

Please examine; if no errors are reported within ten (10) days, the account will be
considered to be correct.

ACCOUNTING FOR DISCOUNTS

SO7 Apply sales and purchases discounts to merchandising transactions.

RELATED TEXT ASSIGNMENTS
Q: 24
SE: 10
E: 14, 15, 16
P: 6
SD: 3

SALES DISCOUNTS

As mentioned earlier, sales discounts for early payment are customary in some industries. Because it usually is not possible to know at the time of the sale whether the customer will pay in time to take advantage of sales discounts, the discounts are recorded only at the time the customer pays. For example, assume that Fenwick Fashions Corporation sells merchandise to a customer on September 20 for $300, on terms of 2/10, n/60. This is the entry at the time of the sale:

A = L + OE
\+
\-

Sept. 20	Accounts Receivable	300	
	Sales		300
	Sold merchandise on credit, terms 2/10, n/60		

KEY POINT: Accounts Receivable must be credited for the full $300 even though only $294 has been received.

The customer can take advantage of the sales discount any time on or before September 30, ten days after the date of the invoice. If the customer pays on September 29, the entry in Fenwick's records would look like this:

A = L + OE
\+   \+

Sept. 29	Cash	294	
	Sales Discounts	6	
	Accounts Receivable		300
	Received payment for Sept. 20 sale; discount taken		

If the customer does not take advantage of the sales discount but waits until November 19 to pay for the merchandise, the entry would be as follows:

A = L + OE
\+
\-

Nov. 19	Cash	300	
	Accounts Receivable		300
	Received payment for Sept. 20 sale; no discount taken		

At the end of the accounting period, the Sales Discounts account has accumulated all the sales discounts taken during the period. Because sales discounts reduce revenues from sales, Sales Discounts is a contra-revenue account with a normal debit balance that is deducted from sales on the income statement.

PURCHASES DISCOUNTS

Merchandise purchases are usually made on credit and sometimes involve **purchases discounts** for early payment. Purchases discounts are discounts taken for early payment for merchandise purchased for resale. They are to the buyer what sales discounts are to the seller. The amount of discounts taken is recorded in a separate account. Assume that Fenwick made a credit purchase of merchandise on November 12 for $1,500 with terms of 2/10, n/30 and returned $200 in merchandise on November 14. When payment is made within the discount period, Fenwick's journal entry looks like this:

A = L + OE
\- \- \+

Nov. 22	Accounts Payable	1,300	
	Purchases Discounts		26
	Cash		1,274
	Paid the invoice of Nov. 12		

Purchase Nov. 12	$1,500	
Less return Nov. 14	200	
Net purchase	$1,300	
Discount: 2%	26	
Cash paid	$1,274	

KEY POINT: Accounts Payable must be debited for the full $1,300 even though only $1,274 has been paid.

If Fenwick does not pay for the purchase within the discount period, the entry would be as follows:

A = L + OE   Dec. 12   Accounts Payable   1,300
– –   Cash   1,300
                           Paid the invoice of Nov. 12,
                           less the return, on due date;
                           no discount taken

Like Purchases Returns and Allowances, Purchases Discounts is a contra-purchases account with a normal credit balance that is deducted from purchases on the income statement. If a company makes only a partial payment on an invoice, most creditors allow the company to take the discount applicable to the partial payment. The discount usually does not apply to freight, postage, taxes, or other charges that might appear on the invoice.

✓ Check out ACE for a Review Quiz at http://accounting.college.hmco.com/students.

Chapter Review

REVIEW OF LEARNING OBJECTIVES

LO1 Identify the management issues related to merchandising businesses.

Merchandising companies differ from service companies in that they earn income by buying and selling goods. The buying and selling of goods adds to the complexity of the business and raises four issues that management must address. First, the series of transactions in which merchandising companies engage (the operating cycle) requires careful cash flow management. Second, to achieve the goal of profitability, management must price goods and control operating costs by using budgets to ensure an adequate income after operating expenses and income taxes have been paid. Third, management must choose whether to use the perpetual or the periodic inventory system. Fourth, management must establish an internal control structure that protects the company's assets—its cash, merchandise inventory, and accounts receivable.

LO2 Define and distinguish the terms of sale for merchandising transactions.

A trade discount is a reduction from the list or catalogue price of a product. A sales discount is a discount given for early payment of a sale on credit. FOB shipping point means that the buyer bears the cost of transportation and that title to the goods passes to the buyer at the shipping origin. FOB destination means that the seller bears the cost of transportation and that title does not pass to the buyer until the goods reach their destination.

LO3 Prepare an income statement and record merchandising transactions under the perpetual inventory system.

The Merchandise Inventory account is continuously adjusted by entering purchases, sales, and other inventory transactions as they occur. Purchases increase the Merchandise Inventory account, and purchases returns decrease it. As goods are sold, their cost is transferred from the Merchandise Inventory account to the Cost of Goods Sold account.

LO4 Prepare an income statement and record merchandising transactions under the periodic inventory system.

When the periodic inventory system is used, the cost of goods sold section of the income statement must include the following elements:

$$\text{Purchases} - \frac{\text{Purchases returns}}{\text{and allowances}} + \frac{\text{Freight}}{\text{in}} = \frac{\text{Net cost of}}{\text{purchases}}$$

$$\frac{\text{Beginning}}{\text{merchandise inventory}} + \frac{\text{Net cost of}}{\text{purchases}} = \frac{\text{Goods}}{\text{available for sale}}$$

$$\frac{\text{Goods}}{\text{available for sale}} - \frac{\text{Ending}}{\text{merchandise inventory}} = \frac{\text{Cost of}}{\text{goods sold}}$$

Under the periodic inventory system, the Merchandise Inventory account stays at the beginning level until the physical inventory is recorded at the end of the accounting period. A Purchases account is used to accumulate purchases of merchandise during the accounting period, and a Purchases Returns and Allowances account is used to accumulate returns of and allowances on purchases.

LO5   Define *internal control* and its basic components, give examples of control activities, and describe the limitations of internal control.

Internal control consists of all the policies and procedures a company uses to ensure the reliability of financial reporting, compliance with laws and regulations, and the effectiveness and efficiency of operations. Internal control has five components: the control environment, risk assessment, information and communication, control activities, and monitoring. Examples of control activities are proper authorization of transactions; recording all transactions to facilitate preparation of financial statements and to establish accountability for assets; use of well-designed documents to ensure proper recording of transactions; physical controls; periodic checks of records and assets; separation of duties into the functions of authorization, operations, custody of assets, and recordkeeping; and use of sound personnel policies. A system of internal control relies on the people who implement it. Thus, the effectiveness of internal control is limited by the people involved. Human error, collusion, and failure to recognize changed conditions all can contribute to a system's failure.

LO6   Apply internal control activities to common merchandising transactions.

Certain procedures strengthen internal control over sales, cash receipts, purchases, and cash disbursements. First, the functions of authorization, recordkeeping, and custody should be kept separate. Second, the accounting system should provide for physical protection of assets (especially cash and merchandise inventory), use of banking services, prompt recording and deposit of cash receipts, and payment by check. Third, the people who have access to cash and merchandise inventory should be specifically designated and their number limited. Fourth, employees who have access to cash or merchandise inventory should be bonded. Fifth, the Cash account should be reconciled each month, and unannounced audits of cash on hand should be made by an individual who does not authorize, handle, or record cash transactions.

SUPPLEMENTAL OBJECTIVE

SO7   Apply sales and purchases discounts to merchandising transactions.

Sales discounts are discounts for early payment. Terms of 2/10, n/30 mean that the buyer can take a 2 percent discount if the invoice is paid within ten days of the invoice date. Otherwise, the buyer is obligated to pay the full amount in 30 days. Discounts on sales are recorded in the Sales Discounts account, and discounts on purchases are recorded in the Purchases Discounts account.

REVIEW OF CONCEPTS AND TERMINOLOGY

The following concepts and terms were introduced in this chapter:

LO5   **Bonding:** The process of carefully checking an employee's background and insuring the company against theft by that person.

LO1   **Cash flow management:** The planning of a company's receipts and payments of cash.

LO6   **Check:** A written order to a bank to pay the amount specified from funds on deposit.

LO6   **Check authorization:** A form prepared by the accounting department after it has compared the receiving report with the purchase order and the invoice. It permits the issuance of a check to pay the invoice.

LO5   **Control activities:** Policies and procedures established by management to ensure that the objectives of internal control are met.

LO5   **Control environment:** The overall attitude, awareness, and actions of management, as reflected in the company's philosophy and operating style, organizational structure, method of assigning authority and responsibility, and personnel policies and practices.

LO1   **Financing period:** The amount of time from the purchase of inventory until it is sold and payment is collected, less the amount of time creditors allow for payment of the inventory. Also called the *cash gap*.

LO2   **FOB destination:** A shipping term that means that the seller bears transportation costs to the place of delivery.

LO2   **FOB shipping point:** A shipping term that means that the buyer bears transportation costs from the point of origin.

LO3   Freight in: The transportation cost of receiving merchandise. Also called *transportation in*.

LO3   Freight Out Expense: The account that accumulates transportation charges on merchandise sold, which are shown as a selling expense. Also called *Delivery Expense*.

LO4   Goods available for sale: The sum of beginning inventory and the net cost of purchases during the period; the total goods available for sale to customers during an accounting period.

LO5   Information and communication: The accounting system established by management and the communication of responsibilities with regard to the accounting system.

LO5   Internal control: All the policies and procedures a company uses to ensure the reliability of financial reporting, compliance with laws and regulations, and the effectiveness and efficiency of operations.

LO6   Invoice: A form sent to the purchaser by the vendor describing the goods delivered, the quantity, price, and terms of payment.

LO1   Merchandise inventory: The goods on hand at any one time that are available for sale to customers.

LO1   Merchandising business: A business that earns income by buying and selling goods.

LO5   Monitoring: Management's regular assessment of the quality of internal control.

LO4   Net cost of purchases: Net purchases plus any freight charges on the purchases.

LO4   Net purchases: Total purchases less any deductions, such as purchases returns and allowances and purchases discounts.

LO1   Operating budget: Management's operating plans as reflected by detailed listings of projected selling expenses and general and administrative expenses.

LO1   Operating cycle: A series of transactions that includes purchases of merchandise inventory for cash or on credit, payment for purchases made on credit, sales of merchandise inventory for cash or on credit, and collection of cash from the sales.

LO1   Periodic inventory system: A system for determining inventory on hand by taking a physical count at the end of an accounting period.

LO1   Perpetual inventory system: A system for determining inventory on hand by keeping continuous records of the quantity and, usually, the cost of individual items as they are bought and sold.

LO1   Physical inventory: An actual count of all merchandise on hand.

LO1   Profitability management: The process of achieving a satisfactory gross margin and maintaining acceptable levels of operating expenses.

LO6   Purchase order: A form prepared by a company's purchasing department and sent to a vendor describing the items ordered; the expected price, terms, and shipping date; and other shipping instructions.

LO6   Purchase requisition: A formal written request for a purchase, prepared by the requesting department in an organization and sent to the purchasing department.

LO4   Purchases: A temporary account used under the periodic inventory system to accumulate the total cost of merchandise purchased for resale during an accounting period.

SO7   Purchases discounts: Discounts taken for prompt payment for merchandise purchased for resale; the Purchases Discounts account is a contra-purchases account.

LO4   Purchases Returns and Allowances: A contra-purchases account used under the periodic inventory system to accumulate cash refunds, credits on account, and other allowances made by suppliers.

LO6   Receiving report: A form prepared by the receiving department of a company describing the quantity and condition of goods received.

LO5   Risk assessment: The identification of areas in which risks of loss of assets or inaccuracies in the accounting records are high.

LO2
SO7
Sales discount: A discount given to a buyer for early payment of a sale made on credit; the Sales Discounts account is a contra-revenue account.

LO3
Sales Returns and Allowances: A contra-revenue account used to accumulate cash refunds, credits on account, and other allowances made to customers who have received defective or otherwise unsatisfactory products.

LO2
Trade discount: A deduction (usually 30 percent or more) off a list or catalogue price that is not recorded in the accounting records.

REVIEW PROBLEM

Merchandising Transactions: Perpetual and Periodic Inventory Systems

LO3
LO4
Dawkins Company engaged in the following transactions during October.

Oct. 1 Sold merchandise to Ernie Devlin on credit, terms n/30, FOB shipping point, $1,050 (cost, $630).
2 Purchased merchandise on credit from Ruland Company, terms n/30, FOB shipping point, $1,900.
2 Paid Custom Freight $145 for freight charges on merchandise received.
6 Purchased store supplies on credit from Arizin Supply House, terms n/30, $318.
9 Purchased merchandise on credit from LNP Company, terms n/30, FOB shipping point, $1,800, including $100 freight costs paid by LNP Company.
11 Accepted from Ernie Devlin a return of merchandise, which was returned to inventory, $150 (cost, $90).
14 Returned for credit $300 of merchandise received on October 2.
15 Returned for credit $100 of store supplies purchased on October 6.
16 Sold merchandise for cash, $500 (cost, $300).
22 Paid Ruland Company for purchase of October 2 less return of October 14.
23 Received full payment from Ernie Devlin for his October 1 purchase, less return on October 11.

REQUIRED ▶
1. Prepare entries in journal form to record the transactions, assuming the perpetual inventory system is used.
2. Prepare entries in journal form to record the transactions, assuming the periodic inventory system is used.

ANSWER TO REVIEW PROBLEM

Accounts that differ under the two systems are highlighted.

1. Perpetual Inventory System

Oct. 1	Accounts Receivable	1,050	
	Sales		1,050
	Sold merchandise on account to Ernie Devlin, terms n/30, FOB shipping point		
	Cost of Goods Sold	630	
	Merchandise Inventory		630
	Transferred cost of merchandise sold to Cost of Goods Sold Account		
2	Merchandise Inventory	1,900	
	Accounts Payable		1,900
	Purchased merchandise on account from Ruland Company, terms n/30, FOB shipping point		
	Freight In	145	
	Cash		145
	Paid freight on previous purchase		

2. Periodic Inventory System

Oct. 1	Accounts Receivable	1,050	
	Sales		1,050
	Sold merchandise on account to Ernie Devlin, terms n/30, FOB shipping point		
2	Purchases	1,900	
	Accounts Payable		1,900
	Purchased merchandise on account from Ruland Company, terms n/30, FOB shipping point		
	Freight In	145	
	Cash		145
	Paid freight on previous purchase		

1. Perpetual Inventory System

Oct. 6 Store Supplies 318
    Accounts Payable 318
    Purchased store supplies
    on account from Arizin
    Supply House, terms n/30

9 Merchandise Inventory 1,700
Freight In 100
    Accounts Payable 1,800
    Purchased merchandise on
    account from LNP Company,
    terms n/30, FOB shipping
    point, freight paid by supplier

11 Sales Returns and Allowances 150
    Accounts Receivable 150
    Accepted return of merchandise
    from Ernie Devlin

Merchandise Inventory 90
    Cost of Goods Sold 90
    Transferred cost of merchandise
    returned to Merchandise
    Inventory account

14 Accounts Payable 300
    Merchandise Inventory 300
    Returned portion of
    merchandise purchased
    from Ruland Company

15 Accounts Payable 100
    Store Supplies 100
    Returned store supplies (not
    merchandise) purchased on
    October 6 for credit

16 Cash 500
    Sales 500
    Sold merchandise for cash

Cost of Goods Sold 300
    Merchandise Inventory 300
    Transferred cost of merchandise
    sold to Cost of Goods Sold
    account

22 Accounts Payable 1,600
    Cash 1,600
    Made payment on account
    to Ruland Company
    $1,900 − $300 = $1,600

23 Cash 900
    Accounts Receivable 900
    Received payment on
    account of Ernie Devlin
    $1,050 − $150 = $900

2. Periodic Inventory System

Store Supplies 318
    Accounts Payable 318
    Purchased store supplies
    on account from Arizin
    Supply House, terms n/30

Purchases 1,700
Freight In 100
    Accounts Payable 1,800
    Purchased merchandise on
    account from LNP Company,
    terms n/30, FOB shipping
    point, freight paid by supplier

Sales Returns and Allowances 150
    Accounts Receivable 150
    Accepted return of merchandise
    from Ernie Devlin

Accounts Payable 300
    Purchases Returns and
    Allowances 300
    Returned portion of
    merchandise purchased
    from Ruland Company

Accounts Payable 100
    Store Supplies 100
    Returned store supplies (not
    merchandise) purchased
    on October 6 for credit

Cash 500
    Sales 500
    Sold merchandise for cash

Accounts Payable 1,600
    Cash 1,600
    Made payment on account
    to Ruland Company
    $1,900 − $300 = $1,600

Cash 900
    Accounts Receivable 900
    Received payment on
    account of Ernie Devlin
    $1,050 − $150 = $900

Chapter Assignments

BUILDING YOUR KNOWLEDGE FOUNDATION

QUESTIONS

1. What four issues must managers of merchandising businesses address?
2. What is the operating cycle of a merchandising business, and why is it important?
3. What are two important elements in achieving a satisfactory profit in a merchandising business?
4. What is an operating budget, and how does it help management improve profitability?
5. What is the difference between a trade discount and a sales discount?
6. Two companies quoted the following prices and terms on 50 units of product:

	Price	Terms
Supplier A	$20 per unit	FOB shipping point
Supplier B	$21 per unit	FOB destination

   Which supplier is quoting the better deal? Explain your answer.
7. Under which inventory system is a Cost of Goods Sold account maintained? Explain why.
8. Discuss this statement: "The perpetual inventory system is the best system because management always needs to know how much inventory it has."
9. Why is it advisable to maintain a Sales Returns and Allowances account when the same result could be obtained by debiting each return or allowance to the Sales account?
10. Is freight in an operating expense? Explain your answer.
11. Under the periodic inventory system, an important figure in computing cost of goods sold is goods available for sale. What are the two main components of goods available for sale, and what is the relationship of ending inventory to goods available for sale?
12. Under the periodic inventory system, how must the amount of inventory at the end of the year be determined?
13. Hornberger Hardware purchased the following items: (a) a delivery truck, (b) two dozen hammers, (c) supplies for its office workers, and (d) a broom for the janitor. Which items should be debited to the Purchases account under the periodic inventory system?
14. What is the difference between the perpetual inventory system and the periodic inventory system?
15. What are the principal differences in the handling of merchandise inventory in the accounting records under the perpetual inventory system and the periodic inventory system?
16. Merchants who accept credit cards from customers must allow the credit card companies a 2 to 6 percent discount on the sales. Why are they willing to do this?
17. Most people think of internal control as a means of making fraud harder to commit and easier to detect. What are some other important purposes of internal control?
18. What are the five components of internal control?
19. What are some examples of control activities?
20. Why is the separation of duties necessary to ensure sound internal control? What does this principle assume about the relationships of employees in a company and the possibility of two or more of them stealing from the company?
21. In a small business, it is sometimes impossible to separate duties completely. What are three other practices that a small business can follow to achieve the objectives of internal control over cash?

22. At Thrifty Variety Store, each sales clerk counts the cash in his or her cash drawer at the end of the day, then removes the cash register tape and prepares a daily cash form, noting any discrepancies. This information is checked by an employee in the cashier's office, who counts the cash, compares the total with the form, and then gives the cash to the cashier. What is the weakness in this system of internal control?

23. How does a movie theater control cash receipts?

24. Is the normal balance of the Sales Discounts account a debit or a credit balance? Is it an asset, liability, expense, or contra-revenue account?

SHORT EXERCISES

SE 1.
LO1 Identification of Management Issues

Identify each of the following decisions as most directly related to (a) cash flow management, (b) profitability management, (c) choice of inventory system, or (d) control of merchandising operations:

1. Determination of how to protect cash from theft or embezzlement
2. Determination of the selling price of goods for sale
3. Determination of policies governing sales of merchandise on credit
4. Determination of whether to use the periodic or the perpetual inventory system

SE 2.
LO2 Terms of Sale

A dealer buys tooling machines from a manufacturer and resells them to its customers.

a. The manufacturer sets a list or catalogue price of $6,000 for a machine. The manufacturer offers its dealers a 40 percent trade discount.

b. The manufacturer sells the machine under terms of FOB shipping point. The cost of shipping is $350.

c. The manufacturer offers a sales discount of 2/10, n/30. The sales discount does not apply to shipping costs.

What is the net cost of the tooling machine to the dealer, assuming it is paid for within ten days of purchase?

SE 3.
LO3 Purchases of Merchandise: Perpetual Inventory System

Record in journal form each of the following transactions, assuming the perpetual inventory system is used:

Aug. 2   Purchased merchandise on credit from Foxx Company, invoice dated August 1, terms n/10, FOB shipping point, $2,300.

3   Received bill from Main Shipping Company for transportation costs on August 2 shipment, invoice dated August 1, terms n/30, $210.

7   Returned damaged merchandise received from Foxx Company on August 2 for credit, $360.

10   Paid in full the amount due to Foxx Company for the purchase of August 2, part of which was returned on August 7.

SE 4.
LO4 Purchases of Merchandise: Periodic Inventory System

Record in journal form the transactions in **SE 3,** assuming the periodic inventory system is used.

SE 5.
LO4 Cost of Goods Sold: Periodic Inventory System

Using the following data and assuming cost of goods sold is $230,000, prepare the cost of goods sold section of a merchandising income statement (periodic inventory system), including computation of the amount of purchases for the month of October:

Freight in	$12,000
Merchandise inventory, Sept. 30, 20xx	33,000
Merchandise inventory, Oct. 31, 20xx	44,000
Purchases	?
Purchases returns and allowances	9,000

SE 6.
LO4 Sales of Merchandise: Periodic Inventory System

Record in journal form the following transactions, assuming the periodic inventory system is used:

Aug. 4   Sold merchandise on credit to Bonds Corporation, terms n/30, FOB destination, $1,200.

5   Paid transportation costs for sale of August 4, $110.

9   Part of the merchandise sold on August 4 was accepted back from Bonds Corporation for full credit and returned to the merchandise inventory, $350.

Sept. 3   Received payment in full from Bonds Corporation for merchandise sold on August 4, less the return on August 9.

SE 7.   Record in journal form the following transaction for Jenny's Cards Store:

LO2   **Credit Card Sales Transaction**

Apr. 19   A tabulation of invoices at the end of the day showed $400 in Visa invoices, which are deposited in a special bank account at full value less 5 percent discount.

SE 8.   Match the check-writing policies for a small business described below to these control activities:

LO5   **Internal Control Activities**
LO6

a. Authorization   e. Periodic independent check
b. Recording transactions   f. Separation of duties
c. Documents and records   g. Sound personnel policies
d. Physical controls

1. The person who writes the checks to pay bills is different from the persons who authorize the payments and who keep the records of the payments.
2. The checks are kept in a locked drawer. The only person who has the key is the person who writes the checks.
3. The person who writes the checks is bonded.
4. Once each month the owner compares and reconciles the amount of money shown in the accounting records with the amount in the bank account.
5. Each check is approved by the owner of the business before it is mailed.
6. A check stub recording pertinent information is completed for each check.
7. Every day, all checks are recorded in the accounting records, using the information on the check stubs.

SE 9.   Internal control is subject to several inherent limitations. Indicate whether each of the following situations is an example of (a) human error, (b) collusion, (c) changed conditions, or (d) cost-benefit considerations:

LO5   **Limitations of Internal Control**

1. Effective separation of duties in a restaurant is impractical because the business is too small.
2. The cashier and the manager of a retail shoe store work together to circumvent the internal controls for the purpose of embezzling funds.
3. The cashier in a pizza shop does not understand the procedures for operating the cash register and thus fails to ring up all sales and to count the cash at the end of the day.
4. At a law firm, computer supplies were mistakenly delivered to the reception area instead of the receiving area because the supplier began using a different means of shipment. As a result, the receipt of supplies was not recorded.

SE 10.   On April 15, Eiji Company sold merchandise to Pinto Company for $1,500 on terms of 2/10, n/30. Record the entries in both Eiji's and Pinto's records for (1) the sale, (2) a return of merchandise on April 20 of $300, and (3) payment in full on April 25. Assume both companies use the periodic inventory system.

SO7   **Sales and Purchases Discounts**

EXERCISES

E 1.   The decisions that follow were made by the management of Cotton Gold Company. Indicate whether each decision pertains primarily to (a) cash flow management, (b) profitability management, (c) choice of inventory system, or (d) control of merchandise operations.

LO1   **Management Issues and Decisions**

1. Decided to mark each item of inventory with a magnetic tag that sets off an alarm if the tag is removed from the store before being deactivated
2. Decided to reduce the credit terms offered to customers from 30 days to 20 days to speed up collection of accounts
3. Decided that the benefits of keeping track of each item of inventory as it is bought and sold would exceed the costs of such a system
4. Decided to raise the price of each item of inventory to achieve a higher gross margin to offset an increase in rent expense
5. Decided to purchase a new type of cash register that can be operated only by a person who knows a predetermined code
6. Decided to switch to a new cleaning service that will provide the same service at a lower cost

LO1 Operating Budget

E 2. The operating budget and actual performance for the six months ended June 30, 20x1, for Kobe Hardware Corporation appear below.

	Budget	Actual
Selling Expenses		
Sales Salaries Expense	$ 90,000	$102,030
Sales Supplies Expense	2,000	1,642
Rent Expense, Selling Space	18,000	18,000
Utilities Expense, Selling Space	12,000	11,256
Advertising Expense	15,000	21,986
Depreciation Expense, Selling Fixtures	6,500	6,778
Total Selling Expenses	$143,500	$161,692
General and Administrative Expenses		
Office Salaries Expense	$ 50,000	$ 47,912
Office Supplies Expense	1,000	782
Rent Expense, Office Space	4,000	4,000
Depreciation Expense, Office Equipment	3,000	3,251
Utilities Expense, Office Space	3,000	3,114
Postage Expense	500	626
Insurance Expense	2,000	2,700
Miscellaneous Expense	500	481
Total General and Administrative Expenses	$ 64,000	$ 62,866
Total Operating Expenses	$207,500	$224,558

1. Prepare an operating report that shows budget, actual, and difference.
2. Discuss the results, identifying which differences most likely should be investigated by management.

LO2 Terms of Sale

E 3. A household appliance dealer buys refrigerators from a manufacturer and resells them to its customers.

a. The manufacturer sets a list or catalogue price of $1,000 for a refrigerator. The manufacturer offers its dealers a 30 percent trade discount.
b. The manufacturer sells the machine under terms of FOB destination. The cost of shipping is $100.
c. The manufacturer offers a sales discount of 2/10, n/30. Sales discounts do not apply to shipping costs.

What is the net cost of the refrigerator to the dealer, assuming it is paid for within ten days of purchase?

LO3 Preparation of the Income Statement: Perpetual Inventory System

E 4. Using the selected account balances at December 31, 20xx, for Tents, Etc. that follow, prepare an income statement for the year ended December 31, 20xx. Show detail of net sales. The company uses the perpetual inventory system, and Freight In has not been included in Cost of Goods Sold.

Account Name	Debit	Credit
Sales		$237,500
Sales Returns and Allowances	$ 11,750	
Cost of Goods Sold	140,000	
Freight In	6,750	
Selling Expenses	21,500	
General and Administrative Expenses	43,500	
Income Taxes	5,000	

E 5.
LO3   Recording Purchases: Perpetual Inventory System

Give the entries to record each of the following transactions under the perpetual inventory system:

a. Purchased merchandise on credit, terms n/30, FOB shipping point, $2,500.
b. Paid freight on the shipment in transaction a, $135.
c. Purchased merchandise on credit, terms n/30, FOB destination, $1,400.
d. Purchased merchandise on credit, terms n/30, FOB shipping point, $2,600, which includes freight paid by the supplier of $200.
e. Returned part of the merchandise purchased in transaction c, $500.
f. Paid the amount owed on the purchase in transaction a.
g. Paid the amount owed on the purchase in transaction d.
h. Paid the amount owed on the purchase in transaction c less the return in e.

E 6.
LO3   Recording Sales: Perpetual Inventory System

On June 15, Ohio Company sold merchandise for $1,300 on terms of n/30 to Whist Company. On June 20, Whist Company returned some of the merchandise for a credit of $300, and on June 25, Whist paid the balance owed. Give Ohio's entries to record the sale, return, and receipt of payment under the perpetual inventory system. The cost of the merchandise sold on June 15 was $750, and the cost of the merchandise returned to inventory on June 20 was $175.

E 7.
LO4   Preparation of the Income Statement: Periodic Inventory System

Using the selected year-end account balances at December 31, 20x2, for the Happ General Store shown below, prepare a 20x2 income statement. Show detail of net sales. The company uses the periodic inventory system. Beginning merchandise inventory was $52,000; ending merchandise inventory is $44,000.

Account Name	Debit	Credit
Sales		$594,000
Sales Returns and Allowances	$ 30,400	
Purchases	229,600	
Purchases Returns and Allowances		8,000
Freight In	11,200	
Selling Expenses	97,000	
General and Administrative Expenses	74,400	
Income Taxes	30,000	

E 8.
LO4   Merchandising Income Statement: Missing Data, Multiple Years

Determine the missing data for each letter in the following three income statements for Iron Wholesale Paper Company (in thousands):

	20x3	20x2	20x1
Sales	$ p	$ h	$286
Sales returns and allowances	24	19	a
Net sales	q	317	b
Merchandise inventory, beginning	r	i	38
Purchases	192	169	c
Purchases returns and allowances	31	j	17
Freight in	s	29	22
Net cost of purchases	189	k	d
Goods available for sale	222	212	182
Merchandise inventory, ending	39	l	42
Cost of goods sold	t	179	e
Gross margin	142	m	126
Selling expenses	u	78	f
General and administrative expenses	39	n	33
Total operating expenses	130	128	g
Income before income taxes	v	o	27
Income taxes	3	2	5
Net income	w	8	22

E 9.
LO4 Recording Purchases: Periodic Inventory System

Using the data in **E 5**, give the entries to record each of the transactions under the periodic inventory system.

E 10.
LO4 Recording Sales: Periodic Inventory System

Using the relevant data in **E 6**, give the entries to record each of the transactions under the periodic inventory system.

E 11.
LO5 Use of Accounting Records in Internal Control

Careful scrutiny of accounting records and financial statements can lead to the discovery of fraud or embezzlement. Each of the following situations may indicate a breakdown in internal control. Indicate the nature of the possible fraud or embezzlement in each of these situations.

1. Wages expense for a branch office was 30 percent higher in 20x2 than in 20x1, even though the office was authorized to employ only the same four employees and raises were only 5 percent in 20x2.
2. Sales returns and allowances increased from 5 percent to 20 percent of sales in the first two months of 20x2, after record sales in 20x1 resulted in large bonuses for the sales staff.
3. Gross margin decreased from 40 percent of net sales in 20x1 to 20 percent in 20x2, even though there was no change in pricing. Ending inventory was 50 percent less at the end of 20x2 than it was at the beginning of the year. There is no immediate explanation for the decrease in inventory.
4. A review of daily records of cash register receipts shows that one cashier consistently accepts more discount coupons for purchases than do the other cashiers.

E 12.
LO5 Control Procedures
LO6

Ned Remy, who operates a small grocery store, has established the following policies with regard to the checkout cashiers:

1. Each cashier has his or her own cash drawer, to which no one else has access.
2. Each cashier may accept checks for purchases under $50 with proper identification. Checks over $50 must be approved by Remy before they are accepted.
3. Every sale must be rung up on the cash register and a receipt given to the customer. Each sale is recorded on a tape inside the cash register.
4. At the end of each day, Remy counts the cash in the drawer and compares it with the amount on the tape inside the cash register.

Match the following conditions for internal control to each of the policies listed above:

a. Transactions are executed in accordance with management's general or specific authorization.
b. Transactions are recorded as necessary to permit preparation of financial statements and maintain accountability for assets.
c. Access to assets is permitted only as allowed by management.
d. At reasonable intervals, the records of assets are compared with the existing assets.

E 13.
LO5 Internal Control Procedures

Lessing Video Store maintains the following policies with regard to purchases of new videotapes at each of its branch stores:

1. Employees are required to take vacations, and the duties of employees are rotated periodically.
2. Once each month a person from the home office visits each branch store to examine the receiving records and to compare the inventory of videos with the accounting records.
3. Purchases of new videos must be authorized by purchase order in the home office and paid for by the treasurer in the home office. Receiving reports are prepared in each branch and sent to the home office.
4. All new personnel receive one hour of training in how to receive and catalogue new videos.
5. The company maintains a perpetual inventory system that keeps track of all videos purchased, sold, and on hand.

Match the following control procedures to each of the above policies. (Some may have several answers.)

a. Authorization
b. Recording transactions
c. Documents and records
d. Limited access
e. Periodic independent verification
f. Separation of duties
g. Sound personnel policies

E 14.
SO7   Sales Involving Discounts

Give the entries to record the following transactions engaged in by Rios Company, which uses the periodic inventory system:

Mar. 1   Sold merchandise on credit to Bee Company, terms 2/10, n/30, FOB shipping point, $1,000.
       3   Accepted a return from Bee Company for full credit, $400.
      10   Received payment from Bee Company for the sale, less the return and discount.
      11   Sold merchandise on credit to Bee Company, terms 2/10, n/30, FOB shipping point, $1,600.
      31   Received payment for amount due from Bee Company for the sale of March 11.

E 15.
SO7   Purchases Involving Discounts

Give the entries to record the following transactions engaged in by Pecan Company, which uses the periodic inventory system:

July 2   Purchased merchandise on credit from Ensur Company, terms 2/10, n/30, FOB destination, invoice dated July 1, $1,600.
      6   Returned some merchandise to Ensur Company for full credit, $200.
     11   Paid Ensur Company for purchase of July 2 less return and discount.
     14   Purchased merchandise on credit from Ensur Company, terms 2/10, n/30, FOB destination, invoice dated July 12, $1,800.
     31   Paid amount owed Ensur Company for purchase of July 14.

E 16.
SO7   Purchases and Sales Involving Discounts

Tanweiczk Company purchased $4,600 of merchandise, terms 2/10, n/30, from A&G Company and paid for the merchandise within the discount period. Give the entries (1) by Tanweiczk Company to record the purchase and payment and (2) by A&G Company to record the sale and receipt of payment. Both companies use the periodic inventory system.

PROBLEMS

P 1.
LO1   Merchandising Income
LO3   Statement: Perpetual Inventory System

At the end of the fiscal year, June 30, 20x3, selected accounts from the adjusted trial balance for Bear Camera Store, Inc., appeared as shown below.

Bear Camera Store, Inc.
Partial Adjusted Trial Balance
June 30, 20x3

Sales		$433,912
Sales Returns and Allowances	$ 11,250	
Cost of Goods Sold	221,185	
Freight In	10,078	
Store Salaries Expense	107,550	
Office Salaries Expense	26,500	
Advertising Expense	18,200	
Rent Expense	14,400	
Insurance Expense	2,800	
Utilities Expense	8,760	
Store Supplies Expense	2,464	
Office Supplies Expense	1,814	
Depreciation Expense, Store Equipment	1,800	
Depreciation Expense, Office Equipment	1,850	
Income Taxes	2,500	

REQUIRED ▶   1. Prepare a multistep income statement for Bear Camera Store, Inc. Freight In should be combined with Cost of Goods Sold. Store Salaries Expense; Advertising Expense;

Store Supplies Expense; and Depreciation Expense, Store Equipment are selling expenses. The other expenses are general and administrative expenses. The company uses the perpetual inventory system. Show details of net sales and operating expenses.

2. Based on your knowledge at this point in the course, how would you use the income statement for Bear Camera Store to evaluate the company's profitability? What other financial statement should be considered and why?

P 2.

LO3 Merchandising Transactions: Perpetual Inventory System

Sweet Company engaged in the following transactions in July 20xx:

July 1 Sold merchandise to Rick Lee on credit, terms n/30, FOB shipping point, $4,200 (cost, $2,520).

3 Purchased merchandise on credit from Cobalt Company, terms n/30, FOB shipping point, $7,600.

5 Paid Mix Freight for freight charges on merchandise received, $580.

6 Purchased store supplies on credit from DGE Supply Company, terms n/20, $1,272.

8 Purchased merchandise on credit from Holt Company, terms n/30, FOB shipping point, $7,200, which includes $400 freight costs paid by Holt Company.

12 Returned some of the merchandise purchased on July 3 for credit, $1,200.

15 Sold merchandise on credit to Bob Wagner, terms n/30, FOB shipping point, $2,400 (cost, $1,440).

16 Returned some of the store supplies purchased on July 6 for credit, $400.

17 Sold merchandise for cash, $2,000 (cost, $1,200).

18 Accepted for full credit a return from Rick Lee and returned merchandise to inventory, $400 (cost, $240).

24 Paid Cobalt Company for purchase of July 3 less return of July 12.

25 Received full payment from Rick Lee for his July 1 purchase less the return on July 18.

REQUIRED ▶ Prepare entries in journal form to record the transactions, assuming use of the perpetual inventory system.

P 3.

LO1 Merchandising Income
LO4 Statement: Periodic Inventory System

The data below are from the adjusted trial balance of Pat's Sports Equipment, Inc., on September 30, 20x5, the fiscal year end. The company's beginning merchandise inventory was $243,666 and ending merchandise inventory is $229,992 for the period.

Pat's Sports Equipment, Inc.
Partial Adjusted Trial Balance
September 30, 20x5

Sales		$1,301,736
Sales Returns and Allowances	$ 33,750	
Purchases	663,555	
Purchases Returns and Allowances		90,714
Freight In	30,234	
Store Salaries Expense	322,650	
Office Salaries Expense	79,500	
Advertising Expense	54,600	
Rent Expense	43,200	
Insurance Expense	8,400	
Utilities Expense	56,280	
Store Supplies Expense	1,392	
Office Supplies Expense	2,442	
Depreciation Expense, Store Equipment	5,400	
Depreciation Expense, Office Equipment	5,550	
Income Taxes	15,000	

REQUIRED ▶ 1. Prepare a multistep income statement for Pat's Sports Equipment, Inc. Store Salaries Expense; Advertising Expense; Store Supplies Expense; and Depreciation Expense,

Store Equipment are selling expenses. The other expenses are general and administrative expenses. The company uses the periodic inventory system. Show details of net sales and operating expenses.

2. Based on your knowledge at this point in the course, how would you use the income statement for Pat's Sports Equipment to evaluate the company's profitability? What other financial statements should be considered and why?

P 4. Use the data in **P 2** for this problem.

LO4   Merchandising Transactions: Periodic Inventory System

REQUIRED ▶ Prepare entries in journal form to record the transactions, assuming use of the periodic inventory system.

P 5. Equipment Services Company provides maintenance services to factories in the Newark, New Jersey, area. The company, which buys a large amount of cleaning supplies, consistently has been over budget in its expenditures for these items. In the past, supplies were left open in the warehouse to be taken each evening as needed by the onsite supervisors. A clerk in the accounting department periodically ordered additional supplies from a long-time supplier. No records were maintained other than to record purchases. Once a year, an inventory of supplies was made for the preparation of the financial statements.

LO5   Internal Control Evaluation
LO6

To solve the budgetary problem, management implemented a new system for controlling and purchasing supplies. A supplies clerk was put in charge of a secured storeroom for cleaning supplies. Supervisors use a purchase requisition to request supplies for the jobs they oversee. Each job receives a predetermined amount of supplies based on a study of its needs. In the storeroom, the supplies clerk notes the levels of supplies and completes the purchase requisition when supplies are needed. The purchase requisition goes to the purchasing clerk, a new position, who is solely responsible for authorizing purchases and who prepares the purchase orders. Supplier prices are monitored constantly to ensure that the lowest price is obtained. When supplies are received, the supplies clerk checks them in and prepares a receiving report, which is sent to accounting, where each payment to a supplier is documented by the purchase requisition, the purchase order, and the receiving report. The accounting department also maintains a record of supplies inventory, supplies requisitioned by supervisors, and supplies received. Once each month, a physical inventory of cleaning supplies in the storeroom is made by the warehouse manager and compared against the supplies inventory records maintained by the accounting department.

REQUIRED ▶ Show how the new system applies or does not apply to the seven control activities described in this chapter. Is each new control activity better than the old system?

P 6. The following is a list of transactions for Image Products, Inc., for the month of March 20xx:

LO4   Merchandising Transactions,
SO7   Including Discounts: Periodic Inventory System

Mar. 1   Sold merchandise on credit to D. Brody, terms 2/10, n/60, FOB shipping point, $2,200.
      3   Purchased merchandise on credit from Isle Company, terms 2/10, n/30, FOB shipping point, $12,800.
      4   Received freight bill for shipment received on March 3, $900.
      6   Sold merchandise for cash, $1,100.
      7   Sold merchandise on credit to R. Guido, terms 2/10, n/60, $2,400.
      9   Purchased merchandise from Maskel Company, terms 1/10, n/30, FOB shipping point, $6,180, which includes freight charges of $400.
     10   Sold merchandise on credit to B. Viola, terms 2/10, n/20, $4,400.
     10   Received check from D. Brody for payment in full for sale of March 1.
     11   Purchased merchandise from Isle Company, terms 2/10, n/30, FOB shipping point, $16,400.
     12   Received freight bill for shipment of March 11, $1,460.
     13   Paid Isle Company for purchase of March 3.
     14   Returned merchandise from the March 9 shipment that was the wrong size and color, for credit, $580.
     16   B. Viola returned some of the merchandise sold to him on March 10 for credit, $400.

Mar. 17 Received payment from R. Guido for half of her purchase on March 7. A discount is allowed on partial payment.

18 Paid Maskel Company balance due on account from transactions on March 9 and 14.

20 In checking the purchase of March 11 from Isle Company, Image Products' accounting department found an overcharge of $800. Isle Company agreed to issue a credit.

21 Paid freight company for freight charges of March 4 and 12.

23 Purchased cleaning supplies on credit from Liu Company, terms n/5, $500.

24 Discovered that some of the cleaning supplies purchased on March 23 had not been ordered. Returned them to Liu Company for credit, $100.

25 Sold merchandise for cash, $1,600.

27 Paid Liu Company for the March 23 purchase less the March 24 return.

28 Received payment in full from B. Viola for transactions on March 10 and 16.

29 Paid Isle Company for purchase of March 11 less allowance of March 20.

31 Received payment for balance of amount owed from R. Guido from transactions of March 7 and 17.

REQUIRED ▶ Prepare entries in journal form to record the transactions, assuming that the periodic inventory system is used.

ALTERNATE PROBLEMS

P 7.

LO1 Merchandising Income
LO3 Statement: Perpetual Inventory System

At the end of the fiscal year, August 31, 20x2, selected accounts from the adjusted trial balance for Holiday Merchandise, Inc., appeared as follows:

Holiday Merchandise, Inc.
Partial Adjusted Trial Balance
August 31, 20x2

Sales		$324,000
Sales Returns and Allowances	$ 4,000	
Cost of Goods Sold	122,800	
Freight In	4,600	
Store Salaries Expense	65,250	
Office Salaries Expense	25,750	
Advertising Expense	48,600	
Rent Expense	4,800	
Insurance Expense	2,400	
Utilities Expense	3,120	
Store Supplies Expense	5,760	
Office Supplies Expense	2,350	
Depreciation Expense, Store Equipment	2,100	
Depreciation Expense, Office Equipment	1,600	
Income Taxes	4,000	

REQUIRED ▶

1. Using the information given, prepare an income statement for Holiday Merchandise, Inc. Combine Freight In with Cost of Goods Sold. Store Salaries Expense; Advertising Expense; Store Supplies Expense; and Depreciation Expense, Store Equipment are selling expenses. The other expenses are general and administrative expenses. The company uses the perpetual inventory system. Show details of net sales and operating expenses.

2. Based on your knowledge at this point in the course, how would you use the income statement for Holiday Merchandise to evaluate the company's profitability? What other financial statement should be considered and why?

P 8.

LO3   Merchandising Transactions: Perpetual Inventory System

Garden Company engaged in the following transactions in October 20xx:

Oct.   7   Sold merchandise on credit to Sonia Mendes, terms n/30, FOB shipping point, $6,000 (cost, $3,600).

8   Purchased merchandise on credit from DaCosta Company, terms n/30, FOB shipping point, $12,000.

9   Paid Jay Company for shipping charges on merchandise purchased on October 8, $508.

10   Purchased merchandise on credit from Paige Company, terms n/30, FOB shipping point, $19,200, including $1,200 freight costs paid by Paige.

13   Purchased office supplies on credit from Hayami Company, terms n/30, $4,800.

14   Sold merchandise on credit to Eliza Samms, terms n/30, FOB shipping point, $4,800 (cost, $2,880).

14   Returned damaged merchandise received from DaCosta Company on October 8 for credit, $1,200.

17   Received check from Sonia Mendes for her purchase of October 7.

18   Returned a portion of the office supplies purchased on October 13 for credit because the wrong items were sent, $800.

19   Sold merchandise for cash, $3,600 (cost, $2,160).

20   Paid Paige Company for purchase of October 10.

21   Paid DaCosta Company the balance from the transactions of October 8 and October 14.

24   Accepted from Eliza Samms a return of merchandise, which was put back in inventory, $400 (cost, $240).

REQUIRED ▶   Prepare entries in journal form to record the transactions, assuming the perpetual inventory system is used.

P 9.

LO1   Merchandising Income
LO4   Statement: Periodic Inventory System

Selected accounts from the adjusted trial balance for Gourmet Gadgets Shop, Inc., as of March 31, 20x4, the end of the fiscal year, are shown below. The merchandise inventory for Gourmet Gadgets Shop was $38,200 at the beginning of the year and $29,400 at the end of the year.

Gourmet Gadgets Shop, Inc.
Partial Adjusted Trial Balance
March 31, 20x4

Sales		$165,000
Sales Returns and Allowances	$ 2,000	
Purchases	70,200	
Purchases Returns and Allowances		2,600
Freight In	2,300	
Store Salaries Expense	32,625	
Office Salaries Expense	12,875	
Advertising Expense	24,300	
Rent Expense	2,400	
Insurance Expense	1,200	
Utilities Expense	1,560	
Store Supplies Expense	2,880	
Office Supplies Expense	1,175	
Depreciation Expense, Store Equipment	1,050	
Depreciation Expense, Office Equipment	800	
Income Taxes	1,000	

REQUIRED ▶   1. Using the information given, prepare an income statement for Gourmet Gadgets Shop, Inc. Store Salaries Expense; Advertising Expense; Store Supplies Expense; and

Depreciation Expense, Store Equipment are selling expenses. The other expenses are general and administrative expenses. The company uses the periodic inventory system. Show details of net sales and operating expenses.

2. Based on your knowledge at this point in the course, how would you use the income statement for Gourmet Gadgets Shop to evaluate the company's profitability? What other financial statements should be considered and why?

P 10.

LO4   **Merchandising Transactions: Periodic Inventory System**

REQUIRED ▶

Use the data in **P 8** for this problem.

Prepare entries in journal form to record the transactions, assuming the periodic inventory system is used.

SKILLS DEVELOPMENT CASES

Conceptual Analysis

SD 1.

LO1   **Cash Flow Management**

Matson Audio and Video Source, Inc., has operated in a middle-size Midwest city for 30 years. The company has always prided itself on individual attention to its customers. It carries a large inventory so it can offer a good selection and deliver purchases quickly. It accepts credit cards and checks in payment but also provides 90 days credit to reliable customers who have purchased from the company in the past. The company maintains good relations with suppliers by paying invoices soon after they are received. In the past year, the company has been strapped for cash and has had to borrow from the bank to pay its bills. An analysis of its financial statements reveals that, on average, inventory is on hand for 70 days before being sold and receivables are held for 90 days before being paid. Accounts payable are paid, on average, in 20 days. What are the operating cycle and the financing period, and how long are Matson's? In what three ways can Matson improve its cash flow management? Make a suggestion for implementing each.

SD 2.

LO1   **Periodic Versus Perpetual Inventory Systems**

Books Unlimited is a well-established chain of 20 bookstores in eastern Michigan. In recent years the company has grown rapidly, adding five new stores in regional malls. Management has relied on the manager of each store to place orders keyed to the market in his or her region; the managers select from a master list of available titles provided by the central office. Every six months, a physical inventory is taken, and financial statements are prepared using the periodic inventory system. At that time, books that have not sold well are placed on sale or, whenever possible, returned to the publisher. As a result of the company's fast growth, there are many new store managers, and management has found that they are not as able to judge the market as are managers of the older, established stores. Thus, management is considering a recommendation to implement a perpetual inventory system and carefully monitor sales from the central office. Do you think Books Unlimited should switch to the perpetual inventory system or stay with the periodic inventory system? Discuss the advantages and disadvantages of each system.

Ethical Dilemma

SD 3.

SO7   **Ethics and Purchases Discounts**

The purchasing power of some customers is such that they can exert pressure on suppliers to go beyond the suppliers' customary allowances. For example, Wal-Mart <www.walmart.com> represents more than 10 percent of annual sales for many suppliers, including Fruit of the Loom <www.fruit.com>, Sunbeam <www.sunbeam.com>, Rubbermaid <www.rubbermaid.com>, and Coleman <www.coleman.com>. *Forbes* magazine reports that while many of these suppliers allow a 2 percent discount if bills are paid within 15 days, "Wal-Mart routinely pays its bills closer to 30 days and takes the 2 percent discount anyway on the gross amount of the invoice, not the net amount, which deducts for [trade] discounts and things like freight costs."[10]

Identify two ways in which Wal-Mart's practice benefits Wal-Mart. Do you think this practice is unethical, or is it just good cash management on the part of Wal-Mart? Are the suppliers harmed by it?

Research Activity

SD 4.

LO1 **Inventory Systems and**
LO3 **Internal Controls**
LO4
LO5
LO6

Go to a retail business, such as a bookstore, a clothing shop, a gift shop, a grocery, a hardware store, or a car dealership, in your local shopping area or a local shopping mall. Ask to speak to someone who is knowledgeable about the store's inventory methods. Find out the answers to the following questions and be prepared to discuss your findings in class:

1. *Inventory systems*   How is each item of inventory identified? Does the business have a computerized or a manual inventory system? Which inventory system, periodic or perpetual, is used? How often do employees take a physical inventory? What procedures are followed in taking a physical inventory? What kinds of inventory reports are prepared or received?
2. *Internal control structure*   How does the company protect against inventory theft and loss? What control activities, including authorization, recording transactions, documents and records, physical controls, periodic checks, separation of duties, and sound personnel policies, does the company use? Can you see these control procedures in use?

Group Activity: Assign teams to carry out the above assignments.

Decision-Making Practice

SD 5.

LO1 **Analysis of Merchandising**
LO3 **Income Statement**
LO4
LO5

In 20x1, Mark Fischer opened a small retail store in a suburban mall. Called Fischer Garb Company, the shop sold designer jeans. Mark Fischer worked 14 hours a day and controlled all aspects of the operation. All sales were for cash or bank credit card. Fischer Garb Company was such a success that in 20x2, Fischer decided to open a second store in another mall. Because the new shop needed his attention, he hired a manager to work in the original store with two sales clerks. During 20x2, the new store was successful, but the operations of the original store did not match the first year's performance.

Concerned about this turn of events, Fischer compared the two years' results for the original store. The figures were as follows:

	20x2	20x1
Net sales	$325,000	$350,000
Cost of goods sold	225,000	225,000
Gross margin	$100,000	$125,000
Operating expenses	75,000	50,000
Income before income taxes	$ 25,000	$ 75,000

In addition, Fischer's analysis revealed that the cost and selling price of jeans were about the same in both years and that the level of operating expenses was roughly the same in both years, except for the new manager's $25,000 salary. Sales returns and allowances were insignificant amounts in both years.

Studying the situation further, Fischer discovered the following facts about the cost of goods sold:

	20x2	20x1
Purchases	$200,000	$271,000
Total purchases allowances	15,000	20,000
Freight in	19,000	27,000
Physical inventory, end of year	32,000	53,000

Still not satisfied, Fischer went through all the individual sales and purchase records for the year. Both sales and purchases were verified. However, the 20x2 ending inventory should have been $57,000, given the unit purchases and sales during the year. After puzzling over all this information, Fischer comes to you for accounting help.

1. Using Fischer's new information, recompute the cost of goods sold for 20x1 and 20x2, and account for the difference in income before income taxes between 20x1 and 20x2.
2. Suggest at least two reasons for the discrepancy in the 20x2 ending inventory. How might Fischer improve the management of the original store?

FINANCIAL REPORTING AND ANALYSIS CASES

Interpreting Financial Reports

FRA 1.

LO1 Comparison of Operating
LO3 Performance
LO4

Wal-Mart <www.walmart.com> and Kmart <www.kmartcorp.com>, two of the largest retailers in the United States, have different approaches to retailing. Their success has been different also. At one time, Kmart was larger than Wal-Mart. Today, Wal-Mart is almost three times as large and Kmart has declared bankruptcy. You can see the difference by analyzing their respective income statements and merchandise inventories. Selected information from their annual reports for the year ended January 31, 2001, is presented below.[11] (All amounts are in millions.)

Wal-Mart: Net sales, $191,329; Cost of goods sold, $150,255; Operating expenses, $31,550; Ending inventory, $21,442

Kmart: Net sales, $37,028; Cost of goods sold, $29,658; Operating expenses, $7,415; Ending inventory, $6,412

REQUIRED ▶

1. Prepare a schedule computing the gross margin and income from operations for both companies as dollar amounts and as percentages of net sales. Also compute inventory as a percentage of the cost of goods sold.
2. From what you know about the different retailing approaches of these two companies, do the gross margins and incomes from operations you computed in 1 seem compatible with these approaches? What is it about the nature of Wal-Mart's operations that produces lower gross margin and lower operating expenses in percentages in comparison to Kmart? Which company's approach was more successful in the fiscal year ending January 31, 2001? Explain your answer.
3. Both companies have chosen a fiscal year that ends on January 31. Why do you suppose they made this choice? How realistic do you think the inventory figures are as indicators of inventory levels during the rest of the year? Which company appears to make the most efficient use of its inventory?

FRA 2.

LO1 Business Objectives and
LO3 Income Statements

Superior Products, Inc., is one of the nation's largest discount retailers, operating 216 stores in 30 states. In a letter to stockholders in the 1999 annual report (fiscal year ended January 31, 2000), the chairman and chief executive officer of the company stated, "Our operating plan for fiscal 2000 (year ended January 30, 2001) calls for moderate sales increases, continued improvement in gross margins, and a continuation of aggressive expense reduction programs." The following data are from the income statements presented in the 2000 annual report (dated January 30, 2001) (in millions):

	Year Ended		
	January 30, 2001	January 31, 2000	February 1, 1999
Net sales	$2,067	$2,142	$2,235
Cost of goods sold	1,500	1,593	1,685
Operating expenses	466	486	502

REQUIRED ▶

Did Superior Products achieve the objectives stated by its chairman? (**Hint:** Prepare an income statement for each year and compute gross margin and operating expenses as percentages of net sales.)

FRA 3.

LO5 Internal Control Lapse

Starbucks Corporation <www.starbucks.com> has accused an employee and her husband of embezzling $3.7 million by billing the company for services from a fictitious consulting firm. The employee and her husband created a phony company called RAD Services Inc. and charged Starbucks for work they never provided. The employee worked in the information technology department. RAD Services Inc. charged

Starbucks for as much as $492,800 in consulting services in a single week.[12] For such a fraud to have taken place, certain control activities were likely not implemented. Identify and describe these activities.

International Company

FRA 4.
LO4   British Terminology for Merchandising Transactions

Harrods <www.harrods.com> is a large British retailer with department stores throughout the United Kingdom and Europe. British and American merchandising terms differ. For instance, in the United Kingdom, the income statement is called the *profit and loss account*, sales is called *turnover*, merchandise inventory is called *stocks*, accounts receivable is called *debtors*, and accounts payable is called *creditors*. Of course, the amounts are stated in terms of the pound (£). In today's business world, it is important to understand terminology employed by professionals from other countries. Explain in your own words why the British may use the terms *profit and loss account, turnover, stocks, debtors,* and *creditors* rather than the American equivalents.

Toys "R" Us Annual Report

FRA 5.
LO1   Operating Cycle and Financing Period

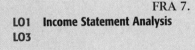

Refer to the Toys "R" Us <www.tru.com> annual report in the Supplement to Chapter 1 and to Figures 1 and 2 in this chapter. Write a memorandum to your instructor briefly describing the Toys "R" Us operating cycle and financing period. This memorandum should identify the most common transactions in the operating cycle as it applies to Toys "R" Us. It should refer to the importance of accounts receivable, accounts payable, and merchandise inventory in the Toys "R" Us financial statements. Complete the memorandum by explaining why the operating cycle and financing period are favorable to the company.

Comparison Case: Toys "R" Us and Walgreen Co.

FRA 6.
LO1   Income Statement Analysis

Refer to the Toys "R" Us <www.tru.com> annual report and the financial statements of Walgreens <www.walgreens.com> in the Supplement to Chapter 1. Determine which company—Toys "R" Us or Walgreens—has more profitable merchandising operations by preparing a schedule that compares the companies based on net sales, cost of sales, gross margin, total operating expenses, and income from operations as a percentage of sales. (*Hint:* You should put the income statements in comparable formats.) In addition, for each company, compute inventory as a percentage of the cost of goods sold. Which company has the highest prices in relation to costs of sales? Which company is more efficient in its operating expenses? Which company manages its inventory better? Overall, on the basis of the income statement, which company is more profitable? Explain your answers.

Fingraph® Financial Analyst™

FRA 7.
LO1   Income Statement Analysis
LO3

Choose any retail company from the list of Fingraph companies on the Needles Accounting Resource Center Web Site at http://accounting.college.hmco.com/students. Access the Microsoft Excel spreadsheets for the company you selected. Using the Fingraph CD-ROM software, display the Income Statements Analysis: Income from Operations in tabular and graphic form for the company.

Write an executive summary that analyzes the change in the company's income from operations from the first to the second year. In preparing the summary, focus on the reasons the change occurred by answering the following questions: Did the company's income from operations improve or decline from the first to the second year? What was the relationship of the change to the change in net sales? Was the change in income from operations primarily due to a change in gross margin or to a change in operating expenses? Suggest some possible reasons for the change in gross margin or operating expenses. Use percentages to support your answer.

Internet Case

FRA 8.

LO1 **Comparison of Traditional**
LO3 **Merchandising with**
       Ecommerce

Ecommerce is a word coined to describe business conducted over the Internet. Ecommerce is similar in some ways to traditional retailing, but it presents new challenges. Choose a company with traditional retail outlets that is also selling over the Internet and go to its web site. Some examples are Wal-Mart <u>www.walmart.com</u>, Kmart <u>www.kmartcorp.com</u>, Toys "R" Us <u>www.tru.com</u>, Barnes & Noble <u>www.bn.com</u>, and Lands' End <u>www.landsend.com</u>. Investigate and list the steps a customer makes to purchase an item on the site. How do these steps differ from those in a traditional retail store? What are some of the accounting challenges in recording Internet transactions? Be prepared to discuss your results in class.

7

Chapter 7 focuses on management of, and accounting for, several types of short-term assets: cash and cash equivalents, short-term investments, accounts receivable, and notes receivable.

Short-Term Financial Assets

LEARNING OBJECTIVES

LO1 Identify and explain the management issues related to short-term financial assets.

LO2 Explain *cash, cash equivalents,* and the importance of electronic funds transfer.

LO3 Identify types of short-term investments and explain the financial reporting implications.

LO4 Define *accounts receivable* and apply the allowance method of accounting for uncollectible accounts.

LO5 Define *promissory note,* and compute and record promissory notes receivable.

SUPPLEMENTAL OBJECTIVE

SO6 Prepare a bank reconciliation.

DECISION POINT
A USER'S FOCUS

Pioneer Corporation <www.pioneer.co.jp> A company must use its assets to maximize income earned while maintaining liquidity. Pioneer Corporation, a leading Japanese manufacturer of electronics for home, commerce, and industry, manages about $2.4 billion in short-term financial assets. **Short-term financial assets** are assets that arise from cash transactions, the investment of cash, and the extension of credit. What is the composition of these assets? Why are they important to Pioneer's management?

Pioneer's short-term financial assets, as reported on the balance sheet in the company's annual report, are shown in the table on the opposite page.[1] These assets make up almost 41 percent of Pioneer's total assets, and they are very important to the company's strategy for meeting its goals. Effective asset management techniques ensure that these assets remain liquid and usable for the company's operations.

A commonly used ratio for measuring the adequacy of short-term financial assets is the quick ratio. The **quick ratio** is the ratio of short-term financial assets to current liabilities. Because Pioneer's current liabilities are (in millions) ¥177,825 ($1,434.1), its quick ratio is 1.39, which is computed as follows:

$$\text{Quick Ratio} = \frac{\text{Short-Term Financial Assets}}{\text{Current Liabilities}}$$

$$= \frac{\$1,995,200,000}{\$1,434,100,000} = 1.39$$

A quick ratio of about 1.0 has historically been the minimum common benchmark. However, it is more important to look at industry characteristics and at the

How does Pioneer Electric, a leading manufacturer of electronics for the home, manage its short-term financial assets?

trends for a particular company to see if the ratio is improving or not. A lower ratio may mean that a company is a very good manager of its short-term financial assets. Pioneer has maintained a quick ratio of over 1.0 for several years. Through good cash manage-ment, the company has not tied up excess funds in quick assets relative to current liabilities. This chapter emphasizes management of, and accounting for, short-term financial assets to achieve liquidity.

Financial Highlights
(In millions)

	Yen	Dollars
Cash and cash equivalents	¥121,127	$ 976.8
Short-term investments	1,598	12.9
Accounts receivable, net of allowances of ¥5,895 ($47.5)	116,594	940.3
Notes receivable	8,079	65.2
Total short-term financial assets	¥247,398	$1,995.2

MANAGEMENT ISSUES RELATED TO SHORT-TERM FINANCIAL ASSETS

LO1 Identify and explain the management issues related to short-term financial assets.

RELATED TEXT ASSIGNMENTS
Q: 1, 2
SE: 1, 2
E: 1, 2
P: 2, 7
SD: 1, 2, 3, 4, 5
FRA: 1, 3, 4, 5, 6

www.homedepot.com

The management of short-term financial assets is critical to the goal of maintaining adequate liquidity. In dealing with short-term financial assets, management must address three key issues: managing cash needs during seasonal cycles, setting credit policies, and financing receivables.

MANAGING CASH NEEDS DURING SEASONAL CYCLES

Most companies experience seasonal cycles of business activity during the year. During some periods, sales are weak; during others, they are strong. There are also periods when expenditures are high and periods when expenditures are low. For toy companies, college textbook publishers, amusement parks, construction companies, and sports equipment companies, the cycles are dramatic, but all companies experience them to some degree.

Seasonal cycles require careful planning of cash inflows, cash outflows, borrowing, and investing. Figure 1 shows the seasonal cycles typical of a home improvement company, such as The Home Depot, Inc. As you can see, cash receipts from sales are highest in the late spring, summer, and fall because that is when most people make home improvements. Sales are relatively low in the winter months. On the other hand, cash expenditures are highest in late winter and spring as the company builds up inventory for spring and summer selling. During the late summer, fall, and winter, the company has excess cash on hand that it needs to invest in a way that will earn a return but still permit access to cash as needed. During the late spring

FIGURE 1
Seasonal Cycles and Cash Requirements for a Home Improvement Company

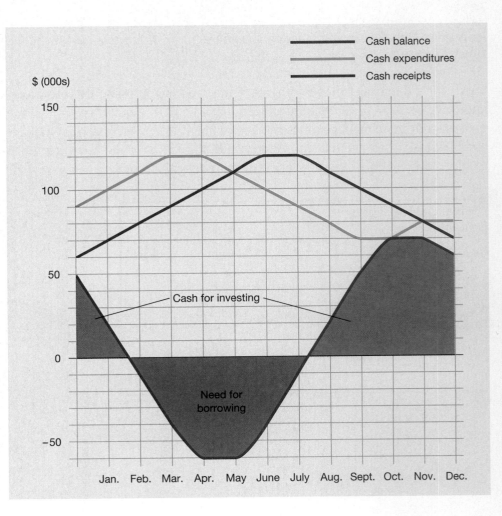

FOCUS ON BUSINESS PRACTICE

What a Difference a Year Makes!

It's hard to know how much cash reserve a company should have. Analysts are often critical of companies that build cash reserves because the cash is not earning as much as other assets might. But having a cash reserve may be a good thing, especially in a cyclical industry like the auto industry. For example, just a year or so ago, the Big Three automakers—General Motors <www.gm.com>, Ford <www.ford.com>, and DaimlerChrysler <www.daimlerchrysler.com>—were awash in cash. However, in little over a year, the three companies went through $28 billion in cash through various purchases, losses, dividends, and share buybacks. Then, with increasing losses from rising costs, big rebates, and 0 percent financing, the companies were suddenly faced with a shortage of cash. As a result, Standard & Poor's lowered their credit ratings, which raises the interest cost of borrowing money. Perhaps the Big Three should have held on to some of that cash.[2]

and early summer, the company needs to plan for short-term borrowing to tide it over until cash receipts pick up later in the year. The discussion in this chapter of accounting for cash and cash equivalents and for short-term investments is directly related to managing the seasonal cycles of a business.

SETTING CREDIT POLICIES

◆ STOP AND THINK!

To increase sales, a company decides to increase its credit terms from 15 days to 30 days. What effect will this change in policy have on receivable turnover, average days' sales uncollected, and cash flows?

Receivable turnover will become smaller because average net accounts receivable will increase relative to sales. Consequently, the average days' sales uncollected will increase. This will have an adverse effect on cash flows because, on average, the company will have to wait longer to receive cash from sales. ■

Companies that sell on credit do so to be competitive and to increase sales. In setting credit terms, management must keep in mind both the terms the company's competitors are offering and the needs of customers. Obviously, companies that sell on credit want to have customers who will pay the debts they incur. To increase the likelihood of selling only to customers who will pay on time, most companies develop control procedures and maintain a credit department. The credit department's responsibilities include the examination of each person or company that applies for credit and the approval or rejection of a credit sale to that customer. Typically, the credit department asks for information about the customer's financial resources and debts. It may also check personal references and credit bureaus for further information. Then, based on the information it has gathered, the credit department decides whether to extend credit to the customer.

Two common measures of the effect of a company's credit policies are **receivable turnover** and **average days' sales uncollected**. The receivable turnover reflects the relative size of a company's accounts receivable and the success of its seasonal conditions and interest rates. It shows how many times, on average, the receivables were turned into cash during the accounting period. The average days' sales uncollected is a related measure that shows, on average, how long it takes to collect accounts receivable.

FOCUS ON BUSINESS PRACTICE

Why Powerful Buyers Can Cause Headaches for Small Businesses

Big buyers often have significant power over small suppliers, and their cash management decisions can cause severe cash flow problems for the little companies that depend on them. For instance, in an effort to control costs and optimize cash flow, Ameritech Corp. <www.ameritech.com> told 70,000 suppliers that it would begin paying its bills in 45 days instead of 30. Other large companies routinely take 90 days or more to pay. Some small suppliers are so anxious to get the big companies' business that they fail to realize the implications of the deals they make until it is too late. When Earthly Elements, Inc., accepted a $10,000 order for dried floral gifts from a national home shopping network, its management was ecstatic because the deal increased sales by 25 percent. But in four months, the resulting cash crunch forced the company to close down. When the shopping network finally paid for the big order six months later, it was too late to revive Earthly Elements.[3]

Turnover ratios usually consist of one balance sheet account and one income statement account. The receivable turnover is computed by dividing net sales by average net accounts receivable. Theoretically, the numerator should be net credit sales, but the amount of net credit sales is rarely made available in public reports, so total net sales is used. Pioneer Corporation, discussed in the Decision Point at the start of the chapter, had net sales in 2001 of $5,052,700,000. Its net trade accounts receivable in 2001 and 2000 were $940,300,000 and $805,564,000, respectively. Its receivable turnover is computed as follows:[4]

$$\text{Receivable Turnover} = \frac{\text{Net Sales}}{\text{Average Net Accounts Receivable}}$$

$$= \frac{\$5,052,700,000}{(\$940,300,000 + \$805,564,000) \div 2}$$

$$= \frac{\$5,052,700,000}{\$872,932,000} = 5.8 \text{ times}$$

To find the average days' sales uncollected, the number of days in a year is divided by the receivable turnover, as follows:

$$\text{Average Days' Sales Uncollected} = \frac{365 \text{ days}}{\text{Receivable Turnover}} = \frac{365 \text{ days}}{5.8} = 62.9 \text{ days}$$

BUSINESS-WORLD EXAMPLE: For many businesses with seasonal sales activity, such as Nordstrom, Dillard, Marshall Field's, and Macy's, the fourth quarter produces more than 25 percent of annual sales. For such businesses, receivables are highest at the balance sheet date, resulting in an artificially low receivable turnover and high average days' sales uncollected.

Pioneer turns its receivables 5.8 times a year, for an average of every 62.9 days. While this turnover period is longer than that of many companies, it is not unusual for electronics companies because their credit terms allow retail outlets to receive and sell products before paying for them. This example demonstrates the need to interpret ratios in light of the specific industry's practice.

As Figure 2 shows, the receivable turnover ratio varies substantially from industry to industry. Grocery stores, for example, have a high turnover because that type of business has few receivables; the turnover in interstate trucking is 10.5 times because the typical credit terms in that industry are 30 days. The turnover in the machinery and computer industries is lower because those industries tend to have longer credit terms.

Figure 3 shows the average days' sales uncollected for the industries listed in Figure 2. Grocery stores, which have the lowest ratio (3.8 days) require the least amount of receivables financing; the computer industry, with average days' sales uncollected of 55.3 days, requires the most.

FIGURE 2
Receivable Turnover for Selected Industries

Source: Data from Dun and Bradstreet, *Industry Norms and Key Business Ratios*, 2000-2001.

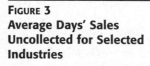

FIGURE 3
Average Days' Sales Uncollected for Selected Industries

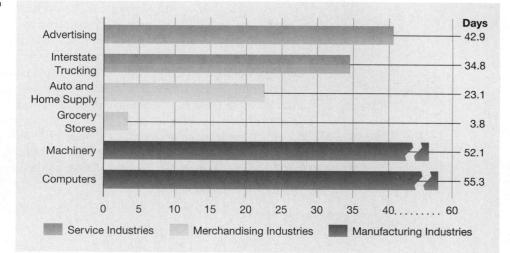

Source: Data from Dun and Bradstreet, *Industry Norms and Key Business Ratios*, 2000-2001.

FINANCING RECEIVABLES

Financial flexibility is important to most companies. Companies that have significant amounts of assets tied up in accounts receivable may be unwilling or unable to wait until cash from the receivables is collected. Many corporations have set up finance companies to help their customers pay for the purchase of their products; for example, Ford has set up Ford Motor Credit Co. (FMCC), General Motors has set up General Motors Acceptance Corp. (GMAC), and Sears has set up Sears Roebuck Acceptance Corp. (SRAC). Some companies borrow funds by pledging their accounts receivable as collateral. If a company does not pay back its loan, the creditor can take the collateral (in this case, the accounts receivable) and convert it to cash to satisfy the loan.

Companies can also raise funds by selling or transferring accounts receivable to another entity, called a **factor**. The sale or transfer of accounts receivable, called **factoring**, can be done with or without recourse. *With recourse* means that the seller of the receivables is liable to the purchaser if a receivable is not collected. *Without recourse* means that the factor that buys the accounts receivable bears any losses from uncollectible accounts. A company's acceptance of credit cards like Visa, MasterCard, or American Express is an example of factoring without recourse because the credit card issuers accept the risk of nonpayment.

The factor, of course, charges a fee for its service. The fee for sales with recourse is usually about 1 percent of the accounts receivable. The fee is higher for sales without recourse because the factor's risk is greater. In accounting terminology, the seller of the receivables with recourse is said to be contingently liable. A **contingent liability** is a potential liability that can develop into a real liability if a particular subsequent event occurs. In this case, the subsequent event would be nonpayment of the receivable by the customer. A contingent liability generally requires disclosure in the notes to the financial statements.

Circuit City Stores, Inc., is one of the nation's largest electronics and appliance retailers. To sell its products, the company offers generous terms through its installment programs, under which customers pay over a number of months. The company is growing rapidly and needs the cash from these installment receivables sooner than the customers have agreed to pay. To generate cash immediately from these receivables, the company sells them through a process called securitization. Under **securitization**, the company groups its receivables in batches and sells them at a discount to companies and investors. When the receivables are paid, the buyers of the receivables receive the full amount; their revenue is the amount of the discount. Circuit City sells all its receivables without recourse, which means that after selling the receivables, it has no further liability, even if the customers do not pay. If

www.ford.com
www.gm.com
www.sears.com

KEY POINT: The receivable turnover and average days' sales uncollected will appear better for a company that factors receivables than for a company that does not factor.

www.circuitcity.com

the receivables were with recourse, it would mean that if a customer did not pay, Circuit City would have to make good on the debt.[5]

Another method of financing receivables is through the **discounting**, or selling, of promissory notes held as notes receivable. Selling notes receivable is called discounting because the bank deducts the interest from the maturity value of the note to determine the proceeds. The holder of the note (usually the payee) endorses the note and delivers it to the bank. The bank expects to collect the maturity value of the note (principal plus interest) on the maturity date but also has recourse against the endorser or seller of the note. If the maker fails to pay, the endorser is liable to the bank for payment. The endorser has a contingent liability in the amount of the discounted notes plus interest that must be disclosed in the notes to the financial statements.

Check out ACE for a Review Quiz at http://accounting.college.hmco.com/students.

CASH AND CASH EQUIVALENTS

LO2 Explain *cash, cash equivalents,* and the importance of electronic funds transfer.

RELATED TEXT ASSIGNMENTS
Q: 3, 4
SE: 3
E: 3
SD: 1
FRA: 4

www.pioneer.co.jp

STOP AND THINK!
A cash register can be considered a type of imprest system. If a cashier in a supermarket started the day with $100 in change, what should the amount of cash in the drawer equal at the end of the day?
The amount of cash in the drawer should equal the total cash sales less any refunds plus $100. ∎

The annual report of Pioneer Corporation refers to *cash and cash equivalents.* Of the two terms, *cash* is the easier to understand. It is the most liquid of all assets and the most readily available to pay debts. On the balance sheet, **cash** normally consists of currency and coins on hand, checks and money orders from customers, and deposits in bank checking and savings accounts. Cash may also include a **compensating balance**, an amount that is not entirely free to be spent. A compensating balance is a minimum amount that a bank requires a company to keep in its bank account as part of a credit-granting arrangement. Such an arrangement restricts cash; in effect, increases the interest of the loan; and reduces a company's liquidity. Therefore, the SEC requires companies to disclose the amount of any compensating balances in a note to the financial statements.

The term *cash equivalents* is a little harder to understand. At times a company may find that it has more cash on hand than it needs to pay current obligations. Excess cash should not remain idle, especially during periods of high interest rates. Thus, management may periodically invest idle funds in time deposits or certificates of deposit at banks and other financial institutions, in government securities (such as U.S. Treasury notes), or in other securities. Such actions are rightfully called investments. However, if the investments have a term of 90 days or less when they are purchased, they are called **cash equivalents** because the funds revert to cash so quickly that they are regarded as cash on the balance sheet. Pioneer Corporation follows this practice. Its policy is stated as follows: "The Company considers all highly liquid investments with a maturity of 90 days or less when purchased to be cash equivalents. Cash equivalents are stated at cost, which approximates market value."[6] A survey of 600 large U.S. corporations found that 53 of them, or 9 percent, used the term *cash* as the balance sheet caption and 510, or 85 percent, used the phrase *cash and cash equivalents* or *cash and equivalents.* Twenty-seven companies, or 5 percent, combined cash with marketable securities.[7] The average amount of cash held can also vary by industry.

Most companies need to keep some currency and coins on hand. Currency and coins are needed for cash registers, for paying expenses that are impractical to pay by check, and for situations that require cash advances—for example, when sales representatives need cash for travel expenses. One way to control a cash fund or cash advances is through the use of an **imprest system**. A common form of imprest system is a petty cash fund, which is established at a fixed amount. Each cash payment from the fund is documented by a receipt. The fund is periodically reimbursed, based on the documented expenditures, by the exact amount necessary to restore its original cash balance. The person responsible for the petty cash fund must

FOCUS ON BUSINESS ETHICS

What About the Unlawful Use of EFT?

Electronic Funds Transfer (EFT) has made it easy to transfer funds around the world. It has facilitated the huge growth in international business, but what about the unlawful use of EFT? To combat the laundering of money by drug dealers, U.S. law requires banks to report cash transactions in excess of $10,000. However, terrorist groups have circumvented this law by electronically transferring amounts of less than $10,000. In response, the Treasury Department has set up rules that require banks to keep records about the sources and recipients of electronic transfers. But it is questionable how much effect this action will have. Since most of the millions of EFT transactions that occur every day look pretty much alike, looking for transactions that support illegal activities is like looking for a needle in a haystack.

ENRICHMENT NOTE:
Periodically, banks detect individuals who are *kiting*. Kiting is the illegal issuing of checks when there is not enough money to cover them. Before one kited check clears the bank, a kited check from another account is deposited to cover it, making an endless circle.

www.walmart.com

www.citigroup.com
www.bankone.com
www.bankofamerica.com

always be able to account for its contents by having cash and receipts whose total equals the originally fixed amount.

All businesses rely on banks to control cash receipts and cash disbursements. Banks serve as safe depositories for cash, negotiable instruments, and other valuable business documents, such as stocks and bonds. The checking accounts that banks provide improve control by minimizing the amount of currency a company needs to keep on hand and by supplying permanent records of all cash payments. Banks also serve as agents in a variety of transactions, such as the collection and payment of certain kinds of debts and the exchange of foreign currencies.

Many companies commonly conduct transactions through a type of electronic communication called **electronic funds transfer (EFT)**. Instead of writing checks to pay for purchases or to repay loans, the company arranges to have cash transferred electronically from its bank to another company's bank. Wal-Mart Stores, Inc., for example, makes 75 percent of its payments to suppliers through EFT. The actual cash, of course, is not transferred. For the banks, an electronic transfer is simply a bookkeeping entry.

In serving customers, banks also offer automated teller machines (ATMs) for making deposits, withdrawing cash, transferring funds among accounts, and paying bills. Large consumer banks like Citibank, BankOne, and Bank of America process hundreds of thousands of ATM transactions each week. Many banks also give customers the option of paying bills over the telephone and with *debit cards*. When a customer makes a retail purchase using a debit card, the amount of the purchase is deducted directly from the buyer's bank account. The bank usually documents debit card transactions for the retailer, but the retailer must develop new internal controls to ensure that the transactions are recorded properly and that unauthorized transfers are not permitted. It is expected that within a few years, 25 percent of all retail activity will be handled electronically.

 Check out ACE for a Review Quiz at http://accounting.college.hmco.com/students.

SHORT-TERM INVESTMENTS

LO3 Identify types of short-term investments and explain the financial reporting implications.

RELATED TEXT ASSIGNMENTS
Q: 5, 6
SE: 4, 5
E: 4, 5
P: 1, 6
SD: 1, 5, 6

When investments have a maturity of more than 90 days but are intended to be held only until cash is needed for current operations, they are called **short-term investments** or **marketable securities**. Investments intended to be held for more than one year are called *long-term investments*. Long-term investments are reported in an investments section of the balance sheet, not in the current assets section. Although long-term investments may be just as marketable as short-term assets, management intends to hold them for an indefinite period of time.

Securities that may be held as short-term or long-term investments fall into three categories, as specified by the Financial Accounting Standards Board: held-to-maturity securities, trading securities, and available-for-sale securities.[8] Trading securities are classified as short-term investments. Held-to-maturity securities and available-for-sale securities may be classified as either short-term or long-term investments, depending on their length to maturity or management's intent to hold them. The three categories of securities when held as short-term investments are discussed here.

HELD-TO-MATURITY SECURITIES

KEY POINT: Any broker costs or taxes paid to acquire securities are part of the cost of the securities.

Held-to-maturity securities are debt securities that management intends to hold to their maturity date and whose cash value is not needed until that date. Such securities are recorded at cost and valued on the balance sheet at cost adjusted for the effects of interest. For example, suppose that on December 1, 20x1, Webber Company pays $97,000 for U.S. Treasury bills, which are short-term debt of the federal government. The bills will mature in 120 days at $100,000. Webber would make the following entry:

20x1

A = L + OE
+
–

Dec. 1   Short-Term Investments   97,000
                Cash   97,000
                    Purchase of U.S. Treasury bills
                    that mature in 120 days

At Webber's year end on December 31, the entry to accrue the interest income earned to date would be as follows:

20x1

A = L + OE
+   +

Dec. 31   Short-Term Investments   750
                Interest Income   750
                    Accrual of interest on U.S. Treasury bills
                    $3,000 × 30/120 = $750

On December 31, the U.S. Treasury bills would be shown on the balance sheet as a short-term investment at their amortized cost of $97,750 ($97,000 + $750). When Webber receives the maturity value on March 31, 20x2, the entry is as follows:

20x2

A = L + OE
+   +
–

Mar. 31   Cash   100,000
                Short-Term Investments   97,750
                Interest Income   2,250
                    Receipt of cash at maturity of
                    U.S. Treasury bills and recognition
                    of related income

TRADING SECURITIES

Trading securities are debt and equity securities bought and held principally for the purpose of being sold in the near term. Debt securities are to be redeemed at a specified time and pay a return in the form of interest. Equity securities are an ownership interest in an entity and are subject to market fluctuations. Return takes the form of dividends and increases in the price of the securities.

Trading securities are frequently bought and sold to generate profits on short-term changes in their prices. Trading securities are classified as current assets on the balance sheet and are valued at fair value, which is usually the same as market value—for example, when securities are traded on a stock exchange or in the over-the-counter market.

An increase or decrease in the fair value of the total trading portfolio (the group of securities held for trading purposes) is included in net income in the accounting period in which the increase or decrease occurs. For example, assume that Franklin Company purchases 10,000 shares of Exxon Mobil Corporation for $900,000 ($90 per share) and 5,000 shares of Texaco Inc. for $300,000 ($60 per share) on October 25, 20x1. The purchase is made for trading purposes; that is, management intends

www.exxonmobil.com

to realize a gain by holding the shares for only a short period. The entry to record the investment at cost follows:

A = L + OE
+
—

20x1
Oct. 25   Short-Term Investments   1,200,000
                Cash   1,200,000
                     Investment in stocks for trading
                     ($900,000 + $300,000 = $1,200,000)

Assume that at year end Exxon Mobil's stock price has decreased to $80 per share and Texaco's has risen to $64 per share. The trading portfolio is now valued at $1,120,000:

Security	Market Value	Cost	Gain (Loss)
Exxon Mobil (10,000 shares)	$ 800,000	$ 900,000	
Texaco (5,000 shares)	320,000	300,000	
Totals	$1,120,000	$1,200,000	($80,000)

Because the current fair value of the portfolio is $80,000 less than the original cost of $1,200,000, an adjusting entry is needed, as follows:

A = L + OE
—   —

20x1
Dec. 31   Unrealized Loss on Investments   80,000
                Allowance to Adjust Short-Term
                Investments to Market   80,000
                     Recognition of unrealized loss
                     on trading portfolio

KEY POINT: The Allowance to Adjust Short-Term Investments to Market account is never changed when securities are sold. It changes only with an adjusting entry at year end.

The unrealized loss will appear on the income statement as a reduction in income. The loss is unrealized because the securities have not been sold; unrealized gains are treated the same way if they occur. The Allowance to Adjust Short-Term Investments to Market account appears on the balance sheet as a contra-asset, as follows:

Short-term investments (at cost) $1,200,000
Less allowance to adjust short-term investments to market   80,000
Short-term investments (at market) $1,120,000

or, more simply,

Short-term investments (at market value, cost is $1,200,000) $1,120,000

If Franklin sells its 5,000 shares of Texaco for $70 per share on March 2, 20x2, a realized gain on trading securities is recorded as follows:

A = L + OE
+   +
—

20x2
Mar. 2   Cash   350,000
                Short-Term Investments   300,000
                Realized Gain on Investments   50,000
                     Sale of 5,000 shares of Texaco
                     for $70 per share; cost was $60 per share

The realized gain will appear on the income statement. Note that the realized gain is unaffected by the adjustment for the unrealized loss at the end of 20x1. The two transactions are treated independently. If the stock had been sold for less than cost, a realized loss on investments would have been recorded. Realized losses also appear on the income statement.

www.bp.com

Let's assume that during 20x2 Franklin buys 2,000 shares of BP Corporation at $64 per share and has no transactions involving Exxon Mobil. Also assume that by December 31, 20x2, the price of Exxon Mobil's stock has risen to $95 per share, or $5 per share more than the original cost, and that BP's stock price has fallen to $58, or $6 less than the original cost. The trading portfolio now can be analyzed as follows:

Security	Market Value	Cost	Gain (Loss)
Exxon Mobil (10,000 shares)	$ 950,000	$ 900,000	
BP (2,000 shares)	116,000	128,000	
Totals	$1,066,000	$1,028,000	$38,000

KEY POINT: The entry to the Allowance to Adjust Short-Term Investments to Market account is equal to the change in the market value. Compute the new allowance, and then compute the amount needed to change the account. The unrealized loss or gain is the other half of the entry.

$$A = L + OE$$
$$+ \qquad +$$

◆ STOP AND THINK!
What would cause an Allowance to Adjust Short-Term Investments to Market account that has a negative (credit) balance at the beginning of the year to have a positive (debit) balance at the end of the year?

The total market value of the portfolio of trading securities would have increased enough during the year to exceed the negative (credit) balance at the beginning of the year. ■

The market value of the portfolio now exceeds the cost by $38,000 ($1,066,000 − $1,028,000). This amount represents the targeted ending balance for the Allowance to Adjust Short-Term Investments to Market account. Recall that at the end of 20x1, that account had a credit balance of $80,000, meaning that the market value of the trading portfolio was less than the cost. The account has no entries during 20x2 and thus retains its balance until adjusting entries are made at the end of the year. The adjustment for 20x2 must be $118,000—enough to result in a debit balance of $38,000 in the allowance account.

20x2

Dec. 31	Allowance to Adjust Short-Term Investments to Market	118,000	
	Unrealized Gain on Investments		118,000
	Recognition of unrealized gain on trading portfolio ($80,000 + $38,000 = $118,000)		

The 20x2 ending balance of the allowance account may be determined as follows:

Allowance to Adjust Short-Term Investments to Market

Dec. 31, 20x2 adj.	118,000	Dec. 31, 20x1 bal.	80,000
Dec. 31, 20x2 bal.	**38,000**		

The balance sheet presentation of short-term investments is as follows:

Short-term investments (at cost)	$1,028,000
Allowance to adjust short-term investments to market	38,000
Short-term investments (at market)	$1,066,000

or, more simply,

Short-term investments (at market value, cost is $1,028,000)	$1,066,000

If the company also holds held-to-maturity securities, they are included in short-term investments at cost adjusted for the effects of interest if they will mature within one year.

AVAILABLE-FOR-SALE SECURITIES

Available-for-sale securities are debt and equity securities that do not meet the criteria for either held-to-maturity or trading securities. They are accounted for in exactly the same way as trading securities, except that the unrealized gain or loss is not reported on the income statement, but as a special item in the stockholders' equity section of the balance sheet. For example, Pioneer Corporation states in its annual report that "all debt securities and marketable equity securities held by the Company are classified as available-for-sale securities, and are carried at their fair values with unrealized gains and losses reported as a component of shareholders' equity."[9] This component is called accumulated other comprehensive income.

www.pioneer.co.jp

DIVIDEND AND INTEREST INCOME

Dividend and interest income for all three categories of investments appears in the other income and expenses section of the income statement.

 Check out ACE for a Review Quiz at http://accounting.college.hmco.com/students.

ACCOUNTS RECEIVABLE

LO4 Define *accounts receivable* and apply the allowance method of accounting for uncollectible accounts.

RELATED TEXT ASSIGNMENTS
Q: 7, 8, 9, 10, 11, 12, 13, 14, 15, 16, 17
SE: 6, 7, 8
E: 6, 7, 8, 9, 10, 11
P: 2, 3, 7
SD: 2, 4
FRA: 1, 2, 4, 7

www.jcpenney.com
www.sears.com

The other major types of short-term financial assets are accounts receivable and notes receivable. Both result from credit sales to customers. Retailers like Sears, Roebuck and Co. have made credit available to nearly every responsible person in the United States. Every field of retail trade has expanded by allowing customers to make payments a month or more after the date of sale. What is not so apparent is that credit has expanded even more in the wholesale and manufacturing industries than at the retail level. The levels of accounts receivable in selected industries are shown in Figure 4.

Accounts receivable are short-term financial assets that arise from sales on credit to customers by wholesalers or retailers. This type of credit is often called **trade credit**. Terms on trade credit usually range from 5 to 60 days, depending on industry practice. For some companies that sell to consumers, **installment accounts receivable** constitute a significant portion of accounts receivable. Installment accounts receivable arise from the sale of goods on terms that allow the buyer to make a series of time payments. Department stores, appliance stores, furniture stores, used car companies, and other retail businesses often offer installment credit. Retailers like J.C. Penney Company, Inc., and Sears, Roebuck and Co. have millions of dollars in installment accounts receivable. Although the payment period may be 24 months or more, installment accounts receivable are classified as current assets if such credit policies are customary in the industry.

On the balance sheet, the title "accounts receivable" is used for amounts arising from credit sales made to customers in the ordinary course of business. If loans or credit sales are made to employees, officers of the corporation, or owners, they should be shown separately, with an asset title like "receivables from employees," because of the increased risk of uncollectibility and conflict of interest.

Normally, individual customer accounts receivable have debit balances, but sometimes customers overpay their accounts either by mistake or in anticipation of future purchases. When these accounts show credit balances, the total of the credits should be shown on the balance sheet as a current liability because the amounts must be refunded if future sales are not made to those customers.

UNCOLLECTIBLE ACCOUNTS AND THE DIRECT CHARGE-OFF METHOD

A company will always have some customers who cannot or will not pay their debts. The accounts owed by such customers are called **uncollectible accounts**, or *bad debts*, and are a loss or an expense of selling on credit. Why does a company sell

FIGURE 4
Accounts Receivable as a Percentage of Total Assets for Selected Industries

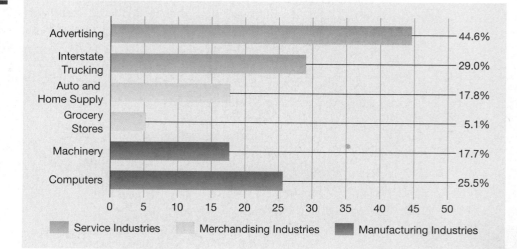

Source: Data from Dun and Bradstreet, *Industry Norms and Key Business Ratios,* 2000-2001.

on credit if it expects that some of its accounts will not be paid? The answer is that the company expects to sell much more than it would if it did not sell on credit, thereby increasing its earnings.

Some companies recognize the loss from an uncollectible account receivable at the time it is determined to be uncollectible by reducing Accounts Receivable directly and increasing Uncollectible Accounts Expense. Many small companies use this method, called the **direct charge-off method**, because it is required in computing taxable income under federal tax regulations. However, companies that follow generally accepted accounting principles do not use it in their financial statements because it does not conform to the matching rule. The direct charge-off is often recorded in a different accounting period from the one in which the sale takes place. Companies that follow GAAP prefer the allowance method, which is explained in the next section.

KEY POINT: The direct charge-off method does not conform to the matching rule.

UNCOLLECTIBLE ACCOUNTS AND THE ALLOWANCE METHOD

KEY POINT: The allowance method relies on an estimate of uncollectible accounts but is in accord with the matching rule.

Under the **allowance method** of accounting for uncollectible accounts, bad debt losses are matched against the sales they help to produce. As mentioned earlier, when management extends credit to increase sales, it knows that it will incur some losses from uncollectible accounts. Those losses are expenses that occur at the time sales on credit are made and should be matched to the revenues they help to generate. Of course, at the time the sales are made, management cannot identify which customers will not pay their debts, nor can it predict the exact amount of money that will be lost. Therefore, to observe the matching rule under generally accepted accounting principles, losses from uncollectible accounts must be estimated, and the estimate becomes an expense in the fiscal year in which the sales are made.

For example, let us assume that Cottage Sales Company made most of its sales on credit during its first year of operation, 20x2. At the end of the year, accounts receivable amounted to $100,000. On December 31, 20x2, management reviewed the collectible status of the accounts receivable. Approximately $6,000 of the $100,000 of accounts receivable were estimated to be uncollectible. Therefore, the uncollectible accounts expense for the first year of operation was estimated to be $6,000. The following adjusting entry would be made on December 31 of that year:

20x2

$A = L + OE$
$\overline{-} \quad \overline{-}$

Dec. 31	Uncollectible Accounts Expense	6,000	
	Allowance for Uncollectible Accounts		6,000
	To record the estimated uncollectible accounts expense for the year		

Uncollectible Accounts Expense appears on the income statement as an operating expense. **Allowance for Uncollectible Accounts** appears on the balance sheet as a contra account that is deducted from accounts receivable.* It reduces the accounts receivable to the amount expected to be realized, or collected, in cash, as follows:

Current assets		
Cash		$ 10,000
Short-term investments		15,000
Accounts receivable	$100,000	
Less allowance for uncollectible accounts	6,000	94,000
Inventory		56,000
Total current assets		$175,000

*The purpose of Allowance for Uncollectible Accounts is to reduce the gross accounts receivable to the amount estimated to be collectible (net realizable value). The purpose of another contra account, Accumulated Depreciation, is *not* to reduce the gross plant and equipment accounts to realizable value. Rather, its purpose is to show how much of the cost of the plant and equipment has been allocated as an expense to previous accounting periods.

FOCUS ON BUSINESS PRACTICE

Selling Goods and Services Is Only Half the Problem.

To be profitable, a company must not only sell goods and services; it must also generate cash flows by collecting on those sales. The latter has been a problem for the five leading North American manufacturers of telecommunications equipment. In the late 1990s, to make sales to start-up telecom companies, these manufacturers made loans of $17 billion to their customers. Nortel Networks <www.nortelnetworks.com> has $4.1 billion in customer financing; Cisco Systems <www.cisco.com>, $2.4 bil-

lion; Lucent Technologies <www.lucent.com>, $5.4 billion; Motorola <www.motorola.com>, $3.8 billion; and Qualcomm <www.qualcomm.com>, $1.18 billion. While not all of these loans are bad debts, many became so when the telecom industry experienced a major recession in 2001. All five companies had to increase their allowances for uncollectible accounts, actions that eliminated previously reported earnings and caused the companies' stock prices to fall.[10]

Accounts receivable may also be shown on the balance sheet as follows:

Accounts receivable (net of allowance for uncollectible
    accounts of $6,000) $94,000

Or they may be shown at "net," with the amount of the allowance for uncollectible accounts identified in a note to the financial statements. The estimated uncollectible amount cannot be identified with any particular customer; therefore, it is credited to a separate contra-asset account—Allowance for Uncollectible Accounts.

The allowance account often has other titles, such as *Allowance for Doubtful Accounts* and *Allowance for Bad Debts*. Once in a while, the older phrase *Reserve for Bad Debts* will be seen, but in modern practice it should not be used. *Bad Debts Expense* is a title often used for Uncollectible Accounts Expense.

ESTIMATING UNCOLLECTIBLE ACCOUNTS EXPENSE

● STOP AND THINK!
How might the receivable turnover and the average days' sales uncollectible ratios reveal that management is consistently underestimating the amount of losses from uncollectible accounts?

A decreasing receivables turnover ratio and an increasing average days' sales uncollectible ratio from period to period, especially in the absence of changes in credit policies, might mean that management is underestimating the amount of losses from uncollectible accounts. ■

As noted, it is necessary to estimate the expense to cover the expected losses for the year. Of course, estimates can vary widely. If management takes an optimistic view and projects a small loss from uncollectible accounts, the resulting net accounts receivable will be larger than if management takes a pessimistic view. The net income will also be larger under the optimistic view because the estimated expense will be smaller. The company's accountant makes an estimate based on past experience and current economic conditions. For example, losses from uncollectible accounts are normally expected to be greater in a recession than during a period of economic growth. The final decision, made by management, on the amount of the expense will depend on objective information, such as the accountant's analyses, and on certain qualitative factors, such as how investors, bankers, creditors, and others may view the performance of the debtor company. Regardless of the qualitative considerations, the estimated losses from uncollectible accounts should be realistic.

The accountant may choose from two common methods for estimating uncollectible accounts expense for an accounting period: the percentage of net sales method and the accounts receivable aging method.

KEY POINT: The percentage of net sales method can be described as the income statement method to emphasize that the percentage of the net sales calculated is the amount expensed. That is, any previous balance in the allowance account is irrelevant in preparing the adjustment.

■ **PERCENTAGE OF NET SALES METHOD**   The **percentage of net sales method** asks the question, How much of this year's net sales will not be collected? The answer determines the amount of uncollectible accounts expense for the year. For example, the following balances represent the ending figures for Hassel Company for 20x9:

Sales		Sales Returns and Allowances	
Dec. 31	645,000	Dec. 31	40,000

Sales Discounts		Allowance for Uncollectible Accounts	
Dec. 31	5,000	Dec. 31	3,600

Below are Hassel's actual losses from uncollectible accounts for the past three years:

Year	Net Sales	Losses from Uncollectible Accounts	Percentage
20x6	$ 520,000	$10,200	1.96
20x7	595,000	13,900	2.34
20x8	585,000	9,900	1.69
Total	$1,700,000	$34,000	2.00

In many businesses, net sales is understood to approximate net credit sales. If there are substantial cash sales, then net credit sales should be used because they generate accounts receivable. Hassel's management believes that uncollectible accounts will continue to average about 2 percent of net sales. The uncollectible accounts expense for the year 20x9 is therefore estimated to be

$$.02 \times (\$645,000 - \$40,000 - \$5,000) = .02 \times \$600,000 = \$12,000$$

The entry to record this estimate is as follows:

A = L + OE	20x9		
− −	Dec. 31	Uncollectible Accounts Expense	12,000	
		Allowance for Uncollectible Accounts		12,000
		To record uncollectible accounts expense		
		at 2 percent of $600,000 net sales		

After the above entry is posted, Allowance for Uncollectible Accounts will have a balance of $15,600:

Allowance for Uncollectible Accounts

		Dec. 31	3,600
		Dec. 31 adj.	12,000
		Dec. 31 bal.	**15,600**

The balance consists of the $12,000 estimated uncollectible accounts receivable from 20x9 sales and the $3,600 estimated uncollectible accounts receivable from previous years.

■ **ACCOUNTS RECEIVABLE AGING METHOD**   The **accounts receivable aging method** asks the question, How much of the year-end balance of accounts receivable will not be collected? Under this method, the year-end balance of Allowance for Uncollectible Accounts is determined directly by an analysis of accounts receivable. The difference between the amount determined to be uncollectible and the actual balance of Allowance for Uncollectible Accounts is the expense for the year. In theory, this method should produce the same result as the percentage of net sales method, but in practice it rarely does.

The **aging of accounts receivable** is the process of listing each customer's receivable account according to the due date of the account. If the customer's account is past due, there is a possibility that the account will not be paid. And that possibility increases as the account extends further beyond the due date. The aging of accounts receivable helps management evaluate its credit and collection policies and alerts it to possible problems.

FOCUS ON INTERNATIONAL BUSINESS

Why Companies in Emerging Economies Must Adapt Accounting Practices

Companies in emerging economies do not always follow the accounting practices accepted in the United States. The Shanghai Stock Exchange is one of the fastest-growing stock markets in the world. Few Chinese companies acknowledge that uncollected receivables are not worth full value even when the receivables have been outstanding for a year or more. It is common practice in the United States to write off receivables more than six months old. Now that Chinese companies like Shanghai Steel Tube and Shanghai Industrial Sewing Machine are making their shares of stock available to outsiders, they must estimate uncollectible accounts in accordance with international accounting standards. Recognition of this expense could easily wipe out annual earnings.[11]

EXHIBIT 1
Analysis of Accounts Receivable by Age

Myer Company
Analysis of Accounts Receivable by Age
December 31, 20xx

Customer	Total	Not Yet Due	1–30 Days Past Due	31–60 Days Past Due	61–90 Days Past Due	Over 90 Days Past Due
A. Arnold	$ 150		$ 150			
M. Benoit	400			$ 400		
J. Connolly	1,000	$ 900	100			
R. Deering	250				$ 250	
Others	42,600	21,000	14,000	3,800	2,200	$1,600
Totals	$44,400	$21,900	$14,250	$4,200	$2,450	$1,600
Estimated percentage uncollectible		1.0	2.0	10.0	30.0	50.0
Allowance for Uncollectible Accounts	$ 2,459	$ 219	$ 285	$ 420	$ 735	$ 800

ENRICHMENT NOTE: The aging method is often superior to the percentage of net sales method during changing economic times. For example, during a recession, more bad debts occur. The aging method automatically reflects the economic change as accounts receivable age because customers are unable to pay. A company using the percentage of net sales method must anticipate the change and modify the percentage it uses.

The aging of accounts receivable for Myer Company is illustrated in Exhibit 1. Each account receivable is classified as being not yet due or as being 1–30 days, 31–60 days, 61–90 days, or over 90 days past due. The estimated percentage uncollectible in each of these catagories is multiplied by the amount in each category in order to determine the estimated, or target, balance of Allowance for Uncollectible Accounts. In total, it is estimated that $2,459 of the $44,400 accounts receivable will not be collected.

Once the target balance for Allowance for Uncollectible Accounts has been found, it is necessary to determine how much the adjustment is. The amount of the adjustment depends on the current balance of the allowance account. Let us assume two cases for the December 31 balance of Myer Company's Allowance for Uncollectible Accounts: (1) a credit balance of $800 and (2) a debit balance of $800.

In the first case, an adjustment of $1,659 is needed to bring the balance of the allowance account to a $2,459 credit balance, calculated as follows:

KEY POINT: When the write-offs in an accounting period exceed the amount of the allowance, a debit balance in the Allowance for Uncollectible Accounts account results.

Targeted balance for allowance for uncollectible accounts	$2,459
Less current credit balance of allowance for uncollectible accounts	800
Uncollectible accounts expense	$1,659

The uncollectible accounts expense is recorded as follows:

A = L + OE

20x2
Dec. 31   Uncollectible Accounts Expense   1,659
                Allowance for Uncollectible Accounts   1,659
                    To bring the allowance for
                    uncollectible accounts to the
                    level of estimated losses

The resulting balance of Allowance for Uncollectible Accounts is $2,459, as follows:

Allowance for Uncollectible Accounts

	Dec. 31	800
	Dec. 31 adj.	1,659
	Dec. 31 bal.	**2,459**

In the second case, because Allowance for Uncollectible Accounts has a debit balance of $800, the estimated uncollectible accounts expense for the year will have to be $3,259 to reach the targeted balance of $2,459. This calculation is as follows:

Targeted balance for allowance for uncollectible accounts	$2,459
Plus current debit balance of allowance for uncollectible accounts	800
Uncollectible accounts expense	$3,259

The uncollectible accounts expense is recorded as follows:

$A = L + OE$
$-\quad -$

20x2				
Dec. 31	Uncollectible Accounts Expense		3,259	
	Allowance for Uncollectible Accounts			3,259
	To bring the allowance for			
	uncollectible accounts to the			
	level of estimated losses			

After this entry, Allowance for Uncollectible Accounts has a credit balance of $2,459:

Allowance for Uncollectible Accounts

Dec. 31	800	Dec. 31 adj.	3,259
		Dec. 31 bal.	**2,459**

■ **COMPARISON OF THE TWO METHODS**   Both the percentage of net sales method and the accounts receivable aging method estimate the uncollectible accounts expense in accordance with the matching rule, but as shown in Figure 5, they do so in different ways. The percentage of net sales method is an income statement

FIGURE 5
Two Methods of Estimating Uncollectible Accounts

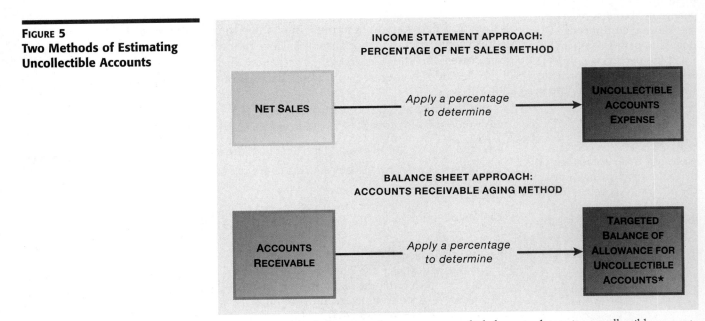

*Add current debit balance or subtract current credit balance to determine uncollectible accounts expense.

KEY POINT: Describing the aging method as the balance sheet method emphasizes that the computation is based on ending accounts receivable, rather than on net sales for the period.

approach. It assumes that a certain proportion of sales will not be collected, and this proportion is the *amount of Uncollectible Accounts Expense* for the accounting period. The accounts receivable aging method is a balance sheet approach. It assumes that a certain proportion of accounts receivable outstanding will not be collected. This proportion is the *targeted balance of the Allowance for Uncollectible Accounts account.* The expense for the accounting period is the difference between the targeted balance and the current balance of the allowance account.

■ **WHY ACCOUNTS WRITTEN OFF WILL DIFFER FROM ESTIMATES** Regardless of the method used to estimate uncollectible accounts, the total of accounts receivable written off in any given year will rarely equal the estimated uncollectible amount. The allowance account will show a credit balance when the total of accounts written off is less than the estimated uncollectible amount. The allowance account will show a debit balance when the total of accounts written off is greater than the estimated uncollectible amount.

WRITING OFF AN UNCOLLECTIBLE ACCOUNT

When it becomes clear that a specific account receivable will not be collected, the amount should be written off to Allowance for Uncollectible Accounts. Remember that the uncollectible amount was already accounted for as an expense when the allowance was established. For example, assume that on January 15, 20x3, R. Deering, who owes Myer Company $250, is declared bankrupt by a federal court. The entry to *write off* this account is as follows:

A = L + OE
+
−

```
20x3
Jan. 15   Allowance for Uncollectible Accounts       250
              Accounts Receivable                            250
              To write off receivable
              from R. Deering as uncollectible;
              Deering declared bankrupt on
              January 15
```

KEY POINT: When writing off an individual account, debit Allowance for Uncollectible Accounts, not Uncollectible Accounts Expense.

Although the write-off removes the uncollectible amount from Accounts Receivable, it does not affect the estimated net realizable value of accounts receivable. The write-off simply reduces R. Deering's account to zero and reduces Allowance for Uncollectible Accounts by a similar amount, as shown below:

	Balances Before Write-off	Balances After Write-off
Accounts receivable	$44,400	$44,150
Less allowance for uncollectible accounts	2,459	2,209
Estimated net realizable value of accounts Receivable	$41,941	$41,941

RECOVERY OF ACCOUNTS RECEIVABLE WRITTEN OFF

Occasionally, a customer whose account has been written off as uncollectible will later be able to pay some or all of the amount owed. When this happens, two journal entries must be made: one to reverse the earlier write-off (which is now incorrect) and another to show the collection of the account. For example, assume that on September 1, 20x3, R. Deering, after his bankruptcy on January 15, notified Myer Company that he could pay $100 of his account and sent a check for $50. The entries to record this transaction are as follows:

	20x3			

A = L + OE
+
−
	Sept. 1	Accounts Receivable
		    Allowance for Uncollectible Accounts
		        To reinstate the portion of
		        the account of R. Deering
		        now considered collectible;
		        originally written off January 15
			100	100

A = L + OE
+
−
	Sept. 1	Cash
		    Accounts Receivable
		        Collection from R. Deering
			50	50

The collectible portion of R. Deering's account must be restored to his account and credited to Allowance for Uncollectible Accounts for two reasons. First, it turned out to be wrong to write off the full $250 on January 15 because only $150 was actually uncollectible. Second, the accounts receivable subsidiary account for R. Deering should reflect his ability to pay a portion of the money he owed despite his declaration of bankruptcy. Documentation of this action will give a clear picture of R. Deering's credit record for future credit action.

✓ Check out ACE for a Review Quiz at http://accounting.college.hmco.com/students.

NOTES RECEIVABLE

LO5 Define *promissory note,* and compute and record promissory notes receivable.

RELATED TEXT ASSIGNMENTS
Q: 18, 19
SE: 9
E: 12, 13, 14, 15
P: 4

A **promissory note** is an unconditional promise to pay a definite sum of money on demand or at a future date. The entity who signs the note and thereby promises to pay is called the *maker* of the note. The entity to whom payment is to be made is called the *payee.*

The promissory note illustrated in Figure 6 is dated May 20, 20x1, and is an unconditional promise by the maker, Samuel Mason, to pay a definite sum, or principal ($1,000), to the payee, Cook County Bank & Trust Company, on the future date of August 18, 20x1. The promissory note bears an interest rate of 8 percent. The payee regards all promissory notes it holds that are due in less than one year as **notes receivable** in the current assets section of the balance sheet. The maker regards them as **notes payable** in the current liabilities section of the balance sheet.

This portion of the chapter is concerned primarily with notes received from customers. The nature of a company's business generally determines how frequently

FIGURE 6
A Promissory Note

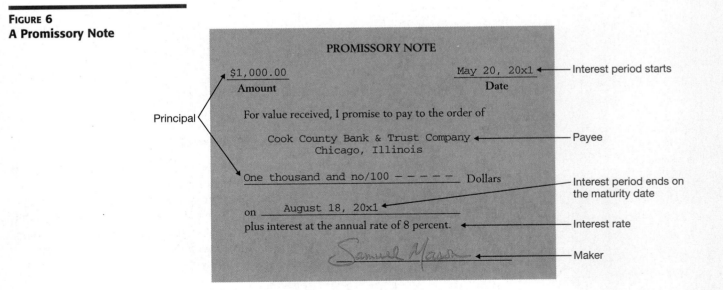

it receives promissory notes from customers. Firms selling durable goods of high value, such as farm machinery and automobiles, will often accept promissory notes. Among the advantages of promissory notes are that they produce interest income and represent a stronger legal claim against a debtor than do accounts receivable. In addition, selling, or discounting, promissory notes to banks is a common financing method. Almost all companies occasionally receive a note, and many companies obtain notes receivable in settlement of past-due accounts.

COMPUTATIONS FOR PROMISSORY NOTES

In accounting for promissory notes, the following terms are important to remember: (1) *maturity date*, (2) *duration of note*, (3) *interest and interest rate*, and (4) *maturity value*.

STUDY NOTE: Another way to compute the duration of notes is to begin with the interest period, as follows:

90	Interest period
−11	days remaining in May (31 − 20)
79	
−30	days in June
49	
−31	days in July
18	due date in August

■ **MATURITY DATE** The **maturity date** is the date on which a promissory note must be paid. This date must either be stated on the note or be determinable from the facts stated on the note. Among the most common statements of maturity date are the following:

1. A specific date, such as "November 14, 20xx"
2. A specific number of months after the date of the note, for example, "three months after date"
3. A specific number of days after the date of the note, for example, "60 days after date"

The maturity date is obvious when a specific date is stated. And when the maturity date is a number of months from the date of the note, one simply uses the same day in the appropriate future month. For example, a note that is dated January 20 and that is due in two months would be due on March 20.

When the maturity date is a specific number of days from the date of the note, however, the exact maturity date must be determined. In computing the maturity date, it is important to exclude the date of the note. For example, a note dated May 20 and due in 90 days would be due on August 18, computed as follows:

Days remaining in May (31 − 20)	11
Days in June	30
Days in July	31
Days in August	18
Total days	90

■ **DURATION OF NOTE** The **duration of note** is the length of time in days between a promissory note's issue date and its maturity date. Knowing the duration of the note is important because interest is calculated for the exact number of days. Identifying the duration is easy when the maturity date is stated as a specific number of days from the date of the note because the two numbers are the same.

FOCUS ON BUSINESS PRACTICE

How Long Is a Year? It Depends.

Most banks use a 365-day year to compute interest for all loans, but some use a 360-day year for commercial loans. For example, the brokerage firm of May SWS Securities <www.maysws.com> of Dallas, Texas, states in its customer loan agreement, "Interest is calculated on a 360-day basis."

In Europe, use of a 360-day year is common. Financial institutions that use the 360-day basis earn slightly more interest than those that use the 365-day basis. In this book, we use a 360-day year to keep the computations simple.

However, if the maturity date is stated as a specific date, the exact number of days must be determined. Assume that a note issued on May 10 matures on August 10. The duration of the note is 92 days, determined as follows:

Days remaining in May (31 − 10)	21
Days in June	30
Days in July	31
Days in August	<u>10</u>
Total days	<u><u>92</u></u>

■ **INTEREST AND INTEREST RATE**   **Interest** is the cost of borrowing money or the return for lending money, depending on whether one is the borrower or the lender. The amount of interest is based on three factors: the principal (the amount of money borrowed or lent), the rate of interest, and the loan's length of time. The formula used in computing interest is as follows:

$$\text{Principal} \times \text{Rate of Interest} \times \text{Time} = \text{Interest}$$

Interest rates are usually stated on an annual basis. For example, the interest on a one-year, 8 percent, $1,000 note would be $80 ($1,000 × 8/100 × 1 = $80). If the term, or time period, of the note is three months instead of a year, the interest charge would be $20 ($1,000 × 8/100 × 3/12 = $20).

When the term of a note is expressed in days, the exact number of days must be used in computing the interest. To keep the computation simple, let us compute interest on the basis of 360 days per year. Therefore, if the term of the above note were 45 days, the interest would be $10, computed as follows: $1,000 × 8/100 × 45/360 = $10.

■ **MATURITY VALUE**   The **maturity value** is the total proceeds of a promissory note—face value plus interest—at the maturity date. The maturity value of a 90-day, 8 percent, $1,000 note is computed as follows:

$$
\begin{aligned}
\text{Maturity Value} &= \text{Principal} + \text{Interest} \\
&= \$1,000 + (\$1,000 \times 8/100 \times 90/360) \\
&= \$1,000 + \$20 \\
&= \$1,020
\end{aligned}
$$

There are also so-called non-interest-bearing notes. The maturity value is the face value, or principal amount. In this case, the principal includes an implied interest cost.

ACCOUNTING ENTRIES FOR PROMISSORY NOTES

The accounting entries for promissory notes receivable fall into four groups: (1) recording receipt of a note, (2) recording collection on a note, (3) recording a dishonored note, and (4) recording adjusting entries.

KEY POINT: The entry to record receipt of a note does not include interest because no interest has yet been earned.

■ **RECORDING RECEIPT OF A NOTE**   Assume that on June 1, a 30-day, 12 percent note is received from a customer, J. Halsted, in settlement of an existing account receivable of $4,000. The entry for this transaction is as follows:

A = L + OE
+
−

June 1	Notes Receivable	4,000	
	Accounts Receivable		4,000
	Received 30-day, 12 percent note in		
	payment of account of J. Halsted		

■ **RECORDING COLLECTION ON A NOTE**   When the note plus interest is collected 30 days later, the entry is as follows:

A = L + OE	July 1	Cash	4,040	
+ +		Notes Receivable		4,000
−		Interest Income		40
		Collected 30-day, 12 percent		
		note from J. Halsted		

STUDY NOTE: Dishonored notes are, in effect, not written off. The amounts are merely transferred to accounts receivable, which can be written off later.

■ **RECORDING A DISHONORED NOTE** When the maker of a note does not pay the note at maturity, the note is said to be dishonored. The holder, or payee, of a **dishonored note** should make an entry to transfer the total amount due from Notes Receivable to an account receivable from the debtor. If J. Halsted dishonors her note on July 1, the following entry would be made:

A = L + OE	July 1	Accounts Receivable	4,040	
+ +		Notes Receivable		4,000
−		Interest Income		40
		30-day, 12 percent note		
		dishonored by J. Halsted		

The interest earned is recorded because although J. Halsted did not pay the note, she is still obligated to pay both the principal and the interest.

Two things are accomplished by transferring a dishonored note receivable into an Accounts Receivable account. First, it leaves only notes that have not matured and are presumably negotiable and collectible in the Notes Receivable account. Second, it establishes a record in the borrower's accounts receivable account that he or she has dishonored a note receivable. Such information may be helpful in deciding whether to extend future credit to the customer.

◆ **STOP AND THINK!**
Under what circumstances would an accrual of interest income on an interest-bearing note receivable not be required at the end of an accounting period?
It would not be required if the interest to date were paid on the last day of the accounting period. ■

■ **RECORDING ADJUSTING ENTRIES** A promissory note received in one period may not be due until a following accounting period. Because the interest on a note accrues by a small amount each day of the note's duration, it is necessary, according to the matching rule, to apportion the interest earned to the periods in which it belongs. For example, assume that on August 31 a 60-day, 8 percent, $2,000 note was received and that the company prepares financial statements monthly. The following adjusting entry is necessary on September 30 to show how the interest earned for September has accrued:

A = L + OE	Sept. 30	Interest Receivable	13.33	
+ +		Interest Income		13.33
		To accrue 30 days' interest		
		earned on a note receivable		
		$2,000 × 8/100 × 30/360 = $13.33		

The Interest Receivable account is a current asset on the balance sheet. When payment of the note plus interest is received on October 30, the following entry is made:*

A = L + OE	Oct. 30	Cash	2,026.67	
+ +		Notes Receivable		2,000.00
−		Interest Receivable		13.33
		Interest Income		13.34
		Receipt of note receivable		
		plus interest		

As can be seen from these transactions, both September and October receive the benefit of one-half the interest earned.

✔ Check out ACE for a Review Quiz at http://accounting.college.hmco.com/students.

*Some firms may follow the practice of reversing the September 30 adjusting entry. Here we assume that a reversing entry is not made.

PREPARING A BANK RECONCILIATION

SO6   Prepare a bank reconciliation.
RELATED TEXT ASSIGNMENTS
SE: 10
E: 16
P: 5, 8

Rarely will the balance of a company's Cash account exactly equal the cash balance shown on the bank statement. Certain transactions shown in the company's records may not have been recorded by the bank, and certain bank transactions may not appear in the company's records. Therefore, a necessary step in internal control is to prove both the balance shown on the bank statement and the balance of Cash in the accounting records. A **bank reconciliation** is the process of accounting for the difference between the balance appearing on the bank statement and the balance of the Cash account in the company's records. This process involves making additions to and subtractions from both balances to arrive at the adjusted cash balance.

The most common transactions shown in the company's records but not entered in the bank's records are the following:

1. *Outstanding checks*   These are checks that the company has issued and recorded but that do not yet appear on the bank statement.

2. *Deposits in transit*   These are deposits mailed or taken to the bank but not received in time to be recorded on the bank statement.

Transactions that may appear on the bank statement but not in the company's records include the following:

1. *Service charges (SC)*   Banks often charge a fee, or service charge, for the use of a checking account. Many banks base the service charge on a number of factors, such as the average balance of the account during the month or the number of checks drawn.

2. *NSF (nonsufficient funds) checks*   An NSF check is a check that the company has deposited but that is not paid when the bank presents it to the issuer's bank. The bank charges the company's account and returns the check so that the company can try to collect the amount due. If the bank has deducted the NSF check from the bank statement but the company has not deducted it from its book balance, an adjustment must be made in the bank reconciliation. The company usually reclassifies the NSF check from Cash to Accounts Receivable because it must now collect from the person or company that wrote the check.

3. *Miscellaneous debits and credits*   Banks also charge for other services, such as stopping payment on checks and printing checks. The bank notifies the depositor of each deduction by including a debit memorandum with the monthly statement. A bank will also sometimes serve as an agent in collecting on promissory notes for the depositor. In such a case, a credit memorandum will be included in the statement, along with a debit memorandum of the service charge.

4. *Interest income*   Banks commonly pay interest on a company's average balance. Accounts that pay interest are sometimes called NOW or money market accounts. Such interest is reported on the bank statement.

An error by either the bank or the depositor will, of course, require immediate correction.

KEY POINT: The ending bank statement balance does not represent the amount that should appear on the balance sheet for cash. There are events and items, such as deposits in transit and outstanding checks, that the bank is unaware of at the cutoff date. This is why a bank reconciliation must be prepared.

■ **ILLUSTRATION OF A BANK RECONCILIATION**   Assume that the October bank statement for Martin Maintenance Company indicates a balance on October 31 of $3,471.07, and that in its records, Martin Maintenance Company has a cash balance on October 31 of $2,415.91. The purpose of a bank reconciliation is to identify the items that make up the difference between these amounts and to determine the correct cash balance. The bank reconciliation for Martin Maintenance is shown in Exhibit 2. The numbered items in the exhibit refer to the following:

1. A deposit in the amount of $276.00 was mailed to the bank on October 31 and has not been recorded by the bank.

EXHIBIT 2
Bank Reconciliation

Martin Maintenance Company
Bank Reconciliation
October 31, 20xx

Balance per bank, October 31		$3,471.07
① Add deposit of October 31 in transit		276.00
		$3,747.07
② Less outstanding checks:		
No. 551	$150.00	
No. 576	40.68	
No. 578	500.00	
No. 579	370.00	
No. 580	130.50	1,191.08
Adjusted bank balance, October 31		**$2,555.89**
Balance per books, October 31		$2,415.91
Add:		
④ Note receivable collected by bank	$280.00	
④ Interest income on note	20.00	
⑦ Interest income	15.62	315.62
		$2,731.53
Less:		
③ Overstatement of deposit of October 6	$ 30.00	
④ Collection fee	5.00	
⑤ NSF check of Arthur Clubb	128.14	
⑥ Service charge	12.50	175.64
Adjusted book balance, October 31		**$2,555.89**

Note: The circled numbers refer to the items listed in the text.

STUDY NOTE: It is possible to place an item in the wrong section of a bank reconciliation and still have it balance. The *correct* adjusted balance must be obtained.

KEY POINT: Even though the September 14 check was deducted on the September 30 reconciliation, it must be deducted again in each subsequent month in which it remains outstanding.

STUDY NOTE: A credit memorandum means that an amount was *added* to the bank balance; a debit memorandum means that an amount was *deducted*.

2. Five checks issued in October or prior months have not yet been paid by the bank, as follows:

Check No.	Date	Amount
551	Sept. 14	$150.00
576	Oct. 30	40.68
578	Oct. 31	500.00
579	Oct. 31	370.00
580	Oct. 31	130.50

3. The deposit for cash sales of October 6 was incorrectly recorded in Martin Maintenance Company's records as $330.00. The bank correctly recorded the deposit as $300.00.

4. Among the returned checks was a credit memorandum showing that the bank had collected a promissory note from A. Jacobs in the amount of $280.00, plus $20.00 in interest on the note. A debit memorandum was also enclosed for the $5.00 collection fee. No entry had been made on Martin Maintenance Company's records.

5. Also returned with the bank statement was an NSF check for $128.14. This check had been received from a customer named Arthur Clubb. The NSF check from Clubb was not reflected in the company's accounting records.

6. A debit memorandum was enclosed for the regular monthly service charge of $12.50. This charge had not yet been recorded by Martin Maintenance Company.

7. Interest earned by the company on the average balance was reported as $15.62.

Note in Exhibit 2 that starting from their separate balances, both the bank and book amounts are adjusted to the amount of $2,555.89. This adjusted balance is the amount of cash owned by the company on October 31 and thus is the amount that should appear on its October 31 balance sheet.

KEY POINT: Notice that only those transactions the company has not recorded before receiving the bank statement are recorded.

■ **RECORDING TRANSACTIONS AFTER RECONCILIATION** The adjusted balance of cash differs from both the bank statement and Martin Maintenance Company's records. The bank balance will automatically become correct when outstanding checks are presented for payment and the deposit in transit is received and recorded by the bank. Entries must be made, however, for the transactions necessary to update the book balance. All the items reported by the bank but not yet recorded by the company must be recorded in the general journal by means of the following entries:

Oct. 31	Cash	300.00	
	Notes Receivable		280.00
	Interest Income		20.00
	Note receivable of $280.00 and interest of $20.00 collected by bank from A. Jacobs		
31	Cash	15.62	
	Interest Income		15.62
	Interest on average bank account balance		
31	Sales	30.00	
	Cash		30.00
	Correction of error in recording a $300.00 deposit as $330.00		
31	Accounts Receivable	128.14	
	Cash		128.14
	NSF check of Arthur Clubb returned by bank		
31	Bank Service Charges Expense	17.50	
	Cash		17.50
	Bank service charge ($12.50) and collection fee ($5.00) for October		

It is acceptable to record these entries in one or two compound entries to save time and space.

✓ Check out ACE for a Review Quiz at http://accounting.college.hmco.com/students.

Chapter Review

REVIEW OF LEARNING OBJECTIVES

LO1 Identify and explain the management issues related to short-term financial assets.

In managing short-term financial assets, management must (1) consider the need for short-term investing and borrowing as the business's balance of cash fluctuates during seasonal cycles, (2) establish credit policies that balance the need for sales with the ability to collect, and (3) assess the need to increase cash flows through the financing of receivables.

LO2 Explain *cash, cash equivalents,* and the importance of electronic funds transfer.

Cash consists of coins and currency on hand, checks and money orders received from customers, and deposits in bank accounts. Cash equivalents are investments that have a term of 90 days or less. Conducting transactions through electronic funds transfer (EFT) is important because of its efficiency. It eliminates much of the paperwork associated with traditional recordkeeping.

LO3 Identify types of short-term investments and explain the financial reporting implications

Short-term investments are classified as held-to-maturity securities, trading securities, or available-for-sale securities. Held-to-maturity securities are debt securities that management intends to hold to the maturity date; they are valued on the balance sheet at cost adjusted for the effects of interest. Trading securities are debt and equity securities bought and held principally for the purpose of being sold in the near term; they are valued at fair value or at market value. Unrealized gains or losses on trading securities appear on the income statement. Available-for-sale securities are debt and equity securities that do not meet the criteria for either held-to-maturity or trading securities. They are accounted for in the same way as trading securities, except that an unrealized gain or loss is reported as a special item in the stockholders' equity section of the balance sheet.

LO4 Define *accounts receivable* and apply the allowance method of accounting for uncollectible accounts.

Accounts receivable are amounts still to be collected from credit sales to customers. Because credit is offered to increase sales, uncollectible accounts associated with credit sales should be charged as expenses in the period in which the sales are made. However, because of the time lag between the sales and the time the accounts are judged uncollectible, the accountant must use the allowance method to match the amount of uncollectible accounts against revenues in any given period.

Uncollectible accounts expense is estimated by either the percentage of net sales method or the accounts receivable aging method. When the first method is used, bad debts are judged to be a certain percentage of sales during the period. When the second method is used, certain percentages are applied to groups of accounts receivable that have been arranged by due dates.

Allowance for Uncollectible Accounts is a contra-asset account to Accounts Receivable. The estimate of uncollectible accounts is debited to Uncollectible Accounts Expense and credited to the allowance account. When an individual account is determined to be uncollectible, it is removed from Accounts Receivable by debiting the allowance account and crediting Accounts Receivable. If the written-off account should later be collected, the earlier entry should be reversed and the collection should be recorded in the normal way.

LO5 Define *promissory note,* and compute and record promissory notes receivable.

A promissory note is an unconditional promise to pay a definite sum of money on demand or at a future date. Companies selling durable goods of high value, such as farm machinery and automobiles, often accept promissory notes. Selling these notes to banks is a common financing method.

In accounting for promissory notes, it is important to know how to calculate the maturity date, duration of note, interest and interest rate, and maturity value. The accounting entries for promissory notes receivable fall into four groups: recording receipt of a note, recording collection on a note, recording a dishonored note, and recording adjusting entries.

SUPPLEMENTAL OBJECTIVE

SO6 Prepare a bank reconciliation.

A bank reconciliation accounts for the difference between the balance that appears on the bank statement and the balance in the company's Cash account. It involves adjusting both balances to arrive at the adjusted cash balance. The bank balance is adjusted for outstanding checks and deposits in transit. The depositor's book balance is adjusted for service charges, NSF checks, interest earned, and miscellaneous debits and credits.

REVIEW OF CONCEPTS AND TERMINOLOGY

The following concepts and terms were introduced in this chapter:

LO4   **Accounts receivable:** Short-term financial assets that arise from sales on credit at the wholesale or retail level.

LO4 Accounts receivable aging method: A method of estimating uncollectible accounts based on the assumption that a predictable proportion of each dollar of accounts receivable outstanding will not be collected.

LO4 Aging of accounts receivable: The process of listing each customer's receivable account according to the due date of the account.

LO4 Allowance method: A method of accounting for uncollectible accounts by expensing estimated uncollectible accounts in the period in which the related sales take place.

LO4 Allowance for Uncollectible Accounts: A contra-asset account that reduces accounts receivable to the amount expected to be collected in cash. Also called *Allowance for Doubtful Accounts* and *Allowance for Bad Debts*.

LO3 Available-for-sale securities: Debt and equity securities that do not meet the criteria for either held-to-maturity or trading securities.

LO1 Average days' sales uncollected: A ratio that shows on average how long it takes to collect accounts receivable; 365 days divided by receivable turnover.

SO6 Bank reconciliation: The process of accounting for the difference between the balance appearing on the bank statement and the balance of the Cash account in the company's records.

LO2 Cash: Coins and currency on hand, checks and money orders from customers, and deposits in bank checking and savings accounts.

LO2 Cash equivalents: Short-term investments that will revert to cash in 90 days or less from the time they are purchased.

LO2 Compensating balance: A minimum amount that a bank requires a company to keep in its bank account as part of a credit-granting arrangement.

LO1 Contingent liability: A potential liability that can develop into a real liability if a particular subsequent event occurs.

LO4 Direct charge-off method: A method of accounting for uncollectible accounts by directly debiting an expense account when bad debts are discovered instead of using the allowance method; this method violates the matching rule but is required for federal income tax computations.

LO1 Discounting: A method of selling notes receivable in which the bank deducts the interest from the maturity value of the note to determine the proceeds.

LO5 Dishonored note: A promissory note that the maker cannot or will not pay at the maturity date.

LO5 Duration of note: The length of time in days between a promissory note's issue date and its maturity date.

LO2 Electronic funds transfer (EFT): The transfer of funds from one bank to another through electronic communication.

LO1 Factor: An entity that buys accounts receivable.

LO1 Factoring: The selling or transferring of accounts receivable.

LO3 Held-to-maturity securities: Debt securities that management intends to hold to their maturity or payment date and whose cash value is not needed until that date.

LO2 Imprest system: A system for controlling small cash disbursements by establishing a fund at a fixed amount and periodically reimbursing the fund by the amount necessary to restore its original cash balance.

LO4 Installment accounts receivable: Accounts receivable that are payable in a series of time payments.

LO5 Interest: The cost of borrowing money or the return for lending money, depending on whether one is the borrower or the lender.

LO3 Marketable securities: Short-term investments intended to be held only until needed to pay current obligations. Also called *short-term investments*.

LO5   **Maturity date:** The date on which a promissory note must be paid.

LO5   **Maturity value:** The total proceeds of a promissory note—principal plus interest—at the maturity date.

LO5   **Notes payable:** Collective term for promissory notes owed by the entity (maker) who promises payment to other entities.

LO5   **Notes receivable:** Collective term for promissory notes held by the entity to whom payment is promised (payee).

LO4   **Percentage of net sales method:** A method of estimating uncollectible accounts based on the assumption that a predictable proportion of each dollar of sales will not be collected.

LO5   **Promissory note:** An unconditional promise to pay a definite sum of money on demand or at a future date.

LO1   **Quick ratio:** A ratio for measuring the adequacy of short-term financial assets; short-term financial assets divided by current liabilities.

LO1   **Receivable turnover:** A ratio for measuring the average number of times receivables were turned into cash during an accounting period; net sales divided by average net accounts receivable.

LO1   **Securitization:** The grouping of receivables into batches for sale at a discount to companies and investors.

LO1   **Short-term financial assets:** Assets that arise from cash transactions, the investment of cash, and the extension of credit.

LO3   **Short-term investments:** Temporary investments of excess cash that are intended to be held only until they are needed to pay current obligations. Also called *marketable securities*.

LO4   **Trade credit:** Credit granted to customers by wholesalers or retailers.

LO3   **Trading securities:** Debt and equity securities bought and held principally for the purpose of being sold in the near term.

LO4   **Uncollectible accounts:** Accounts receivable owed by customers who cannot or will not pay. Also called *bad debts*.

REVIEW PROBLEM

Estimating Uncollectible Accounts, Receivables Analysis, and Notes Receivable Transactions

LO1
LO4
LO5

The Farm Implement Company sells merchandise on credit and also accepts notes for payment. During the year ended June 30, the company had net sales of $1,200,000. At the end of the year, it had Accounts Receivable of $400,000 and a debit balance in Allowance for Uncollectible Accounts of $2,100. In the past, approximately 1.5 percent of net sales has proved uncollectible. Also, an aging analysis of accounts receivable reveals that $17,000 in accounts receivable appears to be uncollectible.

The Farm Implement Company sold a tractor to R. C. Sims. Payment was received in the form of a 90-day, 9 percent, $15,000 note dated March 16. On June 14, Sims dishonored the note. On June 29, the company received payment in full from Sims plus additional interest from the date of the dishonored note.

REQUIRED ▶

K/R

1. Compute Uncollectible Accounts Expense and determine the ending balance of Allowance for Uncollectible Accounts and Accounts Receivable, Net under (a) the percentage of net sales method and (b) the accounts receivable aging method.
2. Compute the receivable turnover and average days' sales uncollected using the data from the accounts receivable aging method in 1 and assuming that the prior year's net accounts receivable were $353,000.
3. Prepare entries in journal form relating to the note received from R. C. Sims.

ANSWER TO REVIEW PROBLEM

1. Uncollectible Accounts Expense computed and balances determined
   a. Percentage of net sales method:

   Uncollectible Accounts Expense = 1.5 percent × $1,200,000 = $18,000

   Allowance for Uncollectible Accounts = $18,000 − $2,100 = $15,900

   Accounts Receivable, Net = $400,000 − $15,900 = $384,100

   b. Accounts receivable aging method:

   Uncollectible Accounts Expense = $2,100 + $17,000 = $19,100

   Allowance for Uncollectible Accounts = $17,000

   Accounts Receivable, Net = $400,000 − $17,000 = $383,000

2. Receivable turnover and average days' sales uncollected computed

$$\text{Receivable Turnover} = \frac{\$1,200,000}{(\$383,000 + \$353,000) \div 2} = 3.3 \text{ times}$$

$$\text{Average Days' Sales Uncollected} = \frac{365 \text{ days}}{3.3} = 110.6 \text{ days}$$

3. Journal entries related to the note prepared

A = L + OE	Mar. 16	Notes Receivable	15,000.00	
+ +		Sales		15,000.00
		Tractor sold to R. C. Sims; terms of note: 90 days, 9 percent		
A = L + OE	June 14	Accounts Receivable	15,337.50	
+ +		Notes Receivable		15,000.00
−		Interest Income		337.50
		The note was dishonored by R. C. Sims Maturity value: $15,000 + ($15,000 × 9/100 × 90/360) = $15,337.50		
A = L + OE	June 29	Cash	15,395.02	
+ +		Accounts Receivable		15,337.50
−		Interest Income		57.52
		Received payment in full from R. C. Sims $15,337.50 + ($15,337.50 × 9/100 × 15/360) $15,337.50 + $57.52 = $15,395.02		

Chapter Assignments

BUILDING YOUR KNOWLEDGE FOUNDATION

QUESTIONS

1. Why does a business need short-term financial assets? What three issues does management face in dealing with short-term financial assets?
2. What is a factor, and what do the terms *factoring with recourse* and *factoring without recourse* mean?
3. What items are included in the Cash account? What is a compensating balance?

4. How do cash equivalents differ from cash? From short-term investments?

5. What are the three kinds of securities held as short-term investments, and how are they valued at the balance sheet date?

6. What are unrealized gains and losses on trading securities? On what statement are they reported?

7. Which of the following items should be in accounts receivable? If an item does not belong in accounts receivable, tell where on the balance sheet it does belong: (a) installment accounts receivable from regular customers, due monthly for three years; (b) debit balances in customers' accounts; and (c) receivables from employees; (d) credit balances in customers' accounts; and (e) receivables from officers of the company.

8. Why does a company sell on credit if it expects that some of the accounts will not be paid? What role does a credit department play in selling on credit?

9. What accounting rule is violated by the direct charge-off method of recognizing uncollectible accounts? Why?

10. According to generally accepted accounting principles, at what point in the cycle of selling and collecting does a loss on an uncollectible account occur?

11. Do the following terms differ in any way: *allowance for bad debts, allowance for doubtful accounts, allowance for uncollectible accounts*?

12. What is the effect on net income of management's taking an optimistic versus a pessimistic view of estimated uncollectible accounts?

13. In what ways is Allowance for Uncollectible Accounts similar to Accumulated Depreciation? In what ways is it different?

14. What is the reasoning behind the percentage of net sales method and the accounts receivable aging method of estimating uncollectible accounts?

15. What is the procedure for estimating uncollectible accounts that also gives management a view of the status of collections and the overall quality of accounts receivable?

16. After adjusting and closing the accounts at the end of the year, suppose that Accounts Receivable is $176,000 and Allowance for Uncollectible Accounts is $14,500. (a) What is the collectible value of Accounts Receivable? (b) If the $450 account of a bankrupt customer is written off in the first month of the new year, what will be the resulting collectible value of Accounts Receivable?

17. Why should an account that has been written off as uncollectible be reinstated if the amount owed is subsequently collected?

18. What is a promissory note? Who is the maker? Who is the payee?

19. What are the maturity dates of the following notes: (a) a three-month note that is dated August 16, (b) a 90-day note that is dated August 16, and (c) a 60-day note that is dated March 25?

SHORT EXERCISES

LO1 Management Issues

SE 1. Indicate whether each of the following actions is related to (a) managing cash needs during seasonal cycles, (b) setting credit policies, or (c) financing receivables:

1. Selling accounts receivable to a factor
2. Borrowing funds for short-term needs during slow periods
3. Conducting thorough checks of new customers' ability to pay
4. Investing cash that is not currently needed for operations

LO1 Short-Term Liquidity Ratios

SE 2. Hobin Company has cash of $20,000, short-term investments of $25,000, net accounts receivable of $45,000, inventory of $44,000, accounts payable of $60,000, and net sales of $360,000. Last year's net accounts receivable were $35,000. Hobin has no current liabilities other than accounts payable.

Compute the following ratios: quick ratio, receivable turnover, and average days' sales uncollected.

SE 3.

LO2 Cash and Cash Equivalents

Compute the amount of cash and cash equivalents on Catta Company's balance sheet if on the balance sheet date, it has currency and coins on hand of $500, deposits in checking accounts of $3,000, U.S. Treasury bills due in 80 days of $30,000, and U.S. Treasury bonds due in 200 days of $50,000.

SE 4.

LO3 Held-to-Maturity Securities

On May 31, Jeans Company invested $49,000 in U.S. Treasury bills. The bills mature in 120 days at $50,000. Prepare entries to record the purchase on May 31; the adjustment to accrue interest on June 30, which is the end of the fiscal year; and the receipt of cash at the maturity date of September 28.

SE 5.

LO3 Trading Securities

Fallow Corporation began investing in trading securities in 20x1. At the end of 20x1, it had the following trading portfolio:

Security	Cost	Market Value
Sara Lee (10,000 shares)	$220,000	$330,000
Skyline (5,000 shares)	100,000	75,000
Totals	$320,000	$405,000

Prepare the necessary year-end adjusting entry on December 31 and the entry for the sale of all the Skyline shares on the following March 23 for $95,000.

SE 6.

LO4 Percentage of Net Sales Method

At the end of October, Soo Company's management estimates the uncollectible accounts expense to be 1 percent of net sales of $2,770,000. Give the entry to record the uncollectible accounts expense, assuming that the Allowance for Uncollectible Accounts has a debit balance of $14,000.

SE 7.

LO4 Accounts Receivable Aging Method

An aging analysis on June 30 of the accounts receivable of Allsides Corporation indicates that uncollectible accounts amount to $43,000. Give the entry to record uncollectible accounts expense under each of the following independent assumptions: (a) Allowance for Uncollectible Accounts has a credit balance of $9,000 before adjustment, and (b) Allowance for Uncollectible Accounts has a debit balance of $7,000 before adjustment.

SE 8.

LO4 Write-off of Accounts Receivable

Mint Company, which uses the allowance method, has an account receivable from Lana Freer of $4,400 that it deems to be uncollectible. Prepare the entries on May 31 to write off the account and on August 13 to record an unexpected receipt of $1,000 from Freer. The company does not expect to collect more from Freer.

SE 9.

LO5 Notes Receivable Entries

On August 25, Landau Company received a 90-day, 9 percent note in settlement of an account receivable in the amount of $10,000. Record the receipt of the note, the accrual of interest at the end of the fiscal year on September 30, and the collection of the note on the due date.

SE 10.

SO6 Bank Reconciliation

Prepare a bank reconciliation from the following information:

a. Balance per bank statement as of June 30, $2,586.58
b. Balance per books as of June 30, $1,318.87
c. Deposits in transit, $348.00
d. Outstanding checks, $1,611.11
e. Interest on average balance, $4.60

EXERCISES

E 1.

LO1 Management Issues

Indicate whether each of the following actions is primarily related to (a) managing cash needs during seasonal cycles, (b) setting credit policies, or (c) financing receivables:

1. Buying a U.S. Treasury bill with cash that is not needed for a few months
2. Comparing receivable turnovers for two years
3. Setting a policy that allows customers to buy on credit
4. Selling notes receivable to a financing company
5. Borrowing funds for short-term needs during the period of the year when sales are low
6. Changing the terms for credit sales in an effort to reduce the average days' sales uncollected

7. Using a factor to provide operating funds
8. Establishing a department whose responsibility is to approve customers' credit

E 2.
LO1 Short-Term Liquidity Ratios

Using the following data from the financial statements of Russo Company, compute the quick ratio, the receivable turnover, and the average days' sales uncollected:

Current assets	
Cash	$ 70,000
Short-term investments	170,000
Notes receivable	240,000
Accounts receivable, net	200,000
Inventory	500,000
Prepaid assets	50,000
Total current assets	$1,230,000
Current liabilities	
Notes payable	$ 300,000
Accounts payable	150,000
Accrued liabilities	20,000
Total current liabilities	$ 470,000
Net sales	$1,600,000
Last period's accounts receivable, net	$ 180,000

E 3.
LO2 Cash and Cash Equivalents

At year end, Taft Company had currency and coins in cash registers of $2,800, money orders from customers of $5,000, deposits in checking accounts of $32,000, U.S. Treasury bills due in 80 days of $90,000, certificates of deposits at the bank that mature in six months of $100,000, and U.S. Treasury bonds due in one year of $50,000. Calculate the amount of cash and cash equivalents that will be shown on the company's year-end balance sheet.

E 4.
LO3 Held-to-Maturity Securities

Vales Company experiences heavy sales in the summer and early fall, after which time it has excess cash to invest until the next spring. On November 1, 20x1, the company invested $194,000 in U.S. Treasury bills. The bills mature in 180 days at $200,000. Prepare entries to record the purchase on November 1; the adjustment to accrue interest on December 31, which is the end of the fiscal year; and the receipt of cash at the maturity date of April 30.

E 5.
LO3 Trading Securities

Epps Corporation, which has begun investing in trading securities, engaged in the following transactions:

Jan.   6   Purchased 7,000 shares of Quaker Oats stock, $30 per share.
Feb. 15   Purchased 9,000 shares of EG&G, $22 per share.

At year end on June 30, Quaker Oats was trading at $40 per share, and EG&G was trading at $18 per share.

Record the entries for the purchases. Then record the necessary year-end adjusting entry. (Include a schedule of the trading portfolio cost and market in the explanation.) Also record the entry for the sale of all the EG&G shares on August 20 for $16 per share. Is the last entry affected by the June 30 adjustment?

E 6.
LO4 Percentage of Net Sales Method

At the end of the year, Simone Enterprises estimates the uncollectible accounts expense to be .7 percent of net sales of $30,300,000. The current credit balance of Allowance for Uncollectible Accounts is $51,600. Prepare the entry in journal form to record the uncollectible accounts expense. What is the balance of Allowance for Uncollectible Accounts after each of these adjustments?

E 7.
LO4 Accounts Receivable Aging Method

Accounts Receivable of Jovic Company shows a debit balance of $52,000 at the end of the year. An aging analysis of the individual accounts indicates estimated uncollectible accounts to be $3,350.

Prepare the entry in journal form to record the uncollectible accounts expense under each of the following independent assumptions: (a) Allowance for Uncollectible Accounts has a credit balance of $400 before adjustment, and (b) Allowance for Uncollectible Accounts has a debit balance of $400 before adjustment. What is the balance of Allowance for Uncollectible Accounts after each of these adjustments?

E 8.

LO4   Aging Method and Net Sales Method Contrasted

At the beginning of 20xx, the balances for Accounts Receivable and Allowance for Uncollectible Accounts were $430,000 and $31,400, respectively. During the year, credit sales were $3,200,000, and collections on account were $2,950,000. In addition, $35,000 in uncollectible accounts were written off.

Using T accounts, determine the year-end balances of Accounts Receivable and Allowance for Uncollectible Accounts. Then make the year-end adjusting entry to record the uncollectible accounts expense and show the year-end balance sheet presentation of Accounts Receivable and Allowance for Uncollectible Accounts under each of the following conditions:

a. Management estimates the percentage of uncollectible credit sales to be 1.2 percent of total credit sales.
b. Based on an aging of accounts receivable, management estimates the end-of-year uncollectible accounts receivable to be $38,700.

Post the results of each of the entries to the T account for Allowance for Uncollectible Accounts.

E 9.

LO4   Aging Method and Net Sales Method Contrasted

During 20x1, Moon Supply Company had net sales of $2,850,000. Most of the sales were on credit. At the end of 20x1, the balance of Accounts Receivable was $350,000, and Allowance for Uncollectible Accounts had a debit balance of $12,000. Moon Supply Company's management uses two methods of estimating uncollectible accounts expense: (a) The percentage of uncollectible sales is 1.5 percent of net sales, and (b) based on an aging of accounts receivable, the end-of-year uncollectible accounts total $35,000. Make the end-of-year adjusting entry to record the uncollectible accounts expense under each method, and tell what the balance of Allowance for Uncollectible Accounts will be after each adjustment. Why are the results different? Which method is likely to be more reliable?

E 10.

LO4   Aging Method and Net Sales Method Contrasted

The Montana Parts Company sells merchandise on credit. During the fiscal year ended July 31, the company had net sales of $4,600,000. At the end of the year, it had Accounts Receivable of $1,200,000 and a debit balance in Allowance for Uncollectible Accounts of $6,800. In the past, approximately 1.4 percent of net sales has proved uncollectible. Also, an aging analysis of accounts receivable reveals that $60,000 of the receivables appear to be uncollectible. Prepare entries in journal form to record uncollectible accounts expense using (a) the percentage of net sales method and (b) the accounts receivable aging method.

What is the resulting balance of Allowance for Uncollectible Accounts under each method? How would your answers under each method change if Allowance for Uncollectible Accounts had a credit balance of $6,800 instead of a debit balance? Why do the methods result in different balances?

E 11.

LO4   Accounts Receivable Transactions

Assuming that the allowance method is used, prepare entries in journal form to record the following transactions:

July 12, 20x4 Sold merchandise to Ezra Lief for $1,800, terms n/10.
Oct. 18, 20x4 Received $600 from Ezra Lief on account.
May   8, 20x5 Wrote off as uncollectible the balance of the Ezra Lief account when he declared bankruptcy.
June 22, 20x5 Unexpectedly received a check for $200 from Ezra Lief.

E 12.

LO5   Interest Computations

Determine the interest on the following notes:

a. $22,800 at 10 percent for 90 days
b. $16,000 at 12 percent for 60 days
c. $18,000 at 9 percent for 30 days
d. $30,000 at 15 percent for 120 days
e. $10,800 at 6 percent for 60 days

E 13.

LO5   Notes Receivable Transactions

Prepare entries in journal form to record the following transactions:

Jan. 16 Sold merchandise to Meier Corporation on account for $36,000, terms n/30.
Feb. 15 Accepted a 90-day, 10 percent, $36,000 note from Meier Corporation in lieu of payment of account.
May   16 Meier Corporation dishonored the note.

June 15   Received payment in full from Meier Corporation, including interest at 10 percent from the date the note was dishonored.

E 14.

LO5   Adjusting Entries: Interest Income

Prepare entries in journal form (assuming reversing entries were not made) to record the following:

Dec. 1   Received a 90-day, 12 percent note for $10,000 from a customer for a sale of merchandise.
     31   Made end-of-year adjustment for interest income.
Mar. 1   Received payment in full for note and interest.

E 15.

LO5   Notes Receivable Transactions

Prepare entries in journal form to record these transactions:

Jan. 5   Accepted a 60-day, 10 percent, $4,800 note dated this day in granting a time extension on the past-due account of N. Tagaki.
Mar. 6   N. Tagaki paid the maturity value of her $4,800 note.
      9   Accepted a 60-day, 12 percent, $3,000 note dated this day in granting a time extension on the past-due account of V. Sonora.
May   8   When asked for payment, V. Sonora dishonored his note.
June 7   V. Sonora paid in full the maturity value of the note plus interest at 12 percent for the period since May 8.

E 16.

SO6   Bank Reconciliation

Prepare a bank reconciliation from the following information:

a. Balance per bank statement as of May 31, $8,454.54
b. Balance per books as of May 31, $6,138.04
c. Deposits in transit, $1,134.42
d. Outstanding checks, $3,455.92
e. Bank service charge, $5.00

PROBLEMS

P 1.

LO3   Held-to-Maturity and Trading Securities

Welcor Distributions follows a policy of investing excess cash until it is needed. During 20x1 and 20x2, the company engaged in the following transactions:

20x1
Feb. 1   Invested $97,000 in 120-day U.S. Treasury bills that had a maturity value of $100,000.
Mar. 30   Purchased 20,000 shares of Ember Company common stock at $16 per share and 12,000 shares of Ray's Fruit, Inc., common stock at $10 per share as trading securities.
June 1   Received maturity value of U.S. Treasury bills in cash.
     10   Received dividends of $.50 per share from Ember Company and $.25 per share from Ray's Fruit, Inc.
     30   Made year-end adjusting entry for trading securities. Market price of Ember Company shares is $13 per share and of Ray's Fruit, Inc., shares is $12 per share.
Dec. 3   Sold all the shares of Ember Company for $12 per share.

20x2
Mar. 17   Purchased 15,000 shares of NSN, Inc., for $9 per share.
May 31   Invested $116,000 in 120-day U.S. Treasury bills that had a maturity value of $120,000.
June 10   Received dividends of $.30 per share from Ray's Fruit, Inc.
     30   Made year-end adjusting entry for held-to-maturity securities.
     30   Made year-end adjusting entry for trading securities. Market price of Ray's Fruit, Inc., shares is $6 per share, and market price of NSN, Inc., shares is $11 per share.

REQUIRED ▶

1. Prepare entries in journal form to record these transactions, assuming that Welcor Distributions' fiscal year ends on June 30.
2. Show the balance sheet presentation of Welcor Distributions' short-term investments on June 30, 20x2.

P 2.

LO1 Methods of Estimating
LO4 Uncollectible Accounts and
Receivables Analysis

Ⓚ/Ⓡ

Boreo Company had an Accounts Receivable balance of $320,000 and a credit balance in Allowance for Uncollectible Accounts of $16,700 at January 1, 20xx. During the year, the company recorded the following transactions:

a. Sales on account, $1,052,000
b. Sales returns and allowances by credit customers, $53,400
c. Collections from customers, $993,000
d. Worthless accounts written off, $19,800

The company's past history indicates that 2.5 percent of its net credit sales will not be collected.

REQUIRED ▶

1. Prepare T accounts for Accounts Receivable and Allowance for Uncollectible Accounts. Enter the beginning balances, and show the effects on these accounts of the items listed above, summarizing the year's activity. Determine the ending balance of each account.
2. Compute Uncollectible Accounts Expense and determine the ending balance of Allowance for Uncollectible Accounts under (a) the percentage of net sales method and (b) the accounts receivable aging method, assuming an aging of the accounts receivable shows that $24,000 may be uncollectible.
3. Compute the receivable turnover and average days' sales uncollected, using the data from the accounts receivable aging method in **2**.
4. How do you explain that the two methods used in **2** result in different amounts for Uncollectible Accounts Expense? What rationale underlies each method?

P 3.

LO4 Accounts Receivable Aging
Method

Magda Fashions Store uses the accounts receivable aging method to estimate uncollectible accounts. On February 1, 20x1, the balance of the Accounts Receivable account was a debit of $446,341, and the balance of Allowance for Uncollectible Accounts was a credit of $43,000. During the year, the store had sales on account of $3,724,000, sales returns and allowances of $63,000, worthless accounts written off of $44,300, and collections from customers of $3,214,000. As part of the end-of-year (January 31, 20x2) procedures, an aging analysis of accounts receivable is prepared. The totals of the analysis, which is partially complete, follow:

Customer Account	Total	Not Yet Due	1–30 Days Past Due	31–60 Days Past Due	61–90 Days Past Due	Over 90 Days Past Due
Balance Forward	$793,791	$438,933	$149,614	$106,400	$57,442	$41,402

To finish the analysis, the following accounts need to be classified:

Account	Amount	Due Date
I. Brock	$10,977	Jan. 15
K. O'Connor	9,314	Feb. 15 (next fiscal year)
B. Davis	8,664	Dec. 20
S. Patel	780	Oct. 1
A. Pina	14,810	Jan. 4
M. Finnette	6,316	Nov. 15
D. Bordo	4,389	Mar. 1 (next fiscal year)
	$55,250	

From past experience, the company has found that the following rates are realistic for estimating uncollectible accounts:

Time	Percentage Considered Uncollectible
Not yet due	2
1–30 days past due	5
31–60 days past due	15
61–90 days past due	25
Over 90 days past due	50

REQUIRED ▶

1. Complete the aging analysis of accounts receivable.
2. Compute the end-of-year balances (before adjustments) of Accounts Receivable and Allowance for Uncollectible Accounts.

3. Prepare an analysis computing the estimated uncollectible accounts.
4. Prepare the entry in journal form to record Magda Fashion Store's estimated uncollectible accounts expense for the year (round the adjustment to the nearest whole dollar).

P 4.
LO5 Notes Receivable Transactions

Pop Importing Company engaged in the following transactions involving promissory notes:

Jan.	14	Sold merchandise to Maxend Company for $37,000, terms n/30.
Feb.	13	Received $8,400 in cash from Maxend Company and received a 90-day, 8 percent promissory note for the balance of the account.
May	14	Received payment in full from Maxend Company.
	15	Received a 60-day, 12 percent note from Monty Smith Company in payment of a past-due account, $12,000.
July	14	When asked to pay, Monty Smith Company dishonored the note.
	20	Received a check from Monty Smith Company for payment of the maturity value of the note and interest at 12 percent for the six days beyond maturity.
	25	Sold merchandise to Cara Kendall Company for $36,000, with payment of $6,000 cash down and the remainder on account.
	31	Received a 45-day, 10 percent, $30,000 promissory note from Cara Kendall Company for the outstanding account receivable.
Sept.	14	When asked to pay, Cara Kendall Company dishonored the note.
	25	Wrote off the Cara Kendall Company account as uncollectible following news that the company had declared bankruptcy.

REQUIRED ▶ Prepare entries in journal form to record the above transactions.

P 5.
SO6 Bank Reconciliation

The following information is available for David Company as of April 30, 20xx:

a. Cash on the books as of April 30 amounted to $114,175.28. Cash on the bank statement for the same date was $141,717.08.
b. A deposit of $14,249.84, representing cash receipts of April 30, did not appear on the bank statement.
c. Outstanding checks totaled $7,293.64.
d. A check for $2,420.00 returned with the statement was recorded as $2,024.00. The check was for advertising.
e. The bank service charge for April amounted to $26.00.
f. The bank collected $36,400.00 for David Company on a note. The face value of the note was $36,000.00
g. An NSF check for $1,140.00 from a customer, Ed Soule, was returned with the statement.
h. The bank mistakenly deducted a check for $800.00 drawn by EKT Corporation.
i. The bank reported a credit of $460.00 for interest on the average balance.

REQUIRED ▶
1. Prepare a bank reconciliation for David Company as of April 30, 20xx.
2. Prepare the necessary entries in journal form from the reconciliation.
3. State the amount of cash that should appear on David Company's balance sheet as of April 30.

ALTERNATE PROBLEMS

P 6.
LO3 Held-to-Maturity and Trading Securities

During certain periods, Yang Company invests its excess cash until it is needed. During 20x1 and 20x2, the company engaged in the following transactions:

20x1
Jan.	16	Invested $146,000 in 120-day U.S. Treasury bills that had a maturity value of $150,000.
Apr.	15	Purchased 10,000 shares of King Tools common stock at $40 per share and 5,000 shares of Mellon Gas common stock at $30 per share as trading securities.
May	16	Received maturity value of U.S. Treasury bills in cash.
June	2	Received dividends of $2.00 per share from King Tools and $1.50 per share from Mellon Gas.

June 30   Made year-end adjusting entry for trading securities. Market price of King Tools shares is $32 per share and of Mellon Gas shares is $35 per share.

Nov. 14   Sold all the shares of King Tools for $42 per share.

20x2

Feb. 15   Purchased 9,000 shares of MKD Communications for $50 per share.

Apr. 1   Invested $195,500 in 120-day U.S. Treasury bills that had a maturity value of $200,000.

June 1   Received dividends of $2.20 per share from Mellon Gas.

    30   Made year-end adjusting entry for held-to-maturity securities.

    30   Made year-end adjusting entry for trading securities. Market price of Mellon Gas shares is $33 per share and of MKD Communications shares is $60 per share.

REQUIRED ▶   1. Prepare entries in journal form to record the preceding transactions, assuming that Yang Company's fiscal year ends on June 30.

2. Show the balance sheet presentation of short-term investments on June 30, 20x2.

P 7.

LO1 Methods of Estimating
LO4 Uncollectible Accounts and
Receivables Analysis

Ⓚ/Ⓡ

On December 31 of last year, the balance sheet of Talon Company had Accounts Receivable of $298,000 and a credit balance in Allowance for Uncollectible Accounts of $20,300. During the current year, Talon Company's records included the following selected activities: (a) sales on account, $1,195,000; (b) sales returns and allowances, $73,000; (c) collections from customers, $1,150,000; and (d) accounts written off as worthless, $16,000. In the past, 1.6 percent of Talon Company's net sales has been uncollectible.

REQUIRED ▶   1. Prepare T accounts for Accounts Receivable and Allowance for Uncollectible Accounts. Enter the beginning balances, and show the effects on these accounts of the items listed above, summarizing the year's activity. Determine the ending balance of each account.

2. Compute Uncollectible Accounts Expense and determine the ending balance of Allowance for Uncollectible Accounts under (a) the percentage of net sales method and (b) the accounts receivable aging method, assuming an aging of the accounts receivable shows that $20,000 may be uncollectible.

3. Compute the receivable turnover and average days' sales uncollected, using the data from the accounts receivable aging method in **2**.

4. How do you explain that the two methods used in **2** result in different amounts for Uncollectible Accounts Expense? What rationale underlies each method?

P 8.

SO6 Bank Reconciliation

The following information is available for Fenton MacIntyre Company as of May 31, 20xx:

a. Cash on the books as of May 31 amounted to $42,754.16. Cash on the bank statement for the same date was $52,351.46.

b. A deposit of $5,220.94, representing cash receipts of May 31, did not appear on the bank statement.

c. Outstanding checks totaled $3,936.80.

d. A check for $1,920.00 returned with the statement was recorded incorrectly in the check register as $1,380.00. The check was for a cash purchase of merchandise.

e. The bank service charge for May amounted to $25.

f. The bank collected $12,240.00 for Fenton MacIntyre Company on a note. The face value of the note was $12,000.00.

g. An NSF check for $183.56 from a customer, Lisa Rideout, was returned with the statement.

h. The bank mistakenly charged to the company account a check for $850.00 drawn by another company.

i. The bank reported that it had credited the account for $240.00 in interest on the average balance for May.

REQUIRED ▶   1. Prepare a bank reconciliation for Fenton MacIntyre Company as of May 31, 20xx.

2. Prepare the entries in journal form necessary to adjust the accounts.

3. State the amount of cash that should appear on Fenton MacIntyre Company's balance sheet as of May 31.

SKILLS DEVELOPMENT CASES

Conceptual Analysis

LO1 Management of Cash
LO2
LO3

SD 1. Collegiate Publishing Company publishes college textbooks in the sciences and humanities. More than 50 percent of Collegiate Publishing's sales occur in July, August, and December. Its cash balances are largest in August, September, and January. During the rest of the year, its cash receipts are low. The company's treasurer keeps the cash in a bank checking account earning little or no interest and pays bills from this account as they come due. To survive periods when cash receipts are low, Collegiate Publishing Company sometimes borrows money, and it repays the loans in the months when cash receipts are largest.

A management consultant has suggested that Collegiate Publishing Company institute a new cash management plan under which cash would be invested in marketable securities as it is received and securities would be sold when the funds are needed. In this way, the company would earn income on the cash and might realize a gain through an increase in the value of the securities, thus reducing the need for borrowing. The president of the company has asked you to assess the plan. Write a memorandum to the president that lays out the accounting implications of the plan for cash and cash equivalents and for the three types of marketable securities. Include in your assessment any disadvantages the plan might have.

LO1 Role of Credit Sales
LO4

SD 2. Mitsubishi Corp. <www.mitsubishi.com>, a broadly diversified Japanese corporation, instituted a credit plan called Three Diamonds for customers who buy its major electronic products, such as large-screen televisions and videotape recorders, from specified retail dealers.[12] Under the plan, approved customers who make purchases in July of one year do not have to make any payments until September of the next year and pay no interest during the intervening months. Mitsubishi pays the dealer the full amount less a small fee, sends the customer a Mitsubishi credit card, and collects from the customer at the specified time.

What was Mitsubishi's motivation for establishing such generous credit terms? What costs are involved? What are the accounting implications?

LO1 Receivables Financing

SD 3. Goldstein Appliances, Inc., is a small manufacturer of washing machines and dryers located in central Michigan. Goldstein sells most of its appliances to large, established discount retail companies that market the appliances under their own names. Goldstein sells the appliances on trade credit terms of n/60. If a customer wants a longer term, however, Goldstein will accept a note with a term of up to nine months. At present, the company is having cash flow troubles and needs $5 million immediately. Its cash balance is $200,000, its accounts receivable balance is $2.3 million, and its notes receivable balance is $3.7 million.

How might Goldstein Appliance's management use its accounts receivable and notes receivable to raise the cash it needs? What are the company's prospects for raising the needed cash?

 Group Activity: Assign to in-class groups and debrief.

Ethical Dilemma

LO1 Ethics, Uncollectible Accounts,
LO4 and Short-Term Objectives

SD 4. Waddell Interiors, a successful retail furniture company, is located in an affluent suburb where a major insurance company has just announced a restructuring that will lay off 4,000 employees. Waddell Interiors sells quality furniture, usually on credit. Accounts Receivable are one of its major assets. Although the company's annual uncollectible accounts losses are not out of line, they represent a sizable amount. The company depends on bank loans for its financing. Sales and net income have declined in the past year, and some customers are falling behind in paying their accounts.

Henry Waddell, the owner of the business, knows that the bank's loan officer likes to see a steady performance. He has therefore instructed the company's controller to underestimate the uncollectible accounts this year to show a small growth in earnings. Waddell believes this action is justified because earnings in future years will average out the losses, and since the company has a history of success, he believes the adjustments are meaningless accounting measures anyway. Are Waddell's actions ethical? Would any parties be harmed by his actions? How important is it to try to be accurate in estimating losses from uncollectible accounts?

 Group Activity: Assign in-class groups to debate the ethical issues of this case.

Research Activity

SD 5.

LO1   Stock and Treasury Investments
LO3

Locate the listing of New York Stock Exchange (NYSE) stocks in a recent issue of *The Wall Street Journal*. Find five companies whose names you recognize (such as IBM, McDonald's, or Ford). Write down the range of each company's stock price for the last year and the current closing price. Also note the dividend, if any, per share. How much did the market values of the common stocks you picked vary in the last year? Do these data demonstrate the need to value short-term investments of this type at market value? How does accounting for short-term investments in these common stocks differ from accounting for short-term investments in U.S. Treasury bills? How are dividends received on investments in these common stocks accounted for?

Be prepared to hand in your notes and to discuss the results of your investigation during class.

Decision-Making Practice

SD 6.

LO3   Accounting for Short-Term Investments

Jackson Christmas Tree Company's business—the growing and selling of Christmas trees—is seasonal. By January 1, after its heavy selling season, the company has cash on hand that will not be needed for several months. It has minimal expenses from January to October and heavy expenses during the harvest and shipping months of November and December. The company's management follows the practice of investing the idle cash in marketable securities, which can be sold as funds are needed for operations. The company's fiscal year ends on June 30.

On January 10 of the current year, Jackson has cash of $597,300 on hand. It keeps $20,000 on hand for operating expenses and invests the rest as follows:

$100,000 three-month Treasury bills	$ 97,800
1,000 shares of Ford Motor Co. ($50 per share)	50,000
2,500 shares of McDonald's ($50 per share)	125,000
2,100 shares of IBM ($145 per share)	304,500
Total short-term investments	$577,300

On February 10 and on May 10, Jackson receives quarterly cash dividends from each company in which it has invested: $.50 per share from Ford Motor Co., $.05 per share from McDonald's, and $.25 per share from IBM. The Treasury bills are redeemed at face value on April 10. On June 1, management sells 500 shares of McDonald's at $55 per share.

On June 30, the market values of the investments are as follows:

Ford Motor Co.	$ 61 per share
McDonald's	$ 46 per share
IBM	$140 per share

Jackson receives another quarterly dividend from each company on August 10. It sells all its remaining shares on November 1 at the following prices:

Ford Motor Co.	$ 55 per share
McDonald's	$ 44 per share
IBM	$160 per share

1. Record the investment transactions that occurred on January 10, February 10, April 10, May 10, and June 1. The Treasury bills are accounted for as held-to-maturity securities, and the stocks are trading securities. Prepare the required adjusting entry on June 30, and record the investment transactions on August 10 and November 1.
2. Explain how the short-term investments would be shown on the balance sheet on June 30.

3. After November 1, what is the balance of Allowance to Adjust Short-Term Investments to Market, and what will happen to this account next June?
4. What is your assessment of Jackson Christmas Tree Company's strategy with regard to idle cash?

FINANCIAL REPORTING AND ANALYSIS CASES

Interpreting Financial Reports

FRA 1.

LO1 Role of Estimates in
LO4 Accounting for Receivables

CompuCredit <www.compucredit.com> is a credit card issuer in Atlanta. It prides itself on making credit cards available to almost anybody in a matter of seconds over the Internet. The cost to the consumer is an interest rate of 28 percent, about double that of companies that provide cards only to customers with good credit. CompuCredit has been successful. It has 1.9 million accounts and achieved an income of over $100 million in a recent year. To arrive at net income, the company estimates that 10 percent of its $1.3 billion in accounts receivable will not be paid; the industry average is 7 percent. Some analysts have been critical of CompuCredit for being too optimistic in its projections of losses.[13]

Why are estimates necessary in accounting for receivables? If CompuCredit were to use the same estimate of losses as other companies in its industry, what would its net income have been for the year? How would one determine if CompuCredit's estimate of losses is reasonable?

FRA 2.

LO4 Accounting for Accounts
Receivable

Dodge Products Co. is a major consumer goods company that sells over 3,000 products in 135 countries. The company's annual report to the Securities and Exchange Commission presented the following data (in thousands) pertaining to net sales and accounts related to accounts receivable for 1999, 2000, and 2001.

	2001	2000	1999
Net sales	$4,910,000	$4,865,000	$4,888,000
Accounts receivable	523,000	524,000	504,000
Allowance for uncollectible accounts	18,600	21,200	24,500
Uncollectible accounts expense	15,000	16,700	15,800
Uncollectible accounts written off	19,300	20,100	17,700
Recoveries of accounts previously written off	1,700	100	1,000

REQUIRED ▶

1. Compute the ratio of Uncollectible Accounts Expense to Net Sales and to Accounts Receivable and the ratio of Allowance for Uncollectible Accounts to Accounts Receivable for 1999, 2000, and 2001.
2. Compute the receivable turnover and average days' sales uncollected for each year, assuming 1998 net accounts receivable were $465,000,000.
3. What is your interpretation of the ratios? Describe management's attitude toward the collectibility of accounts receivable over the three-year period.

International Company

FRA 3.

LO1 Comparison and
Interpretation of Ratios

Philips Electronics N.V. <www.philips.com> and Heineken N.V. <www.heinekencorp.nl> are two well-known Dutch companies. Philips is a large, diversified electronics, music, and media company, and Heineken makes a popular beer. Philips is about three and a half times bigger than Heineken. Its 2001 revenues were 32.3 billion euros, versus 9.1 billion euros for Heineken.

Ratios can help in comparing and understanding companies. For example, the receivable turnovers for Philips and Heineken in 2000 and 2001 were as follows:[14]

	2001	2000
Philips	5.2 times	5.6 times
Heineken	7.7 times	7.9 times

What do the ratios tell you about the credit policies of the two companies? How long does it take each, on average, to collect a receivable? What do the ratios tell about the companies' relative needs for capital to finance receivables? Can you tell which company has a better credit policy? Explain your answers.

Toys "R" Us Annual Report

FRA 4.

LO1 **Analysis of Short-Term**
LO2 **Financial Assets**
LO4

Refer to the Toys "R" Us <www.tru.com> annual report in the Supplement to Chapter 1 to answer the following questions:

1. How much cash and cash equivalents did Toys "R" Us have in 2001? Do you suppose most of that amount is cash in the bank or cash equivalents?
2. Toys "R" Us does not disclose an allowance for uncollectible accounts. How do you explain the lack of disclosure?
3. Compute the quick ratios for 2000 and 2001 and comment on them.
4. Compute receivable turnover and average days' sales uncollected for 2000 and 2001 and comment on Toys "R" Us credit policies. Accounts Receivable in 1999 were $204,000,000.

Comparison Case: Toys "R" Us and Walgreen Co.

FRA 5.

LO1 **Quick Ratio and Seasonality of**
Cash Flows

Refer to the Toys "R" Us <www.tru.com> annual report and the financial statements of Walgreens <www.walgreens.com> in the Supplement to Chapter 1 to answer the following questions:

1. What is the quick ratio for both companies for the last two years? Comment on the results of your calculation. (If you were assigned **FRA 4**, use the calculation from that case for Toys "R" Us.)
2. Do you think the seasonal need for cash is different or the same for Toys "R" Us and Walgreens? Explain. Identify the place in the financial statements where the seasonality of sales is discussed.

Fingraph® Financial Analyst™

FRA 6.

LO1 **Comparison and Analysis of**
Short-Term Financial Assets

Choose any two companies in the same industry from the list of Fingraph companies on the Needles Accounting Resource Center Web Site at http://accounting.college.hmco.com/students. The industry should be one in which accounts receivable is likely to be an important current asset—for example, manufacturing, consumer products, consumer food and beverage, or computers. Retail companies should be avoided because they usually have low accounts receivables. Access the Microsoft Excel spreadsheets for the companies you selected. Click on the URL at the top of each company's spreadsheet for a link to the company's web site and annual report.

1. In the summary of significant accounting policies or notes to the financial statements in the annual reports of the companies you have selected, find any reference to cash and cash equivalents, short-term (marketable) securities, and accounts receivable.
2. Using the Fingraph Financial Analyst CD-ROM software, display and print for the companies you have selected (a) the Current Assets and Current Liabilities Analysis page and (b) the Liquidity and Asset Utilization Analysis page in tabular and graphic form. Prepare a table that compares the quick ratio, receivable turnover, and average days' sales uncollected for both companies for two years.
3. Find and read the liquidity analysis section of management's discussion and analysis in each annual report.
4. Write a one-page executive summary that highlights the accounting policies for short-term financial assets and compares the short-term liquidity position of the two companies. Include your assessment of the companies' relative liquidity, and make reference to management's assessment. Include the Fingraph pages and your table with your report.

Internet Case

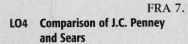

FRA 7.

LO4   Comparison of J.C. Penney and Sears

Access the annual reports of J.C. Penney, Inc. <www.jcpenney.com> and Sears, Roebuck and Co. <www.sears.com> directly, or go to the Needles Accounting Resource Center Student Web Site at http://accounting.college.hmco.com/students for a link to their web sites. Find the accounts receivable and marketable securities (if any) on each company's balance sheet and the notes related to these accounts in the notes to the financial statements. If either company has marketable securities, what is their cost and market value? Does the company currently have a gain or loss on the securities? Which company has the most accounts receivable as a percentage of total assets? What is the percentage of the allowance account to gross accounts receivable for each company? Which company experienced the highest loss rate on its receivables? Why do you think there is a difference? Do the companies finance their receivables? Be prepared to discuss your findings in class.

8

Chapter 8 presents the management issues associated with inventories, including the costing of inventories for financial reporting.

Inventories

Learning Objectives

LO1 Identify and explain the management issues associated with accounting for inventories.

LO2 Define *inventory cost* and relate it to goods flow and cost flow.

LO3 Calculate the pricing of inventory, using the cost basis under the periodic inventory system.

LO4 Apply the perpetual inventory system to the pricing of inventories at cost.

LO5 State the effects of inventory methods and misstatements of inventory on income determination, income taxes, and cash flows.

LO6 Apply the lower-of-cost-or-market (LCM) rule to inventory valuation.

Supplemental Objective

SO7 Estimate the cost of ending inventory using the retail method and gross profit method.

DECISION POINT
A USER'S FOCUS

J.C. Penney Company, Inc. <www.jcpenney.com> Managing inventory for profit is one of management's most complex and challenging tasks. In terms of dollars, the inventory of goods held for sale is one of the largest assets of a merchandising business. As may be seen in the financial highlights on the opposite page, J.C. Penney Company, Inc., a major retailer with department stores in all 50 states and Puerto Rico, devotes more than 25 percent, or $5.3 billion, of its $19.7 billion in assets to inventories. What challenges does J.C. Penney's management face in managing its inventory?

Not only must J.C. Penney's management purchase merchandise that customers will want to buy; it must also have the merchandise available in the right locations at the times when customers want to buy it. Management also must try to minimize the cost of inventory while maintaining quality. To these ends, J.C. Penney maintains purchasing offices in cities throughout the world, including Hong Kong, Taipei, Osaka, Seoul, Bangkok, Singapore, Bombay, and Florence. Further, because of the high cost of borrowing funds and storing inventory, management must control the amount of money tied up in inventory. Important accounting decisions include what assumptions to make about the flow of inventory costs, what prices to put on inventory, what inventory systems to use, and how to protect inventory against loss.

Proper management of inventory has helped J.C. Penney reduce its inventory (and total assets) and increase its level of retail sales. The company still has challenges, however, given the decline in its income

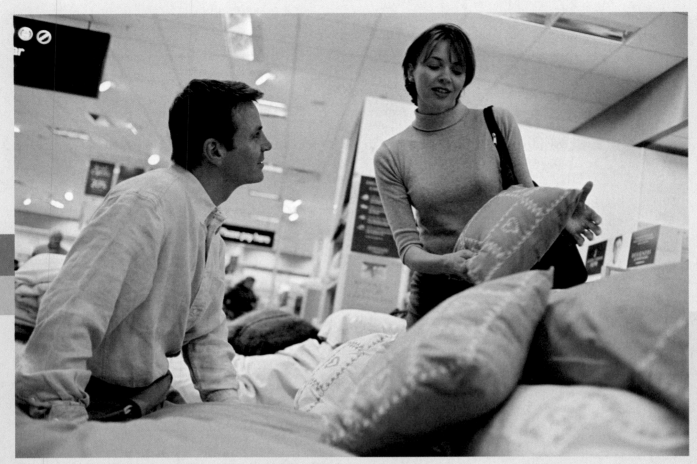

How does J.C. Penney manage its inventory to increase its retail sales?

from operations from a positive $715 million in 1998 to a loss of $886 million in 2000. The company has announced plans to improve the profitability of its core department stores by further improving inventory management, controlling costs, and closing under-performing stores.[1]

Financial Highlights
(In millions)

	2000	1999	1998
Retail sales, net	$31,846	$31,743	$29,761
Cost of goods sold	23,031	22,286	20,621
(Loss)/income from operations	(886)	278	715
Merchandise inventories	5,269	5,947	6,060
Total assets	19,742	20,908	23,600

MANAGEMENT ISSUES ASSOCIATED WITH ACCOUNTING FOR INVENTORIES

LO1 Identify and explain the management issues associated with accounting for inventories.

RELATED TEXT ASSIGNMENTS

Q: 1, 2, 3
SE: 1, 2   www.jcpenney.com
E: 1, 2   www.tru.com
P: 1, 2, 6, 7
SD: 1, 4
FRA: 1, 4, 5, 6, 7   www.itwinc.com

Inventory is considered a current asset because it is normally sold within a year or within a company's operating cycle. For a merchandising business like J.C. Penney or Toys "R" Us, **merchandise inventory** consists of all goods owned and held for sale in the regular course of business.

Inventories are important for manufacturing companies as well. Because manufacturers are engaged in the actual making of products, they have three kinds of inventory: raw materials to be used in the production of goods, partially completed products (often called *work in process*), and finished goods ready for sale. For example, in its annual report for the year 2000, Illinois Tool Works, Inc., disclosed the following inventories:[2]

Financial Highlights
(In thousands)

	2000	1999
Inventories		
Raw materials	$ 350,943	$ 352,992
Work in process	134,044	123,137
Finished goods	696,398	608,083
Total inventories	$1,181,385	$1,084,212

In manufacturing operations, the costs of the work in process and the finished goods inventories include not only the cost of the raw materials that go into the product, but also the cost of the labor used to convert the raw materials to finished goods and the overhead costs that support the production process. Included in this last category are such costs as indirect materials (e.g., paint, glue, and nails), indirect labor (such as the salaries of supervisors), factory rent, depreciation of plant assets, utilities costs, and insurance costs. The methods for maintaining and pricing inventory explained in this chapter are applicable to manufactured goods, but because the details of accounting for manufacturing companies are usually covered as a management accounting topic, this chapter focuses on accounting for merchandising firms.

APPLYING THE MATCHING RULE TO INVENTORIES

The American Institute of Certified Public Accountants states, "A major objective of accounting for inventories is the proper determination of income through the process of matching appropriate costs against revenues."[3] Note that the objective is the proper determination of income through the matching of costs and revenues, not the determination of the most realistic inventory value. These two objectives are sometimes incompatible, in which case the objective of income determination takes precedence.

KEY POINT: Merchandise inventory affects both the income statement and the balance sheet.

The reason inventory accounting is so important to income measurement is linked to the way income is measured on the merchandising income statement. Recall that gross margin is computed as the difference between net sales and cost of goods sold and that cost of goods sold is dependent on the cost assigned to inventory or goods not sold. Because of those relationships, the higher the cost of ending inventory, the lower the cost of goods sold and the higher the resulting gross margin. Conversely, the lower the value assigned to ending inventory, the higher the cost of goods sold and the lower the gross margin. Because the amount of gross margin has a direct effect on the amount of net income, the amount assigned to ending

J.C. Penney Company, Inc.
<www.jcpenney.com>

OBJECTIVES

■ To explain why merchandise inventories represent one of the most important assets of a retail company

■ To understand the difference between goods flow and cost flow

■ To identify and explain four methods of determining inventory cost

■ To define and explain the lower-of-cost-or-market (LCM) rule

BACKGROUND FOR THE CASE

J.C. Penney Company, Inc., as profiled in the Decision Point in this chapter, is a major department store retailer. Merchandise inventories represent a substantial portion of the company's assets. J.C. Penney stores sell fashion at value prices. The company's target customers fall in the middle of the American population. They have a household income ranging from $30,000 to $80,000. The company's goal is "to be the customer's first choice for its products and services." The company faces intense competition not only from other department stores like Sears <www.sears.com> or Macy's <www.macys.com>, but also from discount stores like Target <www.target.com> and specialty stores like The Limited <www.limitedbrands.com>. To a great extent,

J.C. Penney's future success depends on its ability to manage its inventory. Proper management of inventory has helped the company reduce its inventory (and total assets) and increase its level of retail sales, but the company still faces challenges. The company has announced plans to improve the profitability of its core department stores by further improving inventory management, controlling costs, and closing underperforming stores.

For more information about J.C. Penney Company, Inc., visit the company's web site through the Needles Accounting Resource Center Web Site at **http://accounting. college.hmco.com/students**.

REQUIRED

View the video on J.C. Penney Company, Inc., that accompanies this book. As you are watching the video, take notes related to the following questions:

1. Merchandise inventories make up more than 25 percent of J.C. Penney's assets. Explain how inventories affect the profitability of a retailer like J.C. Penney, and give both positive and negative reasons why the level of inventory is important to the company's operations.

2. Explain the difference between goods flow and cost flow as they relate to inventories, and tell which is more important in determining the cost of inventory.

3. Identify and explain the four methods of determining the cost of inventory available to J.C. Penney. Which method does J.C. Penney use?

4. What is the lower-of-cost-or-market (LCM) rule and why is it appropriate for J.C. Penney to use it? Why is LCM considered a conservative approach to inventory valuation?

inventory directly affects the amount of net income. In effect, the value assigned to the ending inventory determines what portion of the cost of goods available for sale is assigned to cost of goods sold and what portion is assigned to the balance sheet as inventory to be carried over into the next accounting period.

ASSESSING THE IMPACT OF INVENTORY DECISIONS

Figure 1 summarizes the choices management has with regard to inventory systems and methods. The decisions usually result in different amounts of reported net income. Thus, the choices affect both the external evaluation of the company by investors and creditors and such internal evaluations as performance reviews, which determine bonuses and executive compensation. Because income is affected, the valuation of inventory may also have a considerable effect on the amount of income taxes paid. Federal income tax authorities have specific regulations about the acceptability of different methods. As a result, management is sometimes faced with balancing the goal of proper income determination with that of minimizing income taxes. Another consideration is that since the choice of inventory valuation method affects the amount of income taxes paid, it also affects a company's cash flows.

FIGURE 1
**Management Choices in
Accounting for Inventories**

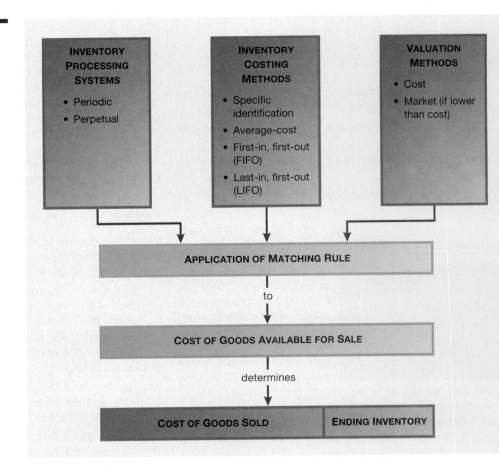

ENRICHMENT NOTE:
Management considers the
behavior of inventory prices
over time when selecting
inventory costing methods.

EVALUATING THE LEVEL OF INVENTORY

The level of inventory has important economic consequences for a company. Ideally, management wants to have a great variety and quantity on hand so that customers have a large choice and do not have to wait for an item to be restocked. Such an inventory policy is not costless, however. The cost of handling and storage and the interest cost of the funds necessary to maintain high inventory levels are usually substantial. On the other hand, low inventory levels may result in disgruntled customers and lost sales. Common measures used in the evaluation of inventory levels are inventory turnover and its related measure, average days' inventory on hand. **Inventory turnover** is a measure similar to receivable turnover. It indicates the number of times a company's average inventory is sold during an accounting period. Inventory turnover is computed by dividing cost of goods sold by average inventory.

ENRICHMENT NOTE:
Some of the costs associated
with carrying inventory are
insurance, property tax, and
storage costs. There is also the
possibility of additional
spoilage and employee theft.

FOCUS ON BUSINESS TECHNOLOGY

Dell's Inventory Turnover Can Make Your Head Spin.

Dell Computer <www.dell.com> turns its inventory every six days. How can it do this when other companies have inventory on hand for 60, 100, or even more days? Technology and good inventory management are a big part of the answer.

Dell's speed from order to delivery sets the industry standard. Consider that a computer ordered by 9 A.M. can be delivered the next day by 9 P.M. How can Dell do this when it doesn't start ordering components and assembling computers until an order is placed? First, Dell's suppliers keep components warehoused just minutes from Dell's factories, making efficient,

just-in-time operations possible. Another time and money saver is the handling of computer monitors. Monitors are no longer shipped first to Dell and then on to buyers. Dell sends an email message to a shipper, such as United Parcel Service <www.ups.com>, and the shipper picks up a monitor from a supplier and schedules it to arrive with the PC. In addition to contributing to a high inventory turnover, this practice saves Dell about $30 per monitor in freight costs. Dell is showing the world how to run a business in the cyber age by selling more than $1 million worth of computers a day on its web site.[4]

FIGURE 2
Inventory Turnover for Selected Industries

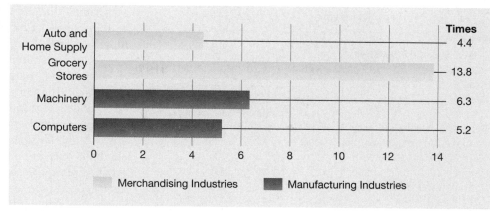

FIGURE 2
Inventory Turnover for Selected Industries

Source: Data from Dun & Bradstreet, *Industry Norms and Key Business Ratios,* 2000–2001.

ENRICHMENT NOTE:
Inventory turnover will be systematically higher if year-end inventory levels are low. For example, Toys "R" Us inventory levels on January 30 are at their lowest point of the year.

For example, J.C. Penney's cost of goods sold was $23,031 million in 2000, and its merchandise inventory was $5,269 million at the end of 2000 and $5,947 million at the end of 1999. Its inventory turnover is computed as follows:

$$\text{Inventory Turnover} = \frac{\text{Cost of Goods Sold}}{\text{Average Inventory}}$$

$$= \frac{\$23,031,000,000}{(\$5,269,000,000 + \$5,947,000,000) \div 2}$$

$$= \frac{\$23,031,000,000}{\$5,608,000,000} = 4.1 \text{ times}$$

The **average days' inventory on hand** indicates the average number of days required to sell the inventory on hand. It is found by dividing the number of days in a year by the inventory turnover, as follows:

$$\text{Average Days' Inventory on Hand} = \frac{\text{Number of Days in a Year}}{\text{Inventory Turnover}}$$

$$= \frac{365 \text{ days}}{4.1 \text{ times}} = 89.0 \text{ days}$$

● **STOP AND THINK!**
Is it good or bad for a retail store to have a large inventory?
It depends. Obviously, a large inventory means customers have choices, and they are less likely to be disappointed because the items they want are out of stock. On the other hand, maintaining a large inventory is expensive, and if the items do not sell, they may have to be sold at discount. The challenge to management is finding the right balance in size of inventory. ■

J.C. Penney turned its inventory over 4.1 times in 2000, or, on average, every 89.0 days. These figures represent an improvement over the previous two years, and they are also reasonable because J.C. Penney is in a business in which fashions change every season, or about every 100 days. Management wants to sell all of each season's inventory within 90 days, even while purchasing inventory for the next season.

There are natural levels of inventory in every industry, as shown for selected merchandising and manufacturing industries in Figures 2 and 3. Nonetheless,

FIGURE 3
Average Days' Inventory on Hand for Selected Industries

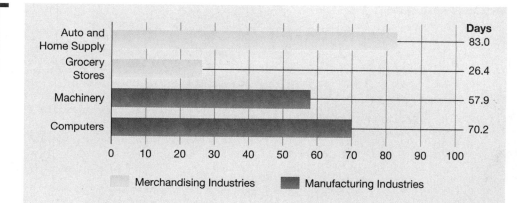

FIGURE 3
Average Days' Inventory on Hand for Selected Industries

Source: Data from Dun & Bradstreet, *Industry Norms and Key Business Ratios,* 2000–2001.

FOCUS ON BUSINESS PRACTICE

What a Headache!

A single seat belt can have as many as 50 parts, and getting them from suppliers used to be a big problem for Autoliv, Inc. <www.autoliv.com>, a Swedish maker of auto safety devices. Autoliv's plant in Indianapolis was encountering constant bottlenecks in dealing with 125 different suppliers. To keep the production lines going required high-priced, rush shipments on a daily basis. To solve the problem, the company began using supply-chain management, keeping in touch with suppliers through the Internet rather than through faxes and phone calls. The new system allows suppliers to monitor the inventory at Autoliv and thus to anticipate problems. It also provides information on quantity and time of recent shipments, as well as continuously updated forecasts of parts that will be needed in the next 12 weeks. With the new system, Autoliv has reduced inventory by 75 percent and rush freight costs by 95 percent.[5]

companies that are able to maintain their inventories at lower levels and still satisfy customer needs are the most successful.

To reduce their levels of inventory, many merchandising and manufacturing companies use supply-chain management in conjunction with a just-in-time operating environment. With **supply-chain management**, a company manages its inventory and purchasing through business-to-business transactions that it conducts over the Internet. In a **just-in-time operating environment**, the company works closely with suppliers to coordinate and schedule shipments so that the shipments arrive just at the time they are needed. The benefits of using supply-chain management in a just-in-time operating environment are that the company has less money tied up in inventory, and the cost associated with carrying the inventory is reduced.

✓ Check out ACE for a Review Quiz at http://accounting.college.hmco.com/students.

INVENTORY COST AND GOODS FLOW

LO2 Define *inventory cost* and relate it to goods flow and cost flow.

RELATED TEXT ASSIGNMENTS
Q: 4, 5, 6
SD: 5
FRA: 1

BUSINESS-WORLD EXAMPLE: When customers order merchandise from a catalogue company, they pay not only the price listed in the catalogue, but also such charges as shipping and insurance. Consequently, the cost is greater than the catalogue price.

According to the AICPA, "The primary basis of accounting for inventories is cost, which has been defined generally as the price paid or consideration given to acquire an asset."[6] This definition of **inventory cost** has generally been interpreted as including the following costs: (1) invoice price less purchases discounts; (2) freight in, including insurance in transit; and (3) applicable taxes and tariffs. There are other costs—for ordering, receiving, and storing—that should in principle also be included in inventory cost. In practice, however, it is so difficult to allocate such costs to specific inventory items that they are usually considered expenses of the accounting period rather than inventory costs.

MERCHANDISE IN TRANSIT

Because merchandise inventory includes all items owned by a company and held for sale, the status of any merchandise in transit, whether the company is selling it or buying it, must be examined to determine if the merchandise should be included in the inventory count. As Figure 4 illustrates, neither the seller nor the buyer has *phys-*

FIGURE 4
Merchandise in Transit

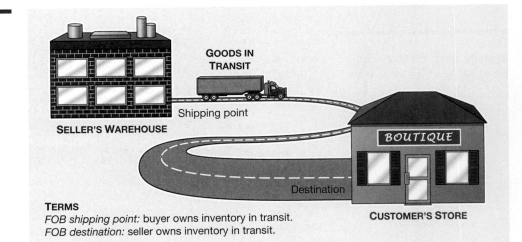

TERMS
FOB shipping point: buyer owns inventory in transit.
FOB destination: seller owns inventory in transit.

ical possession of merchandise in transit. Ownership of goods in transit is determined by the terms of the shipping agreement, which indicate when title passes. Outgoing goods shipped FOB (free on board) destination would be included in the seller's merchandise inventory, whereas those shipped FOB shipping point would not. Conversely, incoming goods shipped FOB shipping point would be included in the buyer's merchandise inventory, but those shipped FOB destination would not.

MERCHANDISE ON HAND NOT INCLUDED IN INVENTORY

KEY POINT: The consignor will count as inventory all merchandise placed (consigned) at other locations.

At the time a company takes a physical inventory, it may have merchandise on hand to which it does not hold title. One category of such goods is merchandise that has been sold and is awaiting delivery to the buyer. Since the sale has been completed, title to the goods has passed to the buyer, and the merchandise should be included in the inventory of the buyer, not of the seller. A second category is goods held on consignment. A **consignment** is merchandise that its owner (known as the *consignor*) places on the premises of another company (the *consignee*) with the understanding that payment is expected only when the merchandise is sold and that unsold items may be returned to the consignor. Title to consigned goods remains with the consignor until the consignee sells the goods. Consigned goods should not be included in the physical inventory of the consignee because they still belong to the consignor.

GOODS FLOW VERSUS COST FLOW

KEY POINT: The assumed flow of costs for inventory pricing does not have to correspond to the natural flow of goods.

The prices of most kinds of merchandise vary during the year. Identical lots of merchandise may have been purchased at different prices. Also, when identical items are bought and sold, it is often impossible to tell which have been sold and which are still in inventory. It is therefore necessary to make an assumption about the order in which items have been sold. Because the assumed order of sale may or may not be the same as the actual order of sale, the assumption is really about the *flow of costs* rather than the *flow of physical inventory*.

⬤ **STOP AND THINK!**

Which is more important from the standpoint of inventory costing: the flow of goods or the flow of costs?

Flow of costs is more important because inventory costing ignores the actual flow of goods and assumes a flow of costs. ∎

The term **goods flow** refers to the actual physical movement of goods in the operations of a company, and the term **cost flow** refers to the association of costs with their *assumed* flow in the operations of a company. The assumed cost flow may or may not be the same as the actual goods flow. The possibility of a difference between cost flow and goods flow may seem strange at first, but it arises because several choices of assumed cost flow are available under generally accepted accounting principles. In fact, it is sometimes preferable to use an assumed cost flow that bears no relationship to goods flow because it gives a better estimate of income, which is the main goal of inventory valuation.

✓ Check out ACE for a Review Quiz at http://accounting.college.hmco.com/students.

METHODS OF PRICING INVENTORY AT COST UNDER THE PERIODIC INVENTORY SYSTEM

LO3 Calculate the pricing of inventory, using the cost basis under the periodic inventory system.

RELATED TEXT ASSIGNMENTS
Q: 7, 8, 9
SE: 3, 4, 5, 6,
E: 3, 4, 5, 7, 9
P: 1, 2, 6, 7
SD: 7

The value assigned to ending inventory is the result of two measurements: quantity and price. Quantity is determined by taking a physical inventory. The pricing of inventory is usually based on the assumed cost flow of the goods as they are bought and sold.

Accountants usually price inventory by using one of the following generally accepted methods, each based on a different assumption of cost flow: (1) specific identification method; (2) average-cost method; (3) first-in, first-out (FIFO) method; and (4) last-in, first-out (LIFO) method. The choice of method depends on the nature of the business, the financial effects of the method, and the cost of implementing the method.

To illustrate the four methods under the periodic inventory system, we use the following data for the month of June:

Inventory Data—June 30

June	1	Inventory	50 units @ $1.00	$ 50
	6	Purchase	50 units @ $1.10	55
	13	Purchase	150 units @ $1.20	180
	20	Purchase	100 units @ $1.30	130
	25	Purchase	150 units @ $1.40	210
Goods available for sale			500 units	$625
Sales			280 units	
On hand June 30			220 units	

Notice that a total of 500 units is available for sale at a total cost of $625. Stated simply, the problem of inventory pricing is to divide the $625 between the 280 units sold and the 220 units on hand. Recall that under the periodic inventory system, the inventory is not updated after each purchase and sale. Thus, it is not necessary to know when the individual sales take place.

SPECIFIC IDENTIFICATION METHOD

If the units in the ending inventory can be identified as coming from specific purchases, the **specific identification method** may be used. This method prices the inventory by identifying the cost of each item in ending inventory. For instance, assume that the June 30 inventory consisted of 50 units from the June 1 inventory, 100 units from the purchase of June 13, and 70 units from the purchase of June 25. The cost assigned to the inventory under the specific identification method would be $268, determined as follows:

Periodic Inventory System—Specific Identification Method

50 units @ $1.00	$ 50	Cost of goods available	
100 units @ $1.20	120	for sale	$625
70 units @ $1.40	98	Less June 30 inventory	268
220 units at a cost of	$268	Cost of goods sold	$357

BUSINESS-WORLD EXAMPLE: Even if it were possible to track each individual inventory item, a company would not do so because it would be excessively expensive to track which items were left in inventory. The cost would clearly exceed the benefit.

The specific identification method may appear logical, and it might be used in the purchase and sale of high-priced articles, such as automobiles and works of art, but it is not used by many companies because of two definite disadvantages. First, it is often difficult and impractical to keep track of the purchase and sale of individual items. Second, when a company deals in items that are identical but that it bought at different costs, deciding which items were sold becomes arbitrary; thus, the company can raise or lower income by choosing the lower- or higher-cost items.

AVERAGE-COST METHOD

Under the **average-cost method**, inventory is priced at the average cost of the goods available for sale during the period. Average cost is computed by dividing the total cost of goods available for sale by the total units available for sale. This gives an average unit cost that is applied to the units in ending inventory. In our illustration, the ending inventory would be $275, or $1.25 per unit, determined as follows:

Periodic Inventory System—Average-Cost Method

Cost of Goods Available for Sale ÷ Units Available for Sale = Average Unit Cost

$625 ÷ 500 units = $1.25

Ending inventory: 220 units @ $1.25 =	$275
Cost of goods available for sale	$625
Less June 30 inventory	275
Cost of goods sold	$350

The average-cost method tends to level out the effects of cost increases and decreases because the cost for the ending inventory calculated under this method is influenced by all the prices paid during the year and by the beginning inventory price. Some, however, criticize the average-cost method because they believe recent costs are more relevant for income measurement and decision making.

FIRST-IN, FIRST-OUT (FIFO) METHOD

The **first-in, first-out (FIFO) method** is based on the assumption that the costs of the first items acquired should be assigned to the first items sold. The costs of the goods on hand at the end of a period are assumed to be from the most recent purchases, and the costs assigned to goods that have been sold are assumed to be from beginning inventory and the earliest purchases. The FIFO method of determining inventory cost may be adopted by any business, regardless of the actual physical flow of goods, because the assumption is made regarding the flow of costs and not the flow of goods.

In our illustration, the June 30 inventory would be $301 when the FIFO method is used. It is computed as follows:

Periodic Inventory System—First-In, First-Out Method

150 units @ $1.40 from purchase of June 25	$210
70 units @ $1.30 from purchase of June 20	91
220 units at a cost of	$301
Cost of goods available for sale	$625
Less June 30 inventory	301
Cost of goods sold	$324

The effect of the FIFO method is to value the ending inventory at the most recent costs and include earlier costs in cost of goods sold. During periods of consistently rising prices, the FIFO method yields the highest possible amount of net income because cost of goods sold will show the earliest costs incurred, which are lower during periods of inflation. Another reason for this result is that businesses tend to increase selling prices as costs rise, even when inventories were purchased before the price rise. The reverse effect occurs in periods of price decreases. Consequently, a major criticism of FIFO is that it magnifies the effects of the business cycle on income.

LAST-IN, FIRST-OUT (LIFO) METHOD

The **last-in, first-out (LIFO) method** of costing inventories is based on the assumption that the costs of the last items purchased should be assigned to the first items sold and that the cost of ending inventory reflects the cost of the merchandise purchased earliest.

Under this method, the June 30 inventory would be $249, computed as follows:

Periodic Inventory System—Last-In, First-Out Method

50 units @ $1.00 from June 1 inventory	$ 50
50 units @ $1.10 from purchase of June 6	55
120 units @ $1.20 from purchase of June 13	144
220 units at a cost of	$249
Cost of goods available for sale	$625
Less June 30 inventory	249
Cost of goods sold	$376

The effect of LIFO is to value inventory at the earliest prices and to include in cost of goods sold the cost of the most recently purchased goods. This assumption, of course, does not agree with the actual physical movement of goods in most businesses.

BUSINESS-WORLD EXAMPLE: The physical flow of goods may sometimes seem to dictate a particular method, such as in a milk producer's operations in which the perishable nature of the product apparently requires a *physical flow* of FIFO. However, the milk producer's management can choose an inventory method based on an assumed *cost flow* that differs from FIFO, such as average-cost or LIFO.

ENRICHMENT NOTE: When you make a FIFO cost flow assumption, you use it even if you can prove that one of the first-purchased items is still in inventory. Let's say that for the first week of January, perfume was packaged in blue boxes, and then the company changed to red packaging. When you price inventory using the FIFO method, you assume the blue boxes (the older merchandise) were sold, even if you have some of them left in inventory.

BUSINESS-WORLD EXAMPLE: Physical flow under LIFO can be likened to the changes in a gravel pile. As gravel on top is sold, more is purchased and added on top. The gravel on the bottom may never be sold. Despite the physical flow of LIFO, any acceptable cost flow assumption may be made.

FIGURE 5
Impact of Cost Flow Assumptions on the Income Statement and Balance Sheet Using the Periodic Inventory System

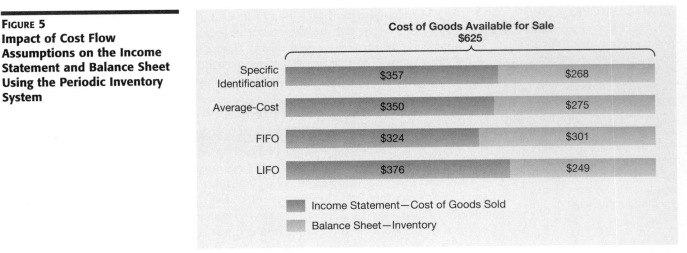

There is, however, a strong logical argument to support LIFO, based on the fact that a certain size of inventory is necessary in a going concern. When inventory is sold, it must be replaced with more goods. The supporters of LIFO reason that the fairest determination of income occurs if the current costs of merchandise are matched against current sales prices, regardless of which physical units of merchandise are sold. When prices are moving either upward or downward, the cost of goods sold will, under LIFO, show costs closer to the price level at the time the goods were sold. As a result, the LIFO method tends to show a smaller net income during inflationary times and a larger net income during deflationary times than other methods of inventory valuation. The peaks and valleys of the business cycle tend to be smoothed out. In inventory valuation, the flow of costs—and hence income determination—is more important than the physical movement of goods and balance sheet valuation.

An argument may also be made against LIFO. Because the inventory valuation on the balance sheet reflects earlier prices, it often gives an unrealistic picture of the current value of the inventory. Such balance sheet measures as working capital and current ratio may be distorted and must be interpreted carefully.

Figure 5 summarizes the impact of the four inventory cost allocation methods on the cost of goods sold as reported on the income statement and on inventory as reported on the balance sheet when a company uses the periodic inventory system. In periods of rising prices, the FIFO method yields the highest inventory valuation, the lowest cost of goods sold, and hence a higher net income; the LIFO method yields the lowest inventory valuation, the highest cost of goods sold, and thus a lower net income.

✔ Check out ACE for a Review Quiz at http://accounting.college.hmco.com/students.

⬥ **STOP AND THINK!**
Under what condition would all four methods of inventory pricing produce exactly the same results?
They would produce the same results if there were no price changes after the purchase of beginning inventory. ■

FOCUS ON BUSINESS PRACTICE

What's a "Category Killer?"

A new type of retail company called the "category killer" seems to ignore the tenets of good inventory management. The category killers include Home Depot <www.homedepot.com>, Barnes & Noble <www.bn.com>, Wal-Mart <www.walmart.com>, Toys "R" Us <www.tru.com>, and Blockbuster Entertainment Corporation <www.blockbuster.com>. These retailers maintain huge inventories of the goods in which they specialize and sell them at such low prices that smaller competitors find it hard to compete. Although the category killers have large amounts of money tied up in inventories, they maintain very sophisticated just-in-time operating environments that require suppliers to meet demanding standards for delivery of products and reduction of inventory costs. Some suppliers are required to stock the shelves and keep track of inventory levels. By minimizing handling and overhead costs and buying at favorably low prices, the category killers achieve great success.

PRICING INVENTORY UNDER THE PERPETUAL INVENTORY SYSTEM

LO4 Apply the perpetual inventory system to the pricing of inventories at cost.

RELATED TEXT ASSIGNMENTS

Q: 10
SE: 7, 8, 9
E: 6, 7
P: 3, 8
SD: 5

The pricing of inventories under the perpetual inventory system differs from pricing under the periodic inventory system. The difference occurs because under the perpetual inventory system, a continuous record of quantities and costs of merchandise is maintained as purchases and sales are made. Under the periodic inventory system, only the ending inventory is counted and priced, and cost of goods sold is determined by deducting the cost of the ending inventory from the cost of goods available for sale. Under the perpetual inventory system, cost of goods sold is accumulated as sales are made and costs are transferred from the Inventory account to the Cost of Goods Sold account. The cost of the ending inventory is the balance of the Inventory account. To illustrate pricing methods under the perpetual inventory system, we use the same data as in the last section, but we add specific sales dates and amounts, as follows:

Inventory Data—June 30

June	1	Inventory	50 units @ $1.00
	6	Purchase	50 units @ $1.10
	10	Sale	70 units
	13	Purchase	150 units @ $1.20
	20	Purchase	100 units @ $1.30
	25	Purchase	150 units @ $1.40
	30	Sale	210 units
	30	Inventory	220 units

Pricing the inventory and cost of goods sold using the specific identification method is the same under the perpetual system as under the periodic system because cost of goods sold and ending inventory are based on the cost of the identified items sold and on hand. The perpetual system facilitates the use of the specific identification method because detailed records of purchases and sales are maintained.

Pricing the inventory and cost of goods sold using the average-cost method differs when the perpetual system is used. Under the periodic system, the average cost is computed for all goods available for sale during the month. Under the perpetual system, an average is computed after each purchase or series of purchases, as follows:

ENRICHMENT NOTE: An automated perpetual system has considerable costs. They include the costs of automating the system, maintaining the system, and taking a physical inventory to check against the perpetual records.

Perpetual Inventory System—Average-Cost Method

June	1	Inventory	50 units @ $1.00	$ 50.00
	6	Purchase	50 units @ $1.10	55.00
	6	Balance	100 units @ $1.05	$105.00
	10	Sale	70 units @ $1.05	(73.50)
	10	Balance	30 units @ $1.05	$ 31.50
	13	Purchase	150 units @ $1.20	180.00
	20	Purchase	100 units @ $1.30	130.00
	25	Purchase	150 units @ $1.40	210.00
	25	Balance	430 units @ $1.28*	$551.50
	30	Sale	210 units @ $1.28	(268.80)
	30	Inventory	220 units @ $1.29*	$282.70
Cost of goods sold			($73.50 + $268.80)	$342.30

*Rounded.

◆ **STOP AND THINK!**

Under the perpetual inventory system, why is the cost of goods sold not determined by deducting the ending inventory from goods available for sale, as it is under the periodic method?

Under the perpetual inventory system, the cost of goods sold and the inventory balance are determined after every transaction. ■

The sum of the costs applied to sales becomes the cost of goods sold, $342.30. The ending inventory is the balance, or $282.70.

When pricing the inventory using the FIFO and LIFO methods, it is necessary to keep track of the components of inventory at each step of the way because as sales are made, the costs must be assigned in the proper order. To apply the FIFO method, the approach is as follows:

Perpetual Inventory System—FIFO Method

June	1	Inventory	50 units @ $1.00		$ 50.00
	6	Purchase	50 units @ $1.10		55.00
	10	Sale	50 units @ $1.00	($ 50.00)	
			20 units @ $1.10	(22.00)	(72.00)
	10	Balance	30 units @ $1.10		$ 33.00
	13	Purchase	150 units @ $1.20		180.00
	20	Purchase	100 units @ $1.30		130.00
	25	Purchase	150 units @ $1.40		210.00
	30	Sale	30 units @ $1.10	($ 33.00)	
			150 units @ $1.20	(180.00)	
			30 units @ $1.30	(39.00)	(252.00)
	30	Inventory	70 units @ $1.30	$ 91.00	
			150 units @ $1.40	210.00	$301.00
Cost of goods sold			($72.00 + $252.00)		$324.00

Note that the ending inventory of $301 and the cost of goods sold of $324 are the same as the figures computed earlier under the periodic inventory system. This will always occur because the ending inventory under both systems consists of the last items purchased—in this case, the entire purchase of June 25 and 70 units from the purchase of June 20.

To apply the LIFO method, the approach is as follows:

Perpetual Inventory System—LIFO Method

June	1	Inventory	50 units @ $1.00		$ 50.00
	6	Purchase	50 units @ $1.10		55.00
	10	Sale	50 units @ $1.10	($ 55.00)	
			20 units @ $1.00	(20.00)	(75.00)
	10	Balance	30 units @ $1.00		$ 30.00
	13	Purchase	150 units @ $1.20		180.00
	20	Purchase	100 units @ $1.30		130.00
	25	Purchase	150 units @ $1.40		210.00
	30	Sale	150 units @ $1.40	($210.00)	
			60 units @ $1.30	(78.00)	(288.00)
	30	Inventory	30 units @ $1.00	$ 30.00	
			150 units @ $1.20	180.00	
			40 units @ $1.30	52.00	$262.00
Cost of goods sold			($75.00 + $288.00)		$363.00

Notice that the ending inventory of $262 includes 30 units from the beginning inventory, all the units from the purchase of June 13, and 40 units from the purchase of June 20.

A comparison of the average-cost, FIFO, and LIFO methods using the perpetual inventory system is shown in Figure 6. The results are the same as under the periodic inventory system, but some amounts have changed. For example, LIFO has

FOCUS ON BUSINESS TECHNOLOGY

More Companies Enjoy LIFO!

Using the LIFO method under the perpetual inventory system is a tedious process, especially if done manually. The development of faster and less expensive computer systems has made it easier for many companies to switch to LIFO and still use the perpetual inventory system. The availability of better technology may partially account for the increasing use of LIFO in the United States and may enable more companies to enjoy LIFO's economic benefits.

FIGURE 6
Impact of Cost Flow Assumptions on the Income Statement and Balance Sheet Using the Perpetual Inventory System

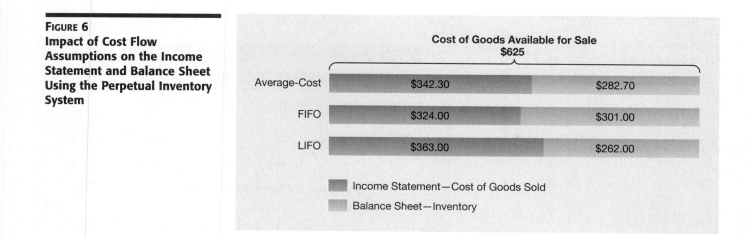

Cost of Goods Available for Sale
$625

Average-Cost	$342.30	$282.70
FIFO	$324.00	$301.00
LIFO	$363.00	$262.00

▮ Income Statement—Cost of Goods Sold

▮ Balance Sheet—Inventory

the lowest inventory valuation regardless of the inventory system used, but the amount is $262 using the perpetual system versus $249 using the periodic system.

✓ Check out ACE for a Review Quiz at http://accounting.college.hmco.com/students.

COMPARISON AND IMPACT OF INVENTORY DECISIONS AND MISSTATEMENTS

LO5 State the effects of inventory methods and misstatements of inventory on income determination, income taxes, and cash flows.

RELATED TEXT ASSIGNMENTS
Q: 11, 12, 13, 14
SE: 10
E: 8, 9, 10
SD: 2, 4, 6, 7
FRA: 1, 2, 3, 4, 5, 8

Exhibit 1 shows how the specific identification, average-cost, FIFO, and LIFO methods of pricing inventory under both the periodic and the perpetual inventory systems affect gross margin. The exhibit uses the same data as before and assumes June sales of $500. Because the specific identification method is based on actual cost, it is the same under both systems.

Keeping in mind that June was a period of rising prices, we can see that LIFO, which charges the most recent, and, in this case, the highest, prices to cost of goods sold, resulted in the lowest gross margin under both systems. Conversely, FIFO, which charges the earliest, and, in this case, the lowest, prices to cost of goods sold,

EXHIBIT 1
Effects of Inventory Systems and Costing Methods on Gross Margin

	Specific Identification Method	Periodic Inventory System Average-Cost Method	First-In, First-Out Method	Last-In, First-Out Method	Perpetual Inventory System* Average-Cost Method	First-In, First-Out Method	Last-In, First-Out Method
Sales	$500	$500	$500	$500	$500	$500	$500
Cost of goods sold							
Beginning inventory	$ 50	$ 50	$ 50	$ 50			
Purchases	575	575	575	575			
Cost of goods available for sale	$625	$625	$625	$625			
Less ending inventory	268	275	301	249	$283†	$301	$262
Cost of goods sold	$357	$350	$324	$376	$342†	$324	$363
Gross margin	$143	$150	$176	$124	$158	$176	$137

*Ending inventory under the perpetual inventory system is provided for comparison only. It is not used in the computation of cost of goods sold.
†Rounded.

FIGURE 7
Inventory Costing Methods
Used by 600 Large Companies

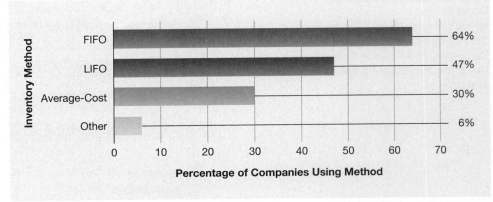

Total percentage exceeds 100 because some companies used different methods for different types of inventory.
Source: "Inventory Costing Methods Used by 600 Large Companies," from *Accounting Trends & Techniques.*
Copyright © 2001 by the American Institute of Certified Public Accountants, Inc. Reprinted with permission.

produced the highest gross margin. The gross margin under the average-cost method is in between the gross margins under LIFO and FIFO. Thus, it is clear that the average-cost method has a less pronounced effect. Note that ending inventory and gross margin under FIFO are the same under both the periodic and the perpetual inventory systems.

During a period of declining prices, the reverse would occur. The LIFO method would produce a higher gross margin than the FIFO method. It is apparent that the method of inventory valuation has the greatest importance during prolonged periods of price changes in one direction, either up or down.

Because the specific identification method depends on the particular items sold, no generalization can be made about the effect of changing prices.

EFFECTS ON THE FINANCIAL STATEMENTS

KEY POINT: The assumption of inventory cost flows is necessary because of changes in merchandise prices.

Each of the four methods of inventory pricing is acceptable for use in published financial statements. The FIFO, LIFO, and average-cost methods are widely used, as can be seen in Figure 7, which shows the inventory costing methods used by 600 large companies. Each method has its advantages and disadvantages, and none can be considered best or perfect. The factors that should be considered in choosing an inventory method are the trend of prices and the effects of each method on financial statements, income taxes, and cash flows.

A basic problem in determining the best inventory measure for a particular company is that inventory affects both the balance sheet and the income statement. As we have seen, the LIFO method is best suited for the income statement because it matches revenues and cost of goods sold. But it is not the best measure of the current balance sheet value of inventory, particularly during a prolonged period of price increases or decreases. FIFO, on the other hand, is best suited to the balance sheet because the ending inventory is closest to current values and thus gives a more realistic view of the current financial assets of a business. Readers of financial statements must be alert to inventory methods and be able to assess their effects.

EFFECTS ON INCOME TAXES

The Internal Revenue Service has developed several rules for valuing inventories for federal income tax purposes. A company has a wide choice of methods, including specific identification, average-cost, FIFO, and LIFO, as well as lower-of-cost-or-market, discussed later in the chapter. But once a method has been chosen, it must be used consistently from one year to the next. The IRS must approve any change in the inventory valuation method for income tax purposes.* This requirement

*A single exception to this rule is that although taxpayers must notify the IRS of a change to LIFO from another method, they do not need to have advance IRS approval.

FOCUS ON BUSINESS PRACTICE

Does a Company's Accounting Method Affect Management's Operating Decisions?

It certainly does when taxes are involved! Research has shown that among firms that use the LIFO inventory method, those with high tax rates are more likely to buy extra inventory at year end than are those with low tax rates.[7] This behavior is predictable because LIFO deducts the most recent purchases, which are likely to have higher costs than earlier purchases, in determining taxable income. This action will result in lower income taxes.

KEY POINT: In periods of rising prices, LIFO results in lower net income and thus lower taxes.

agrees with the consistency convention in accounting, since changes in inventory method may cause income to fluctuate too much and would make income statements hard to interpret from year to year. A company may change its inventory method if there is a good reason for doing so. The nature and effect of the change must be shown on the company's financial statements.

Many accountants believe that using the FIFO and average-cost methods in periods of rising prices causes businesses to report more than their true profit, resulting in the payment of excess income taxes. The profit is overstated because cost of goods sold is understated relative to current prices. The company must buy replacement inventory at higher prices, but additional funds are also needed to pay income taxes. During the rapid inflation of 1979 to 1982, billions of dollars reported as profits and paid in income taxes were believed to be the result of poor matching of current costs and revenues under the FIFO and average-cost methods. Consequently, many companies, believing that prices would continue to rise, switched to the LIFO inventory method.

If a company uses the LIFO method in reporting income for tax purposes, the IRS requires that the same method be used in the accounting records. Also, the IRS will not allow the use of the lower-of-cost-or-market rule if LIFO is used to determine inventory cost. In such a case, only the LIFO cost can be used. This rule, however, does not preclude a company from using lower-of-LIFO-cost-or-market for financial reporting purposes (discussed later in this chapter).

Over a period of rising prices, a business that uses the LIFO method may find that for balance sheet purposes, its inventory is valued at a cost figure far below what it currently pays for the same items. Management must monitor this situation carefully, because if it should let the inventory quantity at year end fall below the beginning-of-the-year level, the company will find itself paying higher income taxes. Higher income before taxes results because the company expenses historical costs of inventory, which are below current costs. When this occurs, it is called a **LIFO liquidation** because sales have reduced inventories below the levels set in prior years; that is, units sold exceed units purchased for the period.

A LIFO liquidation may be prevented by making enough purchases prior to year end to restore the desired inventory level. Sometimes a LIFO liquidation cannot be avoided because products are discontinued or supplies are interrupted, as in the case of a strike. In a recent year, 26 out of 600 large companies reported a LIFO liquidation in which net income was increased because of the matching of older historical cost with present sales dollars.[8]

EFFECTS OF MISSTATEMENTS IN INVENTORY MEASUREMENT

The basic problem of separating goods available for sale into two components—goods sold and goods not sold—is that of assigning a cost to the goods not sold, the ending inventory. The portion of the goods available for sale not assigned to the ending inventory is used to determine the cost of goods sold.

Because the figures for ending inventory and cost of goods sold are related, a misstatement in the inventory figure at the end of the period will cause an equal misstatement in gross margin and income before income taxes in the income statement. The amount of assets and owners' equity on the balance sheet will also be misstated by the same amount. The consequences of overstatement and understatement of inventory are illustrated in the three simplified examples that follow. In each case, beginning inventory, net cost of purchases, and cost of goods available for sale have been stated correctly. In the first example, ending inventory has been stated correctly. In the second example, ending inventory is overstated by $6,000; in the third example, ending inventory is understated by $6,000.

Example 1. Ending Inventory Correctly Stated at $10,000

Cost of Goods Sold for the Year		Income Statement for the Year	
Beginning inventory	$12,000	Net sales	$100,000
Net cost of purchases	58,000	Cost of goods sold	60,000
Cost of goods available for sale	$70,000	Gross margin	$ 40,000
Ending inventory	10,000	Operating expenses	32,000
		Income before income	
Cost of goods sold	$60,000	taxes	$ 8,000

Example 2. Ending Inventory Overstated by $6,000

Cost of Goods Sold for the Year		Income Statement for the Year	
Beginning inventory	$12,000	Net sales	$100,000
Net cost of purchases	58,000	Cost of goods sold	54,000
Cost of goods available for sale	$70,000	Gross margin	$ 46,000
Ending inventory	16,000	Operating expenses	32,000
		Income before income	
Cost of goods sold	$54,000	taxes	$ 14,000

Example 3. Ending Inventory Understated by $6,000

Cost of Goods Sold for the Year		Income Statement for the Year	
Beginning inventory	$12,000	Net sales	$100,000
Net cost of purchases	58,000	Cost of goods sold	66,000
Cost of goods available for sale	$70,000	Gross margin	$ 34,000
Ending inventory	4,000	Operating expenses	32,000
		Income before income	
Cost of goods sold	$66,000	taxes	$ 2,000

KEY POINT: A misstatement in inventory affects not only the current year, but also has the opposite effect on the next year.

KEY POINT: Inventory errors will correct (counterbalance) themselves over a two-year period.

In all three examples, the total cost of goods available for sale was $70,000. The difference in income before income taxes resulted from how this $70,000 was divided between ending inventory and cost of goods sold.

Because the ending inventory in one period becomes the beginning inventory in the following period, it is important to recognize that a misstatement in inventory valuation affects not only the current period but also the following period. Over a two-year period, the errors in income before income taxes will offset, or counterbalance, each other. If we assume that Example 2, represents year 1, for instance, the overstatement of ending inventory in year 1 will cause a $6,000 overstatement of beginning inventory in year 2, resulting in an understatement of income by $6,000 in the second year.

FOCUS ON BUSINESS ETHICS

The Temptation to Overstate Inventories

Net income can be easily manipulated when accounting for inventory. For example, it is easy to overstate or understate inventory by including end-of-the-year purchase and sales transactions in the wrong fiscal year or by simply misstating inventory. In one spectacular case, Rite Aid Corp. <www.riteaid.com>, the large drugstore chain, falsified income by manipulating its computerized inventory system to cover losses from shrinkage, which includes shoplifting, employee theft, and spoilage. In another case, bookkeepers at RentWay, Inc. <www.rentway.com>, a company that rents furniture to apartment dwellers, boosted income artificially over several years by overstating inventory in small increments that were not noticed by top management.[9]

◆ **STOP AND THINK!**

Why is misstatement of inventory one of the most common means of financial statement fraud?

For one thing, the value put on inventory has a direct dollar-for-dollar effect on net income. For another, it is relatively easy to falsify the value placed on the ending inventory and to cover up the falsification. ■

Because the total income before income taxes for the two years is the same, it may appear that one need not worry about inventory misstatements. However, the misstatements violate the matching rule. In addition, management, creditors, and investors make many decisions on an annual basis and depend on the accountant's determination of net income. The accountant has an obligation to make the net income figure for each year as useful as possible.

The effects of misstatements in inventory on income before income taxes are as follows:

Year 1	Year 2
Ending inventory overstated	**Beginning inventory overstated**
Cost of goods sold understated	Cost of goods sold overstated
Income before income taxes overstated	Income before income taxes understated
Ending inventory understated	**Beginning inventory understated**
Cost of goods sold overstated	Cost of goods sold understated
Income before income taxes understated	Income before income taxes overstated

A misstatement in inventory results in a misstatement in income before income taxes of the same amount. Thus, the measurement of inventory is important.

INVENTORY MEASUREMENT AND CASH FLOWS

www.internationalpaper.com

A company's inventory methods affect not only its reported profitability but also its reported liquidity and cash flows. In the case of a large company like International Paper Co., these effects can be complex and material. In a note on inventories, International Paper provides more detail about these effects:

> The last-in, first-out inventory method is used to value most of International Paper's U.S. inventories. Approximately 68% of total raw materials and finished products inventories were valued using this method. If the first-in, first-out method had been used, it would have increased total inventory balances by approximately $264 million and $250 million at December 31, 2000 and 1999, respectively.[10]

By using LIFO, the company usually reports a lower income before taxes. This will have a favorable effect on cash flows because of the lower amount of income taxes to be paid. The reader of the financial statements may determine what International Paper's inventory value would have been if it were valued at current prices under FIFO rather than older prices under LIFO. Thus, a more realistic comparison of the company's liquidity ratios can be made. For example, the more realistic FIFO figure would show a better short-term liquidity position as measured by the current ratio than the LIFO figures reported on the balance sheet would seem to indicate. However, the company's inventory turnover and average days' inventory on hand will be adversely affected if the more realistic FIFO figures are used.

✓ Check out ACE for a Review Quiz at http://accounting.college.hmco.com/students.

VALUING INVENTORY AT THE LOWER OF COST OR MARKET (LCM)

LO6 Apply the lower-of-cost-or-market (LCM) rule to inventory valuation.

RELATED TEXT ASSIGNMENTS
Q: 15, 16
SE: 11
E: 11
SD: 3
FRA: 5

Although cost is usually the most appropriate basis for valuation of inventory, there are times when inventory may properly be shown in the financial statements at less than its cost. If the market value of inventory falls below its cost because of physical deterioration, obsolescence, or decline in price level, a loss has occurred. This loss may be recognized by writing the inventory down to **market**, or current replacement cost, of inventory. For a merchandising company, market is the amount that the company would pay at the present time for the same goods, purchased from the usual suppliers and in the usual quantities. The **lower-of-cost-or-market (LCM) rule**

FOCUS ON BUSINESS PRACTICE

How Bad Can It Get?

Pretty bad! When the lower-of-cost-or-market rule comes into play, it can be an indicator of how bad. For example, when the market for Internet and telecommunications equipment soured in 2001, Cisco Systems, Inc. <www.cisco.com>, found itself faced with probably the largest inventory loss in history. It had to write down to zero almost two-thirds of its $2.5 billion inventory, 80 percent of which consisted of raw materials that would never be made into final product. In another case, through poor management, a downturn in the economy, and underperforming stores, Kmart <www.kmartcorp.com> found itself with a huge amount of excess merchandise, including more than 5,000 truckloads of goods stored in parking lots, which it could not sell except at drastically reduced prices. The company had to mark down its inventory by $1 billion in order to sell it, resulting in a loss for the year.[12]

⬤ **STOP AND THINK!**

Given that the LCM rule is an application of the conservatism convention in the current accounting period, is the effect of this application also conservative in the next period?

It probably is not because a reduction in inventory in the current period resulting in lower net income will cause the beginning inventory in the next period to be smaller and will thus increase income in that period. ∎

STUDY NOTE: Cost must first be determined by the specific identification, FIFO, LIFO, or average-cost method before it can be compared with replacement cost.

requires that when the replacement cost of inventory falls below historical cost, based on one of the conventional inventory costing methods, the inventory is written down to the lower value and a loss is recorded. This rule is an example of the application of the convention of conservatism because the loss is recognized before an actual transaction takes place. Under historical cost accounting, the inventory remains at cost until it is sold. It may help in applying the LCM rule to think of it as the "lower-of-cost-or-replacement-cost" rule.* Approximately 90 percent of 600 large companies report applying the LCM rule to their inventories.[11]

There are two basic methods of valuing inventories at the lower of cost or market accepted both by GAAP and the IRS for federal income tax purposes: (1) the item-by-item method and (2) the major category method. For example, a stereo shop could determine lower of cost or market for each kind of speaker, receiver, and turntable (item by item) or for all speakers, all receivers, and all turntables (major categories).

ITEM-BY-ITEM METHOD

When the **item-by-item method** is used, cost and market values are compared for each item in inventory. Each individual item is then valued at its lower price, as shown in Table 1:

TABLE 1.   Lower of Cost or Market with Item-by-Item Method

		Per Unit		Lower of Cost or Market
	Quantity	Cost	Market	
Category I				
Item a	200	$1.50	$1.70	$ 300
Item b	100	2.00	1.80	180
Item c	100	2.50	2.60	250
Category II				
Item d	300	5.00	4.50	1,350
Item e	200	4.00	4.10	800
Inventory at the lower of cost or market				$2,880

MAJOR CATEGORY METHOD

Under the **major category method**, the total cost and total market values for each category of items are compared. Each category is then valued at its lower amount, as shown in Table 2:

*In some cases, the *realizable value* of the inventory determines the *market value*—the amount for which the goods can be sold—rather than by the amount for which the goods can be replaced. The circumstances in which realizable value determines market value are encountered in practice only occasionally, and the valuation procedures are technical enough to be addressed in a more advanced accounting course.

TABLE 2. Lower of Cost or Market with Major Category Method

		Per Unit		Total		Lower of
	Quantity	Cost	Market	Cost	Market	Cost or Market
Category I						
Item a	200	$1.50	$1.70	$ 300	$ 340	
Item b	100	2.00	1.80	200	180	
Item c	100	2.50	2.60	250	260	
Totals				$ 750	$ 780	$ 750
Category II						
Item d	300	5.00	4.50	$1,500	$1,350	
Item e	200	4.00	4.10	800	820	
Totals				$2,300	$2,170	2,170
Inventory at the lower of cost or market						$2,920

✔ Check out ACE for a Review Quiz at http://accounting.college.hmco.com/students.

VALUING INVENTORY BY ESTIMATION

SO7 Estimate the cost of ending inventory using the retail method and gross profit method.

RELATED TEXT ASSIGNMENTS
Q: 17, 18, 19
E: 12, 13
P: 4, 5
FRA: 5

It is sometimes necessary or desirable to estimate the value of ending inventory. The methods most commonly used for this purpose are the retail method and the gross profit method.

RETAIL METHOD OF INVENTORY ESTIMATION

The **retail method**, as its name implies, is used in retail merchandising businesses to estimate the cost of ending inventory by using the ratio of cost to retail price. There are two principal reasons for its use. First, since preparing financial statements each month requires a knowledge of the cost of inventory, the retail method can be used to estimate the cost without the time or expense of determining the cost of items in the inventory. Second, because items in a retail store normally have a price tag or a universal product code, it is common practice to take the physical inventory at retail from these price tags or codes and to reduce the total value to cost through use of the retail method. The term *at retail* means the amount of the inventory at the marked selling prices of the inventory items.

KEY POINT: When estimating inventory by the retail method, the inventory need not be counted.

When the retail method is used to estimate ending inventory, the records must show the beginning inventory at cost and at retail. The records must also show the amount of goods purchased during the period both at cost and at retail. The net sales at retail is, of course, the balance of the Sales account less returns and allowances. A simple example of the retail method is shown in Table 3.

Goods available for sale is determined both at cost and at retail by listing beginning inventory and net purchases for the period at cost and at their expected selling price, adding freight to the cost column, and totaling. The ratio of these two amounts (cost to retail price) provides an estimate of the cost of each dollar of retail sales value. The estimated ending inventory at retail is then determined by deducting sales for the period from the retail price of the goods that were available for sale during the period. The inventory at retail is then converted to cost on the basis of the ratio of cost to retail.

STUDY NOTE: Freight In is not placed under the Retail column when using the retail method of inventory estimation because businesses automatically price their goods high enough to cover freight charges.

TABLE 3.   Retail Method of Inventory Estimation

	Cost	Retail
Beginning inventory	$ 40,000	$ 55,000
Net purchases for the period (excluding freight in)	107,000	145,000
Freight in	3,000	
Merchandise available for sale	$150,000	$200,000
Ratio of cost to retail price: $\frac{\$150,000}{\$200,000} = 75\%$		
Net sales during the period		160,000
Estimated ending inventory at retail		$ 40,000
Ratio of cost to retail		75%
Estimated cost of ending inventory		$ 30,000

The cost of ending inventory may also be estimated by applying the ratio of cost to retail price to the total retail value of the physical count of the ending inventory. Applying the retail method in practice is often more difficult than this simple example because of such complications as changes in retail price during the year, different markups on different types of merchandise, and varying volumes of sales for different types of merchandise.

GROSS PROFIT METHOD OF INVENTORY ESTIMATION

BUSINESS-WORLD EXAMPLE: It is highly desirable to maintain financial records off site. If records were destroyed, it would be difficult, if not impossible, to reconstruct the data necessary for an insurance claim.

The **gross profit method** (also known as the *gross margin method*) assumes that the ratio of gross margin for a business remains relatively stable from year to year. The gross profit method is used in place of the retail method when records of the retail prices of beginning inventory and purchases are not kept. It is considered acceptable for estimating the cost of inventory for interim reports, but it is not acceptable for valuing inventory in the annual financial statements. It is also useful in estimating the amount of inventory lost or destroyed by theft, fire, or other hazards. Insurance companies often use this method to verify loss claims.

As Table 4 shows, the gross profit method is simple to use. First, figure the cost of goods available for sale in the usual way (add purchases to beginning inventory). Second, estimate the cost of goods sold by deducting the estimated gross margin of 30 percent from sales. Finally, deduct the estimated cost of goods sold from the goods available for sale to arrive at the estimated cost of ending inventory.

TABLE 4.   Gross Profit Method of Inventory Estimation

1. Beginning inventory at cost		$ 50,000
Purchases at cost (including freight in)		290,000
Cost of goods available for sale		$340,000
2. Less estimated cost of goods sold		
Sales at selling price	$400,000	
Less estimated gross margin (30% × 400,000)	120,000	
Estimated cost of goods sold		280,000
3. Estimated cost of ending inventory		$ 60,000

 Check out ACE for a Review Quiz at http://accounting.college.hmco.com/students.

Chapter Review

REVIEW OF LEARNING OBJECTIVES

LO1 Identify and explain the management issues associated with accounting for inventories.

Included in inventory are goods owned, whether produced or purchased, that are held for sale in the normal course of business. Manufacturing companies also include raw materials and work in process. Among the issues management must face in accounting for inventories are allocating the cost of inventories in accordance with the matching rule, assessing the impact of inventory decisions, and evaluating the level of inventory. The objective of accounting for inventories is the proper determination of income through the matching of costs and revenues, not the determination of the most realistic inventory value. Because the valuation of inventory has a direct effect on a company's net income, the choice of inventory systems and methods affects not only the amount of income taxes and cash flows, but also the external and internal evaluation of the company. The level of inventory as measured by the inventory turnover and its related measure, average days' inventory on hand, is important to managing the amount of investment a company needs.

LO2 Define inventory cost and relate it to goods flow and cost flow.

The cost of inventory includes (1) invoice price less purchases discounts; (2) freight in, including insurance in transit; and (3) applicable taxes and tariffs. Goods flow refers to the actual physical flow of merchandise, whereas cost flow refers to the assumed flow of costs in the operations of the business.

LO3 Calculate the pricing of inventory, using the cost basis under the periodic inventory system.

The value assigned to ending inventory is the result of two measurements: quantity and price. Quantity is determined by taking a physical inventory. The pricing of inventory is usually based on the assumed cost flow of the goods as they are bought and sold. One of four assumptions is usually made regarding cost flow. These assumptions are represented by four inventory methods. Inventory pricing can be determined by the specific identification method, which associates the actual cost with each item of inventory, but this method is rarely used. The average-cost method assumes that the cost of inventory is the average cost of goods available for sale during the period. The first-in, first-out (FIFO) method assumes that the costs of the first items acquired should be assigned to the first items sold. The last-in, first-out (LIFO) method assumes that the costs of the last items acquired should be assigned to the first items sold. The inventory method chosen may or may not be equivalent to the actual physical flow of goods.

LO4 Apply the perpetual inventory system to the pricing of inventories at cost.

The pricing of inventories under the perpetual inventory system differs from pricing under the periodic system because under the perpetual system a continuous record of quantities and costs of merchandise is maintained as purchases and sales are made. Cost of goods sold is accumulated as sales are made and costs are transferred from the Inventory account to the Cost of Goods Sold account. The cost of the ending inventory is the balance of the Inventory account. Under the perpetual inventory system, the specific identification method and the FIFO method produce the same results as under the periodic method. The results differ for the average-cost method because an average is calculated after each sale rather than at the end of the accounting period, and for the LIFO method because the cost components of inventory change constantly as goods are bought and sold.

LO5 State the effects of inventory methods and misstatements of inventory on income determination, income taxes, and cash flows.

During periods of rising prices, the LIFO method will show the lowest net income; FIFO, the highest; and average-cost, in between. The opposite effects occur in periods of falling prices. No generalization can be made regarding the specific identification method. The Internal Revenue Service requires that if LIFO is used for tax purposes, it must also be used for financial statements; it also does not allow the lower-of-cost-or-market rule to be applied to the LIFO method. If the value of ending inventory is understated or overstated, a corresponding error—dollar for dollar—will be made in income before income taxes. Furthermore, because the ending inventory of one period is the beginning inventory of the next, the misstatement affects two accounting periods, although the effects are opposite.

LO6 Apply the lower-of-cost-or-market (LCM) rule to inventory valuation.

The lower-of-cost-or-market rule can be applied to the above methods of determining inventory at cost. This rule states that if the replacement cost (market) of the inventory is lower than the inventory cost, the lower figure should be used. Valuation can be determined on an item-by-item or major category basis.

SUPPLEMENTAL OBJECTIVE

SO7 Estimate the cost of ending inventory using the retail method and gross profit method.

Two methods of estimating the value of inventory are the retail method and the gross profit method. Under the retail method, inventory is determined at retail prices and is then reduced to estimated cost by applying a ratio of cost to retail price. Under the gross profit method, cost of goods sold is estimated by reducing sales by estimated gross margin. The estimated cost of goods sold is then deducted from the cost of goods available for sale to estimate the inventory.

REVIEW OF CONCEPTS AND TERMINOLOGY

The following concepts and terms were introduced in this chapter:

LO3 **Average-cost method:** An inventory costing method in which inventory is priced at the average cost of the goods available for sale during the period.

LO1 **Average days' inventory on hand:** The average number of days required to sell the inventory on hand; number of days in a year divided by inventory turnover.

LO2 **Consignment:** Merchandise that its owner (the *consignor*) places on the premises of another company (the *consignee*) with the understanding that payment is expected only when the merchandise is sold and that unsold items may be returned to the consignor.

LO2 **Cost flow:** The association of costs with their assumed flow in the operations of a company.

LO3 **First-in, first-out (FIFO) method:** An inventory costing method based on the assumption that the costs of the first items acquired should be assigned to the first items sold.

LO2 **Goods flow:** The actual physical movement of goods in the operations of a company.

SO7 **Gross profit method:** A method of inventory estimation based on the assumption that the ratio of gross margin for a business remains relatively stable from year to year. Also called *gross margin method*.

LO2 **Inventory cost:** The price paid or consideration given to acquire an asset; includes invoice price less purchases discounts, plus freight in, plus applicable taxes and tariffs.

LO1 **Inventory turnover:** A ratio indicating the number of times a company's average inventory is sold during an accounting period; cost of goods sold divided by average inventory.

LO6 **Item-by-item method:** A lower-of-cost-or-market method of valuing inventory in which cost and market values are compared for each item in inventory and each item is then valued at its lower price.

LO1 **Just-in-time operating environment:** A system of reducing levels of inventory by working closely with suppliers to coordinate and schedule deliveries so that goods arrive just at the time they are needed.

LO3 **Last-in, first-out (LIFO) method:** An inventory costing method based on the assumption that the costs of the last items purchased should be assigned to the first items sold.

LO5 **LIFO liquidation:** The reduction of inventory below previous levels so that income is increased by the amount by which current prices exceed the historical cost of the inventory under LIFO.

LO6 **Lower-of-cost-or-market (LCM) rule:** A method of valuing inventory at an amount less than cost when the replacement cost falls below historical cost.

LO6 **Major category method:** A lower-of-cost-or-market method of valuing inventory in which the total cost and total market values for each category of items are compared and each category is then valued at its lower amount.

LO6 **Market:** Current replacement cost of inventory.

LO1 **Merchandise inventory:** All goods owned and held for sale in the regular course of business.

SO7 **Retail method:** A method of inventory estimation, used in retail merchandising businesses, in which inventory at retail value is reduced by the ratio of cost to retail price.

LO3 **Specific identification method:** An inventory costing method in which the price of inventory is computed by identifying the cost of each item in ending inventory as coming from a specific purchase.

LO1 **Supply-chain management:** A system of managing inventory and purchasing through business-to-business transactions conducted over the Internet.

REVIEW PROBLEM

Periodic and Perpetual Inventory Systems

LO1
LO3 The table below summarizes the beginning inventory, purchases, and sales of Psi
LO4 Company's single product during January.

Date			Beginning Inventory and Purchases Units	Cost	Total	Sales Units
Jan.	1	Inventory	1,400	$19	$26,600	
	4	Sale				300
	8	Purchase	600	20	12,000	
	10	Sale				1,300
	12	Purchase	900	21	18,900	
	15	Sale				150
	18	Purchase	500	22	11,000	
	24	Purchase	800	23	18,400	
	31	Sale				1,350
Totals			4,200		$86,900	3,100

REQUIRED ▶ 1. Assuming that the company uses the periodic inventory system, compute the cost that should be assigned to ending inventory and to cost of goods sold using (a) the average-cost method, (b) the FIFO method, and (c) the LIFO method.
2. Assuming that the company uses the perpetual inventory system, compute the cost that should be assigned to ending inventory and to cost of goods sold using (a) the average-cost method, (b) the FIFO method, and (c) the LIFO method.
K/R 3. Compute inventory turnover and average days' inventory on hand under each of the inventory cost flow assumptions in **1**. What conclusion can be made from this comparison?

ANSWER TO REVIEW PROBLEM

	Units	Amount
Beginning inventory	1,400	$26,600
Purchases	2,800	60,300
Available for sale	4,200	$86,900
Sales	3,100	
Ending inventory	1,100	

Company are as follows:

	2000	1999
Raw materials	$264	$271
Goods in process	48	49
Finished goods	338	365
Inventories at FIFO	650	685
Adjustment to LIFO	(45)	(83)
Total inventories	$605	$602

REQUIRED ▶

1. Prepare a schedule comparing net income for 2000 under the LIFO method with what it would have been under FIFO. Use a corporate income tax rate of 40 percent. Did prices of cocoa and sugar, the principal ingredients of Hershey's products, go up or down in 2000? Explain.

2. Why do you suppose Hershey's management chooses to use the LIFO inventory method? On what economic conditions, if any, do those reasons depend? Given your calculations in **1**, do you believe the economic conditions relevant to Hershey were advantageous for using LIFO in 2000? Explain your answer.

3. Compute inventory turnover and average days' inventory on hand under the LIFO and FIFO methods. What conclusion can be drawn from this comparison?

FRA 2.
LO5   Misstatement of Inventory

Crazy Eddie, Inc. <www.crazyeddie.com>, a discount consumer electronics chain, seemed to be missing $52 million in merchandise inventory. "It was a shock," the new management was quoted as saying. It was also one of the nation's largest swindles. Investors lost $145.6 million when the company declared bankruptcy. A count turned up only $75 million in inventory, compared with $126.7 million reported by former management. Net sales could account for only $6.7 million of the difference. At the time, it was not clear whether bookkeeping errors in prior years or an actual physical loss created the shortfall, although at least one store manager felt it was a bookkeeping error because security was strong. "It would be hard for someone to steal anything," he said. Former management was eventually fined $72.7 million.[16]

REQUIRED ▶

1. What is the effect of the misstatement of inventory on Crazy Eddie's reported earnings in prior accounting periods?

2. Is this a situation you would expect in a company that is experiencing financial difficulty? Explain.

FRA 3.
LO5   LIFO Liquidation

Crane Company <www.crane.com> reported approximately $259 million and $236 million of inventories valued under the LIFO method in 2000 and 1999, respectively. As explained in the company's annual report:

> The reduction of inventory quantities has resulted in a liquidation of LIFO inventories acquired at lower costs prevailing in prior years. Liquidations have reduced cost of sales by $1.3 million in 2000, $2.7 million in 1999, and $.6 million in 1998. Replacement cost would have been higher by $21.4 million and $23.1 million at December 31, 2000 and 1999, respectively.[17]

Assume Crane's average income tax rates for 1999 and 2000 were 40 percent.

REQUIRED ▶

1. Explain why a reduction in the quantity of inventory resulted in an increase in net income. Would the same result have occurred if Crane had used the FIFO method to value inventory? Explain your answer.

2. What is the income tax effect of the LIFO liquidation? Is this a favorable outcome?

International Company

FRA 4.
LO1   Comparison of Inventory
LO5   Levels and Methods

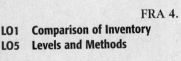

Yamaha Motor Co., Ltd. <www.yamaha-motor.co.jp> and Pioneer Corporation <www.pioneer.co.jp> are two large, diversified Japanese electronics companies. Both use the average-cost method and the lower-of-cost-or-market rule to account for inventories. The following data are for their 2001 fiscal years (in millions of yen):[18]

	Yamaha	Pioneer
Beginning inventory	¥139,625	¥ 91,517
Ending inventory	166,074	84,429
Cost of goods sold	668,992	447,389

Compare the inventory efficiency of Yamaha and Pioneer by computing the inventory turnover and average days' inventory on hand for both companies in 2001. Comment on the results. Most companies in the United States use the LIFO inventory method.

How would inventory method affect your evaluation if you were to compare Pioneer and Yamaha to a U.S. company? What could you do to make the results comparable?

Toys "R" Us Annual Report

FRA 5.

LO1 **Retail Method and Inventory**
LO5 **Ratios**
LO6
SO7

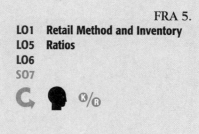

Refer to the note related to inventories in the Toys "R" Us <www.tru.com> annual report in the Supplement to Chapter 1 to answer the following questions: What inventory method(s) does Toys "R" Us use? If LIFO inventories had been valued at FIFO, why would there be no difference? Do you think many of the company's inventories are valued at market? Few companies use the retail method; why do you think Toys "R" Us uses it? Compute and compare the inventory turnover and average days' inventory on hand for Toys "R" Us for 2000 and 2001. Beginning 2000 inventory was $1,902 million.

Comparison Case: Toys "R" Us and Walgreen Co.

FRA 6.

LO1 **Inventory Efficiency**

Refer to the financial statements for Toys "R" Us <www.tru.com> and Walgreens <www.walgreens.com> in the Supplement to Chapter 1. Beginning inventory for 2000 for Toys "R" Us was $1,902 million and for Walgreens, $2,462.6 million. Calculate inventory turnover and average days' inventory on hand for the past two years. If you did **FRA 5**, refer to your answer there for Toys "R" Us. Has either company improved its performance over the past two years? What advantage does the superior company's performance provide to it? Which company appears to make the most efficient use of inventory? Explain.

Fingraph® Financial Analyst™

FRA 7.

LO1 **Comparative Analysis of**
     Inventories and Operating
     Cycle

Select any two companies from the same industry from the list of Fingraph companies on the Needles Accounting Resource Center Web site at http://accounting.college.hmco.com/students. Choose an industry, such as manufacturing, consumer products, consumer food and beverage, or computers, in which inventory is likely to be an important current asset. Access the Microsoft Excel spreadsheets for the companies you selected. Click on the URL at the top of each company's spreadsheet for a link to the company's web site and annual report.

1. In the annual reports of the companies you have selected, read any reference to inventories in the summary of significant accounting policies or notes to the financial statements. What inventory method does the company use? What are the changes in and the relative importance of raw materials, work in process, and finished goods inventories?

2. Using the Fingraph Financial Analyst CD-ROM software, display and print in tabular and graphic form the Liquidity and Asset Utilization Analysis page. Prepare a table that compares the inventory turnover and average days' inventory on hand for both companies for two years. Also include in your table the operating cycle by combining average days' inventory on hand with average days' sales uncollected.

3. Find and read references to inventories in the liquidity analysis section of management's discussion and analysis in each annual report.

4. Write a one-page executive summary that highlights the accounting policies for inventories, the relative importance and changes in raw materials, work in process, and finished goods, and compares the inventory utilization of the two companies, including reference to management's assessment. Comment specifically on the financing implications of the companies' relative operating cycles. Include the Fingraph page and your table with your report.

Internet Case

FRA 8.

LO5 **Effect of LIFO on Income and**
     Cash Flows

Maytag Corporation <www.maytag.com>, an appliance manufacturer, uses the LIFO inventory method. Go to its web site and select "About Maytag." Then select "Financial Center." After finding the income statement and inventory note, calculate what net income would have been had the company used FIFO. Calculate how much cash the company saved for the year and cumulatively by using LIFO. What is the difference between the LIFO and FIFO gross margin and profit margin results? Which reporting alternative is better for the company?

9

Chapter 9 presents the management issues associated with current liabilities, as well as the basic concepts and techniques of the time value of money.

Current Liabilities and the Time Value of Money

LEARNING OBJECTIVES

LO1 Identify the management issues related to recognition, valuation, classification, and disclosure of current liabilities.

LO2 Identify, compute, and record definitely determinable and estimated current liabilities.

LO3 Distinguish *contingent liabilities* from *commitments*.

LO4 Define *interest* and distinguish between simple and compound interest.

LO5 Use compound interest tables to compute the future value of a single sum at compound interest and of an ordinary annuity.

LO6 Use compound interest tables to compute the present value of a single sum due in the future and of an ordinary annuity.

LO7 Apply the concept of the time value of money to simple accounting situations.

DECISION POINT

A USER'S FOCUS

US Airways, Inc. <www.usairways.com> Liabilities are one of the three major parts of the balance sheet. They are legal obligations for the future payment of assets or the future performance of services that result from past transactions. The current and long-term liabilities of US Airways, Inc., which has total assets of almost $8 billion, are shown in the Financial Highlights.[1] Current maturities of long-term debt; accounts payable; accrued aircraft rent; accrued salaries, wages, and vacation; and other accrued expenses will for the most part require an outlay of cash in the next year. Traffic balances payable will require payments to other airlines, but those may be partially offset by amounts owed by other airlines. Unused tickets are tickets already paid for by passengers and represent services that must be performed. Long-term debt will require cash outlays in future years. Altogether these liabilities represent over 75 percent of total assets. How does the decision of US Airways' management to incur so much debt relate to the goals of the business?

Liabilities are important because they are closely related to the goals of profitability and liquidity. Liabilities are sources of cash for operating and financing activities when they are incurred, but they are also obligations that use cash when they are paid. Achieving the appropriate level of liabilities is critical to business success. A company that has too few liabilities may not be earning up to its potential. A company that has too many liabilities, however, may be incurring excessive risks. In the case of US Airways, the company became vulnerable when there was a down-

What factors other than a downturn in air travel caused US Airways to file for bankruptcy?

turn in air travel as occurred in 2001–2002. Because of problems with liquidity, US Airways had to file for bankruptcy in 2002 in order to continue operating. This chapter focuses on the management and accounting issues involving current liabilities, including payroll liabilities and contingent liabilities.

Financial Highlights
(In millions)

Current Liabilities	2001	2000
Current maturities of long-term debt	$ 159	$ 284
Accounts payable	598	506
Traffic balances payable and unused tickets	817	890
Accrued aircraft rent	249	349
Accrued salaries, wages, and vacation	367	319
Other accrued expenses	742	475
Total current liabilities	$2,932	$2,823
Long-term debt, net of current maturities	$3,515	$2,688

MANAGEMENT ISSUES RELATED TO ACCOUNTING FOR CURRENT LIABILITIES

LO1 Identify the management issues related to recognition, valuation, classification, and disclosure of current liabilities.

RELATED TEXT ASSIGNMENTS
Q: 1, 2, 3, 4, 5
SE: 1, 2
E: 1, 2
P: 1
FRA: 1, 3, 4, 5, 6

The primary reason for incurring current liabilities is to meet needs for cash during the operating cycle. The proper identification and management of current liabilities requires an understanding of how these liabilities are recognized, valued, classified, and disclosed.

MANAGING LIQUIDITY AND CASH FLOWS

The operating cycle is the process of converting cash to purchases, to sales, to accounts receivable, and back to cash. Most current liabilities arise in support of this cycle, as when accounts payable arise from purchases of inventory, accrued expenses arise from operating costs, and unearned revenues arise from customers' advance payments. Short-term debt is used to raise cash during periods of inventory buildup or while waiting for collection of receivables. Cash is used to pay current maturities of long-term debt and to pay off liabilities arising from operations.

Failure to manage the cash flows related to current liabilities can have serious consequences for a business. For instance, if suppliers are not paid on time, they may withhold shipments that are vital to a company's operations. Continued failure to pay current liabilities can lead to bankruptcy. To evaluate a company's ability to pay its current liabilities, three measures of liquidity—working capital, the current ratio, and the quick ratio—are often used. Current liabilities are a key component of each of these measures. They typically equal from 25 to 50 percent of total assets.

www.usairways.com

As shown below (in millions of dollars), US Airways' short-term liquidity as measured by working capital was negative in 2000 and 2001:

	Current Assets	−	Current Liabilities	=	Working Capital
2001	$1,793	−	$2,932	=	($1,139)
2000	$2,571	−	$2,823	=	($ 252)

ENRICHMENT NOTE:
Unused tickets are often a significant liability for airlines and other service providers. The receipt of cash is usually incidental to revenue recognition.

This measure highlights the reason why US Airways faced a problem with short-term liquidity. It is common for airlines to have low or negative working capital because unearned ticket revenue is a current liability, but the cash from these ticket sales is quickly consumed in operations. On the assumption that only a small portion of unearned ticket revenues will be repaid to customers, unearned ticket revenue might be excluded from current liabilities for purposes of analysis. The healthiest airlines have positive working capital when unearned ticket revenue is excluded. However, for US Airways, the negative working capital of $1,139 million exceeded the traffic balances and unused tickets of $817 million in 2001.

Another consideration in managing liquidity and cash flows is the amount of time creditors are willing to give a company to pay its accounts payable. Common measures of this time are the **payables turnover** and the **average days' payable**. The payables turnover is the number of times, on average, that accounts payable are paid in an accounting period and shows the relative size of a company's accounts payable. The average days' payable shows how long, on average, a company takes to pay its accounts payables.

www.radioshack.com

For example, RadioShack Corporation, which operates more than 7,000 electronics stores, must carefully plan its purchases and payables. It had accounts payable of $234.8 million in 1999 and in 2000. Its purchases are determined by cost of goods sold adjusted for the change in inventory. An increase in inventory means purchases were more than cost of goods sold; a decrease in inventory means that purchases were less than cost of goods sold. RadioShack's cost of goods sold in 2000 was $2,425.1 million, and its inventory increased by $302.9 million.[2] Its payables turnover is computed as follows:

FIGURE 1
Payables Turnover for Selected Industries

Source: Data from Dun & Bradstreet, *Industry Norms and Key Business Ratios,* 2000–2001.

● **STOP AND THINK!**

Is a decreasing payables turnover good or bad for a company?

Other things being equal, a decreasing payables turnover is good because it means the average days' payable is greater, thus allowing the company more time to pay its bills. The company will not have to borrow as much to finance its operating cycle of inventory turnover and receivables turnover. ■

$$\text{Payables Turnover} = \frac{\text{Cost of Goods Sold} \pm \text{Change in Merchandise Inventory}}{\text{Average Accounts Payable}}$$

$$= \frac{\$2,425.1 + \$302.9}{(\$234.8 + \$234.8) \div 2}$$

$$= \frac{\$2,728.0}{\$234.8} = 11.6 \text{ times}$$

To find the average days' payable, the number of days in a year is divided by the payables turnover:

$$\text{Average Days' Payable} = \frac{365 \text{ days}}{\text{Payables Turnover}} = \frac{365 \text{ days}}{11.6} = 31.5 \text{ days}$$

The payables turnover of 11.6 times and the resulting average days' payable of 31.5 days are consistent with customary 30-day credit terms.

Figures 1 and 2 show the payables turnover and average days' payable for various industries. To get a full picture of a company's operating cycle and liquidity position, these ratios should be considered in relation to the inventory turnover and the receivables turnover and their related days' ratios.

FIGURE 2
Average Days' Payable for Selected Industries

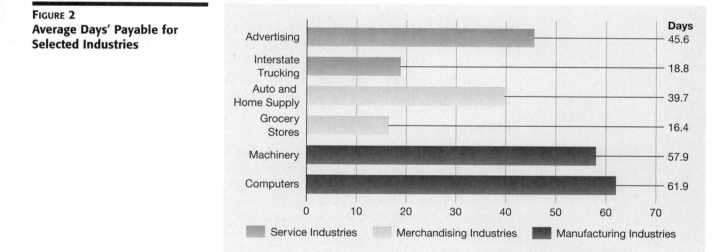

Source: Data from Dun & Bradstreet, *Industry Norms and Key Business Ratios,* 2000–2001.

FOCUS ON BUSINESS PRACTICE

Debt Problems Can Plague Even Well-Known Companies.

In a recent Wall Street horror story that illustrates the importance of managing current liabilities, Xerox Corporation <www.xerox.com>, one of the most storied names in American business, found itself combating rumors that it was facing bankruptcy. Following a statement by Xerox's CEO that the company's financial model was "unsustainable," management was forced to defend the company's liquidity by saying it had adequate funds to continue operations. But in a report filed with the SEC, management acknowledged that it had tapped into its $7 billion line of bank credit for more than $3 billion to pay off short-term debt that was coming due. Unable to secure more money from any other source to pay such debts, Xerox had no choice but to turn to the line of credit from its bank. Had it run out, the company might well have gone bankrupt.[3] Fortunately, Xerox was able to restructure its line of credit to stay in business, but it is still in a perilous position and may have to sell itself to another company to survive.

RECOGNITION OF LIABILITIES

Timing is important in the recognition of liabilities. Failure to record a liability in an accounting period very often goes along with failure to record an expense. The two errors lead to an understatement of expense and an overstatement of income.

A liability is recorded when an obligation occurs. This rule is harder to apply than it might appear. When a transaction obligates a company to make future payments, a liability arises and is recognized, as when goods are bought on credit. However, current liabilities often are not represented by direct transactions. One of the key reasons for making adjusting entries at the end of an accounting period is to recognize unrecorded liabilities. Among these accrued liabilities are salaries payable and interest payable. Other liabilities that can only be estimated, such as taxes payable, must also be recognized through adjusting entries.

On the other hand, companies often enter into agreements for future transactions. For instance, a company may agree to pay an executive $150,000 a year for a period of three years, or a public utility may agree to buy an unspecified quantity of coal at a certain price over the next five years. Such contracts, though they are definite commitments, are not considered liabilities because they are for future—not past—transactions. As there is no current obligation, no liability is recognized.

VALUATION OF LIABILITIES

On the balance sheet, a liability is generally valued at the amount of money needed to pay the debt or at the fair market value of goods or services to be delivered. For most liabilities, the amount is definitely known, but for some, it must be estimated. For example, an automobile dealer who sells a car with a one-year warranty must provide parts and service during the year. The obligation is definite because the sale has occurred, but the amount of the obligation can only be estimated. Such estimates are usually based on past experience and anticipated changes in the business environment. Additional disclosures of the fair value of liabilities may be required in the notes to the financial statements, as explained below.

CLASSIFICATION OF LIABILITIES

The classification of liabilities directly matches the classification of assets. **Current liabilities** are debts and obligations expected to be satisfied within one year or within the normal operating cycle, whichever is longer. Such liabilities are normally paid out of current assets or with cash generated from operations. **Long-term liabilities**, which are liabilities due beyond one year or beyond the normal operating cycle, have a different purpose. They are used to finance long-term assets, such as aircraft in the case of US Airways. The distinction between current and long-term liabilities is important because it affects the evaluation of a company's liquidity.

www.usairways.com

DISCLOSURE OF LIABILITIES

To explain some accounts, supplemental disclosure in the notes to the financial statements may be required. For example, if a company has a large amount of notes payable, an explanatory note may disclose the balances, maturities, interest rates, and other features of the debts. Any special credit arrangements, such as issues of commercial paper and lines of credit, should also be disclosed. For example, Goodyear Tire & Rubber Company, which manufactures and sells tires, vehicle components, industrial rubber products, and rubber-related chemicals, disclosed its credit arrangements in the notes to its financial statements, as follows:

www.goodyear.com

Short Term Debt and Financing Arrangements

At December 31, 2000, the Company had short term committed and uncommitted credit arrangements totaling $2.2 billion, of which $.93 billion were unused. These arrangements are available to the Company or certain of its international subsidiaries through various domestic and international banks at quoted market interest rates. There are no commitment fees or compensating balances associated with these arrangements. In addition, the Company maintains a commercial paper program, whereunder the Company may have up to $1.5 billion outstanding at any one time. Commercial paper totaling $297.7 million was outstanding at December 31, 2000.[4]

This type of disclosure is helpful in assessing whether a company has additional borrowing power, because unused lines of credit allow a company to borrow on short notice, up to the agreed credit limit, with little or no negotiations.

✓ Check out ACE for a Review Quiz at http://accounting.college.hmco.com/students.

ENRICHMENT NOTE:
Financial liabilities, such as loans, notes, and other borrowings, are considered financial instruments. The market value of financial instruments is reported in the notes to the financial statements.

COMMON CATEGORIES OF CURRENT LIABILITIES

LO2 Identify, compute, and record definitely determinable and estimated current liabilities.

RELATED TEXT ASSIGNMENTS
Q: 6, 7, 8, 9, 10, 11, 12, 13, 14, 15, 16
SE: 3, 4, 5, 6, 7
E: 3, 4, 5, 6, 7, 8
P: 1, 2, 3, 4, 6, 7
SD: 1, 2, 4, 5
FRA: 3, 6

Current liabilities fall into two major groups: (1) definitely determinable liabilities and (2) estimated liabilities.

DEFINITELY DETERMINABLE LIABILITIES

Current liabilities that are set by contract or by statute and can be measured exactly are called **definitely determinable liabilities**. The related accounting problems are to determine the existence and amount of each such liability and to see that it is recorded properly. Definitely determinable liabilities include accounts payable, bank loans and commercial paper, notes payable, accrued liabilities, dividends payable, sales and excise taxes payable, current portions of long-term debt, payroll liabilities, and unearned revenues.

KEY POINT: On the balance sheet, the order of presentation for current liabilities is not as strict as for current assets. Generally, Accounts Payable or Notes Payable appears first, and the rest follow.

■ **ACCOUNTS PAYABLE** Accounts payable, sometimes called *trade accounts payable*, are short-term obligations to suppliers for goods and services. The amount in the Accounts Payable account is generally supported by an accounts payable subsidiary ledger, which contains an individual account for each person or company to which money is owed.

www.usairways.com

■ **BANK LOANS AND COMMERCIAL PAPER** Management often establishes a **line of credit** with a bank; this arrangement allows the company to borrow funds when they are needed to finance current operations. For example, US Airways states in a note to its financial statements that "the Company has in place a $190 million 364-day secured revolving credit facility and a $250 million three-year secured revolving credit facility to provide liquidity for its operations."[5] A promissory note for the full amount of the line of credit is signed when the credit is granted, but the company has great flexibility in using the available funds. The company can increase its borrowing up to the limit when it needs cash and reduce the amount borrowed when it generates enough cash of its own. Both the amount borrowed and the interest rate charged by the bank may change daily. The bank may require the company to meet certain financial goals (such as maintaining specific profit margins, current ratios, or debt to equity ratios) to retain the line of credit.

Companies with excellent credit ratings may borrow short-term funds by issuing **commercial paper**, unsecured loans that are sold to the public, usually through professionally managed investment firms. The portion of a line of credit currently borrowed and the amount of commercial paper issued are usually combined with notes payable in the current liabilities section of the balance sheet. Details are disclosed in a note to the financial statements.

CLARIFICATION NOTE:
Only the used portion of the line of credit is recognized as a liability in the financial statements.

■ **NOTES PAYABLE**   Short-term notes payable are obligations represented by promissory notes. These notes may be used to secure bank loans, to pay suppliers for goods and services, and to secure credit from other sources.

The interest may be stated separately on the face of the note (Case 1 in Figure 3), or it may be deducted in advance by discounting it from the face value of the note (Case 2 in Figure 3). The entries to record the note in each case are as follows:

	Case 1—Interest Stated Separately				Case 2—Interest in Face Amount		
Case 1							
A = L + OE	Aug. 31	Cash	5,000	Aug. 31	Cash	4,900	
+ +		Notes Payable	5,000		Discount on Notes Payable	100	
Case 2		Issued 60-day,			Notes Payable		5,000
A = L + OE		12% promissory			Issued 60-day		
+ −		note with interest			promissory note with		
+		stated separately			$100 interest included		
					in face amount		

CLARIFICATION NOTE:
The effective interest rate on the loan in Case 2 is 12.24% ($100/$4,900 ÷ 360/60). Note: For ease of computation 360 days are used to compute interest on notes.

Note that in Case 1 the money received equaled the face value of the note, whereas in Case 2 the money received ($4,900) was less than the face value ($5,000) of the note. The amount of the discount equals the amount of the interest for 60 days. Although the dollar amount of interest on each of these notes is the same, the effective interest rate is slightly higher in Case 2 because the amount received is slightly less ($4,900 in Case 2 versus $5,000 in Case 1). Discount on

FIGURE 3
Two Promissory Notes: One with Interest Stated Separately; One with Interest in Face Amount

CASE 1: INTEREST STATED SEPARATELY

Chicago, Illinois   August 31, 20xx

Sixty days after date I promise to pay First Federal Bank the sum of $5,000 with interest at the rate of 12% per annum.

Sandra Caron
Caron Corporation

CASE 2: INTEREST IN FACE AMOUNT

Chicago, Illinois   August 31, 20xx

Sixty days after date I promise to pay First Federal Bank the sum of $5,000.

Sandra Caron
Caron Corporation

Notes Payable is a contra account to Notes Payable and is deducted from Notes Payable on the balance sheet.

On October 30, when the note is paid, each alternative is recorded as follows:

	Case 1—Interest Stated Separately			Case 2—Interest in Face Amount		

Case 1
A = L + OE
− − −

Case 2
A = L + OE
− − −
A = L + OE
+ −

Oct. 30   Notes Payable   5,000
          Interest Expense   100
              Cash   5,100
              Payment of note
              with interest stated
              separately

$$\$5{,}000 \times \frac{60}{360} \times .12 = \$100$$

Oct. 30   Notes Payable   5,000
              Cash   5,000
              Payment of note
              with interest included
              in face amount

30   Interest Expense   100
          Discount on Notes
          Payable   100
          Interest expense on
          note payable

■ **Accrued Liabilities**   A key reason for making adjusting entries at the end of an accounting period is to recognize and record liabilities that are not already in the accounting records. This practice applies to any type of liability. As you will see, accrued liabilities can include estimated liabilities.

Here the focus is on interest payable, a definitely determinable liability. Interest accrues daily on interest-bearing notes. At the end of the accounting period, an adjusting entry should be made in accordance with the matching rule to record the interest obligation up to that point. Let us again use the example of the two notes presented in Figure 3. If we assume that the accounting period ends on September 30, or 30 days after the issuance of the 60-day notes, the adjusting entries for each case would be as follows:

	Case 1—Interest Stated Separately		Case 2—Interest in Face Amount	

Case 1
A = L + OE
+ −

Case 2
A = L + OE
+ −

KEY POINT: Both of these entries have exactly the same impact on the financial statements.

Sept. 30   Interest Expense   50
              Interest Payable   50
              To record interest
              expense for 30 days
              on note with interest
              stated separately

$$\$5{,}000 \times \frac{30}{360} \times .12 = \$50$$

Sept. 30   Interest Expense   50
              Discount on Notes Payable   50
              To record interest expense
              for 30 days on note with
              interest included in face
              amount

$$\$100 \times \frac{30}{60} = \$50$$

In Case 2, Discount on Notes Payable will now have a debit balance of $50, which will become interest expense during the next 30 days.

■ **Dividends Payable**   Cash dividends are a distribution of earnings by a corporation. The payment of dividends is solely the decision of the corporation's board of directors. A liability does not exist until the board declares the dividends. There is usually a short time between the date of declaration and the date of payment of dividends. During that short time, the dividends declared are considered current liabilities of the corporation.

■ **Sales and Excise Taxes Payable**   Most states and many cities levy a sales tax on retail transactions. There is a federal excise tax on some products, such as automobile tires. A merchant who sells goods subject to these taxes must collect the taxes and forward them periodically to the appropriate government agency. The amount of tax collected represents a current liability until it is remitted to the government. For example, assume that a merchant makes a $100 sale that is subject to a 5 percent sales tax and a 10 percent excise tax. Assuming that the sale takes place on June 1, the entry to record the sale is as follows:

A = L + OE
+   +   +
    +

	June 1	Cash	115	
		Sales		100
		Sales Tax Payable		5
		Excise Tax Payable		10
		Sales of merchandise and collection of sales and excise tax		

The sale is properly recorded at $100, and the taxes collected are recorded as liabilities to be remitted at the proper times to the appropriate government agencies.

■ **CURRENT PORTIONS OF LONG-TERM DEBT**   If a portion of long-term debt is due within the next year and is to be paid from current assets, then that current portion is properly classified as a current liability. For example, suppose that a $500,000 debt is to be paid in installments of $100,000 per year for the next five years. The $100,000 installment due in the current year should be classified as a current liability. The remaining $400,000 should be classified as a long-term liability. Note that no journal entry is necessary. The total debt of $500,000 is simply reclassified when the financial statements are prepared, as follows:

Current liabilities	
Current portion of long-term debt	$100,000
Long-term liabilities	
Long-term debt	400,000

■ **PAYROLL LIABILITIES**   For most organizations, the cost of labor and related payroll taxes is a major expense. In some industries, such as banking and airlines, payroll costs represent more than half of all operating costs. Payroll accounting is important because complex laws and significant liabilities are involved. The employer is liable to employees for wages and salaries and to various agencies for amounts withheld from wages and salaries and for related taxes. The term **wages** refers to payment for the services of employees at an hourly rate. The term **salaries** refers to the compensation of employees who are paid at a monthly or yearly rate.

Because payroll accounting applies only to the employees of an organization, it is important to distinguish between employees and independent contractors. Employees are paid a wage or salary by the organization and are under its direct supervision and control. Independent contractors are not employees of the organization, so they are not accounted for under the payroll system. They offer services to the organization for a fee, but they are not under its direct control or supervision. Certified public accountants, advertising agencies, and lawyers, for example, may act as independent contractors.

Figure 4 provides an illustration of payroll liabilities and their relationship to employee earnings and employer taxes and other costs. Two important observations may be made. First, the amount payable to employees is less than the amount of earnings. This occurs because employers are required by law or are requested by employees to withhold certain amounts from wages and send them directly to government agencies or other organizations. Second, the total employer liabilities exceed employee earnings because the employer must pay additional taxes and make other contributions, such as for pensions and medical care, that increase the cost and liabilities. The most common withholdings, taxes, and other payroll costs are described following Figure 4.

FOCUS ON BUSINESS PRACTICE

Small Businesses Offer Benefits, Too.
A survey of small businesses in the Midwest shows the percentages of respondents that offer the following benefits:[6]

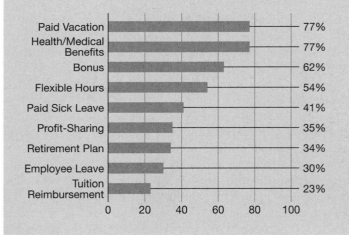

Benefit	Percentage
Paid Vacation	77%
Health/Medical Benefits	77%
Bonus	62%
Flexible Hours	54%
Paid Sick Leave	41%
Profit-Sharing	35%
Retirement Plan	34%
Employee Leave	30%
Tuition Reimbursement	23%

Figure 4
Illustration of Payroll Liabilities

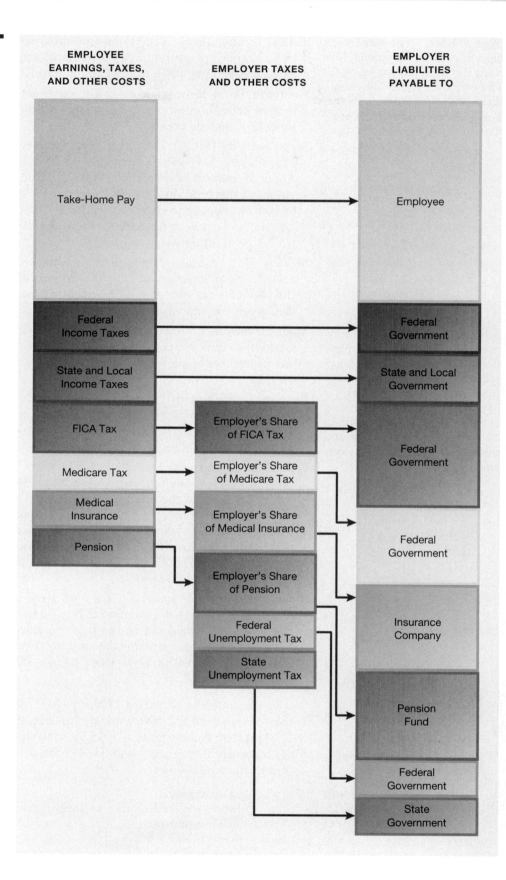

Federal Income Taxes   Federal income taxes are collected on a "pay as you go" basis. Employers are required to withhold appropriate taxes from employees' paychecks and pay them to the United States Treasury.

State and Local Income Taxes   Most states and some local governments have income taxes. In most cases, the procedures for withholding are similar to those for federal income taxes.

Social Security (FICA) Tax   The social security program (the Federal Insurance Contribution Act) offers retirement and disability benefits and survivor's benefits. About 90 percent of the people working in the United States fall under the provisions of this program. The 2002 social security tax rate of 6.2 percent was paid by *both* employee and employer on the first $84,900 earned by an employee during the calendar year. Both the rate and the base to which it applies are subject to change in future years.

Medicare Tax   A major extension of the social security program is Medicare, which provides hospitalization and medical insurance for persons over age 65. In 2002, the Medicare tax rate was 1.45 percent of gross income, with no limit, paid by *both* employee and employer.

Medical Insurance   Many organizations provide medical benefits to employees. Often, the employee contributes a portion of the cost through withholdings from income and the employer pays the rest, usually a greater amount, to the insurance company.

Pension Contributions   Many organizations also provide pension benefits to employees. In a manner similar to that for medical insurance, a portion of the pension contribution is withheld from the employee's income and the rest is paid by the organization to the pension fund.

Federal Unemployment Insurance (FUTA) Tax   This tax is intended to pay for programs to help unemployed workers. It is paid *only* by employers and recently was 6.2 percent of the first $7,000 earned by each employee (this amount may vary from state to state). Against this federal tax, the employer is allowed a credit for unemployment taxes paid to the state. The maximum credit is 5.4 percent of the first $7,000 earned by each employee. Most states set their rate at this maximum. Thus, the FUTA tax most often paid is .8 percent (6.2 percent − 5.4 percent) of the taxable wages.

State Unemployment Insurance Tax   All state unemployment programs provide for unemployment compensation to be paid to eligible unemployed workers. This compensation is paid out of the fund provided by the 5.4 percent of the first $7,000 (or whatever amount the state sets) earned by each employee. In some states, employers with favorable employment records may be entitled to pay less than 5.4 percent.

To illustrate the recording of the payroll, assume that on February 15 total employee wages are $32,500, with withholdings of $5,400 for federal income taxes, $1,200 for state income taxes, $2,015 for social security tax, $471 for Medicare tax, $900 for medical insurance, and $1,300 for pension contributions. The entry to record this payroll follows:

A = L + OE				
+ −	Feb. 15	Wages Expense	32,500	
+		Employees' Federal Income Taxes Payable		5,400
+		Employees' State Income Taxes Payable		1,200
+		Social Security Tax Payable		2,015
+		Medicare Tax Payable		471
+		Medical Insurance Payable		900
+		Pension Contributions Payable		1,300
		Wages Payable		21,214
		To record payroll		

Note that the employees' take-home pay is only $21,214, although $32,500 was earned.

Using the same data, the additional employer taxes and other benefits costs would be recorded as follows, assuming that the payroll taxes correspond to the discussion above and that the employer pays 80 percent of the medical insurance premiums and half of the pension contributions:

A = L + OE
 +   –
    +
    +
    +
    +
    +

Feb. 15	Payroll Taxes and Benefits Expense	9,401	
	Social Security Tax Payable		2,015
	Medicare Tax Payable		471
	Medical Insurance Payable		3,600
	Pension Contributions Payable		1,300
	Federal Unemployment Tax Payable		260
	State Unemployment Tax Payable		1,755
	To record payroll taxes and other costs		

Note that the payroll taxes and benefits increase the total cost of the payroll to $41,901 ($9,401 + $32,500), which exceeds by almost 29 percent the amount earned by employees. This is a typical situation.

■ **UNEARNED REVENUES**   **Unearned revenues** represent obligations for goods or services that the company must provide in a future accounting period in return for an advance payment from a customer. For example, a publisher of a monthly magazine who receives annual subscriptions totaling $240 would make the following entry:

A = L + OE
 +   +

Cash	240	
Unearned Subscriptions		240
Receipt of annual subscriptions		
in advance		

The publisher now has a liability of $240 that will be reduced gradually as monthly issues of the magazine are mailed:

A = L + OE
 –   +

Unearned Subscriptions	20	
Subscription Revenues		20
Delivery of monthly magazine issues		

Many businesses, such as repair companies, construction companies, and special-order firms, ask for a deposit or advance from a customer before they will begin work. Such advances are also current liabilities until the goods or services are actually delivered.

ESTIMATED LIABILITIES

Estimated liabilities are definite debts or obligations whose exact dollar amount cannot be known until a later date. Since there is no doubt about the existence of the legal obligation, the primary accounting problem is to estimate and record the amount of the liability. Examples of estimated liabilities are income taxes, property taxes, product warranties, and vacation pay.

KEY POINT: Estimated liabilities are recorded and presented on the financial statements in the same way as definitely determinable liabilities. The only difference is that estimated liabilities involve some uncertainty in their computation.

FOCUS ON BUSINESS PRACTICE

Those Little Coupons Can Add Up.

Many companies promote their products by issuing coupons that offer "cents off" or other enticements. Since four out of five shoppers use coupons, companies are forced by competition to distribute them. The total value of unredeemed coupons, each of which represents a potential liability for the issuing company, is truly staggering. NCH Promotional Services <www.wattsgroup.com>, a company owned by Dun & Bradstreet, estimates that almost 300 billion coupons are issued annually. Of course, the liability depends on how many of the coupons will actually be redeemed. NCH estimates that number at approximately 6 billion, or about 2 percent. Thus, a big advertiser that puts a cents-off coupon in Sunday papers to reach 60 million people can be faced with liability for 1,200,000 coupons. The total value of coupons redeemed each year is estimated at more than $4 billion.[7]

■ INCOME TAXES The income of a corporation is taxed by the federal government, most state governments, and some cities and towns. The amount of income taxes liability depends on the results of operations. Often the results are not known until after the end of the year. However, because income taxes are an expense in the year in which income is earned, an adjusting entry is necessary to record the estimated tax liability. The entry is as follows:

A = L + OE
    +   −

Dec. 31	Income Taxes Expense	53,000	
	Estimated Income Taxes Payable		53,000
	To record estimated federal income taxes		

Sole proprietorships and partnerships do *not* pay income taxes. Their owners must report their share of the firm's income on their individual tax returns.

ENRICHMENT NOTE: The process of accruing property tax each month could be applied to income taxes if a company desires monthly financial statements.

■ PROPERTY TAX PAYABLE Property taxes are levied on real property, such as land and buildings, and on personal property, such as inventory and equipment. Property taxes are a main source of revenue for local governments. They are usually assessed annually against the property involved. Because the fiscal years of local governments and their assessment dates rarely correspond to a firm's fiscal year, it is necessary to estimate the amount of property tax that applies to each month of the year.

KEY POINT: Recording product warranty expense in the year of the sale follows the matching rule.

■ PRODUCT WARRANTY LIABILITY When a firm places a warranty on its product (or its service) at the time of sale, a liability exists for the length of the warranty. The cost of the warranty is properly debited to an expense account in the period of sale because it is a feature of the product sold and thus is included in the price the customer pays for the product. On the basis of experience, it should be possible to estimate the amount the warranty will cost in the future. Some products will require little warranty service; others may require much. Thus, there will be an average cost per product.

For example, assume a muffler company guarantees that it will replace free of charge any muffler it sells that fails during the time the buyer owns the car. The company charges a small service fee for replacing the muffler. This warranty is an important selling feature for the firm's mufflers. In the past, 6 percent of the mufflers sold have been returned for replacement under the warranty. The average cost of a muffler is $50. Assume that during July, the company sold 350 mufflers. The accrued liability would be recorded as an adjustment at the end of July as shown below:

A = L + OE
    +   −

July 31	Product Warranty Expense	1,050	
	Estimated Product Warranty Liability		1,050
	To record estimated product warranty expense:		
	Number of units sold	350	
	Rate of replacement under warranty	× .06	
	Estimated units to be replaced	21	
	Estimated cost per unit	× $ 50	
	Estimated liability for product warranty	$1,050	

When a muffler is returned for replacement under the warranty, the cost of the muffler is charged against the Estimated Product Warranty Liability account. For example, assume that on December 5, a customer returns with a defective muffler and pays a $20 service fee to have the muffler replaced. Assume that this particular muffler cost $40. The entry is as follows:

A = L + OE
+   −   +
−

Dec. 5	Cash	20	
	Estimated Product Warranty Liability	40	
	Service Revenue		20
	Merchandise Inventory		40
	Replacement of muffler under warranty		

FOCUS ON BUSINESS PRACTICE

Are Frequent-Flier Miles a Liability or a Revenue?

In the early 1980s, American Airlines, Inc. <www.aa.com> developed a frequent-flier program that gives free trips and other awards to customers based on the number of miles they fly on the airline. Since then, many other airlines have instituted similar programs, and it is estimated that 38 million people now participate in them. Today, U.S. airlines have more than 3 trillion "miles" outstanding. Seven to eight percent of all passengers are traveling on free tickets. Estimated liabilities for these tickets have become an important consideration in evaluating an airline's financial position. Complicating the estimate is that almost half the miles have been earned on purchases from hotels, car rental and telephone companies, and Internet service providers like AOL, and through the use of credit cards. In these cases, the companies giving the miles must pay the airlines at the rate of $.02 per mile. Thus, a free ticket obtained with 25,000 miles provides revenue to the airline of $500. In a recent year, airlines took in more than $2 billion from this source.[8]

◆ **STOP AND THINK!**

Do adjusting entries involving estimated liabilities and accruals ever affect cash flows?

They never affect cash flows at the time of the entry, but they may require the payment of a liability in the future. ■

www.usairways.com

■ **VACATION PAY LIABILITY**   In most companies, employees accrue paid vacation as they work during the year. For example, an employee may earn two weeks of paid vacation for each 50 weeks of work. Therefore, the person is paid 52 weeks' salary for 50 weeks' work. Theoretically, the cost of the two weeks' vacation should be allocated as an expense over the whole year so that month-to-month costs will not be distorted. The vacation pay represents 4 percent (two weeks' vacation divided by 50 weeks) of a worker's pay. Every week worked earns the employee a small fraction (4 percent) of vacation pay.

Vacation pay liability can represent a substantial amount of money. As noted in this chapter's Decision Point, US Airways reported at its 2001 year end accrued salaries, wages, and vacation liabilities of $367 million.

Suppose that a company with a vacation policy of two weeks of paid vacation for each 50 weeks of work has a payroll of $21,000, of which $1,000 was paid to employees on vacation for the week ended April 20. Because of turnover and rules regarding term of employment, it is assumed that only 75 percent of employees will ultimately collect vacation pay. The computation of vacation pay expense based on the payroll of employees not on vacation ($21,000 − $1,000) is as follows: $20,000 × 4 percent × 75 percent = $600. The entry to record vacation pay expense for the week ended April 20 is as follows:

A = L + OE				
+ −	Apr. 20	Vacation Pay Expense	600	
		Estimated Liability for Vacation Pay		600
		Estimated vacation pay expense		

At the time employees receive their vacation pay, an entry is made debiting Estimated Liability for Vacation Pay and crediting Cash or Wages Payable. This entry records the $1,000 paid to employees on vacation during August:

A* = L + OE				
− −	Aug. 31	Estimated Liability for Vacation Pay	1,000	
		Cash (or Wages Payable)		1,000
*Assumes cash paid.		Wages of employees on vacation		

The treatment of vacation pay presented in this example may also be applied to other payroll costs, such as bonus plans and contributions to pension plans.

✔ Check out ACE for a Review Quiz at http://accounting.college.hmco.com/students.

CONTINGENT LIABILITIES AND COMMITMENTS

LO3 Distinguish *contingent liabilities* from *commitments*.

RELATED TEXT ASSIGNMENTS
Q: 17, 18
SE: 3
SD: 2, 5
FRA: 2, 3, 5, 6, 7

The FASB requires companies to disclose in a note to their financial statements any contingent liabilities and commitments they may have.

A **contingent liability** is not an existing obligation. Rather, it is a potential liability because it depends on a future event arising out of a past transaction. For instance, a construction company that built a bridge may have been sued by the state for using poor materials. The past transaction is the building of the bridge under contract. The future event is the outcome of the lawsuit, which is not yet known.

KEY POINT: Contingencies are recorded when they are probable and can be reasonably estimated.

The FASB has established two conditions for determining when a contingency should be entered in the accounting records: (1) the liability must be probable, and (2) it can be reasonably estimated.[9] Estimated liabilities like the income taxes liability, warranty liability, and vacation pay liability that we described earlier meet those conditions. Therefore, they are accrued in the accounting records.

www.gm.com

In a survey of 600 large companies, the most common types of contingencies reported were litigation, which can involve many different issues, and environmental concerns.[10] The following description of contingent liabilities comes from the notes in the annual report of General Motors Corp., the world's largest automobile manufacturer:

> Litigation is subject to uncertainties and the outcome of individual litigated matters is not predictable with assurance. Various legal actions, governmental investigations, claims, and proceedings are pending against the Corporation, including those arising out of alleged product defects; employment-related matters; governmental regulations relating to safety, emissions, and fuel economy; product warranties; financial services; dealer, supplier, and other contractual relationships and environmental matters. . . . After discussion with counsel, it is the opinion of management that such liability is not expected to have a material adverse effect on the Corporation's consolidated financial condition or results of operations.[11]

www.usairways.com

● **STOP AND THINK!**

When would a commitment be recognized in the records?

When a transaction has occurred, such as when a purchase agreement is followed up and completed or when a lease payment is made. ■

A **commitment** is a legal obligation that does not meet the technical requirements for recognition as a liability. The most common examples are purchase agreements and leases.[12] For example, in a note to its financial statements, US Airways states: "The Company had 65 A320 aircraft on firm order, 182 aircraft subject to reconfirmation prior to scheduled delivery, and options for 63 additional aircraft." The note goes on to say, "The company leases certain aircraft and ground equipment, in addition to the majority of the ground facilities."[13] It then summarizes the amounts of the lease obligations.

✓ Check out ACE for a Review Quiz at http://accounting.college.hmco.com/students.

THE TIME VALUE OF MONEY

LO4 Define *interest* and distinguish between simple and compound interest.

RELATED TEXT ASSIGNMENTS
Q: 19
SE: 8

"**T**ime is money" is a common expression. It derives from the concept of the **time value of money**, which refers to the effects of the passage of time on holding or not holding money. **Interest** is the specific cost measure of these effects for a given period of time.

The interest associated with the time value of money is an important consideration in any business decision. For example, an individual who holds $100 for one year without putting that $100 in a savings account has forgone the interest that the money could have earned. Thus, there is a cost associated with holding this money equal to the interest that could have been earned. On the other hand, a businessperson who accepts a non-interest-bearing note instead of cash for the sale of merchandise but includes the interest implicitly in the price of the merchandise is not forgoing the interest that could have been earned on that money. These examples illustrate that the timing of the receipt and payment of cash must be considered in making business decisions.

KEY POINT: Compound interest is the most useful concept of interest in business practice.

Simple interest is the interest cost for one or more periods if we assume that the amount on which the interest is computed stays the same from period to period. **Compound interest** is the interest cost for two or more periods if we assume that after each period, the interest of that period is added to the amount on which interest is computed in future periods. In other words, compound interest is interest earned on a principal sum that is increased at the end of each period by the interest of that period. The following two examples illustrate these concepts:

Example of Simple Interest   Joe Sanchez accepts an 8 percent, $30,000 note due in 90 days. How much will he receive in total at that time? Remember that the formula for calculating simple interest is as follows:

$$\text{Interest} = \text{Principal} \times \text{Rate} \times \text{Time}$$
$$= \$30,000 \times 8/100 \times 90/360$$
$$= \$600$$

Therefore, the total that Sanchez will receive is calculated as follows:

$$\text{Total} = \text{Principal} + \text{Interest}$$
$$= \$30,000 + \$600$$
$$= \$30,600$$

◆ STOP AND THINK!

Is a friend who borrows money from you for three years and agrees to pay you the interest due after each year paying simple or compound interest?

Because your friend is paying interest only on the loan, not on the past accumulated interest, he or she is paying simple interest. ■

Example of Compound Interest   Ann Clary deposits $5,000 in a savings account that pays 6 percent interest. She expects to leave the principal and accumulated interest in the account for three years. How much will her account total at the end of three years? Assume that the interest is paid at the end of the year and is added to the principal at that time, and that this total in turn earns interest. The amount at the end of three years can be computed as follows:

(1) Year	(2) Principal Amount at Beginning of Year	(3) Annual Amount of Interest (Col. 2 × 6%)	(4) Accumulated Amount at End of Year (Col. 2 + Col. 3)
1	$5,000.00	$300.00	$5,300.00
2	5,300.00	318.00	5,618.00
3	5,618.00	337.08	5,955.08

At the end of three years, Clary will have $5,955.08 in her savings account. Note that the annual amount of interest increases each year by the interest rate times the interest of the previous year. For example, between year 1 and year 2, the interest increased by $18 ($318 − $300), which equals 6 percent times $300.

✔ Check out ACE for a Review Quiz at http://accounting.college.hmco.com/students.

FUTURE VALUE

LO5 Use compound interest tables to compute the future value of a single sum at compound interest and of an ordinary annuity.

RELATED TEXT ASSIGNMENTS

Q: 20

SE: 8, 9

E: 9, 10, 17, 18

P: 5, 8

Another way to ask the question posed in the example of compound interest is, What is the future value of a single sum ($5,000) at compound interest (6 percent) for three years? **Future value** is the amount an investment will be worth at a future date if invested at compound interest. A businessperson often wants to know future value, but the method of computing future value that we just illustrated is too time-consuming in practice. Imagine how tedious the calculation would be if the example were ten years instead of three. Fortunately, there are tables that simplify solving problems involving compound interest. Table 1, which shows the future value of $1 after a given number of time periods, is an example. This table and the others in this chapter are excerpts from larger tables in the appendix on future value and present value tables.

FUTURE VALUE OF A SINGLE SUM AT COMPOUND INTEREST

Using Table 1 to compute the future value of Ann Clary's savings account, we simply look down the 6 percent column until we reach the line for 3 periods and find

TABLE 1. Future Value of $1 After a Given Number of Time Periods

Period	1%	2%	3%	4%	5%	6%	7%	8%	9%	10%	12%	14%	15%
1	1.010	1.020	1.030	1.040	1.050	1.060	1.070	1.080	1.090	1.100	1.120	1.140	1.150
2	1.020	1.040	1.061	1.082	1.103	1.124	1.145	1.166	1.188	1.210	1.254	1.300	1.323
3	1.030	1.061	1.093	1.125	1.158	1.191	1.225	1.260	1.295	1.331	1.405	1.482	1.521
4	1.041	1.082	1.126	1.170	1.216	1.262	1.311	1.360	1.412	1.464	1.574	1.689	1.749
5	1.051	1.104	1.159	1.217	1.276	1.338	1.403	1.469	1.539	1.611	1.762	1.925	2.011
6	1.062	1.126	1.194	1.265	1.340	1.419	1.501	1.587	1.677	1.772	1.974	2.195	2.313
7	1.072	1.149	1.230	1.316	1.407	1.504	1.606	1.714	1.828	1.949	2.211	2.502	2.660
8	1.083	1.172	1.267	1.369	1.477	1.594	1.718	1.851	1.993	2.144	2.476	2.853	3.059
9	1.094	1.195	1.305	1.423	1.551	1.689	1.838	1.999	2.172	2.358	2.773	3.252	3.518
10	1.105	1.219	1.344	1.480	1.629	1.791	1.967	2.159	2.367	2.594	3.106	3.707	4.046

the factor 1.191. This factor, when multiplied by $1, gives the future value of that $1 at compound interest of 6 percent for three periods (years in this case). Thus, we solve the problem as follows:

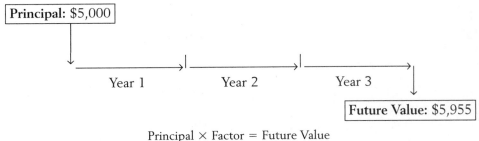

Principal × Factor = Future Value
$5,000 × 1.191 = $5,955

Except for a rounding difference of $.08, the answer is exactly the same as our earlier one.

FUTURE VALUE OF AN ORDINARY ANNUITY

Another common problem involves an **ordinary annuity**, which is a series of equal payments made at the end of equal intervals of time, with compound interest on these payments. For example, assume that at the end of each of the next three years, Ben Katz makes a $200 payment to a savings account that pays 5 percent interest. How much money will he have in his account at the end of the three years? One way of computing the amount is shown in the following table:

(1) Year	(2) Beginning Balance	(3) Interest Earned (5% × Col. 2)	(4) Periodic Payment	(5) Accumulated at End of Period (Col. 2 + Col. 3 + Col. 4)
1	—	—	$200	$200.00
2	$200.00	$10.00	200	410.00
3	410.00	20.50	200	630.50

Katz would have $630.50 in his account at the end of three years, consisting of $600.00 in periodic payments and $30.50 in interest.

This calculation can be simplified by using Table 2. We look down the 5 percent column until we reach period 3 and find the factor 3.153. This factor, when multiplied by $1, gives the future value of a series of three $1 payments at compound interest of 5 percent. Thus, we solve the problem as follows:

TABLE 2. **Future Value of an Ordinary Annuity of $1 Paid in Each Period for a Given Number of Time Periods**

Period	1%	2%	3%	4%	5%	6%	7%	8%	9%	10%	12%	14%	15%
1	1.000	1.000	1.000	1.000	1.000	1.000	1.000	1.000	1.000	1.000	1.000	1.000	1.000
2	2.010	2.020	2.030	2.040	2.050	2.060	2.070	2.080	2.090	2.100	2.120	2.140	2.150
3	3.030	3.060	3.091	3.122	3.153	3.184	3.215	3.246	3.278	3.310	3.374	3.440	3.473
4	4.060	4.122	4.184	4.246	4.310	4.375	4.440	4.506	4.573	4.641	4.779	4.921	4.993
5	5.101	5.204	5.309	5.416	5.526	5.637	5.751	5.867	5.985	6.105	6.353	6.610	6.742
6	6.152	6.308	6.468	6.633	6.802	6.975	7.153	7.336	7.523	7.716	8.115	8.536	8.754
7	7.214	7.434	7.662	7.898	8.142	8.394	8.654	8.923	9.200	9.487	10.09	10.73	11.07
8	8.286	8.583	8.892	9.214	9.549	9.897	10.26	10.64	11.03	11.44	12.30	13.23	13.73
9	9.369	9.755	10.16	10.58	11.03	11.49	11.98	12.49	13.02	13.58	14.78	16.09	16.79
10	10.46	10.95	11.46	12.01	12.58	13.18	13.82	14.49	15.19	15.94	17.55	19.34	20.30

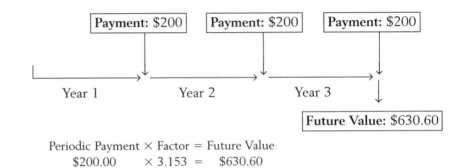

● **STOP AND THINK!**
Why would Mr. Katz be better off if he could begin his payments now instead of at the end of the first year?

Because the first payment would begin earning interest immediately, and the final payment would earn interest for a year. ■

Periodic Payment × Factor = Future Value
$200.00   × 3.153 = $630.60

Except for a rounding difference of $.10, this answer is the same as the one calculated earlier.

✔ Check out ACE for a Review Quiz at http://accounting.college.hmco.com/students.

PRESENT VALUE

LO6 Use compound interest tables to compute the present value of a single sum due in the future and of an ordinary annuity.

RELATED TEXT ASSIGNMENTS
Q: 21, 22
SE: 10
E: 11, 12, 13, 14, 15, 16, 19
P: 4, 5, 8
SD: 6

KEY POINT: Present value is a method of valuing future cash flows.

Suppose that you had the choice of receiving $100 today or one year from today. Intuitively, you would choose to receive the $100 today. Why? You know that if you have the $100 today, you can put it in a savings account to earn interest so that you will have more than $100 a year from today. Therefore, we can say that an amount to be received in the future (future value) is not worth as much today as an amount to be received today (present value) because of the cost associated with the passage of time. In fact, present value and future value are closely related. **Present value** is the amount that must be invested now at a given rate of interest to produce a given future value.

For example, assume that Sue Dapper needs $1,000 one year from now. How much should she invest today to achieve that goal if the interest rate is 5 percent? From earlier examples, the following equation may be established:

Present Value × (1.0 + Interest Rate) = Future Value
Present Value ×   1.05   = $1,000.00
Present Value   = $1,000.00 ÷ 1.05
Present Value   = $952.38

Thus, to achieve a future value of $1,000.00, a present value of $952.38 must be invested. Interest of 5 percent on $952.38 for one year equals $47.62, and these two amounts added together equal $1,000.00.

TABLE 3.   Present Value of $1 to Be Received at the End of a Given Number of Time Periods

Period	1%	2%	3%	4%	5%	6%	7%	8%	9%	10%
1	0.990	0.980	0.971	0.962	0.952	0.943	0.935	0.926	0.917	0.909
2	0.980	0.961	0.943	0.925	0.907	0.890	0.873	0.857	0.842	0.826
3	0.971	0.942	0.915	0.889	0.864	0.840	0.816	0.794	0.772	0.751
4	0.961	0.924	0.888	0.855	0.823	0.792	0.763	0.735	0.708	0.683
5	0.951	0.906	0.863	0.822	0.784	0.747	0.713	0.681	0.650	0.621
6	0.942	0.888	0.837	0.790	0.746	0.705	0.666	0.630	0.596	0.564
7	0.933	0.871	0.813	0.760	0.711	0.665	0.623	0.583	0.547	0.513
8	0.923	0.853	0.789	0.731	0.677	0.627	0.582	0.540	0.502	0.467
9	0.914	0.837	0.766	0.703	0.645	0.592	0.544	0.500	0.460	0.424
10	0.905	0.820	0.744	0.676	0.614	0.558	0.508	0.463	0.422	0.386

PRESENT VALUE OF A SINGLE SUM DUE IN THE FUTURE

When more than one time period is involved, the calculation of present value is more complicated. For example, suppose Don Riley wants to be sure of having $4,000 at the end of three years. How much must he invest today in a 5 percent savings account to achieve this goal? Adapting the above equation, we compute the present value of $4,000 at compound interest of 5 percent for three years in the future:

Year	Amount at End of Year		Divide by		Present Value at Beginning of Year
3	$4,000.00	÷	1.05	=	$3,809.52
2	3,809.52	÷	1.05	=	3,628.11
1	3,628.11	÷	1.05	=	3,455.34

Riley must invest a present value of $3,455.34 to achieve a future value of $4,000.00 in three years. This calculation is also made much easier by using the appropriate table. In Table 3, we look down the 5 percent column until we reach period 3 and find the factor .864. This factor, when multiplied by $1, gives the present value of $1 to be received three years from now at 5 percent interest. Thus, we solve the problem as follows:

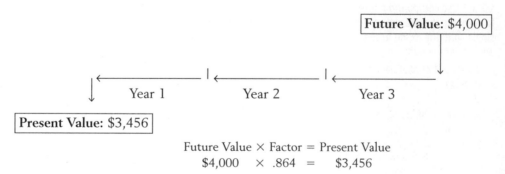

Future Value × Factor = Present Value
$4,000   × .864   = $3,456

Except for a rounding difference of $.66, this result is the same as the one computed earlier.

PRESENT VALUE OF AN ORDINARY ANNUITY

It is often necessary to compute the present value of a series of receipts or payments. When we calculate the present value of equal amounts equally spaced over a period of time, we are computing the present value of an ordinary annuity.

For example, assume that Kathy Foster has sold a piece of property and is to receive $15,000 in three equal annual payments of $5,000, beginning one year from

TABLE 4. Present Value of an Ordinary $1 Annuity Received in Each Period for a Given Number of Time Periods

Period	1%	2%	3%	4%	5%	6%	7%	8%	9%	10%
1	0.990	0.980	0.971	0.962	0.952	0.943	0.935	0.926	0.917	0.909
2	1.970	1.942	1.913	1.886	1.859	1.833	1.808	1.783	1.759	1.736
3	2.941	2.884	2.829	2.775	2.723	2.673	2.624	2.577	2.531	2.487
4	3.902	3.808	3.717	3.630	3.546	3.465	3.387	3.312	3.240	3.170
5	4.853	4.713	4.580	4.452	4.329	4.212	4.100	3.993	3.890	3.791
6	5.795	5.601	5.417	5.242	5.076	4.917	4.767	4.623	4.486	4.355
7	6.728	6.472	6.230	6.002	5.786	5.582	5.389	5.206	5.033	4.868
8	7.652	7.325	7.020	6.733	6.463	6.210	5.971	5.747	5.535	5.335
9	8.566	8.162	7.786	7.435	7.108	6.802	6.515	6.247	5.995	5.759
10	9.471	8.983	8.530	8.111	7.722	7.360	7.024	6.710	6.418	6.145

ENRICHMENT NOTE: Present value is one of the most common techniques used by financial analysts to determine the value today of potential investments.

today. What is the present value of this sale, assuming a current interest rate of 5 percent? This present value may be computed by calculating a separate present value for each of the three payments (using Table 3) and summing the results, as shown in the following table:

Future Receipts (Annuity)				Present Value Factor at 5 Percent (from Table 3)		Present Value
Year 1	Year 2	Year 3				
$5,000			×	.952	=	$ 4,760
	$5,000		×	.907	=	4,535
		$5,000	×	.864	=	4,320
Total Present Value						$13,615

The present value of this sale is $13,615. Thus, there is an implied interest cost (given the 5 percent rate) of $1,385 associated with the payment plan that allows the purchaser to pay in three installments.

We can make this calculation more easily by using Table 4. We look down the 5 percent column until we reach period 3 and find the factor 2.723. This factor, when multiplied by $1, gives the present value of a series of three $1 payments (spaced one year apart) at compound interest of 5 percent. Thus, we solve the problem as follows:

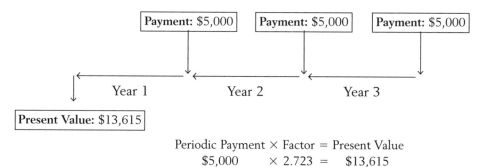

Periodic Payment × Factor = Present Value
$5,000 × 2.723 = $13,615

This result is the same as the one computed earlier.

TIME PERIODS

KEY POINT: The interest rate used when compounding less than one year is the annual rate divided by the number of periods in a year.

In most cases, the compounding period is one year, and the interest rate is stated on an annual basis. However, the left-hand column in Tables 1 to 4 refers not to years but to periods. This wording is intended to accommodate compounding periods of less than one year. Savings accounts that record interest quarterly and bonds that pay interest semiannually are cases in which the compounding period is less than one year. To use the tables in such cases, it is first necessary to (1) divide the annual interest rate by the number of periods in the year, and (2) multiply the number of periods in one year by the number of years.

For example, let us compute the maturity (future) value of a $6,000 note that is to be paid in two years and that carries an annual interest rate of 8 percent. The compounding period is semiannual. Before using Table 1 in this computation, it is necessary to compute the interest rate that applies to each compounding period and the total number of compounding periods. First, the interest rate to use is 4 percent (8% annual rate ÷ 2 periods per year). Second, the total number of compounding periods is 4 (2 periods per year × 2 years). From Table 1, therefore, the maturity value of the note is computed as follows:

$$\text{Principal} \times \text{Factor} = \text{Future Value}$$
$$\$6,000 \quad \times 1.170 = \quad \$7,020$$

The note will be worth $7,020 in two years.

This procedure for determining the interest rate and the number of periods when the compounding period is less than one year may be used with all four tables.

✅ Check out ACE for a Review Quiz at http://accounting.college.hmco.com/students.

APPLICATION OF THE TIME VALUE OF MONEY TO ACCOUNTING

LO7 Apply the concept of the time value of money to simple accounting situations.

RELATED TEXT ASSIGNMENTS
Q: 23
SE: 11
E: 11, 13, 14, 15, 16, 17, 18, 19
P: 4, 5, 8
SD: 3, 6

🔴 **STOP AND THINK!**
Do business decision makers most commonly want to know the future value or the present value of future cash flows?

Although they may want to know the future value of a series of cash flows, they will find present value more useful because decisions are made in the present, which requires knowledge of the present value of future cash flows. ∎

Both future value and present value concepts of the time value of money are widely applicable in the discipline of accounting. The FASB has made them the foundation of its approach to using cash flow information in determining the fair value of assets or liabilities.[14] Here, the purpose is to demonstrate their usefulness in some simple applications. In-depth study of the time value of money is deferred to more advanced courses.

VALUING AN ASSET

An asset is something that will provide future benefits to the company that owns it. Usually, the purchase price of an asset represents the present value of these future benefits. It is possible to evaluate the proposed purchase price by comparing it with the present value of the asset to the company.

For example, Sam Hurst is thinking of buying a new machine that will reduce his annual labor cost by $700 per year. The machine will last eight years. The interest rate that Hurst assumes for making managerial decisions is 10 percent. What is the maximum amount (present value) that Hurst should pay for the machine?

The present value of the machine to Hurst is equal to the present value of an ordinary annuity of $700 per year for eight years at compound interest of 10 percent. Using the factor from Table 4, we compute the value as follows:

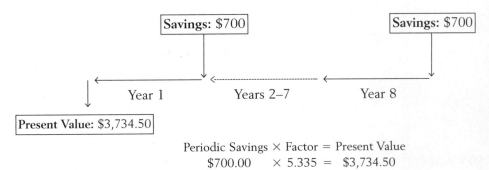

$$\text{Periodic Savings} \times \text{Factor} = \text{Present Value}$$
$$\$700.00 \quad \times 5.335 = \quad \$3,734.50$$

Hurst should not pay more than $3,734.50 for the new machine because this amount equals the present value of the benefits he would receive from owning it.

DEFERRED PAYMENT

To encourage buyers to make a purchase, sellers sometimes agree to defer payment for a sale. This practice is common in the farm implement industry, since farmers often need new equipment in the spring but cannot pay for it until they sell their crops in the fall.

Assume that Plains Implement Corporation sells a tractor to Dana Washington for $50,000 on February 1, agreeing to take payment ten months later, on December 1. When such an agreement is made, the future payment includes not only the sale price, but also an implied (imputed) interest cost. If the prevailing annual interest rate for such transactions is 12 percent compounded monthly, the actual price of the tractor would be the present value of the future payment, computed using the factor from Table 3 (10 periods, 1 percent), as follows:

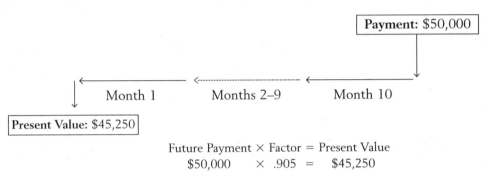

Future Payment × Factor = Present Value
$50,000   × .905 = $45,250

The purchase in Washington's records and the sale in Plains's records are recorded at the present value, $45,250. The balance consists of interest expense or interest income. The entries necessary to record the purchase in Washington's records and the sale in Plains's records are as follows:

	Washington Journal				Plains Journal			

A = L + OE
+   +
	Feb. 1	Tractor
		  Accounts Payable
		    Purchase of tractor
			45,250	45,250	Accounts Receivable
					  Sales
					    Sale of tractor
						45,250	45,250	A = L + OE
								+ +

When Washington pays for the tractor, the entries are as follows:

	Washington Journal				Plains Journal			

A = L + OE
−   −   −
	Dec. 1	Accounts Payable
		Interest Expense
		  Cash
		    Payment on account,
		    including imputed
		    interest expense
			45,250
			4,750
				50,000	Cash
					  Accounts Receivable
					  Interest Income
					    Receipt on account
					    from Washington,
					    including imputed
					    interest earned
						50,000	45,250
							4,750
								A = L + OE
								+ +
								−

INVESTMENT OF IDLE CASH

Let us assume that Childware Corporation, a toy manufacturer, has just completed a successful fall selling season and has $10,000,000 in cash to invest for six months. The company places the cash in a money market account that is expected to pay 12 percent annual interest. Interest is compounded monthly and credited to the company's account each month. How much cash will the company have at the end of six months, and what entries will be made to record the investment and the monthly interest? The future value factor from Table 1 is based on six monthly periods of 1 percent (12 percent divided by 12 months), and the future value is computed as follows:

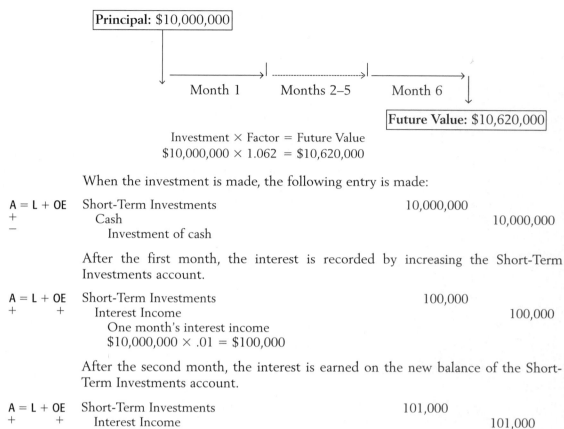

$$\text{Investment} \times \text{Factor} = \text{Future Value}$$
$$\$10,000,000 \times 1.062 = \$10,620,000$$

When the investment is made, the following entry is made:

A = L + OE
+
−

Short-Term Investments	10,000,000	
Cash		10,000,000
Investment of cash		

After the first month, the interest is recorded by increasing the Short-Term Investments account.

A = L + OE
+   +

Short-Term Investments	100,000	
Interest Income		100,000
One month's interest income		
$\$10,000,000 \times .01 = \$100,000$		

After the second month, the interest is earned on the new balance of the Short-Term Investments account.

A = L + OE
+   +

Short-Term Investments	101,000	
Interest Income		101,000
One month's interest income		
$\$10,100,000 \times .01 = \$101,000$		

Entries would continue in a similar manner for four more months, at which time the balance of Short-Term Investments would be about $10,620,000. The actual amount accumulated may vary because the interest rate paid on money market accounts can vary over time as a result of changes in market conditions.

ACCUMULATION OF A FUND FOR LOAN REPAYMENT

When a company owes a large fixed amount due in several years, management would be wise to accumulate a fund to pay off the debt at maturity. When creditors agree to provide a loan, they sometimes require that such a fund be established. In establishing the fund, management must determine how much cash to set aside each period in order to pay the debt. The amount will depend on the estimated rate of interest the investments will earn. Assume that Vason Corporation agrees with a creditor to set aside cash at the end of each year to accumulate enough to pay off a $100,000 note due in five years. Since the first contribution to the fund will be made in one year, five annual contributions will be made by the time the note is due. Assume also that the fund is projected to earn 8 percent, compounded annually. The amount of each annual payment is calculated using Table 2 (5 periods, 8 percent), as follows:

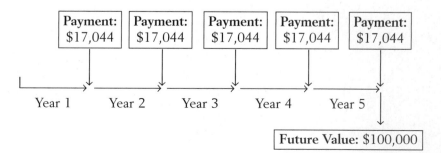

$$\text{Future Value of Fund} \div \text{Factor} = \text{Annual Investment}$$
$$\$100,000 \quad \div \ 5.867 \ = \$17,044 \text{ (rounded)}$$

Each year's contribution to the fund is $17,044. This contribution is recorded as follows:

A = L + OE   Loan Repayment Fund   17,044
+   Cash   17,044
–   Annual contribution to loan repayment fund

OTHER ACCOUNTING APPLICATIONS

There are many other applications of present value in accounting, including imputing interest on non-interest-bearing notes, accounting for installment notes, valuing a bond, and recording lease obligations. Present value is also applied in such areas as pension obligations; premium and discount on debt; depreciation of property, plant, and equipment; capital expenditure decisions; and generally any problem in which time is a factor.

✔ Check out ACE for a Review Quiz at http://accounting.college.hmco.com/students.

Chapter Review

REVIEW OF LEARNING OBJECTIVES

LO1 Identify the management issues related to recognition, valuation, classification, and disclosure of current liabilities.

Liabilities are legal obligations for future payment of assets or future performance of services. They result from past transactions and should be recognized at the time a transaction obligates a company to make future payments. They are valued at the amount of money necessary to satisfy the obligation or at the fair value of goods or services that must be delivered. Liabilities are classified as current or long term. Supplemental disclosure is required when the nature or details of the obligations would help in understanding the liability. Liabilities are an important consideration in assessing a company's liquidity. Key measures are working capital, payables turnover, and average days' payable.

LO2 Identify, compute, and record definitely determinable and estimated current liabilities.

Two principal categories of current liabilities are definitely determinable liabilities and estimated liabilities. Although definitely determinable liabilities, such as accounts payable, notes payable, accrued liabilities, dividends payable, and the current portion of long-term debt, can be measured exactly, the accountant must still be careful not to overlook existing liabilities in these categories. Estimated liabilities, such as liabilities for income taxes, property taxes, and product warranties, definitely exist, but the amounts must be estimated and recorded properly.

LO3 Distinguish *contingent liabilities* from *commitments*.

A contingent liability is a potential liability that arises from a past transaction and is dependent on a future event. Examples of contingent liabilities are lawsuits, income tax disputes, discounted notes receivable, guarantees of debt, and failure to follow government regulations. A commitment is a legal obligation, such as a purchase agreement, that is not recorded as a liability.

LO4 Define *interest* and distinguish between simple and compound interest.

Interest is the cost of using money for a specific period of time. In computing simple interest, the amount on which the interest is computed stays the same from period to period. In computing compound interest, the interest for a period is added to the principal amount before the interest for the next period is computed.

LO5 Use compound interest tables to compute the future value of a single sum at compound interest and of an ordinary annuity.

Future value is the amount an investment will be worth at a future date if invested at compound interest. An ordinary annuity is a series of equal payments made at the end of equal intervals of time, with compound interest on the payments. Use Table 1 in the appendix on future value and present value tables to compute the future value of a single sum and Table 2 in the same appendix to compute the future value of an ordinary annuity.

LO6 Use compound interest tables to compute the present value of a single sum due in the future and of an ordinary annuity.

Present value is the amount that must be invested now at a given rate of interest to produce a given future value. The present value of an ordinary annuity is the present value of a series of payments. Use Table 3 in the appendix on future value and present value tables to compute the present value of a single sum and Table 4 in the same appendix to compute the present value of an ordinary annuity.

LO7 Apply the concept of the time value of money to simple accounting situations.

Present value may be used in evaluating the proposed purchase price of an asset, in computing the present value of deferred payments, in determining the future value of an investment of idle cash, in establishing a fund for loan repayment, and in many other accounting situations in which time is a factor.

REVIEW OF CONCEPTS AND TERMINOLOGY

The following concepts and terms were introduced in this chapter:

LO1   **Average days' payable:** How long, on average, a company takes to pay its accounts payable; 365 days divided by payables turnover.

LO2   **Commercial paper:** Unsecured loans sold to the public, usually through professionally managed investment firms, as a means of borrowing short-term funds.

LO3   **Commitment:** A legal obligation that does not meet the technical requirements for recognition as a liability.

LO4   **Compound interest:** The interest cost for two or more periods if we assume that after each period, the interest of that period is added to the amount on which interest is computed in future periods.

LO3   **Contingent liability:** A potential liability that arises from a past transaction and is dependent on a future event.

LO1   **Current liabilities:** Debts and obligations expected to be satisfied within one year or within the normal operating cycle, whichever is longer.

LO2   **Definitely determinable liabilities:** Current liabilities that are set by contract or statute and that can be measured exactly.

LO2   **Estimated liabilities:** Definite debts or obligations whose exact amounts cannot be known until a later date.

LO5   **Future value:** The amount an investment will be worth at a future date if invested at compound interest.

LO4   **Interest:** The cost associated with the use of money for a specific period of time.

LO1   **Liabilities:** Legal obligations for the future payment of assets or the future performance of services that result from past transactions.

LO2   **Line of credit:** An arrangement with a bank that allows a company to borrow funds as needed.

LO1   **Long-term liabilities:** Debts or obligations due beyond one year or beyond the normal operating cycle.

LO5   **Ordinary annuity:** A series of equal payments made at the end of equal intervals of time, with compound interest on the payments.

LO1   **Payables turnover:** The number of times, on average, that accounts payable are paid in an accounting period; cost of goods sold plus (or minus) change in merchandise inventory divided by average accounts payable.

LO6   **Present value:** The amount that must be invested now at a given rate of interest to produce a given future value.

LO2   **Salaries:** Compensation of employees who are paid at a monthly or yearly rate.

LO4   **Simple interest:** The interest cost for one or more periods if we assume that the amount on which the interest is computed stays the same from period to period.

LO4   **Time value of money:** The effects of the passage of time on holding or not holding money.

LO2 **Unearned revenues:** Revenues received in advance for goods or services that will not be delivered during the current accounting period.

LO2 **Wages:** Payment for services of employees at an hourly rate.

REVIEW PROBLEM

Notes Payable Transactions and End-of-Period Entries

LO2 McLaughlin, Inc., whose fiscal year ends June 30, 20xx, completed the following transactions involving notes payable:

May 11	Purchased a small crane by issuing a 60-day, 12 percent note for $54,000. The face of the note does not include interest.
16	Obtained a $40,000 bank loan to finance a temporary increase in receivables by signing a 90-day, 10 percent note. The face value includes interest.
June 30	Made the end-of-year adjusting entry to accrue interest expense.
30	Made the end-of-year adjusting entry to recognize interest expired on the note.
30	Made the end-of-year closing entry pertaining to interest expense.
July 10	Paid the note plus interest on the crane purchase.
Aug. 14	Paid off the note to the bank.

REQUIRED ▶ Prepare entries in journal form for the above transactions.

ANSWER TO REVIEW PROBLEM

20xx

May 11	Equipment	54,000	
	Notes Payable		54,000
	Purchase of crane with 60-day, 12% note		
16	Cash	39,000	
	Discount on Notes Payable	1,000	
	Notes Payable		40,000
	Loan from bank obtained by signing 90-day, 10% note; discount equals $40,000 × .10 × 90/360 = $1,000		
June 30	Interest Expense	900	
	Interest Payable		900
	To accrue interest expense $54,000 × .12 × 50/360 = $900		
30	Interest Expense	500	
	Discount on Notes Payable		500
	To recognize interest on note $1,000 × 45/90 = $500		
30	Income Summary	1,400	
	Interest Expense		1,400
	To close interest expense		
July 10	Notes Payable	54,000	
	Interest Payable	900	
	Interest Expense	180	
	Cash		55,080
	Payment of note on equipment $54,000 × .12 × 10/360 = $180		
Aug. 14	Notes Payable	40,000	
	Cash		40,000
	Payment of bank loan		
14	Interest Expense	500	
	Discount on Notes Payable		500
	Interest expense on matured note $1,000 − $500 = $500		

Chapter Assignments

BUILDING YOUR KNOWLEDGE FOUNDATION

QUESTIONS

1. What are liabilities?
2. Why is the timing of liability recognition important in accounting?
3. At the end of the accounting period, Janson Company had a legal obligation to accept delivery of and pay for a truckload of hospital supplies the following week. Is this legal obligation a liability?
4. Ned Johnson, a star college basketball player, received a contract from the Midwest Blazers to play professional basketball. The contract calls for a salary of $300,000 a year for four years, dependent on his making the team in each of those years. Should this contract be considered a liability and recorded on the books of the basketball team?
5. What is the rule for classifying a liability as current?
6. What are a line of credit and commercial paper? Where do they appear on the balance sheet?
7. A bank is offering Diane Wedge two alternatives for borrowing $2,000. The first alternative is a $2,000, 12 percent, 30-day note. The second alternative is a $2,000, 30-day note discounted at 12 percent. (a) What entries are required by Diane Wedge to record the two loans? (b) What entries are needed by Wedge to record the payment of the two loans? (c) Which alternative favors Wedge, and why?
8. Where should the Discount on Notes Payable account appear on the balance sheet?
9. When can a portion of long-term debt be classified as a current liability?
10. What are three types of employer-related payroll liabilities?
11. How does an employee differ from an independent contractor?
12. Who pays social security and Medicare taxes?
13. Why are unearned revenues classified as liabilities?
14. What is definite about an estimated liability?
15. Why are income taxes payable considered to be estimated liabilities?
16. When does a company incur a liability for a product warranty?
17. What is a contingent liability, and how does it differ from a commitment?
18. What are some examples of contingent liabilities? For what reason is each a contingent liability?
19. What is the difference between simple and compound interest?
20. What is an ordinary annuity?
21. What is the key variable that distinguishes present value from future value?
22. How does the use of a compounding period of less than one year affect the computation of present value?
23. Why is present value important to accounting? (Illustrate your answer by giving concrete examples of applications in accounting.)

SHORT EXERCISES

LO1 Issues in Accounting for Liabilities

SE 1. Indicate whether each of the following actions relates to (a) managing liquidity and cash flow, (b) recognition of liabilities, (c) valuation of liabilities, (d) classification of liabilities, or (e) disclosure of liabilities:

1. Determining that a liability will be paid in less than one year
2. Estimating the amount of a liability
3. Providing information about when liabilities are due and their interest rates
4. Determining when a liability arises
5. Assessing working capital and payables turnover

LO1 **Measuring Short-Term Liquidity**	SE 2.	Rickland Company has current assets of $130,000 and current liabilities of $80,000, of which accounts payable are $70,000. Rickland's cost of goods sold is $460,000, its merchandise inventory increased by $20,000, and accounts payable were $50,000 the prior year. Calculate Rickland's working capital, payables turnover, and average days' payable.

LO2 **Types of Liabilities**
LO3

SE 3. Indicate whether each of the following is (a) a definitely determinable liability, (b) an estimated liability, (c) a commitment, or (d) a contingent liability:

1. Dividends Payable
2. Pending litigation
3. Income Taxes Payable
4. Current portion of long-term debt
5. Vacation Pay Liability
6. Guaranteed loans of another company
7. Purchase agreement

LO2 **Interest Expense: Interest Not Included in Face Value of Note**

SE 4. On the last day of August, Haas Company borrowed $60,000 on a bank note for 60 days at 10 percent interest. Assume that interest is stated separately. Prepare the following entries in journal form: (1) August 31, recording of note; and (2) October 30, payment of note plus interest.

LO2 **Interest Expense: Interest Included in Face Value of Note**

SE 5. Assume the same facts as in **SE 4,** except that interest of $1,000 is included in the face amount of the note and the note is discounted at the bank on August 31. Prepare the following entries in journal form: (1) August 31, recording of note; and (2) October 30, payment of note and recording of interest expense.

LO2 **Payroll Entries**

SE 6. The following payroll totals for the month of April are from the payroll register of Ciafi Corporation: salaries, $223,000.00; federal income taxes withheld, $31,440.00; social security tax withheld, $13,826.00; Medicare tax withheld, $3,233.50; medical insurance deductions, $6,580.00; and salaries subject to unemployment taxes, $156,600.00. Prepare entries in journal form to record (1) the monthly payroll and (2) employer's payroll expense, assuming social security and Medicare taxes equal to the amounts for employees, a federal unemployment insurance tax of .8 percent, a state unemployment tax of 5.4 percent, and medical insurance premiums for which the employer pays 80 percent of the cost.

LO2 **Product Warranty Liability**

SE 7. Sunchow Corp. manufactures and sells travel clocks. Each clock costs $25 to produce and sells for $50. In addition, each clock carries a warranty that provides for free replacement if it fails during the two years following the sale. In the past, 5 percent of the clocks sold have had to be replaced under the warranty. During October, Sunchow sold 52,000 clocks, and 2,800 clocks were replaced under the warranty. Prepare entries in journal form to record the estimated liability for product warranties during the month and the clocks replaced under warranty during the month.

LO4 **Simple and Compound**
LO5 **Interest**

SE 8. Bailyn Motors, Inc., receives a one-year note that carries a 12 percent annual interest rate on $1,500 for the sale of a used car. Compute the maturity value under each of the following assumptions: (1) Simple interest is charged. (2) The interest is compounded semiannually. (3) The interest is compounded quarterly. (4) The interest is compounded monthly.

LO5 **Future Value Calculations**

SE 9. Find the future value of (1) a single payment of $10,000 at 7 percent for ten years, (2) ten annual payments of $1,000 at 7 percent, (3) a single payment of $3,000 at 9 percent for seven years, and (4) seven annual payments of $3,000 at 9 percent.

LO6 **Present Value Calculations**

SE 10. Find the present value of (1) a single payment of $12,000 at 6 percent for 12 years, (2) 12 annual payments of $1,000 at 6 percent, (3) a single payment of $2,500 at 9 percent for five years, and (4) five annual payments of $2,500 at 9 percent.

LO7 **Valuing an Asset for the Purpose of Making a Purchasing Decision**

SE 11. Tim O'Shea owns a machine shop and has the opportunity to purchase a new machine for $15,000. After carefully studying projected costs and revenues, O'Shea estimates that the new machine will produce a net cash flow of $3,600 annually and will last for eight years. O'Shea feels that an interest rate of 10 percent is adequate for his business.

Calculate the present value of the machine to O'Shea. Does the purchase appear to be a correct business decision?

EXERCISES

LO1 **Issues in Accounting for Liabilities**

E 1. Indicate whether each of the following actions relates to (a) managing liquidity and cash flows, (b) recognition of liabilities, (c) valuation of liabilities, (d) classification of liabilities, or (e) disclosure of liabilities:

1. Setting a liability at the fair market value of goods to be delivered
2. Relating the payment date of a liability to the length of the operating cycle
3. Recording a liability in accordance with the matching rule
4. Providing information about financial instruments on the balance sheet
5. Estimating the amount of "cents-off" coupons that will be redeemed
6. Categorizing a liability as long-term debt
7. Measuring working capital
8. Comparing average days' payable with last year

E 2.

LO1 Measuring Short-Term Liquidity

In 20x1, Telo Company had current assets of $310,000 and current liabilities of $200,000, of which accounts payable were $130,000. Cost of goods sold was $850,000, merchandise inventory increased by $40,000, and accounts payable were $110,000 in the prior year. In 20x2, Telo had current assets of $420,000 and current liabilities of $320,000, of which accounts payable were $150,000. Cost of goods sold was $950,000, and merchandise inventory decreased by $30,000. Calculate Telo's working capital, payables turnover, and average days' payable for 20x1 and 20x2. Assess Telo's liquidity and cash flows in relation to the change in payables turnover from 20x1 to 20x2.

E 3.

LO2 Interest Expense: Interest Not Included in Face Value of Note

On the last day of October, Ready Company borrows $30,000 on a bank note for 60 days at 12 percent interest. Interest is not included in the face amount. Prepare the following entries in journal form: (1) October 31, recording of note; (2) November 30, accrual of interest expense; and (3) December 30, payment of note plus interest.

E 4.

LO2 Interest Expense: Interest Included in Face Value of Note

Assume the same facts as in E 3, except that interest is included in the face amount of the note and the note is discounted at the bank on October 31. Prepare the following entries in journal form: (1) October 31, recording of note; (2) November 30, recognition of interest accrued on note; and (3) December 30, payment of note and recording of interest expense.

E 5.

LO2 Sales and Excise Taxes

Web Page Service billed its customers a total of $980,400 for the month of August, including 9 percent federal excise tax and 5 percent sales tax.

1. Determine the proper amount of service revenue to report for the month.
2. Prepare an entry in journal form to record the revenue and related liabilities for the month.

E 6.

LO2 Payroll Entries

At the end of October, the payroll register for Prairie Tool and Die Corporation contained the following totals: wages, $185,500; federal income taxes withheld, $47,442; state income taxes withheld, $7,818; social security tax withheld, $11,501; Medicare tax withheld, $2,689.75; medical insurance deductions, $6,435; and wages subject to unemployment taxes, $28,620.

Prepare entries in journal form to record the (1) monthly payroll and (2) employer payroll expenses, assuming social security and Medicare taxes equal to the amount for employees, a federal unemployment insurance tax of .8 percent, a state unemployment tax of 5.4 percent, and medical insurance premiums for which the employer pays 80 percent of the cost.

E 7.

LO2 Product Warranty Liability

Hoop Company manufactures and sells electronic games. Each game costs $25 to produce and sells for $45. In addition, each game carries a warranty that provides for free replacement if it fails during the two years following the sale. In the past, 7 percent of the games sold had to be replaced under the warranty. During July, Hoop sold 26,000 games, and 2,800 games were replaced under the warranty.

1. Prepare an entry in journal form to record the estimated liability for product warranties during the month.
2. Prepare an entry in journal form to record the games replaced under warranty during the month.

E 8.

LO2 Vacation Pay Liability

Seacliff Corporation gives three weeks' paid vacation to each employee who has worked at the company for one year. Based on studies of employee turnover and previous experience, management estimates that 65 percent of the employees will qualify for vacation pay this year.

1. Assume that Seacliff's July payroll is $600,000, of which $40,000 is paid to employees on vacation. Figure the estimated employee vacation benefit for the month.
2. Prepare an entry in journal form to record the employee benefit for July.
3. Prepare an entry in journal form to record the pay to employees on vacation.

Note: Tables 1 to 4 in the appendix on future value and present value tables may be used where appropriate to solve Exercises E 9 through E 19.

LO5	**Future Value Calculations**	E 9. Peters receives a one-year note for $3,000 that carries a 12 percent annual interest rate for the sale of a used car. Compute the maturity value under each of the following assumptions: (1) The interest is simple interest. (2) The interest is compounded semi-annually. (3) The interest is compounded quarterly. (4) The interest is compounded monthly.

LO5   Future Value Calculations

E 10. Find the future value of (1) a single payment of $20,000 at 7 percent for ten years, (2) ten annual payments of $2,000 at 7 percent, (3) a single payment of $6,000 at 9 percent for seven years, and (4) seven annual payments of $6,000 at 9 percent.

LO6   Determining an Advance
LO7   Payment

E 11. Heidi Mello is contemplating paying five years' rent in advance. Her annual rent is $9,600. Calculate the single sum that would have to be paid now for the advance rent, if we assume compound interest of 8 percent.

LO6   Present Value Calculations

E 12. Find the present value of (1) a single payment of $24,000 at 6 percent for 12 years, (2) 12 annual payments of $2,000 at 6 percent, (3) a single payment of $5,000 at 9 percent for five years, and (4) five annual payments of $5,000 at 9 percent.

LO6   Present Value of a Lump-Sum
LO7   Contract

E 13. A contract calls for a lump-sum payment of $60,000. Find the present value of the contract, assuming that (1) the payment is due in five years, and the current interest rate is 9 percent; (2) the payment is due in ten years, and the current interest rate is 9 percent; (3) the payment is due in five years, and the current interest rate is 5 percent; and (4) the payment is due in ten years, and the current interest rate is 5 percent.

LO6   Present Value of an Annuity
LO7   Contract

E 14. A contract calls for annual payments of $1,200. Find the present value of the contract, assuming that (1) the number of payments is seven, and the current interest rate is 6 percent; (2) the number of payments is 14, and the current interest rate is 6 percent; (3) the number of payments is seven, and the current interest rate is 8 percent; and (4) the number of payments is 14, and the current interest rate is 8 percent.

LO6   Valuing an Asset for the
LO7   Purpose of Making a
**   Purchasing Decision**

E 15. Hal owns a service station and has the opportunity to purchase a car wash machine for $30,000. After carefully studying projected costs and revenues, Hal estimates that the car wash machine will produce a net cash flow of $5,200 annually and will last for eight years. He determines that an interest rate of 14 percent is adequate for his business. Calculate the present value of the machine to Hal. Does the purchase appear to be a correct business decision?

LO6   Deferred Payment
LO7

E 16. Baj Equipment Corporation sold a precision tool machine with computer controls to Elia Corporation for $800,000 on January 2, agreeing to take payment nine months later, on October 2. Assuming that the prevailing annual interest rate for such a transaction is 16 percent compounded quarterly, what is the actual sale (purchase) price of the machine tool, and what journal entries will be made at the time of the purchase (sale) and at the time of the payment (receipt) on the records of both Elia Corporation and Baj Equipment Corporation?

LO5   Investment of Idle Cash
LO7

E 17. Bald Eagle Publishing Company, a publisher of college textbooks, has just completed a successful fall selling season and has $5,000,000 in cash to invest for nine months, beginning on January 1. The company places the cash in a money market account that is expected to pay 12 percent annual interest compounded monthly. Interest is credited to the company's account each month. How much cash will the company have at the end of nine months, and what entries are made to record the investment and the first two monthly (February 1 and March 1) interest amounts?

LO5   Accumulation of a Fund
LO7

E 18. Rima Corporation borrowed $3,000,000 from an insurance company on a five-year note. Management agreed to set aside enough cash at the end of each year to accumulate the amount needed to pay off the note at maturity. Since the first contribution to the fund will be made in one year, four annual contributions are needed. Assuming that the fund will earn 10 percent compounded annually, how much will the annual contribution to the fund be (round to nearest dollar), and what will be the journal entry for the first contribution?

LO6   Negotiating the Sale of a
LO7   Business

E 19. Neil Fusco is attempting to sell his business to Tiffan Howard. The company has assets of $900,000, liabilities of $800,000, and owners' equity of $100,000. Both parties agree that the proper rate of return to expect is 12 percent; however, they differ on other assumptions. Fusco believes that the business will generate at least $100,000 per year of cash flows for 20 years. Howard thinks that $80,000 in cash flows per year is more reasonable and that only ten years in the future should be considered. Using Table 4 in the appendix on future value and present value tables, determine the range for negotiation by computing the present value of Fusco's offer to sell and of Howard's offer to buy.

PROBLEMS

P 1.

LO1   Identification of Current
LO2   Liabilities

Pete Monaco opened a small television repair shop, Monaco Television Repair, on January 2, 20x0. The shop also sells a limited number of television sets. In January 20x1, Monaco realized he had never filed any tax reports for his business and therefore probably owes a considerable amount of taxes. Since he has limited experience in running a business, he has brought you all his business records, including a checkbook, canceled checks, deposit slips, suppliers' invoices, a notice of annual property taxes of $4,620 due to the city, and a promissory note to his father-in-law for $5,000. He wants you to determine what his business owes the government and other parties.

You analyze all his records and determine the following as of December 31, 20x0:

Unpaid invoices for televisions	$ 18,000
Television sales (excluding sales tax)	88,540
Cost of Televisions Sold	62,250
Workers' salaries	20,400
Repair revenues	120,600
Current assets	32,600
Television inventory	23,500

You learn that the company has deducted $952 from the two employees' salaries for federal income taxes owed to the government. The current social security tax is 6.2 percent on maximum earnings of $84,900 for each employee, and the current Medicare tax is 1.45 percent (no maximum earnings). The FUTA tax is 5.4 percent to the state and .8 percent to the federal government on the first $7,000 earned by each employee, and each employee earned more than $7,000. Monaco has not filed a sales tax report to the state (5 percent of sales).

REQUIRED ▶

1. Given these limited facts, determine Monaco Television Repair's current liabilities as of December 31, 20x0.
2. What additional information would you want from Monaco to satisfy yourself that all current liabilities have been identified?
3. Evaluate Monaco's liquidity by calculating working capital, payables turnover, and average days' payable. Comment on the results. (Assume average accounts payable were the same as year-end accounts payable.)

P 2.

LO2   Notes Payable Transactions
and End-of-Period Entries

Iron Paper Company, whose fiscal year ends December 31, completed the following transactions involving notes payable:

20x3

Nov. 25   Purchased a new loading cart by issuing a 60-day, 10 percent note for $43,200.

Dec. 16   Borrowed $50,000 from the bank to finance inventory by signing a 90-day note. The face value of the note includes interest of $1,500. Proceeds received were $48,500.

31   Made the end-of-year adjusting entry to accrue interest expense.

31   Made the end-of-year adjusting entry to recognize the discount expired on the note.

20x4

Jan. 24   Paid off the loading cart note.

Mar. 16   Paid off the inventory note to the bank.

REQUIRED ▶

1. Prepare entries in journal form for the notes payable transactions.
2. In the transaction of December 16, would the bank be better off making the loan with the interest stated separately instead of included in the $50,000? Why or why not?

P 3.

LO2   Product Warranty Liability

The Gander Company manufactures and sells food processors, which it guarantees for five years. If a processor fails, it is replaced free, but the customer is charged a service fee for handling. In the past, management has found that only 3 percent of the processors sold required replacement under the warranty. The average food processor costs the company $240. At the beginning of September, the account for estimated liability for product warranties had a credit balance of $208,000. During September, 250 processors were returned under the warranty. Service fees of $9,860 were collected for handling. During the month, the company sold 2,800 food processors.

REQUIRED ▶

1. Prepare entries in journal form to record (a) the cost of food processors replaced under warranty and (b) the estimated liability for product warranties for processors sold during the month.

2. Compute the balance of the Estimated Product Warranty Liability account at the end of the month.

3. If the company's product warranty liability is underestimated, what are the effects on current and future years' income?

P 4.

LO2 Non-Interest-Bearing Note
LO6 and Valuing an Asset for the
LO7 Purpose of Making a
Purchasing
Decision

REQUIRED ▶

Part A: Valone Corp., a candy manufacturer, needs a machine to heat chocolate. On January 2, 20x5, Valone purchases a machine to accomplish this task from Delia Company by signing a two-year, non-interest-bearing $32,000 note. Valone currently pays 12 percent interest to borrow money at the bank.

Prepare journal entries in Valone's and Delia's records to (1) record the purchase and the note, (2) adjust the accounts after one year, and (3) record payment of the note after two years (on December 31, 20x6). (Assume that reversing entries are not made by either party.)

Part B: Inquerra owns a printing service and has the opportunity to purchase a high-speed copy machine for $20,000. After carefully studying projected costs and revenues, Inquerra estimates that the copy machine will produce a net cash flow of $3,000 annually and will last for eight years. Inquerra determines that an interest rate of 14 percent is adequate for his business.

REQUIRED ▶

Calculate the present value of the machine to Inquerra. Does the purchase appear to be a correct business decision?

P 5.

LO5 Applications of Time Value of
LO6 Money
LO7

Ingersoll Corporation's management took the following actions, which went into effect on January 2, 20x1. Each involved an application of the time value of money.

a. Established a new retirement plan to take effect in three years and authorized three annual payments of $1,000,000, starting January 2, 20x2, to establish the retirement fund.

b. Approved plans for a new distribution center to be built for $2,000,000 and authorized five annual payments, starting January 2, 20x2, to accumulate the funds for the new center.

c. Bought out the contract of a member of top management for a payment of $100,000 per year for four years beginning January 2, 20x2.

d. Set aside $600,000 for possible losses from lawsuits over a defective product. The lawsuits are not expected to be settled for three years.

REQUIRED ▶

Assuming an annual interest rate of 10 percent and using Tables 1 to 4 in this chapter, answer the following questions:

1. In action **a,** how much will the retirement fund accumulate in three years?
2. In action **b,** how much must the annual payment be to reach the goal?
3. In action **c,** what is the cost (present value) of the buyout?
4. In action **d,** how much will the fund total in three years?

ALTERNATE PROBLEMS

P 6.

LO2 Notes Payable Transactions
and End-of-Period Entries

Alhara Corporation, whose fiscal year ends June 30, completed the following transactions involving notes payable:

20xx

May 11   Signed a 90-day, $132,000 note payable to Maine Bank for a working capital loan. The face value included interest of $3,960. Proceeds received were $128,040.

21   Obtained a 60-day extension on a $36,000 trade account payable owed to a supplier by signing a 60-day, $36,000 note. Interest is in addition to the face value, at the rate of 14 percent.

June 30   Made the end-of-year adjusting entry to accrue interest expense.

30   Made the end-of-year adjusting entry to recognize discount expired on the note.

July 20   Paid off the note plus interest due the supplier.

Aug. 9   Paid the amount due to the bank on the 90-day note.

REQUIRED ▶

1. Prepare journal entries for the notes payable transactions.
2. In the transaction of May 11, would the bank be better off making the loan with the interest stated separately instead of included in the $132,000? Why or why not?

P 7.

LO2 Product Warranty Liability

Suds Up Company is engaged in the retail sale of washing machines. Each machine has a 24-month warranty on parts. If a repair under warranty is required, a charge for the labor is made. Management has found that 20 percent of the machines sold require some work before the warranty expires. Furthermore, the average cost of replacement parts has been $120 per repair. At the beginning of June, the account for the estimated liability for product warranties had a credit balance of $28,600. During June, 112 machines were returned under the warranty. The cost of the parts used in repairing the machines was $17,530, and $18,884 was collected as service revenue for the labor involved. During the month, Suds Up Company sold 450 new machines.

REQUIRED ▶

1. Prepare entries in journal form to record each of the following: (a) the warranty work completed during the month, including related revenue; (b) the estimated liability for product warranties for machines sold during the month.
2. Compute the balance of the Estimated Product Warranty Liability account at the end of the month.
3. If the company's product warranty liability is overestimated, what are the effects on current and future years' income?

P 8.

LO5 Applications of Time Value of
LO6 Money
LO7

The management of Jatz, Inc., took the following actions, which went into effect on January 2, 20x3. Each involved an application of the time value of money.

a. Established in a single payment of $50,000 a contingency fund for the possible settlement of a lawsuit. The suit is expected to be settled in two years.
b. Asked for another fund to be established by a single payment to accumulate to $150,000 in four years.
c. Approved purchase of a parcel of land for future plant expansion. Payments are to start January 2, 20x4, at $100,000 per year for 5 years.
d. Determined that a new building to be built on the property in c would cost $800,000 and authorized five annual payments to be paid starting January 2, 20x4, into a fund for its construction.

REQUIRED ▶

Assuming an annual interest rate of 8 percent and using Tables 1 to 4 in this chapter, answer the following questions:

1. In action **a,** how much will the fund total in two years?
2. In action **b,** how much will need to be deposited initially to accumulate the desired amount?
3. In action **c,** what is the purchase price (present value) of the land?
4. In action **d,** how much would the equal annual payments need to be to accumulate enough money to construct the building?

SKILLS DEVELOPMENT CASES

Conceptual Analysis

SD 1.

LO2 Frequent-Flier Plan

America South Airways instituted a frequent-flier program under which passengers accumulate points toward a free flight based on the number of miles they fly on the airline. One point was awarded for each mile flown, with a minimum of 750 miles being given for any flight. Because of competition in 2001, the company began a bonus plan under which passengers receive triple the normal mileage points. In the past, about 1.5 percent of passenger miles were flown by passengers who had converted points to free flights. With the triple mileage program, it is expected that a 2.5 percent rate will be more appropriate for future years. During 2001, the company had passenger revenues of $966.3 million and passenger transportation operating expenses of $802.8 million before depreciation and amortization. Operating income was $86.1 million. What is the appropriate rate to use to estimate free miles? What would be the effect of the estimated liability for free travel by frequent fliers on 2001 net income? Describe several ways to estimate the amount of this liability. Be prepared to discuss the arguments for and against recognizing this liability.

SD 2.

LO2 Nature and Recognition of an
LO3 Estimated Liability

The decision to recognize and record a liability is sometimes a matter of judgment. People who use General Motors <www.gm.com> credit cards earn rebates toward the purchase or lease of GM vehicles in relation to the amount of purchases they make with their cards. General Motors chooses to treat these outstanding rebates as a commitment in the notes to its financial statements:

> GM sponsors a credit card program . . . that offers rebates that can be applied primarily against the purchase or lease of GM vehicles. The amount of rebates avail-

able to qualified cardholders at December 31, 2000 was $3.8 billion, and $3.7 billion at December 31, 1999 and 1998, respectively.[15]

Using the two criteria established by the FASB for recording a contingency, explain GM's reasoning in treating this liability as a commitment in the notes, where it will likely receive less attention by analysts, rather than including it on the income statement as an expense and on the balance sheet as an estimated liability. Do you agree with this position? (**Hint:** Apply the matching rule.)

LO7 Evaluation of an Auto Lease

SD 3. Ford Credit <www.fordcredit.com> ran an advertisement offering three alternatives for a 24-month lease on a new Lincoln automobile. The three alternatives were zero dollars down and $587 per month for 24 months, $1,975 down and $499 per month for 24 months, or $12,283 down and no payments for 24 months.[16] Assuming that you have enough cash to accept any of the three alternatives and that you determine that a 12 percent annual return compounded monthly is the relevant interest rate for you, use Table 4 in the appendix on future value and present value tables to determine which is the best deal. How would your answer change if the interest rate were higher? If it were lower?

Ethical Dilemma

LO2 Known Legal Violations

SD 4. Chop Shop Restaurant is a large steak restaurant in the suburbs of Chicago. Joe Murray, an accounting student at a nearby college, recently secured a full-time accounting job at the restaurant. He felt fortunate to have a good job that accommodated his class schedule because the local economy was very bad. After a few weeks on the job, Murray realized that his boss, the owner of the business, was paying the kitchen workers in cash and was not withholding federal and state income taxes or social security and Medicare taxes. Murray understands that federal and state laws require these taxes to be withheld and paid to the appropriate agency in a timely manner. He also realizes that if he raises this issue, he could lose his job. What alternatives are available to Murray? What action would you take if you were in his position? Why did you make this choice?

Group Activity: Use in class groups. Debrief by asking each group for an alternative. Then debate the ethics of each alternative.

Research Activity

LO2 Basic Research Skills
LO3

SD 5. Indexes for business periodicals, in which you can look up topics of interest, are available in your school library. Three of the most important of these indexes are the *Business Periodicals Index*, *The Wall Street Journal Index*, and the *Accountants' Index*. Using one or more of these indexes, locate and photocopy two articles related to bank financing, commercial paper, product warranties, airline frequent-flier plans, or contingent liabilities. Keep in mind that you may have to look under related topics to find an article. For example, to find articles about contingent liabilities, you might look under litigation, debt guarantees, or environmental losses. For each of the two articles, write a short summary of the situation and tell how it relates to accounting for the topic as described in the text. Be prepared to discuss your results in class.

Decision-Making Practice

LO6 Basketball Contract
LO7

SD 6. The Cleveland Barons' fifth-year forward Reggie Simpson made the All-Star team in 2001. Simpson has three years left on a contract that is to pay him $2.4 million a year. He wants to renegotiate his contract because other players who have equally outstanding records (although they also have more experience) are receiving as much as $10.5 million per year for five years. Management has a policy of never renegotiating a current contract but is willing to consider extending the contract to additional years. In fact, the Barons have offered Simpson an additional three years at $6.0 million, $9.0 million, and $12.0 million, respectively. In addition, they have added an option year at $15.0 million. Management points out that this package is worth $42.0 million, or $10.5 million per year on average. Simpson is considering this offer and is also considering asking for a bonus to be paid upon the signing of the contract. Write a memorandum to Simpson that comments on management's position and evaluates the offer, assuming a current interest rate of 10 percent. (**Hint:** Use present values.) Propose a range for the signing bonus. Finally, include other considerations that may affect the value of the offer.

FINANCIAL REPORTING AND ANALYSIS CASES

Interpreting Financial Reports

FRA 1.

LO1 Comparison of Two Companies' Ratios with Industry Ratios

Both Sun Microsystems Inc. <www.sun.com> and Cisco Systems <www.cisco.com> are in the computer industry. These data (in thousands) are for their fiscal year ends:[17]

	Sun	Cisco
Accounts payable	$ 1,050,000	$ 644,000
Cost of goods sold	10,049,000	11,221,000
Increase (decrease) in inventory	492,000	452,000

Compare the payables turnover ratio and average days' payable for both companies. Comment on the results. How are cash flows affected by average days' payable? How do Sun Microsystems' and Cisco Systems' ratios compare with the computer industry ratios shown in Figures 1 and 2 in this chapter? (Use year-end amounts for ratios.)

FRA 2.

LO3 Classic Case: Contingent Liabilities

In its 1986 annual report, Texaco, Inc. <www.texaco.com>, one of the world's largest oil companies, reported its loss in the biggest damage judgment rendered to that date:

> **Note 17.** Contingent Liabilities
> Pennzoil Litigation
>
> *State Court Action.* On December 10, 1985, the 151st District Court of Harris County, Texas, entered judgment for Pennzoil Company of $7.5 billion actual damages, $3 billion punitive damages, and approximately $600 million prejudgment interest in *Pennzoil Company v. Texaco, Inc.*, an action in which Pennzoil claims that Texaco, Inc., tortiously interfered with Pennzoil's alleged contract to acquire a 3/7ths interest in Getty. Interest began accruing on the judgment at the simple rate of 10% per annum from the date of judgment. Texaco, Inc., believes that there is no legal basis for the judgment, which it believes is contrary to the evidence and applicable law. Texaco, Inc., is pursuing all available remedies to set aside or to reverse the judgment. . . .
>
> The outcome of the appeal on the preliminary injunction and the ultimate outcome of the Pennzoil litigation are not presently determinable, but could have a material adverse effect on the consolidated financial position and the results of the consolidated operations of Texaco, Inc.[18]

At December 31, 1986, Texaco's retained earnings were $12.882 billion, and its cash and marketable securities totaled $3.0 billion. Its net income for 1986 was $.725 billion.

After a series of court reversals and filing for bankruptcy in 1987, Texaco announced in December 1987 an out-of-court settlement with Pennzoil for $3.0 billion. Although less than the original amount, it is still the largest damage payment in history.

REQUIRED ▶

1. What two conditions established by the FASB must a contingent liability meet before it is recorded in the accounting records? Does the situation described in "Note 17. Contingent Liabilities" meet those conditions? Explain your answer.
2. Do the events of 1987 change your answer to 1? Explain your response.
3. How would the settlement have affected Texaco's retained earnings, cash and marketable securities, and net income?

International Company

FRA 3.

LO1 Classification and Disclosure
LO2 of Current Liabilities and
LO3 Contingent Liabilities

Man Nutzfahrzeuge Aktiengesellschaft <www.mannutzfahrzeuge.de>, a German firm, is one of the world's largest truck companies. Accounting in Germany differs in some respects from that in the United States. A good example is the placement and classification of liabilities. On the balance sheet, Man places liabilities below a detailed stockholders' equity section. Man does not distinguish between current and long-term liabilities; however, a note to the financial statements does disclose the amount of the liabilities due within one year. Those liabilities are primarily what we call *definitely determinable liabilities*, such as loans, accounts payable, and notes payable. Estimated liabilities do not seem to appear in this category. There is an asset category called *current assets*, similar to that used in the United States. In another note to the financial statements, Man lists what it calls *contingent liabilities*, which have not been recorded and do not appear on the balance sheet. These include liabilities for hire and leasing contracts, guarantees of loans of other companies, and warranties on trucks.[19]

What do you think of the idea of combining all liabilities, short-term and long-term, in a single item on the balance sheet? Do you think any of the contingent liabilities should be recorded and shown on the balance sheet?

Toys "R" Us Annual Report

FRA 4.

LO1 **Short-Term Liabilities and Seasonality**

Refer to the balance sheet and the liquidity and capital resources section of management's discussion in the Toys "R" Us annual report <www.tru.com>. Compute the payables turnover for 2001 for Toys "R" Us. How does it compare with the payables turnover ratios for the industries shown in Figure 1? Toys "R" Us is a seasonal business. Would you expect short-term borrowings and accounts payable to be unusually high or unusually low at the balance sheet date of February 2, 2002? How does management use short-term financing to meet its needs for cash during the year?

Comparison Case: Toys "R" Us and Walgreen Co.

FRA 5.

LO1 **Payables Analysis and**
LO3 **Commitments and Contingencies**

Refer to the financial statements and notes for Toys "R" Us <www.tru.com> and Walgreens <www.walgreens.com> in the Supplement to Chapter 1.

1. Compute the payables turnover and average days' payable for Toys "R" Us and Walgreens for the past two years. Accounts payable in 1999 were $1,617 million for Toys "R" Us and $1,130.3 million for Walgreens. The merchandise inventory for Toys "R" Us in 1999 was $2,027 million, and for Walgreens, $2,462.6 million. Which company do you think makes the most use of creditors for financing the needs of the operating cycle?
2. Read each company's note on commitments and contingencies. What commitments and contingencies do the companies have in common? For which company does this information seem to be most important? Why is it important to consider this information in connection with payables analysis?

Fingraph® Financial Analyst™

FRA 6.

LO1 **Comparison of Current**
LO2 **Liabilities and Working**
LO3 **Capital**

Choose any two companies from the list of Fingraph companies on the Needles Accounting Resource Center Web Site at http://accounting.college.hmco.com/students. The industry should be one in which current liabilities are likely to be important, such as the airline, manufacturing, consumer products, or computer industry. Access the Microsoft Excel spreadsheets for the companies you selected. Click the URL at the top of each company's spreadsheet to link to the company's web site and annual report.

1. In the annual reports of the companies you have selected, read the current liability section of the balance sheet and any reference to current liabilities in the summary of significant accounting policies or notes to the financial statements. What are the most important current liabilities for each company? Do any current liabilities appear to be characteristic of the industry? Which current liabilities are definitely determinable, and which appear to be accrued liabilities?
2. Using the Fingraph CD-ROM software, display and print in tabular and graphic form the Current Assets and Current Liabilities Analysis page. Prepare a table that compares the current ratio and working capital for both companies for two years.
3. Find and read references to current liabilities in the liquidity analysis section of management's discussion and analysis in each annual report.
4. Write a one-page executive summary that highlights the most important types of current liabilities for this industry and that compares the current ratio and working capital trends of the two companies, including reference to management's assessment. Include the Fingraph page and your table with your report.

Internet Case

FRA 7.

LO3 **Investigation of Status of Famous Contingencies**

The Texaco <www.texaco.com> case in **FRA 2** involves one of the most famous contingent liabilities in history, but there are other famous ones as well. Others include the suits against tobacco companies, such as RJR Nabisco <www.nabisco.com> and Philip Morris <www.philipmorris.com>, and a suit against Waste Management, Inc. <www.wastemanagement.com>. Investigate the current status of any one of these cases, including Texaco, by going to the company's web site and finding its latest annual report. Look in the notes to the financial statements under "Contingencies." Report what you find about the case, including whether it has been settled or is no longer reported.

Chapter 10 explores the management issues associated with the acquisition, operation, and disposal of property, plant, and equipment, natural resources, and intangible assets, as well as the concepts and techniques of depreciation, depletion, and amortization.

Long-Term Assets

LEARNING OBJECTIVES

LO1 Identify the types of long-term assets and explain the management issues related to accounting for them.

LO2 Distinguish between capital and revenue expenditures, and account for the cost of property, plant, and equipment.

LO3 Define *depreciation* and compute depreciation under the straight-line, production, and declining-balance methods.

LO4 Account for the disposal of depreciable assets.

LO5 Identify the issues related to accounting for natural resources and compute depletion.

LO6 Identify the issues related to accounting for intangible assets, including research and development costs and goodwill.

SUPPLEMENTAL OBJECTIVE

SO7 Apply depreciation methods to problems of partial years, revised rates, groups of similar items, special types of capital expenditures, and cost recovery.

DECISION POINT
A USER'S FOCUS

H. J. Heinz Company <www.heinz.com> The effects of management's decisions regarding long-term assets are most apparent in the areas of reported total assets, net income, and cash flows related to investing activities. How does one learn about the significance of those items to a company? An idea of the extent of a company's long-term assets and their importance can be gained from the financial statements. For example, the list of assets in the Financial Highlights is from the annual report of H. J. Heinz Company, one of the world's largest food companies. Of the company's $9 billion in total assets, property, plant, and equipment represent about 24 percent, and other noncurrent assets represent about 42 percent.

With 66 percent of Heinz's total assets classified as long-term, management's decisions regarding choice of expected useful life and residual value of the assets can have a material impact on the amount expensed on the income statement. The income statement shows that depreciation and amortization expenses associated with those assets are more than $299 million, or about 63 percent of net income. While depreciation and amortization expenses have no cash effect, the statement of cash flows indicates the amount paid for newly purchased property, plant, and equipment and to what extent a company is reinvesting in its operations. Heinz spent more than $411 million on new long-term assets and expensed almost $300 million as depreciation and amortization expense.[1] In addition to annual expense recognition, long-term assets are reviewed annually to determine if the assets have lost some of their service potential,

Why are Heinz's long-term assets important to its financial performance as reflected in the balance sheet, the income statement, and the statement of cash flows?

resulting in asset impairment. Finally, disposals of long-term assets may result in gains or losses on the income statement. Each of these financial-statement issues falls within the scope of accounting for the acquisition, use, and disposal of long-term assets and the related management judgments.

Financial Highlights
(In thousands)

	2001	2000
Property, Plant, and Equipment:		
Land	$ 54,774	$ 45,959
Buildings and leasehold improvements	878,028	860,873
Equipment, furniture, and other	2,947,978	3,440,915
	3,880,780	4,347,747
Less accumulated depreciation	1,712,400	1,988,994
Total property, plant, and equipment, net	$2,168,380	$2,358,753
Other Noncurrent Assets:		
Goodwill (net of amortization: 2001—$334,907 and 2000—$312,433)	$2,077,451	$1,609,672
Trademarks (net of amortization: 2001—$118,254 and 2000—$104,125)	567,692	674,279
Other intangibles (net of amortization: 2001—$157,678 and 2000—$147,343)	120,749	127,779
Other noncurrent assets	984,064	910,225
Total other noncurrent assets	$3,749,956	$3,321,955

MANAGEMENT ISSUES RELATED TO ACCOUNTING FOR LONG-TERM ASSETS

LO1   Identify the types of long-term assets and explain the management issues related to accounting for them.

RELATED TEXT ASSIGNMENTS
Q: 1, 2, 3, 4, 5, 6, 7
SE: 1
E: 1, 2
SD: 1, 6, 7
FRA: 3, 4, 5

STUDY NOTE: For an asset to be classified as property, plant, and equipment, it must be "put in use." This means that it is available for its intended purpose. An emergency generator is "put in use" when it is available for emergencies, even if it is never used.

KEY POINT: A computer used in the office would be considered plant and equipment, whereas an identical computer held for sale to customers would be considered inventory.

● **STOP AND THINK!**
Is carrying value ever the same as market value?

On the date of acquisition, the carrying value equals the current market value. After that, it would be a coincidence if it equaled the market value. ■

Long-term assets are assets that (1) have a useful life of more than one year, (2) are acquired for use in the operation of a business, and (3) are not intended for resale to customers. For many years, it was common to refer to long-term assets as *fixed assets*, but use of this term is declining because the word *fixed* implies that they last forever. The relative importance of long-term assets to various industries is shown in Figure 1. Long-term assets range from 19.8 percent of total assets in the advertising industry to 52.7 percent in interstate trucking.

Although there is no strict rule for defining the useful life of a long-term asset, the most common criterion is that the asset be capable of repeated use for at least a year. Included in this category is equipment used only in peak or emergency periods, such as generators.

Assets not used in the normal course of business should not be included in this category. Thus, land held for speculative reasons or buildings no longer used in ordinary business operations should not be included in the property, plant, and equipment category. Instead, they should be classified as long-term investments.

Finally, if an item is held for resale to customers, it should be classified as inventory—not plant and equipment—no matter how durable it is. For example, a printing press held for sale by a printing press manufacturer would be considered inventory, whereas the same printing press would be considered plant and equipment if a printing company buys it for use in operations.

Long-term assets differ from current assets in that they support the operating cycle instead of being a part of it. They are also expected to benefit the business for a longer period than do current assets. Current assets are expected to be used up or converted to cash within one year or during the operating cycle, whichever is longer. Long-term assets are expected to last beyond that period. Long-term assets and their related expenses are summarized in Figure 2 on page 452.

Generally, long-lived assets are reported at carrying value, as presented in Figure 3 on page 452. **Carrying value** is the unexpired part of the cost of an asset, not its market value; it is also called *book value*. If a long-lived asset loses some or all of its revenue-generating potential before the end of its useful life, the asset may be deemed impaired, and its carrying value reduced. **Asset impairment** occurs when the sum of the expected cash flows from the asset is less than the carrying value of the asset.[2] Reducing carrying value to fair value, as measured by the present value

FIGURE 1
Long-Term Assets as a Percentage of Total Assets for Selected Industries

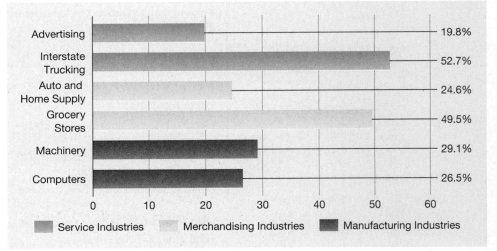

Source: Data from Dun & Bradstreet, *Industry Norms and Key Business Ratios,* 2000–01.

Fermi National Accelerator Laboratory <www.fnal.gov>

OBJECTIVES

- To describe the characteristics of long-term assets
- To identify the four issues that must be addressed in applying the matching rule to long-term assets
- To define depreciation and state the principal causes of depreciation
- To identify the issues related to intangible assets, including research and development

BACKGROUND FOR THE CASE

Fermi National Accelerator Laboratory (Fermilab), located 30 miles west of Chicago, is run by the U.S. Department of Energy. Its primary mission is to advance the understanding of the fundamental nature of matter and energy.

Fermilab operates the world's highest-energy particle accelerator, the Trevatron, or "atom-smasher." Circling through rings of magnets four miles in circumference, particle beams generate experimental conditions equivalent to those that existed in the first quadrillionth of a second after the birth of the universe. This capability to re-create such high energy levels places Fermilab at the frontier of global physics research. The facility provides leadership and resources for qualified experimenters to conduct basic research at the leading edge of high-energy physics and related disciplines. In the year 2000, with Collider Run II, scientists at Fermilab began probing the smallest dimen-

sions that humans have ever examined. These scientists have the opportunity to make discoveries that could answer some important questions in particle physics.

Although a unit of the U.S. government, Fermilab is a financially independent nonprofit corporation with a governing body consisting of the presidents of 87 affiliated research universities. With annual revenues of about $300 million, consisting mostly of government contracts, and annual expenses of about $260 million, Fermilab faces the same management challenges as a for-profit corporation. It must make huge investments in long-term assets. Other than salaries, depreciation is the lab's largest expense. In addition, Fermilab creates intellectual capital through basic research that it shares with U.S. industry to encourage economic development.

For more information about Fermi National Accelerator Laboratory, visit its web site through the Needles Accounting Resource Center Web Site at **http://accounting.college.hmco.com/students** or directly through Fermilab's web site.

REQUIRED

View the video on Fermi National Accelerator Laboratory that accompanies this book. As you are watching the video, take notes related to the following questions:

1. What characteristics distinguish long-term assets? What are some examples of long-term assets at Fermilab?

2. What four issues must be addressed in applying the matching rule to long-term assets?

3. What is depreciation, and what are its two major causes?

4. What are research and development costs, and how does Fermilab account for them? How might this method understate the assets of Fermilab?

---

of future cash flows, is an application of conservatism. All long-term assets are subject to an asset impairment evaluation. A reduction in carrying value as a result of impairment is recorded as a loss.

Because of a slowdown in the growth of Internet, telecommunications, and technology companies, companies like Amazon.com, Cisco Systems, and Lucent Technologies took write-downs totaling billions of dollars. The carrying value of certain long-term tangible and intangible assets no longer exceeded the cash flows that they would help generate, due to declining revenues or slowing revenue growth. The write-downs caused the companies to report operating losses.[3]

DECIDING TO ACQUIRE LONG-TERM ASSETS

The decision to acquire a long-term asset involves a complex process. Methods of evaluating data to make rational decisions in this area are grouped under a topic

FIGURE 2
Classification of Long-Term Assets and Corresponding Expenses

BALANCE SHEET

Long-Term Assets

INCOME STATEMENT

Expenses

Tangible Assets: long-term assets that have physical substance

Land

Plant, Buildings, Equipment (plant assets)

} Land is not expensed because it has an unlimited life.

} **Depreciation:** periodic allocation of the cost of a tangible long-lived asset (other than land and natural resources) over its estimated useful life

Natural Resources: long-term assets purchased for the economic value that can be taken from the land and used up, as with ore, lumber, oil, and gas or other resources contained in the land

Mines

Timberland

Oil and Gas Fields

} **Depletion:** exhaustion of a natural resource through mining, cutting, pumping, or other extraction, and the way in which the cost is allocated

Intangible Assets: long-term assets that have no physical substance but have a value based on rights or advantages accruing to the owner

Patents, Copyrights, Trademarks, Franchises, Leaseholds, Leasehold Improvements, Goodwill

} **Amortization:** periodic allocation of the cost of an intangible asset to the periods it benefits

} Goodwill is not expensed, but its value is reviewed annually.

called capital budgeting, which is usually covered as a managerial accounting topic. However, an awareness of the general nature of the problem is helpful in understanding the accounting issues related to long-term assets. To illustrate the acquisition decision, let us assume that Irena Markova, M.D., is considering the purchase of a $5,000 computer system for her office. She estimates that if she purchases the computer, she can reduce the hours of a part-time employee sufficiently to save net

FIGURE 3
Carrying Value of Long-Term Assets on the Balance Sheet

Plant Assets	Natural Resources	Intangible Assets
Less Accumulated Depreciation	Less Accumulated Depletion	Less Accumulated Amortization
Carrying Value	Carrying Value	Carrying Value

cash flows of $2,000 per year for four years and that the computer will be worth $1,000 at the end of that period. These data are summarized as follows:

	20x1	20x2	20x3	20x4
Acquisition cost	($5,000)			
Net annual savings in cash flows	$2,000	$2,000	$2,000	$2,000
Disposal price				1,000
Net cash flows	($3,000)	$2,000	$2,000	$3,000

To place the cash flows on a comparable basis, it is helpful to use present value tables, such as Tables 3 and 4 in the appendix on future value and present value tables. Assuming that the appropriate interest rate is 10 percent compounded annually, the purchase may be evaluated as follows:

		Present Value
Acquisition cost	Present value factor = 1.000	
	1.000 × $5,000	($5,000)
Net annual savings in cash flows	Present value factor = 3.170	
	(Table 4: 4 periods, 10%)	
	3.170 × $2,000	6,340
Disposal price	Present value factor = .683	
	(Table 3: 4 periods, 10%)	
	.683 × $1,000	683
Net present value		$2,023

As long as the net present value is positive, Dr. Markova will earn at least 10 percent on the investment. In this case, the return is greater than 10 percent because the net present value is a positive $2,023. Based on this analysis, Dr. Markova makes the decision to purchase. However, there are other important considerations that have to be taken into account, such as the costs of training and maintenance, and the possibility that because of unforeseen circumstances, the savings may not be as great as expected. In Dr. Markova's case, the decision to purchase is likely to be a good one because the net present value is both positive and large relative to the investment.

Information about a company's acquisitions of long-term assets may be found under investing activities in the statement of cash flows. For example, in referring to this section of its 2001 annual report, the management of H.J. Heinz Company makes the following statement:

www.heinz.com

> Capital expenditures totaled $411.3 million compared to $452.4 million last year. . . . This year's capital expenditures were concentrated in North American Grocery & Foodservice and Europe. Last year's capital expenditures were concentrated across all major segments.[4]

FINANCING LONG-TERM ASSETS

In addition to deciding whether to acquire a long-term asset, management must decide how to finance the asset if it is acquired. Some companies are profitable enough to pay for long-term assets out of cash flows from operations, but when financing is needed, some form of long-term arrangement related to the life of the asset is usually most appropriate. For example, an automobile loan generally spans 4 or 5 years, whereas a mortgage on a house may span as many as 30 years.

For a major long-term acquisition, a company may issue capital stock, long-term notes, or bonds. A good place to study a company's long-term financing is in the financing activities section of the statement of cash flows. For instance, in discussing www.ford.com this section, Ford Motor Company's management states, "Automotive debt at December 31, 2000 totaled $12 billion, which was 39 percent of total capitalization (stockholders' equity and Automotive debt), up from 30 percent of total capitalization a year ago."[5]

APPLYING THE MATCHING RULE TO LONG-TERM ASSETS

Accounting for long-term assets requires the proper application of the matching rule through the resolution of two important issues. The first is how much of the total cost to allocate to expense in the current accounting period. The second is how much to retain on the balance sheet as an asset to benefit future periods. To resolve these issues, four important questions about the acquisition, use, and disposal of each long-term asset must be answered (see Figure 4):

1. How is the cost of the long-term asset determined?
2. How should the expired portion of the cost of the long-term asset be allocated against revenues over time?
3. How should subsequent expenditures, such as repairs and additions, be treated?
4. How should disposal of the long-term asset be recorded?

STUDY NOTE: Useful life is measured by the service units a business expects to receive from an asset. It should not be confused with physical life, which is often much longer. If the management of a new business is having difficulty determining an asset's estimated useful life, it may obtain help from trade magazines. Nearly every industry has at least one.

Because of the long life of long-term assets and the complexity of the transactions relating to them, management has many choices and estimates to make. For example, acquisition cost may be complicated by group purchases, trade-ins, or construction costs. In addition, to allocate the cost of the asset to future periods effectively, management must estimate how long the asset will last and what it will be worth at the end of its use. In making such estimates, it is helpful to think of a long-term asset as a bundle of services to be used in the operation of the business over a period of years. A delivery truck may provide 100,000 miles of service over its life. A piece of equipment may have the potential to produce 500,000 parts. A building may provide shelter for 50 years. As each of those assets is purchased, the company is paying in advance for 100,000 miles, the capacity to produce 500,000 parts, or 50 years of service. In essence, each asset is a type of long-term prepaid expense. The accounting problem is to spread the cost of the services over the useful life of the

FIGURE 4
Issues of Accounting for Long-Term Assets

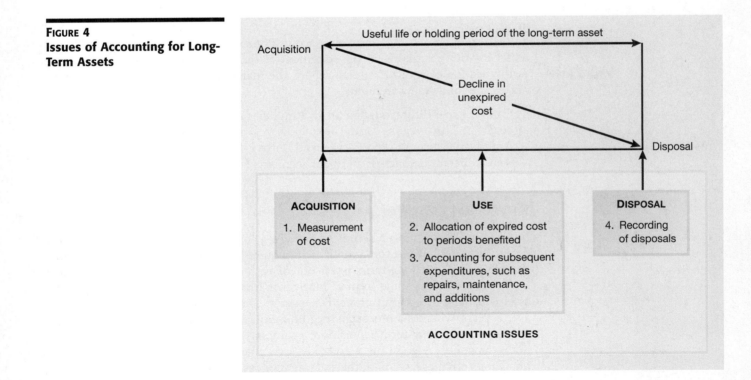

asset. As the services benefit the company over the years, the cost becomes an expense rather than an asset.

✓ Check out ACE for a Review Quiz at http://accounting.college.hmco.com/students.

ACQUISITION COST OF PROPERTY, PLANT, AND EQUIPMENT

LO2 Distinguish between capital and revenue expenditures, and account for the cost of property, plant, and equipment.

RELATED TEXT ASSIGNMENTS
Q: 8, 9, 10
SE: 2, 3
E: 3, 4, 5, 14
P: 1, 6
SD: 4, 5, 6
FRA: 3

STUDY NOTE: Although dyeing a carpet may make it look almost new, it is not considered a capital expenditure because even though the carpet looks better, its fibers are not stronger, and it probably will not last significantly longer than it would have before the color was changed.

STUDY NOTE: The cost of mailing lists may be recorded as an asset because the mailing lists will be used over and over and will benefit future accounting periods.

KEY POINT: Expenditures necessary to prepare an asset for its intended use are a cost of the asset.

Expenditure refers to a payment or an obligation to make future payment for an asset, such as a truck, or a service, such as a repair. Expenditures may be classified as capital expenditures or revenue expenditures. A **capital expenditure** is an expenditure for the purchase or expansion of a long-term asset. Capital expenditures are recorded in the asset accounts because they benefit several future accounting periods. A **revenue expenditure** is an expenditure related to the repair, maintenance, and operation of a long-term asset. Revenue expenditures are recorded in the expense accounts because their benefits are realized in the current period.

THE IMPORTANCE OF CLASSIFYING EXPENDITURES CORRECTLY

Careful distinction between capital and revenue expenditures is important to the proper application of the matching rule. For example, if the purchase of an automobile is mistakenly recorded as a revenue expenditure, the total cost of the automobile is recorded as an expense on the income statement. As a result, current net income is reported at a lower amount (understated), and in future periods net income will be reported at a higher amount. If, on the other hand, a revenue expenditure, such as the painting of a building, were charged to an asset account, the expense of the current period would be understated. Current net income would be overstated by the same amount, and the net income of future periods would be understated.

Determining when a payment is an expense and when it is an asset is a matter of judgment in which management takes a leading role. For example, inconsistencies have existed in accounting for the costs of computer programs that run the systems for businesses. Some companies immediately write off the cost as an expense, whereas others treat it as a long-term intangible asset and amortize it year after year. As companies spend billions of dollars a year on this type of software, this is an important variable in the profitability of many companies. Although the AICPA has issued new rules to try to bring more standardization to these accounting issues, considerable latitude does still exist, such as in determining how long the economic life of the software will be.[6]

GENERAL APPROACH TO ACQUISITION COSTS

The acquisition cost of property, plant, and equipment includes all expenditures reasonable and necessary to get the asset in place and ready for use. For example, the cost of installing and testing a machine is a legitimate cost of the machine. However, if the machine is damaged during installation, the cost of repairs is an operating expense and not an acquisition cost.

Cost is easiest to determine when a purchase is made for cash. In that case, the cost of the asset is equal to the cash paid for the asset plus expenditures for freight, insurance while in transit, installation, and other necessary related costs. If a debt is incurred in the purchase of the asset, the interest charges are not a cost of the asset, but a cost of borrowing the money to buy the asset. They are therefore an operating expense. An exception to this principle is that interest costs incurred during the construction of an asset are properly included as a cost of the asset.[7]

Expenditures like freight, insurance while in transit, and installation are included in the cost of the asset because they are necessary if the asset is to function. Following the matching rule, they are allocated to the useful life of the asset rather than charged as expenses in the current period.

For practical purposes, many companies establish policies defining when an expenditure should be recorded as an expense or an asset. For example, small expenditures for items that would normally be treated as assets may be treated as expenses because the amounts involved are not material in relation to net income. Thus, a wastebasket, which might last for years, would be recorded as a supplies expense rather than as a depreciable asset.

Some of the problems of determining the cost of long-lived plant assets are discussed in the next sections.

KEY POINT: Many costs may be incurred to prepare land for its intended use and condition. All such costs are a cost of land.

■ **LAND**   There are often expenditures in addition to the purchase price of land that should be debited to the Land account. Some examples are commissions to real estate agents; lawyers' fees; accrued taxes paid by the purchaser; costs of preparing the land to build on, such as the costs of tearing down old buildings and draining, clearing, and grading the land; and assessments for local improvements, such as putting in streets and sewage systems. The cost of landscaping is usually debited to the Land account because such improvements are relatively permanent. Land is not subject to depreciation because it does not have a limited useful life.

ENRICHMENT NOTE: The costs of tearing down existing buildings can be major. For example, companies may spend millions of dollars imploding buildings so they can remove them and build new ones.

Let us assume that a company buys land for a new retail operation. It pays a net purchase price of $170,000, pays brokerage fees of $6,000 and legal fees of $2,000, pays $10,000 to have an old building on the site torn down, receives $4,000 salvage from the old building, and pays $1,000 to have the site graded. The cost of the land is $185,000:

Net purchase price		$170,000
Brokerage fees		6,000
Legal fees		2,000
Tearing down old building	$10,000	
Less salvage	4,000	6,000
Grading		1,000
Total cost		$185,000

■ **LAND IMPROVEMENTS**   Some improvements to real estate, such as driveways, parking lots, and fences, have a limited life and are thus subject to depreciation. They should be recorded in an account called Land Improvements rather than in the Land account.

■ **BUILDINGS**   When an existing building is purchased, its cost includes the purchase price plus all repairs and other expenditures required to put it in usable condition. Buildings are subject to depreciation because they have a limited useful life. When a business constructs its own building, the cost includes all reasonable and necessary expenditures, such as those for materials, labor, part of the overhead and other indirect costs, architects' fees, insurance during construction, interest on construction loans during the period of construction, lawyers' fees, and building permits. If outside contractors are used in the construction, the net contract price plus other expenditures necessary to put the building in usable condition are included in the cost.

ENRICHMENT NOTE: The electrical wiring and plumbing of a dental chair are included in the cost of the asset since they are a necessary cost of preparing the asset for use.

■ **EQUIPMENT**   The cost of equipment includes all expenditures connected with purchasing the equipment and preparing it for use. Those expenditures include the invoice price less cash discounts; freight, including insurance; excise taxes and tariffs; buying expenses; installation costs; and test runs to ready the equipment for operation. Equipment is subject to depreciation.

FOCUS ON BUSINESS ETHICS

Is It an Asset or Expense? The Answer Matters.

Determining whether an expenditure is a long-term asset or an expense is not always as clear-cut as some might imagine. Management has considerable leeway in how to record transactions, but the financial statements must be prepared in accordance with generally accepted accounting principles and the result cannot be deceptive. If management's choices are questioned, the results can sometimes have drastic consequences.

For example, *The Wall Street Journal* reported that the chief financial officer of WorldCom used an unorthodox and unusually aggressive technique to account for one of the long-distance company's biggest expenses. The company recorded charges paid to local telephone networks to complete calls as long-term assets instead of operating expenses. This increased income in the year in question by deferring the costs to a future year, effectively turning a net loss for the year into a net income. In total, the company says that at least $3.8 billion was accounted for in this way. As a result of the report, the company's stock price dropped from a high of $64.50 to less than one dollar. The SEC filed civil fraud charges against WorldCom, saying the company "falsely portrayed itself as a profitable business."[8] Criminal charges may follow and the company will likely face bankruptcy.

This and other notable cases show that accounting is not a passive part of business that can be manipulated at will, but must be taken seriously. The financial statements must reveal the substance of the business's activities.

● **STOP AND THINK!**

What incentive does a company have to allocate more of a group purchase price to the land than to the building?

A higher land valuation has the effect of increasing income because a smaller building valuation results in a lower amount to depreciate over its useful life. ■

■ **GROUP PURCHASES** Land and other assets are sometimes purchased for a lump sum. Because land is a nondepreciable asset that has an unlimited life, it must have a separate ledger account, and the lump-sum purchase price must be apportioned between the land and the other assets. For example, assume that a building and the land on which it is situated are purchased for a lump-sum payment of $85,000. The apportionment can be made by determining the price of each if purchased separately and applying the appropriate percentages to the lump-sum price. Assume that appraisals yield estimates of $10,000 for the land and $90,000 for the building if purchased separately. In that case, 10 percent of the lump-sum price, or $8,500, would be allocated to the land, and 90 percent, or $76,500, would be allocated to the building, as follows:

	Appraisal	Percentage	Apportionment
Land	$ 10,000	10% ($10,000 ÷ $100,000)	$ 8,500 ($85,000 × 10%)
Building	90,000	90% ($90,000 ÷ $100,000)	76,500 ($85,000 × 90%)
Totals	$100,000	100%	$85,000

✓ Check out ACE for a Review Quiz at http://accounting.college.hmco.com/students.

ACCOUNTING FOR DEPRECIATION

LO3 Define *depreciation* and compute depreciation under the straight-line, production, and declining-balance methods.

RELATED TEXT ASSIGNMENTS
Q: 11, 12, 13, 14, 15, 16
SE: 4, 5, 6
E: 5, 6, 7
P: 2, 3, 7, 8
SD: 1, 2, 6
FRA: 1, 3, 5, 6

The AICPA describes depreciation accounting as follows:

The cost of a productive facility is one of the costs of the services it renders during its useful economic life. Generally accepted accounting principles require that this cost be spread over the expected useful life of the facility in such a way as to allocate it as equitably as possible to the periods during which services are obtained from the use of the facility. This procedure is known as depreciation accounting, a system of accounting which aims to distribute the cost or other basic value of tangible capital assets, less salvage (if any), over the estimated useful life of the unit . . . in a systematic and rational manner. It is a process of allocation, not of valuation.[9]

This description contains several important points. First, all tangible assets except land have a limited useful life. Because of this, their costs must be distributed as expenses over the years they benefit. Physical deterioration and obsolescence are the major causes of the limited useful life of a depreciable asset. The

physical deterioration of tangible assets results from use and from exposure to the elements, such as wind and sun. Periodic repairs and a sound maintenance policy may keep buildings and equipment in good operating order and extract the maximum useful life from them, but every machine or building at some point must be discarded. Repairs do not eliminate the need for depreciation. **Obsolescence** is the process of becoming out of date. Because of fast-changing technology and fast-changing demands, machinery and even buildings often become obsolete before they wear out. Accountants do not distinguish between physical deterioration and obsolescence because they are interested in the length of an asset's useful life, not in what limits that useful life.

Second, the term *depreciation*, as used in accounting, does not refer to an asset's physical deterioration or decrease in market value over time. Depreciation means the allocation of the cost of a plant asset to the periods that benefit from the services of that asset. The term is used to describe the gradual conversion of the cost of the asset into an expense.

Third, depreciation is not a process of valuation. Accounting records are kept in accordance with the cost principle; they are not indicators of changing price levels. It is possible that because of an advantageous purchase and specific market conditions, the market value of a building may rise. Nevertheless, depreciation must continue to be recorded because it is the result of an allocation, not a valuation, process. Eventually, the building will wear out or become obsolete regardless of interim fluctuations in market value.

FACTORS THAT AFFECT THE COMPUTATION OF DEPRECIATION

Four factors affect the computation of depreciation: (1) cost, (2) residual value, (3) depreciable cost, and (4) estimated useful life.

■ **COST**   As explained earlier in the chapter, cost is the net purchase price plus all reasonable and necessary expenditures to get the asset in place and ready for use.

■ **RESIDUAL VALUE**   The **residual value** of an asset is its estimated net scrap, salvage, or trade-in value as of the estimated date of disposal. Other terms often used to describe residual value are *salvage value* and *disposal value*.

■ **DEPRECIABLE COST**   The **depreciable cost** of an asset is its cost less its residual value. For example, a truck that costs $12,000 and has a residual value of $3,000 would have a depreciable cost of $9,000. Depreciable cost must be allocated over the useful life of the asset.

■ **ESTIMATED USEFUL LIFE**   **Estimated useful life** is the total number of service units expected from a long-term asset. Service units may be measured in terms of years

FOCUS ON BUSINESS PRACTICE

The Useful Life of an Aircraft Is How Long?

Most airlines depreciate airplanes over an estimated useful life of 10 to 20 years. But how long will a properly maintained airplane really last? Western Airlines <www.westernairlines.com> paid $3.3 million for a new Boeing 737 in July 1968. More than 78,000 flights and 30 years later, this aircraft was still flying for Vanguard Airlines <www.flyvanguard.com>, a no-frills airline. Among the other airlines that have owned this aircraft during the course of its life are Piedmont, Delta <www.delta.com>, and US Airways <www.usairways.com>.

Virtually every part of the plane has been replaced over the years. Boeing believes the plane could theoretically make double the number of flights before it is retired.

The useful lives of many types of assets can be extended indefinitely if the assets are correctly maintained, but proper accounting in accordance with the matching rule requires depreciation over a "reasonable" useful life. Each airline that owned the plane would have accounted for the plane in this way.

the asset is expected to be used, units expected to be produced, miles expected to be driven, or similar measures. In computing the estimated useful life of an asset, an accountant should consider all relevant information, including (1) past experience with similar assets, (2) the asset's present condition, (3) the company's repair and maintenance policy, (4) current technological and industry trends, and (5) local conditions, such as weather.

Depreciation is recorded at the end of the accounting period by an adjusting entry that takes the following form:

A = L + OE   Depreciation Expense, Asset Name → *Income Statement*   xxx
_   _   Accumulated Depreciation, Asset Name → *Balance sheet*   xxx
contra ←   To record depreciation for the period
asset ←

METHODS OF COMPUTING DEPRECIATION

Many methods are used to allocate the cost of plant assets to accounting periods through depreciation. Each is proper for certain circumstances. The most common methods are (1) the straight-line method, (2) the production method, and (3) an accelerated method known as the declining-balance method.

CLARIFICATION NOTE:
The straight-line depreciation method should be used when approximately equal asset benefit is obtained each year.

■ **STRAIGHT-LINE METHOD** When the **straight-line method** is used to calculate depreciation, the depreciable cost of the asset is spread evenly over the estimated useful life of the asset. The straight-line method is based on the assumption that depreciation depends only on the passage of time. The depreciation expense for each period is computed by dividing the depreciable cost (cost of the depreciating asset less its estimated residual value) by the number of accounting periods in the asset's estimated useful life. The rate of depreciation is the same in each year. Suppose, for example, that a delivery truck costs $10,000 and has an estimated residual value of $1,000 at the end of its estimated useful life of five years. The annual depreciation would be $1,800 under the straight-line method, calculated as follows:

KEY POINT: Residual value and useful life are, at best, educated guesses.

$$\frac{\text{Cost} - \text{Residual Value}}{\text{Estimated Useful Life}} = \frac{\$10,000 - \$1,000}{5 \text{ years}} = \$1,800 \text{ per year}$$

The depreciation for the five years would be as follows:

Depreciation Schedule, Straight-Line Method

	Cost	Yearly Depreciation	Accumulated Depreciation	Carrying Value
Date of purchase	$10,000	—	—	$10,000
End of first year	10,000	$1,800	$1,800	8,200
End of second year	10,000	1,800	3,600	6,400
End of third year	10,000	1,800	5,400	4,600
End of fourth year	10,000	1,800	7,200	2,800
End of fifth year	10,000	1,800	9,000	1,000

There are three important points to note from the depreciation schedule for the straight-line depreciation method. First, the depreciation is the same each year. Second, the accumulated depreciation increases uniformly. Third, the carrying value decreases uniformly until it reaches the estimated residual value.

■ **PRODUCTION METHOD** The **production method** of depreciation is based on the assumption that depreciation is solely the result of use and that the passage of time plays no role in the depreciation process. If we assume that the delivery truck in the previous example has an estimated useful life of 90,000 miles, the depreciation cost per mile would be determined as follows:

$$\frac{\text{Cost} - \text{Residual Value}}{\text{Estimated Units of Useful Life}} = \frac{\$10,000 - \$1,000}{90,000 \text{ miles}} = \$.10 \text{ per mile}$$

If we assume that the use of the truck was 20,000 miles for the first year, 30,000 miles for the second, 10,000 miles for the third, 20,000 miles for the fourth, and 10,000 miles for the fifth, the depreciation schedule for the delivery truck would be as follows:

Depreciation Schedule, Production Method

	Cost	Miles	Yearly Depreciation	Accumulated Depreciation	Carrying Value
Date of purchase	$10,000	—	—	—	$10,000
End of first year	10,000	20,000	$2,000	$2,000	8,000
End of second year	10,000	30,000	3,000	5,000	5,000
End of third year	10,000	10,000	1,000	6,000	4,000
End of fourth year	10,000	20,000	2,000	8,000	2,000
End of fifth year	10,000	10,000	1,000	9,000	1,000

There is a direct relation between the amount of depreciation each year and the units of output or use. Also, the accumulated depreciation increases each year in direct relation to units of output or use. Finally, the carrying value decreases each year in direct relation to units of output or use until it reaches the estimated residual value.

Under the production method, the unit of output or use employed to measure the estimated useful life of each asset should be appropriate for that asset. For example, the number of items produced may be an appropriate measure for one machine, but the number of hours of use may be a better measure for another. The production method should be used only when the output of an asset over its useful life can be estimated with reasonable accuracy.

■ **DECLINING-BALANCE METHOD**   An **accelerated method** of depreciation results in relatively large amounts of depreciation in the early years of an asset's life and smaller amounts in later years. Such a method, which is based on the passage of time, assumes that many kinds of plant assets are most efficient when new, and so provide more and better service in the early years of their useful life. It is consistent with the matching rule to allocate more depreciation to earlier years than to later years if the benefits or services received in the earlier years are greater than those received later.

An accelerated method also recognizes that fast-changing technologies cause some equipment to become obsolescent and lose service value rapidly. Thus, it is realistic to allocate more to depreciation in earlier years than in later ones. Another argument in favor of an accelerated method is that repair expense is likely to be greater in later years than in earlier years. Thus, the total of repair and depreciation expense remains fairly constant over a period of years. This result naturally assumes that the services received from the asset are roughly equal from year to year.

The **declining-balance method** is the most common accelerated method of depreciation. Under this method, depreciation is computed by applying a fixed rate to the carrying value (the declining balance) of a tangible long-lived asset, resulting in higher depreciation charges during the early years of the asset's life. Though any fixed rate can be used, the most common rate is a percentage equal to twice the straight-line depreciation percentage. When twice the straight-line rate is used, the method is usually called the **double-declining-balance method**.

In our earlier example, the delivery truck had an estimated useful life of five years. Consequently, under the straight-line method, the depreciation rate for each year was 20 percent (100 percent ÷ 5 years).

Under the double-declining-balance method, the fixed rate is 40 percent (2 × 20 percent). This fixed rate is applied to the *remaining carrying value* at the end of each year. Estimated residual value is not taken into account in figuring depreciation except in a year when calculated depreciation exceeds the amount necessary to

KEY POINT: Under the double-declining-balance method, depreciation in the last year rarely equals the exact amount needed to reduce carrying value to residual value. Depreciation in the last year is limited to the amount necessary to reduce carrying value to residual value.

PARENTHETICAL NOTE:
An asset remains on the books as long as it is in use. Even if the asset is fully depreciated, the company should not remove it from the books until it is taken out of service.

◆ **STOP AND THINK!**
Which depreciation method would best reflect the risk of obsolescence from rapid technological changes?

An accelerated depreciation method is best. Companies facing rapid technological change use it to minimize the risk of obsolescence. ∎

bring the carrying value down to the estimated residual value. The depreciation schedule for this method is as follows:

Depreciation Schedule, Double-Declining-Balance Method

	Cost	Yearly Depreciation		Accumulated Depreciation	Carrying Value
Date of purchase	$10,000	—		—	$10,000
End of first year	10,000	(40% × $10,000)	$4,000	$4,000	6,000
End of second year	10,000	(40% × $6,000)	2,400	6,400	3,600
End of third year	10,000	(40% × $3,600)	1,440	7,840	2,160
End of fourth year	10,000	(40% × $2,160)	864	8,704	1,296
End of fifth year	10,000		296*	9,000	1,000

*Depreciation limited to amount necessary to reduce carrying value to residual value:
$296 = $1,296 (previous carrying value) − $1,000 (residual value).

Note that the fixed rate is always applied to the carrying value at the end of the previous year. The depreciation is greatest in the first year and declines each year after that. Finally, the depreciation in the last year is limited to the amount necessary to reduce carrying value to residual value.

■ **COMPARISON OF THE THREE METHODS**   A visual comparison may provide a better understanding of the three depreciation methods described above. Figure 5 compares yearly depreciation and carrying value under the three methods. In the left-hand graph, which shows yearly depreciation, straight-line depreciation is uniform at $1,800 per year over the five-year period. However, the double-declining-balance method begins at an amount greater than straight-line ($4,000) and decreases each year to amounts that are less than straight-line (ultimately, $296). The production method does not generate a regular pattern because of the random fluctuation of the depreciation from year to year. The three yearly depreciation patterns are reflected in the graph of carrying value. In that graph, each method starts in the same place (cost of $10,000) and ends at the same place (residual value of $1,000). It is the patterns during the useful life of the asset that differ for each method. For instance, the carrying value under the straight-line method is always greater than that under the double-declining-balance method, except at the beginning and end of useful life.

FIGURE 5
Graphic Comparison of Three Methods of Determining Depreciation

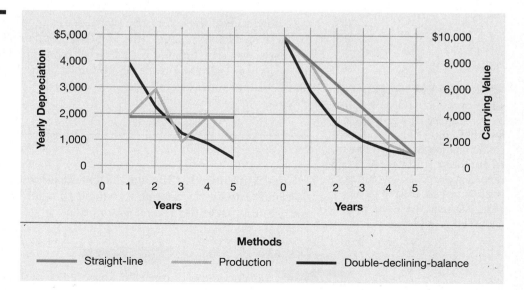

Methods

—— Straight-line   ‑‑‑‑ Production   —— Double-declining-balance

FOCUS ON BUSINESS PRACTICE

Accelerated Methods Save Money!

An AICPA study of 600 large companies found that the overwhelming majority used the straight-line method of depreciation for financial reporting purposes, as shown in Figure 6. Only about 15 percent used some type of accelerated method, and 6 percent used the production method. These figures tend to be misleading about the importance of accelerated depreciation methods, however, especially when it comes to income taxes. Federal income tax laws allow either the straight-line method or an accelerated method, and for tax purposes, about 75 percent of the 600 companies studied preferred an accelerated method. Companies use different methods of depreciation for good reason. The straight-line method can be advantageous for financial reporting because it can produce the highest net income, and an accelerated method can be beneficial for tax purposes because it can result in lower income taxes.

FIGURE 6
Depreciation Methods Used by 600 Large Companies for Financial Reporting

CLARIFICATION NOTE: For financial reporting purposes, the objective is to measure performance accurately. For tax purposes, the objective is to minimize tax liability.

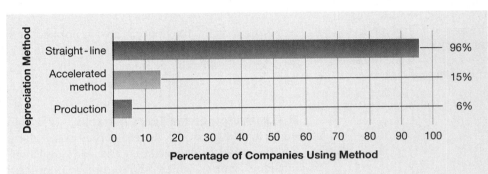

Total percentage exceeds 100 because some companies used different methods for different types of depreciable assets.

Source: From *Accounting Trends & Techniques.* Copyright © 2000 by the American Institute of Certified Public Accountants, Inc. Reprinted with permission.

Check out ACE for a Review Quiz at http://accounting.college.hmco.com/students.

DISPOSAL OF DEPRECIABLE ASSETS

LO4   Account for the disposal of depreciable assets.

RELATED TEXT ASSIGNMENTS
Q: 17, 18
SE: 7, 8
E: 8, 9
P: 4
FRA: 6

ENRICHMENT NOTE: Plant assets may also be disposed of by involuntary conversion (e.g., fire, theft, mud slide, flood) or condemnation by a governmental authority. For financial reporting purposes, involuntary conversions are treated in the same way as if the assets were discarded or sold.

When plant assets are no longer useful because they are worn out or obsolete, they may be discarded, sold, or traded in on the purchase of new plant and equipment. For accounting purposes, a plant asset may be disposed of in one of three ways: It may be (1) discarded, (2) sold for cash, or (3) exchanged for another asset. To illustrate how each of these cases is recorded, assume that MGC Company purchased a machine on January 2, 20x0, for $6,500 and planned to depreciate it on a straight-line basis over an estimated useful life of ten years. The residual value at the end of ten years was estimated to be $500. On January 2, 20x7, the balances of the relevant accounts appear as follows:

Machinery		Accumulated Depreciation, Machinery	
6,500			4,200

On September 30, 20x7, management disposes of the asset. The next few sections illustrate the accounting treatment to record depreciation for the partial year and the disposal under several assumptions.

DISCARD OR SALE OF PLANT ASSETS

When a plant asset is discarded or disposed of in some other way, it is first necessary to record depreciation expense for the partial year up to the date of disposal. This step is required because the asset was used until that date and, under the matching rule, the accounting period should receive the proper allocation of depreciation expense.

In this illustration, MGC Company disposes of the machinery on September 30. The entry to record the depreciation for the first nine months of 20x7 (nine-twelfths of a year) is as follows:

A = L + OE
−   −

Sept. 30	Depreciation Expense, Machinery	450	
	Accumulated Depreciation, Machinery		450
	To record depreciation up to date of		
	disposal		

$$\frac{\$6,500 - \$500}{10} \times \frac{9}{12} = \$450$$

KEY POINT: When it disposes of an asset, a company must do two things. First, it must bring the depreciation up to date. Second, it must remove all evidence of ownership of the asset, including the contra account Accumulated Depreciation.

The relevant accounts appear as follows after the entry is posted:

Machinery		Accumulated Depreciation, Machinery	
6,500			4,650

After updating the depreciation, it is then necessary to remove the carrying value of the asset as shown in the following sections.

■ **DISCARDED PLANT ASSETS** A plant asset rarely lasts exactly as long as its estimated life. If it lasts longer than its estimated life, it is not depreciated past the point at which its carrying value equals its residual value. The purpose of depreciation is to spread the depreciable cost of an asset over the estimated life of the asset. Thus, the total accumulated depreciation should never exceed the total depreciable cost. If an asset remains in use beyond the end of its estimated life, its cost and accumulated depreciation remain in the ledger accounts. Proper records will thus be available for maintaining control over plant assets. If the residual value is zero, the carrying value of a fully depreciated asset is zero until the asset is disposed of. If such an asset is discarded, no gain or loss results.

In the illustration, however, the discarded equipment has a carrying value of $1,850 at the time of its disposal. The carrying value is computed from the T accounts above as machinery of $6,500 less accumulated depreciation of $4,650. A loss equal to the carrying value should be recorded when the machine is discarded, as follows:

A = L + OE
−   −
+

Sept. 30	Accumulated Depreciation, Machinery	4,650	
	Loss on Disposal of Machinery	1,850	
	Machinery		6,500
	Discarded machine no longer used		
	in the business		

Gains and losses on disposals of plant assets are classified as other revenues and expenses on the income statement.

● **STOP AND THINK!**
When would the disposal of long-term assets result in no gain or loss?

If cash received for the assets equals their residual value, then no gain or loss occurs. ■

■ **PLANT ASSETS SOLD FOR CASH** The entry to record a plant asset sold for cash is similar to the one just illustrated, except that the receipt of cash should also be recorded. The following entries show how to record the sale of a machine under three assumptions about the selling price. In the first case, the $1,850 cash received is exactly equal to the $1,850 carrying value of the machine; therefore, no gain or loss occurs.

A = L + OE
+
+
−

Sept. 30	Cash	1,850	
	Accumulated Depreciation, Machinery	4,650	
	Machinery		6,500
	Sale of machine for carrying value;		
	no gain or loss		

In the second case, the $1,000 cash received is less than the carrying value of $1,850, so a loss of $850 is recorded.

A = L + OE
+
+
−

Sept. 30	Cash	1,000	
	Accumulated Depreciation, Machinery	4,650	
	Loss on Sale of Machinery	850	
	Machinery		6,500
	Sale of machine at less than carrying value; loss of $850 ($1,850 − $1,000) recorded		

KEY POINT: For an asset discarded or sold for cash, the gain (loss) on disposal of the asset equals cash received minus carrying value.

In the third case, the $2,000 cash received exceeds the carrying value of $1,850, so a gain of $150 is recorded.

A = L + OE
+   +
+
−

Sept. 30	Cash	2,000	
	Accumulated Depreciation, Machinery	4,650	
	Gain on Sale of Machinery		150
	Machinery		6,500
	Sale of machine at more than the carrying value; gain of $150 ($2,000 − $1,850) recorded		

EXCHANGES OF PLANT ASSETS

Businesses also dispose of plant assets by trading them in on the purchase of other plant assets. Exchanges may involve similar assets, such as an old machine traded in on a newer model, or dissimilar assets, such as a cement mixer traded in on a truck. In either case, the purchase price is reduced by the amount of the trade-in allowance.

Basically, accounting for exchanges of plant assets is similar to accounting for sales of plant assets for cash. If the trade-in allowance received is greater than the carrying value of the asset surrendered, there has been a gain. If the allowance is less, there has been a loss. There are special rules for recognizing these gains and losses, depending on the nature of the assets exchanged:

Exchange	Losses Recognized	Gains Recognized
For financial accounting purposes		
Of dissimilar assets	Yes	Yes
Of similar assets	Yes	No
For income tax purposes		
Of dissimilar assets	Yes	Yes
Of similar assets	No	No

CLARIFICATION NOTE: For assets to be similar, they must be used for similar purposes. A desktop computer, for example, is similar to a laptop computer. Dissimilar assets, such as a truck and a cement mixer, are not used for similar purposes.

PARENTHETICAL NOTE: Recognizing losses but not gains on similar assets follows the convention of conservatism.

KEY POINT: For exchanges of dissimilar assets, the gain or loss on exchange equals the trade-in allowance minus carrying value of the old asset.

For both financial accounting and income tax purposes, both gains and losses are recognized when a company exchanges dissimilar assets. Assets are dissimilar when they perform different functions or do not meet specific monetary and business criteria for being considered similar assets. For financial accounting purposes, most exchanges are considered exchanges of dissimilar assets. In rare cases, when exchanges meet the specific criteria for exchanges of similar assets, the gains are not recognized. In these cases, you could think of the trade-in as an extension of the life and usefulness of the original machine. Instead of recognizing a gain at the time of the exchange, the company records the new machine at the sum of the carrying value of the older machine plus any cash paid.[10]

For income tax purposes, similar assets are defined as those performing the same function. Neither gains nor losses on exchanges of these assets are recognized in computing a company's income tax liability. Thus, in practice, accountants face cases in which both gains and losses are recognized (exchanges of dissimilar assets), cases in which losses are recognized and gains are not (exchanges of similar assets for financial reporting purposes), and cases in which neither gains nor losses are recognized (exchanges of similar assets for income tax purposes). Since all these options are used in practice, they are all illustrated in the following sections.

■ **Loss on the Exchange Recognized**   A loss is recognized for financial accounting purposes on all exchanges in which a material loss occurs. To illustrate the recognition of a loss, let us assume that the firm in our earlier example exchanges the machine for a newer, more modern machine on the following terms:

CLARIFICATION NOTE:
There is no relationship between carrying value and trade-in value. Carrying value is original cost minus accumulated depreciation to date, whereas trade-in value is fair market value on the date of the exchange.

List price of new machine	$12,000
Trade-in allowance for old machine	(1,000)
Cash payment required	$11,000

In this case, the trade-in allowance ($1,000) is less than the carrying value ($1,850) of the old machine. The loss on the exchange is $850 ($1,850 − $1,000). The following journal entry records this transaction under the assumption that the loss is to be recognized:

A = L + OE
+
+
−
−

Sept. 30	Machinery (new)	12,000	
	Accumulated Depreciation, Machinery	4,650	
	Loss on Exchange of Machinery	850	
	Machinery (old)		6,500
	Cash		11,000
	Exchange of machines		

KEY POINT: For income tax purposes, gains and losses on the exchange of similar assets are not recognized.

■ **Loss on the Exchange Not Recognized**   In the previous example, in which a loss was recognized, the new asset was recorded at the purchase price of $12,000 and a loss of $850 was recorded. If the transaction involves similar assets and is to be recorded for income tax purposes, the loss should not be recognized. In this case, the cost basis of the new asset will reflect the effect of the unrecorded loss. The cost basis is computed by adding the cash payment to the carrying value of the old asset:

Carrying value of old machine	$ 1,850
Cash paid	11,000
Cost basis of new machine	$12,850

Note that no loss is recognized in the entry to record this transaction:

A = L + OE
+
+
−
−

Sept. 30	Machinery (new)	12,850	
	Accumulated Depreciation, Machinery	4,650	
	Machinery (old)		6,500
	Cash		11,000
	Exchange of machines		

Note that the new machinery is reported at the purchase price of $12,000 plus the unrecognized loss of $850. The nonrecognition of the loss on the exchange is, in effect, a postponement of the loss. Since depreciation of the new machine will be computed based on a cost of $12,850 instead of $12,000, the "unrecognized" loss results in more depreciation each year on the new machine than if the loss had been recognized.

■ **Gain on the Exchange Recognized**   Gains on exchanges are recognized for accounting purposes when dissimilar assets are involved. To illustrate the recognition of a gain, we continue with our example, assuming the following terms and assuming the machines being exchanged serve different functions:

KEY POINT: For exchanges of assets, the cash payment on the exchange equals list price of the new asset minus trade-in allowance of the old asset.

List price of new machine	$12,000
Trade-in allowance for old machine	(3,000)
Cash payment required	$ 9,000

Here, the trade-in allowance ($3,000) exceeds the carrying value ($1,850) of the old machine by $1,150. Thus, there is a gain on the exchange, assuming that the price of the new machine has not been inflated to allow for an excessive trade-in value. In other words, a gain exists if the trade-in allowance represents the fair market value of the old machine. Assuming that this condition is true, the entry to record the transaction is as follows:

A = L + OE
+   +
+
−
−

Sept. 30	Machinery (new)	12,000	
	Accumulated Depreciation, Machinery	4,650	
	Gain on Exchange of Machinery		1,150
	Machinery (old)		6,500
	Cash		9,000
	Exchange of machines		

■ **GAIN ON THE EXCHANGE NOT RECOGNIZED** When similar assets are exchanged, gains are not recognized for either accounting or income tax purposes. The cost basis of the new machine must reflect the effect of the unrecorded gain. This cost basis is computed by adding the cash payment to the carrying value of the old asset, as follows:

Carrying value of old machine	$ 1,850
Cash paid	9,000
Cost basis of new machine	$10,850

The entry to record the transaction is as follows:

A = L + OE
+
+
−
−

Sept. 30	Machinery (new)	10,850	
	Accumulated Depreciation, Machinery	4,650	
	Machinery (old)		6,500
	Cash		9,000
	Exchange of machines		

As with the nonrecognition of losses, the nonrecognition of the gain on an exchange is, in effect, a postponement of the gain. In this illustration, when the new machine is eventually discarded or sold, its cost basis will be $10,850 instead of its original price of $12,000. Since depreciation will be computed on the cost basis of $10,850, the "unrecognized" gain is reflected in lower depreciation each year on the new machine than if the gain had been recognized.

✔ Check out ACE for a Review Quiz at http://accounting.college.hmco.com/students.

ACCOUNTING FOR NATURAL RESOURCES

LO5 Identify the issues related to accounting for natural resources and compute depletion.

RELATED TEXT ASSIGNMENTS
Q: 19, 20
SE: 9
E: 10
FRA: 5

CLARIFICATION NOTE:
Natural resources are not intangible assets. Natural resources are correctly classified as components of property, plant, and equipment.

Natural resources are shown on the balance sheet as long-term assets with such descriptive titles as Timberlands, Oil and Gas Reserves, and Mineral Deposits. The distinguishing characteristic of these assets is that they are converted to inventory by cutting, pumping, mining, or other extraction methods. Natural resources are recorded at acquisition cost, which may include some costs of development. As the resource is extracted and converted to inventory, the asset account must be proportionally reduced. The carrying value of oil reserves on the balance sheet, for example, is reduced by a small amount for each barrel of oil pumped. As a result, the original cost of the oil reserves is gradually reduced, and depletion is recognized in the amount of the decrease.

DEPLETION

The term *depletion* is used to describe not only the exhaustion of a natural resource but also the proportional allocation of the cost of a natural resource to the units extracted. The costs are allocated in a way that closely resembles the production method used to calculate depreciation. When a natural resource is purchased or developed, there must be an estimate of the total units that will be available, such

$$A = L + OE$$
$$- \quad -$$

as barrels of oil, tons of coal, or board-feet of lumber. The depletion cost per unit is determined by dividing the cost of the natural resource (less residual value, if any) by the estimated number of units available. The amount of the depletion cost for each accounting period is then computed by multiplying the depletion cost per unit by the number of units extracted and sold. For example, for a mine having an estimated 1,500,000 tons of coal, a cost of $1,800,000, and an estimated residual value of $300,000, the depletion charge per ton of coal is $1:

$$\frac{\$1,800,000 - \$300,000}{1,500,000 \text{ tons}} = \$1 \text{ per ton}$$

Thus, if 115,000 tons of coal are mined and sold during the first year, the depletion charge for the year is $115,000. This charge is recorded as follows:

Dec. 31	Depletion Expense, Coal Deposits	115,000	
	Accumulated Depletion, Coal Deposits		115,000
	To record depletion of coal mine: $1 per ton for 115,000 tons mined and sold		

On the balance sheet, data for the mine would be presented as follows:

Coal deposits	$1,800,000	
Less accumulated depletion	115,000	$1,685,000

Sometimes a natural resource is not sold in the year it is extracted. It is important to note that it would then be recorded as a depletion *expense* in the year it is *sold*. The part not sold is considered inventory.

DEPRECIATION OF CLOSELY RELATED PLANT ASSETS

The extraction of natural resources generally requires special on-site buildings and equipment (e.g., conveyors and drilling and pumping devices). If the useful life of those assets is longer than the estimated time it will take to deplete the resource, a special problem arises. Because such long-term assets are often abandoned and have no useful purpose once all the resources have been extracted, they should be depreciated on the same basis as the depletion is computed. For example, if machinery with a useful life of ten years is installed on an oil field that is expected to be depleted in eight years, the machinery should be depreciated over the eight-year period, using the production method. That way, each year's depreciation will be proportional to the year's depletion. If one-sixth of the oil field's total reserves is pumped in one year, then the depreciation should be one-sixth of the machinery's cost minus the residual value. If the useful life of a long-term plant asset is less than the expected life of the depleting resource, the shorter life should be used to compute depreciation. In such cases, or when an asset will not be abandoned once the reserves have been fully depleted, other depreciation methods, such as straight-line or declining-balance, are appropriate.

DEVELOPMENT AND EXPLORATION COSTS IN THE OIL AND GAS INDUSTRY

The costs of exploring and developing oil and gas resources can be accounted for under one of two methods. Under **successful efforts accounting**, the cost of successful exploration—for example, producing an oil well—is a cost of the resource. It should be recorded as an asset and depleted over the estimated life of the resource. The cost of an unsuccessful exploration—such as the cost of a dry well—is written off immediately as a loss. Because of these immediate write-offs, successful efforts accounting is considered the more conservative method and is used by most large oil companies.

Exploration-minded independent oil companies, on the other hand, argue that the cost of dry wells is part of the overall cost of the systematic development of an oil field and is thus a part of the cost of producing wells. Under this **full-costing** method, all costs, including the cost of dry wells, are recorded as assets and depleted over the estimated life of the producing resources. This method tends to improve a company's earnings performance in its early years. Either method is permitted by the Financial Accounting Standards Board.[11]

✓ Check out ACE for a Review Quiz at http://accounting.college.hmco.com/students.

ACCOUNTING FOR INTANGIBLE ASSETS

LO6 Identify the issues related to accounting for intangible assets, including research and development costs and goodwill.

RELATED TEXT ASSIGNMENTS
Q: 21, 22, 23, 24, 25, 26
SE: 10
E: 11
P: 5
SD: 3, 5, 6
FRA: 2, 3, 5, 6

www.heinz.com

KEY POINT: Generally, intangible assets, including goodwill, are recorded only when purchased. An exception is the cost of internally developed computer software after a working prototype has been developed.

The purchase of an intangible asset is a special kind of capital expenditure. An intangible asset is long term, but it has no physical substance. Its value comes from the long-term rights or advantages it offers to its owner. The most common examples—goodwill, trademarks, brand names, copyrights, patents, licenses or franchises, leaseholds, leasehold improvements, technology, noncompete covenants, and customer lists—are described in Table 1. Some current assets, such as accounts receivable and certain prepaid expenses, have no physical substance, but they are not classified as intangible assets because they are short term. Intangible assets are both long term and nonphysical.

Figure 7 shows the percentage of companies that report the various types of intangible assets. For some companies, intangible assets make up a substantial portion of total assets. As noted in the Decision Point at the beginning of the chapter, goodwill, trademarks, and other intangible assets of H.J. Heinz Company amount to over $2.7 billion, or 31 percent of total assets. How these assets are accounted for will have a substantial effect on Heinz's performance.

Intangible assets are accounted for at acquisition cost—that is, the amount that was paid for them. Some intangible assets, such as goodwill and trademarks, may be acquired at little or no cost. Even though they may have great value and be needed for profitable operations, they should not appear on the balance sheet unless they have been purchased from another party at a price established in the marketplace.

The accounting issues connected with intangible assets, other than goodwill, are the same as those connected with other long-lived assets. The Accounting Principles Board, in its *Opinion No. 17*, lists them as follows:

1. Determining an initial carrying amount

2. Accounting for that amount after acquisition under normal business conditions—that is, through periodic write-off or amortization—in a manner similar to depreciation

FIGURE 7
Intangible Assets Separately Reported by 600 Large Companies

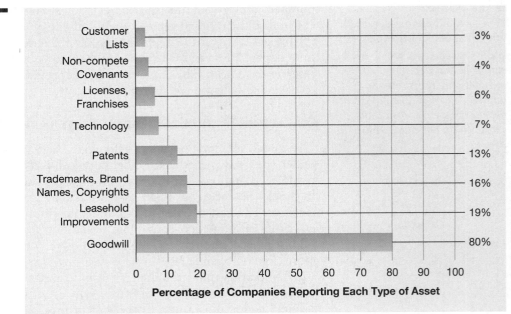

Source: Data from *Accounting Trends and Technology,* 2001

TABLE 1. Accounting for Intangible Assets

Type	Description	Accounting Treatment
Goodwill	The excess of the amount paid for the purchase of a business over the fair market value of the net assets.	Debit Goodwill for the acquisition cost, and perform impairment review annually.
Trademark, brand name	A registered symbol or name that can be used only by its owner to identify a product or service.	Debit Trademark or Brand Name for the acquisition cost, and amortize it over a reasonable life, not to exceed 40 years.
Copyright	An exclusive right granted by the federal government to reproduce and sell literary, musical, and other artistic materials and computer programs for a period of the author's life plus 70 years.	Record at acquisition cost, and amortize over the useful life, which is often much shorter than the legal life, but not to exceed 40 years. For example, the cost of paperback rights to a popular novel would typically be amortized over a useful life of two to four years.
Patent	An exclusive right granted by the federal government for a period of 20 years to make a particular product or use a specific process. A design may be granted a patent for 14 years.	The cost of successfully defending a patent in a patent infringement suit is added to the acquisition cost of the patent. Amortize over the useful life, which may be less than the legal life.
License, franchise	A right to an exclusive territory or market, or the right to use a formula, technique, process, or design.	Debit License or Franchise for the acquisition cost, and amortize it over a reasonable life, not to exceed 40 years.
Leasehold	A right to occupy land or buildings under a long-term rental contract. For example, Company A, which owns the right to use but does not want to use a retail location, sells or subleases to Company B the right to use it for ten years in return for one or more rental payments. Company B has purchased a leasehold.	Debit Leasehold for the amount of the rental payment, and amortize it over the remaining life of the lease. Payments to the lessor during the life of the lease should be debited to Lease Expense.
Leasehold improvements	Improvements to leased property that become the property of the lessor (the owner of the property) at the end of the lease.	Debit Leasehold Improvements for the cost of improvements, and amortize the cost of the improvements over the remaining life of the lease.
Technology	Capitalized costs associated with software developed for sale, lease, or internal use.	Record the amount of capitalizable software production costs, and amortize over the estimated economic life of the product.
Noncompete covenant	A contract limiting the rights of others to compete in a specific industry or line of business for a specified period.	Record at the acquisition cost, and amortize over the contract period.
Customer list	A list of customers or subscribers.	Debit Customer Lists for amount paid, and amortize over the expected life.

FOCUS ON BUSINESS PRACTICE

Take a Closer Look at Subscriber Lists!

One of the most valuable intangible assets some companies have is a list of subscribers. For example, the Newark Morning Ledger Co., a newspaper chain, purchased a chain of Michigan newspapers whose list of 460,000 subscribers was valued at $68 million. The U.S. Supreme Court upheld the company's right to amortize the value of the subscriber list because the company showed that the list had a limited useful life. The Internal Revenue Service had argued that the list had an indefinite life and therefore could not provide tax deductions through amortization. This ruling will benefit other types of businesses that purchase everything from bank deposits to pharmacy prescription files.[13]

CLARIFICATION NOTE:
Useful life refers to how long an intangible asset will be contributing income to a firm.

3. Accounting for that amount if the value declines substantially and permanently[12]

In addition to these three problems, an intangible asset, because it has no physical substance, may sometimes be impossible to identify. For these reasons, its value and its useful life may be quite hard to estimate.

The Accounting Principles Board has decided that a company should record as assets the costs of intangible assets acquired from others. However, the company should record as expenses the costs of developing intangible assets. Also, intangible assets that have a determinable useful life, such as patents, copyrights, and leaseholds, should be written off through periodic amortization over that useful life in much the same way that plant assets are depreciated. Even though some intangible assets, such as brand names and trademarks, have no measurable limit on their lives, they should still be amortized over a reasonable length of time.

To illustrate these procedures, assume that Soda Bottling Company purchases a patent on a unique bottle cap for $18,000. The entry to record the patent would include $18,000 in the asset account Patents. Note that if Soda Bottling Company had developed the bottle cap internally instead of purchasing it from others, the costs of developing the cap, such as salaries of researchers, supplies used in testing, and costs of equipment, would have been expensed as incurred.

Assume now that Soda's management determines that although the patent for the bottle cap will last for 20 years, the product using the cap will be sold only for the next six years. The entry to record the annual amortization expense would be for $3,000 ($18,000 ÷ 6 years). Note that the Patents account is reduced directly by the amount of the amortization expense. This is in contrast to the treatment of other long-term asset accounts, for which depreciation or depletion is accumulated in separate contra accounts.

If the patent becomes worthless before it is fully amortized, the remaining carrying value is written off as a loss by removing it from the Patents account.

RESEARCH AND DEVELOPMENT COSTS

Most successful companies carry out research and development (R&D) activities, often within a separate department. Among these activities are development of new products, testing of existing and proposed products, and pure research. The costs of these activities are substantial expenditures for many companies. In a recent year, General Motors spent $6.6 billion on research and development, or about 4 percent of its revenues.[14] R&D costs can be even greater in high-tech fields like pharmaceuticals. For example, Abbott Laboratories recently spent $1.4 billion, or almost 10 percent of revenues, on R&D, and Roche Group spent almost $4 billion, or 14 percent of revenues.[15]

www.gm.com

www.abbott.com
www.roche.com

FOCUS ON INTERNATIONAL BUSINESS

Lack of Comparability Is a Real Problem!

Worldwide variability in accounting practice causes problems for those who want to compare the financial statements of companies from different countries. For example, the method of accounting for R&D costs differs, depending on the country in which a company files its financial report. In Germany, Mexico, and the United States, a company must expense its R&D costs, whereas in France, Australia, and Japan, a company may expense R&D or capitalize it (record it as an asset) if it meets certain criteria. Companies complying with the European Directives (European laws affecting financial reporting) have a choice of expensing or capitalizing R&D costs, but companies complying with International Accounting Standards (IAS) must expense research costs and capitalize development costs that meet certain conditions.[16]

In the past, some companies recorded as assets R&D costs that could be directly traced to the development of specific patents, formulas, or other rights. Other costs, such as those for testing and pure research, were treated as expenses of the accounting period and deducted from income. Since then, the Financial Accounting Standards Board has stated that all R&D costs should be treated as revenue expenditures and charged to expense in the period in which they are incurred.[17] The board argues that it is too hard to trace specific costs to specific profitable developments. Also, the costs of research and development are continuous and necessary for the success of a business and so should be treated as current expenses. To support this conclusion, the board cites studies showing that 30 to 90 percent of all new products fail and that 75 percent of new-product expenses go to unsuccessful products. Thus, their costs do not represent future benefits.

COMPUTER SOFTWARE COSTS

The costs that companies incur in developing computer software for sale or lease or for their own internal use are considered research and development costs until the product has proved technologically feasible. Thus, costs incurred before that point should be charged to expense when incurred. A product is deemed technologically feasible when a detailed working program has been designed. Once that occurs, all software production costs are recorded as assets, such as Technology, and are amortized over the estimated economic life of the product using the straight-line method. If at any time the company cannot expect to realize from a software product the amount of its unamortized costs on the balance sheet, the asset should be written down to the amount expected to be realized.[18]

LEASEHOLD IMPROVEMENTS

As noted in Table 1, improvements to leased property that become the property of the lessor (the owner of the property) at the end of the lease are called leasehold improvements. Such improvements are common for both small and large businesses. A study of large companies showed that 19 percent list leasehold improvements separately; the percentage is likely to be much higher for small businesses, since they generally operate in leased premises.[19] The improvement costs are amortized over the remaining term of the lease or the useful life of the improvement, whichever is shorter. Leasehold improvements are often classified as tangible assets in the property, plant, and equipment section of the balance sheet but are included in the intangible asset section because the improvements revert to the lessor at the end of the lease and are therefore more of a right than a tangible asset.

GOODWILL

● **STOP AND THINK!**

Why would a company spend millions of dollars on goodwill?

The company must be paying for anticipated superior earnings and believes it will more than recoup the goodwill it purchased. ■

The term *goodwill* means different things to different people. In most cases, goodwill is taken to mean the good reputation of a company. From an accounting standpoint, goodwill exists when a purchaser pays more for a business than the fair market value of the net assets if purchased individually. Because the purchaser has paid more than the fair market value of the physical assets, there must be intangible assets. If the company being purchased does not have patents, copyrights, trademarks, or other identifiable intangible assets of value, the excess payment is assumed to be for goodwill. Goodwill exists because most businesses are worth more as going concerns than as collections of assets. Goodwill reflects all the factors that allow a company to earn a higher-than-market rate of return on its assets, including customer satisfaction, good management, manufacturing efficiency, the advantages of holding a monopoly, good locations, and good employee relations. The payment above and beyond the fair market value of the tangible assets and other specific intangible assets is properly recorded in the Goodwill account.

The FASB has stated that purchased goodwill is an asset to be reported as a separate line item on the balance sheet and is subject to an annual impairment review. The impairment review requires a company to determine the reporting-unit level

FOCUS ON BUSINESS PRACTICE

Wake up, Goodwill Is Growing!

As Figure 7 shows, 80 percent of 600 large companies separately report goodwill as an asset. Because much of the growth of these companies has come through purchasing other companies, goodwill as a percentage of total assets has also grown. For some, the amount of goodwill is material:[20]

	Goodwill (in billions)	Percentage of Total Assets
Lucent Technologies <www.lucent.com>	$9,945	20.4
Sara Lee Corporation <www.saralee.com>	$2,621	22.6
Tribune Company <www.tribune.com>	$8,496	57.9

KEY POINT: Goodwill equals purchase price minus adjusted net asset value.

on which goodwill is to be tested and the specific methodology to calculate the fair value of the reporting unit. If the fair value of goodwill is less than its carrying value on the balance sheet, then goodwill is considered impaired. Impairment results in reducing goodwill to its fair value and reporting the impairment charge on the income statement. A company can perform the fair value measurement for each reporting unit at any time as long as the measurement date is consistent from year to year.[21]

Goodwill should not be recorded unless it is paid for in connection with the purchase of a whole business. The amount to be recorded as goodwill can be determined by writing the identifiable net assets up to their fair market values at the time of purchase and subtracting the total from the purchase price. For example, assume that the owners of Company A agree to sell the company for $11,400,000. If the net assets (total assets − total liabilities) are fairly valued at $10,000,000, then the amount of the goodwill is $1,400,000 ($11,400,000 − $10,000,000). If the fair market value of the net assets is later determined to be more or less than $10,000,000, an entry is made in the accounting records to adjust the assets to the fair market value. The goodwill would then represent the difference between the adjusted net assets and the purchase price of $11,400,000.

Check out ACE for a Review Quiz at http://accounting.college.hmco.com/students.

SPECIAL PROBLEMS OF DEPRECIATING PLANT ASSETS

SO7 Apply depreciation methods to problems of partial years, revised rates, groups of similar items, special types of capital expenditures, and cost recovery.

RELATED TEXT ASSIGNMENTS
Q: 27, 28, 29, 30, 31, 32
E: 12, 13, 14, 15
P: 3, 8
FRA: 1

The illustrations used so far in this chapter have been simplified to explain the concepts and methods of depreciation. In actual business practice, there is often a need to (1) calculate depreciation for partial years, (2) revise depreciation rates based on new estimates of useful life or residual value, (3) group like items when calculating depreciation, (4) account for special types of capital expenditures, and (5) use the accelerated cost recovery method for tax purposes. The next sections discuss these five cases.

DEPRECIATION FOR PARTIAL YEARS

So far, most illustrations of depreciation methods have assumed that plant assets were purchased at the beginning or end of an accounting period. Usually, however, businesses buy assets when they are needed and sell or discard them when they are no longer useful or needed. The time of year is normally not a factor in the decision. Consequently, it is often necessary to calculate depreciation for partial years.

For example, assume that a piece of equipment is purchased for $3,600 and that it has an estimated useful life of six years and an estimated residual value of $600. Assume also that it is purchased on September 5 and that the yearly accounting period ends on December 31. Depreciation must be recorded for four months, September through December, or four-twelfths of the year. This factor is applied to the calculated depreciation for the entire year. The four months' depreciation under the straight-line method is calculated as follows:

$$\frac{\$3,600 - \$600}{6 \text{ years}} \times 4/12 = \$167$$

For the other depreciation methods, most companies compute the first year's depreciation and then multiply by the partial year factor. For example, if the company used the double-declining-balance method on the preceding equipment, the depreciation on the asset would be computed as follows:

$$\$3,600 \times 1/3 \times 4/12 = \$400$$

Typically, the depreciation calculation is rounded off to the nearest whole month because a partial month's depreciation is rarely material and the calculation is easier. In this case, depreciation was recorded from the beginning of September even though the purchase was made on September 5.

For all methods, the remainder (eight-twelfths) of the first year's depreciation is recorded in the next annual accounting period together with four-twelfths of the second year's depreciation.

REVISION OF DEPRECIATION RATES

Because a depreciation rate is based on an estimate of an asset's useful life, the periodic depreciation charge is seldom precise. It is sometimes very inadequate or excessive. This situation may result from an underestimate or overestimate of the asset's useful life or from a wrong estimate of the residual value. What action should be taken when it is found that after several years of use, a piece of equipment will last less time—or longer—than originally thought? Sometimes, it is necessary to revise the estimate of useful life so that the periodic depreciation expense increases or decreases. Then, to reflect the revised situation, the remaining depreciable cost of the asset is spread over the remaining years of useful life.

With this technique, the annual depreciation expense is increased or decreased to reduce the asset's carrying value to its residual value at the end of its remaining useful life. For example, assume that a delivery truck was purchased for $7,000 and has a residual value of $1,000. At the time of the purchase, the truck was expected to last six years, and it was depreciated on the straight-line basis. However, after two years of intensive use, it is determined that the truck will last only two more years, but that its estimated residual value at the end of the two years will still be $1,000. In other words, at the end of the second year, the truck's estimated useful life is reduced from six years to four years. At that time, the asset account and its related accumulated depreciation account would appear as follows:

Delivery Truck		Accumulated Depreciation, Delivery Truck	
Cost 7,000		Depreciation, year 1	1,000
		Depreciation, year 2	1,000

The remaining depreciable cost is computed as follows:

Cost	minus	Depreciation Already Taken	minus	Residual Value
$7,000	–	$2,000	–	$1,000 = $4,000

The new annual periodic depreciation charge is computed by dividing the remaining depreciable cost of $4,000 by the remaining useful life of two years. Therefore, the new periodic depreciation charge is $2,000. The annual adjusting entry for depreciation for the next two years would be as follows:

A = L + OE

Dec. 31	Depreciation Expense, Delivery Truck	2,000	
	Accumulated Depreciation, Delivery Truck		2,000
	To record depreciation expense for the year		

This method of revising depreciation is used widely in industry. It is also supported by *Opinion No. 9* and *Opinion No. 20* of the Accounting Principles Board of the AICPA.

GROUP DEPRECIATION

To say that the estimated useful life of an asset, such as a piece of equipment, is six years means that the average piece of equipment of that type is expected to last six years. In reality, some pieces may last only two or three years, and others may last eight or nine years, or longer. For this reason, and for reasons of convenience, large companies group similar items, such as trucks or pieces of office equipment, to calculate depreciation. This method is called **group depreciation**. Group depreciation is widely used in all fields of industry and business. A survey of large businesses indicated that 65 percent used group depreciation for all or part of their plant assets.[22]

SPECIAL TYPES OF CAPITAL EXPENDITURES

Companies make capital expenditures not only for plant assets, natural resources, and intangible assets but also for additions and betterments. An **addition** is an enlargement to the physical layout of a plant asset. As an example, if a new wing is added to a building, the benefits from the expenditure will be received over several years, and the amount paid for it should be debited to the asset account. A **betterment** is an improvement that does not add to the physical layout of a plant asset. Installation of an air-conditioning system is an example of a betterment that will offer benefits over a period of years; therefore, its cost should be charged to an asset account.

> **ENRICHMENT NOTE:**
> Other examples of betterments include replacing stairs with an escalator in a department store and paving a gravel parking lot.

Revenue expenditures for plant equipment include the repairs necessary to keep an asset in good working condition. Repairs fall into two categories: ordinary repairs and extraordinary repairs. **Ordinary repairs** are necessary to maintain an asset in good operating condition. Trucks must have periodic tune-ups, their tires and batteries must be regularly replaced, and other routine repairs must be made. Offices and halls must be painted regularly, and broken tiles or woodwork must be replaced. Such repairs are a current expense.

> **ENRICHMENT NOTE:**
> Putting a new motor in a cement mixer and replacing the roof on a building, thereby extending its life, are other examples of extraordinary repairs.

Extraordinary repairs are repairs of a more significant nature—they affect the estimated residual value or estimated useful life of an asset. For example, a boiler for heating a building may be given a complete overhaul, at a cost of several thousand dollars, that will extend its useful life by five years. Typically, extraordinary repairs are recorded by debiting the Accumulated Depreciation account, under the assumption that some of the depreciation previously recorded has now been eliminated. The effect of this reduction in the Accumulated Depreciation account is to increase the carrying value of the asset by the cost of the extraordinary repair. Consequently, the new carrying value of the asset should be depreciated over the new estimated useful life.

Let us assume that a machine that cost $10,000 has no residual value and an estimated useful life of ten years. After eight years, the accumulated depreciation under the straight-line method is $8,000, and the carrying value is $2,000 ($10,000 − $8,000). At that point, the machine is given a major overhaul costing $1,500. This expenditure extends the machine's useful life three years beyond the original ten years. The entry for the extraordinary repair would be as follows:

A = L + OE	Jan. 4	Accumulated Depreciation, Machinery	1,500	
+		Cash		1,500
−		Extraordinary repair		
		to machinery		

The annual periodic depreciation for each of the five years remaining in the machine's useful life would be calculated as follows:

Carrying value before extraordinary repairs	$2,000
Extraordinary repairs	1,500
Total	$3,500

$$\text{Annual periodic depreciation} = \frac{\$3,500}{5 \text{ years}} = \$700$$

If the machine remains in use for the five years expected after the major overhaul, the total of the five annual depreciation charges of $700 will exactly equal the new carrying value, including the cost of the extraordinary repair.

COST RECOVERY FOR FEDERAL INCOME TAX PURPOSES

The Tax Reform Act of 1986 is arguably the most sweeping revision of federal tax laws since the original enactment of the Internal Revenue Code in 1913. First, it allows a company to expense the first $17,500 (which increases to $25,000 by tax year 2003) of equipment expenditures rather than recording them as an asset. Second, it allows a new method of writing off expenditures recorded as assets, the **Modified Accelerated Cost Recovery System (MACRS)**. MACRS discards the concepts of estimated useful life and residual value. Instead, it requires that a cost recovery allowance be computed (1) on the unadjusted cost of property being recovered, and (2) over a period of years prescribed by the law for all property of similar types. The accelerated method prescribed under MACRS for most property other than real estate is 200 percent declining balance with a half-year convention (only one half-year's depreciation is allowed in the year of purchase, and one half-year's depreciation is taken in the last year). In addition, the period over which the cost may be recovered is specified. Recovery of the cost of property placed in service after December 31, 1986, is calculated as prescribed in the 1986 law.

Congress hoped that MACRS would encourage businesses to invest in new plant and equipment by allowing them to write off such assets rapidly. MACRS accelerates the write-off of these investments in two ways. First, the prescribed recovery periods are often shorter than the estimated useful lives used for calculating depreciation for the financial statements. Second, the accelerated method allowed under the new law enables businesses to recover most of the cost of their investments early in the depreciation process.

CLARIFICATION NOTE: MACRS depreciation is used for tax purposes only. It cannot be used for financial reporting.

Tax methods of depreciation are not usually acceptable for financial reporting under generally accepted accounting principles because the recovery periods are shorter than the depreciable assets' estimated useful lives.

Chapter Review

REVIEW OF LEARNING OBJECTIVES

LO1 Identify the types of long-term assets and explain the management issues related to accounting for them.

Long-term assets are assets that are used in the operation of a business, are not intended for resale, and have a useful life of more than one year. Long-term assets are either tangible or intangible. In the former category are land, plant assets, and natural resources. In the latter are trademarks, patents, franchises, goodwill, and other rights. The accounting issues associated with long-term assets relate to the decision to acquire the assets, the means of financing the assets, and the methods of accounting for the assets.

LO2 Distinguish between capital and revenue expenditures, and account for the cost of property, plant, and equipment.

It is important to distinguish between capital expenditures, which are recorded as assets, and revenue expenditures, which are recorded as expenses. The error of classifying one as the other will have an important effect on net income. The acquisition cost of property, plant, and equipment includes all expenditures that are reasonable and necessary to get such an asset in place and ready for use. Among these expenditures are purchase price, installation cost, freight charges, and insurance during transit.

LO3 Define *depreciation* and compute depreciation under the straight-line, production, and declining-balance methods.

Depreciation is the periodic allocation of the cost of a plant asset over its estimated useful life. It is recorded by debiting Depreciation Expense and crediting a related contra-asset account called Accumulated Depreciation. Factors that affect the computation of depreciation are cost, residual value, depreciable cost, and estimated useful life. Depreciation is commonly computed by the straight-line method, the production method, or an accelerated method. The straight-line method is related directly to the passage of time, whereas the production method is related directly to use. An accelerated method, which results in relatively large amounts of depreciation in earlier years and reduced amounts in later years, is based on the assumption that plant assets provide greater economic benefit in their earlier years than in later years. The most common accelerated method is the declining-balance method.

LO4 Account for the disposal of depreciable assets.

Long-term depreciable assets may be disposed of by being discarded, sold, or exchanged. When long-term assets are disposed of, it is necessary to record the depreciation up to the date of disposal and to remove the carrying value from the accounts by removing the cost from the asset account and the depreciation to date from the accumulated depreciation account. If a long-term asset is sold at a price that differs from its carrying value, the gain or loss should be recorded and reported on the income statement. In recording exchanges of similar plant assets, a gain or loss may arise. Losses, but not gains, should be recognized at the time of the exchange. When a gain is not recognized, the new asset is recorded at the carrying value of the old asset plus any cash paid. For income tax purposes, neither gains nor losses are recognized in the exchange of similar assets. When dissimilar assets are exchanged, gains and losses are recognized under both accounting and income tax rules.

LO5 Identify the issues related to accounting for natural resources and compute depletion.

Natural resources are depletable assets that are converted to inventory by cutting, pumping, mining, or other forms of extraction. Natural resources are recorded at cost as long-term assets. They are allocated as expenses through depletion charges as the resources are sold. The depletion charge is based on the ratio of the resource extracted to the total estimated resource. A major issue related to this subject is accounting for oil and gas reserves.

LO6 Identify the issues related to accounting for intangible assets, including research and development costs and goodwill.

The purchase of an intangible asset should be treated as a capital expenditure and recorded at acquisition cost, which in turn should be amortized over the useful life of the asset. The FASB requires that research and development costs be treated as revenue expenditures and charged as expenses in the periods of expenditure. Software costs are treated as research and development costs and expensed until a feasible working program is developed, after which time the costs may be capitalized and amortized over a reasonable estimated life. Goodwill is the excess of the amount paid for the purchase of a business over the fair market value of the net assets and is usually related to the superior earning potential of the business. It should be recorded only if paid for in connection with the purchase of a business, and it should be reviewed annually for possible impairment.

SUPPLEMENTAL OBJECTIVE

SO7 Apply depreciation methods to problems of partial years, revised rates, groups of similar items, special types of capital expenditures, and cost recovery.

In actual business practice, many factors affect depreciation calculations. It may be necessary to calculate depreciation for partial years because assets are bought and sold throughout the year, or to revise depreciation rates because of changed conditions. Because it is often difficult to estimate the useful life of a single item, and because it is more convenient, many large businesses group similar items for purposes of depreciation. Companies must also consider certain special capital expenditures when calculating depreciation. For example, expenditures for additions and betterments are capital expenditures. Extraordinary repairs, which increase the residual value or extend the life of an asset, are also treated as capital expenditures, but ordinary repairs are revenue expenditures. For income tax purposes, rapid write-offs of depreciable assets are allowed under the Modified Accelerated Cost Recovery System. Such rapid write-offs are not usually acceptable for financial accounting because the shortened recovery periods violate the matching rule.

REVIEW OF CONCEPTS AND TERMINOLOGY

The following concepts and terms were introduced in this chapter:

LO3   **Accelerated method:** A method of depreciation that allocates relatively large amounts of the depreciable cost of an asset to earlier years and reduced amounts to later years.

SO7   **Addition:** An enlargement to the physical layout of a plant asset.

LO1 **Amortization:** The periodic allocation of the cost of an intangible asset to the periods it benefits.

LO1 **Asset impairment:** Loss of revenue-generating potential of a long-lived asset before the end of its useful life; the difference between an asset's carrying value and its fair value, as measured by the present value of the expected cash flows.

SO7 **Betterment:** An improvement that does not add to the physical layout of a plant asset.

LO6 **Brand name:** A registered name that can be used only by its owner to identify a product or service.

LO2 **Capital expenditure:** An expenditure for the purchase or expansion of a long-term asset, recorded in an asset account.

LO1 **Carrying value:** The unexpired part of the cost of an asset, not its market value. Also called *book value*.

LO6 **Copyright:** An exclusive right granted by the federal government to reproduce and sell literary, musical, and other artistic materials and computer programs for a period of the author's life plus 70 years.

LO6 **Customer list:** A list of customers or subscribers.

LO3 **Declining-balance method:** An accelerated method of depreciation in which depreciation is computed by applying a fixed rate to the carrying value (the declining balance) of a tangible long-lived asset.

LO1 **Depletion:** The exhaustion of a natural resource through mining, cutting, pumping, or other extraction, and the way in which the cost is allocated.

LO3 **Depreciable cost:** The cost of an asset less its residual value.

LO1 **Depreciation:** The periodic allocation of the cost of a tangible long-lived asset (other than land and natural resources) over its estimated useful life.

LO3 **Double-declining-balance method:** An accelerated method of depreciation in which a fixed rate equal to twice the straight-line percentage is applied to the carrying value (the declining balance) of a tangible long-lived asset.

LO3 **Estimated useful life:** The total number of service units expected from a long-term asset.

LO2 **Expenditure:** A payment or an obligation to make future payment for an asset or a service.

SO7 **Extraordinary repairs:** Repairs that affect the estimated residual value or estimated useful life of an asset thereby increasing its carrying value.

LO6 **Franchise:** The right or license to an exclusive territory or market.

LO5 **Full-costing:** A method of accounting for the costs of exploring and developing oil and gas resources in which all costs are recorded as assets and depleted over the estimated life of the producing resources.

LO6 **Goodwill:** The excess of the cost of a group of assets (usually a business) over the fair market value of the net assets if purchased individually.

SO7 **Group depreciation:** The grouping of similar items to calculate depreciation.

LO1 **Intangible assets:** Long-term assets with no physical substance whose value is based on rights or advantages accruing to the owner.

LO6 **Leasehold:** A right to occupy land or buildings under a long-term rental contract.

LO6 **Leasehold improvements:** Improvements to leased property that become the property of the lessor at the end of the lease.

LO6 **License:** The right to use a formula, technique, process, or design.

LO1 **Long-term assets:** Assets that have a useful life of more than one year, are acquired for use in the operation of a business, and are not intended for resale. Less commonly called *fixed assets*.

SO7   **Modified Accelerated Cost Recovery System (MACRS):** A mandatory system of depreciation for income tax purposes, enacted by Congress in 1986, that requires a cost recovery allowance to be computed (1) on the unadjusted cost of property being recovered, and (2) over a period of years prescribed by the law for all property of similar types.

LO1   **Natural resources:** Long-term assets purchased for the economic value that can be taken from the land and used up.

LO6   **Noncompete covenant:** A contract limiting the rights of others to compete in a specific industry or line of business for a specified period.

LO3   **Obsolescence:** The process of becoming out of date, which is a factor in the limited useful life of tangible assets.

SO7   **Ordinary repairs:** Repairs necessary to maintain an asset in good operating condition, which are recorded as current period expenses.

LO6   **Patent:** An exclusive right granted by the federal government for a period of 20 years to make a particular product or use a specific process or design.

LO3   **Physical deterioration:** Limitations on the useful life of a depreciable asset resulting from use and from exposure to the elements.

LO3   **Production method:** A method of depreciation that assumes depreciation is solely the result of use and that allocates depreciation based on the units of output or use during each period of an asset's useful life.

LO3   **Residual value:** The estimated net scrap, salvage, or trade-in value of a tangible asset at the estimated date of disposal. Also called *salvage value* or *disposal value*.

LO2   **Revenue expenditure:** An expenditure related to repair, maintenance, and operation of a long-term asset, recorded by a debit to an expense account.

LO3   **Straight-line method:** A method of depreciation that assumes depreciation depends only on the passage of time and that allocates an equal amount of depreciation to each accounting period in an asset's useful life.

LO5   **Successful efforts accounting:** A method of accounting for the costs of exploring and developing oil and gas resources in which successful exploration is recorded as an asset and depleted over the estimated life of the resource and all unsuccessful efforts are immediately written off as losses.

LO1   **Tangible assets:** Long-term assets that have physical substance.

LO6   **Technology:** Capitalized costs associated with software developed for sale, lease, or internal use and amortized over the estimated economic life of the software.

LO6   **Trademark:** A registered symbol or brand name that can be used only by its owner to identify a product or service.

REVIEW PROBLEM

Comparison of Depreciation Methods

LO3   Norton Construction Company purchased a cement mixer on January 2, 20x1, for $14,500. The mixer was expected to have a useful life of five years and a residual value of $1,000. The company engineers estimated that the mixer would have a useful life of 7,500 hours. It was used 1,500 hours in 20x1, 2,625 hours in 20x2, 2,250 hours in 20x3, 750 hours in 20x4, and 375 hours in 20x5. Norton Construction Company's year end is December 31.

REQUIRED ▶   1. Compute the depreciation expense and carrying value for 20x1 to 20x5, using the following methods: (a) straight-line, (b) production, and (c) double-declining-balance.

2. Prepare the adjusting entry to record the depreciation for 20x1 that you calculated in 1(a).

3. Show the balance sheet presentation for the cement mixer after the entry in **2** on December 31, 20x1.
4. What conclusions can you draw from the patterns of yearly depreciation?

ANSWER TO REVIEW PROBLEM

1. Depreciation computed:

Depreciation Method	Year	Computation	Depreciation	Carrying Value
a. Straight-line	20x1	$13,500 × 1/5	$2,700	$11,800
	20x2	13,500 × 1/5	2,700	9,100
	20x3	13,500 × 1/5	2,700	6,400
	20x4	13,500 × 1/5	2,700	3,700
	20x5	13,500 × 1/5	2,700	1,000
b. Production	20x1	$13,500 × $\dfrac{1,500}{7,500}$	$2,700	$11,800
	20x2	13,500 × $\dfrac{2,625}{7,500}$	4,725	7,075
	20x3	13,500 × $\dfrac{2,250}{7,500}$	4,050	3,025
	20x4	13,500 × $\dfrac{750}{7,500}$	1,350	1,675
	20x5	13,500 × $\dfrac{375}{7,500}$	675	1,000
c. Double-declining-balance	20x1	$14,500 × .4	$5,800	$ 8,700
	20x2	8,700 × .4	3,480	5,220
	20x3	5,220 × .4	2,088	3,132
	20x4	3,132 × .4	1,253*	1,879
	20x5		879*[†]	1,000

*Rounded.

[†] Remaining depreciation to reduce carrying value to residual value ($1,879 − $1,000 = $879).

2. Adjusting entry prepared—straight-line method:

20x1			
Dec. 31	Depreciation Expense, Cement Mixer	2,700	
	Accumulated Depreciation, Cement Mixer		2,700
	To record depreciation expense, straight-line method		

3. Balance sheet presentation for 20x1 shown:

Property, plant, and equipment
Cement mixer $14,500
Less accumulated depreciation   2,700
  $11,800

4. Conclusions drawn from depreciation patterns: The pattern of depreciation for the straight-line method differs significantly from that for the double-declining-balance method. In the earlier years, the amount of depreciation under the double-declining-balance method is significantly greater than the amount under the straight-line method. In the later years, the opposite is true. The carrying value under the straight-line method is greater than that under the double-declining-balance method at the end of all years except the fifth year. Depreciation under the production method differs from that under the other methods in that it follows no regular pattern. It varies with the amount of use. Consequently, depreciation is greatest in 20x2 and 20x3, which are the years of greatest use. Use declined significantly in the last two years.

Chapter Assignments

BUILDING YOUR KNOWLEDGE FOUNDATION

QUESTIONS

1. What are the characteristics of long-term assets?

2. Which of the following items would be classified as plant assets on the balance sheet? (a) A truck held for sale by a truck dealer, (b) an office building that was once the company headquarters but is now to be sold, (c) a typewriter used by a secretary of the company, (d) a machine that is used in manufacturing operations but is now fully depreciated, (e) pollution-control equipment that does not reduce the cost or improve the efficiency of a factory, (f) a parking lot for company employees.

3. Why is land different from other long-term assets?

4. What do accountants mean by the term *depreciation*, and what is its relationship to depletion and amortization?

5. What is asset impairment, and how does it affect the valuation of long-term assets?

6. How do cash flows relate to the decision to acquire a long-term asset, and how does the useful life of an asset relate to the means of financing it?

7. Why is it useful to think of a plant asset as a bundle of services?

8. What is the distinction between revenue expenditures and capital expenditures, why is it important, and what in general is included in the cost of a long-term asset?

9. Which of the following expenditures stemming from the purchase of a computer system would be charged to the asset account? (a) The purchase price of the equipment, (b) interest on the debt incurred to purchase the equipment, (c) freight charges, (d) installation charges, (e) the cost of special communications outlets at the computer site, (f) the cost of repairing a door that was damaged during installation, (g) the cost of adjustments to the system during the first month of operation.

10. Hale's Grocery obtained bids on the construction of a receiving dock at the back of its store. The lowest bid was $22,000. The company decided to build the dock itself, however, and was able to do so for $20,000, which it borrowed. The activity was recorded as a debit to Buildings for $22,000 and credits to Notes Payable for $20,000 and Gain on Construction for $2,000. Do you agree with the entry?

11. A firm buys technical equipment that is expected to last twelve years. Why might the equipment have to be depreciated over a shorter period of time?

12. A company purchased a building five years ago. The market value of the building is now greater than it was when the building was purchased. Explain why the company should continue depreciating the building.

13. Evaluate the following statement: "A parking lot should not be depreciated because adequate repairs will make it last forever."

14. Is the purpose of depreciation to determine the value of equipment? Explain your answer.

15. Contrast the assumption underlying the straight-line depreciation method with the assumption underlying the production depreciation method.

16. What is the principal argument supporting an accelerated depreciation method?

17. If a plant asset is sold during the year, why should depreciation be computed for the partial year prior to the date of the sale?

18. If a plant asset is discarded before the end of its useful life, how is the amount of loss measured?

19. Old Stake Mining Company computes the depletion rate of ore to be $2 per ton. During 20xx the company mined 400,000 tons of ore and sold 370,000 tons. What is the total depletion expense for the year?

20. Under what circumstances can a mining company depreciate its plant assets over a period of time that is less than their useful lives?

21. Because accounts receivable have no physical substance, can they be classified as intangible assets?

22. Under what circumstances can a company have intangible assets that do not appear on the balance sheet?

23. How does the Financial Accounting Standards Board recommend that research and development costs be treated?

24. After spending three years developing a new software program for designing office buildings, Archi Draw Company recently completed the detailed working program. How does accounting for the costs of software development differ before and after the completion of a successful working program?

25. How is accounting for software development costs similar to and different from accounting for research and development costs?

26. Under what conditions should goodwill be recorded? Should it remain in the records permanently once it is recorded?

27. What basic procedure should be followed in revising a depreciation rate?

28. On what basis can depreciation be taken on a group of assets rather than on individual items?

29. What will be the effect on future years' income of charging an addition to a building to repair expense?

30. In what ways do an addition, a betterment, and an extraordinary repair differ?

31. How does an extraordinary repair differ from an ordinary repair? What is the accounting treatment for each?

32. What is the difference between depreciation for accounting purposes and the Modified Accelerated Cost Recovery System for income tax purposes?

SHORT EXERCISES

LO1 Management Issues

SE 1. Indicate whether each of the following actions is primarily related to (a) acquisition of long-term assets, (b) financing of long-term assets, or (c) choosing methods and estimates related to long-term assets:

1. Deciding between common stock and long-term notes for the raising of funds
2. Relating the acquisition cost of a long-term asset to the cash flows generated by the asset
3. Determining how long an asset will benefit the company
4. Deciding to use cash flows from operations to purchase long-term assets
5. Determining how much an asset will sell for when it is no longer useful to the company

LO2 Determining Cost of Long-Term Assets

SE 2. Parsons Auto purchased a neighboring lot for a new building and parking lot. Indicate whether each of the following expenditures is properly charged to (a) Land, (b) Land Improvements, or (c) Buildings.

1. Paving costs
2. Architects' fee for building design
3. Cost of clearing the property
4. Cost of the property

5. Building construction costs
6. Lights around the property
7. Building permit
8. Interest on the construction loan

LO2 Group Purchase

SE 3. Apse Company purchased property with a warehouse and parking lot for $750,000. An appraiser valued the components of the property if purchased separately as follows:

Land	$200,000	25%	$187,500
Land improvements	100,000	12.5%	$193,750
Building	500,000	62.5%	$468,750
Total	$800,000		

Determine the cost to be assigned to each component.

LO3 Straight-Line Method

SE 4. Canondale Fitness Center purchased a new step machine for $5,500. The apparatus is expected to last four years and have a residual value of $500. What will be the depreciation expense for each year under the straight-line method?

LO3 Production Method	**SE 5.**	Assuming that the step machine in **SE 4** has an estimated useful life of 8,000 hours and was used for 2,400 hours in year 1, for 2,000 hours in year 2, for 2,200 hours in year 3, and for 1,400 hours in year 4, how much would depreciation expense be in each year?
LO3 Double-Declining-Balance Method	**SE 6.**	Assuming that the step machine in **SE 4** is depreciated using the double-declining-balance method, how much would depreciation expense be in each year?

LO4   Disposal of Plant Assets: No Trade-In

SE 7. Midwest Printing had a piece of equipment that cost $8,100 and on which $4,500 of accumulated depreciation had been recorded. The equipment was disposed of on January 4, the first day of business of the current year.

1. Calculate the carrying value of the equipment.
2. Calculate the gain or loss on the disposal under each of the following assumptions:

   a. It was discarded as having no value.
   b. It was sold for $1,500 cash.
   c. It was sold for $4,000 cash.

LO4   Disposal of Plant Assets: Trade-In

SE 8. For each of the following assumptions and referring to the equipment mentioned in **SE 7,** compute the gain (loss) on the exchange, the cash payment required, and the amount at which the new equipment would be recorded:

1. The equipment was traded in on dissimilar equipment that had a list price of $12,000. A $3,800 trade-in was allowed, and the balance was paid in cash. Gains and losses are to be recognized.
2. The equipment was traded in on dissimilar equipment that had a list price of $12,000. A $1,750 trade-in was allowed, and the balance was paid in cash. Gains and losses are to be recognized.
3. Same as **2,** except the items are similar and gains and losses are not to be recognized.

LO5   Natural Resources

SE 9. Tierra Company purchased land containing an estimated 4,000,000 tons of ore for $8,000,000. The land will be worth $1,200,000 without the ore after eight years of active mining. Although the equipment needed for the mining will have a useful life of 20 years, it is not expected to be usable and will have no value after the mining on this site is complete. Compute the depletion charge per ton and the amount of depletion expense for the first year of operation, assuming that 600,000 tons of ore were mined and sold. Also, compute the first-year depreciation on the mining equipment using the production method, assuming a cost of $9,600,000 with no residual value.

LO6   Intangible Assets: Computer Software

SE 10. Kabira created a new software application for PCs. Its costs during research and development were $500,000, and its costs after the working program was developed were $350,000. Although its copyright may be amortized over 40 years, management believes that the product will be viable for only five years. How should the costs be accounted for? At what value will the software appear on the balance sheet after one year?

EXERCISES

LO1   Management Issues

E 1. Indicate whether each of the following actions is primarily related to (a) acquisition of long-term assets, (b) financing of long-term assets, or (c) choosing methods and estimates related to long-term assets:

1. Deciding to use the production method of depreciation
2. Allocating costs on a group purchase
3. Determining the total units a machine will produce
4. Deciding to borrow funds to purchase equipment
5. Estimating the savings a new machine will produce and comparing the amount to cost
6. Deciding whether to rent or buy a piece of equipment

LO1   Purchase Decision—Present Value Analysis

E 2. Management is considering the purchase of a new machine for a cost of $12,000. It is estimated that the machine will generate positive net cash flows of $3,000 per year for five years and will have a disposal price at the end of that time of $1,000. Assuming an interest rate of 9 percent, determine if management should purchase the machine. Use Tables 3 and 4 in the appendix on future value and present value tables to determine the net present value of the new machine.

LO2   Determining Cost of Long-Term Assets

E 3. Macoma Manufacturing purchased land next to its factory to be used as a parking lot. Expenditures incurred by the company were as follows: purchase price, $150,000; broker's fees, $12,000; title search and other fees, $1,100; demolition of a shack on the property, $4,000; general grading of property, $2,100; paving parking lots, $20,000; lighting for parking lots, $16,000; and signs for parking lots, $3,200. Determine the amounts that should be debited to the Land account and the Land Improvements account.

LO2 Group Purchase

E 4. Lilly Cerith purchased a car wash for $480,000. If purchased separately, the land would have cost $120,000, the building $270,000, and the equipment $210,000. Determine the amount that should be recorded in the new business's records for land, building, and equipment.

LO2 Cost of Long-Term Asset
LO3 and Depreciation

E 5. Ron MacGinty purchased a used tractor for $35,000. Before the tractor could be used, it required new tires, which cost $2,200, and an overhaul, which cost $2,800. Its first tank of fuel cost $150. The tractor is expected to last six years and have a residual value of $4,000. Determine the cost and depreciable cost of the tractor and calculate the first year's depreciation under the straight-line method.

LO3 Depreciation Methods

E 6. Murex Oil Company purchased a drilling truck for $90,000. Murex expected the truck to last five years or 200,000 miles, with an estimated residual value of $15,000 at the end of that time. During 20x5, the truck was driven 48,000 miles. Murex's year end is December 31. Compute the depreciation for 20x5 under each of the following methods, assuming that the truck was purchased on January 13, 20x4: (1) straight-line, (2) production, and (3) double-declining-balance. Using the amount computed in **3**, prepare the entry in journal form to record depreciation expense for the second year and show how the Drilling Truck account would appear on the balance sheet.

LO3 Double-Declining-Balance Method

E 7. Triton Burglar Alarm Systems Company purchased a word processor for $2,240. It has an estimated useful life of four years and an estimated residual value of $240. Compute the depreciation charge for each of the four years using the double-declining-balance method.

LO4 Disposal of Plant Assets

E 8. A piece of equipment that cost $32,400 and on which $18,000 of accumulated depreciation had been recorded was disposed of on January 2, the first day of business of the current year. For each of the following assumptions, compute the gain (loss) on the disposal or exchange. In addition, for assumptions **4, 5** and **6**, compute the cash payment required and the amount at which the new equipment would be recorded.

1. It was discarded as having no value.
2. It was sold for $6,000 cash.
3. It was sold for $18,000 cash.
4. It was traded in on dissimilar equipment having a list price of $48,000. A $16,200 trade-in was allowed, and the balance was paid in cash. Gains and losses are to be recognized.
5. It was traded in on dissimilar equipment having a list price of $48,000. A $7,500 trade-in was allowed, and the balance was paid in cash. Gains and losses are to be recognized.
6. Same as **5**, except the items are similar and gains and losses are not to be recognized.

LO4 Disposal of Plant Assets

E 9. Church Company purchased a computer on January 2, 20x1, at a cost of $5,000. It is expected to have a useful life of five years and a residual value of $500. Assuming that the computer is disposed of on July 1, 20x4, record the partial year's depreciation for 20x4 using the straight-line method, and record the disposal under each of the following assumptions:

1. The computer is discarded.
2. The computer is sold for $800.
3. The computer is sold for $2,200.
4. The computer is exchanged for a new computer with a list price of $9,000. A $1,200 trade-in is allowed on the cash purchase. The accounting approach to gains and losses is followed.
5. Same as **4**, except a $2,400 trade-in is allowed.
6. Same as **4**, except the income tax approach is followed.
7. Same as **5**, except the income tax approach is followed.
8. Same as **4**, except the computer is exchanged for dissimilar office equipment.
9. Same as **5**, except the computer is exchanged for dissimilar office equipment.

LO5 Natural Resource Depletion and Depreciation of Related Plant Assets

E 10. Dosinia Mining Company purchased land containing an estimated 10 million tons of ore for a cost of $8,800,000. The land without the ore is estimated to be worth $1,600,000. The company expects that all the usable ore can be mined in 10 years. Buildings costing $800,000 with an estimated useful life of 30 years were erected on the site.

Equipment costing $960,000 with an estimated useful life of 10 years was installed. Because of the remote location, neither the buildings nor the equipment has an estimated residual value. During its first year of operation, the company mined and sold 800,000 tons of ore.

1. Compute the depletion charge per ton.
2. Compute the depletion expense that Dosinia Mining should record for the year.
3. Determine the depreciation expense for the year for the buildings, making it proportional to the depletion.
4. Determine the depreciation expense for the year for the equipment under two alternatives: (a) making the expense proportional to the depletion and (b) using the straight-line method.

LO6   Amortization of Copyrights and Trademarks

E 11. 1. Morro Publishing Company purchased the copyright to a basic computer textbook for $20,000. The usual life of a textbook is about four years. However, the copyright will remain in effect for another 50 years. Calculate the annual amortization of the copyright.

2. Starling Company purchased a trademark from a well-known supermarket for $160,000. The management of the company argued that because the trademark's value would last forever and might even increase, no amortization should be charged. Calculate the minimum amount of annual amortization that should be charged, according to guidelines of the appropriate Accounting Principles Board opinion.

SO7   Depreciation Methods and Partial Years

E 12. Using the data given for Murex Oil Company in **E 6,** compute the depreciation for calendar year 20x4 under each of the following methods, assuming that the truck was purchased on July 1, 20x4, and was driven 20,000 miles during 20x4: (1) straight-line, (2) production, and (3) double-declining-balance.

SO7   Revision of Depreciation Rates

E 13. Saints Hospital purchased a special x-ray machine. The machine, which cost $311,560, was expected to last ten years, with an estimated residual value of $31,560. After two years of operation (and depreciation charges using the straight-line method), it became evident that the x-ray machine would last a total of only seven years. The estimated residual value, however, would remain the same. Given this information, determine the new depreciation charge for the third year on the basis of the revised estimated useful life.

LO2   Special Types of Capital
SO7   Expenditures

E 14. Tell whether each of the following transactions related to an office building is a revenue expenditure (RE) or a capital expenditure (CE). In addition, indicate whether each transaction is an ordinary repair (OR), an extraordinary repair (ER), an addition (A), a betterment (B), or none of these (N).

1. The hallways and ceilings in the building are repainted at a cost of $8,300.
2. The hallways, which have tile floors, are carpeted at a cost of $28,000.
3. A new wing is added to the building at a cost of $175,000.
4. Furniture is purchased for the entrance to the building at a cost of $16,500.
5. The air-conditioning system is overhauled at a cost of $28,500. The overhaul extends the useful life of the air-conditioning system by ten years.
6. A cleaning firm is paid $200 per week to clean the newly installed carpets.

SO7   Extraordinary Repairs

E 15. Kaolin Manufacturing has an incinerator that originally cost $187,200 and now has accumulated depreciation of $132,800. The incinerator has completed its 15th year of service in an estimated useful life of 20 years. At the beginning of the 16th year, the company spent $42,800 repairing and modernizing the incinerator to comply with pollution-control standards. Therefore, the incinerator is now expected to last 10 more years instead of 5. It will not, however, have more capacity than it did in the past or a residual value at the end of its useful life.

1. Prepare the entry in journal form to record the cost of the repair.
2. Compute the carrying value of the incinerator after the entry.
3. Prepare the entry to record straight-line depreciation for the current year.

PROBLEMS

LO2   Determining Cost of Assets

P 1. Sonia Computers constructed a new training center in 20x2. You have been hired to manage the training center. A review of the accounting records shows the following expenditures debited to an asset account called Training Center:

Attorney's fee, land acquisition	$ 17,450
Cost of land	299,000
Architect's fee, building design	51,000
Building	510,000
Parking lot and sidewalk	67,800
Electrical wiring, building	82,000
Landscaping	27,500
Cost of surveying land	4,600
Training equipment, tables, and chairs	68,200
Installation of training equipment	34,000
Cost of grading the land	7,000
Cost of changes in building to soundproof rooms	29,600
Total account balance	$1,198,150

During the center's construction, an employee of Sonia Computers worked full time overseeing the project. He spent two months on the purchase and preparation of the site, six months on the construction, one month on land improvements, and one month on equipment installation and training room furniture purchase and setup. His salary of $32,000 during this ten-month period was charged to Administrative Expense. The training center was placed in operation on November 1.

REQUIRED ▶ Prepare a schedule with the following four column (Account) headings: Land, Land Improvements, Building, and Equipment. Place each of the above expenditures in the appropriate column. Total the columns.

P 2.

LO3 Comparison of Depreciation Methods

Hart Manufacturing Company purchased a robot for $720,000 at the beginning of year 1. The robot has an estimated useful life of four years and an estimated residual value of $60,000. The robot, which should last 20,000 hours, was operated 6,000 hours in year 1; 8,000 hours in year 2; 4,000 hours in year 3; and 2,000 hours in year 4.

REQUIRED ▶
1. Compute the annual depreciation and carrying value for the robot for each year assuming the following depreciation methods: (a) straight-line, (b) production, and (c) double-declining-balance.
2. Prepare the adjusting entry in journal form that would be made each year to record the depreciation calculated under the straight-line method.
3. Show the balance sheet presentation for the robot after the adjusting entry in year 2 using the straight-line method.
4. What conclusions can you draw from the patterns of yearly depreciation and carrying value in 1?

P 3.

LO3 Depreciation Methods and
SO7 Partial Years

Ada Pinkston purchased a laundry company. In addition to the washing machines, Pinkston installed a tanning machine and a refreshment center. Because each type of asset performs a different function, Pinkston has decided to use different depreciation methods. Data on each type of asset are summarized in the table below. The tanning machine was operated for 2,100 hours in 20x5, 3,000 hours in 20x6, and 2,400 hours in 20x7.

Asset	Date Purchased	Cost	Installation Cost	Residual Value	Estimated Life	Depreciation Method
Washing machines	3/5/x5	$15,000	$2,000	$2,600	4 years	Straight-line
Tanning machine	4/1/x5	34,000	3,000	1,000	7,500 hours	Production
Refreshment center	10/1/x5	3,400	600	600	10 years	Double-declining-balance

REQUIRED ▶ Assume the fiscal year ends December 31. Compute the depreciation expense for each item and the total depreciation expense for 20x5, 20x6, and 20x7. Round your answers to the nearest dollar and present them in a table with the headings shown below.

			Depreciation		
Asset	Year	Computations	20x5	20x6	20x7

P 4.

LO4 Recording Disposals

Robles Construction Company purchased a road grader for $29,000. The machine is expected to have a useful life of five years and a residual value of $2,000.

REQUIRED ▶ Prepare entries in journal form to record the disposal of the road grader at the end of the second year, after the depreciation is recorded, assuming that the straight-line method is used and making the following separate assumptions:

a. The road grader is sold for $20,000 cash.
b. The road grader is sold for $16,000 cash.
c. The road grader is traded in on a dissimilar piece of machinery costing $33,000, a trade-in allowance of $20,000 is given, the balance is paid in cash, and gains or losses are recognized.
d. The road grader is traded in on a dissimilar piece of machinery costing $33,000, a trade-in allowance of $16,000 is given, the balance is paid in cash, and gains or losses are recognized.
e. Same as **c**, except it is traded for a similar road grader and Robles Construction Company follows accounting rules for the recognition of gains or losses.
f. Same as **d**, except it is traded for a similar road grader and Robles Construction Company follows accounting rules for the recognition of gains or losses.
g. Same as **c**, except it is traded for a similar road grader and gains or losses are not recognized for income tax purposes.
h. Same as **d**, except it is traded for a similar road grader and gains or losses are not recognized for income tax purposes.

P 5.

LO6 Amortization of License, Leasehold, and Leasehold Improvements

Part A: On January 2, Future Play, Inc., purchased the exclusive license to make dolls based on the characters in a popular new television series called "Sky Pirates." The license cost $2,100,000, and there was no termination date on the rights. Immediately after signing the contract, the company sued a rival firm that claimed it had already received the exclusive license to the series characters. Future Play successfully defended its rights at a cost of $360,000.

During the first year and the next, Future Play marketed toys based on the series. Because a successful television series lasts about five years, the company felt it could market the toys for three more years. However, before the third year of the series could get under way, a controversy arose between its two stars and its producer. As a result, the stars refused to work the third year, and the show was canceled, rendering the exclusive rights worthless.

REQUIRED ▶ Prepare entries in journal form to record the following: (a) purchase of the exclusive license; (b) successful defense of the license; (c) amortization expense, if any, for the first year; and (d) write-off of the license as worthless.

Part B: Pamela Newell purchased a six-year sublease on a building from the estate of the former tenant. It was a good location for her business, and the annual rent of $3,600, which had been established ten years before, was low. The cost of the sublease was $9,450.

To use the building, Newell had to make certain alterations. She moved some panels at a cost of $1,700 and installed others for $6,100. She also added carpet, lighting fixtures, and a sign at costs of $2,900, $3,100, and $1,200, respectively. All items except the carpet would last for at least twelve years. The expected life of the carpet was six years. None of the improvements would have a residual value.

REQUIRED ▶ Prepare entries in journal form to record the following: (a) the payment for the sublease; (b) the payments for the alterations, panels, carpet, lighting fixtures, and sign; (c) the lease payment for the first year; (d) the amortization expense, if any, associated with the sublease; and (e) the amortization expense, if any, associated with the alterations, panels, carpet, lighting fixtures, and sign.

ALTERNATE PROBLEMS

P 6.

LO2 Determining Cost of Assets

Olive Company began operation on January 2 of 20x5. At the end of the year, the company's auditor discovered that all expenditures involving long-term assets had been debited to an account called Fixed Assets. An analysis of the Fixed Assets account, which had a year-end balance of $5,289,944, disclosed that it contained the following items:

Cost of land	$ 633,200
Surveying costs	8,200
Transfer of title and other fees required by the county	1,840
Broker's fees for land	42,288
Attorney's fees associated with land acquisition	14,096
Cost of removing timber from land	100,800
Cost of grading land	8,400
Cost of digging building foundation	69,200
Architect's fee for building and land improvements (80 percent building)	129,600
Cost of building construction	1,420,000
Cost of sidewalks	22,800
Cost of parking lots	108,800
Cost of lighting for grounds	160,600
Cost of landscaping	23,600
Cost of machinery	1,978,000
Shipping cost on machinery	110,600
Cost of installing machinery	352,400
Cost of testing machinery	44,200
Cost of changes in building to comply with safety regulations pertaining to machinery	25,080
Cost of repairing building that was damaged in the installation of machinery	17,800
Cost of medical bill for injury received by employee while installing machinery	4,800
Cost of water damage to building during heavy rains prior to opening the plant for operation	13,640
Account balance	$5,289,944

Olive Company sold the timber it cleared from the land to a firewood dealer for $10,000. This amount was credited to Miscellaneous Income.

During the construction period, two of Olive's supervisors devoted full time to the construction project. They earn annual salaries of $96,000 and $84,000, respectively. They spent two months on the purchase and preparation of the land, six months on the construction of the building (approximately one-sixth of which was devoted to improvements on the grounds), and one month on machinery installation. The plant began operation on October 1, and the supervisors returned to their regular duties. Their salaries were debited to Factory Salaries Expense.

REQUIRED ▶ Prepare a schedule with the following column headings: Land, Land Improvements, Buildings, Machinery, and Expense. Place each of the above expenditures in the appropriate column. Negative amounts should be shown in parentheses. Total the columns.

P 7.

LO3 Comparison of Depreciation Methods

Hours Construction Company purchased a new crane for $360,500 at the beginning of year 1. The crane has an estimated residual value of $35,000 and an estimated useful life of six years. The crane is expected to last 10,000 hours. It was used 1,800 hours in year 1; 2,000 in year 2; 2,500 in year 3; 1,500 in year 4; 1,200 in year 5; and 1,000 in year 6.

REQUIRED ▶ 1. Compute the annual depreciation and carrying value for the new crane for each of the six years (round to nearest dollar where necessary) under each of the following methods: (a) straight-line, (b) production, and (c) double-declining-balance.
2. Prepare the adjusting entry that would be made each year to record the depreciation calculated under the straight-line method.
3. Show the balance sheet presentation for the crane after the adjusting entry in year 2 using the straight-line method.
4. What conclusions can you draw from the patterns of yearly depreciation and carrying value in 1?

P 8.

LO3 Depreciation Methods and
SO7 Partial Years

Thant Company operates three types of equipment. Because of the equipment's varied functions, company accounting policy requires the application of three different depreciation methods. Data on this equipment are summarized in the table that follows.

Equipment	Date Purchased	Cost	Installation Cost	Estimated Residual Value	Estimated Life	Depreciation Method
1	1/12/x1	$171,000	$ 9,000	$18,000	10 years	Double-declining-balance
2	7/9/x1	191,100	15,900	21,000	10 years	Straight-line
3	10/2/x1	290,700	8,100	33,600	20,000 hours	Production

Equipment 3 was used for 2,000 hours in 20x1; for 4,200 hours in 20x2; and for 3,200 hours in 20x3.

REQUIRED ▶ Assuming that the fiscal year ends December 31, compute the depreciation expense on each type of equipment and the total depreciation expense for 20x1, 20x2, and 20x3 by filling in a table with the headings shown below.

		Depreciation		
Equipment No.	Computations	20x1	20x2	20x3

SKILLS DEVELOPMENT CASES

Conceptual Analysis

SD 1.

LO1 Nature of Depreciation and
LO3 Amortization and Estimated
Useful Lives

A change in the estimated useful lives of long-term assets can have a significant effect. For instance, General Motors Corp. <www.gm.com> states,

> In the third quarter of 1987, the Corporation revised the estimated service lives of its plants and equipment and special tools retroactive to January 1, 1987. These revisions, which were based on 1987 studies of actual useful lives and periods of use, recognized current estimates of service lives of the assets and had the effect of reducing 1987 depreciation and amortization charges by $1,236.6 million or $2.53 per share of $1⅔ par value common stock.[23]

General Motors' income before income taxes for the year was $2,005.4 million. Discuss the purpose of depreciation and amortization. What is estimated service life, and on what basis did General Motors change the estimates of the service lives of plants and equipment and special tools? What was the effect of this change on the corporation's income before income taxes? Is it likely that the company is in better condition economically as a result of the change? Does the company have more cash at the end of the year as a result? (Ignore income tax effects.)

SD 2.

LO3 Change of Depreciation
Method

Polaroid Corporation <www.polaroid.com>, a manufacturer of instant cameras and film, changed from an accelerated depreciation method for financial reporting purposes to the straight-line method for assets acquired after January 1, 1997. As noted in Polaroid's 1997 annual report:

> The company changed its method of depreciation for financial reporting for the cost of buildings, machinery, and equipment acquired on or after January 1, 1997, from a primarily accelerated method to the straight-line method.[24]

What reasons can you give for Polaroid's choosing to switch to a straight-line method of depreciation? Discuss which of the two depreciation methods is more conservative. Polaroid's deteriorating financial position led it to declare bankruptcy in 2001. Could this accounting change have been a signal that the company was in trouble?

SD 3.

LO6 Brands

Hilton Hotels Corporation <www.hilton.com> and Marriott International <www.marriott.com> provide hospitality services. Hilton Hotels' well-known brands include Hilton, Doubletree, Hampton Inn, Embassy Suites, Red Lion Hotels and Inns, and Homewood Suites. Marriott also owns or manages properties with recognizable brand names, such as Marriott Hotels, Resorts and Suites; Ritz-Carlton; Renaissance Hotels; Residence Inn; Courtyard; and Fairfield Inn.

On its balance sheet, Hilton Hotels Corporation includes brands (net of amortization) of $1,048 million, or 11.3 percent of total assets. Marriott International, however, does not list brands among its intangible assets.[25] What principles of accounting for intangibles would cause Hilton to record brands as an asset while Marriott does not? How will these differences in accounting for brands generally affect the net income and return on assets of these two competitors?

Ethical Dilemma

LO2 Ethics and Allocation of Acquisition Costs

SD 4. Signal Company has purchased land and a warehouse for $18,000,000. The warehouse is expected to last 20 years and to have a salvage value equal to 10 percent of its cost. The chief financial officer (CFO) and the controller are discussing the allocation of the purchase price. The CFO believes that the largest amount possible should be assigned to the land because this action will improve reported net income in the future. Depreciation expense will be lower because land is not depreciated. He suggests allocating one-third, or $6,000,000, of the cost to the land. This results in depreciation expense each year of $540,000 [($12,000,000 − $1,200,000) ÷ 20 years]. The controller disagrees, arguing that the smallest amount possible, say one-fifth of the purchase price, should be allocated to the land, thereby saving income taxes, since the depreciation, which is tax deductible, will be greater. Under this plan, annual depreciation would be $648,000 [($14,400,000 − $1,440,000) ÷ 20 years]. The annual tax savings at a 30 percent tax rate is $32,400 [($648,000 − $540,000) × .30]. How will this decision affect the company's cash flows? Ethically, how should the purchase cost be allocated? Who will be affected by the decision?

Group Activity: Divide the class into groups and have each develop the position of the CFO or controller for presentation and debate.

LO2 Ethics of Aggressive
LO6 Accounting Policies

SD 5. Is it ethical to choose aggressive accounting practices to advance a company's business? During the 1990s, America Online (AOL) <www.aol.com>, the largest Internet service provider in the United States, was one of the hottest stocks on Wall Street. After its initial stock offering in 1992, its stock price shot up several thousand percent. Accounting is very important to a company like AOL because earnings enable it to sell shares of stock and raise more cash to fund its growth. In its early years, AOL was one of the most aggressive companies in its choice of accounting principles. AOL's strategy called for building the largest customer base in the industry. Consequently, it spent many millions of dollars each year marketing its services to new customers. Such costs are usually recognized as operating expenses in the year in which they are incurred. However, AOL treated these costs as long-term assets, called "deferred subscriber acquisition costs," and expensed them over several years, because it said the average customer was going to stay with the company for three years or more. The company also recorded research and development costs as "product development costs" and amortized them over five years. Both of these practices are justifiable theoretically, but they are not common practice. If the standard, more conservative practice had been followed, the company would have had a net loss in every year it has been in business.[26] This result would have greatly limited AOL's ability to raise money and grow.

Explain in your own words AOL management's rationale for adopting the accounting policies that it did. What could go wrong with such a plan? How would you evaluate the ethics of AOL's actions? Who benefits from the actions? Who is harmed by these actions?

Research Activity

LO1 Individual Field Trip
LO2
LO3
LO6

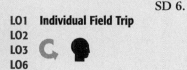

SD 6. Visit a fast-food restaurant. Make a list of all the intangible and property, plant, and equipment assets you can identify. For each one, identify one management issue that relates to that asset. In addition, give examples of at least one capital expenditure and one revenue expenditure that is applicable to property, plant, and equipment assets. Bring your list to class for discussion.

Decision-Making Practice

SD 7.

**LO1   Purchase Decision and Time
Value of Money**

Morningside Machine Works has obtained a subcontract to manufacture parts for a new military aircraft. The parts are to be delivered over the next five years, and the company will be paid as the parts are delivered.

To make the parts, Morningside Machine Works will have to purchase new equipment. Two types are available. Type A is conventional equipment that can be put into service immediately; Type B requires one year to be put into service but is more efficient than Type A. Type A requires an immediate cash investment of $1,000,000 and will produce enough parts to provide net cash receipts of $340,000 each year for the five years. Type B may be purchased by signing a two-year non-interest-bearing note for $1,346,000. It is projected that Type B will produce net cash receipts of zero in year 1, $500,000 in year 2, $600,000 in year 3, $600,000 in year 4, and $200,000 in year 5. Neither type of equipment can be used on other contracts or will have any useful life remaining at the end of the contract. Morningside currently pays an interest rate of 16 percent to borrow money.

1. What is the present value of the investment required for each type of equipment? (Use Table 3 in the appendix on future value and present value tables.)
2. Compute the net present value of each type of equipment based on your answer in 1 and the present value of the net cash receipts projected to be received. (Use Tables 3 and 4 in the appendix on future value and present value tables.)
3. Write a memorandum to the board of directors that recommends the option that appears to be best for Morningside. Explain your reasoning and include 1 and 2 as attachments.

FINANCIAL REPORTING AND ANALYSIS CASES

Interpreting Financial Reports

FRA 1.

**LO3   Effects of Change in
S07   Accounting Method**

Depreciation expense is a significant cost for companies in which plant assets are a high proportion of assets. The amount of depreciation expense in a given year is affected by estimates of useful life and choice of depreciation method. In 2002, Century Steelworks Company, a major integrated steel producer, changed the estimated useful lives for its major production assets. It also changed the method of depreciation for other steel-making assets from straight-line to the production method.

The company's 2002 annual report states, "A recent study conducted by management shows that actual years-in-service figures for our major production equipment and machinery are, in most cases, higher than the estimated useful lives assigned to these assets. We have recast the depreciable lives of such assets so that equipment previously assigned a useful life of 8 to 26 years now has an extended depreciable life of 10 to 32 years."

The report goes on to explain that the new production method of depreciation "recognizes that depreciation of production equipment and machinery correlates directly to both physical wear and tear and the passage of time. The production method of depreciation, which we have now initiated, more closely allocates the cost of these assets to the periods in which products are manufactured."

The report summarizes the effects of both actions on the year 2002 as shown in the following table:

Incremental Increase in Net Income	In Millions	Per Share
Lengthened lives	$11.0	$ .80
Production method		
Current year	7.3	.53
Prior years	2.8	.20
Total increase	$21.1	$1.53

During 2002, Century Steelworks reported a net loss of $83,156,500 ($6.03 per share). Depreciation expense for 2002 was $87,707,200.

In explaining the changes the company has made, the controller of Century Steelworks was quoted in an article in *Business Journal* as follows: "There is no reason for Century Steelworks to continue to depreciate our assets more conservatively than our competitors do." But the article also quotes an industry analyst who argues that by slowing its method of depreciation, Century Steelworks could be viewed as reporting lower-quality earnings.

REQUIRED ▶

1. Explain the accounting treatment when there is a change in the estimated lives of depreciable assets. What circumstances must exist for the production method to produce the effect it did in relation to the straight-line method? What would Century Steelworks' net income or loss have been if the changes had not been made? What might have motivated management to make the changes?

2. What does the controller of Century Steelworks mean when he says that Century had been depreciating "more conservatively than our competitors do"? Why might the changes at Century Steelworks indicate, as the analyst asserts, "lower-quality earnings"? What risks might Century face as a result of its decision to use the production method of depreciation?

International Company

FRA 2.
LO6   Accounting for Goodwill: U.S. and IAS rules

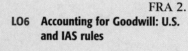

For most pharmaceutical companies, intangible assets, such as goodwill, patents, licenses, and trademarks, make up a significant percentage of total assets. For example, for Roche Group <www.roche.com>, intangible assets constitute 22.8 percent of total assets, and for Baxter International <www.baxter.com>, 14.2 percent.[27] For both companies, goodwill represents the largest portion of intangible assets.

Before 2000, Roche Group, a Swiss company, charged any goodwill resulting from acquisitions against equity immediately. However, in 2000, in accordance with a change in International Accounting Standards (IAS), Roche began recording goodwill as an asset and amortizing it over a period of up to 20 years. This IAS change brought U.S. and IAS companies into closer agreement on accounting for goodwill. At that time, companies like Baxter International, which comply with U.S. GAAP, recorded goodwill resulting from acquisitions as an asset and amortized it over periods not to exceed 40 years. However, as of 2002, U.S. companies, while continuing to record purchased goodwill as an asset, were no longer required to amortize any existing or new goodwill. Both IAS and U.S. GAAP require companies to apply the impairment test annually to ensure that goodwill is not overvalued.

REQUIRED ▶

What impact did accounting for goodwill under IAS and U.S. GAAP have on cash flows and net income in the year 2002? In your opinion, which accounting treatment for goodwill (U.S. or IAS) is better? State your reasons.

Toys "R" Us Annual Report

FRA 3.
LO1   Long-Term Assets
LO2
LO3
LO6

1. Refer to the balance sheets and to the note on property and equipment in the notes to the financial statements in the Toys "R" Us <www.tru.com> annual report to answer the following questions: What percentage of total assets in the most recent year was property and equipment? What is the most significant type of property and equipment? Does Toys "R" Us have a significant investment in land? What other kinds of things are included in the property and equipment category? (Ignore leased property under capital leases for now.)

2. Refer to the summary of significant accounting policies and to the note on property and equipment in the Toys "R" Us annual report. What method of depreciation does Toys "R" Us use? How long does management estimate its buildings to last as compared with furniture and equipment? What does this say about the company's need to remodel its stores?

3. Refer again to the note on property and equipment. What are leaseholds and leasehold improvements? How significant are these items, and what are their effects on the earnings of the company?

Comparison Case: Toys "R" Us and Walgreen Co.

FRA 4.

LO1   **Long-Term Assets and Cash Flows**

Refer to the annual report of Toys "R" Us <www.tru.com> and to the financial statements of Walgreens <www.walgreens.com> in the Supplement to Chapter 1 to answer the following:

1. Prepare a table that shows the net amount each company spent on property and equipment (from the statement of cash flows), the total property and equipment (from the balance sheet), and the percentage of the first figure to the second for each of the past two years. Which company grew its property and equipment at a faster rate?

2. Which other note to the financial statements is helpful in evaluating the cash flows related to property and equipment? (**Hint:** In what way do Toys "R" Us and Walgreens gain use of property and equipment other than by purchase?) How important is this method of obtaining use of assets to these companies? Which company makes greater use of the method?

Fingraph® Financial Analyst™

FRA 5.

LO1   **Comparison of Long-Term**
LO3   **Assets**
LO5
LO6

Choose any two companies from the list of Fingraph companies on the Needles Accounting Resource Center Web Site at http://accounting.college.hmco.com/students. The industry should be one in which long-term assets are likely to be important, such as the airline, manufacturing, consumer products, consumer food and beverage, or computer industry. Access the Microsoft Excel spreadsheets for the companies you selected. For parts 1, 3, and 4, click on the URL at the top of each company's spreadsheet for a link to the company's web site and annual report.

1. In the annual reports of the companies you have selected, read the long-term asset section of the balance sheet and any reference to long-term assets in the summary of significant accounting policies or notes to the financial statements. What are the most important long-term assets for each company? What depreciation methods do the companies use? Do any long-term assets appear to be characteristic of the industry? What intangible assets do the companies have, and how important are they?

2. Using the Fingraph CD-ROM software, display and print in tabular and graphic form the Balance Sheet Analysis page. Prepare a table that compares the gross and net amounts for property, plant, and equipment.

3. Locate the statements of cash flows in the two companies' annual reports. Prepare another table that compares depreciation (and amortization) expense from the operating activities section with the net purchases of property, plant, and equipment (net capital expenditures) from the investing activities section for two years. Does depreciation (and amortization) expense exceed replacement of long-term assets? Are the companies expanding or reducing their property, plant, and equipment?

4. Find and read references to long-term assets and capital expenditures in management's discussion and analysis in each annual report.

5. Write a one-page executive summary that highlights the most important long-term assets and the accounting policies for long-term assets, and that compares the investing activities of the two companies, including reference to management's assessment. Include the Fingraph page and your tables with your report.

Internet Case

FRA 6.

LO3   **SEC and Forms 10-K**
LO4
LO6

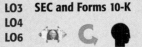

Public corporations are required not only to communicate with their stockholders by means of an annual report but also to submit an annual report to the Securities and Exchange Commission (SEC). The annual report to the SEC is called a Form 10-K and is a source of the latest information about a company. Through the Needles Accounting Resource Center Web Site at http://accounting.college.hmco.com/students, access the SEC's EDGAR files to locate either H.J. Heinz Company's <www.heinz.com> or Ford Motor Company's <www.ford.com> Form 10-K. Find the financial statements and the notes to the financial statements. Scan through the notes to the financial statements and prepare a list of information related to long-term assets, including intangibles. For instance, what depreciation methods does the company use? What are the useful lives of its property, plant, and equipment? What intangible assets does the company have? Does the company have goodwill? How much does the company spend on research and development? In the statement of cash flows, how much did the company spend on new property, plant, and equipment (capital expenditures)? Summarize your results and be prepared to discuss them as well as your experience in using the SEC's EDGAR database.

 Group Activity: Divide students into groups according to the company researched and have each group compile a comprehensive list of information about its company.

Chapter 11 covers the management issues related to sources of long-term financing, with an emphasis on bond liabilities.

Long-Term Liabilities

LEARNING OBJECTIVES

LO1 Identify the management issues related to issuing long-term debt.

LO2 Identify and contrast the major characteristics of bonds.

LO3 Record the issuance of bonds at face value and at a discount or premium.

LO4 Use present values to determine the value of bonds.

LO5 Amortize bond discounts and bond premiums using the straight-line and effective interest methods.

LO6 Record bonds issued between interest dates and year-end adjustments.

SUPPLEMENTAL OBJECTIVES

SO7 Account for the retirement of bonds and the conversion of bonds into stock.

SO8 Explain the basic features of mortgages payable, long-term leases, and pensions and other postretirement benefits as long-term liabilities.

DECISION POINT

A USER'S FOCUS

AT&T Corporation <www.att.com> During 2000, AT&T Corporation more than doubled its debt financing. How much to borrow and how much debt should be financed long term are two questions management must consider. What is the impact of AT&T's higher debt level on its capital structure and its interest-paying ability?

Decisions related to the issuance of long-term debt are among the most important that management has to make because, next to the success or failure of a company's operations, how the company finances its operations is the most important factor in the company's long-term viability. Long-term liabilities, or long-term debt, are obligations of a business that are due to be paid after one year or beyond the operating cycle, whichever is longer. AT&T's capital structure includes a large amount of long-term debt, as shown by the figures for 2000 in the Financial Highlights.[1] Total liabilities are greater than stockholders' equity, and the debt to equity ratio is 1.1 ($129,432 ÷ $112,791). What factors might have influenced AT&T's management to incur a large amount of debt?

In the past, AT&T was the nation's largest long-distance telephone company. The investments in power lines, transformers, computers, and other types of property, plant, and equipment required for this business are enormous. These are mostly long-term assets, and the most sensible way to finance them is through long-term financing. When the business was protected from competition, management could reasonably predict sufficient earnings and cash flow to meet the debt and interest obligations. Now that AT&T

Now that AT&T is facing competition for its markets, why must management reassess the company's long-term liabilities?

is facing open competition for its markets, the company must reassess not only the kind of business it is but also the amount and kinds of debt it carries. The amount and type of debt a company incurs depends on many factors, including the nature of the business, its competitive environment, the state of the financial markets, and the predictability of its earnings.

Financial Highlights: Capital Structure
(In millions)

Liabilities	
Total current liabilities	$ 50,867
Long-term debt	$ 33,092
Long-term benefit-related liabilities	3,670
Deferred income taxes	36,713
Other long-term liabilities and deferred credits	5,090
Total long-term liabilities	$ 78,565
Total liabilities	$129,432
Stockholders' equity	112,791
Total liabilities and stockholders' equity	$242,223

MANAGEMENT ISSUES RELATED TO ISSUING LONG-TERM DEBT

LO1   Identify the management issues related to issuing long-term debt.

RELATED TEXT ASSIGNMENTS
Q: 1
SE: 1
E: 1
SD: 6
FRA: 1, 3, 4, 5, 6

KEY POINT: Although carrying a lot of debt is risky, there are some advantages to issuing bonds instead of stock. First, bond interest expense is tax-deductible for the issuing corporation, whereas dividends paid on stock are not. Second, issuing bonds is a way to raise capital without diluting ownership of the corporation. The challenge is to determine the optimal balance between stocks and bonds so that the advantages of each can be enjoyed.

www.continental.com

Profitable operations and short-term credit seldom provide sufficient cash for a growing business. Growth often requires investment in long-term assets and in research and development and other activities that will produce income in future years. To finance such assets and activities, the company requires funds that will be available for longer periods. Two key sources of long-term funds are the issuance of capital stock and the issuance of long-term debt in the form of bonds, notes, mortgages, and leases. The management issues related to issuing long-term debt are (1) whether to take on long-term debt, (2) how much long-term debt to carry, (3) what types of long-term debt to incur, and (4) how to handle debt repayment.

THE DECISION TO ISSUE LONG-TERM DEBT

A key decision for management is whether to rely solely on stockholders' equity—capital stock issued and retained earnings—for long-term funds for the business or to rely partially on long-term debt for those funds. Since long-term debts represent financial commitments that must be paid at maturity and interest or other payments that must be paid periodically, common stock would seem to have two advantages over long-term debt: it does not have to be paid back, and dividends on common stock are usually paid only if the company earns sufficient income. Long-term debt does, however, have some advantages over common stock, including the following:

1. **Stockholder control.** Since bondholders and other creditors do not have voting rights, common stockholders do not relinquish any control of the company.

2. **Tax effects.** The interest on debt is tax-deductible, whereas dividends on common stock are not. For example, if a corporation pays $100,000 in interest and the income tax rate is 30 percent, the net cost to the corporation is $70,000 because it will save $30,000 on its income taxes. To pay $100,000 in dividends, the company would have to earn $142,857 before taxes ($100,000 ÷ .70).

3. **Financial leverage.** If a corporation is able to earn more on its assets than it pays in interest on debt, the excess will increase its earnings for stockholders. This concept is called **financial leverage** or *trading on the equity*. For example, if a company is able to earn 12 percent, or $120,000, on a $1,000,000 investment financed by long-term 10 percent notes, it will earn $20,000 before taxes ($120,000 − $100,000). Financial leverage makes heavily debt-financed investments in office buildings and shopping centers attractive to investors, who hope to earn a return that exceeds the cost of the interest on the underlying debt. The debt to equity ratio is considered an overall measure of the financial leverage of a company.

Despite these advantages, using debt financing is not always in a company's best interest. First, since cash is required to make periodic interest payments and to pay back the principal amount of the debt at the maturity date, a company whose plans for earnings do not pan out, whose operations are subject to ups and downs, or whose cash flow is weak can be in danger. If the company fails to meet its obligations, it can be forced into bankruptcy by creditors. In other words, a company may become overcommitted. Consider, for example, the heavily debt-financed airline industry. Both TWA and Continental Airlines filed for bankruptcy protection because they could not make payments on their long-term debt and other liabilities. (While in bankruptcy both firms restructured their debt and interest payments, but only Continental survived.) And Swiss Air and Midway Airlines shut down all operations because of insufficient cash to pay creditors and employees. Second, financial leverage can work against a company if the earnings from its investments do not exceed its interest payments. This happened during the savings and loan crisis when long-term debt was used to finance the construction of office buildings that subsequently could not be leased for enough money to cover interest payments.

FOCUS ON INTERNATIONAL BUSINESS

Pushed to the Brink of Failure

Due to recent declines in passenger revenue, a record number of airlines are shutting down operations, operating under bankruptcy protection, seeking purchase by another airline, or relying on government loan guarantees for their short-term survival. Air Afrique, Canada 3000, Swiss Air, and Midway Airlines have been among those hardest hit.[2] Subsequently, TWA and US Airways joined the group as the largest airline bankruptcies.

In a weak economy, the large amount of debt financing that airlines use to fund operations and purchases of aircraft adds to their troubles. With lower cash flows, the airlines find it harder to make payments of interest and principal on debt, thereby increasing the risk of default.

HOW MUCH DEBT TO CARRY

The amount of total debt that companies carry varies widely. Many companies carry less than 100 percent of their stockholders' equity. However, as can be seen from Figure 1, the average debt to equity for these selected industries exceeds 100 percent of stockholders' equity. The range is from about 114 percent to 182 percent of equity. Clearly the use of debt financing varies widely across industries. Firms that own a high percentage of long-term assets would be looking to long-term financing as an option. We saw previously that AT&T has a debt to equity ratio of 1.1 times. Financial leverage makes it advantageous to have long-term debt so long as the company earns a satisfactory income and is able to make interest payments and repay the debt at maturity. Since failure to make timely interest payments could force a company into bankruptcy, it is important for companies to assess the risk of default or nonpayment of interest or principal.

www.att.com

A common measure of how much risk a company is undertaking with its debt is the **interest coverage ratio**. It measures the degree of protection a company has from default on interest payments. For AT&T, which in 2000 had income before taxes of $2,608 million and interest expense of $3,183 million, this ratio is computed as follows:

$$\text{Interest Coverage Ratio} = \frac{\text{Income Before Taxes} + \text{Interest Expense}}{\text{Interest Expense}}$$

$$= \frac{\$2,608,000,000 + \$3,183,000,000}{\$3,183,000,000}$$

$$= 1.8 \text{ times}$$

This ratio shows that the interest expense for AT&T was covered 1.8 times in 2000. AT&T's interest coverage ratio was much higher in 1999 (6.7 times) and 1998 (20.5 times). The company's income before taxes in 2000 was 74 percent lower, and its

FIGURE 1
Average Debt to Equity for Selected Industries

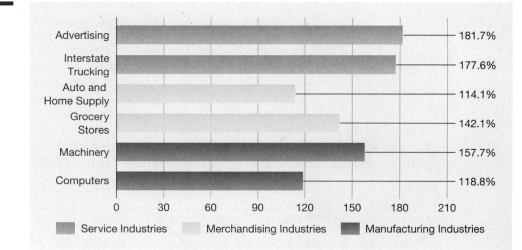

Source: Data from Dun & Bradstreet, *Industry Norms and Key Business Ratios,* 2000–2001.

◆ STOP AND THINK!

How does a lender assess the risk that a borrower may default—that is, not pay interest and principal when due?

The lender reviews the enterprise's current earnings and cash flows as well as its debt to equity and interest coverage ratios. The analysis may also include a historical comparison that reflects both good and poor economic times. The lender can then judge how well the company has met its past debt obligations. ■

www.att.com

interest expense was 80 percent higher, resulting in the dramatic decline in interest coverage. Interest expense increased as a result of almost $10 billion of new long-term debt financing, not because of rising interest rates. The risk for lenders increased substantially, and a lower debt rating is likely if earnings before taxes do not return to levels of previous years.

TYPES OF LONG-TERM DEBT

Long-term bonds (most of which are also called debentures) are the most common type of long-term debt. They can have many different characteristics, including the time until repayment, amount of interest, whether the company can elect to repay early, and whether they can be converted into common stock or other securities. But there are many other types of long-term debt, such as long-term notes, mortgages, and long-term leases. AT&T, for example, has a mixture of long-term obligations, as shown by the following excerpt from its 2000 annual report:[3]

Financial Highlights: Long-Term Obligations

(This table shows the outstanding long-term debt obligations, in millions, at December 31.)

Interest Rates (b)	Maturities	2000
Debentures and Notes		
4.00%–6.00%	2001–2018	$ 6,639
6.25%–6.50%	2001–2029	6,660
6.55%–7.50%	2001–2037	7,840
7.53%–8.50%	2001–2097	5,267
8.60%–11.13%	2001–2045	7,320
Variable rate	2001–2054	2,794
Total debentures and notes		36,520
Other		360
Less: Unamortized discount—net		64
Total long-term obligations		36,816
Less: Currently maturing long-term debt		3,724
Net long-term obligations		$33,092

To structure long-term financing to the best advantage of their companies, managers must know the characteristics of the various types of long-term debt.

TIMING OF LONG-TERM DEBT REPAYMENT

Ability to repay debt influences a company's debt rating and the cost of borrowing additional funds. Management must plan its cash flows carefully to ensure that it will have sufficient funds to repay long-term debt when it comes due. If this is done well and on a consistent basis, then a company can achieve the best debt rating and benefit from the lowest interest cost. To show the potential effects of long-term debt on future cash flows, the notes to a company's financial statements provide a schedule of debt repayment over the next five years. For example, in its notes, AT&T disclosed the following information detailing the cash payments required for 2001 through 2005 and later:[4]

www.att.com

2001	2002	2003	2004	2005	Later years
$3,724	$2,661	$3,093	$4,112	$4,182	$19,044

The total of these cash payments, $36,816 million, equals the amount of total long-term obligations on AT&T's balance sheet of December 31, 2000.

 Check out ACE for a Review Quiz at http://accounting.college.hmco.com/students.

THE NATURE OF BONDS

LO2 Identify and contrast the major characteristics of bonds.

RELATED TEXT ASSIGNMENTS
Q: 2, 3
SD: 4, 6
FRA: 6, 7

ENRICHMENT NOTE: An investor who purchases debt securities, such as bonds or notes, is a creditor of the organization, not an owner.

TERMINOLOGY NOTE:
Do not confuse the terms *indenture* and *debenture*. They sound alike, but an indenture is a bond contract, whereas a debenture is an unsecured bond.

STUDY NOTE: Bonds are quoted as a percentage of face value; stocks are quoted as a dollar amount.

A **bond** is a security, usually long term, representing money that a corporation or other entity borrows from the investing public. (Bonds are also issued by the U.S. government, state and local governments, and foreign countries to raise money.) A bond must be repaid at a specified time and requires periodic payments of interest.* Interest is usually paid semiannually (twice a year). Bonds must not be confused with stocks. Because stocks are shares of ownership, stockholders are owners. Bondholders are creditors. Bonds are promises to repay the amount borrowed, called the *principal*, and interest at a specified rate on specified future dates.

Often, a bondholder receives a **bond certificate** as evidence of the organization's debt. In most cases, the face value (denomination) of the bond is $1,000 or some multiple of $1,000. A **bond issue** is the total value of bonds issued at one time. For example, a $1,000,000 bond issue could consist of a thousand $1,000 bonds. Because a bond issue can be bought and held by many investors, the organization usually enters into a supplementary agreement called a **bond indenture**. The bond indenture defines the rights, privileges, and limitations of the bondholders. It generally describes such things as the maturity date of the bonds, interest payment dates, and interest rate. It may also cover repayment plans and restrictions.

The prices of bonds are stated in terms of a percentage of face value. A bond issue quoted at 103½ means that a $1,000 bond costs $1,035 ($1,000 × 1.035). When a bond sells at exactly 100, it is said to sell at face or par value. When it sells above 100, it is said to sell at a premium; below 100, at a discount. A $1,000 bond quoted at 87.62 would be selling at a discount and would cost the buyer $876.20.

A bond indenture can be written to fit the financing needs of an individual organization. As a result, the bonds being issued in today's financial markets have many different features. Several of the more important ones are described in the following paragraphs.

SECURED OR UNSECURED BONDS

STUDY NOTE: A debenture of a solid company actually might be a less risky investment than a secured bond of an unstable company.

Bonds can be either secured or unsecured. If issued on the general credit of the organization, they are **unsecured bonds** (also called *debenture bonds*). **Secured bonds** give the bondholders a pledge of certain assets as a guarantee of repayment. The security identified by a secured bond can be any specific asset of the organization or a general category of asset, such as property, plant, or equipment.

TERM OR SERIAL BONDS

STUDY NOTE: An advantage of issuing serial bonds is that the organization retires the bonds over a period of years, rather than all at once.

When all the bonds of an issue mature at the same time, they are called **term bonds**. For instance, an organization may decide to issue $1,000,000 worth of bonds, all due 20 years from the date of issue. When the bonds in an issue mature on different dates, the bonds are called **serial bonds**. An example of serial bonds would be a $1,000,000 issue that calls for retiring $200,000 of the principal every five years. This arrangement means that after the first $200,000 payment is made, $800,000 of the bonds would remain outstanding for the next five years. In other words, $1,000,000 is outstanding for the first five years, $800,000 for the second five years, and so on. An organization may issue serial bonds to ease the task of retiring its debt.

*At the time this chapter was written, the market interest rates on corporate bonds were volatile. Therefore, the examples and problems in this chapter use a variety of interest rates to demonstrate the concepts.

FOCUS ON INTERNATIONAL BUSINESS

Choice of Bank Debt Cripples Japanese Firms.

When U.S. companies need cash, one ready source is a bond issue, but this source of funds is not available in many other countries. For instance, surprising as it may seem, Japan, with one of the world's largest economies and financial systems, has only a fledgling corporate bond market. Whereas corporate bonds account for 31 percent of U.S. corporate debt, only 57 of the 2,500 publicly listed companies in Japan have any domestic bonds outstanding. Japanese companies have traditionally relied on loans from big Japanese banks when they need cash. Reliance on bank debt has caused problems for Japanese companies because, as a result of the collapse of the real estate industry in Japan, Japanese banks do not have the funds to lend them.[5] Similar problems have occurred recently in other Asian countries.

◆ **STOP AND THINK!**

If a company with a high debt to equity ratio wants to increase its debt when the economy is weak, what kind of bond might it issue?

It would most likely issue a secured bond because, rather than being issued on the company's general credit, certain assets are pledged as a guarantee of repayment. ■

REGISTERED OR COUPON BONDS

Most bonds issued today are **registered bonds**. The names and addresses of the owners of such bonds must be recorded with the issuing organization. The organization keeps a register of the owners and pays interest by check to the bondholders of record on the interest payment date. **Coupon bonds** generally are not registered with the organization; instead, they bear interest coupons stating the amount of interest due and the payment date. The bondholder removes the coupons from the bonds on the interest payment dates and presents them at a bank for collection.

 Check out ACE for a Review Quiz at http://accounting.college.hmco.com/students.

ACCOUNTING FOR BONDS PAYABLE

LO3 Record the issuance of bonds at face value and at a discount or premium.

RELATED TEXT ASSIGNMENTS
Q: 4, 5
SE: 2, 3, 5, 7
E: 2, 3, 4, 5, 10, 12
P: 1, 2, 3, 4, 5, 6, 7, 8
SD: 1, 5

When the board of directors of a public corporation decides to issue bonds, the company must submit the appropriate legal documents to the Securities and Exchange Commission for permission to borrow the funds. The SEC reviews the corporation's financial health and the specific terms of the bond agreement. Once approved, the company has a limited time in which to issue the authorized bonds. It is not necessary to make an entry for the bond authorization, but most companies prepare a memorandum in the Bonds Payable account describing the issue. This note lists the number and value of bonds authorized, the interest rate, the interest payment dates, and the life of the bonds.

Once the bonds are issued, the corporation must pay interest to the bondholders over the life of the bonds (in most cases, semiannually) and the principal of the bonds at maturity.

BALANCE SHEET DISCLOSURE OF BONDS

KEY POINT: Bonds payable are presented on the balance sheet as either a current or a long-term liability, depending on the maturity date and method of retiring the bonds.

Bonds payable and unamortized discounts or premiums (which we explain later) are typically shown on a company's balance sheet as long-term liabilities. However, if the maturity date of the bond issue is one year or less and the bonds will be retired using current assets, bonds payable should be listed as a current liability. If the issue is to be paid with segregated assets or replaced by another bond issue, the bonds should still be shown as a long-term liability.

Important provisions of the bond indenture are reported in the notes to the financial statements, as illustrated by the Financial Highlights excerpted from the AT&T annual report. Often reported with them is a list of all bond issues, the kinds of bonds, any securities connected with the bonds, interest payment dates, maturity dates, and interest rates.

www.att.com

BONDS ISSUED AT FACE VALUE

Suppose that the Vason Corporation has authorized the issuance of $100,000 of 9 percent, five-year bonds on January 1, 20x0. According to the bond indenture, interest is to be paid on January 1 and July 1 of each year. Assume that the bonds are sold on January 1, 20x0, for their face value. The entry to record the issuance is as follows:

A = L + OE
+   +

20x0			
Jan. 1	Cash	100,000	
	Bonds Payable		100,000
	Sold $100,000 of 9%, 5-year bonds		
	at face value		

STUDY NOTE: When calculating semiannual interest, do not use the annual rate (9 percent in this case) by mistake. Rather, use half the annual rate.

As stated above, interest is paid on January 1 and July 1 of each year. Therefore, the corporation would owe the bondholders $4,500 interest on July 1, 20x0:

$$\text{Interest} = \text{Principal} \times \text{Rate} \times \text{Time}$$

$$= \$100,000 \times .09 \times \frac{6}{12} \text{ year}$$

$$= \$4,500$$

The interest paid to the bondholders on each semiannual interest payment date (January 1 or July 1) would be recorded as follows:

A* = L + OE
−   −
*assumes cash paid

Bond Interest Expense	4,500	
Cash (or Interest Payable)		4,500
Paid (or accrued) semiannual interest		
to bondholders of 9%, 5-year bonds		

FACE INTEREST RATE AND MARKET INTEREST RATE

KEY POINT: A bond sells at face value when the face interest rate of the bond is identical to the market interest rate for similar bonds on the date of issue.

KEY POINT: When bonds with an interest rate different from the market rate are issued, they sell at a discount or premium. The discount or premium acts as an equalizing factor.

When issuing bonds, most organizations try to set the face interest rate as close as possible to the market interest rate. The **face interest rate** is the rate of interest paid to bondholders based on the face value, or principal, of the bonds. The rate and amount are fixed over the life of the bond. An organization must decide in advance what the face interest rate will be to allow time to file with regulatory bodies, publicize the issue, and print the certificates.

The **market interest rate** is the rate of interest paid in the market on bonds of similar risk. It is also referred to as the *effective interest rate*. The market interest rate fluctuates daily. Because an organization has no control over the market interest rate, it often differs from the face interest rate on the issue date. As a result, the issue price of the bonds does not always equal their face value. If the market interest rate is higher than the face interest rate, the issue price will be less than the face value and the bonds are said to be issued at a **discount**. The discount equals the excess of

FOCUS ON BUSINESS PRACTICE

Check Out Those Bond Prices!

The price of many bonds can be found daily in business publications like *The Wall Street Journal*. For instance, shown to the right are the quotations for a number of AT&T <www.att.com> bonds. The first is a bond with a face interest rate of 7⅛ percent that is due in 2002. The current yield is 7.1 percent based on the closing price of 100¹⁄₁₆. The volume of $1,000 bonds traded was 138, and the last sale was up by ¹⁄₁₆ point from the previous day's last sales.

Corporation bond price/change (1/4/02), from *Wall Street Journal*. Copyright 2002 by Dow Jones & Co. Inc. Reproduced with permission of Dow Jones & Co. Inc. in the format textbook via Copyright Clearance Center.

Bonds	Cur Yld	Vol	Close		Net Chg
ATT 7⅛02	7.1	138	100¹⁄₁₆	1	¹⁄₁₆
ATT 6½02	6.4	130	101½	1	²⁵⁄₃₂
ATT 6¾04	6.6	5	102⅜	1	¼
ATT 5⅝04	5.5	155	101¾	1	½
ATT 7½06	7.2	49	104¾	1	⅛
ATT 7¾07	7.4	184	105½	1	1
ATT 6s09	6.2	26	96¼	1	½
ATT 8⅛22	7.9	95	103⅛	1	⅛
ATT 8⅛24	7.9	93	103	1	½
ATT 8.35s25	8.0	85	104⅜	1	⅞
ATT 6½29	7.3	223	88¾	1	¾
ATT 8⅝31	8.3	640	104	2	⅜

the face value over the issue price. On the other hand, if the market interest rate is lower than the face interest rate, the issue price will be more than the face value and the bonds are said to be issued at a **premium**. The premium equals the excess of the issue price over the face value.

BONDS ISSUED AT A DISCOUNT

Suppose that the Vason Corporation issues $100,000 of 9 percent, five-year bonds at 96.149 on January 1, 20x0, when the market interest rate is 10 percent. In this case, the bonds are being issued at a discount because the market interest rate exceeds the face interest rate. The following entry records the issuance of the bonds at a discount:

KEY POINT: The carrying amount is always the face value of the bonds plus the unamortized premium or less the unamortized discount. The carrying amount always approaches the face value over the life of the bond.

20x0			
A = L + OE	Jan. 1	Cash	96,149	
+ +		Unamortized Bond Discount	3,851	
−	*Contra* ← Bonds Payable		100,000
	liability account	Sold $100,000 of 9%, 5-year bonds at 96.149		

Face amount of bonds	$100,000	
Less purchase price of bonds ($100,000 × .96149)	96,149	
Unamortized bond discount	$ 3,851	

In the entry, Cash is debited for the amount received ($96,149), Bonds Payable is credited for the face amount ($100,000) of the bond liability, and the difference ($3,851) is debited to Unamortized Bond Discount. If a balance sheet is prepared right after the bonds are issued at a discount, the liability for bonds payable is reported as follows:

KEY POINT: The unamortized bond discount is subtracted from bonds payable on the balance sheet. The carrying value will be below the face value until the maturity date.

Long-term liabilities		
9% bonds payable, due 1/1/x5	$100,000	
Less unamortized bond discount	3,851	$96,149

Unamortized bond discount is a contra-liability account: its balance is deducted from the face amount of the bonds to arrive at the carrying value, or present value, of the bonds. The bond discount is described as unamortized because it will be amortized (written off) over the life of the bonds.

BONDS ISSUED AT A PREMIUM

◆ **STOP AND THINK!**
What determines whether bonds are issued at a discount, premium, or face value?
The relationship between the prevailing market rate of interest and the face interest rate on the issue date is the determinant. ■

When bonds have a face interest rate above the market rate for similar investments, they are issued at a price above the face value, or at a premium. For example, assume that the Vason Corporation issues $100,000 of 9 percent, five-year bonds for $104,100 on January 1, 20x0, when the market interest rate is 8 percent. This means that investors will purchase the bonds at 104.1 percent of their face value. The issuance would be recorded as follows:

20x0			
A = L + OE	Jan. 1	Cash	104,100	
+ +		Unamortized Bond Premium		4,100
+		Bonds Payable		100,000
		Sold $100,000 of 9%, 5-year bonds at 104.1 ($100,000 × 1.041)		

KEY POINT: The unamortized bond premium is *added* to bonds payable on the balance sheet. The carrying value will be above the face value until the maturity date.

Right after this entry is made, bonds payable would be presented on the balance sheet as follows:

Long-term liabilities		
9% bonds payable, due 1/1/x5	$100,000	
Unamortized bond premium	4,100	$104,100

Focus on Business Practice

100-Year Bonds Are Not for Everyone.

In 1993, interest rates on long-term debt were at historically low levels, which induced some companies to attempt to lock in those low costs for long periods. One of the most aggressive companies in that regard was The Walt Disney Company <www.disney.go.com>, which issued $150 million of 100-year bonds at a yield of only 7.5 percent. It was the first time since 1954 that 100-year bonds had been issued. Among the others that followed Walt Disney's lead by issuing 100-year bonds were the Coca-Cola Company <www.coca-cola.com>, Columbia HCA Healthcare <www.hcahealthcare.com>, Bell South <www.bellsouth.com>, IBM <www.ibm. com>, and even the People's Republic of China. Some analysts wondered if even Mickey Mouse could survive 100 years. Investors who purchase such bonds take a financial risk because if interest rates rise, which would seem likely, then the market value of the bonds will decrease.[6]

The carrying value of the bonds payable is $104,100, which equals the face value of the bonds plus the unamortized bond premium. The cash received from the bond issue is also $104,100. This means that the purchasers were willing to pay a premium of $4,100 to buy these bonds because their face interest rate was higher than the market interest rate.

BOND ISSUE COSTS

KEY POINT: A separate Bond Issue Costs account is usually established and amortized over the life of the issue.

Most bonds are sold through underwriters, who receive a fee for taking care of the details of marketing the issue or for taking a chance on receiving the selling price. Such costs are connected with the issuance of bonds. Because bond issue costs benefit the whole life of a bond issue, it makes sense to spread the costs over that period. It is generally accepted practice to establish a separate account for bond issue costs and to amortize them over the life of the bonds. However, issue costs decrease the amount of money a company receives from a bond issue. They have the effect, then, of raising the discount or lowering the premium on the issue. As a result, bond issue costs can be spread over the life of the bonds through the amortization of a discount or premium. Because this method simplifies recordkeeping, we assume in the text and problems of this book that all bond issue costs increase the discounts or decrease the premiums of bond issues.

 Check out ACE for a Review Quiz at http://accounting.college.hmco.com/students.

USING PRESENT VALUE TO VALUE A BOND

LO4 Use present values to determine the value of bonds.

RELATED TEXT ASSIGNMENTS
SE: 4
E: 6, 7, 8, 13

Present value is relevant to the study of bonds because the value of a bond is based on the present value of two components of cash flow: (1) a series of fixed interest payments and (2) a single payment at maturity. The amount of interest a bond pays is fixed over its life. However, the market interest rate varies from day to day. Thus, the amount investors are willing to pay for a bond changes as well.

Assume, for example, that a bond has a face value of $10,000 and pays fixed interest of $450 every six months (a 9 percent annual rate). The bond is due in five years. If the market interest rate today is 14 percent, what is the present value of the bond?

To determine the present value of the bond, we use Table 4 in the appendix on future value and present value tables to calculate the present value of the periodic interest payments of $450, and we use Table 3 in the same appendix to calculate the present value of the single payment of $10,000 at maturity. Since interest payments are made every six months, the compounding period is half a year. Because of this, it is necessary to convert the annual rate to a semiannual rate of 7 percent (14 percent divided by two six-month periods per year) and to use ten periods (five

STUDY NOTE: The amount buyers are willing to pay for an investment is normally based on what they expect to receive in return, taken at present value. In the case of a bond, the theoretical value equals the present value of the periodic interest payments plus the present value of the maturity value. The discount rate is set at the market rate (what investors are looking for), not at the face rate.

years multiplied by two six-month periods per year). Using this information, we compute the present value of the bond as follows:

Present value of 10 periodic payments at 7% (from Table 4 in the appendix on future value and present value tables): $450 × 7.024	$3,160.80
Present value of a single payment at the end of 10 periods at 7% (from Table 3 in the appendix on future value and present value tables): $10,000 × .508	5,080.00
Present value of $10,000 bond	$8,240.80

The market interest rate has increased so much since the bond was issued (from 9 percent to 14 percent) that the value of the bond is only $8,240.80 today. That amount is all investors would be willing to pay at this time for a bond that provides income of $450 every six months and a return of the $10,000 principal in five years.

If the market interest rate falls below the face interest rate, say to 8 percent (4 percent semiannually), the present value of the bond will be greater than the face value of $10,000:

 STOP AND THINK!

Why do bond prices vary over time?

Bond price is the present value of the principal and interest cash flows at the market interest rate; therefore, as the market interest rate changes over time, bond prices will change. ■

Present value of 10 periodic payments at 4% (from Table 4 in the appendix on future value and present value tables): $450 × 8.111	$ 3,649.95
Present value of a single payment at the end of 10 periods at 4% (from Table 3 in the appendix on future value and present value tables): $10,000 × .676	6,760.00
Present value of $10,000 bond	$10,409.95

✓ Check out ACE for a Review Quiz at http://accounting.college.hmco.com/students.

AMORTIZATION OF BOND DISCOUNTS AND PREMIUMS

LO5 Amortize bond discounts and bond premiums using the straight-line and effective interest methods.

RELATED TEXT ASSIGNMENTS

Q: 6, 7
SE: 2, 3, 7
E: 2, 3, 4, 5, 9, 12
P: 1, 2, 3, 4, 5, 6, 7, 8
SD: 2

A bond discount or premium represents the amount by which the total interest cost is higher or lower than the total interest payments. To record interest expense properly and ensure that at maturity the carrying value of bonds payable equals its face value, systematic reduction of the bond discount or premium over the bond term is required. That is, the discount or premium has to be amortized over the life of the bonds. This is accomplished by using either the straight-line method or the effective interest method.

AMORTIZING A BOND DISCOUNT

In the example on page 502, Vason Corporation issued $100,000 of five-year bonds at a discount because the market interest rate of 10 percent exceeded the face interest rate of 9 percent. The bonds were sold for $96,149, resulting in an unamortized bond discount of $3,851. Because this discount affects interest expense in each year of the bond issue, the bond discount should be amortized (reduced gradually) over the life of the issue. This means that the unamortized bond discount will decrease gradually over time, and that the carrying value of the bond issue (face value less unamortized discount) will increase gradually. By the maturity date of the bond, the carrying value of the issue will equal its face value, and the unamortized bond discount will be zero. In the following sections, the total interest cost is calculated, and the bond discount is amortized using the straight-line and the effective interest methods.

KEY POINT: A bond discount is considered a component of total interest cost because a bond discount represents the amount in excess of the issue price that the corporation must pay on the maturity date.

[handwritten note: amortization + (interest on face value = total interest cost.]

■ **CALCULATION OF TOTAL INTEREST COST** When bonds are issued at a discount, the effective (or market) interest rate paid by the company is greater than the face interest rate on the bonds. The reason is that the interest cost to the company is the stated interest payments *plus* the amount of the bond discount. That is, although the company does not receive the full face value of the bonds on issue, it still must pay back the full face value at maturity. The difference between the issue price and the face value must be added to the total interest payments to arrive at the actual interest expense. The full cost to the corporation of issuing the bonds at a discount is as follows:

Cash to be paid to bondholders	
Face value at maturity	$100,000
Interest payments ($100,000 × .09 × 5 years)	45,000
Total cash paid to bondholders	$145,000
Less cash received from bondholders	96,149
Total interest cost	$ 48,851

Or, alternatively:

Interest payments ($100,000 × .09 × 5 years)	$ 45,000
Bond discount	3,851
Total interest cost	$ 48,851

The total interest cost of $48,851 is made up of $45,000 in interest payments and the $3,851 bond discount, so the bond discount increases the interest paid on the bonds from the face interest rate to the market interest rate. The *market (effective) interest rate* is the real interest cost of the bond over its life.

For each year's interest expense to reflect the market interest rate, the discount must be allocated over the remaining life of the bonds as an increase in the interest expense each period. The process of allocation is called *amortization of the bond discount*. Thus, interest expense for each period will exceed the actual payment of interest by the amount of the bond discount amortized over the period.

Some companies and governmental units issue bonds that do not require periodic interest payments. These bonds, called **zero coupon bonds**, are simply a promise to pay a fixed amount at the maturity date. They are issued at a large discount because the only interest earned by the buyer or paid by the issuer is the discount. For example, a five-year, $100,000 zero coupon bond issued at a time when the market rate is 14 percent, compounded semiannually, would sell for only $50,800. That amount is the present value of a single payment of $100,000 at the end of five years. The discount of $49,200 ($100,000 − $50,800) is the total interest cost; it is amortized over the life of the bond.

KEY POINT: The discount on a zero coupon bond represents the interest that will be paid (in its entirety) on the maturity date.

■ **STRAIGHT-LINE METHOD** The **straight-line method** assumes equal amortization of the bond discount for each interest period. Suppose that the interest payment dates for the Vason Corporation bond issue are January 1 and July 1. The amount of the bond discount amortized and the interest expense for each semiannual period are calculated in four steps:

1. Total Interest Payments = Interest Payments per Year × Life of Bonds
$$= 2 \times 5 = 10$$

2. Amortization of Bond Discount per Interest Period $= \dfrac{\text{Bond Discount}}{\text{Total Interest Payments}}$

$$= \frac{\$3,851}{10} = \$385*$$

*Rounded.

3. Cash Interest Payment = Face Value × Face Interest Rate × Time

$$= \$100,000 \times .09 \times 6/12 = \$4,500$$

4. Interest Expense per Interest Period = Interest Payment + Amortization of Bond Discount

$$= \$4,500 + \$385 = \$4,885$$

On July 1, 20x0, the first semiannual interest date, the entry would be as follows:

A* = L + OE
−   +   −
*assumes cash paid

(every entry over 5 year period) Know

20x0			
July 1	Bond Interest Expense	4,885	
	Unamortized Bond Discount		385
	Cash (or Interest Payable)		4,500
	Paid (or accrued) semiannual interest to bondholders and amortized the discount on 9%, 5-year bonds		

Notice that the bond interest expense is $4,885, but the amount paid to the bondholders is the $4,500 face interest payment. The difference of $385 is the credit to Unamortized Bond Discount. This lowers the debit balance of the Unamortized Bond Discount account and raises the carrying value of the bonds payable by $385 each interest period. Assuming that no changes occur in the bond issue, this entry will be made every six months for the life of the bonds. When the bond issue matures, there will be no balance in the Unamortized Bond Discount account, and the carrying value of the bonds will be $100,000—exactly equal to the amount due the bondholders.

The straight-line method has long been used, but it has a certain weakness. Because the carrying value goes up each period and the bond interest expense stays the same, the rate of interest falls over time. Conversely, when the straight-line method is used to amortize a premium, the rate of interest rises over time. Therefore, the Accounting Principles Board has ruled that the straight-line method can be used only when it does not lead to a material difference from the effective interest method.[7] An amount is material if it affects a decision on the evaluation of the company.

◆ **STOP AND THINK!**
When is it acceptable to use the straight-line method to amortize a bond discount or premium?

It is acceptable only when it does not produce a result materially different from that produced by the effective interest method. ■

■ **EFFECTIVE INTEREST METHOD**   To compute the interest and amortization of a bond discount for each interest period under the **effective interest method**, a constant interest rate is applied to the carrying value of the bonds at the beginning of the interest period. This constant rate equals the market rate, or effective rate, at the time the bonds were issued. The amount to be amortized each period is the difference between the interest computed by using the market rate and the actual interest paid to bondholders.

As an example, we use the same facts presented earlier—a $100,000 bond issue at 9 percent, with a five-year maturity and interest to be paid twice a year. The market, or effective, interest rate at the time the bonds were issued was 10 percent. The bonds were sold for $96,149, a discount of $3,851. The interest and amortization of the bond discount are shown in Table 1.

The amounts in the table (using period 1) were computed as follows:

Column A: The carrying value of the bonds is their face value less the unamortized bond discount ($100,000 − $3,851 = $96,149).

Column B: The interest expense to be recorded is the effective interest. It is found by multiplying the carrying value of the bonds by the effective (market) interest rate for one-half year ($96,149 × .10 × ½ = $4,807).

Column C: The interest paid in the period is a constant amount computed by multiplying the face value of the bonds by their face interest rate by the interest time period ($100,000 × .09 × ½ = $4,500).

Column D: The discount amortized is the difference between the effective interest expense to be recorded and the interest to be paid on the interest payment date ($4,807 − $4,500 = $307).

TABLE 1. Interest and Amortization of a Bond Discount: Effective Interest Method

	A	B	C	D	E	F
Semiannual Interest Period	Carrying Value at Beginning of Period	Semiannual Interest Expense at 10% to Be Recorded* (5% × A)	Semiannual Interest Payment to Bondholders (4½% × $100,000)	Amortization of Bond Discount (B − C)	Unamortized Bond Discount at End of Period (E − D)	Carrying Value at End of Period (A + D)
0					$3,851	$ 96,149
1	$96,149	$4,807	$4,500	$307	3,544	96,456
2	96,456	4,823	4,500	323	3,221	96,779
3	96,779	4,839	4,500	339	2,882	97,118
4	97,118	4,856	4,500	356	2,526	97,474
5	97,474	4,874	4,500	374	2,152	97,848
6	97,848	4,892	4,500	392	1,760	98,240
7	98,240	4,912	4,500	412	1,348	98,652
8	98,652	4,933	4,500	433	915	99,085
9	99,085	4,954	4,500	454	461	99,539
10	99,539	4,961†	4,500	461	—	100,000

*Rounded to the nearest dollar.

†Last period's interest expense equals $4,961 ($4,500 + $461); it does not equal $4,977 ($99,539 × .05) because of the cumulative effect of rounding.

Column E: The unamortized bond discount is the balance of the bond discount at the beginning of the period less the current period amortization of the discount ($3,851 − $307 = $3,544). The unamortized discount decreases each interest payment period because it is amortized as a portion of interest expense.

Column F: The carrying value of the bonds at the end of the period is the carrying value at the beginning of the period plus the amortization during the period ($96,149 + $307 = $96,456). Notice that the sum of the carrying value and the unamortized discount (Column F + Column E) always equals the face value of the bonds ($96,456 + $3,544 = $100,000).

The entry to record the interest expense is exactly like the one used when the straight-line method is applied. However, the amounts debited and credited to the various accounts are different. Using the effective interest method, the entry for July 1, 20x0, would be as follows:

A* = L + OE
−   +   −
*assumes cash paid

20x0			
July 1	Bond Interest Expense	4,807	
	Unamortized Bond Discount		307
	Cash (or Interest Payable)		4,500
	Paid (or accrued) semiannual interest to bondholders and amortized the discount on 9%, 5-year bonds		

KEY POINT: The bond interest expense recorded exceeds the amount of interest paid because of the amortization of the bond discount. The matching rule dictates that the discount be amortized over the life of the bond.

Notice that it is not necessary to prepare an interest and amortization table to determine the amortization of a discount for any one interest payment period. It is necessary only to multiply the carrying value by the effective interest rate and subtract the interest payment from the result. For example, the amount of discount to be amortized in the seventh interest payment period is $412, calculated as follows: ($98,240 × .05) − $4,500.

■ **VISUAL SUMMARY OF THE EFFECTIVE INTEREST METHOD**   The effect on carrying value and interest expense of the amortization of a bond discount using the effective

FIGURE 2
Carrying Value and Interest Expense—Bonds Issued at a Discount

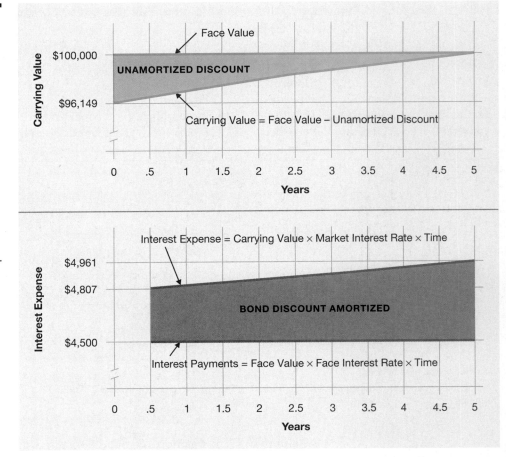

KEY POINT: The bond interest expense *increases* each period because the carrying value of the bonds (the principal on which the interest is calculated) increases each period.

interest method can be seen in Figure 2 (which is based on the data from Table 1). Notice that initially the carrying value (the issue price) is less than the face value, but that it gradually increases toward the face value over the life of the bond issue. Notice also that interest expense exceeds interest payments by the amount of the bond discount amortized. Interest expense increases gradually over the life of the bond because it is based on the gradually increasing carrying value (multiplied by the market interest rate).

AMORTIZING A BOND PREMIUM

In our example of bonds issued at a premium, Vason Corporation issued $100,000 of five-year bonds at a premium because the market interest rate of 8 percent was less than the face interest rate of 9 percent. The bonds were sold for $104,100, which resulted in an unamortized bond premium of $4,100. Like a discount, a premium must be amortized over the life of the bonds so that it can be matched to its effects on interest expense during that period. In the following sections, the total interest cost is calculated, and the bond premium is amortized using the straight-line and the effective interest methods.

■ **CALCULATION OF TOTAL INTEREST COST**   Because the bondholders paid more than face value for the bonds, the premium of $4,100 ($104,100 − $100,000) represents an amount that the bondholders will not receive at maturity. The premium is in effect a reduction, in advance, of the total interest paid on the bonds over the life of the bond issue. The total interest cost over the issue's life can be computed as follows:

KEY POINT: The bond interest expense recorded is less than the amount of the interest paid because of the amortization of the bond premium. The matching rule dictates that the premium be amortized over the life of the bond.

KEY POINT: A bond premium is deducted from interest payments in calculating total interest cost because a bond premium represents an amount over the face value of a bond that the corporation never has to return to the bondholders. In effect, it reduces the higher-than-market interest the corporation is paying on the bond.

Cash to be paid to bondholders

Face value at maturity		$100,000
Interest payments ($100,000 × .09 × 5 years)		45,000
Total cash paid to bondholders		$145,000
Less cash received from bondholders		104,100
Total interest cost		$ 40,900

Or, alternatively:

Interest payments ($100,000 × .09 × 5 years)		$ 45,000
Less bond premium		4,100
Total interest cost		$ 40,900

Notice that the total interest payments of $45,000 exceed the total interest cost of $40,900 by $4,100, the amount of the bond premium.

■ **STRAIGHT-LINE METHOD**   Under the straight-line method, the bond premium is spread evenly over the life of the bond issue. As with bond discounts, the amount of the bond premium amortized and the interest expense for each semiannual period are computed in four steps:

1. Total Interest Payments = Interest Payments per Year × Life of Bonds
$$= 2 \times 5 = 10$$

2. Amortization of Bond Premium per Interest Period $= \dfrac{\text{Bond Premium}}{\text{Total Interest Payments}}$
$$= \frac{\$4,100}{10} = \$410$$

3. Cash Interest Payment = Face Value × Face Interest Rate × Time
$$= \$100,000 \times .09 \times \%_2 = \$4,500$$

4. Interest Expense per Interest Period = Interest Payment − Amortization of Bond Premium
$$= \$4,500 - \$410 = \$4,090$$

On July 1, 20x0, the first semiannual interest date, the entry would be as follows:

A* = L + OE

*assumes cash paid

20x0			
July 1	Bond Interest Expense	4,090	
	Unamortized Bond Premium	410	
	Cash (or Interest Payable)		4,500
	Paid (or accrued) semiannual interest to bondholders and amortized the premium on 9%, 5-year bonds		

Notice that the bond interest expense is $4,090, but the amount received by the bondholders is the $4,500 face interest payment. The difference of $410 is the debit to Unamortized Bond Premium. This lowers the credit balance of the Unamortized Bond Premium account and the carrying value of the bonds payable by $410 each interest period. Assuming that the bond issue remains unchanged, the same entry will be made on every semiannual interest date over the life of the bond issue. When the bond issue matures, there will be no balance in the Unamortized Bond Premium account, and the carrying value of the bonds payable will be $100,000, exactly equal to the amount due the bondholders.

STUDY NOTE: Whether a bond is sold at a discount or a premium, its carrying value will equal its face value on the maturity date.

As noted earlier, the straight-line method should be used only when it does not lead to a material difference from the effective interest method.

■ **EFFECTIVE INTEREST METHOD**   Under the straight-line method, the effective interest rate changes constantly, even though the interest expense is fixed, because

TABLE 2.   Interest and Amortization of a Bond Premium: Effective Interest Method

	A	B	C	D	E	F
Semiannual Interest Period	Carrying Value at Beginning of Period	Semiannual Interest Expense at 8% to Be Recorded* (4% × A)	Semiannual Interest Payment to Bondholders (4½% × $100,000)	Amortization of Bond Premium (C − B)	Unamortized Bond Premium at End of Period (E − D)	Carrying Value at End of Period (A − D)
0					$4,100	$104,100
1	$104,100	$4,164	$4,500	$336	3,764	103,764
2	103,764	4,151	4,500	349	3,415	103,415
3	103,415	4,137	4,500	363	3,052	103,052
4	103,052	4,122	4,500	378	2,674	102,674
5	102,674	4,107	4,500	393	2,281	102,281
6	102,281	4,091	4,500	409	1,872	101,872
7	101,872	4,075	4,500	425	1,447	101,447
8	101,447	4,058	4,500	442	1,005	101,005
9	101,005	4,040	4,500	460	545	100,545
10	100,545	3,955†	4,500	545	—	100,000

*Rounded to the nearest dollar.

†Last period's interest expense equals $3,955 ($4,500 − $545); it does not equal $4,022 ($100,545 × .04) because of the cumulative effect of rounding.

the effective interest rate is determined by comparing the fixed interest expense with a carrying value that changes as a result of amortizing the discount or premium. To apply a fixed interest rate over the life of the bonds based on the actual market rate at the time of the bond issue requires the use of the effective interest method. Under this method, the interest expense decreases slightly each period (see Table 2, Column B) because the amount of the bond premium amortized increases slightly (Column D). This occurs because a fixed rate is applied each period to the gradually decreasing carrying value (Column A).

The first interest payment is recorded as follows:

	20x0			
A* = L + OE	July 1	Bond Interest Expense	4,164	
− − −		Unamortized Bond Premium	336	
*assumes cash paid		Cash (or Interest Payable)		4,500
		Paid (or accrued) semiannual interest to bondholders and amortized the premium on 9%, 5-year bonds		

FOCUS ON BUSINESS TECHNOLOGY

Speed Up the Calculations!

Interest and amortization tables like those in Tables 1 and 2 are ideal applications for computer spreadsheet software, such as Lotus and Microsoft Excel. Once the tables have been constructed with the proper formula in each cell, only five variables must be entered to produce the entire table. These variables are the face value of the bonds, selling price, life of the bonds, face interest rate, and market interest rate.

Notice that the unamortized bond premium (Column E) decreases gradually to zero as the carrying value decreases to the face value (Column F). To find the amount of premium amortized in any one interest payment period, subtract the effective interest expense (the carrying value times the effective interest rate, Column B) from the interest payment (Column C). In semiannual interest period 5, for example, the amortization of premium is $393, which is calculated in the following manner: $4,500 − ($102,674 × .04).

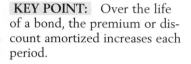

FIGURE 3
Carrying Value and Interest Expense—Bonds Issued at a Premium

KEY POINT: Over the life of a bond, the premium or discount amortized increases each period.

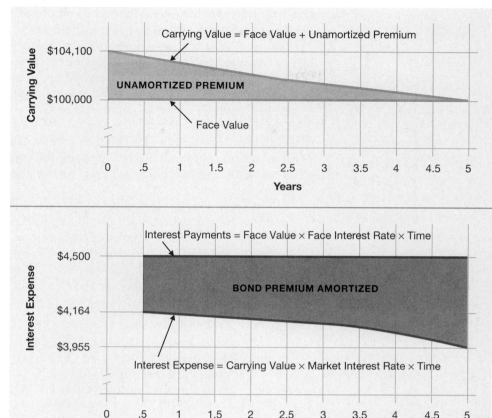

■ **VISUAL SUMMARY OF THE EFFECTIVE INTEREST METHOD** The effect on carrying value and interest expense of the amortization of a bond premium using the effective interest method can be seen in Figure 3 (which is based on data from Table 2). Notice that initially the carrying value (issue price) is greater than the face value, but that it gradually decreases toward the face value over the life of the bond issue. Notice also that interest payments exceed interest expense by the amount of the premium amortized and that interest expense decreases gradually over the life of the bond because it is based on the gradually decreasing carrying value (multiplied by the market interest rate).

✔ Check out ACE for a Review Quiz at http://accounting.college.hmco.com/students.

OTHER BONDS PAYABLE ISSUES

LO6 Record bonds issued between interest dates and year-end adjustments.

RELATED TEXT ASSIGNMENTS
Q: 8
SE: 3, 5, 6, 7
E: 4, 5, 9, 10, 11, 12
P: 1, 2, 3, 5, 6, 7, 8

Several other issues arise in accounting for bonds payable. Among them are the sale of bonds between interest payment dates and the year-end accrual of bond interest expense.

SALE OF BONDS BETWEEN INTEREST DATES

Bonds may be issued on an interest payment date, as in the previous examples, but they are often issued between interest payment dates. The generally accepted method of handling bonds issued in this manner is to collect from investors the interest that would have accrued for the partial period preceding the issue date.

Then, when the first interest period is completed, the corporation pays investors the interest for the entire period. Thus, the interest collected when bonds are sold is returned to investors on the next interest payment date.

There are two reasons for following this procedure. The first is a practical one. If a company issued bonds on several different days and did not collect the accrued interest, records would have to be maintained for each bondholder and date of purchase. In such a case, the interest due each bondholder would have to be computed on the basis of a different time period. Clearly, large bookkeeping costs would be incurred under this kind of system. On the other hand, if accrued interest is collected when the bonds are sold, the corporation can pay the interest due for the entire period on the interest payment date, eliminating the extra computations and costs.

The second reason for collecting accrued interest in advance is that when that amount is netted against the full interest paid on the interest payment date, the resulting interest expense represents the amount for the time the money was borrowed. For example, assume that the Vason Corporation sold $100,000 of 9 percent, five-year bonds for face value on May 1, 20x0, rather than on January 1, 20x0, the issue date. The entry to record the sale of the bonds is as follows:

$A = L + OE$
$+ \quad + \quad +$

20x0			
May 1	Cash	103,000	
	Bond Interest Expense		3,000
	Bonds Payable		100,000
	Sold 9%, 5-year bonds at face value plus 4 months' accrued interest $100,000 \times .09 \times \frac{4}{12} = \$3,000$		

ENRICHMENT POINT:
This is one of the few times an expense account is credited (other than when it is closed). The ledger account demonstrates that the net effect is the recording of two months' interest (May and June).

$A^* = L + OE$
$- \quad - \quad -$

*assumes cash paid

As shown, Cash is debited for the amount received, $103,000 (the face value of $100,000 plus four months' accrued interest of $3,000). Bond Interest Expense is credited for the $3,000 of accrued interest, and Bonds Payable is credited for the face value of $100,000.

When the first semiannual interest payment date arrives, this entry is made:

20x0			
July 1	Bond Interest Expense	4,500	
	Cash (or Interest Payable)		4,500
	Paid (or accrued) semiannual interest $100,000 \times .09 \times \frac{6}{12} = \$4,500$		

Notice that the entire half-year interest is both debited to Bond Interest Expense and credited to Cash because the corporation pays bond interest only once every six months, in full six-month amounts. This process is illustrated in Figure 4. The actual interest expense for the two months that the bonds were outstanding is $1,500. This amount is the net balance of the $4,500 debit to Bond Interest Expense on July 1 less the $3,000 credit to Bond Interest Expense on May 1. You can see these steps clearly in the following T account:

Bond Interest Expense			
Bal.	0	May 1	3,000
July 1	4,500		
Bal.	1,500		

YEAR-END ACCRUAL OF BOND INTEREST EXPENSE

Bond interest payment dates rarely correspond with a company's fiscal year. Therefore, an adjustment must be made at the end of the accounting period to

FIGURE 4
Effect on Bond Interest Expense When Bonds Are Issued Between Interest Dates

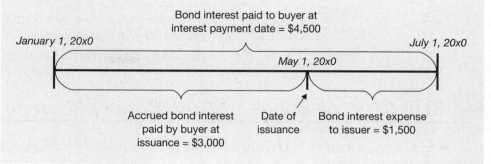

accrue the interest expense on the bonds from the last payment date to the end of the fiscal year. Further, if there is any discount or premium on the bonds, it must also be amortized for the fractional period.

Remember that in the example of bonds issued at a premium, Vason Corporation issued $100,000 in bonds on January 1, 20x0, at 104.1 percent of face value. Suppose the company's fiscal year ends on September 30, 20x0. In the period since the interest payment and amortization of the premium on July 1, three months' worth of interest has accrued, and the following adjusting entry under the effective interest method must be made:

KEY POINT: Remember that adjusting entries never affect cash.

$$A = L + OE$$
$$+ \quad -$$
$$-$$

20x0
Sept. 30	Bond Interest Expense	2,075.50	
	Unamortized Bond Premium	174.50	
	Interest Payable		2,250.00
	To record accrual of interest on 9% bonds payable for 3 months and amortization of one-half of the premium for the second interest payment period		

CLARIFICATION NOTE: The matching rule dictates that both the accrued interest and the amortization of a premium or discount be recorded at year end.

This entry covers one-half of the second interest period. Unamortized Bond Premium is debited for $174.50, which is one-half of $349, the amortization of the premium for the second period from Table 2. Interest Payable is credited for $2,250, three months' interest on the face value of the bonds ($100,000 × .09 × $\frac{3}{12}$). The net debit figure of $2,075.50 ($2,250.00 − $174.50) is the bond interest expense for the three-month period.

When the January 1, 20x1, payment date arrives, the entry to pay the bondholders and amortize the premium is as follows:

$$A = L + OE$$
$$- \quad - \quad -$$

20x1
Jan. 1	Bond Interest Expense	2,075.50	
	Interest Payable	2,250.00	
	Unamortized Bond Premium	174.50	
	Cash		4,500.00
	Paid semiannual interest, including interest previously accrued, and amortized the premium for the period since the end of the fiscal year		

● **STOP AND THINK!**
Why must the accrual of bond interest expense be recorded?

Bond interest expense must be accrued at the close of each accounting period to ensure proper matching of all the borrowing costs associated with bonds payable. Interest payment dates rarely coincide with the end of the accounting period. ■

As shown here, one-half ($2,250) of the amount paid ($4,500) was accrued on September 30. Unamortized Bond Premium is debited for $174.50, the remaining amount to be amortized for the period ($349.00 − $174.50). The resulting bond interest expense is the amount that applies to the three-month period from October 1 to December 31.

Bond discounts are recorded at year end in the same way as bond premiums. The difference is that the amortization of a bond discount increases interest expense instead of decreasing it as a premium does.

✓ Check out ACE for a Review Quiz at http://accounting.college.hmco.com/students.

RETIREMENT OF BONDS · *Know concepts only*

SO7 Account for the retirement of bonds and the conversion of bonds into stock.

RELATED TEXT ASSIGNMENTS
Q: 9, 10
SE: 8, 9
E: 13, 14, 15
P: 4, 5
FRA: 2

ENRICHMENT NOTE:
When interest rates drop, corporations frequently refinance their bonds at the lower rate, much like homeowners who refinance their mortgage loans when interest rates go down. Even though a call premium is usually paid to extinguish the bonds, the interest saved makes the refinancing cost-effective in the long run.

Usually, bonds are paid when due—on the stated maturity date. However, it can be advantageous not to wait until maturity, as is sometimes the case with callable bonds and convertible bonds.

CALLABLE BONDS

Callable bonds give the issuer the right to buy back and retire the bonds at a specified **call price,** usually above face value, before maturity. Such bonds give the company flexibility in financing its operations. For example, if bond interest rates drop, the company can call its bonds and reissue debt at a lower interest rate. A company might also call its bonds if it has earned enough to pay off the debt, if the reason for having the debt no longer exists, or if it wants to restructure its debt to equity ratio. The bond indenture states the time period and the prices at which the bonds can be redeemed. The retirement of a bond issue before its maturity date is called **early extinguishment of debt**.

Let's assume that Vason Corporation can call or retire at 105 the $100,000 of bonds it issued at a premium (104.1) and that it decides to do so on July 1, 20x3. (To simplify the example, the retirement is made on an interest payment date.) Because the bonds were issued on January 1, 20x0, the retirement takes place on the seventh interest payment date. Assume that the entry for the required interest payment and the amortization of the premium has been made. The entry to retire the bonds is as follows:

A = L + OE
−   −   −

	20x3			
	July 1	Bonds Payable	100,000	
		Unamortized Bond Premium	1,447	
		Loss on Retirement of Bonds	3,553	
		Cash		105,000
		Retired 9% bonds at 105		

In this entry, the cash paid is the face value times the call price ($100,000 × 1.05 = $105,000). The unamortized bond premium can be found in Column E of Table 2. The loss on retirement of bonds occurs because the call price of the bonds is greater than the carrying value ($105,000 − $101,447 = $3,553).

STUDY NOTE: The goal is to eliminate from the books any reference to the bonds being retired.

Sometimes, a rise in the market interest rate can cause the market value of bonds to fall considerably below their face value. If it has the cash to do so, the company may find it advantageous to purchase the bonds on the open market and retire them, rather than wait and pay them off at face value. A gain is recognized for the difference between the purchase price of the bonds and the carrying value of the retired bonds. For example, assume that because of a rise in interest rates, Vason Corporation is able to purchase the $100,000 bond issue on the open market at 85. The entry would be as follows:

A = L + OE
−   −   +

	20x3			
	July 1	Bonds Payable	100,000	
		Unamortized Bond Premium	1,447	
		Cash		85,000
		Gain on Retirement of Bonds		16,447
		Purchased and retired		
		9% bonds at 85		

CONVERTIBLE BONDS

Bonds that can be exchanged for common stock or other securities of the corporation are called **convertible bonds**. Convertibility enables an investor to make more money if the market price of the common stock rises, because the value of the bonds then rises. However, if the common stock price does not rise, the investor still holds the bonds and receives both the periodic interest payments and the principal at the maturity date.

Several factors related to the issuance of convertible bonds are favorable to the company. First, the interest rate is usually less than the company would have to offer if the bonds were not convertible. An investor is willing to give up some current interest for the prospect that the value of the stock will increase and therefore the value of the bonds will also increase. Another advantage is that management will not have to give up any current control of the company. Unlike stockholders, bondholders do not have voting rights. A third benefit is tax savings. Interest paid on bonds is fully deductible for income tax purposes, whereas cash dividends on common stock are not. Fourth, the company's income will be affected favorably if the company earns a return that exceeds the interest cost of the bonds. Finally, the convertible feature offers financial flexibility. If the market value of the stock rises to a level at which the bond is worth more than face value, management can avoid repaying the bonds by calling them for redemption, thereby forcing the bondholders to convert their bonds into common stock. The bondholders will agree to convert because no gain or loss results from the transaction.

One major disadvantage of bonds is that interest must be paid semiannually. Inability to make an interest payment could force the company into bankruptcy. Common stock dividends are declared and paid only when the board of directors decides to do so. Another disadvantage of bonds is that when the bonds are converted, they become new outstanding common stock. These new shares give the bondholders stockholders' rights and reduce the proportional ownership of the existing stockholders.

When a bondholder wishes to convert bonds into common stock, the common stock is recorded at the carrying value of the bonds. The bond liability and the associated unamortized discount or premium are written off the books. For this reason, no gain or loss on the transaction is recorded. For example, suppose that Vason Corporation's bonds are not called on July 1, 20x3. Instead, the corporation's bondholders decide to convert all the bonds to $8 par value common stock under a convertible provision of 40 shares of common stock for each $1,000 bond. The entry would be as follows:

A = L + OE
−   +
−   +

20x3			
July 1	Bonds Payable	100,000	
	Unamortized Bond Premium	1,447	
	Common Stock		32,000
	Paid-in Capital in Excess of Par		
	Value, Common		69,447
	Converted 9% bonds payable into		
	$8 par value common stock at a rate		
	of 40 shares for each $1,000 bond		

STUDY POINT: The credits to the contributed capital accounts are based on the carrying value of the bonds converted. As a result, no gain or loss is recognized. If only a portion of the bonds had been converted, proportionate shares of the balances in Bonds Payable and Unamortized Bond Premium would be eliminated.

The unamortized bond premium is found in Column E of Table 2. At a rate of 40 shares for each $1,000 bond, 4,000 shares will be issued, with a total par value of $32,000 (4,000 × $8). The Common Stock account is credited for the amount of the par value of the stock issued. In addition, Paid-in Capital in Excess of Par Value, Common is credited for the difference between the carrying value of the bonds and the par value of the stock issued ($101,447 − $32,000 = $69,447). No gain or loss is recorded.

✓ Check out ACE for a Review Quiz at http://accounting.college.hmco.com/students.

OTHER LONG-TERM LIABILITIES

SO8 Explain the basic features of mortgages payable, long-term leases, and pensions and other post-retirement benefits as long-term liabilities.

RELATED TEXT ASSIGNMENTS
Q: 11, 12, 13, 14, 15
SE: 10
E: 16, 17
SD: 3, 6
FRA: 4, 6

A company may have other long-term liabilities besides bonds. The most common are mortgages payable, long-term leases, and pensions and other postretirement benefits.

MORTGAGES PAYABLE

A **mortgage** is a long-term debt secured by real property. It is usually paid in equal monthly installments. Each monthly payment includes interest on the debt and a reduction in the debt. Table 3 shows the first three monthly payments on a $50,000, 12 percent mortgage. The mortgage was obtained on June 1, and the monthly payments are $800. According to the table, the entry to record the July 1 payment would be as follows:

$$A = L + OE$$
$$- \quad - \quad -$$

July 1	Mortgage Payable	300	
	Mortgage Interest Expense	500	
	Cash		800
	Made monthly mortgage payment		

Notice from the entry and from Table 3 that the July 1 payment represents interest expense of $500 ($50,000 × .12 × ½) and a reduction in the debt of $300 ($800 − $500). Therefore, the unpaid balance is reduced to $49,700 by the July payment. August's interest expense is slightly less than July's because of the decrease in the debt.

LONG-TERM LEASES

A company can obtain new operating assets in several ways. One way is to borrow money and buy the asset. Another is to rent the equipment on a short-term lease. A third way is to obtain the equipment on a long-term lease. The first two methods do not create accounting problems. In the first case, the asset and liability are recorded at the amount paid, and the asset is subject to periodic depreciation. In the second case, the lease is short term in relation to the useful life of the asset, and the risks of ownership remain with the lessor. This type of agreement is called an **operating lease**. It is proper accounting procedure to treat operating lease payments as an expense and to debit the amount of each monthly payment to Rent Expense.

The third alternative, a long-term lease, is one of the fastest-growing ways of financing operating equipment in the United States today. It has several advantages.

TABLE 3. Monthly Payment Schedule on a $50,000, 12 Percent Mortgage

	A	B	C	D	E
Payment Date	Unpaid Balance at Beginning of Period	Monthly Payment	Interest for 1 Month at 1% on Unpaid Balance* (1% × A)	Reduction in Debt (B − C)	Unpaid Balance at End of Period (A − D)
June 1					$50,000
July 1	$50,000	$800	$500	$300	49,700
Aug. 1	49,700	800	497	303	49,397
Sept. 1	49,397	800	494	306	49,091

*Rounded to the nearest dollar.

TABLE 4. Payment Schedule on a 16 Percent Capital Lease

	A	B	C	D
Year	Lease Payment	Interest (16%) on Unpaid Obligation* (D × 16%)	Reduction of Lease Obligation (A − B)	Balance of Lease Obligation (D − C)
Beginning				$14,740
1	$ 4,000	$2,358	$ 1,642	13,098
2	4,000	2,096	1,904	11,194
3	4,000	1,791	2,209	8,985
4	4,000	1,438	2,562	6,423
5	4,000	1,028	2,972	3,451
6	4,000	549†	3,451	—
	$24,000	$9,260	$14,740	

*Computations are rounded to the nearest dollar.

†The last year's interest equals $549 ($4,000 − $3,451); it does not exactly equal $552 ($3,451 × .16) because of the cumulative effect of rounding.

For instance, a long-term lease requires no immediate cash payment, the rental payment is deducted in full for tax purposes, and it costs less than a short-term lease. Acquiring the use of plant assets under long-term leases does create several accounting challenges, however. Often, such leases cannot be canceled. Also, their duration may be about the same as the useful life of the asset. Finally, they stipulate that the lessee has the option to buy the asset at a nominal price at the end of the lease. The lease is much like an installment purchase because the risks of ownership are transferred to the lessee. Both the lessee's available assets and its legal obligations (liabilities) increase because the lessee must make a number of payments over the life of the asset.

The Financial Accounting Standards Board has described this kind of long-term lease as a **capital lease**. The term reflects the provisions of such a lease, which make the transaction more like a purchase or sale on installment. The FASB has ruled that in the case of a capital lease, the lessee must record an asset and a long-term liability equal to the present value of the total lease payments during the lease term. In doing so, the lessee must use the present value at the beginning of the lease.[8] Much like a mortgage payment, each lease payment consists partly of interest expense and partly of repayment of debt. Further, depreciation expense is figured on the asset and entered on the records of the lessee.

Suppose, for example, that Isaacs Company enters into a long-term lease for a machine used in its manufacturing operations. The lease terms call for an annual payment of $4,000 for six years, which approximates the useful life of the machine (see Table 4). At the end of the lease period, the title to the machine passes to Isaacs. This lease is clearly a capital lease and should be recorded as an asset and a liability according to FASB *Statement No. 13*.

A lease is a contract that provides for a periodic payment for the right to use an asset or assets. Present value techniques can be used to place a value on the asset and on the corresponding liability associated with a capital lease. If Isaacs's interest cost is 16 percent, the present value of the lease payments can be computed as follows:

Periodic Payment × Factor (Table 4 in the appendix on future value and present value tables: 16%, 6 periods) = Present Value

$4,000 × 3.685   = $14,740

TERMINOLOGY NOTE: From the lessee's point of view, a lease is treated as either an operating lease or a capital lease. An operating lease is a true lease and is treated as such. A capital lease, however, is in substance an installment purchase, and the leased asset and related liability must be recognized at their present value.

KEY POINT: Under a capital lease, the lessee must record depreciation, using any allowable method. Depreciation is *not* recorded under an operating lease, however, because the leased asset is not recognized on the lessee's books.

The entry to record the lease contract is as follows:

A = L + OE
+   +

Capital Lease Equipment	14,740	
Capital Lease Obligations		14,740
To record capital lease on machinery		

Capital Lease Equipment is classified as a long-term asset; Capital Lease Obligations is classified as a long-term liability. Each year, Isaacs must record depreciation on the leased asset. Using straight-line depreciation, a six-year life, and no salvage value, the following entry would record the depreciation:

A = L + OE
−   −

Depreciation Expense, Capital Lease Equipment	2,457	
Accumulated Depreciation, Capital Lease		
Equipment		2,457
To record depreciation expense on capital lease		

The interest expense for each year is computed by multiplying the interest rate (16 percent) by the amount of the remaining lease obligation. Table 4 shows these calculations. Using the data in the table, the first lease payment would be recorded as follows:

A = L + OE
−   −   −

Interest Expense (Column B)	2,358	
Capital Lease Obligations (Column C)	1,642	
Cash		4,000
Made payment on capital lease		

PENSIONS

Most employees who work for medium-sized and large companies are covered by some sort of pension plan. A **pension plan** is a contract between a company and its employees in which the company agrees to pay benefits to the employees after they retire. Many companies pay the full cost of the pension, but frequently the employees also contribute part of their salary or wages. The contributions from both parties are typically paid into a **pension fund**, from which benefits are paid to retirees. In most cases, pension benefits consist of monthly payments to retired employees and other payments upon disability or death.

There are two kinds of pension plans. Under a *defined contribution plan*, the employer is required to contribute an annual amount specified by an agreement between the company and its employees or by a resolution of the board of directors. Retirement payments depend on the amount of pension payments the accumulated contributions can support. Under a *defined benefit plan*, the employer's annual contribution is the amount required to fund pension liabilities arising from employment in the current year, but the exact amount will not be determined until the retirement and death of the current employees. Under a defined benefit plan, the amount of future benefits is fixed, but the annual contributions vary depending on assumptions about how much the pension fund will earn. Under a defined contribution plan, each year's contribution is fixed, but the benefits vary depending on how much the pension fund earns.

Accounting for annual pension expense under a defined contribution plan is simple. After the required contribution is determined, Pension Expense is debited and a liability (or Cash) is credited.

Accounting for annual expense under a defined benefit plan is one of the most complex topics in accounting; thus, the intricacies are reserved for advanced courses. In concept, however, the procedure is simple. First, the amount of pension expense is determined. Then, if the amount of cash contributed to the fund is less than the pension expense, a liability results, which is reported on the balance sheet. If the amount of cash paid to the pension plan exceeds the pension expense, a prepaid expense arises and appears on the asset side of the balance sheet. For example, the annual report for Philip Morris Companies, Inc., includes among assets on the balance sheet a prepaid pension of $628 million.[9]

ENRICHMENT NOTE:
Companies prefer defined contribution plans because the employees assume the risk that their pension assets will earn a sufficient return to meet their retirement needs.

www.philipmorris.com

ENRICHMENT NOTE: Accounting for a defined benefit plan is far more complex than accounting for a defined contribution plan. Fortunately, accountants can rely on the calculations of professional actuaries, whose expertise includes the mathematics of pension plans.

In accordance with the FASB's *Statement No. 87*, all companies should use the same actuarial method to compute pension expense.[10] However, because actuarial methods require the estimation of many factors, such as the average remaining service life of active employees, the long-run return on pension plan assets, and future salary increases, the computation of pension expense is not simple. In addition, terminology further complicates pension accounting. In nontechnical terms, the pension expense for the year includes not only the cost of the benefits earned by people working during the year but also interest costs on the total pension obligation (which are calculated on the present value of future benefits to be paid) and other adjustments. Those costs are reduced by the expected return on the pension fund assets.

Since 1989, all employers whose pension plans do not have sufficient assets to cover the present value of their pension benefit obligations (on a termination basis) must record the amount of the shortfall as a liability on their balance sheets. The investor no longer has to read the notes to the financial statements to learn whether the pension plan is fully funded. However, if a pension plan does have sufficient assets to cover its obligations, then no balance sheet reporting is required or permitted.

OTHER POSTRETIREMENT BENEFITS

KEY POINT: Other postretirement benefits should be expensed when earned by the employee, not when received after retirement. This practice conforms to the matching rule.

Many companies provide retired employees not only with pensions but also with health care and other benefits. In the past, these **other postretirement benefits** were accounted for on a cash basis; that is, they were expensed when the benefits were paid, after an employee had retired. The FASB has concluded, however, that those benefits are earned by the employee and that, in accordance with the matching rule, they should be estimated and accrued during the period of time the employee is working.[11]

The estimates must take into account assumptions about retirement age, mortality, and, most significantly, future trends in health care benefits. Like pension benefits, such future benefits should be discounted to the current period. A field test conducted by the Financial Executives Research Foundation determined that the change to accrual accounting increased postretirement benefits by two to seven times the amount recognized on a cash basis.

✓ Check out ACE for a Review Quiz at http://accounting.college.hmco.com/students.

Chapter Review

REVIEW OF LEARNING OBJECTIVES

LO1 Identify the management issues related to issuing long-term debt.

Long-term debt is used to finance long-term assets and business activities that have long-term earnings potential, such as property, plant, and equipment and research and development. In issuing long-term debt, management must decide (1) whether to take on long-term debt, (2) how much long-term debt to carry, (3) what types of long-term debt to incur, and (4) how to handle debt repayment. Among the advantages of long-term debt financing are that (1) common stockholders do not relinquish any control, (2) interest on debt is tax deductible, and (3) financial leverage may increase earnings. Disadvantages of long-term financing are that (1) interest and principal must be repaid on schedule, and (2) financial leverage can work against a company if an investment is not successful.

LO2 Identify and contrast the major characteristics of bonds.

A bond is a security that represents money borrowed from the investing public. When a corporation issues bonds, it enters into a contract, called a bond indenture, with the bondholders. The bond indenture identifies the major conditions of the bonds. A corporation can issue several types of bonds, each having different characteristics. For example, a bond issue may or may not require security (secured versus unsecured bonds). It may be payable at a single time (term bonds) or at several times (serial bonds). And the holder may receive interest automatically (registered bonds) or may have to return coupons to receive interest payable (coupon bonds).

LO3 Record the issuance of bonds at face value and at a discount or premium.

When bonds are issued, the bondholders pay an amount equal to, less than, or greater than the bonds' face value. Bondholders pay face value for bonds when the interest rate on the bonds approximates the market rate for similar investments. The issuing corporation records the bond issue at face value as a long-term liability in the Bonds Payable account.

Bonds are issued at an amount less than face value when their face interest rate is lower than the market rate for similar investments. The difference between the face value and the issue price is called a discount and is debited to Unamortized Bond Discount.

When the face interest rate on bonds is greater than the market interest rate on similar investments, investors are willing to pay more than face value for the bonds. The difference between the issue price and the face value is called a premium and is credited to Unamortized Bond Premium.

LO4 Use present values to determine the value of bonds.

The value of a bond is determined by summing the present values of (1) the series of fixed interest payments of the bond issue and (2) the single payment of the face value at maturity. Tables 3 and 4 in the appendix on future value and present value tables should be used in making these computations.

LO5 Amortize bond discounts and bond premiums using the straight-line and effective interest methods.

When bonds are sold at a discount or a premium, the interest rate is adjusted from the face rate to an effective rate that is close to the market rate when the bonds were issued. Therefore, bond discounts or premiums have the effect of increasing or decreasing the interest expense on the bonds over their life. Under these conditions, it is necessary to amortize the discount or premium over the life of the bonds by using either the straight-line method or the effective interest method.

The straight-line method allocates a fixed portion of the bond discount or premium each interest period to adjust the interest payment to interest expense. The effective interest method, which is used when the effects of amortization are material, results in a constant rate of interest on the carrying value of the bonds. To find interest and the amortization of discounts or premiums, the effective interest rate is applied to the carrying value of the bonds (face value minus the discount or plus the premium) at the beginning of the interest period. The amount of the discount or premium to be amortized is the difference between the interest figured by using the effective rate and that obtained by using the face rate. The results of using the effective interest method on bonds issued at a discount or a premium are summarized below and compared with issuance at face value.

	Bonds Issued At		
	Face Value	Discount	Premium
Trend in carrying value over bond term	Constant	Increasing	Decreasing
Trend in interest expense over bond term	Constant	Increasing	Decreasing
Interest expense versus interest payments	Interest expense = interest payments	Interest expense > interest payments	Interest expense < interest payments
Classification of bond discount or premium	Not applicable	Contra-liability (deducted from Bonds Payable)	Liability (added to Bonds Payable)

LO6 Record bonds issued between interest dates and year-end adjustments.

When bonds are sold on dates between the interest payment dates, the issuing corporation collects from investors the interest that has accrued since the last interest payment date. When the next interest payment date arrives, the corporation pays the bondholders interest for the entire interest period.

When the end of a corporation's fiscal year does not fall on an interest payment date, the corporation must accrue bond interest expense from the last interest payment date to the end of the company's fiscal year. This accrual results in the inclusion of the interest expense in the year incurred.

SUPPLEMENTAL OBJECTIVES

SO7 Account for the retirement of bonds and the conversion of bonds into stock.

Callable bonds can be retired before maturity at the option of the issuing corporation. The call price is usually an amount greater than the face value of the bonds, in which case the corporation recognizes a loss on the retirement of the bonds. A gain can be recognized on the early extinguishment of debt when a company purchases its bonds on the open market at a price below carrying value. This happens when a rise in the market interest rate causes the market value of the bonds to fall below face value.

Convertible bonds allow the bondholder to convert bonds to common stock in the issuing corporation. In this case, the common stock issued is recorded at the carrying value of the bonds being converted. No gain or loss is recognized.

SO8 Explain the basic features of mortgages payable, long-term leases, and pensions and other postretirement benefits as long-term liabilities.

A mortgage is a long-term debt secured by real property. It usually is paid in equal monthly installments. Each payment is partly interest expense and partly debt repayment. If a long-term lease is a capital lease, the risks of ownership lie with the lessee. Like a mortgage payment, each lease payment is partly interest and partly a reduction of debt. For a capital lease, both an asset and a long-term liability should be recorded. The liability should be equal to the present value at the beginning of the lease of the total lease payments over the lease term. The recorded asset is subject to depreciation. Pension expense must be recorded in the current period. Other postretirement benefits should be estimated and accrued while the employee is still working.

REVIEW OF CONCEPTS AND TERMINOLOGY

The following concepts and terms were introduced in this chapter:

LO2 **Bond:** A security, usually long term, representing money that a corporation or other entity borrows from the investing public.

LO2 **Bond certificate:** Evidence of an organization's debt to a bondholder.

LO2 **Bond indenture:** A supplementary agreement to a bond issue that defines the rights, privileges, and limitations of bondholders.

LO2 **Bond issue:** The total value of bonds issued at one time.

SO7 **Callable bonds:** Bonds that an organization can buy back and retire at a call price before maturity.

SO7 **Call price:** A specified price, usually above face value, at which a corporation may buy back and retire bonds before maturity.

SO8 **Capital lease:** A long-term lease in which the risk of ownership lies with the lessee and whose terms resemble those of a purchase or sale on installment.

SO7 **Convertible bonds:** Bonds that can be exchanged for common stock or other securities of the corporation.

LO2 **Coupon bonds:** Bonds that are usually not registered with the issuing organization but instead bear interest coupons stating the amount of interest due and the payment date.

LO3 **Discount:** The amount by which the face value of a bond exceeds the issue price, which occurs when the market interest rate is higher than the face interest rate.

SO7 **Early extinguishment of debt:** The retirement of a bond issue before its maturity date.

LO5 **Effective interest method:** A method of amortizing bond discounts or premiums that applies a constant interest rate (the market rate at the time the bonds were issued) to the carrying value of the bonds at the beginning of each interest period.

LO3 **Face interest rate:** The rate of interest paid to bondholders based on the face value of the bonds.

LO1 **Financial leverage:** The ability to increase earnings for stockholders by earning more on assets than is paid in interest on debt incurred to finance the assets. Also called *trading on the equity.*

LO1 **Interest coverage ratio:** A measure of the degree of protection a company has from default on interest payments; income before taxes plus interest expense divided by interest expense.

LO3 **Market interest rate:** The rate of interest paid in the market on bonds of similar risk. Also called *effective interest rate.*

SO8 **Mortgage:** A long-term debt secured by real property.

SO8 **Operating lease:** A short-term lease in which the risks of ownership remain with the lessor and whose payments are recorded as rent expense.

SO8 **Other postretirement benefits:** Health care and other nonpension benefits paid to a worker after retirement but earned while the employee is still working.

SO8 **Pension fund:** A fund established through contributions by an employer, and often by employees, from which payments are made to employees after retirement or on disability or death.

SO8 **Pension plan:** A contract between a company and its employees under which the company agrees to pay benefits to the employees after they retire.

LO3 **Premium:** The amount by which the issue price of a bond exceeds its face value, which occurs when the market interest rate is lower than the face interest rate.

LO2 **Registered bonds:** Bonds for which the names and addresses of bondholders are recorded with the issuing organization.

LO2 **Secured bonds:** Bonds that give the bondholders a pledge of certain assets as a guarantee of repayment.

LO2 **Serial bonds:** Bonds in an issue that mature on different dates.

LO5 **Straight-line method:** A method of amortizing bond discounts or premiums that allocates the discount or premium equally over each interest period of the life of a bond.

LO2 **Term bonds:** Bonds in an issue that mature at the same time.

LO2 **Unsecured bonds:** Bonds issued on the general credit of an organization. Also called *debenture bonds.*

LO5 **Zero coupon bonds:** Bonds that do not pay periodic interest but that promise to pay a fixed amount on the maturity date.

REVIEW PROBLEM

Interest and Amortization of a Bond Discount, Bond Retirement, and Bond Conversion

LO3
LO5
SO7
When the Merrill Manufacturing Company was expanding its metal window division, it did not have enough capital to finance the expansion. So, management sought and received approval from the board of directors to issue bonds. The company planned to issue $5,000,000 of 8 percent, five-year bonds in 20x1. Interest would be paid on June 30 and December 31 of each year. The bonds would be callable at 104, and each $1,000 bond would be convertible into 30 shares of $10 par value common stock.

On January 1, 20x1, the bonds were sold at 96 because the market rate of interest for similar investments was 9 percent. The company decided to amortize the bond discount by using the effective interest method. On July 1, 20x3, management called and retired half the bonds, and investors converted the other half into common stock.

REQUIRED ▶
1. Prepare an interest and amortization schedule for the first five interest periods.
2. Prepare the entries in journal form to record the sale of the bonds, the first two interest payments, the bond retirement, and the bond conversion.

ANSWER TO REVIEW PROBLEM

1. Schedule prepared for the first five interest periods:

Interest and Amortization of Bond Discount

Semiannual Interest Payment Date	Carrying Value at Beginning of Period	Semiannual Interest Expense* (9% × ½)	Semiannual Interest Payment (8% × ½)	Amortization of Discount	Unamortized Bond Discount at End of Period	Carrying Value at End of Period
Jan. 1, 20x1					$200,000	$4,800,000
June 30, 20x1	$4,800,000	$216,000	$200,000	$16,000	184,000	4,816,000
Dec. 31, 20x1	4,816,000	216,720	200,000	16,720	167,280	4,832,720
June 30, 20x2	4,832,720	217,472	200,000	17,472	149,808	4,850,192
Dec. 31, 20x2	4,850,192	218,259	200,000	18,259	131,549	4,868,451
June 30, 20x3	4,868,451	219,080	200,000	19,080	112,469	4,887,531

*Rounded to the nearest dollar.

2. Entries made in journal form:

20x1

Jan. 1	Cash	4,800,000	
	Unamortized Bond Discount	200,000	
	Bonds Payable		5,000,000
	Sold $5,000,000 of 8%, 5-year bonds at 96		
June 30	Bond Interest Expense	216,000	
	Unamortized Bond Discount		16,000
	Cash		200,000
	Paid semiannual interest and amortized the discount on 8%, 5-year bonds		
Dec. 31	Bond Interest Expense	216,720	
	Unamortized Bond Discount		16,720
	Cash		200,000
	Paid semiannual interest and amortized the discount on 8%, 5-year bonds		

20x3

July 1	Bonds Payable	2,500,000	
	Loss on Retirement of Bonds	156,235	
	Unamortized Bond Discount		56,235
	Cash		2,600,000
	Called $2,500,000 of 8% bonds and retired them at 104 $112,469 × ½ = $56,235*		
1	Bonds Payable	2,500,000	
	Unamortized Bond Discount		56,234
	Common Stock		750,000
	Paid-in Capital in Excess of Par Value, Common		1,693,766
	Converted $2,500,000 of 8% bonds into common stock: 2,500 × 30 shares = 75,000 shares 75,000 shares × $10 = $750,000 $112,469 − $56,235 = $56,234 $2,500,000 − ($56,234 + $750,000) = $1,693,766		

*Rounded.

Chapter Assignments

BUILDING YOUR KNOWLEDGE FOUNDATION

QUESTIONS

1. What are the advantages and disadvantages of issuing long-term debt?
2. What are a bond certificate, a bond issue, and a bond indenture? What information is in a bond indenture?
3. What are the essential differences between (a) secured and debenture bonds, (b) term and serial bonds, and (c) registered and coupon bonds?
4. Napier Corporation sold $500,000 of 5 percent $1,000 bonds on the interest payment date. What would the proceeds from the sale be if the bonds were issued at 95, at 100, and at 102?
5. If you were about to buy bonds on which the face interest rate was less than the market interest rate, would you expect to pay more or less than par value for the bonds?
6. Why does the amortization of a bond discount increase interest expense to an amount greater than interest paid? Why does the amortization of a premium have the opposite effect?
7. When the effective interest method of amortizing a bond discount or premium is used, why does the amount of interest expense change from period to period?
8. When bonds are issued between interest dates, why is it necessary for the issuer to collect an amount equal to accrued interest from the buyer?
9. Why would a company want to exercise the call provision of a bond when it can wait to pay off the debt?
10. What are the advantages of convertible bonds to the company issuing them and to the investor?
11. What are the two components of a uniform monthly mortgage payment?
12. What is a capital lease? Why should an accountant record both an asset and a liability in connection with this type of lease? What items should appear on the income statement as the result of a capital lease?
13. What is a pension plan? What is a pension fund?
14. What is the difference between a defined contribution plan and a defined benefit plan? In general, how is expense determined under each plan? What assumptions must be made to account for the expenses of a defined benefit plan?
15. What are other postretirement benefits, and how is the matching rule applied?

SHORT EXERCISES

LO1 Bond Versus Common Stock Financing

SE 1. Indicate whether each of the following is an advantage or a disadvantage of using long-term bond financing rather than issuing common stock:

1. Interest paid on bonds is tax deductible.
2. Investments are sometimes not as successful as planned.
3. Financial leverage can have a negative effect when investments do not earn as much as the interest payments on the related debt.
4. Bondholders do not have voting rights in a corporation.
5. Positive financial leverage may be achieved.

**LO3 Entries for Interest Using
LO5 the Straight-Line Method**

SE 2. On April 1, 20x1, Agaki Corporation issued $4,000,000 in 8.5 percent, five-year bonds at 98. The semiannual interest payment dates are April 1 and October 1. Prepare entries in journal form for the issue of the bonds by Agaki on April 1, 20x1, and the first two interest payments on October 1, 20x1, and April 1, 20x2. Use the straight-line method and ignore year-end accruals.

	SE 3.	On March 1, 20xx, Westward Freight Company sold $100,000 of its 9.5 percent, 20-year bonds at 106. The semiannual interest payment dates are March 1 and September 1. The market interest rate is about 8.9 percent. The company's fiscal year ends August 31. Prepare entries in journal form to record the sale of the bonds on March 1, the accrual of interest and amortization of premium on August 31, and the first interest payment on September 1. Use the effective interest method to amortize the premium.

LO3 Entries for Interest Using the
LO5 Effective Interest Method
LO6

SE 4. Cap Art, Inc., is considering the sale of two bond issues. Choice A is a $400,000 bond issue that pays semiannual interest of $32,000 and is due in 20 years. Choice B is a $400,000 bond issue that pays semiannual interest of $30,000 and is due in 15 years. Assume that the market interest rate for each bond is 12 percent. Calculate the amount that Cap Art will receive if both bond issues occur. (Calculate the present value of each bond issue and sum.)

LO4 Valuing Bonds Using Present Value

SE 5. League Company is authorized to issue $900,000 in bonds on June 1. The bonds carry a face interest rate of 8 percent, with interest to be paid on June 1 and December 1. Prepare entries in journal form for the issue of the bonds under the independent assumptions that (a) the bonds are issued on September 1 at 100 and (b) the bonds are issued on June 1 at 103.

LO3 Entries for Bond Issues
LO6

SE 6. Eisley Corporation sold $200,000 of 9 percent, ten-year bonds for face value on September 1, 20xx. The issue date of the bonds was May 1, 20xx. The company's fiscal year ends on December 31, and this is its only bond issue. Record the sale of the bonds on September 1 and the first semiannual interest payment on November 1, 20xx. What is the bond interest expense for the year ended December 31, 20xx?

LO6 Sale of Bonds Between Interest Dates

SE 7. On October 1, 20x1, Knight Corporation issued $500,000 of 9 percent bonds at 96. The bonds are dated October 1 and pay interest semiannually. The market rate of interest is 10 percent, and the company's year end is December 31. Prepare the entries to record the issuance of the bonds, the accrual of the interest on December 31, 20x1, and the payment of the first semiannual interest on April 1, 20x2. Assume that the company does not use reversing entries and uses the effective interest method to amortize the bond discount.

LO3 Year-End Accrual of Bond
LO5 Interest
LO6

SE 8. The Ross Corporation has outstanding $800,000 of 8 percent bonds callable at 104. On December 1, immediately after the payment of the semiannual interest and the amortization of the bond discount were recorded, the unamortized bond discount equaled $21,000. On that date, $480,000 of the bonds were called and retired. Prepare the entry to record the retirement of the bonds on December 1.

SO7 Entry for Bond Retirement

SE 9. The Hui Corporation has $1,000,000 of 6 percent bonds outstanding. There is $20,000 of unamortized discount remaining on the bonds after the March 1, 20x2, semiannual interest payment. The bonds are convertible at the rate of 20 shares of $10 par value common stock for each $1,000 bond. On March 1, 20x2, bondholders presented $600,000 of the bonds for conversion. Prepare the entry to record the conversion of the bonds.

SO7 Entry for Bond Conversion

SE 10. Sedaka Corporation purchased a building by signing a $300,000 long-term mortgage with monthly payments of $2,400. The mortgage carries an interest rate of 8 percent. Prepare a monthly payment schedule showing the monthly payment, the interest for the month, the reduction in debt, and the unpaid balance for the first three months. (Round to the nearest dollar.)

SO8 Mortgage Payable

EXERCISES

E 1. Compute the interest coverage ratios for 20x4 and 20x5 from the partial income statements of Ivy Wall Company that appear below. State whether the ratio improved or worsened over time.

LO1 Interest Coverage Ratio

	20x5	20x4
Income from operations	$23,890	$18,460
Interest expense	5,800	3,300
Income before income taxes	$18,090	$15,160
Income taxes	5,400	4,500
Net income	$12,690	$10,660

E 2.

LO3   Entries for Interest Using the
LO5   Straight-Line Method

Agga Corporation issued $4,000,000 in 10.5 percent, ten-year bonds on February 1, 20x1, at 104. The semiannual interest payment dates are February 1 and August 1. Prepare entries in journal form for the issue of bonds by Agga on February 1, 20x1, and the first two interest payments on August 1, 20x1, and February 1, 20x2. Use the straight-line method and ignore year-end accruals.

E 3.

LO3   Entries for Interest Using
LO5   the Straight-Line Method

Famina Corporation issued $8,000,000 in 8.5 percent, five-year bonds on March 1, 20x1, at 96. The semiannual interest payment dates are March 1 and September 1. Prepare entries in journal form for the issue of the bonds by Famina on March 1, 20x1, and the first two interest payments on September 1, 20x1, and March 1, 20x2. Use the straight-line method and ignore year-end accruals.

E 4.

LO3   Entries for Interest Using the
LO5   Effective Interest Method
LO6

The Whistle Toy Company sold $500,000 of 9.5 percent, 20-year bonds on April 1, 20xx, at 106. The semiannual interest payment dates are April 1 and October 1. The market interest rate is 8.9 percent. The company's fiscal year ends September 30. Prepare entries in journal form to record the sale of the bonds on April 1, the accrual of interest and amortization of premium on September 30, and the first interest payment on October 1. Use the effective interest method to amortize the premium.

E 5.

LO3   Entries for Interest Using
LO5   the Effective Interest Method
LO6

On March 1, 20x1, the Eddy Corporation issued $1,200,000 of 10 percent, five-year bonds. The semiannual interest payment dates are March 1 and September 1. Because the market rate for similar investments was 11 percent, the bonds had to be issued at a discount. The discount on the issuance of the bonds was $48,670. The company's fiscal year ends February 28. Prepare entries in journal form to record the bond issue on March 1, 20x1; the payment of interest and the amortization of the discount on September 1, 20x1; the accrual of interest and the amortization of the discount on February 28, 20x2; and the payment of interest on March 1, 20x2. Use the effective interest method. (Round answers to the nearest dollar.)

E 6.

LO4   Valuing Bonds Using Present
Value

Octogon, Inc., is considering the sale of two bond issues. Choice A is an $800,000 bond issue that pays semiannual interest of $64,000 and is due in 20 years. Choice B is an $800,000 bond issue that pays semiannual interest of $60,000 and is due in 15 years. Assume that the market interest rate for each bond is 12 percent. Calculate the amount that Octogon, Inc., will receive if both bond issues are made. (**Hint:** Calculate the present value of each bond issue and sum.)

E 7.

LO4   Valuing Bonds Using Present
Value

Use the present value tables in the appendix on future value and present value tables to calculate the issue price of a $1,200,000 bond issue in each of the following independent cases, assuming that interest is paid semiannually:

a. A ten-year, 8 percent bond issue; the market interest rate is 10 percent.
b. A ten-year, 8 percent bond issue; the market interest rate is 6 percent.
c. A ten-year, 10 percent bond issue; the market interest rate is 8 percent.
d. A 20-year, 10 percent bond issue; the market interest rate is 12 percent.
e. A 20-year, 10 percent bond issue; the market interest rate is 6 percent.

E 8.

LO4   Zero Coupon Bonds

The state of Idaho needs to raise $100,000,000 for highway repairs. Officials are considering issuing zero coupon bonds, which do not require periodic interest payments. The current market interest rate for the bonds is 10 percent. What face value of bonds must be issued to raise the needed funds, assuming the bonds will be due in 30 years and compounded annually? How would your answer change if the bonds were due in 50 years? How would both answers change if the market interest rate were 8 percent instead of 10 percent?

E 9.

LO5   Entries for Interest Payments
LO6   Using the Effective Interest
Method

The long-term debt section of the Sanchos Corporation's balance sheet at the end of its fiscal year, December 31, 2001, was as follows:

Long-term liabilities
  Bonds payable—8%, interest payable
    1/1 and 7/1, due 12/31/13 $1,000,000
    Less unamortized bond discount   80,000 $920,000

Prepare entries in journal form relevant to the interest payments on July 1, 2002, December 31, 2002, and January 1, 2003. Assume a market interest rate of 10 percent.

E 10.

LO3   Entries for Bond Issue
LO6

Water Symphonics, Inc., is authorized to issue $1,800,000 in bonds on June 1. The bonds carry a face interest rate of 9 percent, which is to be paid on June 1 and December 1. Prepare entries in journal form for the issue of the bonds by Water Symphonics, Inc., under the assumptions that (a) the bonds are issued on September 1 at 100 and (b) the bonds are issued on June 1 at 105.

E 11.
LO6 Sale of Bonds Between Interest Dates

Margi Corporation sold $400,000 of 12 percent, ten-year bonds at face value on September 1, 20xx. The issue date of the bonds was May 1, 20xx.

1. Record the sale of the bonds on September 1 and the first semiannual interest payment on November 1, 20xx.
2. The company's fiscal year ends on December 31, and this is its only bond issue. What is the bond interest expense for the year ended December 31, 20xx?

E 12.
LO3 Year-End Accrual of Bond
LO5 Interest
LO6

Lon Corporation issued $1,000,000 of 9 percent bonds on October 1, 20x1, at 96. The bonds are dated October 1 and pay interest semiannually. The market interest rate is 10 percent, and Lon's fiscal year ends on December 31. Prepare the entries to record the issuance of the bonds, the accrual of the interest on December 31, 20x1, and the first semiannual interest payment on April 1, 20x2. Assume the company does not use reversing entries and uses the effective interest method to amortize the bond discount.

E 13.
LO4 Time Value of Money and
SO7 Early Estinguishment of Debt

Brown, Inc., has a $1,400,000, 8 percent bond issue that was issued a number of years ago at face value. There are now ten years left on the bond issue, and the market interest rate is 16 percent. Interest is paid semiannually.

1. Using present value tables, figure the current market value of the bond issue.
2. Record the retirement of the bonds, assuming the company purchases the bonds on the open market at the calculated value.

E 14.
SO7 Entry for Bond Retirement

The Pucinski Corporation has outstanding $1,600,000 of 8 percent bonds callable at 104. On September 1, immediately after recording the payment of the semiannual interest and the amortization of the discount, the unamortized bond discount equaled $42,000. On that date, $960,000 of the bonds were called and retired. Prepare the entry to record the retirement of the bonds on September 1.

E 15.
SO7 Entry for Bond Conversion

The Daglar Corporation has $400,000 of 6 percent bonds outstanding. There is $20,000 of unamortized discount remaining on these bonds after the July 1, 20x8, semiannual interest payment. The bonds are convertible at the rate of 40 shares of $5 par value common stock for each $1,000 bond. On July 1, 20x8, bondholders presented $300,000 of the bonds for conversion. Prepare the entry to record the conversion of the bonds.

E 16.
SO8 Mortgage Payable

Fiery Corporation purchased a building by signing a $150,000 long-term mortgage with monthly payments of $2,000. The mortgage carries an interest rate of 12 percent.

1. Prepare a monthly payment schedule showing the monthly payment, the interest for the month, the reduction in debt, and the unpaid balance for the first three months. (Round to the nearest dollar.)
2. Prepare entries in journal form to record the purchase and the first two monthly payments.

E 17.
SO8 Recording Lease Obligations

Foxx Corporation has leased a piece of equipment that has a useful life of 12 years. The terms of the lease are $43,000 per year for 12 years. Foxx currently is able to borrow money at a long-term interest rate of 15 percent. Round answers to the nearest dollar.)

1. Calculate the present value of the lease.
2. Prepare the entry to record the lease agreement.
3. Prepare the entry to record depreciation of the equipment for the first year using the straight-line method.
4. Prepare the entries to record the lease payments for the first two years.

PROBLEMS

P 1.
LO3 Bond Transactions–Straight-
LO5 Line Method
LO6   **REQUIRED ▶**

Gala Corporation has $30,000,000 of 10.5 percent, 20-year bonds dated June 1, with interest payment dates of May 31 and November 30. The company's fiscal year ends on December 31. It uses the straight-line method to amortize bond premiums or discounts.

1. Assume the bonds are issued at 103 on June 1. Prepare entries in journal form for June 1, November 30, and December 31.
2. Assume the bonds are issued at 97 on June 1. Prepare entries in journal form for June 1, November 30, and December 31.
3. Assume the bonds are issued at face value plus accrued interest on August 1. Prepare entries in journal form for August 1, November 30, and December 31.

P 2.

LO3   Bond Transactions–Effective
LO5   Interest Method
LO6

Paco Corporation has $16,000,000 of 9.5 percent, 25-year bonds dated March 1, with interest payable on March 1 and September 1. The company's fiscal year ends on November 30. It uses the effective interest method to amortize bond premiums or discounts. (Round amounts to the nearest dollar.)

REQUIRED ▶

1. Assume the bonds are issued at 102.5 on March 1 to yield an effective interest rate of 9.2 percent. Prepare entries in journal form for March 1, September 1, and November 30.
2. Assume the bonds are issued at 97.5 on March 1 to yield an effective interest rate of 9.8 percent. Prepare entries in journal form for March 1, September 1, and November 30.
3. Assume the bonds are issued on June 1 at face value plus accrued interest. Prepare entries in journal form for June 1, September 1, and November 30.

P 3.

LO3   Bonds Issued at a Discount
LO5   and a Premium
LO6

Reiser Corporation issued bonds twice during 20x4. A summary of the transactions involving the bonds follows.

20x4

Jan.   1   Issued $3,000,000 of 9.9 percent, 10-year bonds dated January 1, 20x4, with interest payable on June 30 and December 31. The bonds were sold at 102.6, resulting in an effective interest rate of 9.4 percent.

Mar.   1   Issued $2,000,000 of 9.2 percent, 10-year bonds dated March 1, 20x4, with interest payable March 1 and September 1. The bonds were sold at 98.2, resulting in an effective interest rate of 9.5 percent.

June 30   Paid semiannual interest on the January 1 issue and amortized the premium, using the effective interest method.

Sept.   1   Paid semiannual interest on the March 1 issue and amortized the discount, using the effective interest method.

Dec. 31   Paid semiannual interest on the January 1 issue and amortized the premium, using the effective interest method.

        31   Made an end-of-year adjusting entry to accrue interest on the March 1 issue and to amortize two-thirds of the discount applicable to the second interest period.

20x5

Mar.   1   Paid semiannual interest on the March 1 issue and amortized the remainder of the discount applicable to the second interest period.

REQUIRED ▶

Prepare entries in journal form to record the bond transactions. (Round amounts to the nearest dollar.)

P 4.

LO3   Bond Interest and
LO5   Amortization Table, and
SO7   Bond Retirements

In 20x1, the Boston Corporation was authorized to issue $60,000,000 of six-year unsecured bonds. The bonds carried a face interest rate of 9 percent, payable semiannually on June 30 and December 31. The bonds were callable at 105 any time after June 30, 20x4. All of the bonds were issued on July 1, 20x1 at 95.568, a price yielding an effective interest rate of 10 percent. On July 1, 20x4, the company called and retired half the outstanding bonds.

REQUIRED ▶

1. Prepare a table similar to Table 1 to show the interest and amortization of the bond discount for 12 interest payment periods, using the effective interest method. (Round results to the nearest dollar.)
2. Calculate the amount of loss on early retirement of one-half of the bonds on July 1, 20x4.

P 5.

LO3   Comprehensive Bond
LO5   Transactions
LO6
SO7

The Ingolls Corporation, a company whose fiscal year ends on June 30, engaged in the following long-term bond transactions over a three-year period:

20x3

Nov.   1   Issued $40,000,000 of 12 percent debenture bonds at face value plus accrued interest. Interest is payable on January 31 and July 31, and the bonds are callable at 104.

20x4

Jan. 31   Made the semiannual interest payment on the 12 percent bonds.
June 30   Made the year-end accrual of interest payment on the 12 percent bonds.
July   1   Issued $20,000,000 of 10 percent, 15-year convertible bonds at 105. Interest is payable on June 30 and December 31, and each $1,000 bond is convertible into 30 shares of $10 par value common stock. The market rate of interest is 9 percent.

July 31   Made the semiannual interest payment on the 12 percent bonds.
Dec. 31   Made the semiannual interest payment on the 10 percent bonds and amortized the bond premium.

20x5
Jan.   31   Made the semiannual interest payment on the 12 percent bonds.
Feb.   28   Called and retired all of the 12 percent bonds, including accrued interest.
June 30   Made the semiannual interest payment on the 10 percent bonds and amortized the bond premium.
July   1   Accepted for conversion into common stock all of the 10 percent bonds.

REQUIRED ▶ Prepare entries in journal form to record the bond transactions, making all necessary accruals and using the effective interest method. (Round all calculations to the nearest dollar.)

ALTERNATE PROBLEMS

P 6.
LO3 Bond Transactions–Straight-
LO5 Line Method
LO6

Raol Corporation has $4,000,000 of 9.5 percent, 25-year bonds dated March 1, with interest payable on March 1 and September 1. The company's fiscal year ends on November 30, and it uses the straight-line method to amortize bond premiums or discounts.

REQUIRED ▶
1. Assume the bonds are issued at 103.5 on March 1. Prepare entries in journal form for March 1, September 1, and November 30.
2. Assume the bonds are issued at 96.5 on March 1. Prepare entries in journal form for March 1, September 1, and November 30.
3. Assume the bonds are issued on June 1 at face value plus accrued interest. Prepare entries in journal form for June 1, September 1, and November 30.

P 7.
LO3 Bond Transactions–Effective
LO5 Interest Method
LO6

Dubchec Corporation has $10,000,000 of 10.5 percent, 20-year bonds dated June 1, with interest payment dates of May 31 and November 30. The company's fiscal year ends December 31. It uses the effective interest method to amortize bond premiums or discounts.

REQUIRED ▶
1. Assume the bonds are issued at 103 on June 1 to yield an effective interest rate of 10.1 percent. Prepare entries in journal form for June 1, November 30, and December 31. (Round amounts to the nearest dollar.)
2. Assume the bonds are issued at 97 on June 1 to yield an effective interest rate of 10.9 percent. Prepare entries in journal form for June 1, November 30, and December 31. (Round amounts to the nearest dollar.)
3. Assume the bonds are issued at face value plus accrued interest on August 1. Prepare entries in journal form for August 1, November 30, and December 31. (Round amounts to the nearest dollar.)

P 8.
LO3 Bonds Issued at a Discount
LO5 and a Premium
LO6

Fils Corporation issued bonds twice during 20x3. The transactions were as follows:

20x3
Jan.   1   Issued $1,000,000 of 9.2 percent, 10-year bonds dated January 1, 20x3, with interest payable on June 30 and December 31. The bonds were sold at 98.1, resulting in an effective interest rate of 9.5 percent.
Apr.   1   Issued $2,000,000 of 9.8 percent, 10-year bonds dated April 1, 20x3, with interest payable on March 31 and September 30. The bonds were sold at 102, resulting in an effective interest rate of 9.5 percent.
June 30   Paid semiannual interest on the January 1 issue and amortized the discount, using the effective interest method.
Sept. 30   Paid semiannual interest on the April 1 issue and amortized the premium, using the effective interest method.
Dec. 31   Paid semiannual interest on the January 1 issue and amortized the discount, using the effective interest method.
        31   Made an end-of-year adjusting entry to accrue interest on the April 1 issue and to amortize half the premium applicable to the second interest period.

20x4
Mar. 31   Paid semiannual interest on the April 1 issue and amortized the premium applicable to the second half of the second interest period.

REQUIRED ▶ Prepare entries in journal form to record the bond transactions. (Round amounts to the nearest dollar.)

SKILLS DEVELOPMENT CASES

Conceptual Analysis

SD 1.

LO3 **Bond Interest Rates and Market Prices**

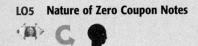

Safeway Inc. <www.safeway.com> is one of the largest food and drug retailers in North America. Among its long-term liabilities is a bond due in 2004 that carries a face interest rate of 9.65 percent. Recently this bond sold on the New York Stock Exchange at 108⅜. Does this bond sell at a discount or a premium? Assuming the bond was originally issued at face value, have interest rates risen or declined since the date of issue? Do you expect the market rate of interest on this bond to be more or less than 9.65 percent? Does the current market price affect either the amount that the company pays in semi-annual interest or the amount of interest expense for the same period? Explain your answers.

SD 2.

LO5 **Nature of Zero Coupon Notes**

The Wall Street Journal reported, "Financially ailing Trans World Airlines has renegotiated its agreement to sell its 40 landing and takeoff slots and three gates at O'Hare International Airport to American Airlines." Instead of receiving a lump-sum cash payment in the amount of $162.5 million, TWA elected to receive a zero coupon note from American <www.aa.com> that would be paid off in monthly installments over a 20-year period. Since the 240 monthly payments totaled $500 million, TWA placed a value of $500 million on the note and indicated that the bankruptcy court would not have accepted the lower lump-sum cash payment.

How does this zero coupon note differ from the zero coupon bonds that we described earlier in this chapter? Explain the difference between the $162.5 million cash payment and the $500 million note. Do you think TWA was right in placing a $500 million price on the sale?[12]

SD 3.

SO8 **Lease Financing**

FedEx Corporation <www.fedex.com>, known for overnight delivery and distribution of high-priority goods and documents throughout the world, has an extensive fleet of aircraft and vehicles. In its 2001 annual report, the company stated that it "utilizes certain aircraft, land, facilities, and equipment under capital and operating leases which expire at various dates through 2038. In addition, supplemental aircraft are leased under agreements which generally provide for cancellation upon 30 days' notice." The annual report further stated that the minimum commitments for capital leases and noncancelable operating leases for 2002 were $15,416,000 and $1,246,936,000, respectively.[13] What is the difference between a capital lease and an operating lease? How do the accounting procedures for the two types of leases differ? How do you interpret management's reasoning in acquiring some aircraft under capital leases and others under operating leases? Why do you think the management of FedEx leases most of its aircraft instead of buying them?

Ethical Dilemma

SD 4.

LO2 **Bond Indenture and Ethical Reporting**

CellWorks Technology, Inc., a biotech company, has a $24,000,000 bond issue outstanding. The bond indenture has several restrictive provisions, including requirements that current assets exceed current liabilities by a ratio of 2 to 1 and that income before income taxes exceed the annual interest on the bonds by a ratio of 3 to 1. If those requirements are not met, the bondholders can force the company into bankruptcy. The company is still awaiting Food and Drug Administration (FDA) approval of its new product CMZ-12, a cancer treatment drug. Management had been counting on sales of CMZ-12 this year to meet the provisions of the bond indenture. As the end of the fiscal year approaches, the company does not have sufficient current assets or income before taxes to meet the requirements. Roger Landon, the chief financial officer, proposes, "Since we can assume that FDA approval will occur early next year, I suggest we book sales and receivables from our major customers now in anticipation of next year's sales. This action will increase our current assets and our income before taxes. It is essential that we do this to save the company. Look at all the people who will be hurt if we don't do it."

Is Landon's proposal acceptable accounting? Is it ethical? Who could be harmed by it? What steps might management take?

Research Activity

SD 5.
LO3   Reading the Bond Markets

Obtain a recent issue of *The Wall Street Journal* and turn to the page on which the New York Exchange Bonds are listed. Notice, first, the Dow Jones Bond Averages of 20 bonds, ten utilities, and ten industrials. Are the averages above or below 100? Is this a premium or a discount? Is the market interest rate above or below the face rate of the average bond? Now, choose three bonds from those listed—one that sells at a discount, one that sells at a premium, and one that sells for approximately 100. For each bond, write the name of the company, the face interest rate, the year the bond is due, the current yield (market rate of interest), and the current closing market price. (Some bonds have the letters *cv* in the Yield column, which means the bonds are convertible into common stock and the yield may not be meaningful.) For each bond, explain the relationships between the face interest rate, the current yield, and the closing price. What other factors affect the current yield of a bond? Be prepared to discuss your findings in class.

Decision-Making Practice

SD 6.
LO1   Issuance of Long-Term Bonds
LO2   Versus Leasing
SO8

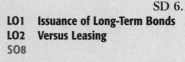

The Weiss Chemical Corporation plans to build or lease a new plant that will produce liquid fertilizer for the agricultural market. The plant is expected to cost $800,000,000 and will be located in the southwestern United States. The company's chief financial officer, Sharon Weiss, has spent the last several weeks studying different means of financing the plant. From her talks with bankers and other financiers, she has decided that there are two basic choices: the plant can be financed through the issuance of a long-term bond or through a long-term lease. Details for the two options are as follows:

1. Issue $800,000,000 of 25-year, 16 percent bonds secured by the new plant. Interest on the bonds would be payable semiannually.
2. Sign a 25-year lease for an existing plant calling for lease payments of $65,400,000 on a semiannual basis.

Weiss wants to know what the effect of each choice will be on the company's financial statements. She estimates that the useful life of the plant is 25 years, at which time it is expected to have an estimated residual value of $80,000,000.

Weiss plans a meeting to discuss the alternatives. Write a short memorandum to her identifying the issues that should be considered at this meeting. (**Note:** You are not asked to make any calculations, discuss the factors, or recommend an action.)

FINANCIAL REPORTING AND ANALYSIS CASES

Interpreting Financial Reports

FRA 1.
LO1   Debt Repayment

During economic recessions, occupancy rates of hotels generally decline, and the hotels are forced to reduce their room prices. The impact on a hotel's cash flows may be such that it is unable to pay its debts when they come due. A recent study of the financial statements of 3,300 hotels by the Hospitality Research Group found that 16 percent of hotels were unable to generate enough cash from operations to make debt repayments in 2000. The group estimates that this figure will increase to 20.9 percent in 2001 and 36.5 percent in 2002.[14] What alternative sources of cash might be available to hotels whose cash flows from operations are inadequate to cover debt repayments?

FRA 2.
SO7   Characteristics of Convertible
Debt

Amazon.com, Inc. <www.amazon.com>, gained renown as an online marketplace for books, records, and other products. Although the increase in its stock price was initially meteoric, the company has yet to earn a profit. To support its enormous growth, the company issued $1,250,000,000 in 4¾ percent convertible notes due in 2009 at face value. Interest is payable on February 1 and August 1. The notes are convertible into common stock at a price of $156 per share, which is 27 percent above the market price of $123 for the common stock on the date of issue. The market value of Amazon.com's common stock has been quite volatile; earlier it was $200 per share.[15]

REQUIRED ▶   What reasons can you suggest for Amazon.com's management choosing notes that are convertible into common stock rather than simply issuing nonconvertible notes or issuing common stock directly? Are there any disadvantages to this approach? If the price of the company's common stock returns to $200 per share, what would be the total theoretical value of the notes? If the holders of the notes were to elect to convert the notes into common stock, what would be the effect on the company's debt to equity ratio, and what would be the effect on the percentage ownership of the company by other stockholders?

International Company

FRA 3.

LO1 Comparison of Interest Coverage

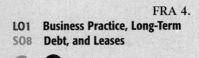

Japanese companies have historically relied more on debt financing and are more highly leveraged than U.S. companies. For instance, NEC Corporation <www.nec.com> and Sanyo Electric Co. <www.sanyo.com>, two large Japanese electronics companies, had debt to equity ratios of about 4.3 and 3.5, respectively, in 2001. From the selected data from the companies' annual reports shown below (in millions of yen), compute the interest coverage ratios for the two companies for the two years. Comment on the riskiness of the companies and on the trends they show.[16]

	NEC		Sanyo	
	2001	2000	2001	2000
Interest expense	63,873	70,211	26,427	27,914
Income before income taxes	92,323	30,183	73,484	36,953

Group Activity: Assign the two companies to different groups to calculate the ratios and discuss the results. Debrief by discussing the advantages and disadvantages of a debt-laden capital structure.

Toys "R" Us Annual Report

FRA 4.

LO1 Business Practice, Long-Term
SO8 Debt, and Leases

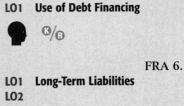

Refer to the financial statements and the notes to the financial statements in the Toys "R" Us <www.tru.com> annual report to answer the following questions:

1. Is it the practice of Toys "R" Us to own or lease most of its property and equipment?
2. Does Toys "R" Us lease property predominantly under capital leases or under operating leases? How much was rental expense for operating leases in 2001?

Comparison Case: Toys "R" Us and Walgreen Co.

FRA 5.

LO1 Use of Debt Financing

Refer to the annual report of Toys "R" Us <www.tru.com> and the financial statements of Walgreens <www.walgreens.com>. Calculate the debt to equity ratio and the interest coverage ratio for both companies' most recent two years. Evaluate and comment on the relative performance of the two companies with regard to debt financing. Which company has more risk of not being able to meet its interest obligations? Explain.

FRA 6.

LO1 Long-Term Liabilities
LO2
SO8

Fingraph® Financial Analyst™

Select any two companies from the same industry from the list of Fingraph companies on the Needles Accounting Resource Center Web Site at http://accounting. college.hmco.com/students. Access the Microsoft Excel spreadsheets for the companies you selected. For parts 1, 3, and 4, click on the URL at the top of each company's spreadsheet for a link to the company's web site and annual report.

1. In the annual reports of the companies you have selected, identify the long-term liabilities on the balance sheet and read any reference to long-term liabilities in the summary of significant accounting policies or notes to the financial statements. There is likely to be a separate note for each type of long-term liability. What are the most important long-term liabilities for each company?
2. Using the Fingraph CD-ROM software, display and print in tabular and graphic form the Balance Sheet Analysis page. Prepare a table that compares the debt to equity and interest coverage ratios for both companies for two years.
3. Read the statements of cash flows in both annual reports. Have the companies been increasing or decreasing their long-term debt? If increasing, what were each com-

pany's most important sources of long-term financing over the past two years? If decreasing, which liabilities are being decreased?

4. Find and read references to long-term liabilities in management's discussion and analysis in each annual report.

5. Write a one-page executive summary that highlights the most important types of long-term liabilities for these companies, identifies their accounting policies for specific long-term liabilities, and compares their debt to equity and interest coverage trends. The summary should refer to management's assessment. Include the Fingraph page and your table with your report.

Internet Case

FRA 7.

LO2   Bond Rating Changes

Go to the Needles Accounting Resource Center Web Site at http://accounting. college.hmco.com/students. Under Web Links, select Standard & Poor's or access their web site directly at <www.standardandpoors.com>. In times of economic or industry recessions, it is common to see downward revisions of bond ratings. From the Standard & Poor's list of companies with lowered bond ratings, identify three whose names you recognize. For each company, give reasons that you believe contributed to the ratings downgrade.

Chapter 12 focuses on long-term equity financing, including the types of equity securities and transactions that affect the stockholders' equity section of the balance sheet, such as stock issues, dividends, and treasury stock purchases.

Contributed Capital

LEARNING OBJECTIVES

LO1 Identify and explain the management issues related to contributed capital.

LO2 Identify the components of stockholders' equity.

LO3 Account for cash dividends.

LO4 Identify the characteristics of preferred stock, including the effect on distribution of dividends.

LO5 Account for the issuance of stock for cash and other assets.

LO6 Account for treasury stock.

DECISION POINT
A USER'S FOCUS

Cisco Systems, Inc. <www.cisco.com> One way corporations raise new capital is by issuing stock. Cisco Systems, Inc., a major manufacturer, of telecommunications equipment, issued over $3.7 billion of common stock in a recent three-year period, as shown in the Financial Highlights on the opposite page.[1] Why does Cisco Systems' management choose to issue common stock to satisfy some of its needs for new capital? What are some of the advantages and disadvantages of this approach?

Financing with common stock has several advantages. First, it is less risky than financing with bonds because dividends on common stock are not paid unless the board of directors decides to pay them. Cisco Systems does not currently pay any dividends. In contrast, if the interest on bonds is not paid, a company can be forced into bankruptcy. Second, when a company does not pay a cash dividend, the cash generated by profitable operations can be invested in the company's operations. Third, a company may need the proceeds of a common stock issue to maintain or improve the balance between liabilities and stockholders' equity. By issuing common stock in 2001, Cisco Systems offset the impact on stockholders' equity of a $1 billion net loss in 2001. The balance between total liabilities and total equity remains a relatively low 30 percent.

On the other hand, issuing common stock comes with certain disadvantages. Unlike the interest on bonds, dividends paid on stock are not tax-deductible. Furthermore, when it issues more stock, the corpora-

Why does Cisco Systems, Inc. choose to issue common stock to satisfy some of its needs for new capital?

tion dilutes its ownership. This means that the current stockholders must yield some control to the new stockholders. It is important for accountants to understand the nature and characteristics of corporations as well as the process of accounting for a stock issue and other types of stock transactions.

Financial Highlights

(In millions)

	2001	2000	1999
Issuance of common stock	$1,262	$1,564	$947

MANAGEMENT ISSUES RELATED TO CONTRIBUTED CAPITAL

LO1 Identify and explain the management issues related to contributed capital.

RELATED TEXT ASSIGNMENTS

Q: 1, 2, 3, 4, 5, 6, 7, 8, 9
SE: 1, 2, 3, 4
E: 1
P: 1, 2, 3, 4, 5, 6, 7, 8
SD: 1, 4, 5, 6
FRA: 1, 4, 5, 6, 7

A corporation is defined as a body of persons granted a charter recognizing them as a separate legal entity having its own rights, privileges, and liabilities distinct from those of its members.[2] In other words, a corporation is a legal entity separate and distinct from its owners.

The management of contributed capital is a critical component in the financing of a corporation. Important issues faced by management in the area of contributed capital are managing under the corporate form of business, using equity financing, determining dividend policies, evaluating performance using return on equity, and using stock options as compensation.

MANAGING UNDER THE CORPORATE FORM OF BUSINESS

Although sole proprietorships and partnerships outnumber corporations in the United States, corporations dominate the economy in total dollars of assets and output of goods and services. Corporations are well suited to today's trends toward large organizations, international trade, and professional management. Figure 1 shows the amount and sources of new funds raised by corporations in recent years.

FIGURE 1
Sources of Capital Raised by Corporations in the United States

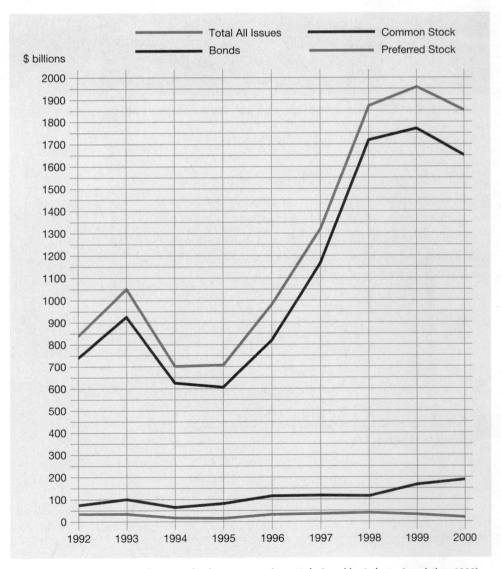

Source: Data from *Securities Industry Yearbook 1999–2000* (New York: Securities Industry Association, 1999), p. 895.

Lotus Development Corporation
<www.lotus.com>

OBJECTIVES

- To become familiar with the advantages of a corporation, especially in equity financing
- To identify the ways investors obtain return on investment in a corporation
- To show how stock buybacks affect return on equity as a measure of profitability

BACKGROUND FOR THE CASE

The story of software giant Lotus Development Corporation is a prototype of the recent history of high-technology com-

panies. When Lotus was founded in the early 1980s, its landmark spreadsheet program The program was an overnight sensation at corporations because of its ability to make rapid calculations based on mathematical relationships in large databases. The program went far beyond the rudimentary spreadsheets that preceded it by incorporating a database module and graphics capability. In October 1983, investors stampeded for the company's initial public offering of 2.6 million shares at $18 per share, for a total of $46.8 million. For several years, the company had no real competition. By 1992, it had sold more than 11 million units of Lotus 1-2-3, but it was unable to solidify its position by developing any new blockbuster products. Microsoft gained on Lotus and eventually passed it with its spreadsheet program Excel. Finally, Lotus developed a hit "groupware" product called Lotus Notes, which boosts productivity by enabling workers to share information and collaborate electronically on complex tasks. For example, the large audit firm Pricewaterhouse-Coopers <www.pwcglobal.com> networks more than 2,000 auditors all over the world and the knowledge of

experts in various parts of the firm via Lotus Notes. Other big companies, such as Citigroup <www.citigroup.com>, Ford <www.ford.com>, and Unilever <www.unilever.com> also use Lotus Notes. The success of Lotus Notes attracted the notice of IBM <www.ibm.com>, which had failed to develop its own groupware product. In 1995, IBM made a hostile takeover bid for Lotus and bought out the company. In fewer than 15 years, Lotus had gone from an intriguing start-up to a mature company with sales of more than $1 billion and, finally, to being a takeover candidate for a giant competitor.

For more information about Lotus, which is now a division of IBM, visit the company's or IBM's web site through the Needles Accounting Resource Center Web Site at **http://accounting.college.hmco.com/students**.

REQUIRED

View the video on Lotus Development Corporation that accompanies this book. As you are watching the video, take notes related to the following questions:

1. All corporations must raise equity capital in the form of common stock. In your own words, what is common stock? What is the relationship of par value to market value of common stock? What is an initial public offering (IPO)? Why was Lotus's IPO important in the company's early history?

2. Investors in corporations want to receive an adequate return on their investment. What are the ways in which investors can receive a return? In what way did Lotus's shareholders receive a return?

3. From 1991 to 1993, Lotus's board of directors authorized the repurchase of 7,700,000 shares of the company's approximately 44,000,000 shares. What impact did the repurchase of these shares have on the investors' return? What role did the takeover by IBM play in achieving an adequate return for Lotus's shareholders?

4. Return on equity is a common measure of management's ability to meet the company's profitability goal. What role do common stock buybacks (purchases of treasury stock) play in a company's increasing return on equity?

The amount raised increased dramatically after 1995. In 2000, the amount of new corporate capital was $1,851.0 billion, of which $1,646.6 billion, or 89 percent, came from new bond issues; $189.1 billion, or 10 percent, came from new common stock issues; and $15.4 billion, or 1 percent, came from preferred stock issues.

In managing a corporation, the advantages and disadvantages of this form of business must be considered. Some of the advantages are as follows:

- **Separate Legal Entity**   A corporation is a separate legal entity. As such, it can buy, sell, or own property; sue and be sued; enter into contracts; hire and fire employees; and be taxed.

- **Limited Liability**   Because a corporation is a separate legal entity, it is responsible for its own actions and liabilities. This means that a corporation's creditors can satisfy their claims only against the assets of the corporation, not against the personal property of the corporation's owners. Because the owners are not responsible for the corporation's debts, their liability is limited to the amount of their investment. The personal property of sole proprietors and partners, however, generally is available to creditors.

- **Ease of Capital Generation**   It is fairly easy for a corporation to raise capital because shares of ownership in the business are available to a great number of potential investors for a small amount of money. As a result, a single corporation can be owned by many people.

- **Ease of Transfer of Ownership**   A share of stock, a unit of ownership in a corporation, is transferable. A stockholder can normally buy and sell shares without affecting the corporation's activities or needing the approval of other owners.

- **Lack of Mutual Agency**   There is no mutual agency in the corporate form of business. If a stockholder, acting as an owner, tries to enter into a contract for the corporation, the corporation is not bound by the contract. But in a partnership, because of mutual agency, all the partners can be bound by one partner's actions.

- **Continuous Existence**   Because a corporation is a separate legal entity, an owner's death, incapacity, or withdrawal does not affect the life of the corporation. The life of a corporation is set by its charter and regulated by state laws.

- **Centralized Authority and Responsibility**   The board of directors represents the stockholders and delegates the responsibility and authority for the day-to-day operation of the corporation to a single person, usually the president. Operating power is not divided among the many owners of the business. The president may delegate authority over certain segments of the business to others, but he or she is held accountable to the board of directors. If the board is dissatisfied with the performance of the president, it can replace him or her.

- **Professional Management**   Large corporations are owned by many people, the vast majority of whom are unequipped to make timely decisions about business operations. So, in most cases, management and ownership are separate. This allows a corporation to hire the best talent available to manage the business.

The disadvantages of a corporation are as follows:

- **Government Regulation**   Corporations must meet the requirements of state laws. As "creatures of the state," corporations are subject to greater control and regulation by the state than are other forms of business. They must file many reports with the state in which they are chartered. Also, publicly held corporations must file reports with the Securities and Exchange Commission and with the stock exchanges. Meeting those requirements is very costly.

- **Taxation**   A major disadvantage of the corporate form of business is **double taxation**. Because a corporation is a separate legal entity, its earnings are subject to federal and state income taxes, which may be as much as 35 percent of corporate earnings. If any of the corporation's after-tax earnings are then paid out as dividends, the earnings are taxed again as income to the stockholders. In contrast, the earnings of sole proprietorships and partnerships are taxed only once, as personal income to the owners.

- **Limited Liability**   Although limited liability is an advantage of incorporation, it also can be a disadvantage. Limited liability restricts the ability of a small corporation to borrow money. Because creditors can lay claim only to the assets of the corporation, they limit their loans to the level secured by those assets or ask stockholders to guarantee the loans personally.

- **Separation of Ownership and Control**   Just as limited liability can be a drawback, so can the separation of ownership and control. Management sometimes makes decisions that are not good for the corporation as a whole. Poor communication can also make it hard for stockholders to exercise control over the corporation or even to recognize that management's decisions are harmful.

USING EQUITY FINANCING

A **share of stock** is a unit of ownership in a corporation. A **stock certificate** is issued to the owner. It shows the number of shares of the corporation's stock that the stockholder owns. Stockholders can transfer their ownership at will. When they do, they must sign their stock certificate and send it to the corporation's secretary. In large corporations that are listed on the organized stock exchanges, stockholders' records are hard to maintain. Such companies can have millions of shares of stock, thousands of which change ownership every day. Therefore, they often appoint independent registrars and transfer agents (usually banks and trust companies) to help perform the secretary's duties. The outside agents are responsible for transferring the corporation's stock, maintaining stockholders' records, preparing a list of stockholders for stockholders' meetings, and paying dividends.

When a corporation applies for a charter, the articles of incorporation specify the maximum number of shares of stock the corporation is allowed to issue. This number represents **authorized stock**. Most corporations are authorized to issue more shares of stock than are necessary at the time of organization, which allows for future stock issues to raise additional capital. For example, Cisco Systems has 20 billion shares of stock authorized and only 7.3 billion shares issued. If Cisco Systems needs cash to expand in the future, it can sell its unissued shares. If a corporation issues all of its authorized stock, it cannot issue more stock without a change in its state charter.

www.cisco.com

KEY POINT: Par value is usually a small amount, $.01 up to $10. The amount is arbitrary and has primarily legal significance.

The charter also shows the par value of the stock that has been authorized. **Par value** is an arbitrary amount assigned to each share of stock. It must be recorded in the capital stock accounts and constitutes the legal capital of a corporation. **Legal capital** equals the number of shares issued times the par value; it is the minimum amount that can be reported as contributed capital. Par value usually bears little if any relationship to the market value or book value of the shares. The par value of Cisco Systems' common stock is only $.001 per share, and its legal capital is $7.3 million (7.3 billion shares × $.001). When a corporation is formed, a memorandum entry may be made in the general journal giving the number and description of authorized shares.

ENRICHMENT NOTE:
In effect, the underwriter buys the stock from the corporation at a set price. The stock price in the secondary markets can be above or below the commitment to the corporation. Thus, the underwriter can gain or lose on the transaction and is exposed to a certain amount of risk.

www.gs.com

■ **INITIAL PUBLIC OFFERING** To help with the initial issue of capital stock, called an **initial public offering (IPO)**, a corporation often uses an **underwriter**—an intermediary between the corporation and the investing public. For a fee—usually less than 1 percent of the selling price—the underwriter guarantees the sale of the stock. The corporation records the amount of the net proceeds of the offering—what the public paid less the underwriter's fees, legal and printing expenses, and any other direct costs of the offering—in its capital stock and additional paid-in capital accounts. When Goldman, Sachs, & Co., the renowned 130-year-old investment bank, recently went public, it had one of the largest IPOs ever recorded, amounting to about $3.6 billion.

■ **START-UP AND ORGANIZATION COSTS** The costs of forming a corporation are called **start-up and organization costs**. Such costs, which are incurred before the corporation begins operations, include state incorporation fees and attorneys' fees for drawing up the articles of incorporation. They also include the cost of printing stock certificates, accountants' fees for services rendered in registering the firm's initial stock, and other expenditures that are necessary for the formation of the corporation.

KEY POINT: Start-up and organization costs are expensed when incurred.

Theoretically, start-up and organization costs benefit the entire life of the corporation. For that reason, a case can be made for recording them as intangible assets and amortizing them over the years of the life of the corporation. However, the life of a corporation normally is not known, so accountants expense start-up and organization costs as they are incurred.[3]

FIGURE 2
Stock Quotations on the New York Stock Exchange

NYSE COMPOSITE TRANSACTIONS

YTD % CHG	52 WEEKS HI	LO	STOCK (SYM)	DIV	YLD %	PE	VOL 100S	LAST	NET CHG
+ 3.7	21.46	14.75	AT&T **T** s	.15	.8	9	111752	18.82	−0.09
▼ −18.0	27.30	11.29	AT&T Wrls **AWE**	...	...	...	160850	11.79	+0.33
−11.0	25.40	14.51	AVX Cp **AVX**	.15	.7	31	3978	20.99	−0.19
− 3.9	34.75	15.40	✦ AXA ADS **AXA** s	.50e	2.5	...	3966	20.20	+0.55
− 0.1	25.79	14.20	AZZ **AZZ**	.16	.8	13	44	21.09	+0.29
− 8.3	19.50	13.55	AaronRent **RNT**	.04	.3	18	1615	14.95	−0.65
− 6.3	16.50	10.50	AaronRent A **RNTA**	.04	.3	15	508	12.65	+2.15
+10.2	18.95	6.10	ABB ADS **ABB** n	...	...	...	85	10.37	−0.13
+ 0.8	25.12	23.06	AbbeyNtl **SUA**	1.75	7.0	...	130	24.99	+0.01
+ 2.2	25.85	24.75	AbbeyNtl ADS **ANBB** n	...	...	...	905	25.75	+0.05
+ 1.7	25.80	24	AbbeyNtl 7 1/4% **SUD**	1.81	7.1	...	30	25.33	+0.01
▲+ 2.0	25.70	24.70	AbbeyNtl Nts **SXA** n	.49e	1.9	...	457	25.60	+0.15
...	57.17	42.25	AbbottLab **ABT**	.84	1.5	52	26990	55.77	−0.12
− 5.9	47.50	16.21	Abercrombie A **ANF**	...	...	15	16297	24.97	−0.49
+ 0.7	9.21	6.06	Abitibi g **ABY**	.40g	...	...	798	7.37	−0.03
+ 2.4	7.22	5.80	✦ AcadiaRlty **AKR**	.48	7.4	13	104	6.50	+0.11
− 5.7	28.34	11.61	Accenture **ACN** n	...	...	...	39870	25.39	+0.45
+ 2.2	6.05	3.70	✦ Acceptlns **AIF**	...	...	dd	136	5.20	+0.02
+ 2.3	18.46	8.50	AckrlyGp **AK**	.02	.1	11	378	17.90	+0.27

Source: Stock quotations on the New York Stock Exchange (1/16/02), from *Wall Street Journal*. Copyright 2002 by Dow Jones & Co. Inc. Reproduced with permission of Dow Jones & Co. Inc. in the format texbook via Copyright Clearance Center.

DETERMINING DIVIDEND POLICIES

A **dividend** is a distribution among stockholders of the assets that a corporation's earnings have generated. Each stockholder receives these assets, usually cash, in proportion to the number of shares of stock held. The board of directors has sole authority to declare dividends, but the dividend policies are influenced by senior managers, who usually serve as members of the board. Receiving dividends from a corporation is one of two ways in which stockholders can earn a return on their investment in the company. The other way is to sell their shares of stock for more than they paid for them.

Investors evaluate the amount of dividends received with the ratio **dividends yield**. Dividends yield measures the current return to an investor in the form of dividends and is computed by dividing the dividends per share by the market price per share. For instance, the dividends yield (shown in Figure 2) for Abbott Laboratories, a large, successful pharmaceutical company, is computed as follows:

www.abbott.com

$$\text{Dividends Yield} = \frac{\text{Dividends per Share}}{\text{Market Price per Share}} = \frac{\$.84}{\$55.77} = 1.5\%$$

Since the yield on corporate bonds exceeds 7 percent, the shareholders of Abbott Labs must expect some of their return to come from increases in the price of the shares.

A measure of investors' confidence in a company's future is the **price/earnings (P/E) ratio**, which is calculated by dividing the market price per share by the earnings per share. The price/earnings ratio will vary as market price per share fluctuates daily and the amount of earnings per share changes. Figure 2 shows a P/E ratio of 52 for Abbott Labs. It was computed using the most recent annual earnings per share, as follows:

$$\text{Price/Earnings (P/E) Ratio} = \frac{\text{Market Price per Share}}{\text{Earnings per Share}} = \frac{\$55.77}{\$1.08} = 52 \text{ times}$$

Since the market price is 52 times earnings, investors are paying a high price in relation to earnings. They do so in the expectation that this drug company will continue

ENRICHMENT NOTE: Due to the rise in prices of stocks during the 1990s, the average dividends yield has declined and the average P/E ratio has increased.

to be successful. Caution must be taken in interpreting high P/E ratios because unusually low earnings can produce a high result.

www.apple.com
Companies usually pay dividends to stockholders only when they have had profitable operations. For example, Apple Computer, Inc., paid a dividend beginning in 1987 but suspended its dividend payments in 1996 to conserve cash after large operating losses in 1995. Factors other than earnings affect the decision to pay dividends. First, a company may change its dividend policy to bring it into line with the prevailing industry policy. For example, despite positive earnings, AT&T Corporation slashed its dividends 83 percent. This action put AT&T's policy more in line with the policies of its peers in the telecommunications industry, most of which do not pay dividends.[4] Second, the expected volatility of earnings is a factor. If a company has years of good earnings followed by years of poor earnings, the board may want to keep dividends low to avoid giving a false impression of sustained high earnings. For years, General Motors Corporation followed the practice of having a fairly stable dividend yield and paying a bonus dividend in especially good years. Third, the level of dividends affects cash flows. Some companies may not have the cash to pay higher dividends because operations are not generating cash at the level of earnings or because the companies are investing the cash in future operations. For instance, Abbott Labs pays a dividend of $.84 per share on earnings of $1.08 per share. Management believes a portion of the cash generated by the earnings is better spent for other purposes, such as researching and developing new drugs that will generate revenue in the future. It is partly due to Abbott's investment in new products that stockholders are willing to pay a high price for its stock. In recent years, because the tax rates are more favorable to capital gains made by selling shares than to dividend income, many investors have shown a preference for companies like Cisco Systems that have strong earnings growth but that pay no dividends.

www.att.com

www.gm.com

www.cisco.com

EVALUATING PERFORMANCE USING RETURN ON EQUITY

Return on equity is the most important ratio associated with stockholders' equity because it is a common measure of management's performance. For instance, when *Business Week* and *Forbes* rate companies on their success, return on equity is the major basis of their evaluations. Also, the compensation of top executives is often tied to return on equity benchmarks. This ratio is computed for Abbott Labs from information in the company's 2000 annual report, as follows:[5]

www.abbott.com

$$\text{Return on Equity} = \frac{\text{Net Income}}{\text{Average Stockholders' Equity}}$$

$$= \frac{\$2,785,977,000}{(\$7,427,595,000 + \$8,570,906,000) \div 2}$$

$$= 34.8\%$$

KEY POINT: A company can improve its return on equity by increasing net income or by reducing average stockholders' equity.

Abbott Labs' healthy return on equity of 34.8 percent depends, of course, on the amount of net income the company earns. But it also depends on the level of stockholders' equity, which depends, in turn, on management decisions about the amount of stock the company sells to the public. Management can keep the stockholders' equity at a minimum by financing the business with cash flows from operations and with debt instead of with stock. However, the use of debt to finance the business increases a company's risk because the interest and principal of the debt must be paid in a timely manner. In the case of common stock, dividends may be suspended if there is a cash shortage. Abbott Labs has a debt to equity ratio of 78.3% and thus is taking advantage of the leverage provided by debt.

In addition, management can reduce the number of shares in the hands of the public by buying back the company's shares on the open market. The cost of these shares, which are called *treasury stock*, has the effect of reducing the amount of stockholders' equity and thereby increasing the return on equity. Many companies follow this practice instead of paying or increasing dividends. Their reason for doing

FOCUS ON BUSINESS PRACTICE

When Are Stock Options Worthless? Apparently Never!

Stock options are supposed to reward employees for good performance. They also act as an incentive for continued good performance, thus aligning the interests of owners and employees. When stock prices rise, the rewards can be handsome; some executives have made staggering sums on stock options. For example, the CEO of Cisco Systems <www.cisco.com> made $156 million in option-related profits in fiscal 2000, dwarfing his salary of about $1.3 million. To keep employees happy when stock prices decline, companies often change the stock-option rules to accommodate them. When their stock prices fell, Amazon <www.amazon.com>, Sprint Corp. <www.sprint.com>, and Real Networks Inc. <www.realnetworks.com> repriced options at a lower value or allowed employees to turn in worthless options to be issued later at a lower price. Yet other companies let employees cancel already exercised options. Actions like these anger owners who believe employees should be held accountable for the company's poor performance and not rewarded for unsatisfactory results.[6]

so is that it puts money into the hands of stockholders in the form of market price appreciation without creating a commitment to higher dividends in the future. For example, during the three years ended 2000, Abbott Labs purchased its common stock at a cost of $1.3 billion.[7] Abbott Labs' stock repurchases improved the company's return on equity, increased its earnings per share, and lowered its price/earnings ratio.

USING STOCK OPTIONS AS COMPENSATION

● **STOP AND THINK!**

Why do companies like to give options as compensation?

Companies do not have to record compensation expense on stock options, which can improve profitability. (There is a proposal to change this rule.) Also, salaries require a cash outflow, but stock options do not. Finally, companies get a tax deduction for the difference between the option price and the market price on the exercise date. Tax deductions decrease taxes owed and increase cash flows. ■

More than 97 percent of public companies encourage the ownership of their common stock through a **stock option plan**, which is an agreement to issue stock to employees according to specified terms.[8] In most cases, the stock option plan gives employees the right to purchase stock in the future at a fixed price. This type of plan, which is usually offered only to management personnel, both compensates and motivates management because the market value of a company's stock is tied to the company's performance. As the market value of the stock goes up, the difference between the option price and the market price grows, which increases management's compensation. Another key benefit of stock options for corporations is a tax deduction for the amount of compensation expense, which lowers income taxes owed.

On the date stock options are granted, the fair value of the options must be estimated, and the amount in excess of the exercise price must be either recorded as compensation expense over the grant period or reported in the notes to the financial statements.[9] If a company chooses to record compensation expense, additional paid-in capital will increase as a result. Almost all companies report the excess of fair value over exercise price in the notes to the financial statements. The notes must include the impact on net income and earnings per share of not recording compensation expense in the income statement.

If note disclosure is the preferred method of reporting compensation costs, then when an option eventually is exercised and the stock is issued, the entry is the same as for issuance of common stock to any outsider. For example, assume that on July 1, 20x1, a company grants its key management personnel the option to purchase 50,000 shares of $10 par value common stock at its then-current market value of $15 per share. Suppose that one of the firm's vice presidents exercises the option to purchase 2,000 shares on March 30, 20x4, when the market price is $25 per share. Although the vice president has a gain of $20,000 (the $50,000 market value less the $30,000 option price), no compensation expense is recorded. Estimation of the fair value of options at the grant date is the subject of more advanced courses.*

✔ Check out ACE for a Review Quiz at http://accounting.college.hmco.com/students.

*Stock options are discussed here in the context of employee compensation. They can also be important features of complex corporate capitalization arrangements.

COMPONENTS OF STOCKHOLDERS' EQUITY

LO2 Identify the components of stockholders' equity.

RELATED TEXT ASSIGNMENTS
Q: 16
SE: 5
E: 2, 3, 4
P: 1, 4, 5, 6, 8
SD: 1, 5, 6
FRA: 1, 3, 4, 6

In a corporation's balance sheet, the owners' claims to the business are called *stockholders' equity*. Look at the sample stockholders' equity section of a balance sheet that follows.

Stockholders' Equity			
Contributed capital			
Preferred stock, $50 par value, 1,000 shares authorized, issued, and outstanding			$ 50,000
Common stock, $5 par value, 30,000 shares authorized, 20,000 shares issued and outstanding		$100,000	
Paid-in capital in excess of par value, common		50,000	150,000
Total contributed capital			$200,000
Retained earnings			60,000
Total stockholders' equity			$260,000

Notice that the equity section of the corporate balance sheet is divided into two parts: (1) contributed capital and (2) retained earnings. Contributed capital represents the stockholders' investments in the corporation. Retained earnings are the earnings of the corporation since its inception, less any losses, dividends, or transfers to contributed capital. Retained earnings are not a pool of funds to be distributed to the stockholders; instead, they represent the stockholders' claim to the assets from earnings reinvested in the corporation.

In keeping with the convention of full disclosure, the contributed-capital part of the stockholders' equity section of the balance sheet gives a great deal of information about the corporation's stock: the kinds of stock; their par value; and the number of shares authorized, issued, and outstanding.

A corporation can issue two basic types of stock: common stock and preferred stock. If only one kind of stock is issued by the corporation, it is called **common stock**. Common stock is the company's **residual equity**. This means that all creditors' and usually preferred stockholders' claims to the company's assets rank ahead of those of the common stockholders in case of liquidation. Because common stock is generally the only stock that carries voting rights, it represents the means of controlling the corporation.

The second kind of stock a company can issue is called **preferred stock**. Preferred stock has preference over common stock in one or more areas. These "preferences" will be described later in the chapter. Both common stock and preferred stock are sold to raise money. But investors in preferred stock and investors in common stock have different investment goals; preferred stock investors place more value on one or more of the preferences attached to the preferred stock.

The **issued stock** of a corporation is the shares sold or otherwise transferred to stockholders. For example, a corporation can be authorized to issue 500,000 shares of stock but may choose to issue only

KEY POINT: A corporation may have more shares issued than it has outstanding because it has repurchased some shares, which are called *treasury stock*.

FOCUS ON INTERNATIONAL BUSINESS

Hot New European Stock Markets Have Cooled!

In 1996, to bring capital to cash-starved growth-stock companies, Europe's stock exchanges began setting up a series of four new exchanges, including France's Nouveau Marche and Germany's Neuer Markt. More than 160 companies went public via this "Euro new market" network. Most owners of these stocks are individual investors, rather than institutional fund managers, as is the case in the United States. The new markets rose quickly, causing a good deal of excitement.[10] However, when they failed to meet expectations, they seemed to fall even faster than they had risen. Case in point, Germany has announced the closing of the Neuer Markt.

FIGURE 3
Relationship of Authorized, Unissued, Issued, Outstanding, and Treasury Shares

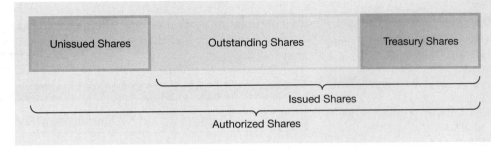

STOP AND THINK!
Why are issued shares not the same amount as authorized shares?

Authorized shares usually far exceed a corporation's need for immediate capital. Issuing fewer shares than authorized provides a corporation with greater flexibility in raising additional contributed capital in the future. ■

300,000 shares when the company is organized. The holders of those 300,000 shares own 100 percent of the corporation. The remaining 200,000 shares of stock are unissued shares. No rights or privileges are associated with them until they are issued.

Outstanding stock is stock that has been issued and is still in circulation. A share of stock is not outstanding if the issuing corporation has repurchased it or if a stockholder has given it back to the company that issued it, so a company can have more shares issued than are currently outstanding. Issued shares that are bought back and held by the corporation are called *treasury stock*, which we discuss in detail later in this chapter. The relationship of authorized, issued, unissued, outstanding, and treasury shares is illustrated in Figure 3.

 Check out ACE for a Review Quiz at http://accounting.college.hmco.com/students.

DIVIDENDS

LO3   Account for cash dividends.
RELATED TEXT ASSIGNMENTS
Q: 10, 11
SE: 6
E: 5, 6
P: 1, 4, 5, 6, 8
SD: 5
FRA: 3, 7

ENRICHMENT NOTE:
Some reasons that the board of directors of a corporation with sufficient cash and retained earnings might not declare a dividend include the following: the cash is needed for expansion; the board of directors wants to liquidate debt and improve the overall financial position of the company; there are major uncertainties threatening the corporation (such as a pending lawsuit or a possible workers' strike); and the economy is poor, and the board of directors decides it would be prudent to keep resources for difficult times.

Dividends can be paid quarterly, semiannually, annually, or at other times decided on by the board. Most states do not allow the board to declare a dividend that exceeds retained earnings. When a dividend that exceeds retained earnings is declared, the corporation is, in essence, returning to the stockholders part of their contributed capital. It is called a **liquidating dividend** and is usually paid when a company is going out of business or reducing its operations. Having sufficient retained earnings in itself does not justify the distribution of a dividend. If cash or other readily distributable assets are not available for distribution, the company might have to borrow money to pay a dividend—an action most boards of directors want to avoid.

Three important dates are associated with dividends. In order of occurrence, they are (1) the date of declaration, (2) the date of record, and (3) the date of payment. The **date of declaration** is the date on which the board of directors formally declares that a dividend is going to be paid. The **date of record** is the date on which ownership of the stock of a company, and therefore of the right to receive a dividend, is determined. Individuals who own the stock on the date of record will receive the dividend. Between that date and the date of payment, the stock is said to be **ex-dividend**. If the owner on the date of record later sells the shares of stock, the right to the cash dividend remains with that person; it does not transfer with the shares to the second owner. The **date of payment** is the date on which the dividend is paid to the stockholders of record.

To illustrate accounting for cash dividends, we assume that the board of directors has decided that sufficient cash is available to pay a $56,000 cash dividend to the common stockholders. The process has two steps. First, the board declares the dividend as of a certain date. Second, the dividend is paid. Assume that the dividend is declared on February 21, 20xx, for stockholders of record on March 1, 20xx, to be paid on March 11, 20xx. Here are the entries to record the declaration and payment of the cash dividend:

Date of Declaration

A = L + OE
   +   −

Feb. 21	Cash Dividends Declared		56,000	
	Cash Dividends Payable			56,000
	Declared cash dividend			
	to common stockholders			

⬢ Stop and Think!

If an investor sells shares after the declaration date but before the date of record, does the seller still receive the dividend?

Yes, but it comes in the form of a higher price for the stock, not in a dividend distribution. After the declaration date, the stock price adjusts upward to include the dividend declared. As a result, the seller receives the dividend even though on the distribution date, the check for the dividend will go to the buyer. ∎

Date of Record

Mar. 1   No entry is required. This date is used simply to determine the owners of the stock who will receive the dividends. After this date (starting March 2), the shares are ex-dividend.

Date of Payment

A = L + OE
   −   −

Mar. 11	Cash Dividends Payable		56,000	
	Cash			56,000
	Paid cash dividends			
	declared on February 21			

Notice that the liability for the dividend is recorded on the date of declaration because the legal obligation to pay the dividend is established on that date. No entry is required on the date of record. The liability is liquidated, or settled, on the date of payment. The Cash Dividends Declared account is a temporary stockholders' equity account that is closed at the end of the accounting period by debiting Retained Earnings and crediting Cash Dividends Declared. Retained Earnings are thereby reduced by the total dividends declared during the period.

 Check out ACE for a Review Quiz at http://accounting.college.hmco.com/students.

THE CHARACTERISTICS OF PREFERRED STOCK

LO4   Identify the characteristics of preferred stock, including the effect on distribution of dividends.

  RELATED TEXT ASSIGNMENTS
  Q: 11, 12, 13
  SE: 7
  E: 3, 7, 8
  P: 2, 4, 5, 7, 8
  SD: 2, 5
  FRA: 2, 7

KEY POINT: Preferred stock has many different characteristics. They are rarely exactly the same from company to company.

Most preferred stock has one or more of the following characteristics: preference as to dividends, preference as to assets of the business in liquidation, convertibility, and a callable option. In fact, a corporation may offer several different classes of preferred stock, each with distinctive characteristics to attract different investors.

PREFERENCE AS TO DIVIDENDS

Preferred stocks ordinarily have a preference over common stock in the receipt of dividends; that is, the holders of preferred shares must receive a certain amount of dividends before the holders of common shares can receive dividends. The amount that preferred stockholders must be paid before common stockholders can be paid is usually stated in dollars per share or as a percentage of the par value of the preferred shares. For example, a corporation can issue a preferred stock and pay an annual dividend of $4 per share, or it might issue a preferred stock at $50 par value and pay a yearly dividend of 8 percent of par value, also $4 per share.

Preferred stockholders have no guarantee of ever receiving dividends. The company must have earnings and the board of directors must declare dividends on preferred shares before any liability arises. The consequences of not declaring a dividend to preferred stockholders in the current year vary according to the exact terms under which the shares were issued. In the case of **noncumulative preferred stock**, if the board of directors fails to declare a dividend to preferred stockholders in a given year, the company is under no obligation to make up the missed dividend in future years. In the case of **cumulative preferred stock**, however, the fixed dividend amount per share accumulates from year to year, and the whole amount must be paid before any dividends on common stock can be paid. Dividends not paid in the year they are due are called **dividends in arrears**.

Assume that a corporation has been authorized to issue 10,000 shares of $100 par value, 5 percent cumulative preferred stock and that the shares have been issued and are outstanding. If no dividends were paid in 20x1, at the end of the year there would be preferred dividends of $50,000 (10,000 shares × $100 × .05 = $50,000) in arrears. If dividends are paid in 20x2, the preferred stockholders' dividends in arrears plus the 20x2 preferred dividends must be paid before any dividends on common stock can be paid.

Dividends in arrears are not recognized as liabilities because no liability exists until the board declares a dividend. A corporation cannot be sure it is going to make a profit, so, of course, it cannot promise dividends to stockholders. However, if a company has dividends in arrears, the amount should be reported either in the body of the financial statements or in a note. The following note appeared in a steel company's annual report:

> On January 1, 20xx, the company was in arrears by $37,851,000 ($1.25 per share) on dividends to its preferred stockholders. The company must pay all dividends in arrears to preferred stockholders before paying any dividends to common stockholders.

Suppose that on January 1, 20x1, a corporation issued 10,000 shares of $10 par, 6 percent cumulative preferred stock and 50,000 shares of common stock. The first year's operations resulted in income of only $4,000. The corporation's board of directors declared a $3,000 cash dividend to the preferred stockholders. The dividend picture at the end of 20x1 was as follows:

20x1 dividends due preferred stockholders ($100,000 × .06)	$6,000
Less 20x1 dividends declared to preferred stockholders	3,000
20x1 preferred stock dividends in arrears	$3,000

Now suppose that in 20x2 the corporation earned income of $30,000 and wanted to pay dividends to both the preferred and the common stockholders. Because the preferred stock is cumulative, the corporation must pay the $3,000 in arrears on the preferred stock, plus the current year's dividends on its preferred stock, before it can distribute a dividend to the common stockholders. For example, assume that the corporation's board of directors declared a $12,000 dividend to be distributed to preferred and common stockholders. It would be distributed as follows:

20x2 declaration of dividends	$12,000
Less 20x1 preferred stock dividends in arrears	3,000
Available for 20x2 dividends	$ 9,000
Less 20x2 dividends due preferred stockholders ($100,000 × .06)	6,000
Remainder available to common stockholders	$ 3,000

This is the entry when the dividend is declared:

A = L + OE	Dec. 31	Cash Dividends Declared	12,000	
+ −		Cash Dividends Payable		12,000
		Declared a $9,000 cash dividend to preferred stockholders and a $3,000 cash dividend to common stockholders		

PREFERENCE AS TO ASSETS

Many preferred stocks have preference in terms of the assets of the corporation in the case of liquidation. If the corporation's existence is terminated, the preferred stockholders have a right to receive the par value of their stock or a larger stated liquidation value per share before the common stockholders receive any share of the

FOCUS ON BUSINESS PRACTICE

Why Did Microsoft Issue Preferred Stock?

Preferred stock represents a flexible means of achieving goals that cannot be achieved with common stock. For example, Microsoft Corporation <www.microsoft.com> issued almost $1 billion in preferred stock even though the company probably did not need the cash.[11] Since Microsoft does not pay and has no plans to pay a dividend on its common stock, this preferred stock satisfies the desire of investors who want to own Microsoft stock but who want to buy stocks that pay a dividend. The preferred stock pays a fixed dividend and is convertible into common stock or convertible notes. If it is not converted, the company guarantees it can be redeemed at face value for cash in three years. In return for this flexibility and low risk, the company puts a limit of 25 to 30 percent on the gain that can be realized from converting the preferred stock into common stock. As a Microsoft vice president put it, "If you own the preferred, you get a dividend yield and downside protection, but the upside is capped."[12]

ENRICHMENT NOTE:
When a preferred shareholder converts to common stock, he or she gains voting rights but loses the dividend and liquidation preference. Conversion back to preferred stock is not an option.

⬥ **STOP AND THINK!**
Why would a company want to issue callable preferred stock?
Callable preferred stock gives the company greater flexibility. The company can eliminate the related dividends at some future date by redeeming the shares at a specified call price. ∎

corporation's assets. This preference can also extend to any dividends in arrears owed to the preferred stockholders.

CONVERTIBLE PREFERRED STOCK

A corporation can make its preferred stock more attractive to investors by adding convertibility. People who hold **convertible preferred stock** can exchange their shares of preferred stock for shares of the company's common stock at a ratio stated in the preferred stock contract. Convertibility appeals to investors for two reasons. First, like all preferred stockholders, owners of convertible preferred stock are more likely to receive regular dividends than are common stockholders. Second, if the market value of a company's common stock rises, the conversion feature allows the preferred stockholders to share in the increase. The rise in value would come either through increases in the value of the preferred stock or through conversion to common stock.

For example, suppose that a company issues 1,000 shares of 8 percent, $100 par value convertible preferred stock for $100 per share. Each share of stock can be converted into five shares of the company's common stock at any time. The market value of the common stock is now $15 per share. In the past, an owner of the common stock could expect dividends of about $1 per share per year. The owner of one share of preferred stock, on the other hand, now holds an investment that is approaching a value of $100 on the market and is more likely to receive dividends than is the owner of common stock.

Assume that in the next several years, the corporation's earnings increase, and the dividends paid to common stockholders rise to $3 per share. Assume also that the market value of a share of common stock rises from $15 to $30. Preferred stockholders can convert each of their preferred shares into five common shares and increase their dividends from $8 on each preferred share to the equivalent of $15 ($3 on each of five common shares). Further, the market value of each share of preferred stock will be close to the $150 value of the five shares of common stock because each share can be converted into five shares of common stock.

CALLABLE PREFERRED STOCK

Most preferred stock is **callable preferred stock**. That is, it can be redeemed or retired at the option of the issuing corporation at a price stated in the preferred stock contract. A stockholder must surrender nonconvertible preferred stock to the corporation when asked to do so. If the preferred stock is convertible, the stockholder can either surrender the stock to the corporation or convert it into common stock when the corporation calls the stock. The *call price*, or redemption price, is usually higher than the par value of the stock. For example, a $100 par value preferred stock might be callable at $103 per share. When preferred stock is called and surrendered, the stockholder is entitled to (1) the par value of the stock, (2) the call premium, (3) any dividends in arrears, and (4) a portion of the current period's dividend, prorated by the proportion of the year to the call date.

A corporation may call its preferred stock for several reasons. First, it may want to force conversion of the preferred stock to common stock because the cash dividend paid on the equivalent common stock is lower than the dividend paid on the preferred shares. Second, it may be able to replace the outstanding preferred stock on the current market with a preferred stock at a lower dividend rate or with long-term debt, which can have a lower after-tax cost. Third, the corporation may simply be profitable enough to retire the preferred stock.

 Check out ACE for a Review Quiz at http://accounting.college.hmco.com/students.

ACCOUNTING FOR STOCK ISSUANCE

LO5   Account for the issuance of stock for cash and other assets.

RELATED TEXT ASSIGNMENTS
Q: 14
SE: 8, 9
E: 4, 9, 10
P: 1, 4, 5, 6, 8
SD: 5
FRA: 1, 7

KEY POINT: Legal capital is the minimum amount that can be reported as contributed capital. For the protection of creditors, dividends that would reduce capital below the amount of legal capital cannot be declared.

KEY POINT: When stock is issued with no par and no stated value, all proceeds represent legal capital and are recorded as capital stock. Because stock may be issued at different prices, the legal capital per share varies.

⬢ **STOP AND THINK!**
What relevance does par value or stated value have to a financial ratio, such as return on equity or debt to equity?

Return on equity and debt to equity are computed using total stockholders' equity, which includes par or stated value. Financial analysis does not generally find par or stated value of any relevance. ■

A share of capital stock may be either par or no-par. The value of par stock is stated in the corporate charter and must be printed on each share of stock. Par value can be $.01, $1, $5, $100, or any other amount established by the organizers of the corporation. The par values of common stocks tend to be lower than those of preferred stocks.

As noted earlier, par value is the amount per share that is entered into a corporation's capital stock accounts and that makes up the legal capital of the corporation. A corporation cannot declare a dividend that would cause stockholders' equity to fall below the legal capital of the firm. Therefore, the par value is a minimum cushion of capital that protects the corporation's creditors. Any amount in excess of par value received from the issuance of stock is recorded in the Paid-in Capital in Excess of Par Value account and represents a portion of the company's contributed capital.

No-par stock is capital stock that does not have a par value. There are several reasons for issuing stock without a par value. One is that some investors confuse par value with the market value of stock instead of recognizing it as an arbitrary figure. Another reason is that most states do not allow an original stock issue below par value and thereby limit a corporation's flexibility in obtaining capital.

No-par stock can be issued with or without a stated value. The board of directors of a corporation issuing no-par stock may be required by state law to place a **stated value** on each share of stock or may choose to do so as a matter of convenience. The stated value can be any value set by the board unless the state specifies a minimum amount, which is sometimes the case. The stated value can be set before or after the shares are issued if the state law is not specific.

If a company issues no-par stock without a stated value, all proceeds are recorded in the Capital Stock account. That amount becomes the corporation's legal capital unless a different amount is specified by state law. Because additional shares of the stock can be issued at different prices, the per-share credit to the Capital Stock account will not be uniform. This is a key way in which no-par stock without a stated value differs from par value stock or no-par stock with a stated value.

When no-par stock with a stated value is issued, the shares are recorded in the Capital Stock account at the stated value. Any amount received in excess of the stated value is recorded in the Paid-in Capital in Excess of Stated Value account. The amount in excess of the stated value is part of the corporation's contributed capital. However, the stated value is normally considered to be the legal capital of the corporation.

PAR VALUE STOCK

When par value stock is issued, the appropriate capital stock account (usually Common Stock or Preferred Stock) is credited for the par value regardless of whether the proceeds are more or less than the par value. For example, assume that Bradley Corporation is authorized to issue 20,000 shares of $10 par value common stock and issues 10,000 shares at $10 per share on January 1, 20xx. The entry to record the stock issue at par value would be as follows:

A = L + OE				
+ +	Jan. 1	Cash	100,000	
		Common Stock		100,000
		Issued 10,000 shares of $10 par value common stock for $10 per share		

Cash is debited for $100,000 (10,000 shares × $10), and Common Stock is credited for an equal amount because the stock was sold for par value.

When stock is issued for a price greater than par, the proceeds in excess of par are credited to a capital account called Paid-in Capital in Excess of Par Value,

Common. For example, assume that the 10,000 shares of Bradley common stock sold for $12 per share on January 1, 20xx. The entry to record the issuance of the stock at the price in excess of par value would be as follows:

A = L + OE
  +   +
        +

Jan. 1	Cash	120,000	
	Common Stock		100,000
	Paid-in Capital in Excess of		
	Par Value, Common		20,000
	Issued 10,000 shares of $10 par value common stock for $12 per share		

KEY POINT: Common stock and paid-in capital in excess of par value are separated for legal purposes. Their effect on the company's balance sheet is the same.

Cash is debited for the proceeds of $120,000 (10,000 shares × $12), and Common Stock is credited for the total par value of $100,000 (10,000 shares × $10). Paid-in Capital in Excess of Par Value, Common is credited for the difference of $20,000 (10,000 shares × $2). The amount in excess of par value is part of the corporation's contributed capital and will be included in the stockholders' equity section of the balance sheet. The stockholders' equity section for Bradley Corporation immediately following the stock issue would appear as follows:

Contributed capital	
Common stock, $10 par value, 20,000 shares authorized, 10,000 shares issued and outstanding	$100,000
Paid-in capital in excess of par value, common	20,000
Total contributed capital	$120,000
Retained earnings	—
Total stockholders' equity	$120,000

If a corporation issues stock for less than par, an account called Discount on Capital Stock is debited for the difference. The issuance of stock at a discount rarely occurs; it is illegal in many states.

NO-PAR STOCK

As mentioned earlier, stock can be issued without a par value. However, most states require that all or part of the proceeds from the issuance of no-par stock be designated as legal capital, which cannot be withdrawn except in liquidation. The purpose of this requirement is to protect the corporation's assets for creditors. Assume that Bradley Corporation's capital stock is no-par common and that 10,000 shares are issued on January 1, 20xx, at $15 per share. The $150,000 (10,000 shares × $15) in proceeds would be recorded as shown in the following entry:

A = L + OE
  +   +

Jan. 1	Cash	150,000	
	Common Stock		150,000
	Issued 10,000 shares of no-par common stock for $15 per share		

KEY POINT: When no-par stock has a stated value, the stated value serves the same purpose as par value.

Because the stock does not have a stated or par value, all proceeds of the issue are credited to Common Stock and are part of the company's legal capital.

Most states allow the board of directors to put a stated value on no-par stock, and that value represents the corporation's legal capital. Assume that Bradley's board puts a $10 stated value on its no-par stock. The entry to record the issue of 10,000 shares of no-par common stock with a $10 stated value for $15 per share would appear as follows:

A = L + OE
  +   +
        +

Jan. 1	Cash	150,000	
	Common Stock		100,000
	Paid-in Capital in Excess of		
	Stated Value, Common		50,000
	Issued 10,000 shares of no-par common stock with $10 stated value for $15 per share		

Notice that the legal capital credited to Common Stock is the stated value decided by the board of directors. Notice also that the account Paid-in Capital in Excess of Stated Value, Common is credited for $50,000. The $50,000 is the difference between the proceeds ($150,000) and the total stated value ($100,000). Paid-in Capital in Excess of Stated Value is presented on the balance sheet in the same way as Paid-in Capital in Excess of Par Value.

ISSUANCE OF STOCK FOR NONCASH ASSETS

KEY POINT: Even though the board of directors has the right to determine the fair market value of property that is exchanged for stock, it cannot establish the amount arbitrarily. It must do so in a prudent fashion, using all the information at its disposal.

Stock can be issued for assets or services other than cash. The problem is to determine the dollar amount that should be recorded for the exchange. The generally preferred rule is to record the transaction at the fair market value of what the corporation is giving up—in this case, the stock. If the fair market value of the stock cannot be determined, the fair market value of the assets or services received can be used. Transactions of this kind usually involve the use of stock to pay for land or buildings or for the services of attorneys and others who helped organize the company.

When there is an exchange of stock for noncash assets, the board of directors has the right to determine the fair market value of the property. Suppose that when Bradley Corporation was formed on January 1, 20xx, its attorney agreed to accept 100 shares of its $10 par value common stock for services rendered. At the time the stock was issued, its market value could not be determined. However, for similar services the attorney would have billed the company $1,500. The entry to record the noncash transaction is as follows:

A = L + OE	Jan. 1 Start-up and Organization Expense	1,500	
+ +	Common Stock		1,000
+	Paid-in Capital in Excess of		
	Par Value, Common		500
	Issued 100 shares of $10 par		
	value common stock for attorney's		
	services		

Now suppose that two years later Bradley Corporation exchanged 1,000 shares of its $10 par value common stock for a piece of land. At the time of the exchange, the stock was selling on the market for $16 per share. The following entry records the exchange:

A = L + OE	Jan. 1 Land	16,000	
+ +	Common Stock		10,000
+	Paid-in Capital in Excess of		
	Par Value, Common		6,000
	Issued 1,000 shares of $10 par value		
	common stock with a market value		
	of $16 per share for a piece of land		

✔ Check out ACE for a Review Quiz at http://accounting.college.hmco.com/students.

ACCOUNTING FOR TREASURY STOCK

LO6 Account for treasury stock.

RELATED TEXT ASSIGNMENTS

Q: 15, 16
SE: 10, 11
E: 2, 6, 11, 12
P: 3, 4, 5, 8
SD: 3, 4
FRA: 4, 6, 7

Treasury stock is capital stock, either common or preferred, that the issuing company has reacquired. The company normally gets the stock back by purchasing the shares on the market. It is common for companies to buy and hold their own stock. In a recent year, 410, or 68 percent, of 600 large companies held treasury stock.[13] Although the purchase of treasury stock can be a severe drain on cash, a company may purchase its own stock for several reasons:

1. It may want stock to distribute to employees through stock option plans.

2. It may be trying to maintain a favorable market for its stock.

3. It may want to increase its earnings per share or stock price per share.

4. It may want to have additional shares of stock available for such activities as purchasing other companies.

5. It may want to prevent a hostile takeover.

A treasury stock purchase reduces the assets and stockholders' equity of the company. It is not considered a purchase of assets, as the purchase of shares in another company would be. Treasury stock is capital stock that has been issued but is no longer outstanding. Treasury shares can be held for an indefinite period, reissued, or retired. Like unissued stock, treasury stock has no rights until it is reissued. It does not have voting rights, rights to cash dividends and stock dividends, or rights to share in assets during liquidation of the company, and it is not considered to be outstanding in the calculation of book value. However, there is one major difference between unissued shares and treasury shares: A share of stock that originally was issued at par value or greater and fully paid for, and that then was reacquired as treasury stock, can be reissued at less than par value without negative consequences.

KEY POINT: Treasury stock is not the same as unissued stock. Treasury stock represents shares that have been issued but are no longer outstanding. Unissued shares, on the other hand, have never been in circulation.

PURCHASE OF TREASURY STOCK

When treasury stock is purchased, it is normally recorded at cost. The transaction reduces the firm's assets as well as stockholders' equity. For example, assume that on September 15 Caprock Corporation purchases 1,000 shares of its common stock on the market at a price of $50 per share. The purchase would be recorded as follows:

A = L + OE
−   −

Sept. 15	Treasury Stock, Common	50,000	
	Cash		50,000
	Acquired 1,000 shares of the company's common stock for $50 per share		

The treasury shares are recorded at cost. The par value, stated value, or original issue price of the stock is ignored.

The stockholders' equity section of Caprock's balance sheet shows the cost of the treasury stock as a deduction from the total of contributed capital and retained earnings:

ENRICHMENT NOTE: Since treasury stock reduces stockholders' equity—the denominator of the return on equity ratio—the return on equity will increase when treasury shares are purchased even though there is no increase in earnings.

Contributed capital	
Common stock, $5 par value, 100,000 shares authorized, 30,000 shares issued, 29,000 shares outstanding	$ 150,000
Paid-in capital in excess of par value, common	30,000
Total contributed capital	$ 180,000
Retained earnings	900,000
Total contributed capital and retained earnings	$1,080,000
Less treasury stock, common (1,000 shares at cost)	50,000
Total stockholders' equity	$1,030,000

Notice that the number of shares issued, and therefore the legal capital, has not changed, although the number of outstanding shares has decreased as a result of the transaction.

SALE OF TREASURY STOCK

Treasury shares can be sold at cost, above cost, or below cost. For example, assume that on November 15, Caprock Corporation sells its 1,000 treasury shares for $50 per share. The following entry records the transaction:

A = L + OE
+   +

Nov. 15	Cash	50,000	
	Treasury Stock, Common		50,000
	Reissued 1,000 shares of treasury stock for $50 per share		

When treasury shares are sold for an amount greater than their cost, the excess of the sales price over cost should be credited to Paid-in Capital, Treasury Stock. No gain should be recorded. For example, suppose that on November 15, Caprock sells its 1,000 treasury shares for $60 per share. The entry for the reissue would be as follows:

A = L + OE	Nov. 15	Cash	60,000	
+ +		Treasury Stock, Common		50,000
+		Paid-in Capital, Treasury Stock		10,000
		Sold 1,000 shares of treasury stock for $60 per share; cost was $50 per share		

KEY POINT: Gains and losses on the reissue of treasury stock are never recognized as such. Instead, the accounts Retained Earnings and Paid-in Capital, Treasury Stock are used.

If treasury shares are sold below their cost, the difference is deducted from Paid-in Capital, Treasury Stock. When this account does not exist or its balance is insufficient to cover the excess of cost over the reissue price, Retained Earnings absorbs the excess. No loss is recorded. For example, suppose that on September 15, Caprock bought 1,000 shares of its common stock on the market at a price of $50 per share. The company sold 400 shares on October 15 for $60 per share and the remaining 600 shares on December 15 for $42 per share. The entries for these transactions are as follows:

A = L + OE	Sept. 15	Treasury Stock, Common	50,000	
− −		Cash		50,000
		Purchased 1,000 shares of treasury stock at $50 per share		

A = L + OE	Oct. 15	Cash	24,000	
+ +		Treasury Stock, Common		20,000
+		Paid-in Capital, Treasury Stock		4,000
		Sold 400 shares of treasury stock for $60 per share; cost was $50 per share		

A = L + OE	Dec. 15	Cash	25,200	
+		Paid-in Capital, Treasury Stock	4,000	
−		Retained Earnings	800	
+		Treasury Stock, Common		30,000
		Sold 600 shares of treasury stock for $42 per share; cost was $50 per share		

STUDY NOTE: Retained Earnings is debited only when the Paid-in Capital, Treasury Stock account has been depleted. In this case, the credit balance of $4,000 is exhausted completely before Retained Earnings absorbs the excess.

In the entry for the December 15 transaction, Retained Earnings is debited for $800 because the 600 shares were sold for $4,800 less than cost. That amount is $800 greater than the $4,000 of paid-in capital generated by the sale of the 400 shares of treasury stock on October 15.

FOCUS ON BUSINESS PRACTICE

When Are Share Buybacks a Bad Idea?

Corporate America set share repurchase records in 2000 of $123 billion. As recently as 1991, share repurchases totaled only $10 billion. Hewlett-Packard <www.hp.com>, AT&T <www.att.com>, Intel <www.intel.com>, and Microsoft <www.microsoft.com> spent billions to boost their stock prices—but to no avail.

According to renowned investor Warren Buffet, share buybacks are ill-advised when companies buy high and sell low. Such action is the exact opposite of good investment theory (to buy when stocks are cheap and to sell when prices rise).

But in 2000, to avoid increased shares outstanding and the resulting lower earnings per share, companies were buying stock at record high prices and then selling it to employees at much lower prices.

Another bad idea is to borrow money to buy back stock. In 2000, many companies were borrowing money to repurchase stock, thereby increasing their debt to equity ratio. These companies are now suffering credit rating reductions and severe stock price declines.[14]

RETIREMENT OF TREASURY STOCK

If a company determines that it will not reissue treasury stock, it can, with the approval of its stockholders, retire the stock. When shares of stock are retired, all items related to those shares are removed from the related capital accounts. When treasury stock whose acquisition price is less than the original contributed capital is retired, the difference is recognized in Paid-in Capital, Retirement of Stock. If the acquisition price is more than was received when the stock was first issued, the difference is a reduction in stockholders' equity and is debited to Retained Earnings. For instance, suppose that instead of selling the 1,000 shares of treasury stock it purchased for $50,000, Caprock Corporation decides to retire the shares on November 15. Assuming that the $5 par value common stock was originally issued at $6 per share, this entry records the retirement:

A = L + OE
−
−
−
+

Nov. 15	Common Stock	5,000	
	Paid-in Capital in Excess of		
	Par Value, Common	1,000	
	Retained Earnings	44,000	
	Treasury Stock, Common		50,000
	Retired 1,000 shares that		
	cost $50 per share and were		
	issued originally at $6 per share		

✓ Check out ACE for a Review Quiz at http://accounting.college.hmco.com/students.

Chapter Review

REVIEW OF LEARNING OBJECTIVES

LO1 Identify and explain the management issues related to contributed capital.

The management of contributed capital is a critical component in the financing of a corporation. The issues faced by management in the area of contributed capital are managing under the corporate form of business, using equity financing, determining dividend policies, evaluating performance using return on equity, and using stock options as compensation.

LO2 Identify the components of stockholders' equity.

Stockholders' equity consists of contributed capital and retained earnings. Contributed capital includes two basic types of stock: common stock and preferred stock. When only one type of security is issued, it is common stock. Common stockholders have voting rights; they also share in the earnings of the corporation. Preferred stock, like common stock, is sold to raise capital. But the investors in preferred stock have different objectives. To attract such investors, corporations usually give them a preference—in terms of receiving dividends and assets—over common stockholders.

Retained earnings, the other component of stockholders' equity, represents the claim of stockholders to the assets of the company resulting from profitable operations. These are earnings that have been invested in the corporation.

LO3 Account for cash dividends.

The liability for payment of cash dividends arises on the date of declaration by the board of directors. The declaration is recorded with a debit to Cash Dividends Declared and a credit to Cash Dividends Payable. The date of record requires no entry; it is the date on which ownership of the stock, and thus of the right to receive a dividend, is determined. Date of payment is recorded with a debit to Cash Dividends Payable and a credit to Cash.

LO4 Identify the characteristics of preferred stock, including the effect on distribution of dividends.

The dividend on preferred stock is generally figured first; the remainder goes to common stock. If the preferred stock is cumulative and in arrears, the amount in arrears must be allocated to preferred stockholders before any allocation is made to common stockholders. In addition, certain preferred stock is convertible. Preferred stock is often callable at the option of the corporation.

LO5 Account for the issuance of stock for cash and other assets.

A corporation's stock is normally issued for cash and other assets. Most states require that stock be issued at a minimum value called *legal capital*. Legal capital is represented by the par or stated value of the stock.

When stock is issued for cash at par or stated value, Cash is debited and Common Stock or Preferred Stock is credited. When stock is sold at an amount greater than par or stated value, the excess is recorded in Paid-in Capital in Excess of Par or Stated Value.

Stock is sometimes issued for noncash assets. In these cases, the board of directors must decide how to value the stock. The general rule is to record the stock at its market value. If this value cannot be determined, the fair market value of the asset received is used to record the transaction.

LO6 Account for treasury stock.

Treasury stock is stock that the issuing company has reacquired. A company may buy its own stock for several reasons, including a desire to create stock option plans, maintain a favorable market for the stock, increase earnings per share, or purchase other companies. Treasury stock is similar to unissued stock in that it does not have rights until it is reissued. However, treasury stock can be resold at less than par value without penalty. The accounting treatment for treasury stock is as follows:

Treasury Stock Transaction	Accounting Treatment
Purchase of treasury stock	Debit Treasury Stock and credit Cash for the cost of the shares.
Sale of treasury stock at the same price as the cost of the shares	Debit Cash and credit Treasury Stock for the cost of the shares.
Sale of treasury stock at an amount greater than the cost of the shares	Debit Cash for the reissue price of the shares, and credit Treasury Stock for the cost of the shares and Paid-in Capital, Treasury Stock for the excess.
Sale of treasury stock at an amount less than the cost of the shares	Debit Cash for the reissue price; debit Paid-in Capital, Treasury Stock for the difference between the reissue price and the cost of the shares; and credit Treasury Stock for the cost of the shares. If Paid-in Capital, Treasury Stock does not exist or its balance is not large enough to cover the difference, Retained Earnings should absorb the difference.
Retirement of treasury stock	Debit Common Stock and Paid-in Capital in Excess of Par Value for the original issue price and Retained Earnings for the remainder to bring the total to the cost of the treasury stock. Credit Treasury Stock for its total cost.

REVIEW OF CONCEPTS AND TERMINOLOGY

The following concepts and terms were introduced in this chapter:

LO1 **Authorized stock:** The maximum number of shares a corporation can issue without a change in its state charter.

LO4 **Callable preferred stock:** Preferred stock that can be redeemed or retired at a stated price at the option of the issuing corporation.

LO2 **Common stock:** Shares of stock that carry voting rights but that rank below preferred stock in terms of dividends and the distribution of assets.

LO4 **Convertible preferred stock:** Preferred stock that can be exchanged for common stock at the option of the holder.

LO1 **Corporation:** A separate legal entity having its own rights, privileges, and liabilities distinct from those of its owners.

LO4 **Cumulative preferred stock:** Preferred stock on which unpaid dividends accumulate over time and must be satisfied before a dividend can be paid to common stockholders.

LO3 **Date of declaration:** The date on which the board of directors declares a dividend.

LO3 **Date of payment:** The date on which payment of a dividend is made.

LO3 **Date of record:** The date on which ownership of stock for the purpose of receiving a dividend is determined.

LO1 **Dividend:** The distribution of a corporation's assets (usually cash generated by past earnings) to its stockholders.

LO4 **Dividends in arrears:** Past dividends on cumulative preferred stock that remain unpaid.

LO1 **Dividends yield:** Current return to stockholders in the form of dividends; dividends per share divided by market price per share.

LO1 **Double taxation:** Taxation of corporate earnings twice—once as income of the corporation and once as income to stockholders based on the dividends they receive.

LO3 **Ex-dividend:** A description of capital stock between the date of record and the date of payment, when the right to a dividend already declared on the stock remains with the person who sells the stock and does not transfer to the person who buys it.

LO1 **Initial public offering (IPO):** A company's first issue of capital stock to the public.

LO2 **Issued stock:** The shares of stock sold or otherwise transferred to stockholders.

LO1 **Legal capital:** The number of shares of stock issued times the par value; the minimum amount that can be reported as contributed capital.

LO3 **Liquidating dividend:** A dividend that exceeds retained earnings; usually paid when a corporation goes out of business or reduces its operations.

LO4 **Noncumulative preferred stock:** Preferred stock that does not oblige the issuer to make up a missed dividend in a subsequent year.

LO5 **No-par stock:** Capital stock that does not have a par value.

LO2 **Outstanding stock:** Stock that has been issued and is still in circulation.

LO1 **Par value:** An arbitrary amount assigned to each share of stock; constitutes the legal capital of a corporation.

LO2 **Preferred stock:** Stock that has preference over common stock, usually in terms of dividends and the distribution of assets.

LO1 **Price/earnings (P/E) ratio:** A measure of confidence in a company's future; market price per share divided by earnings per share.

LO2 **Residual equity:** The common stock of a corporation.

LO1 **Return on equity:** A measure of management performance; net income divided by average stockholders' equity.

LO1 **Share of stock:** A unit of ownership in a corporation.

LO1 **Start-up and organization costs:** The costs of forming a corporation.

LO5 **Stated value:** A value assigned by the board of directors of a corporation to no-par stock.

LO1 **Stock certificate:** A document issued to a stockholder indicating the number of shares of stock the stockholder owns.

LO1 **Stock option plan:** An agreement to issue stock to employees according to specified terms.

LO6 **Treasury stock:** Capital stock, either common or preferred, that the issuing company has reacquired but has not subsequently resold or retired.

LO1 **Underwriter:** An intermediary between the corporation and the investing public who facilitates an issue of stock or other securities for a fee.

REVIEW PROBLEM

Stock Journal Entries and Stockholders' Equity

LO1
LO2
LO3
LO4
LO5
LO6

The Beta Corporation was organized in 20x1 in the state of Arizona. Its charter authorized the corporation to issue 1,000,000 shares of $1 par value common stock and an additional 25,000 shares of 4 percent, $20 par value cumulative convertible preferred stock. Here are the transactions related to the company's stock during 20x1:

Feb.   1   Issued 100,000 shares of common stock for $125,000.

       15   Issued 3,000 shares of common stock for accounting and legal services. The services were billed to the company at $3,600.

Mar. 15   Issued 120,000 shares of common stock to Edward Jackson in exchange for a building and land appraised at $100,000 and $25,000, respectively.

Apr.   2   Purchased 20,000 shares of common stock for the treasury at $1.25 per share from a person who changed his mind about investing in the company.

July   1   Issued 25,000 shares of preferred stock for $500,000.

Sept. 30   Sold 10,000 of the shares in the treasury for $1.50 per share.

Dec. 31   The board declared dividends of $24,910 payable on January 15 to stockholders of record on January 8. Dividends included preferred stock cash dividends for one-half year.

For the period ended December 31, 20x1, the company reported net income of $40,000 and earnings per common share of $.14. At December 31, the market price per common share was $1.60.

REQUIRED ▶

1. Record these transactions in journal form. In the explanation for the December 31 entry to record dividends, show dividends payable for each class of stock.

2. Prepare the stockholders' equity section of the Beta Corporation balance sheet as of December 31, 20x1. (**Hint:** Use net income and dividends to calculate retained earnings.)

K/R 3. Calculate dividends yield on common stock, price/earnings ratio of common stock, and return on equity.

ANSWER TO REVIEW PROBLEM

1. Entries prepared in journal form:

Feb.	1	Cash	125,000	
		Common Stock		100,000
		Paid-in Capital in Excess of		
		Par Value, Common		25,000
		Issued 100,000 shares of		
		$1 par value common		
		stock for $1.25 per share		
	15	Start-up and Organization Expense	3,600	
		Common Stock		3,000
		Paid-in Capital in Excess of		
		Par Value, Common		600
		Issued 3,000 shares of		
		$1 par value common stock		
		for billed accounting and		
		legal services of $3,600		
Mar.	15	Building	100,000	
		Land	25,000	
		Common Stock		120,000
		Paid-in Capital in Excess of		
		Par Value, Common		5,000
		Issued 120,000 shares of		
		$1 par value common stock		
		for a building and land		
		appraised at $100,000 and		
		$25,000, respectively		

Apr.	2	Treasury Stock, Common	25,000	
		Cash		25,000
		Purchased 20,000 shares of common stock for the treasury at $1.25 per share		
July	1	Cash	500,000	
		Preferred Stock		500,000
		Issued 25,000 shares of $20 par value preferred stock for $20 per share		
Sept. 30		Cash	15,000	
		Treasury Stock, Common		12,500
		Paid-in Capital, Treasury Stock		2,500
		Sold 10,000 shares of treasury stock at $1.50 per share; original cost was $1.25 per share		
Dec. 31		Cash Dividends Declared	24,910	
		Cash Dividends Payable		24,910
		Declared a $24,910 cash dividend to preferred and common stockholders		

Total dividend $24,910
Less preferred stock cash
  dividend
  $500,000 × .04 × 6/12   10,000
Common stock cash dividend $14,910

2. Stockholders' equity section of the balance sheet prepared:

Beta Corporation
Balance Sheet
December 31, 20x1

Stockholders' Equity

Contributed capital		
Preferred stock, 4 percent cumulative convertible, $20 par value, 25,000 shares authorized, issued, and outstanding		$500,000
Common stock, $1 par value, 1,000,000 shares authorized, 223,000 shares issued, and 213,000 shares outstanding	$223,000	
Paid-in capital in excess of par value, common	30,600	
Paid-in capital, treasury stock	2,500	256,100
Total contributed capital		$756,100
Retained earnings		15,090*
Total contributed capital and retained earnings		$771,190
Less treasury stock, common (10,000 shares, at cost)		12,500
Total stockholders' equity		$758,690

*Retained Earnings = $40,000 − $24,910 = $15,090.

3. Dividends yield on common stock, price/earnings ratio of common stock, and return on equity calculated:

$$\text{Dividends per Share} = \$14,910 \text{ Common Stock Dividend}$$
$$\div \; 213,000 \text{ Common Shares Outstanding} = \$.07$$

$$\text{Dividends Yield} = \frac{\text{Dividends per Share}}{\text{Market Price per Share}} = \frac{\$.07}{\$1.60} = 4.4\%$$

$$\text{Price/Earnings (P/E) Ratio} = \frac{\text{Market Price per Share}}{\text{Earnings per Share}} = \frac{\$1.60}{\$.14} = 11.4 \text{ times}$$

The opening balance of stockholders' equity on February 1, 20x1, was $125,000.

$$\text{Return on Equity} = \frac{\text{Net Income}}{\text{Average Stockholders' Equity}}$$

$$= \frac{\$40,000}{(\$758,690 + \$125,000) \div 2}$$

$$= 9.1\%$$

Chapter Assignments

BUILDING YOUR KNOWLEDGE FOUNDATION

QUESTIONS

1. What management issues are related to contributed capital?
2. Identify and explain several advantages of the corporate form of business.
3. Identify and explain several disadvantages of the corporate form of business.
4. What is dividends yield, and what do investors learn from it?
5. What is the price/earnings (P/E) ratio, and what does it measure?
6. What are the start-up and organization costs of a corporation?
7. What is the proper accounting treatment of start-up and organization costs?
8. What is a stock option plan, and why would a company have one?
9. What is the legal capital of a corporation, and what is its significance?
10. Describe the significance of the following dates as they relate to dividends: (a) date of declaration, (b) date of record, and (c) date of payment.
11. Explain the accounting treatment of cash dividends.
12. What are dividends in arrears, and how should they be disclosed in the financial statements?
13. Define the terms *cumulative*, *convertible*, and *callable* as they apply to preferred stock.
14. How is the value of stock determined when stock is issued for noncash assets?
15. Define *treasury stock* and explain why a company would purchase its own stock.
16. What is the proper classification of the accounts listed below on the balance sheet? Indicate whether stockholders' equity accounts are contributed capital, retained earnings, or contra stockholders' equity.

   a. Common Stock
   b. Treasury Stock
   c. Paid-in Capital, Treasury Stock
   d. Paid-in Capital in Excess of Par Value, Common
   e. Paid-in Capital in Excess of Stated Value, Common
   f. Retained Earnings

SHORT EXERCISES

LO1 Management Issues

SE 1. Indicate whether each of the following actions is related to (a) managing under the corporate form of business, (b) using equity financing, (c) determining dividend policies, or (d) evaluating performance using return on equity:

1. Considering whether to make a distribution to stockholders
2. Controlling day-to-day operations
3. Determining whether to issue preferred or common stock
4. Compensating management based on the company's meeting or exceeding the targeted return on equity
5. Issuing shares
6. Transferring shares without the approval of other owners

LO1 Advantages and Disadvantages of a Corporation

SE 2. Identify whether each of the following characteristics is an advantage or a disadvantage of the corporate form of business:

1. Ease of transfer of ownership
2. Taxation
3. Separate legal entity
4. Lack of mutual agency
5. Government regulation
6. Continuous existence

LO1 Effect of Start-up and Organization Costs

SE 3. At the beginning of 20x3, Shea Company incurred the following start-up and organization costs: (1) attorneys' fees with a market value of $5,000, paid with 3,000 shares of $1 par value common stock, and (2) incorporation fees paid of $3,000. Calculate total start-up and organization costs. What will be the effect of these costs on the balance sheet and income statement?

LO1 Exercise of Stock Options

SE 4. On June 6, Heda Cord exercised her option to purchase 10,000 shares of Acton Company $1 par value common stock at an option price of $4. The market price per share was $4 on the grant date and $18 on the exercise date. Record the transaction on Acton's books.

LO2 Stockholders' Equity

SE 5. Prepare the stockholders' equity section of Cappo Corporation's balance sheet from the following accounts and balances on December 31, 20xx:

Account	Balance Debit	Balance Credit
Common Stock, $10 par value, 60,000 shares authorized, 40,000 shares issued, and 39,000 shares outstanding		$400,000
Paid-in Capital in Excess of Par Value, Common		200,000
Retained Earnings		30,000
Treasury Stock, Common (1,000 shares, at cost)	$15,000	

LO3 Cash Dividends

SE 6. Lister Corporation has authorized 100,000 shares of $1 par value common stock, of which 80,000 are issued and 70,000 are outstanding. On May 15, the board of directors declared a cash dividend of $.10 per share payable on June 15 to stockholders of record on June 1. Prepare the entries, as necessary, for each of the three dates.

LO4 Preferred Stock Dividends with Dividends in Arrears

SE 7. The Mattoon Corporation has 1,000 shares of $100, 8 percent cumulative preferred stock outstanding and 20,000 shares of $1 par value common stock outstanding. In the company's first three years of operation, its board of directors paid cash dividends as follows: 20x3, none; 20x4, $20,000; and 20x5, $40,000. Determine the total cash dividends and dividends per share paid to the preferred and common stockholders during each of the three years.

LO5 Issuance of Stock

SE 8. Briar Company is authorized to issue 100,000 shares of common stock. The company sold 5,000 shares at $12 per share. Prepare entries in journal form to record the sale of stock for cash under each of the following independent alternatives: (1) The stock has a par value of $5, and (2) the stock has no par value but a stated value of $1 per share.

LO5 Issuance of Stock for Noncash Assets

SE 9. Rhinecliff Corporation issued 8,000 shares of its $1 par value common stock in exchange for land that had a fair market value of $50,000. Prepare in journal form the entries necessary to record the issuance of the stock for the land under each of these conditions: (1) The stock was selling for $7 per share on the day of the transaction; (2) management attempted to place a value on the common stock but could not do so.

LO6 Treasury Stock Transactions

SE 10. Prepare in journal form the entries necessary to record the following stock transactions of the Osaka Company during 20xx:

Oct.   1   Purchased 1,000 shares of its own $2 par value common stock for $20 per share, the current market price.
        17   Sold 250 shares of treasury stock purchased on October 1 for $25 per share.
        21   Sold 400 shares of treasury stock purchased on October 1 for $18 per share.

LO6 Retirement of Treasury Stock

SE 11. On October 28, 20xx, the Osaka Company (**SE 10**) retired the remaining 350 shares of treasury stock. The shares were originally issued at $5 per share. Prepare the necessary entry in journal form.

Exercises

LO1 Dividends Yield and Price/Earnings Ratio

E 1. In 20x5, Pallas Corporation earned $2.20 per share and paid a dividend of $1.00 per share. At year end, the price of its stock was $33 per share. Calculate the dividends yield and the price/earnings ratio.

LO2 Stockholders' Equity
LO6

E 2. The following accounts and balances are from the records of Relay Corporation on December 31, 20xx:

Account	Balance Debit	Balance Credit
Preferred Stock, $100 par value, 9 percent cumulative, 20,000 shares authorized, 12,000 shares issued and outstanding		$1,200,000
Common Stock, $12 par value, 90,000 shares authorized, 60,000 shares issued, and 57,000 shares outstanding		720,000
Paid-in Capital in Excess of Par Value, Common		388,000
Retained Earnings		46,000
Treasury Stock, Common (3,000 shares, at cost)	$60,000	

Prepare a stockholders' equity section for Relay Corporation's balance sheet.

LO2 Characteristics of Common
LO4 and Preferred Stock

E 3. Indicate whether each of the following characteristics is more closely associated with common stock (C) or preferred stock (P):

1. Often receives dividends at a set rate
2. Is considered the residual equity of a company
3. Can be callable
4. Can be convertible
5. More likely to have dividends that vary in amount from year to year
6. Can be entitled to receive dividends not paid in past years
7. Likely to have full voting rights
8. Receives assets first in liquidation
9. Generally receives dividends before other classes of stock

LO2 Stock Entries Using
LO5 T Accounts; Stockholders' Equity

E 4. The Wendt Hospital Supply Corporation was organized in 20xx. It was authorized to issue 100,000 shares of no-par common stock with a stated value of $5 per share, and 20,000 shares of $100 par value, 6 percent noncumulative preferred stock. On March 1, the company issued 60,000 shares of its common stock for $15 per share and 8,000 shares of its preferred stock for $100 per share.

1. Record the issuance of the stock in T accounts.
2. Prepare the stockholders' equity section of Wendt Hospital Supply Corporation's balance sheet as it would appear immediately after the company issued the common and preferred stock.

LO3 Cash Dividends

E 5. Espinoza Corporation secured authorization from the state for 200,000 shares of $10 par value common stock. It has 160,000 shares issued and 140,000 shares outstanding. On June 5, the board of directors declared a $.50 per share cash dividend to be paid on June 25 to stockholders of record on June 15. Prepare entries in journal form to record these events.

**LO3 Cash Dividends
LO6**

E 6. Stein Corporation has 500,000 authorized shares of $1 par value common stock, of which 400,000 are issued, including 40,000 shares of treasury stock. On October 15, the board of directors declared a cash dividend of $.25 per share payable on November 15 to stockholders of record on November 1. Prepare entries in journal form for each of the three dates.

**LO4 Cash Dividends with
Dividends in Arrears**

E 7. The Anselm Corporation has 10,000 shares of its $100 par value, 7 percent cumulative preferred stock outstanding, and 50,000 shares of its $1 par value common stock outstanding. In Anselm's first four years of operation, its board of directors paid cash dividends as follows: 20x3, none; 20x4, $120,000; 20x5, $140,000; 20x6, $140,000. Determine the dividends per share and total cash dividends paid to the preferred and common stockholders during each of the four years.

**LO4 Cash Dividends on Preferred
and Common Stock**

E 8. The Cormer Corporation pays dividends at the end of each year. The dividends that it paid for 20x3, 20x4, and 20x5 were $80,000, $60,000, and $180,000, respectively. Calculate the total amount of dividends the Cormer Corporation paid in each of these years to its common and preferred stockholders under both of the following capital structures: (1) 20,000 shares of $100 par, 6 percent noncumulative preferred stock and 60,000 shares of $10 par common stock; (2) 10,000 shares of $100 par, 7 percent cumulative preferred stock and 60,000 shares of $10 par common stock. No dividends were in arrears at the beginning of 20x3.

LO5 Issuance of Stock

E 9. Big Sky Company is authorized to issue 200,000 shares of common stock. On August 1, the company issued 10,000 shares at $25 per share. Prepare entries in journal form to record the issuance of stock for cash under each of the following alternatives:

1. The stock has a par value of $25.
2. The stock has a par value of $10.
3. The stock has no par value.
4. The stock has a stated value of $1 per share.

**LO5 Issuance of Stock for Noncash
Assets**

E 10. On July 1, 20xx, Floron, a new corporation, issued 20,000 shares of its common stock to finance a corporate headquarters building. The building has a fair market value of $600,000 and a book value of $400,000. Because Floron is a new corporation, it is not possible to establish a market value for its common stock. Record the issuance of stock for the building, assuming the following conditions: (1) the par value of the stock is $10 per share; (2) the stock is no-par stock; and (3) the stock has a stated value of $4 per share.

LO6 Treasury Stock Transactions

E 11. Record in T accounts the following stock transactions of Tablani Company, which represent all the company's treasury stock transactions during 20xx:

May 5   Purchased 400 shares of its own $2 par value common stock for $20 per share, the current market price.
       17   Sold 150 shares of treasury stock purchased on May 5 for $22 per share.
       21   Sold 100 shares of treasury stock purchased on May 5 for $20 per share.
       28   Sold the remaining 150 shares of treasury stock purchased on May 5 for $19 per share.

**LO6 Treasury Stock Transactions
Including Retirement**

E 12. Record in T accounts the following stock transactions of Theodakis Corporation, which represent all its treasury stock transactions for the year:

June 1   Purchased 2,000 shares of its own $30 par value common stock for $70 per share, the current market price.
       10   Sold 500 shares of treasury stock purchased on June 1 for $80 per share.
       20   Sold 700 shares of treasury stock purchased on June 1 for $58 per share.
       30   Retired the remaining shares purchased on June 1. The original issue price was $42 per share.

PROBLEMS

P 1.

LO1 **Start-up and Organization**
LO2 **Costs, Stock and Dividend**
LO3 **Entries Using T Accounts, and**
LO5 **Stockholders' Equity**

On March 1, 20xx, Yang Corporation began operations with a charter from the state that authorized 100,000 shares of $2 par value common stock. Over the next quarter, the firm engaged in the following transactions:

Mar. 1   Issued 30,000 shares of common stock, $100,000.
      2   Paid fees associated with obtaining the charter and starting up and organizing the corporation, $12,000.
Apr. 10   Issued 13,000 shares of common stock, $65,000.
May 31   The board of directors declared a $.10 per share cash dividend to be paid on June 15 to shareholders of record on June 10.

REQUIRED ▶

1. Record the above transactions in T accounts.
2. Prepare the stockholders' equity section of Yang Corporation's balance sheet on May 31, 20xx. Net income earned during the first quarter was $15,000.

P 2.

LO1 **Preferred and Common Stock**
LO4 **Dividends and Dividends Yield**

The Sisken Corporation had the following stock outstanding from 20x3 through 20x6:

Preferred stock: $50 par value, 8 percent cumulative, 10,000 shares authorized, issued, and outstanding

Common stock: $5 par value, 200,000 shares authorized, issued, and outstanding

The company paid $30,000, $30,000, $94,000, and $130,000 in dividends during 20x3, 20x4, 20x5, and 20x6, respectively. The market price per common share was $7.25 and $8.00 per share at year end 20x5 and 20x6, respectively.

REQUIRED ▶

1. Determine the dividends per share and the total dividends paid to common stockholders and preferred stockholders in 20x3, 20x4, 20x5, and 20x6.
2. Perform the same computations, with the assumption that the preferred stock was noncumulative.
3. Calculate the 20x5 and 20x6 dividends yield for common stock, using the dividends per share computed in **2.**
4. How are cumulative preferred stock and noncumulative preferred stock similar to long-term bonds? How do they differ from long-term bonds?

P 3.

LO1 **Treasury Stock Transactions**
LO6

The Bender Company was involved in the following treasury stock transactions during 20xx:

Jan. 10   Purchased 52,000 shares of its $2 par value common stock on the market for $40 per share.
      20   Sold 16,000 shares of the treasury stock for $42 per share.
Feb. 8   Sold 12,000 shares of the treasury stock for $38 per share.
      16   Sold 20,000 shares of the treasury stock for $34 per share.
Mar. 14   Purchased an additional 8,000 shares for $36 per share.
      25   Retired all the remaining shares of treasury stock. All shares originally were issued at $16 per share.

REQUIRED ▶

1. Record these transactions in journal form.
2. What effect does the purchase of treasury stock have on return on equity? Why might management prefer to buy treasury stock rather than pay dividends?

P 4.

LO1 **Comprehensive Stockholders'**
LO2 **Equity Transactions and**
LO3 **Financial Ratios**
LO4
LO5
LO6

Aradia, Inc., was organized and authorized to issue 10,000 shares of $100 par value, 9 percent preferred stock and 100,000 shares of no-par, $10 stated value common stock on July 1, 20xx. Stock-related transactions for Aradia were as follows:

July 1   Issued 20,000 shares of common stock at $22 per share.
      1   Issued 1,000 shares of common stock at $22 per share for services rendered in connection with the organization of the company.
      2   Issued 4,000 shares of preferred stock at par value for cash.
     10   Issued 5,000 shares of common stock for land on which the asking price was $120,000. Market value of the stock was $24. Management wishes to record the land at full market value of the stock.
Aug. 2   Purchased 3,000 shares of its common stock at $26 per share.
     10   Declared a cash dividend for one month on the outstanding preferred stock and $.04 per share on common stock outstanding, payable on August 22 to stockholders of record on August 12.
     12   Date of record for cash dividends.
     22   Paid cash dividends.

REQUIRED ▶

1. Record the transactions in T accounts.
2. Prepare the stockholders' equity section of the balance sheet as it would appear on August 31, 20xx. Net income for July and August was $50,000.
3. Calculate dividends yield, price/earnings ratio, and return on equity. Assume earnings per common share are $1.97 and market price per common share is $25. For beginning stockholders' equity, use the balance at the close of business on July 1, 20xx.

P 5.

LO1 Comprehensive Stockholders'
LO2 Equity Transactions and
LO3 T Accounts
LO4
LO5
LO6

In January 20xx, the Handori Corporation was organized and authorized to issue 2,000,000 shares of no-par common stock and 50,000 shares of 5 percent, $50 par value, noncumulative preferred stock. The stock-related transactions for the first year's operations were as follows:

Jan. 19   Sold 15,000 shares of the common stock for $31,500. State law requires a minimum of $1 stated value per share.

21   Issued 5,000 shares of common stock to attorneys and accountants for services valued at $11,000 and provided during the organization of the corporation.

Feb. 7   Issued 30,000 shares of common stock for a building that had an appraised value of $78,000.

Mar. 22   Purchased 10,000 shares of its common stock at $3 per share.

July 15   Issued 5,000 shares of common stock to employees under a stock option plan that allows any employee to buy shares at the current market price, which is now $3 per share.

Aug. 1   Sold 2,500 shares of treasury stock for $4 per share.

Sept. 1   Declared a cash dividend of $.15 per common share to be paid on September 25 to stockholders of record on September 15.

15   Cash dividends date of record.

25   Paid cash dividends to stockholders of record on September 15.

Oct. 30   Issued 4,000 shares of common stock for a piece of land. The stock was selling for $3 per share, and the land had a fair market value of $12,000.

Dec. 15   Issued 2,200 shares of preferred stock for $50 per share.

REQUIRED ▶

1. Record the above transactions in T accounts. Prepare T accounts for Cash; Land; Building; Cash Dividends Payable; Preferred Stock; Common Stock; Paid-in Capital in Excess of Stated Value, Common; Paid-in Capital, Treasury Stock; Retained Earnings; Treasury Stock, Common; Cash Dividends Declared; and Start-up and Organization Expense.
2. Prepare the stockholders' equity section of Handori Corporation's balance sheet as of December 31, 20xx. Net income earned during the year was $100,000.

ALTERNATE PROBLEMS

P 6.

LO1 Start-up and Organization
LO2 Costs, Stock and Dividend
LO3 Entries, and Stockholders'
LO5 Equity

Queens Corporation began operations on September 1, 20xx. The corporation's charter authorized 300,000 shares of $8 par value common stock. Queens Corporation engaged in the following transactions during its first quarter:

Sept. 1   Issued 50,000 shares of common stock, $500,000.

1   Paid an attorney $32,000 to help start up and organize the corporation and obtain a corporate charter from the state.

Oct.   2   Issued 80,000 shares of common stock, $960,000.

Nov. 30   Declared a cash dividend of $.40 per share to be paid on December 15 to stockholders of record on December 10.

REQUIRED ▶

1. Prepare entries in journal form to record the above transactions.
2. Prepare the stockholders' equity section of Queens Corporation's balance sheet on November 30, 20xx. Net income for the quarter was $80,000.

P 7.

LO1 Preferred and Common Stock
LO4 Dividends and Dividends Yield

The Lazerano Corporation had both common stock and preferred stock outstanding from 20x2 through 20x4. Information about each stock for the three years is as follows:

Type	Par Value	Shares Outstanding	Other
Preferred	$100	40,000	7% cumulative
Common	20	600,000	

The company paid $140,000, $800,000, and $1,100,000 in dividends for 20x2 through 20x4, respectively. The market price per common share was $15 and $17 per share at the end of years 20x3 and 20x4, respectively.

REQUIRED ▶

1. Determine the dividends per share and total dividends paid to the common and preferred stockholders each year.
2. Assuming that the preferred stock was noncumulative, repeat the computations performed in **1**.
3. Calculate the 20x3 and 20x4 dividends yield for common stock using dividends per share computed in **2**.
4. How are cumulative preferred stock and noncumulative preferred stock similar to long-term bonds? How do they differ from long-term bonds?

P 8.

LO1 **Comprehensive Stockholders'**
LO2 **Equity Transactions**
LO3
LO4
LO5
LO6

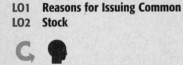

Czeczh, Inc., was organized and authorized to issue 10,000 shares of $100 par value, 9 percent preferred stock and 100,000 shares of no-par, $5 stated value common stock on July 1, 20xx. Stock-related transactions for Czeczh are as follows:

July	1	Issued 20,000 shares of common stock at $11 per share.
	1	Issued 1,000 shares of common stock at $11 per share for services rendered in connection with the organization of the company.
	2	Issued 2,000 shares of preferred stock at par value for cash.
	10	Issued 5,000 shares of common stock for land on which the asking price was $70,000. Market value of the stock was $12. Management wishes to record the land at full market value of the stock.
Aug.	2	Purchased 3,000 shares of its common stock at $13 per share.
	10	Declared a cash dividend for one month on the outstanding preferred stock and $.02 per share on common stock outstanding, payable on August 22 to stockholders of record on August 12.
	12	Date of record for cash dividends.
	22	Paid cash dividends.

REQUIRED ▶

1. Record the transactions in journal form.
2. Prepare the stockholders' equity section of the balance sheet as it would appear on August 31, 20xx. Net income for July and August was $25,000.

Skills Development Cases

Conceptual Analysis

SD 1.

LO1 **Reasons for Issuing Common**
LO2 **Stock**

In a recent year, Avaya, Inc. <www.avaya.com>, an East Coast telecommunications company, issued 34,300,000 shares of common stock for a total of $212,000,000.[15] As a growing company, Avaya could have raised this significant amount of money by issuing long-term bonds, but the company's bond rating had recently been lowered. What are some advantages of issuing common stock as opposed to bonds? What are some disadvantages?

SD 2.

LO4 **Reasons for Issuing Preferred**
 Stock

Preferred stock is a hybrid security; it has some of the characteristics of stock and some of the characteristics of bonds. Historically, preferred stock has not been a popular means of financing. In the past few years, however, it has become more attractive to companies and individual investors alike, and investors are buying large amounts because of high yields. Large preferred stock issues have been made by such banks as Chase <www.chase.com>, Citibank <www.citigroup.com>, HSBC Bank USA <www.us.hsbc.com>, and Wells Fargo <www.wellsfargo.com>, as well as by other companies. The dividends yields on these stocks are over 9 percent, higher than the interest rates on bonds of comparable risk.[16] Especially popular are preferred equity redemption convertible stocks, or PERCs, which are automatically convertible into common stock after three years if the company does not call them first and retire them. What reasons can you give for the popularity of preferred stock, and of PERCs in particular, when the tax-deductible interest on bonds is lower? Discuss from both the company's and the investor's standpoint.

SD 3.

LO6 **Purposes of Treasury Stock**

Many companies in recent years have bought back their common stock. For example, IBM <www.ibm.com>, with large cash holdings, spent almost $27 billion over five years repurchasing its stock. What are the reasons companies buy back their own shares? What is the effect of common stock buybacks on earnings per share, return on equity, return on assets, debt to equity, and the current ratio?

Ethical Dilemma

SD 4.

LO1 Ethics, Management
LO6 Compensation, and Treasury
Stock

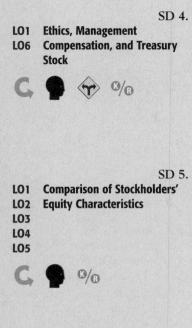

Compensation of senior management is often tied to earnings per share or return on equity. Treasury stock purchases have a favorable impact on both these measures. In the recent buyback boom, many companies borrowed money to purchase treasury shares, resulting in a higher debt to equity ratio. In some cases, the motivation for the borrowing and repurchase of shares was the desire of executives to secure their year-end cash bonuses. Did these executives act ethically? Were their actions in the best interests of stockholders? Why or why not? How might such behavior be avoided in the future?

Research Activity

SD 5.

LO1 Comparison of Stockholders'
LO2 Equity Characteristics
LO3
LO4
LO5

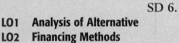

Select the annual reports of three corporations from sources in your library or from the Fingraph® Financial Analyst™ CD-ROM software that accompanies this text. You can choose them from the same industry or at random, at the direction of your instructor. (**Note:** You may be asked to use these companies again in the Research Activity cases in later chapters.) Prepare a table with a column for each corporation. Then answer the following questions for each corporation: Does it have preferred stock? If so, what are the preferred stock's par value and dividend, and is the stock cumulative or convertible? Is the common stock par value or no-par? What is its par value or stated value? What cash dividends, if any, did the corporation pay in the past year? What is the dividends yield? From the notes to the financial statements, determine whether the corporation has an employee stock option plan. If so, what are some of its provisions? What is the return on equity? Be prepared to discuss the characteristics of the stocks and dividends of the three corporations in class.

Decision-Making Practice

SD 6.

LO1 Analysis of Alternative
LO2 Financing Methods

Northeast Servotech Corporation, which offers services to the computer industry, has expanded rapidly in recent years. Because of its profitability, the company has been able to grow without obtaining external financing. This fact is reflected in its current balance sheet, which contains no long-term debt. The liabilities and stockholders' equity sections of the balance sheet on March 31, 20xx, appear below.

Northeast Servotech Corporation
Balance Sheet
March 31, 20xx

Liabilities		
Current liabilities		$ 500,000
Stockholders' Equity		
Common stock, $10 par value, 500,000 shares authorized, 100,000 shares issued and outstanding	$1,000,000	
Paid-in capital in excess of par value, common	1,800,000	
Retained earnings	1,700,000	
Total stockholders' equity		4,500,000
Total liabilities and stockholders' equity		$5,000,000

The company now has the opportunity to double its size by purchasing the operations of a rival company for $4,000,000. If the purchase goes through, Northeast

Servotech will become one of the top companies in its specialized industry. The problem for management is how to finance the purchase. After much study and discussion with bankers and underwriters, management has prepared the following three financing alternatives to present to the board of directors, which must authorize the purchase and the financing:

Alternative A   The company could issue $4,000,000 of long-term debt. Given the company's financial rating and the current market rates, management believes the company will have to pay an interest rate of 12 percent on the debt.

Alternative B   The company could issue 40,000 shares of 8 percent, $100 par value preferred stock.

Alternative C   The company could issue 100,000 additional shares of $10 par value common stock at $40 per share.

Management explains to the board that the interest on the long-term debt is tax-deductible and that the applicable income tax rate is 40 percent. The board members know that a dividend of $.80 per share of common stock was paid last year, up from $.60 and $.40 per share in the two years before that. The board has had a policy of regular increases in dividends of $.20 per share. The board believes each of the three financing alternatives is feasible and now wants to study the financial effects of each alternative.

1. Prepare a schedule to show how the liabilities and stockholders' equity sections of Northeast Servotech's balance sheet would look under each alternative, and compute the debt to equity ratio (total liabilities ÷ total stockholders' equity) for each.
2. Compute and compare the cash needed to pay the interest or dividends for each kind of new financing, net of income taxes, in the first year.
3. How might the cash needed to pay for the financing change in future years under each alternative?
4. Prepare a memorandum to the board of directors that evaluates the alternatives in order of preference based on cash flow effects, giving arguments for and against each one.

Group Activity: Assign the alternatives to different groups to analyze and present to members of the class who act as the board of directors.

FINANCIAL REPORTING AND ANALYSIS CASES

Interpreting Financial Reports

FRA 1.

LO1 **Effect of Stock Issue**
LO2
LO5

Netscape Communications Corporation <www.netscape.com>, now part of AOL–Time Warner, is a leading provider of software that links people and information over the Internet and intranets. It is one of the great success stories of the Internet age. When Netscape went public with an IPO, it issued stock at $14 per share. In its second year as a public company, Netscape announced a common stock issue in an ad in *The Wall Street Journal:*

6,440,000 Shares
NETSCAPE
Common Stock
Price $53¾ a share

If Netscape sold all these shares at the offering price of $53.75, the net proceeds before issue costs would have been $346.15 million.

Shown at the top of the next page is a portion of the stockholders' equity section of the balance sheet adapted from Netscape's annual report, which was issued prior to this stock offering.

REQUIRED ▶

1. Assume the net proceeds from the sale of 6,440,000 shares at $53.75 were $342.6 million after issue costs. Record the stock issuance on Netscape's accounting records in journal form.
2. Prepare the portion of the stockholders' equity section of the balance sheet shown above after the issue of the common stock, based on the information given. Round all answers to the nearest thousand.

Stockholders' Equity (In thousands)	
Common stock, $.0001 par value, 200,000,000 shares authorized, 81,063,158 shares issued and outstanding	$ 8
Additional paid-in capital	196,749
Accumulated deficit	(16,314)

3. Based on your answer in **2,** did Netscape have to increase its authorized shares to undertake this stock issue?

4. What amount per share did Netscape receive and how much did Netscape's underwriters receive to help in issuing the stock if investors paid $53.75 per share? What do underwriters do to earn their fee?

FRA 2.

LO4   **Effect of Deferring Preferred Dividends**

US Airways <www.usairways.com> had indefinitely deferred the quarterly dividend on its $358 million of cumulative convertible 9¼ percent preferred stock.[17] According to a US Airways spokesperson, the company did not want to "continue to pay a dividend while the company is losing money." Others interpreted the action as "an indication of a cash crisis situation."

At the time, Berkshire Hathaway <www.berkshirehathaway.com>, the large company run by Warren Buffett and the owner of the preferred stock, was not happy, but US Airways was able to turn around, become profitable, and return to paying its cumulative dividends on preferred stock. Berkshire Hathaway was able to convert the preferred stock into 9.24 million common shares of US Airways' common stock at $38.74 per share at a time when the market value had risen to $62.[18]

What is cumulative convertible preferred stock? Why is deferring dividends on those shares a drastic action? What is the impact on profitability and liquidity? Why did using preferred stock instead of long-term bonds as a financing method probably save the company from bankruptcy? What was Berkshire Hathaway's gain on its investment at the time of the conversion?

International Company

FRA 3.

LO2   **Stockholders' Equity and**
LO3   **Dividends**

Roche Group <www.roche.com> is a giant Swiss pharmaceutical company. Its stockholders' equity shows how little importance common stock, which the Swiss call *share capital*, typically has in the financing of Swiss companies:[19]

	2001	2000
Shareholders' equity (in millions of Swiss francs)		
Share capital	160	160
Retained earnings	32,273	31,614
Total shareholders' equity	32,433	31,774

When Swiss companies need financing, they often rely on debt financing from large Swiss banks and other debt markets. With only 160 million Swiss francs (1.6 million shares) in share capital, Roche has had few stock issues in its history. In contrast, the company has over 42 billion Swiss francs in liabilities. Roche has been profitable, having built up retained earnings of more than 32 billion Swiss francs over the years. The company also pays a substantial dividend that totaled 981 million Swiss francs in 2001.

Calculate the dividends per share and dividends yield assuming a share price of 118.5 Swiss francs. Assuming that dividends and net income were the only factors that affected retained earnings during 2001, how much did Roche earn in 2001 in U.S. dollars (use an exchange rate of 1.7 Swiss francs to the dollar)? What was Roche's return on equity? Comment on Roche's dividend policy and its level of earnings.

Toys "R" Us Annual Report

FRA 4.

LO1 **Stockholders' Equity**
LO2
LO6

Refer to the Toys "R" Us <www.tru.com> annual report to answer the following questions:

1. What type of capital stock does Toys "R" Us have? What is the par value? How many shares were authorized, issued, and outstanding at the end of fiscal 2001?
2. What is the dividends yield for Toys "R" Us and its relationship to the investors' total return? Does the company rely mostly on stock or on earnings for its stockholders' equity?
3. Does the company have a stock option plan? To whom do the stock options apply? Do employees have significant stock options? Given the market price of the stock shown in the report, do these options represent significant value to the employees?
4. Calculate and discuss the price/earnings ratio and return on equity for 2000 and 2001. The average share price for the fourth quarter was $20.60 and $21.13 for 2000 and 2001, respectively.

Comparison Case: Toys "R" Us and Walgreen Co.

FRA 5.

LO1 **Return on Equity, Treasury Stock, and Dividends Policy**

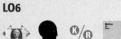

Refer to the annual report of Toys "R" Us <www.tru.com> and the financial statements and notes of Walgreens <www.walgreens.com> in the Supplement to Chapter 1.

1. Compute the return on equity for both companies for the most recent two years.
2. Did either company purchase treasury stock during these years? How will the purchase of treasury stock affect return on equity and earnings per share?
3. Did either company issue stock during these years? What are the details?
4. Compare the dividend policy of the two companies.

Fingraph® Financial Analyst™

FRA 6.

LO1 **Comparative Analysis of**
LO2 **Stockholders' Equity**
LO6

Select any two companies from the list of Fingraph companies on the Needles Accounting Resource Center Web Site at http://accounting.college.hmco.com/students. Access the Microsoft Excel spreadsheets for the companies you selected.

1. In the Fingraph spreadsheet for each company, identify the equity section of the balance sheet information. Do the companies have more than one kind of capital stock? Do the companies have treasury stock?
2. Using the Fingraph CD-ROM software, prepare a page of text that summarizes the price/earnings ratio and dividends yield for each company.
3. Using the Fingraph CD-ROM software, prepare a page of text that summarizes the financing section of each company's statement of cash flows.
4. Write a one-page executive summary that highlights the types of capital stock and the significance of treasury stock for these companies. Mention the extent to which they raised cash from recent stock issues or used cash to repurchase capital stock. Describe the impact on total equity. Also compare the price/earnings ratio and dividends yield trends of the two companies. Include your Fingraph pages with your report.

Internet Case

FRA 7.

LO1 **Comparison of Financing of**
LO3 **Internet Companies**
LO4
LO5
LO6

Many Internet start-up companies have gone public in recent years. These companies are generally unprofitable and require a great deal of cash to finance expansion. They also reward their employees with stock options. Choose any two of the following Internet companies: Amazon.com <www.amazon.com>, Yahoo! <www.yahoo.com>, eBay Inc.

<www.ebay.com>, or AOL-Time Warner <www.aoltw.com>. Go to the web sites of the two companies you have selected. In their latest annual reports, look at the financing section of the statement of cash flows for the last three years. How have these two companies financed their businesses? Have they issued stock or long-term debt? Have they purchased treasury stock, paid dividends, or issued stock under stock option plans? Are the companies profitable (see net income or earnings at the top of the statement)? Are your findings in line with your expectations about these Internet companies? Find each company's stock price, either on its web site or in a newspaper, and compare it with the average issue price of that company's past stock issues. Summarize your findings and conclusions.

Chapter 13 focuses on the components of the corporate income statement and the statement of stockholders' equity within the context of evaluating quality of earnings. The chapter also covers earnings per share, stock dividends, stock splits, and book value per share.

The Corporate Income Statement and the Statement of Stockholders' Equity

LEARNING OBJECTIVES

LO1 Prepare a corporate income statement and identify the issues related to evaluating the quality of earnings.

LO2 Show the relationships among income taxes expense, deferred income taxes, and net of taxes.

LO3 Describe the disclosure on the income statement of discontinued operations, extraordinary items, and accounting changes.

LO4 Compute earnings per share.

LO5 Prepare a statement of stockholders' equity.

LO6 Account for stock dividends and stock splits.

LO7 Calculate book value per share.

DECISION POINT

A USER'S FOCUS

AMR Corporation <www.amrcorp.com> AMR Corporation, American Airlines' parent company, is one of the two largest airline companies in the United States. Its operating results are of interest to many people, but interpreting these results is not always easy. Net earnings per share is the "bottom line" by which many investors judge a company's success or failure. But the bottom line can be misleading. Corporate income statements may contain increases and decreases made at the discretion of management that cause the bottom line to vary. For instance, consider AMR's performance for the three-year period from 1998 to 2000, as measured in earnings per share.[1] As shown in the Financial Highlights, net earnings per share decreased steadily from $7.78 in 1998 to $5.43 in 2000. Discontinued operations contributed to the decrease in each of the three years, and the company had an extraordinary loss in 2000. As a result, income from operations was lower than the "bottom-line" numbers and is a better indicator of the company's future operations. In this chapter, we examine the components of the corporate income statement and the statement of stockholders' equity with a view to understanding their impact on a company's future operations.

Why was American Airlines' income from operations lower than its "bottom-line" numbers?

Financial Highlights			
Earnings per Share: Basic	2000	1999	1998
Income from continuing operations	$ 5.20	$ 4.30	$ 6.60
Discontinued operations	0.30	2.16	1.18
Extraordinary loss	(0.07)	—	—
Net earnings	$ 5.43	$ 6.46	$ 7.78

PERFORMANCE MEASUREMENT: QUALITY OF EARNINGS ISSUES

LO1 Prepare a corporate income statement and identify the issues related to evaluating the quality of earnings.

RELATED TEXT ASSIGNMENTS
Q: 1, 2, 3, 4, 5
SE: 1, 2
E: 1, 2, 3
P: 1, 2, 3, 6
SD: 1, 2, 4
FRA: 1, 4, 6, 7

The Financial Accounting Standards Board (FASB) has taken the position that income for a period should be all-inclusive, comprehensive income, which is different from net income.[2] **Comprehensive income** is the change in a company's equity from sources other than owners during a period; it includes net income, changes in unrealized investment gains and losses, and other items affecting equity. Companies are reporting comprehensive income and its components as a separate financial statement or as a part of another financial statement.

In a recent survey of 600 large companies, 519 reported comprehensive income. Of these, 81 percent reported comprehensive income on the statement of stockholders' equity, 13 percent reported it on a separate statement, and only 6 percent reported it on the income statement.[3] In the illustration of comprehensive income later in this chapter, we follow the most common practice and show it as a part of the statement of stockholders' equity.

THE CORPORATE INCOME STATEMENT

www.aimr.org

Net income is the most commonly used measure of earnings because current and expected earnings are important factors in evaluating a company's performance and analyzing its prospects. In fact, a survey of 2,000 members of the Association for Investment Management and Research indicated that the two most important economic measures in evaluating common stocks were expected changes in earnings per share and expected return on equity;[4] net income is a key component of both measures. The corporate income statement is the statement that shows how a company's net income is derived.

KEY POINT: It is important to know which items included in earnings are recurring and which are one-time items. Income from continuing operations before nonoperating items gives a clear signal about future results. In assessing the company's future earnings potential, nonoperating items are excluded because they are not expected to continue.

Net income or loss for a period includes all revenues, expenses, gains, and losses over the period, with the exception of prior period adjustments. Thus, the corporate income statement may consist of several components, as illustrated in Exhibit 1. When a company has both continuing and discontinued operations, the operating income section is called **income from continuing operations**. Income from continuing operations before income taxes is affected by choices of accounting methods and estimates and may contain such items as gains and losses, write-downs, and restructurings. The income taxes expense section of the statement is also subject to special accounting rules. The lower part of the statement may contain such nonoperating items as discontinued operations, extraordinary gains and losses, and effects of accounting changes. Another item that may appear in this section is the write-off of goodwill when its value has been impaired. Finally, earnings per share information appears at the bottom of the statement. We discuss these components of the corporate income statement in more detail later in the chapter.

FOCUS ON BUSINESS PRACTICE

Why Do Investors Study Quality of Earnings?

Analysts for Twentieth Century Mutual Funds, a major investment company, now merged with American Century Services Corp. <www.americancentury.com>, make adjustments to a company's reported financial performance to create a more accurate picture of the company's ongoing operations. Assume a paper company reports earnings of $1.30 per share, which makes year-to-year comparisons unusually strong. Upon further investigation, however, it is found that the per share number includes a one-time gain on the sale of assets of $.25 per share. Twentieth Century would list the company in its data base as earning only $1.05 per share. "These kinds of adjustments help assure long-term decisions aren't based on one-time events."[5]

Because of the importance of net income, or the "bottom line," in measuring a company's prospects, there is significant interest in evaluating the quality of the net income figure, or the **quality of earnings**. The quality of a company's earnings refers to the substance of earnings and their sustainability into future accounting periods. For example, if earnings increase because of a gain on the sale of an asset, analysts may not view this portion of earnings as sustainable. The quality of earnings may be affected by the accounting methods and estimates the company's management chooses and by the gains and losses, the write-downs and restructurings, and the nature of the nonoperating items reported on the income statement. Since management has choices in the content and positioning of these income-statement categories, there is the potential for man-

EXHIBIT 1
Corporate Income Statement

Junction Corporation
Income Statement
For the Year Ended December 31, 20x1

Operating items before income taxes →	Revenues	$925,000
	Costs and expenses	(550,000)
	Gain on sale of assets	150,000
	Write-downs of assets	(25,000)
	Restructurings	(75,000)

Income taxes →	Income from continuing operations before income taxes	$425,000
	Income taxes expense	144,500

	Income from continuing operations		$280,500
	Discontinued operations		
	Income from operations of discontinued segment (net of taxes, $35,000)	$90,000	
	Loss on disposal of segment (net of taxes, $42,000)	(73,000)	17,000

Nonoperating items →	Income before extraordinary items and cumulative effect of accounting change	$297,500
	Extraordinary gain (net of taxes, $17,000)	43,000
	Subtotal	$340,500
	Cumulative effect of a change in accounting principle (net of taxes, $5,000)	(6,000)
	Net income	$334,500

Earnings per share information →	Earnings per common share:	
	Income from continuing operations	$ 2.81
	Discontinued operations (net of taxes)	.17
	Income before extraordinary items and cumulative effect of accounting change	$ 2.98
	Extraordinary gain (net of taxes)	.43
	Cumulative effect of accounting change (net of taxes)	(.06)
	Net income	$ 3.35

(handwritten margin note: Know sequence)

ENRICHMENT NOTE:
Management is responsible for the content of financial statements. Financial statements report on the performance of management. When a group is responsible for reporting on its own activity, usually the best or most favorable position will be reported.

aging earnings to achieve specific income targets. Thus, it is critical for users of income statements to understand these factors and take them into consideration when evaluating a company's performance.

CHOICE OF ACCOUNTING METHODS AND ESTIMATES

Choices of accounting methods and estimates affect a firm's operating income. To assure proper matching of revenues and expenses, accounting requires cost allocations and estimates of data that will not be known with certainty until some future date. For example, accountants estimate the useful life of assets when they are acquired. However, technological obsolescence could shorten the expected useful life, and excellent maintenance and repairs could lengthen it. The actual useful life will not be known with certainty until some future date. The estimate affects both current and future operating income.

Because there is considerable latitude in assumptions underlying estimates, management and other financial statement users must be aware of the impact of accounting estimates on reported operating income. Estimates include percentage of uncollectible accounts receivable, sales returns, useful life, residual or salvage value, total units of production, total recoverable units of natural resources, amortization period, expected warranty claims, and expected environmental cleanup costs.

These estimates are not equally important to all firms. Their relative importance depends on the industry in which a firm operates. For example, the estimate of uncollectible receivables for a credit card firm, such as American Express, or a financial services firm, such as Bank of America, can have a material impact on earnings, but the estimate of useful life may be less important because depreciable assets represent only a small percentage of total assets. Toys "R" Us has very few receivables, but it has substantial investment in depreciable assets; thus, estimates of useful life and residual value are much more important than the estimate of uncollectible accounts receivable.

The choice of methods also affects a firm's operating income. Generally accepted accounting methods include uncollectible receivable methods (percentage of net sales and aging of accounts receivable), inventory methods (last-in, first-out [LIFO]; first-in, first-out [FIFO]; and average-cost), depreciation methods (accelerated, production, and straight-line), and revenue recognition methods. These methods are designed to match revenues and expenses. Costs are allocated based on a determination of the benefits to the current period (expenses) versus the benefits to future periods (assets). The expenses are estimates, and the period or periods benefited cannot be demonstrated conclusively. The estimates are also subjective, because in practice it is hard to justify one method of estimation over another.

For these reasons, management, the accountant, and the financial statement user need to understand the possible effects of different accounting procedures on net income and financial position. Some methods and estimates are more conservative than others because they tend to produce a lower net income in the current period. For example, suppose that two companies have similar operations, but one uses FIFO for inventory costing and straight-line (SL) for computing depreciation, whereas the other uses LIFO for inventory costing and double-declining-balance (DDB) for computing depreciation. The income statements of the two companies might appear as follows:

www.americanexpress.com
www.bankofamerica.com

www.tru.com

KEY POINT: Two companies in the same industry may have comparable earnings quantity but not comparable earnings quality. To assess the quality of reported earnings, one must know the methods and estimates used to compute income. GAAP allow several methods and estimates, all yielding different results.

	FIFO and SL	LIFO and DDB
Net sales	$925,000	$925,000
Goods available for sale	$400,000	$400,000
Less ending inventory	60,000	50,000
Cost of goods sold	$340,000	$350,000
Gross margin	$585,000	$575,000
Less depreciation expense	$ 40,000	$ 80,000
Less other expenses	170,000	170,000
Total operating expenses	$210,000	$250,000
Income from continuing operations before special items and income taxes	$375,000	$325,000

The income from continuing operations before special items and income taxes (operating income) for the firm using LIFO and DDB is lower because in periods of rising prices, the LIFO inventory costing method produces a higher cost of goods sold, and, in the early years of an asset's useful life, accelerated depreciation yields a higher depreciation expense. The result is lower operating income. However, future operating income is expected to be higher. It is also important that the choice of accounting method does not affect cash flows except for possible differences in income taxes caused by the use of one method instead of another.

The $50,000 difference in operating income stems only from the differences in accounting methods. Differences in the estimated lives and residual values of the plant assets could lead to an even greater variation. In practice, of course, differences in net income occur for many reasons, but the user must be aware of the discrepancies that can occur as a result of the accounting methods chosen by management. In general, an accounting method or estimate that results in lower current earnings is considered to produce a better quality of operating income.

The existence of such alternatives could cause problems in the interpretation of financial statements were it not for the conventions of full disclosure and consistency. As noted in an earlier chapter, full disclosure requires that management explain the significant accounting policies used in preparing the financial statements in a note to the statements. Consistency requires that the same accounting procedures be followed from year to year. If a change in procedure is made, the nature of the change and its monetary effect must be explained in a note.

GAINS AND LOSSES

When a company sells or otherwise disposes of operating assets or marketable securities, a gain or loss generally results. These gains or losses appear in the operating portion of the income statement, but they usually represent one-time events. They are not sustainable, ongoing operations, and management often has some choice as to their timing. Thus, from an analyst's point of view, they should be ignored when considering operating income.

WRITE-DOWNS AND RESTRUCTURINGS

Management has considerable latitude in deciding when an asset is no longer of value to the company. If the value of an asset is impaired, management may decide to record a write-down. A **write-down**, also referred to as a *write-off*, is the recording of a decrease in the value of an asset below the carrying value on the balance sheet and the reduction of income in the current period by the amount of the decrease. If operations have changed, management may decide to record a restructuring. A **restructuring** is the estimated cost associated with a change in a company's operations, usually involving the closing of facilities and the laying off of personnel. Both write-downs and restructurings reduce current operating income and boost future income by shifting future costs to the current accounting period.

Write-downs and restructurings are important to consider because they often are an indication of bad management decisions in the past, such as paying too much for the assets of another company or making operational changes that do not work out. Companies sometimes take all possible losses in the current year so that future years will be "clean" of these costs. Such "big baths," as they are called, commonly occur when a company is having a bad year. They also often occur in years when there is a change in management. The new management takes a "big bath" in the current year so it can show improved results in future years.

Write-downs and restructurings are common. In a recent year, 27 percent of 600 large companies had write-downs, and 26 percent had restructurings. Another 24 percent had write-downs or charges involving intangible assets.[6] As discussed in the chapter on long-term assets, goodwill is subject to an annual impairment test to determine if its current fair value is below cost.

NATURE OF NONOPERATING ITEMS

The nonoperating items that appear on the income statement, such as discontinued operations, extraordinary gains and losses, and effects of accounting changes, can also significantly affect the bottom line, or net income. In fact, in Exhibit 1, earnings

<aside>
⬢ **STOP AND THINK!**

Is it unethical for new management to take a "big bath" in order to enhance future performance?

It is not unethical as long as new management stays within the accounting rules and properly discloses its actions. An investor or analyst must be aware of these actions and take them into consideration when evaluating the company's performance. ■
</aside>

FOCUS ON BUSINESS ETHICS

Whistle-Blowing

External users of financial statements depend on management's honesty and openness in disclosing factual information about a company. In the vast majority of cases, management's reports are reliable, but there are exceptions. Whistle-blowers—employees who step forward to disclose such exceptions and other types of wrongdoing they observe in their companies—run various risks, including losing their jobs, with no assurance that their actions will have any effect. In the recent Enron

case, the largest bankruptcy in U.S. history, the whistle-blower was a company accountant who, well before the firm's collapse, informed her CEO and the firm's external auditors of Enron's questionable accounting practices. Although her warnings were ignored then, they made headlines during the SEC and congressional investigations, as well as the criminal prosecutions that followed the collapse.[7]

ENRICHMENT NOTE:
Discontinued operations, extraordinary items, and cumulative effects of a change in accounting principle are more likely to occur in large, public corporations. A knowledge of these items is important when analyzing **www.sears.com** the financial results of such companies. These items do not occur as frequently in small, private corporations.

per common share for income from continuing operations are $2.81, but net income per share is $3.35 when all the nonoperating items are taken into consideration.

For practical reasons, the calculations of trends and ratios are based on the assumption that net income and other components are comparable from year to year and from company to company. However, in making interpretations, the astute analyst will always look beyond the ratios to the quality of the components. For example, write-downs, restructurings, and nonoperating items, if the charges are large enough, can have a significant effect on a company's return on equity.

A company may boost income by including one-time gains. For example, Sears, Roebuck and Co. used a gain from the change of an accounting principle to bolster its net income by $136 million or by $.35 per share. Without the gain, earnings per share (EPS) would have decreased from $3.12 to $2.92, not increased as Sears reported.[8] The quality of Sears's earnings is, in fact, lower than it might appear on the surface. Unless analysts are prepared to go beyond the "bottom line" in analyzing and interpreting financial reports, they can come to the wrong conclusions.

EFFECT OF QUALITY OF EARNINGS ON CASH FLOWS AND PERFORMANCE MEASURES

The reason for considering quality of earnings issues is to assess their effects on cash flows and performance measures. Generally speaking, except for possible income tax effects, none of the gains and losses, asset write-downs, restructurings, and nonoperating items has any effect on cash flows. The cash expenditures for these items were made previously. For this reason, the focus of analysis is on sustainable earnings, which generally have a relationship to future cash flows.

Since management's performance and compensation are often linked to return on assets or return on equity, it is important to understand the nature of both the numerator and denominator of these performance measures. Most commonly, the numerator in these ratios is net income. However, when a company has a complex income statement with items that affect quality of earnings, such as those discussed above, it is important not to take net income at face value. Consider the example of Junction Corporation in Exhibit 1. The reported net income is $334,500, whereas income from continuing operations is $280,500. Even the latter amount is a questionable measure of sustainable earnings because of the gain, write-down, and restructuring, which collectively added $50,000 to income from continuing operations before income taxes. With a tax rate of 34 percent, the sustainable earnings after income taxes are probably close to $247,500 [$280,500 − ($50,000 × .66)].

It also pays to examine how quality of earnings issues affect the denominator of the return on assets and return on equity ratios. If a company has a write-down or restructuring of assets, in addition to a reduction in net income, there is also a reduction in assets and in stockholders' equity, which tends to improve these ratios in current and future years. This contributes to the motivation to take "big-bath" write-offs in years that are poor anyway so that it will be easier to show improvement in future ratios.

 Check out ACE for a Review Quiz at http://accounting.college.hmco.com/students.

INCOME TAXES EXPENSE

LO2   Show the relationships among income taxes expense, deferred income taxes, and net of taxes.

RELATED TEXT ASSIGNMENTS
Q: 6, 7
SE: 3
E: 3, 4, 5
P: 2, 3, 6
SD: 4
FRA: 2

ENRICHMENT NOTE:
Most people think it is illegal to keep accounting records on a different basis from income tax records. However, the Internal Revenue Code and GAAP often do not agree. To work with two conflicting sets of guidelines, the accountant must keep two sets of records.

ENRICHMENT NOTE: The federal income tax is progressive. That is, the rate increases as taxable income increases.

Corporations determine their taxable income (the amount on which taxes are paid) by subtracting allowable business deductions from includable gross income. The federal tax laws determine which business expenses may be deducted and which cannot be deducted from taxable gross income. (Rules for calculating and reporting taxable income in specialized industries, such as banking, insurance, mutual funds, and cooperatives, are highly technical and may vary significantly from the ones we discuss in this chapter.)

Table 1 shows the tax rates that apply to a corporation's taxable income. A corporation with taxable income of $70,000 would have a federal income tax liability of $12,500: $7,500 (the tax on the first $50,000 of taxable income) plus $5,000 (25 percent of the $20,000 earned in excess of $50,000).

Income taxes expense is the expense recognized in the accounting records on an accrual basis that applies to income from continuing operations. This expense may or may not equal the amount of taxes actually paid by the corporation and recorded as income taxes payable in the current period. The amount payable is determined from taxable income, which is measured according to the rules and regulations of the income tax code.

For the sake of convenience, most small businesses keep their accounting records on the same basis as their tax records, so that the income taxes expense on the income statement equals the income taxes liability to be paid to the U.S. Treasury. This practice is acceptable when there is no material difference between the income on an accounting basis and the income on an income tax basis. However, the purpose of accounting is to determine net income in accordance with generally accepted accounting principles, not to determine taxable income and tax liability.

Management has an incentive to use methods that minimize the firm's tax liability, but accountants, who are bound by accrual accounting and the materiality concept, cannot let tax procedures dictate their method of preparing financial statements if the result would be misleading. As a consequence, there can be a material

TABLE 1.   Tax Rate Schedule for Corporations, 2001

Taxable Income		Tax Liability	
Over	But Not Over		Of the Amount Over
—	$ 50,000	0 + 15%	—
$ 50,000	75,000	$ 7,500 + 25%	$ 50,000
75,000	100,000	13,750 + 34%	75,000
100,000	335,000	22,250 + 39%	100,000
335,000	10,000,000	113,900 + 34%	335,000
10,000,000	15,000,000	3,400,000 + 35%	10,000,000
15,000,000	18,333,333	5,150,000 + 38%	15,000,000
18,333,333	—	6,416,667 + 35%	18,333,333

Note: Tax rates are subject to change by Congress.

difference between accounting income and taxable income, especially in larger businesses. This discrepancy can result from differences in the timing of the recognition of revenues and expenses under the two accounting methods. Some possible variations are shown below.

	Accounting Method	**Tax Method**
Expense recognition	Accrual or deferral	At time of expenditure
Accounts receivable	Allowance	Direct charge-off
Inventories	Average-cost	FIFO
Depreciation	Straight-line	Modified Accelerated Cost Recovery System

DEFERRED INCOME TAXES

KEY POINT: The discrepancy between GAAP-based tax expense and Internal Revenue Code-based tax liability produces the need for the Deferred Income Taxes account.

The accounting method used to accrue income taxes expense on the basis of accounting income whenever there are differences between accounting and taxable income is called **income tax allocation**. The account used to record the difference between the income taxes expense and income taxes payable is called **Deferred Income Taxes**. For example, Junction Corporation shows income taxes expense of $144,500 on its income statement in Exhibit 1, but it has actual income taxes payable to the U.S. Treasury of $92,000. The following entry records the estimated income taxes expense applicable to income from continuing operations using the income tax allocation procedure:

$A = L + OE$
$+ \quad -$
$\quad +$

Dec. 31	Income Taxes Expense	144,500	
	Income Taxes Payable		92,000
	Deferred Income Taxes		52,500
	To record estimated current and deferred income taxes		

● **STOP AND THINK!**
What is an argument against the recording of deferred income taxes?

Because the recording of deferred income taxes depends on future actions of management, which may or may not happen, critics of deferred taxes argue that the income taxes for a particular year should simply be the amount of income taxes paid. Thus, each year is allowed to stand on its own. ■

In other years, it is possible for Income Taxes Payable to exceed Income Taxes Expense, in which case the same entry is made except that Deferred Income Taxes is debited.

The Financial Accounting Standards Board has issued specific rules for recording, measuring, and classifying deferred income taxes.[9] Deferred income taxes are recognized for the estimated future tax effects resulting from temporary differences in the valuation of assets, liabilities, equity, revenues, expenses, gains, and losses for tax and financial reporting purposes. Temporary differences include revenues and expenses or gains and losses that are included in taxable income before or after they are included in financial income. In other words, the recognition point for revenues, expenses, gains, and losses is not the same for tax and financial reporting. For example, advance payments for goods and services, such as magazine subscriptions, are not recognized in financial income until the product is shipped, but for tax purposes they are usually recognized as revenue when cash is received. The result is that taxes paid exceed taxes expense, which creates a deferred income taxes asset (or prepaid taxes).

STUDY NOTE: Deferred Income Taxes is classified as a liability when it has a credit balance and as an asset when it has a debit balance. It is further classified as either current or long-term depending on when it is expected to reverse.

Classification of deferred income taxes as current or noncurrent depends on the classification of the related asset or liability that created the temporary difference. For example, the deferred income taxes asset mentioned above would be classified as current if unearned subscription revenue is classified as a current liability. On the other hand, the temporary difference arising from depreciation is related to a long-term depreciable asset. Therefore, the resulting deferred income taxes would be classified as long-term. However, if a temporary difference is not related to an asset or liability, then it is classified as current or noncurrent based on its expected date of reversal. Temporary differences and the classification of deferred income taxes that results are covered in depth in more advanced courses.

Each year, the balance of the Deferred Income Taxes account is evaluated to determine whether it still accurately represents the expected asset or liability in light of legislated changes in income tax laws and regulations. If changes have occurred, an adjusting entry to bring the account balance into line with current laws is required. For example, a decrease in corporate income tax rates, like the one that occurred in 1987, means that a company with a deferred income taxes liability will pay less in taxes in future years than the amount indicated by the credit balance of its Deferred Income Taxes account. As a result, the company would debit Deferred Income Taxes to reduce the liability and credit Gain from Reduction in Income Tax Rates. This credit increases the reported income on the income statement. If the tax rate increases in future years, a loss would be recorded and the deferred income taxes liability would be increased.

In any given year, the amount a company pays in income taxes is determined by subtracting (or adding, as the case may be) the deferred income taxes for that year, as reported in the notes to the financial statements, from (or to) income taxes expense, which is reported in the financial statements. In subsequent years, the amount of deferred income taxes can vary based on changes in tax laws and rates.

Some understanding of the importance of deferred income taxes to financial reporting can be gained from studying a survey of the financial statements of 600 large companies. About 65 percent reported deferred income taxes with a credit balance in the long-term liability section of the balance sheet.[10]

NET OF TAXES

The phrase **net of taxes**, as used in Exhibit 1, means that the effect of applicable taxes (usually income taxes) has been considered in determining the overall effect of an item on the financial statements. The phrase is used on the corporate income statement when a company has items that must be disclosed in a separate section. Each such item should be reported net of the applicable income taxes to avoid distorting the income taxes expense associated with ongoing operations and the resulting net operating income. For example, assume that a corporation with operating income before income taxes of $120,000 has a total tax expense of $66,000 and that the total income includes a gain of $100,000 on which a tax of $30,000 is due. Also assume that the gain is not part of normal operations and must be disclosed separately on the income statement as an extraordinary item (explained later). This is how the income taxes expense would be reported on the income statement:

Operating income before income taxes	$120,000
Income taxes expense	36,000
Income before extraordinary item	$ 84,000
Extraordinary gain (net of taxes, $30,000)	70,000
Net income	$154,000

If all the income taxes expense were deducted from operating income before income taxes, both the income before extraordinary item and the extraordinary gain would be distorted.

A company follows the same procedure in the case of an extraordinary loss. For example, assume the same facts as before except that the total income taxes expense is only $6,000 because of a $100,000 extraordinary loss. The result is a $30,000 tax savings, shown as follows:

Operating income before income taxes	$120,000
Income taxes expense	36,000
Income before extraordinary item	$ 84,000
Extraordinary loss (net of taxes, $30,000)	(70,000)
Net income	$ 14,000

In Exhibit 1, the total of the income tax items for Junction Corporation is $149,500. That amount is allocated among five statement components, as follows:

Income taxes expense on income from continuing operations	$144,500
Income taxes on income from a discontinued segment	35,000
Income tax savings on the loss on the disposal of the segment	(42,000)
Income taxes on the extraordinary gain	17,000
Income tax savings on the cumulative effect of a change in accounting principle	(5,000)
Total income taxes expense	$149,500

✔ Check out ACE for a Review Quiz at http://accounting.college.hmco.com/students.

NONOPERATING ITEMS

LO3 Describe the disclosure on the income statement of discontinued operations, extraordinary items, and accounting changes.

RELATED TEXT ASSIGNMENTS
Q: 8, 9, 10
E: 3
P: 2, 3, 6
SD: 2, 4
FRA: 4, 6

www.amrcorp.com

⬣ **STOP AND THINK!**
Why is it useful to disclose discontinued operations separately on the income statement?

Users of financial statements want to assess the effects of past performance on the future performance of a company. Separating discontinued operations on the income statement helps accomplish that objective. ▪

Nonoperating items are items not related to the company's normal operations. They appear in a separate section of the income statement because they are considered one-time items that will not affect future results. There are three principal kinds of nonoperating items: discontinued operations, extraordinary items, and accounting changes.

DISCONTINUED OPERATIONS

Large companies in the United States usually have many **segments**. A segment may be a separate major line of business or serve a separate class of customer. For example, a company that makes heavy drilling equipment may also have another line of business, such as the manufacture of mobile homes. A large company may discontinue or otherwise dispose of certain segments of its business that do not fit its future plans or are not profitable. **Discontinued operations** are segments of a business that are no longer part of its ongoing operations. Generally accepted accounting principles require that gains and losses from discontinued operations be reported separately on the income statement. Such separation makes it easier to evaluate the ongoing activities of the business. For example, the Financial Highlights in the Decision Point in this chapter show that AMR's discontinued operations are a significant factor in its "bottom-line" earnings per share. The discontinued operations are AMR's Sabre reservation services, one of the steadiest and most profitable parts of the company's business, which it is divesting to the shareholders of the company. For the analyst, this important piece of information means that in the future, the company is going to be more dependent on the volatile airline business.

In Exhibit 1, the disclosure of discontinued operations has two parts. One part shows that after the decision to discontinue, the income from operations of the disposed segment was $90,000 (net of $35,000 taxes). The other part shows that the loss from the disposal of the segment was $73,000 (net of $42,000 tax savings). Computation of the gains or losses is covered in more advanced accounting courses. We have described the disclosure to give a complete view of the corporate income statement.

EXTRAORDINARY ITEMS

In its *Opinion No. 30*, the Accounting Principles Board defines **extraordinary items** as "events or transactions that are distinguished by their unusual nature *and* by the infrequency of their occurrence."[11] Unusual and infrequent occurrences are explained in the opinion as follows:

Unusual Nature—the underlying event or transaction should possess a high degree of abnormality and be of a type clearly unrelated to, or only incidentally related to, the ordinary and typical activities of the entity, taking into account the environment in which the entity operates.

KEY POINT: To qualify as extraordinary, an event must be unusual (not in the ordinary course of business) and must not be expected to occur again in the foreseeable future. Occasionally, it is not clear whether an event meets these two criteria, and the decision then becomes a matter of judgment.

Infrequency of Occurrence—the underlying event or transaction should be of a type that would not reasonably be expected to recur in the foreseeable future, taking into account the environment in which the entity operates.[12]

If an item is both unusual and infrequent (and material in amount), it should be reported separately from continuing operations on the income statement. The disclosure allows readers to identify gains or losses in income that would not be expected to happen again soon. Items usually treated as extraordinary include (1) an uninsured loss from flood, earthquake, fire, or theft; (2) a gain or loss resulting from the passage of a new law; and (3) the expropriation (taking) of property by a foreign government.

Gains or losses from extraordinary items should be reported on the income statement after discontinued operations. And they should be shown net of applicable taxes. In a recent year, 74 (12 percent) of 600 large companies reported extraordinary items on their income statements.[13] In Exhibit 1, the extraordinary gain was $43,000 after applicable taxes of $17,000.

ACCOUNTING CHANGES

ENRICHMENT NOTE: A change in accounting method (principle) violates the convention of consistency. Such a change is allowed, however, when it can be demonstrated that the new method will produce more useful financial statements. The effect of the change is disclosed just above net income on the income statement.

ETHICAL CONSIDERATION: Some accounting changes can produce a significant increase in net income without an accompanying improvement in performance. The user of financial statements should be aware that some businesses implement an accounting change solely for the increase in net income that results.

In a departure from the consistency convention, a company is allowed to make accounting changes if current procedures are incorrect or inappropriate. For example, a change from the FIFO to the LIFO inventory method can be made if there is adequate justification for the change. Adequate justification usually means that if the change occurs, the financial statements will better show the financial activities of the company. A company's desire to lower the amount of income taxes it pays is not considered adequate justification for an accounting change. If justification does exist and an accounting change is made, generally accepted accounting principles require the disclosure of the change in the financial statements.

The **cumulative effect of an accounting change** is the effect that the new accounting principle would have had on net income in prior periods if it had been applied instead of the old principle. This effect is shown on the income statement immediately after extraordinary items.[14] For example, assume that in the five years prior to 20x1, Junction Corporation had used the straight-line method to depreciate its machinery. This year, the company retroactively changed to the double-declining-balance method of depreciation. The controller computed the cumulative effect of the change in depreciation charges (net of taxes) as $6,000, as follows:

Cumulative, five-year double-declining-balance depreciation	$29,000
Less cumulative, five-year straight-line depreciation	18,000
Before tax effect	$11,000
Income tax savings	5,000
Cumulative effect of accounting change	$ 6,000

FOCUS ON INTERNATIONAL BUSINESS

Were Preussag's Year-End Results Really "Remarkable"?

The big German travel company Preussag <www.preussag.com> reported that the year 2000 was "a remarkable year" in which the company achieved "all-time high" results and "profit rose by 16.5 percent." The financial reports reveal that profits would not have been so remarkable if the effects of four voluntary accounting changes had not been taken into account. Profits would have increased by only 6.7 percent if Preussag had not made these changes. The company began recognizing revenue from holiday packages at the beginning of the holiday instead of at the stage of completion, but it began deferring the cost of brochures over future tourist seasons. In addition, the cost of "empty-leg flights" at the beginning and the end of each tourist season are now amortized over the season. Finally the inventory method was changed from LIFO to the average-cost method. None of these cosmetic changes affect future cash flows or change the company's operations for the better.[15]

Relevant information about the accounting change is shown in the notes to the financial statements. The change results in $11,000 of depreciation expense for prior years being deducted in the current year, in addition to the current year's depreciation costs included in the $550,000 costs and expenses section of the income statement. This expense must be shown in the current year's income statement as a reduction in income (see Exhibit 1). In a recent year, 62, or 10 percent, of 600 large companies reported changes in accounting procedures.[16] Further study of accounting changes is left to more advanced accounting courses.

✔ Check out ACE for a Review Quiz at http://accounting.college.hmco.com/students.

EARNINGS PER SHARE

LO4 Compute earnings per share.

RELATED TEXT ASSIGNMENTS

Q: 11, 12, 13
SE: 4
E: 3, 6
P: 2, 3, 6
FRA: 6, 7

www.3m.com

Readers of financial statements use earnings per share information to judge a company's performance and to compare it with the performance of other companies. Because such information is so important, the Accounting Principles Board concluded that earnings per share of common stock should be presented on the face of the income statement.[17] As shown in Exhibit 1, the information is usually disclosed just below the net income.

An earnings per share amount is always shown for (1) income from continuing operations, (2) income before extraordinary items and the cumulative effect of accounting changes, (3) the cumulative effect of accounting changes, and (4) net income. If the statement shows a gain or loss from discontinued operations or a gain or loss on extraordinary items, earnings per share amounts can also be presented for them.

The following per share data from the income statement of Minnesota Mining and Manufacturing Company (3M) show why it is a good idea to study the components of earnings per share:[18]

Ⓚ/Ⓡ

ENRICHMENT NOTE:
Earnings per share is a measure of a corporation's profitability. It is one of the most closely watched financial statement ratios in the business world. Its disclosure on the income statement is required.

Financial Highlights

	2000	1999	1998
Earnings per share—basic			
Income before extraordinary loss and cumulative effect of accounting change	$ 4.69	$ 4.39	$ 3.01
Extraordinary loss	—	—	(.10)
Cumulative effect of accounting change	(.19)	—	—
Net income	$ 4.50	$ 4.39	$ 2.91

Note that net income was influenced by special items in 1998 and 2000: An extraordinary loss decreased income from continuing operations by $.10 per share in 1998, and the cumulative effect of an accounting change decreased earnings by $.19 in 2000. In 1999, the company had no special items; thus, 100 percent of 3M's basic earnings per share were attributable to continuing operations.

Basic earnings per share is net income applicable to common stock divided by the weighted-average number of common shares outstanding. To compute this figure, one must determine if the number of common shares outstanding changed during the year, and if the company paid preferred stock dividends.

When a company has only common stock and has the same number of shares outstanding throughout the year, the earnings per share computation is simple. From Exhibit 1, we know that Junction Corporation reported net income of

● **STOP AND THINK!**
What is one action a company can take to improve its earnings per share without improving its earnings or net income?

Many companies attempt to improve their earnings per share by reducing the number of shares outstanding through buybacks of their own stock. ■

$334,500. Assume that the company had 100,000 shares of common stock outstanding for the entire year. The earnings per share of common stock is computed as follows:

$$\text{Earnings per Share} = \frac{\$334,500}{100,000} = \$3.35 \text{ per share}$$

If the number of shares outstanding changes during the year, it is necessary to figure the weighted-average number of shares outstanding for the year. Suppose that during various periods of the year, Junction Corporation had the following amounts of common shares outstanding: January–March, 100,000 shares; April–September, 120,000 shares; and October–December, 130,000 shares. The weighted-average number of common shares outstanding and basic earnings per share would be found this way:

100,000 shares × ³⁄₁₂ year	25,000
120,000 shares × ⁶⁄₁₂ year	60,000
130,000 shares × ³⁄₁₂ year	32,500
Weighted-average common shares outstanding	117,500

$$\text{Basic Earnings per Share} = \frac{\text{Net Income}}{\text{Weighted-Average Common Shares Outstanding}}$$

$$= \frac{\$334,500}{117,500 \text{ shares}} = \$2.85 \text{ per share}$$

If a company has nonconvertible preferred stock outstanding, the dividend for that stock must be subtracted from net income before earnings per share for common stock are computed. Suppose that Junction Corporation has preferred stock on which the annual dividend is $23,500. Earnings per share on common stock would be $2.65 [($334,500 − $23,500) ÷ 117,500 shares].

Companies with a capital structure in which there are no bonds, stocks, or stock options that can be converted into common stock are said to have a **simple capital structure**. The earnings per share for these companies is computed as shown above. Some companies, however, have a **complex capital structure**, which includes exercisable stock options or convertible preferred stocks and bonds. Those convertible securities have the potential of diluting the earnings per share of common stock. *Potential dilution* means that a stockholder's proportionate share of ownership in a company could be reduced through the conversion of stocks or bonds or the exercise of stock options, which would increase the total number of shares the company has outstanding.

For example, suppose that a person owns 10,000 shares of a company, which equals 2 percent of the outstanding shares of 500,000. Now suppose that holders of convertible bonds convert the bonds into 100,000 shares of stock. The person's 10,000 shares would then equal only 1.67 percent (10,000 ÷ 600,000) of the outstanding shares. In addition, the added shares outstanding would lower earnings per share and would most likely lower market price per share.

Because stock options and convertible preferred stocks or bonds have the potential to dilute earnings per share, they are referred to as **potentially dilutive securities**. When a company has a complex capital structure, it must report two earnings per share figures: basic earnings per share and diluted earnings per share.[19] **Diluted earnings per share** are calculated by adding all potentially dilutive securities to the denominator of the basic earnings per share calculation. This figure shows stockholders the maximum potential effect of dilution on their ownership position in the company.

The difference between basic and diluted earnings per share can be significant. For example, consider the results reported by AMR Corporation:

KEY POINT: A company with potentially dilutive securities (such as convertible preferred stock or bonds) has a complex capital structure and must present two earnings per share figures—basic and diluted. The latter figure is the more conservative of the two.

www.amrcorp.com

Financial Highlights			
	2000	1999	1998
Basic earnings per share	$5.43	$6.46	$7.78
Diluted earnings per share	5.03	6.26	7.52

Note that while both measures of earnings per share are decreasing, basic earnings per share are greater by 3–8 percent.[20] The basic earnings per share is used in various ratios, including the price/earnings ratio.

The computation of diluted earnings per share is a complex process and is reserved for more advanced courses.

✓ Check out ACE for a Review Quiz at http://accounting.college.hmco.com/students.

THE STATEMENT OF STOCKHOLDERS' EQUITY

LO5 Prepare a statement of stockholders' equity.

RELATED TEXT ASSIGNMENTS
Q: 14, 15, 16
SE: 5, 6, 7
E: 7, 8
P: 4, 5, 7, 8
SD: 4, 5
FRA: 1, 3, 4, 6, 7

⬢ **STOP AND THINK!**
In Exhibit 2, what is the total amount of comprehensive income?

The total amount of comprehensive income includes all changes in stockholders' equity not involving the owners. In Exhibit 2, it is the net income of $270,000 and accumulated other comprehensive income (foreign currency translation adjustment) of ($10,000), or $260,000. ∎

KEY POINT: The statement of stockholders' equity is a labeled calculation of the change in each stockholders' equity account over the period.

KEY POINT: In accounting, a deficit is a negative (debit) balance in Retained Earnings. It is not the same thing as a net loss, which reflects the performance in just one accounting period.

The **statement of stockholders' equity**, also called the *statement of changes in stockholders' equity*, summarizes the changes in the components of the stockholders' equity section of the balance sheet. More and more companies are using this statement in place of the statement of retained earnings because it reveals much more about the year's stockholders' equity transactions. In the statement of stockholders' equity in Exhibit 2, for example, the first line shows the beginning balance of each account in the stockholders' equity section. Each subsequent line discloses the effects of transactions on those accounts. Tri-State earned net income of $270,000 and had a foreign currency translation loss of $10,000, reported as accumulated other comprehensive income. These two items together resulted in comprehensive income of $260,000. The statement also shows that during 20x1 Tri-State Corporation issued 5,000 shares of common stock for $250,000, had a conversion of $100,000 of preferred stock into common stock, declared and issued a 10 percent stock dividend on common stock, had a net purchase of treasury shares of $24,000, and paid cash dividends on both preferred and common stock. The ending balances of the accounts are presented at the bottom of the statement. Those accounts and balances make up the stockholders' equity section of Tri-State's balance sheet on December 31, 20x1, as shown in Exhibit 3.

RETAINED EARNINGS

Notice that in Exhibit 2 the Retained Earnings column has the same components as the statement of retained earnings. The **retained earnings** of a company are the part of stockholders' equity that represents stockholders' claims to assets arising from the earnings of the business. Retained earnings equal a company's profits since the date of its inception, less any losses, dividends to stockholders, or transfers to contributed capital.

It is important to remember that retained earnings are not the assets themselves. The existence of retained earnings means that assets generated by profitable operations have been kept in the company to help it grow or meet other business needs. A credit balance in Retained Earnings is *not* directly associated with a specific amount of cash or designated assets. Rather, such a balance means that assets as a whole have been increased.

Retained Earnings can carry a debit balance. Generally, this happens when a company's dividends and subsequent losses are greater than its accumulated profits from operations. In such a case, the firm is said to have a **deficit** (debit balance) in Retained Earnings. A deficit is shown in the stockholders' equity section of the balance sheet as a deduction from contributed capital.

EXHIBIT 2
Statement of Stockholders' Equity

Tri-State Corporation
Statement of Stockholders' Equity
For the Year Ended December 31, 20x1

	Preferred Stock $100 Par Value 8% Convertible	Common Stock $10 Par Value	Paid-in Capital in Excess of Par Value, Common	Retained Earnings	Treasury Stock	Accumulated Other Comprehensive Income	Total
Balance, December 31, 20x0	$400,000	$300,000	$300,000	$600,000	—		$1,600,000
Net income				270,000			270,000
Foreign currency translation adjustment						($10,000)	(10,000)
Issuance of 5,000 shares of common stock		50,000	200,000				250,000
Conversion of 1,000 shares of preferred stock to 3,000 shares of common stock	(100,000)	30,000	70,000				—
10 percent stock dividend on common stock, 3,800 shares		38,000	152,000	(190,000)			—
Purchase of 500 shares of treasury stock					($24,000)		(24,000)
Cash dividends							
Preferred stock				(24,000)			(24,000)
Common stock				(47,600)			(47,600)
Balance, December 31, 20x1	$300,000	$418,000	$722,000	$608,400	($24,000)	($10,000)	$2,014,400

EXHIBIT 3
Stockholders' Equity Section of a Balance Sheet

KEY POINT: The ending balances on the statement of stockholders' equity are transferred to the stockholders' equity section of the balance sheet.

Tri-State Corporation
Stockholders' Equity
December 31, 20x1

Contributed capital		
Preferred stock, $100 par value, 8 percent convertible, 10,000 shares authorized, 3,000 shares issued and outstanding		$ 300,000
Common stock, $10 par value, 100,000 shares authorized, 41,800 shares issued, 41,300 shares outstanding	$418,000	
Paid-in capital in excess of par value, common	722,000	1,140,000
Total contributed capital		$1,440,000
Retained earnings		608,400
Total contributed capital and retained earnings		$2,048,400
Less treasury stock, common (500 shares, at cost)	$ 24,000	
Foreign currency translation adjustment	10,000	34,000
Total stockholders' equity		$2,014,400

FOCUS ON INTERNATIONAL BUSINESS

Why Are Reserves Common in Other Countries?

Restrictions on retained earnings, called *reserves*, are much more common in some foreign countries than in the United States. In Sweden, for instance, reserves are used to respond to fluctuations in the economy. The Swedish tax code allows companies to set up contingency reserves for the purpose of maintaining financial stability. Appropriations to those reserves reduce taxable income and income taxes. The reserves become taxable when they are reversed, but they are available to absorb losses should they occur. For example, Skandia Group <www.skandia.com>, a large Swedish insurance company, reported a net income of only SK2,826 million in 2000, considerably less than the SK3,456 million in 1999. An examination of its statement of stockholders' equity shows restricted reserves in 2000 of SK10.2 billion. Skandia also increased its dividends in 2000 to SK512 million and still had SK9.5 billion in unrestricted reserves.[21]

RESTRICTION ON RETAINED EARNINGS

A corporation may be required or may want to restrict all or a portion of its retained earnings. A **restriction on retained earnings** means that dividends can be declared only to the extent of the *unrestricted* retained earnings. The following are reasons a company might restrict retained earnings:

1. *A contractual agreement.* For example, bond indentures may place a limitation on the dividends the company can pay.

2. *State law.* Many states do not allow a corporation to distribute dividends or purchase treasury stock if doing so reduces equity to a level that would impair the legal capital of the company.

3. *Voluntary action by the board of directors.* Often, a board decides to retain assets in the business for future needs. For example, the company may want to limit dividends to save enough money for a new building or to offset a possible future loss of assets resulting from a lawsuit.

A restriction on retained earnings does not change the total retained earnings or stockholders' equity of the company. It simply divides retained earnings into two parts: restricted and unrestricted. The unrestricted amount represents earnings kept in the business that the company can use for dividends and other purposes. Also, the restriction of retained earnings does not restrict cash or other assets in any way. It simply explains to the readers of the financial statements that a certain amount of assets generated by earnings will remain in the business for the purpose stated. It is still management's job to make sure enough cash or assets are on hand to fulfill the purpose. The removal of a restriction does not necessarily mean that the board of directors can then declare a dividend.

The most common way to disclose restricted retained earnings is by reference to a note to the financial statements. For example:

Retained earnings (Note 15) $900,000

Note 15:
Because of plans to expand the capacity of the company's clothing division, the board of directors has restricted retained earnings available for dividends by $300,000.

✅ Check out ACE for a Review Quiz at http://accounting.college.hmco.com/students.

ACCOUNTING FOR STOCK DIVIDENDS AND STOCK SPLITS

LO6 Account for stock dividends and stock splits.

RELATED TEXT ASSIGNMENTS
Q: 17, 18
SE: 6, 8, 9
E: 9, 10, 11
P: 4, 5, 7, 8
SD: 3, 4, 5
FRA: 6

Two common transactions that can modify the content of stockholders' equity are stock dividends and stock splits.

STOCK DIVIDENDS

A **stock dividend** is a proportional distribution of shares among a corporation's stockholders. Unlike a cash dividend, it involves no distribution of assets, so it has no effect on a firm's assets and liabilities. A board of directors may declare a stock dividend for several reasons:

1. It may want to give stockholders some evidence of the company's success without paying a cash dividend, which would affect working capital.

2. It may want to reduce the stock's market price by increasing the number of shares outstanding. (This goal is, however, more often met by a stock split.)

3. It may want to make a nontaxable distribution to stockholders. Stock dividends that meet certain conditions are not considered income, so they are not taxed.

4. It may wish to increase the company's permanent capital by transferring an amount from retained earnings to contributed capital.

The total stockholders' equity is not affected by a stock dividend. The effect of a stock dividend is to transfer a dollar amount from retained earnings to contributed capital on the date of declaration. The amount transferred is the fair market value (usually, the market price) of the additional shares to be issued. The laws of most states specify the minimum value of each share transferred under a stock dividend, which is normally the minimum legal capital (par or stated value). However, generally accepted accounting principles state that market value reflects the economic effect of small stock distributions (less than 20 to 25 percent of a company's outstanding common stock) better than par or stated value does. For this reason, market price should be used to account for small stock dividends.[22]

To illustrate how to account for a stock dividend, let us assume that Caprock Corporation has the following stockholders' equity structure:

Contributed capital		
Common stock, $5 par value, 100,000 shares		
authorized, 30,000 shares issued and outstanding		$ 150,000
Paid-in capital in excess of par value, common		30,000
Total contributed capital		$ 180,000
Retained earnings		900,000
Total stockholders' equity		$1,080,000

Suppose that the board of directors declares a 10 percent stock dividend on February 24, distributable on March 31 to stockholders of record on March 15, and that the market price of the stock on February 24 is $20 per share. The entries to record the declaration and distribution of the stock dividend are as follows:

Date of Declaration

A = L + OE	Feb. 24	Stock Dividends Declared	60,000	
−		Common Stock Distributable		15,000
+		Paid-in Capital in Excess of Par		
+		Value, Common		45,000
		Declared a 10 percent stock dividend		
		on common stock, distributable on		
		March 31 to stockholders of record		
		on March 15:		
		30,000 shares × .10 = 3,000 shares		
		3,000 shares × $20/share = $60,000		
		3,000 shares × $5/share = $15,000		

KEY POINT: For a small stock dividend, the portion of retained earnings transferred is determined by multiplying the number of shares to be distributed by the stock's market price on the date of declaration.

Date of Record

Mar. 15   No entry required.

Date of Distribution

A = L + OE	Mar. 31	Common Stock Distributable	15,000	
−		Common Stock		15,000
+		Distributed a stock dividend of		
		3,000 shares		

The effect of this stock dividend is to permanently transfer the market value of the stock, $60,000, from retained earnings to contributed capital and to increase the

KEY POINT: The declaration of a stock dividend results
in a reshuffling of stockholders'
equity. That is, a portion of
retained earnings is converted
into contributed capital (by
closing the Stock Dividends
Declared account). Total stockholders' equity is not affected.
Retained earnings are transferred at the time of the
recording (date of declaration)
and not at the closing of the
Stock Dividends Declared
account.

KEY POINT: Common
Stock Distributable is a contributed capital (stockholders'
equity) account, not a liability.
When the shares is issued,
this account is converted to the
Common Stock account.

number of shares outstanding by 3,000. The Stock Dividends Declared account is
used to record the total amount of the stock dividend. Retained Earnings is reduced
by the amount of the stock dividend when the Stock Dividends Declared account
is closed to Retained Earnings at the end of the accounting period. Common
Stock Distributable is credited for the par value of the stock to be distributed
(3,000 × $5 = $15,000).

In addition, when the market value is greater than the par value of the stock,
Paid-in Capital in Excess of Par Value, Common must be credited for the amount
by which the market value exceeds the par value. In this case, the total market value
of the stock dividend ($60,000) exceeds the total par value ($15,000) by $45,000.
No entry is required on the date of record. On the distribution date, the common
stock is issued by debiting Common Stock Distributable and crediting Common
Stock for the par value of the stock ($15,000).

Common Stock Distributable is not a liability account because there is no obligation to distribute cash or other assets. The obligation is to distribute additional
shares of capital stock. If financial statements are prepared between the date of declaration and the date of distribution, Common Stock Distributable should be
reported as part of contributed capital:

Contributed capital	
Common stock, $5 par value, 100,000 shares	
authorized, 30,000 shares issued and outstanding	$ 150,000
Common stock distributable, 3,000 shares	15,000
Paid-in capital in excess of par value, common	75,000
Total contributed capital	$ 240,000
Retained earnings	840,000
Total stockholders' equity	$1,080,000

⬢ **STOP AND THINK!**
When a stockholder receives
shares of stock in a stock dividend, why should (s)he not
consider the value of the shares
as income?

*Spending the value of the stock
dividend would reduce the stockholder's proportionate ownership
of the company and the stockholder's net worth, as if the stockholder had sold some of his or
her shares of stock.* ■

Three points can be made from this example. First, the total stockholders'
equity is the same before and after the stock dividend. Second, the assets of the corporation are not reduced as they are with a cash dividend. Third, the proportionate
ownership in the corporation of any individual stockholder is the same before and
after the stock dividend.

To illustrate these points, assume that a stockholder owns 1,000 shares before
the stock dividend. After the 10 percent stock dividend is distributed, this stockholder would own 1,100 shares, as illustrated below.

Stockholders' Equity	Before Dividend	After Dividend
Common stock	$ 150,000	$ 165,000
Paid-in capital in excess of par value, common	30,000	75,000
Total contributed capital	$ 180,000	$ 240,000
Retained earnings	900,000	840,000
Total stockholders' equity	$1,080,000	$1,080,000
Shares outstanding	30,000	33,000
Stockholders' equity per share	$ 36.00	$ 32.73

Stockholders' Investment

	Before Dividend	After Dividend
Shares owned	1,000	1,100
Shares outstanding	30,000	33,000
Percentage of ownership	3⅓%	3⅓%
Proportionate investment ($1,080,000 × .03⅓)	$36,000	$36,000

Both before and after the stock dividend, the stockholders' equity totals $1,080,000
and the stockholder owns 3⅓ percent of the company. The proportionate investment (stockholders' equity times percentage ownership) remains at $36,000.

KEY POINT: When a large (greater than 20 to 25 percent) stock dividend is declared, the transfer from retained earnings is based on the stock's par or stated value, not on its market value.

All stock dividends have an effect on the market price of a company's stock. But some stock dividends are so large that they have a material effect. For example, a 50 percent stock dividend would cause the market price of the stock to drop about 33 percent because the increase is now one-third of shares outstanding. The AICPA has decided that large stock dividends, those greater than 20 to 25 percent, should be accounted for by transferring the par or stated value of the stock on the date of declaration from retained earnings to contributed capital.[23]

STOCK SPLITS

KEY POINT: Stock splits and stock dividends reduce earnings per share because they increase the number of shares. Cash dividends have no effect on earnings per share.

www.gillette.com

A **stock split** occurs when a corporation increases the number of issued shares of stock and reduces the par or stated value proportionally. A company may plan a stock split when it wants to lower the stock's market value per share and increase the demand for the stock at this lower price. This action may be necessary if the market value per share has become so high that it hinders the trading of the stock or if the company wants to signal to the market its success in achieving its operating goals. The Gillette Company achieved these strategic objectives in a recent year by declaring a 2-for-1 stock split and raising its cash dividend. The market viewed these actions positively, pushing Gillette's share price from $77 to $106. After the stock split, the number of shares outstanding doubled, thereby cutting the share price in half and also the dividend per share. Most important, each stockholder's total wealth was unchanged as a result of the stock split.

ENRICHMENT NOTE: Stock splits greater than 2 for 1 are unusual. Splits such as 3 for 2 or 4 for 3 are far more common. On occasion, companies whose stock sells for a very low price will perform a reverse stock split, which reduces the number of shares and increases the market price.

To illustrate a stock split, suppose that Caprock Corporation has 30,000 shares of $5.00 par value stock outstanding. The market value is $70.00 per share. The corporation plans a 2-for-1 split. This split will lower the par value to $2.50 and increase the number of shares outstanding to 60,000. A stockholder who previously owned 400 shares of the $5.00 par stock would own 800 shares of the $2.50 par stock after the split. When a stock split occurs, the market value tends to fall in proportion to the increase in outstanding shares of stock. For example, a 2-for-1 stock split would cause the price of the stock to drop by approximately 50 percent, to about $35.00. It would also halve earnings per share and cash dividends per share (if the board does not increase the dividend). The lower price and the increase in shares tend to promote the buying and selling of shares.

A stock split does not increase the number of shares authorized. Nor does it change the balances in the stockholders' equity section of the balance sheet. It simply changes the par value and the number of shares issued, both shares outstanding and shares held as treasury stock. Therefore, an entry is not necessary. However, it is appropriate to document the change by making a memorandum entry in the general journal, such as the following:

July 15   The 30,000 shares of $5 par value common stock issued and outstanding were split 2 for 1, resulting in 60,000 shares of $2.50 par value common stock issued and outstanding.

FOCUS ON BUSINESS PRACTICE

Do Stock Splits Help Increase a Company's Market Price?

Stock splits tend to follow the market. When the market went up dramatically in 1998, 1999, and 2000, there were record numbers of stock splits—more than 1,000 per year. At the height of the market in early 2000, stock splitters included such diverse companies as Alcoa <www.alcoa.com>, Apple Computer <www.apple.com>, Chase Manhattan <www.chase.com>, Intel <www.intel.com>, Nvidia <www.nvidia.com>, Juniper Networks <www.juniper.net>, and Tiffany & Co. <www.tiffany.com>. Some analysts liken stock splits to the air a pastry chef whips into a mousse: it doesn't make it any sweeter, just frothier. There is no fundamental reason a stock should go up because of a stock split. When Rambus Inc. <www.rambus.com>, a developer of high-speed memory technology, announced a four-for-one split on March 10, 2000, its stock rose more than 50 percent, to $471 per share.[24] But when the market deflated in 2001, its stock dropped to less than $10 per share. Research shows that stock splits have no long-term effect on stock prices.

The change for the Caprock Corporation is as follows:

Before Stock Split

Contributed capital

Common stock, $5 par value, 100,000 shares authorized, 30,000 shares issued and outstanding	$ 150,000
Paid-in capital in excess of par value, common	30,000
Total contributed capital	$ 180,000
Retained earnings	900,000
Total stockholders' equity	$1,080,000

After Stock Split

Contributed capital

Common stock, $2.50 par value, 100,000 shares authorized, 60,000 shares issued and outstanding	$ 150,000
Paid-in capital in excess of par value, common	30,000
Total contributed capital	$ 180,000
Retained earnings	900,000
Total stockholders' equity	$1,080,000

KEY POINT: A stock split affects only the common stock calculation. In this case, there are twice as many shares after the split, but par value is now half of what it was.

KEY POINT: As long as the newly outstanding shares do not exceed the previously authorized shares, permission from the state is not needed for a stock split.

Although the amount of stockholders' equity per share is half as much, each stockholder's proportionate interest in the company remains the same.

If the number of split shares will exceed the number of authorized shares, the board of directors must secure state and stockholders' approval before it can issue additional shares.

✔ Check out ACE for a Review Quiz at http://accounting.college.hmco.com/students.

BOOK VALUE

L07 Calculate book value per share.

RELATED TEXT ASSIGNMENTS
Q: 19
SE: 10
E: 12
P: 4, 5, 7, 8
SD: 4, 5
FRA: 5, 6

KEY POINT: Book value per share represents the equity of one share of stock in the net assets (assets minus liabilities) of a corporation. It can apply to both common and preferred stock.

K/R

The word *value* is associated with shares of stock in several ways. Par value or stated value is set when the stock is authorized and establishes the legal capital of a company. Neither par value nor stated value has any relationship to a stock's book value or market value. The **book value** of a company's stock represents the total assets of the company less its liabilities. It is simply the stockholders' equity of the company or, to look at it another way, the company's net assets. The **book value per share** therefore represents the equity of the owner of one share of stock in the net assets of the corporation. That value, of course, does not necessarily equal the amount the shareholder would receive if the company were sold or liquidated. It differs in most cases because assets are usually recorded at historical cost, not at the current value at which they could be sold.

When a company has only common stock outstanding, book value per share is calculated by dividing the total stockholders' equity by the total common shares outstanding. In computing the shares outstanding, common stock distributable is included. Treasury stock (shares previously issued and now held by the company), however, is not included. For example, suppose that Caprock Corporation has total stockholders' equity of $1,030,000 and 29,000 shares outstanding after recording the purchase of treasury shares. The book value per share of Caprock's common stock is $35.52 ($1,030,000 ÷ 29,000 shares).

If a company has both preferred and common stock, the determination of book value per share is not so simple. The general rule is that the call value (or par value, if a call value is not specified) of the preferred stock plus any dividends in arrears is subtracted from total stockholders' equity to determine the equity pertaining to common stock. As an illustration, refer to the stockholders' equity section of Tri-

What is the effect of a stock dividend or a stock split on book value per share?

Both a stock dividend and a stock split reduce the book value per share because they increase the number of shares outstanding without changing the total of stockholders' equity. ■

State Corporation's balance sheet in Exhibit 3. Assuming that no dividends are in arrears and that the preferred stock is callable at $105, the equity pertaining to common stock is calculated as follows:

Total stockholders' equity	$2,014,400
Less equity allocated to preferred shareholders	
(3,000 shares × $105)	315,000
Equity pertaining to common shareholders	$1,699,400

There are 41,300 shares of common stock outstanding (41,800 shares issued less 500 shares of treasury stock). The book values per share are computed as follows:

Preferred Stock: $315,000 ÷ 3,000 shares = $105 per share
Common Stock: $1,699,400 ÷ 41,300 shares = $41.15 per share

If we assume the same facts except that the preferred stock is 8 percent cumulative and that one year of dividends is in arrears, the stockholders' equity would be allocated as follows:

Total stockholders' equity		$2,014,400
Less: Call value of outstanding preferred shares	$315,000	
Dividends in arrears ($300,000 × .08)	24,000	
Equity allocated to preferred shareholders		339,000
Equity pertaining to common shareholders		$1,675,400

The book values per share are then as follows:

Preferred Stock: $339,000 ÷ 3,000 shares = $113 per share
Common Stock: $1,675,400 ÷ 41,300 shares = $40.57 per share

Undeclared preferred dividends fall into arrears on the last day of the fiscal year (the date shown on the financial statements). Also, dividends in arrears do not apply to unissued preferred stock.

✔ Check out ACE for a Review Quiz at http://accounting.college.hmco.com/students.

Chapter Review

REVIEW OF LEARNING OBJECTIVES

LO1 Prepare a corporate income statement and identify the issues related to evaluating the quality of earnings.

The operating income section on the income statement of a corporation with both continuing and discontinued operations is called income from continuing operations. Income from continuing operations before income taxes is affected by choices of accounting methods and estimates and may contain such items as gains and losses, write-downs, and restructurings. The income taxes expense section of the statement is also subject to special accounting rules. The lower part of the statement may contain such nonoperating items as discontinued operations, extraordinary gains and losses, and effects of accounting changes. Earnings per share information appears at the bottom of the statement. The quality of a company's earnings refers to the substance of earnings and their sustainability into future accounting periods. The quality of earnings may be affected by the accounting methods and estimates the company's management chooses and by the gains and losses, the write-downs and restructurings, and the nature of the nonoperating items reported on the income statement. The reason for considering quality of earnings issues is to assess their effects on cash flows and performance measures. Generally speaking, except for possible income tax effects, none of the gains and losses, asset write-downs, restructurings, and nonoperating items has any effect on cash flows. Quality of earnings issues can affect key performance ratios like return on assets and return on equity.

LO2 Show the relationships among income taxes expense, deferred income taxes, and net of taxes.

Income taxes expense is the taxes applicable to income from operations on an accrual basis. Income tax allocation is necessary when differences between accrual-based accounting income and taxable income cause a material difference between income taxes expense as shown on the income statement and actual income tax liability. The difference between income taxes expense and income taxes payable is debited or credited to an account called Deferred Income Taxes. *Net of taxes* is a phrase used to indicate that the effect of income taxes has been considered when showing an item on the income statement.

LO3 Describe the disclosure on the income statement of discontinued operations, extraordinary items, and accounting changes.

Because of their unusual nature, a gain or loss on discontinued operations and on extraordinary items and the cumulative effect of accounting changes must be disclosed on the income statement separately from continuing operations and net of income taxes. Relevant information about any accounting change is shown in the notes to the financial statements.

LO4 Compute earnings per share.

Stockholders and other readers of financial statements use earnings per share data to evaluate a company's performance and to compare it with the performance of other companies. Therefore, earnings per share data are presented on the face of the income statement. The amounts are computed by dividing the income applicable to common stock by the number of common shares outstanding for the year. If the number of shares outstanding has varied during the year, then the weighted-average number of common shares outstanding should be used in the computation. When the company has a complex capital structure, both basic and diluted earnings per share must be disclosed on the face of the income statement.

LO5 Prepare a statement of stockholders' equity.

A statement of stockholders' equity shows changes over the period in each component of the stockholders' equity section of the balance sheet. This statement reveals much more about the transactions that affect stockholders' equity than does the statement of retained earnings.

LO6 Account for stock dividends and stock splits.

A stock dividend is a proportional distribution of shares among a corporation's stockholders. Here is a summary of the key dates and accounting treatment of stock dividends:

Key Date	Stock Dividend
Date of declaration	Debit Stock Dividends Declared for the market value of the stock to be distributed (if it is a small stock dividend), and credit Common Stock Distributable for the stock's par value and Paid-in Capital in Excess of Par Value, Common for the excess of the market value over the stock's par value.
Date of record	No entry.
Date of distribution	Debit Common Stock Distributable and credit Common Stock for the par value of the stock that has been distributed.

A stock split is usually undertaken to reduce the market value of a company's stock and improve the demand for the stock. Because there is normally a decrease in the par value of the stock in proportion to the number of additional shares issued, a stock split has no effect on the dollar amounts in the stockholders' equity accounts. The split should be recorded in the general journal by a memorandum entry only.

LO7 Calculate book value per share.

Book value per share is the stockholders' equity per share. It is calculated by dividing stockholders' equity by the number of common shares outstanding plus shares distributable. When a company has both preferred and common stock, the call or par value of the preferred stock plus any dividends in arrears is deducted from total stockholders' equity before dividing by the common shares outstanding.

REVIEW OF CONCEPTS AND TERMINOLOGY

The following concepts and terms were introduced in this chapter:

LO4   **Basic earnings per share:** The net income applicable to common stock divided by the weighted-average number of common shares outstanding.

LO7   **Book value:** The total assets of a company less its liabilities; stockholders' equity or net assets.

LO7   **Book value per share:** The equity of the owner of one share of stock in the net assets of the corporation.

LO4   **Complex capital structure:** A capital structure that includes exercisable stock options or convertible preferred stocks and bonds.

LO1   **Comprehensive income:** The change in a company's equity from sources other than owners during a period; it includes net income, changes in unrealized investment gains and losses, and other items affecting equity.

LO3   **Cumulative effect of an accounting change:** The effect that a different accounting principle would have had on the net income of prior periods if it had been used instead of the old principle.

LO2   **Deferred Income Taxes:** The account used to record the difference between the Income Taxes Expense and Income Taxes Payable accounts.

LO5   **Deficit:** A debit balance in the Retained Earnings account.

LO4   **Diluted earnings per share:** The net income applicable to common stock divided by the sum of the weighted-average number of common shares outstanding plus potentially dilutive securities.

LO3   **Discontinued operations:** Segments of a business that are no longer part of its ongoing operations.

LO3   **Extraordinary items:** Events or transactions that are both unusual in nature and infrequent in occurrence.

LO1   **Income from continuing operations:** The operating income section of the income statement when a company has both continuing and discontinued operations.

LO2   **Income tax allocation:** An accounting method used to accrue income taxes expense on the basis of accounting income whenever there are differences between accounting and taxable income.

LO2   **Net of taxes:** A phrase indicating that the effect of applicable taxes (most often, income taxes) has been considered in determining the overall effect of an item on the financial statements.

LO4   **Potentially dilutive securities:** Stock options and convertible preferred stocks or bonds, which have the potential to dilute earnings per share.

LO1   **Quality of earnings:** The substance of earnings and their sustainability into future accounting periods.

LO5   **Restriction on retained earnings:** The required or voluntary identification of a portion of retained earnings that cannot be used to declare dividends.

LO1   **Restructuring:** The estimated cost associated with a change in a company's operations, usually involving the closing of facilities and the laying off of personnel.

LO5   **Retained earnings:** Stockholders' claims to assets arising from the earnings of the business; the accumulated earnings of a corporation from its inception, minus any losses, dividends, or transfers to contributed capital.

LO3   **Segments:** Distinct parts of business operations, such as a line of business or a class of customer.

LO4   **Simple capital structure:** A capital structure in which there are no stocks, bonds, or stock options that can be converted into common stock.

LO5 **Statement of stockholders' equity:** A financial statement that summarizes changes in the components of the stockholders' equity section of the balance sheet. Also called *statement of changes in stockholders' equity.*

LO6 **Stock dividend:** A proportional distribution of shares among a corporation's stockholders.

LO6 **Stock split:** An increase in the number of outstanding shares of stock accompanied by a proportionate reduction in the par or stated value.

LO1 **Write-down:** The recording of a decrease in the value of an asset below the carrying value on the balance sheet and the reduction of income in the current period by the amount of the decrease. Also called *write-off.*

REVIEW PROBLEM

Comprehensive Stockholders' Equity Transactions

LO5
LO6
LO7

The stockholders' equity of the Szatkowski Company on June 30, 20x1, was as follows:

Contributed capital	
Common stock, no par value, $6 stated value, 1,000,000 shares authorized, 250,000 shares issued and outstanding	$1,500,000
Paid-in capital in excess of stated value, common	820,000
Total contributed capital	$2,320,000
Retained earnings	970,000
Total stockholders' equity	$3,290,000

Stockholders' equity transactions for the next fiscal year were as follows:

a. The board of directors declared a 2-for-1 stock split.
b. The board of directors obtained authorization to issue 50,000 shares of $100 par value, 6 percent noncumulative preferred stock, callable at $104.
c. Issued 12,000 shares of common stock for a building appraised at $96,000.
d. Purchased 8,000 shares of the company's common stock for $64,000.
e. Issued 20,000 shares of preferred stock for $100 per share.
f. Sold 5,000 shares of treasury stock for $35,000.
g. Declared cash dividends of $6 per share on preferred stock and $.20 per share on common stock.
h. Declared a 10 percent stock dividend on common stock. The market value was $10 per share. The stock dividend is distributable after the end of the fiscal year.
i. Closed Net Income for the year, $340,000.
j. Closed the Cash Dividends Declared and Stock Dividends Declared accounts to Retained Earnings.

Because of a loan agreement, the company is not allowed to reduce retained earnings below $100,000. The board of directors determined that this restriction should be disclosed in the notes to the financial statements.

REQUIRED ▶

1. Record the stockholders' equity components of the preceding transactions in T accounts. Indicate when there is no entry.
2. Prepare the stockholders' equity section of the company's balance sheet on June 30, 20x2, including appropriate disclosure of the restriction on retained earnings.
3. Compute the book values per share of common stock on June 30, 20x1 and 20x2, and of preferred stock on June 30, 20x2, using end-of-year shares outstanding.

ANSWER TO REVIEW PROBLEM

1. Entries in T accounts:
   a. No entry: memorandum in journal
   b. No entry: memorandum in journal

Preferred Stock		
	e.	2,000,000

Common Stock		
	Beg. bal.	1,500,000
	c.	36,000
	End. Bal	1,536,000

Common Stock Distributable		
	h.	152,700

Paid-in Capital in Excess of Stated Value, Common		
	Beg. bal.	820,000
	c.	60,000
	h.	356,300
	End. Bal.	1,236,300

Retained Earnings			
f.	5,000	Beg. bal.	970,000
j.	730,800	i.	340,000
		End. bal.	574,200

Treasury Stock, Common			
d.	64,000	f.	40,000
End. Bal.	24,000		

Cash Dividends Declared			
g.	221,800*	j.	221,800

Stock Dividend Declared			
h.	509,000**	j.	509,000

*20,000 × $6 = $120,000
509,000 × $.20 = $101,800
Total = $221,800

**509,000 shares × .10 × $10 = $509,000

2. Stockholders' equity section of the balance sheet:

Szatkowski Company
Stockholders' Equity
June 30, 20x2

Contributed capital		
Preferred stock, $100 par value, 6 percent noncumulative, 50,000 shares authorized, 20,000 shares issued and outstanding		$2,000,000
Common stock, no par value, $3 stated value, 1,000,000 shares authorized, 512,000 shares issued, 509,000 shares outstanding	$1,536,000	
Common stock distributable, 50,900 shares	152,700	
Paid-in capital in excess of stated value, common	1,236,300	2,925,000
Total contributed capital		$4,925,000
Retained earnings (Note x)		574,200
Total contributed capital and retained earnings		$5,499,200
Less treasury stock, common (3,000 shares, at cost)		24,000
Total stockholders' equity		$5,475,200

Note x: The board of directors has restricted retained earnings available for dividends by the amount of $100,000 as required under a loan agreement.

3. Book values:
   June 30, 20x1
   Common Stock: $3,290,000 ÷ 250,000 shares = $13.16 per share

June 30, 20x2
    Preferred Stock: Call price of $104 per share equals book value per share
    Common Stock:
        ($5,475,200 − $2,080,000) ÷ (509,000 shares + 50,900 shares) =
        $3,395,200 ÷ 559,900 shares = $6.06 per share

Chapter Assignments

BUILDING YOUR KNOWLEDGE FOUNDATION

QUESTIONS

1. What is comprehensive income? How does it differ from net income?

2. What is quality of earnings, and what are four ways in which quality of earnings may be affected?

3. Why would the reader of financial statements be interested in management's choice of accounting methods and estimates? Give an example.

4. What is the difference between a write-down and a restructuring, and where do they appear on the corporate income statement?

5. In the first quarter of 1994, AT&T, the giant telecommunications company, reported a net loss because it reduced its income by $1.3 billion, or $.96 per share, as a result of changing its method of accounting for disability and severance payments. Without this charge, the company would have earned $1.15 billion, or $.85 per share. Where on the corporate income statement do you find the effects of changes in accounting principles? As an analyst, how would you treat this accounting change?

6. "Accounting income should be geared to the concept of taxable income because the public understands that concept." Comment on this statement, and tell why income tax allocation is necessary.

7. Nabisco had about $1.3 billion of deferred income taxes in 1996, equal to about 11 percent of total liabilities. This percentage had risen or remained steady for many years. Given management's desire to put off the payment of taxes as long as possible, the long-term growth of the economy and inflation, and the definition of a liability (probable future sacrifice of economic benefits arising from present obligations), make an argument for not accounting for deferred income taxes.

8. Why should a gain or loss on discontinued operations be disclosed separately on the income statement?

9. Explain the two major criteria for extraordinary items. How should extraordinary items be disclosed in the financial statements?

10. When an accounting change occurs, what disclosures must be made in the financial statements?

11. How are earnings per share disclosed in the financial statements?

12. When does a company have a simple capital structure? A complex capital structure?

13. What is the difference between basic and diluted earnings per share?

14. What is the difference between the statement of stockholders' equity and the stockholders' equity section of the balance sheet?

15. When does a company have a deficit in retained earnings?

16. What is the purpose of a restriction on retained earnings? Why might a company have restrictions on its retained earnings?

17. Explain how the accounting treatment of stock dividends differs from that of cash dividends.

18. What is the difference between a stock dividend and a stock split? What is the effect of each on the capital structure of the corporation?

19. Would you expect a corporation's book value per share to equal its market value per share? Why or why not?

SHORT EXERCISES

LO1 Quality of Earnings

SE 1. Each of the items listed below is a quality of earnings issue. Indicate whether the item is (a) an accounting method, (b) an accounting estimate, or (c) a nonoperating item. For any item for which the answer is (a) or (b), indicate which alternative is usually the more conservative choice.

1. LIFO versus FIFO
2. Extraordinary loss
3. 10-year useful life versus 15-year useful life
4. Effect of change in accounting principle
5. Straight-line versus accelerated method
6. Discontinued operations
7. Immediate write-off versus amortization
8. Increase versus decrease in percentage of uncollectible accounts

LO1 Corporate Income Statement

SE 2. Assume that Brown Company's chief financial officer gave you the following information: Net Sales, $720,000; Cost of Goods Sold, $350,000; Loss from Discontinued Operations (net of income tax benefit of $70,000), $200,000; Loss on Disposal of Discontinued Operations (net of income tax benefit of $16,000), $50,000; Operating Expenses, $130,000; Income Taxes Expense on Continuing Operations, $100,000. From this information, prepare the company's income statement for the year ended June 30, 20xx. (Ignore earnings per share information.)

LO2 Corporate Income Tax Rate Schedule

SE 3. Using the corporate tax rate schedule in Table 1, compute the income tax liability for taxable income of (1) $400,000 and (2) $20,000,000.

LO4 Earnings per Share

SE 4. During 20x1, Halle Corporation reported a net income of $669,200. On January 1, Halle had 360,000 shares of common stock outstanding. The company issued an additional 240,000 shares of common stock on August 1. In 20x1, the company had a simple capital structure. During 20x2, there were no transactions involving common stock, and the company reported net income of $870,000. Determine the weighted-average number of common shares outstanding for 20x1 and 20x2. Also, compute earnings per share for 20x1 and 20x2.

LO5 Statement of Stockholders' Equity

SE 5. Refer to the statement of stockholders' equity for Tri-State Corporation in Exhibit 2 to answer the following questions: (1) At what price per share were the 5,000 shares of common stock sold? (2) What was the conversion price per share of the common stock? (3) At what price was the common stock selling on the date of the stock dividend? (4) At what price per share was the treasury stock purchased?

LO5 Effects of Stockholders'
LO6 Equity Actions

SE 6. Tell whether each of the following actions will increase, decrease, or have no effect on total assets, total liabilities, and total stockholders' equity:

1. Declaration of a stock dividend
2. Declaration of a cash dividend
3. Stock split
4. Restriction of retained earnings
5. Purchase of treasury stock

LO5 Restriction of Retained Earnings

SE 7. Jade Company has a lawsuit filed against it. The board took action to restrict retained earnings in the amount of $2,500,000 on May 31, 20x1, pending the outcome of the suit. On May 31, the company had retained earnings of $3,725,000. Show how the restriction on retained earnings would be disclosed as a note to the financial statements.

LO6 Stock Dividends

SE 8. On February 15, Red Mountain Corporation's board of directors declared a 2 percent stock dividend applicable to the outstanding shares of its $10 par value common stock, of which 200,000 shares are authorized, 130,000 are issued, and 20,000 are held in the treasury. The stock dividend was distributable on March 15 to stockholders of record on March 1. On February 15, the market value of the common stock was $15 per share. On March 30, the board of directors declared a $.50 per share cash dividend. No other stock transactions have occurred. Record, as necessary, the transactions of February 15, March 1, March 15, and March 30.

LO6 Stock Split

SE 9. On August 10, the board of directors of Torrelli International declared a 3-for-1 stock split of its $9 par value common stock, of which 800,000 shares were authorized and 250,000 were issued and outstanding. The market value on that date was $60 per share. On the same date, the balance of paid-in capital in excess of par value, common was $6,000,000, and the balance of retained earnings was $6,500,000. Prepare the stockholders' equity section of the company's balance sheet after the stock split. What journal entry, if any, is needed to record the stock split?

LO7 Book Value for Preferred and Common Stock

SE 10. Using data from the stockholders' equity section of Gem Corporation's balance sheet shown below, compute the book value per share for both the preferred and the common stock.

Contributed capital		
Preferred stock, $100 par value, 8 percent cumulative, 10,000 shares authorized, 500 shares issued and outstanding*		$ 50,000
Common stock, $10 par value, 100,000 shares authorized, 40,000 shares issued and outstanding	$400,000	
Paid-in capital in excess of par value, common	516,000	916,000
Total contributed capital		$ 966,000
Retained earnings		275,000
Total stockholders' equity		$1,241,000

*The preferred stock is callable at $104 per share, and one year's dividends are in arrears.

EXERCISES

LO1 Effect of Alternative Accounting Methods

E 1. At the end of its first year of operations, a company calculated its ending merchandise inventory according to three different accounting methods, as follows: FIFO, $95,000; average-cost, $90,000; LIFO, $86,000. If the company used the average-cost method, its net income for the year would be $34,000.

1. Determine net income if the company used the FIFO method.
2. Determine net income if the company used the LIFO method.
3. Which method is more conservative?
4. Will the consistency convention be violated if the company chooses to use the LIFO method?
5. Does the full-disclosure convention require disclosure of the inventory method used in the financial statements?

LO1 Corporate Income Statement

E 2. Assume that the Silver Furniture Company's chief financial officer gave you the following information: net sales, $1,900,000; cost of goods sold, $1,050,000; extraordinary gain (net of income taxes of $3,500), $12,500; loss from discontinued operations (net of income tax benefit of $30,000), $50,000; loss on disposal of discontinued operations (net of income tax benefit of $13,000), $35,000; selling expenses, $50,000; administrative expenses, $40,000; income taxes expense on continuing operations, $300,000. From this information, prepare the company's income statement for the year ended June 30, 20xx. (Ignore earnings per share information.)

LO1 Corporate Income Statement
LO2
LO3
LO4

E 3. The following items are components of Aconite Corporation's income statement for the year ended December 31, 20x1:

Sales	$555,000
Cost of goods sold	(275,000)
Operating expenses	(112,500)
Restructuring	(55,000)
Total income taxes expense for period	(82,350)
Income from operations of a discontinued segment	80,000
Gain on disposal of segment	70,000
Extraordinary gain on retirement of bonds	36,000
Cumulative effect of a change in accounting principle	(24,000)
Net income	$192,150
Earnings per share	$.96

Recast the income statement in proper multistep form, including allocating income taxes to appropriate items (assume a 30 percent income tax rate) and showing earnings per share figures (200,000 shares outstanding).

LO2 Corporate Income Tax Rate Schedule

E 4. Using the corporate tax rate schedule in Table 1, compute the income tax liability for the following situations:

Situation	Taxable Income
A	$ 70,000
B	85,000
C	320,000

LO2 Income Tax Allocation

E 5. The Amarillo Corporation reported the following accounting income before income taxes, income taxes expense, and net income for 20x2 and 20x3:

	20x2	20x3
Income before income taxes	$280,000	$280,000
Income taxes expense	88,300	88,300
Net income	$191,700	$191,700

On the balance sheet, deferred income taxes liability increased by $38,400 in 20x2 and decreased by $18,800 in 20x3.

1. How much did Amarillo Corporation actually pay in income taxes for 20x2 and 20x3?
2. Prepare entries in journal form to record income taxes expense for 20x2 and 20x3.

LO4 Earnings per Share

E 6. During 20x3, the La Jeune Corporation reported a net income of $1,529,500. On January 1, La Jeune had 700,000 shares of common stock outstanding. The company issued an additional 420,000 shares of common stock on October 1. In 20x3, the company had a simple capital structure. During 20x4, there were no transactions involving common stock, and the company reported net income of $2,016,000.

1. Determine the weighted-average number of common shares outstanding each year.
2. Compute earnings per share for each year.

LO5 Restriction of Retained Earnings

E 7. The board of directors of the Solwar Company has approved plans to acquire another company during the coming year. The acquisition should cost approximately $550,000. The board took action to restrict retained earnings of the company in the amount of $550,000 on July 17, 20x4. On July 31, the company had retained earnings of $975,000. Show how the restriction on retained earnings would be disclosed in a note to the financial statements.

LO5 Statement of Stockholders' Equity

E 8. The stockholders' equity section of Molloy Corporation's balance sheet on December 31, 20x4, appears as follows:

Contributed capital	
Common stock, $2 par value, 500,000 shares authorized, 400,000 shares issued and outstanding	$ 800,000
Paid-in capital in excess of par value, common	1,200,000
Total contributed capital	$2,000,000
Retained earnings	4,200,000
Total stockholders' equity	$6,200,000

Prepare a statement of stockholders' equity for the year ended December 31, 20x5, assuming the following transactions occurred in sequence during 20x5:

a. Issued 10,000 shares of $100 par value, 9 percent cumulative preferred stock at par after obtaining authorization from the state.
b. Issued 40,000 shares of common stock in connection with the conversion of bonds having a carrying value of $600,000.
c. Declared and issued a 2 percent common stock dividend. The market value on the date of declaration was $14 per share.
d. Purchased 10,000 shares of common stock for the treasury at a cost of $16 per share.
e. Earned net income of $460,000.
f. Declared and paid the full year's dividend on preferred stock and a dividend of $.40 per share on common stock outstanding at the end of the year.
g. Had foreign currency translation adjustment of minus $100,000.

LO6 Journal Entries: Stock Dividends

E 9. The Halcyon Company has 30,000 shares of its $1 par value common stock outstanding. Record in journal form the following transactions as they relate to the company's common stock:

July 17 Declared a 10 percent stock dividend on common stock to be distributed on August 10 to stockholders of record on July 31. Market value of the stock was $5 per share on this date.
      31 Record date.
Aug. 10 Distributed the stock dividend declared on July 17.
Sept. 1 Declared a $.50 per share cash dividend on common stock to be paid on September 16 to stockholders of record on September 10.

LO6 Stock Split

E 10. The Chu Company currently has 500,000 shares of $1 par value common stock authorized with 200,000 shares outstanding. The board of directors declared a 2-for-1 split on May 15, when the market value of the common stock was $2.50 per share. The retained earnings balance on May 15 was $700,000. Paid-in capital in excess of par value, common on this date was $20,000. Prepare the stockholders' equity section of the company's balance sheet before and after the stock split. What entry, if any, would be necessary to record the stock split?

LO6 Stock Split

E 11. On January 15, the board of directors of Extell International declared a 3-for-1 stock split of its $12 par value common stock, of which 800,000 shares were authorized and 200,000 were issued and outstanding. The market value on that date was $45 per share. On the same date, the balance of paid-in capital in excess of par value, common was $4,000,000, and the balance of retained earnings was $8,000,000. Prepare the stockholders' equity section of the company's balance sheet before and after the stock split. What entry, if any, is needed to record the stock split?

LO7 Book Value for Preferred and Common Stock

E 12. Below is the stockholders' equity section of the Vault Corporation's balance sheet. Determine the book value per share for both the preferred and the common stock.

Contributed capital		
Preferred stock, $100 per share, 6 percent cumulative, 10,000 shares authorized, 200 shares issued and outstanding*		$ 20,000
Common stock, $5 par value, 100,000 shares authorized, 10,000 shares issued, 9,000 shares outstanding	$50,000	
Paid-in capital in excess of par value, common	28,000	78,000
Total contributed capital		$ 98,000
Retained earnings		95,000
Total contributed capital and retained earnings		$193,000
Less treasury stock, common (1,000 shares at cost)		15,000
Total stockholders' equity		$178,000

*The preferred stock is callable at $105 per share, and one year's dividends are in arrears.

PROBLEMS

LO1 Effect of Alternative Accounting Methods

P 1. Cobley Company began operations in 20xx. At the beginning of the year, the company purchased plant assets of $450,000, with an estimated useful life of ten years and no salvage value. During the year, the company had net sales of $650,000, salaries expense of $100,000, and other expenses of $40,000, excluding depreciation. In addition, Cobley Company purchased inventory as follows:

Jan. 15	400 units at $200	$ 80,000
Mar. 20	200 units at $204	40,800
June 15	800 units at $208	166,400
Sept. 18	600 units at $206	123,600
Dec. 9	300 units at $210	63,000
Total	2,300 units	$473,800

At the end of the year, a physical inventory disclosed 500 units still on hand. The managers of Cobley Company know they have a choice of accounting methods, but they are unsure how those methods will affect net income. They have heard of the FIFO and LIFO inventory methods and the straight-line and double-declining-balance depreciation methods.

REQUIRED ▶

1. Prepare two income statements for Cobley Company, one using the FIFO and straight-line methods and the other using the LIFO and double-declining-balance methods. Ignore income taxes.
2. Prepare a schedule accounting for the difference in the two net income figures obtained in **1**.
3. What effect does the choice of accounting method have on Cobley's inventory turnover? What conclusions can you draw?
4. How does the choice of accounting methods affect Cobley's return on assets? Assume the company's only assets are cash of $40,000, inventory, and plant assets. Use year-end balances to compute the ratios. Is your evaluation of Cobley's profitability affected by the choice of accounting methods?

P 2.

LO1 **Corporate Income Statement**
LO2
LO3
LO4

K/R

Income statement information for the Lee Corporation during 20x3 is as follows:

a. Administrative expenses, $110,000.
b. Cost of goods sold, $440,000.
c. Restructuring charge, $125,000.
d. Cumulative effect of a change in inventory methods that decreased income (net of taxes, $28,000), $60,000.
e. Extraordinary loss from a storm (net of taxes, $10,000), $20,000.
f. Income taxes expense, continuing operations, $42,000.
g. Net sales, $1,015,000.
h. Selling expenses, $190,000.

REQUIRED ▶

1. Prepare Lee Corporation's income statement for 20x3, including earnings per share, assuming a weighted average of 200,000 shares of common stock outstanding for 20x3.
2. What is a restructuring charge, and why is it deducted before income from operations before income taxes?

P 3.

LO1 **Corporate Income Statement**
LO2 **and Evaluation of Business**
LO3 **Operations**
LO4

K/R

During 20x3, Buhr Corporation engaged in a number of complex transactions to improve the business—selling off a division, retiring bonds, and changing accounting methods. The company has always issued a simple single-step income statement, and the accountant has accordingly prepared the December 31 year-end income statements for 20x2 and 20x3, as shown below.

Buhr Corporation
Income Statements
For the Years Ended December 31, 20x3 and 20x2

	20x3	20x2
Net sales	$3,500,000	$4,200,000
Cost of goods sold	(1,925,000)	(2,100,000)
Operating expenses	(787,500)	(525,000)
Income taxes expense	(576,450)	(472,500)
Income from operations of a discontinued segment	560,000	
Gain on disposal of discontinued segment	490,000	
Extraordinary gain on retirement of bonds	252,000	
Cumulative effect of a change in accounting principle	(168,000)	
Net income	$1,345,050	$1,102,500
Earnings per share	$ 6.73	$ 5.51

Thomas Buhr, the president of Buhr Corporation, is pleased to see that both net income and earnings per share increased by 22 percent from 20x2 to 20x3 and intends to announce to the company's stockholders that the plan to improve the business has been successful.

REQUIRED ▶ 1. Recast the 20x3 and 20x2 income statements in proper multistep form, including allocating income taxes to appropriate items (assume a 30 percent income tax rate) and showing earnings per share figures (200,000 shares outstanding).
2. What is your assessment of Buhr Corporation's plan and business operations in 20x3?

P 4.

LO5   Dividends, Stock Splits, and
LO6   Stockholders' Equity
LO7

Ⓚ/Ⓡ

The stockholders' equity section of Brandon Linen Mills, Inc., as of December 31, 20x2, was as follows:

Contributed capital	
Common stock, $6 par value, 500,000 shares	
authorized, 80,000 shares issued and outstanding	$ 480,000
Paid-in capital in excess of par value, common	150,000
Total contributed capital	$ 630,000
Retained earnings	480,000
Total stockholders' equity	$1,110,000

A review of the stockholders' equity records of Brandon Linen Mills, Inc., disclosed the following transactions during 20x3:

Mar. 25   The board of directors declared a 5 percent stock dividend to stockholders of record on April 20 to be distributed on May 1. The market value of the common stock was $11 per share.
Apr. 20   Date of record for the stock dividend.
May   1   Issued the stock dividend.
Sept. 10   Declared a 3-for-1 stock split.
Dec. 15   Declared a 10 percent stock dividend to stockholders of record on January 15 to be distributed on February 15. The market price on this date is $3.50 per share.

REQUIRED ▶ 1. Record the stockholders' equity components of the transactions for Brandon Linen Mills, Inc., in T accounts.
2. Prepare the stockholders' equity section of the company's balance sheet as of December 31, 20x3. Assume net income for 20x3 is $47,000.
3. Calculate book value per share before and after the above transactions.

P 5.

LO5   Dividends, Stock Splits, and
LO6   Stockholders' Equity
LO7

Ⓚ/Ⓡ

The balance sheet of the O'Connor Woolen Company disclosed the following stockholders' equity as of September 30, 20x3:

Contributed capital	
Common stock, $2 par value, 1,000,000 shares	
authorized, 300,000 shares issued and outstanding	$ 600,000
Paid-in capital in excess of par value, common	370,000
Total contributed capital	$ 970,000
Retained earnings	350,000
Total stockholders' equity	$1,320,000

The following stockholders' equity transactions were completed during the next fiscal year in the order presented:

20x3
Dec. 17   Declared a 10 percent stock dividend to be distributed January 20 to stockholders of record on January 1. The market value per share on the date of declaration was $4.

20x4
Jan.   1   Date of record.
      20   Distributed the stock dividend.
Apr. 14   Declared a $.25 per share cash dividend. The cash dividend is payable May 15 to stockholders of record on May 1.
May   1   Date of record.

May 15   Paid the cash dividend.
June 17   Split its stock 2 for 1.
Sept. 15   Declared a cash dividend of $.10 per share payable October 10 to stockholders of record on October 1.

On September 14, the board of directors restricted retained earnings for plant expansion in the amount of $175,000. The restriction should be shown in the notes to the financial statements.

REQUIRED ▶ 1. Record the above transactions in journal form.
2. Prepare the stockholders' equity section of the company's balance sheet as of September 30, 20x4, with an appropriate disclosure of the restriction of retained earnings. Assume net income for the year is $150,000.
3. Calculate book value per share before and after the transactions.

ALTERNATE PROBLEMS

P 6.

LO1 Corporate Income Statement
LO2
LO3
LO4

Ⓚ/ⓡ

Information concerning operations of the Norris Weather Gear Corporation during 20xx is as follows:

a. Administrative expenses, $90,000.
b. Cost of goods sold, $420,000.
c. Write-down of assets, $75,000.
d. Cumulative effect of an accounting change in depreciation methods that increased income (net of taxes, $20,000), $42,000.
e. Extraordinary loss from an earthquake (net of taxes, $36,000), $60,000.
f. Sales (net), $975,000.
g. Selling expenses, $80,000.
h. Income taxes expense applicable to continuing operations, $105,000.

REQUIRED ▶ 1. Prepare the corporation's income statement for the year ended December 31, 20xx, including earnings per share information. Assume a weighted average of 100,000 common shares outstanding during the year.
2. What is a write-down, and why is it deducted before income from operations?

P 7.

LO5 Dividends, Stock Splits, and
LO6 Stockholders' Equity
LO7

Ⓚ/ⓡ

The stockholders' equity section of the balance sheet of Goodson Corporation as of December 31, 20x4, was as follows:

Contributed capital
  Common stock, $4 par value, 500,000 shares authorized,
    200,000 shares issued and outstanding .... $ 800,000
  Paid-in capital in excess of par value, common 1,000,000

  Total contributed capital $1,800,000
Retained earnings 1,200,000

Total stockholders' equity $3,000,000

The following transactions occurred in 20x5 for Goodson Corporation:

Feb. 28   The board of directors declared a 10 percent stock dividend to stockholders of record on March 25 to be distributed on April 5. The market value on this date is $16.
Mar. 25   Date of record for stock dividend.
Apr.   5   Issued stock dividend.
Aug.   3   Declared a 2-for-1 stock split.
Nov. 20   Purchased 18,000 shares of the company's common stock at $8 per share for the treasury.
Dec. 31   Declared a 5 percent stock dividend to stockholders of record on January 25 to be distributed on February 5. The market value per share was $9.

REQUIRED ▶ 1. Record the stockholders' equity components of the transactions for Goodson Corporation in T accounts.
2. Prepare the stockholders' equity section of the company's balance sheet as of December 31, 20x5. Assume net income for 20x5 is $108,000.
3. Calculate book value per share before and after the above transactions.

LO5 **Dividends, Stock Splits, and**
LO6 **Stockholders' Equity**
LO7

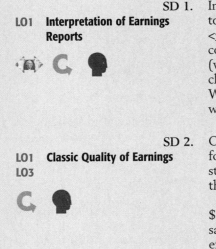

P 8. The stockholders' equity section of the Blue Furniture Restoration Company's balance sheet as of December 31, 20x2, was as follows:

Contributed capital
Common stock, $1 par value, 3,000,000 shares
authorized, 500,000 shares issued and outstanding ..... $ 500,000
Paid-in capital in excess of par value, common 200,000

Total contributed capital ..... $ 700,000
Retained earnings 540,000

Total stockholders' equity $1,240,000

The company engaged in the following stockholders' equity transactions during 20x3:

Mar. 5 Declared a $.20 per share cash dividend to be paid on April 6 to stockholders of record on March 20.
20 Date of record.
Apr. 6 Paid the cash dividend.
June 17 Declared a 10 percent stock dividend to be distributed August 17 to stockholders of record on August 5. The market value of the stock was $7 per share.
Aug. 5 Date of record.
17 Distributed the stock dividend.
Oct. 2 Split its stock 3 for 1.
Dec. 27 Declared a cash dividend of $.05 payable January 27, 20x4, to stockholders of record on January 14, 20x4.

On December 9, the board of directors restricted retained earnings for a pending lawsuit in the amount of $100,000. The restriction should be shown in the notes to the firm's financial statements.

REQUIRED ▶ 1. Record the 20x3 transactions in journal form.
2. Prepare the stockholders' equity section of the company's balance sheet as of December 31, 20x3, with an appropriate disclosure of the restriction on retained earnings. Assume net income for the year is $200,000.
3. Calculate book value per share before and after the above transactions.

SKILLS DEVELOPMENT CASES

Conceptual Analysis

SD 1.
LO1 **Interpretation of Earnings Reports**

In a recent year, analysts expected International Business Machines (IBM) <www.ibm.com> to earn $1.32 per share. The company actually earned $1.33. Microsoft Corporation <www.microsoft.com> was expected to earn $.43 per share, but it earned only $.41. The corporate income statements of these companies show that Microsoft had a special charge (with corresponding liability) of $660 million, or $.06 per share, based on settlement of a class-action law suit filed on behalf of consumers, whereas IBM had no such a charge.[25] Who did better, Microsoft or IBM? Use quality of earnings to support your answer. Also, what is the effect of Microsoft's special charge on current and future cash flows?

SD 2.
LO1 **Classic Quality of Earnings**
LO3

On Tuesday, January 19, 1988, IBM <www.ibm.com> reported greatly increased earnings for the fourth quarter of 1987. Despite this reported gain in earnings, the price of IBM's stock on the New York Stock Exchange declined by $6 per share to $111.75. In sympathy with this move, most other technology stocks also declined.[26]

IBM's fourth-quarter net earnings rose from $1.39 billion, or $2.28 a share, to $2.08 billion, or $3.47 a share, an increase of 49.6 percent and 52.2 percent over the same period a year earlier. Management declared that these results demonstrated the effectiveness of IBM's efforts to become more competitive and that, despite the economic uncertainties of 1988, the company was planning for growth.

The apparent cause of the stock price decline was that the huge increase in income could be traced to nonrecurring gains. Investment analysts pointed out that IBM's high earnings stemmed primarily from such factors as a lower tax rate. Despite most analysts' expectations of a tax rate between 40 and 42 percent, IBM's was a low 36.4 percent, down from the previous year's 45.3 percent. Analysts were also disappointed in IBM's revenue growth. Revenues within the United States were down, and much of the company's growth in revenues came through favorable currency translations, increases that might not be repeated. In fact, some estimates of IBM's fourth-quarter earnings attributed $.50 per share to currency translations and another $.25 to tax-rate changes.

Other factors contributing to IBM's rise in earnings were one-time transactions, such as the sale of Intel Corporation stock and bond redemptions, along with a corporate stock buyback program that reduced the amount of stock outstanding in the fourth quarter by 7.4 million shares.

The analysts were concerned about the quality of IBM's earnings. Identify four quality of earnings issues reported in the case and the analysts' concern about each. In percentage terms, what is the impact of the currency changes on fourth-quarter earnings? Comment on management's assessment of IBM's performance. Do you agree with management? (Optional question: What has IBM's subsequent performance been?) Be prepared to discuss your answers in class.

Ethical Dilemma

SD 3.

LO6 Ethics and Stock Dividends

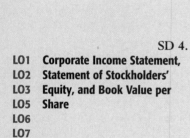

For 20 years Bass Products Corporation, a public corporation, has followed the practice of paying a cash dividend every quarter and has promoted itself to investors as a stable, reliable company. Recent competition from Asian companies has negatively affected its earnings and cash flows. As a result, Sandra Bass, president of the company, is proposing that the board of directors declare a stock dividend of 5 percent this year instead of a cash dividend. She says, "This will maintain our consecutive dividend record and will not require any cash outflow." What is the difference between a cash dividend and a stock dividend? Why does a corporation usually distribute either kind of dividend, and how does each affect the financial statements? Is the action that Sandra Bass has proposed ethical?

Research Activity

SD 4.

LO1 Corporate Income Statement,
LO2 Statement of Stockholders'
LO3 Equity, and Book Value per
LO5 Share
LO6
LO7

Select the annual reports of three corporations, using one or more of the following sources: your library, the Internet, or the Needles Accounting Resource Center web site at http://accounting.college.hmco.com/students. You may choose companies from the same industry or at random, at the direction of your instructor. (If you completed the related research activity in the chapter on contributed capital, use the same three companies.) Prepare a table with a column for each corporation. Then, for any year covered by the balance sheet, the statement of stockholders' equity, and the income statement, answer the following questions: Does the company own treasury stock? Did it buy or retire any treasury stock? Did it declare a stock dividend or a stock split? What other transactions appear in the statement of stockholders' equity? Has the company deferred any income taxes? Were there any discontinued operations, extraordinary items, or accounting changes? Compute the book value per common share for the company. In *The Wall Street Journal* or the financial section of another daily newspaper, find the current market price of each company's common stock and compare it with the book value you computed. Should there be any relationship between the two values? Be prepared to discuss your answers in class.

Decision-Making Practice

SD 5.

LO5 Analyzing Effects of
LO6 Stockholders' Equity
LO7 Transactions

Metzger Steel Corporation (MSC) is a small specialty steel manufacturer located in northern Alabama. It has been owned by the Metzger family for several generations. Arnold Metzger is a major shareholder in MSC by virtue of his having inherited 200,000 shares of common stock in the company. Metzger has not shown much interest in the business because of his enthusiasm for archaeology, which takes him to far parts of the world. However, when he received the minutes of the last board of directors meeting, he questioned a number of transactions involving stockholders' equity. He asks you, as a person with a knowledge of accounting, to help him interpret the effect of these transactions on his interest in MSC.

You begin by examining the stockholders' equity section of MSC's December 31, 20x1, balance sheet:

Metzger Steel Corporation
Stockholders' Equity
December 31, 20x1

Contributed capital	
Common stock, $10 par value, 5,000,000 shares	
authorized, 1,000,000 shares issued and outstanding	$10,000,000
Paid-in capital in excess of par value, common	25,000,000
Total contributed capital	$35,000,000
Retained earnings	20,000,000
Total stockholders' equity	$55,000,000

Then you read the relevant parts of the minutes of the board of directors meeting on December 15, 20x2:

Item A   The president reported the following transactions involving the company's stock during the last quarter:

October 15. Sold 500,000 shares of authorized common stock through the investment banking firm of T.R. Kendall at a net price of $50 per share.

November 1. Purchased 100,000 shares for the corporate treasury from Lucy Metzger at a price of $55 per share.

Item B   The board declared a 2-for-1 stock split (accomplished by halving the par value and doubling each stockholder's shares), followed by a 10 percent stock dividend. The board then declared a cash dividend of $2 per share on the resulting shares. Cash dividends are declared on outstanding shares and shares distributable. All these transactions are applicable to stockholders of record on December 20 and are payable on January 10. The market value of MSC stock on the board meeting date after the stock split was estimated to be $30.

Item C   The chief financial officer stated that he expected the company to report net income for the year of $4,000,000.

1. Prepare a stockholders' equity section of MSC's balance sheet as of December 31, 20x2, that reflects the above transactions. (**Hint:** Use T accounts to analyze the transactions. Also use a T account to keep track of the shares of common stock outstanding.)
2. Write a memorandum to Arnold Metzger that shows the book value per share and Metzger's percentage of ownership at the beginning and end of the year. Explain the difference and state whether Metzger's position has improved during the year. Tell why or why not and state how Metzger may be able to maintain his percentage of ownership.

FINANCIAL REPORTING AND ANALYSIS CASES

Interpreting Financial Reports

FRA 1.

LO1 **Interpretation of Statement**
LO5 **of Stockholders' Equity**

The consolidated statement of stockholders' equity for Jackson Electronics, Inc., a manufacturer of a broad line of electrical components, is presented at the top of the next page.

REQUIRED ▶

This statement of stockholders' equity has nine summary transactions. Show that you understand it by preparing an entry in journal form with an explanation for each. In each

Jackson Electronics, Inc.
Consolidated Statement of Stockholders' Equity
(In thousands)

	Preferred Stock	Common Stock	Paid-in Capital in Excess of Par Value, Common	Retained Earnings	Treasury Stock, Common	Accumulated Other Comprehensive Income	Total
Balance at September 30, 20x1	$2,756	$3,902	$14,149	$119,312	($ 942)		$139,177
Net income	—	—	—	18,753	—		18,753
Unrealized gain on available for sale securities						$12,000	12,000
Redemption and retirement of preferred stock (27,560 shares)	(2,756)	—	—	—	—		(2,756)
Stock options exercised (89,000 shares)	—	89	847	—	—		936
Purchases of common stock for treasury (501,412 shares)	—	—	—	—	(12,552)		(12,552)
Issuance of common stock (148,000 shares) in exchange for convertible subordinated debentures	—	148	3,635	—	—		3,783
Issuance of common stock (715,000 shares) for cash	—	715	24,535	—	—		25,250
Issuance of 500,000 shares of common stock in exchange for investment in Electrix Company shares	—	500	17,263	—	—		17,763
Cash dividends—common stock ($.80 per share)	—	—	—	(3,086)	—		(3,086)
Balance at September 30, 20x2	$ —	$5,354	$60,429	$134,979	($13,494)	$12,000	$199,268

case, if applicable, determine the average price per common share. At times, you will have to make assumptions about an offsetting part of the entry. For example, assume debentures (long-term bonds) are recorded at face value and that employees pay cash for stock purchased under company incentive plans. Also, define comprehensive income and determine the amount for Jackson Electronics.

Group Activity: Assign each transaction to a different group to develop the entry and present the explanation to the class.

FRA 2.
LO2 Analysis of Income Taxes from Annual Report

In its 2000 annual report, The Washington Post Company <www.washingtonpost.com>, a newspaper publishing and television broadcasting company based in Washington, D.C., provided the following data about its current and deferred income tax provisions (in millions):[27]

	2000	
	Current	Deferred
U.S. federal	$ 77.5	$ 4.9
Foreign	1.0	—
State	22.6	(12.7)
	$101.1	($7.8)

REQUIRED ▶

1. What was the 2000 income taxes expense? Record in journal form the overall income tax liability for 2000, using income tax allocation procedures.
2. In the long-term liability section of its balance sheet, The Washington Post Company shows deferred income taxes of $117.7 million in 2000 versus $114.0 million in 1999. This shows an increase in the amount of deferred income taxes. How do such deferred income taxes arise? What would cause deferred income taxes to increase? Give an example of this process. Given the definition of a liability, do you see a potential problem with the company's classifying deferred income taxes as a liability?

International Company

FRA 3.

LO5   Restriction of Retained Earnings

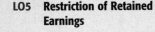

In some countries, including Japan, the availability of retained earnings for the payment of dividends is restricted. The following disclosure appeared in the annual report of Yamaha Motor Company, Ltd. <www.yamaha.com>, the Japanese motorcycle manufacturer:[28]

> The Commercial Code of Japan provides that an amount not less than 10 percent of the total of cash dividends and bonuses [paid] to directors and corporate auditors be appropriated as a legal reserve until such reserve equals 25 percent of stated capital. The legal reserve may be used to reduce a deficit or may be transferred to stated capital, but is not available as dividends.

"Stated capital" is equivalent to common stock. For Yamaha, this legal reserve amounted to ¥34.4 billion, or $290 million. How does this practice differ from that in the United States? Why do you think it is government policy in Japan? Do you think it is a good idea?

Toys "R" Us Annual Report

FRA 4.

LO1   Corporate Income Statement,
LO3   Statement of Stockholders'
LO5   Equity, and Book Value per Share

Refer to the Toys "R" Us <www.tru.com> annual report to answer the following questions:

1. Does Toys "R" Us have discontinued operations, extraordinary items, or cumulative effects from accounting changes? Would you say the income statement for Toys "R" Us is relatively simple or relatively complex?
2. What transactions most commonly affect the stockholders' equity section of the balance sheet of Toys "R" Us? Examine the statements of stockholders' equity.

Comparison Case: Toys "R" Us and Walgreen Co.

FRA 5.

LO7   Book Value and Market Value

Refer to the annual report for Toys "R" Us <www.tru.com> and the financial statements for Walgreens <www.walgreens.com> in the Supplement to Chapter 1. Compute the 2001 and 2000 book value per share for both companies and compare the results to the average stock price of each in the fourth quarter of 2001 as shown in the notes to the financial statements. How do you explain the differences in book value per share, and how do you interpret their relationship to market prices?

Fingraph® Financial Analyst™

FRA 6.

LO1   Stockholders' Equity Analysis
LO3
LO4
LO5
LO6
LO7

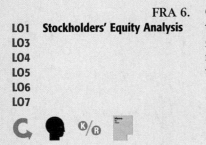

Choose any two companies in the same industry from the list of Fingraph companies on the Needles Accounting Resource Center Student Web Site at http://accounting. college.hmco.com/students. Access the Microsoft Excel spreadsheets for the companies you selected. Click on the URL at the top of each company's spreadsheet for a link to the company's web site and annual report.

1. In the annual reports of the companies you have selected, find the corporate income statement and summary of significant accounting policies (usually the first note to the financial statements). Did the companies report any discontinued operations, extraordinary items, or accounting changes? What percentage impact did these items have on earnings per share? Summarize the methods and estimates each company uses in a table. If the company changed its accounting methods, was the change the

result of a new accounting standard or a voluntary choice by management? Evaluate the quality of earnings for each company.

2. Did the companies provide a statement of stockholders' equity or summarize changes in stockholders' equity in the notes only? Did the companies declare any stock dividends or stock splits? Calculate book value per common share.

3. Find in the financial section of your local paper the current market prices of the companies' common stock. Discuss the difference between market price per share and book value per share.

4. Find and read references to earnings per share in management's discussion and analysis in each annual report.

5. Write a one-page executive summary that highlights the quality of earnings for these companies, the relationship of book value and market value, and the existence or absence of stock splits or dividends, including reference to management's assessment. Include your table with your report.

Internet Case

FRA 7.
LO1 Comparison of Comprehensive
LO4 Income Disclosures
LO5

When the FASB ruled that public companies should report comprehensive income, it did not issue specific guidelines for how this amount and its components should be disclosed. Choose two companies in the same industry from the Needles Accounting Resource Center Web Site at http://accounting.college.hmco.com/students. Using web links, go to the annual reports on the web sites of the two companies you have selected. In the latest annual report, look at the financial statements. How have your two companies reported comprehensive income—as a part of the income statement, a part of stockholders' equity, or a separate statement? What items create a difference between net income and comprehensive income? Is comprehensive income greater or less than net income? Is comprehensive income more volatile than net income? Which measure of income is used to compute basic earnings per share?

Chapter 14 presents the statement of cash flows and explains the changes in cash flows from operating, investing, and financing activities. The chapter also focuses on how to analyze the statement of cash flows to determine a company's cash-generating ability and its free cash flow.

The Statement of Cash Flows

LEARNING OBJECTIVES

LO1 State the principal purposes and uses of the statement of cash flows, and identify its components.

LO2 Analyze the statement of cash flows.

LO3 Use the indirect method to determine cash flows from operating activities.

LO4 Determine cash flows from investing activities.

LO5 Determine cash flows from financing activities.

DECISION POINT
A USER'S FOCUS

Marriott International, Inc. <www.marriott.com>
Marriott International, Inc., is a world leader in lodging and contract hotel services. The balance sheet, income statement, and statement of stockholders' equity presented in Marriott's annual report give an excellent picture of the company's philosophy and performance.

Although these three financial statements are essential to the evaluation of any company, they do not tell the entire story. A fourth statement, the statement of cash flows, contains some additional information, as shown in the Financial Highlights on page 612.[1] This statement shows how much cash the company's operations generated during the past three years and how much cash investing and financing activities used or provided.

Marriott feels that maintaining adequate cash flows is important to the future of the company. In fact, Marriott's emphasis on cash flows is reflected in its compensation plan for top executives. A review of the plan indicates that cash flows, at the firm or business group level, are the financial measure given the greatest weight in determining compensation. Why would Marriott emphasize cash flows to such an extent?

Strong cash flows are essential to management's key goal of liquidity. If cash flows exceed the amount needed for operations and expansion, the company will not have to borrow additional funds. The excess cash flows will be available to reduce the company's debt and improve its financial position by lowering its debt to equity ratio. Another reason for the emphasis

What does Marriott's statement of cash flows reveal about the company's success in providing top-notch lodging and hotel services?

on cash flows may be the belief that strong cash flows from operations generate shareholder value and increase the market value of the company's stock.

The statement of cash flows demonstrates management's commitments in ways that are not readily apparent in the other financial statements. For example, it can show whether management's focus is on the short term or the long term. This statement, which is required by the FASB, satisfies the board's long-held position that a primary objective of financial statements is to provide investors and creditors with information about a company's cash flows.[2]

Financial Highlights: Consolidated Statement of Cash Flows

Marriott International, Inc., and Subsidiaries

(In millions)

	2000	1999	1998
OPERATING ACTIVITIES			
Net income	$ 479	$ 400	$ 390
Adjustments to reconcile to cash provided by operations:			
Depreciation and amortization	195	162	140
Income taxes	133	87	76
Timeshare activity, net	(195)	(102)	28
Other	48	19	(22)
Working capital changes:			
Accounts receivable	(53)	(126)	(104)
Inventories	(4)	(17)	15
Other current assets	28	(38)	(16)
Accounts payable and accruals	219	326	98
Cash provided by operations	850	711	605
INVESTING ACTIVITIES			
Capital expenditures	(1,095)	(929)	(937)
Acquisitions	—	(61)	(48)
Dispositions	742	436	332
Loan advances	(389)	(144)	(48)
Loan collections and sales	93	54	169
Other	(377)	(143)	(192)
Cash used in investing activities	(1,026)	(787)	(724)
FINANCING ACTIVITIES			
Commercial paper, net	46	355	426
Issuance of long-term debt	338	366	868
Repayment of long-term debt	(26)	(63)	(473)
Redemption of convertible subordinated debt	—	(120)	—
Issuance of Class A common stock	58	43	15
Dividends paid	(55)	(52)	(37)
Purchase of treasury stock	(340)	(354)	(398)
Advances to Old Marriott	—	—	(100)
Cash provided by financing activities	21	175	301
(DECREASE) INCREASE IN CASH AND EQUIVALENTS	(155)	99	182
CASH AND EQUIVALENTS, beginning of year	489	390	208
CASH AND EQUIVALENTS, end of year	$ 334	$ 489	$ 390

VIDEO CASE

Goodyear Tire & Rubber Company

<www.goodyear.com>

OBJECTIVES

- To state the purposes of the statement of cash flows
- To identify the three components of the statement of cash flows
- To identify the reasons why cash flows from operating activities usually differ from net income
- To understand the importance of cash flows from investing and financing activities

BACKGROUND FOR THE CASE

Goodyear was founded in 1898 by Frank Seiberling, who borrowed $3,500 to start a bicycle tire factory and  subsequently began making tires for horseless carriages. Today, Goodyear is the world's largest tire and rubber company, with factories in 28 countries and more than 100,000 employees. In a recent year, sales exceeded $14 billion. In addition to producing Goodyear tires, the company makes Dunlop, Kelly, Fulda, Lee, Sava, and Debica tires and rubber products for the automotive and industrial markets.

Goodyear's goal is to be ranked by all measures as the best tire and rubber company in the world. It intends to accomplish this by doing the following:

- having fast and profitable growth in all core businesses.
- achieving a number one or two market position.
- making strategic acquisitions and expansions.
- being the lowest cost producer.

To achieve these objectives, especially "fast and profitable growth" and "strategic acquisitions and expansions," Goodyear will need adequate funding. Management expects the funding to come from strong cash flows; divestiture of underperforming, nonstrategic assets; and debt issues. Within this framework, management must maintain the company's financial health and a strong balance sheet, with a debt to debt plus equity ratio of 25 to 30 percent.

Understanding Goodyear's performance in meeting the challenge of achieving adequate funding requires an ability to read and understand the statement of cash flows.

For more information about Goodyear Tire & Rubber Company, visit the company's web site through the Needles Accounting Resource Center Web Site at **http://accounting.college.hmco.com/students**.

REQUIRED

1. What are the purposes and three main components of the statement of cash flows?

2. What is the most important amount in the statement of cash flows? Why is it the most important?

3. What is the relationship of cash flows from operating activities to net income for Goodyear, and how do you account for the difference?

4. What are Goodyear's principal investing and financing activities?

OVERVIEW OF THE STATEMENT OF CASH FLOWS

LO1   State the principal purposes and uses of the statement of cash flows, and identify its components.

RELATED TEXT ASSIGNMENTS
Q: 1, 2, 3, 4, 5, 6
SE: 1, 8
E: 1
P: 1, 5
SD: 1, 2, 3
FRA: 3

The **statement of cash flows** shows how a company's operating, investing, and financing activities have affected cash during an accounting period. It explains the net increase (or decrease) in cash during the period. For purposes of preparing this statement, **cash** is defined as including both cash and cash equivalents. The FASB defines **cash equivalents** as short-term, highly liquid investments, including money market accounts, commercial paper, and U.S. Treasury bills. A company maintains cash equivalents to earn interest on cash that would otherwise remain unused temporarily. Suppose, for example, that a company has $1,000,000 that it will not need for 30 days. To earn a return on this amount, the company may place the cash in an account that earns interest (such as a money market account), it may lend the cash to another corporation by purchasing that corporation's short-term notes (commercial paper), or it may purchase a short-term obligation of the U.S. government (Treasury bills). In this context, short-term refers to original maturities of 90 days or less. Since cash and cash equivalents are considered the same, transfers between the Cash account and cash equivalents are not treated as cash receipts or cash payments. In effect, cash equivalents are combined with the Cash account on the statement of cash flows.

KEY POINT: Money market accounts, commercial paper (short-term notes), and U.S. Treasury bills are considered cash equivalents because they are highly liquid, temporary (90 days or less) holding places for cash not currently needed to operate the business. They can be quickly converted into cash if the need arises.

◆ **STOP AND THINK!**

Which statement is more useful—the income statement or the statement of cash flows?

The statements are equally useful. The income statement relates most directly to the goal of profitability, whereas the statement of cash flows is more closely tied to the goal of liquidity. ■

KEY POINT: Management uses the statement of cash flows to make various investing and financing decisions. Investors and creditors, on the other hand, use the statement primarily to assess cash flow prospects.

KEY POINT: Operating activities arise from the day-to-day sale of goods and services, investing activities involve long-term assets and investments, and financing activities deal with stockholders' equity accounts and debt (borrowing).

Cash equivalents should not be confused with short-term investments or marketable securities, which are not combined with the Cash account on the statement of cash flows. Purchases of marketable securities are treated as cash outflows and sales of marketable securities as cash inflows on the statement of cash flows. In this chapter, we assume that cash includes cash and cash equivalents.

PURPOSES OF THE STATEMENT OF CASH FLOWS

The primary purpose of the statement of cash flows is to provide information about a company's cash receipts and cash payments during an accounting period. A secondary purpose of the statement is to provide information about a company's operating, investing, and financing activities during the accounting period. Some information about those activities may be inferred from other financial statements, but it is on the statement of cash flows that all the transactions affecting cash are summarized.

INTERNAL AND EXTERNAL USES OF THE STATEMENT OF CASH FLOWS

The statement of cash flows is useful internally to management and externally to investors and creditors. Management uses the statement to assess liquidity, to determine dividend policy, and to evaluate the effects of major policy decisions involving investments and financing. In other words, management may use the statement to determine if short-term financing is needed to pay current liabilities, to decide whether to raise or lower dividends, and to plan for investing and financing needs.

Investors and creditors find the statement useful in assessing the company's ability to manage cash flows, to generate positive future cash flows, to pay its liabilities, to pay dividends and interest, and to anticipate its need for additional financing. Also, they may use the statement to explain the differences between net income on the income statement and the net cash flows generated from operations. In addition, the statement shows both the cash and the noncash effects of investing and financing activities during the accounting period.

CLASSIFICATION OF CASH FLOWS

The statement of cash flows classifies cash receipts and cash payments into the categories of operating, investing, and financing activities. The components of these activities are illustrated in Figure 1 and summarized below.

1. **Operating activities** include the cash effects of transactions and other events that enter into the determination of net income. Included in this category as cash inflows are cash receipts from customers for goods and services, interest and dividends received on loans and investments, and sales of trading securities. Included as cash outflows are cash payments for wages, inventory, expenses, interest, taxes, and purchases of trading securities. In effect, the income statement is changed from an accrual to a cash basis.

2. **Investing activities** include the acquisition and sale of long-term assets and marketable securities, other than trading securities or cash equivalents, and the making and collecting of loans. Cash inflows include the cash received from selling long-term assets and marketable securities and from collecting loans. Cash outflows include the cash expended for purchases of long-term assets and marketable securities and the cash lent to borrowers.

3. **Financing activities** include obtaining resources from stockholders and providing them with a return on their investments, and obtaining resources from creditors and repaying the amounts borrowed or otherwise settling the obligations. Cash inflows include the proceeds from issues of stocks and from short-term and long-term borrowing. Cash outflows include the repayments of loans (excluding interest) and payments to owners, including cash dividends. Treasury stock transactions are also considered financing activities. Repayments of

FIGURE 1
Classification of Cash Inflows and Cash Outflows

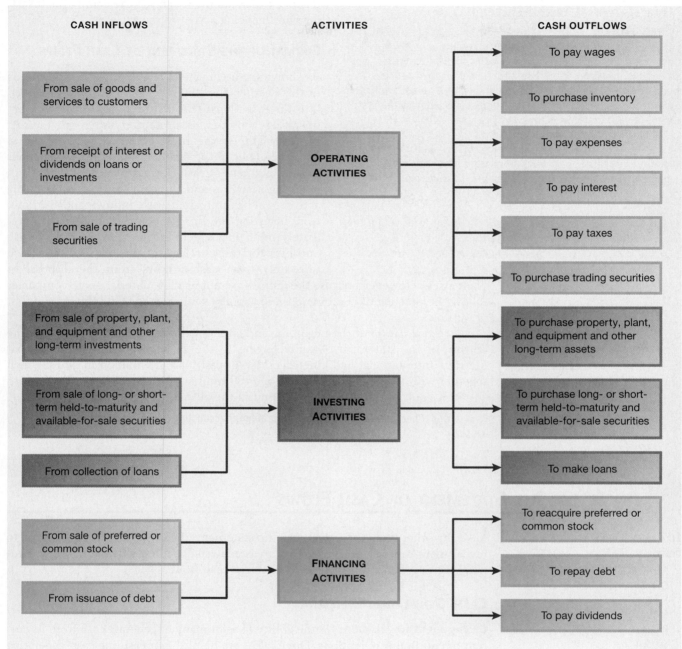

accounts payable or accrued liabilities are not considered repayments of loans under financing activities; they are classified as cash outflows under operating activities.

Companies occasionally engage in significant **noncash investing and financing transactions** involving only long-term assets, long-term liabilities, or stockholders' equity. For instance, a company might exchange a long-term asset for a long-term liability, settle a debt by issuing capital stock, or take out a long-term mortgage for the purchase of land and a building. Such transactions represent significant investing and financing activities, but they would not be reflected on the statement of cash flows because they do not involve either cash inflows or outflows. However, because such transactions will affect future cash flows, the FASB has determined

FOCUS ON INTERNATIONAL BUSINESS

How Universal Is the Statement of Cash Flows?

Despite the importance of the statement of cash flows in assessing the liquidity of companies in the United States, considerable variation in its use and format has existed in other countries. For example, the principal directives related to financial reporting for the European Union do not address the statement of cash flows. In many countries, the statement shows the change in working capital instead of the change in cash and cash equivalents. However, international accounting standards require the statement of cash flows, and international financial markets expect it to be presented. As a result, most multinational companies include the statement in their financial reports. Most European countries will adopt the statement of cash flows by 2006, when the European Union will require the use of international accounting standards.

www.marriott.com

that they should be disclosed in a separate schedule as part of the statement of cash flows. In this way, the reader of the statement can see the company's investing and financing activities more clearly.

FORMAT OF THE STATEMENT OF CASH FLOWS

As shown in the Financial Highlights at the beginning of this chapter, the statement of cash flows is divided into three sections. The first section, cash flows from operating activities, is presented using the indirect method. This is the most common method and is explained later in the chapter. The other two sections of the statement of cash flows are the cash flows from investing activities and the cash flows from financing activities. The individual cash inflows and outflows from investing and financing activities are shown separately in their respective categories. Normally, cash outflows for the purchase of plant assets are shown separately from cash inflows from the disposal of plant assets. However, because the inflows are not usually material, some companies follow the practice of combining these two lines in order to show the net amount of outflow.

A reconciliation of the beginning and ending balances of cash appears near the bottom of the statement. Again referring to the Financial Highlights, note that Marriott International had a net decrease in cash of $155 million in 2000, which together with the beginning balance of $489 million results in $334 million of cash and cash equivalents on hand at the end of the year.

✓ Check out ACE for a Review Quiz at http://accounting.college.hmco.com/students.

ANALYZING THE STATEMENT OF CASH FLOWS

LO2 Analyze the statement of cash flows.

RELATED TEXT ASSIGNMENTS
Q: 7, 8
SE: 2, 3
E: 2
P: 2, 3, 4, 6, 7
SD: 3, 4
FRA: 1, 2, 3, 4, 5, 6

www.marriott.com

Like the other financial statements, the statement of cash flows can be analyzed to reveal significant relationships. Two areas analysts examine when studying a company are cash-generating efficiency and free cash flow.

CASH-GENERATING EFFICIENCY

Cash-generating efficiency is the ability of a company to generate cash from its current or continuing operations. Three ratios are helpful in measuring cash-generating efficiency: cash flow yield, cash flows to sales, and cash flows to assets. We compute these ratios for Marriott International in 2000 using data from the Financial Highlights at the beginning of this chapter and those presented below.[3] All dollar amounts are stated in millions.

Financial Highlights for Marriott International
(In millions of dollars)

	2000	1999	1998
Net Sales	$10,017	$8,739	$7,968
Total Assets	8,237	7,324	6,233

ENRICHMENT NOTE: The cash flow yield enables users to assess whether sufficient cash flows underlie earnings. Serious questions would be raised if cash flow yield was less than 1.0. For example, receivables and inventories might be growing too fast, perhaps signaling a slowdown in sales growth or a problem in managing receivables collection or inventory levels.

Cash flow yield is the ratio of net cash flows from operating activities to net income, computed as follows:

$$\text{Cash Flow Yield} = \frac{\text{Net Cash Flows from Operating Activities}}{\text{Net Income}}$$

$$= \frac{\$850}{\$479}$$

$$= 1.8 \text{ times}$$

Marriott International has a good cash flow yield of 1.8 times; that is, the corporation's operating activities are generating about 80 percent more cash flow than net income. If special items, such as discontinued operations, appear on the income statement and are material, income from continuing operations should be used as the denominator.

Cash flows to sales is the ratio of net cash flows from operating activities to sales, computed as follows:

$$\text{Cash Flows to Sales} = \frac{\text{Net Cash Flows from Operating Activities}}{\text{Net Sales}}$$

$$= \frac{\$850}{\$10,017}$$

$$= 8.5\%$$

KEY POINT: The change in cash shown in the comparative balance sheets provides a check figure for the statement of cash flows.

Marriott generates cash flows to sales of 8.5 percent. The company generated a positive but relatively small percentage of net cash from sales.

Cash flows to assets is the ratio of net cash flows from operating activities to average total assets, computed as follows:

$$\text{Cash Flows to Assets} = \frac{\text{Net Cash Flows from Operating Activities}}{\text{Average Total Assets}}$$

$$= \frac{\$850}{(\$8,237 + \$7,324) \div 2}$$

$$= 10.9\%$$

● STOP AND THINK!
If cash flow yield is less than 1.0, would cash flows to sales and cash flows to assets be greater or less than profit margin and return on assets, respectively?

Cash flows to sales and cash flows to assets would be less than profit margin and return on assets, respectively, because a cash flow yield of 1.0 means that cash flows from operations are less than net income. Both are numerators in ratios that have the same denominators. ■

The cash flows to assets ratio is higher than the cash flows to sales ratio because Marriott International has a good asset turnover ratio (sales ÷ average total assets) of approximately 1.3 times (10.9% ÷ 8.5%). Cash flows to sales and cash flows to assets are closely related to the profitability measures of profit margin and return on assets. They exceed those measures by the amount of the cash flow yield ratio because cash flow yield is the ratio of net cash flows from operating activities to net income.

Although Marriott's cash flow yield and cash flows to assets are relatively good, its efficiency at generating cash flows from operating activities, as measured by cash flows to sales, could be improved.

FREE CASH FLOW

www.marriott.com

In 2000, Marriott had a net cash outflow of $1,026 million for investing activities, which could indicate that the company was expanding. However, that figure mixes capital expenditures for plant assets, which reflect management's expansion of operations, with the acquisition of hotel chains and loan advances and collections. Cash flows from financing activities provided $21 million, but that figure combines financing activities associated with long-term debt and stocks with dividends paid to stockholders. While something can be learned by looking at those broad

FOCUS ON BUSINESS PRACTICE

What Do You Mean, "Free Cash Flow"?

Because the statement of cash flows has been around for less than 20 years, no generally accepted analyses have yet been developed. For example, the term *free cash flow* is commonly used in the business press, but there is no agreement on its definition. An article in *Forbes* defines *free cash flow* as "cash available after paying out capital expenditures and dividends, *but before taxes and interest*"[4] [emphasis added]. An article in

The Wall Street Journal defines it as "operating income less maintenance-level capital expenditures."[5] The definition with which we are most in agreement is the one used in *Business Week:* free cash flow is net cash flows from operating activities less net capital expenditures and dividends. This "measures truly discretionary funds—company money that an owner could pocket without harming the business."[6]

KEY POINT: Free cash flow should be interpreted in light of the company's overall need for cash. For instance, the purchase of treasury stock will reduce the amount of cash that is free for operating uses.

categories, many analysts find it more informative to go beyond them to focus on a computation called free cash flow.

Free cash flow is the amount of cash that remains after deducting the funds a company must commit to continue operating at its planned level. The commitments must cover current or continuing operations, interest, income taxes, dividends, and net capital expenditures. Cash requirements for current or continuing operations, interest, and income taxes must be paid or the company's creditors and the government can take legal action. Although the payment of dividends is not strictly required, dividends normally represent a commitment to stockholders. If these payments are reduced or eliminated, stockholders will be unhappy and the price of the company's stock will fall. Net capital expenditures represent management's plans for the future.

If free cash flow is positive, it means that the company has met all its planned cash commitments and has cash available to reduce debt or to expand. A negative free cash flow means that the company will have to sell investments, borrow money, or issue stock in the short term to continue at its planned level. If free cash flow remains negative for several years, a company may not be able to raise cash by issuing stock or bonds.

Since cash commitments for current or continuing operations, interest, and income taxes are incorporated in cash flows from current operations, free cash flow for Marriott is computed as follows (in millions):

$$\text{Free Cash Flow} = \frac{\text{Net Cash Flows from Operating Activities} - \text{Dividends}}{- \text{ Purchases of Plant Assets} + \text{Sales of Plant Assets}}$$

$$= \$850 - \$55 - \$1,095 + \$742$$

$$= \$442$$

FOCUS ON BUSINESS PRACTICE

Cash Flows Tell All.

In early 2001, the telecommunications industry began one of the biggest market crashes in history. Could it have been predicted? The telecommunications industry depends on heavy capital expenditures in equipment, such as cable lines and computers. When the cash flows from sales of 41 telecommunications companies are compared with their capital expenditures (a negative component of free cash flow) over the six years preceding the crash, an interesting pattern emerges. In the first three years, both cash flows from sales and capital expenditures were about 20 percent of sales. In other words,

free cash flows were neutral, with operations generating enough cash flows to cover capital expenditures. In the next three years, these measures diverged. Cash flows to sales stayed at about 20 percent of sales, but the companies increased capital expenditure dramatically, to 35 percent of sales. Thus, free cash flows turned very negative, and almost half of capital expenditures had to be financed by debt instead of operations, making these companies more vulnerable to the downturn in the economy that occurred in 2001.[7]

Purchases and sales of plant assets appear in the investing activities section of the statement of cash flows. Marriott reported both capital expenditures and dispositions of property and equipment. Dividends are found in the financing activities section. Marriott had positive free cash flow of $442 million due primarily to its strong operating cash flow of $850 million and $742 million cash received on disposal of property and equipment. The cash provided by financing activities was the lowest in three years, only $21 million, and was possible because of increasing cash provided by operations. The company repaid long-term debt of $26 million while issuing new debt of $338 million. Marriott also issued common stock in the amount of $58 million and purchased treasury stock for $340 million. The result is that financing activities were a positive $21 million.

Cash flows can vary from year to year, so it is best to look at trends in cash flow measures over several years when analyzing a company's cash flows. Marriott's cash flow yield has shown little variation over the past three years. Management summed this up in the company's annual report:

Cash from Operations
The company's operating cash flow is stable, and typically does not fluctuate widely within an economic cycle.[8]

✓ Check out ACE for a Review Quiz at http://accounting.college.hmco.com/students.

PREPARING THE STATEMENT OF CASH FLOWS: OPERATING ACTIVITIES

LO3 Use the indirect method to determine cash flows from operating activities.

RELATED TEXT ASSIGNMENTS
Q: 9, 10, 11
SE: 4, 5, 8
E: 3, 4, 5, 9
P: 2, 3, 4, 6, 7
SD: 1, 4
FRA: 3, 5

KEY POINT: The direct and indirect methods relate only to the operating activities section of the statement of cash flows. They are both acceptable for financial reporting purposes.

To demonstrate the preparation of the statement of cash flows, we will work through an example step by step. The data for this example are presented in Exhibits 1 and 2, which show Ryan Corporation's balance sheets for December 31, 20x4 and 20x3, and its 20x4 income statement. Exhibit 1 shows the balance sheet accounts that we use for analysis and whether the change in each account is an increase or a decrease. Exhibit 2 contains data about transactions that affected noncurrent accounts. The company's accountants would identify those transactions from the records.

The first step in preparing the statement of cash flows is to determine cash flows from operating activities. The income statement indicates a business's success or failure in earning an income from its operating activities. However, because the income statement is prepared on an accrual basis, it does not reflect the inflow and outflow of cash from those activities. Revenues are recorded even though the cash for them may not have been received, and expenses are recorded even though the cash for them may not have been expended. Thus, to arrive at cash flows from operations, the figures on the income statement must be converted from an accrual basis to a cash basis.

There are two methods of converting the income statement from an accrual basis to a cash basis: the direct method and the indirect method. Under the **direct method**, each item on the income statement is adjusted from the accrual basis to the cash basis. The result is a statement that begins with cash receipts from sales and interest and deducts cash payments for purchases, operating expenses, interest payments, and income taxes to arrive at net cash flows from operating activities. The **indirect method**, on the other hand, does not require the individual adjustment of each item on the income statement; it lists only those adjustments necessary to convert net income to cash flows from operations.

The direct and indirect methods always produce the same net figure. The direct method is more easily understood by the average reader because it results in a more straightforward presentation of operating cash flows than does the indirect method. However, the indirect method is the overwhelming choice of most companies and

EXHIBIT 1
Comparative Balance Sheets with Changes in Accounts Indicated

	Ryan Corporation Comparative Balance Sheets December 31, 20x4 and 20x3			
	20x4	**20x3**	**Change**	**Increase or Decrease**
Assets				
Current assets				
Cash	$ 46,000	$ 15,000	$ 31,000	Increase
Accounts receivable (net)	47,000	55,000	(8,000)	Decrease
Inventory	144,000	110,000	34,000	Increase
Prepaid expenses	1,000	5,000	(4,000)	Decrease
Total current assets	$238,000	$185,000	$ 53,000	
Investments available for sale	$115,000	$127,000	($ 12,000)	Decrease
Plant assets				
Plant assets	$715,000	$505,000	$210,000	Increase
Accumulated depreciation	(103,000)	(68,000)	(35,000)	Increase
Total plant assets	$612,000	$437,000	$175,000	
Total assets	$965,000	$749,000	$216,000	
Liabilities				
Current liabilities				
Accounts payable	$ 50,000	$ 43,000	$ 7,000	Increase
Accrued liabilities	12,000	9,000	3,000	Increase
Income taxes payable	3,000	5,000	(2,000)	Decrease
Total current liabilities	$ 65,000	$ 57,000	$ 8,000	
Long-term liabilities				
Bonds payable	295,000	245,000	50,000	Increase
Total liabilities	$360,000	$302,000	$ 58,000	
Stockholders' Equity				
Common stock, $5 par value	$276,000	$200,000	$ 76,000	Increase
Paid-in capital in excess of par value, common	214,000	115,000	99,000	Increase
Retained earnings	140,000	132,000	8,000	Increase
Treasury stock	(25,000)	0	(25,000)	Increase
Total stockholders' equity	$605,000	$447,000	$158,000	
Total liabilities and stockholders' equity	$965,000	$749,000	$216,000	

KEY POINT: The indirect method begins with net income and adjusts up or down to produce net cash flows from operating activities.

accountants. A survey of large companies shows that 99 percent use this method.[9] The indirect method is superior to the direct method from the analysts' perspective because its format begins with net income and derives cash flows from operations. The analyst can readily identify the factors that cause cash flows from operations. Further, from the company's standpoint, the indirect method is easier and less expensive to prepare. For these reasons, we use the indirect method in this book.

EXHIBIT 2
Income Statement and Other Information on Noncurrent Accounts

Ryan Corporation
Income Statement
For the Year Ended December 31, 20x4

Net sales		$698,000
Cost of goods sold		520,000
Gross margin		$178,000
Operating expenses (including depreciation expense of $37,000)		147,000
Operating income		$ 31,000
Other income (expenses)		
Interest expense	($23,000)	
Interest income	6,000	
Gain on sale of investments	12,000	
Loss on sale of plant assets	(3,000)	(8,000)
Income before income taxes		$ 23,000
Income taxes		7,000
Net income		$ 16,000

Other transactions affecting noncurrent accounts during 20x4:

1. Purchased investments in the amount of $78,000.
2. Sold investments that cost $90,000 for $102,000.
3. Purchased plant assets in the amount of $120,000.
4. Sold plant assets that cost $10,000 with accumulated depreciation of $2,000 for $5,000.
5. Issued $100,000 of bonds at face value in a noncash exchange for plant assets.
6. Repaid $50,000 of bonds at face value at maturity.
7. Issued 15,200 shares of $5 par value common stock for $175,000.
8. Purchased treasury stock in the amount of $25,000.
9. Paid cash dividends in the amount of $8,000.

As illustrated in Figure 2, the indirect method focuses on items from the income statement that must be adjusted to reconcile net income to net cash flows from operating activities. The items that require adjustment are those that affect net income but not net cash flows from operating activities. They include depreciation and amortization, gains and losses, and changes in the balances of current asset and current liability accounts. The reconciliation of Ryan Corporation's net income to

FIGURE 2
Indirect Method of Determining Net Cash Flows from Operating Activities

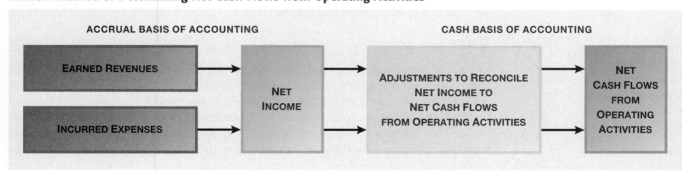

EXHIBIT 3
Schedule of Cash Flows from Operating Activities: Indirect Method

Ryan Corporation
Schedule of Cash Flows from Operating Activities
For the Year Ended December 31, 20x4

Cash flows from operating activities		
Net income		$16,000
Adjustments to reconcile net income to net		
cash flows from operating activities		
Depreciation	$37,000	
Gain on sale of investments	(12,000)	
Loss on sale of plant assets	3,000	
Changes in current assets and current liabilities		
Decrease in accounts receivable	8,000	
Increase in inventory	(34,000)	
Decrease in prepaid expenses	4,000	
Increase in accounts payable	7,000	
Increase in accrued liabilities	3,000	
Decrease in income taxes payable	(2,000)	14,000
Net cash flows from operating activities		$30,000

● **STOP AND THINK!**
If a company has positive earnings, can cash flows from operating activities ever be negative?

If a company has large gains, large increases in current assets, or decreases in current liabilities, the results could overwhelm the earnings and create negative cash flows from operating activities. ■

net cash flows from operating activities is shown in Exhibit 3. Each adjustment is discussed in the following sections.

DEPRECIATION

Cash payments for plant assets, intangibles, and natural resources occur when the assets are purchased and are reflected as investing activities on the statement of cash flows at that time. When depreciation expense, amortization expense, and depletion expense appear on the income statement, they simply indicate allocations of the costs of the original purchases to the current accounting period; they do not affect net cash flows in the current period. The amount of such expenses can usually be found by referring to the income statement or a note to the financial statements. For Ryan Corporation, the income statement reveals depreciation expense of $37,000, which would have been recorded as follows:

KEY POINT: Operating expenses on the income statement include depreciation expense, which does not require a cash outlay.

$$A = L + OE$$
$$- \quad -$$

Depreciation Expense	37,000	
Accumulated Depreciation		37,000
To record annual depreciation on plant assets		

The recording of depreciation involved no outlay of cash even though depreciation expense appears on the income statement. Thus, to derive cash flows from operations, an adjustment for depreciation is needed to increase net income by the amount of depreciation recorded.

GAINS AND LOSSES

STUDY NOTE: Gains and losses by themselves do not represent cash flows; they are merely bookkeeping adjustments. For example, when a long-term asset is sold, it is the *proceeds* (cash received), not the gain or loss, that constitute cash flow.

Gains and losses that appear on the income statement also do not affect cash flows from operating activities and need to be removed from this section of the statement of cash flows. The cash receipts generated by the disposal of the assets that resulted in the gains or losses are shown in the investing section of the statement of cash flows. Thus, gains and losses are removed from net income (preventing double counting) to reconcile net income to cash flows from operating activities. For example, on its income statement, Ryan Corporation showed a $12,000 gain on the sale of investments, and this is subtracted from net income to reconcile net income to net cash flows from operating activities. The reason for this is that the $12,000 is already included (added) in the investing activities section as part of the $102,000 cash from the sale of the investment. Because the gain is included in the calculation of net income, the $12,000 gain needs to be subtracted to prevent double counting. Also, Ryan Corporation showed a $3,000 loss on the sale of plant assets. Following the same logic, the $3,000 loss is already reflected in the $5,000 sale of plant assets in the investing activities section. Thus, the $3,000 is added to net income to reconcile net income to net cash flows from operating activities.

CHANGES IN CURRENT ASSETS

Decreases in current assets other than cash have positive effects on cash flows, and increases in current assets have negative effects on cash flows. A decrease in a current asset frees up invested cash, thereby increasing cash flow. An increase in a current asset consumes cash, thereby decreasing cash flow. For example, refer to the balance sheets and income statement for Ryan Corporation in Exhibits 1 and 2. Note that net sales in 20x4 were $698,000 and that Accounts Receivable decreased by $8,000. Thus, cash received from sales was $706,000, calculated as follows:

$$\$706,000 = \$698,000 + \$8,000$$

Collections were $8,000 more than sales recorded for the year. This relationship may be illustrated as follows:

	Accounts Receivable		
	Beg. Bal. 55,000	706,000 ⟶	Cash Receipts from Customers
Sales to Customers ⟶	698,000		
	End. Bal. 47,000		

Thus, to reconcile net income to net cash flows from operating activities, the $8,000 decrease in Accounts Receivable is added to net income.

Inventory may be analyzed in the same way. For example, Exhibit 1 shows that Inventory increased by $34,000 from 20x3 to 20x4. This means that Ryan Corporation expended $34,000 more in cash for purchases than was included in cost of goods sold on the income statement. As a result of this expenditure, net income is higher than the net cash flows from operating activities, so $34,000 must be deducted from net income. Using the same logic, the decrease of $4,000 in Prepaid Expenses is added to net income to reconcile net income to net cash flows from operations.

CHANGES IN CURRENT LIABILITIES

Changes in current liabilities have the opposite effects on cash flows from those of changes in current assets. Increases in current liabilities are added to net income, and decreases in current liabilities are deducted from net income to reconcile net income to net cash flows from operating activities. An increase in a current liability represents a postponement of a cash payment, which frees up cash and increases cash flow in the current period. A decrease in current liabilities consumes cash, thereby decreasing cash flow. For example, Exhibit 1 shows that Ryan Corporation had a $7,000 increase in accounts payable from 20x3 to 20x4. This means that Ryan Corporation paid $7,000 less to creditors than the amount of purchases indicates in cost of goods sold on the income statement. This relationship may be visualized as follows:

	Accounts Payable		
Cash Payments to Suppliers ⟵	547,000	Beg. Bal. 43,000	
		554,000* ⟵	Purchases
		End. Bal. 50,000	

*Purchases = Cost of Goods Sold ($520,000) + Increase in Inventory ($34,000).

FOCUS ON BUSINESS PRACTICE

What's Your "Burn Rate"?

Why would a company have a total market value less than the amount of cash it has on hand? The answer is "burn rate." Burn rate is the pace at which companies use cash in their operations. A major contributor to the market crash of the stocks of dot-com companies was the difficulty these firms had in generating enough revenue to produce positive cash flows from operations. For example, when investors thought Webvan Group, Inc., the Internet grocer, would be the delivery service model of the future, the company was valued as high as $11.4 billion. However, as Webvan's burn rate reached $55 million a month, its market value dropped to a mere $132 million, even though the company had $212 million in cash.[10] The company was never able to generate sufficient revenues and soon declared bankruptcy.

As a result, $7,000 is added to net income to reconcile net income to net cash flows from operating activities. By the same logic, the increase of $3,000 in accrued liabilities is added to net income, and the decrease of $2,000 in income taxes payable is deducted from net income.

SCHEDULE OF CASH FLOWS FROM OPERATING ACTIVITIES

In summary, Exhibit 3 shows that by using the indirect method, net income of $16,000 has been adjusted by reconciling items totaling $14,000 to arrive at net cash flows from operating activities of $30,000. This means that although net income was $16,000, Ryan actually had net cash flows of $30,000 available from operating activities to use for purchasing assets, reducing debts, or paying dividends.

The effects of items on the income statement that do not affect cash flows may be summarized as follows:

	Add to or Deduct from Net Income
Depreciation expense	Add
Amortization expense	Add
Depletion expense	Add
Losses	Add
Gains	Deduct

The adjustments for increases and decreases in current assets and current liabilities may be summarized as follows:

	Add to Net Income	Deduct from Net Income
Current assets		
Accounts receivable (net)	Decrease	Increase
Inventory	Decrease	Increase
Prepaid expenses	Decrease	Increase
Current liabilities		
Accounts payable	Increase	Decrease
Accrued liabilities	Increase	Decrease
Income taxes payable	Increase	Decrease

✓ Check out ACE for a Review Quiz at http://accounting.college.hmco.com/students.

PREPARING THE STATEMENT OF CASH FLOWS: INVESTING ACTIVITIES

LO4 Determine cash flows from investing activities.

RELATED TEXT ASSIGNMENTS
Q: 12, 13, 14
SE: 6, 8
E: 6, 7, 8, 9
P: 2, 3, 4, 6, 7
SD: 4
FRA: 3, 5

To determine cash flows from investing activities, each account involving cash receipts and cash payments from investing activities is examined individually. The objective is to explain the change in each account balance from one year to the next.

Investing activities center on the long-term assets shown on the balance sheet, but they also include transactions affecting short-term investments from the current assets section of the balance sheet and investment gains and losses from the income statement. The balance sheets in Exhibit 1 show that Ryan Corporation had long-term assets of investments and plant assets, but no short-term investments. The income statement in Exhibit 2 shows that Ryan had investment-related items in the form of a gain on the sale of investments and a loss on the sale of plant assets.

The schedule at the bottom of Exhibit 2 lists the following five items pertaining to investing activities in 20x4:

1. Purchased investments in the amount of $78,000.
2. Sold investments that cost $90,000 for $102,000.
3. Purchased plant assets in the amount of $120,000.
4. Sold plant assets that cost $10,000 with accumulated depreciation of $2,000 for $5,000.
5. Issued $100,000 of bonds at face value in a noncash exchange for plant assets.

The following sections analyze the accounts related to investing activities to determine their effects on Ryan Corporation's cash flows.

INVESTMENTS

The objective here is to explain Ryan Corporation's $12,000 decrease in investments, all of which are classified as available-for-sale securities. This is accomplished by analyzing the increases and decreases in the Investments account to determine the effects on the Cash account. Purchases increase investments, and sales decrease investments.

Item 1 in Ryan's list of investing activities shows purchases of $78,000 during 20x4. This transaction is recorded as follows:

$A = L + OE$
$+$
$-$

Investments	78,000	
Cash		78,000
Purchase of investments		

The entry shows that the effect of this transaction is a $78,000 decrease in cash flows.

Item 2 in the list shows that Ryan sold investments that cost $90,000 for $102,000, resulting in a gain of $12,000. This transaction is recorded in the following way:

$A = L + OE$
$+$ $+$
$-$

Cash	102,000	
Investments		90,000
Gain on Sale of Investments		12,000
Sale of investments for a gain		

The effect of this transaction is a $102,000 increase in cash flows. Note that the gain on sale of investments is included in the $102,000. This is why we excluded it in computing cash flows from operations. If it had been included in that section, it would have been counted twice.

The $12,000 decrease in the Investments account (unrelated to the $12,000 gain above) during 20x4 has now been explained, as seen in the following T account:

Investments			
Beg. Bal.	127,000	Sales	90,000
Purchases	78,000		
End. Bal.	115,000		

The cash flow effects from these transactions are shown in the investing activities section on the statement of cash flows as follows:

Purchase of investments	($ 78,000)
Sale of investments	102,000

Notice that purchases and sales are listed separately as cash outflows and inflows to give readers of the statement a complete view of investing activity. Some companies prefer to combine them into a single net amount.

If Ryan Corporation had short-term investments or marketable securities, the analysis of cash flows would be the same.

PLANT ASSETS

In the case of plant assets, it is necessary to explain the changes in both the Plant Assets account and the related Accumulated Depreciation account. According to Exhibit 1, Ryan Corporation's plant assets increased by $210,000, and accumulated depreciation increased by $35,000. Purchases increase plant assets, and sales decrease plant assets. Accumulated depreciation is increased by the amount of depreciation expense and decreased by the removal of the accumulated depreciation associated with plant assets that are sold. Three items listed in Exhibit 2 affect plant assets. Item **3** in the list indicates that Ryan Corporation purchased plant assets totaling $120,000 during 20x4, as shown by the following entry:

A = L + OE
+
−

Plant Assets	120,000	
Cash		120,000
Purchase of plant assets		

This transaction results in a cash outflow of $120,000.

Item **4** states that Ryan Corporation sold for $5,000 plant assets that cost $10,000 and had accumulated depreciation of $2,000, which resulted in a loss of $3,000. The entry to record this transaction is as follows:

A = L + OE
+
+   −
−

Cash	5,000	
Accumulated Depreciation	2,000	
Loss on Sale of Plant Assets	3,000	
Plant Assets		10,000
Sale of plant assets at a loss		

KEY POINT: Even though Ryan had a loss on the sale, it realized a positive cash flow of $5,000, which will be reported in the investing activities section of the statement of cash flows. When the indirect approach is used, the loss is eliminated with an "add-back" to net income.

Note that in this transaction the positive cash flow is equal to the amount of cash received, or $5,000. The loss on the sale of plant assets is included here, and excluded from the operating activities section (see page 623), by adjusting net income for the amount of the loss. The amount of a loss or gain on the sale of an asset is determined by the amount of cash received and does not represent a cash outflow or inflow.

The disclosure of these two transactions in the investing activities section of the statement of cash flows is as follows:

| Purchase of plant assets | ($120,000) |
| Sale of plant assets | 5,000 |

Cash outflows and cash inflows are listed separately here, though companies sometimes combine them into a single net amount, as they do the purchase and sale of investments.

Item **5** on the list of Ryan's investing activities is a noncash exchange that affects two long-term accounts, Plant Assets and Bonds Payable. It is recorded as follows:

A = L + OE
+   +

Plant Assets	100,000	
Bonds Payable		100,000
Issued bonds at face value for plant assets		

Although this transaction does not involve an inflow or outflow of cash, it is a significant transaction involving both an investing activity (the purchase of plant assets) and a financing activity (the issue of bonds payable). Because one purpose of the statement of cash flows is to show important investing and financing activities, the transaction is listed in a separate schedule, either at the bottom of the statement of cash flows or accompanying the statement, as follows:

Schedule of Noncash Investing and Financing Transactions

| Issue of bonds payable for plant assets | $100,000 |

Through our analysis of the preceding transactions and the depreciation expense for plant assets, we have now accounted for all the changes in the Plant Assets accounts, as shown in the following T accounts:

Plant Assets

Beg. Bal.	505,000	Sale		10,000
Cash Purchase	120,000			
Noncash Purchase	100,000			
End. Bal.	715,000			

Accumulated Depreciation

Sale	2,000	Beg. Bal.		68,000
		Dep. Exp.		37,000
		End. Bal.		103,000

Had the balance sheet included specific plant asset accounts (e.g., Buildings and Equipment and related accumulated depreciation accounts) or other long-term asset accounts (e.g., Intangibles), the analysis would have been the same.

✔ Check out ACE for a Review Quiz at http://accounting.college.hmco.com/students.

PREPARING THE STATEMENT OF CASH FLOWS: FINANCING ACTIVITIES

LO5 Determine cash flows from financing activities.

RELATED TEXT ASSIGNMENTS
Q: 13, 14
SE: 7, 8
E: 8, 9
P: 2, 3, 4, 6, 7
SD: 4
FRA: 3, 5

KEY POINT: Financing activities involve stockholders' equity accounts and short- and long-term borrowings. Because dividends paid involve retained earnings, they are appropriately included in this category.

The procedure for determining cash flows from financing activities is like the analysis of investing activities, including treatment of related gains or losses, but the accounts analyzed are short-term borrowings, long-term liabilities, and stockholders' equity accounts. Cash dividends from the statement of stockholders' equity must also be considered. Since Ryan Corporation does not have short-term borrowings, we deal only with long-term liabilities and stockholders' equity accounts. These items from Exhibit 2 pertain to Ryan's financing activities in 20x4:

5. Issued $100,000 of bonds at face value in a noncash exchange for plant assets.
6. Repaid $50,000 of bonds at face value at maturity.
7. Issued 15,200 shares of $5 par value common stock for $175,000.
8. Purchased treasury stock for $25,000.
9. Paid cash dividends in the amount of $8,000.

BONDS PAYABLE

Exhibit 1 shows that Bonds Payable increased by $50,000 in 20x4. This account is affected by items **5** and **6**. Item **5** was analyzed in connection with plant assets. As noted above, it is reported on the schedule of noncash investing and financing transactions, but it must be remembered here in preparing the T account for Bonds Payable. Item **6** results in a cash outflow, which is recorded as follows:

A = L + OE
‒   ‒

Bonds Payable	50,000	
Cash		50,000
Repayment of bonds at face value at maturity		

This cash outflow is shown in the financing activities section of the statement of cash flows as follows:

Repayment of bonds   ($50,000)

The following T account explains the change in Bonds Payable:

Bonds Payable

Repayment	50,000	Beg. Bal.		245,000
		Noncash Issue		100,000
		End. Bal.		295,000

If Ryan Corporation had any notes payable, the analysis would be the same.

COMMON STOCK

Like the Plant Asset account and its related accounts, related stockholders' equity accounts should be analyzed together. For example, Paid-in Capital in Excess of Par Value, Common should be examined with Common Stock. In 20x4, Ryan Corporation's Common Stock account increased by $76,000, and Paid-in Capital in Excess of Par Value, Common increased by $99,000. Those increases are explained by item 7 in the list in Exhibit 2, which states that Ryan issued 15,200 shares of common stock for $175,000. The entry to record the cash inflow is as follows:

$$A = L + OE$$
$$+ \quad\quad +$$
$$+$$

Cash	175,000	
Common Stock		76,000
Paid-in Capital in Excess of Par Value, Common		99,000
Issued 15,200 shares of $5 par value common stock		

STUDY NOTE: The purchase of treasury stock would also qualify as a financing activity, but would appear as a cash outflow.

This cash inflow is shown in the financing activities section of the statement of cash flows as follows:

Issue of common stock $175,000

The following analysis of this transaction is all that is needed to explain the changes in the two accounts during 20x4:

Common Stock		Paid-in Capital in Excess of Par Value, Common	
Beg. Bal. 200,000		Beg. Bal. 115,000	
Issue 76,000		Issue 99,000	
End. Bal. 276,000		End. Bal. 214,000	

RETAINED EARNINGS

At this point, we have dealt with several items that affect retained earnings. For instance, we used Ryan's net income in the analysis of cash flows from operating activities. The only other item affecting Ryan's retained earnings is the payment of $8,000 in cash dividends (item 9 in Exhibit 2), which is recorded as follows:

$$A = L + OE$$
$$- \quad\quad -$$

Retained Earnings	8,000	
Cash		8,000
Cash dividends for 20x4		

Ryan Corporation would have declared the dividend before paying it and therefore would have debited the Cash Dividends Declared account instead of Retained Earnings, but after paying the dividend and closing the Cash Dividends Declared account to Retained Earnings, the effect is as shown. Cash dividends are displayed in the financing activities section of the statement of cash flows as follows:

KEY POINT: It is dividends paid, not dividends declared, that appear on the statement of cash flows.

Dividends paid   ($8,000)

The following T account shows the change in the Retained Earnings account:

Retained Earnings			
Dividends	8,000	Beg. Bal.	132,000
		Net Income	16,000
		End. Bal.	140,000

TREASURY STOCK

As noted in the chapter on contributed capital, many companies buy back their own stock on the open market. These buybacks use cash, as this entry shows:

$$A = L + OE$$
$$- \quad\quad -$$

Treasury Stock	25,000	
Cash		25,000

This use of cash is classified in the statement of cash flows as a financing activity as follows:

● STOP AND THINK!
In computing free cash flow,
what is an argument for treating purchases of treasury stock
like dividend payments?

*Both purchases of treasury stock
and dividend payments represent
payments to stockholders. Each
diverts cash from productive use
in the business (as assets), and
thus each reduces free cash flow.* ■

Purchase of treasury stock   ($25,000)

The T account for this transaction is as follows:

Treasury Stock	
Purchase 25,000	

At this point in the analysis, we have analyzed all income statement items, explained all balance sheet changes, and taken all additional information into account. The resulting information may now be assembled into a statement of cash flows for Ryan Corporation, which is presented in Exhibit 4.

EXHIBIT 4
Statement of Cash Flows:
Indirect Method

Ryan Corporation
Statement of Cash Flows
For the Year Ended December 31, 20x4

Cash flows from operating activities		
Net income		$ 16,000
Adjustments to reconcile net income to net		
cash flows from operating activities		
Depreciation	$ 37,000	
Gain on sale of investments	(12,000)	
Loss on sale of plant assets	3,000	
Changes in current assets and current liabilities		
Decrease in accounts receivable	8,000	
Increase in inventory	(34,000)	
Decrease in prepaid expenses	4,000	
Increase in accounts payable	7,000	
Increase in accrued liabilities	3,000	
Decrease in income taxes payable	(2,000)	14,000
Net cash flows from operating activities		$ 30,000
Cash flows from investing activities		
Purchase of investments	($ 78,000)	
Sale of investments	102,000	
Purchase of plant assets	(120,000)	
Sale of plant assets	5,000	
Net cash flows from investing activities		(91,000)
Cash flows from financing activities		
Repayment of bonds	($ 50,000)	
Issue of common stock	175,000	
Dividends paid	(8,000)	
Purchase of treasury stock	(25,000)	
Net cash flows from financing activities		92,000
Net increase (decrease) in cash		$ 31,000
Cash at beginning of year		15,000
Cash at end of year		$ 46,000

Schedule of Noncash Investing and Financing Transactions

Issue of bonds payable for plant assets	$100,000

✔ Check out ACE for a Review Quiz at http://accounting.college.hmco.com/students.

Chapter Review

REVIEW OF LEARNING OBJECTIVES

LO1 State the principal purposes and uses of the statement of cash flows, and identify its components.

The statement of cash flows explains the changes in cash and cash equivalents from one accounting period to the next by showing cash inflows and outflows from the operating, investing, and financing activities of a company for an accounting period. For the statement of cash flows, *cash* is defined as including both cash and cash equivalents. The primary purpose of the statement is to provide information about a firm's cash receipts and cash payments during an accounting period. A secondary purpose is to provide information about a firm's operating, investing, and financing activities. The statement is useful to management and to investors and creditors in assessing the liquidity of a business, including its ability to generate future cash flows and to pay debts and dividends.

Cash flows may be classified as stemming from (1) operating activities, which include the cash effects of transactions and other events that enter into the determination of net income; (2) investing activities, which include the acquisition and sale of marketable securities and property, plant, and equipment, and the making and collecting of loans, excluding interest; or (3) financing activities, which include obtaining resources from stockholders and creditors and providing the former with a return on their investments and the latter with repayment. Noncash investing and financing transactions are also important because they affect future cash flows; these exchanges of long-term assets or liabilities are of interest to investors and creditors when evaluating the financing and investing activities of a business.

LO2 Analyze the statement of cash flows.

In analyzing a firm's statement of cash flows, analysts tend to focus on cash-generating efficiency and free cash flow. Cash-generating efficiency is a firm's ability to generate cash from its current or continuing operations. Three ratios used in measuring cash-generating efficiency are cash flow yield, cash flows to sales, and cash flows to assets. Free cash flow is the cash that remains after deducting the funds a firm must commit to continue operating at its planned level. Such commitments must cover current or continuing operations, interest, income taxes, dividends, and net capital expenditures.

LO3 Use the indirect method to determine cash flows from operating activities.

Under the indirect method, net income is adjusted for all noncash effects and for items that need to be converted from an accrual to a cash basis to arrive at a cash flow basis, as follows:

Cash flows from operating activities
Net income   xxx
  Adjustments to reconcile net income to net cash
   flows from operating activities
   (list of individual items)   xxx   xxx
Net cash flows from operating activities   xxx

LO4 Determine cash flows from investing activities.

Cash flows from investing activities are determined by identifying the cash flow effects of the transactions that affect each account relevant to investing activities. Such accounts include all long-term assets and short-term marketable securities.

LO5 Determine cash flows from financing activities.

The procedure for determining cash flows from financing activities is almost identical to that for investing activities. The difference is that the accounts involved are short-term borrowings, long-term liabilities, and stockholders' equity. The effects of gains and losses reported on the income statement must also be considered. After the changes in the balance sheet accounts from one accounting period to the next have been explained, all the cash flow effects should have been identified.

REVIEW OF CONCEPTS AND TERMINOLOGY

The following concepts and terms were introduced in this chapter:

LO1 **Cash:** For purposes of the statement of cash flows, both cash and cash equivalents.

LO1 **Cash equivalents:** Short-term (90 days or less), highly liquid investments, including money market accounts, commercial paper, and U.S. Treasury bills.

LO2 **Cash flows to assets:** The ratio of net cash flows from operating activities to average total assets.

LO2 **Cash flows to sales:** The ratio of net cash flows from operating activities to sales.

LO2 **Cash flow yield:** The ratio of net cash flows from operating activities to net income.

LO2 **Cash-generating efficiency:** The ability of a company to generate cash from its current or continuing operations.

LO3 **Direct method:** The procedure for converting the income statement from an accrual basis to a cash basis by separately adjusting each item on the income statement.

LO1 **Financing activities:** Business activities that involve obtaining resources from stockholders and creditors and providing the former with a return on their investments and the latter with repayment.

LO2 **Free cash flow:** The amount of cash that remains after deducting the funds a company must commit to continue operating at its planned level; net cash flows from operating activities minus dividends paid minus net capital expenditures.

LO3 **Indirect method:** The procedure for converting the income statement from an accrual basis to a cash basis by adjusting net income for items that do not affect cash flows, including depreciation, amortization, depletion, gains, losses, and changes in current assets and current liabilities.

LO1 **Investing activities:** Business activities that involve the acquisition and sale of long-term assets and marketable securities, other than trading securities or cash equivalents, and the making and collecting of loans.

LO1 **Noncash investing and financing transactions:** Significant investing and financing transactions involving only long-term assets, long-term liabilities, or stockholders' equity that do not affect current cash inflows or outflows.

LO1 **Operating activities:** Business activities that involve the cash effects of transactions and other events that enter into the determination of net income.

LO1 **Statement of cash flows:** A financial statement that shows how a company's operating, investing, and financing activities have affected cash during an accounting period.

REVIEW PROBLEM

The Statement of Cash Flows

LO2
LO3 Northwest Corporation's 20x5 income statement appears below. Its comparative balance sheets for 20x5 and 20x4 are presented on the next page.
LO4
LO5

Northwest Corporation
Income Statement
For the Year Ended December 31, 20x5

Net sales		$1,650,000
Cost of goods sold		920,000
Gross margin		$ 730,000
Operating expenses (including depreciation expense of $12,000 on buildings and $23,100 on equipment, and amortization expense of $4,800)		470,000
Operating income		$ 260,000
Other income (expenses)		
Interest expense	($ 55,000)	
Dividend income	3,400	
Gain on sale of investments	12,500	
Loss on disposal of equipment	(2,300)	(41,400)
Income before income taxes		$ 218,600
Income taxes		52,200
Net income		$ 166,400

Northwest Corporation
Comparative Balance Sheets
December 31, 20x5 and 20x4

	20x5	20x4	Change	Increase or Decrease
Assets				
Cash	$ 105,850	$ 121,850	($16,000)	Decrease
Accounts receivable (net)	296,000	314,500	(18,500)	Decrease
Inventory	322,000	301,000	21,000	Increase
Prepaid expenses	7,800	5,800	2,000	Increase
Long-term investments	36,000	86,000	(50,000)	Decrease
Land	150,000	125,000	25,000	Increase
Buildings	462,000	462,000	—	—
Accumulated depreciation, buildings	(91,000)	(79,000)	(12,000)	Increase
Equipment	159,730	167,230	(7,500)	Decrease
Accumulated depreciation, equipment	(43,400)	(45,600)	2,200	Decrease
Intangible assets	19,200	24,000	(4,800)	Decrease
Total assets	$1,424,180	$1,482,780	($58,600)	
Liabilities and Stockholders' Equity				
Accounts payable	$ 133,750	$ 233,750	($100,000)	Decrease
Notes payable (current)	75,700	145,700	(70,000)	Decrease
Accrued liabilities	5,000	—	5,000	Increase
Income taxes payable	20,000	—	20,000	Increase
Bonds payable	210,000	310,000	(100,000)	Decrease
Mortgage payable	330,000	350,000	(20,000)	Decrease
Common stock, $10 par value	400,000	340,000	60,000	Increase
Paid-in capital in excess of par value, common	90,000	50,000	40,000	Increase
Retained earnings	209,730	93,330	116,400	Increase
Treasury stock	(50,000)	(40,000)	(10,000)	Increase
Total liabilities and stockholders' equity	$1,424,180	$1,482,780	($ 58,600)	

The company's records for 20x5 provide the following additional information:

a. Long-term investments (available-for-sale securities) that cost $70,000 were sold at a gain of $12,500; additional long-term investments were made in the amount of $20,000.

b. Five acres of land to build a parking lot were purchased for $25,000.

c. Equipment that cost $37,500 with accumulated depreciation of $25,300 was sold at a loss of $2,300; new equipment costing $30,000 was purchased.

d. Notes payable in the amount of $100,000 were repaid; an additional $30,000 was borrowed by signing notes payable.

e. Bonds payable in the amount of $100,000 were converted into 6,000 shares of common stock.

f. The Mortgage Payable account was reduced by $20,000.

g. Cash dividends declared and paid were $50,000.

h. Treasury stock was purchased for $10,000.

REQUIRED ▶

1. Prepare a statement of cash flows using the indirect method.
2. Compute cash flow yield, cash flows to sales, cash flows to assets, and free cash flow for 20x5.

ANSWER TO REVIEW PROBLEM

1. Statement of cash flows using the indirect method:

Northwest Corporation
Statement of Cash Flows
For the Year Ended December 31, 20x5

Cash flows from operating activities

Net income		$166,400
Adjustments to reconcile net income		
to net cash flows from operating activities		
Depreciation expense, buildings	$ 12,000	
Depreciation expense, equipment	23,100	
Amortization expense, intangible assets	4,800	
Gain on sale of investments	(12,500)	
Loss on disposal of equipment	2,300	
Changes in current assets and current		
liabilities		
Decrease in accounts receivable	18,500	
Increase in inventory	(21,000)	
Increase in prepaid expenses	(2,000)	
Decrease in accounts payable	(100,000)	
Increase in accrued liabilities	5,000	
Increase in income taxes payable	20,000	(49,800)
Net cash flows from operating activities		$116,600

Cash flows from investing activities

Sale of long-term investments	$ 82,500[a]	
Purchase of long-term investments	(20,000)	
Purchase of land	(25,000)	
Sale of equipment	9,900[b]	
Purchase of equipment	(30,000)	
Net cash flows from investing activities		17,400

Cash flows from financing activities

Repayment of notes payable	($100,000)	
Issuance of notes payable	30,000	
Reduction in mortgage	(20,000)	
Dividends paid	(50,000)	
Purchase of treasury stock	(10,000)	
Net cash flows from financing activities		(150,000)

Net increase (decrease) in cash		($ 16,000)
Cash at beginning of year		121,850
Cash at end of year		$105,850

Schedule of Noncash Investing and Financing Transactions

Conversion of bonds payable into common stock	$100,000

[a]$70,000 + $12,500 (gain) = $82,500
[b]$37,500 − $25,300 = $12,200 (book value) − $2,300 (loss) = $9,900

2. Cash flow yield, cash flows to sales, cash flows to assets, and free cash flow for 20x5:

$$\text{Cash Flow Yield} = \frac{\$116,600}{\$166,400} = .7 \text{ times}$$

$$\text{Cash Flows to Sales} = \frac{\$116,600}{\$1,650,000} = 7.1\%$$

$$\text{Cash Flows to Assets} = \frac{\$116,600}{(\$1,424,180 + \$1,482,780) \div 2} = 8.0\%$$

$$\text{Free Cash Flow} = \$116,600 - \$50,000 - \$25,000 - \$30,000 + \$9,900$$
$$= \$21,500$$

Chapter Assignments

BUILDING YOUR KNOWLEDGE FOUNDATION

QUESTIONS

1. In the statement of cash flows, what does cash include?

2. To earn a return on cash on hand during 20x3, Sallas Corporation transferred $45,000 from its checking account to a money market account, purchased a $25,000 Treasury bill, and invested $35,000 in common stocks. How will each of these transactions affect the statement of cash flows?

3. What are the purposes of the statement of cash flows?

4. Why is the statement of cash flows needed when most of the information in it is available from a company's comparative balance sheets and income statement?

5. What are the three classifications of cash flows? Give some examples of each.

6. Why is it important to disclose certain noncash transactions? How should they be disclosed?

7. Define *cash-generating efficiency* and identify three ratios that measure it.

8. Define *free cash flow* and identify its components. What do *positive* and *negative* free cash flows mean?

9. What is the basic difference between the direct method and the indirect method of determining cash flows from operations?

10. In determining net cash flows from operating activities (assuming the indirect method is used), what are the effects on cash generated by the following items: (a) an increase in accounts receivable, (b) a decrease in inventory, (c) an increase in accounts payable, (d) a decrease in wages payable, (e) depreciation expense, and (f) amortization of patents?

11. In 20x1, Cell-Borne Corporation had a net loss of $12,000 but positive cash flows from operations of $9,000. What conditions might have caused this situation?

12. What is the proper treatment on the statement of cash flows of a transaction in which a building that cost $50,000 with accumulated depreciation of $32,000 was sold at a loss of $5,000?

13. What is the proper treatment on the statement of cash flows of (a) a transaction in which buildings and land were purchased by the issuance of a mortgage for $234,000 and (b) a conversion of $50,000 in bonds payable into 2,500 shares of $6 par value common stock?

14. Glen Corporation has the following other income and expense items: interest expense, $12,000; interest income, $3,000; dividend income, $5,000; and loss on the

retirement of bonds, $6,000. Where does each of these items appear on the statement of cash flows, or how does the item affect the statement?

SHORT EXERCISES

SE 1.
LO1 Classification of Cash Flow Transactions

Stahl Corporation engaged in the transactions listed below. Identify each as (a) an operating activity, (b) an investing activity, (c) a financing activity, (d) a noncash transaction, or (e) none of the above.

1. Sold land.
2. Declared and paid a cash dividend.
3. Paid interest.
4. Issued common stock for plant assets.
5. Issued preferred stock.
6. Borrowed cash on a bank loan.

SE 2.
LO2 Cash-Generating Efficiency Ratios and Free Cash Flow

In 20x2, Portillo Corporation had year-end assets of $550,000, net sales of $790,000, net income of $90,000, net cash flows from operating activities of $180,000, purchases of plant assets of $120,000, and sales of plant assets of $20,000, and it paid dividends of $40,000. In 20x1, year-end assets were $500,000. Calculate the cash-generating efficiency ratios of cash flow yield, cash flows to sales, and cash flows to assets. Also calculate free cash flow.

SE 3.
LO2 Cash-Generating Efficiency Ratios and Free Cash Flow

Examine the cash flow measures in part **2** of the review problem in this chapter. Discuss the meaning of these ratios.

SE 4.
LO3 Computing Cash Flows from Operating Activities: Indirect Method

Global Market Corporation had a net income of $33,000 during 20x4. During the year, the company had depreciation expense of $14,000. Accounts Receivable increased by $11,000, and Accounts Payable increased by $5,000. Those were the company's only current assets and current liabilities. Use the indirect method to determine net cash flows from operating activities.

SE 5.
LO3 Computing Cash Flows from Operating Activities: Indirect Method

During 20x4, Cheng Corporation had a net income of $72,000. Included on its income statement were depreciation expense of $8,000 and amortization expense of $900. During the year, Accounts Receivable decreased by $4,100, Inventories increased by $2,700, Prepaid Expenses decreased by $500, Accounts Payable decreased by $7,000, and Accrued Liabilities decreased by $850. Use the indirect method to determine net cash flows from operating activities.

SE 6.
LO4 Cash Flows from Investing Activities and Noncash Transactions

During 20x3, Okee Company purchased land for $750,000. It paid $250,000 in cash and signed a $500,000 mortgage for the rest. The company also sold a building that originally cost $180,000, on which it had $140,000 of accumulated depreciation, for $190,000 cash, making a gain of $150,000. Prepare the cash flows from investing activities and schedule of noncash investing and financing transactions sections of the statement of cash flows.

SE 7.
LO5 Cash Flows from Financing Activities

During 20x4, Dakota Company issued $1,000,000 in long-term bonds at 96, repaid $150,000 of bonds at face value, paid interest of $80,000, and paid dividends of $50,000. Prepare the cash flows from the financing activities section of the statement of cash flows.

SE 8.
LO1
LO3 Identifying Components of the Statement of Cash Flows
LO4
LO5

Assuming the indirect method is used to prepare the statement of cash flows, tell whether each of the following items would appear (a) in cash flows from operating activities, (b) in cash flows from investing activities, (c) in cash flows from financing activities, (d) in the schedule of noncash investing and financing transactions, or (e) not on the statement of cash flows at all:

1. Dividends paid
2. Cash receipts from sales
3. Decrease in accounts receivable
4. Sale of plant assets
5. Gain on sale of investment
6. Issue of stock for plant assets
7. Issue of common stock
8. Net income

EXERCISES

E 1.
LO1 Classification of Cash Flow Transactions

Trout Corporation engaged in the transactions listed below. Identify each transaction as (a) an operating activity, (b) an investing activity, (c) a financing activity, (d) a noncash transaction, or (e) not on the statement of cash flows. (Assume the indirect method is used.)

1. Declared and paid a cash dividend.
2. Purchased a long-term investment.
3. Increased accounts receivable.
4. Paid interest.
5. Sold equipment at a loss.
6. Issued long-term bonds for plant assets.
7. Increased dividends receivable on securities held.
8. Issued common stock.
9. Declared and issued a stock dividend.
10. Repaid notes payable.
11. Decreased wages payable.
12. Purchased a 60-day Treasury bill.
13. Purchased land.

E 2.
LO2 Cash-Generating Efficiency Ratios and Free Cash Flow

In 20x5, Ignatz Corporation had year-end assets of $4,800,000, net sales of $6,600,000, net income of $560,000, net cash flows from operating activities of $780,000, dividends of $240,000, and net capital expenditures of $820,000. In 20x4, year-end assets were $4,200,000.

Calculate the cash-generating efficiency ratios of cash flow yield, cash flows to sales, and cash flows to assets. Also calculate free cash flow.

E 3.
LO3 Cash Flows from Operating Activities: Indirect Method

The condensed single-step income statement for the year ended December 31, 20x2, of Gro-More Chem Company, a distributor of farm fertilizers and herbicides, appears as follows:

Sales		$6,500,000
Less: Cost of goods sold	$3,800,000	
Operating expenses (including depreciation of $410,000)	1,900,000	
Income taxes	200,000	5,900,000
Net income		$ 600,000

Selected accounts from Gro-More Chem Company's balance sheets for 20x2 and 20x1 are as follows:

	20x2	20x1
Accounts receivable	$1,200,000	$850,000
Inventory	420,000	510,000
Prepaid expenses	130,000	90,000
Accounts payable	480,000	360,000
Accrued liabilities	30,000	50,000
Income taxes payable	70,000	60,000

Present in good form a schedule of cash flows from operating activities using the indirect method.

E 4.
LO3 Computing Cash Flows from Operating Activities: Indirect Method

During 20x1, Germaine Corporation had a net income of $41,000. Included on its income statement were depreciation expense of $2,300 and amortization expense of $300. During the year, Accounts Receivable increased by $3,400, Inventories decreased by $1,900, Prepaid Expenses decreased by $200, Accounts Payable increased by $5,000, and Accrued Liabilities decreased by $450. Determine net cash flows from operating activities using the indirect method.

E 5.
LO3 Preparing a Schedule of Cash Flows from Operating Activities: Indirect Method

For the year ended June 30, 20xx, net income for Pine Corporation was $7,400. Depreciation expense was $2,000. During the year, Accounts Receivable increased by $4,400, Inventories increased by $7,000, Prepaid Rent decreased by $1,400, Accounts Payable increased by $14,000, Salaries Payable increased by $1,000, and Income Taxes Payable decreased by $600. Use the indirect method to prepare a schedule of cash flows from operating activities.

E 6.

LO4 Computing Cash Flows from Investing Activities: Investments

FBR Company's T account for long-term available-for-sale investments at the end of 20x3 is as follows:

Investments

Beg. Bal.	38,000	Sales	39,000
Purchases	58,000		
End Bal.	57,000		

In addition, FBR's income statement shows a loss on the sale of investments of $6,500. Compute the amounts to be shown as cash flows from investing activities and show how they are to appear in the statement of cash flows.

E 7.

LO4 Computing Cash Flows from Investing Activities: Plant Assets

The T accounts for plant assets and accumulated depreciation for FBR Company at the end of 20x3 are as follows:

Plant Assets

Beg. Bal.	65,000	Disposals	23,000
Purchases	33,600		
End. Bal.	75,600		

Accumulated Depreciation

Disposals	14,700	Beg. Bal.	34,500
		Depreciation	10,200
		End. Bal.	30,000

In addition, FBR Company's income statement shows a gain on sale of plant assets of $4,400. Compute the amounts to be shown as cash flows from investing activities and show how they are to appear on the statement of cash flows.

E 8.

LO4 Determining Cash Flows from
LO5 Investing and Financing Activities

All transactions involving Notes Payable and related accounts of Wix Company during 20x4 are as follows:

Cash	18,000	
Notes Payable		18,000
Bank loan		
Patent	30,000	
Notes Payable		30,000
Purchase of patent by issuing note payable		
Notes Payable	5,000	
Interest Expense	500	
Cash		5,500
Repayment of note payable at maturity		

Determine the amounts of the transactions affecting financing activities and show how they are to appear on the statement of cash flows for 20x4.

E 9.

LO3 Preparing the Statement of
LO4 Cash Flows: Indirect Method
LO5

Margol Corporation's 20x4 income statement appears below. Its comparative balance sheets for June 30, 20x4 and 20x3 are on the next page.

Margol Corporation
Income Statement
For the Year Ended June 30, 20x4

Sales	$468,000
Cost of goods sold	312,000
Gross margin	$156,000
Operating expenses	90,000
Operating income	$ 66,000
Interest expense	5,600
Income before income taxes	$ 60,400
Income taxes	24,600
Net income	$ 35,800

Margol Corporation
Comparative Balance Sheets
June 30, 20x4 and 20x3

	20x4	20x3
Assets		
Cash	$139,800	$ 25,000
Accounts receivable (net)	42,000	52,000
Inventory	86,800	96,800
Prepaid expenses	6,400	5,200
Furniture	110,000	120,000
Accumulated depreciation, furniture	(18,000)	(10,000)
Total assets	$367,000	$289,000
Liabilities and Stockholders' Equity		
Accounts payable	$ 26,000	$ 28,000
Income taxes payable	2,400	3,600
Notes payable (long-term)	74,000	70,000
Common stock, $10 par value	230,000	180,000
Retained earnings	34,600	7,400
Total liabilities and stockholders' equity	$367,000	$289,000

The following information is also available: The company issued a $44,000 note payable for purchase of furniture; sold furniture that cost $54,000 with accumulated depreciation of $30,600 at carrying value; recorded depreciation on the furniture during the year, $38,600; repaid a note in the amount of $40,000; issued $50,000 of common stock at par value; and declared and paid dividends of $8,600.

Prepare Margol Corporation's statement of cash flows for the year 20x4 using the indirect method.

PROBLEMS

LO1   Classification of Cash Flow Transactions

P 1.   Analyze each transaction listed in the table that follows and place X's in the appropriate columns to indicate the transaction's classification and its effect on cash flows using the indirect method.

Transaction	Cash Flow Classification				Effect on Cash Flows		
	Operating Activity	Investing Activity	Financing Activity	Noncash Trans-action	Increase	Decrease	No Effect
1. Incurred a net loss.							
2. Declared and issued a stock dividend.							
3. Paid a cash dividend.							
4. Decreased accounts receivable.							
5. Increased inventory.							
6. Retired long-term debt with cash.							
7. Sold available-for-sale securities at a loss.							
8. Issued stock for equipment.							
9. Decreased prepaid insurance.							
10. Purchased treasury stock with cash.							
11. Retired a fully depreciated truck (no gain or loss).							
12. Increased interest payable.							
13. Decreased dividends receivable on investment.							
14. Sold treasury stock.							
15. Increased income taxes payable.							
16. Transferred cash to money market account.							
17. Purchased land and building with a mortgage.							

LO2   Statement of Cash Flows:
LO3   Indirect Method
LO4
LO5

P 2.   Maron Corporation's comparative balance sheets as of December 31, 20x5 and 20x4 and its income statement for the year ended December 31, 20x5 are presented on the next page.

During 20x5, Maron Corporation sold furniture and fixtures that cost $35,600, on which it had accumulated depreciation of $28,800, at a gain of $7,000. The corporation also purchased furniture and fixtures in the amount of $39,600; paid a $20,000 note payable and borrowed $40,000 on a new note; converted bonds payable in the amount of $100,000 into 2,000 shares of common stock; and declared and paid $6,000 in cash dividends.

REQUIRED ▶   1. Using the indirect method, prepare a statement of cash flows for Maron Corporation. Include a supporting schedule of noncash investing transactions and financing transactions.

Maron Corporation
Comparative Balance Sheets
December 31, 20x5 and 20x4

	20x5	20x4
Assets		
Cash	$164,800	$ 50,000
Accounts receivable (net)	165,200	200,000
Merchandise inventory	350,000	450,000
Prepaid rent	2,000	3,000
Furniture and fixtures	148,000	144,000
Accumulated depreciation, furniture and fixtures	(42,000)	(24,000)
Total assets	$788,000	$823,000
Liabilities and Stockholders' Equity		
Accounts payable	$143,400	$200,400
Income taxes payable	1,400	4,400
Notes payable (long-term)	40,000	20,000
Bonds payable	100,000	200,000
Common stock, $20 par value	240,000	200,000
Paid-in capital in excess of par value, common	181,440	121,440
Retained earnings	81,760	76,760
Total liabilities and stockholders' equity	$788,000	$823,000

Maron Corporation
Income Statement
For the Year Ended December 31, 20x5

Net sales		$1,609,000
Cost of goods sold		1,127,800
Gross margin		$ 481,200
Operating expenses (including depreciation expense of $46,800)		449,400
Income from operations		$ 31,800
Other income (expenses)		
Gain on sale of furniture and fixtures	$ 7,000	
Interest expense	(23,200)	(16,200)
Income before income taxes		$ 15,600
Income taxes		4,600
Net income		$ 11,000

2. What are the primary reasons for Maron Corporation's large increase in cash from 20x4 to 20x5, despite its low net income?
3. Compute and assess cash flow yield and free cash flow for 20x5.

P 3.

LO2 **Statement of Cash Flows:**
LO3 **Indirect Method**
LO4
LO5

The comparative balance sheets for Pierre Fabrics, Inc., for December 31, 20x3, and 20x2 appear below.

Pierre Fabrics, Inc.
Comparative Balance Sheets
December 31, 20x3 and 20x2

	20x3	20x2
Assets		
Cash	$ 38,560	$ 27,360
Accounts receivable (net)	102,430	75,430
Inventory	112,890	137,890
Prepaid expenses	—	20,000
Land	25,000	—
Building	137,000	—
Accumulated depreciation, building	(15,000)	—
Equipment	33,000	34,000
Accumulated depreciation, equipment	(14,500)	(24,000)
Patents	4,000	6,000
Total assets	$423,380	$276,680
Liabilities and Stockholders' Equity		
Accounts payable	$ 10,750	$ 36,750
Notes payable (current)	10,000	—
Accrued liabilities	—	12,300
Mortgage payable	162,000	—
Common stock, $10 par value	180,000	150,000
Paid-in capital in excess of par value, common	57,200	37,200
Retained earnings	3,430	40,430
Total liabilities and stockholders' equity	$423,380	$276,680

Additional information about Pierre Fabrics' operations during 20x3 is as follows: net loss, $28,000; building and equipment depreciation expense amounts, $15,000 and $3,000, respectively; equipment that cost $13,500 with accumulated depreciation of $12,500 sold for a gain of $5,300; equipment purchases, $12,500; patent amortization, $3,000; purchase of patent, $1,000; funds borrowed by issuing notes payable, $25,000; notes payable repaid, $15,000; land and building purchased for $162,000 by signing a mortgage for the total cost; 3,000 shares of $10 par value common stock issued for a total of $50,000; and cash dividend paid, $9,000.

REQUIRED ▶
1. Using the indirect method, prepare a statement of cash flows for Pierre Fabrics, Inc.
2. Why did Pierre Fabrics have an increase in cash in a year in which it recorded a net loss of $28,000? Discuss and interpret.
3. Compute and assess cash flow yield and free cash flow for 20x3.

P 4.

LO2 **Statement of Cash Flows:**
LO3 **Indirect Method**
LO4
LO5

The comparative balance sheets for Maggio Masonry, Inc., for December 31, 20x3 and 20x2 are presented on the next page. During 20x3, the company had net income of $96,000 and building and equipment depreciation expenses of $80,000 and $60,000, respectively. It amortized intangible assets in the amount of $20,000; purchased

Maggio Masonry, Inc.
Comparative Balance Sheets
December 31, 20x3 and 20x2

	20x3	20x2
Assets		
Cash	$ 257,600	$ 305,600
Accounts receivable (net)	738,800	758,800
Inventory	960,000	800,000
Prepaid expenses	14,800	26,800
Long-term investments	440,000	440,000
Land	361,200	321,200
Building	1,200,000	920,000
Accumulated depreciation, building	(240,000)	(160,000)
Equipment	480,000	480,000
Accumulated depreciation, equipment	(116,000)	(56,000)
Intangible assets	20,000	40,000
Total assets	$4,116,400	$3,876,400
Liabilities and Stockholders' Equity		
Accounts payable	$ 470,800	$ 660,800
Notes payable (current)	40,000	160,000
Accrued liabilities	10,800	20,800
Mortgage payable	1,080,000	800,000
Bonds payable	1,000,000	760,000
Common stock	1,300,000	1,300,000
Paid-in capital in excess of par value, common	80,000	80,000
Retained earnings	254,800	194,800
Treasury stock	(120,000)	(100,000)
Total liabilities and stockholders' equity	$4,116,400	$3,876,400

investments for $116,000; sold investments for $150,000, on which it recorded a gain of $34,000; issued $240,000 of long-term bonds at face value; purchased a warehouse and land through a $320,000 mortgage; paid $40,000 to reduce the mortgage; borrowed $60,000 by issuing notes payable; repaid notes payable in the amount of $180,000; declared and paid cash dividends in the amount of $36,000; and purchased treasury stock in the amount of $20,000.

REQUIRED ▶

1. Using the indirect method, prepare a statement of cash flows for Maggio Masonry, Inc.
2. Why did Maggio Masonry experience a decrease in cash in a year in which it had a net income of $96,000? Discuss and interpret.
3. Compute and assess cash flow yield and free cash flow for 20x3.

ALTERNATE PROBLEMS

P 5.

LO1 Classification of Cash Flow Transactions

Analyze each transaction listed in the table that follows and place X's in the appropriate columns to indicate the transaction's classification and its effect on cash flows using the indirect method.

Transaction	Cash Flow Classification				Effect on Cash Flows		
	Operating Activity	Investing Activity	Financing Activity	Noncash Trans- action	Increase	Decrease	No Effect
1. Earned a net income.							
2. Declared and paid a cash dividend.							
3. Issued stock for cash.							
4. Retired long-term debt by issuing stock.							
5. Increased accounts payable.							
6. Decreased inventory.							
7. Increased prepaid insurance.							
8. Purchased a long-term investment with cash.							
9. Sold trading securities at a gain.							
10. Sold a machine at a loss.							
11. Retired fully depreciated equipment.							
12. Decreased interest payable.							
13. Purchased available-for-sale securities (long-term).							
14. Decreased dividends receivable.							
15. Decreased accounts receivable.							
16. Converted bonds to common stock.							
17. Purchased 90-day Treasury bill.							

LO2 Statement of Cash Flows:
LO3 Indirect Method
LO4
LO5

P 6.   Sulyat Corporation's income statement for 20x7 appears below.

Sulyat Corporation
Income Statement
For the Year Ended June 30, 20x7

Net sales		$1,040,900
Cost of goods sold		656,300
Gross margin		$ 384,600
Operating expenses (including depreciation expense of $60,000)		189,200
Income from operations		$ 195,400
Other income (expenses)		
Loss on sale of equipment	($ 4,000)	
Interest expense	(37,600)	(41,600)
Income before income taxes		$ 153,800
Income taxes		34,200
Net income		$ 119,600

Sulyat Corporation's comparative balance sheets as of June 30, 20x7 and 20x6 are as follows:

Sulyat Corporation
Comparative Balance Sheets
June 30, 20x7 and 20x6

	20x7	20x6
Assets		
Cash	$167,000	$ 20,000
Accounts receivable (net)	100,000	120,000
Inventory	180,000	220,000
Prepaid expenses	600	1,000
Property, plant, and equipment	628,000	552,000
Accumulated depreciation, property, plant, and equipment	(183,000)	(140,000)
Total assets	$892,600	$773,000
Liabilities and Stockholders' Equity		
Accounts payable	$ 64,000	$ 42,000
Notes payable (due in 90 days)	30,000	80,000
Income taxes payable	26,000	18,000
Mortgage payable	360,000	280,000
Common stock, $5 par value	200,000	200,000
Retained earnings	212,600	153,000
Total liabilities and stockholders' equity	$892,600	$773,000

During 20x7, Sulyat Corporation sold equipment that cost $24,000, on which it had accumulated depreciation of $17,000, at a loss of $4,000. The corporation also purchased land and a building for $100,000 through an increase of $100,000 in Mortgage Payable; made a $20,000 payment on the mortgage; repaid notes but borrowed an additional $30,000 through the issuance of a new note payable; and declared and paid a $60,000 cash dividend.

REQUIRED ▶

1. Using the indirect method, prepare a statement of cash flows. Include a supporting schedule of noncash investing and financing transactions.
2. What are the primary reasons for Sulyat Corporation's large increase in cash from 20x6 to 20x7?
3. Compute and assess cash flow yield and free cash flow for 20x7.

P 7.

LO2 **Statement of Cash Flows:**
LO3 **Indirect Method**
LO4
LO5

The comparative balance sheets for Fernandez Fashions, Inc., for December 31, 20x3 and 20x2 appear on the next page. Additional information about Fernandez Fashions' operations during 20x3 is as follows: net income, $56,000; building and equipment depreciation expense amounts, $30,000 and $6,000, respectively; equipment that cost $27,000 with accumulated depreciation of $25,000 sold at a gain of $10,600; equipment purchases, $25,000; patent amortization, $6,000; purchase of patent, $2,000; funds borrowed by issuing notes payable, $50,000; notes payable repaid, $30,000; land and building purchased for $324,000 by signing a mortgage for the total cost; 3,000 shares of $20 par value common stock issued for a total of $100,000; cash dividend paid $18,000; and treasury stock purchased, $15,000.

Fernandez Fashions, Inc.
Comparative Balance Sheets
December 31, 20x3 and 20x2

	20x3	20x2
Assets		
Cash	$174,120	$ 54,720
Accounts receivable (net)	204,860	150,860
Inventory	225,780	275,780
Prepaid expenses	—	40,000
Land	50,000	—
Building	274,000	—
Accumulated depreciation, building	(30,000)	—
Equipment	66,000	68,000
Accumulated depreciation, equipment	(29,000)	(48,000)
Patents	8,000	12,000
Total assets	$943,760	$553,360
Liabilities and Stockholders' Equity		
Accounts payable	$ 21,500	$ 73,500
Notes payable	20,000	—
Accrued liabilities (current)	—	24,600
Mortgage payable	324,000	—
Common stock, $20 par value	370,000	310,000
Paid-in capital in excess of par value, common	114,400	74,400
Retained earnings	118,860	80,860
Treasury stock	(25,000)	(10,000)
Total liabilities and stockholders' equity	$943,760	$553,360

REQUIRED ▶

1. Using the indirect method, prepare a statement of cash flows for Fernandez Fashions, Inc.
2. Why did Fernandez Fashions have an increase in cash of $119,400 when it recorded net income of $56,000? Discuss and interpret.
3. Compute and assess cash flow yield and free cash flow for 20x3.

SKILLS DEVELOPMENT CASES

Conceptual Analysis

SD 1.

LO1 EBITDA and the Statement of
LO3 Cash Flows

When Fleetwood Enterprises, Inc. <www.fleetwood.com>, a large producer of recreational vehicles and manufactured housing, warned that it might not be able to generate enough cash to satisfy debt requirements and could be in default of a loan agreement, its cash flow, defined in the financial press as "EBITDA" (earnings before interest, taxes, depreciation, and amortization), was a negative $2.7 million. The company would have had to generate $17.7 million in the next accounting period to comply with the loan terms.[11] To what section of the statement of cash flows does EBITDA most closely relate? Is EBITDA a good approximation for this section of the statement of cash flows?

Explain your answer, which should include an identification of the major differences between EBITDA and the section of the statement of cash flows you chose.

Ethical Dilemma

LO1   Ethics and Cash Flow Classifications

SD 2. Chemical Waste Treatment, Inc., a fast-growing company that disposes of chemical wastes, has an $800,000 line of credit at its bank. One section in the credit agreement says that the ratio of cash flows from operations to interest expense must exceed 3.0. If this ratio falls below 3.0, the company must reduce the balance outstanding on its line of credit to one-half the total line if the funds borrowed against the line of credit exceed one-half of the total line.

After the end of the fiscal year, the company's controller informs the president: "We will not meet the ratio requirements on our line of credit in 20x2 because interest expense was $1.2 million and cash flows from operations were $3.2 million. Also, we have borrowed 100 percent of our line of credit. We do not have the cash to reduce the credit line by $400,000." The president says, "This is a serious situation. To pay our ongoing bills, we need our bank to increase our line of credit, not decrease it. What can we do?" "Do you recall the $500,000 two-year note payable for equipment?" replied the controller. "It is now classified as 'Proceeds from Notes Payable' in cash flows provided from financing activities in the statement of cash flows. If we move it to cash flows from operations and call it 'Increase in Payables,' it would increase cash flows from operations to $3.7 million and put us over the limit." "Well, do it," ordered the president. "It surely doesn't make any difference where it is on the statement. It is an increase in both places. It would be much worse for our company in the long term if we failed to meet this ratio requirement."

What is your opinion of the president's reasoning? Is the president's order ethical? Who benefits and who is harmed if the controller follows the president's order? What are management's alternatives? What would you do?

 **Group Activity.** Assign in-class groups to develop a position in support of or against the president's reasoning and have them defend that position in a debate.

Research Activity

**LO1   Basic Research Skills
LO2**

SD 3. Find the statement of cash flows in the annual reports of three corporations, using sources in your library or the Fingraph® Financial Analyst™ CD-ROM software that accompanies this text. You may choose corporations from the same industry or at random, at the direction of your instructor. (If you did a Research Activity in a previous chapter, use the same three companies.)

For any year covered by these companies' statements of cash flows, answer the following questions: Does the company use the direct or the indirect method? Is its net income more or less than its net cash flows from operating activities? What are the major causes of differences between net income and net cash flows from operating activities? Compute cash flow efficiency ratios and free cash flow for each company. Does the dividend appear secure? Did the company make significant capital expenditures during the year? How did the company finance the expenditures? Do you notice anything unusual about the investing and financing activities of these three companies? Do the investing and financing activities provide any insights into management's plan for each company? If so, what are they?

Be prepared to discuss your findings in class.

Decision-Making Practice

**LO2   Analysis of Cash Flow
LO3   Difficulty
LO4
LO5**

SD 4. Lou Klein, certified public accountant, has just given his employer May Hashimi, the president of Hashimi Print Gallery, Inc., the income statement that appears at the top of the next page.

Hashimi Print Gallery, Inc.
Income Statement
For the Year Ended December 31, 20x4

Net sales	$884,000
Cost of goods sold	508,000
Gross margin	$376,000
Operating expenses (including depreciation expense of $20,000)	204,000
Operating income	$172,000
Interest expense	24,000
Income before income taxes	$148,000
Income taxes	28,000
Net income	$120,000

After examining the statement, Hashimi said to Klein, "Lou, the statement seems to be well done, but what I need to know is why I don't have enough cash to pay my bills this month. You show that I earned $120,000 in 20x4, but I have only $24,000 in the bank. I know I bought a building on a mortgage and paid a cash dividend of $48,000, but what else is going on?" Klein replied, "To answer your question, we have to look at comparative balance sheets and prepare another type of statement. Take a look at these balance sheets." The statement handed to Hashimi follows.

Hashimi Print Gallery, Inc.
Comparative Balance Sheets
December 31, 20x4 and 20x3

	20x4	20x3
Assets		
Cash	$ 24,000	$ 40,000
Accounts receivable (net)	178,000	146,000
Inventory	240,000	180,000
Prepaid expenses	10,000	14,000
Building	400,000	—
Accumulated depreciation	(20,000)	—
Total assets	$832,000	$380,000
Liabilities and Stockholders' Equity		
Accounts payable	$ 74,000	$ 96,000
Income taxes payable	6,000	4,000
Mortgage payable	400,000	—
Common stock	200,000	200,000
Retained earnings	152,000	80,000
Total liabilities and stockholders' equity	$832,000	$380,000

1. To what statement is Klein referring? From the information given, prepare the additional statement using the indirect method.
2. Hashimi Print Gallery, Inc., has a cash problem despite profitable operations. Why is this the case?

FINANCIAL REPORTING AND ANALYSIS CASES

Interpreting Financial Reports

FRA 1.

LO2   Anatomy of a Disaster

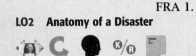

On October 16, 2001, Kenneth Lay, chairman and CEO of Enron Corporation <www.enron.com>, announced the company's earnings for the first nine months of 2001 as follows:

> Our 26 percent increase in recurring earnings per diluted share shows the very strong results of our core wholesale and retail energy businesses and our natural gas pipelines. The continued excellent prospects in these businesses and Enron's leading market position make us very confident in our strong earnings outlook.[12]

Less than six months later, the company filed for the biggest bankruptcy in U.S. history. Its stock dropped to less than $1 per share, and a major financial scandal was underway. Presented on the opposite page is Enron's statement of cash flows for the first nine months of 2001 and 2000 (restated to correct the previous accounting errors). Assume you report to an investment analyst who has asked you to analyze this statement for clues as to why the company went under.

1. For the two time periods shown, compute the cash-generating efficiency ratios of cash flow yield, cash flows to sales (Enron's revenues were $133,762 million in 2001 and $55,494 million in 2000), and cash flows to assets (use total assets of $61,783 million for 2001 and $64,926 million for 2000). Also compute free cash flows for the two years.
2. Prepare a memorandum to the investment analyst that assesses Enron's cash-generating efficiency in light of the chairman's remarks and that evaluates its available free cash flow, taking into account its financing activities. Identify significant changes in operating items and any special operating items that should be considered. Include your computations as an attachment.

International Company

FRA 2.

LO2   Cash-Generating Efficiency Ratios and Free Cash Flow

The following data pertain to two of Japan's best-known and most successful companies, Sony Corporation <www.sony.com> and Canon, Inc. <www.usacanon.com>.[13] (Numbers are in billions of yen.)

	Sony Corporation		Canon, Inc.	
	2000	1999	2000	1999
Net sales	¥6,238	¥6,415	¥2,781	¥2,622
Net income	122	179	134	70
Average total assets	6,579	6,351	2,711	2,658
Net cash flows from operating activities	597	663	347	309
Dividends	21	25	15	15
Net capital expenditures	374	340	165	144

Calculate the ratios of cash flow yield, cash flows to sales, and cash flows to assets, as well as free cash flow, for the two years for both Sony Corporation and Canon, Inc.

Enron Corporation
Statement of Cash Flows
For the Nine Months Ending September 30, 2001 and 2002

	2001	2000
	(In millions)	
Cash Flows from Operating Activities		
Reconciliation of net income to net cash provided by operating activities		
Net income	$ 225	$ 797
Cumulative effect of accounting changes, net of tax	(19)	0
Depreciation, depletion and amortization	746	617
Deferred income taxes	(134)	8
Gains on sales of non-trading assets	(49)	(135)
Investment losses	768	0
Changes in components of working capital		
Receivables	987	(3,363)
Inventories	1	339
Payables	(1,764)	2,899
Other	464	(455)
Trading investments		
Net margin deposit activity	(2,349)	541
Other trading activities	173	(555)
Other, net	198	(566)
Net Cash Provided by (Used in) Operating Activities	$ (753)	$ 127
Cash Flows from Investing Activities		
Capital expenditures	(1,584)	(1,539)
Equity investments	(1,172)	(858)
Proceeds from sales of non-trading investments	1,711	222
Acquisition of subsidiary stock	0	(485)
Business acquisitions, net of cash acquired	(82)	(773)
Other investing activities	(239)	(147)
Net Cash Used in Investing Activities	$(1,366)	$(3,580)
Cash Flows from Financing Activities		
Issuance of long-term debt	4,060	2,725
Repayment of long-term debt	(3,903)	(579)
Net increase in short-term borrowings	2,365	1,694
Issuance of common stock	199	182
Net redemption of company-obligated preferred securities of subsidiaries	0	(95)
Dividends paid	(394)	(396)
Net (acquisition) disposition of treasury stock	(398)	354
Other financing activities	(49)	(12)
Net Cash Provided by Financing Activities	$ 1,880	$ 3,873
Increase (Decrease) in Cash and Cash Equivalents	$ (239)	$ 420
Cash and Cash Equivalents, Beginning of Period	1,240	333
Cash and Cash Equivalents, End of Period	$ 1,001	$ 753

Source: Adapted from Enron Corporation, SEC filings, 2001.

Which company is most efficient in generating cash flow? Which company has the best year-to-year trend? Which company do you think will most probably need external financing?

Toys "R" Us Annual Report

FRA 3.

LO1
LO2 **Analysis of the Statement of Cash Flows**
LO3
LO4
LO5

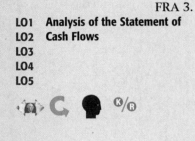

Refer to the statement of cash flows in the Toys "R" Us <www.tru.com> annual report to answer the following questions:

1. Does Toys "R" Us use the indirect method of reporting cash flows from operating activities? Other than net earnings, what are the most important factors affecting the company's cash flows from operating activities? Explain the trend of each of these factors.
2. Based on the cash flows from investing activities, would you say that Toys "R" Us is a contracting or an expanding company? Explain.
3. Has Toys "R" Us used external financing? If so, where did it come from?

Comparison Case: Toys "R" Us and Walgreen Co.

FRA 4.

LO2 **Cash Flows Analysis**

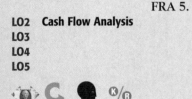

Refer to the annual report of Toys "R" Us <www.tru.com> and the financial statements of Walgreens <www.walgreens.com> in the Supplement to Chapter 1. Calculate for two years each company's cash flow yield, cash flows to sales ratio, cash flows to assets ratio, and free cash flows. In 1999, Walgreens' total assets were $5,906,700,000. Discuss and compare the trends of the cash-generating ability of both Toys "R" Us and Walgreens. Comment on each company's change in cash and cash equivalents over the two-year period.

Fingraph® Financial Analyst™

FRA 5.

LO2 **Cash Flow Analysis**
LO3
LO4
LO5

Choose any two companies in the same industry from the list of Fingraph companies on the Needles Accounting Resource Center Web Site at http://accounting.college.hmco.com/students. Access the Microsoft Excel spreadsheets for the companies you selected. Click on the URL at the top of each company's spreadsheet for a link to the company's web site and annual report.

1. In the annual reports of the companies you have selected, find the statement of cash flows. Do the companies use the direct or indirect method of preparing the statement?
2. Using the Fingraph CD-ROM software, display and print in tabular and graphic form the Statement of Cash Flows: Operating Activities Analysis page. Prepare a table that compares the cash flow yield, cash flows to sales, and cash flows to assets ratios for both companies for two years. Are the ratios moving in the same direction or opposite ones? Study the operating activities sections of the statements to determine the main causes of differences between the net income and cash flows from operations. How do the companies compare?
3. Using the Fingraph CD-ROM software, display and print in tabular and graphic form the Statement of Cash Flows: Investing and Financing Activities Analysis page. Prepare a table that compares the free cash flow for both companies for two years. How do the companies compare? Are the companies growing or contracting? Study the investing and financing activities sections of the statements to determine the main causes of differences between the companies.
4. Find and read references to cash flows in the liquidity analysis section of management's discussion and analysis in each annual report.
5. Write a one-page executive summary that reports your findings from parts 1–4, including your assessment of the companies' comparative liquidity. Include the Fingraph pages and your tables with your report.

Internet Case

LO2   Follow-up Analysis of Cash Flows

FRA 6.

Go to Marriott International's web site <www.marriott.com> and find the statement of cash flows in its latest annual report. Compare it with the 2000 statement at the beginning of this chapter by (1) identifying major changes in operating, investing, and financing activities; (2) reading management's financial review of cash flows; and (3) calculating the cash flow ratios (cash flow yield, cash flows to sales, cash flows to assets) and free cash flow for the most recent year. How does Marriott's cash flow performance differ between these two years? Be prepared to discuss your conclusions in class.

Chapter 15 focuses on financial performance evaluation by internal and external users. The chapter describes the tools and techniques of financial analysis and ratio analysis.

Financial Performance Evaluation

DECISION POINT

A USER'S FOCUS

Sun Microsystems <www.sun.com> Sun Microsystems is a global leader in providing products and services for computer networking. A committee of its board of directors has developed a compensation package for top management that is linked to, among other things, financial performance measures, some of which are presented in the Financial Highlights. These measures are, in turn, linked to creating shareholder value. How does Sun Microsystems make these links?

The company's executive compensation package consists primarily of the following three components:

- Base salary
- Long-term incentives
- Annual incentive bonus

Executives' base salaries are competitive within the industry, and long-term incentives are tied to stock options that will become more valuable if the stock price goes up, thereby creating shareholder value. Of the three components, the annual incentive bonus is most closely linked to financial performance in any given year. Even though the company was profitable and its revenues increased in 2001, no annual incentive bonuses were awarded because growth in revenues and in earnings per share was below the company's plan. These results contrast sharply with those in 2000, when financial performance was outstanding and several executives received bonuses in excess of $1 million.[1]

Thus, at Sun Microsystems, as at many other companies that demand outstanding results, financial performance is an important factor in management

How is financial performance tied to the annual incentive bonuses that executives at Sun hope to receive?

compensation. Managers who work in such an environment must understand the comprehensive framework that internal and external users of financial statements commonly employ to evaluate a company's results. This chapter presents that framework.

Financial Highlights
(In millions except earnings per share)

	2001	2000	1999
Net revenues	$18,250	$15,721	$11,806
Net income	927	1,854	1,030
Earnings per share—basic	0.28	0.59	0.33

FINANCIAL PERFORMANCE EVALUATION BY INTERNAL AND EXTERNAL USERS

LO1 Describe and discuss financial performance evaluation by internal and external users.

RELATED TEXT ASSIGNMENTS
Q: 1, 2
SE: 1
E: 1

◆ **STOP AND THINK!**
Why is it essential that management compensation, including bonuses, be linked to financial goals and strategies that achieve shareholder value?

If the overall financial plan is expected to increase the owners' wealth, then aligning managers' compensation and bonuses with achieving or exceeding these financial targets encourages managers to act in their own and the owners' best interests. ■

Financial performance evaluation, also called *financial statement analysis*, comprises all the techniques users of financial statements employ to show important relationships in an organization's financial statements and to relate them to important financial objectives. Users of financial statements who perform financial performance evaluations fall into two categories: internal users and external users. Both groups have a strong interest in financial performance. Internal users include top managers, who set and strive to achieve financial performance objectives, middle-level managers of business processes, and employee stockholders. External users are creditors and investors who want to assess management's accomplishment of financial objectives, as well as customers who have cooperative agreements with the company.

INTERNAL USERS

Setting financial performance objectives is a major function of management's plan to achieve the company's strategic goals. All strategic and operating plans established by management must eventually be stated in terms of financial objectives. A primary objective of management is to increase the wealth of the owners or stockholders of the business, but this objective must be divided into categories. A complete financial plan should have balanced financial performance objectives in all the following categories:

Business Objectives	Links to Financial Performance
Liquidity	Ability to pay bills when due and to meet unexpected needs for cash
Profitability	Ability to earn a satisfactory net income
Long-term solvency	Ability to survive for many years
Cash flow adequacy	Ability to generate sufficient cash through operating, investing, and financing activities
Market strength	Ability to increase the wealth of owners

Management's main responsibility is to put into action and to carry out its plan to achieve the financial performance objectives. Management must constantly monitor key financial performance measures, determine the cause of any deviations in the measures, and propose corrective actions. Annual measures provide data for long-term trend analysis. Management develops monthly, quarterly, and annual reports that compare actual performance with objectives for key financial measures in each of the above categories. These reports should be formatted to highlight key performance measures.

EXTERNAL USERS

Creditors make loans in the form of trade accounts, notes, or bonds. They expect them to be repaid according to specified terms and to receive interest on the notes and bonds payable. Investors buy capital stock, from which they hope to receive dividends and an increase in value. Both groups face risks. The creditor faces the risk that the debtor will fail to pay back the loan. The investor faces the risks that dividends will be reduced or not paid and that the market price of the stock will drop. For both groups, the goal is to achieve a return that makes up for the risk. In general, the greater the risk taken, the greater the return required as compensation.

Any one loan or any one investment can turn out badly. As a result, most creditors and investors put their funds into a **portfolio**, which is a group of loans or investments. The portfolio is designed to average the returns and the risks. Nevertheless, individual decisions about the loans or stock in the portfolio must still be made. It is in making those individual decisions that financial performance evaluation is most useful. Creditors and investors use financial performance evaluation in two general ways: to judge past performance and current position, and to judge future potential and the risk connected with that potential.

KEY POINT: Past performance is a measure of certainty, whereas trends and projections entail varying degrees of risk and uncertainty.

■ **ASSESSMENT OF PAST PERFORMANCE AND CURRENT POSITION**   Past performance is often a good indicator of future performance. Therefore, an investor or creditor looks at the trends of past sales, expenses, net income, cash flow, and return on investment not only as means of judging management's past performance but also as possible indicators of future performance. In addition, an evaluation of current position will tell, for example, what assets the business owns and what liabilities it must pay. It will also tell what the company's cash position is, how much debt it has in relation to equity, and what levels of inventories and receivables exist. Knowing a company's past performance and current position is often important in judging future potential and the related risk.

■ **ASSESSMENT OF FUTURE POTENTIAL AND RELATED RISK**   Information about the past and present is useful only to the extent that it bears on decisions about the future. An investor evaluates the potential earning ability of a company because that ability will affect the market price of the company's stock and the amount of dividends the company will pay. A creditor evaluates the potential debt-paying ability of the company.

The riskiness of an investment or loan depends on how easy it is to predict future profitability or liquidity. If an investor can predict with confidence that a company's earnings per share will be between $2.50 and $2.60 in the next year, the investment is less risky than if the earnings per share are expected to fall between $2.00 and $3.00. For example, the potential associated with an investment in an established and stable electric utility, or a loan to it, is relatively easy to predict on the basis of the company's past performance and current position. The potential associated with investment in a small Internet firm, on the other hand, may be much harder to predict. For this reason, the investment in or loan to the electric utility carries less risk than the investment in or loan to the small Internet company.

Often, in return for taking a greater risk, an investor in the small Internet company will demand a higher expected return (increase in market price plus dividends) than will an investor in the established utility company. Also, a creditor of the Internet company will demand a higher interest rate and possibly more assurance of repayment (a secured loan, for instance) than a creditor of the utility company. The higher interest rate reimburses the creditor for assuming a higher risk.

✓ Check out ACE for a Review Quiz at http://accounting.college.hmco.com/students.

STANDARDS FOR FINANCIAL STATEMENT ANALYSIS

LO2   Describe and discuss the standards for financial performance evaluation.

RELATED TEXT ASSIGNMENTS
Q: 3, 4
SE: 1
E: 1
SD: 1
FRA: 6

When analyzing financial statements, decision makers must judge whether the relationships they find are favorable or unfavorable. Three commonly used standards of comparison are rule-of-thumb measures, past performance of the company, and industry norms.

RULE-OF-THUMB MEASURES

Many financial analysts, investors, and lenders employ general standards, or rule-of-thumb measures, for key financial ratios. For example, most analysts today agree

www.dunandbradstreet.com

ENRICHMENT NOTE:
Rules of thumb evolve and change as the environment changes. Not long ago, an acceptable current ratio was higher than today's 2:1.

that a current ratio (current assets divided by current liabilities) of 2:1 is acceptable. The credit-rating firm of Dun & Bradstreet, in its *Industry Norms and Key Business Ratios*, offers such rules of thumb as the following:

Current debt to tangible net worth   Ordinarily, a business begins to pile up trouble when this relationship exceeds 80 percent.

Inventory to net working capital   Ordinarily, this relationship should not exceed 80 percent.

Although such measures may suggest areas that need further investigation, there is no proof that the specified levels are applicable to all companies. A company with a current ratio higher than 2:1 may have a poor credit policy (resulting in accounts receivable being too large), too much inventory, or poor cash management. Another company may have a ratio lower than 2:1 but still have excellent management in all three of those areas. Thus, rule-of-thumb measures must be used with great care.

PAST PERFORMANCE OF THE COMPANY

An improvement over rule-of-thumb measures is the comparison of financial measures or ratios of the same company over time. Such a comparison gives the analyst some basis for judging whether the measure or ratio is getting better or worse. It may also be helpful in showing possible future trends. However, trends reverse at times, so such projections must be made with care. Another problem with trend analysis is that past performance may not be enough to meet present needs. For example, even if a company has improved its return on total investment from 3 percent one year to 4 percent the next, the 4 percent return may, in fact, not be adequate for the company's needs.

INDUSTRY NORMS

⬢ **STOP AND THINK!**
How are past performance and industry norms useful in evaluating a company's performance?

A company's past performance indicates whether performance is improving. Industry norms tell how well a company is performing in relation to its peer group. ∎

One way of making up for the limitations of using past performance as a standard is to use industry norms. Such norms show how a company compares with others in the same industry. For example, suppose that companies in an industry have an average rate of return on total investment of 8 percent. In such a case, 3 and 4 percent returns on investment are probably not adequate. Industry norms can also be used to judge trends. Suppose that a company's profit margin dropped from 12 to 10 percent because of a downward turn in the economy. If the average drop in profit margin of other companies in the same industry was from 12 to 4 percent, this norm would indicate that the company had done relatively well. Sometimes, instead of industry averages, data for the industry leader or a specific competitor are used for analysis.

Using industry norms as standards has three limitations. First, companies in the same industry may not be strictly comparable. Consider two companies in the oil industry. One purchases oil products and markets them through service stations. The other, an international company, discovers, produces, refines, and markets its own oil products. Because of their different operations, these two companies cannot be compared.

KEY POINT: Each segment represents an investment that the home office or parent company evaluates and reviews frequently. The segment can remain an active investment or be replaced by a more attractive one.

Second, many large companies today operate in more than one industry or segment. Some of these **diversified companies**, or *conglomerates*, operate in many unrelated industries. The individual segments of a diversified company generally have different rates of profitability and different degrees of risk. In analyzing the consolidated financial statements of such companies, it is often impossible to use industry norms as standards. There are simply no comparable companies. A requirement of the Financial Accounting Standards Board, presented in *Statement No. 131*, provides

EXHIBIT 1
Selected Segment Information for Goodyear Tire & Rubber Co.

(In millions)	2000	1999	1998
Sales			
North American Tire	$ 7,111.3	$ 6,648.6	$ 6,507.9
European Union Tire	3,198.1	2,642.7	2,139.8
Eastern Europe, Africa, and Middle East Tire	793.0	812.9	867.4
Latin American Tire	1,047.9	948.1	1,269.8
Asia Tire	524.6	593.2	519.3
Total Tires	**12,674.9**	**11,645.5**	**11,304.2**
Engineered Products	1,174.2	1,234.8	1,301.8
Chemical Products	1,129.7	949.8	993.0
Total Segment Sales	**14,978.8**	**13,830.1**	**13,599.0**
Income			
North American Tire	$ 260.7	$ 26.3	$ 314.2
European Union Tire	88.7	188.0	199.7
Eastern Europe, Africa, and Middle East Tire	54.6	49.8	102.4
Latin American Tire	69.8	67.7	186.1
Asia Tire	17.9	26.0	7.5
Total Tires	**491.7**	**357.8**	**809.9**
Engineered Products	43.1	70.4	111.7
Chemical Products	64.2	116.4	132.7
Total Segment Income	**599.0**	**544.6**	**1,054.3**
Assets			
North American Tire	$ 5,268.5	$ 5,046.6	$ 4,136.7
European Union Tire	3,088.1	3,336.1	1,690.0
Eastern Europe, Africa, and Middle East Tire	903.6	897.1	898.1
Latin American Tire	796.5	820.7	993.8
Asia Tire	668.5	725.5	744.0
Total Tires	**10,725.2**	**10,826.0**	**8,462.6**
Engineered Products	736.8	712.4	717.5
Chemical Products	742.9	689.6	625.1
Total Segment Assets	**12,204.9**	**12,228.0**	**9,805.2**

Source: Goodyear Tire & Rubber Co., *Annual Report,* 2000.

a partial solution to this problem. It states that diversified companies must report profit or loss, certain revenue and expense items, and assets for each of their segments. Depending on how the company is organized for assessing performance, segment information may be reported for operations in different industries or different geographical areas, or for major customers.[2]

www.goodyear.com

Exhibit 1 shows an example of segment reporting. Goodyear Tire & Rubber Co., well known as a tire manufacturer, also has significant engineered and chemical products divisions. The data on sales, income, and assets for these segments,

FOCUS ON BUSINESS ETHICS

Take the Numbers with a Grain of Salt.

Traditionally, pro-forma statements presented financial statements as they would appear after certain agreed-upon transactions, such as mergers or acquisitions, took place. In recent years, pro-forma statements have become more widely used as a way for companies to present a better picture of their operations than would be the case under GAAP. According to a survey by the National Investor Relations Institute, 57 percent of companies across a range of industries use pro-forma reporting.[3] In one quarter, Amazon.com <www.amazon.com> reported a "pro-forma operating" loss of $49 million and a "pro-forma

net" loss of $76 million; had the company used GAAP, it would have reported a net loss of $234 million. Among many other examples, JDS Uniphase <www.jdsu.com> reported a "pro-forma" gain of $.14 per share, when, in fact, its net loss using GAAP was $1.13 per share. Pro-forma statements, which are unaudited, have come to mean whatever a company's management wants them to mean. Thus, the analyst should rely exclusively on financial statements that are prepared using GAAP and that are audited by an independent CPA.[4]

shown in Exhibit 1, allow the analyst to compute important profitability performance measures, such as profit margin, asset turnover, and return on assets, for each segment and to compare them with the appropriate industry norms.

The third limitation of industry norms is that companies in the same industry with similar operations may use different acceptable accounting procedures. That is, they may use different methods to value inventories and different methods to depreciate assets. Even so, if little information about a company's past performance is available, industry norms probably offer the best available standards for judging current performance—as long as they are used with care.

 Check out ACE for a Review Quiz at http://accounting.college.hmco.com/students.

SOURCES OF INFORMATION

LO3 Identify the sources of information for financial performance evaluation.

RELATED TEXT ASSIGNMENTS
Q: 5
SE: 2
E: 1
SD: 2, 3, 4, 5
FRA: 6

The external analyst is often limited to using publicly available information about a company. The major sources of information about publicly held corporations are reports published by the company, SEC reports, business periodicals, and credit and investment advisory services.

REPORTS PUBLISHED BY THE COMPANY

The annual report of a publicly held corporation is an important source of financial information. The main parts of an annual report from a financial analyst's perspective are management's analysis of the past year's operations; the financial statements; the notes to the financial statements, which include a summary of significant accounting policies; the auditors' report; and financial highlights for a five- or ten-year period.

Most publicly held companies also publish **interim financial statements** each quarter. Those reports present limited information in the form of condensed financial statements, which need not be subjected to a full audit by the independent auditor. The financial community watches the interim statements closely for early signs of important changes in a company's earnings trend.

SEC REPORTS

Publicly held corporations in the United States must file annual reports, quarterly reports, and current reports with the Securities and Exchange Commission (SEC).

FOCUS ON BUSINESS TECHNOLOGY

Find It on the Internet.

Performance reports and other financial information, including stock quotes, reference data, and news about companies and markets, are available instantaneously through such Internet services as CompuServe <www.compuserve.com>, America Online, <www.aol.com>, Yahoo <www.yahoo.com>, and Wall Street Journal Interactive Edition <http://online.wsj.com>.

With access to these online services and those of brokers like Charles Schwab & Co., Inc. <www.schwab.com>, which allow customers to use their own computers to buy and sell stock and other securities, individuals today can avail themselves of resources equivalent to those used by many professional analysts.

● **STOP AND THINK!**

Why would ratios that include one balance sheet account and one income statement or statement of cash flows account, such as receivable turnover or return on assets, be questionable if they came from quarterly or other interim financial reports?

On quarterly financial statements, all numbers on the income statement and statement of cash flows are for less than one year, whereas the balance sheet figures are full values similar to those at year end. Thus, any ratios that use data from the income statement or statement of cash flows as their basis will be less than they might be on a full-year basis. ■

www.moodys.com
www.standardpoor.com
www.dunandbradstreet.com

www.rmahq.com

www.pepsi.com

If they have more than $10 million in assets and more than 500 shareholders, they must file these reports electronically at www.sec.gov/edgar.shtml, where anyone can access them free of charge.

The Securities and Exchange Commission requires companies to use a standard form, called Form 10-K, for the annual report. Form 10-K contains more information than the annual reports published by companies. For that reason, it is a valuable source of information.

Companies file their quarterly reports with the SEC on Form 10-Q. This report presents important facts about interim financial performance.

The current report, filed on Form 8-K must be submitted to the SEC within a few days of the date of certain significant events, such as the sale or purchase of a division of the company or a change in the company's auditors. The current report is often the first indicator of important changes that may affect a company's financial performance in the future.

BUSINESS PERIODICALS AND CREDIT AND INVESTMENT ADVISORY SERVICES

Financial analysts must keep up with current events in the financial world. Probably the best source of financial news is *The Wall Street Journal*, which is published every business day and is the most complete financial newspaper in the United States. Some helpful magazines, published every week or every two weeks, are *Forbes*, *Barron's*, *Fortune*, and the *Financial Times*.

For further details about the financial history of companies, the publications of such services as Moody's Investors Service, Inc., and Standard & Poor's are useful. Data on industry norms, average ratios and relationships, and credit ratings are available from such agencies as The Dun & Bradstreet Corp. In its publication entitled *Industry Norms and Key Business Ratios*, Dun & Bradstreet offers an annual analysis of 14 ratios for each of 125 industry groups, classified as retailing, wholesaling, manufacturing, and construction. *Annual Statement Studies*, published by the Risk Management Association (formerly Robert Morris Associates), presents many facts and ratios for 223 different industries. A number of private services are also available for a yearly fee.

An example of specialized financial reporting readily available to the public is Mergent's *Handbook of Dividend Achievers*, which profiles companies that have increased their dividends consistently over the past ten years. A listing from that publication—for PepsiCo Inc.—is shown in Exhibit 2. A wealth of information about the company is summarized on one page, including the market action of its stock; its business operations, recent developments, and prospects; earnings and dividend data; and annual financial data for the past ten years. The kind of data contained in these summaries is used in many of the analyses and ratios explained in this chapter.

 Check out ACE for a Review Quiz at http://accounting.college.hmco.com/students.

EXHIBIT 2
Listing from Mergent's *Handbook of Dividend Achievers*

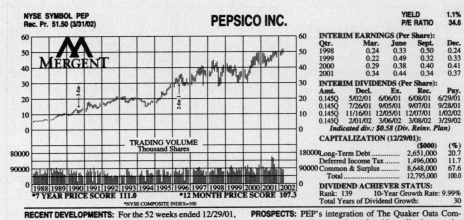

NYSE SYMBOL PEP
Rec. Pr. 51.50 (3/31/02)

PEPSICO INC.

YIELD 1.1%
P/E RATIO 34.6

INTERIM EARNINGS (Per Share):

Qtr.	Mar.	June	Sept.	Dec.
1998	0.24	0.33	0.50	0.24
1999	0.22	0.49	0.32	0.33
2000	0.29	0.38	0.40	0.41
2001	0.34	0.44	0.34	0.37

INTERIM DIVIDENDS (Per Share):

Amt.	Decl.	Ex.	Rec.	Pay.
0.145Q	5/02/01	6/06/01	6/08/01	6/29/01
0.145Q	7/26/01	9/05/01	9/07/01	9/28/01
0.145Q	11/16/01	12/05/01	12/07/01	1/02/02
0.145Q	2/01/02	3/06/02	3/08/02	3/29/02

Indicated div.: $0.58 (Div. Reinv. Plan)

CAPITALIZATION (12/29/01):

	($000)	(%)
Long-Term Debt	2,651,000	20.7
Deferred Income Tax	1,496,000	11.7
Common & Surplus	8,648,000	67.6
Total	12,795,000	100.0

TRADING VOLUME
Thousand Shares

DIVIDEND ACHIEVER STATUS:
Rank: 139   10-Year Growth Rate: 9.99%
Total Years of Dividend Growth: 30

1988|1989|1990|1991|1992|1993|1994|1995|1996|1997|1998|1999|2000|2001|2002
*7 YEAR PRICE SCORE 111.0   *12 MONTH PRICE SCORE 107.3
*NYSE COMPOSITE INDEX=100

RECENT DEVELOPMENTS: For the 52 weeks ended 12/29/01, net income was $2.66 billion versus $2.54 billion in the year-earlier period, which included 53 weeks. Results for 2001 and 2000 included after-tax other asset impairment and restructuring charges of $19.0 million and $111.0 million, respectively. Results for 2001 also included after-tax merger-related charges of $322.0 million. Net sales rose 5.7% to $26.94 billion from $25.48 billion the year before. Comparisons were made with restated 2000 results.

PROSPECTS: PEP's integration of The Quaker Oats Company is proceeding as planned, with realized synergies expected at the high end of the previously announced range of $140.0 million to $175.0 million. Meanwhile, new product introductions will be key to top-line growth in 2002. Roll-outs for 2002 include new salty snack platforms such as Munchies Snack Mix, Go Snacks and Ruffles 3D's, as well as Diet Code Red, and Mountain Dew's new energy drink, called AMP.

BUSINESS

PEPSICO INC. operates on a worldwide basis within the soft drinks, juice and snack-foods businesses. The Pepsi-Cola segment, which accounted for 23.9% of sales in 2001, manufactures concentrates, and markets PEPSI, PEPSI-COLA, DIET PEPSI, PEPSI ONE, MOUNTAIN DEW, MUG, FRUITWORKS, SIERRA MIST, AQUAFINA, MIRINDA, SLICE and allied brands worldwide, and 7-UP internationally. The Tropicana segment, 14.9%, manufactures and sells its products under trademarks such as TROPICANA PURE PREMIUM, and TROPICANA SEASONS BEST. The Frito-Lay segment, 53.8%, manufactures, markets, sells and distributes a varied line of salty and sweet snack foods. Trademarks include LAY'S, DORITOS, CHEETOS, ROLD GOLD and WOW! Quaker Foods, 7.4%, manufactures, markets and sells products that include ready-to-eat and hot cereals. On 8/2/01, PEP completed its acquisition of The Quaker Oats Company. As of 12/31/01, PEP maintained economic ownership of about 42.0% in The Pepsi Bottling Group.

ANNUAL FINANCIAL DATA

	12/29/01	12/30/00	12/25/99	12/26/98	12/27/97	12/28/96	12/30/95
Earnings Per Share	⑧1.47	1.48	④1.37	③1.31	①0.95	⑧0.72	①1.00
Cash Flow Per Share	2.07	2.13	2.06	2.12	1.65	1.79	2.08
Tang. Book Val. Per Share	2.17	1.91	1.47	...	0.72	...	...
Dividends Per Share	0.57	0.55	0.53	0.51	0.48	0.43	0.38
Dividend Payout %	38.8	37.2	38.7	38.9	50.5	59.7	38.0

INCOME STATEMENT (IN MILLIONS):

Total Revenues	26,935.0	20,438.0	20,367.0	22,348.0	20,917.0	31,645.0	30,421.0
Costs & Expenses	21,832.0	16,253.0	16,517.0	18,530.0	17,149.0	27,380.0	25,694.0
Depreciation & Amort.	1,082.0	960.0	1,032.0	1,234.0	1,106.0	1,719.0	1,740.0
Operating Income	4,021.0	3,225.0	2,818.0	2,584.0	2,662.0	2,546.0	2,987.0
Net Interest Inc./(Exp.)	d152.0	d145.0	d245.0	d321.0	d353.0	d499.0	d555.0
Income Before Income Taxes	4,029.0	3,210.0	3,656.0	2,263.0	2,309.0	2,047.0	2,432.0
Income Taxes	1,367.0	1,027.0	1,606.0	270.0	818.0	898.0	826.0
Net Income	⑧2,662.0	2,183.0	④2,050.0	③1,993.0	①1,491.0	⑧1,149.0	①1,606.0
Cash Flow	3,740.0	3,143.0	3,082.0	3,227.0	2,597.0	2,868.0	3,346.0
Average Shs. Outstg. (000)	1,807,000	1,475,000	1,496,000	1,519,000	1,570,000	1,606,000	1,608,000

BALANCE SHEET (IN MILLIONS):

Cash & Cash Equivalents	1,649.0	1,330.0	1,056.0	394.0	2,883.0	786.0	1,498.0
Total Current Assets	5,853.0	4,604.0	4,173.0	4,362.0	6,251.0	5,139.0	5,546.0
Net Property	6,876.0	5,438.0	5,266.0	7,318.0	6,261.0	10,191.0	9,870.0
Total Assets	21,695.0	18,339.0	17,551.0	22,660.0	20,101.0	24,512.0	25,432.0
Total Current Liabilities	4,998.0	3,935.0	3,788.0	7,914.0	4,257.0	5,139.0	5,230.0
Long-Term Obligations	2,651.0	2,346.0	2,812.0	4,028.0	4,946.0	8,439.0	8,509.0
Net Stockholders' Equity	8,648.0	7,249.0	6,881.0	6,401.0	6,936.0	6,623.0	7,313.0
Net Working Capital	855.0	669.0	385.0	d3,552.0	1,994.0	...	316.0
Year-end Shs. Outstg. (000)	1,756,000	1,446,000	1,455,000	1,471,000	1,502,000	1,545,000	1,576,000

STATISTICAL RECORD:

Operating Profit Margin %	14.9	15.8	13.8	11.6	12.7	8.0	9.8
Net Profit Margin %	9.9	10.7	10.1	8.9	7.1	3.6	5.3
Return on Equity %	30.8	30.1	29.8	31.1	21.5	17.3	22.0
Return on Assets %	12.3	12.8	11.7	8.8	7.4	4.7	6.3
Debt/Total Assets %	12.2	12.8	16.0	17.8	24.6	34.4	33.5
Price Range	50.46-40.25	49.94-29.69	42.56-30.13	44.81-27.56	41.31-28.25	35.88-27.25	29.38-16.94
P/E Ratio	34.3-27.4	33.7-20.1	31.1-22.0	34.2-21.0	43.5-29.7	49.8-37.8	29.4-16.9
Average Yield %	1.3	1.4	1.5	1.4	1.4	1.4	1.6

Statistics are as originally reported. Adj. for 2-for-1 stk. split, 5/96. ① Incl. non-recur. chrgs. of $290.0 mill.; bef. disc. oper. gain of $651.0 mill. ② Incl. non-recur. chrgs. 1/31/96, $716.0 mill.; chrg. 12/31/95, $520.0 mill. ③ Incl. non-recur. chrg. of $288.0 mill. ④ Incl. non-recur. chrg. of $65.0 mill. ⑤ Incl. aft.-tax merger-rel. chrgs. of $322.0 mill. and asset impairmnt. & restruct. chrgs. of $19.0 mill. ⑧ Refl. 10/6/97 spin-off of TRICON Global Restaurants.

OFFICERS:
S. S. Reinemund, Chmn., C.E.O.
R. S. Morrison, Vice-Chmn.
I. K. Nooyi, Pres., C.F.O.

INVESTOR CONTACT: Susan V. Watson, V.P., Inv. Rel., (914) 253-3035

PRINCIPAL OFFICE: 700 Anderson Hill Road, Purchase, NY 10577-1444

TELEPHONE NUMBER: (914) 253-2000
FAX: (914) 253-2070
WEB: www.pepsico.com
NO. OF EMPLOYEES: 143,000 (approx.)
SHAREHOLDERS: 227,000 (approx.)
ANNUAL MEETING: In May
INCORPORATED: DE, Sept., 1919; reincorp., NC, Dec., 1986

INSTITUTIONAL HOLDINGS:
No. of Institutions: 1,076
Shares Held: 1,145,439,909
% Held: 65.5

INDUSTRY: Bottled and canned soft drinks (SIC: 2086)

TRANSFER AGENT(S): The Bank of New York, Newark, NJ

Source: Sample listing from *Handbook of Dividend Achievers, 2001.* Reprinted by permission of Mergent, Inc.

TOOLS AND TECHNIQUES OF FINANCIAL ANALYSIS

LO4 Apply horizontal analysis, trend analysis, vertical analysis, and ratio analysis to financial statements.

RELATED TEXT ASSIGNMENTS

Q: 6, 7, 8, 9

SE: 3, 4, 5   www.sun.com

E: 2, 3, 4

P: 1

SD: 6

FRA: 1

Few numbers are very significant when looked at individually. It is their relationship to other numbers or their change from one period to another that is important. The tools of financial analysis are intended to show relationships and changes. Among the more widely used tools are horizontal analysis, trend analysis, vertical analysis, and ratio analysis. To illustrate how these tools are used, we devote the rest of this chapter to a comprehensive financial analysis of Sun Microsystems, Inc. Sun Microsystems was formed in 1982 and, as noted in this chapter's Decision Point, it has emerged as a global leader in network computing. It developed many of the networking technologies that are the basis of the Internet and corporate intranets, including the widely adopted Java technology.

HORIZONTAL ANALYSIS

Generally accepted accounting principles require the presentation of comparative financial statements that give financial information for the current year and the previous year. A common starting point for studying such statements is **horizontal analysis**, which computes changes from the previous year to the current year in both dollar amounts and percentages. The percentage change relates the size of the change to the size of the dollar amounts involved.

Exhibits 3 and 4 present the comparative balance sheets and income statements of Sun Microsystems and show both the dollar and percentage changes. The percentage change is computed as follows:

$$\text{Percentage Change} = 100 \times \left(\frac{\text{Amount of Change}}{\text{Base Year Amount}} \right)$$

The **base year** in any set of data is always the first year to be considered. For example, when studying data from 2000 and 2001, 2000 is the base year. As the balance sheets in Exhibit 3 show, between 2000 and 2001, Sun Microsystems' total current assets increased by $1,057 million, from $6,877 million to $7,934 million, or by 15.4 percent. This is computed as follows:

$$\text{Percentage Change} = 100 \times \left(\frac{\$1,057 \text{ million}}{\$6,877 \text{ million}} \right) = 15.4\%$$

The company's total current liabilities also increased—by $600 million, or 13.2 percent—in this two-year period. When examining such changes, it is important to consider both the dollar amount of the change as well as the percentage change in each component. For example, the difference between the percentage increase in warranty reserve (48.8 percent) and deferred revenues and customer deposits (41.7 percent) is not great. However, the dollar increase in deferred revenues and customer deposits is more than five times the dollar increase in warranty reserve ($538 million versus $103 million).

Sun Microsystems' balance sheets for this period also show an increase in total assets of $4,029 million, or 28.5 percent, which included an increase of $602 million, or 28.7 percent, in property, plant, and equipment, net. In addition, they show that stockholders' equity increased by $3,277 million, or 44.8 percent. All of this indicates that Sun Microsystems is a rapidly growing company.

The most important findings from the income statements in Exhibit 4 are that net revenues increased by $2,529 million, or 16.1 percent; operating income decreased by $1,082 million, or 45.2 percent; and net income decreased by $927 million, or 50.0 percent. These extremely negative results occurred in part because net revenues grew at a slower rate (16.1 percent) than cost of sales (33.0 percent) and operating expenses (19.4 percent).

ENRICHMENT NOTE:
Traditional horizontal analysis presents trends in terms of nominal dollars. Advanced analysis might adjust data over several time periods to remove any inflation effect or price-level changes.

EXHIBIT 3
Comparative Balance Sheets with Horizontal Analysis

Sun Microsystems, Inc.
Consolidated Balance Sheets
June 30, 2001 and 2000

(Dollar amounts in millions)	2001	2000	Increase (Decrease) Amount	Increase (Decrease) Percentage
Assets				
Current assets:				
Cash and cash equivalents	$ 1,472	$ 1,849	($377)	(20.4)
Short-term investments	387	626	(239)	(38.2)
Accounts receivable, net of allowances				
of $410 in 2001 and $534 in 2000	2,955	2,690	265	9.9
Inventories	1,049	557	492	88.3
Deferred tax assets	1,102	673	429	63.7
Prepaids and other current assets	969	482	487	101.0
Total current assets	$ 7,934	$ 6,877	$1,057	15.4
Property, plant and equipment, net	2,697	2,095	602	28.7
Long-term investments	4,677	4,496	181	4.0
Goodwill, net of accumulated amortization				
of $349 in 2001 and $88 in 2000	2,041	163	1,878	1,152.1
Other assets, net	832	521	311	59.7
Total assets	$18,181	$14,152	$4,029	28.5
Liabilities and Stockholders' Equity				
Current liabilities:				
Short-term borrowings	$ 3	$ 7	$ (4)	(57.1)
Accounts payable	1,050	924	126	13.6
Accrued payroll-related liabilities	488	751	(263)	(35.0)
Accrued liabilities and other	1,374	1,155	219	9.0
Deferred revenues and customer deposits	1,827	1,289	538	41.7
Warranty reserve	314	211	103	48.8
Income taxes payable	90	209	(119)	(56.9)
Total current liabilities	$ 5,146	$ 4,546	$ 600	13.2
Deferred income taxes	744	577	167	28.9
Long-term debt and other obligations	1,705	1,720	(15)	(0.9)
Stockholders' equity	10,586	7,309	3,277	44.8
Total liabilities and stockholders' equity	$18,181	$14,152	$4,029	28.5

Source: Sun Microsystems, Inc., *Annual Report,* 2001.

TREND ANALYSIS

A variation of horizontal analysis is **trend analysis**, in which percentage changes are calculated for several successive years instead of for two years. Trend analysis, with its long-run view, is important because it may point to basic changes in the nature of a business. In addition to presenting comparative financial statements, most companies present a summary of key data for five or more years. Exhibit 5 (page 664)

EXHIBIT 4
Comparative Income Statements with Horizontal Analysis

Sun Microsystems, Inc.
Consolidated Income Statements
For the Years Ended June 30, 2001 and 2000

(Dollar amounts in millions, except per share amounts)	2001	2000	Increase (Decrease) Amount	Percentage
Net revenues	$18,250	$15,721	$ 2,529	16.1
Cost of sales	10,041	7,549	2,492	33.0
Gross margin	$ 8,209	$ 8,172	$ 37	0.5
Operating expenses				
Research and Development	$ 2,016	$ 1,630	$ 386	23.7
Selling, general and administrative	4,544	4,072	472	11.6
Goodwill amortization	261	65	196	301.5
Purchased in-process R&D	77	12	65	541.7
Total operating expenses	$ 6,898	$ 5,779	$ 1,119	19.4
Operating Income	$ 1,311	$ 2,393	($ 1,082)	(45.2)
Gain (loss) on investments	(90)	208	(298)	(143.3)
Interest income	463	254	209	82.3
Interest expense	(100)	(84)	(16)	19.0
Income before taxes	$ 1,584	$ 2,771	($ 1,187)	(42.8)
Provision for income taxes	603	917	(314)	(34.2)
Income Before Cumulative Effect	$ 981	$ 1,854	$ (873)	(47.1)
Cumulative effect of change in accounting principle	(54)		(54)	NA
Net income	$ 927	$ 1,854	$ 927	(50.0)
Net income per common share—basic	$0.28	$0.59	($0.31)	(52.2)
Net income per common share—diluted	$0.27	$0.55	($0.28)	(50.9)
Shares used in calculation of net income per common share—basic	3,234	3,151	83	2.6
Shares used in calculation of net income per common share—diluted	3,417	3,379	38	1.1

shows a trend analysis of Sun Microsystems' five-year summary of net revenues and operating income.

Trend analysis uses an **index number** to show changes in related items over time. For index numbers, the base year is equal to 100 percent. Other years are measured in relation to that amount. For example, the 2001 index for Sun Microsystems' net revenues is figured as follows (dollar amounts in millions):

$$\%\ \ \text{Index} = 100 \times \left(\frac{\text{Index Year Amount}}{\text{Base Year Amount}} \right)$$

$$= 100 \times \left(\frac{\$18,250}{\$8,661} \right) = 210.7\%$$

EXHIBIT 5
Trend Analysis

ENRICHMENT NOTE:
Trend analysis is usually done for a five-year period to reflect the general five-year economic cycle that affects the U.S. economy. Cycles of other lengths exist and are tracked by the National Bureau of Economic Research. Trend analysis needs to use the appropriate cycle time to cover the complete cycle's impact on the business being studied.

Sun Microsystems, Inc.
Net Revenues and Operating Income
Trend Analysis

	2001	2000	1999	1998	1997
Dollar values (in millions)					
Net revenues	$18,250	$15,721	$11,806	$9,862	$8,661
Operating income	1,311	2,393	1,520	1,114	1,033
Trend analysis (in percentages)					
Net revenues	210.7	181.5	136.3	113.9	100.0
Operating income	126.9	231.7	147.1	107.8	100.0

Source: Sun Microsystems, Inc., *Annual Report,* 2001.

The trend analysis in Exhibit 5 shows that net revenues at Sun Microsystems increased over the five-year period, as did operating income in every year except 2001, when it declined dramatically. Figure 1 illustrates these trends.

VERTICAL ANALYSIS

In **vertical analysis**, percentages are used to show the relationship of the different parts to a total in a single statement. The analyst sets a total figure in the statement equal to 100 percent and computes each component's percentage of that total. (The figure would be total assets or total liabilities and stockholders' equity on the balance sheet, and net revenues or net sales on the income statement.) The resulting statement of percentages is called a **common-size statement**. Common-size balance sheets and common-size income statements for Sun Microsystems are shown in pie-chart form in Figures 2 and 3, and in financial statement form in Exhibits 6 and 7.

Vertical analysis is useful for comparing the importance of specific components in the operation of a business. Also, comparative common-size statements can be used to identify important changes in the components from one year to the next.

FIGURE 1
Graph of Trend Analysis Shown in Exhibit 5

◆ **STOP AND THINK!**
In a five-year trend analysis, why do the dollar values remain the same for their respective years while the percentages usually change when a new five-year period is chosen?

In a five-year trend analysis for a new five-year period, the base year changes. Unless two successive base years have exactly the same dollar values, the trend analysis percentages will be different each year. ■

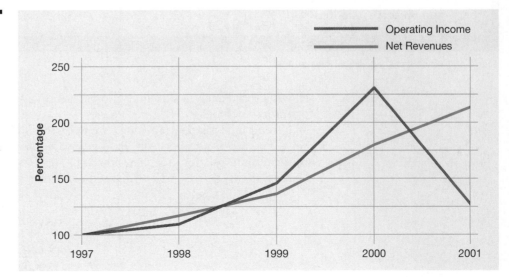

FIGURE 2
Common-Size Balance Sheets Presented Graphically

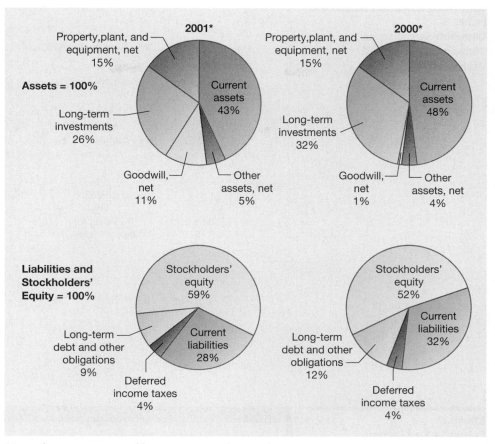

* Rounding causes some additions not to total precisely.

EXHIBIT 6
Common-Size Balance Sheets

Sun Microsystems, Inc.
Common-Size Balance Sheets
June 30, 2001 and 2000

	2001*	2000*
Assets		
Current assets	43.6%	48.6%
Property, plant and equipment, net	14.8	14.8
Long-term investments	25.7	31.8
Goodwill, net	11.2	1.2
Other assets, net	4.6	3.7
Total assets	100.0%	100.0%
Liabilities and Stockholders' Equity		
Current liabilities	28.3%	32.1%
Deferred income taxes	4.1	4.1
Long-term debt and other obligations	9.4	12.2
Stockholders' equity	58.2	51.6
Total liabilities and stockholders' equity	100.0%	100.0%

*Amounts do not precisely total 100 percent in all cases due to rounding.
Source: Sun Microsystems, Inc., *Annual Report,* 2001.

Figure 3
Common-Size Income Statements Presented Graphically

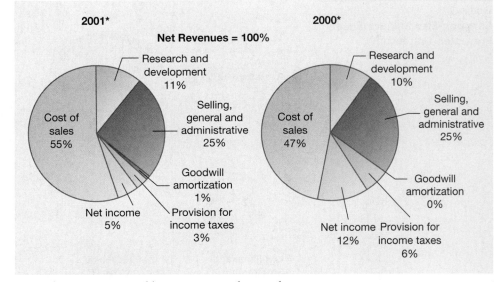

* Rounding causes some additions not to total precisely.
Note: Not all items are presented.

Exhibit 7
Common-Size Income Statements

Sun Microsystems, Inc.
Common-Size Income Statements
For the Years Ended June 30, 2001 and 2000

	2001*	2000*
Net revenues	100.0%	100.0%
Cost of sales	55.0	48.0
Gross margin	45.0%	52.0%
Operating expenses:		
Research and development	11.0%	10.4%
Selling, general, and administrative	24.9	25.9
Goodwill amortization	1.4	0.4
Purchased in-process R&D	0.5	0.1
Total operating expenses	37.8%	36.8%
Operating income	7.2%	15.2%
Other income (expense)	1.5	2.4
Income before income taxes	8.7%	17.6%
Provision for income taxes	3.3	5.8
Income before cumulative effect of change in accounting principle	5.4%	11.8%
Cumulative effect of change in accounting principle	(0.3)	—
Net income	5.1%	11.8%

*Rounding causes some additions and subtractions not to total precisely.
Source: Sun Microsystems, Inc., Annual Report, 2001.

The main conclusions to be drawn from this analysis are that current assets and current liabilities make up a large portion of Sun Microsystems' financial structure and that the company has few long-term liabilities. The graphs in Figure 2 and the common-size balance sheets in Exhibit 6 show that the composition of assets at Sun Microsystems shifted from long-term investments and current assets toward goodwill. In the relationship of liabilities and stockholders' equity, there was a shift from total liabilities to stockholders' equity.

The common-size income statements in Exhibit 7, illustrated in Figure 3, show that Sun Microsystems reduced its selling, general, and administrative expenses from 2000 to 2001 by 1.0 percent of revenues (25.9% − 24.9%). This reduction was offset by an increase in goodwill amortization of 1.0 percent (1.4% − 0.4%).

Common-size statements are often used to make comparisons between companies. They allow an analyst to compare the operating and financing characteristics of two companies of different size in the same industry. For example, the analyst might want to compare Sun Microsystems with other companies in terms of percentage of total assets financed by debt or in terms of selling, general, and administrative expenses as a percentage of net revenues. Common-size statements would show those and other relationships.

RATIO ANALYSIS

Ratio analysis is a technique of financial performance evaluation that identifies meaningful relationships between the components of the financial statements. To be most meaningful, the interpretation of ratios must include a study of the underlying data. Ratios are useful guides or shortcuts in evaluating a company's financial position and operations and in comparing financial data for several years or for several companies. The primary purpose of ratios is to point out areas needing further investigation. To interpret ratios correctly, an analyst must have a general understanding of the company and its environment. Ratios may be expressed in several ways. For example, a ratio of net income of $100,000 to sales of $1,000,000 may be stated as:

1. Net income is 1/10 or 10 percent of sales.

2. The ratio of sales to net income is 10 to 1 (10:1), or sales are 10 times net income.

3. For every dollar of sales, the company has an average net income of 10 cents.

✅ Check out ACE for a Review Quiz at http://accounting.college.hmco.com/students.

COMPREHENSIVE ILLUSTRATION OF RATIO ANALYSIS

LO5 Apply ratio analysis to financial statements in a comprehensive evaluation of a company's financial performance.

RELATED TEXT ASSIGNMENTS
Q: 10, 11, 12, 13, 14, 15
SE: 6, 7, 8, 9, 10
E: 5, 6, 7, 8, 9
P: 2, 3, 4, 5, 6
SD: 1, 6
FRA: 2, 3, 4, 5   www.sun.com

To illustrate how analysts apply ratio analysis to a company's financial statements in order to evaluate the company's financial situation, we will perform a comprehensive ratio analysis of Sun Microsystems' financial performance for 2000 and 2001. In the discussion and analysis section in Sun Microsystems' annual report, management states: "While we reported significant growth in our products net revenues on a year-over-year basis, all of this growth occurred in the first half of fiscal 2001. . . . If the current macro economic conditions persist, we expect demand, and therefore products net revenue in the first half of fiscal 2002, will be less than the comparable period in fiscal 2001."[5] These statements provide the context for evaluating Sun Microsystems' liquidity, profitability, long-term solvency, cash flow adequacy, and market strength. Most data for the analyses come from the financial statements presented in Exhibits 3 and 4. Other data are presented as needed.

EVALUATING LIQUIDITY

STOP AND THINK!

Why does a decrease in receivable turnover or inventory turnover create the need for cash from operating activities?

When receivable turnover or inventory turnover decreases, it means that the company has more average days' receivable or more average days' inventory on hand to finance. Consequently, the company needs more cash to pay for the increase in receivables or inventory. ■

Liquidity is a company's ability to pay bills when they are due and to meet unexpected needs for cash. All the ratios that relate to liquidity involve working capital or some part of it, because it is out of working capital that debts are paid. The objective of liquidity is also closely related to the cash flow ratios.

The liquidity ratios from 2000 to 2001 for Sun Microsystems are presented in Exhibit 8. The **current ratio** and the **quick ratio** are measures of short-term debt-paying ability. The principal difference between the two is that the numerator of the current ratio includes inventories and prepaid expenses. Inventories take longer to convert to cash than do the current assets included in the numerator of the quick ratio. The quick ratio was 1.1 times in 2000 and 0.9 times in 2001. The current ratio was 1.5 times in both years primarily because current assets and current liabilities grew at similar rates. However, the composition of current assets shows a decline in quick ratio assets offset by increases in the remaining current assets.

Two major components of current assets, receivables and inventory, show improving trends. The relative size of the accounts receivable and the effectiveness of credit policies are measured by the **receivable turnover**, which rose from 6.3 times in 2000 to 6.5 times in 2001. The related ratio of **average days' sales uncollected** decreased by about one day, from 57.9 days in 2000 to 56.2 days in 2001. The major change in this category of ratios is in the inventory turnover. The **inventory turnover**, which measures the relative size of inventories, worsened. Inventory turnover decreased from 17.4 times in 2000 to 12.5 times in 2001. This results in an unfavorable increase in **average days' inventory on hand**, from 21.0 days in 2000 to 29.2 days in 2001. When taken together this means that Sun Microsystems' **operating cycle**, or the time it takes to sell products and collect for them, increased from 78.9 days in 2000 (57.9 days + 21.0 days or the average days' sales uncollected plus the average days' inventory on hand) to 85.4 days in 2001 (56.2 days + 29.2 days). Related to the operating cycle is the number of days the company takes to pay its accounts payable. The **payables turnover** increased from 9.3 times in 2000 to 10.7 times in 2001. This results in average days' payable of 39.2 days in 2000 and 34.1 days in 2001. Thus, if the **average days' payable** is subtracted from the operating cycle, the financing period, or days of financing required, are 39.7 days in 2000 and 51.3 days in 2001, a significant decline (see Figure 4). Overall, Sun Microsystems' liquidity declined.

EVALUATING PROFITABILITY

Profitability relates to a company's ability to earn a satisfactory income so that investors and stockholders will continue to provide capital to the company. Profitability is also closely linked to liquidity because earnings ultimately produce

FIGURE 4
Financing Period for Sun Microsystems, 2001

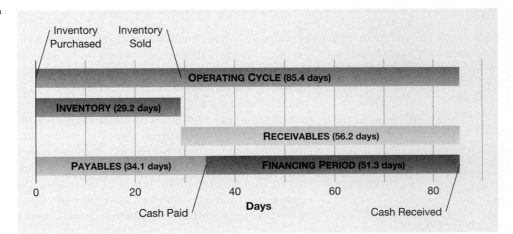

Exhibit 8
Liquidity Ratios of Sun Microsystems, Inc.

(Dollar amounts in millions)	2001	2000

Current ratio: Measure of short-term debt-paying ability

$$\frac{\text{Current Assets}}{\text{Current Liabilities}} \qquad \frac{\$7,934}{\$5,146} = 1.5 \text{ times} \qquad \frac{\$6,877}{\$4,546} = 1.5 \text{ times}$$

Quick ratio: Measure of short-term debt-paying ability

$$\frac{\text{Cash} + \text{Marketable Securities} + \text{Receivables}}{\text{Current Liabilities}}$$

$$\frac{\$1,472 + \$387 + \$2,955}{\$5,146} \qquad \frac{\$1,849 + \$626 + \$2,690}{\$4,546}$$

$$= \frac{\$4,814}{\$5,146} = 0.9 \text{ times} \qquad = \frac{\$5,165}{\$4,546} = 1.1 \text{ times}$$

Receivable turnover: Measure of relative size of accounts receivable and effectiveness of credit policies

$$\frac{\text{Net Sales}}{\text{Average Accounts Receivable}} \qquad \frac{\$18,250}{(\$2,955 + \$2,690) \div 2} \qquad \frac{\$15,721}{\$2,690 + \$2,287^* \div 2}$$

$$= \frac{\$18,250}{\$2,823} = 6.5 \text{ times} \qquad = \frac{\$15,721}{\$2,489} = 6.3 \text{ times}$$

Average days' sales uncollected: Measure of average days taken to collect receivables

$$\frac{\text{Days in Year}}{\text{Receivable Turnover}} \qquad \frac{365 \text{ days}}{6.5 \text{ times}} = 56.2 \text{ days} \qquad = \frac{365 \text{ days}}{6.3 \text{ times}} = 57.9 \text{ days}$$

Inventory turnover: Measure of relative size of inventory

$$\frac{\text{Costs of Goods Sold}}{\text{Average Inventory}} \qquad \frac{\$10,041}{(\$1,049 + \$557) \div 2} \qquad \frac{\$7,549}{\$557 + \$308^* \div 2}$$

$$= \frac{\$10,041}{\$803} = 12.5 \text{ times} \qquad = \frac{\$7,549}{\$433} = 17.4 \text{ times}$$

Average days' inventory on hand: Measure of average days taken to sell inventory

$$\frac{\text{Days in Year}}{\text{Inventory Turnover}} \qquad \frac{365 \text{ days}}{12.5 \text{ times}} = 29.2 \text{ days} \qquad = \frac{365 \text{ days}}{17.4 \text{ times}} = 21.0 \text{ days}$$

Payables turnover: Measure of relative size of accounts payable

$$\frac{\text{Costs of Goods Sold} +/- \text{Change in Inventory}}{\text{Average Accounts Payable}}$$

$$\frac{\$10,041 + \$492}{(\$1,050 + \$924) \div 2} \qquad \frac{\$7,549 + \$249^*}{(\$924 + \$754^*) \div 2}$$

$$= \frac{\$10,533}{\$987} = 10.7 \text{ times} \qquad = \frac{\$7,798}{\$839} = 9.3 \text{ times}$$

Average days' payable: Measure of average days taken to pay accounts payable

$$\frac{\text{Days in Year}}{\text{Payables Turnover}} \qquad = \frac{365 \text{ days}}{10.7 \text{ times}} = 34.1 \text{ days} \qquad = \frac{365 \text{ days}}{9.3 \text{ times}} = 39.2 \text{ days}$$

*1999 figures are derived from the statement of cash flows in Sun Microsystems' annual report.
Source: Sun Microsystems, Inc., *Annual Report,* 2001.

FOCUS ON BUSINESS PRACTICE

There's More Than One Way to Measure Profitability.

Efforts to link management compensation to the company's performance measures and to the creation of shareholder wealth are increasing. One such measure compares the company's return on assets with the cost of debt and equity capital. If the return on assets exceeds the cost of financing the assets with debt and equity, then management is indeed creating value for the shareholders. This measure is referred to in various ways. The originators refer to it as *Economic Value Added*, or *EVA®*. Coca-Cola <www.coca-cola.com>, which uses this measure to evaluate management performance, calls it by its more generic name, *economic profit*. In its annual report, Coca-Cola reports economic profit along with other key financial measures, such as free cash flow and return on equity.

KEY POINT: Profit often is expressed in different ways in accounting literature. Examples are income before income taxes, income after income taxes, and net operating income. Being aware of the content of net income data in profitability ratios enables analysts to draw appropriate conclusions about the results of ratio computation.

cash flow. For this reason, evaluating profitability is important to both investors and creditors. The profitability ratios of Sun Microsystems, Inc., are shown in Exhibit 9.

Profit margin, which measures the net income produced by each dollar of sales, decreased from 11.8 to 5.1 percent. **Asset turnover**, which measures how efficiently assets are used to produce sales, decreased from 1.4 to 1.1 times. The result is a decrease in the company's earning power, or **return on assets**, from 16.4 percent in 2000 to 5.7 percent in 2001. These computations show the relationships:

Profit Margin		Asset Turnover		Return on Assets
$\dfrac{\text{Net Income}}{\text{Net Sales}}$	$\times$	$\dfrac{\text{Net Sales}}{\text{Average Total Assets}}$	$=$	$\dfrac{\text{Net Income}}{\text{Average Total Assets}}$
2000 11.8%	$\times$	1.4	$=$	16.4%
2001 5.1%	$\times$	1.1	$=$	5.7%

ENRICHMENT NOTE: In both asset turnover and return on assets, the analysis is improved if only productive assets are used in the calculations. For example, unfinished new plant construction or investments in obsolete or nonoperating plants could be removed from the asset base to give a better picture of the productivity of assets.

(The small difference in the two sets of return on assets figures results from the rounding of the ratios.) The profitability of stockholders' investments, or **return on equity**, also declined, from 30.5 percent in 2000 to 10.4 percent in 2001.

Although we have used net income in computing profitability ratios for Sun Microsystems, net income is not always a good indicator of a company's sustainable earnings. For instance, if a company has discontinued operations, then income from continuing operations may be a better measure of sustainable earnings. For a company that has one-time items on the income statement, such as restructurings, gains, or losses, income from operations before these items may be a better measure. Some analysts like to use earnings before interest and taxes, or EBIT, for the earnings measure because it excludes the effects of the company's borrowings and the tax rates from the analysis. Whatever figure one uses for earnings, it is important to try to determine the effects of various components on future operations.

EVALUATING LONG-TERM SOLVENCY

KEY POINT: Liquidity is a firm's ability to meet its current obligations, whereas solvency is a firm's ability to meet its maturing obligations as they come due, without losing the ability to continue operations.

Long-term solvency has to do with a company's ability to survive for many years. The aim of long-term solvency analysis is to detect early signs that a company is headed for financial difficulty. Studies have indicated that accounting ratios can show as much as five years in advance that a company may fail.[6] Declining profitability and liquidity ratios are key indicators of possible business failure. Two other ratios that analysts often consider when assessing long-term solvency are debt to equity and interest coverage, which are shown in Exhibit 10.

Increasing amounts of debt in a company's capital structure mean that the company is becoming more heavily leveraged. This condition negatively affects long-term solvency because it represents increasing legal obligations to pay interest periodically and the principal at maturity. Failure to make those payments can result in bankruptcy. The **debt to equity ratio** measures capital structure and leverage by showing the amount of a company's assets provided by creditors in relation to the amount provided by stockholders. Sun Microsystems' debt to equity ratio was only .9 times in 2000 and .7 times in 2001. Recall from Exhibit 3 that the company has primarily short-term debt and little long-term debt. It also has ample current assets,

EXHIBIT 9
Profitability Ratios of Sun Microsystems, Inc.

(Dollar amounts in millions)	2001	2000

Profit margin: Measure of net income produced by each dollar of sales

$$\frac{\text{Net Income}}{\text{Net Sales}} \qquad \frac{\$927}{\$18,250} = 5.1\% \qquad \frac{\$1,854}{\$15,721} = 11.8\%$$

Asset turnover: Measure of how efficiently assets are used to produce sales

$$\frac{\text{Net Sales}}{\text{Average Total Assets}} \qquad \frac{\$18,250}{(\$18,181+\$14,152) \div 2} \qquad \frac{\$15,721}{(\$14,152+\$8,499^*) \div 2}$$

$$= \frac{\$18,250}{\$16,167} = 1.1 \text{ times} \qquad = \frac{\$15,721}{\$11,326} = 1.4 \text{ times}$$

Return on assets: Measure of overall earning power or profitability

$$\frac{\text{Net Income}}{\text{Average Total Assets}} \qquad \frac{\$927}{\$16,167} = 5.7\% \qquad \frac{\$1,854}{\$11,326} = 16.4\%$$

Return on equity: Measure of the profitability of stockholders' investments

$$\frac{\text{Net Income}}{\text{Average Stockholders' Equity}} \qquad \frac{\$927}{(\$10,586 + \$7,309) \div 2} \qquad \frac{\$1,854}{(\$7,309 + \$4,867^*) \div 2}$$

$$= \frac{\$927}{\$8,948} = 10.4\% \qquad = \frac{\$1,854}{\$6,088} = 30.5\%$$

*1999 figures are from the 11-year financial history and the statement of stockholders' equity in Sun Microsystems' annual report.
Source: Sun Microsystems, Inc., *Annual Report,* 2001.

EXHIBIT 10
Long-Term Solvency Ratios of Sun Microsystems, Inc.

(Dollar amounts in millions)	2001	2000

Debt to equity ratio: Measure of capital structure and leverage

$$\frac{\text{Total Liabilities}}{\text{Stockholders' Equity}} \qquad \frac{\$7,595}{\$10,586} = .7 \text{ times} \qquad \frac{\$6,843}{\$7,309} = .9 \text{ times}$$

Interest coverage ratio: Measure of creditors' protection from default on interest payments

$$\frac{\text{Income Before Income Taxes + Interest Expense}}{\text{Interest Expense}} \qquad \frac{\$1,584 + \$100}{\$100} \qquad \frac{\$2,771 + \$84}{\$84}$$

$$= 16.8 \text{ times} \qquad = 34.0 \text{ times}$$

Source: Sun Microsystems, Inc., *Annual Report,* 2001.

as reflected by the current ratio. All these are positive indications of the company's long-term solvency. Sun Microsystems' management sums up the company's position as follows: "We believe our level of financial resources is a significant competitive factor in our industry and we may choose at any time to raise additional capital through debt or equity financing to strengthen our financial position, facilitate growth, and provide us with additional flexibility to take advantage of business opportunities that may arise."[7]

If debt is risky, why have any? The answer is that the level of debt is a matter of balance. Despite its riskiness, debt is a flexible means of financing certain business operations. Sun Microsystems is using debt to finance a temporary increase in inventory. The interest paid on that debt is deductible for income tax purposes, whereas dividends on stock are not. Because debt usually carries a fixed interest charge, the cost of financing can be limited, and leverage can be used to advantage. If the company is able to earn a return on assets greater than the cost of interest, it makes an overall profit. In addition, there are advantages to being a debtor in periods of inflation because the debt, which is a fixed dollar amount, can be repaid with cheaper dollars. However, the company runs the risk of not earning a return on assets equal to the cost of financing those assets, thereby incurring a loss.

The **interest coverage ratio** measures the degree of protection creditors have from a default on interest payments. Because of its small amount of long-term debt, Sun Microsystems had interest coverage ratios of 34.0 times in 2000 and 16.8 times in 2001. Interest coverage, though declining, is not a problem for the company.

ENRICHMENT NOTE:
Because of innovative financing plans and other means of acquiring assets, a beneficial modern-day ratio is the fixed charges ratio. This ratio includes interest, lease payments, and all other fixed obligations that must be met through earnings.

EVALUATING CASH FLOW ADEQUACY

Because cash flows are needed to pay debts when they are due, cash flow measures are closely related to liquidity and long-term solvency. Sun Microsystems' cash flow adequacy ratios are presented in Exhibit 11. By most measures, the company's ability to generate positive operating cash flows declined from 2000 to 2001. Key to those decreases is that net cash flows from operating activities had a large decrease, from $3,754 million in 2000 to $2,089 million in 2001, while net sales and average total assets increased. **Cash flow yield**, or the relationship of cash flows from operating activities to net income, increased from 2.0 to 2.3 because net income declined faster than net cash flows from operating activities. **Cash flows to sales**, or the ability of sales to generate operating cash flows, decreased from 23.9 to 11.4 percent. **Cash flows to assets**, or the ability of assets to generate operating cash flows, decreased from 33.1 to 12.9 percent.

Free cash flow, the cash generated after providing for commitments, also decreased but remains positive even though capital expenditures increased while net cash flows from operating activities decreased. Another factor is that the company pays no dividends. Management's comment with regard to cash flows in the future is, "We believe that the liquidity provided by existing cash, cash equivalents, and non-strategic investments, along with our borrowing arrangements and cash generated from operations, will provide sufficient capital to meet our requirements for at least the next 12 months."[8]

EVALUATING MARKET STRENGTH

The market price of a company's stock is of interest to the analyst because it represents what investors as a whole think of the company at a point in time. Market price is the price at which the stock is bought and sold. It provides information about how investors view the potential return and risk connected with owning the company's stock. Market price by itself is not very informative for this purpose, however. Companies differ in number of outstanding shares and amount of underlying earnings and dividends. Thus, market price must be related to earnings by considering the price/earnings ratio and the dividends yield. Those ratios for Sun Microsystems appear in Exhibit 12 and have been computed using the market prices for Sun Microsystems' stock at the end of 2000 and 2001.

EXHIBIT 11
Cash Flow Adequacy Ratios of Sun Microsystems, Inc.

(Dollar amounts in millions)	2001	2000

Cash flow yield: Measure of the ability to generate operating cash flows in relation to net income

Net Cash Flows from
  Operating Activities

    Net Income

$$\frac{\$2,089^*}{\$927} = 2.3 \text{ times} \qquad \frac{\$3,754^*}{\$1,854} = 2.0 \text{ times}$$

Cash flows to sales: Measure of the ability of sales to generate operating cash flows

Net Cash Flows from
  Operating Activities

    Net Sales

$$\frac{\$2,089^*}{\$18,250} = 11.4\% \qquad \frac{\$3,754^*}{\$15,721} = 23.9\%$$

Cash flows to assets: Measure of the ability of assets to generate operating cash flows

Net Cash Flows from
  Operating Activities

  Average Total Assets

$$\frac{\$2,089^*}{(\$18,181 + \$14,152) \div 2} \qquad \frac{\$3,754^*}{(\$14,152 + \$8,499^\dagger) \div 2}$$

$$= \frac{\$2,089}{\$16,167} = 12.9\% \qquad = \frac{\$3,754}{\$11,326} = 33.1\%$$

Free cash flow: Measure of cash generated or cash deficiency after providing for commitments

Net Cash Flows from Operating
  Activities − Dividends −
    Net Capital Expenditures

$\$2,089^* - \$0 - \$1,292^*$

$= \$797$

$\$3,754^* - \$0 - \$982^*$
$= \$2,772$

*These figures are from the statements of cash flows in Sun Microsystems' annual report.
†The 1999 figure is from the 11-year financial history in Sun Microsystems' annual report.
Source: Sun Microsystems, Inc., *Annual Report,* 2001.

EXHIBIT 12
Market Strength Ratios of Sun Microsystems, Inc.

	2001	2000

Price/earnings ratio: Measure of investor confidence in a company

Market Price per Share

  Earnings per Share

$$\frac{\$18.21^*}{\$.28} = 65.0 \text{ times} \qquad \frac{\$43.47^*}{\$.59} = 73.7 \text{ times}$$

Dividends yield: Measure of a stock's current return to an investor

Dividends per Share

Market Price per Share

Sun Microsystems does not pay a dividend.

*Market price is from Sun Microsystems' annual report.
Source: Sun Microsystems, Inc., *Annual Report,* 2001.

The **price/earnings (P/E) ratio**, which measures investor confidence in a company, is the ratio of the market price per share to earnings per share. The P/E ratio is useful in comparing the relative values placed on the earnings of different companies and in comparing the value placed on a company's shares in relation to the overall market. With a lower P/E ratio, the investor obtains more underlying earnings per dollar invested.

Sun Microsystems' P/E ratio decreased from 73.7 times in 2000 to 65.0 times in 2001, which signals that investors have less confidence in the company. The **dividends yield** measures a stock's current return to an investor in the form of dividends. Because Sun Microsystems pays no dividend, it may be concluded that investors expect their return to come from increases in the stock's market value.

SUMMARY OF THE FINANCIAL ANALYSIS OF SUN MICROSYSTEMS, INC.

Our analysis clearly shows that Sun Microsystems' financial condition declined from 2000 to 2001, as measured by its liquidity, profitability, long-term solvency, and cash flow adequacy ratios. This performance resulted in a lower market price per share.

✓ Check out ACE for a Review Quiz at http://accounting.college.hmco.com/students.

Chapter Review

REVIEW OF LEARNING OBJECTIVES

LO1 Describe and discuss financial performance evaluation by internal and external users.

Creditors and investors, as well as managers, use financial performance evaluation to judge the past performance and current position of a company, and also to judge its future potential and the risk associated with it. Creditors use the information gained from their analysis to make reliable loans that will be repaid with interest. Investors use the information to make investments that will provide a return that is worth the risk.

LO2 Describe and discuss the standards for financial performance evaluation.

Three commonly used standards for financial performance evaluation are rule-of-thumb measures, the company's past performance, and industry norms. Rule-of-thumb measures are weak because of the lack of evidence that they can be widely applied. The past performance of a company can offer a guideline for measuring improvement but is not helpful in judging performance relative to other companies. Although the use of industry norms overcomes this last problem, its disadvantage is that firms are not always comparable, even in the same industry.

LO3 Identify the sources of information for financial performance evaluation.

The main sources of information about publicly held corporations are company-published reports, such as annual reports and interim financial statements; SEC reports; business periodicals; and credit and investment advisory services.

LO4 Apply horizontal analysis, trend analysis, vertical analysis, and ratio analysis to financial statements.

Horizontal analysis involves the computation of changes in both dollar amounts and percentages from year to year. Trend analysis is an extension of horizontal analysis in that it calculates percentage changes for several years. The changes are computed by setting a base year equal to 100 and calculating the results for subsequent years as percentages of that base year. Vertical analysis uses percentages to show the relationship of the component parts to a total in a single statement. The resulting financial statements, which are expressed entirely in percentages, are called common-size statements. Ratio analysis is a technique of financial performance evaluation that identifies meaningful relationships between the components of the financial statements.

LO5 Apply ratio analysis to financial statements in a comprehensive evaluation of a company's financial performance.

A comprehensive ratio analysis includes the evaluation of a company's liquidity, profitability, long-term solvency, cash flow adequacy, and market strength. The ratios for measuring these characteristics are shown in Exhibits 8 to 12.

REVIEW OF CONCEPTS AND TERMINOLOGY

The following concepts and terms were introduced in this chapter:

LO5   **Asset turnover:** Net sales divided by average total assets; a measure of how efficiently assets are used to produce sales.

LO5   **Average days' inventory on hand:** Days in the year divided by inventory turnover; a measure that shows the average number of days taken to sell inventory.

LO5   **Average days' payable:** Days in the year divided by payables turnover; a measure that shows the average number of days taken to pay accounts payable.

LO5   **Average days' sales uncollected:** Days in the year divided by receivable turnover; a measure that shows the number of days, on average, that a company must wait to receive payment for credit sales.

LO4   **Base year:** In financial analysis, the first year to be considered in any set of data.

LO5   **Cash flows to assets:** Net cash flows from operating activities divided by average total assets; a measure of the ability of assets to generate operating cash flows.

LO5   **Cash flows to sales:** Net cash flows from operating activities divided by net sales; a measure of the ability of sales to generate operating cash flows.

LO5   **Cash flow yield:** Net cash flows from operating activities divided by net income; a measure of a company's ability to generate operating cash flows in relation to net income.

LO4   **Common-size statement:** A financial statement in which the components of a total figure are stated in terms of percentages of that total.

LO5   **Current ratio:** Current assets divided by current liabilities; a measure of short-term debt-paying ability.

LO5   **Debt to equity ratio:** Total liabilities divided by stockholders' equity; a measure that shows the relationship of debt financing to equity financing, or the extent to which a company is leveraged.

LO2   **Diversified companies:** Companies that operate in more than one industry. Also called *conglomerates*.

LO5   **Dividends yield:** Dividends per share divided by market price per share; a measure of a stock's current return to an investor.

LO1   **Financial performance evaluation:** All the techniques used to show important relationships in financial statements and to relate them to important financial objectives. Also called *financial statement analysis*.

LO5   **Free cash flow:** Net cash flows from operating activities minus dividends minus net capital expenditures; a measure of cash generated or cash deficiency after providing for commitments.

LO4   **Horizontal analysis:** A technique for analyzing financial statements that involves the computation of changes from the previous to the current year in both dollar amounts and percentages.

LO4   **Index number:** In trend analysis, a number that shows changes in related items over time, which is calculated by setting the base year equal to 100 percent.

LO5   **Interest coverage ratio:** Income before income taxes plus interest expense divided by interest expense; a measure of the degree of protection creditors have from default on interest payments.

LO3   **Interim financial statements:** Financial statements issued for a period of less than one year, usually a quarter or a month.

LO5   **Inventory turnover:** The cost of goods sold divided by average inventory; a measure of the relative size of inventory.

LO5   **Operating cycle:** Average days' inventory on hand plus average days' sales uncollected; the time it takes to sell products and collect for them.

LO5   **Payables turnover:** Cost of goods sold plus or minus change in inventory divided by average accounts payable; a measure of the relative size of accounts payable.

LO1   **Portfolio:** A group of loans or investments designed to average the returns and risks of a creditor or investor.

LO5   **Price/earnings (P/E) ratio:** Market price per share divided by earnings per share; a measure of investor confidence in a company and a means of comparing stock values.

LO5   **Profit margin:** Net income divided by net sales; a measure that shows the percentage of each revenue dollar that contributes to net income.

LO5   **Quick ratio:** The more liquid current assets—cash, marketable securities or short-term investments, and receivables—divided by current liabilities; a measure of short-term debt-paying ability.

LO4   **Ratio analysis:** A technique of financial performance evaluation that identifies meaningful relationships between the components of the financial statements.

LO5   **Receivable turnover:** Net sales divided by average accounts receivable; a measure of the relative size of accounts receivable and the effectiveness of credit policies.

LO5   **Return on assets:** Net income divided by average total assets; a measure of overall earning power, or profitability, that shows the amount earned on each dollar of assets invested.

LO5   **Return on equity:** Net income divided by average stockholders' equity; a measure of how much income was earned on each dollar invested by stockholders.

LO4   **Trend analysis:** A type of horizontal analysis in which percentage changes are calculated for several successive years instead of for two years.

LO4   **Vertical analysis:** A technique for analyzing financial statements that uses percentages to show the relationships of the different parts to a total in a single statement.

REVIEW PROBLEM

Comparative Analysis of Two Companies

LO5

K/R

Maggie Washington is considering an investment in one of two fast-food restaurant chains because she believes the trend toward eating out more often will continue. She has narrowed her choices to Quik Burger and Big Steak, whose balance sheets and income statements are presented on the opposite page.

The statements of cash flows show that net cash flows from operations were $2,200,000 for Quik Burger and $3,000,000 for Big Steak. Net capital expenditures were $2,100,000 for Quik Burger and $1,800,000 for Big Steak. Dividends of $500,000 were paid by Quik Burger and $600,000 by Big Steak. The market prices of the stocks of Quik Burger and Big Steak were $30 and $20, respectively. Financial information pertaining to prior years is not readily available to Maggie Washington. Assume that all notes payable of these two companies are current liabilities and that all their bonds payable are long-term liabilities.

REQUIRED ▶   Conduct a comprehensive ratio analysis of Quik Burger and Big Steak and compare the results. Perform the analysis by following the steps outlined below. Use end-of-year balances for averages, assume no change in inventory, and round all ratios and percentages to one decimal place.

1. Prepare an analysis of liquidity.
2. Prepare an analysis of profitability.
3. Prepare an analysis of long-term solvency.
4. Prepare an analysis of cash flow adequacy.
5. Prepare an analysis of market strength.
6. Indicate in each analysis the company that apparently had the more favorable ratio. (Consider differences of .1 or less to be neutral.)
7. In what ways would having access to prior years' information aid this analysis?

Balance Sheets
December 31, 20xx
(in thousands)

	Quik Burger	Big Steak
Assets		
Cash	$ 2,000	$ 4,500
Accounts receivable (net)	2,000	6,500
Inventory	2,000	5,000
Property, plant, and equipment (net)	20,000	35,000
Other assets	4,000	5,000
Total assets	$30,000	$56,000
Liabilities and Stockholders' Equity		
Accounts payable	$ 2,500	$ 3,000
Notes payable	1,500	4,000
Bonds payable	10,000	30,000
Common stock, $1 par value	1,000	3,000
Paid-in capital in excess of par value, common	9,000	9,000
Retained earnings	6,000	7,000
Total liabilities and stockholders' equity	$30,000	$56,000

Income Statements
For the Year Ended December 31, 20xx
(in thousands, except per share amounts)

	Quik Burger	Big Steak
Net sales	$53,000	$86,000
Costs and expenses		
Cost of goods sold	$37,000	$61,000
Selling expenses	7,000	10,000
Administrative expenses	4,000	5,000
Total costs and expenses	$48,000	$76,000
Income from operations	$ 5,000	$10,000
Interest expense	1,400	3,200
Income before income taxes	$ 3,600	$ 6,800
Income taxes	1,800	3,400
Net income	$ 1,800	$ 3,400
Earnings per share	$ 1.80	$ 1.13

ANSWER TO REVIEW PROBLEM

Ratio Name	Quik Burger	Big Steak	6. Company with More Favorable Ratio*

1. Liquidity analysis

a. Current ratio

$$\frac{\$2,000 + \$2,000 + \$2,000}{\$2,500 + \$1,500}$$

$$= \frac{\$6,000}{\$4,000} = 1.5 \text{ times}$$

$$\frac{\$4,500 + \$6,500 + \$5,000}{\$3,000 + \$4,000}$$

$$= \frac{\$16,000}{\$7,000} = 2.3 \text{ times} \quad \text{Big Steak}$$

b. Quick ratio

$$\frac{\$2,000 + \$2,000}{\$2,500 + \$1,500}$$

$$= \frac{\$4,000}{\$4,000} = 1.0 \text{ times}$$

$$\frac{\$4,500 + \$6,500}{\$3,000 + \$4,000}$$

$$= \frac{\$11,000}{\$7,000} = 1.6 \text{ times} \quad \text{Big Steak}$$

c. Receivable turnover

$$\frac{\$53,000}{\$2,000} = 26.5 \text{ times}$$

$$\frac{\$86,000}{\$6,500} = 13.2 \text{ times} \quad \text{Quik Burger}$$

d. Average days' sales uncollected

$$\frac{365}{26.5} = 13.8 \text{ days}$$

$$\frac{365}{13.2} = 27.7 \text{ days} \quad \text{Quik Burger}$$

e. Inventory turnover

$$\frac{\$37,000}{\$2,000} = 18.5 \text{ times}$$

$$\frac{\$61,000}{\$5,000} = 12.2 \text{ times} \quad \text{Quik Burger}$$

f. Average days' inventory on hand

$$\frac{365}{18.5} = 19.7 \text{ days}$$

$$\frac{365}{12.2} = 29.9 \text{ days} \quad \text{Quik Burger}$$

g. Payables turnover

$$\frac{\$37,000 + 0}{\$2,500} = 14.8 \text{ times}$$

$$\frac{\$61,000 + 0}{\$3,000} = 20.3 \text{ times} \quad \text{Big Steak}$$

h. Average days' payable

$$\frac{365}{14.8} = 24.7 \text{ days}$$

$$\frac{365}{20.3} = 18.0 \text{ days} \quad \text{Big Steak}$$

2. Profitability analysis

a. Profit margin

$$\frac{\$1,800}{\$53,000} = 3.4\%$$

$$\frac{\$3,400}{\$86,000} = 4.0\% \quad \text{Big Steak}$$

b. Asset turnover

$$\frac{\$53,000}{\$30,000} = 1.8 \text{ times}$$

$$\frac{\$86,000}{\$56,000} = 1.5 \text{ times} \quad \text{Quik Burger}$$

c. Return on assets

$$\frac{\$1,800}{\$30,000} = 6.0\%$$

$$\frac{\$3,400}{\$56,000} = 6.1\% \quad \text{Neutral}$$

d. Return on equity

$$\frac{\$1,800}{\$1,000 + \$9,000 + \$6,000}$$

$$= \frac{\$1,800}{\$16,000} = 11.3\%$$

$$\frac{\$3,400}{\$3,000 + \$9,000 + \$7,000}$$

$$= \frac{\$3,400}{\$19,000} = 17.9\% \quad \text{Big Steak}$$

3. Long-term solvency analysis

a. Debt to equity ratio

$$\frac{\$2,500 + \$1,500 + \$10,000}{\$1,000 + \$9,000 + \$6,000}$$

$$= \frac{\$14,000}{\$16,000} = .9 \text{ times}$$

$$\frac{\$3,000 + \$4,000 + \$30,000}{\$3,000 + \$9,000 + \$7,000}$$

$$= \frac{\$37,000}{\$19,000} = 1.9 \text{ times} \quad \text{Quik Burger}$$

*This analysis indicates the company with the apparently more favorable ratio. Class discussion may focus on conditions under which different conclusions may be drawn.

Ratio Name	Quik Burger	Big Steak	6. Company with More Favorable Ratio
b. Interest coverage ratio	$\dfrac{\$3,600 + \$1,400}{\$1,400}$ $= \dfrac{\$5,000}{\$1,400} = 3.6$ times	$\dfrac{\$6,800 + \$3,200}{\$3,200}$ $= \dfrac{\$10,000}{\$3,200} = 3.1$ times	Quik Burger

4. **Cash flow adequacy analysis**

Ratio Name	Quik Burger	Big Steak	Company with More Favorable Ratio
a. Cash flow yield	$\dfrac{\$2,200}{\$1,800} = 1.2$ times	$\dfrac{\$3,000}{\$3,400} = .9$ times	Quik Burger
b. Cash flows to sales	$\dfrac{\$2,200}{\$53,000} = 4.2\%$	$\dfrac{\$3,000}{\$86,000} = 3.5\%$	Quik Burger
c. Cash flows to assets	$\dfrac{\$2,200}{\$30,000} = 7.3\%$	$\dfrac{\$3,000}{\$56,000} = 5.4\%$	Quik Burger
d. Free cash flow	$\$2,200 - \$500 - \$2,100$ $= (\$400)$	$\$3,000 - \$600 - \$1,800$ $= \$600$	Big Steak

5. **Market strength analysis**

Ratio Name	Quik Burger	Big Steak	Company with More Favorable Ratio
a. Price/earnings ratio	$\dfrac{\$30}{\$1.80} = 16.7$ times	$\dfrac{\$20}{\$1.13} = 17.7$ times	Big Steak
b. Dividends yield	$\dfrac{\$500,000/1,000,000}{\$30} = 1.7\%$	$\dfrac{\$600,000/3,000,000}{\$20} = 1.0\%$	Quik Burger

7. **Usefulness of prior years' information**
Prior years' information would be helpful in two ways. First, turnover, return, and cash flows to assets ratios could be based on average amounts. Second, a trend analysis could be performed for each company.

Chapter Assignments

BUILDING YOUR KNOWLEDGE FOUNDATION

QUESTIONS

1. How are the objectives of investors and creditors in using financial performance evaluation similar? How do they differ?
2. What role does risk play in making loans and investments?
3. What standards of comparison are commonly used to evaluate financial statements, and what are their relative merits?
4. Why would a financial analyst compare the ratios of Steelco, a steel company, with the ratios of other companies in the steel industry? What factors might invalidate such a comparison?
5. Where can investors find information about a publicly held company in which they are thinking of investing?
6. Why would an investor want to see both horizontal and trend analyses of a company's financial statements?
7. What does the following sentence mean: "Based on 1990 equaling 100, net income increased from 240 in 1997 to 260 in 1998"?

8. What is the difference between horizontal and vertical analysis?

9. What is the purpose of ratio analysis?

10. In a period of high interest rates, why are receivable turnover and inventory turnover especially important?

11. The following statements were made on page 35 of the November 6, 1978, issue of *Fortune* magazine: "Supermarket executives are beginning to look back with some nostalgia on the days when the standard profit margin was 1 percent of sales. Last year the industry overall margin came to a thin 0.72 percent." How could a supermarket earn a satisfactory return on assets with such a small profit margin?

12. Company A and Company B both have net incomes of $1,000,000. Is it possible to say that these companies are equally successful? Why or why not?

13. Circo Company has a return on assets of 12 percent and a debt to equity ratio of .5. Would you expect return on equity to be more or less than 12 percent?

14. What amount is common to all cash flow adequacy ratios? To what other groups of ratios are the cash flow adequacy ratios most closely related?

15. The market price of Company J's stock is the same as that of Company Q's. How might you determine whether investors are equally confident about the future of these companies?

SHORT EXERCISES

LO1 Objectives and Standards
LO2 of Financial Performance
Evaluation

SE 1. Indicate whether each of the following items is (a) an objective or (b) a standard of comparison of financial statement analysis:

1. Industry norms
2. Assessment of a company's past performance
3. The company's past performance
4. Assessment of future potential and related risk
5. Rule-of-thumb measures

LO3 Sources of Information

SE 2. For each piece of information listed below, indicate whether the *best* source would be (a) reports published by the company, (b) SEC reports, (c) business periodicals, or (d) credit and investment advisory services.

1. Current market value of a company's stock
2. Management's analysis of the past year's operations
3. Objective assessment of a company's financial performance
4. Most complete body of financial disclosures
5. Current events affecting the company

LO4 Trend Analysis

SE 3. Using 20x0 as the base year, prepare a trend analysis for the following data, and tell whether the results suggest a favorable or unfavorable trend. (Round your answers to one decimal place.)

	20x2	20x1	20x0
Net sales	$158,000	$136,000	$112,000
Accounts receivable (net)	43,000	32,000	21,000

LO4 Horizontal Analysis

SE 4. The comparative income statements and balance sheets of SiteWorks, Inc., appear on the opposite page. Compute the amount and percentage changes for the income statements, and comment on the changes from 20x0 to 20x1. (Round the percentage changes to one decimal place.)

LO4 Vertical Analysis

SE 5. Express the comparative balance sheets of SiteWorks, Inc., as common-size statements, and comment on the changes from 20x0 to 20x1. (Round computations to one decimal place.)

LO5 Liquidity Analysis

SE 6. Using the information for SiteWorks, Inc., in **SE 4** and **SE 5,** compute the current ratio, quick ratio, receivable turnover, average days' sales uncollected, inventory turnover, average days' inventory on hand, payables turnover, and average days' payable for 20x0 and 20x1. Inventories were $4,000 in 19x9, $5,000 in 20x0, and $7,000 in 20x1. Accounts Receivable were $6,000 in 19x9, $8,000 in 20x0, and $10,000 in 20x1. Accounts Payable were $9,000 in 19x9, $10,000 in 20x0, and $12,000 in 20x1. The company had no marketable securities or prepaid assets. Comment on the results. (Round computations to one decimal place.)

SiteWorks, Inc.
Comparative Income Statements
For the Years Ended December 31, 20x1 and 20x0

	20x1	20x0
Net sales	$180,000	$145,000
Cost of goods sold	112,000	88,000
Gross margin	$ 68,000	$ 57,000
Operating expenses	40,000	30,000
Operating income	$ 28,000	$ 27,000
Interest expense	7,000	5,000
Income before income taxes	$ 21,000	$ 22,000
Income taxes	7,000	8,000
Net income	$ 14,000	$ 14,000
Earnings per share	$ 1.40	$ 1.40

SiteWorks, Inc.
Comparative Balance Sheets
December 31, 20x1 and 20x0

	20x1	20x0
Assets		
Current assets	$ 24,000	$ 20,000
Property, plant, and equipment (net)	130,000	100,000
Total assets	$154,000	$120,000
Liabilities and Stockholders' Equity		
Current liabilities	$ 18,000	$ 22,000
Long-term liabilities	90,000	60,000
Stockholders' equity	46,000	38,000
Total liabilities and stockholders' equity	$154,000	$120,000

SE 7.
LO5 Profitability Analysis

Using the information for SiteWorks, Inc., in **SE 4** and **SE 5,** compute the profit margin, asset turnover, return on assets, and return on equity for 20x0 and 20x1. In 19x9, total assets were $100,000 and total stockholders' equity was $30,000. Comment on the results. (Round computations to one decimal place.)

SE 8.
LO5 Long-Term Solvency Analysis

Using the information for SiteWorks, Inc., in **SE 4** and **SE 5,** compute the debt to equity ratio and the interest coverage ratio for 20x0 and 20x1. Comment on the results. (Round computations to one decimal place.)

SE 9.
LO5 Cash Flow Adequacy Analysis

Using the information for SiteWorks, Inc., in **SE 4, SE 5,** and **SE 7,** compute the cash flow yield, cash flows to sales, cash flows to assets, and free cash flow for 20x0 and 20x1. Net cash flows from operating activities were $21,000 in 20x0 and $16,000 in 20x1. Net capital expenditures were $30,000 in 20x0 and $40,000 in 20x1. Cash dividends were $6,000 in both years. Comment on the results. (Round computations to one decimal place.)

SE 10.

LO5   Market Strength Analysis

Using the information for SiteWorks, Inc., in **SE 4, SE 5,** and **SE 9,** compute the price/earnings ratio and dividends yield for 20x0 and 20x1. The company had 10,000 shares of common stock outstanding in both years. The price of SiteWorks' common stock was $30 in 20x0 and $20 in 20x1. Comment on the results. (Round computations to one decimal place.)

EXERCISES

E 1.

LO1   Objectives, Standards, and
LO2   Sources of Information for
LO3   Financial Performance
Evaluation

Identify each of the following as (a) an objective of financial statement analysis, (b) a standard for financial statement analysis, or (c) a source of information for financial statement analysis:

1. Average ratios of other companies in the same industry
2. Assessment of the future potential of an investment
3. Interim financial statements

4. Past ratios of the company
5. SEC Form 10-K
6. Assessment of risk
7. A company's annual report

E 2.

LO4   Horizontal Analysis

Compute the amount and percentage changes for the following balance sheets, and comment on the changes from 20x3 to 20x4. (Round the percentage changes to one decimal place.)

Trumpet Company
Comparative Balance Sheets
December 31, 20x4 and 20x3

	20x4	20x3
Assets		
Current assets	$ 37,200	$ 25,600
Property, plant, and equipment (net)	218,928	194,400
Total assets	$256,128	$220,000
Liabilities and Stockholders' Equity		
Current liabilities	$ 22,400	$ 6,400
Long-term liabilities	70,000	80,000
Stockholders' equity	163,728	133,600
Total liabilities and stockholders' equity	$256,128	$220,000

E 3.

LO4   Trend Analysis

Using 20x3 as the base year, prepare a trend analysis of the following data, and tell whether the situation shown by the trends is favorable or unfavorable. (Round your answers to one decimal place.)

	20x7	20x6	20x5	20x4	20x3
Net sales	$25,520	$23,980	$24,200	$22,880	$22,000
Cost of goods sold	17,220	15,400	15,540	14,700	14,000
General and administrative expenses	5,280	5,184	5,088	4,896	4,800
Operating income	3,020	3,396	3,572	3,284	3,200

E 4.

LO4   Vertical Analysis

Express the comparative income statements that follow as common-size statements, and comment on the changes from 20x5 to 20x6. (Round computations to one decimal place.)

Trumpet Company
Comparative Income Statements
For the Years Ended December 31, 20x4 and 20x3

	20x4	20x3
Net sales	$424,000	$368,000
Cost of goods sold	254,400	239,200
Gross margin	$169,600	$128,800
Selling expenses	$106,000	$ 73,600
General expenses	50,880	36,800
Total operating expenses	$156,880	$110,400
Operating income	$ 12,720	$ 18,400

LO5   Liquidity Analysis

E 5. Partial comparative balance sheet and income statement information for Helig Company is as follows:

	20x4	20x3
Cash	$ 6,800	$ 5,200
Marketable securities	3,600	8,600
Accounts receivable (net)	22,400	17,800
Inventory	27,200	24,800
Total current assets	$ 60,000	$ 56,400
Accounts payable	$ 20,000	$ 14,100
Net sales	$161,280	$110,360
Cost of goods sold	108,800	101,680
Gross margin	$ 52,480	$ 8,680

In 20x2, the year-end balances for Accounts Receivable and Inventory were $16,200 and $25,600, respectively. Accounts Payable was $15,300 in 20x2 and is the only current liability. Compute the current ratio, quick ratio, receivable turnover, average days' sales uncollected, inventory turnover, average days' inventory on hand, payables turnover, and average days' payable for each year. (Round computations to one decimal place.) Comment on the change in the company's liquidity position, including its operating cycle and required days of financing from 20x3 to 20x4.

LO5   Turnover Analysis

E 6. Main Tuxedo Shop has been in business for four years. Because the company has recently had a cash flow problem, management wonders whether there is a problem with receivables or inventories. Here are selected figures from the company's financial statements (in thousands):

	20x4	20x3	20x2	20x1
Net sales	$288	$224	$192	$160
Cost of goods sold	180	144	120	96
Accounts receivable (net)	48	40	32	24
Merchandise inventory	56	44	32	20
Accounts payable	25	20	15	10

Compute the receivable turnover, inventory turnover, and payables turnover for each of the four years, and comment on the results relative to the cash flow problem that Main Tuxedo Shop has been experiencing. Merchandise inventory was $22,000, accounts receivable was $22,000, and accounts payable was $8,000 in 20x0. (Round computations to one decimal place.)

LO5   Profitability Analysis

E 7. D.J. Company had total assets of $640,000 in 20x2, $680,000 in 20x3, and $760,000 in 20x4. Its debt to equity ratio was .67 times in all three years. In 20x3, the company had net income of $77,112 on revenues of $1,224,000. In 20x4, the company had net income of $98,952 on revenues of $1,596,000. Compute the profit margin, asset turnover, return on assets, and return on equity for 20x3 and 20x4. Comment on the apparent cause of the increase or decrease in profitability. (Round the percentages and other ratios to one decimal place.)

E 8.

LO5   Long-Term Solvency and Market Strength Ratios

An investor is considering investing in the long-term bonds and common stock of Companies M and N. Both companies operate in the same industry. In addition, both companies pay a dividend per share of $4 and have a yield of 10 percent on their long-term bonds. Other data for the two companies are as follows:

	Company M	Company N
Total assets	$2,400,000	$1,080,000
Total liabilities	1,080,000	594,000
Income before income taxes	288,000	129,600
Interest expense	97,200	53,460
Earnings per share	3.20	5.00
Market price of common stock	40	47.50

Compute the debt to equity, interest coverage, price/earnings (P/E), and dividends yield ratios, and comment on the results. (Round computations to one decimal place.)

E 9.

LO5   Cash Flow Adequacy Analysis

Using the data below from the financial statements of Cheng, Inc., compute the company's cash flow yield, cash flows to sales, cash flows to assets, and free cash flow. (Round computations to one decimal place.)

Net sales	$6,400,000
Net income	704,000
Net cash flows from operating activities	912,000
Total assets, beginning of year	5,780,000
Total assets, end of year	6,240,000
Cash dividends	240,000
Net capital expenditures	596,000

PROBLEMS

P 1.

LO4   Horizontal and Vertical Analyses

Ⓚ/Ⓡ

The condensed comparative income statements and balance sheets for Rochelle Corporation follow.

Rochelle Corporation
Comparative Income Statements
For the Years Ended December 31, 20x5 and 20x4

	20x5	20x4
Net sales	$1,600,800	$1,485,200
Costs and expenses		
Cost of goods sold	$ 908,200	$ 792,400
Selling expenses	260,200	209,200
Administrative expenses	280,600	231,000
Total costs and expenses	$1,449,000	$1,232,600
Income from operations	$ 151,800	$ 252,600
Interest expense	50,000	40,000
Income before income taxes	$ 101,800	$ 212,600
Income taxes	28,000	70,000
Net income	$ 73,800	$ 142,600
Earnings per share	$ 1.23	$ 2.38

Rochelle Corporation
Comparative Balance Sheets
December 31, 20x5 and 20x4

	20x5	20x4
Assets		
Cash	$ 62,200	$ 54,400
Accounts receivable (net)	145,000	85,400
Inventory	245,200	215,600
Property, plant, and equipment (net)	1,155,400	1,015,000
Total assets	$1,607,800	$1,370,400
Liabilities and Stockholders' Equity		
Accounts payable	$ 209,400	$ 144,600
Notes payable	100,000	100,000
Bonds payable	400,000	220,000
Common stock, $10 par value	600,000	600,000
Retained earnings	298,400	305,800
Total liabilities and stockholders' equity	$1,607,800	$1,370,400

REQUIRED ▶ Perform the following analyses. (Round all ratios and percentages to one decimal place.)

1. Prepare schedules showing the amount and percentage changes from 20x4 to 20x5 for the comparative income statements and the balance sheets.
2. Prepare common-size income statements and balance sheets for 20x4 and 20x5.
3. Comment on the results in **1** and **2** by identifying favorable and unfavorable changes in the components and composition of the statements.

P 2.

LO5 Effects of Transactions on Ratios

Jamal Corporation, a clothing retailer, engaged in the transactions listed in the first column of the table below. Opposite each transaction is a ratio and space to mark the effect of each transaction on the ratio.

Transaction	Ratio	Effect		
		Increase	Decrease	None
a. Issued common stock for cash.	Asset turnover			
b. Declared cash dividend.	Current ratio			
c. Sold treasury stock.	Return on equity			
d. Borrowed cash by issuing note payable.	Debt to equity ratio			
e. Paid salaries expense.	Inventory turnover			
f. Purchased merchandise for cash.	Current ratio			
g. Sold equipment for cash.	Receivable turnover			
h. Sold merchandise on account.	Quick ratio			
i. Paid current portion of long-term debt.	Return on assets			
j. Gave sales discount.	Profit margin			
k. Purchased marketable securities for cash.	Quick ratio			
l. Declared 5% stock dividend.	Current ratio			
m. Purchased a building.	Free cash flow			

REQUIRED ▶ Place an X in the appropriate column to show whether the transaction increased, decreased, or had no effect on the indicated ratio.

LO5   Ratio Analysis

Ⓚ/Ⓡ

P 3. Data for Rochelle Corporation in 20x5 and 20x4 follow. These data should be used in conjunction with the data in **P 1.**

	20x5	20x4
Net cash flows from operating activities	$128,000	$198,000
Net capital expenditures	$238,000	$76,000
Dividends paid	$62,800	$70,000
Number of common shares	60,000	60,000
Market price per share	$40	$60

Selected balances at the end of 20x3 were accounts receivable (net), $105,400; inventory, $198,800; total assets, $1,295,600; accounts payable, $134,400; and stockholders' equity, $753,200. All Rochelle's notes payable were current liabilities; all its bonds payable were long-term liabilities.

REQUIRED ▶ Perform a ratio analysis following the steps outlined below. Round all answers to one decimal place, and consider changes of .1 or less to be neutral. After making the calculations, indicate whether each ratio improved or deteriorated from 20x4 to 20x5 (use *F* for favorable and *U* for unfavorable).

1. Prepare a liquidity analysis by calculating for each year the (a) current ratio, (b) quick ratio, (c) receivable turnover, (d) average days' sales uncollected, (e) inventory turnover, (f) average days' inventory on hand, (g) payables turnover, and (h) average days' payable.
2. Prepare a profitability analysis by calculating for each year the (a) profit margin, (b) asset turnover, (c) return on assets, and (d) return on equity.
3. Prepare a long-term solvency analysis by calculating for each year the (a) debt to equity ratio and (b) interest coverage ratio.
4. Prepare a cash flow adequacy analysis by calculating for each year the (a) cash flow yield, (b) cash flows to sales, (c) cash flows to assets, and (d) free cash flow.
5. Prepare a market strength analysis by calcualting for each year the (a) price/earnings ratio and (b) dividends yield.
6. Based on your analysis, assess Rochelle's performance in each of the following areas: liquidity, profitability, long-term solvency, and cash flow adequacy. Explain your evaluations.

LO5   Comprehensive Ratio Analysis of Two Companies

Ⓚ/Ⓡ

P 4. Juanita Maxwell has decided to invest some of her savings in common stock. She feels that the chemical industry has good growth prospects, and she has narrowed her choice to two companies in that industry. As a final step in making the choice, she has decided to perform a comprehensive ratio analysis of the two companies, Reynard and Bouche. Income statement and balance sheet data for these two companies follow.

	Reynard	Bouche
Net sales	$9,486,200	$27,287,300
Costs and expenses		
Cost of goods sold	$5,812,200	$18,372,400
Selling expenses	1,194,000	1,955,700
Administrative expenses	1,217,400	4,126,000
Total costs and expenses	$8,223,600	$24,454,100
Income from operations	$1,262,600	$ 2,833,200
Interest expense	270,000	1,360,000
Income before income taxes	$ 992,600	$ 1,473,200
Income taxes	450,000	600,000
Net income	$ 542,600	$ 873,200
Earnings per share	$ 1.55	$ .87

	Reynard	Bouche
Assets		
Cash	$ 126,100	$ 514,300
Marketable securities (at cost)	117,500	1,200,000
Accounts receivable (net)	456,700	2,600,000
Inventories	1,880,000	4,956,000
Prepaid expenses	72,600	156,600
Property, plant, and equipment (net)	5,342,200	19,356,000
Intangibles and other assets	217,000	580,000
Total assets	$8,212,100	$29,362,900
Liabilities and Stockholders' Equity		
Accounts payable	$ 517,400	$ 2,342,000
Notes payable	1,000,000	2,000,000
Income taxes payable	85,200	117,900
Bonds payable	2,000,000	15,000,000
Common stock, $1 par value	350,000	1,000,000
Paid-in capital in excess of par value, common	1,747,300	5,433,300
Retained earnings	2,512,200	3,469,700
Total liabilities and stockholders' equity	$8,212,100	$29,362,900

During the year, Reynard paid a total of $140,000 in dividends, and its current price per share is $20. Bouche paid a total of $600,000 in dividends during the year, and its current market price per share is $9. Reynard had net cash flows from operations of $771,500 and net capital expenditures of $450,000. Bouche had net cash flows from operations of $843,000 and net capital expenditures of $1,550,000.

Information pertaining to these companies' prior years is not readily available. Assume that all their notes payable are current liabilities and that all their bonds payable are long-term liabilities.

REQUIRED ▶ Conduct a comprehensive ratio analysis of Reynard and of Bouche following the steps outlined below. (Round all ratios and percentages except earnings per share to one decimal place.)

1. Prepare a liquidity analysis by calculating for each company the (a) current ratio, (b) quick ratio, (c) receivable turnover, (d) average days' sales uncollected, (e) inventory turnover, (f) average days' inventory on hand, (g) payables turnover, and (h) averages days' payables.
2. Prepare a profitability analysis by calculating for each company the (a) profit margin, (b) asset turnover, (c) return on assets, and (d) return on equity.
3. Prepare a long-term solvency analysis by calculating for each company the (a) debt to equity ratio and (b) interest coverage ratio.
4. Prepare a cash flow adequacy analysis by calculating for each company the (a) cash flow yield, (b) cash flows to sales, (c) cash flows to assets, and (d) free cash flow.
5. Prepare an analysis of market strength by calculating for each company the (a) price/earnings ratio and (b) dividends yield.
6. Compare the two companies by inserting the ratio calculations from 1 through 5 in a table with the following column headings: Ratio Name, Reynard, Bouche, and Company with More Favorable Ratio. Indicate in the last column which company had the more favorable ratio in each case.
7. How could the analysis be improved if information about these companies' prior years were available?

ALTERNATE PROBLEMS

LO5　Effects of Transactions on Ratios

⑯/ⓡ

P 5. Mankato Corporation engaged in the transactions listed in the first column of the following table. Opposite each transaction is a ratio and space to indicate the effect of each transaction on the ratio.

		Effect		
Transaction	Ratio	Increase	Decrease	None
a. Sold merchandise on account.	Current ratio			
b. Sold merchandise on account.	Inventory turnover			
c. Collected on accounts receivable.	Quick ratio			
d. Wrote off an uncollectible account.	Receivable turnover			
e. Paid on accounts payable.	Current ratio			
f. Declared cash dividend.	Return on equity			
g. Incurred advertising expense.	Profit margin			
h. Issued stock dividend.	Debt to equity ratio			
i. Issued bonds payable.	Asset turnover			
j. Accrued interest expense.	Current ratio			
k. Paid previously declared cash dividend.	Dividends yield			
l. Purchased treasury stock.	Return on assets			
m. Recorded depreciation expense.	Cash flow yield			

REQUIRED ▶ Place an X in the appropriate column to show whether the transaction increased, decreased, or had no effect on the indicated ratio.

LO5　Ratio Analysis

⑯/ⓡ

P 6. The condensed comparative income statements and balance sheets of Lisle Corporation follow. All figures are in thousands of dollars, except earnings per share.

Lisle Corporation
Comparative Income Statements
For the Years Ended December 31, 20x6 and 20x5

	20x6	20x5
Net sales	$1,638,400	$1,573,200
Costs and expenses		
Cost of goods sold	$1,044,400	$1,004,200
Selling expenses	238,400	259,000
Administrative expenses	223,600	211,600
Total costs and expenses	$1,506,400	$1,474,800
Income from operations	$ 132,000	$ 98,400
Interest expense	32,800	19,600
Income before income taxes	$ 99,200	$ 78,800
Income taxes	31,200	28,400
Net income	$ 68,000	$ 50,400
Earnings per share	$ 1.70	$ 1.26

Lisle Corporation
Comparative Balance Sheets
December 31, 20x6 and 20x5

	20x6	20x5
Assets		
Cash	$ 40,600	$ 20,400
Accounts receivable (net)	117,800	114,600
Inventory	287,400	297,400
Property, plant, and equipment (net)	375,000	360,000
Total assets	$820,800	$792,400
Liabilities and Stockholders' Equity		
Accounts payable	$133,800	$238,600
Notes payable	100,000	200,000
Bonds payable	200,000	—
Common stock, $5 par value	200,000	200,000
Retained earnings	187,000	153,800
Total liabilities and stockholders' equity	$820,800	$792,400

Additional data for Lisle Corporation in 20x6 and 20x5 are as follows:

	20x6	20x5
Net cash flows from operating activities	$106,500,000	$86,250,000
Net capital expenditures	$22,500,000	$16,000,000
Dividends paid	$22,000,000	$17,200,000
Number of common shares	40,000,000	40,000,000
Market price per share	$9	$15

Selected balances (in thousands) at the end of 20x4 were accounts receivable (net), $103,400; inventory, $273,600; total assets, $732,800; accounts payable $193,300; and stockholders' equity, $320,600.

All Lisle Corporation's notes payable were current liabilities. All its bonds payable were long-term liabilities.

REQUIRED ▶ Perform a ratio analysis following the steps outlined below. Round percentages and ratios to one decimal place, and consider changes of .1 or less to be neutral. After making the calculations, indicate whether each ratio had a favorable (F) or unfavorable (U) change from 20x5 to 20x6.

1. Conduct a liquidity analysis by calculating for each year the (a) current ratio, (b) quick ratio, (c) receivable turnover, (d) average days' sales uncollected, (e) inventory turnover, and (f) average days' inventory on hand.
2. Conduct a profitability analysis by calculating for each year the (a) profit margin, (b) asset turnover, (c) return on assets, and (d) return on equity.
3. Conduct a long-term solvency analysis by calculating for each year the (a) debt to equity ratio and (b) interest coverage ratio.
4. Conduct a cash flow adequacy analysis by calculating for each year the (a) cash flow yield, (b) cash flows to sales, (c) cash flows to assets, and (d) free cash flow.
5. Conduct a market strength analysis by calculating for each year the (a) price/earnings ratio and (b) dividends yield.
6. Based on your analysis, assess Lisle's performance in each of the following areas: liquidity, profitability, long-term solvency, and cash flow adequacy. Explain your evaluations.

SKILLS DEVELOPMENT CASES

Conceptual Analysis

SD 1.

LO2 Standards for Financial
LO5 Performance Evaluation

Helene Curtis, a well-known, publicly owned corporation, became a take-over candidate and sold out in the 1990s after years of poor profit performance. As early as 1978, *Forbes* observed, "By almost any standard, Chicago-based Helene Curtis rates as one of America's worst-managed personal care companies. In recent years its return on equity has hovered between 10% and 13%, well below the industry average of 18% to 19%. Net profit margins of 2% to 3% are half that of competitors. . . . As a result, while leading names like Revlon <www.revlon.com> and Avon <www.avon.com> are trading at three and four times book value, Curtis trades at less than two-thirds book value."[9] Considering that many companies in other industries were happy with a return on equity of 10 percent to 13 percent, why is this analysis so critical of Curtis's performance? Assuming that Curtis could have doubled its profit margin, what other information would be necessary to project the resulting return on stockholders' investment? Why did Revlon's and Avon's stocks trade for more than Curtis's? Be prepared to discuss your answers in class.

SD 2.

LO3 Using Segment Information

Refer to Exhibit 1, which shows the segment information of Goodyear Tire & Rubber Company <www.goodyear.com>. In what business segments does Goodyear operate? What is the relative size of its business segments in terms of sales and income in the most recent year shown? Which segment is most profitable in terms of return on assets? In which region of the world is the tires segment largest, and which tire segment is most profitable in terms of return on assets?

SD 3.

LO3 Using Investors' Services

Refer to Exhibit 2, which contains the PepsiCo Inc. <www.pepsi.com> listing from Mergent's *Handbook of Dividend Achievers*. Assume that an investor has asked you to assess PepsiCo's recent history and prospects. Write a memorandum to the investor that addresses the following points:

1. PepsiCo's earnings history. (What has been the general relationship between PepsiCo's return on assets and its return on equity over the last seven years? What does this tell you about the way the company is financed? What figures back up your conclusion?)
2. The trend of PepsiCo's stock price and price/earnings ratio for the seven years shown.
3. PepsiCo's prospects, including developments likely to affect the company's future.

Ethical Dilemma

SD 4.

LO3 Management of Earnings

Management of most companies is very sensitive to the fact that analysts watch key performance measures, such as whether a firm is meeting earnings targets. A slight weakening of analysts' confidence can severely affect the price of a company's stock. The SEC has been cracking down on companies that manipulate earnings to achieve financial goals. For instance, some time ago, the SEC filed a complaint against W. R. Grace & Co. <www.grace.com> for releasing $1.5 million from reserves into earnings in order to meet earnings targets. Grace officials claimed that the amount was immaterial and that the company was in accord with accounting rules for booking an immaterial item. (The amount was about 1.5 percent of net income.) The SEC, on the other hand, argued that it was a matter of principle: "Does anyone think that it's acceptable to intentionally book an error [false transaction] for the purpose of making earnings targets?" But some think such action on the part of the SEC will harm confidence in business.[10] Do you think it is unethical for a company's management to increase earnings periodically through the use of one-time transactions, such as adjustments of reserves or sale of assets, on which it has a profit?

Research Activity

SD 5.

LO3 Using Investors' Services

Find *Moody's Investors Service* or *Standard & Poor's Industry Guide* in your library. Locate reports on three corporations. You may choose the corporations at random or from the same industry, as directed by your instructor. (If you did a related research activity in a previous chapter, use the same three companies.) Write a summary of what you learned about each company's financial performance, including the performance measures that it uses and its prospects for the future. Be prepared to discuss your findings in class.

Decision-Making Practice

SD 6.

LO4   **Effect of a One-Time Item on**
LO5   **a Loan Decision**

Apple a Day, Inc., and Unforgettable Edibles, Inc., are food catering businesses that operate in the same metropolitan area. Their customers include *Fortune* 500 companies, regional firms, and individuals. The two firms reported similar profit margins for the current year, and both base bonuses for managers on the achievement of a target profit margin and return on equity. Each firm has submitted a loan request to you, a loan officer for City National Bank. They have provided you with the following information:

	Apple a Day	Unforgettable Edibles
Net sales	$625,348	$717,900
Cost of goods sold	225,125	287,080
Gross margin	$400,223	$430,820
Operating expenses	281,300	371,565
Operating income	$118,923	$ 59,255
Gain on sale of real estate	—	81,923
Interest expense	(9,333)	(15,338)
Income before income taxes	$109,590	$125,840
Income taxes	25,990	29,525
Net income	$83,600	$96,315
Average stockholders' equity	$312,700	$390,560

1. Perform a vertical analysis and prepare a common-size income statement for each firm. Compute profit margin and return on equity.
2. Discuss these results, the bonus plan for management, and loan considerations. Identify the company that is the better loan risk.

FINANCIAL REPORTING AND ANALYSIS CASES

Interpreting Financial Reports

FRA 1.

LO4   **Trend Analysis**

H. J. Heinz Company <www.heinz.com> is a global company engaged in several lines of business, including food service, infant foods, condiments, pet foods, and weight control food products. Below is a five-year summary of operations and other related data for Heinz.[11] (Dollars are expressed in thousands.)

Five-Year Summary of Operations and Other Related Data
H. J. Heinz Company and Subsidiaries

	2001	2000	1999	1998	1997
Summary of operations					
Sales	$9,430,422	$9,407,949	$9,299,610	$9,209,284	$9,397,007
Cost of products sold	5,883,618	5,788,565	5,944,867	5,711,213	6,385,091
Interest expense	552,957	269,748	258,815	258,616	274,746
Provision for income taxes	178,140	573,123	360,790	453,415	177,193
Net income (before special items)	494,918	890,553	474,341	801,566	301,871
Other related data					
Dividends paid: Common	537,290	513,756	484,817	452,966	416,923
Total assets	9,035,150	8,850,697	8,053,634	8,023,421	8,437,787
Total debt	4,885,687	4,112,401	3,376,413	5,806,905	5,997,366
Shareholders' equity	1,373,727	1,595,856	1,803,004	2,216,516	2,440,921

REQUIRED ▶   Prepare a trend analysis for Heinz with 1997 as the base year and discuss the results. Identify important trends and state whether the trends are favorable or unfavorable. Discuss significant relationships among the trends.

International Company

FRA 2.

LO5   Comparison of International Companies' Operating Cycles

Ratio analysis enables one to compare the performance of companies whose financial statements are presented in different currencies. Selected data from 2000 for two large pharmaceutical companies—one American, Pfizer, Inc. <www.pfizer.com>, and one Swiss, Roche <www.roche.com>—are presented below (in millions).[12]

	Pfizer, Inc. (U.S.)	Roche (Swiss)
Net Sales	$29,574	SF28,672
Cost of Goods Sold	4,907	9,163
Accounts Receivable	5,489	5,519
Inventories	2,702	5,754
Accounts Payable	1,719	2,215

Accounts receivable in 1999 were $5,368 for Pfizer and SF6,178 for Roche. Inventories in 1999 were $2,588 for Pfizer and SF6,546 for Roche. Accounts payable in 1999 were $1,889 for Pfizer and SF2,378 for Roche.

For each company, calculate the receivable, inventory, and payables turnovers and the respective days associated with each. Then determine the operating cycle for each company and the days of financing required for current operations. Compare the results.

Group Activity: Divide the class into groups to make the calculations. Assign the analysis of Pfizer to half of the groups, and the analysis of Roche to the other half. Have the groups compare results and discuss as a class.

Toys "R" Us Annual Report

FRA 3.

LO5   Comprehensive Ratio Analysis

Using data from the Toys "R" Us <www.tru.com> annual report, conduct a comprehensive ratio analysis that compares the company's performance in 2001 and 2000. If you have computed ratios for Toys "R" Us in previous chapters, you may prepare a table that summarizes the ratios for 2001 and 2000 and show calculations only for the ratios not previously calculated. If this is the first ratio analysis you have done for Toys "R" Us, show all your computations. In either case, after each group of ratios, comment on the performance of Toys "R" Us. Round your calculations to one decimal place. Prepare and comment on the following categories of ratios:

Liquidity analysis: current ratio, quick ratio, receivable turnover, average days' sales uncollected, inventory turnover, average days' inventory on hand, payables turnover, and average days' payable. (Accounts Receivable, Inventory, and Accounts Payable were [in millions] $182, $2,027, and $1,617, respectively, in 1999.)

Profitability analysis: profit margin, asset turnover, return on assets, and return on equity. (Comment on the effect of the restructuring in 2001 on the company's profitability.)

Long-term solvency analysis: debt to equity ratio and interest coverage ratio.

Cash flow adequacy analysis: cash flow yield, cash flows to sales, cash flows to assets, and free cash flow.

Market strength analysis: price/earnings ratio and dividends yield.

Comparison Case: Toys "R" Us and Walgreen Co.

FRA 4.

LO5   Comparison of Key Financial Performance Measures

Refer to the annual report of Toys "R" Us <www.tru.com> and the financial statements for Walgreens <www.walgreens.com> in the Supplement to Chapter 1. Calculate the following key financial performance measures for the two most recent years:

Liquidity: operating cycle
                        days of financing needed

Profitability: profit margin
                        asset turnover
                        return on assets

Long-term solvency: debt to equity ratio

Cash flow adequacy: cash flow yield
                         free cash flow

Evaluate and comment on the relative performance of the two companies with respect to each of the above categories. (**Note:** Total assets for Walgreens in 1999 were $5,906.7 million.)

Fingraph® Financial Analyst™

FRA 5.

**LO5   Comprehensive Financial
Performance Evaluation**

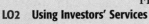

Choose any company from the list of Fingraph companies on the Needles Accounting Resource Center Web Site at http://accounting.college.hmco.com/students. Access the Microsoft Excel spreadsheets for the company you selected.

1. Using the Fingraph CD-ROM software, display and print the following pages for the company you have selected:

   a. Balance Sheet Analysis
   b. Current Assets and Current Liabilities Analysis
   c. Liquidity and Asset Utilization Analysis
   d. Income from Operations Analysis
   e. Statement of Cash Flows: Operating Activities Analysis
   f. Statement of Cash Flows: Investing and Financing Activities Analysis
   g. Market Strength Analysis

2. Prepare an executive summary that describes the company's financial condition and performance over the past two years. Attach the pages you printed in support of your analysis.

Internet Case

FRA 6.

**LO2   Using Investors' Services
LO3**

Go to the web site for Moody's Investors Service <www.moodys.com>. Click on "ratings," which will show revisions of debt ratings issued by Moody's in the past few days. Choose a rating that has been upgraded or downgraded and read the short press announcement related to it. What reasons does Moody's give for the change in rating? What is Moody's assessment of the future of the company or institution? What financial performance measures are mentioned in the article? Summarize your findings and be prepared to share them in class.

16

Chapter 16 covers two topics: (1) accounting for investments by one company in the capital stock or bonds of another, including consolidated financial statements, and (2) international accounting, including the effects of changing rates of exchange and diverse international accounting standards.

Long-Term Investments and International Accounting

LEARNING OBJECTIVES

LO1 Identify the classifications of long-term investments in bonds and stocks and apply the cost-adjusted-to-market and equity methods as appropriate.

LO2 Identify the uses of consolidated financial statements, prepare a consolidated balance sheet at acquisition date using the purchase method, and prepare a consolidated income statement.

LO3 Define *exchange rate* and record transactions that are affected by changes in foreign exchange rates.

LO4 Describe the restatement of a foreign subsidiary's financial statements in U.S. dollars.

LO5 Describe the progress toward international accounting standards.

DECISION POINT

A USER'S FOCUS

PepsiCo, Inc. <www.pepsico.com> PepsiCo, Inc., has been expanding rapidly in the beverage and snack food markets both domestically and abroad. Because it is difficult to develop new brands in these highly competitive markets, PepsiCo has bought other companies with established brands. For instance, in recent years, it has purchased Tropicana Products, South Beach Beverage Company, and Quaker Oats. The latter was the biggest U.S. merger of 2001. PepsiCo did not buy Quaker Oats for its famous oat cereal, but for its popular beverage brand Gatorade. To raise money for these purchases, the company sold 62 percent of its ownership of PepsiCo Bottling Company. As a result of the purchases, PepsiCo, though still trailing Coca-Cola <www.coca-cola.com> in the cola wars, leads the noncola market with a 25 percent market share.[1] Such transactions are common in today's business world. How are they reflected in a company's financial statements?

The Financial Highlights, taken from PepsiCo's annual report, show just two of their effects. "Investments in non-consolidated affiliates" are investments in companies in which PepsiCo has less than 50 percent ownership, as in the case of PepsiCo Bottling Company. Goodwill is the result of PepsiCo's having bought a controlling share in another company, as in the case of South Beach Beverage Company. As you can see, these assets represent a significant part of PepsiCo's overall asset base. Readers of financial statements must understand the implications that

Why is PepsiCo's purchase of Quaker Oats for its popular brand Gatorade considered a long-term investment?

such items have for a company's financial performance. This chapter explains these items and expands the discussion to issues related to international accounting.

Financial Highlights
(Dollar amounts in millions)

	2000		1999	
	Amount	Percentage	Amount	Percentage
Investments in non-consolidated affiliates	$2,978	16.2%	$2,846	16.2%
Goodwill	3,576	19.5	3,745	21.3
Total assets	18,339	100.0	17,551	100.0

LONG-TERM INVESTMENTS IN BONDS AND STOCKS

LO1 Identify the classifications of long-term investments in bonds and stocks and apply the cost-adjusted-to-market and equity methods as appropriate.

RELATED TEXT ASSIGNMENTS

Q: 1, 2, 3, 4, 5, 6   www.pepsico.com
SE: 1, 2, 3, 4
E: 1, 2, 3, 4
P: 1, 2, 6, 7
SD: 3, 5
FRA: 5, 6

Companies make long-term investments for a variety of reasons. For instance, PepsiCo makes investments in operations critical to the distribution of its products, such as its investments in PepsiCo Bottling Company. It also makes investments to expand its markets, as in its purchases of Tropicana, South Beach Beverage, and Quaker Oats. These are stock investments, but a company can also make long-term investments in bonds. Investments in bonds can be a way of ensuring that an affiliate company has sufficient long-term capital, or it can simply be a way of making a relatively secure investment. The following sections discuss the classifications of bonds and stocks and the methods used to account for such investments.

LONG-TERM INVESTMENTS IN BONDS

Like all investments, investments in bonds are recorded at cost, which, in this case, is the price of the bonds plus the broker's commission. When bonds are purchased between interest payment dates, the purchaser must also pay an amount equal to the interest that has accrued on the bonds since the last interest payment date. Then, on the next interest payment date, the purchaser receives an interest payment for the whole period. The payment for accrued interest should be recorded as a debit to Interest Income, which will be offset by a credit to Interest Income when the semiannual interest is received.

Subsequent accounting for a corporation's long-term bond investments depends on the classification of the bonds. If the company plans at some point to sell the bonds, they are classified as **available-for-sale securities**. If the company plans to hold the bonds until they are paid off on their maturity date, they are considered **held-to-maturity securities**. Except in industries like insurance and banking, it is unusual for companies to buy the bonds of other companies with the express purpose of holding them until they mature, which can be in 10 to 30 years. Thus, most long-term bond investments are available-for-sale securities. Such bonds are accounted for at fair value, much as equity or stock investments are; fair value is usually the market value. When bonds are intended to be held to maturity, they are accounted for not at fair value but at cost, adjusted for the amortization of their discount or premium. The procedure is similar to accounting for long-term bond liabilities, except that separate accounts for discounts and premiums are not used.

KEY POINT: The fair value of bonds is closely related to interest rates. An increase in interest rates lowers the fair value of bonds, and vice versa.

LONG-TERM INVESTMENTS IN STOCKS

All long-term investments in stocks are recorded at cost, in accordance with generally accepted accounting principles. The treatment of the investment in the accounting records after the initial purchase depends on the extent to which the investing company can exercise *significant influence* or *control* over the operating and

FOCUS ON BUSINESS ETHICS

Are You an Insider?

In the United States, *insider trading,* or making use of inside information for personal gain, is unethical and illegal. The officers and employees of a public company are not allowed to buy or sell shares of stock in their own company in advance of the release of significant information; only after the information is released to the stockholders and the general public can insiders make such trades. The Securities and Exchange Commission <www.sec.gov> vigorously prosecutes any individual, whether employed by the company in question or not, who buys or sells shares of a publicly held company based on information not yet available to the public. This is not always true in other countries. Until recently, insider trading was not illegal in Germany, but with the goal of expanding its securities markets, Germany recently reformed its securities laws. It established the Federal Authority for Securities Trading (FAST), in part to oversee insider trading activities. However, only 7 FAST staff members handle these investigations, as compared with the more than 50 staff members who handle SEC investigations.[2] Other countries continue to permit insider trading.

TABLE 1. Accounting Treatments of Long-Term Investments in Stocks

Level of Ownership	Percentage of Ownership	Accounting Treatment
Noninfluential and noncontrolling	Less than 20%	Cost initially; investment adjusted subsequent to purchase for changes in market value
Influential but noncontrolling	Between 20% and 50%	Equity method; investment valued subsequently at cost plus investor's share of income (or minus investor's share of loss) minus dividends received
Controlling	More than 50%	Financial statements consolidated

KEY POINT: Influence and control are related specifically to equity holdings, not debt holdings.

financial policies of the other company. The Accounting Principles Board (APB) defined these important terms in its *Opinion No. 18.*

Significant influence is an investing firm's ability to affect the operating and financial policies of the company whose shares it owns, even though it holds 50 percent or less of the voting stock. Indications of significant influence include representation on the board of directors, participation in policymaking, and material transactions, exchange of managerial personnel, and technological dependency between the two companies. For the sake of uniformity, the APB decided that without proof to the contrary, ownership of 20 percent or more of the voting stock should be presumed to confer significant influence.* Ownership of less than 20 percent of the voting stock does not confer significant influence.

Control is an investing firm's ability to decide the operating and financial policies of the other company. Control exists when the investor owns more than 50 percent of the voting stock of the company in which it has invested.

Thus, in the absence of information to the contrary, a noninfluential and noncontrolling investment would be less than 20 percent ownership. An influential but noncontrolling investment would be 20 to 50 percent ownership. And a controlling investment would be more than 50 percent ownership. The accounting treatment differs for each kind of investment. Table 1 summarizes these treatments.

■ **NONINFLUENTIAL AND NONCONTROLLING INVESTMENT** Available-for-sale securities are debt or equity securities that are not classified as trading or held-to-maturity securities. When equity securities are involved, a further criterion is that they be noninfluential and noncontrolling investments of less than 20 percent of the voting stock. The Financial Accounting Standards Board requires a **cost-adjusted-to market method** for accounting for available-for-sale securities. Under this method, available-for-sale securities must be recorded initially at cost and thereafter adjusted

*The Financial Accounting Standards Board pointed out in its *Interpretation No. 35* (May 1981) that this rule is not a rigid one. All relevant facts and circumstances should be examined to determine whether significant influence exists. The FASB noted five circumstances that may negate significant influence: (1) The company files a lawsuit against the investor or a complaint with a government agency; (2) the investor tries but fails to become a director; (3) the investor agrees not to increase its holdings; (4) the company is operated by a small group that ignores the investor's wishes; (5) the investor tries but fails to obtain company information that is not available to other stockholders.

periodically through the use of an allowance account to reflect changes in the market value.[3]

Available-for-sale securities are classified as long term if management intends to hold them for more than one year. When accounting for long-term available-for sale securities, the unrealized gain or loss resulting from the adjustment is not reported on the income statement. Instead, it is reported as a special item in the stockholders' equity section of the balance sheet and in comprehensive income disclosure.

At the end of each accounting period, the total cost and the total market value of these long-term stock investments must be determined. If the total market value is less than the total cost, the difference must be credited to a contra-asset account called Allowance to Adjust Long-Term Investments to Market. Because of the long-term nature of the investment, the debit part of the entry, which represents a decrease in value below cost, is treated as a temporary decrease and does not appear as a loss on the income statement. It is shown in a contra-stockholders' equity account called Unrealized Loss on Long-Term Investments.* Thus, both of these accounts are balance sheet accounts. If the market value exceeds the cost, the allowance account is added to Long-Term Investments, and the unrealized gain appears as an addition to stockholders' equity.

When long-term investments in stock are sold, the difference between the sale price and the cost of the stock is recorded and reported as a realized gain or loss on the income statement. Dividend income from such investments is recorded by a debit to Cash and a credit to Dividend Income. For example, assume the following facts about the long-term stock investments of Coleman Corporation:

June 1, 20x3	Paid cash for the following long-term investments: 10,000 shares of Durbin Corporation common stock (representing 2 percent of outstanding stock) at $25 per share; 5,000 shares of Kotes Corporation common stock (representing 3 percent of outstanding stock) at $15 per share.
Dec. 31, 20x3	Quoted market prices at year end: Durbin common stock, $21; Kotes common stock, $17.
Apr. 1, 20x4	Change in policy required sale of 2,000 shares of Durbin common stock at $23.
July 1, 20x4	Received cash dividend from Kotes equal to $.20 per share.
Dec. 31, 20x4	Quoted market prices at year end: Durbin common stock, $24; Kotes common stock, $13.

KEY POINT: On April 1, 20x4, a *change in policy* requires the sale. This points out that intent is often the only difference between long-term investments and short-term investments.

Entries to record these transactions are as follows:

Investment

20x3

A = L + OE
+
–

June 1 Long-Term Investments   325,000
            Cash   325,000
            Investments in Durbin common
            stock (10,000 shares × $25 =
            $250,000) and Kotes common stock
            (5,000 shares × $15 = $75,000)

Year-End Adjustment

20x3

A = L + OE
–   –

Dec. 31 Unrealized Loss on Long-Term Investments   30,000
              Allowance to Adjust Long-Term
              Investments to Market   30,000
              To record reduction of long-term
              investment to market

*If the decrease in market value of the long-term investment is deemed permanent, a different procedure is followed to record the decline. A loss account on the income statement is debited instead of the Unrealized Loss account.

Company	Shares	Market Price	Total Market	Total Cost
Durbin	10,000	$21	$210,000	$250,000
Kotes	5,000	17	85,000	75,000
			$295,000	$325,000

KEY POINT: *Total* cost and *total* market or fair value are used to determine the adjustment.

Total Cost − Total Market Value = $325,000 − $295,000 = $30,000

Sale

A = L + OE
+
−

20x4
Apr. 1 Cash   46,000
       Loss on Sale of Investments   4,000
           Long-Term Investments   50,000
            Sale of 2,000 shares of Durbin
            common stock
            2,000 × $23 = $46,000
            2,000 × $25 = 50,000
            Loss $ 4,000

Dividend Received

A = L + OE
+   +

20x4
July 1 Cash   1,000
       Dividend Income   1,000
           Receipt of cash dividend from Kotes stock
           5,000 × $.20 = $1,000

Year-End Adjustment

A = L + OE
+   +

20x4
Dec. 31 Allowance to Adjust Long-Term
        Investments to Market   12,000
          Unrealized Loss on Long-Term
          Investments   12,000
           To record the adjustment in long-
           term investment so it is reported
           at market

The adjustment equals the previous balance ($30,000 from the December 31, 20x3, entry) minus the new balance ($18,000), or $12,000. The new balance of $18,000 is the difference at the present time between the total market value and the total cost of all investments. It is figured as follows:

Company	Shares	Market Price	Total Market	Total Cost
Durbin	8,000	$24	$192,000	$200,000
Kotes	5,000	13	65,000	75,000
			$257,000	$275,000

Total Cost − Total Market Value = $275,000 − $257,000 = $18,000

The Allowance to Adjust Long-Term Investments to Market and the Unrealized Loss on Long-Term Investments are reciprocal contra accounts, each with the same dollar balance, as shown by the effects of these transactions on the T accounts:

Contra-Asset Account		Contra-Stockholders' Equity Account	
Allowance to Adjust Long-Term Investments to Market		Unrealized Loss on Long-Term Investment	
20x4 12,000	20x3 30,000	20x3 30,000	20x4 12,000
	Bal. 20x4 18,000	Bal. 20x4 18,000	

The Allowance account reduces long-term investments by the amount by which the cost of the investments exceeds market; the Unrealized Loss account reduces stockholders' equity by a similar amount. The opposite effects will exist if market value exceeds cost, resulting in an unrealized gain.

■ **INFLUENTIAL BUT NONCONTROLLING INVESTMENT** As we have noted, ownership of 20 percent or more of a company's voting stock is considered sufficient to influence the company's operations. When this is the case, the stock investment should be accounted for using the **equity method**. The equity method presumes that an investment of 20 percent or more is not a passive investment and that the investor should therefore share proportionately in the success or failure of the company. The three main features of this method are as follows:

1. The investor records the original purchase of the stock at cost.

2. The investor records its share of the company's periodic net income as an increase in the Investment account, with a corresponding credit to an income account. Similarly, it records its share of a periodic loss as a decrease in the Investment account, with a corresponding debit to a loss account.

3. When the investor receives a cash dividend, the asset account Cash is increased, and the Investment account is decreased.

To illustrate the equity method of accounting, we assume the following facts about an investment by Vassor Corporation: On January 1 of the current year, Vassor acquired 40 percent of the voting common stock of Block Corporation for $180,000. With this share of ownership, Vassor can exert significant influence over Block's operations. During the year, Block reported net income of $80,000 and paid cash dividends of $20,000. Vassor recorded these transactions as follows:

Investment

A = L + OE	Investment in Block Corporation	180,000	
+	Cash		180,000
−	Investment in Block Corporation common stock		

Recognition of Income

A = L + OE	Investment in Block Corporation	32,000	
+ +	Income, Block Corporation Investment		32,000
	Recognition of 40% of income reported		
	by Block Corporation		
	40% × $80,000 = $32,000		

Receipt of Cash Dividend

A = L + OE	Cash	8,000	
+	Investment in Block Corporation		8,000
−	Cash dividend from Block Corporation		
	40% × $20,000 = $8,000		

The balance of the Investment in Block Corporation account after these transactions is $204,000, as shown here:

Investment in Block Corporation

Investment	180,000	Dividend received	8,000
Share of Income	32,000		
Balance	204,000		

■ **CONTROLLING INVESTMENT** Some investing firms that own less than 50 percent of the voting stock of a company exercise such powerful influence that for all practical purposes, they control the policies of the other company. Nevertheless, ownership of more than 50 percent of the voting stock is required for accounting recognition

⬢ **STOP AND THINK!**

When a company uses the equity method to record its proportionate share of the income and dividends of a company in which it has invested, what are the cash flow effects?

There are no cash flow effects. However, any dividends received are received in cash. Usually, the income is greater than the dividends. ■

STUDY POINT: Under the equity method, dividends received are credited to the Investment account because the dividends represent a return from or a decrease in the investment in Block Corporation.

FOCUS ON INTERNATIONAL BUSINESS

Accounting for International Joint Ventures

When U.S. companies make investments abroad, they often find it wise or necessary to partner with a local company or with the government of the country. Some countries require that their citizens own a minimum percentage of each business. In other countries—among them, Brazil, China, India, and the former Soviet Socialist Republics—the government has traditionally had a share of ownership. Such business arrangements are usually called *joint ventures*. Since the resulting enterprise is jointly owned, it is appropriate to treat the U.S. company's status as "influential but noncontrolling." Thus, the most appropriate accounting method for these arrangements is the equity method.

ENRICHMENT NOTE:
Parents and subsidiaries are separate legal entities even though they combine their financial reports at year end.

of control. When a firm has a controlling interest, a parent-subsidiary relationship is said to exist. The investing company is known as the **parent company**; the other company is a **subsidiary**. Because the two corporations are separate legal entities, each prepares separate financial statements. However, owing to their special relationship, they are viewed for public financial reporting purposes as a single economic entity. For this reason, they must combine their financial statements into a single set of statements called **consolidated financial statements**.

Accounting for consolidated financial statements is complex and is usually the subject of an advanced accounting course. However, most large public corporations have subsidiaries and must prepare consolidated financial statements. It is therefore important to have some understanding of accounting for consolidations.

 Check out ACE for a Review Quiz at http://accounting.college.hmco.com/students.

CONSOLIDATED FINANCIAL STATEMENTS

LO2 Identify the uses of consolidated financial statements, prepare a consolidated balance sheet at acquisition date using the purchase method, and prepare a consolidated income statement.

RELATED TEXT ASSIGNMENTS
Q: 4, 5, 6, 7, 8, 9, 10, 11, 12
SE: 4, 5, 6, 7, 8
E: 4, 5, 6, 7, 8
P: 3, 4
FRA: 1, 4, 6   www.pepsico.com
www.ibm.com

Most major corporations find it convenient for economic, legal, tax, or other reasons to operate in parent-subsidiary relationships. When we speak of a large company, such as PepsiCo or IBM, we generally think of the parent company, not of its many subsidiaries. When considering investment in such a firm, however, the investor wants a clear financial picture of the total economic entity. The main purpose of consolidated financial statements is to give such a view of the parent and subsidiary firms by treating them as if they were one company. On a consolidated balance sheet, the Inventory account includes the inventory held by the parent and all its subsidiaries. Similarly, on the consolidated income statement, the Sales account is the total revenue from sales by the parent and all its subsidiaries. This overview helps management, stockholders, and creditors of the parent company judge the company's progress in meeting its goals.

According to a 1987 ruling of the Financial Accounting Standards Board (*Statement No. 94*), all subsidiaries in which the parent owns a controlling interest (more than 50 percent) must be consolidated with the parent for financial reporting purposes.[4] As a result, the financial statements of all majority-owned subsidiaries are, with few exceptions, now consolidated with the parent company's financial statements for external reporting purposes. Some companies, such as General Electric, present both consolidated statements and separate statements for their subsidiaries in their annual reports.

KEY POINT: As separate entities, the parent and the subsidiary maintain individual accounting records. Work sheet eliminations remove only duplications that occur in consolidation and the effects of intercompany transactions.

CONSOLIDATED BALANCE SHEET

In preparing consolidated financial statements under the **purchase method**, similar accounts from the separate statements of the parent and the subsidiaries are combined. Some accounts result from transactions between the parent and the subsidiary. Examples are debt owed by one of the entities to the other and sales and purchases between the two entities. When considering the group of companies as a single business, it is not appropriate to include these accounts in the group financial

FOCUS ON BUSINESS PRACTICE

Anatomy of a Purchase

When one company purchases another, the transaction often involves an exchange of stock. For instance, when PepsiCo <www.pepsico.com> purchased Quaker Oats in 2001, the transaction was as follows:

> Quaker shareholders will receive 2.3 shares of PepsiCo capital stock. . . . Based on the closing price of PepsiCo stock of $42.375, the proposed tax-free transaction would be valued at $97.625 per Quaker share. . . . These PepsiCo capital shares exchanged for Quaker shares will represent approximately 18% of the outstanding shares of PepsiCo capital stock after the merger.[5]

At the time of the announcement, Quaker shares were selling for about $88. Thus, Quaker shareholders had a gain of about $9 per share and ended up owning 18 percent of PepsiCo—a good deal for them.

statements; the purchases and sales are only transfers between different parts of the business, and the payables and receivables do not represent amounts due to or receivable from outside parties. For this reason, it is important that certain **eliminations** be made. These eliminations avoid the duplication of accounts and reflect the financial position and operations from the standpoint of a single entity. Eliminations appear only on the work sheets used in preparing consolidated financial statements. They are never shown in the accounting records of either the parent or the subsidiary. There are no consolidated journals or ledgers.

Another good example of accounts that result from transactions between the two entities is the Investment in Subsidiary account on the parent's balance sheet and in the stockholders' equity section of the subsidiary. When the balance sheets of the two companies are combined, these accounts must be eliminated to avoid duplicating these items in the consolidated financial statements.

To illustrate the preparation of a consolidated balance sheet under the purchase method, we use the following balance sheets for Parent and Subsidiary Companies:

Accounts	Parent Company	Subsidiary Company
Cash	$100,000	$25,000
Other assets	760,000	60,000
Total assets	$860,000	$85,000
Liabilities	$ 60,000	$10,000
Common stock	600,000	55,000
Retained earnings	200,000	20,000
Total liabilities and stockholders' equity	$860,000	$85,000

■ **100 PERCENT PURCHASE AT BOOK VALUE** Suppose that Parent Company purchases 100 percent of the stock of Subsidiary Company for an amount exactly equal to Subsidiary's book value. The book value of Subsidiary Company is $75,000 ($85,000 − $10,000). Parent Company would record the purchase as shown below:

A = L + OE
+
−

Investment in Subsidiary Company	75,000	
Cash		75,000
Purchase of 100 percent of Subsidiary		
Company at book value		

It is helpful to use a work sheet like the one shown in Exhibit 1 in preparing consolidated financial statements. Note that the balance of Parent Company's Cash account is now $25,000 and that Investment in Subsidiary Company is shown as an

EXHIBIT 1
Work Sheet for Preparing a Consolidated Balance Sheet

Parent and Subsidiary Companies
Work Sheet for Consolidated Balance Sheet
As of Acquisition Date

Accounts	Balance Sheet, Parent Company	Balance Sheet, Subsidiary Company	Eliminations		Consolidated Balance Sheet
			Debit	Credit	
Cash	25,000	25,000			50,000
Investment in subsidiary company	75,000			(1) 75,000	
Other assets	760,000	60,000			820,000
Total assets	860,000	85,000			870,000
Liabilities	60,000	10,000			70,000
Common stock	600,000	55,000	(1) 55,000		600,000
Retained earnings	200,000	20,000	(1) 20,000		200,000
Total liabilities and stockholders' equity	860,000	85,000	75,000	75,000	870,000

(1) Elimination of intercompany investment.

asset in Parent Company's balance sheet, reflecting the purchase of the subsidiary. To prepare a consolidated balance sheet, it is necessary to eliminate the investment in the subsidiary, as shown in elimination entry 1 in Exhibit 1. This entry accomplishes two things. First, it eliminates the double counting that would take place when the net assets of the two companies are combined. Second, it eliminates the stockholders' equity section of Subsidiary Company.

The theory underlying consolidated financial statements is that parent and subsidiary are a single entity. The stockholders' equity section of the consolidated balance sheet is the same as that of Parent Company. So, after eliminating the Investment in Subsidiary Company account and the stockholders' equity of the subsidiary, we can take the information from the right-hand column in Exhibit 1 and present it in the following form:

Parent and Subsidiary Companies
Consolidated Balance Sheet
As of Acquisition Date

Cash	$ 50,000	Liabilities	$ 70,000
Other assets	820,000	Common stock	600,000
		Retained earnings	200,000
		Total liabilities and	
Total assets	$870,000	stockholders' equity	$870,000

EXHIBIT 2
Work Sheet Showing Elimination When Purchase Is for Less than 100 Percent Ownership

Accounts	Balance Sheet, Parent Company	Balance Sheet, Subsidiary Company	Eliminations		Consolidated Balance Sheet
			Debit	Credit	
Parent and Subsidiary Companies					
Work Sheet for Consolidated Balance Sheet					
As of Acquisition Date					
Cash	32,500	25,000			57,500
Investment in subsidiary company	67,500			(1) 67,500	
Other assets	760,000	60,000			820,000
Total assets	860,000	85,000			877,500
Liabilities	60,000	10,000			70,000
Common stock	600,000	55,000	(1) 55,000		600,000
Retained earnings	200,000	20,000	(1) 20,000		200,000
Minority interest				(1) 7,500	7,500
Total liabilities and stockholders' equity	860,000	85,000	75,000	75,000	877,500

(1) Elimination of intercompany investment. Minority interest equals 10 percent of subsidiary's stockholders' equity.

KEY POINT: When the elimination entry is made, all of the subsidiary's stockholders' equity is eliminated. The percentage not owned by the parent company is assigned to minority interest.

■ **LESS THAN 100 PERCENT PURCHASE AT BOOK VALUE**   A parent company does not have to purchase 100 percent of a subsidiary to control it. If it purchases more than 50 percent of the subsidiary's voting stock, it will have legal control. In the consolidated financial statements, therefore, the total assets and liabilities of the subsidiary are combined with those of the parent. However, it is still necessary to account for the interests of the stockholders of the subsidiary company who own less than 50 percent of the voting stock. These are the minority stockholders, and their **minority interest** must appear on the consolidated balance sheet as an amount equal to their percentage of ownership times the net assets of the subsidiary.

Suppose that Parent Company buys, for $67,500, only 90 percent of Subsidiary Company's voting stock. In this case, the portion of the company purchased has a book value of $67,500 (90% × $75,000). The work sheet used for preparing the consolidated balance sheet appears in Exhibit 2. The elimination is made in the same way as in Exhibit 1, except that the minority interest must be accounted for. All of the Investment in Subsidiary Company ($67,500) is eliminated against all of Subsidiary Company's stockholders' equity ($75,000). The difference ($7,500, or 10% × $75,000) is set as minority interest.

There are two ways to classify minority interest on the consolidated balance sheet. One is to place it between long-term liabilities and stockholders' equity. The other is to consider the stockholders' equity section as consisting of (1) minority interest and (2) Parent Company's stockholders' equity, as shown here:

Minority interest	$ 7,500
Common stock	600,000
Retained earnings	200,000
Total stockholders' equity	$807,500

■ PURCHASE AT MORE OR LESS THAN BOOK VALUE   The purchase price of a business depends on many factors, such as the current market price, the relative strength of the buyer's and seller's bargaining positions, and the prospects for future earnings. Thus, it is only by chance that the purchase price of a subsidiary will equal the book value of the subsidiary's equity. Usually, it will not. For example, a parent company may pay more than the book value of a subsidiary to purchase a controlling interest if the assets of the subsidiary are understated. In that case, the recorded historical cost less depreciation of the subsidiary's assets may not reflect current market values. The parent may also pay more than book value if the subsidiary has something that the parent wants, such as an important technical process, a new and different product, or a new market. On the other hand, the parent may pay less than book value for its share of the subsidiary's stock if the subsidiary's assets are not worth their depreciated cost. Or the subsidiary may have suffered heavy losses, causing its stock to sell at rather low prices.

The Accounting Principles Board has provided the following guidelines for consolidating a purchased subsidiary and its parent when the parent pays more than book value for its investment in the subsidiary:

> First, all identifiable assets acquired . . . and liabilities assumed in a business combination . . . should be assigned a portion of the cost of the acquired company, normally equal to their fair values at date of acquisition.
>
> Second, the excess of the cost of the acquired company over the sum of the amounts assigned to identifiable assets acquired less liabilities assumed should be recorded as goodwill.[6]

To illustrate the application of these principles, we assume that Parent Company purchases 100 percent of Subsidiary Company's voting stock for $92,500, or $17,500 more than book value. Parent Company considers $10,000 of the $17,500 to be due to the increased value of Subsidiary's other assets and $7,500 of the $17,500 to be due to the overall strength that Subsidiary Company would add to Parent Company's organization. The work sheet used for preparing the consolidated balance sheet appears in Exhibit 3. All of the Investment in Subsidiary Company ($92,500) has been eliminated against all of Subsidiary Company's stockholders' equity ($75,000). The excess of cost over book value ($17,500) has been debited in the amounts of $10,000 to Other Assets and $7,500 to a new account called **Goodwill**, or *Goodwill from Consolidation*.

The amount of goodwill is determined as follows:

Cost of investment in subsidiary	$92,500
Book value of subsidiary	75,000
Excess of cost over book value	$17,500
Portion of excess attributable to undervalued long-term assets of subsidiary	10,000
Portion of excess attributable to goodwill	$ 7,500

On the consolidated balance sheet, goodwill appears as an asset representing the portion of the excess of the cost of the investment over book value that cannot be allocated to any specific asset. Other assets appears on the consolidated balance sheet at the combined total of $830,000 ($760,000 + $60,000 + $10,000).

When the parent company pays less than book value for its investment in the subsidiary, Accounting Principles Board *Opinion No. 16* requires that the excess of book value over cost of the investment be used to lower the carrying value of the subsidiary's long-term assets. The reasoning behind this is that market values of long-lived assets (other than marketable securities) are among the least reliable of estimates, since a ready market does not usually exist for such assets. In other words, the Accounting Principles Board advises against using negative goodwill, except in very special cases.

Goodwill is carried on the balance sheet at cost and is subject to an annual impairment test, as explained in the chapter on long-term assets.

KEY POINT: Regardless of the circumstances, the Investment in Subsidiary Company account must be eliminated completely and should not appear on the consolidated balance sheet.

KEY POINT: Goodwill is recorded in financial records when the purchase price of a business exceeds the fair market value of the net assets purchased.

KEY POINT: In these examples, neither company has goodwill on its balance sheet, but goodwill is "created" when consolidated statements are prepared.

● STOP AND THINK!
Under what conditions would a company have both minority interest and goodwill in a consolidation?

Both minority interest and goodwill would occur if the purchase was for less than 100 percent ownership (resulting in minority interest) and the price was more than book value (resulting in goodwill). ■

EXHIBIT 3
Work Sheet Showing Elimination When Purchase Cost Is Greater than Book Value

Accounts	Balance Sheet, Parent Company	Balance Sheet, Subsidiary Company	Eliminations		Consolidated Balance Sheet
			Debit	Credit	
Cash	7,500	25,000			32,500
Investment in subsidiary company	92,500			(1) 92,500	
Other assets	760,000	60,000	(1) 10,000		830,000
Goodwill	—	—	(1) 7,500		7,500
Total assets	860,000	85,000			870,000
Liabilities	60,000	10,000			70,000
Common stock	600,000	55,000	(1) 55,000		600,000
Retained earnings	200,000	20,000	(1) 20,000		200,000
Total liabilities and stockholders' equity	860,000	85,000	92,500	92,500	870,000

Parent and Subsidiary Companies
Work Sheet for Consolidated Balance Sheet
As of Acquisition Date

(1) Elimination of intercompany investment. Excess of cost over book value ($92,500 − $75,000 = $17,500) is allocated to Other Assets ($10,000) and to Goodwill ($7,500).

■ **INTERCOMPANY RECEIVABLES AND PAYABLES**   If either the parent or the subsidiary company owes money to the other, there will be a receivable on the creditor company's individual balance sheet and a payable on the debtor company's individual balance sheet. When a consolidated balance sheet is prepared, both the receivable and the payable should be eliminated because from the viewpoint of the consolidated entity, neither the asset nor the liability exists. In other words, it does not make sense for a company to owe money to itself. The eliminating entry is made on the work sheet by debiting the payable and crediting the receivable for the amount of the intercompany loan.

CONSOLIDATED INCOME STATEMENT

The consolidated income statement for a consolidated entity is prepared by combining the revenues and expenses of the parent and subsidiary companies. The procedure is the same as that for preparing a consolidated balance sheet. That is, intercompany transactions are eliminated to prevent double counting of revenues and expenses. The following intercompany transactions affect the consolidated income statement: (1) sales and purchases of goods and services between parent and subsidiary (purchases for the buying company and sales for the selling company); (2) income and expenses related to loans, receivables, or bond indebtedness between parent and subsidiary; and (3) other income and expenses from intercompany transactions.

To illustrate the eliminating entries, we assume that Parent Company made sales of $120,000 in goods to Subsidiary Company, which in turn sold all the goods to others. Subsidiary Company paid Parent Company $2,000 interest on a loan from the parent.

EXHIBIT 4
Work Sheet for Preparing a Consolidated Income Statement

Parent and Subsidiary Companies
Work Sheet for Consolidated Income Statement
For the Year Ended December 31, 20xx

Accounts	Income Statement, Parent Company	Income Statement, Subsidiary Company	Eliminations		Consolidated Income Statement
			Debit	Credit	
Sales	430,000	200,000	(1) 120,000		510,000
Other revenues	60,000	10,000	(2) 2,000		68,000
Total revenues	490,000	210,000			578,000
Cost of goods sold	210,000	150,000		(1) 120,000	240,000
Other expenses	140,000	50,000		(2) 2,000	188,000
Total costs and expenses	350,000	200,000			428,000
Net income	140,000	10,000	122,000	122,000	150,000

(1) Elimination of intercompany sales and purchases.
(2) Elimination of intercompany interest income and interest expense.

KEY POINT: Intercompany sales or purchases are not revenues or expenses to the consolidated entity. They are only paper transactions to provide for an exchange between affiliates. True revenues and expenses occur only when transactions are with parties outside the firm.

The work sheet in Exhibit 4 shows how to prepare a consolidated income statement. The purpose of the eliminating entries is to treat the two companies as a single entity. Thus, it is important to include in Sales only those sales made to outsiders and to include in Cost of Goods Sold only those purchases made from outsiders. This goal is met with the first eliminating entry, which eliminates the $120,000 of intercompany sales and purchases by a debit of that amount to Sales and a credit of that amount to Cost of Goods Sold. As a result, only sales to outsiders ($510,000) and purchases from outsiders ($240,000) are included in the Consolidated Income Statement column. The intercompany interest income and expense are eliminated by a debit to Other Revenues and a credit to Other Expenses.

Public corporations also prepare consolidated statements of stockholders' equity and consolidated statements of cash flows. For examples of these statements, see the Toys "R" Us annual report in the Supplement to Chapter 1.

www.tru.com

✓ Check out ACE for a Review Quiz at http://accounting.college.hmco.com/students.

INTERNATIONAL ACCOUNTING

LO3 Define *exchange rate* and record transactions that are affected by changes in foreign exchange rates.

RELATED TEXT ASSIGNMENTS
Q: 13, 14
SE: 9, 10
E: 9, 10
P: 5
SD: 1, 2, 4
FRA: 3

www.pepsico.com

As businesses grow, they naturally look for new sources of supply and new markets in other countries. Today, it is common for businesses to operate in more than one country, and many of these so-called **multinational** or **transnational corporations** operate throughout the world.

The extent of a company's international operations can be found in its annual report in the segment information note to the financial statements. The annual report will also contain a description of the company's international operations.

For example, the Frito Lay segment of PepsiCo, Inc., obtains more than one-third of its $13 billion in revenues from countries outside the United States.

TABLE 2.   Extent of Foreign Revenues for Selected U.S. Companies

Company	Foreign Revenues (millions)	Total Revenues (millions)	Foreign Revenues (percentage)
Exxon Mobil <www.exxonmobil.com>	$158,403	$228,439	69.3
IBM <www.ibm.com>	50,377	87,548	57.5
Ford <www.ford.com>	51,691	170,064	30.4
General Motors <www.gm.com>	48,233	184,632	26.1
PepsiCo <www.pepsico.com>	7,259	20,438	35.5

Source: Form 10-K of each company.

PepsiCo's annual report contains the following description of this division's international operations:

> Frito-Lay International manufactures, markets, sells and distributes salty and sweet snacks. Products include Walkers brand snack foods in the United Kingdom, Smith's brand snack foods in Australia, Sabritas brand snack foods and Alegro and Gamesa brand sweet snacks in Mexico. Many of our U.S. brands have been introduced internationally such as Lay's and Ruffles brand potato chips, Doritos and Tostitos brand tortilla chips, Fritos brand corn chips and Cheetos brand cheese-flavored snacks. Principal international snack markets include Mexico, the United Kingdom, Brazil, Spain, the Netherlands, Australia and South Africa.[7]

www.ibm.com

www.nestle.com

www.michelin.com
www.unilever.com
www.sony.com

Table 2 shows the extent of the foreign revenues of five large U.S. corporations. IBM, for example, has operations in 80 countries and receives almost 60 percent of its sales from outside the United States. Other industrial countries, such as Switzerland, France, Germany, Great Britain, the Netherlands, and Japan, have also given rise to numerous worldwide corporations. Nestlé, the large Swiss food company, makes 98 percent of its sales outside Switzerland. Other companies that make more than half their sales outside their home countries include Michelin, the French tire maker; Unilever, the British/Netherlands consumer products company; and Sony, the Japanese electronics company. More than five hundred companies are listed on at least one stock exchange outside their home countries.

KEY POINT: Foreign investment in U.S. companies is widespread, as is U.S. investment in foreign companies.

Sophisticated investors no longer restrict their investment activities to domestic securities markets. Many Americans invest in foreign securities markets, and non-Americans invest heavily in the stock market in the United States. Figure 1 shows that from 1980 to 1999, the total value of securities traded on the world's stock markets increased over twentyfold, with the U.S. share of the pie declining from 55 to 51 percent.

EFFECTS OF FOREIGN BUSINESS TRANSACTIONS

KEY POINT: Conducting international business causes two accounting problems for U.S. companies. First, the use of different currencies creates a translation problem. Second, foreign companies often do not follow U.S. accounting standards, which creates comparability problems.

Foreign business transactions have two major effects on accounting. First, most sales or purchases of goods and services in other countries involve different currencies. Thus, one currency needs to be translated into another, using exchange rates.* An **exchange rate** is the value of one currency stated in terms of another. For example, an English company purchasing goods from a U.S. company and paying in U.S. dollars must exchange British pounds for U.S. dollars before making payment. In effect, currencies are goods that can be bought and sold. Table 3 lists the exchange rates of several currencies in terms of dollars. It shows the exchange rate for the British

---

*At the time this chapter was written, exchange rates were fluctuating rapidly. The examples, exercises, and problems in this book use exchange rates in the general range for the countries involved.

FIGURE 1
Value of Securities Traded on the World's Stock Markets

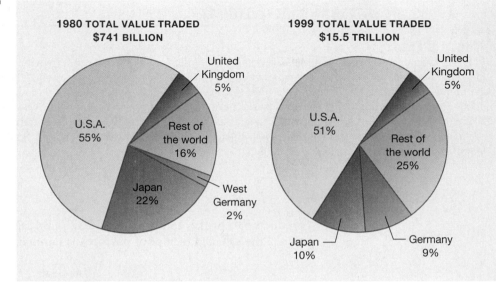

Source: International Finance Corporation, *Emerging Stock Markets Factbook,* © 2000.

● **STOP AND THINK!**

Why is this recent headline—"Weak Euro Gives U.S. Companies Fiscal Indigestion"—true for some U.S. companies but not for others?

A weak euro means the dollar is strong (the dollar buys more euros). This makes American goods more expensive to sell in international markets and foreign goods less expensive to purchase. Thus, a weak euro hurts American companies that export and helps American companies that import. ■

KEY POINT: A U.S. company must use dollars to record sales and purchases in its records.

KEY POINT: When both parties to a transaction deal in the same currency, no foreign currency problem exists. When the parties deal in different currencies, however, the fluctuating exchange rates create a need for special accounting procedures.

pound as $1.41. Like the price of any good or service, these prices change daily according to supply and demand. Accounting for these price changes in recording foreign transactions and preparing financial statements for foreign subsidiaries are discussed in the next two sections.

The second major effect of international business on accounting is that financial standards differ from country to country, which makes it difficult to compare companies from different countries. The obstacles to achieving comparability and some of the progress in solving the problem are discussed later in this chapter.

ACCOUNTING FOR TRANSACTIONS IN FOREIGN CURRENCIES

A U.S. manufacturer may expand by selling its product to foreign customers, or it may lower its product cost by buying a less expensive part from a source in another country. In previous chapters, all purchases and sales were recorded in dollars, and it was assumed that the dollar is a uniform measure in the same way that the inch and the centimeter are. But in the international marketplace, a transaction may take place in Japanese yen, British pounds, or some other currency. The values of these currencies in relation to the dollar rise and fall daily. Thus, if there is a delay between the date of sale or purchase and the date of receipt or payment, the amount of cash involved may differ from that originally agreed upon.

■ **FOREIGN SALES**   When a domestic company sells merchandise abroad, it may bill either in its own country's currency or in the foreign currency. If the billing and payment are both in the domestic currency, no accounting problem arises. For example, assume that a U.S. maker of precision tools sells $160,000 worth of its

TABLE 3.   Partial Listing of Foreign Exchange Rates

Country	Price in $ U.S.	Country	Price in $ U.S.
Britain (pound)	1.41	Hong Kong (dollar)	.13
Canada (dollar)	.63	Japan (yen)	.008
Europe (euro)	.86	Mexico (peso)	.11

Source: The Wall Street Journal, January 31, 2002.

FOCUS ON INTERNATIONAL BUSINESS

What's a Euro?

In 2002, European countries, with the exception of the United Kingdom and Denmark, adopted a single currency called the euro, thus eliminating the French franc, German mark, and other European currencies. While individuals have had to adjust to the new coins and bills, the change has affected companies as well. For example, PepsiCo <www.pepsico.com> identified a number of issues raised by the euro. Among these were "the need to adapt computer and financial systems, business processes and equipment, such as vending machines, to accommodate euro-denominated transactions and the impact of one currency on pricing." PepsiCo also noted that "due to numerous uncertainties, we cannot reasonably estimate the long-term effects."[8]

products to a British company and bills the British company in dollars. The entry to record the sale and receipt of payment is familiar:

Date of Sale

A = L + OE	Accounts Receivable, British company	160,000	
+ +	Sales		160,000

Date of Receipt

A = L + OE	Cash	160,000	
+ −	Accounts Receivable, British company		160,000

KEY POINT: Exchange gains and losses occur when there is a timing difference between sale and receipt and a change in the exchange rate occurs. The larger the time span, the more likely it is that a difference will occur.

However, if the U.S. company bills the British company in British pounds and accepts payment in pounds, the U.S. company may incur an **exchange gain or loss**. A gain or loss will occur if the exchange rate between dollars and pounds changes between the date of sale and the date of receipt. Since gains and losses tend to offset one another, a single account is used during the year to accumulate the activity. The net exchange gain or loss is reported on the income statement. For example, assume that the sale of $160,000 above was billed at £100,000, reflecting an exchange rate of 1.60 (that is, $1.60 per pound) on the sale date. Now assume that by the date of receipt, the exchange rate has fallen to 1.50. The entries to record the transactions follow:

Date of Sale

A = L + OE	Accounts Receivable, British company	160,000	
+ +	Sales		160,000
	£100,000 × $1.60 = $160,000		

Date of Receipt

A = L + OE	Cash	150,000	
+ −	Exchange Gain or Loss	10,000	
−	Accounts Receivable, British company		160,000
	£100,000 × $1.50 = $150,000		

The U.S. company has incurred an exchange loss of $10,000 because it agreed to accept a fixed number of British pounds in payment for its products, , and the value of each pound dropped before the payment was made. Had the value of the pound in relation to the dollar increased, the U.S. company would have made an exchange gain.

■ **FOREIGN PURCHASES** The same logic applies to purchases as to sales, except that the relationship of exchange gains and losses to changes in exchange rates is reversed. For example, assume that the U.S. toolmaker purchases parts from a

Japanese supplier for $15,000. If the purchase and payment are made in U.S. dollars, no accounting problem arises.

Date of Purchase

A = L + OE				
+	−	Purchases	15,000	
		Accounts Payable, Japanese company		15,000

Date of Payment

A = L + OE				
−	−	Accounts Payable, Japanese company	15,000	
		Cash		15,000

However, the Japanese company may bill the U.S. company in yen and be paid in yen. If so, the U.S. company will incur an exchange gain or loss if the exchange rate changes between the date of purchase and the date of payment. For example, assume that the transaction is for ¥2,500,000 and that the exchange rates on the dates of purchase and payment are $.0090 and $.0085 per yen, respectively. The entries are as follows:

Date of Purchase

A = L + OE				
+	−	Purchases	22,500	
		Accounts Payable, Japanese company		22,500
		¥2,500,000 × $.0090 = $22,500		

Date of Payment

A = L + OE				
−	− +	Accounts Payable, Japanese company	22,500	
		Exchange Gain or Loss		1,250
		Cash		21,250
		¥2,500,000 × $.0085 = $21,250		

In this case, the U.S. company received an exchange gain of $1,250 because it agreed to pay a fixed ¥2,500,000, and between the dates of purchase and payment, the exchange value of the yen decreased in relation to the dollar.

■ **REALIZED VERSUS UNREALIZED EXCHANGE GAIN OR LOSS** The preceding illustrations dealt with completed transactions (in the sense that payment was made). In each case, the exchange gain or loss was recognized on the date of receipt or payment. If financial statements are prepared between the sale or purchase and the receipt or payment and exchange rates have changed, there will be unrealized gains or losses. The Financial Accounting Standards Board's *Statement No. 52* requires that exchange gains and losses "be included in determining net income for the period in which the exchange rate changes."[9] The requirement includes interim (quarterly) statements and applies whether or not a transaction is complete.

This ruling has caused much debate. Critics charge that it gives too much weight to fleeting changes in exchange rates, causing random changes in earnings that hide long-run trends. Others believe that the use of current exchange rates to value receivables and payables as of the balance sheet date is a major step toward economic reality (current values). To illustrate, we use the preceding case, in which a U.S. company buys parts from a Japanese supplier. We assume that the transaction has not been completed by the balance sheet date, when the exchange rate is $.0080 per yen:

KEY POINT: Cash flows are not affected by unrealized exchange gains and losses. The cash effect is ultimately determined when the transactions are complete and exchange gains or losses are realized.

Date		Exchange Rate ($ per Yen)
Date of purchase	Dec. 1	.0090
Balance sheet date	Dec. 31	.0080
Date of payment	Feb. 1	.0085

The accounting effects of the unrealized gain are as follows:

	Dec. 1	Dec. 31	Feb. 1
Purchase recorded in U.S. dollars (billed as ¥2,500,000)	$22,500	$22,500	$22,500
Dollars to be paid to equal ¥2,500,000 (¥2,500,000 × exchange rate)	22,500	20,000	21,250
Unrealized gain (or loss)	—	$ 2,500	
Realized gain (or loss)			$ 1,250

A = L + OE
    +   −
	Dec. 1	Purchases
		    Accounts Payable, Japanese company
			22,500	22,500

A = L + OE
    −   +
	Dec. 31	Accounts Payable, Japanese company
		    Exchange Gain or Loss
			2,500	2,500

A = L + OE
    −   −   −
	Feb. 1	Accounts Payable, Japanese company
		    Exchange Gain or Loss
		    Cash
			20,000
			1,250
				21,250

In this case, the original sale was billed in yen by the Japanese company. Following the rules of *Statement No. 52*, an exchange gain of $2,500 is recorded on December 31, and an exchange loss of $1,250 is recorded on February 1. Even though these large fluctuations do not affect the net exchange gain of $1,250 for the whole transaction, the effect on each year's income statements may be important.

✓ Check out ACE for a Review Quiz at http://accounting.college.hmco.com/students.

RESTATEMENT OF FOREIGN SUBSIDIARY FINANCIAL STATEMENTS

LO4   Describe the restatement of a foreign subsidiary's financial statements in U.S. dollars.

RELATED TEXT ASSIGNMENTS
Q: 15
FRA: 3

⬢ **STOP AND THINK!**
Why do the financial statements of foreign subsidiaries need to be restated?

They need to be restated because they are in a currency other than the U.S. dollar, and the dollar must be used when the statements are consolidated with the U.S. parent company's financial statements. ■

Companies often expand by establishing or buying foreign subsidiaries. If a company owns more than 50 percent of a foreign subsidiary and thus exercises control, then the foreign subsidiary should be included in the consolidated financial statements. The reporting of foreign subsidiaries is covered by FASB *Statement No. 52*. The consolidation procedure is the same as the one we described for domestic subsidiaries, except that the statements of the foreign subsidiary must be restated in the reporting currency before consolidation takes place. The **reporting currency** is the currency in which the consolidated financial statements are presented, which for U.S. companies is usually the U.S. dollar. Clearly, it makes no sense to combine the assets of a Mexican subsidiary stated in pesos with the assets of the U.S. parent company stated in dollars. Thus, **restatement** in the currency of the parent company is necessary.

The method of restatement depends on the foreign subsidiary's **functional currency**, which is the currency of the place where the subsidiary carries on most of its business. Generally, it is the currency in which a company earns and spends its cash. The functional currency used depends on the kind of foreign operation in which the subsidiary takes part.

There are two broad types of foreign operation. Type I includes those that are fairly self-contained and integrated within a certain country or economy. Type II includes those that are mainly a direct and integral part or extension of the parent company's operations. As a rule, Type I subsidiaries use the currency of the country in which they are located, and Type II subsidiaries use the currency of the parent company. If the parent is a U.S. company, the functional currency of a Type I subsidiary will be the currency of the country where the subsidiary carries on its business, and the functional currency of a Type II subsidiary will be the U.S. dollar. *Statement No. 52* makes an exception when a Type I subsidiary operates in a country where there is hyperinflation (as a rule of thumb, more than 100 percent cumulative inflation over three years), such as Brazil or Argentina. In such a case, the subsidiary is treated as a Type II subsidiary, with the functional currency being the U.S. dollar. Restatements in these situations do not affect cash flows because they are done simply for the convenience of preparing consolidated statements.

✓ Check out ACE for a Review Quiz at http://accounting.college.hmco.com/students.

INTERNATIONAL ACCOUNTING STANDARDS

LO5 Describe the progress toward international accounting standards.

RELATED TEXT ASSIGNMENTS
Q: 16, 17
FRA: 2

International investors need to compare the financial position and results of operations of companies from different countries. At present, however, few standards of accounting are recognized worldwide.[10] For example, LIFO is the most popular method of valuing inventory in the United States, but it is not acceptable in most European countries. Historical cost is strictly followed in Germany, replacement cost is used by some companies in the Netherlands, and a mixed system, allowing lower of cost or market in some cases, is used in the United States and Britain. Even the formats of financial statements differ from country to country. In Britain and France, for example, the order of the balance sheets is almost the reverse of that in the United States. In those countries, property, plant, and equipment is the first listing in the assets section.

A number of major problems stand in the way of setting international standards. One is that accountants and users of accounting information have not been able to agree on the goals of financial statements. Differences in the way the accounting profession has developed in various countries, in the laws regulating

FOCUS ON INTERNATIONAL BUSINESS

How Do U.S. and U.K. GAAP Compare?

Many foreign companies that do business in the United States have started showing in the notes to their financial statements the major differences between income calculated under their countries' accounting rules and income calculated under U.S. GAAP. One of these companies is Cadbury Schweppes <www.cadburyschweppes.com>, the large British candy and beverage firm. The Financial Highlights presented here are adapted from that company's annual report.[11]

U.K. and U.S. GAAP differ significantly in accounting for intangibles, such as brand names, trademarks, and goodwill. For example, brand names carried as assets must be written off over time as amortization costs in the United States but not in the United Kingdom. Purchased goodwill may be written off against stockholders' equity in the United Kingdom, but until 2001, it had to be capitalized and amortized in the United States. Other differences relate to the timing of the recognition of property transactions and one-time charges, such as restruc-

turings. In addition, the United Kingdom does not generally require deferred taxation accounting, whereas the United States does.

The disclosures provided in the notes to Cadbury Schweppes's financial statements are very helpful in calculating the firm's profitability ratios and comparing them with those of U.S. companies.

Financial Highlights
(In millions of pounds)

	2000	1999
Income attributable to shareholders under U.K. GAAP	496	642
U.S. GAAP adjustments:		
Amortisation of goodwill and trademarks	(102)	(89)
Restructuring costs	9	—
Depreciation of capitalised interest	3	(6)
Pension costs	7	3
Exceptional item/Disposal gain adjustment	(22)	23
Timing of recognition of foreign currency hedges	2	(3)
SAYE/LTIP	(9)	—
Other items	(5)	—
Taxation on above adjustments	—	2
Deferred taxation	4	22
Net income under U.S. GAAP	383	594

companies, and in governmental and other requirements present other hurdles. Further difficulties are created by differences among countries in the basic economic factors affecting financial reporting, inconsistencies in practices recommended by the accounting profession in different countries, and the influence of tax laws on financial reporting.

Probably the best hopes for finding areas of agreement among different countries are the International Accounting Standards Board (IASB) and the International Federation of Accountants (IFAC).

The role of the IASB is to contribute to the development and adoption of accounting principles that are relevant, balanced, and comparable throughout the world by formulating and publicizing accounting standards and encouraging their observance in the presentation of financial statements.[12] The standards issued by the IASB are generally followed by large multinational companies that are clients of international accounting firms. The IASB has been especially helpful to companies in developing economies that do not have the financial history or resources to develop accounting standards. The IASB is currently engaged in a major project to improve financial reporting worldwide by introducing a set of international accounting standards that will be acceptable to the world's securities regulators, such as the SEC in the United States. If successful, the effort should make it easier for companies to raise equity capital and list their stocks in other countries.

The IFAC, formed in 1977, also includes most of the world's accountancy organizations. It fully supports the work of the IASB and recognizes the IASB as the sole body with responsibility and authority to issue pronouncements on international accounting standards. The IFAC's principal role is to assure quality audits and financial statements prepared in accordance with international accounting standards. It attempts to accomplish this objective by issuing international auditing standards and monitoring the practice of international firms.

The European Community is also attempting to harmonize accounting standards. One of its directives requires certain minimum, uniform reporting and disclosure standards for financial statements. Other directives deal with uniform rules for preparing consolidated financial statements and qualifications of auditors. More importantly, the European Community has agreed to require international accounting standards beginning in 2005 for all companies that seek financing across borders. This is an important step for recognition of international accounting standards and for the goal of a single European market. It will leave the United States as the only major market that does not accept international accounting standards.

The road to international harmony is not easy. However, there is reason for optimism because an increasing number of countries are recognizing the appropriateness of uniform accounting standards in international trade and commerce.

✔ Check out ACE for a Review Quiz at http://accounting.college.hmco.com/students.

ENHANCEMENT NOTE:
The two most important sets of accounting standards are U.S. GAAP and IASB international accounting standards. Which of these two will ultimately prevail as the world standard is yet to be determined.

◆ **STOP AND THINK!**
Why would some European companies prefer to use U.S. GAAP rather than international accounting standards?
It is easier for European companies to trade their stocks on U.S. stock exchanges if they follow U.S. GAAP. At present, international accounting standards are not accepted in the United States. ■

Chapter Review

REVIEW OF LEARNING OBJECTIVES

LO1 Identify the classifications of long-term investments in bonds and stocks and apply the cost-adjusted-to-market and equity methods as appropriate.

Long-term investments in bonds fall into two categories: available-for-sale securities, which are recorded at cost and subsequently accounted for at fair value; and held-to-maturity securities, which are accounted for at the amortized cost. Long-term stock investments fall into three categories: noninfluential and noncontrolling investments, which represent less than 20 percent ownership; influential but noncontrolling investments, which represent 20 percent to 50 percent ownership; and controlling investments, which represent more than 50 percent ownership.

The cost-adjusted-to-market method is used to account for noninfluential and noncontrolling investments in stock. Under this method, investments are initially recorded at cost and then adjusted to market value. The equity method is used to account for influential but noncontrolling investments. Under this method, the investment is initially recorded at cost and then adjusted for the investor's share of the company's net income or loss and subsequent dividends.

LO2 Identify the uses of consolidated financial statements, prepare a consolidated balance sheet at acquisition date using the purchase method, and prepare a consolidated income statement.

The FASB requires that consolidated financial statements be prepared when an investing company has legal and effective control over another company. Control exists when the parent company owns more than 50 percent of the voting stock of the subsidiary. Consolidated financial statements are useful to investors and others because they treat the parent company and its subsidiaries as an integrated economic unit.

When a consolidated balance sheet is prepared at the date of acquisition, a work sheet entry is made to eliminate the investment from the parent company's financial statements and the stockholders' equity section of the subsidiary's financial statements. The assets and liabilities of the two companies are combined. If the parent owns less than 100 percent of the subsidiary, minority interest equal to the percentage of the subsidiary owned by minority stockholders multiplied by the stockholders' equity in the subsidiary appears on the consolidated balance sheet. If the cost of the parent's investment in the subsidiary is greater than the subsidiary's book value, an amount equal to the excess of cost over book value is allocated to undervalued subsidiary assets and to goodwill. If the cost of the parent's investment in the subsidiary is less than book value, the excess of book value over cost should be used to reduce the book value of the subsidiary's long-term assets (other than long-term marketable securities).

When consolidated income statements are prepared, intercompany sales, purchases, interest income, interest expense, and other income and expenses from intercompany transactions must be eliminated to avoid double counting of these items.

LO3 Define *exchange rate* and record transactions that are affected by changes in foreign exchange rates.

An *exchange rate* is the value of one currency stated in terms of another. A domestic company may make sales or purchases abroad in either its own country's currency or a foreign currency. If a transaction (sale or purchase) and its resolution (receipt or payment) are made in the domestic currency, no accounting problem arises. However, if the transaction and its resolution are made in a foreign currency and the exchange rate changes between the time of the transaction and its resolution, an exchange gain or loss will occur and should be recorded.

LO4 Describe the restatement of a foreign subsidiary's financial statements in U.S. dollars.

Foreign financial statements are converted to U.S. dollars by multiplying the appropriate exchange rates by the amounts in the foreign financial statements. In general, the rates that apply depend on whether the subsidiary is separate and self-contained (Type I) or an integral part of the parent company (Type II).

LO5 Describe the progress toward international accounting standards.

There has been some progress toward establishing international accounting standards, especially through the efforts of the International Accounting Standards Board, the International Federation of Accountants, and the European Community. However, there still are serious inconsistencies in financial reporting among countries. These inconsistencies make the comparison of financial statements from different countries difficult.

REVIEW OF CONCEPTS AND TERMINOLOGY

The following concepts and terms were introduced in this chapter:

LO1 **Available-for-sale securities:** Investments in debt or equity securities that a company plans to sell at some point.

LO1 **Consolidated financial statements:** Financial statements that reflect the combined operations of a parent company and its subsidiaries.

LO1 **Control:** An investing company's ability to decide the operating and financial policies of another firm because it owns more than 50 percent of that firm's voting stock.

LO1 **Cost-adjusted-to-market method:** A method of accounting for available-for-sale securities at cost adjusted for changes in the market value of the securities.

LO2 **Eliminations:** Entries made on consolidation work sheets to eliminate transactions between parent and subsidiary companies.

LO1 **Equity method:** A method of accounting for influential but noncontrolling long-term investments in which the investment is initially recorded at cost and then adjusted for the investor's share of the company's net income or loss and subsequent dividends.

LO3   Exchange gain or loss: A gain or loss due to exchange rate fluctuation that is reported on the income statement.

LO3   Exchange rate: The value of one currency stated in terms of another.

LO4   Functional currency: The currency of the place where a subsidiary carries on most of its business.

LO2   Goodwill: The amount paid for a subsidiary that exceeds the fair value of the subsidiary's assets less its liabilities; also called *goodwill from consolidation*.

LO1   Held-to-maturity securities: Investments in debt or equity securities that a company plans to hold until their maturity date.

LO2   Minority interest: The amount recorded on a consolidated balance sheet that represents the holdings of owners of less than 50 percent of a subsidiary's voting stock.

LO3   Multinational (transnational) corporations: Companies that operate in more than one country.

LO1   Parent company: A company that has a controlling interest in another firm.

LO2   Purchase method: A method of accounting for controlling investments in which similar accounts from the parent's and subsidiaries' statements are combined.

LO4   Reporting currency: The currency used in consolidated financial statements.

LO4   Restatement: The stating of one currency in terms of another.

LO1   Significant influence: An investing company's ability to affect the operating and financial policies of the firm in which it has invested, even though it holds 50 percent or less of the voting stock.

LO1   Subsidiary: A firm in which another company owns a controlling interest.

REVIEW PROBLEM

Consolidated Balance Sheet: Less than 100 Percent Ownership

LO2   In a cash transaction, Taylor Company purchased 90 percent of the outstanding stock of Schumacher Company for $763,200 on June 30, 20xx. Directly after the acquisition, the separate balance sheets of the companies appeared as follows:

	Taylor Company	Schumacher Company
Assets		
Cash	$ 400,000	$ 48,000
Accounts receivable	650,000	240,000
Inventory	1,000,000	520,000
Investment in Schumacher Company	763,200	—
Plant and equipment (net)	1,500,000	880,000
Other assets	50,000	160,000
Total assets	$4,363,200	$1,848,000
Liabilities and Stockholders' Equity		
Accounts payable	$ 800,000	$ 400,000
Long-term debt	1,000,000	600,000
Common stock	2,000,000	800,000
Retained earnings	563,200	48,000
Total liabilities and stockholders' equity	$4,363,200	$1,848,000

The following additional information is available: (1) Schumacher Company's other assets represent a long-term investment in Taylor Company's long-term debt. The debt was purchased for an amount equal to Taylor's carrying value of the debt. (2) Taylor Company owes Schumacher Company $100,000 for services rendered.

REQUIRED ▶   Prepare a work sheet for preparing a consolidated balance sheet as of the acquisition date.

ANSWER TO REVIEW PROBLEM

Taylor and Schumacher Companies
Work Sheet for Consolidated Balance Sheet
June 30, 20xx

Accounts	Balance Sheet, Taylor Company	Balance Sheet, Schumacher Company	Eliminations Debit	Eliminations Credit	Consolidated Balance Sheet
Cash	400,000	48,000			448,000
Accounts receivable	650,000	240,000		(3) 100,000	790,000
Inventory	1,000,000	520,000			1,520,000
Investment in					
Schumacher Company	763,200	—		(1) 763,200	
Plant and equipment (net)	1,500,000	880,000			2,380,000
Other assets	50,000	160,000		(2) 160,000	50,000
Total assets	4,363,200	1,848,000			5,188,000
Accounts payable	800,000	400,000	(3) 100,000		1,100,000
Long-term debt	1,000,000	600,000	(2) 160,000		1,440,000
Common stock	2,000,000	800,000	(1) 800,000		2,000,000
Retained earnings	563,200	48,000	(1) 48,000		563,200
Minority interest	—	—		(1) 84,800	84,800
Total liabilities and					
stockholders' equity	4,363,200	1,848,000	1,108,000	1,108,000	5,188,000

(1) Elimination of intercompany investment. Minority interest equals 10 percent of Schumacher Company's stockholders' equity [10% × ($800,000 + $48,000) = $84,800].

(2) Elimination of intercompany long-term debt.

(3) Elimination of intercompany receivables and payables.

Chapter Assignments

BUILDING YOUR KNOWLEDGE FOUNDATION

QUESTIONS

1. Why are the concepts of significant influence and control important in accounting for long-term investments?

2. For each of the following categories of long-term investments, briefly describe the applicable percentage of ownership and accounting treatment: (a) noninfluential

and noncontrolling investment, (b) influential but noncontrolling investment, and (c) controlling investment.

3. What is a parent-subsidiary relationship?

4. Would the stockholders of American Home Products Corporation be more interested in the consolidated financial statements of the overall company than in the statements of its many subsidiaries? Explain.

5. Merchant's summary of significant accounting policies also contained this statement: "*Investments.* Investments in companies in which Merchant has significant influence in management are on the equity basis." What is the equity method of accounting for investments, and why did Merchant use it in this case?

6. The 2000 annual report of Merchant Corporation included the following statement in its summary of significant accounting policies: "*Principles applied in consolidation.* Majority-owned subsidiaries are consolidated, except for leasing and finance companies and those subsidiaries not considered to be material." What accounting rule does this practice violate, and why?

7. Why should intercompany receivables, payables, sales, and purchases be eliminated in the preparation of consolidated financial statements?

8. The following item appears on Merchant's consolidated balance sheet: "Minority Interest—$50,000." Explain how this item arose and where you would expect to find it on the consolidated balance sheet.

9. Why may the price paid to acquire a controlling interest in a subsidiary company exceed the subsidiary's book value?

10. The following item also appears on Merchant's consolidated balance sheet: "Goodwill from Consolidation—$70,000." Explain how this item arose and where you would expect to find it on the consolidated balance sheet.

11. Subsidiary Corporation has a book value of $100,000, of which Parent Corporation purchases 100 percent for $115,000. None of the excess of cost over book value is attributed to tangible assets. What is the amount of goodwill from consolidation?

12. Subsidiary Corporation, a wholly-owned subsidiary, has total sales of $500,000, $100,000 of which were made to Parent Corporation. Parent Corporation has total sales of $1,000,000. What is the amount of sales on the consolidated income statement?

13. What does it mean to say that the exchange rate for the euro in terms of the U.S. dollar is .95? If a bottle of French perfume costs 50 euros, how much will it cost in dollars?

14. If a U.S. company does business with a foreign company and all their transactions take place in the foreign currency, which company may incur exchange gains or losses, and why?

15. What is the difference between a functional currency and a reporting currency?

16. If you as an investor were trying to evaluate the relative performance of General Motors, Volkswagen, and Toyota Motors from their published financial statements, what problems might you encounter (other than a language problem)?

17. What are some of the obstacles to uniform international accounting standards, and what efforts are being made to overcome them?

SHORT EXERCISES

LO1 Cost-Adjusted-to-Market Method

SE 1. On December 31, 20x1, the market value of Cedar Deck Company's portfolio of long-term available-for-sale securities was $320,000. The cost of these securities was $285,000. Prepare the entry to adjust the portfolio to market at year end, assuming that the company did not have any long-term investments prior to 20x1.

LO1 Cost-Adjusted-to-Market Method

SE 2. Refer to your answer to **SE 1.** Assume that on December 31, 20x2, the cost of Cedar Deck Company's portfolio of long-term available-for-sale securities was $640,000 and that its market value was $600,000. Prepare the entry to record the 20x2 year-end adjustment.

LO1 Equity Method

SE 3. Sturchio Company owns 30 percent of Raymond Company. In 20x1, Raymond Company earned $120,000 and paid $80,000 in dividends. Prepare entries in journal form for Sturchio Company's records on December 31 to reflect this information. Assume that the dividends are received on December 31.

SE 4.
LO1 Methods of Accounting for
LO2 Long-Term Investments

For each of the investments listed below, tell which of the following methods should be used for external financial reporting: (a) cost-adjusted-to-market method, (b) equity method, (c) consolidation of parent and subsidiary financial statements.

1. 49 percent investment in Motir Corporation
2. 51 percent investment in Saris Corporation
3. 5 percent investment in Ransor Corporation

SE 5.
LO2 Purchase of 100 Percent at
Book Value

Maple House Corporation buys 100 percent ownership of Winter Sweets Corporation for $50,000. At the time of the purchase, Winter Sweets' stockholders' equity consists of $10,000 in common stock and $40,000 in retained earnings, and Maple House's stockholders' equity consists of $100,000 in common stock and $200,000 in retained earnings. After the purchase, what would be the amount, if any, of the following accounts on the consolidated balance sheet: Goodwill, Minority Interest, Common Stock, and Retained Earnings?

SE 6.
LO2 Purchase of Less than 100
Percent at Book Value

Assume the same facts as in **SE 5** except that Maple House purchased 80 percent of Winter Sweets Corporation for $40,000. After the purchase, what would be the amount, if any, of the following accounts on the consolidated balance sheet: Goodwill, Minority Interest, Common Stock, and Retained Earnings?

SE 7.
LO2 Purchase of 100 Percent at
More than Book Value

Assume the same facts as in **SE 5** except that the purchase of 100 percent of Winter Sweets Corporation was for $60,000. After the purchase, what would be the amount, if any, of the following accounts on the consolidated balance sheet: Goodwill, Minority Interest, Common Stock, and Retained Earnings? Assume that the fair value of Winter Sweets' net assets equals their book value.

SE 8.
LO2 Intercompany Transactions

T Company owns 100 percent of C Company. The following are accounts from the balance sheets and income statements of both companies:

	T Company	C Company
Accounts Receivable	$ 230,000	$150,000
Accounts Payable	180,000	90,000
Sales	1,200,000	890,000
Cost of Goods Sold	710,000	540,000

What would be the combined amount of each of the above accounts on the consolidated financial statements assuming the following additional information: (1) C Company sold to T Company merchandise at cost in the amount of $270,000; (2) T Company sold all the merchandise it bought from C Company to customers, but it still owes C Company $60,000 for the merchandise.

SE 9.
LO3 Recording Sales: Fluctuating
Exchange Rate

Prepare an entry to record a sale by a U.S. company on account on September 12 in the amount of C$ 420,000 to a Canadian company. Also, record the subsequent collection in full in Canadian dollars on October 12. On September 12 the exchange rate was $.60 per C$ 1, and on October 12 it was $.50 per C$ 1.

SE 10.
LO3 Recording Purchases:
Fluctuating Exchange Rate

Prepare an entry to record a purchase by a U.S. company on account on September 12 in the amount of C$ 420,000 from a Canadian company. Also record the subsequent payment in full in Canadian dollars on October 12. On September 12 the exchange rate was $.60 per C$ 1, and on October 12 it was $.50 per C$ 1.

EXERCISES

E 1.
LO1 Long-Term Investments

Fenster Corporation has the following portfolio of long-term available-for-sale securities at year end:

Company	Percentage of Voting Stock Held	Cost	Year-End Market Value
A Corporation	4	$160,000	$190,000
B Corporation	12	750,000	550,000
C Corporation	5	60,000	110,000
Total		$970,000	$850,000

Both the Unrealized Loss on Long-Term Investments account and the Allowance to Adjust Long-Term Investments to Market account currently have a balance of $80,000 from the last accounting period. Prepare the year-end adjustment to reflect the information listed.

E 2.
LO1 Long-Term Investments: Cost-Adjusted-to-Market and Equity Methods

On January 1, O'Byrne Corporation purchased, as long-term investments, 8 percent of the voting stock of Magda Corporation for $500,000 and 45 percent of the voting stock of Sumari Corporation for $2 million. During the year, Magda Corporation had earnings of $200,000 and paid dividends of $80,000. Sumari Corporation had earnings of $600,000 and paid dividends of $400,000. The market value of neither investment changed during the year. Which of these investments should be accounted for using the cost-adjusted-to-market method? Which should be accounted for using the equity method? At what amount should each investment be carried on the balance sheet at year end? Give a reason for each choice.

E 3.
LO1 Long-Term Investments: Equity Method

On January 1, 20xx, Orcola Corporation acquired 40 percent of the voting stock of Visnjics Corporation, an amount sufficient to exercise significant influence over Visnjics Corporation's activities, for $2,400,000 in cash. On December 31, Orcola determined that Visnjics paid dividends of $400,000 but incurred a net loss of $200,000 for 20xx. Prepare journal entries in Orcola Corporation's records to reflect this information.

E 4.
LO1 Methods of Accounting for
LO2 Long-Term Investments

Diversified Corporation has the following long-term investments:

1. 60 percent of the common stock of Tunis Corporation
2. 13 percent of the common stock of Iron Dale, Inc.
3. 50 percent of the nonvoting preferred stock of Perton Corporation
4. 100 percent of the common stock of its financing subsidiary, DJD, Inc.
5. 35 percent of the common stock of the French company Rue de la Variété
6. 70 percent of the common stock of the Canadian company Nova Scotia Fisheries

For each of these investments, tell which of the following methods should be used for external financial reporting, and why:

a. Cost-adjusted-to-market method
b. Equity method
c. Consolidation of parent and subsidiary financial statements

E 5.
LO2 Elimination Entry for a Purchase at Book Value

Panda Manufacturing Company purchased 100 percent of the common stock of Soule Manufacturing Company for $300,000. Soule's stockholders' equity included common stock of $200,000 and retained earnings of $100,000. Prepare the eliminating entry in journal form that would appear on the work sheet for consolidating the balance sheets of these two entities as of the acquisition date.

E 6.
LO2 Elimination Entry and Minority Interest

The stockholders' equity section of Carney Corporation's balance sheet appeared as follows on December 31:

Common stock, $10 par value, 40,000 shares authorized and issued	$400,000
Retained earnings	48,000
Total stockholders' equity	$448,000

Souris Manufacturing Company owns 80 percent of Carney's voting stock and paid $11.20 per share. In journal form, prepare the entry (including minority interest) to eliminate Souris's investment and Carney's stockholders' equity that would appear on the work sheet used in preparing the consolidated balance sheet for the two firms.

E 7.
LO2 Consolidated Balance Sheet with Goodwill

On September 1, 20x1, A Company purchased 100 percent of the voting stock of B Company for $960,000 in cash. The separate condensed balance sheets immediately after the purchase were as follows:

	A Company	B Company
Other assets	$2,206,000	$1,089,000
Investment in B Company	960,000	—
Total assets	$3,166,000	$1,089,000
Liabilities	$ 871,000	$ 189,000
Common stock	1,000,000	300,000
Retained earnings	1,295,000	600,000
Total liabilities and stockholders' equity	$3,166,000	$1,089,000

Prepare a work sheet for preparing the consolidated balance sheet immediately after A Company acquired control of B Company. Assume that any excess cost of

A Company's investment in the subsidiary over book value is attributable to goodwill from consolidation.

E 8.

LO2 Preparation of Consolidated Income Statement

Barr Company has owned 100 percent of Guido Company since 20x0. The income statements of these two companies for the year ended December 31, 20x1, follow.

	Barr Company	Guido Company
Net sales	$3,000,000	$1,200,000
Cost of goods sold	1,500,000	800,000
Gross margin	$1,500,000	$ 400,000
Less: Selling expenses	$ 500,000	$ 100,000
General and administrative expenses	600,000	200,000
Total operating expenses	$1,100,000	$ 300,000
Income from operations	$ 400,000	$ 100,000
Other income	120,000	—
Net income	$ 520,000	$ 100,000

The following is additional information: (1) Guido Company purchased $560,000 of inventory from Barr Company, which it had sold to Guido customers by the end of the year. (2) Guido Company leased its building from Barr Company for $120,000 per year. Prepare a consolidated income statement work sheet for the two companies for the year ended December 31, 20x1. Ignore income taxes.

E 9.

LO3 Recording International Transactions: Fluctuating Exchange Rate

Wooster Corporation purchased a special-purpose machine from Konigsberg Corporation on credit for E 50,000. At the date of purchase, the exchange rate was $.90 per euro. On the date of the payment, which was made in euros, the value of the euro was $.95. Prepare entries in journal form to record the purchase and payment in Wooster Corporation's accounting records.

E 10.

LO3 Recording International Transactions: Fluctuating Exchange Rate

U.S. Corporation made a sale on account to U.K. Company on November 15 in the amount of £300,000. Payment was to be made in British pounds on February 15. U.S. Corporation's fiscal year is the same as the calendar year. The British pound was worth $1.70 on November 15, $1.58 on December 31, and $1.78 on February 15. Prepare entries in journal form to record the sale, year-end adjustment, and collection on U.S. Corporation's books.

PROBLEMS

P 1.

LO1 Long-Term Investment Transactions

On January 2, 20x3, the Fleider Company made several long-term investments in the voting stock of various companies. It purchased 10,000 shares of Malo at $2.00 a share, 15,000 shares of Tsu at $3.00 a share, and 6,000 shares of Rantana at $4.50 a share. Each investment represents less than 20 percent of the voting stock of the company. The remaining securities transactions of Fleider during 20x3 were as follows:

May 15 Purchased with cash 6,000 shares of Voss stock for $3.00 per share. This investment represents less than 20 percent of the Voss voting stock.

July 16 Sold the 10,000 shares of Malo stock for $1.80 per share.

Sept. 30 Purchased with cash 5,000 additional shares of Tsu for $3.20 per share. This investment still represents less than 20 percent of the voting stock.

Dec. 31 The market values per share of the stock in the Long-Term Investments account were as follows: Tsu, $3.25; Rantana, $4.00; and Voss, $2.00.

Fleider's transactions in securities during 20x4 were as follows:

Feb. 1 Received a cash dividend from Tsu of $.10 per share.

July 15 Sold the 6,000 Rantana shares for $4.00 per share.

Aug.   1   Received a cash dividend from Tsu of $.10 per share.
Sept. 10   Purchased 3,000 shares of Ryan for $7.00 per share. This investment represents less than 20 percent of the voting stock of the company.
Dec. 31   The market values per share of the stock in the Long-Term Investments account were as follows: Tsu, $3.25; Voss, $2.50; and Ryan, $6.50.

REQUIRED ▶

1. Prepare entries in journal form to record all Fleider Company's transactions in long-term investments during 20x3 and 20x4.
2. Assume that Fleider increased its ownership in Tsu to 25 percent and its ownership in Ryan to 60 percent in 20x5. How would these actions affect the methods used to account for the investments?

P 2.
LO1 Long-Term Investments: Equity Method

Cathay Corporation owns 35 percent of the voting stock of Mitgang Corporation. The Investment account on Cathay's books as of January 1, 20xx, was $360,000. During 20xx, Mitgang reported the following quarterly earnings and dividends:

Quarter	Earnings	Dividends Paid
1	$ 80,000	$ 50,000
2	120,000	50,000
3	60,000	50,000
4	(40,000)	50,000
	$220,000	$200,000

Because of the percentage of voting shares Cathay owns, it can exercise significant influence over the operations of Mitgang Corporation. Therefore, Cathay Corporation must account for the investment using the equity method.

REQUIRED ▶

1. Prepare the entries in journal form that Cathay Corporation must make each quarter to record its share of earnings and dividends.
2. Prepare a T account for Cathay's investment in Mitgang, and enter the beginning balance, the relevant entries from 1, and the ending balance.
3. What is the effect on cash flow of Cathay's ownership of Mitgang, and where would it appear on the statement of cash flows?

P 3.
LO2 Consolidated Balance Sheet: Less than 100 Percent Ownership

The Rivera Corporation purchased 80 percent of the voting stock of the Toona Corporation for $410,400 in cash. The balance sheets of the two companies immediately after the acquisition appear below.

	Rivera Corporation	Toona Corporation
Assets		
Cash	$ 75,000	$ 30,000
Accounts receivable	180,000	100,000
Inventory	800,000	350,000
Investment in Toona Corporation	410,400	—
Property, plant, and equipment (net)	1,250,000	500,000
Other assets	50,000	20,000
Total assets	$2,765,400	$1,000,000
Liabilities and Stockholders' Equity		
Accounts payable	$ 200,000	$ 75,000
Salaries payable	25,000	10,000
Taxes payable	10,000	2,000
Bonds payable	650,000	400,000
Common stock	1,250,000	450,000
Retained earnings	630,400	63,000
Total liabilities and stockholders' equity	$2,765,400	$1,000,000

The following additional information is available: (1) The Other Assets account on Toona Corporation's balance sheet represents an investment in Rivera's Bonds Payable. The investment in Rivera's bonds was made at an amount equal to Rivera's carrying value of the bonds. (2) Of the Accounts Receivable of Rivera Corporation, $25,000 is due from Toona.

REQUIRED ▶ Prepare a work sheet for a consolidated balance sheet as of the acquisition date.

P 4.

LO2 Consolidated Balance Sheet: Cost Exceeding Book Value

The balance sheets of Nickels and Cartters Corporations as of December 31, 20xx, are as follows:

	Nickels Corporation	Cartters Corporation
Assets		
Cash	$ 300,000	$ 60,000
Accounts receivable	350,000	300,000
Inventory	125,000	300,000
Investment in Cartters Corporation	400,000	—
Property, plant, and equipment (net)	675,000	425,000
Other assets	10,000	25,000
Total assets	$1,860,000	$1,110,000
Liabilities and Stockholders' Equity		
Accounts payable	$ 375,000	$ 250,000
Salaries payable	150,000	135,000
Bonds payable	175,000	400,000
Common stock	750,000	250,000
Retained earnings	410,000	75,000
Total liabilities and stockholders' equity	$1,860,000	$1,110,000

REQUIRED ▶ Prepare a consolidated balance sheet work sheet for the two companies, assuming that Nickels purchased 100 percent of the common stock of Cartters for $400,000 immediately prior to December 31, 20xx, and that $35,000 of the excess of cost over book value is attributable to the increased value of Cartters Corporation's inventory. The rest of the excess is considered goodwill.

P 5.

LO3 International Transactions

Dolfsky Import/Export Company, whose year end is October 31, engaged in the following transactions (exchange rates in parentheses):

Aug. 12 Sold goods to a Mexican firm for $20,000; terms n/30 in U.S. dollars (peso = $.131).

24 Purchased goods from a Japanese firm for $40,000; terms n/20 in yen (yen = $.0080).

Sept. 2 Sold goods to a British firm for $48,000; terms n/30 in pounds (pound = $1.60).

11 Received payment in full for August 12 sale (peso = $.128).

13 Paid for the goods purchased on August 24 (yen = $.0088).

21 Purchased goods from an Italian firm for $28,000; terms n/10 in U.S. dollars (euro = $.90).

30 Purchased goods from a Japanese firm for $35,200; terms n/60 in yen (yen = $.0088).

Oct. 2 Paid for the goods purchased on September 21 (euro = $.85).

3 Received payment in full for the goods sold on September 2 (pound = $1.50).

8 Sold goods to a French firm for $66,000; terms n/30 in euros (euro = $.88).

19 Purchased goods from a Mexican firm for $37,000; terms n/30 in U.S. dollars (peso = $.135).

Oct. 31   Made year-end adjusting entries for incomplete foreign exchange transactions (euro = $.85; peso = $.130; pound = $1.40; yen = $.0100).

Nov. 9   Received payment for the goods sold on October 8 (euro = $.87).

    18   Paid for the goods purchased on October 19 (peso = $.132).

    28   Paid for the goods purchased on September 30 (yen = $.0090).

REQUIRED ▶   Prepare entries in journal form for these transactions.

ALTERNATE PROBLEMS

P 6.

LO1 Long-Term Investment Transactions

Fallon Corportion made the following transactions in its Long-Term Investments account over a two-year period:

20x2

Apr. 1   Purchased with cash 20,000 shares of Levine Company stock for $76 per share.

June 1   Purchased with cash 15,000 shares of Brown Corporation stock for $36 per share.

Sept. 1   Received a $.50 per share dividend from Levine Company.

Nov. 1   Purchased with cash 25,000 shares of Dault Corporation stock for $55 per share.

Dec. 31   Market values per share of shares held in the Long-Term Investments account were as follows: Levine Company, $70; Brown Corporation, $16; and Dault Corporation, $61.

20x3

Feb. 1   Because of unfavorable prospects for Brown Corporation, Brown stock was sold for cash at $20 per share.

May 1   Purchased with cash 10,000 shares of Honey Corporation for $112 per share.

Sept. 1   Received $1 per share dividend from Levine Company.

Dec. 31   Market values per share of shares held in the Long-Term Investments account were as follows: Levine Company, $80; Dault Corporation, $70; and Honey Corporation, $100.

REQUIRED ▶

1. Prepare entries to record these transactions. Assume that all investments represent less than 20 percent of the voting stock of the company whose stock was acquired.
2. Assume that Fallon increased its ownership in Honey to 28 percent and its ownership in Dault to 55 percent in 20x4. How would these actions affect the methods used to account for the investments?

P 7.

LO1 Long-Term Investments: Equity Method

Bon Company owns 40 percent of the voting stock of Macree Company. The Investment account for this company on Bon's balance sheet had a balance of $300,000 on January 1, 20xx. During 20xx, the Macree Company reported the following quarterly earnings and dividends paid:

Quarter	Earnings	Dividends Paid
1	$ 40,000	$20,000
2	30,000	20,000
3	80,000	20,000
4	(20,000)	20,000
	$130,000	$80,000

Bon Company exercises a significant influence over the operations of Macree Company and therefore uses the equity method to account for its investment.

REQUIRED ▶

1. Prepare the journal entries that Bon Company must make each quarter in accounting for its investment in Macree.
2. Prepare a T account for the investment in Macree Company's common stock. Enter the beginning balance, relevant portions of the entries made in 1, and the ending balance.
3. What is the effect on cash flow of Bon's ownership of Macree, and where would it appear on the statement of cash flows?

SKILLS DEVELOPMENT CASES

Conceptual Analysis

SD 1.

LO3 Effects of Changes in Exchange Rates

Compagnie Générale des Etablissements Michelin <www.michelin.com>, the famous French manufacturer of Michelin tires, is one of the world's largest tiremakers. The company also owns the former U.S. tiremaker Uniroyal Goodrich Tire Company. In recent years, Michelin's sales of tires made in France, exported to the United States, and sold in dollars have been enhanced by a relatively strong dollar. Explain why a strong dollar relative to the euro would lead to an increase in Michelin's sales. Why are sales of Uniroyal Goodrich in the United States not relevant to a discussion of the effects of a strong dollar?

SD 2.

LO3 Effects of Changes in Exchange Rates

Japan Airlines Co. Ltd. <www.japanair.com>, one of the world's top-ranking airlines, has an extensive global network of passenger and cargo services. The company engages in sales and purchase transactions throughout the world. At the end of the year, it has receivables and payables in many currencies that must be translated into yen so that its consolidated financial statements can be prepared. The company's annual report notes that these receivables and payables are translated at the applicable year-end rates. What will be the effects (exchange gain or loss) under each of the following assumptions about changes in the exchange rates that occurred after the transactions that gave rise to the receivables or payables? (1) Receivables exceed payables, and, on average, the yen has risen relative to other currencies. (2) Receivables exceed payables, and, on average, the yen has fallen relative to other currencies. (3) Payables exceed receivables, and, on average, the yen has risen relative to other currencies. (4) Payables exceed receivables, and, on average, the yen has fallen relative to other currencies. Suggest some ways in which Japan Airlines can minimize the effects of the fluctuations in exchange rates as they relate to receivables and payables.

Ethical Dilemma

SD 3.

LO1 Insider Trading

Refer to the Focus on Business Ethics box about insider trading in this chapter to answer the following questions:

1. What does insider trading mean?
2. Why do you think insider trading is illegal in the United States and Germany?
3. Why do you think insider trading is permissible in some other countries?
4. Do you think the prohibition of insider trading in the United States is the correct approach? Why or why not?

 *Group Activity:* Divide the class into groups to discuss the above questions. Also ask them to consider why definitions of unethical behavior differ from country to country. Debrief in class.

Research Activity

SD 4.

LO3 Reading and Analyzing Foreign Currency Markets

On its "foreign exchange" page, *The Wall Street Journal* publishes a table that shows the exchange rates of the currencies of about 50 countries with the U.S. dollar. Choose the currency of any country in which you are interested. Write down the value of that currency in U.S. dollar equivalents for one day in the first week of each month for the past six months, as reported in *The Wall Street Journal*'s exchange rate tables. Prepare a chart that shows the variation in exchange rate for the currency over this time period. Assuming that you run a company that exports goods to the country you choose, would you find the change in exchange rate over the past six months favorable or unfavorable? Assuming that you run a company that imports goods from the country you chose, would you find the change in exchange rate over the past six months favorable or unfavorable? Explain your answers and tell what business practices you would follow to offset any adverse effects of exchange rate fluctuations. Be prepared to discuss your results in class.

Decision-Making Practice

SD 5.

LO1 Accounting for Investments

Gulf Coast Corporation is a successful oil and gas exploration business in the southwestern United States. At the beginning of 20xx, the company made investments in three companies that perform services in the oil and gas industry. The details of each of these investments follow.

Gulf Coast purchased 100,000 shares of Marsh Service Corporation at a cost of $16 per share. Marsh has 1.5 million shares outstanding, and during 20xx paid dividends of $.80 per share on earnings of $1.60 per share. At the end of the year, Marsh's shares were selling for $24 per share.

Gulf Coast also purchased 2 million shares of Crescent Drilling Company at $8 per share. Crescent has 10 million shares outstanding. In 20xx, Crescent paid a dividend of $.40 per share on earnings of $.80 per share. During the year, the president of Gulf Coast was appointed to Crescent's board of directors. At the end of the year, Crescent's stock was selling for $12 per share.

In another action, Gulf Coast purchased 1 million of Logan Oil Field Supplies Company's 5 million outstanding shares at $12 per share. The president of Gulf Coast sought membership on Logan's board of directors but was rebuffed when a majority of shareholders stated they did not want to be associated with Gulf Coast. Logan paid a dividend of $.80 per share and reported a net income of only $.40 per share for the year. By the end of the year, its stock price had dropped to $4 per share.

1. What principal factors must you consider to determine how to account for Gulf Coast's investments? Should they be shown on the balance sheet as short-term or long-term investments? What factors affect this decision?
2. For each investment, make entries in journal form for (a) initial investment, (b) receipt of cash dividend, and (c) recognition of income (if appropriate).
3. What adjusting entry (if any) is required at the end of the year?
4. Assuming that Gulf Coast sells its investment in Logan after the first of the year for $6 per share, what journal entry would be made? Assuming no other transactions occur and that the market value of Gulf Coast's investment in Marsh exceeds cost by $2,400,000 at the end of the second year, what adjusting entry (if any) would be required?

FINANCIAL REPORTING AND ANALYSIS CASES

Interpreting Financial Reports

FRA 1.

LO2 Effects of Consolidating Finance Subsidiaries

National Stores Corporation is one of the largest owners of discount appliance stores in the United States. It owns Bi-Lo Superstores and several other discount chains. The company has a wholly owned finance subsidiary to handle its accounts receivable. Condensed balance sheets for National Stores and its finance subsidiary are shown below (in millions). The fiscal year ends January 31, 2003.

	National Stores Corporation	Finance Subsidiary
Assets		
Current assets (except accounts receivable)	$ 866	$ 1
Accounts receivable (net)	293	869
Property, equipment, and other assets	933	—
Investment in finance subsidiary	143	—
Total assets	$2,235	$870
Liabilities and Stockholders' Equity		
Current liabilities	$ 717	$ 10
Long-term liabilities	859	717
Stockholders' equity	659	143
Total liabilities and stockholders' equity	$2,235	$870

Total sales to customers were $4 billion. The Financial Accounting Standards Board's *Statement No. 94* requires all majority-owned subsidiaries to be consolidated in the parent company's financial statements. National Stores' management believes it is misleading to consolidate the finance subsidiary because it distorts the real operations of the company. You are asked to assess the effects of the statement on National Stores' financial position.

REQUIRED ▶

1. Prepare a consolidated balance sheet for National Stores Corporation and its finance subsidiary.
2. Demonstrate the effects of *Statement No. 94* by computing the following ratios for National Stores before and after the consolidation in **1**: receivable turnover, average days' sales uncollected, and debt to equity (use year-end balances).
3. What are some of the other ratios that will be affected by the implementation of *Statement No. 94*? Does consolidation assist investors and creditors in assessing the risk of investing in National Stores' securities or lending the company money? Relate your answer to your calculations in **2**. What do you think of management's position?

International Company

FRA 2.
LO5   Differences Between U.S. and U.K. Accounting Principles

Cable & Wireless, plc <www.cwplc.com>, is a major global communications company that provides business networks and mobile communications in Europe, the Caribbean, and Asia. This company publishes its financial statements in accordance with GAAP in the United Kingdom but includes in its annual report a very interesting summary of the differences that would result if selected financial data were presented in accordance with GAAP in the United States, as shown below (in millions).[13]

	Per UK GAAP		Per US GAAP	
	2001	2000	2001	2000
Stockholders' Equity	£15,380	£8,096	£22,992	£16,191
Net Income as Reported Under UK GAAP			£ 2,632	
US GAAP Adjustments				
Amortisation of goodwill and other intangible assets			£ 51	
Customer acquisition costs			7	
Restructuring costs			69	
Partial depreciation			6	
Equity accounting			—	
Capitalisation of interest			(80)	
Deferred tax—full provision			160	
—tax effect of other US GAAP reconciling items			147	
Pension costs			(19)	
Cumulative exchange gain on sale of foreign fixed asset investments			(24)	
Gain on sale of subsidiary			4,511	
Loss on marketable securities			(4,618)	
Capacity sales			(213)	
Impairment			—	
Stock based compensation			(3)	
Other			(8)	
Minority interests			100	
Net Income Under US GAAP			£ 2,718	

Assume that an investment analyst has asked you to evaluate Cable & Wireless's profitability. Prepare a memorandum that shows the calculation of return on equity for 2001 under U.K. GAAP and U.S. GAAP. Indicate which country's GAAP shows better results. Explain the role of goodwill and intangibles in this difference. (**Hint:** Recall that purchased goodwill is shown as an asset and is subject to an impairment test in the United States, whereas it is deducted from stockholders' equity and does not appear on the income statement in the United Kingdom.) Identify two other important differences between U.K. and U.S. GAAP. Also comment on whether accounting principles appear to be more conservative under U.K. or U.S. GAAP.

Toys "R" Us Annual Report

FRA 3.

LO3   Disclosure of International
LO4   Operations and Effects of
        Foreign Exchange

Refer to the Toys "R" Us <www.tru.com> annual report to answer the following questions:

1. From the note to the financial statements on segments, what percentages of Toys "R" Us sales and operating income are international? Is the international segment growing? Does the company earn a higher return of operating income on identifiable assets on its Toys "R" Us U.S. segment or on its international segment?
2. The note on seasonal financing and long-term debt reports that Toys "R" Us borrowed funds using euro bonds and has a Swiss franc note payable. Will a strong or weak dollar be more favorable to Toys "R" Us in repaying these loans? Explain.

Comparison Case: Toys "R" Us and Walgreen Co.

FRA 4.

LO2   Consolidation and Investment
        Practices

Refer to the annual report of Toys "R" Us <www.tru.com> and the financial statements of Walgreens <www.walgreens.com> in the Supplement to Chapter 1. Find each company's policy on consolidations in the notes to the financial statements. Discuss and compare the practices and extent of disclosure of the two companies. Does either company have other investments? If so, how are they accounted for?

Fingraph® Financial Analyst™

FRA 5.

LO1   Long-Term Investment
        Analysis

Choose any two companies in the same industry from the list of Fingraph companies on the Needles Accounting Resource Center Web Site at http://accounting.college.hmco.com/students. Access the Microsoft Excel spreadsheets for the companies you selected. Click on the URL at the top of each company's spreadsheet for a link to the company's web site and annual report.

1. In the annual reports of the companies you selected, find the balance sheet accounts and notes to the financial statements associated with long-term investments. What type of long-term investments does each company have? Are the investments valued at cost or market? What is the difference between cost and market value? Did the companies report unrealized gains and losses on their investments? Summarize in a table the types of investments, how they are valued, and the amounts of cost and market value and unrealized gains and losses.
2. Find the income statements for the companies you selected. Did the companies report any interest or dividend income? If so, what are these amounts? An examination of the notes may be necessary.
3. Write a one-page executive summary that highlights the types of long-term investments and their valuation, and the impact on net income in the current year. The summary should refer to management's assessment. Include your table as an attachment to the summary.

Internet Case

FRA 6.

LO1   Comparison of Two Recent
LO2   Acquisitions

Mergers and acquisitions are in the news almost every day. Go to the web site for MSNBC <www.msnbc.com> and scan recent headlines to locate two articles related to one company's purchasing or making an offer to purchase another. Read the articles and summarize the nature of the actual or proposed acquisition. What are the companies' names? What industry are they in? What is the dollar amount of the acquisition? How will the acquisition be paid for—in cash, stock, or a combination? In what ways are the acquisitions similar? How do they differ? Be prepared to present your findings in class.

Appendix A

The Merchandising Work Sheet and Closing Entries

This appendix shows how to prepare the work sheet and closing entries for merchandising companies. The work sheet for a merchandising company is basically the same as for a service business (for an example, see the work sheet for Joan Miller Advertising Agency in the chapter on accounting information systems). However, it includes the additional accounts needed to handle merchandising transactions. The treatment of these accounts differs depending on whether a company uses the periodic or the perpetual inventory system.

THE PERIODIC INVENTORY SYSTEM

When a merchandising company uses the periodic inventory system, the accounts generally include Sales, Sales Returns and Allowances, Sales Discounts, Purchases, Purchases Returns and Allowances, Purchases Discounts, Freight In, and Merchandise Inventory. Except for Merchandise Inventory, these accounts are treated in much the same way as revenue and expense accounts for a service company. They are transferred to the Income Summary account in the closing process. On the work sheet, they are extended to the Income Statement columns.

Merchandise Inventory requires special treatment under the periodic inventory system because purchases of merchandise are accumulated in the Purchases account. No entries are made to the Merchandise Inventory account during the accounting period. Its balance at the end of the period, before adjusting and closing entries, is the same as it was at the beginning of the period. Thus, its balance at this point represents beginning merchandise inventory. Remember also that the cost of goods sold is determined by adding beginning merchandise inventory to net cost of purchases and then subtracting ending merchandise inventory. The objectives of handling merchandise inventory in the closing entries at the end of the period are to (1) remove the beginning balance from the Merchandise Inventory account, (2) enter the ending balance into the Merchandise Inventory account, and (3) enter the beginning inventory as a debit and the ending inventory as a credit to the Income Summary account to calculate net income. The following T accounts, which use figures for Fenwick Fashions Corporation from the chapter on merchandising operations, show how these objectives can be met:

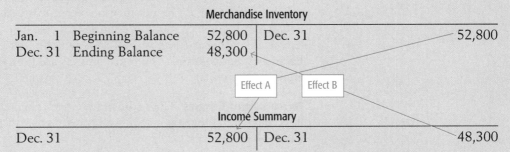

In this example, merchandise inventory was $52,800 at the beginning of the year and $48,300 at the end of the year. Effect A removes the $52,800 from Merchandise Inventory, leaving a zero balance, and transfers it to Income Summary. In Income Summary, the $52,800 is, in effect, added to net purchases because, like expenses, the balance of the Purchases account is debited to Income Summary in a closing entry. Effect B establishes the ending balance of Merchandise Inventory, $48,300, and enters it as a credit in the Income Summary account. The credit entry in Income Summary has the effect of deducting the ending inventory from goods available for sale because both purchases and beginning inventory are entered on the debit side. In other words, beginning merchandise inventory and purchases are debits to Income Summary, and ending merchandise inventory is a credit to Income Summary. The work sheet for Fenwick Fashions Corporation is shown in Exhibit 1 and is discussed below.

■ **TRIAL BALANCE COLUMNS**   The first step in the preparation of the work sheet is to enter the balances from the ledger accounts into the Trial Balance columns. You are already familiar with this procedure.

■ **ADJUSTMENTS COLUMNS**   The adjusting entries are entered in the Adjustments columns just as they are for service companies. No adjusting entry is made for merchandise inventory. After the adjusting entries are entered on the work sheet, the columns are totaled to prove that total debits equal total credits.

■ **OMISSION OF ADJUSTED TRIAL BALANCE COLUMNS**   These two columns, which appear in the work sheet for a service company, can be omitted. They are optional and are used when there are many adjusting entries to record. When only a few adjusting entries are required, as is the case for Fenwick Fashions, these columns are not necessary and may be omitted to save time.

■ **INCOME STATEMENT AND BALANCE SHEET COLUMNS**   After the Trial Balance columns have been totaled, the adjustments entered, and the equality of the columns proved, the balances are extended to the Income Statement and Balance Sheet columns. As on the work sheet for a service company, you begin with the Cash account at the top of the sheet and move sequentially down, one account at a time, entering each account balance in the correct Income Statement or Balance Sheet column.

The "problem" extension here is in the Merchandise Inventory row. The beginning inventory balance of $52,800 (which is already in the trial balance) is extended to the debit column of the Income Statement columns, as shown in Exhibit 1. This procedure has the effect of adding beginning inventory to net purchases because the Purchases account is also in the debit column of the Income Statement columns. The ending inventory balance of $48,300 (which is determined by the physical inventory and is not in the trial balance) is then inserted in the credit column of the Income Statement columns. This procedure has the effect of subtracting the ending inventory from goods available for sale in order to calculate the cost of goods sold. Finally, the ending merchandise inventory ($48,300) is inserted in the debit side of the Balance Sheet columns because it will appear on the balance sheet.

After all the items have been extended into the correct columns, the four columns are totaled. The net income or net loss is the difference between the debit and credit Income Statement columns. In this case, Fenwick Fashions Corporation has earned a net income of $24,481, which is extended to the credit side of the Balance Sheet columns. The four columns are then added to prove that total debits equal total credits.

■ **ADJUSTING ENTRIES**   The adjusting entries from the work sheet are now entered into the general journal and posted to the ledger. The procedure is the same as for a service company.

■ **CLOSING ENTRIES**   Exhibit 2 shows the closing entries for Fenwick Fashions. Notice that Merchandise Inventory is credited for the amount of beginning inventory ($52,800) in the first entry and debited for the amount of the ending inventory ($48,300) in the second entry. Otherwise, these closing entries are similar to those for a service company except that the merchandising accounts also must be closed to Income Summary. All income statement accounts with debit balances, including the merchandising accounts of Sales Returns and Allowances, Sales

EXHIBIT 1
Work Sheet for Fenwick Fashions Corporation: Periodic Inventory System

Fenwick Fashions Corporation
Work Sheet
For the Year Ended December 31, 20xx

Account Name	Trial Balance Debit	Trial Balance Credit	Adjustments Debit	Adjustments Credit	Income Statement Debit	Income Statement Credit	Balance Sheet Debit	Balance Sheet Credit
Cash	29,410						29,410	
Accounts Receivable	42,400						42,400	
Merchandise Inventory	52,800				52,800	48,300	48,300	
Prepaid Insurance	17,400			(a) 5,800			11,600	
Store Supplies	2,600			(b) 1,540			1,060	
Office Supplies	1,840			(c) 1,204			636	
Land	4,500						4,500	
Building	20,260						20,260	
Accumulated Depreciation, Building		5,650		(d) 2,600				8,250
Office Equipment	8,600						8,600	
Accumulated Depreciation, Office Equipment		2,800		(e) 2,200				5,000
Accounts Payable		25,683						25,683
Common Stock		50,000						50,000
Retained Earnings		68,352						68,352
Dividends	20,000						20,000	
Sales		246,350				246,350		
Sales Returns and Allowances	2,750				2,750			
Sales Discounts	4,275				4,275			
Purchases	126,400				126,400			
Purchases Returns and Allowances		5,640				5,640		
Purchases Discounts		2,136				2,136		
Freight In	8,236				8,236			
Sales Salaries Expense	22,500				22,500			
Freight Out Expense	5,740				5,740			
Advertising Expense	10,000				10,000			
Office Salaries Expense	26,900				26,900			
	406,611	406,611						
Insurance Expense, Selling			(a) 1,600		1,600			
Insurance Expense, General			(a) 4,200		4,200			
Store Supplies Expense			(b) 1,540		1,540			
Office Supplies Expense			(c) 1,204		1,204			
Depreciation Expense, Building			(d) 2,600		2,600			
Depreciation Expense, Office Equipment			(e) 2,200		2,200			
Income Taxes Expense			(f) 5,000		5,000			
Income Taxes Payable				(f) 5,000				5,000
			18,344	18,344	277,945	302,426	186,766	162,285
Net Income					24,481			24,481
					302,426	302,426	186,766	186,766

EXHIBIT 2
Closing Entries for a Merchandising Concern: Periodic Inventory System

		General Journal			Page 10
Date		Description	Post. Ref.	Debit	Credit
20xx Dec.	31	*Closing entries:* Income Summary		277,945	
		Merchandise Inventory			52,800
		Sales Returns and Allowances			2,750
		Sales Discounts			4,275
		Purchases			126,400
		Freight In			8,236
		Sales Salaries Expense			22,500
		Freight Out Expense			5,740
		Advertising Expense			10,000
		Office Salaries Expense			26,900
		Insurance Expense, Selling			1,600
		Insurance Expense, General			4,200
		Store Supplies Expense			1,540
		Office Supplies Expense			1,204
		Depreciation Expense, Building			2,600
		Depreciation Expense, Office Equipment			2,200
		Income Taxes Expense			5,000
		To close temporary expense and revenue accounts with debit balances and to remove the beginning inventory			
	31	Merchandise Inventory		48,300	
		Sales		246,350	
		Purchases Returns and Allowances		5,640	
		Purchases Discounts		2,136	
		Income Summary			302,426
		To close temporary expense and revenue accounts with credit balances and to establish the ending inventory			
	31	Income Summary		24,481	
		Retained Earnings			24,481
		To close the Income Summary account			
	31	Retained Earnings		20,000	
		Dividends			20,000
		To close the Dividends account			

Discounts, Purchases, and Freight In, and beginning Merchandise Inventory are credited in the first entry. The total of these accounts ($277,945) equals the total of the debit column in the Income Statement columns of the work sheet. All income statement accounts with credit balances—Sales, Purchases Returns and Allowances, and Purchases Discounts—and ending Merchandise Inventory are debited in the second entry. The total of these accounts ($302,426) equals the total of the Income Statement credit column in the work sheet. The third entry closes the Income Summary account and transfers net income to Retained Earnings. The fourth entry closes the Dividends account to Retained Earnings.

THE PERPETUAL INVENTORY SYSTEM

Exhibit 3 shows the work sheet for Fenwick Fashions Corporation, assuming the company uses the perpetual inventory system. Under this system, purchases of

EXHIBIT 3
Work Sheet for Fenwick Fashions Corporation: Perpetual Inventory System

Fenwick Fashions Corporation
Work Sheet
For the Year Ended December 31, 20xx

Account Name	Trial Balance Debit	Trial Balance Credit	Adjustments Debit	Adjustments Credit	Income Statement Debit	Income Statement Credit	Balance Sheet Debit	Balance Sheet Credit
Cash	29,410						29,410	
Accounts Receivable	42,400						42,400	
Merchandise Inventory	48,300						48,300	
Prepaid Insurance	17,400			(a) 5,800			11,600	
Store Supplies	2,600			(b) 1,540			1,060	
Office Supplies	1,840			(c) 1,204			636	
Land	4,500						4,500	
Building	20,260						20,260	
Accumulated Depreciation, Building		5,650		(d) 2,600				8,250
Office Equipment	8,600						8,600	
Accumulated Depreciation, Office Equipment		2,800		(e) 2,200				5,000
Accounts Payable		25,683						25,683
Common Stock		50,000						50,000
Retained Earnings		68,352						68,352
Dividends	20,000						20,000	
Sales		246,350				246,350		
Sales Returns and Allowances	2,750				2,750			
Sales Discounts	4,275				4,275			
Cost of Goods Sold	123,124				123,124			
Freight In	8,236				8,236			
Sales Salaries Expense	22,500				22,500			
Freight Out Expense	5,740				5,740			
Advertising Expense	10,000				10,000			
Office Salaries Expense	26,900				26,900			
	398,835	398,835						
Insurance Expense, Selling			(a) 1,600		1,600			
Insurance Expense, General			(a) 4,200		4,200			
Store Supplies Expense			(b) 1,540		1,540			
Office Supplies Expense			(c) 1,204		1,204			
Depreciation Expense, Building			(d) 2,600		2,600			
Depreciation Expense, Office Equipment			(e) 2,200		2,200			
Income Taxes Expense			(f) 5,000		5,000			
Income Taxes Payable				(f) 5,000				5,000
			18,344	18,344	221,869	246,350	186,766	162,285
Net Income					24,481			24,481
					246,350	246,350	186,766	186,766

EXHIBIT 4
Closing Entries for a Merchandising Concern: Perpetual Inventory System

Date		Description	Post. Ref.	Debit	Credit
20xx		*Closing entries:*			
Dec.	31	Income Summary		221,869	
		Sales Returns and Allowances			2,750
		Sales Discounts			4,275
		Cost of Goods Sold			123,124
		Freight In			8,236
		Sales Salaries Expense			22,500
		Freight Out Expense			5,740
		Advertising Expense			10,000
		Office Salaries Expense			26,900
		Insurance Expense, Selling			1,600
		Insurance Expense, General			4,200
		Store Supplies Expense			1,540
		Office Supplies Expense			1,204
		Depreciation Expense, Building			2,600
		Depreciation Expense, Office Equipment			2,200
		Income Taxes Expense			5,000
		To close temporary expense and revenue accounts with debit balances			
	31	Sales		246,350	
		Income Summary			246,350
		To close temporary revenue account with credit balance			
	31	Income Summary		24,481	
		Retained Earnings			24,481
		To close the Income Summary account			
	31	Retained Earnings		20,000	
		Dividends			20,000
		To close the Dividends account			

General Journal — Page 10

merchandise are recorded directly in the Merchandise Inventory account and costs are transferred from the Merchandise Inventory account to the Cost of Goods Sold account as merchandise is sold. Thus, the Merchandise Inventory account is up to date at the end of the accounting period and is not involved in the closing process. Note that the ending merchandise inventory in Exhibit 3 is $48,300 in both the Trial Balance and the Balance Sheet columns.

Exhibit 4 shows the closing entries for Fenwick Fashions under the perpetual inventory system. The Cost of Goods Sold account is closed to Income Summary along with the expense accounts because it has a debit balance. There are no entries to the Merchandise Inventory account. Also, there is no Purchases Returns and Allowances account under the perpetual inventory system, and Freight In is accounted for separately but is combined with Cost of Goods Sold on the income statement.

PROBLEMS

P 1.

Work Sheet, Financial Statements, and Closing Entries for a Merchandising Company: Periodic Inventory System

The following trial balance is from the ledger of David's Music Store, Inc., at the end of its annual accounting period:

David's Music Store, Inc.
Trial Balance
November 30, 20x4

Cash	$ 18,075	
Accounts Receivable	27,840	
Merchandise Inventory	88,350	
Store Supplies	5,733	
Prepaid Insurance	4,800	
Store Equipment	111,600	
Accumulated Depreciation, Store Equipment		$ 46,800
Accounts Payable		36,900
Common Stock		30,000
Retained Earnings		95,982
Dividends	36,000	
Sales		306,750
Sales Returns and Allowances	2,961	
Purchases	189,600	
Purchases Returns and Allowances		58,965
Purchases Discounts		4,068
Freight In	6,783	
Sales Salaries Expense	64,050	
Rent Expense	10,800	
Other Selling Expenses	7,842	
Utilities Expense	5,031	
	$579,465	$579,465

REQUIRED ▶

1. Enter the trial balance on a work sheet and complete the work sheet using the following information: ending merchandise inventory, $99,681; ending store supplies inventory, $912; unexpired prepaid insurance, $600; estimated depreciation on store equipment, $12,900; sales salaries payable, $240; accrued utilities expense, $450; and estimated income taxes expense, $15,000.
2. Prepare an income statement, a statement of retained earnings, and a balance sheet. Sales salaries expense; other selling expenses; store supplies expense; and depreciation expense, store equipment are selling expenses.
3. From the work sheet, prepare the closing entries.

P 2.

Work Sheet, Financial Statements, and Closing Entries for a Merchandising Company: Perpetual Inventory System

The trial balance on the next page is from the ledger of Marjie's Party Costumes Corporation at the end of its annual accounting period.

REQUIRED ▶

1. Enter the trial balance for Marjie's Party Costumes on a work sheet and complete the work sheet using the following information: ending store supplies inventory, $550; expired insurance, $2,400; estimated depreciation on store equipment, $5,000; sales salaries payable, $650; accrued utilities expense, $100; and estimated income taxes expense, $20,000.

Marjie's Party Costumes Corporation
Trial Balance
June 30, 20x4

Cash	$ 7,050	
Accounts Receivable	24,830	
Merchandise Inventory	88,900	
Store Supplies	3,800	
Prepaid Insurance	4,800	
Store Equipment	151,300	
Accumulated Depreciation, Store Equipment		$ 25,500
Accounts Payable		38,950
Common Stock		50,000
Retained Earnings		111,350
Dividends	24,000	
Sales		475,250
Sales Returns and Allowances	4,690	
Cost of Goods Sold	231,840	
Freight In	10,400	
Sales Salaries Expense	64,600	
Rent Expense	48,000	
Other Selling Expenses	32,910	
Utilities Expense	3,930	
	$701,050	$701,050

2. Prepare an income statement, a statement of retained earnings, and a balance sheet. Sales salaries expense; other selling expenses; store supplies expense; and depreciation expense, store equipment are selling expenses.
3. From the work sheet, prepare closing entries.

Appendix B

Special-Purpose Journals

Most business transactions—90 to 95 percent—fall into one of four categories. Each kind of transaction can be recorded in a special-purpose journal:

Transaction	Special-Purpose Journal	Posting Abbreviation
Sale of merchandise on credit	Sales journal	S
Purchase on credit	Purchases journal	P
Receipt of cash	Cash receipts journal	CR
Disbursement of cash	Cash payments journal	CP

The general journal is used to record transactions that do not fall into any of these special categories. (The posting abbreviation is **J**.)

Using special-purpose journals greatly reduces the work involved in entering and posting transactions in the general ledger. For example, in most cases, instead of posting every debit and credit for each transaction, only the total amounts of the transactions are posted. In addition, labor can be divided by assigning each journal to a different employee. This division of labor is important in establishing good internal control. Special-purpose journals thus promote efficiency, economy, and control. The concepts that underly these journals also underlie the programs that drive computerized general ledger accounting systems.

SALES JOURNAL

The *sales journal* is designed to handle all credit sales. Cash sales are recorded in the cash receipts journal. Exhibit 1 illustrates a page from a typical sales journal and related ledger accounts. The page records six sales transactions involving five customers. Notice how the sales journal saves time:

1. Only one line is needed to record each transaction. Each entry consists of a debit to a customer in Accounts Receivable. The corresponding credit to Sales is understood.

2. The account names do not have to be written out because each entry automatically is debited to Accounts Receivable and credited to Sales.

3. No explanations are necessary because the function of the sales journal is to record credit sales only.

4. Only one amount—the total credit sales for the month—has to be posted. It is posted twice: once as a debit to Accounts Receivable and once as a credit to Sales. You can see the time this saves for the six transactions listed in Exhibit 1. Imagine the time saved when there are hundreds of sales transactions.

■ **CONTROLLING ACCOUNTS AND SUBSIDIARY LEDGERS** Every entry in the sales journal represents a debit to a customer's account in Accounts Receivable. Throughout the book, we've posted all such transactions to Accounts Receivable. However, a single entry in Accounts Receivable does not tell us how much each customer has bought and how much each customer has paid or still owes. In practice, almost all companies that sell to customers on credit keep an individual accounts receivable record for each customer. If the company has 6,000 credit customers, there are 6,000 accounts receivable. To include all these accounts in the general ledger with the other asset, liability, and stockholders' equity accounts would make it very bulky. Consequently, most companies place individual customers' accounts in a separate ledger, called a *subsidiary ledger*. In the accounts receivable subsidiary

EXHIBIT 1
Sales Journal and Related Ledger Accounts

Sales Journal   Page 1

Date		Account Debited	Invoice Number	Post. Ref.	Amount (Debit Accounts Receivable/ Credit Sales)
July	1	Peter Clark	721	✓	750
	5	Georgetta Jones	722	✓	500
	8	Eugene Cumberland	723	✓	335
	12	Maxwell Gertz	724	✓	1,165
	18	Peter Clark	725	✓	1,225
	25	Michael Powers	726	✓	975
					4,950
					(114/411)

Post total at **end of month.**

Accounts Receivable   114

Date	Post. Ref.	Debit	Credit	Balance Debit	Balance Credit
July 31	S1	4,950		4,950	

Sales   411

Date	Post. Ref.	Debit	Credit	Balance Debit	Balance Credit
July 31	S1		4,950		4,950

ledger, customers' accounts are filed either alphabetically or numerically (if account numbers are used).

When a company puts its individual customers' accounts in an accounts receivable subsidiary ledger, it still must maintain an Accounts Receivable account in the general ledger. This account "controls" the subsidiary ledger and is called a *controlling account* or *control account*. It controls in the sense that its balance must equal the total of the individual account balances in the subsidiary ledger. The balance of the controlling account on the balance sheet date appears as Accounts Receivable on the balance sheet. For transactions that involve accounts receivable, such as credit sales, entries must be posted to the individual customers' accounts daily. Postings to the controlling account in the general ledger are made at least once a month. If a wrong amount has been posted, the sum of customers' account balances in the subsidiary accounts receivable ledger will not equal the balance of the corresponding controlling account in the general ledger. When these amounts do not match, the accountant must find the error and correct it.

Exhibit 2 shows how controlling accounts work. The single controlling account in the general ledger summarizes all the individual accounts in the subsidiary ledger. Most companies use an accounts payable subsidiary ledger as well.

■ **SUMMARY OF THE SALES JOURNAL PROCEDURE**   Exhibit 2 illustrates the procedure for using a sales journal:

1. Enter each sales invoice in the sales journal on a single line. Record the date, the customer's name, the invoice number, and the amount. No column is needed for the terms if the terms on all sales are the same.

2. At the end of each day, post each individual sale to the customer's account in the accounts receivable subsidiary ledger. As each sale is posted, place a check-

EXHIBIT 2
Relationship of Sales Journal, General Ledger, and Accounts Receivable Subsidiary Ledger and the Posting Procedure

Sales Journal   Page 1

Date		Account Debited	Invoice Number	Post. Ref.	Amount (Debit Accounts Receivable/ Credit Sales)
July	1	Peter Clark	721	✓	750
	5	Georgetta Jones	722	✓	500
	8	Eugene Cumberland	723	✓	335
	12	Maxwell Gertz	724	✓	1,165
	18	Peter Clark	725	✓	1,225
	25	Michael Powers	726	✓	975
					4,950
					(114/411)

Post total at **end of month** to general ledger accounts.

Post individual amounts **daily** to subsidiary ledger accounts.

General Ledger

Accounts Receivable   114

Date	Post. Ref.	Debit	Credit	Balance Debit	Balance Credit
July 31	S1	4,950		4,950	

Sales   411

Date	Post. Ref.	Debit	Credit	Balance Debit	Balance Credit
July 31	S1		4,950		4,950

Accounts Receivable Subsidiary Ledger

Peter Clark

Date		Post. Ref.	Debit	Credit	Balance
July	1	S1	750		750
	18	S1	1,225		1,975

Eugene Cumberland

Date		Post. Ref.	Debit	Credit	Balance
July	8	S1	335		335

Continue posting to Maxwell Gertz, Georgetta Jones, and Michael Powers.

mark (or customer account number, if used) in the Post. Ref. (posting reference) column of the sales journal to indicate that it has been posted. In the Post. Ref. column of each customer's account, place an *S* and the sales journal page number (*S1* means Sales Journal—Page 1) to indicate the source of the entry.

3. At the end of the month, sum the Amount column in the sales journal to determine the total credit sales, and post the total to the general ledger accounts (debit Accounts Receivable and credit Sales). Place the numbers of the accounts debited and credited beneath the total in the sales journal to indicate that this step has been completed. In the general ledger, indicate the source of the entry in the Post. Ref. column of each account.

4. Verify the accuracy of the posting by adding the account balances of the accounts receivable subsidiary ledger and comparing the total with the balance

EXHIBIT 3
Schedule of Accounts Receivable

Mitchell's Used Car Sales	
Schedule of Accounts Receivable	
July 31, 20xx	
Peter Clark	$1,975
Eugene Cumberland	335
Maxwell Gertz	1,165
Georgetta Jones	500
Michael Powers	975
Total Accounts Receivable	$4,950

of the Accounts Receivable controlling account in the general ledger. You can do this by listing the accounts in a schedule of accounts receivable, like the one in Exhibit 3, in the order in which the accounts are maintained. This step is performed after posting collections on account in the cash receipts journal.

■ **SALES TAXES** Other columns can be added to the sales journal. Many cities and states require retailers to collect a sales tax from their customers and periodically remit the total collected to the city or state. In this case, an additional column is needed in the sales journal to record the credit to Sales Taxes Payable on credit sales. The form of the entry is shown in Exhibit 4.

PURCHASES JOURNAL

The *purchases journal* is used to record purchases on credit. It can take the form of either a single-column journal or a multicolumn journal. In the single-column journal shown in Exhibit 5, only credit purchases of merchandise for resale to customers are recorded. This kind of transaction is recorded with a debit to Purchases and a credit to Accounts Payable. When the single-column purchases journal is used, credit purchases of items other than merchandise are recorded in the general journal. Cash purchases are never recorded in the purchases journal; they are recorded in the cash payments journal, which we explain later.

Like the Accounts Receivable account, the Accounts Payable account in the general ledger is generally used as a controlling account. So that the company knows how much it owes each supplier, it keeps a separate account for each supplier in an accounts payable subsidiary ledger.

The procedure for using the purchases journal is much like that for using the sales journal:

1. Enter each purchase invoice in the purchases journal on a single line. Record the date, the supplier's name, the invoice date, the terms (if given), and the amount. It is not necessary to record the shipping terms in the terms column because they do not affect the payment date.

2. At the end of each day, post each individual purchase to the supplier's account in the accounts payable subsidiary ledger. As each purchase is posted, place a checkmark in the Post. Ref. column of the purchases journal to show that it has been posted. Also place a *P* and the page number of the purchases journal (*P1* stands for Purchases Journal—Page 1) in the Post. Ref. column of each supplier's account to show the source of the entry.

3. At the end of the month, sum the Amount column in the purchases journal, and post the total to the general ledger accounts (a debit to Purchases and a credit to Accounts Payable). Place the numbers of the accounts debited and credited beneath the totals in the purchases journal to show that this step has

EXHIBIT 4
Section of a Sales Journal with a Column for Sales Taxes

				Debit	Credits	
					Sales	
					Taxes	
		Invoice	Post.	Accounts	Payable	
Date	Account Debited	Number	Ref.	Receivable		Sales
Aug. 1	Ralph P. Hake	727	✓	206	6	200

Sales Journal — Page 2

EXHIBIT 5
Relationship of Single-Column Purchases Journal to the General Ledger and the Accounts Payable Subsidiary Ledger

Purchases Journal — Page 1

Date	Account Credited	Date of Invoice	Term	Post. Ref.	Amount (Debit Purchases/ Credit Accounts Payable)
July 1	Jones Chevrolet	7/1	2/10, n/30	✓	2,500
2	Marshall Ford	7/2	2/15, n/30	✓	300
3	Dealer Sales	7/3	n/30	✓	700
12	Thomas Auto	7/11	n/30	✓	1,400
17	Dealer Sales	7/17	2/10, n/30	✓	3,200
19	Thomas Auto	7/17	n/30	✓	1,100
					9,200
					(511/212)

Post individual amounts **daily.**

Post total at **end of month.**

General Ledger

Accounts Payable 212

Date	Post. Ref.	Debit	Credit	Balance Debit	Balance Credit
July 31	P1		9,200		9,200

Purchases 511

Date	Post. Ref.	Debit	Credit	Balance Debit	Balance Credit
July 31	P1	9,200		9,200	

Accounts Payable Subsidiary Ledger

Dealer Sales

Date	Post. Ref.	Debit	Credit	Balance
July 3	P1		700	700
17	P1		3,200	3,900

Jones Chevrolet

Date	Post. Ref.	Debit	Credit	Balance
July 1	P1		2,500	2,500

Continue posting to Marshall Ford and Thomas Auto.

EXHIBIT 6
A Multicolumn Purchases Journal

					Credit		Debits			Other Accounts		
Date	Account Credited	Date of Invoice	Terms	Post. Ref.	Accounts Payable	Purchases	Freight In	Store Supplies	Office Supplies	Account	Post. Ref.	Amount
July 1	Jones Chevrolet	7/1	2/10, n/30	✓	2,500	2,500						
2	Marshall Ford	7/2	2/15, n/30	✓	300	300						
2	Shelby Car Delivery	7/2	n/30	✓	50		50					
3	Dealer Sales	7/3	n/30	✓	700	700						
12	Thomas Auto	7/11	n/30	✓	1,400	1,400						
17	Dealer Sales	7/17	2/10, n/30	✓	3,200	3,200						
19	Thomas Auto	7/17	n/30	✓	1,100	1,100						
25	Osborne Supply	7/21	n/10	✓	187			145	42			
28	Auto Supply	7/28	n/10	✓	200					Parts	120	200
					9,637	9,200	50	145	42			200
					(212)	(511)	(514)	(132)	(133)			(✓)

Purchases Journal — Page 1

been carried out. In the general ledger, indicate the source of the entry in the Post. Ref. column of each account.

4. Check the accuracy of the posting by adding the account balances of the accounts payable subsidiary ledger and comparing the total with the balance of the Accounts Payable controlling account in the general ledger. This step can be done by preparing a schedule of accounts payable from the subsidiary ledger.

The single-column purchases journal can be expanded to record credit purchases of items other than merchandise by adding separate debit columns for other accounts that are used often. For example, the multicolumn purchases journal in Exhibit 6 has columns for Freight In, Store Supplies, Office Supplies, and Other Accounts. Here, the total credits to Accounts Payable ($9,637) equal the total debits to Purchases, Freight In, Store Supplies, Office Supplies, and Parts ($9,200 + $50 + $145 + $42 + $200). Again, the individual transactions in the Accounts Payable column are posted daily to the accounts payable subsidiary ledger, and the totals of each column in the purchases journal are posted monthly to the corresponding general ledger accounts.

CASH RECEIPTS JOURNAL

All transactions involving receipts of cash are recorded in the *cash receipts journal*. Examples of these transactions are cash from cash sales and cash from credit customers in payment of their accounts. Although all cash receipts are alike in that they require a debit to Cash, they differ in that they require a variety of credit entries. Thus, the cash receipts journal must have several columns. The account numbers are entered in the Post. Ref. column, and the amounts are posted daily to the appropriate account in the general ledger.

The cash receipts journal shown in Exhibit 7 has three debit columns and three credit columns. The three debit columns are as follows:

1. *Cash*   Each entry must have an amount in this column because each transaction involves a receipt of cash.

EXHIBIT 7
Relationship of the Cash Receipts Journal to the General Ledger and the Accounts Receivable Subsidiary Ledger

Cash Receipts Journal — Page 1

		Account Debited/Credited	Post. Ref.	Debits — Cash	Debits — Sales Discounts	Debits — Other Accounts	Credits — Accounts Receivable	Credits — Sales	Credits — Other Accounts
July	1	Common Stock	311	20,000					20,000
	5	Sales		1,200				1,200	
	8	Georgetta Jones	✓	490	10		500		
	13	Sales		1,400				1,400	
	16	Peter Clark	✓	750			750		
	19	Sales		1,000				1,000	
	20	Equipment	151	500					500
	24	Notes Payable	213	5,000					5,000
	26	Sales		1,600				1,600	
	28	Peter Clark	✓	588	12		600		
				32,528	22		1,850	5,200	25,500
				(111)	(412)		(114)	(411)	(✓)

Post individual amounts in Accounts Receivable Susidiary Ledger column **daily.**

Post totals at **end of month.**

Total not posted.

Post individual amounts in Other Accounts column **daily.**

General Ledger

Cash   111

Date	Post. Ref.	Debit	Credit	Balance Debit	Balance Credit
July 31	CR1	32,528		32,528	

Accounts Receivable   114

Date	Post. Ref.	Debit	Credit	Balance Debit	Balance Credit
July 31	S1	4,950		4,950	
31	CR1		1,850	3,100	

Equipment   151

Date	Post. Ref.	Debit	Credit	Balance Debit	Balance Credit
Bal.				500	
July 20	CR1		500	—	

Accounts Receivable Subsidiary Ledger

Peter Clark

Date	Post. Ref.	Debit	Credit	Balance
July 1	S1	750		750
16	CR1		750	—
18	S1	1,225		1,225
28	CR1		600	625

Georgetta Jones

Date	Post. Ref.	Debit	Credit	Balance
July 5	S1	500		500
8	CR1		500	—

Continue posting to Notes Payable and Common Stock.

Continue posting to Sales and Sales Discounts.

2. *Sales Discounts*   This company allows a 2 percent discount for prompt payment. Therefore, it is useful to have a column for sales discounts. Notice that in the transactions of July 8 and 28, the debits to Cash and Sales Discounts equal the credits to Accounts Receivable.

3. *Other Accounts*   The Other Accounts column (sometimes called *Sundry Accounts*) is used for transactions that involve both a debit to Cash and a debit to some account other than Sales Discounts.

These are the credit columns:

1. *Accounts Receivable*   This column is used to record collections on account from customers. The name of the customer is written in the Account Debited/ Credited column so that the payment can be entered in the corresponding account in the accounts receivable subsidiary ledger. Posting to the individual accounts receivable accounts is usually done daily so that each customer's balance is up to date.

2. *Sales*   This column is used to record all cash sales during the month. Retail firms that use cash registers would make an entry at the end of each day for the total sales from each cash register for that day. The debit, of course, is in the Cash debit column.

3. *Other Accounts*   This column is used for the credit portion of any entry that is neither a cash collection from accounts receivable nor a cash sale. The name of the account to be credited is indicated in the Account Debited/Credited column. For example, the transactions of July 1, 20, and 24 involve credits to accounts other than Accounts Receivable or Sales. These individual postings should be done daily (or weekly if there are just a few of them). If a company finds that it consistently is crediting a certain account in the Other Accounts column, it can add another credit column to the cash receipts journal for that particular account.

The procedure for posting the cash receipts journal, as shown in Exhibit 7, is as follows:

1. Post the transactions in the Accounts Receivable column daily to the individual accounts in the accounts receivable subsidiary ledger. The amount credited to the customer's account is the same as that credited to Accounts Receivable. A checkmark in the Post. Ref. column of the cash receipts journal indicates that the amount has been posted, and a *CR1* (Cash Receipts Journal—Page 1) in the Post. Ref. column of each subsidiary ledger account indicates the source of the entry.

2. Post the debits/credits in the Other Accounts columns daily, or at convenient short intervals during the month, to the general ledger accounts. Write the account number in the Post. Ref. column of the cash receipts journal as the individual items are posted to indicate that the posting has been done, and write *CR1* in the Post. Ref. column of the general ledger account to indicate the source of the entry.

3. At the end of the month, total the columns in the cash receipts journal. The sum of the Debits column totals must equal the sum of the Credits column totals:

Debits Column Totals		Credits Column Totals	
Cash	$32,528	Accounts Receivable	$ 1,850
Sales Discounts	22	Sales	5,200
Other Accounts	0	Other Accounts	25,500
Total Debits	$32,550	Total Credits	$32,550

This step is called *crossfooting*.

4. Post the Debits column totals as follows:
   a. *Cash*   Posted as a debit to the Cash account.
   b. *Sales Discounts*   Posted as a debit to the Sales Discounts account.

5. Post the Credits column totals as follows:
   a. *Accounts Receivable*   Posted as a credit to the Accounts Receivable controlling account.
   b. *Sales*   Posted as a credit to the Sales account.

6. Write the account numbers below each column in the cash receipts journal as they are posted to indicate that these steps have been completed. *CR1* is written in the Post. Ref. column of each account in the general ledger to indicate the source of the entry.

7. Notice that the total of the Other Accounts column is not posted because each entry was posted separately when the transaction occurred. The individual accounts were posted in step **2**. Place a checkmark at the bottom of the column to show that postings in that column have been made and that the total is not posted.

CASH PAYMENTS JOURNAL

All transactions involving payments of cash are recorded in the *cash payments journal* (also called the *cash disbursements journal*). Examples of these transactions are cash purchases and payments of obligations resulting from earlier purchases on credit. The form of the cash payments journal is much like that of the cash receipts journal.

The cash payments journal shown in Exhibit 8 has three credit columns and two debit columns.

The credit columns for the cash payments journal are as follows:

1. *Cash*   Each entry must have an amount in this column because each transaction involves a payment of cash.

2. *Purchases Discounts*   When purchases discounts are taken, they are recorded in this column.

3. *Other Accounts*   This column is used to record credits to accounts other than Cash or Purchases Discounts. Notice that the July 31 transaction shows a purchase of Land for $15,000, with a check for $5,000 and a note payable for $10,000.

The debit columns are as follows:

1. *Accounts Payable*   This column is used to record payments to suppliers that have extended credit to the company. Each supplier's name is written in the Payee column so that the payment can be entered in the supplier's account in the accounts payable subsidiary ledger.

2. *Other Accounts*   Cash can be expended for many reasons. Therefore, an Other Accounts or Sundry Accounts column is needed in the cash payments journal. The title of the account to be debited is written in the Account Credited/Debited column, and the amount is entered in the Other Accounts debit column. If a company finds that a particular account appears often in the Other Accounts column, it can add another debit column to the cash payments journal.

The procedure for posting the cash payments journal, shown in Exhibit 8, is as follows:

1. Post the transactions in the Accounts Payable column daily to the individual accounts in the accounts payable subsidiary ledger. Place a checkmark in the Post. Ref. column of the cash payments journal to indicate that the posting has been made.

2. Post the debits/credits in the Other Accounts debit/credit columns to the general ledger daily or at convenient short intervals during the month. Write the account number in the Post. Ref. column of the cash payments journal as the individual items are posted to indicate that the posting has been completed and

EXHIBIT 8
Relationship of the Cash Payments Journal to the General Ledger and the Accounts Payable Subsidiary Ledger

Cash Payments Journal   Page 1

Date	Ck. No.	Payee	Account Credited/Debited	Post. Ref.	Credits Cash	Credits Purchases Discounts	Credits Other Accounts	Debits Accounts Payable	Debits Other Accounts
July 2	101	Sondra Tidmore	Purchases	511	400				400
6	102	Daily Journal	Advertising Expense	612	200				200
8	103	Siviglia Agency	Rent Expense	631	250				250
11	104	Jones Chevrolet		✓	2,450	50		2,500	
16	105	Charles Kuntz	Salaries Expense	611	600				600
17	106	Marshall Ford		✓	294	6		300	
24	107	Grabow & Co.	Prepaid Insurance	119	480				480
27	108	Dealer Sales		✓	3,136	64		3,200	
30	109	A&B Equipment Company	Office Equipment Service Equipment	144 146	900				400 500
31	110	Burns Real Estate	Notes Payable Land	213 141	5,000		10,000		15,000
					13,710	120	10,000	6,000	17,830
					(111)	(512)	(✓)	(212)	(✓)

> Post individual amounts in Other Accounts column **daily.**

> Post individual amounts in Accounts Payable Subsidiary Ledger column **daily.**

> Post totals at **end of month.**

> Totals not posted.

General Ledger

Cash   111

Date	Post. Ref.	Debit	Credit	Balance Debit	Balance Credit
July 31	CR1	32,528		32,528	
31	CP1		13,710	18,818	

Prepaid Insurance   119

Date	Post. Ref.	Debit	Credit	Balance Debit	Balance Credit
July 24	CP1	480		480	

> Continue posting to Land, Office Equipment, Service Equipment, Notes Payable, Purchases, Salaries Expense, Advertising Expense, and Rent Expense.

> Continue posting to Purchases Discounts and Accounts Payable.

Accounts Payable Subsidiary Ledger

Dealer Sales

Date	Post. Ref.	Debit	Credit	Balance
July 3	P1		700	700
17	P1		3,200	3,900
27	CP1	3,200		700

Jones Chevrolet

Date	Post. Ref.	Debit	Credit	Balance
July 1	P1		2,500	2,500
11	CP1	2,500		—

Marshall Ford

Date	Post. Ref.	Debit	Credit	Balance
July 2	P1		300	300
17	CP1	300		—

CP1 (Cash Payments Journal—Page 1) in the Post. Ref. column of each general ledger account.

3. At the end of the month, the columns are footed and crossfooted. That is, the sum of the Credits column totals must equal the sum of the Debits column totals, as follows:

Credits Column Totals		Debits Column Totals	
Cash	$13,710	Accounts Payable	$ 6,000
Purchases Discounts	120	Other Accounts	17,830
Other Accounts	10,000		
Total Credits	$23,830	Total Debits	$23,830

4. At the end of the month, post the column totals for Cash, Purchases Discounts, and Accounts Payable to their respective accounts in the general ledger. Write the account number below each column in the cash payments journal as it is posted to indicate that this step has been completed and *CP1* in the Post. Ref. column of each general ledger account. Place a checkmark under the total of each Other Accounts column in the cash payments journal to indicate that the postings in the column have been made and that the total is not posted.

GENERAL JOURNAL

Adjusting and closing entries are recorded in the general journal. Transactions that do not involve sales, purchases, cash receipts, or cash payments should also be recorded in the general journal. Usually, there are only a few of these transactions. Two examples of entries that do not fit in a special-purpose journal are a return of merchandise bought on account and an allowance from a supplier for credit.

These entries are shown in Exhibit 9. Notice that the entries include a debit or a credit to a controlling account (Accounts Payable or Accounts Receivable). The name of the customer or supplier also is given here. When this kind of debit or credit is made to a controlling account in the general ledger, the entry must be posted twice: once to the controlling account and once to the individual account in the subsidiary ledger. This procedure keeps the subsidiary ledger equal to the controlling account. Notice that the July 26 transaction is posted by a debit to Sales Returns and Allowances in the general ledger (shown by the account number 413), a credit to the Accounts Receivable controlling account in the general ledger (account number 114), and a credit to the Maxwell Gertz account in the accounts receivable subsidiary ledger (checkmark).

EXHIBIT 9
Transactions Recorded in the General Journal

	General Journal				Page 1
Date	Description	Post. Ref.	Debit	Credit	
July 25	Accounts Payable, Thomas Auto	212/✓	1,400		
	Purchases Returns and Allowances	513		1,400	
	Returned used car for credit; invoice date: 7/11				
26	Sales Returns and Allowances	413	35		
	Accounts Receivable, Maxwell Gertz	114/✓		35	
	Allowance for faulty tire				

PROBLEMS

P 1.

Cash Receipts and Cash Payments Journals

The items below detail all cash transactions by O'Shea Company for the month of October. The company uses multicolumn cash receipts and cash payments journals similar to those illustrated in this appendix.

Oct. 1   The owner, Michael O'Shea, invested $50,000 cash and $24,000 in equipment in the business in exchange for common stock.
2   Paid rent to Bell Agency, $600, with check no. 75.
3   Cash sales, $2,200.
6   Purchased store equipment for $5,000 from Quadrangle Company, with check no. 76.
7   Purchased merchandise for cash, $6,500, from Fillet Company, with check no. 77.
8   Paid Said Company invoice, $1,800, less 2 percent discount, with check no. 78 (assume that a payable has already been recorded).
9   Paid advertising bill, $350, to WKBD, with check no. 79.
10   Cash sales, $3,910.
12   Received $800 on account from R. Sol.
13   Purchased used truck for cash, $3,520, from Linexx Company, with check no. 80.
19   Received $4,180 from Silber Company, in settlement of a $4,000 note plus interest.
20   Received $1,078 ($1,100 less $22 cash discount) from Yi Li.
21   Declared and paid O'Shea a dividend, $2,000, by issuing check no. 81.
23   Paid Rolod Company invoice, $2,500, less 2 percent discount, with check no. 82.
26   Paid Dusk Company for freight on merchandise received, $60, with check no. 83.
27   Cash sales, $4,800.
28   Paid B. Ricardo monthly salary, $1,400, with check no. 84.
31   Purchased land from M. Lon for $20,000, paying $5,000 with check no. 85 and signing a note payable for $15,000.

REQUIRED ▶

1. Enter the preceding transactions in the cash receipts and cash payments journals.
2. Foot and crossfoot the journals.

P 2.

Purchases and General Journals

The following items represent the credit transactions for Maglotz Company during the month of August. The company uses a multicolumn purchases journal and a general journal similar to those illustrated in this appendix.

Aug. 2   Purchased merchandise from Lemon Company, $1,400.
5   Purchased truck to be used in the business from Correa Company, $8,000.
8   Purchased office supplies from Rulers Company, $400.
12   Purchased filing cabinets from Rulers Company, $550.
14   Purchased merchandise, $1,400, and store supplies, $200, from Kessin Company.
17   Purchased store supplies from Lemon Company, $100, and office supplies from Tuvail Company, $50.
20   Purchased merchandise from Kessin Company, $1,472.
24   Purchased merchandise from Lemon Company, $2,452; the $2,452 invoice total included shipping charges, $232.
26   Purchased office supplies from Rulers Company, $150.
29   Purchased merchandise from Kessin Company, $290.
30   Returned defective merchandise purchased from Kessin Company on August 20 for full credit, $432.

REQUIRED ▶

1. Enter the preceding transactions in the purchases journal and the general journal.

Assume that all terms are n/30 and that invoice dates are the same as the transaction dates. Use Page 1 for all references.

2. Foot and crossfoot the purchases journal.

3. Open these general ledger accounts: Store Supplies (116), Office Supplies (117), Trucks (142), Office Equipment (144), Accounts Payable (211), Purchases (511), Purchases Returns and Allowances (512), and Freight In (513). Open accounts payable subsidiary ledger accounts as needed. Post from the journals to the ledger accounts.

Comprehensive Use of Special-Purpose Journals

P 3. During October, Fontana Refrigeration Company completed the following transactions:

Oct. 1 Received merchandise from Tark Company, $5,000, invoice dated September 29, terms 2/10, n/30, FOB shipping point.
3 Issued check no. 230 to Walters Realtors for October rent, $4,000.
4 Received merchandise from La Rock Manufacturing, $10,800, invoice dated October 1, terms 2/10, n/30, FOB shipping point.
6 Issued check no. 231 to Rabbit Company for repairs, $1,120.
7 Received $800 credit memorandum pertaining to October 4 shipment from La Rock Manufacturing for return of unsatisfactory merchandise.
8 Issued check no. 232 to Emerald Company for freight charges on October 1 and October 4 shipments, $368.
9 Sold merchandise to R. Kuldip, $2,000, terms 1/10, n/30, invoice no. 725.
10 Issued check no. 233 to Tark Company for full payment less discount.
11 Sold merchandise to A. Imoto for $2,500, terms 1/10, n/30, invoice no. 726.
12 Issued check no. 234 to La Rock Manufacturing for balance of account less discount.
13 Purchased advertising on credit from WRRT, invoice dated October 13, $900, terms n/20.
15 Issued credit memorandum to A. Imoto for $100 for merchandise returned.
16 Cash sales for the first half of the month, $19,340. (To shorten this problem, cash sales are recorded only twice a month instead of daily, as they would be in actual practice.)
17 Sold merchandise to N. Floy, $1,400, terms 1/10, n/30, invoice no. 727.
18 Received check from R. Kuldip for October 9 sale less discount.
19 Received check from A. Imoto for balance of account less discount.
20 Received merchandise from Tark Company, $5,600, invoice dated October 19, terms 2/10, n/30, FOB shipping point.
21 Received freight bill from Summers Company for merchandise received on October 20, invoice dated October 19, $1,140, terms n/5.
22 Issued check no. 235 for advertising purchase of October 13.
24 Received merchandise from La Rock Manufacturing, $7,200, invoice dated October 23, terms 2/10, n/30, FOB shipping point.
25 Issued check no. 236 for freight charge of October 21.
26 Sold merchandise to R. Kuldip, $1,600, terms 1/10, n/30, invoice no. 728.
28 Received credit memorandum from La Rock Manufacturing for defective merchandise received October 24, $600.
29 Issued check no. 237 to Western Company for purchase of office equipment, $700.
30 Issued check no. 238 to Tark Company for half of October 20 purchase less discount.
30 Received check in full from N. Floy, no discount allowed.
31 Cash sales for the last half of the month, $23,120.
31 Issued check no. 239, payable to Payroll Account, for monthly sales salaries, $8,600.

REQUIRED ▶ 1. Prepare a sales journal, a multicolumn purchases journal, a cash receipts journal, a cash payments journal, and a general journal for Fontana Refrigeration Company similar to the ones illustrated in this appendix. Use Page 1 for all journal references.
2. Open the following general ledger accounts: Cash (111), Accounts Receivable (112), Office Equipment (141), Accounts Payable (211), Sales (411), Sales Discounts (412), Sales Returns and Allowances (413), Purchases (511), Purchases Discounts (512), Purchases Returns and Allowances (513), Freight In (514), Sales Salaries Expense (521), Advertising Expense (522), Rent Expense (531), and Repairs Expense (532).

3. Open the following accounts receivable subsidiary ledger accounts: No. Floy, A. Imoto, and R. Kuldip.
4. Open the following accounts payable subsidiary ledger accounts: La Rock Manufacturing, Summers Company, Tark Company, and WRRT.
5. Enter the transactions in the journals and post as appropriate.
6. Foot and crossfoot the journals, and make the end-of-month postings.
7. Prepare a trial balance of the general ledger and prove the control balances of Accounts Receivable and Accounts Payable by preparing schedules of accounts receivable and accounts payable.

Appendix C

Accounting for Unincorporated Businesses

Throughout the book, we have focused on accounting for the corporate form of business. In this appendix, our focus is on accounting for sole proprietorships and partnerships.

ACCOUNTING FOR SOLE PROPRIETORSHIPS

A *sole proprietorship* is a business owned by one person. For the individual, this business form can be a convenient way of separating business activities from personal interests. Legally, however, the proprietorship is the same economic unit as the individual. The sole proprietor receives all the profits or losses and is liable for all the obligations of the business. Proprietorships represent the largest number of businesses in the United States, but typically they are the smallest in size. The life of a proprietorship ends when the owner wishes it to or at the owner's death or incapacity.

When someone invests in his or her own company, the amount of the investment is recorded in a capital account. For example, the entry to record the initial investment of $10,000 by Clara Hooper in her new mail-order business would be a debit to the Cash account for $10,000 and a credit to the Clara Hooper, Capital account for $10,000.

During the period, Hooper will probably withdraw assets from the business for personal living expenses. Since legally there is no separation between the owner and the sole proprietorship, it is not necessary to make a formal declaration of a withdrawal, as would be required in the case of corporate dividends. The withdrawal of $500 by Hooper is recorded as a debit to the Clara Hooper, Withdrawals account for $500 and a credit to the Cash account for $500.

Revenue and expense accounts for sole proprietorships are closed out to Income Summary in the same way as they are for corporations. Income Summary, however, is closed to the Capital account instead of to Retained Earnings. For example, the closing entries that follow assume a net income of $1,000 and withdrawals of $500:

Income Summary	1,000	
Clara Hooper, Capital		1,000
To close Income Summary in		
a sole proprietorship		
Clara Hooper, Capital	500	
Clara Hooper, Withdrawals		500
To close Withdrawals		

ACCOUNTING FOR PARTNERSHIPS

The Uniform Partnership Act, which has been adopted by a majority of the states, defines a *partnership* as "an association of two or more persons to carry on as co-owners of a business for profit." Normally, partnerships are formed when owners of small businesses wish to combine capital or managerial talents for some common business purpose. Partnerships are treated as separate entities in accounting, but legally there is no economic separation between them and their owners. They differ in many ways from the other forms of business. Here we describe some of their important characteristics.

■ **VOLUNTARY ASSOCIATION**   A partnership is a voluntary association of individuals rather than a legal entity in itself. Therefore, a partner is responsible under the law for his or her partners' actions within the scope of the business. A partner also has unlimited liability for the debts of the partnership. Because of these potential liabilities, a partner must be allowed to choose the people who join the partnership.

■ **PARTNERSHIP AGREEMENT**   A partnership is easy to form. Two or more competent people simply agree to be partners in some common business purpose. This agreement is known as a *partnership agreement*. The partnership agreement does not have to be in writing. However, it is good business practice to have a written document that clearly states the details of the partnership, including the name, location, and purpose of the business; the names of the partners and their respective duties; the investments of each partner; the method of distributing income and losses; and procedures for the admission and withdrawal of partners, the withdrawal of assets allowed each partner, and the liquidation (termination) of the business.

■ **LIMITED LIFE**   Because a partnership is formed by an agreement between partners, it has a *limited life*. It may be dissolved when a new partner is admitted; a partner withdraws, goes bankrupt, is incapacitated (to the point that he or she cannot perform as obligated), retires, or dies; or the terms of the partnership agreement are met (e.g., when the project for which the partnership was formed is completed). The partnership agreement can be written to cover each of these situations, thus allowing the partnership to continue legally.

■ **MUTUAL AGENCY**   Each partner is an agent of the partnership within the scope of the business. Because of this *mutual agency*, any partner can bind the partnership to a business agreement as long as he or she acts within the scope of the company's normal operations. For example, a partner in a used-car business can bind the partnership through the purchase or sale of used cars. But this partner cannot bind the partnership to a contract for buying men's clothing or any other goods that are not related to the used-car business.

■ **UNLIMITED LIABILITY**   Each partner has personal *unlimited liability* for all the debts of the partnership. If a partnership cannot pay its debts, creditors must first satisfy their claims from the assets of the business. If these assets are not enough to pay all debts, the creditors can seek payment from the personal assets of each partner. If a partner's personal assets are used up before the debts are paid, the creditors can claim additional assets from the remaining partners who are able to pay. Each partner, then, can be required by law to pay all the debts of the partnership.

■ **CO-OWNERSHIP OF PARTNERSHIP PROPERTY**   When individuals invest property in a partnership, they give up the right to their separate use of the property. The property becomes an asset of the partnership and is owned jointly by the partners.

■ **PARTICIPATION IN PARTNERSHIP INCOME**   Each partner has the right to share in the company's income and the responsibility to share in its losses. The partnership agreement should state the method of distributing income and losses to each partner. If the agreement describes how income should be shared but does not mention losses, losses are distributed in the same way as income. If the agreement does not describe the method of income and loss distribution, the partners must by law share income and losses equally.

ACCOUNTING FOR PARTNERS' EQUITY

The owners' equity of a partnership is called *partners' equity*. In accounting for partners' equity, it is necessary to maintain separate Capital and Withdrawals accounts for each partner and to divide the income and losses of the company among the partners. In the partners' equity section of the balance sheet, the balance of each partner's Capital account is listed separately:

Liabilities and Partners' Equity

Total liabilities		$28,000
Partners' equity		
Desmond, capital	$25,000	
Frank, capital	34,000	
Total partners' equity		59,000
Total liabilities and partners' equity		$87,000

Each partner invests cash, other assets, or both in the partnership according to the partnership agreement. Noncash assets should be valued at their fair market value on the date they are transferred to the partnership. The assets invested by a partner are debited to the proper account, and the total amount is credited to the partner's Capital account.

To show how partners' investments are recorded, let's assume that Jerry Adcock and Rose Villa have agreed to combine their capital and equipment in a partnership to operate a jewelry store. According to their partnership agreement, Adcock will invest $28,000 cash and $47,000 of equipment, and the partnership will assume a note payable on the equipment of $10,000. The entry to record one partner's initial investment is as follows:

20x3			
July 1	Cash	28,000	
	Equipment	47,000	
	Note Payable		10,000
	Jerry Adcock, Capital		65,000
	Initial investment of Jerry		
	Adcock in Adcock and Villa		

DISTRIBUTION OF PARTNERSHIP INCOME AND LOSSES

A partnership's income and losses can be distributed according to whatever method the partners specify in the partnership agreement. Income in this form of business normally has three components: return to the partners for the use of their capital (called *interest on partners' capital*), compensation for services the partners have rendered (partners' salaries), and other income for any special contributions individual partners may make to the partnership or risks they may take. The breakdown of total income into its three components helps clarify how much each partner has contributed to the firm.

Distributing income and losses among partners can be accomplished by using stated ratios or capital balance ratios or by paying the partners' salaries and interest on their capital and sharing the remaining income according to stated ratios. *Salaries* and *interest* here are not *salaries expense* or *interest expense* in the ordinary sense of the terms. They do not affect the amount of reported net income. Instead, they refer to ways of determining each partner's share of net income or loss on the basis of time spent and money invested in the partnership.

■ **STATED RATIOS** One method of distributing income and losses is to give each partner a stated ratio of the total income or loss. If each partner is making an equal contribution to the firm, each can assume the same share of income and losses. It is important to understand that an equal contribution to the firm does not necessarily mean an equal capital investment in the firm. One partner may be devoting more time and talent to the firm, whereas another may have made a larger capital investment. And if the partners contribute unequally to the firm, unequal stated ratios can be appropriate. Let's assume that Adcock and Villa had a net income last year of $140,000 and that the stated ratio for Adcock is 60 percent and for Villa, 40 percent. The computation of each partner's share of the income and the journal entry to show the distribution based on these ratios are as follows:

Adcock ($140,000 × .60)	$ 84,000
Villa ($140,000 × .40)	56,000
Net income	$140,000

20x4			
June 30	Income Summary	140,000	
	Jerry Adcock, Capital		84,000
	Rose Villa, Capital		56,000
	Distribution of income for the year to the partners' Capital accounts		

■ **CAPITAL BALANCE RATIOS**   If invested capital produces the most income for the partnership, then income and losses may be distributed according to *capital balance*. One way of distributing income and losses here is to use a ratio based on each partner's capital balance at the beginning of the year. For example, suppose that at the start of the fiscal year, July 1, 20x3, Jerry Adcock, Capital showed a $65,000 balance and Rose Villa, Capital showed a $60,000 balance. The total partners' equity in the firm, then, was $125,000. Each partner's capital balance at the beginning of the year divided by the total partners' equity at the beginning of the year is that partner's beginning capital balance ratio:

	Beginning Capital Balance	Beginning Capital Balance Ratio
Jerry Adcock	$ 65,000	65 ÷ 125 = .52 = 52%
Rose Villa	60,000	60 ÷ 125 = .48 = 48%
	$125,000	

The income that each partner should receive when distribution is based on beginning capital balance ratios is figured by multiplying the total income by each partner's capital ratio. If we assume that income for the year was $140,000, Jerry Adcock's share of that income was $72,800, and Rose Villa's share was $67,200:

Jerry Adcock	$140,000 × .52 =	$ 72,800
Rose Villa	$140,000 × .48 =	67,200
		$140,000

■ **SALARIES, INTEREST, AND STATED RATIOS**   Partners generally do not contribute equally to a firm. To make up for unequal contributions, a partnership agreement can allow for partners' salaries, interest on partners' capital balances, or a combination of both in the distribution of income. Again, salaries and interest of this kind are not deducted as expenses before the partnership income is determined. They represent a method of arriving at an equitable distribution of income or loss.

Salaries allow for differences in the services that partners provide the business. However, they do not take into account differences in invested capital. To allow for capital differences, each partner can receive, in addition to salary, a stated interest on his or her invested capital. Suppose that Jerry Adcock and Rose Villa agree to annual salaries of $8,000 and $7,000, respectively, as well as 10 percent interest on their beginning capital balances, and to share any remaining income equally. The calculations for Adcock and Villa, assuming income of $140,000, are shown at the top of the next page.

If the partnership agreement allows for the distribution of salaries or interest or both, the amounts must be allocated to the partners even if profits are not enough to cover the salaries and interest. In fact, even if the company has a loss, these allocations still must be made. The negative balance, or loss, after the allocation of salaries and interest must be distributed according to the stated ratio in the partnership agreement, or equally if the agreement does not mention a ratio.

	Income of Partner		Income Distributed
	Adcock	Villa	
Total Income for Distribution			$140,000
Distribution of Salaries			
Adcock	$ 8,000		
Villa		$ 7,000	(15,000)
Remaining Income After Salaries			$125,000
Distribution of Interest			
Adcock ($65,000 × .10)	6,500		
Villa ($60,000 × .10)		6,000	(12,500)
Remaining Income After Salaries and Interest			$112,500
Equal Distribution of Remaining Income			
Adcock ($112,500 × .50)	56,250		
Villa ($112,500 × .50)		56,250	(112,500)
Remaining Income			—
Income of Partners	$70,750	$69,250	$140,000

For example, let's assume that Adcock and Villa agreed to the following conditions, with much higher annual salaries, for the distribution of income and losses:

	Salaries	Interest	Beginning Capital Balance
Adcock	$70,000	10 percent of beginning	$65,000
Villa	60,000	capital balances	60,000

The computations for the distribution of the income and loss, again assuming income of $140,000, are as follows:

	Income of Partner		Income Distributed
	Adcock	Villa	
Total Income for Distribution			$140,000
Distribution of Salaries			
Adcock	$70,000		
Villa		$60,000	(130,000)
Remaining Income After Salaries			$ 10,000
Distribution of Interest			
Adcock ($65,000 × .10)	6,500		
Villa ($60,000 × .10)		6,000	(12,500)
Negative Balance After Salaries and Interest			($ 2,500)
Equal Distribution of Negative Balance*			
Adcock ($2,500 × .50)	(1,250)		
Villa ($2,500 × .50)		(1,250)	2,500
Remaining Income			—
Income of Partners	$75,250	$64,750	$140,000

*Notice that the negative balance is distributed equally because the agreement does not indicate how income and losses should be distributed after salaries and interest are paid.

DISSOLUTION OF A PARTNERSHIP

Dissolution of a partnership occurs whenever there is a change in the original association of partners. When a partnership is dissolved, the partners lose their authority to continue the business as a going concern. This does not mean that the business operation necessarily is ended or interrupted, but it does mean—from a legal and accounting standpoint—that the separate entity ceases to exist. The remaining partners can act for the partnership in finishing the affairs of the business or in forming a new partnership that will be a new accounting entity. The dissolution of a partnership takes place through, among other events, the admission of a new partner, the withdrawal of a partner, or the death of a partner.

■ **ADMISSION OF A NEW PARTNER**   The admission of a new partner dissolves the old partnership because a new association has been formed. Dissolving the old partnership and creating a new one requires the consent of all the original partners and the ratification of a new partnership agreement. An individual can be admitted to a partnership in one of two ways: by purchasing an interest in the partnership from one or more of the original partners, or by investing assets in the partnership.

Purchasing an Interest from a Partner   When a person purchases an interest in a partnership from an original partner, the transaction is a personal one between these two people. However, the interest purchased must be transferred from the Capital account of the selling partner to the Capital account of the new partner.

Suppose that Jerry Adcock decides to sell his interest of $70,000 in Adcock and Villa to Richard Davis for $100,000 on August 31, 20x5, and that Rose Villa agrees to the sale. The entry to record the sale on the partnership books looks like this:

20x5

Aug. 31	Jerry Adcock, Capital	70,000	
	Richard Davis, Capital		70,000
	Transfer of Jerry Adcock's equity to Richard Davis		

Notice that the entry records the book value of the equity, not the amount Davis pays. The amount Davis pays is a personal matter between him and Adcock.

Investing Assets in a Partnership   When a new partner is admitted through an investment in the partnership, both the assets and the partners' equity in the firm increase. This is because the assets the new partner invests become partnership assets, and as partnership assets increase, partners' equity increases.

For example, assume that Richard Davis wants to invest $75,000 for a one-third interest in the partnership of Adcock and Villa. The Capital accounts of Jerry Adcock and Rose Villa are $70,000 and $80,000, respectively. The assets of the firm are valued correctly. So, the partners agree to sell Davis a one-third interest in the firm for $75,000. Davis's $75,000 investment equals a one-third interest in the firm after the investment is added to the previously existing capital of the partnership:

Jerry Adcock, Capital	$ 70,000
Rose Villa, Capital	80,000
Davis's investment	75,000
Total capital after Davis's investment	$225,000
One-third interest = $225,000 ÷ 3 =	$ 75,000

The entry to record Davis's investment is as follows:

20x5

Aug. 31	Cash	75,000	
	Richard Davis, Capital		75,000
	Admission of Richard Davis for a one-third interest in the company		

Bonus to the Old Partners   A partnership is sometimes so profitable or otherwise advantageous that a new investor is willing to pay more than the actual dollar interest he or she receives in the partnership. Suppose an individual pays $100,000 for an $80,000 interest in a partnership. The $20,000 excess of the payment over the interest purchased is a *bonus* to the original partners. The bonus must be distributed to the original partners according to the partnership agreement. When the agreement does not cover the distribution of bonuses, it should be distributed to the original partners in accordance with the method of distributing income and losses.

Assume that the Adcock and Villa Company has operated for several years and that the partners' capital balances and the stated ratios for distribution of income and loss are as follows:

Partners	Capital Balances	Stated Ratios
Adcock	$160,000	55%
Villa	140,000	45%
	$300,000	100%

Richard Davis wants to join the firm. He offers to invest $100,000 on December 1 for a one-fifth interest in the business and income. The original partners agree to the offer. This is the computation of the bonus to the original partners:

Partners' equity in the original partnership		$300,000
Cash investment by Richard Davis		100,000
Partners' equity in the new partnership		$400,000
Partners' equity assigned to Richard Davis ($400,000 × ⅕)		$ 80,000
Bonus to the original partners		
Investment by Richard Davis	$100,000	
Less equity assigned to Richard Davis	80,000	$ 20,000
Distribution of bonus to original partners		
Jerry Adcock ($20,000 × .55)	$ 11,000	
Rose Villa ($20,000 × .45)	9,000	$ 20,000

This is the entry that records Davis's admission to the partnership:

```
20x5
Dec. 1   Cash                                       100,000
             Jerry Adcock, Capital                            11,000
             Rose Villa, Capital                               9,000
             Richard Davis, Capital                          80,000
                Investment by Richard Davis for
                a one-fifth interest in the firm,
                and the bonus distributed to the
                original partners
```

Bonus to the New Partner   There are several reasons why a partnership might want a new partner. A partnership in financial trouble might need additional cash. Or the partners might want to expand the firm's markets and need more capital for this purpose than they themselves can provide. Also, the partners might know a person who would bring a unique talent to the firm. Under these conditions, a new partner may be admitted to the partnership with the understanding that part of the original partners' capital will be transferred (credited) to the new partner's Capital account as a bonus.

■ **WITHDRAWAL OF A PARTNER**   Generally, a partner has the right to withdraw from a partnership in accord with legal requirements. However, to avoid disputes when a partner does decide to withdraw or retire from the firm, the partnership agreement should describe the procedures to be followed. The agreement should specify

(1) whether an audit will be performed, (2) how the assets will be reappraised, (3) how a bonus will be determined, and (4) by what method the withdrawing partner will be paid.

A partner who wants to withdraw from a partnership can do so in one of several ways. The partner can sell his or her interest to another partner or to an outsider with the consent of the remaining partners, or the partner can withdraw assets equal to his or her capital balance, less than his or her capital balance (in this case, the remaining partners receive a bonus), or greater than his or her capital balance (in this case, the withdrawing partner receives a bonus). Bonuses upon withdrawal of a partner are allocated in much the same way as bonuses that arise when a new partner is admitted.

■ **DEATH OF A PARTNER**   When a partner dies, the partnership is dissolved because the original association has changed. The partnership agreement should state the actions to be taken. Normally, the books are closed, and financial statements are prepared. These actions are necessary to determine the capital balance of each partner on the date of the death. The agreement also may indicate whether an audit should be conducted, assets appraised, and a bonus recorded, as well as the procedures for settling with the deceased partner's heirs. The remaining partners may purchase the deceased's equity, sell it to outsiders, or deliver certain business assets to the estate. If the firm intends to continue, a new partnership must be formed.

LIQUIDATION OF A PARTNERSHIP

Liquidation of a partnership is the process of ending the business—of selling enough assets to pay the partnership's liabilities and distributing any remaining assets among the partners. Liquidation is a special form of dissolution. When a partnership is liquidated, the business will not continue. As the assets of the business are sold, any gain or loss should be distributed to the partners according to the stated ratios. As cash becomes available, it must be applied first to outside creditors, then to loans from partners, and finally to the partners' capital balances. Any deficits in partners' capital accounts must be made up from personal assets.

PROBLEMS

Partnership Formation and Distribution of Income

P 1. In January 20x3, Ed Rivers and Bob Bascomb agreed to produce and sell chocolate candies. Rivers contributed $240,000 in cash to the business. Bascomb contributed the building and equipment, valued at $220,000 and $140,000, respectively. The partnership had an income of $84,000 during 20x3 but was less successful during 20x4, when income was only $40,000.

REQUIRED ▶

1. Prepare the entry to record the investment of both partners in the partnership.
2. Determine the share of income for each partner in 20x3 and 20x4 under each of the following conditions: (a) The partners agreed to share income equally. (b) The partners failed to agree on an income-sharing arrangement. (c) The partners agreed to share income according to the ratio of their original investments. (d) The partners agreed to share income by allowing interest of 10 percent on their original investments and dividing the remainder equally. (e) The partners agreed to share income by allowing salaries of $40,000 for Rivers and $28,000 for Bascomb, and dividing the remainder equally. (f) The partners agreed to share income by paying salaries of $40,000 to Rivers and $28,000 to Bascomb, allowing interest of 9 percent on their original investments, and dividing the remainder equally.

Admission and Withdrawal of a Partner

P 2. Margaret, Tracy, and Lou are partners in Woodwork Company. Their capital balances as of July 31, 20x4, are as follows:

Margaret, Capital	Tracy, Capital	Lou, Capital
45,000	15,000	30,000

Each partner has agreed to admit Vonice to the partnership.

Prepare the entries to record Vonice's admission to or Margaret's withdrawal from the partnership under each of the following conditions: (a) Vonice pays Margaret $12,500 for 20 percent of Margaret's interest in the partnership. (b) Vonice invests $20,000 cash in the partnership and receives an interest equal to her investment. (c) Vonice invests $30,000 cash in the partnership for a 20 percent interest in the business. A bonus is to be recorded for the original partners on the basis of their capital balances. (d) Vonice invests $30,000 cash in the partnership for a 40 percent interest in the business. The original partners give Vonice a bonus according to the ratio of their capital balances on July 31, 20x4. (e) Margaret withdraws from the partnership, taking $52,500. The excess of withdrawn assets over Margaret's partnership interest is distributed according to the balances of the Capital accounts. (f) Margaret withdraws by selling her interest directly to Vonice for $60,000.

Appendix D

Future Value and Present Value Tables

Table 1 provides the multipliers necessary to compute the future value of a *single* cash deposit made at the *beginning* of year 1. Three factors must be known before the future value can be computed: (1) the time period in years, (2) the stated annual rate of interest to be earned, and (3) the dollar amount invested or deposited.

Example—Table 1. Determine the future value of $5,000 deposited now that will earn 9 percent interest compounded annually for five years. From Table 1, the necessary multiplier for five years at 9 percent is 1.539, and the answer is

$$\$5,000 \times 1.539 = \$7,695$$

TABLE 1. Future Value of $1 After a Given Number of Time Periods

Periods	1%	2%	3%	4%	5%	6%	7%	8%	9%	10%	12%	14%	15%
1	1.010	1.020	1.030	1.040	1.050	1.060	1.070	1.080	1.090	1.100	1.120	1.140	1.150
2	1.020	1.040	1.061	1.082	1.103	1.124	1.145	1.166	1.188	1.210	1.254	1.300	1.323
3	1.030	1.061	1.093	1.125	1.158	1.191	1.225	1.260	1.295	1.331	1.405	1.482	1.521
4	1.041	1.082	1.126	1.170	1.216	1.262	1.311	1.360	1.412	1.464	1.574	1.689	1.749
5	1.051	1.104	1.159	1.217	1.276	1.338	1.403	1.469	1.539	1.611	1.762	1.925	2.011
6	1.062	1.126	1.194	1.265	1.340	1.419	1.501	1.587	1.677	1.772	1.974	2.195	2.313
7	1.072	1.149	1.230	1.316	1.407	1.504	1.606	1.714	1.828	1.949	2.211	2.502	2.660
8	1.083	1.172	1.267	1.369	1.477	1.594	1.718	1.851	1.993	2.144	2.476	2.853	3.059
9	1.094	1.195	1.305	1.423	1.551	1.689	1.838	1.999	2.172	2.358	2.773	3.252	3.518
10	1.105	1.219	1.344	1.480	1.629	1.791	1.967	2.159	2.367	2.594	3.106	3.707	4.046
11	1.116	1.243	1.384	1.539	1.710	1.898	2.105	2.332	2.580	2.853	3.479	4.226	4.652
12	1.127	1.268	1.426	1.601	1.796	2.012	2.252	2.518	2.813	3.138	3.896	4.818	5.350
13	1.138	1.294	1.469	1.665	1.886	2.133	2.410	2.720	3.066	3.452	4.363	5.492	6.153
14	1.149	1.319	1.513	1.732	1.980	2.261	2.579	2.937	3.342	3.798	4.887	6.261	7.076
15	1.161	1.346	1.558	1.801	2.079	2.397	2.759	3.172	3.642	4.177	5.474	7.138	8.137
16	1.173	1.373	1.605	1.873	2.183	2.540	2.952	3.426	3.970	4.595	6.130	8.137	9.358
17	1.184	1.400	1.653	1.948	2.292	2.693	3.159	3.700	4.328	5.054	6.866	9.276	10.760
18	1.196	1.428	1.702	2.026	2.407	2.854	3.380	3.996	4.717	5.560	7.690	10.580	12.380
19	1.208	1.457	1.754	2.107	2.527	3.026	3.617	4.316	5.142	6.116	8.613	12.060	14.230
20	1.220	1.486	1.806	2.191	2.653	3.207	3.870	4.661	5.604	6.728	9.646	13.740	16.370
21	1.232	1.516	1.860	2.279	2.786	3.400	4.141	5.034	6.109	7.400	10.800	15.670	18.820
22	1.245	1.546	1.916	2.370	2.925	3.604	4.430	5.437	6.659	8.140	12.100	17.860	21.640
23	1.257	1.577	1.974	2.465	3.072	3.820	4.741	5.871	7.258	8.954	13.550	20.360	24.890
24	1.270	1.608	2.033	2.563	3.225	4.049	5.072	6.341	7.911	9.850	15.180	23.210	28.630
25	1.282	1.641	2.094	2.666	3.386	4.292	5.427	6.848	8.623	10.830	17.000	26.460	32.920
26	1.295	1.673	2.157	2.772	3.556	4.549	5.807	7.396	9.399	11.920	19.040	30.170	37.860
27	1.308	1.707	2.221	2.883	3.733	4.822	6.214	7.988	10.250	13.110	21.320	34.390	43.540
28	1.321	1.741	2.288	2.999	3.920	5.112	6.649	8.627	11.170	14.420	23.880	39.200	50.070
29	1.335	1.776	2.357	3.119	4.116	5.418	7.114	9.317	12.170	15.860	26.750	44.690	57.580
30	1.348	1.811	2.427	3.243	4.322	5.743	7.612	10.060	13.270	17.450	29.960	50.950	66.210
40	1.489	2.208	3.262	4.801	7.040	10.290	14.970	21.720	31.410	45.260	93.050	188.900	267.900
50	1.645	2.692	4.384	7.107	11.470	18.420	29.460	46.900	74.360	117.400	289.000	700.200	1,084.000

Where r is the interest rate and n is the number of periods, the factor values for Table 1 are

$$FV\ factor = (1 + r)^n$$

Situations requiring the use of Table 2 are similar to those requiring Table 1 except that Table 2 is used to compute the future value of a *series* of *equal* annual deposits at the end of each period.

Example—Table 2. What will be the future value at the end of 30 years if $1,000 is deposited each year on January 1, beginning in year 1, assuming 12 percent interest compounded annually? The required multiplier from Table 2 is 241.3, and the answer is

$$\$1,000 \times 241.3 = \$241,300$$

The factor values for Table 2 are

$$FVa\ factor = \frac{(1 + r)^n - 1}{r}$$

TABLE 2. Future Value of $1 Paid in Each Period for a Given Number of Time Periods

Periods	1%	2%	3%	4%	5%	6%	7%	8%	9%	10%	12%	14%	15%
1	1.000	1.000	1.000	1.000	1.000	1.000	1.000	1.000	1.000	1.000	1.000	1.000	1.000
2	2.010	2.020	2.030	2.040	2.050	2.060	2.070	2.080	2.090	2.100	2.120	2.140	2.150
3	3.030	3.060	3.091	3.122	3.153	3.184	3.215	3.246	3.278	3.310	3.374	3.440	3.473
4	4.060	4.122	4.184	4.246	4.310	4.375	4.440	4.506	4.573	4.641	4.779	4.921	4.993
5	5.101	5.204	5.309	5.416	5.526	5.637	5.751	5.867	5.985	6.105	6.353	6.610	6.742
6	6.152	6.308	6.468	6.633	6.802	6.975	7.153	7.336	7.523	7.716	8.115	8.536	8.754
7	7.214	7.434	7.662	7.898	8.142	8.394	8.654	8.923	9.200	9.487	10.090	10.730	11.070
8	8.286	8.583	8.892	9.214	9.549	9.897	10.260	10.640	11.030	11.440	12.300	13.230	13.730
9	9.369	9.755	10.160	10.580	11.030	11.490	11.980	12.490	13.020	13.580	14.780	16.090	16.790
10	10.460	10.950	11.460	12.010	12.580	13.180	13.820	14.490	15.190	15.940	17.550	19.340	20.300
11	11.570	12.170	12.810	13.490	14.210	14.970	15.780	16.650	17.560	18.530	20.650	23.040	24.350
12	12.680	13.410	14.190	15.030	15.920	16.870	17.890	18.980	20.140	21.380	24.130	27.270	29.000
13	13.810	14.680	15.620	16.630	17.710	18.880	20.140	21.500	22.950	24.520	28.030	32.090	34.350
14	14.950	15.970	17.090	18.290	19.600	21.020	22.550	24.210	26.020	27.980	32.390	37.580	40.500
15	16.100	17.290	18.600	20.020	21.580	23.280	25.130	27.150	29.360	31.770	37.280	43.840	47.580
16	17.260	18.640	20.160	21.820	23.660	25.670	27.890	30.320	33.000	35.950	42.750	50.980	55.720
17	18.430	20.010	21.760	23.700	25.840	28.210	30.840	33.750	36.970	40.540	48.880	59.120	65.080
18	19.610	21.410	23.410	25.650	28.130	30.910	34.000	37.450	41.300	45.600	55.750	68.390	75.840
19	20.810	22.840	25.120	27.670	30.540	33.760	37.380	41.450	46.020	51.160	63.440	78.970	88.210
20	22.020	24.300	26.870	29.780	33.070	36.790	41.000	45.760	51.160	57.280	72.050	91.020	102.400
21	23.240	25.780	28.680	31.970	35.720	39.990	44.870	50.420	56.760	64.000	81.700	104.800	118.800
22	24.470	27.300	30.540	34.250	38.510	43.390	49.010	55.460	62.870	71.400	92.500	120.400	137.600
23	25.720	28.850	32.450	36.620	41.430	47.000	53.440	60.890	69.530	79.540	104.600	138.300	159.300
24	26.970	30.420	34.430	39.080	44.500	50.820	58.180	66.760	76.790	88.500	118.200	158.700	184.200
25	28.240	32.030	36.460	41.650	47.730	54.860	63.250	73.110	84.700	98.350	133.300	181.900	212.800
26	29.530	33.670	38.550	44.310	51.110	59.160	68.680	79.950	93.320	109.200	150.300	208.300	245.700
27	30.820	35.340	40.710	47.080	54.670	63.710	74.480	87.350	102.700	121.100	169.400	238.500	283.600
28	32.130	37.050	42.930	49.970	58.400	68.530	80.700	95.340	113.000	134.200	190.700	272.900	327.100
29	33.450	38.790	45.220	52.970	62.320	73.640	87.350	104.000	124.100	148.600	214.600	312.100	377.200
30	34.780	40.570	47.580	56.080	66.440	79.060	94.460	113.300	136.300	164.500	241.300	356.800	434.700
40	48.890	60.400	75.400	95.030	120.800	154.800	199.600	259.100	337.900	442.600	767.100	1,342.000	1,779.000
50	64.460	84.580	112.800	152.700	209.300	290.300	406.500	573.800	815.100	1,164.000	2,400.000	4,995.000	7,218.000

TABLE 3.   **Present Value of $1 to Be Received at the End of a Given Number of Time Periods**

Periods	1%	2%	3%	4%	5%	6%	7%	8%	9%	10%	12%
1	0.990	0.980	0.971	0.962	0.952	0.943	0.935	0.926	0.917	0.909	0.893
2	0.980	0.961	0.943	0.925	0.907	0.890	0.873	0.857	0.842	0.826	0.797
3	0.971	0.942	0.915	0.889	0.864	0.840	0.816	0.794	0.772	0.751	0.712
4	0.961	0.924	0.888	0.855	0.823	0.792	0.763	0.735	0.708	0.683	0.636
5	0.951	0.906	0.883	0.822	0.784	0.747	0.713	0.681	0.650	0.621	0.567
6	0.942	0.888	0.837	0.790	0.746	0.705	0.666	0.630	0.596	0.564	0.507
7	0.933	0.871	0.813	0.760	0.711	0.665	0.623	0.583	0.547	0.513	0.452
8	0.923	0.853	0.789	0.731	0.677	0.627	0.582	0.540	0.502	0.467	0.404
9	0.914	0.837	0.766	0.703	0.645	0.592	0.544	0.500	0.460	0.424	0.361
10	0.905	0.820	0.744	0.676	0.614	0.558	0.508	0.463	0.422	0.386	0.322
11	0.896	0.804	0.722	0.650	0.585	0.527	0.475	0.429	0.388	0.350	0.287
12	0.887	0.788	0.701	0.625	0.557	0.497	0.444	0.397	0.356	0.319	0.257
13	0.879	0.773	0.681	0.601	0.530	0.469	0.415	0.368	0.326	0.290	0.229
14	0.870	0.758	0.661	0.577	0.505	0.442	0.388	0.340	0.299	0.263	0.205
15	0.861	0.743	0.642	0.555	0.481	0.417	0.362	0.315	0.275	0.239	0.183
16	0.853	0.728	0.623	0.534	0.458	0.394	0.339	0.292	0.252	0.218	0.163
17	0.844	0.714	0.605	0.513	0.436	0.371	0.317	0.270	0.231	0.198	0.146
18	0.836	0.700	0.587	0.494	0.416	0.350	0.296	0.250	0.212	0.180	0.130
19	0.828	0.686	0.570	0.475	0.396	0.331	0.277	0.232	0.194	0.164	0.116
20	0.820	0.673	0.554	0.456	0.377	0.312	0.258	0.215	0.178	0.149	0.104
21	0.811	0.660	0.538	0.439	0.359	0.294	0.242	0.199	0.164	0.135	0.093
22	0.803	0.647	0.522	0.422	0.342	0.278	0.226	0.184	0.150	0.123	0.083
23	0.795	0.634	0.507	0.406	0.326	0.262	0.211	0.170	0.138	0.112	0.074
24	0.788	0.622	0.492	0.390	0.310	0.247	0.197	0.158	0.126	0.102	0.066
25	0.780	0.610	0.478	0.375	0.295	0.233	0.184	0.146	0.116	0.092	0.059
26	0.772	0.598	0.464	0.361	0.281	0.220	0.172	0.135	0.106	0.084	0.053
27	0.764	0.586	0.450	0.347	0.268	0.207	0.161	0.125	0.098	0.076	0.047
28	0.757	0.574	0.437	0.333	0.255	0.196	0.150	0.116	0.090	0.069	0.042
29	0.749	0.563	0.424	0.321	0.243	0.185	0.141	0.107	0.082	0.063	0.037
30	0.742	0.552	0.412	0.308	0.231	0.174	0.131	0.099	0.075	0.057	0.033
40	0.672	0.453	0.307	0.208	0.142	0.097	0.067	0.046	0.032	0.022	0.011
50	0.608	0.372	0.228	0.141	0.087	0.054	0.034	0.021	0.013	0.009	0.003

Table 3 is used to compute the value today of a single amount of cash to be received sometime in the future. To use Table 3, you must first know (1) the time period in years until funds will be received, (2) the stated annual rate of interest, and (3) the dollar amount to be received at the end of the time period.

Example—Table 3. What is the present value of $30,000 to be received 25 years from now, assuming a 14 percent interest rate? From Table 3, the required multiplier is .038, and the answer is

$$\$30,000 \times .038 = \$1,140$$

14%	15%	16%	18%	20%	25%	30%	35%	40%	45%	50%	Periods
0.877	0.870	0.862	0.847	0.833	0.800	0.769	0.741	0.714	0.690	0.667	1
0.769	0.756	0.743	0.718	0.694	0.640	0.592	0.549	0.510	0.476	0.444	2
0.675	0.658	0.641	0.609	0.579	0.512	0.455	0.406	0.364	0.328	0.296	3
0.592	0.572	0.552	0.516	0.482	0.410	0.350	0.301	0.260	0.226	0.198	4
0.519	0.497	0.476	0.437	0.402	0.328	0.269	0.223	0.186	0.156	0.132	5
0.456	0.432	0.410	0.370	0.335	0.262	0.207	0.165	0.133	0.108	0.088	6
0.400	0.376	0.354	0.314	0.279	0.210	0.159	0.122	0.095	0.074	0.059	7
0.351	0.327	0.305	0.266	0.233	0.168	0.123	0.091	0.068	0.051	0.039	8
0.308	0.284	0.263	0.225	0.194	0.134	0.094	0.067	0.048	0.035	0.026	9
0.270	0.247	0.227	0.191	0.162	0.107	0.073	0.050	0.035	0.024	0.017	10
0.237	0.215	0.195	0.162	0.135	0.086	0.056	0.037	0.025	0.017	0.012	11
0.208	0.187	0.168	0.137	0.112	0.069	0.043	0.027	0.018	0.012	0.008	12
0.182	0.163	0.145	0.116	0.093	0.055	0.033	0.020	0.013	0.008	0.005	13
0.160	0.141	0.125	0.099	0.078	0.044	0.025	0.015	0.009	0.006	0.003	14
0.140	0.123	0.108	0.084	0.065	0.035	0.020	0.011	0.006	0.004	0.002	15
0.123	0.107	0.093	0.071	0.054	0.028	0.015	0.008	0.005	0.003	0.002	16
0.108	0.093	0.080	0.060	0.045	0.023	0.012	0.006	0.003	0.002	0.001	17
0.095	0.081	0.069	0.051	0.038	0.018	0.009	0.005	0.002	0.001	0.001	18
0.083	0.070	0.060	0.043	0.031	0.014	0.007	0.003	0.002	0.001		19
0.073	0.061	0.051	0.037	0.026	0.012	0.005	0.002	0.001	0.001		20
0.064	0.053	0.044	0.031	0.022	0.009	0.004	0.002	0.001			21
0.056	0.046	0.038	0.026	0.018	0.007	0.003	0.001	0.001			22
0.049	0.040	0.033	0.022	0.015	0.006	0.002	0.001				23
0.043	0.035	0.028	0.019	0.013	0.005	0.002	0.001				24
0.038	0.030	0.024	0.016	0.010	0.004	0.001	0.001				25
0.033	0.026	0.021	0.014	0.009	0.003	0.001					26
0.029	0.023	0.018	0.011	0.007	0.002	0.001					27
0.026	0.020	0.016	0.010	0.006	0.002	0.001					28
0.022	0.017	0.014	0.008	0.005	0.002						29
0.020	0.015	0.012	0.007	0.004	0.001						30
0.005	0.004	0.003	0.001	0.001							40
0.001	0.001	0.001									50

The factor values for Table 3 are

$$\text{PV factor} = (1 + r)^{-n}$$

Table 3 is the reciprocal of Table 1.

TABLE 4.   Present Value of $1 Received Each Period for a Given Number of Time Periods

Periods	1%	2%	3%	4%	5%	6%	7%	8%	9%	10%	12%
1	0.990	0.980	0.971	0.962	0.952	0.943	0.935	0.926	0.917	0.909	0.893
2	1.970	1.942	1.913	1.886	1.859	1.833	1.808	1.783	1.759	1.736	1.690
3	2.941	2.884	2.829	2.775	2.723	2.673	2.624	2.577	2.531	2.487	2.402
4	3.902	3.808	3.717	3.630	3.546	3.465	3.387	3.312	3.240	3.170	3.037
5	4.853	4.713	4.580	4.452	4.329	4.212	4.100	3.993	3.890	3.791	3.605
6	5.795	5.601	5.417	5.242	5.076	4.917	4.767	4.623	4.486	4.355	4.111
7	6.728	6.472	6.230	6.002	5.786	5.582	5.389	5.206	5.033	4.868	4.564
8	7.652	7.325	7.020	6.733	6.463	6.210	5.971	5.747	5.535	5.335	4.968
9	8.566	8.162	7.786	7.435	7.108	6.802	6.515	6.247	5.995	5.759	5.328
10	9.471	8.983	8.530	8.111	7.722	7.360	7.024	6.710	6.418	6.145	5.650
11	10.368	9.787	9.253	8.760	8.306	7.887	7.499	7.139	6.805	6.495	5.938
12	11.255	10.575	9.954	9.385	8.863	8.384	7.943	7.536	7.161	6.814	6.194
13	12.134	11.348	10.635	9.986	9.394	8.853	8.358	7.904	7.487	7.103	6.424
14	13.004	12.106	11.296	10.563	9.899	9.295	8.745	8.244	7.786	7.367	6.628
15	13.865	12.849	11.938	11.118	10.380	9.712	9.108	8.559	8.061	7.606	6.811
16	14.718	13.578	12.561	11.652	10.838	10.106	9.447	8.851	8.313	7.824	6.974
17	15.562	14.292	13.166	12.166	11.274	10.477	9.763	9.122	8.544	8.022	7.120
18	16.398	14.992	13.754	12.659	11.690	10.828	10.059	9.372	8.756	8.201	7.250
19	17.226	15.678	14.324	13.134	12.085	11.158	10.336	9.604	8.950	8.365	7.366
20	18.046	16.351	14.878	13.590	12.462	11.470	10.594	9.818	9.129	8.514	7.469
21	18.857	17.011	15.415	14.029	12.821	11.764	10.836	10.017	9.292	8.649	7.562
22	19.660	17.658	15.937	14.451	13.163	12.042	11.061	10.201	9.442	8.772	7.645
23	20.456	18.292	16.444	14.857	13.489	12.303	11.272	10.371	9.580	8.883	7.718
24	21.243	18.914	16.936	15.247	13.799	12.550	11.469	10.529	9.707	8.985	7.784
25	22.023	19.523	17.413	15.622	14.094	12.783	11.654	10.675	9.823	9.077	7.843
26	22.795	20.121	17.877	15.983	14.375	13.003	11.826	10.810	9.929	9.161	7.896
27	23.560	20.707	18.327	16.330	14.643	13.211	11.987	10.935	10.027	9.237	7.943
28	24.316	21.281	18.764	16.663	14.898	13.406	12.137	11.051	10.116	9.307	7.984
29	25.066	21.844	19.189	16.984	15.141	13.591	12.278	11.158	10.198	9.370	8.022
30	25.808	22.396	19.600	17.292	15.373	13.765	12.409	11.258	10.274	9.427	8.055
40	32.835	27.355	23.115	19.793	17.159	15.046	13.332	11.925	10.757	9.779	8.244
50	39.196	31.424	25.730	21.482	18.256	15.762	13.801	12.234	10.962	9.915	8.305

Table 4 is used to compute the present value of a *series* of *equal* annual cash flows.

Example—Table 4. Arthur Howard won a contest on January 1, 20x4, in which the prize was $30,000, payable in 15 annual installments of $2,000 each December 31, beginning in 20x4. Assuming a 9 percent interest rate, what is the present value of Howard's prize on January 1, 20x4? From Table 4, the required multiplier is 8.061, and the answer is:

$$\$2,000 \times 8.061 = \$16,122$$

The factor values for Table 4 are

$$\text{PVa factor} = \frac{1 - (1 + r)^{-n}}{r}$$

Table 4 is the columnar sum of Table 3. Table 4 applies to *ordinary annuities*, in which the first cash flow occurs one time period beyond the date for which the present value is computed.

14%	15%	16%	18%	20%	25%	30%	35%	40%	45%	50%	Periods
0.877	0.870	0.862	0.847	0.833	0.800	0.769	0.741	0.714	0.690	0.667	1
1.647	1.626	1.605	1.566	1.528	1.440	1.361	1.289	1.224	1.165	1.111	2
2.322	2.283	2.246	2.174	2.106	1.952	1.816	1.696	1.589	1.493	1.407	3
2.914	2.855	2.798	2.690	2.589	2.362	2.166	1.997	1.849	1.720	1.605	4
3.433	3.352	3.274	3.127	2.991	2.689	2.436	2.220	2.035	1.876	1.737	5
3.889	3.784	3.685	3.498	3.326	2.951	2.643	2.385	2.168	1.983	1.824	6
4.288	4.160	4.039	3.812	3.605	3.161	2.802	2.508	2.263	2.057	1.883	7
4.639	4.487	4.344	4.078	3.837	3.329	2.925	2.598	2.331	2.109	1.922	8
4.946	4.772	4.607	4.303	4.031	3.463	3.019	2.665	2.379	2.144	1.948	9
5.216	5.019	4.833	4.494	4.192	3.571	3.092	2.715	2.414	2.168	1.965	10
5.453	5.234	5.029	4.656	4.327	3.656	3.147	2.752	2.438	2.185	1.977	11
5.660	5.421	5.197	4.793	4.439	3.725	3.190	2.779	2.456	2.197	1.985	12
5.842	5.583	5.342	4.910	4.533	3.780	3.223	2.799	2.469	2.204	1.990	13
6.002	5.724	5.468	5.008	4.611	3.824	3.249	2.814	2.478	2.210	1.993	14
6.142	5.847	5.575	5.092	4.675	3.859	3.268	2.825	2.484	2.214	1.995	15
6.265	5.954	5.669	5.162	4.730	3.887	3.283	2.834	2.489	2.216	1.997	16
6.373	6.047	5.749	5.222	4.775	3.910	3.295	2.840	2.492	2.218	1.998	17
6.467	6.128	5.818	5.273	4.812	3.928	3.304	2.844	2.494	2.219	1.999	18
6.550	6.198	5.877	5.316	4.844	3.942	3.311	2.848	2.496	2.220	1.999	19
6.623	6.259	5.929	5.353	4.870	3.954	3.316	2.850	2.497	2.221	1.999	20
6.687	6.312	5.973	5.384	4.891	3.963	3.320	2.852	2.498	2.221	2.000	21
6.743	6.359	6.011	5.410	4.909	3.970	3.323	2.853	2.498	2.222	2.000	22
6.792	6.399	6.044	5.432	4.925	3.976	3.325	2.854	2.499	2.222	2.000	23
6.835	6.434	6.073	5.451	4.973	3.981	3.327	2.855	2.499	2.222	2.000	24
6.873	6.464	6.097	5.467	4.948	3.985	3.329	2.856	2.499	2.222	2.000	25
6.906	6.491	6.118	5.480	4.956	3.988	3.330	2.856	2.500	2.222	2.000	26
6.935	6.514	6.136	5.492	4.964	3.990	3.331	2.856	2.500	2.222	2.000	27
6.961	6.534	6.152	5.502	4.970	3.992	3.331	2.857	2.500	2.222	2.000	28
6.983	6.551	6.166	5.510	4.975	3.994	3.332	2.857	2.500	2.222	2.000	29
7.003	6.566	6.177	5.517	4.979	3.995	3.332	2.857	2.500	2.222	2.000	30
7.105	6.642	6.234	5.548	4.997	3.999	3.333	2.857	2.500	2.222	2.000	40
7.133	6.661	6.246	5.554	4.999	4.000	3.333	2.857	2.500	2.222	2.000	50

An *annuity due* is a series of equal cash flows for N time periods, but the first payment occurs immediately. The present value of the first payment equals the face value of the cash flow; Table 4 then is used to measure the present value of $N - 1$ remaining cash flows.

Example—Table 4. Determine the present value on January 1, 20x4, of 20 lease payments; each payment of $10,000 is due on January 1, beginning in 20x4. Assume an interest rate of 8 percent.

$$\text{Present value} = \text{Immediate payment} + \left\{ \frac{\text{Present value of 19 subsequent}}{\text{payments at 8\%}} \right.$$

$$= \$10,000 + (\$10,000 \times 9.604) = \$106,040$$

Endnotes

Chapter 1

1. Walgreen Co., *Annual Report*, 2001.
2. *Statement of Financial Accounting Concepts No. 1*, "Objectives of Financial Reporting by Business Enterprises" (Norwalk, Conn.: Financial Accounting Standards Board, 1978), par. 9.
3. Ibid.
4. Christopher D. Ittner, David F. Larcker, and Madhav V. Rajan, "The Choice of Performance Measures in Annual Bonus Contracts," *The Accounting Review*, April 1997.
5. Walgreen Co., *Annual Report*, 2001.
6. Kathy Williams and James Hart, "Microsoft: Tooling the Information Age," *Management Accounting*, May 1996, p. 42.
7. *Statement of the Accounting Principles Board No. 4*, "Basic Concepts and Accounting Principles Underlying Financial Statements of Business Enterprises" (New York: American Institute of Certified Public Accountants, 1970), par. 138.
8. Touche Ross & Co., "Ethics in American Business" (New York: Touche Ross & Co., 1988), p. 7.
9. "Global Ethics Codes Gain Importance as a Tool to Avoid Litigation and Fines," *The Wall Street Journal*, August 19, 1999.
10. *Statement Number IC*, "Standards of Ethical Conduct for Management Accountants" (Montvale, N.J.: Institute of Management Accountants, 1983, revised 1997).
11. J.C. Penney Company, Inc., *Annual Report*, 1995.
12. Nikhil Deogun, "Coca-Cola Reports 27% Drop in Profits Hurt by Weakness in Foreign Markets," *The Wall Street Journal*, January 27, 1999.
13. Southwest Airlines Co., *Annual Report*, 1996.
14. Queen Sook Kim, "Lechters Inc. Files for Chapter 11, Arranges Financing," *The Wall Street Journal*, May 22, 2001.
15. Charles Schwab Corporation, *Annual Report*, 2001.
16. Robert Frank, "Facing a Loss, Lego Narrates a Sad Toy Story," *The Wall Street Journal*, January 22, 1999.

Chapter 2

1. "Boeing Scores a Deal to Sell 15 Planes for Long-Haul Routes," *The Wall Street Journal*, October 5, 2000.
2. The Boeing Co., *Annual Report*, 1994.
3. Craig S. Smith, "China Halts New Purchases of Jets," *The Wall Street Journal*, February 9, 1999.
4. The Boeing Co., *Annual Report*, 2000.
5. Patricia Kranz, "Rubles? Who Needs Rubles?" *BusinessWeek*, April 13, 1998; Andrew Higgins, "Lacking Money to Pay, Russian Firms Survive on Deft Barter System," *The Wall Street Journal*, August 27, 1998.
6. Intel Corp., *Annual Report*, 2000.
7. Shawn Young, "Lucent Revises Its Revenue Downward," *The Wall Street Journal*, December 22, 2000.
8. Nike, Inc., *Annual Report*, 2000.
9. Mellon Bank, *Annual Report*, 2000.
10. Ajinomoto Company, *Annual Report*, 2000.

Chapter 3

1. Kelly Services, *Annual Report*, 2000.
2. *Statement of Financial Accounting Concepts No. 1*, "Objectives of Financial Reporting by Business Enterprises" (Norwalk, Conn.: Financial Accounting Standards Board, 1978), par. 44.
3. "Revenue Recognition in Financial Statements," *Staff Accounting Bulletin No. 10* (Securities and Exchange Commission, 1999).
4. Thomas J. Phillips Jr., Michael S. Luehlfing, and Cynthia M. Daily, "The Right Way to Recognize Revenue," *Journal of Accountancy*, June 2001.
5. Michael Schroeder and Elizabeth MacDonald, "SEC Expects More Big Cases on Accounting," *The Wall Street Journal*, December 24, 1998.
6. PricewaterhouseCoopers presentation, 1999.
7. Lyric Opera of Chicago, *Annual Report*, 2001.
8. The Walt Disney Company, *Annual Report*, 2001.
9. H. J. Heinz Company, *Annual Report*, 2001.
10. Takashimaya Company, Limited, *Annual Report*, 2000.

Chapter 4

1. Hershey Foods Corp., Form 10-Q, September 30, 2001.
2. News item, *Crain's Chicago Business*, October 2001.
3. News item, *The Wall Street Journal*, July 29, 1999.
4. Michael Totty, "The Next Phase," *The Wall Street Journal*, May 21, 2001.
5. Frank Potter, "Event-to-Knowledge: A New Metric for Finance Department Efficiency," *Strategic Finance*, July 2001.
6. Adapted from H & R Block, Inc., *Annual Report*, 2001.
7. Nestlé S.A., *Annual Report*, 2000.

Chapter 5

1. General Mills, Inc., *Annual Report*, 2001.
2. "Objectives of Financial Reporting by Business Enterprises," *Statement of Financial Accounting Concepts No. 1* (Norwalk, Conn.: Financial Accounting Standards Board, 1978), pars. 32–54.
3. "Qualitative Characteristics of Accounting Information," *Statement of Financial Accounting Concepts No. 1* (Norwalk, Conn.: Financial Accounting Standards Board, 1980), par. 20.
4. Accounting Principles Board, "Accounting Changes," *Opinion No. 20* (New York: American Institute of Certified Public Accountants, 1971), par. 17.
5. Securities and Exchange Commission, *Staff Accounting Bulletin No. 99*, 1999.
6. Ray J. Groves, "Here's the Annual Report. Got a Few Hours?" *The Wall Street Journal Europe*, August 26–27, 1994.
7. Roger Lowenstein, "Investors Will Fish for Footnotes in 'Abbreviated' Annual Reports," *The Wall Street Journal*, September 14, 1995.
8. General Mills, *Annual Report*, 2001.
9. Ibid.
10. National Commission on Fraudulent Financial Reporting, *Report of the National Commission on Fraudulent Financial Reporting* (Washington, D.C., 1987), p. 2.
11. Arthur Levitt, "The Numbers Game," NYU Center for Law and Business, September 28, 1998.
12. "Ex-chairman of Cendant Is Indicted," *The Wall Street Journal*, March 1, 2001; "SEC Sues Former Sunbeam Executive," *Chicago Tribune*, May 16, 2001; "Enron: A Wake-up Call," *The Wall Street Journal*, December 4, 2001; "SEC List of Accounting-Fraud Probes Grows," *The Wall Street Journal*, July 6, 2001.
13. *Accounting Research and Terminology Bulletin*, final edition (New York: American Institute of Certified Public Accountants, 1961), p. 20.
14. "Debt vs. Equity: Whose Call Counts," *BusinessWeek*, July 19, 1999.
15. Roger Lowenstein, "The '20% Club' No Longer Is Exclusive," *The Wall Street Journal*, May 4, 1995.
16. "SEC Probes Lucent Accounting Practices," *The Wall Street Journal*, February 9, 2001.
17. Albertson's Inc., *Annual Report*, 2001; Great Atlantic & Pacific Tea Company, *Annual Report*, 2001.
18. GlaxoSmithKline PLC, *Annual Report*, 2000.
19. Toys "R" Us, *Annual Report*, 1987.

Chapter 6

1. Target, *Annual Report*, 2001.
2. Ibid.
3. "Shop Online—Pickup at the Store," *BusinessWeek*, June 12, 2000; Nick Wingfield, "As Web Sales Grow Mail-Order Sellers Are Benefiting the Most," *The Wall Street Journal*, May 2, 2001.
4. Joel Millman, "Here's What Happens to Many Lovely Gifts After Santa Rides Off," *The Wall Street Journal*, December 26, 2001.
5. Matthew Rose, "Magazine Revenue at Newsstands Falls in Worst Year Ever," *The Wall Street Journal*, May 15, 2001.
6. Circuit City Stores, *Annual Report*, 2001.
7. *Professional Standards*, vol. 1 (New York: American Institute of Certified Public Accountants, June 1, 1999), Sec. AU 322.07.
8. "1998 Fraud Survey," KPMG Peat Marwick, 1998.
9. *Professional Standards*, vol. 1, Sec. AU 325.16.
10. Matthew Schifrin, "The Big Squeeze," *Forbes*, March 11, 1996.
11. Wal-Mart Stores, Inc., *Annual Report*, 2000; Kmart Corp., *Annual Report*, 2000.
12. Amy Merrick, "Starbucks Accuses Employee, Husband of Embezzling $37 Million from Firm," *The Wall Street Journal*, November 20, 2000.

Chapter 7

1. Pioneer Corporation, *Annual Report*, 2001.
2. "So Much for Detroit's Cash Cushion," *BusinessWeek*, November 5, 2001.
3. Michael Selz, "Big Customers' Late Bills Choke Small Suppliers," *The Wall Street Journal*, June 22, 1994.
4. Pioneer Corporation, *Annual Report*, 2001.
5. Circuit City Stores, Inc., *Annual Report*, 2001.
6. Pioneer Corporation, *Annual Report*, 2001.
7. *Accounting Trends & Techniques* (New York: American Institute of CPAs, 2000), p. 130.
8. *Statement of Financial Accounting Standards No. 115*, "Accounting for Certain Investments in Debt and Equity Securities" (Norwalk, Conn.: Financial Accounting Standards Board, 1993).
9. Pioneer Corporation, *Annual Report*, 2001.
10. "Bad Loans Rattle Telecom Vendors," *BusinessWeek*, February 19, 2001.
11. Craig S. Smith, "Chinese Companies Writing Off Old Debt," *The Wall Street Journal*, December 28, 1995.
12. Information based on promotional brochures of Mitsubishi Electric Corp.
13. Elizabeth McDonald, "Unhatched Chickens," *Forbes*, February 19, 2001.
14. Philips Electronics N.V., *Annual Report*, 2001; Heineken N.V., *Annual Report*, 2001.

Chapter 8

1. J.C. Penney Company, Inc., *Annual Report*, 2000.
2. Illinois Tool Works, Inc., *Annual Report*, 2000.
3. American Institute of Certified Public Accountants, *Accounting Research Bulletin No. 43* (New York: AICPA, 1953), ch. 4.
4. Gary McWilliams, "Whirlwind on the Web," *BusinessWeek*, April 7, 1997.
5. Karen Lundebaard, "Bumpy Ride," *The Wall Street Journal*, May 21, 2001.
6. American Institute of Certified Public Accountants, *Accounting Research Bulletin No. 43* (New York: AICPA, 1953), ch. 4.
7. Micah Frankel and Robert Trezevant, "The Year-End LIFO Inventory Purchasing Decision: An Empirical Test," *The Accounting Review*, April 1994.
8. American Institute of Certified Public Accountants, *Accounting Trends & Techniques* (New York: AICPA, 2001).
9. "As Rite Aid Grew, CEO Seemed Unable to Manage His Empire," *The Wall Street Journal*, October 20, 1999; "RentWay Details Improper Bookkeeping," *The Wall Street Journal*, June 8, 2001.

10. International Paper Company, *Annual Report*, 2001.
11. American Institute of Certified Public Accountants, *Accounting Trends & Techniques* (New York: AICPA, 2001).
12. "Cisco's Numbers Confound Some," *International Herald Tribune*, April 19, 2001; "Kmart Posts $67 Million Loss Due to Markdowns," *The Wall Street Journal*, November 10, 2000.
13. American Institute of Certified Public Accountants, *Accounting Trends & Techniques* (New York: AICPA, 2001).
14. Exxon Mobil, *Annual Report*, 2000.
15. Adapted from Hershey Foods Corp., *Annual Report*, 2000.
16. "SEC Case Judge Rules Crazy Eddie Principals Must Pay $72.7 Million," *The Wall Street Journal*, May 11, 2000.
17. Crane Company, *Annual Report*, 2000.
18. Pioneer Corporation, *Annual Report*, 2001; Yamaha Motor Co., Ltd., *Annual Report*, 2001.

Chapter 9

1. US Airways, Inc., *Annual Report*, 2000.
2. RadioShack Corporation, *Annual Report*, 2000.
3. Pamela L. Moore, "How Xerox Ran Short of Black Ink," *BusinessWeek*, October 30, 2000.
4. Goodyear Tire & Rubber Company, *Annual Report*, 2000.
5. US Airways, Inc., *Annual Report*, 2000.
6. Andersen Enterprise Group, cited in *Crain's Chicago Business*, July 5, 1999.
7. Raju Narisetti, "P&G Ad Chief Plots Demise of the Coupon," *The Wall Street Journal*, April 17, 1996; Renae Merle, "Slowdown Is Business Boon for Coupon Seller Valassis," *The Wall Street Journal*, May 1, 2001.
8. Scott McCartney, "Free Airline Miles Become a Potent Tool for Selling Everything," *The Wall Street Journal*, April 16, 1996; "You've Got Miles," *BusinessWeek*, March 6, 2000.
9. *Statement of Financial Accounting Standards No. 5*, "Accounting for Contingencies" (Norwalk, Conn.: Financial Accounting Standards Board, 1975).
10. American Institute of Certified Public Accountants, *Accounting Trends & Techniques*, 1998, p. 73.
11. General Motors Corp., *Annual Report*, 2000.
12. American Institute of Certified Public Accountants, *Accounting Trends & Techniques*, 2001.
13. US Airways, Inc., *Annual Report*, 2000.
14. *Statement of Financial Accounting Concepts No. 7*, "Using Cash Flow Information and Present Value in Accounting Measurement" (Norwalk, Conn.: Financial Accounting Standards Board, 2000).
15. General Motors Corp., *Annual Report*, 2000.
16. Advertisement, *Chicago Tribune*, February 15, 1994.
17. Sun Micosystems Inc., *Annual Report*, 2001; Cisco Systems, *Annual Report*, 2001.
18. Texaco, Inc., *Annual Report*, 1986.
19. Man Nutzfahrzeuge Aktiengesellschaft, *Annual Report*, 1997.

Chapter 10

1. H. J. Heinz Company, *Annual Report*, 2001.
2. *Statement of Financial Accounting Standards No. 144*, "Accounting for the Impairment or Disposal of Long-Lived Assets" (Norwalk, Conn.: Financial Accounting Standards Board, 2001).
3. David Henry, "The Numbers Game," *BusinessWeek*, May 14, 2001.
4. H. J. Heinz Company, *Annual Report*, 2001.
5. Ford Motor Company, *Annual Report*, 2001.
6. *Statement of Position No. 98-1*, "Accounting for the Costs of Computer Software Developed or Planned for Internal Use" (New York: American Institute of Certified Public Accountants, 1996).
7. *Statement of Financial Accounting Standards No. 34*, "Capitalization of Interest Cost" (Norwalk, Conn.: Financial Accounting Standards Board, 1979), par. 9–11.
8. Jared Sandberg, Deborah Solomon, and Rebecca Blumenstein, "Inside WorldCom's Unearthing of a Vast Accounting Scandal," *The Wall Street Journal*, June 27, 2002.

9. *Financial Accounting Standards: Original Pronouncements as of July 1, 1977* (Norwalk, Conn.: Financial Accounting Standards Board, 1977), ARB No. 43, Ch. 9, Sec. C, par. 5.

10. Accounting Principles Board, *Opinion No. 29*, "Accounting for Nonmonetary Transactions" (New York: American Institute of Certified Public Accountants, 1973); Emerging Issues Task Force, *EITF Issue Summary 86-29*, "Nonmonetary Transactions: Magnitude of Boot and the Exceptions to the Use of Fair Value" (Norwalk, Conn.: Financial Accounting Standards Board, 1986).

11. *Statement of Financial Accounting Standards No. 25*, "Suspension of Certain Accounting Requirements for Oil and Gas Producing Companies" (Norwalk, Conn.: Financial Accounting Standards Board, 1979).

12. Adapted from Accounting Principles Board, *Opinion No. 17*, "Intangible Assets" (New York: American Institute of Certified Public Accountants, 1970), par. 2.

13. "What's in a Name?" *Time*, May 3, 1993.

14. General Motors, *Annual Report*, 2000.

15. Abbott Laboratories, *Annual Report*, 2000; Roche Group, *Annual Report*, 2000.

16. Allan B. Afterman, *International Accounting, Financial Reporting and Analysis* (New York: Warren, Gorham & Lamont, 1995).

17. *Statement of Financial Accounting Standards No. 2*, "Accounting for Research and Development Costs" (Norwalk, Conn.: Financial Accounting Standards Board, 1974), par. 12.

18. *Statement of Financial Accounting Standards No. 86*, "Accounting for the Costs of Computer Software to be Sold, Leased, or Otherwise Marketed" (Norwalk, Conn.: Financial Accounting Standards Board, 1985).

19. *Accounting Trends & Techniques*, 2001.

20. Lucent Technologies, *Annual Report*, 2000; Sara Lee Corporation, *Annual Report*, 2000; Tribune Company, *Annual Report*, 2000.

21. *Statement of Financial Accounting Standards No. 144*, "Accounting for the Impairment or Disposal of Long-Lived Assets" (Norwalk, Conn.: Financial Accounting Standards Board, 2001).

22. Edward P. McTague, "Accounting for Trade-Ins of Operational Assets," *National Public Accountant* (January 1986), p. 39.

23. General Motors Corp., *Annual Report*, 1987.

24. Polaroid Corporation, *Annual Report*, 1997.

25. Hilton Hotels Corporation, *Annual Report*, 2000; Marriott International, *Annual Report*, 2000.

26. "Stock Gives Case the Funds He Needs to Buy New Technology," *BusinessWeek*, April 15, 1996.

27. Roche Group, *Annual Report*, 2000; Baxter International, Inc., *Annual Report*, 2000.

Chapter 11

1. AT&T Corporation, *Annual Report*, 2000.

2. "Canadian Airline's Demise Adds to Industry Woes," *The Washington Post*, November 16, 2001; "A Striking End for Air Afrique," British Broadcasting Company, November 26, 2001; "Small Airlines Adapting Quicker," Associated Press, November 22, 2001; "Swiss Air Rescue Hopes Brighten," British Broadcasting Company, November 21, 2001.

3. AT&T Corporation, *Annual Report*, 2000.

4. Ibid.

5. Quentin Hardy, "Japanese Companies Need to Raise Cash, but First a Bond Market Must Be Built," *The Wall Street Journal*, October 20, 1992.

6. Bill Barnhart, "Bond Bellwether," *Chicago Tribune*, December 4, 1996.

7. Accounting Principles Board, *Opinion No. 21*, "Interest on Receivables and Payables" (New York: American Institute of Certified Public Accountants, 1971), par. 15.

8. *Statement of Financial Accounting Standards No. 13*, "Accounting for Leases" (Norwalk, Conn.: Financial Accounting Standards Board, 1976), par. 10.

9. Philip Morris Companies, Inc., *Annual Report*, 2000.

10. *Statement of Financial Accounting Standards No. 87*, "Employers' Accounting for Pensions" (Norwalk, Conn.: Financial Accounting Standards Board, 1985).

11. *Statement of Financial Accounting Standards No. 106*, "Employers' Accounting for Postretirement Benefits Other than Pensions" (Norwalk, Conn.: Financial Accounting Standards Board, 1990).

12. Stanley Ziemba, "TWA, American Revise O'Hare Gate Agreement," *The Wall Street Journal*, May 13, 1992.

13. FedEx Corporation, *Annual Report*, 2001.

14. "More Hotels Won't Be Able to Pay Debt from Operations, Study Says," *The Wall Street Journal*, October 30, 2001.

15. Amazon.com, Press Release, January 28, 1999.

16. NEC Corporation, *Annual Report*, 2001; Sanyo Electric Co., *Annual Report*, 2001.

Chapter 12

1. Cisco Systems, Inc., *Annual Report*, 2001.

2. Copyright © 2000 by Houghton Mifflin Company. Reproduced by permission from *The American Heritage Dictionary of the English Language, Fourth Edition*.

3. *Statement of Position No. 98-5*, "Report on the Costs of Start up Activities" (New York: American Institute of Certified Public Accountants, 1998).

4. Deborah Solomon, "AT&T Slashes Dividends 83%, Cuts Forecasts," *The Wall Street Journal*, December 21, 2000.

5. Abbott Laboratories, *Annual Report*, 2000.

6. Ruth Simon and Ianthe Jeanne Dugan, "Options Overdose," *The Wall Street Journal*, June 4, 2001.

7. Abbott Laboratories, *Annual Report*, 2000.

8. American Institute of Certified Public Accountants, *Accounting Trends & Techniques* (New York: AICPA, 2001).

9. *Statement of Accounting Standards No. 123*, "Accounting for Stock-Based Compensation" (Norwalk, Conn.: Financial Accounting Standards Board, 1995).

10. Suzanne McGee, "Europe's New Markets for IPOs of Growth Start-Ups Fly High," *The Wall Street Journal*, February 22, 1999.

11. Microsoft Corporation, Inc., *Annual Report*, 1997.

12. G. Christian Hill, "Microsoft Plans Preferred Issue of $750 Million," *The Wall Street Journal*, December 3, 1996.

13. American Institute of Certified Public Accountants, *Accounting Trends & Techniques* (New York: AICPA, 2001).

14. Robert McGough, Suzanne McGee, and Cassell Bryan-Low, "Buyback Binge Now Creates Big Hangover," *The Wall Street Journal*, December 18, 2000.

15. "Avaya Prices Public Offering of Common Stock" and "Avaya Completes Sale of Approximately $200 Million Common Stock," *The Wall Street Journal Online*, March 22, 2002.

16. Tom Herman, "Preferreds' Rich Yields Blind Some Investors to Risks," *The Wall Street Journal*, March 24, 1992.

17. Stanley Ziemba, "USAir Defers Dividends on Preferred Stock," *Chicago Tribune*, September 30, 1994.

18. Susan Carey, "US Airways to Redeem Preferred Owned by Berkshire Hathaway," *The Wall Street Journal*, February 4, 1998.

19. Roche Group, *Annual Report*, 2001.

Chapter 13

1. AMR Corporation, *Annual Report*, 2000.

2. *Statement of Financial Accounting Standards No. 130*, "Reporting Comprehensive Income" (Norwalk, Conn.: Financial Accounting Standards Board, 1997).

3. American Institute of Certified Public Accountants, *Accounting Trends & Techniques* (New York: American Institute of Certified Public Accountants, 2001).

4. Cited in *The Week in Review* (Deloitte Haskins & Sells), February 28, 1985.

5. "Up to the Minute, Down to the Wire," *Twentieth Century Mutual Funds Newsletter*, 1996.

6. American Institute of Certified Public Accountants, *Accounting Trends & Techniques* (New York: American Institute of Certified Public Accountants, 2001).

7. Robert Manor and Melita Marie Garza, "Company's Accounting May Prove Hard to Criminalize," *Chicago Tribune*, January 11, 2002.

8. Sears, Roebuck and Co., *Annual Report*, 1997.

9. *Statement of Financial Accounting Standards No. 109*, "Accounting for Income Taxes" (Norwalk, Conn.: Financial Accounting Standards Board, 1992).

10. American Institute of Certified Public Accountants, *Accounting Trends & Techniques* (New York: American Institute of Certified Public Accountants, 2001).

11. Accounting Principles Board, *Opinion No. 30*, "Reporting the Results of Operations" (New York: American Institute of Certified Public Accountants, 1973), par. 20.

12. Ibid.

13. American Institute of Certified Public Accountants, *Accounting Trends & Techniques* (New York: American Institute of Certified Public Accountants, 1999).

14. Accounting Principles Board, *Opinion No. 20*, "Accounting Changes" (New York: American Institute of Certified Public Accountants, 1971), par. 20.

15. David Cairns International, *IAS Survey Update*, July 2001.

16. American Institute of Certified Public Accountants, *Accounting Trends & Techniques* (New York: American Institute of Certified Public Accountants, 2001).

17. Accounting Principles Board, *Opinion No. 15*, "Earnings per Share" (New York: American Institute of Certified Public Accountants, 1969), par. 12.

18. Minnesota Mining and Manufacturing Company, *Annual Report*, 2000.

19. *Statement of Financial Accounting Standards No. 128*, "Earnings per Share and the Disclosure of Information About Capital Structure" (Norwalk, Conn.: Financial Accounting Standards Board, 1997).

20. AMR Corporation, *Annual Report*, 2000.

21. Skandia Group, *Annual Report*, 2000.

22. *Accounting Research Bulletin No. 43* (New York: American Institute of Certified Public Accountants, 1953), chap. 7, sec. B, par. 10.

23. Ibid., par. 13.

24. Robert O'Brien, "Techs' Chill Fails to Stem Stock Splits," *The Wall Street Journal*, June 8, 2000.

25. Rebecca Buckman, "Microsoft Posts Hefty 18% Revenue Rise," *Wall Street Journal*, January 18, 2002; William M. Bulkeley, "IBM Reports 13% Decline in Net Income," *The Wall Street Journal*, January 18, 2002.

26. "Technology Firms Post Strong Earnings but Stock Prices Decline Sharply," *The Wall Street Journal*, January 21, 1988; Donald R. Seace, "Industrials Plunge 57.2 Points—Technology Stocks' Woes Cited," *The Wall Street Journal*, January 21, 1988.

27. The Washington Post Company, *Annual Report*, 2000.

28. Yamaha Motor Company, Ltd., *Annual Report*, 2001.

Chapter 14

1. Marriott International, Inc., *Annual Report*, 2000.

2. *Statement of Financial Accounting Standards No. 95*, "Statement of Cash Flows" (Norwalk, Conn.: Financial Accounting Standards Board, 1987); *Statement of Financial Accounting Concepts No. 1*, "Objectives of Financial Reporting for Business Enterprises" (Norwalk, Conn.: Financial Accounting Standards Board, 1978), par. 37–39.

3. Marriott International, Inc., *Annual Report*, 2000.

4. Gary Slutsker, "Look at the Birdie and Say: 'Cash Flow,'" *Forbes*, October 25, 1993.

5. Jonathan Clements, "Yacktman Fund Is Bloodied but Unbowed," *The Wall Street Journal*, November 8, 1993.

6. Jeffrey Laderman, "Earnings, Schmearnings—Look at the Cash," *BusinessWeek*, July 24, 1989.

7. "Deadweight on the Markets," *BusinessWeek*, February 19, 2001.

8. Marriott International, Inc., *Annual Report*, 2000.

9. American Institute of Certified Public Accountants, *Accounting Trends & Techniques* (New York: AICPA, 2001).

10. Pallavi Gogoi, "Cash-Rich, So?" *BusinessWeek*, March 19, 2001.

11. "Cash Flow Shortfall in Quarter May Lead to Default on Loan," *The Wall Street Journal*, September 4, 2001.

12. Enron Corporation, *Press Release*, October 16, 2001.

13. Sony Corporation, *Annual Report*, 2000; Canon, Inc., *Annual Report*, 2000.

Chapter 15

1. Sun Microsystems, *Proxy Statement*, 2001.

2. *Statement of Financial Accounting Standards No. 131*, "Segment Disclosures" (Norwalk, Conn.: Financial Accounting Standards Board, 1997).

3. Phyllis Plitch, "Firms Embrace Pro Forma Way on Earnings," *The Wall Street Journal*, January 22, 2002.

4. David Henry, "The Numbers Game," *BusinessWeek*, May 14, 2001.

5. Sun Microsystems, Inc. *Annual Report*, 2001.

6. William H. Beaver, "Alternative Accounting Measures as Indicators of Failure," *Accounting Review*, January 1968; Edward Altman, "Financial Ratios, Discriminant Analysis and the Prediction of Corporate Bankruptcy," *Journal of Finance*, September 1968.

7. Sun Microsystems, Inc., "Management's Discussion and Analysis," *Annual Report*, 2001.

8. Ibid.

9. *Forbes*, November 13, 1978, p. 154.

10. Elizabeth MacDonald, "Firms Say SEC Earnings Scrutiny Goes Too Far," *The Wall Street Journal*, February 1, 1999.

11. H. J. Heinz Company, *Annual Report*, 2001.

12. Pfizer, Inc., *Annual Report*, 2000; Roche Group, *Annual Report*, 2000.

Chapter 16

1. PepsiCo, Inc., *Annual Report*, 2000.

2. Greg Steinmetz and Cacilie Rohwedder, "SAP Insider Probe Points to Reforms Needed in Germany," *The Wall Street Journal*, May 8, 1997.

3. *Statement of Financial Accounting Standards No. 115*, "Accounting for Certain Investments in Debt and Equity Securities" (Norwalk, Conn.: Financial Accounting Standards Board, 1993).

4. *Statement of Financial Accounting Standards No. 94*, "Consolidation of All Majority-Owned Subsidiaries" (Norwalk, Conn.: Financial Accounting Standards Board, 1987).

5. PepsiCo, Inc., *Annual Report*, 2000.

6. Accounting Principles Board, *Opinion No. 16*, "Business Combinations" (New York: Accounting Principles Board, 1970), par. 87.

7. PepsiCo., Inc., *Annual Report*, 2000.

8. Ibid.

9. *Statement of Financial Accounting Standards No. 52*, "Foreign Currency Translation" (Norwalk, Conn.: Financial Accounting Standards Board, 1981), par. 15.

10. *Financial Reporting: An International Survey* (New York: Price Waterhouse, May 1995).

11. Cadbury Schweppes, *Annual Report*, 2000.

12. "International Accounting Standards Committee Objectives and Procedures," *Professional Standards* (New York: American Institute of Certified Public Accountants, 1988), vol. B, sec. 9000, par. 24–27.

13. Cable & Wireless, plc, *Annual Report*, 1996.

Company Name Index

Subject Index

Print and Electronic Supplements for Instructors

Instructor's Solutions Manual. The manual contains answers to all text exercises, problems, and cases, as well as a transition guide listing the changes from the seventh edition to the 2004 edition of the text.

Electronic Solutions. This online resource, which contains solutions from the printed Instructor's Solutions Manual, allows instructors to manipulate the numbers in the classroom or to distribute solutions electronically.

Solutions Transparencies. More than 800 transparencies provide solutions for every exercise, problem, and case in the text, including the appendixes.

Course Manual. Available on the HMClassPrep with HMTesting Instructor CD-ROM, the Course Manual is filled with practical advice and teaching tips. It contains a planning matrix and time/difficulty chart for every chapter, and chapter-by-chapter instructional materials and review quizzes.

NEW! PowerPoint Slides. A brand new set of PowerPoint slides is available on the HMClassPrep with HMTesting Instructor CD-ROM. They can also be downloaded from the Needles Accounting Resource Center Web Site at http://accounting.college.hmco.com/instructors. The new slides are concise, contain lots of examples of transactions, and explain the accounting process in clear, easy-to-follow steps.

Video Cases. Six video cases are available on the HMClassPrep with HMTesting Instructor CD-ROM. They include Intel (Chapter 1), **NEW!** J.C. Penney (Chapter 6), **NEW!** Claire's Stores (Chapter 8), Fermi National Accelerator Laboratory (Chapter 10), Lotus Development Corporation (Chapter 12), and **NEW!** Goodyear Tire & Rubber Company (Chapter 14). A corresponding text case relates each video to the themes of the chapter.

Test Bank with Achievement Test Masters and Answers. This test bank provides more than 3,000 true-false, multiple choice, short essay, and critical-thinking questions, as well as exercises and problems.

NEW! HMClassPrep with HMTesting Instructor CD-ROM. This CD contains the computerized version of the Test Bank. It allows instructors to select, edit, and add questions, or generate randomly selected questions to produce a test master for easy duplication. The 2004 edition of the computerized test bank also contains algorithms and the option to compile tests using key terms from the text. Online Testing and Gradebook functions allow instructors to administer tests via their local area network or the Web, set up classes, record grades from tests or assignments, analyze grades, and compile class and individual statistics. The instructor CD also contains the Solutions Manual, the complete Course Manual, PowerPoint slides, Video Cases, check figures for end-of-chapter problems, and web links to the Accounting Transaction Tutor and the Needles Accounting Resource Center Web Site.

Needles Accounting Resource Center Instructor Web Site. This site (http://accounting.college.hmco.com/instructors) includes downloadable PowerPoint slides of text presentation materials and text illustrations, Electronic Solutions, PowerPoint slides, accounting issues essays, check figures for the end-of-chapter problems, and links to other valuable text resources.

NEW! Essays. Now available on the Needles Accounting Resource Center Web Site is a series of 16 short essays (one for each chapter) that present timely accounting issues. Each essay has two sets of questions and suggested answers. Students can answer the first set by reading the essay and related text chapter. The second set requires students to do additional research. Instructors can use these essays for exams or as extra credit assignments.

Blackboard Course Cartridges. These cartridges provide flexible, efficient, and creative ways to present learning materials and manage distance learning courses. Specific resources include chapter overviews, check figures for in-text problems, practice quizzes, PowerPoint slides, and Excel Solutions. In addition to course management benefits, instructors may make use of an electronic grade book, receive papers from students enrolled in the course via the Internet, and track student use of the communication and collaboration functions.

WebCT e-Packs. These e-packs provide instructors with a flexible, Internet-based education platform. The WebCT e-packs come with a full array of features to enrich the online learning experience, including online quizzes, bulletin board, chat tool, whiteboard, and other functionality. The e-packs contain text-specific resources, including chapter overviews, check figures, practice quizzes, PowerPoint slides, and Excel Solutions.

Solutions Manual for Soft-Tec Practice Case. This manual provides the solutions for the Soft-Tec Practice Case, which can be solved manually or on a computer.